THE EXPEDITIONS OF
John Charles Frémont

John Charles Frémont as he looked about 1849. From a print in
Walter Colton's *Three Years in California* (New York, 1850).

THE EXPEDITIONS OF
John Charles
Frémont

VOLUME 1
Travels from 1838 to 1844

EDITED BY

DONALD JACKSON AND MARY LEE SPENCE

UNIVERSITY OF ILLINOIS PRESS

URBANA, CHICAGO, AND LONDON

THE EXPEDITIONS OF
John Charles Frémont

ADVISORY COMMITTEE

Allan Nevins (chairman)
Herman R. Friis
Robert W. Johannsen
Dale L. Morgan

ACKNOWLEDGMENTS

The preparation of the first volume and Map Portfolio of Frémont's travels began in 1965. Since then the editors have solicited advice and assistance from scores of persons and institutions all over the United States—and a few abroad. To each we are profoundly grateful, but we must be content to name specifically only those institutions which provided funds for research and publication.

The National Historical Publications Commission gave its early endorsement to the undertaking, and provided not only search facilities in the National Archives but also funds for the payment of wages. The Research Board of the University of Illinois gave generously, as always, for the cost of wages, travel, photocopies, and other necessities. The University of Illinois Press, going beyond its traditional role as publisher, became an actual sponsor of the project, providing released time for the senior editor, office space for both editors, and other considerations.

We are also grateful to Miss Jessie Benton Frémont, of Washington, D.C., the granddaughter of John Charles Frémont, for representing the family in granting us permission to use certain papers not in government repositories.

30 June 1970

DONALD JACKSON
MARY LEE SPENCE

CONTENTS

THE EXPEDITION OF 1843–44 TO OREGON AND CALIFORNIA

ILLUSTRATIONS

MAPS

INTRODUCTION

The career of John Charles Frémont was marred by disasters large and small, but his successes were monumental. His character was flawed by vanity and by hunger for recognition and financial gain, but there was enough toughness of spirit to carry him five times across the plains and Rockies under conditions of intense privation, leading bands of courageous men. In his lifetime some good men loved him and others despised or mistrusted him. Even today there are strongly differing points of view about his motives and his methods, but there is less dispute about his place in the history of his century.

Frémont's activities in the West, and his published reports, affected the lives of thousands of migrants who plied the Oregon and California trails. His success as an explorer, his interest in politics, and his marriage to the daughter of Senator Thomas Hart Benton of Missouri made him a familiar and sometimes influential figure in Washington. He played a major role in the conquest of California, only to be court-martialed for his early failure to recognize Stephen Watts Kearny as governor. He was the first presidential standard bearer of the newly formed Republican Party in 1856. His commission as major general in the Civil War, and his handling of his two brief commands, involved him in controversy and earned him the disfavor of Abraham Lincoln.

After acquiring great riches in the development of gold mines on the Mariposa grant in California, he lost the Mariposa and much of his wealth in financial schemes after the Civil War. At last he was surviving by means of sinecures—such as the governorship of Arizona Territory—and the income from the writings of his wife, Jessie Benton Frémont. When he died on 13 July 1890 he was nearly a pauper. Frémont's proudest legacy was what he had done before the age of forty, exploring the West and making it known—through his narratives—to a nation hungry to know.

These volumes will deal with those first forty years of his life, and how they affected the future of the nation.

If one factor alone sets Frémont apart from his most notable predecessors in the field of U.S. exploration, it is the accident of time. He was ready, and the public was ready, to turn all eyes to the West and discover what it had to hold for the mass of men. If Lewis and Clark had been able to carry out their travels under such strong public scrutiny, they, too, might have been considered "dashing figures." They lacked the aid of a blustering press agent such as Thomas Hart Benton (although having President Thomas Jefferson as a sponsor was not bad), but mainly they lacked an impatient public. *Their* public was curious, patient, proud, but with no thought in 1804–6 of an Oregon Trail, an ox team and wagon, or a new life waiting beyond the Mississippi or the Rockies.

Although time was on Frémont's side, and he had strong supporters in Secretary of War Joel Poinsett and Senator Benton, he brought attributes of his own to the making of the Frémont legend. He brought audacity, courage, and a quick mind which had absorbed a good deal of knowledge in the fields of natural history, geography, and surveying. He also brought Jessie into the picture—a beautiful and talented girl, inheritor of her father's concern for power and prestige, and with an ability to write which would provide young Frémont with a lifelong amanuensis and ghost-writer.

Senator Benton aided the young explorer in many ways, but no one can say that he freely gave his daughter in marriage; young John Charles accomplished that on his own. Together, John Charles and Jessie comprised a team such as one does not find again in U.S. history, perhaps until another truly dashing pair—George Armstrong Custer and his wife Elizabeth—appear upon the scene. And to stretch the analogy just a bit, Charles and Anne Morrow Lindbergh come to mind in more recent times.

Back again to the importance of the period, and the social and political climate in which Frémont was to operate. It is well known that his expeditions, especially the first two, often followed the trails of other wagon trains. It is important, though, to say *some* wagon trains, and very early ones at that. We present a note (p. 173n) which indicates how really early in the migration period his operations began. Only two emigrant trains had preceded him: the John Bartleson party to California in 1841, and the Elijah White party to Oregon in 1842.

It is almost impossible to overstate the enthusiasm with which the nation greeted the printed reports of the first two western expeditions. The first publication, which in our edition begins on p. 168, introduced a new kind of intelligence from the West: readable narrative combined with competent maps, both produced from personal observation. But it carried the reader only to the Rockies. It was the second report (p. 426), with its description of the route via Laramie, Fort Hall, and Walla Walla to the lush Oregon valleys, then on through the length of California and back across the southwestern deserts, that made Frémont's reputation secure.

It seemed natural that members of the Congress should wish the two reports issued as one volume, with a single map of the entire area covered. The records of Congress contain many a letter or memorandum (some of which we cite) dealing with delays in publication, changes in printing orders, urgent requests for copies before they were finished. There was a dispute in the House over whether members of the previous Congress, not re-elected, should receive copies—and the new Congress resolved that they should not. And there were unconfirmed reports that members of Congress or their employees were selling copies to the public.

The many editions issued by trade publishers were not long in coming. By 1846, L. W. Hall in Syracuse had issued a version with no maps or illustrations. At least two Washington publishers (Taylor, Wilde, & Co., and H. Polkinhorn) published their own editions, as did H. E. Phinney in Cooperstown, N.Y. Foreign editions included those of Wiley & Putnam, London, in 1846, and a German version in 1847.

The two Washington publishing houses which had been awarded the contract for the combined report were Gales and Seaton, printers of the *Daily National Intelligencer,* and Blair and Rives, publishers of the *Congressional Globe.* Both of these publishers, having early access to the report, hastened to print extracts and reviews. The *Intelligencer,* for example, ran a total of twenty-three columns between 7 and 26 August 1845. On 28 August it followed with three columns, including an evaluation of the second expedition and some remarks on the third, which was then in progress.

A laudatory review appeared in the July 1845 issue of the *United States Magazine and Democratic Review,* in which Lewis and Clark were compared unfavorably to Frémont:

The honorary reward of Brevet Captain has been bestowed upon him. Lewis and Clark received something more substantial,—double pay, sixteen hundred acres of land each, promotion to generals, appointment of governors, commission to treat with Indians, and copy-right in their Journal. Certainly as first explorers, they were entitled to great merit; but they lack the science which Capt. Frémont carried into his expeditions; and, returning on the same line by which they went out, their discoveries lack the breadth and variety which distinguish his. His work was lacking [i.e., needed] to complete the view of the great region from the Mississippi to the Pacific ocean; and it has come at the exact moment that it was most wanted, and will be most useful. Great events are pending of which Oregon is the subject. . . . We assume to say that the publication of this Report will increase the emigration to Oregon, and will sharpen the appetite of two great nations [Great Britain and the U.S.] for the possession of a river whose mouth happens to be the only outlet to the sea. . . .

The reviewer's allusions to Lewis and Clark could have profited by a bit more research, but his enthusiasm for Frémont typified the mood of the country.

Other great events were to follow: the third expedition, resulting in Frémont's involvement in the conquest of California; his court-martial, which did little damage to his own public image and gave California an untold wealth of publicity; and then the unsuccessful campaign for the presidency.

Perhaps the loss of the election marked the moment when the bright star began to fade. Perhaps it was the Civil War, during which he proved to be no military man. Somehow the years sped by, riches came and went, and at last he was old. It is certain that he died poor, but less certain that he died entirely bitter—for there were bright memories to temper the unhappy ones and much achievement mingled with his many failures. Among his effects at the time of his death was a scrap of paper bearing a poem he had written near the end of his life as he was crossing the Continental Divide on a train. Part of it reads:

> Long years ago I wandered here,
> In the midsummer of the year,
>   Life's summer too.
> A score of horsemen here we rode,
> The mountain-world its glories showed,
>   All fair to view.

. . . .

Now changed the scene, and changed the eyes
That here once looked on glowing skies
   When summer smiled.
These riven trees and wind-swept plain
Now shew the winter's dread domain—
   Its fury wild.

    .   .   .   .

The buoyant hopes and busy life
Have ended all in hateful strife
   And baffled aim.
The world's rude contact killed the rose,
No more its shining radiance shows
   False roads to fame.

    .   .   .   .

Where still some grand peaks mark the way
Touched by the light of parting day
   And memory's sun.
Backward amid the twilight glow
Some lingering spots yet brightly show
   On roads hard won.

The verses recalled much, and Jessie saved them. Then she penned a sentence of her own which summed up the labors of a valiant traveler and the pride of a devoted wife. "Railroads followed the lines of his journeyings—a nation followed his maps to their resting place—and cities have risen on the ashes of his lonely campfires."[1]

PARENTAGE AND EARLY YEARS

When John Charles Frémont was born, 21 January 1813, his parents already had scandalized their community and moved away in disgrace. The fact that they never married was to plague Frémont all his life, but particularly during the presidential race of 1856

---

[1] The poem is in the library of the Southwest Museum, Los Angeles, and Jessie's quotation is from a draft manuscript, "Great Events during the Life of Major General John C. Frémont," Bancroft Library, Berkeley. Hereafter, libraries and other repositories will be referred to by the symbols used in the *National Union Catalog* of the Library of Congress (see listing on pp. xliii–xliv).

when the word "illegitimate" came frequently to the lips of his political enemies.

The father was Charles Fremon, a Frenchman from the neighborhood of Lyons, said to have made his way to Virginia from Santo Domingo. One biographer says he was on his way to join an aunt in Santo Domingo, about 1800, when he was captured by an English man-of-war and held prisoner for a few years.[2] Exactly when Fremon came to Virginia is not known, but by the spring of 1808 he seems to have been teaching French in the fashionable academy operated by L. H. Girardin and David Doyle, near Richmond. When he was dismissed after a year on the grounds that he was not a fit person to give instruction to young ladies, he opened a night school for the French language and tutored in private homes. He later rejoined Girardin at a new location.[3]

By this time he had rented a small house from John Pryor and had soon alienated the affections of Mrs. Pryor, the former Ann Beverly Whiting, who was a good deal younger than her husband. One source says the two lovers actually hoped for Pryor's death so that they might marry. Richmond society was rocked by the scandal

---

[2] BIGELOW, 11–12. This 1856 campaign biography was prepared from material assembled by Jessie. Some of the problems she encountered, particularly with regard to JCF's mother, are reflected in letters to Elizabeth Blair Lee, 2 July [1856], and to John Bigelow, 7 July [1856], in the Blair-Lee Papers, NjP, and Bigelow Collection, NN. Pierre-Georges Roy, a Canadian archivist, believes that JCF's father was actually Louis-René Frémont of Québec, who established himself in Virginia. See ROY [1] and [2]. It is not clear when the "t" was added to the name; in early newspaper advertisements the father's name is "Fremon." In fact, receipts for French and dancing lessons in the Wayne-Stites Anderson Papers, GHi, are signed "Jean Charles Fremon" though Charles Fremon seems to have been the common form. Young Frémont was variously called "J.C.," "J. Charles," or "Charles" in his early years. He did not begin to use the accented form of "Frémont" until he began his association with the French scientist Joseph N. Nicollet.

[3] In an advertisement in the Richmond *Enquirer* of 8 March 1808, Girardin mentions "a well-qualified native of France" as his assistant. Moncure Robinson (1802–91), an eminent engineer, claimed that he studied French under Charles Fremon at the College of William and Mary (OSBORNE). It is more likely that he studied under Fremon at Girardin's academy, which he attended—as did also Thomas Jefferson's grandson, T. Jefferson Randolph. For Fremon's dismissal, see letter of David Doyle to L. H. Girardin in the Virginia *Patriot,* 23 Aug. 1811. For Fremon's proprietorship of his own school and his reaffiliation with Girardin, see advertisements in the Richmond *Enquirer,* 24, 27, and 31 Oct. and 10 and 14 Nov. 1809; 12 June, 27 July, and 11 Sept. 1810.

in July 1811. Girardin and his current partner, John Wood, lost their academy and feuded publicly over the responsibility for the hiring of Fremon. Finally Mrs. Pryor left her husband's bed and board and went with Fremon to Williamsburg, Norfolk, and then Charleston.

In a divorce petition some months later, Pryor charged that his wife had left the house voluntarily. But Ann wrote her brother-in-law that she had been "turned out of doors at night and in an approaching storm" and threatened with "the most cruel and violent treatment" if she remained in the house. She also wrote that she and Fremon were poor, "but we can be content with little, for I have found that happiness consists not in riches." Pryor's intention of applying to the Virginia legislature for a divorce was widely circulated, and of course Ann hoped that he would succeed. But the House of Delegates rejected the petition 13 December 1811 without giving a reason.[4]

By the fall of 1811, the Fremons, as we shall now call the pair although apparently they were never able to marry, were in Savannah, Ga. During the next year Charles tried a number of ways to make ends meet: he gave French lessons, worked in a dancing academy, took in boarders, opened his own dancing school, gave cotillion parties, and opened a livery stable at his residence.

So it was that John Charles Frémont was born into a nomadic

---

[4] John Pryor was a veteran officer of the Revolution who kept livery stables in Richmond and gave the city its first amusement resort, Haymarket Gardens. In 1811, he was "far advanced in years," according to his divorce petition, and BIGELOW, 20, says he was sixty-two when he married seventeen-year-old Ann Whiting in 1796. But he was vigorous enough to take the field against the British in 1813, and did not die until 1823 (Richmond *Enquirer,* 9 Feb. 1813, and P. C. CLARK). Ann Beverly Whiting was the daughter of the wealthy Thomas Whiting, a burgess for Gloucester in 1775–76, and Elizabeth Sewell. She was born shortly before the death of her father, whose will was dated 15 Oct. 1780. In 1796, with her "full consent" and that of her stepfather and guardian, Maj. Samuel Carey, she was married to Pryor. See BIGELOW, 13–20, and Pryor's manuscript petition for divorce of 1 Dec. 1811, Vi. For further details of the elopement and attempted divorce, see letter of John Wood to the public, Virginia *Patriot,* 26 July 1811; letter of David Doyle to Girardin, *Patriot,* 23 Aug. 1811; advertisements by Wood and Girardin regarding their separation, Richmond *Enquirer,* 12 and 16 July 1811. No surviving copy has been found of a twenty-eight-page pamphlet published by Girardin, "pregnant with calumny and slander" according to Wood. Ann's letter to John Lowry, 28 Aug. 1811, was abstracted by Pryor in support of his divorce petition. For the negative decision on the divorce, see *Journal* of the Virginia House of Delegates, 1811–12.

family of unstable finances on 21 January 1813. His nurse was Hannah, a family slave who had apparently been recovered after running away the previous year. We know little about the next few years in the life of the family. They left Savannah, and a daughter, who died in infancy, was born in Nashville in 1814. From there the Fremons apparently wandered to Norfolk, where a second daughter and a second son were born in 1815 and 1817. After Charles Fremon died in 1818, his widow and her small children stayed for a time in Virginia, and John Charles received his first schooling there. They were in Charleston by 1823, and in 1826 young John Charles had entered the law office of John W. Mitchell. Gone now was the family hope that he would become an Episcopal minister, though in June 1827 he was confirmed in St. Paul's Church by Bishop Bowen for St. Philip's congregation.[5]

The earliest Frémont document which has come to our attention derives from his service with attorney Mitchell. It is a subpoena issued by Mitchell to several persons and given to sixteen-year-old John Charles to serve. An endorsement on the reverse side reads:

J. C. Fremont being duly sworn deponeth that he served on the within named witnesses personally this writ & gave them tickets— except the witness Alphy Berney whom he could not find.

Sworn to before me 14 July 1828   J. Charles Fremont
J. W. Mitchell[6]

---

[5] For sparse information about the Fremons during this period, see advertisements in the *Columbian Museum & Savannah Advertiser,* 3 Oct. 1811, and in the *Republican and Savannah Evening Ledger,* 7 Dec., 1811; 2 Jan. and 31 Oct. 1812; 13 Feb. 1813. The assumption that the Fremons never married is based on the fact that Pryor did not die until 1823, five years after Fremon's death. There is no record that Pryor ever received his divorce. The MEMOIRS and BIGELOW do not mention the birth of a child named Ann in Nashville, but see ROY [1]. BIGELOW indicates that the youngest daughter (and for him the only daughter) was born in Nashville. He does not name her or the younger son. ROY gives their names as Elizabeth and Thomas-Archibald, but JCF's letter to his mother on 8 June 1838 (our Doc. No. 3) refers to "Frank," presumably his brother.

A chronology of JCF's life in the New York *Times,* 21 July 1856, puts him in school in Virginia in 1820, in school in Charleston in 1823, and in Mitchell's law office in 1826. His confirmation in St. Paul's is substantiated by records inspected for us 6 Oct. 1966 by Sam T. Cobb, rector of St. Philip's.

[6] Subpoena of 10 July 1828, in Mitchell's hand, with JCF's signature on the endorsement, IU.

Mitchell apparently concluded that the pulpit, rather than the bar, might be the better profession for John Charles after all, and took him to the school of J. Roberton, who prepared boys for the College of Charleston. It is from Roberton that we have our first description of the youth. If the memory of an elderly scholar some twenty-three years later can be relied upon, he was a boy of medium size, "graceful in manners, rather slender, but well formed, and upon the whole, what I would call handsome; of a keen, piercing eye, and a noble forehead seemingly the very seat of genius." To Roberton's astonishment, Frémont within a year had read Caesar, Nepos, Sallust, six books of Virgil, nearly all of Horace, two books of Livy, Graeca Minora, part of Graeca Majora, and four books of Homer's *Iliad*. He also made much progress in mathematics.[7]

Frémont, who seems to have continued working in Mitchell's law office while reading the classics and doing his calculations, entered the junior class in the College of Charleston in May 1829. The college records for 1830 list him as Charles or C. J. Fremont in the Scientific Department. The records also show that he was away during the first three months of 1830, "teaching in the country by permission." He resumed his studies in April, but as the year advanced his absences became frequent as he spent more and more time with a Creole family who had a beguiling, black-eyed daughter named Cecilia. He had fallen deeply in love, and though the college faculty was patient because of his recent good scholarship and his abundant promise, he was finally dismissed 5 February 1831 for "incorrigible negligence." He missed graduation by three months. But about five years later he applied to the trustees for a B.A. degree and his request was granted.[8]

That his career seemed in jeopardy was of little concern; he treated the period of freedom from studies as a holiday: "The days

---

[7] ROBERTON, 3–5. He does not mention JCF by name but the identity of the student is almost certain; Roberton is quoted in BIGELOW, the MEMOIRS, and in an item on JCF in the New York *Times*, 27 June 1856. The Benton Papers, MoSHi, contain two letters from Jessie to Roberton, one of which expresses the hope that he will repeat his visits to the Frémonts and another assuring him and "his inquiring friend" that JCF was born and reared in the Protestant Episcopal Church.

[8] For JCF's college record, see the journal of the College of Charleston, weekly record, Jan. 1830–Feb. 1831, and for his receipt of the B.A. degree, the journal of the proceedings of the trustees, 19 March 1838, p. 263. One of the trustees of the college when JCF received his belated degree was his friend Joel Poinsett (EASTERBY, 261).

went by on wings. In the summer we [Frémont and the two boys in the Creole family] ranged about in the woods, or on the now historic islands, gunning or picnicking, the girls dangerously near the breakers on the bar. I remember as in a picture, seeing the beads of perspiration on the forehead of my friend Henry as he tugged frantically at his oar when we had found ourselves one day in the suck of Drunken Dick, a huge breaker that to our eyes appeared monstrous as he threw his spray close to the boat. For us it was really pull Dick pull Devil."

Evenings were also spent with Cecilia and her brothers, though occasionally he absented himself to study a work on astronomy or to read a chronicle of men "who had made themselves famous by brave and noble deeds, or infamous by cruel and base acts."[9]

The family's poverty would not permit Frémont too long a holiday. He obtained positions as a teacher of mathematics in various schools (including John A. Wooten's private school), and also took charge of an "Apprentices' Library," a collection of books with some added instructional facilities, and labored as a private surveyor.[10] The death of his sister Elizabeth in 1832, and the departure of his brother to try a career on the stage, awoke John Charles to sterner realities and ended this desultory phase of his life.

He now began to come into association with a number of distinguished men. The first to exert an influence upon his career was Joel Poinsett (1799–1851), whose home was on the outskirts of Charleston. Poinsett had been minister to Mexico, and now during Frémont's teaching days was a principal leader of the Union men of South Carolina in the nullification controversy of 1830–32. From him, and from Thomas Hart Benton later, Frémont imbibed the Unionist views, as opposed to sectional interests, which remained with him all his life. It was certainly through Poinsett's influence, but not with his approval, that he obtained a civilian post as teacher of mathematics to the midshipmen on board the *U.S.S. Natchez*, which had been sent to Charleston to uphold the power of the federal government to collect the tariffs declared null and void by the state of South Carolina. When compromise averted a possible outbreak of war between the state and federal governments in April 1833, the *Natchez* returned to Hampton Roads. The next month,

---

[9] The period spent by JCF with the Creole family is discussed in MEMOIRS, 20–21.

[10] NEVINS, 17; BENTON [2]; New York *Times,* 21 July 1856.

under the command of Capt. John P. Zantzinger, she sailed with Frémont abroad for a two-year cruise in South American waters.[11]

Frémont, who drew $25.00 a month plus rations, maintained that the cruise had no future bearing on his career, though he "saw more of the principal cities and people than a traveller usually does." The routine of the ship, on which David G. Farragut was one of the lieutenants, was broken by a couple of duels while the vessel was anchored off Rio de Janeiro. In the first, one of the principals was killed; in the other, Frémont and Decatur Hurst, the seconds, put only powder in the pistols and then rowed the duelists across the bay. Finding "a narrow strip of sandy beach about forty yards long between the water and the mountain," they positioned their men and gave the word to fire. Of course the men remained upright and Frémont and Hurst were able to carry them "triumphantly back to the ship, nobody hurt and nobody wiser."[12]

In 1835, Congress provided for several professorships of mathematics in the Navy at $1,200 a year. Frémont received such an appointment on 13 June 1835, with pay retroactive to 3 March. When the *Natchez* docked at New York, he went home to Charleston and wrote the following letter to Secretary of Navy Mahlon Dickerson:

It will not perhaps be unknown to you that, when the U.S. Ship Natchez arrived at New York, I was attached to her as Professor of Mathematics. Immediately after information of the passage of the "Navy Bill" had been received on the Brazilian Station, I received from Commodore James Renshaw—to whose ship the Natchez, I had been attached as Schoolmaster from the commencement of her cruise—an appointment as "Professor of Mathematics in the Navy of the United States," bearing date June 13th 1835. Desirous of being again ordered to sea, I am somewhat at a loss to know if you will deem the above circumstances sufficient for that purpose, or whether references, with testimonials of character and qualifications, will be thought previously requisite. Should such be the case, I shall be happy to forward them to the Department, immediately on receiving a notification to that effect. I should, however, suppose that the fact of having been appointed to my station by Commodore Renshaw

---

[11] DNA-45, muster roll of the *U.S.S. Natchez*, 1833–35, p. 68.

[12] See MEMOIRS, 23. JCF says that Decatur Hurst was a nephew of Commodore Stephen Decatur and later died from wounds sustained in a duel in Africa. CALLAHAN lists a William D. Hurst but not a Decatur Hurst. The duelists were Robert P. Lovell, Poinsett's nephew, and Enoch G. Parrott (1815–79), senior officer during much of the blockade of Charleston in the Civil War.

will be deemed sufficient, and it may not be disadvantageous to me to state that I received from him, when the Natchez was on the eve of departure, an offer of being ordered to another ship of the squadron. It being to you, Sir, a matter of indifference to what ship I am ordered, it will not, I imagine, be considered out of rule respectfully to request that in the event of being successful in my application, I may be attached to the frigate United States, which vessel I understand will be shortly sent to the Mediterranean. My situation not permitting me long to remain unemployed, permit me to say, that, should it entirely suit your convenience, I would be much gratified to be favored with an early answer to this communication.[13]

Dickerson acknowledged Frémont's request for an appointment, saying that "When the public interest shall require the services of a Professor of Mathematics, it will give me pleasure to recur to your application." Impatiently, Frémont wrote again on 16 January 1836, sending Dickerson several enclosures including a testimonial from Captain Zantzinger. Again Dickerson acknowledged the letter without offering much hope. But in April he authorized Frémont to take the examination for professor of mathematics, and sent him to Baltimore for that purpose. He passed an examination conducted by Professors Edward C. Ward and P. I. Rodriquez, who reported: "Mr. J. C. Freemont was found qualified, & we take great pleasure in stating that he is a gentleman whose talents will be very beneficial to the Midshipmen of the navy."[14]

That was in June. By October there still had been no assignment, and again Frémont wrote to Dickerson:

Having been informed that several vessels are on the eve of sailing from the harbors of Norfolk & New York I have thought the present a fit opportunity respectfully to request that I may be appointed to one of them. Should it suit your convenience to send me an appointment I should be much gratified to find it for the Mediterranean—a wish which I am only induced to express because I understand no selections have as yet been made. A communication, with which I had the honor to be favoured from yourself immediately subsequent to having passed an examination at Balte, informs me that I shall be sent to sea as soon as my services may be required. I should in consequence not have applied at

---

[13] JCF to Dickerson, 31 Oct. 1835 (MeHi—Fogg Collection).

[14] Dickerson to JCF, 23 April 1836, DNA-45, Gen. Lbk, 22:252; memorandum of the report of Ward and Rodriquez on the examination of professors of mathematics, 3 June 1836, DNA-45, Gen. Lbk, 22:331; MEMOIRS, 23.

present but that I am led to believe such applications customary at the times when ships are being fitted out for sea.[15]

Dickerson annotated the letter by instructing his clerk: "Inform him that a Professor of Mathematics is already detailed for the North Carolina but it may be in my power in a short time to assign you duty in a Cruising Vessel." He struck out the words "probably in a Ship destined to cruise on the Coast of Brazil."

Not until 4 April 1837 did Dickerson write Frémont the long-awaited orders to duty. "You will proceed to Boston and report to Com. [John] Downes for duty as Professor of Mathematics on board the U.S.S. Independence." But a year and a half of waiting had been too much, and the necessity of earning a living had already forced Frémont to seek other opportunities. He declined the appointment.[16]

We have been able to trace in sketchy fashion Frémont's brief naval career. More hazy, however, is his service as a surveyor for Captain William G. Williams of the U.S. Corps of Topographical Engineers, who had been ordered to assist William G. McNeill in a survey of a route for the projected Charleston, Louisville, and Cincinnati Railroad. This road would have done much to link the states of the West and Northwest with those of the South. Leading spirits in the enterprise were Frémont's benefactor Poinsett and Robert Young Hayne, a prominent South Carolina politician who later became president of the railroad company.

Frémont found the work congenial: "We were engaged in running experimental lines, and the plotting of the field notes sometimes kept us up until midnight. Our quarters were sometimes at a village inn and more frequently at some farmer's house, where milk and honey and many good things were welcome to an appetite sharpened by all day labor on foot and a tramp of several miles backward and forward, morning and evening. . . . The summer weather in the mountains was fine, the cool water abundant, and the streams lined with azaleas. . . . The survey was a kind of picnic with work enough to give it zest, and we were all sorry when it was over."[17]

---

[15] JCF to Dickerson, 19 Oct. 1836, DNA-45, Misc. LR, No. 69.

[16] Dickerson to JCF, 4 April 1837, DNA-45, Letters to Officers, Ships of War, 24:33.

[17] MEMOIRS, 23–24. See also J. J. Abert to W. G. Williams, 17 March 1836, DNA-77, LS, 2:63; and the joint report of the chief and associate engineers of the Charleston, Louisville, and Cincinnati Railroad, 7 Oct. 1837, Senate Doc. 158, 25th Cong., 2nd sess., U.S. Serial 316.

After the work on the railroad survey was suspended, Frémont again was employed with Captain Williams as his assistant engineer in the survey of the territory occupied by the Cherokee Indians. The land lay mainly in Georgia, though some cut across into North Carolina and Tennessee. Because the Cherokees were bitterly opposed to the federal government's policy of transferring the major tribes to the area west of the Mississippi River, the War Department felt that a survey would aid military purposes if war broke out, or facilitate the distribution of land among the frontiersmen if it did not. It was a strenuous survey of forest and mountain country made hurriedly in mid-winter, but here, Frémont wrote many years later, "I found the path which I was 'destined to walk.' Through many of the years to come the occupation of my prime of life was to be among Indians and in waste places."[18]

In December 1837, Frémont applied for a commission in the U.S. Corps of Topographical Engineers (Captain Williams had already written a supporting letter). In February 1838, Williams was instructed to come to Washington as soon as his survey was completed and to bring Frémont with him. In March, with the job done, Frémont spent a few days in Charleston and then proceeded to Washington. His friend Poinsett, now Secretary of War, requested that the twenty-five-year-old Frémont be assigned as a civilian assistant to the distinguished French scientist Joseph Nicolas Nicollet, who was about to embark upon an examination of the northern territory lying between the Mississippi and Missouri rivers. While he was away on the first of his two expeditions with Nicollet, Frémont's commission as a lieutenant in the Topographical Corps was approved.[19]

From this point in Fremont's life, the documents tell the story.

---

[18] MEMOIRS, 50. It is difficult to say just how long JCF worked on the Cherokee survey in 1837–38, as the documents are few. Some of the field notebooks in which he kept his raw surveying data are in DNA-77, and there is one voucher which may not cover his complete service. Dated 19 April 1838, it lists payment for "Salary as Asst. Engr. in the Cherokee Nation N.C. &c. for 43 days, viz. from the 6th March to the 18th April 1838 inclusively at $1200.00 per annum, $141.04." It appears to have been JCF's final payment, but may not have been the only one. DNA-217, Records of the Third Auditor, Acct. No. 3649, Voucher No. 158.

[19] The foregoing summary of JCF's early years is not intended as a complete biography. For a more detailed account of this period, see NEVINS, 1–28.

THE DOCUMENTS AND THE PROJECT

"It is not a cheerful task, that of going over and destroying old letters and papers, but it is better than having them get into wrong hands. . . . I will be thankful when I am all through with it for it is very hard to burn up the letters of those we love."[20] So wrote Frémont's daughter Elizabeth in 1907 as she pillaged what was left of her parents' literary remains. It is an old story, and a source of anguish to the historian. But papers tend to survive all their natural enemies: not only fire, flood, and mildew but the busy destructiveness of descendants. And so public a figure as Frémont must of necessity lodge a great many documents in relatively safe places.

Of the mauscript materials available to the student of Frémont and his times, most are in the National Archives and the Library of Congress. Of the several smaller collections elsewhere, a few were placed in the public trust by members of the family. There are, as far as we can discern, no papers of John Charles or Jessie Benton Frémont still in family hands, but there are many in private collections. All these sources—the public repositories and private holdings—have been searched as thoroughly as possible for what is substantial and informative. A man with as many business, political, and military interests as Frémont could not avoid producing much trivia. No sensible editor would undertake a complete edition of Frémont papers. He would seize most gratefully upon every shred which bears upon the expeditions of 1838–54, for such documents are not plentiful. For other activities of Frémont, however, he would find it necessary to be selective—even in regard to such vital events as the Bear Flag Revolt.

In this series we combine unpublished manuscript materials with Frémont's published reports and selections from his *Memoirs*. The previously published works have never been thoroughly annotated, and the hitherto unpublished letters and documents provide much new material for such annotation.

The published documents upon which Frémont's reputation came to rest in his own lifetime are here listed chronologically. Joseph N. Nicollet's map, but not the *Report,* is included, and both are dis-

---

[20] Elizabeth Benton Frémont to Sarah McDowell Preston, 6 Aug. 1907 (KyU—Preston Family Papers).

cussed elsewhere as a factor in Frémont's development as an explorer and scientific observer.

1. *Northern Boundary of Missouri,* H.R. Doc. 38, 27th Cong., 3rd sess., U.S. Serial 420. A report of Frémont's explorations of the Des Moines River, as high as the Raccoon Fork, in 1841. The manuscript version is used as a text in the present volume.

2. *A Report on an Exploration of the Country Lying between the Missouri River and the Rocky Mountains on the Line of the Kansas and Great Platte Rivers,* Sen. Doc. 243, 27th Cong., 3rd sess., U.S. Serial 416.

3. *Report of the Exploring Expedition to the Rocky Mountains in the Year 1842, and to Oregon and North California in the Years 1843–44,* Sen. Exec. Doc. 174, 28th Cong., 2nd sess., U.S. Serial 461.

4. *Message of the President of the United States Communicating the Proceedings of the Court Martial in the Trial of Lieutenant Colonel Frémont,* Sen. Exec. Doc. 33, 30th Cong., 1st sess., U.S. Serial 507.

5. *Geographical Memoir upon Upper California, in Illustration of His Map of Oregon and California,* Sen. Misc. Doc. 148, 30th Cong., 1st sess., U.S. Serial 511.

6. *Memoirs of My Life,* vol. 1 (no others issued), Chicago and New York, 1887. Originally published in ten parts in paper wrappers.

Unfortunately the *Memoirs* carry the story of Frémont's life only to 1847—through the conquest of California and his appointment by Robert F. Stockton as governor of that territory. "I close the page," he wrote, "because my path of life led out from among the grand and lovely features of nature, and its pure and wholesome air, into the poisoned atmosphere and jarring circumstances of conflict among men, made subtle and malignant by clashing interests." The principal events of his remaining forty-three years of life his wife tried to chronicle, often with a view also to justifying his sometimes controversial decisions and behavior, in "Great Events during the Life of Major General John C. Frémont." Intended as a sequel to the *Memoirs,* the manuscript was never published.

Although the publication of the *Memoirs,* which draws at times *verbatim* on the official *Reports* of his first two expeditions, was undoubtedly prompted by economic necessity, a book recounting his daring and colorful achievements had long been envisioned. Theodore Talbot, about to set out in 1845 on the third expedition, wrote to his mother that "Capt. Frémont intends publishing his 3 reports, the two previous and the coming one, in one large and handsomely illustrated volume."[21] At one time, too, according to Mrs. Frémont, her husband and Senator Benton conceived a joint editorship of the letters written by, to, and about Frémont from 1842 to 1854, but many of the letters were burned in the fire that destroyed Benton's home in February 1855.[22]

Frémont had long been conscious of Baron Alexander von Humboldt's wish for "truth in representing nature," and as early as 1842 had attempted to record his explorations photographically. On both the first and second expeditions he had carried daguerreotype cameras, and though he was unable to use them successfully they do represent the first instances of the employment of a camera on western expeditions sent out by the government. Edward M. Kern accompanied the third expedition as an artist and on the fifth Solomon Nunes Carvalho, an authority in the whole field of photography and daguerreotyping, spent hours making "views." Carvalho's plates survived the storms of the Sierras and the perils of an ocean voyage and were brought back by Frémont to New York, where Mathew Brady was engaged to copy them by the wet process so that paper prints could be made. The paper prints, in turn, were used as copy by artists and engravers in preparing plates to illustrate Frémont's proposed book; for he now entered into a contract with George Childs of Philadelphia to bring out the journals of the various expeditions as a companion book of American travel to the Arctic journeys of Dr. Elisha Kent Kane, then being published so profitably by the same house. The campaign of 1856 interrupted the work.[23]

Soon after the election, work on the proposed book was begun again, and Jessie wrote Elizabeth Blair Lee: "Say to your Father that the election looks ages back now that we are so interested in the book and if he could see the beautiful pictures that are growing under Mr. [James] Hamilton's brush he would like us turn his back on the 'busy world' & fly to the mountains on canvas." In April she wrote Mrs. Lee, "The book grows finely—not the text yet but the illustrations and all the preparatory work." And in May, Mrs. Blair re-

---

[21] Theodore Talbot to Adelaide Talbot [St. Louis], 30 May 1845 (DLC—Talbot Papers).

[22] Jessie B. Frémont to R. [U.?] Johnson, Los Angeles, 28 Aug. 1890 (James S. Copley Collection, La Jolla, Calif.).

[23] MEMOIRS, xvi.

ceived the following note: "We are at work on the book which is our baby and pet—the summer plans are not fairly fixed as yet, we keep this house by the month for the convenience of having the artists work under Mr. Frémont's supervision. They have Lizzie's former bedroom & have made a grand collection of oily rags and bad smelling bottles and paints but the results are beautiful. Frank & Mr. Frémont grow young together over imaginary buffalo hunts located in certain valleys which look out upon them like nature from the canvas."

On the same day in May she wrote Lizzie Lee, "All the astronomical & tedious part of the work is now finished as far as Mr. Frémont goes into it." A bit later she wrote, "Jacob [presumably Jacob Dodson, the Negro who had been JCF's servant on the 1845 expedition] came on with me & I have had my pen in hand as much as five hours & a half at a time—We finish with him today—that much work is done."[24]

But the writing was interrupted by Frémont's going to California and Jessie to Europe. After the return of both in the late fall of 1857, another attempt was made at writing, but soon all the Frémonts were packing for California and the Mariposa. And while Jessie hoped "that Mr. Frémont will write as well as direct his work there," the book was not finished, the contract was canceled, and George Childs had to be reimbursed for all the expenditures he had made. The Civil War and the business schemes following it gave no leisure for writing.[25]

---

[24] See letters of Jessie B. Frémont to Elizabeth Blair Lee, Thursday night [1857?], 7 April 1857, 4 May [1857?], 2 [June?] 1857, and to Mrs. Blair, 4 May 1857, all in NjP—Blair-Lee Papers.

[25] Jessie B. Frémont to Elizabeth Blair Lee, 15 Dec. [1857?]. JCF gave George Childs notes as a guaranty that he would be paid for the expenditures on the book, and on 9 Feb. 1864 Childs sought the aid of Maj. Simon Stevens to obtain an early settlement of the notes. Childs wrote, "I hope you are arranging the Frémont matter so that I can surely get the balance next week. Impress upon the General that it is of *vital importance* for me to have the amount this month" (PPAmP). Childs eventually sold the notes to Drexels (see George W. Childs to [Simon Stevens], Philadelphia, 20 Jan. 1865, NHi). So common was the knowledge that Frémont was preparing a book that Gouverneur Warren, in his *Memoir to Accompany the Map of the Territory of the United States from the Mississippi River to the Pacific Ocean,* at p. 50 noted: "In press [1859] Colonel J. C. Frémont's Explorations, prepared by the author, and embracing all his expeditions. —Childs & Peterson, publishers, No. 602 Arch Street, Philadelphia."

Jessie Benton Frémont, from the portrait by T. Buchanan Read
Courtesy of the Southwest Museum

When the Frémonts left for Arizona in 1878, the boxes containing materials for the books were placed in safes below the pavement at Morrell's and were thus saved when fire destroyed that warehouse and the many other Frémont treasures stored in it. In 1886, perhaps inspired by the success of General Grant's *Personal Memoirs,* work was resumed. The Frémonts took a house in Washington so that Mrs. Frémont could use the facilities of the Library of Congress, and her daughter Lily typed copy. Fire at the publishers, Belford and Clark and Co., once more threatened the book, but the plates were not destroyed and publication was delayed only a few weeks. Commercially the work was a disappointment, but after Frémont's death, Jessie—with the aid of her son Frank—continued what she hoped would constitute the second volume of the *Memoirs.* She wrote Mrs. George Browne, "I have such fine offers, which will complete the General's work, make money for Lil and give me a living object."[26]

Such is the long history of the making of the *Memoirs.*

In many ways, an edition of Frémont's papers is not a documentation of the man, but rather of the events in which he participated. Occasionally we draw from the journals and letters of other participants in these events. The disastrous fourth expedition of 1848, for example, could not be thoroughly presented in any other fashion. And the letters of Jessie Benton Frémont are often more important than those of her husband in illuminating the Frémont legend. Indeed it may be said that because so many of Frémont's letters were composed and set to paper by Jessie, the documentary history of these two persons is but a single subject of study.

ON THE ANNOTATION OF BOTANICAL MATTERS

The historical editor is taxed to make a meaningful contribution to the botanical aspects of an expedition. He cannot tell the systematic botanist anything—indeed, must turn to him for counsel—and can give little aid to the untrained reader. As a minimum, he can attempt to give a recent scientific name, and perhaps a commonly accepted colloquial name, to the plants enumerated in the text.

---

[26] Jessie Benton Frémont to Nell, Los Angeles, 27 Jan. 1891 (CU-B—Frémont Papers).

Even this modest assignment becomes difficult. Taxonomists are continually producing new combinations, referring plants to new genera, with the result that many possibilities confront the editor who is looking for the "correct" modern designation. The task is made harder by the fact that collectors of an earlier day, and even the scientists who analyzed their findings, followed no stabilized pattern. "For want of anything better the men in the field employed descriptive phrases or had recourse to colloquial names; misapplied the Latin names of plants with which they were familiar to others which to them appeared to be the same; employed Latin epithets (at times misspelled) which subsequently, because of priority or other rulings, came to be regarded as synonyms" (MC KELVEY, 1097).

After bringing our own mediocre botanical knowledge to bear on JCF's narrative, we turned for expert counsel to Professor Joseph Ewan, Tulane University, and his able research assistant, Nesta Dunn Ewan. These two were able to solve many of the problems that had puzzled us, and our gratitude to them is sincere and substantial. Because we turned to them while they were researching at the Royal Botanic Gardens, Kew, England, far from such resources as were available for the writing of Professor Ewan's *Rocky Mountain Naturalists* (Denver, Colo., 1950), and other works on American botany, our request was all the more inconvenient.

When JCF's mention of a plant by common or scientific name is in virtually modern terminology, we let it stand without augmentation. When a brief identification, either in brackets or in a note, will keep the narrative going without undue intrusion, we use that device. And when a matter requires special comment, a somewhat longer note is used. Our chief botanical aid, however, is the index. Here we have placed every significant mention of a plant, by binomial or common name, followed by the accepted modern equivalent. Thus, when both JCF's narrative and our running annotation fails the reader, he may try the index.

Vernacular names are given to species when such are available, but frequently the common name of the genus has necessarily been substituted. Plants in the montane area, especially, may have no specific common names, and such generic names as aster, ragwort, and goldenrod prevail.

EDITORIAL PROCEDURES

The Documents

The original text is followed as closely as the demands of typography will permit, with several departures based on common sense and the current practice of scholars. In the matter of capitalization the original is followed, unless the writer's intention is not clear, in which case we resort to modern practice. Occasionally in the interests of clarity, a long, involved sentence, usually penned or dictated by a bare literate, is broken into two sentences. Missing periods at the ends of sentences are supplied, dashes terminating sentences are supplanted by periods, and superfluous dashes after periods are omitted. In abbreviations, raised letters are brought down and a period supplied if modern usage calls for one. Words underscored in manuscripts are italicized. The complimentary closing is run in with the preceding paragraph, and a comma is used if no other end punctuation is present. The acute accent mark on the *e* in Frémont is supplied when it appears in the document and omitted where it does not appear, but it is used in all of our own headings and references to Frémont, even in the pre-1838 period. It was probably Frémont's association with the French scientist, Joseph N. Nicollet, that brought the accented *e* to the signature. Procedures for dealing with missing or illegible words, conjectural readings, etc. are shown in the list of symbols, pp. xliii–xliv. When in doubt as to how to proceed in a trivial matter, modern practice is silently followed; if the question is more important, the situation is explained in a note.

When a related document or letter is used, that is, not one directly to or from Frémont, extraneous portions are deleted and the deletion is indicated by a symbol. If a manuscript contains only a brief reference to the pertinent subject, we are more likely to quote the passage in a note to some related letter than to print it as a separate document.

Because Jessie B. Frémont wrote and signed so many of her husband's letters, we have felt that there should be some indication of this to the reader. Our solution to the problem is set forth in the list of symbols.

The Notes

The first manuscript indicated is the one from which the transcription has been made; other copies, if known, are listed next. If endorsements or addresses are routine, their presence is merely noted, but if they contribute useful information, they are quoted in full. For example, see the endorsement on Frémont's application for a mountain howitzer for his third expedition, Vol. 1, Doc. No. 130.

Material taken from printed texts is so indicated (printed, LARKIN, 4:239–41), but no attempt is made to record other printed versions.

Senders, receivers, and persons referred to in the manuscripts are briefly identified at first mention. For senders and receivers, this identification is made in the first paragraph of the notes and no reference number is used. The reader can easily find the identification of an individual by locating in the index the page on which he is first mentioned.

No source is cited for the kind of biographical information to be found in standard directories, genealogies, and similar aids.

Names of authors in SMALL CAPITALS are citations to sources listed in the bibliography on pp. 807–17. This device enables us to keep many long titles and other impedimenta out of the notes. In the case of two or more works by the same author, a number is assigned as in J. D. MC DERMOTT [1]. When a published work is being discussed, not merely cited, we often list it fully by author and title in the notes.

To avoid the constant repetition of the Frémont names, we have freely used the initials JCF and JBF for John Charles and Jessie.

Washington D.C. Sep.: 15th 1841

Dear Sir

Your esteemed favor of 11th Curr.t came safely to hand yesterday. I am quite glad to receive intelligence of the Box, respecting which I had begun to feel some anxiety — May I so far trespass on your kindness as to beg that you will have it sent to this place per Rail Road, accompanied by Charges. I hope you will excuse the trouble I sincerely regret giving & which I could not well avoid ——

It gives me pleasure to hear that Mr. Nicollet's health is improving so much — I trust that you are regaining yours as rapidly & with the warmest regards for Yourself remain

Very truly & respectfully
Yr Sir Yours
J. C. Fremont

Ramsay Crooks Esq.r
President Amer. fur C.o
New York

A letter by Frémont, in his handwriting

My dear Sir:

Among the plants, and not among those where it grew, was an unnumbered specimen of the tall cedar of the Californian Mts. Did you see it? Can you tell me if I may call it a cedar in popular writing? Six feet & over in diameter — 130 feet high — and the berries have very much a juniper flavor.

Yours Truly,
J. C. Frémont.

Monday morning
April 20th.

It may be some assistance to your memory to ~~suggest~~ that you called the plates I wrote to you of, last night, new species.

A letter by Frémont, in the handwriting of Jessie Benton Frémont

SYMBOLS

C	California State Library, Sacramento
CLSM	Southwest Museum, Los Angeles
CSmH	Henry E. Huntington Library, San Marino
CoU	University of Colorado, Boulder
CU-B	Bancroft Library, University of California, Berkeley
DLC	Library of Congress
GHi	Georgia Historical Society, Savannah
IU	University of Illinois, Urbana
KyLoF	Filson Club Library, Louisville, Ky.
KyU	University of Kentucky, Lexington
MeHi	Maine Historical Society, Portland
MnHi	Minnesota Historical Society, St. Paul
MH-G	Harvard University, Gray Herbarium Library, Cambridge, Mass.
MoSB	Missouri Botanical Garden Library, St. Louis
MoSHi	Missouri Historical Society, St. Louis
NcU	University of North Carolina, Chapel Hill
NHi	New York Historical Society Library, New York
NjP	Princeton University Library, Princeton, N.J.
NN	New York Public Library, New York
NNNBG	New York Botanical Garden, Bronx Park, New York
PHi	Historical Society of Pennsylvania, Philadelphia
PPAmP	American Philosophical Society, Philadelphia
Vi	Virginia State Library, Richmond

National Archives Record Groups

DNA-45	Naval Records Collection of the Office of Naval Records and Library

DNA-49	Records of the General Land Office
DNA-75	Records of the Bureau of Indian Affairs
DNA-77	Records of the Office of the Chief of Engineers
DNA-94	Records of the Adjutant General's Office
DNA-107	Records of the Office of the Secretary of War
DNA-156	Records of the Chief of Ordnance, War Department
DNA-217	Records of the United States General Accounting Office (T-135 denotes a collection of microfilm documents in this Record Group.)

Other Symbols and Editorial Aids

AD	Autograph document
ADS	Autograph document, signed
ADS-JBF	Autograph document, Frémont's name signed by Jessie
AL	Autograph letter
ALS	Autograph letter, signed
ALS-JBF	Autograph letter, Frémont's name signed by Jessie
D	Document
DS	Document, signed
DS-JBF	Document, Frémont's name signed by Jessie
JBF	Jessie Benton Frémont
JCF	John Charles Frémont
Lbk	Letterbook copy
LR	Letter received
LS	Letter sent
RC	Receiver's copy
RG	Record Group
SC	Sender's copy
[ ]	Word or phrase supplied or corrected. Editorial remarks within text are italicized and enclosed in square brackets.
[?]	Conjectural reading, or conjectural identification of an addressee.
[. . .]	A word or two missing or illegible. Longer omissions are specified in footnotes.
< >	Word or phrase deleted from manuscript, usually by sender. The words are set in italics.
. . . .	Unrelated matter deleted by the editor. The symbol stands alone, centered on a separate line.

Early Years
and the 1842 Expedition
to South Pass

1. J. J. Abert to Frémont

Bureau of Topogrl Engrs
Washington April 16th 1838.

Sir

I am authorized by the Hon. Secretary of War to inform you that you will be employed as a Civil Engineer under the law of 30th April 1824, and that you will be and are hereby assigned as an Assistant to J. N. Nicol[l]et, Esqre.[1]

Mr. Nicol[l]et is now on his way to St. Louis, Missouri. You will repair to that place without delay and report to him for orders. With the view of relieving him in his important duties from all unnecessary details, you will act as disbursing agent to the expedition, but you will make only such expenditures as he shall authorize. For this purpose a requisition for One Thousand dollars will be this day made in your favour. Additional funds will be supplied on your estimates and will be sent to such places as you shall indicate.

Enclosed is a copy of the regulations on the subject of accounts, and you will also receive herewith sets of blank vouchers and forms.

Your compensation will be four dollars per day, to commence this day, with an additional allowance of ten cents per mile for your travelling expenses. Respectfully,

J. J. Abert. Lt.Cl. Tl. Eng.

Lbk (DNA-77, LS, 2:512). John James Abert (1788–1863) had attended West Point, practiced law, made geodetic and topographic surveys in the eastern U.S., and was now chief of the Bureau of Topographical Engineers. Serving on this assignment from 1834 to 1861, he was to oversee most of the extensive surveys of the West during this period.

1. Joseph Nicolas Nicollet (1786–1843), French astronomer and geographer, had come to the U.S. from Paris in 1832 for the purpose of "making a scientific tour and with the view of contributing to the progressive increase of knowledge in the physical geography of North America" (NICOLLET, 3). He soon had established a reputation as a highly skilled and original scientist, enjoying the respect of such men as Ferdinand Rudolph Hassler, director of the new U.S. Coast and Geodetic Survey. By 1835 he had become interested in making the first accurate survey of the Mississippi River. He traveled widely —to New Orleans, St. Louis, and other cities of the Mississippi Valley—surveying and establishing stations to aid in the determination of altitudes. In 1836, he visited the headwaters of the Mississippi—the region around Lake Itasca in Minnesota—and did some preliminary mapping which was to culminate later in his important map, "Hydrographic Basin of the Upper Mississippi River."

Thus far, he had financed all his own work. Now, through the influence of Secretary of War Poinsett, the Bureau of Topographical Engineers was to pay for Nicollet's further expeditions and the preparation of the map. Nicollet documents in this volume are selected only to show the role of JCF in the expeditions of 1838 and 1839, and can do little to depict the scope of Nicollet's work. His map, but not his historic *Report Intended to Illustrate a Map of the Hydrographical Basin of the Upper Mississippi River,* is reproduced in this volume. He deserves his own biographer, or an editor who will annotate the *Report* and accompanying map as a contribution to the history of science in the U.S. For a paper summarizing his life and work, see "Joseph N. Nicollet, Geographer," by Martha Coleman Bray, in J. F. MC DERMOTT [1].

2. Excerpt from the *Memoirs*

[1838]

The Cherokee survey was over. I remained at home only just long enough to enjoy the pleasure of the return to it, and to rehabituate myself to old scenes. While I was trying to devise and settle upon some plan for the future, my unforgetful friend, Mr. Poinsett, had also been thinking for me. He was now Secretary of War, and, at his request, I was appointed by President [Martin] Van Buren a second lieutenant[1] in the United States Topographical Corps, and ordered to Washington. Washington was greatly different then from the beautiful capital of to-day. Instead of many broad, well-paved, and leafy avenues, Pennsylvania Avenue about represented the town. There were not the usual resources of public amusement. It was a lonesome place for a young man knowing but one person in the city, and there was no such attractive spot as the Battery by

4

the sea at Charleston, where a stranger could go and feel the freedom of both eye and thought.

Shut in to narrow limits, the mind is driven in upon itself and loses its elasticity; but the breast expands when, upon some hill-top, the eye ranges over a broad expanse of country, or in face of the ocean. We do not value enough the effect of space for the eye; it reacts on the mind, which unconsciously expands to larger limits and freer range of thought. So I was low in my mind and lonesome until I learned, with great relief, that I was to go upon a distant survey into the West. But that first impression of flattened lonesomeness which Washington had given me has remained with me to this day.

About this time, a distinguished French savant had returned from a geographical exploration of the country about the sources of the Mississippi, the position of which he first established. That region and its capabilities were then but little known, and the results of his journey were of so interesting a nature that they had attracted public notice and comment. Through Mr. Poinsett, Mr. Nicollet was invited to come to Washington, with the object of engaging him to make a complete examination of the great prairie region between the Mississippi and Missouri Rivers, as far north as the British line, and to embody the whole of his labors in a map and general report for public use.

Mr. Nicollet had left France, intending to spend five years in geographical researches in this country. His mind had been drawn to the early discoveries of his countrymen, some of which were being obliterated and others obscured in the lapse of time. He anticipated great pleasure in renewing the memory of these journeys, and in rescuing them all from the obscurity into which they had fallen. A member of the French Academy of Sciences, he was a distinguished man in the circles to which Arago and other savants of equal rank belonged.[2] Not only had he been trained in science, but he was habitually schooled to the social observances which make daily intercourse attractive, and become invaluable where hardships are to be mutually borne and difficulties overcome and hazards met. His mind was of the higher order. A musician as well as a mathematician, it was harmonious and complete.

The Government now arranged with him to extend his surveys south and west of the country which he had already explored. Upon this survey I was ordered to accompany him as his assistant.

5

It was a great pleasure to me to be assigned to this duty. By this time I had gone through some world-schooling and was able to take a sober view of the realities of life. I had learned to appreciate fully the rare value of the friendly aid which had opened up for me such congenial employment, and I resolved that, if it were in me to do so, I would prove myself worthy of it. The years of healthy exercise which I had spent in open air had hardened my body, and the work I had been engaged in was kindred to that which I was now to have. Field work in a strange region, in association with a man so distinguished, was truly an unexpected good fortune, and I went off from Washington full of agreeable anticipation.

At St. Louis I joined Mr. Nicollet.[3] This was the last large city on the western border, and the fitting-out place for expeditions over the uninhabited country. The small towns along the western bank of the Missouri made for two or three hundred miles a sort of fringe to the prairies. At St. Louis I met for the first time General Robert E. Lee, then a captain in the United States Engineer Corps, charged with improvements of the Mississippi River.[4] He was already an interesting man. His agreeable, friendly manner to me as a younger officer when I was introduced to him, left a more enduring impression than usually goes with casual introductions.

In St. Louis Mr. Nicollet had a pleasant circle of friends among the old French residents. They were proud of him as a distinguished countryman, and were gratified with his employment by the American Government, which in this way recognized his distinction and capacity. His intention, in the prosecution of his larger work to revive the credit due to early French discoverers, was pleasing to their national pride.

His acquaintances he made mine, and I had the pleasure and advantage to share in the amiable intercourse and profuse hospitality which in those days characterized the society of the place. He was a Catholic, and his distinction, together with his refined character, made him always a welcome guest with his clergy. And I may say in the full sense of the word, that I "assisted" often at the agreeable suppers in the refectory. The pleasure of these grew in remembrance afterward, when hard and scanty fare and sometimes starvation and consequent bodily weakness made visions in the mind, and hunger made memory dwell upon them by day and dream of them by night.

Such social evenings followed almost invariably the end of the day's preparations. These were soon now brought to a close with the kindly and efficient aid of the Fur Company's[5] officers. Their personal experience made them know exactly what was needed on the proposed voyage, and both stores and men were selected by them; the men out of those in their own employ. These were principally practised *voyageurs,* accustomed to the experiences and incidental privations of travel in the Indian country.

The aid given by the house of Chouteau was, to this and succeeding expeditions, an advantage which followed them throughout their course to their various posts among the Indian tribes.

Our destination now was a trading post on the west bank of the Mississippi, at the mouth of the St. Peter's, now better known as the Minisotah River. This was the residence of Mr. Henry Sibley,[6] who was in charge of the Fur Company's interests in the Mississippi Valley. He gave us a frontier welcome[7] and heartily made his house our headquarters. This was the point of departure at which the expedition began its work. It was on the border line of civilization. On the left or eastern bank of the river were villages and settlements of the whites, and the right was the Indian country which we were about to visit. Fort Snelling was on the high bluff point opposite between the Mini-sotah and the Mississippi. Near by was a Sioux Indian village, and usually its Indians were about the house grounds. Among these I saw the most beautiful Indian girl I have ever met, and it is a tribute to her singular beauty that after so many years I remember still the name of "Ampetu-washtoy"—"the Beautiful day."

The house had much the character of a hunting-lodge. There were many dogs around about, and two large wolfhounds, Lion and Tiger, had the run of the house and their quarters in it. Mr. Sibley was living alone, and these fine dogs made him friendly companions, as he belonged to the men who love dogs and horses. For his other dogs he had built within the enclosure a lookout about fifteen feet high. Around its platform the railing was usually bordered with the heads of dogs resting on their paws and looking wistfully out over the prairie, probably reconnoitering for wolves. Of the two hounds Tiger had betrayed a temper of such ferocity, even against his master, as eventually cost him his life. Lion, though a brother, had, on the contrary, a companionable and affectionate disposition and almost human intelligence, which in his case brought about a separation from his old home.

7

On the marriage of Mr. Sibley, Lion so far resented the loss of his first place that he left the house, swam across the Mississippi, and went to the Fort, where he ended his days. Always he was glad to meet his master when he came over, keeping close by him and following him to the shore, though all persuasion failed to make him ever recross the river to the home where he had been supplanted; but his life-size portrait still hangs over the fireplace of Mr. Sibley's library. These dogs were of the rare breed of the Irish wolfhound, and their story came up as an incident in a correspondence, stretching from Scotland to Mini-sotah, on the question as to whether it had not become extinct; growing out of my happening to own a dog inheriting much of that strain.

Cut off from the usual resources, Mr. Sibley had naturally to find his in the surroundings. The prominent feature of Indian life entered into his, and hunting became rather an occupation than an amusement. But his hunting was not the tramp of a day to some neighboring lake for wild fowl, or a ride on the prairie to get a stray shot at a wolf. These hunting expeditions involved days' journeys to unfrequented ranges where large game was abundant, or in winter to the neighborhood of one of his trading-posts, where in event of rough weather the stormy days could be passed in shelter. He was fully six feet in height, well and strongly built, and this, together with his skill as a hunter, gave him a hold on the admiration and respect of the Indians.

In all this stir of frontier life Mr. Nicollet felt no interest and took no share; horse and dog were nothing to him. His manner of life had never brought him into their companionship, and the congenial work he now had in charge engrossed his attention and excited his imagination. His mind dwelt continually upon the geography of the country, the Indian names of lakes and rivers and their signification, and upon whatever tradition might retain of former travels by early French explorers.

Some weeks had now been spent in completing that part of the outfit which had been referred to this place. The intervening time had been used to rate the chronometers and make necessary observations of the latitude and longitude of our starting-point.

MEMOIRS, 30–34. For a discussion of the *Memoirs* and how they came to be written, see the introduction, pp. xxxii–xxxvi. Since much of that work is a duplication of other JCF publications, such as FREMONT [2] and FREMONT [3], the *Memoirs* will not appear intact in the present series. Only extracts will be used, as above, where other documents do not provide continuity.

1. Although JCF was first employed as a civilian (see Doc. No. 1), his appointment as second lieutenant in the Corps of Topographical Engineers came soon—on 7 July 1838—and his letter of acceptance was written 1 Jan. 1839. See DNA-94, 5309 ACP 1879 John C. Fremont.

2. Nicollet was not a member of the French Academy of Sciences, and Dominique François Arago (1786–1853) had helped to block his election (ARAGO, 194). Arago was an astronomer who eventually became secretary of the academy.

3. In a letter of 17 May 1838, registered in the bureau but not found, JCF reported his arrival in St. Louis. He was warmly welcomed by Nicollet, who had been worrying lest he not arrive in time to serve the expedition as disbursing officer. This apprehension had prompted Nicollet to seek the advice of Capt. Ethan Allen Hitchcock on the keeping of records (Hitchcock to Nicollet, 15 May 1838, DLC—Nicollet Papers).

4. Superintending the improvement of St. Louis harbor, and of the Missouri and Upper Mississippi rivers, was the first important independent Army assignment of Robert E. Lee (1807–70). He was particularly concerned with such obstructions to navigation as the rapids near the mouth of the Des Moines, and near Rock Island, Ill.

5. Because the Chouteau enterprises will appear frequently in this and ensuing volumes, a brief outline of their various forms seems desirable. The public called it the American Fur Company, though legally speaking the business was known after 1838 as P. Chouteau, Jr., and Company. SUNDER nicely avoids confusion by calling it Chouteau's American Fur Company.

In 1826, an alliance had been formed between John Jacob Astor's great American Fur Company, and Bernard Pratte and Company, of St. Louis, under which the management of the affairs of the Western Department of the American Fur Company were placed in Pratte's hands. Upon Astor's retirement in 1834, the Western Department was purchased by the St. Louis house —which now called itself Pratte, Chouteau and Company. The Northern Department, retaining the name of the American Fur Company, was sold to a company of which merchant and fur trader Ramsay Crooks was the principal partner.

In St. Louis in 1838, Pratte dropped from active participation in the company, and the name, in becoming P. Chouteau, Jr., and Company, merely reflected the power and the business and financial acumen of the leading shareholder, Pierre Chouteau, Jr. (1789–1865). In 1843, Crooks relinquished the Minnesota trade and Chouteau picked it up. In this manner the company built a trading area which came to extend over an immense territory, embracing the whole country watered by the Upper Mississippi and Missouri rivers, as well as the tributaries of the latter (CHITTENDEN, 1:322, 364, 366; SUNDER, 3–17).

6. Henry Hastings Sibley (1811–91) was associated with Ramsay Crooks in the Northern Department of the American Fur Company, and would later become a partner with Chouteau. He was to have a long and notable career in business and politics, becoming Minnesota's first territorial delegate and state governor (SIBLEY [2] and JORSTAD).

7. Indian agent Lawrence Taliaferro noted in his journal that the steamer *Burlington* arrived at Fort Snelling 25 May 1838 with the Nicollet party (MnHi).

9

3. Frémont to Mrs. Ann B. Hale

ST. PETERS upper Mississip
June 6th '38

We shall leave this place, Dear Mother, on Saturday morning, on an expedition up the river St. Peters & shall not return here under 3 months. During that period you will receive no news from me as there is no post communication whatever, after leaving this place. You must however answer this and write also from time to time as there is a possibility of our returning sooner & at all events I shall be glad to find letters here when we do return. I have requested the Post Master of St. Louis to forward to Charleston any letters wh. may reach his office to my address. I do this in order that you may receive Capt. [William G.] Williams letter of information relative to the deposit [in] the Bank of the Metropolis at Washington. I shall write to him (the Captain) to-day a request that he will [. . .] the advice to my address in Charleston so that you will be sure to receive the necessary information. Enclosed I send you my signature to a blank & I suppose you will take Mr. McCrady's[1] advice respecting the manner of obtaining the deposit. I had a letter recently from the gentleman who is to deposit with Capt. Williams the amt. of $60.00. The other amt. of $146.14, I presume the Capt. has already deposited. Write particularly to me on this subject. In writing to me the best plan will be to put simply my name on the letter without direction & enclose it or them in an envelope to Mr. Poinsett with a request that he will forward them. Get Mr. McCrady to do this for you. This method was recommended to Mr. Nicollet by the Department as the proper method for letters to reach us. I like Mr. Nicollet very much though he is inclined to spare neither himself nor us as regards labor, he yet takes every means to make us comfortable. He is a real Frenchman in this & you know exactly what they are. He has provided a nice little store of Coffee, Chocolate, Tea, prepared Soup &c in addition to the more substantial articles of food. He has got a store of medicine too & makes me take some pills occasionally. As far as regards Science I am improving under him daily & my health under the influence of this delicious climate has become excellent. In addition to myself Mr. N. has with him on his own account a young gentleman of N.Y. whose name is Flandin & a German Botanist, a Mr. Geyer,[2] both very amiable & agreeable. We journey up this river in a large boat manned with 9 men. As soon as we reach the point at which we leave the river, we put ourselves, provisions, instruments, tents &c into wagons & with our company of 13 in all, take to the prairies. I anticipate an interesting & delightful expedition. In the mean time I trust you are enjoying good health & will make yourself happy until we meet again. Is Frank[3] with you? If he is make him & his wife both put something in your letter to me. I wd. like them to write separate letters, but I don't like to send too large a package to Mr. P. Give my love to all our friends but particularly to Lane. Tell her if [she] sees or communicates with Mr. Poinsett to tell him not to forget to put me in the Topl. Corps. I must stop now & leave room for blanks.

Yr. Affectionate Son—Ch.

Copy, reproduced from a typescript in MnHi; original not available. Endorsed, "Fort Snelling June 9 [?]"; addressed, "Mrs. Ann B. Hale Care of Edwd. McCrady Esqr. Charleston S. Carolina." JCF's mother had remarried, but no information concerning her third husband or the date of the marriage has come to hand. In 1844, Jessie Benton Frémont refers to her as a widow— all alone except for her son. Certainly no husband was present at her burial on 20 Sept. 1847, and JCF took the body to Charleston for interment. See St. Thaddeus' Church [Aiken, S.C.], church record book for 1847, p. 379, and the diary or journal of the Rev. John Hamilton Cornish, Southern Historical Collection, NcU.

1. Though Edward McCrady (1802–92) was some eleven years older than the explorer, JCF claimed him as a friend and named a stream in California and Oregon after him (MEMOIRS, 483). McCrady was appointed U.S. district attorney for the Charleston area in 1839, at the request of Joel R. Poinsett. In 1856, politics and the publication of an old private letter brought a rift in the friendship (see Jessie's manuscript, "Great Events during the Life of Major General John C. Frémont," CU-B).

2. J. Eugene Flandin was a youth of nineteen, the son of New York merchant Pierre Flandin. After serving with Nicollet on this expedition he returned to New York to visit his family with the idea of going out again with Nicollet in 1839, but he only went as far as St. Louis (see Doc. No. 20). However, his association with Frémont lasted for several years; the New York Times, 19 Feb. 1852, reported that he had engineered the sale of JCF's Mariposa estate to Thomas Denny Sargent for a million dollars. Charles A. Geyer (1809–53) had come from Dresden in 1834 to explore the plant life of North America. He had met Nicollet at St. Louis after an expedition up the Missouri, and was asked to accompany him on both the 1838 and 1839 ventures. Although he lost his principal collection of plants, Nicollet's Report does contain Geyer's list of plants as edited by botanist John Torrey. See also NUTE, DRURY [1], and MC KELVEY.

3. Frank is JCF's younger brother. He left home at fifteen to pursue a career on the stage, but several years later an injury received during a riot in Buffalo, N.Y., forced him to return to his mother in Charleston. He died

in 1840 or 1841, before the birth of his daughter Nina, who became JCF's ward (BIGELOW, 29; MEMOIRS, 56; E. B. FRÉMONT, 62, 106, 182). The girl named Lane, mentioned a few lines later, is unidentified.

4. Frémont to Joel R. Poinsett

ST. PETERS, Upper Mississippi
8 June 1838

DEAR SIR

Our preparations are at last entirely completed & tomorrow we follow the steps of the Pilgrim of Science into the Prairie Wilderness. I can scarcely tell you how delighted I am in having been placed under him in this Expedition. Every day—almost every hour I feel myself sensibly advancing in professional knowledge & the confused ideas of Science & Philosophy wh my mind has been occupied are momently arranging themselves into order & clearness. I admire Mr. Nicollet very much, not only for his extraordinary & highly cultivated capacity, but for his delightful manner—his delicacy & his almost extravagant enthusiasm in the object of his present enterprise wh he seems to think the sole object of his existence. The unsettled & excited state of the Indians has been the cause of great difficulty in procuring men: even old voyageurs & hunters being at this time afraid to venture among them. Mr. Nicollet's good management however & his intimate acquaintance with the character of the people have overcome all difficulties & I have found new occasion to admire him for the rigid economy at which these arrangements have been made. Every instant of our time has however been occupied in astronomical & Geological observations—so closely indeed that we have scarcely been able to avail ourselves of the kind hospitality & attentions of the Garrison at Fort Snelling & at this moment I write in the haste of a stolen interval. Mr. Nicollet I am aware has made you acquainted with all details connected with the expedition & I can add, I presume, nothing to what Mr. Taliaferro[1] & others have communicated to you relative to the Indians. Our party, tho' small, is well armed, at least sufficiently so to secure us in the event of an accidental rencontre & Mr. Nicollet's knowledge of the Indians justifies us in believing that we shall meet with no serious difficulty. Everything wh could facilitate our business & all manner of kindnesses have been offered to us by Mr. H.H. Sibley, one of the Partners of the American N.W. Fur Comp., residing at this place.[2] We are living with him & shall probably do so whenever we chance to be at this place in the intervals of our excursions. He has been obliged to withdraw several of his posts on account of the bad conduct of the Indians. At Lake Travers, one of the Posts withdrawn, one of his clerks has been killed, another wounded & numbers of horses & cattle destroyed.

I hope that your health has been by this time thoroughly restored. In company wh Capt. Williams I called on you when at Washington, but you had not yet sufficiently recovered to receive visits, which I extremely regretted. I was anxious among other things to tell you of the extreme solicitude wh your illness had excited throughout the South—it must have been extremely gratifying to you. I certainly think that this delightful [. . .] be extremely beneficial to you. Will you have the kindness to present my regards to Mrs. Poinsett? I shall find something in this country to add to her collection & I will certainly allow myself the pleasure of bringing them to her on my return. I am, most Respectfully, Dear Sir, yr obt Servt.

C. Fremont

ALS, RC (PHi—Poinsett Papers). Addressed from "Fort Snelling June 19" to "Hon. Joel R. Poinsett. Secretary of War. Washington City D.C."
1. Lawrence Taliaferro (1794–1871), the Indian agent at St. Peters (Fort Snelling), spent many years trying to keep peace between the Sioux and their traditional enemies, the Chippewas. He left the agency in 1840.
2. It was Sibley who procured the *voyageurs* for Nicollet and became responsible as agent of the American Fur Company for their reimbursement (see Memo. of Agreement between H. H. Sibley and certain *voyageurs*, [June 1838], MnHi, and our Doc. No. 13, voucher no. 8).

5. Excerpt from the *Memoirs*

[1838]

At length we set out.[1] As our journey was to be over level and unbroken country the camp material was carried in one-horse carts, driven by Canadian voyageurs, the men usually employed by the Fur Company in their business through this region. M. de Montmort,[2] a French gentleman attached to the legation at Washington, and Mr. Eugene Flandin, a young gentleman belonging to a French family of New York, accompanied the party as friends of Mr. Nicollet. These were pleasant travelling companions, and both looked up to Mr. Nicollet with affectionate deference and admiration. No botanist had been allowed to Mr. Nicollet by the Government, but he had for himself employed Mr. Charles Geyer, a botanist recently from Germany, of unusual practical knowledge in his profession and of companionable disposition.

The proposed surveys of this northwestern region naturally divided themselves into two: the present one, at this point connecting with Mr. Nicollet's surveys of the upper Mississippi, was to extend westward to the waters of the Missouri Valley; the other, intended for the operations of the succeeding year, was to include the valley of the Missouri River, and the northwestern prairies as far as to the British line.

Our route lay up the Mini-sotah for about a hundred and fifteen miles, to a trading-post at the lower end of the *Traverse des Sioux;* the prairie and river valley being all beautiful and fertile country. We travelled along the southern side of the river, passing on the way several Indian camps, and establishing at night the course of the river by astronomical observations. The *Traverse des Sioux* is a crossing-place about thirty miles long, where the river makes a large rectangular bend, coming down from the northwest and turning abruptly to the northeast; the streams from the southeast, the south, and southwest flowing into a low line of depression to where they gather into a knot at the head of this bend, and into its lowest part as into a bowl. In this great elbow of the river is the Marah-tanka or Big Swan Lake, the summer resort of the Sissiton Sioux. Our way over the crossing lay between the lake and the river. At the end of the *Traverse* we returned to the right shore at the mouth of the Waraju or Cottonwood River, and encamped near the principal village of the Sissitons. Their lodges were pitched in a beautiful situation, under large trees. It needs only the slightest incident to throw an Indian village into a sudden excitement which is startling to a stranger. We are occupied quietly among the Indians, Mr. Nicollet, as usual, surrounded by them, with the aid of the interpreter getting them to lay out the form of the lake and the course of the streams entering the river near by, and, after repeated pronunciations, entering their names in his note-book; Geyer, followed by some Indians, curiously watching him while digging up plants; and I, more numerously attended, pouring out the quicksilver for the artificial horizon, each in his way busy at work; when suddenly everything started into motion, the Indians running tumultuously to a little rise which commanded a view of the prairie, all clamor and excitement. The commotion was caused by the appearance of two or three elk on the prairie horizon. Those of us who were strangers, and ignorant of their usages, fancied there must be at least a war-party in sight.

From this point we travelled up the Waraju River and passed a few days in mapping the country around the Pelican Lakes, and among the lower spurs of the *Coteau des Prairies,* a plateau which separates the waters of the Mississippi and Missouri Rivers. This is the single elevation separating the prairies of the two rivers. Approaching it, the blue line which it presents, marked by wooded ravines in contrast with the green prairie which sweeps to its feet, suggested to the *voyageurs* the name they gave it, of the Prairie Coast. At this elevation, about fifteen hundred feet above the sea, the prairie air was invigorating, the country studded with frequent lakes was beautiful, and the repose of a few days was refreshing to men and animals after the warmer and moister air of the lower valley. Throughout this region, the rivers and lakes, and other noticeable features of the country, bear French and Indian names, Sioux or Chippewa, and sometimes Shayan [Cheyenne]. Sometimes they perpetuate the memory of an early French discoverer, or rest upon some distinguishing local character of stream or lake; and sometimes they record a simple incident of chase or war which in their limited history were events.

We now headed for our main object in this direction, the Red Pipe Stone Quarry, which was to be the limit of our western travel; from there we were to turn directly north. All this country had been a battle-ground between the Sioux and Sacs and Foxes. Crossing the high plains over which our journey now lay, we became aware that we were followed by a party of Indians. Guard at night was necessary. But it was no light thing, after a day's work of sketching the country, to stand guard the night through, as it now fell to me among others to do. When we would make the noon halt I promptly took my share of it under the shade of a cart in deep sleep, which the fragrant breeze of the prairie made delightful.

Our exaggerated precautions proved useless, as the suspected hostile party were only friendly Sioux who, knowing nothing about us, were on their side cautiously watching us.

The Indians have a belief that the Spirit of the Red Pipe Stone speaks in thunder and lightning whenever a visit is made to the Quarry. With a singular coincidence such a storm broke upon us as we reached it, and the confirmation of the legend was pleasing to young Renville[3] and the Sioux who had accompanied us.

As we came into the valley the storm broke away in a glow of sunshine on the line of red bluff which extended for about three miles. The day after our arrival the party of Indians we had been watching came in. We spent three friendly days together; they were after the red pipe stone, and we helped them, by using gunpowder, to uncover the rock.

It was in itself a lovely place, made interesting by the mysterious character given to it by Indian tradition, and because of the fact that the existence of such a rock is not known anywhere else. It is on the land of the Sissiton Sioux, but the other Indians make to it annual pilgrimages, as it is from this they make their images and pipes. This famous stone, where we saw it, was in a layer about a foot and a half thick, overlaid by some twenty-six feet of red-colored indurated sand-rock; the color diminishing in intensity from the base to the summit. The water in the little valley had led the buffalo through it in their yearly migration from north to south, and the tradition is that their trail wore away the surface and uncovered the stone.

There was a detached pedestal standing out a few feet away from the bluff, and about twenty-five feet high. It was quite a feat to spring to this from the bluff, as the top was barely a foot square and uneven, and it required a sure foot not to go further. This was a famous place of the country, and nearly all of us, as is the custom in famous places the world over, carved our names in the stone. It speaks for the enduring quality of this rock that the names remain distinct to this day.

When the position had been established and other objects of the visit accomplished, we took up the northern line of march for the *Lac qui parle,* the trading-post and residence of the Renville family.

On our way we passed through and mapped the charming lake country of the *Coteau des Prairies.*

The head of the Renville family,[4] a French Canadian, was a border chief. Between him and the British line was an unoccupied region of some seven hundred miles. Over all the Indian tribes which ranged these plains he had a controlling influence; they obeyed himself and his son, who was a firm-looking man of decided character. Their good will was a passport over this country.

The hospitable reception which is the rule of the country met us here. I take pleasure in emphasizing and dwelling on this, because it is apart from the hospitality of civilized life. There is lively satisfaction on both sides. The advent of strangers in an isolated place brings novelty and excitement, and to the stranger arriving, there is great enjoyment in the change from privations and watchful unrest, to the quiet safety and profusion of plenty in such a frontier home. Our stay here was made very agreeable. We had abundance of milk and fresh meat and vegetables, all seasoned with a traveller's appetite and a hearty welcome.

To gratify us a game of Lacrosse was played with spirit and skill by the Indians. Among the players was a young half-breed of unusual height, who was incomparably the swiftest runner among them. He was a relation of the Renvilles and seemed to have some recognized family authority, for during the play he would seize an Indian by his long hair and hurl him backward to the ground to make room for himself, the other taking it as matter of course.

Some time was spent here in visiting the various lakes near by, fixing their position and gathering information concerning the character of the country and its Indians. This over, and the limit of the present journey attained, we turned our faces eastward and started back to the mouth of the St. Peter's.

While Mr. Nicollet was occupied in making a survey of the Lesueur River, and identifying localities and verifying accounts of preceding travellers, I was sent to make an examination of the Mankato or Blue Earth River, which bore upon the subjects he had in view. The eastern division of the expedition now closed with our return to Mr. Sibley's.

Among the episodes which gave a livelier coloring to the instructive part of this campaign, was a hunting expedition on which I went with Mr. Sibley.[5] With him also went M. Faribault,[6] a favorite companion of his on such occasions. It was a royal hunt. He took with him the whole of Red Dog's village—men, women, and children. The hunting-ground was a number of days' journey to the south, in Ioway, where game was abundant; many deer and some elk. It was in November, when the does are in their best condition. The country was well timbered and watered, stretches of prairie interspersed with clumps and lines of woods.

Early in the morning the chief would indicate the camping-ground for the night, and the men sally out for the hunt. The women, with the camp equipage, would then make direct for the spot pointed out, ordinarily some grove about nine miles distant. Toward nightfall the hunters came in with their game.

The day's tramp gave a lively interest to the principal feature which the camp presented; along the woods bright fires, where fat venison was roasting on sticks before them, or stewing with corn or wild rice in pots hanging from tripods; squaws busy over the cooking and children rolling about over the ground. No sleep is better or more restoring than follows such a dinner, earned by such a day.

On the march one day, a squaw dropped behind, but came into camp a little later than the others, bringing a child a few hours old. By circumstance of birth he should have become a mighty hunter, but long before he reached man's age he had lost birthright, he and his tribe, and I doubt if he got even the mess of pottage for which Esau bartered his. During the hunt we had the experience of a prairie fire. We were on a detached excursion, Sibley, Faribault and I. After midnight we were aroused from a sound sleep by the crackling noise, and springing to our feet, found ourselves surrounded, without a minute to lose. Gathering in our animals, we set fire to the grass near our tent, transferring quickly animals and baggage to the cleared ground. The fire swept past, and in a few seconds struck a grove of aspens near by and leaped up the trees, making a wall of flame that sent a red glow into the sky brighter even than the waves of fire that rolled over the prairie. We lost nothing, only tent and belongings a little blackened with the smouldering grass; but the harm was to the woods and the game.

The work of the year and in this quarter was now finished, and we returned to St. Louis, to prepare for the survey of the more western division in the succeeding year.

MEMOIRS, 34–38.

1. The route which JCF now describes took the expedition southwest from Fort Snelling, at present Minneapolis and St. Paul, Minn., along the Minnesota River to the vicinity of Mankato, then westward to the Cottonwood River near New Ulm. Ascending the Cottonwood and its tributaries, the party reached the Lake Shetek complex in Murray County—and one of the smaller

lakes in the group is now called Lake Fremont. After visiting the pipestone quarry at Pipestone, Minn., the expedition headed north toward Lac qui Parle. JCF says the party traveled due north over the high plains, but the map issued with Nicollet's *Report* shows the group swinging to the west as far as the Big Sioux River, then approaching Lac qui Parle from the west. From this point the route followed the Minnesota back down to Fort Snelling, except for a couple of diversions which JCF mentions.

2. The Count de Montmort was attached to the French legation in Washington until 1841. It is clear that he traveled with Nicollet during a part of this expedition, but he returned to Washington sometime in 1838. He did not go out again in the spring of 1839 (ALMANAC, 1840, 1841). Besides Flandin, there appears to have been still another French adventurer with the expedition. According to the vouchers for the 1838 expedition, a captain named Belligny traveled with the party for about forty days—paying his own way. It is not certain where Belligny joined Nicollet. In a letter of 2 July 1838, Frederick Gebhardt and Co. of New York introduced Gaspard de Belligny to Ramsay Crooks, saying he was from Lyons and wished to tour the U.S. and see the Indians, and asked for letters to Detroit and St. Louis for him. (AMER. FUR CO., 1: item 4721). Another letter, written 20 Aug. 1838 by Gabriel Franchère (MnHi—Sibley Papers) calls Belligny "a French gentleman who travels the country for his amusement and information." But by the time these letters were written the work of the expedition was well under way. There is no documentation for JCF's statement (p. 53) that Belligny was with the 1839 expedition.

3. Joseph Renville, Jr., son of Joseph Renville of Lac qui Parle, served as guide and interpreter to Nicollet. For his services and the use of Renville's wagons and horses he was given a horse and a $40.00 double-barreled gun (see voucher no. 14, our p. 40, and ACKERMANN).

4. Joseph Renville (1779–1846) had been in the Sioux country most of his life (his mother was a Sioux) and had served as an interpreter in 1805–6 when Zebulon Pike explored the Upper Mississippi. After serving as a British army captain in the War of 1812, he entered the service of the Hudson's Bay Company, then helped to organize the Columbia Fur Company. When his company was sold he moved to Lac qui Parle, built a trading post, and spent the rest of his life there (ACKERMANN; CHITTENDEN, 1:323–37).

5. The hunting expedition described here may not have occurred until 1839. Taliaferro saw JCF with the Nicollet party 28 Oct. 1838 bound for St. Louis, according to his journal (MnHi). On the other hand, Nicollet had to wait for JCF at Prairie du Chien the following autumn when, presumably, he was hunting with Sibley. Sibley himself says that he accompanied JCF to Prairie du Chien after the hunt—but he erroneously dates it 1840 (SIBLEY [3]). Although he does not mention Frémont in the letter he wrote to his father from Prairie du Chien on 5 Nov. 1839, Sibley does say he had just arrived in that river town from having conducted "a party of Sioux down to the Red Cedar River (a tributary of the Lower Iowa) on the west of the Mississippi on a hunting excursion" of one month (MnHi—Sibley Papers). He had come to Prairie du Chien to meet Ramsay Crooks, who incidentally arrived back in St. Louis in time to go east with Nicollet.

6. Alexander Faribault (1806–82) was long a prominent factor for the American Fur Company, established several trading posts in the Cannon River area, and founded the city of Faribault, Minn. He became a representative in the territorial legislature in 1851 (SIBLEY [2]; MINN. COLL., vol. 14).

6. Frémont to Henry H. Sibley

LAC QUI PARLE, Sioux Country
16 July '38

DEAR SIR

I avail myself of the opportunity offered by Mr. Browns departure this afternoon to acquaint you with the success of the expedition thus far & at the same time so express my regret that in our contemplated excursion to the Devil's Lake we cannot hope to enjoy the society of yourself, Capt. Scott, Marryatt &c. The chief of the Yanctons who has been waiting for us here & who accompanies us in a visit to Lac Travers & the Riviere a Jaques says that unless we are fond of walking it will not be wise to go to Lac du Diable at present. The Indians from the Missouri 460 Lodge of Tetons & 300 of the Yanctons are there at present—amounting as we are told to probably 4000 warriors, all with the old hate of the Americans & the small-pox. They will winter there so that it is not probable that Marryatt will give us next summer anything in [James Fenimore] Cooper's line, tho' I am sure that he has told you something of such a design. I would give much to know if you are determined to carry your plan into execution & go there in September. Mr. Nicollet they tell us cannot with any sort of prudence go now, tho' as we shall shortly be within 8 days journey of the Lake I should not be surprised if his anxiety to visit that section of the country induced him to attempt it. We will be somewhat emboldened too by the favorable circumstances which have hitherto attended us. Until yesterday we had not had two hours rain in all our journey skies without a cloud the nights delightfully cool & the thermometer sometimes as low as 45° + not an evening lost to astronomical observations. The scenery too was occasionally surpassingly beautiful—& I never tho' something of a Traveller had my love of the beautiful in nature more completely gratified than when we reached the Pelican group of Lakes. It is altogether of the character which the French term gracieux & I believe we have nothing so in our language to express it more justly—we afterwards met with Lake scenery more beautiful perhaps but with me none excited such emotions as the first. We have visited the pipe Quarry & I should have been satisfied if we had made the journey merely for the purpose of seeing it. I could compare it to nothing perhaps more justly than to the Ruins of some Porphyritic city standing on the verge of a desolate plain which had once been covered with luxuriant farms & splendid villas—we passed the 5 lodges without difficulty & are now quiet here but busily at work for a day or two. Mr. Nicollet begged me in writing for myself to write for him also, with his regards he sends you a Box of Sardines & part of a saucisson—the sardines I can assure you are really excellent & you must enjoy them. Will you have the kindness to present my regards to the Officers of the Garrison particularly to Major Plympton's & Lieut. Smith's families. Remember me if you please to the gentlemen of your family. We shall be with you about the 15th of next month. With much respect, Yours truly,

C. FREMONT

P.S. We find it hard that you sent us not even a word by Mr. Brown —not one word—all the party join in presenting their regards to you —you were too much occupied with [. . .] to think of us—excuse haste, etc.

ALS, RC (MnHi—Sibley Papers). Addressed to Sibley at St. Peters. Persons mentioned in this letter include Joseph Renshaw Brown (1805–70), a trader with the Sioux who had come to Minnesota as a boy with the troops that built Fort Snelling; Capt. Martin Scott (1788–1847), who was stationed at Fort Snelling from about 1821 to 1840 (WILLIAMS [2]); Capt. Frederick Marryat (1792–1848), British author who stopped for a brief time with Sibley when he visited the U.S. in 1837–38 and gave an account of his tour in *A Diary in America* (London, 1838); Maj. Joseph Plympton (d. 1860), the commandant at Fort Snelling, 1837–41; and Lieut. E. Kirby Smith, stationed there in 1837 and 1838.

7. Frémont to Joel R. Poinsett

ST. PETERS Wisconsin Territory
Sepr. 5th 1838—

DEAR SIR

I hasten to give you immediately on our arrival a brief account of our recent campaign. We have returned without having a single tale of danger or suffering to relate—no one sick no accident—we have not even starved a little & starvation is the most common accident in this country. On the contrary we are here in fine health & exuberant spirits & in the exultation of the most complete success. I should be glad to relate to you some of the many interesting incidents of our journey, but in the narrow limits of a letter it is impossible to do justice to any of the events wh. which every day was crowded. It seemed as if it were the will of Providence that the magnificent country we have traversed should no longer be without an inhabitant, so highly favored by circumstances that it seemed as if an invisible hand smoothed & prepared our way. Mr. Nicollet has several times suffered such an opinion to escape him, for mingled with his zeal for science & warmed by the enthusiasm characteristic of his countrymen, he cherishes the most exalted religious feeling. For 39 days out of a journey of 85, we travelled on without the loss of an hour & meeting wh. scarcely 2 hours rain—during the bright skies whose heat was tempered by winds like those from the sea sweeping over the prairies & cloudless nights, offering us every facility for our numerous astronomical observations. Told before our departure that dangers wd. beset every step, wh. gloomy accounts of hostile tribes whose country we were obliged to traverse—we were every where received with the warmest demonstrations of welcome & hospitality. On our arrival in the indian country proper, Mr. Nicollet sent a messenger to a formidable tribe which lay in our route, of his intention to pass thro' their country. With our messenger returned their chief, a man nearly 7 ft. in height & in proportion a study for a statuary. "I heard of your arrival," said he, "& tho' wounded I could not rest in my Lodge, but have flown to welcome you to our country. You are going to visit that country & where you go our enemies throng. I must go with you. My first wish is to die for the whites." You may be sure that his proffer of friendship was warmly met, but we told him how impossible it was for him to travel in such a state & at last induced him reluctantly to abandon his intention. "But I give you then my Son," said he,—"he is to me the dearest thing on earth, but my heart will be rejoiced if he dies fighting for the whites." "I will answer for his life with mine," said Mr. N. & I believe that each present formed a silent determination to bring back that indian or remain on the prairie wh him. We had a council on that evening, when Mr. N. explained to the indians the purpose of his coming among them. He was already known to them as the Great French Spirit. "I come, as you know, from the nation beyond the great Salt Lake whose chief many years ago was your Father. My Grandfather then came to visit the Sioux & to do them some good & the Sioux all treated him well. My people & yours were then brothers. My an-

cestors returned to their own country, but they did not forget their
brethren the Sioux & spoke often of them to their children. Their
children did not forget the words of the old men & they are anxious
to hear from their friends the Sioux & to know if they are happy &
have plenty of Buffalos. So I have come to know these things. But I
went first to shake the hand wh your great Father at Washington, &
he said, "Go to my children the Sioux. They live so far from me that
I do not know what they want. Go & look at their country & count
their lodges. Take them something to eat & do them some good, &
tell my children that I send you to them & that when you come back
& bring good words of them, I will make their Fires very large as
they were long ago, & my children shall be happy." It was affecting
to hear that chief's reply, spoken with natural eloquence & an abrupt
energy peculiar to the savage & always startling to the listener. He
spoke of his nation, of the earlier and happier periods of its history
& contrasted these with its present poverty & rapid decay. "Then,"
said he, "the Buffalo covered the plains. Our enemies fled before us
& the blaze of our Fires was seen from afar, but they have dwindled
away until their light is almost extinguished. There is no more
games & my people are few & our enemies press us on every side.
We thought that we were to die when the snow comes but you come
& bring us life. Our sky was covered with clouds & dark with storm,
but you came & again the sun shines bright in the blue heavens & we
are happy." Mr. N. has always labored to prevent these people from
going to war. "I give you this powder," he wd. tell them, "to kill
game for the support of your women & children & to pay your debts
to the Traders, but do not dare to go to war with it—with it you
will be successful in the chase, but your scalp will hang in your
enemy's lodge if you carry it with you to war." He always represented himself [to] these people as specially sent by the President to
enquire into their condition with a view of improving it—endeavoring in every way to promote the interests of the U. States. The tact &
judgment displayed in his intercourse wh them has been eminently
successful, & I could not dwell too much upon his superb management of the expedition—not an article lost or broken throughout our
long journey, not a horse injured or stolen, a set of the most ungov-
ernable men in the world reduced in less than a week to perfect
order & obedience, the whole party cheerful & contented & all conducted wh the strictest regard to economy, superintending in person
the most trifling details of duty—giving, himself, the Reveillé at 4 in

the morning, travelling all day pencil in hand sketching & noting everything—physical and descriptive Geography, Geology, Meteorology, terrestrial magnetism, study of the resources of the country in relation to its future political condition—nothing but the most extraordinary devotion to the cause of science could have supported him under such unremitted labor—night came but brought wh it no cessation of toil, our astronomical observations were frequently protracted beyond the turn of the night & every fourth night one of the officers kept watch until daylight. Mr. N. taking his turn among the rest—"C'est bien," he wd. sometimes say with exultation, when after the toils were over, we stood to converse a little at our midnight fires, our frames exhausted & our blood fevered with the merciless attacks of the mosquitoes—c'est bien n'est-ce pas? so much is *done*. No matter what happens, if we die tonight, we shall have done something good for science.

After having explored the Coteaux des Prairies in length 140 miles, visited extensively the region of the Red Pipe Stone quarry & the region watered by the Blue Earth Riv. & its numerous Forks, we go now to take advantage of the few days that remain of the favorable season to explore the wild & broken region that lies immediately west of the Mississippi & south of the St. Peters.

I have the pleasure to thank you for my appointment to the Topl. Engineers. Major Plympton informed me of it on my arrival here & showed me my name on the list. I do not transmit to the Department an acceptance form, because I have not yet received any communication on that subject—indeed we are all, expecially Mr. Nicollet, extremely disappointed in having received no letters from any quarter on our arrival after a somewhat long absence.

We have been transacting our money affairs thro' the Am. Fur Co. & as we close our business with that company at *St. Louis,* we have to request that two or three thousand dollars may be transmitted to that place, which we shall probably reach in the latter days of October. Mr. N. told me that it is not necessary to make a formal requisition. I leave this letter with Mr. H. Sibley, of the Am. Fur Co., to be forwarded by the first steamboat. Very Respectfully Dear Sir, Your Obt. Servt.

C. FREMONT

ALS, RC (PHi—Poinsett Papers).

8. J. J. Abert to Pratte, Chouteau and Company

Bureau of Top. Engineers
WASHINGTON, Octr. 18th. 1838.

GENTLEMEN,

Your letter of the 5th inst. has been duly received.

By the enclosed extract from the instructions to Lieut. Freemont, who is with Mr. Nicollet, you will perceive that he is the disbursing agent of the expedition, and that all its accounts will have to be settled by him. As Mr. Nicollet was fully aware of this arrangement before he left St. Louis, that he did not apprize you of it could have been only from an oversight. Lieut. Freemonts application for funds will be immediately complied with. He will adjust your account if approved by Mr. Nicollet, but as neither of these gentlemen are probably fully aware of the exactness required by our accounting officers in the final adjustments of accounts, you will pardon me in suggesting the propriety of your charges being sustained by special statements of quantities & prices. Very respectfully,

J. J. ABERT, C.T.E.

Lbk (DNA-77, LS, 2:627).

9. Fragment of a Frémont Journal

[22–26 Oct. 1838]

Oct. 22d. 1838. This morning an Indian from M. Nicollet—to my great surprise he is at Sibley's—has made a voyage full of success but attended wh. hardship—12 jours [. . .] par la faim et l'incendre des prairies—says that in 3 days at farthest he will start to join me—despatched Baptisier[1] at 8 a.m. to Wells,[2] ½ days journey on Lake Pepin, in search of Flour, Sugar, &c. Evening—this day passed as the others, in walking among the neighboring hills, reading &c. Snow still covers the high prairies. I find nothing remarkable in Geology, Limestone & Sandstone with some handsome conglomerates & occasionally a granite Boulder. I believe that I have forgotten to mention in its proper place a large granite Boulder on the shore of Lake

Pepin when the wind compelled me to encamp during the 13th & 14th ult. The soil being excellent, all the vegetables I have seen are very large & fairly flavoured, Turnips, Potatoes, carrots &c. Roque[3] might have a beautiful & comfortable farm, he has Cows, Oxen, Horses, all the material—but the spirit of Indian indolence seems to pervade all here & provided there is enough to satisfy the wants of the present moment, they do not look beyond. 4 Indian Lodges encamped here yesterday & they have been a little troublesome to us today—they began to congregate around our fire at supper time, but our good cook routed them, & they betook themselves to Roque's family fire & in a few moments more than a Dozen were assembled there—their kettle hanging over the fire & a close array of wild Ducks en appolas encircling it.

Oct. 23d. The day has opened beautifully—a bright spring sun shining in a clear sky for the first time since the 10th ult. The lake & the river, notwithstanding its swift current, smooth as a mirror. Above and below this place the river freezes, but immediately in front of the house, never. Why? After Breakfast walked wh. Flandin on the road by wh. Baptisier was to return & ascended one of the mountains near the entrance of the lake & walked for a short distance along the [*three words illegible*] snow on summit. Flandin took off his coat on reaching the summit (instead of Buttoning it) & lost a little work on astronomy, a present from M. Verrot[4] of Balt. Fine view here—think that the Riv. aux Boeufs is a mouth of the Riv. des Sauteurs—the whole intervening space from the Cote to latter being occupied by channels & marais—very nearly the same as the Riv. aux Embarras & the Riv. à l'eau Blanche. Day passed as usual, much pleased wh. "La Perfectibilité humaine." Towards Evening Maxime[5] returned wh. 6 fine Ducks & shortly after came Baptisier—he had purchased Flour, Coffee, tea & sugar to the amount of 4.50 & had lost, he said, 2.50. I was informed after his departure yesterday that he never lost an opportunity to become intoxicated & he had enjoyed this at Wells'. Supped well & slept well. After supper sat up some time listening to Augustin's account of Indian feuds &c.

Oct. 24. Mr. N. not yet arrived. Rains constantly wh. high wind from the north during the night but wh. the morning the rain—the sun broke out gloriously among the clouds, though the wind rose higher. It sweeps down river wh. is so ruffled as to look like a rapid today, & the little lake is angry & white. 1 P.M. have returned from a walk to the hills. The snow still lies in sheltered places—the wind is blowing Keenly & the sky covered wh. dark, hard clouds threatening snow. Maxime has retd. from the chase bringing wh. him 10 Ducks & a large & very fat Goose. I take much pleasure in listening to his narrations of these expeditions. The colour of the goose is body gray, neck & head black, the latter having a white band. About 5 O'clock a party of Americans, 5 in number came to the house & requested permission to stay the night, which was cold, raw & windy—granted of course—displayed a full measure of that troublesome curiosity & intolerable ill manners *peculiar* to the [*several words cut from paper*] very much annoyed by them. They were from the Mile or Chippeway river bound to the Prairie du Chien—they left us next morning after breakfast.

Oct. 25 Thursday. M. N. not arrived. Spent the day in reading, mapping & walking. Maxime start[ed] for the chase at daylight this morning & return[ed] at Breakfast time wh. 2 very fat Geese & 2 [. . .]. The Post Boy arrived—informed us that Mr. N. had passed Danton's[6] on the 23rd—he will certainly arrive tomorrow.

Oct. 26. Prepared a fine breakfast in expectation of enjoying the society of our friends at that meal. Th[ey] did not come. After Breakfast walked to the summit of a mountain overlooking the lake, about 2 miles hence. Just as I reached the summit, saw the Barge on the lake at foot of hill—they were under sail & reached the house before me. Messrs. Geyer & Montmort looking well. Mr. N. very thin. Mr. Montmort escaped drowning in the morning. Mr. N's remark [. . .] alive to *want of calculation*. Are all men unjust? Much excited—walked in the cold wind for an hour or so, wh. had a cooling effect. Will the resolutions formed in that hour be adhered to? Returned to the house. Maxime not yet arrived—hope he will come in time for supper.[7]

AD (CLSM). This fragment of JCF's record of the 1838 expedition is found in a small notebook, the cover of which bears the initials "C. F." and the title, in his hand, "Cahier d'Observations Astronomique." The document contains astronomical data in JCF's hand.

1. Probably Jean Baptiste Gea, who appears in the financial vouchers for Nov. 1838.

2. James Wells (d. 1863) was a prominent trader when Sibley went to Minnesota in 1834 (SIBLEY [3]).

3. Probably Augustin Rocque, a trader whose house was about three miles below Lake Pepin—said to have been the only house in 1834 between Prairie du Chien and the mouth of the Minnesota River (SIBLEY [3]).

4. Jean Marcel Pierre Auguste Verot (1805–76), of the Sulpician order, taught at St. Mary's Seminary in Baltimore where Nicollet had stayed. He

became vicar-apostolic of Florida in 1858 and bishop of St. Augustine in 1870.

5. Maxime Maxwell, listed in the 1838 financial vouchers as a *voyageur*.

6. Samuel Dentan and Daniel Gavin, missionaries from Lausanne, had established themselves at the head of Lake Pepin where a small band of Sioux lived in what was commonly known as Red Wing's village (FOLWELL, 1:203–4).

7. Two days later, agent Taliaferro noted in his journal that his steamboat overtook the Nicollet party of seven on a barge below Mt. Trempeleau. "We could not hail or have a word with them as I wished" (MnHi).

10. J. J. Abert to Frémont

Bureau of Topogrl. Engineers
WASHINGTON, Oct. 26th 1838

SIR,

A requisition for three thousand dollars has been this day made in your favor. The amount will be sent to you at St. Louis. Respectfully,

J. J. ABERT C.T.E.

Lbk (DNA-77, LS, 3:5).

11. J. J. Abert to Pratte, Chouteau and Company

Bureau of Topogrl. Engineers
WASHINGTON, Novr. 12th 1838.

GENTLMN.

Your letter of the 31 Octr. [*not found*] has this moment been received.

I cannot see what possible difference it can make by whom or through whom your advances on account of the expedition under Mr. Nicollet are paid. In case of advance of money, the advance will be refunded, in case of sales of goods, the goods will be paid for, but for the reason in my last & its inclosure Lt. Fremont was made the monied agent of the expedition. All this was known (to Mr. Nicollet) before his departure and, of course, before you had advanced a dollar. Mr. Nicollets drafts will without doubt be paid by Lt. Fremont, and to enable him to meet these and other engagements of the expedition, a requisition for $3000 to be placed at his disposal at St. Louis was made on the 26th of October.

On many days previous to the departure of Mr. Nicollet from this place and for many after, the illness of Mr. Poinsett was such, that no business intercourse was had with him. The expedition was therefore organized entirely by this office, in a way presumed to coincide with his views, and in conformity with the general custom in such cases. But in my letter to you of the 18th you are informed that Lt. Fremonts application for funds would be immediately complied with. He will adjust your accounts if approved by Mr. Nicollet. Mr. Nicollet could of course approve of your cash advances on his draft, there could therefore be no difficulty or delay in the adjustment. And to prevent the possibility of delay, in anticipation of the wants of the expedition, the amount of $3000 as before stated was sent on the 26th of last month. You will perceive therefore that to meet your cash advances every arrangement has already been made & without any knowledge in this office of the assurances of the Secretary to which you refer, those assurances have been fully met.

It was not possible for the Department to send funds to you in order to meet Mr. Nicollets drafts on your firm; it could only have paid such drafts drawn on the Department in your favour. Then the draft would have been charged to Nicollet and he would have had to have accounted for the expenditures of the amount. Had the money have been sent to you to meet Nicollet's drafts then you would have been charged with the amount on the book of the Treasury, and you would have had to have accounts for the expenditure. Either of these courses would have put Mr. Nicollet or yourself to great inconvenience. On these accounts Lt. Fremont was made the agent, and as he was directed to pay any account that Mr. Nicollet should approve it preserves the customary form and kept Mr. Nicollet at the head. I have made these explanations to satisfy you that the arrangement is proper and that every proper result be relied upon with confidence.

J. J. ABERT Cl. Tl. En.

Lbk (DNA-77, LS, 3:10–11).

29

12. Joseph N. Nicollet to F. R. Hassler

ST. LOUIS, 26 December 1838

MY DEAR FRIEND,

Mr. Charles Fremont, who will give you this letter, is the lieutenant of the topographic corps who accompanied me in my expedition as first assistant. I present him to you as a special friend, very eager to make your acquaintance, and very capable of appreciating your great work. He will give you all the details of my campaign which was very happy, and will explain to you the reasons which keep me here another several weeks. I am in a hurry to see you again and am exceedingly vexed at the forced delay I face in getting myself immediately to Washington. It was impossible to give you word of myself earlier, having been constantly away from all means of communication with civilization. I had news of you through Col. Abert, when I arrived at the place where mail awaited me. But nothing more recent than the month of August. I am making a vow that we will find each other under the same roof to spend together those moments of conversation that are so dear to me. In the hope of seeing you again soon, I abstain from writing you more lengthily, having much to do to send off Mr. Fremont to Washington with all my paperwork.

Adieu, my dear friend, my best to all your family, and to you more than ever,

J. N. NICOLLET

ALS, RC (NN—Hassler Papers). Addressed. The original is in French. Ferdinand Rudolph Hassler (1770–1843) had come to the U.S. from Switzerland in 1805 and was now superintendent of the U.S. Coast and Geodetic Survey. He would soon be inviting his good friend Nicollet, and young JCF, to make some nighttime astronomical observations atop his house in Washington (CAJORI; NEVINS, 48–50).

13. Financial Records, 1838

[31 Dec. 1838]

Editorial note: The value of financial records in historical documentation is nearly self-evident. In the case of exploring expeditions, these records provide more than just fiscal information: they list equipment and supplies, and the suppliers dealt with; they present a rough chronology of an expedition; and they provide a usually reliable roster of the personnel and the period of employment for each man. It is not uncommon for the name of an *engagé* or other employee to appear nowhere but in the financial records.

It is necessary, however, to be selective in presenting such records. The most useful items are the individual vouchers which go to make up the quarterly reports of the man charged with disbursing the funds. We shall concentrate upon these, citing other documents when they provide useful information. And we shall do a good deal of normalizing and summarizing, feeling that a slavish attempt to reproduce all the myriad bits of documentation in utter faithfulness to capitalization, spelling, and format cannot serve any historiographic purpose.

In some cases, wording has been simplified or omitted but the meaning has not been altered. Prices of individual items are usually omitted if they can easily be determined by the total price.

JCF's accounts are fairly complete in the National Archives, usually compiled on a yearly basis—each quarter occasionally reported separately—and with all the documents folded in thirds and tied with ribbon. Each of these packets is a "consolidated file," containing, besides the vouchers which represent JCF's disbursements, various summaries, abstracts of disbursements, and a statement of account current. Supporting letters are sometimes present, and will be quoted or given in full when they contribute information.

JCF's accounts for the four quarters of 1838 are in DNA-217, Third Auditor's Reports and Accounts, Account No. 10954.

Voucher No. 1, St. Louis, 17 May 1838
U.S. to Henry Chouteau

15 May 1838

Bill for medicine chest	19.87
2½ bbls. biscuit @ 2.50, keg 25¢	9.00
100 lbs. dried beef @ 12½¢, box 25¢	12.75
3½ *tablettes de bouillon*	14.00
117 lbs. sausages	15.00
4 boxes sardines 6.00, and 10 lbs. chocolate 7.50	13.50
2 lbs. arrowroot @ .75, box .75	2.25

4 lbs. tea	4.00
Lantern, candles, sugar, tobacco, etc.	11.50
10 lbs. Mocha coffee	2.20
8 hams, 101½ lbs.	12.68
1 keg butter	7.00
1 doz. port wine	12.00
4 bottles Cognac brandy	4.00
Sugar	8.50
34 lbs. salt	1.02
Box 50¢, 3 tin canisters 1.00, drayage 25¢	1.75
17 May 1838	
1 box sperm candles, 36 lbs. @ 45¢, box 25¢	16.45
	167.47

Rect. 17 May by J. Richardson. Certified by JCF. Endorsed by J. F. A. Sanford: "I certify that J. Richardson is an Employe in the service of H. Chouteau Grocer & Compy. Merchants, St. Louis, Mo., and as such, is in the habit of receipting for any money due to Chouteau. Merchants in that country always give their clerks this authority." In an unknown hand: "The Bill & receipt for Medicine Chest wanting $19.87." Later endorsement by JCF: "The man from whom the Medicine Chest was purchased could not be found on our return to St. Louis, from the Western Country, & as it was actually purchased *by me* from Mr. Chouteau, I supposed that his receipt would be regarded as satisfactory. C. Fremont." Henri P. Chouteau (1805–55), a wholesale grocer and commission and forwarding merchant, was located at 39 N. Front Street, St. Louis, in 1839 (J. F. MC DERMOTT [2], 176). John F. A. Sanford was associated with P. Chouteau, Jr., and Company, acting mainly as a liaison between St. Louis and the East (SUNDER, 6–7).

Many of the vouchers accumulated valuable information in the process of being receipted, certified, and endorsed. In such cases, the information will be noted. But many are routinely receipted at the place and on the date drawn, by the person to whom the money was owing, and are routinely certified by JCF as having "been received by me and used, or intended to be used, etc." Where nothing is to be learned from the receipting, certification, and endorsement, they are omitted.

Voucher No. 2, St. Peters, 13 Sept. 1838
U.S. to American Fur Company

16 July through 3 Aug.
Sundry articles furnished Mr. Nicollet at Lac qui Parle, viz.:

Binding and lead	10.13
1 sheep, 6.00, 9 lbs. shot, 10 lbs. tobacco	10.75
45 lbs. lead, 10 lbs. tobacco, 20 lbs. pemmican	10.62
45 lbs. sugar, 4 plates, 4 spoons, and 4 forks	12.25

canoe, 15.00, 30 lbs. flour, 2.10	17.10
1 basket and bag for mess	4.00
soap	3.00
	67.85

Rect. 13 Sept. 1838 at St. Peters by H. H. Sibley, as agent for the American Fur Company.

Voucher No. 3, St. Peters, 13 Sept. 1838
U.S. to American Fur Company

10 Sept. 1838

To advances of sundry necessaries to men at Lac qui Parle	15.20
less: by amount received for 1 wooden canoe	12.00
	3.20

Rect. 13 Sept. 1838 by H. H. Sibley as agent for the American Fur Company. Certified by JCF and endorsed by him: "The particulars of the Bill are of such a nature that they could not be specified in detail, such as a pound of beef to one man, a few potatoes to another & so on with the rest. C. Fremont."

Voucher No. 4, St. Peters, 13 Sept. 1838
U.S. to Stambaugh and Sibley

5 June 1838

For articles furnished Mr. Nicollet's expedition at Fort
Snelling

115 lbs. bacon 28.75, 2 lbs. tea 3.00, 4 lbs. coffee 1.00	32.75
20 lbs. rice, 2.50, 3 bed cords 1.50	4.00
1 pair shoe brushes 50¢, 2 boxes blacking 25¢	.75
6 tin cups 75¢, 1 set knives and forks 4.00, 6 spoons 1.38	6.13
½ doz. teaspoons 50¢, ½ doz. plates 6/, 1 tin pan 75¢	2.00
1 frying pan 1.50, 1 tea pot 1.00, 1 tea kettle 4.50	7.00
2 lbs. candles 1.00, 2 bars soap 12/, 1 tin basin 69¢	3.19
1 candlestick 62¢, 1 loaf salt, 44¢, 1 teapot 1.00	2.06
1 piece tape 25¢, 1 fish line 25¢	.50
29 Aug.	
6 lead pencils 90¢, 1½ quires paper 75¢	1.65
1 Sept.	
2¾ gals. wine to me	5.50
1 bottle port wine 1.00 Paid Mrs. Campbell for washing 1.87	2.87
	68.40

Rect. 13 Sept. 1838 at St. Peters by H. H. Sibley as agent for the American Fur Company. Certified by JCF. Endorsed: "I certify that H. H. Sibley whose name is affixed to the within receipt, is the agent of the Am. Fur Co. West Depart. and that he is authorized to receipt for them, or Stambaugh & Sibley. J. F. A. Sanford." Samuel C. Stambaugh and Sibley were partners in the sutlership at Fort Snelling. Stambaugh, the former publisher of a county newspaper in Pennsylvania, had been appointed to the Indian agency at Green Bay in 1832. When his appointment was rejected by the Senate, President Andrew Jackson sent him to Wisconsin as a special agent (JONES, 186; MARTIN). Mrs. Campbell may be Marguerite Menager Campbell, the wife of Scott Campbell, who was an interpreter at Fort Snelling for some twenty-five years (WILLIAMS [1], 134; HOFFMANN, 35–37, 42).

Voucher No. 5, St. Peters, 13 Sept. 1838
U.S. to American Fur Company

17 June

For sundries furnished Mr. Nicollet at Traverse des Sioux, viz:

3 pieces fancy calico, 96⅔ yds.	24.00
1 tin kettle 14/, 1 gun $6.00	7.75
2 tin pans 10/, 1 piece ribbon 6/	2.00
10 lbs. powder @ 5/, 32 lbs. lead @ 10¢	9.45
10 lbs. tobacco, 1¼ coffee	2.25
30 lbs. flour @ 6¢, 2 lbs. sugar @ 20¢	2.20
4¼ lbs. rice @ 1/; amt. paid Provencalle per request 12.00	12.53
8 lbs. tobacco @ 20¢, 12 lbs. lead @ 10¢	2.80
12 lbs. salt @ 5¢, 1 cod line 8/	1.60
	64.58

Rect. 13 Sept. 1838 at St. Peters by H. H. Sibley as agent for the American Fur Company. Certified by JCF. Auditor's comment on endorsement sheet: "The Bill & Receipt for the Amt. paid Provencalle wanting, $12.00." Added comment by JCF: "The same remarks applicable to this as to other bills of Am. Fur Compy. Agents. C. F." Louis Provencalle (ca. 1780–ca. 1850) was a Minnesota trader for more than twenty-five years. He was in charge of the post at Traverse des Sioux when Sibley made his first inspection there in 1835 (BABCOCK).

Voucher No. 6, St. Peters, 13 Sept. 1838
U.S. to American Fur Company

25 Aug. 1838

6 lbs. powder 4.50, 13 lbs. lead 13/	6.13
20 lbs flour 1.50, 2 lbs. tobacco 6/	2.25
1 keg powder, 25 lbs. 13.00, 1 bag corn 4.00	17.00
½ yd. ticking 1/, thread 6¢, paid for bark canoe 35.00	35.19

½ bag corn 2.00, 26 lbs. bacon 6.50	8.50
1 lb. turtle twine 5/, 1 lb. candles 2/, 22 lbs. flour 1.65	2.53
Repairing frying pan 6/, 2 lbs. Tobacco 4/	1.25
paid Benjamin Dyonne 81 days service @ 1.00	81.00
hire of 6 horses & carts 57 days from 18 June to 13 Aug., and of 2 horses & carts 63 days from 18 June to 19 Aug., in all 468 days @ 75¢ per diem	351.00
Paid Joseph Laframboise for a calf furnished by him	10.00
Paid Mrs. Perry for washing	7.13
	521.98

Rect. 13 Sept. 1838 at St. Peters by H. H. Sibley as agent for the American Fur Company. Certified by JCF. Auditor's note states bills and receipts lacking for canoe and for money to Dyonne and Laframboise. Endorsement by JCF: "These things were, as others, purchased of the Am. Fur Compy. from whom the receipt was obtained. C.F." The name of Benjamin Dyomme appears frequently in the ledgers and daybooks of the American Fur Company, 1835–45. Joseph Laframboise had been an American Fur Company agent at Lake of the Two Woods on the Coteau des Prairies in 1835, but that post was now abandoned and he was serving as a guide to Nicollet. SIBLEY [3] and WILSON provide information on his life and trading activities. Mrs. Perry is probably Mary Ann Perry (d. 1859), wife of Swiss watchmaker Abraham Perry, who had come to Fort Snelling in 1827 (WILLIAMS [1], 66–67, 101). But as Sophy Perry collected the money (Mendota Day Book, 23 June 1838, Sibley Papers) it is possible that "Mrs. Perry" is the daughter-in-law of the elder Perrys, though we suspect she is one of Mary Ann's six daughters collecting the money for her mother.

Voucher No. 7, St. Peters, [ ] Sept. 1838
U.S. to American Fur Company

28 May 1838

2 barrels flour 22.00, 1 barrel pork 22.00	44.00
freight of 1300 lbs. to Traverse des Sioux	6.50
30 May	
2 lbs tobacco 8/, 1 bag shot 2.75	3.75
1 2-quire blank book 12/, 23 yds. mosquito netting 8.63	10.13
8 yds. cotton 20/, thread 2/, knife 6/, needles 2/	3.75
4 June	
thread 2/, 2 yds. stroud 6.00, 8 lbs. tobacco 1.60	7.85
8 June	
14 lbs. sugar 2.80, 3 pair 3-pt. blankets 30.00	32.80
1 pair 2½-pt. blankets 9.00, 12 bushel corn 18.00, 6 bags 12/	28.50
4 barrels flour 44.00, 3 barrels pork 66.00, large kettle 3.00	113.00

6 guns 58.50, 1 crow bar 3.00	61.50
3 drills & hammer 3.00, 1 axe 3.00, 1 yd. cotton 2/, 1 hatchet 6/	7.00
paid for making mosquito bar 1.50, 1 quire ruled cap paper 4/	2.00
1 patent gimlet 1/6, 36 lbs. navy bread 3.60, 40 lbs. flour 3.00	6.79
	327.57

Rect. [   ] Sept. 1838 at St. Peters by H. H. Sibley as agent for the American Fur Company. Certified by JCF.

Voucher No. 8, St. Peters, [   ] *Sept. 1838*
U.S. to American Fur Company

4 June 1838

40 lbs. pork 7.50, 20 flints 3/, 12 gun worms 6/	8.63

30 June

1 barrel flour 12.00, 1 barrel pork 24.00, 57 lbs. sugar 11.50	47.50
2 bags corn 240 lbs. 7.50, 2 bags to contain 4/	8.00

9 July

amount of Majese Ascaud's [Arcand's] wages 25 days @ 1.00	25.00

9 Aug.

2 lbs. soap	.37

25 Aug.

Service of Joseph Laframboise as guide and interpreter 78 days @ 2.50 per diem	195.00
Paid Laframboise for use of horse for 43 days	43.00
James Clewett services as voyageur 83 days @ 1.00	83.00
Eusebe Lanctot same, 87 days	87.00
Maxime Maxwell same, 81 days	81.00
Pierre Boucher same, 86½ days	86.50
Joseph Brunelle same, 80½ days	80.50
François Dezirie for services as cook	100.25
	845.75

Rect. [   ] Sept. 1838 at St. Peters by H. H. Sibley as agent for the American Fur Company. Certified by JCF. Auditor's note inquires about absence of supporting documents. Endorsement by JCF: "The same remarks are applicable to this as to other bills from agent of American Fur Compy. C. F." Arcand, Lanctot, and Boucher are not identified, although their names appear frequently in the ledgers and daybooks kept at Mendota. Brunelle, a *voyageur* and scout, was said to be more than one hundred years old when he died in

1912 (letter of L. J. Carpenter, 11 Feb. 1935, Historical Information File, MnHi). James Reuben Clewett (b. 1810), an Englishman, came to Minnesota from Canada as a *voyageur* and clerk for the American Fur Company, working first at the post below Lake Pepin and later at Lake Traverse (WILLIAMS [1], 88–89). François Dezirie is undoubtedly Desiré Fronchet, who boasted of having been a soldier under Napoleon. He may have served in the U.S. Army at Fort Snelling, and in 1836 had been employed by Nicollet during the expedition to the headwaters of the Mississippi (NICOLLET, 92; JONES, 169; WILLIAMS [1], 63).

Voucher No. 9, Prairie du Chien, 26 Nov. 1838
U.S. to American Fur Company

19 Nov.

3 blank books 6/, 9 steel pens & 2 handles 12/	3.75
8 skeins twine 1/, 1 box caps 3/, 1 lb. shot 1/	1.50
1 pair blue blankets 3½ pt.	16.00
1 fine pen knife	1.50
26 Nov.	
paid H. Francis for board of party	20.25
Cash paid Lieut. Fremont	500.00
	543.00

Rect. at Prairie du Chien 26 Nov. 1838 by H. L. Dousman as agent for the American Fur Company. Certified by JCF. Auditor's note states the $500.00 will be credited to account of JCF for first quarter 1839. Subvoucher lacking for amount paid H. Francis. Endorsement by JCF: "This is a bill of Mr. Dousman's which I knew to be correct, and paid under the supposition that he was the only person with whom I could be considered as dealing. C. F." Hercules L. Dousman (1800–1868) was a partner of Joseph Rolette at the American Fur Company station. The two men made the establishment a powerful one, controlling trade over a wide area to the north and west (SIBLEY [1]). H. Francis is not identified.

Voucher No. 10, St. Louis, 3 Jan. 1839
U.S. to Pratte, Chouteau and Company

For advances to J. N. Nicollet on account of
   Exploring expedition
24 May 1838

Paid for sundry articles of merchandise for Indian presents	317.23
Paid for tent	26.50
1 June	
Paid for sundry merchandise as presents to Renville's family	
at Lake Traverse	73.86

24 Sept.

Paid draft in favor of H. Sibley	1899.33
18 Nov.	
Paid draft in favor of H. L. Dousman	1312.40
17 Dec.	
Paid draft in favor of H. L. Dousman	539.50
Paid postage	.50
31 Dec.	
Paid draft in favor of Lt. Fremont	500.00
	4669.32

Rect. at St. Louis, 3 Jan. 1839, by Pratte, Chouteau and Co. Certified by JCF. Auditor's note indicates subvouchers lacking. Endorsement by JCF: "As Mr. Chouteau was the only person concerned with me in the transactions specified on the face of the acct. I did not think it necessary to require of him certificates as to the amount which he paid for the several articles on the bill. C. F."

Voucher No. 11, St. Louis, 1 Jan. 1839
U.S. to John Charles Frémont

1838

Transportation of party, instruments and baggage under the command of J. N. Nicollet from Prairie du Chien to St. Louis	300.47
1 chronometer guard chain	8.00
Repair of sextant	2.50
2 thermometers	5.00
	315.97

Rect. at St. Louis 1 Jan. 1839 by JCF. Certified by JCF. Auditor notes that subvouchers are missing. Endorsement by JCF: "The expenditures for transportation of the party &c. were made little by little in a wild country and to a people unacquainted with such things as accounts. Vouchers in form for every expenditure could only have been obtained at the sacrifice of public interest by the delay which it would have occasioned. The guard chain, thermometers, and repair of sextant were paid by Mr. Nicollet whose certificate is hereunto annexed. C. Fremont." Endorsement by Nicollet certifying to his purchase of the equipment.

Voucher No. 12, Washington, 1 Feb. 1839
U.S. to John Charles Frémont

1838

To services rendered in the capacity of assistant engineer

in a geographical expedition under command of J. N. Nicollet from 15 April to 31 Dec. inclusively at four dollars per diem   1036.00
To travelling expenses at 10 cents per mile, 2520 miles, viz.: from Washington to St. Louis, thence to Fort Snelling, and from St. Louis to Washington   252.00
                                                                        1288.00

Rect. 1 Feb. 1839 at Washington, D.C., by JCF. Certified by JCF.

Voucher No. 13, Prairie du Chien, 7 Nov. 1838
U.S. to American Fur Company

14 Sept.

1 cod line 8/, 1 bed cord 5/, 1 bbl. flour 14.00, 1 bbl. pork 26.00	41.63
1 box blacking 2/, 1 auger 6/, 1 drawing knife 10/	2.25
1 hand saw 16/, 3 tin dippers 9/, rope 8/	4.13
24 lbs bacon 6.00, difference on robes, 2.00, 22 lbs. flour 1.65	9.65

17 Sept.

Paid A. Ferribault for horse 120.00, 9 lbs pork 1.38	121.38

5 Oct.

Paid Indian guide, Nez Coupee	10.00

20 Oct.

Amt. of account with Stambaugh & Sibley	42.35
difference on blankets 3.00, corn and pork	5.50
1 bushel potatoes 4/, looking glass 2/, 20 lbs. sugar 4.00	4.75
Hire of horse, 3 carts, 3 harness, 36½ days	54.50
1 mule killed by Indians or stolen	30.50
Paid D. Ferribault for 33 days service as interpreter @ 2.50	82.50
1 bbl. pork 30.00, 1 bushel potatoes 4/, 5 lbs. pork 6/, 5 lbs. salt 2/	31.50
Paid A. Ferribault for 33 days hire of horse @ 6/	24.75
	465.39

Rect. at Prairie du Chien 7 Nov. 1838 by H. L. Dousman as agent for the American Fur Company. Certified by JCF. Auditor notes lack of subvouchers for several items. Endorsement by JCF: "As to those things for which subvouchers are required, I can only say that Mr. Dousman was the man from whom the *actual purchase* was made and I cannot see that it is requisite that I should furnish the receipt of the person from whom he purchased. C. Fremont."

39

David Faribault (d. ca. 1886) was the young son of Jean Baptiste Faribault. Like his father and his brothers, Alexander and Oliver, he also became a trader.

Voucher No. 14, Prairie du Chien, 7 Nov. 1838
U.S. to American Fur Company

9 Sept. 1838

4 lbs. tobacco 12/, 1 lb. twine 5/, 2 quires paper 8/	3.13
4 papers matches 8/, 2 fish lines 2/, 10 lbs. flour 6/, 6 lbs. pork 90¢	2.91

13 Sept.

soap 7/6, 1 pair brushes 6/, 1 box blacking 2/, 1 lb twine 6/	2.56

14 Sept.

1 horse 50.00 and double barreled gun 40.00, presented to J. Renville Jr. for services as guide and interpreter and for loan of wagons, horses, etc.	90.00
32 lbs. tobacco 8.00, 2 kettles 34/, 6 forks 18/, 6 spoons 3/	14.88
1 sickle 12/, 6 tin cups 6/, 2 lbs. nails 3/, 3¼ yds. cotton 8/	3.63
1 frying pan 6/, 2 bags 4/, 1 axe helve 2/	1.50
1 bbl. flour 13.00, 1 bbl. mess pork 30.00	43.00
1 plough line 3/, pd. Mrs. Latourville for mending, 5.00	5.38
1 blue cloth capot 6.00, 1 yd. ribbon 13¢	6.13
paid wages of men with provisions during Mr. Nicollet's stay at St. Peters	43.00
	216.12

Rect. at Prairie du Chien 7 Nov. 1838 by H. L. Dousman as agent for the American Fur Company. Certified by JCF. Auditor questions lack of sub-vouchers. Endorsement by JCF: "With the exception of the sanction of the Secy. of War for the present to Renville this acct. is of the same nature of the others of Mr. Dousman's. C. F." Mrs. Latourville is not identified.

Voucher No. 15, Prairie du Chien, [ ] Nov. 1838
U.S. to American Fur Company

3 Nov.

2 pocket flasks @ 4/, 3 quires paper 3/	2.13
paid Joseph Rolette for 1 wood canoe	20.00
12 mackerels @ 1/, 3 lbs. rice @ 22/, 2 loaves bread @ 1/.	2.12
1 lb. chocolate 3/, 2 thermometers @ 22/, 1 bottle ink 3/	6.25
2 steel pens @ 1/, 3 lead pencils @ 1/	.63

9 Nov.

5 steel pens & handles 6/, 1 sheet drawing paper 1/	.87
4 lead pencils @ 1/, 1 doz. quills 3/	.88
2 cakes soap 5/, 1 yd. diaper 2/, 1½ yds. gauze 6/, 1 lb. soap 2/	1.88
1 scarlet belt 4/, 4 lbs. lead 4/, 1 plough line 3/	1.37
14 sheets envelope paper	.25
Sundry provisions and supplies furnished to the party	70.25
	106.63

Rect. at Prairie du Chien [ ] Nov. 1838 by H. L. Dousman as agent for the American Fur Company. Certified by JCF. Endorsed by JCF: "The same remarks are applicable to this as to the other bill of Mr. Dousman's for $465.39. C. F." Joseph Rolette (1781–1842), a fur trader and land speculator at Prairie du Chien, was associated with Hercules L. Dousman in the American Fur Company after 1826 (DICT. WIS. BIOG.). Zebulon Pike met him (and archly declined a gift of brandy, coffee, and sugar) during his expedition of 1805–6.

Voucher No. 16, Prairie du Chien, [ ] Nov. 1838
U.S. to American Fur Company

20 Oct.

Paid D. Ferribault for a blanket 6.00 and a double barreled gun 20.00, presented to Indian guide	26.00

[ ] Nov.

Paid the following for services

George Cournoyer	61.00
Joseph Brunelle	80.75
Jean Baptiste Gea	70.00
Maxime Maxwell	73.00
Chs. Prevost	51.51
Pierre Lanoix	60.00
Louis Quenon	74.25
Paid Louis Rock for services as guide and interpreter 37 days @ 1.50, and for powder, lead, and potatoes, 72.75. Credit 1 double-barrelled gun 45.00	27.75
	524.26

Rect. at Prairie du Chien [ ] Nov. 1838 by H. L. Dousman as agent for the American Fur Company. Certified by JCF. Auditor's note questions lack of subvouchers. Endorsement by JCF: "Same explanation as to other accts. of Mr. D's. C. F." George Cournoyer was listed as a resident of St. Paul in 1850 (WILLIAMS [1], 267). Louis Rock [Rocque] was the son of Augustin Rocque, the trader living below Lake Pepin. Prevost, Lanoix, and Quenon not identified; but obviously Nicollet thought highly of Lanoix as he requested that Sibley bring him and George Cournoyer to Lac qui Parle (Nicollet to Sibley, St. Louis, 18 March 1839, MnHi—Sibley Papers). Gea is referred to elsewhere as "Baptisier."

Voucher No. 17 [not present]

Voucher No. 18, St. Louis, 6 Dec. 1838
U.S. to J. N. Nicollet

Bill A [see below]	51.75
Bill B [see below]	46.00
1. India rubber, for canoe coverings, to secure provisions, instruments, etc.	32.50
2. Transportation of instruments and baggage from Baltimore to St. Louis, by stages and steamboats	48.50
3. Nautical almanac, American almanac	6.50
4. Paid to watchmaker for a chronometer box, to secure a valuable chronometer that belongs to U.S.	2.25
N.B. 1 to 4, no receipts. At the time I paid out those articles I was ignorant of the rules to be observed on keeping public accounts, and the accounting officer of the expedition had not yet joined with me.	187.50

Rect. at St. Louis 6 Dec. 1838 by J. N. Nicollet. Certified by JCF.

Bill A, U.S. to George Engelmann, M.D., 17 May 1838	
Vaccine matter	19.00
Camphor, peppermint and other drugs	2.25
apparatus for geological surveys (hammers, chisel, punch, and a big knife)	9.50
paper, 8 reams, for preserving plants	18.00
boxing up the same	1.00
	51.75

Bill B, U.S. to J. & S. Hawken, 17 May 1838	
One fine American fowling piece, double barrel, with leather case	46.00

For a note on Dr. George Engelmann, of St. Louis, see under Doc. No. 31. The Hawken brothers, Jacob (1786–1849) and Samuel (b. 1792), were St. Louis gunmakers whose "Hawken rifle" was famous from the Alleghenies to the Rockies. It was the weapon in common use by the American Fur Company (SCHARF, 1:809–10).

Voucher No. 19, Baltimore, 18 April 1838
U.S. to James Green

12 April

Repairing barometer	12.00
repairing microscope	.75
repairing magnetic compass, brass needle	1.50
2 mountain barometers	50.00
2 cases for same	5.50
6 pocket thermometers	15.00
6 dark glasses	2.25
3 magnifiers	2.25
	89.25
discount	2.00
	87.25

Certified by J. N. Nicollet. Dr. George Engelmann noted that for forty years he had used instruments made by James Green, of Baltimore and New York (BEK, pt. 4, p. 85). In 1840, Green was located at 1 S. Liberty Street, Baltimore.

1. In addition to the vouchers presented above, one small subvoucher is present, a bill from the steamboat *Burlington* for freight from St. Louis to St. Peters, 924 pounds @ 1.00 per cwt, totaling $13.86. Rect. at St. Peters 26 May 1838 in a clerk's hand.

The collection of vouchers assembled here represents JCF's first encounter with the rigorous requirements of the War Department in the keeping of accounts. Not only was he new at the task, but he had a natural aversion to such niceties which was to bring him into conflict with bookkeepers and auditors throughout all his service for the government. Given Nicollet's own naïve approach to such formalities, the two men combined must have put despair into the hearts of the Washington staff. Colonel Abert was to find many an occasion to justify, to the auditors, the informality of JCF's accounts. He first attempted it in a letter (filed with these accounts) of 16 Dec. 1840 to Secretary of War Joel R. Poinsett: "The U.S. had no funds for the Survey, and this [American Fur] Company had to advance and pay for everything, which it did at the request of the War Department. The high character of this Company for integrity, puts that point beyond question. And in reference to items in the bills of the Company, in which they charge an amount as being paid for an article, and which is objected to for the want of a subvoucher, it appears to me that this is an exactness without adequate object. The remark in the bill, if it proves anything, proves that the Company had not the article for sale, procured it for the U.S. and charged for it no more than it cost them. . . . The Company are not manufacturers. Everything they sell was bought from some one, but articles procured by them and not in their line were furnished to the U.S. without profit. No subvoucher was in my judgment, more necessary in such cases than for any other article." By way of further explanation, Abert wrote to the Treasury Department:

"There is a circumstance connected with the expenditures under Lieut. Fremont, and of which the Comptroller was probably not aware, which places the American Fur Company so frequently in the attitude of an original paymaster. It is, that having no funds at the time, appropriated for the expedition, it was sustained entirely (and at the request of the War Department) by the resources and means of that company. In fact, that company supplied every thing and had to await an appropriation before it was paid" (Lbk, DNA-77, LS, 4:319).

JCF was still explaining, in a letter of 26 Feb. 1841 to the Second Comptroller of the Treasury (filed with the above financial accounts), why he did not have proper receipts from the *engagés* who were paid by Pierre Chouteau, Jr. "The causes, arising from the nature of the service in an uncivilized region, which led to so loose a method of keeping accounts, and my own inexperience in such matters, I have, heretofore, explained in remarks accompanying the several vouchers for my expenditures. . . ."

14. Frémont to J. J. Abert

St. Louis 1 Jany. 1839

Sir

I have the honor to accept the appointment which has been conferred upon me of 2d Lieutenant in the Corps of Topographical Engineers. Respectfully Sir Your Obt. Servt.,

C. Fremont

ALS, RC (DNA-94, 5309 ACP file 1879 John C. Fremont). Endorsed; recd. 26 Jan. 1839.

15. J. J. Abert to Frémont

Bureau of Topl. Engrs.
Washington, Jany. 4th 1839

Sir,

I have received your letter of the 21st[1] and congratulate you on your safe return to St. Louis. This with one from Prairie du Chien at the termination of your first expedition, and the two brought by Mr. Montmort are the only letters which have been received from either

Mr. Nicollet or yourself since your departure, last spring, from St. Louis.

I hope you may not be so truly unfortunate as to lose the Geological and botanical collection.

If you should have occasion to make a draft in order to close your accounts with Pratt Chouteau & Co. please to draw it on this Bureau. Respectfully,

J. J. ABERT. Cl. T. E.

Lbk (DNA-77, LS, 3:40).
1. JCF's 21 Dec. 1838 letter, referred to here by Abert, was listed in the Register of Letters Received, but is no longer present in the National Archives. This is true also of his 19 Nov. 1838 letter, written from Prairie du Chien, in which he reported Nicollet was ill.

16. J. J. Abert to Frémont

Bureau Topl. Enginrs.
WASHINGTON, March 2d 1839

SIR

You will repair to St. Louis as soon as practicable, & there joining Mr. Nicollet, will aid him in his geographl. operations.

The experience which you have had with your accts., will, I hope, prevent the encountering of similar difficulties hereafter, & impress upon your mind the necessity of bills in detail and receipts. You can procure the materials for a small flag and have it made.

The Secretary agrees to the recommendation of Mr. Nicollet in reference to Mess. Geyers & Flandin & you are therefore authorized to pay them for the expedition of the present year a compensation of two dollars per day to each in full for their services.

In addition to the requisition for $500 to be paid to you at this place, another for $1500 has been this day made in your favour to be sent to St. Louis & Mess. Pratt Chouteau & Co. will be written to & requested to credit your demands to the amount of $5000.

Whether Mess. Pratt Chouteau & Co. credit to you will be liquidated by sending money to St. Louis, or by authorizing you to draw on the Bureau for the amt. when the expedition has terminated cannot now be decided, but will be by the time you will close your acct. with them.

The compensation to Mr. Nicollet & to Mess. Geyer and Flandin will be paid by you, as required by them, as far as practicable out of the funds sent to you & for which you will have credit with Mess. Pratt Chouteau & Co.

The plan of the expedition for the present year, as indicated in a letter from Mr. Nicollet to you, of the 9th of Jany. (on file in this office) is fully approved by the Secretary.[1] Respectfy,

J. J. ABERT. Cl. T. E.

Lbk (DNA-77, LS, 3:98–99).
1. JCF submitted Nicollet's plan for the 1839 operation in a letter to the bureau, 23 Feb. 1839. It was registered as received, but is no longer present. What Nicollet proposed was to continue the operation now being called "Military and Geographical Survey of the Country West of the Mississippi and North of the Missouri." He and JCF were preparing to depart in the spring, first ascending the Missouri by steamboat. Since the vessel was scheduled to leave St. Louis in March, it was necessary for the bureau to send them off before funds had been appropriated (see Doc. No. 17). Documents which follow are selected to outline the course of the expedition and JCF's role in it, but Nicollet's official *Report* is not presented.

17. J. J. Abert to Pratte, Chouteau and Company

Bureau of Topl. Engineers
WASHINGTON March 2d 1839

GENTN.

I am directed by the Hon. Secrety. of War to inform you that he has approved of the expedition to the West for the present year, as indicated by Mr. Nicollet, & I am also authorized to request you to meet the demands of the expedition for an amount of $5000. Lt. Fremont is the disbursing agent of the expedition.

In liquidating such advances & credits as you shall give, the Dept. will either transmit funds to you at St. Louis or authorize Lt. Fremont to draw bills on the Dept., payable here, after the expedition has terminated, but I cannot now say which course it will be in its power to adopt. I am however at liberty to assure you that it will adopt whichever course shall be found agreeable to you & which shall not militate against the necessary regulations of the Treasury Dept. Respectfully,

J. J. ABERT, Cl. T. E.

Lbk (DNA-77, LS, 3:98). Once again it became necessary for the government to rely upon private interests to finance an expedition. Having received authorization from the Secretary of War and assurances from Congress that the necessary appropriations would be made, Abert was embarrassed by a substantial oversight. After the adjournment of Congress, while the expedition was under way, it was found that the appropriation for the survey had "escaped attention." In his annual report of 30 Dec. 1839, it was necessary for Abert to plead for the money, and to suggest that funds be provided for additional surveys. "Our operations have been heretofore limited to the region north of the Missouri and west of the Mississippi but not extending westwardly to the Rocky mountains. It is extremely desirable that means to fill up the hiatus south of the Missouri and to extend the observations to the Rocky mountains should now be granted. It would really be questioning the known intelligence of the country were one to reason upon the advantages of correct geographical knowledge, or of the national benefit of obtaining now in time of peace, a knowledge of so vast a region bordering upon so extensive a line of our settlements inhabited by a numerous, warlike and well-armed race . . ." (Abert to Sec. of War, DNA-77, LS, 3:399–400). Thus the Bureau of Topographical Engineers began to maneuver for the authority which would send JCF to the Rockies in 1842.

18. J. J. Abert to Joseph N. Nicollet

Bureau of Topl Engins.
WASHINGTON, Mrch 4th 1839

SIR

I am directed by the Hon. Secretary of War to inform you that your plan of operations for the ensuing year as indicated in your letter of the 9th Jany. to Lt. Fremont is fully approved. Arrangements to make the same effectual have been adopted as you will be apprized by a letter of the 2d. instt. to Lt. Fremont sent open to you for your perusal.

The circulars you desire to have from the commandg. general and from the Commissioner of Indian Affairs are herewith inclosed. Respectfy,

J. J. ABERT Cl. T. E.

Lbk (DNA-77, LS, 3:100). The nature of the circulars Nicollet had asked for is not known.

19. J. J. Abert to Frémont

Bureau of Topl. Engineers
WASHINGTON, March 5th 1839

SIR.

Before your departure with the expedition of the present year, you will transmit to the Bureau your accounts & vouchers to the time of your present expenditures, in order that the balances with which you stand charged may be reduced as much as possible, and in order to save from the hazard of the contemplated expedition the evidences of the expenditures which you have already made.

In addition to the advice given in my letter of the 2d instt. in reference to your accounts allow me also to advise that you provide yourself with full explanation of expenditures of an unusual kind, and correct statements of the circumstances under which presents are made to Indians that in all cases in which the discretionary authority of the Department has to be invoked in favour of a voucher every desirable explanation may be submitted to its consideration. Respectfy,

J. J. ABERT Cl. T. E.

Lbk (DNA-77, LS, 3:101).

20. Frémont to Henry H. Sibley

ST. LOUIS April 4th. 1839

My DEAR SIR

We leave this place today in the steamboat Antelope for the Missouri River, intending if possible to be at Lac qui Parle by the end of June where Mr. Nicollet requests me to say, he shall be most happy to see you.

He intends proceeding from that place directly to Devil's Lake. Our party will be composed of the same persons as last year with the exception of Mr. Flandin who came with us as far as St. Louis but left us there having a fine opportunity of going to Europe where he may spend some few years.[1]

We have left in charge of Messrs. P. Chouteau & Co. a case directed to you in which you will find two Boxes of Cigars, which we send you to smoke with your friends, as I have heard of no steamboat going up your way & suppose you must be in want of Cigars—also a small Box directed to J. Renville at Lac qui Parle. All the gentlemen of our party unite in tending you their warmest remembrances & hope to see you in July at Renvilles. You must not fail to come—previously to that time you will hear from us again in which we will be able to fix a more definite period. Very Respy. yr. obt. servt.,

C. FREMONT

ALS, RC (MnHi—Sibley Papers). Addressed to Sibley at Fort Snelling. Endorsed.

1. If Flandin did go to Europe, he had returned by 1843, for in that year he was in his father's New York store furnishing foodstuffs to JCF for his second western expedition (DNA-217, T-135, voucher no. 2, 3 March 1843).

21. George M. Brooke to Frémont

FORT CRAWFORD April 4th 1839.

MY DEAR SIR

I had the pleasure, to receive, this morning, your letter of the 19th Ultimo, and have sent the things by the [Lamden?] accordingly, and hope they may arrive in time. I have enclosed the bill of lading, in this letter, as it is sent by a friend of mine, who will put it in the post office, as I do not know, at what house you may lodge. I am sorry to say, that I did not succeed, in the transfer of Lt. [?], and of course, that we have been deprived of their society. I regret to inform you, of the death of Capt. Lacey[1] on the 1st Inst.

We have been well enough, this winter, no visitors & very little news.

Please make my best regards to Mr. Nicollet, and the Gentlemen, with you. Wishing you all, a pleasant, and safe tour I remain very much yr. friend,

GEO. M. BROOKE

ALS, RC (CU-B—Fremont Papers). Addressed, "For Lt. C. Fremont, to the care of Pratte & Chouteau, St. Louis" with the added notation, "Favd. by Mr.

W. Wright." Wright operated a ferry across the Wisconsin near Prairie du Chien. Brig.-Gen. George M. Brooke, who was to sit on the court-martial board which tried JCF in 1847–48, was at this time commanding Fort Crawford, the military post at Prairie du Chien. He may have met the young lieutenant in 1838, when the Nicollet expedition stopped at his post, although he was absent from the fort during the spring of 1838 and again in November when JCF was there (MAHAN, 218–19).

1. Capt. Edgar Martin Lacey, 5th Infantry, commanded Fort Crawford in Nov. 1838 while General Brooke was absent (MAHAN, 332). He died 2 April 1839, according to HEITMAN.

22. Excerpt from the *Memoirs*

[1839]

A partial equipment for the expedition to the northwest prairies was obtained in St. Louis. Arrangements had previously been made at *Lac qui parle,* during the preceding journey, for a reinforcement of men to meet the party at an appointed time on Rivière à Jacques [James River], a tributary to the Missouri River. At St. Louis five men were engaged, four of them experienced in prairie and mountain travel; one of them Etienne Provost, known as *l'homme des montagnes.* The other man was Louis Zindel, who had seen service as a non-commissioned officer of Prussian artillery, and was skilled in making rockets and fireworks.[1] We left St. Louis early in April, 1839, on board the Antelope, one of the American Fur Company's steamboats, which, taking its customary advantage of the annual rise in the Missouri from the snows of the Rocky Mountains, was about starting on its regular voyage to the trading-post on the upper waters of the river.[2]

For nearly two months and a half we were struggling against the current of the turbid river, which in that season of high waters was so swift and strong that sometimes the boat would for moments stand quite still, seeming to pause to gather strength, until the power of steam asserted itself and she would fight her way into a smooth reach. In places the river was so embarrassed with snags that it was difficult to thread a way among them in face of the swift current and treacherous channel, constantly changing. Under these obstacles we usually laid up at night, making fast to the shore at some convenient place, where the crew could cut a supply of wood for the next day. It was a pleasant journey, as little disturbed as on the ocean. Once above the settlements of the lower Missouri, there were no sounds to disturb the stillness but the echoes of the high-pressure steam-pipe, which travelled far along and around the shores, and the incessant crumbling away of the banks and bars, which the river was steadily undermining and destroying at one place to build up at another. The stillness was an impressive feature, and the constant change in the character of the river shores offered always new interest as we steamed along. At times we travelled by high perpendicular escarpments of light colored rock, a gray and yellow marl, made picturesque by shrubbery or trees; at others the river opened out into a broad delta-like expanse, as if it were approaching the sea. At length, on the seventieth day we reached Fort Pierre, the chief post of the American Fur Company.[3] This is on the right or western bank of the river, about one thousand and three hundred miles from St. Louis. On the prairie, a few miles away, was a large village of Yankton Sioux. Here we were in the heart of the Indian country and near the great Buffalo ranges. Here the Indians were sovereign.

This was to be our starting-point for an expedition northward over the great prairies, to the British line. Some weeks were spent in making the remaining preparations, in establishing the position and writing up journals, and in negotiations with the Indians. After the usual courtesies had been exchanged our first visit to their village was arranged. On our way we were met by thirty of the principal chiefs, mounted and advancing in line. A noble-looking set of men showing to the best advantage, their fine shoulders and breasts being partly uncovered. We were conducted by them to the village, where we were received with great ceremony by other chiefs, and all their people gathered to meet us. We were taken into a large and handsome lodge and given something to eat, an observance without which no Indian welcome is complete. The village covered some acres of ground, and the lodges were pitched in regular lines. These were large, of about twenty skins or more. The girls were noticeably well clothed, wearing finely dressed skins nearly white, much embroidered with beads and porcupine quills dyed many colors; and stuffs from the trading-post completed their dress. These were the best formed and best looking Indians of the plains, having the free bearing belonging with their unrestrained life in sunshine and open air. Their mode of life had given them the uniform and smooth development of breast and limb which indicates power, without knots of exaggerated muscle, and the copper-bronze of their skins, burnt in by many suns, increased the statue-like effect. The buffalo and other game being near, gave them abundant food and means to obtain from the trading-post what to them were luxuries.

Having made the customary and expected presents which ratified the covenants of good will and free passage over their country, we left the village, escorted half-way by the chiefs.

A few days after our visit to the village, one of the chiefs came to the fort, bringing with him a pretty girl of about eighteen, handsomely dressed after the manner I have described. Accompanied by her and the interpreter, he came to the room opening on the court where we were employed over our sketch-books and maps, and formally offered her to Mr. Nicollet as a wife for him. This placed our chief for a moment in an embarrassing position. But, with ready and crafty tact he explained to the chief that he already had one, and that the Great Father would not permit him to have two. At the same time suggesting that the younger chief, designating me, had none. This put me in a worse situation. But being at bay, I promptly replied that I was going far away and not coming back, and did not like to take the girl away from her people; that it might bring bad luck; but that I was greatly pleased with the offer, and to show that I was so, would give the girl a suitable present. Accordingly, an attractive package of scarlet and blue cloths, beads, a mirror, and other trifles was made up, and they left us; the girl quite satisfied with her trousseau, and he with other suitable presents made him. Meantime we had been interested by the composure of the girl's manner, who during the proceedings had been quietly leaning against the door-post, apparently not ill-pleased with the matrimonial conference.

All was now ready. The rating of the chronometers had been verified. Our observations had placed Fort Pierre in latitude, 44° 23' 28", longitude, 100° 12' 30", and elevation above the sea 1456 feet. Horses, carts, and provisions had been obtained at the fort and six men added to the party; Mr. May, of Kentucky, and a young man from Pembinah had joined us. They were on their way to the British Colony of the Red River of the North. William Dixon and Louison Frenière had been engaged as interpreters and guides. Both of these were half-breeds, well known as fine horsemen and famous hunters, as well as most experienced guides. The party now consisted of nineteen persons, thirty-three horses, and ten carts. With Mr. Nicollet, Mr. Geyer, who was again our botanist, and myself, was an officer of

the French army, Captain Belligny, who wished to use so good an occasion to see the Indian country.[4] We reached the eastern shore with
all our equipage in good order, and made camp for the night at the
foot of the river hills opposite the fort. The hills leading to the prairie plateau, about five hundred feet above the river, were rough and
broken into ravines. We had barely reached the upland when the
hunters came galloping in, and the shout of *la vache! la vache!* rang
through the camp, everyone repeating it, and everyone excited.

A herd of buffalo had been discovered, coming down to water. In
a few moments the buffalo horses were saddled and the hunters
mounted, each with a smooth-bore, single or double-barrelled gun,
a handkerchief bound fillet-like around the head, and all in the
scantiest clothing. Conspicuous among them were Dixon and Louison. To this latter I then, and thereafter, attached myself.

My horse was a good one, an American, but grass-fed and prairie-
bred. Whether he had gained his experience among the whites or
Indians I do not know, but he was a good hunter and knew about
buffalo, and badger holes as well, and when he did get his foot into
one it was not his fault.

Now I was to see the buffalo. This was an event on which my
imagination had been dwelling. I was about to realize the tales the
mere telling of which was enough to warm the taciturn Renville
into enthusiastic expression, and to rouse all the hunter in the ex-
citable Frenière.

The prairie over which we rode was rolling, and we were able to
keep well to leeward and out of sight of the herd. Riding silently up
a short slope, we came directly upon them. Not a hundred yards below us was the great, compact mass of animals, moving slowly
along, feeding as they went, and making the loud incessant grunting noise peculiar to them. There they were.

The moment's pause that we made on the summit of the slope
was enough to put the herd in motion. Instantly as we rose the hill,
they saw us. There was a sudden halt, a confused wavering movement, and then a headlong rout; the hunters in their midst. How I
got down that short hillside I never knew. From the moment I saw
the herd I never saw the ground again until all was over. I remember, as the charge was made, seeing the bulls in the rear turn, then
take a few bounds forward, and then, turning for a last look, join
the headlong flight.

As they broke into the herd the hunters separated. For some instants I saw them as they showed through the clouds of dust, but I scarcely noticed them. I was finding out what it was to be a prairie hunter. We were only some few miles from the river, hardly clear of the breaks of the hills, and in places the ground still rough. But the only things visible to me in our flying course were the buffalo and the dust, and there was tumult in my breast as well as around me. I made repeated ineffectual attempts to steady myself for a shot at a cow after a hard struggle to get up with her; and each time barely escaped a fall. In such work a man must be able to forget his horse, but my horsemanship was not yet equal to such a proof. At the outset, when the hunters had searched over the herd and singled out each his fattest cow, and made his dash upon her, the herd broke into bands which spread over the plain. I clung to that where I found myself, unwilling to give up, until I found that neither horse nor man could bear the strain longer. Only some straggling groups were in sight, loping slowly off, seemingly conscious that the chase was over. I dismounted and reloaded, and sat down on the grass for a while to give us both a rest. I could nowhere see any of my companions, and, except that it lay somewhere to the south of where I was, I had no idea where to look for the camp. The sun was getting low, and I decided to ride directly west, thinking that I might reach the river hills above the fort while there was light enough for me to find our trail of the morning. In this way I could not miss the camp, but for the time being I was lost.

My horse was tired and I rode slowly. He was to be my companion and reliance in a long journey, and I would not press him. The sun went down, and there was no sign that the river was near. While it was still light an antelope came circling round me, but I would not fire at him. His appearance and strange conduct seemed uncanny but companionable, and the echo to my gun might not be a pleasant one. Long after dark I struck upon a great number of paths, deeply worn, and running along together in a broad roadway. They were leading directly toward the river, and I supposed, to the fort. With my anxieties all relieved I was walking contentedly along, when I suddenly recognized that these were buffalo-trails leading to some accustomed great watering-place. The discovery was something of a shock, but I gathered myself together and walked on. I had been for some time leading my horse. Toward midnight I reached the breaks of the river hills at a wooded ravine, and just then I saw a rocket shoot up into the sky, far away to the south.

That was camp, but apparently some fifteen miles distant, impossible for me to reach by the rough way in the night around the ravines. So I led my horse to the brink of the ravine, and going down I found water, which, *à plusieurs reprises,* I brought up to him, using my straw hat for a bucket. Taking off his saddle and bridle, and fastening him by his long lariat to one of the stirrups, I made a pillow of the saddle and slept soundly until morning. He did not disturb me much, giving an occasional jerk to my pillow, just enough to let me see that all was right.

At the first streak of dawn I saddled up. I had laid my gun by my side in the direction where I had seen the rocket, and riding along that way, the morning was not far advanced when I saw three men riding toward me at speed. They did not slacken their pace until they came directly up against me, when the foremost touched me. It was Louison Frenière. A reward had been promised by Mr. Nicollet to the first who should touch me, and Louison won it. And this was the end of my first buffalo hunt.

The camp gathered around all glad to see me. To be lost on the prairie in an Indian country is a serious accident, involving many chances, and no one was disposed to treat it lightly. Our party was made up of men experienced in prairie and in mountain travel, exposed always to unforeseen incidents.

When Frenière left the camp in search of me he had no hesitation about where to look. In the rolling country over which the hunt lay it would have been merely an accident to find either camp or water. He knew I would not venture the chance, but would strike directly for the river; and so in leaving camp he kept the open ground along the heads of the ravines, confident that he would either find me or my trail. He was sure I would remain on the open ground at the first water I found. He knew, too, as I did not, that from the Fort the valley of the river trended to the northwest, by this increasing the distance I had to travel; still farther increased by a large bend in which the river sweeps off to the westward. On the maps in common use it was nearly north and south, and had it really been so in fact I should have reached the breaks while it was still light enough for me to see the Fort or recognize our crossing-place, and perhaps to find my way to the camp. All the same I had made an experience and it had ended well.

The camp equipage being carried in carts, and not packed upon mules, the gearing up was quickly done; but meanwhile I had time for a fine piece of fat buffalo-meat standing already roasted on a stick before the fire, and a tin cup of good coffee. My horse and I did a fair share of walking on this day's march, and at every unusually good spot of grass I took the bit from his mouth and let him have the chance to recruit from the night before.

We were now on the upland of the *Coteau du Missouri,* here 1,960 feet above the sea. Travelling to the northeastward our camp for the night was made by a fork of the Medicine Bow River [Medicine Creek], the last running water our line would cross until we should reach the waters of the Rivière à Jacques on the eastern slopes of the plateau. On the open plains water is found only in ponds; not always permanent, and not frequent.

From the top of the hill [Medicine Butte] which gives its name to the stream where we had encamped the view was over great stretches of level prairie, fading into the distant horizon, and unbroken except by the many herds of buffalo which made on it dark spots that looked like groves of timber; here and there puffs of dust rising from where the bulls were rolling or fighting. On these high plains the buffalo feed contentedly, and good buffalo grass usually marks the range where they are found. The occasional ponds give them water, and, for them, the rivers are never far away.

This was the Fourth of July.[5] I doubt if any boy in the country found more joy in his fireworks than I did in my midnight rocket with its silent message. Water and wood to-night were abundant, and with plenty in camp and buffalo all around we celebrated our independence of the outside world.

Some days were now occupied in making the crossing of the plateau; our line being fixed by astronomical positions, and the level prairie required no sketching. I spent these days with Frenière among the buffalo. Sometimes when we had gotten too far ahead of our caravan it was an enjoyment to lie in careless ease on the grass by a pond and be refreshed by the breeze which carried with it the fragrance of the prairie. Edged with grasses growing into the clear water, and making a fresh border around them, these resting-spots are rather lakelets than ponds.

The grand simplicity of the prairie is its peculiar beauty, and its occurring events are peculiar and of their own kind. The uniformity is never sameness, and in his exhilaration the voyager feels even the occasional field of red grass waving in the breeze pleasant to his eye.

And whatever the object may be—whether horseman, or antelope, or buffalo—that breaks the distant outline of the prairie, the surrounding circumstances are of necessity always such as to give it a special interest. The horseman may prove to be enemy or friend, but the always existing uncertainty has its charm of excitement in the one case, and the joy of the chase in the other. There is always the suspense of the interval needed to verify the strange object; and, long before the common man decides anything, the practised eye has reached certainty. This was the kind of lore in which Frenière was skilled, and with him my prairie education was continued under a master. He was a reckless rider. Never troubling himself about impediments, if the shortest way after his buffalo led through a pond through it he plunged. Going after a band on one of these days we came upon a long stretch of shallow pond that we had not seen, and which was thickly sown with boulders half hidden in tall grass and water. As I started to go around he shouted, "In there—in! *Tout droit! faut pas craindre le cheval.*" And in we went, floundering through, happily without breaking bones of ourselves or our horses. It was not the horse that I was afraid of; I did not like that bed of rocks and water.

Crossing the summit level of the plateau we came in sight of the beautiful valley, here about seventy miles broad, of the *Rivière à Jacques,* its scattered wooded line stretching as far as the eye could reach. Descending the slope we saw in the distance ahead moving objects, soon recognized as horsemen; and before these could reach us a clump of lodges came into view. They proved to be the encampment of about a hundred Indians, to whom Dixon and Frenière were known as traders of the Fur Company. After an exchange of friendly greetings our camp was pitched near by. Such a rare meeting is an exciting break in the uneventful Indian life; and the making of presents gave a lively expression to the good feeling with which they received us, and was followed by the usual Indian rejoicing. After a conference in which our line of travel was indicated, the chief offered Mr. Nicollet an escort, the country being uncertain, but the offer was declined. The rendezvous for our expected reinforcement was not far away, and Indians with us might only prove the occasion for an attack in the event of meeting an unfriendly band. They had plenty of good buffalo-meat and the squaws had gathered in a quantity of the *pommes des prairies,* or prairie turnips

(*Psoralia esculenta*), which is their chief vegetable food, and abundant on the prairie. They slice and dry this for ordinary and winter use.

Travelling down the slope of the coteau, in a descent of 750 feet we reached the lake of "The Scattered Small Wood," a handsome but deceptive bit of water, agreeable to the eye, but with an unpleasant brackish taste.

About two years ago I received a letter, making of me some inquiries concerning this beautiful lake country of the Northwest. In writing now of the region over which I had travelled, I propose to speak of it as I had seen it, preserving as far as possible its local coloring of the time; shutting out what I may have seen or learned of the changes years have wrought. But, since the time of which I am writing, I have not seen this country. Looking over it, in the solitude where I left it, its broad valleys and great plains untenanted as I saw and describe them, I think that the curiosity and interest with which I read this letter, will also be felt by any who accompany me along these pages. Under this impression, and because the writer of the letter had followed our trail to this point—the *"Lake of the Scattered Small Wood"*—I give it here:

"Iowa City, Ia., February 13, 1884.

. . . . "This I write feeling that as you have devoted your life to engineering and scientific pursuits, it will be at least a gratification to receive a letter upon such subjects as are connected with what you have done. It has been my fortune to locate and construct railway lines for the Chicago & Northwestern Railway in Minnesota and Dakota, in doing which I have surveyed not less than three thousand miles of line, and in so doing have passed over a very large extent of the surface of that region. While doing this work I have been led to inquire into the climate of that remarkable region. I visited many places which you in 1838 discovered and named. Among these are Lakes Benton and Hendricks, the first about twenty miles north of the famous 'Red Pipe Stone Quarry,' a very fine sheet of water, along the south shore of which I located the railroad, and there has sprung up a fine town called Lake Benton. West of this, in Dakota, and on the west side of the Big Sioux River, is a lake region, to many of the lakes in which you gave names, and it is to this locality that I wish to particularly call your attention. These lakes bear the names of Thompson, Whitewood, Preston, Te-tonka-ha, Abert (now changed to Albert), Poinsett, and Kampeska. The last named is at the head of the Big Sioux, and Poinsett a few miles to the southward.

"When I constructed the Dakota Central Railway in 1879–80, all these lakes excepting Thompson, Poinsett, and Kampeska, were dry; and it took me a long time and no small research to ascertain when they last held water. They had been known to be dry for the twenty-five years preceding 1879, or at least persons who had lived there or in the vicinity for twenty-five years said that the lakes were dry when they came into the locality, and had, with numerous smaller ones, been dry ever since; and all who knew about them had a theory that they had dried up long since, and that they never would fill again; but I found old Frenchmen who had seen these lakes full of water in 1843–46, and I, in studying over the matter, found that you had seen and named them in 1836–38 [1838–39], and I would thank you very much if you will take the time and trouble to describe them to me as you saw them then.

"I came very near locating the railroad line through Lake Preston, for the head men of the railroad company believed that it had dried up for all time; but on my presenting the testimony of certain reliable voyageurs, they allowed me to go around it. It was well that they did, for the winter of 1880–81 gave a snow-fall such as had not been seen since the years 1843–44, and in the spring of 1881 all these lakes filled up, bank full, and have continued so ever since. I had the pleasure of comparing my engineer's levels for elevation above the sea with your barometer determination at Fort Pierre on the Missouri River. Your altitude was 1,450 feet, mine was 1,437, the difference 13 feet. My determination is within the limits of ± 6 feet. The distance over which my levels were taken was 680 miles, and were well checked. I also followed up your trail as you marched from Fort Pierre northeasterly to the 'Scattered Small Wood Lake.' I was so successful as to verify your barometer reading in several instances by checking with mine, and in no case found over 15 feet difference between us, and that always in the same relation as at Fort Pierre. Hoping that you will excuse this long letter, and that you may be able to tell me if those lakes were dry when you saw them, or otherwise, and add any other information you see fit,

"I am, truly yours,
"C. W. Irish,[6] C. E. "

59

The next day we reached the Rivière à Jacques, at the *Talle de Chênes,* a clump of oaks which was the rendezvous where our expected reinforcement was to meet us. The river valley here is about seventy miles wide. Observations made during the four days that we remained at the Talle de Chênes place it in latitude 45° 16′ 34″, longitude 98° 7′ 45″, and the elevation above the sea 1,341 feet. At the end of this time, no one appearing, the party again took up the line of march, and, following the right bank, on the evening of the 14th encamped near the mouth of Elm River. This river and its forks are well timbered, and for the reason that they furnish firewood and shelter, Indian hunting parties make it their winter crossing-place on the way westward after buffalo on the Missouri plateau.

On the high plains the winter storms are dangerous. Many tales are told of hunters caught out in a *poudrerie* with no timber near, when it is impossible to see one's way, and every landmark is obliterated or hidden by the driving snow. At such times the hunter has no other resource than to dig for himself a hole in the snow, leaving only a breathing-place above his head, and to remain in it wrapped in his blankets until the storm passes over; when, putting on the dry socks and moccasins which he always carries, he makes for the nearest wood.

The buffalo herds, when caught in such storms and no timber in sight, huddle together in compact masses, all on the outside crowding and fighting to get to the inside; and so, kept warm by the struggling, incessant motion, the snow meanwhile being stamped away under their feet, protect themselves from the fiercest storms.

For several days we travelled up the valley of the *Jacques,* making astronomical stations, and collecting material for Mr. Nicollet's map. Occasionally, to the same end, I was detached, with Dixon or Frenière, on topographical excursions, which gave me a good general knowledge of the country along the route. At the *Butte aux Os* (Bone Hill), in latitude 46° 27′ 37″, longitude 98° 8′ elevation above the sea 1,400 feet, we left the *Rivière à Jacques,* or *Chan-sansan,* its valley extending apparently far in a course to west of north, and in a few miles we reached the height of land which separates it from the Shayen [Sheyenne] River. This is a tributary to the Red River of the North, and was formerly the home of the Shayens, to-day written Cheyennes. In the incessant wars between the various tribes of this region the Shayens were driven from their country over the Missouri River south to where they now are.

The summit of the plateau was only 1,460 feet above the sea. Here we regained the great prairie plains, and here we saw in their magnificent multitudes the grand buffalo herds on their chief range. They were moving southwestwardly, apparently toward the plains of the upper Missouri. For three days we were in their midst, travelling through them by day and surrounded by them at night. We could not avoid them. Evidently some disturbing cause had set them in motion from the north. It was necessary to hobble some of our animals and picket them all, and keep them close in to prevent any of them from making off with the buffalo, when they would have been irretrievably lost. Working through the herds it was decided, in order to get more out of their way, to make a temporary halt for a day or two on the *Tampa,* a small stream flowing into the Shayen. On the second day after, Dixon and Frenière came in with three Indians from a party which had been reconnoitring our camp. They belonged to a hunting village of some three hundred lodges, who were out making buffalo-meat and were just about arranging for a grand *"surround."* It would have been dangerous to risk breaking in upon this, as might easily happen in our ignorance of the locality and their plans. To avert mischief Frenière, on the third day, rode over to the village with a message requesting their chiefs to indicate the time and route for our march. In consequence we were invited to come on to their encampment. Pushing our way through the crowds of buffalo, we were met in the afternoon by two of the chiefs who escorted us to the village and pointed out the place for our camp. We found the encampment made up of about three hundred lodges of various tribes—Yanktons, Yankton[ais], and Sissitons—making about two thousand Indians.

The representations of our guides had insured us a most friendly reception. We were invited to eat in the lodges of different chiefs; the choicest, fattest pieces of buffalo provided for us, and in return they were invited to eat at our camp. The chiefs sat around in a large circle on buffalo robes or blankets, each provided with a deep soup plate and spoon of tin. The first dish was a generous *pot-au-feu,* principally of fat buffalo meat and rice. No one would begin until all the plates were filled. When all was ready the feast began. With the first mouthful each Indian silently laid down his spoon, and each looked at the other. After a pause of bewilderment the interpreter succeeded in having the situation understood. Mr. Nicollet had put among our provisions some Swiss cheese, and to give flavor to the soup a liberal portion of this had been put into the kettles. Until this strange flavor was accounted for the Indians thought they were being poisoned; but, the cheese being shown to them, and explanation made, confidence was restored; and by the aid of several kettles of water well sweetened with molasses, and such other tempting *delicatessen* as could be produced from our stores, the dinner party went on and terminated in great good humor and general satisfaction.

The next day they made their surround. This was their great summer hunt when a provision of meat was made for the year, the winter hunting being in smaller parties. The meat of many fat cows was brought in, and the low scaffolds on which it was laid to be sun-dried were scattered over all the encampment. No such occasion as this was to be found for the use of presents, and the liberal gifts distributed through the village heightened their enjoyment of the feasting and dancing, which was prolonged through the night. Friendly relations established, we continued our journey.

Having laid down the course of the river by astronomical stations, during three days' travel; we crossed to the left bank and directed our road toward the Devil's Lake, which was the ultimate object of the expedition. The Indian name of the lake is Mini-wakan, the Enchanted Water; converted by the whites into Devil's Lake.

Our observations placed the river where we left it in latitude 47° 46′ 29″, longitude 98° 13′ 30″, and elevation above the sea 1,328 feet; the level of the bordering plateaus being about one hundred and sixty feet above the river.

In our journey along this river, mosquitoes had infested the camp in such swarms and such pertinacity that the animals would quit feeding and come up to the fires to shelter themselves in the smoke. So virulent were they that to eat in any quiet was impossible, and we found it necessary to use the long green veils, which to this end had been recommended to us by the fur traders. Tied around our straw hats the brims kept the veils from our faces, making a space within which the plates could be held; and behind these screens we contrived to eat without having the food uncomfortably flavored by mosquito sauce piquante.

After a short day's march of fourteen miles we made our first camp on this famous war and hunting ground, four miles from the *Mini-wakan*. Early in the day's march we had caught sight of the woods and hills bordering the lake, among them being conspicuous a heart-shaped hill near the southern shore. The next day after an hour's march we pitched our camp at the head of a deep bay not far from this hill. To this the Indians have given the name of the *"Heart of the Enchanted Water,"* by the whites translated "Heart of the Devil's Lake."

At a wooden lake of fresh water near last night's camp on the plateau we had found traces of a large encampment which had been recently abandoned. The much-trodden ground and trails all round showed that a large party had been here for several weeks. From many cart-wheel tracks and other signs our guides recognized it as a hunting camp of the *Métis,* or *Bois-Brulés,* of the Red River of the North; and the deep ruts cut by the wheels showed that the carts had received their full load, and that the great hunt of the year was over. It was this continuous and widespread hunt that had put in motion the great herds through which we had passed.

Among other interesting features of the northwest we had heard much from our guides about these people and their buffalo hunts; and to have just missed them by a few days only was quite a disappointment.

The home of the Half-breeds is at Pembina in British North America. They are called indifferently *Métis* or Half-breeds, *Bois-Brulés,* and *Gens libres* or Free People of the North. The Half-breeds themselves are in greater part the descendants of French Canadian traders and others who, in the service of the Fur Company, and principally of the Northwest Company of Montreal, had been stationed at their remote forts, or scattered over the northwest Indian country in gathering furs. These usually took local wives from among the Indian women of the different tribes, and their half Indian children grew up to a natural life of hunting and kindred pursuits, in which their instincts gave them unusual skill.

The Canadian *engagés* of the company who had remained in the country after their term of service had expired were called Free Canadians; and, from their association with the Half-breeds came also the name of *Gens libres.* They were prominently concerned in a singular event which occurred in British America about a quarter of a century before the time of which I am writing. In the rivalry between the Hudson's Bay Company and the Northwest Fur and Trading Company of Montreal, the Half-breeds were used by the Northwest Company in their successful attempts to destroy a Scotch colony which had been planted by the Earl of Selkirk[7] on the Red

River of the North at its confluence with the Assiniboine, about forty miles above Lake Winnipeg. The colony was founded upon a grant of land made to the Earl by the Hudson's Bay Company in 1811; and about a hundred immigrants were settled at the Forks in 1812, reaching to some two hundred in 1814. This was called the Kildonan settlement, from a parish in the County of Sutherland which had been the home of the immigrants. In August of 1815 it was entirely broken up by the Northwest Company, and the settlers driven away and dispersed. During the following winter and spring the colony was re-established, and in prosperous condition when it was attacked by a force of Half-breeds, under officers of the Northwest Company, and some twenty unresisting persons killed; including Mr. [Robert] Semple, the Governor of the Hudson's Bay Company and five of his officers. In the course of this contest there were acts of a savage brutality, not repugnant, perhaps, to the usages of the Indian country where they were perpetrated, but unknown among civilized men. The opposition made to the colony by the Northwest Company was for the declared reason that "Colonization was unfavorable to the Fur Trade:" their policy was to hold the great part of a continent as a game preserve for the benefit solely of their trade.

The colony was revived when the Northwest was merged in the Hudson's Bay Company, and reoccupied its old site at the Forks of Red River; the settlements extending gradually southward along the banks of the river. The grants of land which had been made to the colonists by the Earl of Selkirk held good under the general grant made to him by the Hudson's Bay Company in 1811, and have been so maintained.

Meantime the Half-breeds had been increasing in number; and, as the buffalo have receded before the settlements in British America, they made their hunting expeditions to the plains around the Devil's Lake. With them, the two important events of the year are the buffalo hunts which they come to these plains to make. They bring with them carts built to carry each the meat of ten buffalo, which they make into *pemmican*. This consists of the meat dried by fire or sun, coarsely pounded and mixed with melted fat, and packed into skin sacks. It is of two qualities; the ordinary pemmican of commerce, being the meat without selection, and the finer, in small sacks, consisting of the choicest parts kneaded up with the marrow.

Buffalo tongues, pemmican, and robes, constitute chiefly their trade and support.

When making their hunts the party is usually divided; one-half to hunt, the other to guard the camp. Years ago they were much harassed by the Indians of the various tribes who frequented these buffalo grounds as much to fight as to hunt. But as a result of these conflicts with the Half-breeds the Indians were always obliged to go into mourning; and gradually they had learned to fight shy of these people and of late years had ceased to molest them. They are good shots and good riders, and have a prairie-wide reputation for skill in hunting and bravery in fighting.

We remained on the Devil's Lake over a week, during which three stations were made along the southern shore, giving for the most northern latitude 47° 59′ 29″, and for longitude 98° 28′. Our barometer gave for the top of the "Enchanted Hill" 1,766 feet above the sea, for the plateau 1,486 feet, and for the lake 1,476 feet. It is a beautiful sheet of water, the shores being broken into pleasing irregularity by promontories and many islands. As in some other lakes on the plateau, the water is brackish, but there are fish in it; and it is doubtless much freshened by the rains and melting snows of the spring. No outlet was found, but at the southern end there are low grounds by which at the season of high waters the lake may discharge into the Shayen River. This would put it among the sources of the Red River. The most extended view of its waters obtainable from any of the surrounding hills seemed to reach about forty miles in a northwesterly direction. Accompanied by Dixon or Frenière, I was sent off on several detached excursions to make out what I could of the shape and size of the lake. On one of these I went for a day's journey along the western shore, but was unable in the limited time to carry my work to the northern end. Toward nightfall we found near the shore good water and made there our camp in open ground. Nothing disturbed our rest for several hours, when we were roused by a confused heavy trampling and the usual grunting sounds which announced buffalo. We had barely time to get our animals close in and to throw on dry wood and stir up the fire before the herd was upon us. They were coming to the lake for water, and the near ones being crowded forward by those in the rear and disregarding us, they were nigh going directly over us. By shouting and firing our pieces, we succeeded in getting them to make a little space, in which they kept us as they crowded down into the lake. The brackish, salty water, is what these animals like, and to turn the course of such a herd from water at night would be impossible.

Unwieldy as he looks, the buffalo bull moves with a suddenness and alertness that make him at close quarters a dangerous antagonist. Frenière and I being together one day, we discovered a bull standing in the water of a little lake near the shore, and we rode up to see what he was doing there alone. "He may be sick," said Frenière. As we approached we noticed that he was watching us inquiringly, his head high up, with intention, as a bull in an arena. As we got abreast of him within a few yards, he made two or three quick steps toward us and paused. *"Oho! bonjour camarade,"* Frenière called out, and moved his horse a little away. My attention for an instant was diverted to my *riata,* which was trailing, when the bull made a dash at us. I made an effort to get out of his range, but my horse appeared to think that it was in the order of proceeding for me first to fire. A rough graze to his hind quarters which staggered him made him see that the bull had decided to take this particular affair into his own hands, or horns, and under the forcible impression he covered a rod or two of ground with surprising celerity; the bull meanwhile continuing his course across the prairie without even turning his head to look at us. Concluding that it was not desirable to follow up our brief acquaintance, we too continued our way. A good hunter does not kill merely for the sake of killing.

The outward line of the expedition being closed, our route was now turned eastward across the plateau toward the valley of the Red River of the North. The first night was passed at a small fresh-water lake near the Lake of the Serpents, which is salt; and on August 7th we encamped again on the Shayen-oju. Continuing east, we crossed next day the height of land at an elevation of 1,500 feet above sea level, and a few miles farther came in view of the wide-spread valley of the Red River, its green wooded line extending far away to the north on its way to British America. From this point, travelling southerly, a week was spent in sketching and determining positions among the head-waters of its tributaries; and on August 14th we descended again to the valley of the Shayen and recrossed that river at an elevation of 1,228 feet above the sea, its course not many miles below curving northeast to the Red River. Two days later we reached the Lake of the Four Hills, about a hundred feet above the river. This lake is near the foot of the ascent to the *Réipahan,* or

Head of the Coteau des Prairies. We ascended the slope to the highest point at the head of the Coteau, where the elevation was 2,000
feet above the sea and the width of the Coteau about twenty miles.
In its extension to the south it reaches, in about a hundred and fifty
miles, a breadth of forty miles; sloping abruptly on the west to the
great plains of the *Riviere à Jacques*, and on the east to the prairies
of the Mini-sotah River. Here we spent several days in the basin of
the beautiful lakes which make the head-waters of the Mini-sotah of
the Mississippi River, and the Tchankasndata or Sioux River of the
Missouri. The two groups of lakes are near together, occupying apparently the same basin, with a slight rise between; the Mini-sotah
group being the northern. They lie in a depression or basin, from
150 to 300 feet below the rim of the Coteau, full of clear living water,
often partially wooded; and, having sometimes a sandy beach or
shore strewed with boulders, they are singularly charming natural
features. These were pleasant camping-grounds—wood was abundant, the water was good, and there were fish in the lakes.

From the lake region we descended 800 or 900 feet to the lower
prairies, and took up our march for the residence of our friends the
Renvilles.

Some well employed time was devoted here to make examinations
of the Big Stone and other lakes, and to making observations and
collecting materials to render Mr. Nicollet's projected map of this
region as nearly complete as practicable. In all these excursions we
had the effective aid of the Renvilles, whose familiar knowledge of
the country enabled us to economize both labor and time.

The autumn was far advanced when we took our leave of this
post. That year the prairie flowers had been exceptional in luxuriance and beauty. The rich lowlands near the house were radiant
with asters and golden-rod, and memory chanced to associate these
flowers, as the last thing seen, with the place. Since then I have not
been in that country or seen the Renvilles; but still I never see the
golden-rod and purple asters in handsome bloom, without thinking
of that hospitable refuge on the far northern prairies.

Some additional examinations on the water-shed of the Mini-sotah
and along the Mississippi closed the labors of these expeditions; and
at nightfall early in November I landed at *Prairie du Chien* in a
bark canoe, with a detachment of our party.[8] A steamboat at the
landing was firing up and just about starting for St. Louis, but we
thought it would be pleasant to rest a day or two and enjoy comfort-

able quarters while waiting for the next boat. But the next boat was in the spring, for next morning it was snowing hard, and the river was frozen from bank to bank. I had time enough while there to learn two things: one, how to skate; the other, the value of a day.

After some weeks of wagon journey through Illinois, in a severe winter, we reached St. Louis; when, after the party had been cared for, I went on to Washington to assist Mr. Nicollet in working up the material collected in the expeditions.

MEMOIRS, 38–54.

1. Etienne Provost (ca. 1782–1850), one of the best known of the mountain men of his time. His name is spelled many ways (as in Provo, Utah), and as he did not write, we do not know his preference. He was with the Chouteau-DeMun trading venture to the Rockies in 1815–17, exploiting the fur resources of the Platte and upper Arkansas rivers. A few years later he had moved to the Great Basin, and he has been credited with the discovery of Great Salt Lake—though men from the Hudson's Bay Company may have preceded him. He had contacts with William H. Ashley but was never associated with him as a partner, and was employed by the American Fur Company for a number of years. He ascended the Missouri with John James Audubon in 1843. For biographies, see ANDERSON, 343–51, and L. HAFEN [3], 6:371–85. Louis Zindel was a new immigrant when he signed on with Nicollet. Upon returning to St. Louis he opened a grocery store at 128 Market Street, but joined JCF again in 1843 for his expedition to California and Oregon. He made tents for the expedition of 1845 but did not join it, and later moved to Keokuk, Iowa, to continue in the grocery trade. From an examination of the vouchers, it seems probable that the other three men who signed on at St. Louis were Joseph Fournaise, François Latulippe, and Joseph Chartran.

2. The *Antelope* was making her second voyage up the Missouri, having gone as far as Fort Union the previous year. But she drew too much water for the shallow reaches of the upper river, and on this trip she would fall 400 miles short of her destination—Fort Union again (SUNDER, 21). Besides the Nicollet party, she carried fur company officials John F. A. Sanford, William Laidlaw, and James Kipp. The famed missionary, Father Pierre-Jean de Smet, would board at Council Bluffs to ride as far as the Vermillion River (NICOLLET, 41–42). A second vessel, the *Pirate,* which started up river ahead of the *Antelope* carrying supplies for the Nicollet party, struck a snag and sank a few miles below Council Bluffs. A chart of the river prepared by Nicollet and JCF, now in the Nicollet Papers, DLC, indicates the location of the wreck.

3. At the present site of Pierre, S.D. While there is no journal of the voyage to this point, the large-scale charts of the river give a good account of the trip, as they show dates and places of encampment.

4. The men mentioned by JCF include William F. P. May (ca. 1797–1855), an independent fur trader for more than thirty years on the upper Missouri, the Platte, and apparently in the Santa Fe trade (CHRISTOPHER & HAFEN). William Dickson, a son of fur trader Robert Dickson, served as an Indian interpreter among the Sioux at times, and in 1835 was in charge of an American Fur Company post near the James River. JCF notes its location on the

charts of the river in the DNA. Louison Frenière had been hired 10 July 1838 by P. D. Papin as a clerk and interpreter. He was a Sioux half-breed, later to serve as interpreter for the upper Missouri agency. It is doubtful that Captain Belligny was on this expedition (see Doc. No. 5, note 2).

5. Near Blunt, in Hughes County, S.D. The expedition will now strike off to the northeast, passing south of the Scatterwood Lakes in Faulk County, and reaching the James River 10 July. By 14 July they will reach Sand Lake in Brown County, cross into present North Dakota on 16 July, and two days later leave the James and strike out northeast toward the Sheyenne River. Then they will proceed northward, first along the Sheyenne and then overland (passing a lake which they will name Lake Jessie when they eventually make their map) and arriving in the Devils Lake area of North Dakota on 27 July. From here the party will head south again, following along the eastern side of the Coteau, to the headwaters of the Minnesota. The Nicollet map does not show dates or routes from this point, but JCF says the party visited again with the Renvilles at Lac qui Parle, investigating lakes in the area, and that the autumn was well advanced when they started down the Minnesota for Fort Snelling. For detailed comment on the route in the Dakotas, see STEVENS.

6. Charles W. Irish (1834–1904), pioneer settler in Iowa City, not only surveyed and supervised the construction of many railroad lines, but also served under President Grover Cleveland as chief of the Bureau of Irrigation. He later became deputy mining surveyor of Nevada (see obituary notice, *Annals of Iowa*, ser. 3, 6 [1903–5]:639).

7. Thomas Douglas, fifth Earl of Selkirk (1771–1820).

8. Nicollet had reached Prairie du Chien before 14 Oct. and was expecting to descend the Mississippi with JCF, who would arrive in two or three days (Nicollet to P. Chouteau, Jr., and Co., 14 Oct. 1839, MoSHi). The coming of winter, however, seems to have forced him to proceed to St. Louis without Frémont as he feared ice would close the river as it had in Nov. 1838 (see letters of Nicollet to Sibley, Washington, 26 April 1840, and Hercules L. Dousman to Sibley, 20 Nov. 1838, MnHi—Sibley Papers).

23. Financial Records, 1839

[31 Dec. 1839]

Quarter Ending 31 March 1839

Voucher No. 1, Baltimore, 9 Feb. 1839
U.S. to Brantz Mayer

1 Troughton's reflecting circle and stand   150.00

Brantz Mayer (1809–79), a Baltimore lawyer, historian, and one of the founders of the Maryland Historical Society.

Voucher No. 2, New York, 27 Feb. 1839
U.S. to A. Bininger & Co.

20 lbs Dresden chocolate	20.00
1 boxes sardines	7.50
1 Stilton cheese	6.25
2 boxes Andoulettes	4.00
3 lbs Bermuda arrowroot	3.31
8 bottles superior old port	8.00
4 bottles brandy	4.00
2 bottles raspberry brandy	1.50
2 bottles fleur d'orange	1.25
	55.81

In 1846–47, A. Bininger & Co. was a firm of grocers at 141 Broadway, New York.

Voucher No. 3, New York, 27 Feb. 1839
U.S. to E. & G. W. Blunt

1 chronometer balance watch by Amdd [?] & Dent, No. 4632	220.00

Edmund and George W. Blunt specialized in books and charts, and handled all nautical instruments of American manufacture. In 1846–47, the firm was located at 179 Water Street, New York.

Voucher No. 4 (U.S. to E. & G. W. Blunt) [*not present*]

Voucher No. 5, New York, 27 Feb. 1839
U.S. to E. & G. W. Blunt

1 camera lucida	18.00

Voucher No. 6, New York, 27 Feb. 1839
U.S. to E. & G. W. Blunt

1 English nautical almanac for 1839	2.50
1 American nautical almanac for 1839	1.50
1 English nautical almanac for 1840	2.50
	6.50

Voucher No. 7, New York, 27 Feb. 1839
U.S. to E. & G. W. Blunt

1 variation chart	3.00

Voucher No. 8, Baltimore, 4 March 1839
U.S. to James Green

8 pocket thermometers	16.00
2 of the same	5.00
1 compass in gimbals	5.00
5 lbs. quicksilver	8.75
	34.75

Voucher No. 9, [Baltimore], 4 March 1839
U.S. to Edward Jenkins and Sons

20 yards gum elastic cloth	25.00

In 1839, the Baltimore firm of Edward Jenkins and Sons, "importers of saddlery," was at 147 and 148 Baltimore Street. Some sixty years later the firm was still in business, located at 21 Hanover.

Voucher No. 10, Baltimore, 4 March 1839
U.S. to Fielding Lucas, Jr.

2 airtight ink stands	2.00
1 doz. Cohen's pencils	1.25
$\frac{3}{4}$ ea. 3H and 4H Jackson's pens	$2.62\frac{1}{2}$
9 pieces India rubber	$.37\frac{1}{2}$
1 bunch quills	1.00
4 2-quire cap quartos	1.50
1 3-quire cap No. 1 paper	1.50
1 quire super quarto port [folio]	$.37\frac{1}{2}$
1 each 2- and 3-quire demi quarto	3.00
2 small blank books	.75
logarithm tables, Callet	5.00
	$19.37\frac{1}{2}$

Fielding Lucas, Jr. (1781–1854), a publisher of fine books and maps, supplier of "every article used in books, newspaper, and job offices," had earlier been a partner in the Baltimore firm of Conrad, Lucas, and Co., book publishers. See FOSTER.

Voucher No. 11, Baltimore, 5 March 1839
U.S. to Stockton, Falls & Co.

Freight of instruments and stores from Baltimore to Wheeling   13.00

In 1842, the general stage offices of Stockton and Falls and Co. were at the Baltimore & Ohio depot on Pratt Street.

Voucher No. 12, St. Louis, 20 March 1839
U.S. to Collier & Pettus

153 lbs. dried beef	19.89
4 half bbls. pilot bread	10.00
1 box	.50
	30.39

Collier & Pettus were wholesale grocers and forwarding and commission merchants, 14 Front Street, St. Louis.

Voucher No. 13, St. Louis, 22 March 1839
U.S. to S. W. Meech

$\frac{1}{4}$ ream blue wove cap	1.50
$\frac{1}{4}$ ream white letter	1.38
2 quires envelope paper	.75
1 4-quire half-bound record	1.50
1 2-quire 1/bound blanks	2.00
1 card steel pens	1.00
1 box wafers	.13
1 screw top ink stand	.75
4 bottles Japan ink	1.00
6 reams mapping paper	12.00
2 rulers	.50
4 papers of ink powder	.50
1 4-quire demy record	4.00
4 binder's boards covered with leather	3.00
covering two boards with leather	.75
2 binder's boards	.25
binding 2 vols. geology & botany	1.87
box for packing mapping paper	1.00
	33.88

S. W. Meech was proprietor of the Franklin Bookstore, St. Louis.

Voucher No. 14, St. Louis, 22 March 1839
U.S. to Mueller & Kingpeter

21 March 1839

1 trunk	4.50
1 case for telescope	2.25
6 straps for herbarium	1.50
	8.25

This St. Louis firm was listed in 1840–41 as Miller & Kinzpeter, saddlers and harnessmakers, at 53 S. Second Street.

Voucher No. 15, St. Louis, 21 March 1839
U.S. to A. W. Kruger

1 German cavalry bridle, martingale and crupper   15.00

A. W. Kruger not identified.

Voucher No. 16, St. Louis, 22 March 1839
U.S. to H. L. Zierlein

1 rifle   20.00

Henry L. Zierlein (1799–1864), a Prussian, became one of the first German hardware merchants in St. Louis.

Voucher No. 17, St. Louis, 23 March 1839
U.S. to J. N. Nicollet

On account of services rendered as chief of the North West Exploring Expedition   1000.00

Voucher No. 18, St. Louis, 19 March 1839
U.S. to R. Simpson

24 lbs. chocolate   4.80

This merchant may be Dr. Robert Simpson (1785–1873), who operated a store in this period but who earlier had served in the Army as a surgeon. He had come to the Mississippi Valley in 1809 from Maryland, ordered to serve the troops at the newly constructed Fort Madison. After resigning in 1812 he started a medical practice in St. Louis, and also operated a drug store. See SCHARF, 2:1520; BILLON, 244, 341; JACKSON [3], 25–26.

Voucher No. 19, St. Louis, 23 March 1839
U.S. to J. E. Flandin

Transportation of stores and instruments from New York to
Baltimore   3.75

Voucher No. 20, St. Louis, 25 March 1839
U.S. to Charles Reshiner

23 Jan. 1839
1 sextant cleaned and varnished	20.00
1 magnifying glass and movement	5.00
1 mahogany box	8.00
2 barometers filled, and new tubes	5.00

15 Feb.
1 brass frame to magnifying glass	.75
1 magnifying glass with wood frame	1.00

16 March
1 artificial horizon repaired	1.00
cleaning vertical circle	3.00

22 March
cleaning telescope	.75
magnifying glass and tube to small sextant	2.50
2 leather cases for barometers	4.00
2 leather cases altered	1.00
1 leather case for sextant	4.00
	56.00

We have not identified Charles Reshiner or Ryhiner, or F. Ryhiner (see
voucher no. 15 below).

Voucher No. 21, St. Louis, 25 March 1839
U.S. to Chas. A. Geyer

For services   100.00

Endorsed by JCF: "Mr. Geyer was appointed by the War Department as
assistant to J. N. Nicollet Esqr., appointment bearing date 1st March 1839."
In another hand: "at $2.00 per day from the 10th March to the 29th April
inclusive." Another endorsement by JCF: "The amount was paid in advance
to enable Mr. Geyer to procure his outfit. . . ."

Voucher No. 22, St. Louis, 25 March 1839
U.S. to H. Helgenberg

1 sledge hammer	2.50
1 small hammer	1.00
1 small grubbing hoe	2.00
2 stone chisels	2.00
1 pruning [?] rod	1.50
	9.00

Certified: "I certify that the above amount is Correct. C. Frémont." Both the certification and signature are in the hand of Jessie Benton Frémont, and probably were not added until at least late 1841. Henry Helgenberg first appears in a St. Louis directory in 1842, listed as a grocer on Carondelet Avenue between Bridge and Wood.

Voucher No. 23, St. Louis, 22 March 1839
U.S. to Charles A. Geyer

For services 16.00, drayage 1.00   17.00

With endorsements similar to those for no. 21, indicating service at 2.00 per day from 1 to 8 March inclusive.

Voucher No. 24, St. Louis, 28 March 1839
U.S. to J. N. Nicollet

On account of services rendered as chief of the North West
Exploring Expedition.   100.00

Voucher No. 25, St. Louis, 29 March 1839
U.S. to J. S. Page

1 cord and tassels for flag $.87\frac{1}{2}$

No firm by this name is listed in the St. Louis directory for 1838–39, and it may be an error for J. S. Pease & Company—importers and dealers in hardware, cutlery, etc. at 20 N. First Street.

Voucher No. 26, St. Louis, 29 March 1839
U.S. to Henry Chouteau

1 box hams and bacon	43.50
1 keg butter	11.20
1 box port wine, 12 bottles	8.00

1 box sperm candles	14.88
drayage	.25
	77.83

Voucher No. 27, St. Louis, 29 March 1839
U.S. to Chouteau & Barlow

25 March 1839

3 bed cords	1.50
2 tea kettles	3.50
2 [boxes] percussion caps	1.25
2 frying pans	2.00
2 cork screws	.75
2 doz. knives and forks	4.00
3 loaves sugar	4.10
1 tin cup	.75
4 canisters	2.00
1 [ ] plates	1.00
2 coffee pots	3.00
2 lanterns	1.00
3 lbs. saleratus	.75
2 doz. matches	1.00
1 doz. spoons	1.12
2 wash basins	.75
2 sauce pans	2.00
1 saw	1.25
2 spades	2.50
	34.22

Chouteau and Barlow, grocers and dry goods and commission merchants, were at Front and Market Streets, St. Louis, in 1838–39.

Voucher No. 28, St. Louis, 29 March 1839
U.S. to E. & J. C. Bredell

| 1 crimson scarf | 1.75 |

Edward and John C. Bredell, brothers, were dry goods merchants at Main and Market Streets, St. Louis.

Voucher No. 29, St. Louis, 29 March 1839
U.S. to Gaty, Coonce & Beltshoover

[An illegible voucher involving materials for making rockets, including brass items, three rammers, and other items, totaling 28.75].

Samuel Gaty (b. 1811) was chief partner in a foundry firm known variously as Gaty & Coonce; Gaty, Coonce & Morton; and Gaty, Coonce & Beltshoover. Gaty made the first casting in St. Louis and the first steam engine west of the Mississippi (SCHARF, 1:666–68).

Voucher No. 30, St. Louis, 30 March 1839
U.S. to Mrs. E. Lyons

Making 2 mosquito bars	3.00
making liner for same	1.50
making scarf for flag	1.00
	5.50

In 1840, an E. Lyons family ran a fancy goods store at 24 Market Street, St. Louis.

Voucher No. 31, St. Louis, 29 March 1839
U.S. to Taylor & Marshall

½ yard Tibet merino	1.25

In 1841, Taylor and Marshall were dealers in staple and fancy dry goods, Main and Pine Streets, St. Louis.

Voucher No. 32, St. Louis, 30 March 1839
U.S. to George Engelmann, M.D.

Set of chemical tests in a box with blowpipe	8.50
6 [. . .]	18.00
medicines, emetics, pills	3.50
bottle of camphor	1.50
	31.50

Voucher No. 33, St. Louis, 30 March 1839
U.S. to Jaccard & Co.

Cleaning and repairing one gold patent duplex watch	8.00
3 common keys	.37½

1 guard chain	.37½
2 watch glasses	2.00
cleaning and repairing silver watch	4.00
	14.75

Until 1848, Louis Jaccard was a principal owner of the jewelry house of Jaccard & Co., St. Louis (SCHARF, 2:1320).

Second, Third, and Fourth Quarters, 1839

Voucher No. 1, St. Louis, 1 April 1839
U.S. to Carstens & Schuetze

[Illegible bill, including 15 lbs. saltpeter for 3.00, and 2 lbs. sulfur.]   4.81

Carstens and Schuetze, 168 Main Street, St. Louis, were wholesale druggists and apothecaries.

Voucher No. 2, St. Louis, 1 April 1839
U.S. to S. Wing & Co.

30 tin grenade cases   11.25

S. Wing & Co., 21 N. First Street, is listed as tin manufacturer and dealer in the St. Louis directory for 1842.

Voucher No. 3, St. Louis, Mo., 2 April 1839
U.S. to Mead & Adriance

2 pair gilt flag tassels   7.00

In 1839, Mead and Adriance were dealers in clocks, watches, jewelry, and military and fancy goods, at the corner of First and Pine Streets, St. Louis.

Voucher No. 4, St. Louis, 3 April 1839
U.S. to George Engelmann, M.D.

2 bottles soda of tartaric acid	2.00
sharpening lancets	.25
	2.25

Voucher No. 5, St. Louis, 3 April 1839
U.S. to Grimsley & Young

2 Spanish saddles	15.00
1 bridle	2.50
1 black leather belt	.50
	18.00

Grimsley and Young made saddles, harness, and trunks for the wholesale and retail trade, 37 Main Street, St. Louis.

Voucher No. 6, St. Louis, 4 April 1839
U.S. to J. E. Flandin

To cash advanced for paper, etc.	2.00
cleaning rifle	2.50
tent poles	11.00
drayage	1.50
powder	.75
	16.75

Voucher No. 7, St. Louis, 5 April 1839
U.S. to J. E. Flandin

gun and case	55.00
compensation for service from 4 March to 5 April @ 2.00	66.00
	121.00

Voucher No. 8, Fort Pierre, 25 June 1839
U.S. to J. Baptiste Dorion

1 bay horse	140.00

Jean Baptiste Dorion, the interpreter at Fort Pierre when the Nicollet party stopped there, was the son of Pierre Dorion (ca. 1750–1810), who served with Lewis and Clark, and the brother of Pierre Dorion, Jr., who guided the Astorians to Oregon and was killed there by Indians in 1813 (ROBINSON, 13:46–48).

Voucher No. 9, Lac du Brochet, 18 Aug. 1839
U.S. to Louison Frenier

For services rendered as guide, 61 days @ 2.50	152.50

Frenière's mark witnessed by William Dickson.

Voucher No. 10, Lac du Brochet, 18 Aug. 1839
U.S. to Pierre Dorion

For services as hunter, 61 days @ 1.00 per diem   61.00

Dorion's mark witnessed by William Dickson. Dorion was the son of Jean Baptiste, who is identified under voucher no. 8.

Voucher No. 11, Coteau du Prairie, 22 Aug. 1839
U.S. to Wm. Dickson

For service as interpreter and guide, 96 days @ 4.00	384.00
1 bridle	2.00
	386.00

Voucher No. 12, Traverse des Sioux, 13 Sept. 1839
U.S. to Joseph Renville

1 3-pt. blanket	7.00
1-3/4 [. . .]	6.50
$\frac{2}{3}$ yds. same	2.00
107 lbs. lead	13.37$\frac{1}{2}$
50 lbs. powder	37.50
80 lbs. beef	6.40
100 lbs. flour	6.50
4 lbs. white sugar	1.00
equipment	30.00
1 *canneau* [?]	15.00
10 lbs. tobacco	2.50
3 lbs. tobacco	.75
50 lbs. meal	3.25
30 lbs. lard	7.50
15 lbs. sugar	3.75
For 7 days of service as guide and interpreter from 5 Sept. through 11 Sept. @ 2.50	17.50
	160.52

Voucher No. 13, St. Peters, 1 Nov. 1839
U.S. to American Fur Company

Shoeing 1 horse 3.00, 1 cast steel axe with handle 3.37	6.37
2 lbs. sugar 40¢, $\frac{1}{2}$ lb. tea 5/, 28 lbs. pork 4.20	5.22
2$\frac{1}{2}$ lbs. soap 5/, cash 80.00, 4 lbs. tobacco 1.00	81.63

1 hemp bed cord 5/, 6 lbs. shot 6/, 20 lbs. sugar 4.00	5.38
15 lbs. pemmican 2.10, 50 lbs. pork 7.50	9.60
96 lbs. flour 7.00, ½ gallon molasses 6.00	7.75
4 lbs. coffee 80¢, 1 3-pt. blanket 6.00, 1 surcingle 8/	7.80
Amount paid for hire of 1 man with horse and cart from St. Peters to Prairie du Chien with allowance of time for return, say 50 days @ 2.00 per day	100.00
	223.75

Rect. by H. H. Sibley for the American Fur Company.

Voucher No. 14, Prairie du Chien, 3 Nov. 1839
U.S. to American Fur Company

113 lbs. pork @ 12½¢, 8 lbs. coffee @ 25¢	16.13
40 loaves bread @ 12½¢, 25 lbs. sugar 4.25	9.25
1 quire paper 50¢, 1 gal. pease 25¢	.75
1 box matches, 25¢, 1 lb. tea 1.25	1.50
paid Augt. Rock for provisions	5.00
1 paper tacks 25¢, 1 lb. cut nails	.44
amount paid M. Richards for provisions	38.00
	71.07

Rect. by H. L. Dousman for the American Fur Company. M. Richards, in the last line, is not identified—but a man named Milo Richards was selected for the grand jury at the 3 Jan. 1842 meeting of the Crawford County Board of Commissioners (wis. his. rec. sur., 95).

Voucher No. 15, St. Louis, 2 Dec. 1839
U.S. to Estate of C. Ryhiner

Repair 1 telescope	3.00

Rect. by F. Ryhiner, administrator.

Voucher No. 16, St. Louis, 6 Dec. 1839
U.S. to L. Zindel

For services rendered, 17 days @ 1.00, from 18 Nov. to 5 Dec. inclusive	17.00

Voucher No. 17, Pittsburgh, 17 Dec. 1839
U.S. to May & Hannas

Freight on 12 packs from St. Louis to Pittsburgh	10.00
2 packing boxes	1.50
receiving, forwarding & drayage on 17 packs	2.00
	13.50

In 1839, May and Hannas were wholesale grocers and commission and forwarding merchants in Pittsburgh.

Voucher No. 18, Pittsburgh, 18 Dec. 1839
U.S. to L. Ackerman

Transportation per stage coach of instruments and one trunk containing manuscripts and field notes	15.00

L. Ackerman not identified.

Voucher No. 19, St. Louis, 18 Dec. 1839
U.S. to Charles A. Geyer

For services rendered as assistant to J. N. Nicollet from 28 April to 14 Dec. 1839 @ 2.00 per diem	462.00

Subvoucher, St. Louis, 4 Dec. 1839
U.S. to P. Chouteau, Jr., and Company

For advances at St. Louis to Lt. Fremont on a/c of
Exploring Expedition
19 March 1839

To cash paid Lt. Fremont's order	600.00
To cash paid Flandin	50.00
To cash paid the same	83.00
To cash paid the same	15.00
To cash paid Dorion	39.00
To cash paid Frenière	102.00
To cash paid for advertising lost boxes	6.00
To cash paid Dousman	600.00
To cash paid Dickson	386.00
To cash paid Lt. Fremont's order	200.00
To cash paid same	2000.00
To wages paid Jacques Fournaise	165.00

To wages paid François Latulippe	185.00
To wages paid Joseph Chartran	191.00
To wages paid Louis Zindell	207.00
To wages paid Etienne Provost	778.00
To cash paid Lt. Fremont's order	300.00
	5907.00

Rect. at St. Louis 4 Dec. 1839 by Pierre Chouteau, Jr., and certified by JCF. Endorsed in the auditor's office: "Private with the exception of an item for advertising boxes." Persons not previously identified include Joseph Fournaise, who may be Jacques Fournais, *dit* Pino. Fournais went to the mountains in 1827 for W. H. Ashley & Co. and was with Robert Campbell in the Flathead country in 1827–28. He apparently was a man of extreme age at his death at Kansas City in 1871, perhaps as old as 124 years, and reportedly had been refused service with Andrew Jackson in the War of 1812 because of his age (ASHLEY, 290–91). Warren Ferris described some of his unusual experiences in Indian country without a weapon (FERRIS, 221–30). François Latulippe, who is carried in the Chouteau ledgers both as Latulipe Monbleau and François Latulipe, would join JCF's expedition in 1842 as a *voyageur* and go as far as Fort John on the Platte River. See pp. 182–84. Joseph Chartran, whom we have not identified, is listed elsewhere as Joseph Chartrand.

The location of the foregoing documents is DNA-217, Third Auditor's Reports and Accounts, Acct. No. 10954.

24. Frémont to Joel R. Poinsett

BALTIMORE, Jany 3d '40

DEAR SIR

Expecting to find Mr. Nicollet detained by his friends at this place I left Washington on the 27th ult. to tell him how much time was pressing & how pleased you would be to see him. Up to this time, however, he has not made his appearance & we have received no letter nor any other intelligence from him. Remembering that I left him in bad health, not yet recovered from a rather severe attack, & knowing that he would not fail to do the same for me, I would certainly set out in search, but that my funds are so completely low as to prevent me. He may be sick at some little roadside inn & wd. be glad to see a friend.

I can do nothing in the way of work without him and therefore I think I am excusable in remaining here until his arrival & shall do so if I do not receive an order to the contrary. I was hoping that

Mrs. Poinsett's Buffalo tongues would have been in time for the New Year Dinner, but the state of the roads, I suppose, prevented their arrival. I hope that she is well. Will you have the kindness to present to her my respectful regards with my New Year wishes for the enjoyment of uninterrupted health & happiness?

I am receiving a great deal of very agreeable attention here. Some of their friendship for Mr. N. is reflected on me, I suppose. I hope soon to be able to give you notice of his arrival. Very Respectfully Dear Sir, Your Obt. Servt.

CHARLES FREMONT

ALS, RC (PHi—Poinsett Papers). Addressed and endorsed.

25. Frémont to J. J. Abert

WASHINGTON CITY Novr. 10th 1840

SIR,

It becomes necessary for us soon to give up the rooms which we now occupy in the Coast Survey & Weights and Measures building, which will oblige us to hire rooms for our own work. I have made the requisite enquiries and find that rooms can be obtained on $4\frac{1}{2}$ street for $18 per month each.

We shall want three rooms and the necessary fuel, and I have now to submit the application to your consideration. Very respectfully &c.

CHS. FREMONT

Copy (DNA-217, Third Auditor's Reports and Accounts, Acct. No. 12245). Endorsed: "Col. Abert respectfully recommends no greater allowance than $10 for each room per month, $10 for an attendant with the requisite fuel. . . . Approved, J. R. P[oinsett]."

26. J. J. Abert to Frémont

Bureau of Topogrl. Engrs.
WASHINGTON, Novbr. 19th 1840

SIR

Your letter of the 10th instt. has been duly submitted to the War Department, and in reply I am authorized to state that you can engage three rooms at a charge not exceeding ten dollars for each room per month. An attendant upon the rooms at a charge not exceeding ten dollars pr. month, and you can also procure the necessary fuel. The expenditures on these accounts will have to be paid out of the appropriation for the Survey upon which you are employed. The entire balance left in the Treasury is $1742.20 and I am particularly charged to direct that on no account is the balance to be exceeded, so as to create arrearages in case no additional appropriations should be made. Respectfully,

J. J. ABERT Cl. T. E.

Lbk (DNA-77, LS, 4:296–97).

27. Financial Records, 1840

[31 Dec. 1840]

First, Second, and Third Quarters, 1840

Voucher No. 1, St. Louis, [1 July 1840]
U.S. to Charles A. Geyer

For services rendered to the U.S. as assistant to J. N. Nicollet from 14 Dec. 1839 to 1 July 1840 @ 2.00 per diem	396.00
For transportation as follows:	
Fort Pierre to Oak Wood on the James River, 118 mi.	11.80
Oak Wood to Devil's Lake, 362 mi.	36.20
Devil's Lake to Lac qui Parle, 520 mi.	52.00
Lac qui Parle to St. Peters, 470 mi.	47.00
St. Peters to St. Louis, 694 mi.	69.40
	612.40

Voucher No. 2, St. Louis, 19 Nov. 1839
U.S. to Joseph Fournaise

For services to J. N. Nicollet as an engagé, 1 March to 16
Nov. 1839 @ 1.00 per diem   261.00
Less cash received on account   163.13
                                                                       ———
                                                                        97.87

Signed with Fournaise's mark and witnessed by M[ichel] S[ylvestre] Cerré,
a member of a family well known in the fur trade of the West. Cerré had
been a member of the "French Company" or P. D. Papin Co. which Kenneth
McKenzie eliminated from the trade in 1830. He had also been principal assistant to Captain Bonneville (CHITTENDEN, 1:309, 405; ABEL, xxvi, 202). After
1835, Cerré's time was spent mainly in St. Louis. In 1848, he was the only
Whig representative from that city elected to the state legislature. He served
as sheriff of St. Louis County from Aug. 1858 until his death in 1860 (ANDER-
SON, 281–83).

Voucher No. 3, St. Louis, 19 Nov. 1839
U.S. to Francis Latulipe

For services to J. N. Nicollet as an engagé, 1 March to 16
Nov. 1839 @ 1.00 per diem   261.00
Less cash received on account   96.50
                                                                       ———
                                                                       164.50

Signed with Latulippe's mark and witnessed by M. S. Cerré.

Voucher No. 4, St. Louis, 19 Nov. 1839
U.S. to Joseph Chartrand

For services to J. N. Nicollet as an engagé, 1 March to 16
Nov. 1839   261.00
Less cash received on account   152.00
                                                                       ———
                                                                       109.00

Signed with Chartrand's mark and witnessed by M. S. Cerré.

Voucher No. 5, St. Louis, 19 Nov. 1839
U.S. to Louis Zindel

For services to J. N. Nicollet as an engagé, 1 March to 16
Nov. 1839   261.00
Less cash received on account   56.00
                                                                       ———
                                                                       205.00

Signed with Zindel's mark and witnessed by M. S. Cerré.

Voucher No. 6, St. Louis, 20 Nov. 1839
U.S. to Etienne Provinceau [Provost]

For services to J. N. Nicollet as a guide, 1 March to 16 Nov.
  1839 @ 3.00 per diem   783.00
Less cash received on account   33.00
                                            750.00

Voucher No. 7, St. Louis, 20 Nov. 1839
U.S. to J. N. Nicollet

To amount expended in the purchase of provisions and
  other necessaries required in a survey of the Mississippi
  during a portion of the months of October and November 1839   183.00

Endorsed by Nicollet: "These expenditures were for a separate Survey under me, and were for provisions & hire of hands, provisions bought as wanted
from the inhabitants. I certify that the expenses were actually made as stated,
that vouchers could not have been procured but in a few cases and that I was
not aware of their necessity, and that the amount charged was paid on public
account."

Voucher No. 8, St. Louis, 23 Nov. 1839
U.S. to J. N. Nicollet

On account of geographical surveys west of the Mississippi   2000.00

Voucher No. 9, St. Louis, 29 Nov. 1839
U.S. to P. Chouteau, Jr., and Company

For sundries furnished Lt. Fremont at Fort Pierre:

226 lbs. sugar	113.00
112 lbs. coffee	56.00
2¼ lbs. tea	6.75
368 lbs. tobacco	184.00
10 3-pt. blue blankets	100.00
2 3-pt. H. B. [Hudson Bay] blankets	20.00
8 2½ pt. H. B. blankets	64.00
5 2-pt. white blankets	35.00
58 pieces dry meat	29.00
211 lbs. lead	52.75
28½ lbs. powder	21.38
21 lbs. balls	5.25

3 buffalo robes	9.00
8 bu. white agate beads	32.00
¼ lb. fine garnishing 25¢, 20 bu. blue beads $40.00	40.25
20 bu. white beads 40.00, 12 bu. blue agate beads 48.00	88.00
10 bu. barley corn 30.00, 4 strings beads 2.00	32.00
25 lbs. biscuit 5.00, 8 lbs. thread 20.00	25.50
6 lbs. fish hooks 6.00, 12½ doz. Crambo combs 12.13	18.13
2 gross Indian awls 8.00, 2 gross gun worms 5.00	13.00
19 snaffle bridles	23.75
5 half-plate bridles	17.50
2 full-plate bridles	6.67
¼ lb. candle wick 25¢, 30-¾ lbs. arrow points 10.38	10.63
1 piece [. . .] cloth	60.75
1 yd. blue stroud 2.50, 1 piece cloth 10.00	12.50
1 piece scarlet cloth	65.25
14¼ yds. red flannel 14.25, 1 yd. fine blue cloth 7.00	21.25
6 pair scissors 3.00, 1 box soap 14.10	17.10
3 surcingles 3.00 1 fort [?] flag 50.00	53.00
1 American ensign 15.00, 1 capot 16.00	31.00
3 leather halters 6.00, 173 yds. calico 86.50	92.50
2 wooden bowls 2.00, 1 padlock 1.00	3.00
2 japanned kettles 13.75, 2 tin kettles 5.00	18.75
1 iron chain 3.00, 11 large cords 5.00, 1 drawing knife 1.75	9.75
2 shirts 3.50, 5 lbs. tallow 75¢, 2 pieces stirrup iron 3.00	7.25
1 barrel navy bread, 24.00, 3 parchments, 3.00	27.00
12³⁄₁₂ doz. knives	76.50
6 chopping axes 18.00, 1 Assiniboin lance 3.00	21.00
8 lbs. sturgeon line 24.00, 4 doz. looking glasses 6.00	30.00
10¾ lbs. vermillion	43.00
3 gross coat buttons 12.00, 1 doz. small [?] 3.00	15.00
3 gross finger rings 9.00, 2 elk skins 5.00	14.00
3 antelope skins 5.00, 5 bu. corn & bags 15.50	20.50
150 lbs. salt 18.75, 6 lbs. gun flints 12.00	30.75
6 pieces ribbon 18.00, ¾ gross Highland gartering 5.00	23.00
3 [?] brass nails	6.00
5 lbs. verdigris 15.00, 5 doz. fire steels 10.00	25.00
75 lbs. nails 18.75, 10 papers hawk bells 15.00	33.75
12 papers needles 3.00, 1 leather bag 1.00	4.00
2 grizzly bear skins 6.00, 3 black silk handkerchiefs 6.00	12.00

9 undressed cowskins	18.00
1 large skin	5.00
1 ermine [?]	1.96
paid Dorion	32.00
paid L. Frenier	30.00
paid H. Tillot [*not identified*]	3.00
3 kegs for sugar 1.25, 1 bag 50¢, 1 packing box 4.00	5.75
1 keg for coffee 2.00, 1 10-gallon keg 2.00	4.00
	1876.87

Voucher No. 10, St. Louis, 29 Nov. 1839
U.S. to P. Chouteau, Jr., and Company

15 March	
36 yds. mosquito netting	9.00
28 March	
65 yds. bed ticking	18.25
6 barrels flour	48.00
110 lbs. sugar	11.00
100 lbs. rice	8.50
13 lbs. tea	9.75
150 lbs. powder	48.00
125 lbs. shot	12.00
160 lbs. small bar lead	10.40
2 lbs. pepper	.33
3 hatchets	2.25
4 sickles	2.00
6 axes with handles	12.00
2 barrels lyed corn, 7 bushels	7.87
2 April	
2 pieces Russia sheeting	18.00
3 barrels mess pork	72.00
2 kegs white lead	6.00
5 gals. linseed oil	7.25
37 oz. red lead, keg 25¢	4.88
1 bottle Japan varnish	.75
drayage	1.25
	309.48

Voucher No. 11, St. Louis, 29 Nov. 1839
U.S. to the Steamboat Antelope

5 April
For freight and passage of Lt. Fremont and party:

freight to Fort Pierre	322.20
4 cabin passages	300.00
6 men on deck	120.00
	742.20

Certified by E. Chouteau, master.

Voucher No. 12, St. Louis, 4 Dec. 1839
U.S. to Papin & Halsey (for P. Chouteau, Jr., and Company)

For sundries furnished Lt. Fremont at Fort Pierre:
1 Sept.

4 carts and harness complete	220.00
4 mules 320.00, 1 horse 70.00	390.00
4 Indian horses	240.00
4 Northwest guns	80.00
1 fowling gun 25.00, 3 powder horns 1.50	26.50
2 months' time of 5 men @ 25.00 per month	250.00
62 days' hire of 6 carts, 3 horses, 3 mules, and harness, each cart per day 1.50	558.00
62 days' hire of 2 used guns and 3 horns	2.75
62 days' hire of 3 Northwest guns	15.00
	1782.25

Certified by P. D. Papin and JCF, and receipted by Pierre Chouteau, Jr., and Co. Pierre Didier Papin (b. 1798) was an agent of Chouteau at Fort Pierre, along with Jacob Halsey (d. 1842). Papin would be assigned to take charge of Fort Laramie in 1845, and thus have further dealings with JCF.

Voucher No. 13, Washington, 8 July 1840
U.S. to J. N. Nicollet

For transportation from Washington to St. Louis, 911 mi.
In Northwest Territory from 9 June to 26 Aug., 78 days
  at 18 mi. per day, 1404 mi.
From 14 Sept. to 26 Oct., 43 days at 18 mi. per day, 774 mi.
From St. Peters to St. Louis, 694 mi.
Fort Pierre to Oak Wood on James River, 118 mi.

James River to Devil's Lake 362 mi.
Devil's Lake to Lac qui Parle, 520 mi.
Lac qui Parle to St. Peters, 470 mi.
St. Peters to St. Louis, 694 mi.
St. Louis to Washington, 911 mi.

| | Total, 6858 mi. @ 10¢ per mi. | 685.80 |

Endorsed by JCF: "The number of miles daily made in the N. W. Terry. could not be exactly ascertained. An average was taken. C. Fremont."

Voucher No. 14, Washington, 8 July 1840
U.S. to J. N. Nicollet

For services rendered in making geographical surveys of the country west of the Mississippi, from 7 April 1838 to 7 July 1840, inclusive, 823 days @ 8.00 per diem	6584.00
Amount recd. of Lt. C. Fremont on account	1000.00
Amount recd. of Lt. C. Fremont on account	100.00
Amount recd. of Lt. C. Fremont on account	2000.00
	3484.00

Voucher No. 15, Washington, 21 July 1840
U.S. to Ludolph Müller

For services as assistant calculator on reduction of maps from North West Surveys for 70 days, from 12 May to 20 July @ 2.00 per diem	140.00

Ludolph Müller, whom JCF hired to assist him with the preparation of the Nicollet map, does not appear in the various Washington, D.C., directories for the 1830s and 1840s.

Voucher No. 16, Washington, 19 Aug. 1840
U.S. to William Fischer

10 Aug.

1 card mapping pens	1.25
1 stick India ink	.37½
½ doz. Roohs pencils	1.00
china cup	.06½
	2.68½

William Fischer, stationer, was located at Stationer's Hall, Washington, D.C. JCF has made a small error in addition, and the total should be $2.69.

Voucher No. 17, Washington, 20 Aug. 1840
U.S. to Geo. & T. Parker

7 June
1 box candles   17.61
20 Aug.
1 box candles   17.48
                                                         ———
                                                            35.08

In 1843, George and T. Parker were grocers on the north side of the Centre Market Place, between Seventh and Eighth W., Washington.

Voucher No. 18, Washington, 20 Aug. 1840
U.S. to Franck Taylor

1 Colton's map of Iowa   2.75
1 Colton's map of Missouri   .62½
                                                         ———
                                                            3.37½

Franck Taylor, a book dealer, advertised in the *Daily National Intelligencer,* 24 Dec. 1839, that he was "four doors east of Gadsby's Hotel."

Voucher No. 19, Washington, 30 Sept. 1840
U.S. to Ludolph Müller

For services as assistant to J. N. Nicollet from 1 Aug. to 30
Sept. @ 2.00 per diem   122.00

Fourth Quarter, 1840

Voucher No. 1, Washington, 28 Sept. 1840
U.S. to Post Office Department

Postage on one letter weighing 2 oz.   2.00

Voucher No. 2, Washington, 1 Oct. 1840
U.S. to J. N. Nicollet

For services rendered as superintendent of the government
surveys in the Northwestern Country, from 8 July to
30 Sept. 1840 @ 8.00 per diem   680.00

Voucher No. 3, Washington, 30 Nov. 1840
U.S. to Thomas Triplett

29 Oct.

6 yds. cotton for a map	1.00
pasting paper on same	2.00
6 yds. linen for maps	2.00
pasting paper on same	4.00
sewing the linen for the maps	.50
6 yds. linen	1.87½
1 paste brush	1.00
	12.37½

Thomas Triplett, a bookbinder, was on Massachusetts Avenue between Sixth and Seventh in 1846.

Voucher No. 4, Washington, 20 Dec. 1840
U.S. to William King, Jr.

For repairing 3 instrument boxes   8.25

William King, Jr., may be the son of the cabinet maker William King, listed in Benjamin Homan's Directory of Georgetown, D.C., as being on Congress Street, near Water [31st near K Street].

Voucher No. 5, Washington, 30 Dec. 1840
U.S. to C. M. Eakin

For 1 box of colors to be used in construction of map of North
Western Surveys   7.50

Constant M. Eakin was an assistant in the Coast Survey.

Voucher No. 6, Washington, 30 Dec. 1840
U.S. to Ludolph Müller

For 37 days work, assisting in the office on detail drawings,
from 24 Nov. to 30 Dec. 1840 @ 2.00 per diem   74.00

Voucher No. 7, Washington, 31 Dec. 1840
U.S. to Charles Renard

12 sheets drawing paper for maps	11.00
6 yds. linen	1.50
sewing for 2 maps	1.12½

bookbinder work	$1.62\frac{1}{2}$
tacks	.10
	15.35

Charles Renard, according to CAJORI, 179, was also one of Ferdinand R. Hassler's assistants.

The documents presented above are in DNA-217, Third Auditor's Reports and Accounts, Acct. No. 10954.

28. J. J. Abert to Joel R. Poinsett

Bureau of Topol. Engrs.
WASHINGTON, Jany. 25th 1841

SIR

I have the honor to acknowledge your direction to report upon that part of a Resolution of the Military Committee of the House of Representatives in reference to the amount required to extend the Surveys, and to publish the map lately made by Mr. Nicollet.

For the amount required to extend the Survey, allow me to refer to the estimate which accompanied the annual report from this office, 12th Novbr. 1840, in which there is an item:

"for continuing the military and geographical surveys west of the Mississippi . . . $20,000.00."

In reference to the cost of publishing the map already made, I submit a letter from Mr. Stone.[1] The map ought to be engraved on the same scale on which it is drawn, for, if reduced, justice will not be done to the work, as many highly interesting details would have to be omitted. I hope, therefore, that no reduction of the Scale will be authorized.

In a work of the importance of this involving as well the reputation of the War Department by which it was directed, as that of the officer by whom the Survey has been made, it is proper that some person should be held responsible for its accuracy. I hope, therefore, that any direction to print the same will also contain authority for its being done under the direction of this office.

The map should be engraved, as the best, the most economical, and the most creditable method of exhibiting work of that character; the price stated by Mr. Stone is not beyond a rigid valuation of a moderate compensation for the materials, talents and labors which the engraving will require; and as the plates will belong to the U.S., future editions of the map can be issued, at no greater cost than for the labor of printing and for the paper required, and future additions can be engraved upon the same plates.

There is a report in preparation which should accompany the map, and for the printing of which it is also desirable to have authority.

The direction might be to have these laid before Congress during its next session, as it is not possible to have them in time for the present. Very respectfully,

J. J. ABERT
Cl. C. T. E.

Lbk (DNA-77, LS, 4:359–60).
1. W. J. Stone (1798–1865), London-born engraver and lithographer who spent more than fifty years in Washington. The estimate he sent to Abert has not been found.

29. Joel R. Poinsett to Levi Woodbury

February 26-1841

SIR,

I have the honor to request that certain township plats on file in the General Land Office, which will be designated by the bearer, Lieut. Fremont, may be delivered to him to be used for a few days, to aid in filling up the details of a map of the North Western territory, now being constructed under the direction of this department.

JRP.

Lbk (DNA-107, LS, 23:224). Levi Woodbury (1789–1851) was Secretary of the Treasury and would soon serve as a U.S. senator from New Hampshire.

30. J. J. Abert to Frémont

Bureau of Topographical Eng.
WASHINGTON, June 4th. 1841

SIR.

You will repair without delay to the mouth of the Rac[c]oon fork of the Des Moines, in order to determine that position, and the Topography of the adjacent country. You will also make a survey of the Des Moines, from the Rac[c]oon fork to its mouth.

As this information is wanted for the map of the Western Country now being made, you will infuse all the industry in your power in the execution of the duty; and if practicable, be back to this city early in August. Respectfully,

J. J. ABERT
Col. C. T. E.

Lbk (DNA-77, LS, 4:480). In the role of legend-makers, the Frémonts perpetuated the story that JCF had been sent to survey the Des Moines River to get him away from Washington and the charms of young Jessie Benton. His campaign biographer, John Bigelow, mentions a "mysterious but inexorable order" to survey the river (BIGELOW, 34), and JCF's own memoirs say, "Whether or not this detachment from Washington originated with Mr. Nicollet or not I do not know, but I was loath to go" (MEMOIRS, 68). Actually the boundary between Missouri and Iowa Territory was in dispute and perhaps Benton hoped JCF's survey of the lower course of the Des Moines would bolster the expansionist claims of the Missourians. Furthermore, the Nicollet map would be more valuable with such a survey. The area around the Raccoon Forks (where the Raccoon joins the Des Moines) had been surveyed by the 1st Dragoons when exploring for a wagon road between Fort Leavenworth and Fort Snelling in 1838. Field notes and a journal kept by one of the surveying officers are in DNA-77, Box 64. But there apparently was no continuous and extensive survey of the entire river below the forks, although Lieut. Albert M. Lea (1808–91) had been in the area with the Dragoons in 1835 and had done some mapping. His *Notes on the Wisconsin Territory, Particularly with Reference to the Iowa District or Black Hawk Purchase* was published in Philadelphia in 1836.

One further survey, ordered by Abert in Dec. 1840, had limited objectives and a small budget, and appears to have been concerned mainly with obstructions to navigation, which in itself had boundary overtones. See the report of Capt. William B. Guion, of the Topographical Engineers, 9 Oct. 1841, DNA-77, LR, 2:70.

If, as the story goes, Senator Thomas Hart Benton had JCF sent out of Washington so that he might forget about Jessie, there is a note of irony in the incident. When JCF submitted his report on the Des Moines in the following spring (see Doc. No. 37), the entire document except the maps was in Jessie's hand.

31. Joseph N. Nicollet to Frémont

MY DEAR FREMONT,

I have received with joy your letter dated St. Louis, 23rd of June past, and I was happy to learn that all was going according to your wishes to assure the success of your short and interesting mission. I assure you that your absence is no less sad to me here than mine had been to you in St. Louis. I thank you for the touching memento of your friendship. No day passes when I do not accompany you in heart and thought in all your moves. I calculate your arrival in Racoon fork, and I see with sorrow that the moon is going, and that we won't have much distance from the moon to the stars, unless you can stand upright after midnight. But you have the distances in the sun during the day, and I know you won't lose them. I am glad that you have taken Mr. Geyer to help you. You had not left Baltimore when the idea came to me and I would have written to St. Louis to give you the idea, if I had not thought that Mr. Geyer was probably involved in work and that he could not have accepted your offer. I am deeply distressed with what you tell me of his situation. Unfortunately, I cannot do all that you ask me for him. I can do only half, and I am writing to Mr. Chouteau to give him the sum of 100 dollars for me, until I can do something more. It would not be convenient for me to send this money to his landlord, and for the sake of Geyer I should not do it, either. It would be better for him to arrange his own affairs without his landlord knowing what goes on between us, between friends. Besides, I would not have another way of sending this money except by Mr. Chouteau, with whom I have an account, and who will advance me the sum. But Mr. Chouteau, to whom I am writing for this, doesn't know for what reason I am sending this sum to Mr. Geyer, thus the latter need have no qualms in presenting himself to receive it and give an acknowledgment. I am writing a short note to Mr. Geyer, being very hurried, but explain all of this to him and tell him that it is with great pleasure that I come to his aid, but with great regret not to be able to do more.[1] Moreover, I shall see Mr. Geyer in the month of September next. My health, while better, is not strong, and I need two months of leave, that I will take sometime after your return here, for it is indispensable that one of the two of us be here.

We have worked very hard, I don't go out anymore, all continues to be fine, even very fine, with our superiors, the Col. and Mr. Bell.[2] The revision of the copy of the map took us 26 days. All the names are written; it lacks only your work on the Desmoines, and to finish the topography. I will not change anything of your admirable Missouri. Two small errors in your drawing, and two errors in the computations reconciled the whole business. I can't tell you the chagrin I felt at first in destroying the beautiful Piece of the Missouri. Later, what joy! when I saw that nothing would be changed. The Map has not yet come back from Stone's, and Mr. Scammon[3] has still not been able to do anything on the topography. But it will soon be here. Don't forget that I am counting on you for my Coteau des Prairies and the Missouri and Mississippi rivers. So come as promptly as possible, everyone here and in Baltimore asks for you, even at Mr. B . . . 's,[4] each time I go there. The young ladies arrived the day before yesterday, in the evening, ten days later than they were expected, because of the *Grandma* who died the moment when they were to start out to return to Washington. *Everything is fine, you are happily and impatiently awaited.*

I am beginning to enjoy the pleasure of thinking that you are at the end of your work, and that you have succeeded at least in the *main points.* Mr. Chouteau will be glad to see you again. He spent two weeks here. Have you gathered any fossils? I would be pleased if Mr. Geyer could gather some around St. Louis, such as Gravel, Fluorspar, with some specimens of the rock to which they belong, all *labeled* in order of superposition. If he can do that for me, pay, I beg you, expenses and his time for me. I would also like some specimens of the limestone on which the city of St. Louis rests, from Market Street all the way to the bottom of the Mississippi, if it's possible. I need that to complete my collection, having lost part of that which I had gathered in 1837.

You haven't told me anything of the commissions which I gave you for our friend, Dr. Engelmann.[5] Give him my best, and tell him that I will bring him his Barometer. Mr. Goebel's [record of] the eclipse [is not] necessary to me, but I would be relieved to have the local information that I asked him in order to put his observatory on the map and to make his work known.[6] I haven't heard anything about that yet. I am at the end of my paper, I would like to chat with you again, but I don't recall anything of importance. If anything comes to me, I will write you again. I await you with open arms to embrace and to congratulate you. All the best,

J. N. Nicollet

Ask our friend Dr. Engelmann to send the enclosed note to Mr. Goebel.

ALS, RC (IU—Frémont Papers). This letter, in French, was presented to the University of Illinois by Allan Nevins, who received it from the Frémont family. Addressed, "Lieut. Chs. Fremont of the Topographical Corps St. Louis (Mo.)."

1. The gist of this passage seems to be that botanist Charles A. Geyer is in financial difficulties, although it is not completely clear whether Nicollet is lending or giving him $100.00. Taking Geyer along on the Des Moines River survey seems to have been JCF's idea. Although Geyer obviously went for the sake of making plant collections, JCF could only hire him as an *engagé* and boat hand (see Doc. No. 36) at $1.50 per day.

2. Colonel Abert and John Bell, who served briefly as Secretary of War under President Harrison in 1841.

3. Lieut. Eliakim Scammon (d. 1894), of the Corps of Topographical Engineers.

4. The home of Senator Thomas Hart Benton. The last sentence in the paragraph is, of course, a veiled reference to the friendship between JCF and Jessie.

5. A German emigrant, Dr. George Engelmann (1809–84) practiced medicine in St. Louis but was mainly known as a botanist and pioneer meteorologist. He corrresponded widely with other scientists, and his strategic location at the edge of the frontier put him in an excellent position to observe and participate in scientific advances in new geographical areas.

6. David Goebel (1787–1872) had come to Missouri from Coburg, Germany, in 1834, becoming a farmer, teacher, and surveyor. The information which Nicollet mentions is apparently to be found in a notebook now at the State Historical Society of Missouri, containing astronomical observations, barometric pressures, and thermometric readings made in eastern Missouri from 1840 to 1844 (*Mo. Hist. Rev.*, 35:613).

32. Frémont to Ramsay Crooks

Washington City
August 12th 1841

My Dear Sir.

Mr. [John F. A.] Sanford has had the kindness to take charge of a very interesting collection of minerals which he proposes to forward to us through you. Mr. Nicollet joins me in requesting that you will have the kindness to send it to the care of the Revd. Mr. Raymond,[1] President of St. Mary's College, Baltimore, Md. In presenting his warm regards to you Mr. N. desires me to say that he expects to have the pleasure of seeing you about the 20th in New York. He has had a severe attack of illness & his health is at present quite bad. Annexed I send you a Draft for the amt. you had the kindness to advance for which I beg leave to repeat my acknowledgements. Most Respectfully & truly Yr. Obt. Servt.

J. CH. FREMONT

ALS, RC (NHi—American Fur Company Papers). Addressed, "Ramsay Crooks Esqre. Rear 39 Ann St. New York N.Y." Endorsed; recd. 14 Aug. and answered 14 Aug. Crooks' reply acknowledged receipt of a check for $100 and assured JCF that the minerals would be sent to Baltimore when they arrived (Lbk, 17:134).

1. Father Gilbert Raymond, later president—in 1850—of St. Charles' College for boys, fifteen miles from Baltimore (CATH. ALMANAC).

33. Frémont to Ramsay Crooks

WASHINGTON D.C. Sepr. 15th. 1841

DEAR SIR

Your esteemed favor of 11th Currt. came safely to hand yesterday. I am quite glad to receive intelligence of the Box, respecting which I had begun to feel some anxiety. May I so far trespass on your kindness as to beg that you will have it sent to this place per Rail Road, accompanied by Charges? I hope you will excuse the trouble I sincerely regret giving & which I could not well avoid.

It gives me pleasure to hear that Mr. Nicollet's health is improving so much. I trust that you are regaining yours as rapidly & with the warmest regards for yourself remain Very truly & Respectfully Dr. Sir Yours,

J. C. FRÉMONT

ALS, RC (NHi—American Fur Company Papers). Addressed; endorsed; recd. 19 Sept., answered 5 Oct. Crooks' letter of 11 Sept. advised JCF that fur company agents in New Orleans had received a box addressed from St. Louis, and were shipping it on to New York. He asked for instructions about the disposal of the package and made brief comments on Nicollet's recent visit to New York and the improved state of the scientist's health (Lbk, 17:254). On 5 Oct., Crooks was able to inform JCF that the box had arrived, that it had been sent on to Washington, and that the charges were $1.25 (Lbk, 17:348).

34. J. J. Abert to Frémont

Bureau to Topographical Engineers
WASHINGTON, Octr. 10th. 1841

SIR,

Your letter of the 9th inst. has just been received. The Resolution of the Senate, in reference to the Map to which you allude, places the Superintendance of its publication under this office; your course therefore, in reporting your fears upon the subject is correct and approved.

The work of the drawing should long since have been removed to this office, that a knowledge of its progress, as well as that of the Engraver, could have been known.

You will therefore, without delay, remove your work as indicated, where the Engraver will be sent for, and the matter of your letter fully enquired into. Very Respectfully, &c.

J. J. ABERT
Col. C. T. E.

Lbk (DNA-77, LS, 5:37). JCF's letter of 9 Oct., to which this is a reply, is not registered in the bureau's records and has not been found.

35. Ferdinand H. Gerdes to Frémont

WASHINGTON 7 Novb. 1841

MY DEAR MR. FREMONT.

Your letter dated Balto. I have received in due time, and, would not have delayed my answer on this particular occasion for an hour, if it had not been for breaking up my camp and leaving for Washington. I have arrived here on Friday morning, and now I hasten to offer you my best congratulations and beg you to accept my most sincere wishes for your future happiness. Perhaps you have noticed, Mr. Fremont, that I am not very fond of much and big talk, but so much I can assure you, that none of your friends—(you have permitted me to class myself amongst them)—feel a warmer interest for you then I do, that no one wishes more truly and cordial, that those expectations of a blessed domestic happiness, w[h]ich you naturally must have formed, may *soon* and continually be realized. I hope you will not think it to great a liberty, when I repeat the words *"soon"*. —Although my dear Mr. Fr. I can not judge in this particular case clearly, yet I would venture to say, that any delay of an open declaration, w[h]ich some time or another must follow, makes your excuse less well, as this declaration itself, much more difficult. Beside the possibility of an accidental discovery is very strong!—Why don't you go, manly and open as you are, forward and put things by a single step to right—never mind in what this step consists—only act now and you will *soon* get over little disturbances w[h]ich might arise at first. Nothing very serious *can* happen now more to you— the prize is secured and the rest will soon be smoothed by help of time and mutual affection and love.

If I am mistaken in my suggestion, it is for want of information, and then I beg to forgive me. It is friendship that makes me write so. Anyhow, I symp[ath]ize with you—and entertain no fears for a fortunate conclusion.

I arrived here on Friday morning and am perfectly happy in the society of my lovely girl. I don't like it much you beat me so decidedly, but I hope now to follow soon, and then if I should go out in Spring again, I will not have to leave her behind me. I had no time in Balto. to call on you, beside I did not know your residence alto' supposing it be Barnums.

Mrs. Cummings and Mary[1] desire to be remembered to you and I conclude with the assurance of friendship and personal esteem. Yours very truly,

F. H. Gerdes

When walking last night with my Mary & Mrs. C. we met Mrs. F. I had a glimpse at her, and thought she looked very well and happy. Excuse all the blots, neither pen nor ink are good for anything.

ALS, RC (CU-B—Frémont Papers). Addressed, "Lieut. J. C. Freemont U.S. Topogr. Engineers Baltimore." From Baltimore the letter was forwarded to Charleston, S.C.

The letter requires a longer note than its importance might indicate. It is one of the few extant personal letters to JCF in this period, and has been quoted before (as in NEVINS, 69–70), but the writer has not previously been identified. His signature is very poor and has usually been rendered "F. W. Gody." Because he mentions "breaking up my camp and leaving for Washington," it is not surprising that he has been considered a frontiersman whom JCF may have met in the Mississippi or Missouri valleys. He is obviously of JCF's generation and feels qualified to speak of such personal matters as the secret marriage of the Frémonts.

The writer's reference to "Mrs. Cummings and Mary" wishing to be remembered to JCF, and the fact that he had been out walking "with my Mary & Mrs. C.," provided the first lead. The financial records had already revealed that JCF was renting rooms for the work of the Survey from Mary J. Cummings. It occurred to us that the writer of the letter might be courting a girl named Mary, the daughter of JCF's landlady. So we instituted a search of marriage records in the District of Columbia for several months after the letter was written, and found that on 26 May 1842 Miss Mary Cummings had indeed been married—to Ferdinand H. Gerdes. And then the signature began to look like "F. H. Gerdes."

Born in Germany, young Gerdes (1809–84) was an assistant in the U.S. Coast and Geodetic Survey. He was engaged in primary triangulation in New Jersey and Maryland, and in topographical work on the Delaware River, between 1841 and 1844. And of course he would have had a further occasion to become acquainted with JCF through his superintendent, F. R. Hassler. During the Civil War, Gerdes served on special duty with the Gulf Squadron under Farragut, then did surveying in western waters. For an obituary notice, see COAST AND GEODETIC SURVEY, 15–16.

JCF and the seventeen-year-old Jessie Benton were married secretly on 19 Oct. 1841 by a Catholic priest, Father Van Horseigh, after two Protestant clergymen had refused to perform the ceremony. For Senator Benton's rage on returning from a western trip and finding the couple married, and for his refusal to permit a second marriage by a Protestant minister as Jessie's mother wished, see the letters of Jessie to Elizabeth Blair Lee, 23 July [1856], NjP—Blair-Lee Papers, and Sarah Simpson (Hart) Thompson to Nathaniel Hart, 19 Jan. 1842, KyLoF—Edmund T. Halsey Collection. Mrs. Simpson writes that Benton would not let Jessie remain in his house. "The marriage was published & Frémont took his wife to his lodgings." At Mrs. Benton's request, intermediaries finally got the senator to treat the couple with "passing civility."

36. Financial Records, 1841

First Quarter, 1841

Voucher No. 1, Washington, 28 Feb. 1841
U.S. to J. N. Nicollet

For services rendered as superintendent of Northwestern
Surveys from 1 Oct. 1840 to 28 Feb. 1841, 151 days at 8.00
per diem.   1208.00

Voucher No. 2, Washington, 13 March 1841
U.S. to A. Shepherd

$\frac{1}{2}$ ton of coal delivered   6.25

Endorsed by JCF: "The above expenditure was authorized by the Secretary
of War. See letter from Col. J. J. Abert appended to Voucher No. 4." The
letter is our Doc. No. 26. A. Shepherd advertised in the *Daily National Intelligencer,* 1 Sept. 1841, that he sold coal, firewood, and building lumber on
Seventh Street, Washington.

Voucher No. 3, Washington, 20 March 1841
U.S. to Mary J. Cummings

For 3 rooms at 30 dollars per month from 20 Nov. 1840 to 20
March 1841.   120.00

Endorsement by JCF same as with preceding voucher.

Voucher No. 4, Washington, 25 March 1841
U.S. to Geo. McDuell

2 Nov.
1 cord hickory wood   7.00
2 cords green oak   11.00
1 cord seasoned oak   5.50
27 Nov.
$\frac{3}{4}$ ton coal   6.75
28 Nov.
$\frac{3}{4}$ ton coal   6.75
$\frac{3}{4}$ ton coal   6.75
1 cord pine wood   4.50

30 Nov.
1 cord oak   5.50
26 Dec.
¾ ton coal   6.75
28 Dec.
¾ ton coal   6.75
25 Jan.
1½ tons coal   13.50
Sawing and portage   5.75
                                                                      ─────────
                                                                                 86.50

George McDuell had a wood and coal yard "on the Tiber or Canal," near Fourteenth Street, Washington.

Voucher No. 5, Washington, 31 March 1841
U.S. to Christopher Kraft

For 4 months' attendance upon rooms from 20 Nov. 1840 to
20 March 1841, @ 10 per month   40.00

Christopher Kraft, a servant, not further identified.

Second Quarter, 1841

Voucher No. 1, Washington, 20 May 1841
U.S. to John Hitz

2 doz. fillers   .25
crucibles of different sizes and descriptions   3.35
iron muffle supports and muffles   2.25
chemical reagents, furnaces, coal and all the necessary labo-
  ratory implements   39.50
                                                                      ─────────
                                                                                 45.35

John Hitz, a Swiss emigrant and formerly employed in the gold mines of Virginia, had been engaged by Ferdinand R. Hassler in 1835 to make the brass that was necessary for the standards (CAJORI, 159).

Voucher No. 2, Washington, 20 May 1841
U.S. to John Hitz

For services rendered to the United States as assistant to J. N.
  Nicollet in analysing the ores and minerals of the North
  Western Expedition, for 15 days from 3 May to 17 May @
  4.00 per day.   60.00

Voucher No. 3, Baltimore, 31 May 1841
U.S. to James Green

30 Jan.	
1 dipping needle apparatus, stand and case	115.00
1 magnetic needle	2.00
1 double magnifier	1.50
29 May	
repairing mountain barometer	7.00
repairing barometer in tripod	7.00
	132.50

Voucher No. 4, Washington, 31 May 1841
U.S. to J. N. Nicollet

For services rendered the U.S. as superintendent of Northwestern Surveys, from 1 March to 31 May 1841, 92 days @ 8.00 per day.   736.00

Voucher No. 5, Baltimore, 8 June 1841
U.S. to James Green

1 June	
1½ lbs. mercury	3.00
1 thermometer	2.00
1 compass	2.50
	7.50

Voucher No. 6, Washington, 7 June 1841
U.S. to William Fischer

31 May	
6 sheets antiquarian for engraving maps	6.00
4 June	
4 sheets antiquarian for same	4.00
	10.00

Voucher No. 7, Washington, 21 June 1841
U.S. to Dinnies & Radford

2 blank books, quarto	2.00
1 blank book	.50
1 penknife	.50

6 lead pencils	.62
1 paper ink powder	.12
	3.74

This voucher was probably drawn in St. Louis, not Washington, where Dinnies and Radford offered books, stationery, and pianos for sale.

Voucher No. 8, St. Louis, 22 July 1841
U.S. to Steamboat Monsoon

For 2 sick passengers   4.00

Endorsed by JCF: "I certify that the two men for whom transportation was paid as above were in the service of the United States."

Voucher No. 9, St. Louis, 23 June 1841
U.S. to Edward Ploudre

1 gray horse sixteen hands high   75.00

Edward Ploudre not identified.

Voucher No. 10, St. Louis, 23 June 1841
U.S. to Jacob Kenner

For making 1 box to serve as case for mercurial horizon	1.62
repairing gun	.75
making box for geological specimens	.75
	3.12

Jacob Kenner not identified.

Voucher No. 11, St. Louis, 23 June 1841
U.S. to J. J. Humbert

1 mosquito bar   9.00

John J. Humbert, upholsterer, born in Frankfurt-am-Main and living in St. Louis by 1836 (VAN RAVENSWAAY).

Voucher No. 12, St. Louis, 23 June 1841
U.S. to Adolphus Meier

21 June
1 measuring tape	2.50
½ doz. knives and forks	.75
½ doz. iron tablespoons	.44

1 axe and handle, 1 hatchet	3.25
1 frying pan, 1 teakettle	1.75
2 [. . .]	1.25
2 [. . .]	.37
1 tin lanthorn	.50
4 cups	.25
1 wash basin	.50
4 tin plates	.50
1 screwdriver	.25
1 box	.50
Drayage	.50
	13.31

Adolphus Meier & Co., importer of hardware and cutlery, guns, pistols, and looking glasses, 23 Main Street, St. Louis.

Voucher No. 13, St. Louis, 23 June 1841
U.S. to Angelrodt, Eggers & Barth

6 lbs. sperm candles	3.00
25 lbs. coffee	3.75
4 lbs Imp. tea	5.00
2½ lbs. soap	.25
16 lbs. sugar	2.91
50 lbs. rice	3.25
1 can rifle powder	1.00
½ barrel crackers	2.50
34 lbs. chewing tobacco	8.50
4 lbs. chocolate	1.00
1 box	.25
6 boxes matches	.19
1 ream paper	2.75
	34.35

Angelrodt, Eggers, and Barth, 165 Main Street, St. Louis, were importers and dealers in groceries, liquors, wines, and cigars.

Voucher No. 14, St. Louis, 25 June 1841
U.S. to Jaccard & Co.

cleaning and repairing chronometer	5.00
1 card steel pens	1.00
	6.00

Voucher No. 15, St. Louis, 25 June 1841
U.S. to Grimsley & Young

1 Spanish saddle	7.00
1 fine bridle	4.50
1 martingale	1.00
	12.50

Voucher No. 16, St. Louis, 25 June 1841
U.S. to B. W. Ayres

Keeping 1 horse 2 days, 23 to 25 June, @ 50¢ per diem   1.00

B. W. Ayres kept the Green Tree Tavern at 68 Second, St. Louis.

Voucher No. 17, St. Louis, 25 June 1841
U.S. to Grimsley & Young

3 side hobbles   2.25

Voucher No. 18, St. Louis, 25 June 1841
U.S. to Jacob Blattner

1 spyglass made by Franzenhofer, Munich   50.00

Jacob Blattner made and sold an assortment of mathematical, optical, and physical instruments. In 1841, he moved his establishment from Chestnut to 34 Olive Street, St. Louis.

Voucher No. 19, Churchville, Mo., 26 June 1841
U.S. to Steamboat Monsoon

Passage for one from St. Louis to Churchville	5.00
2 deck passages for Chas. A. Geyer and C. Lambert [?]	4.00
Freight on 8 packages merchandise	.75
	9.75

For a note on Clément Lambert, see under voucher no. 3, third quarter, below.

Voucher No. 20, Washington, 5 June 1841
U.S. to Polkinhorn & Campbell

1 leather cover for sextant   3.50

Polkinhorn and Campbell are listed as harness and trunk makers in the Washington directory for 1843.

Voucher No. 21, Washington, 20 June 1841
U.S. to Jane Cummings

Hire of 3 rooms and servant to attend same at 40.00 per
month for 3 months, 20 March to 20 June 1841   120.00

Third Quarter, 1841

Voucher No. 1, Churchville, Mo., 20 July 1841
U.S. to L. B. Mitchell

For furnishing a wagon, 2 mules and driver for transporta-
tion of party engaged in the Survey of the Des Moines
River, from Churchville, Mo., to the trading post of the
American Fur Co. in the Sac and Fox Indian country.   34.93
For additional transportation of two men between same
places who were likewise engaged in same Survey.   20.00
                                                     ———————
                                                       54.93

Endorsed by JCF: "In both cases a customary allowance was made to defray
expenses of wagon, horses, &c. during their return from the trading post." A
man named L. B. Mitchell crossed the plains to California in 1850 in company with A. W. Harlan, who was emigrating from southeast Iowa (HARLAN).

Voucher No. 2, Churchville, Mo., 21 July 1841
U.S. to Pacḳesayso (Sauḳ Indian)

For services as boatman for 21 days from 4 July to 24 July
1841 @ .75 per diem   15.75

Signed with Packesayso's mark; no witness.

Voucher No. 3, St. Louis, 23, July 1841
U.S. to Clément Lambert

For services to the U.S. as engagé on the Survey of the Des
Moines River, 33 days @ 1.75 per diem, 23 June to 22 July
1841   52.50
For extra duty as cook for the party @ 50¢ per diem, 3 July
to 20 July   8.00
                                                     ———————
                                                       60.50

After serving JCF as *engagé* and cook on the Des Moines River survey,
Clément Lambert served on the 1842 expedition as a camp conductor; in 1845,

he aided in preparations for JCF's third western expedition but did not accompany it. Well known as a mountaineer and guide, he was about seventy-four when he died in Decatur City, Nebr. See his obituary in the St. Louis *Missouri Republican*, 8 March 1880.

Voucher No. 4, St. Louis, 23 July 1841
U.S. to P. Chouteau, Jr., and Company

22 June

1 pair 4-pt. blue blankets furnished to Lt. J. C. Fremont on his expedition to the Des Moines River	12.50

Voucher No. 5, St. Louis, 24 July 1841
U.S. to P. Chouteau, Jr., and Company

For the following articles furnished to Lt. Fremont for expedition to the Des Moines River:

8 lbs. shot 1.00, $\frac{3}{4}$ lb. powder 1.63, salt 25¢	2.88
36½ yds. bed ticking 13.69, 2 tin pans 1.25, 2 same 50¢	15.44
Tin cups, tin kettle, fire steel	.67
[*illegible*]	6.12
8¼ lbs. lead 1.06, 1 barrel flour 8.00	9.06
65 lbs. flour 2.60, 139 lbs. pork 15.90	18.50
paid for making tent	4.50
1 dressed skin 1.00, 1 bear skin 2.00	3.00
18 lbs. lard 2.25, 1 canoe 10.00	12.25
18 days use of a mule 18.00, 18 days use of wagon 5.00	23.00
5 lbs. sugar 63¢, 20 lbs. flour 80¢, 8 lbs. lard 1.00	2.43
transportation of party from mouth of the Des Moines to Sauk and Fox village	10.00
paid Lt. Fremont	25.00
hire of the following men:	
Packesayso	11.00
Cameron for self & horse	20.00
Vessar [Vauchard?] for services as pilot	36.00
A. Netherson [?]	24.00
	223.85

Filed with voucher no. 24 is a memorandum of 22 Feb. 1842 from JCF, explaining the lack of subvouchers for some of his expenditures and detailing once more his relationship with the American Fur Company through Pierre Chouteau, Jr. The memorandum is in Jessie Benton Frémont's hand, but signed by JCF. "The funds to defray the expenses of the Des Moines survey were deposited as usual in the Bank at St. Louis, & on leaving that place for the Des Moines river, I was furnished by the house of Chouteau & Co. with letters to the agent in the Indian country requesting him to furnish me with men & other necessaries. On my return to St. Louis at the close of the Survey, payment was made for the assistance obtained in men & provisions above, to the house of Chouteau & Co., & a voucher taken accordingly. . . ." The men named in the voucher are not further identified, though it is clear that "Vessar" operated the trading house on the Des Moines which JCF mentions in his report (our Doc. No. 37). Two brothers who were traders, Louis and Charles Vauchard, are frequently mentioned in the David Adams Papers, MoSHi.

Voucher No. 6, St. Louis, 24 July 1841
U.S. to Charles A. Geyer

For services rendered the U.S. as an engagé and boat hand on the Survey of the Des Moines River from 22 June to 22 July, 31 days @ 1.50 per diem.   46.50

To amount expended in purchase of provisions for party during march from Churchville, Mo., to the Indian agency on the Des Moines   1.50

                                                                            48.00

Voucher No. 7, Washington, 19 Aug. 1841
U.S. to J. N. Nicollet

For services rendered the U.S. as superintendent of North Western Surveys, from 1 to 31 July 1841, 31 days @ 8.00 per diem   248.00

Voucher No. 8, Washington, 19 Aug. 1841
U.S. to J. N. Nicollet

For services rendered the U.S. as superintendent of North Western Surveys, from 1 to 30 June 1841, 30 days @ 8.00 per diem   240.00

Voucher No. 9, Washington, 20 Sept. 1841
U.S. to Jane Cummings

To hire of 3 rooms and servant at 40 per month, 3 months from 20 June to 20 Sept. 1841   120.00

Endorsed by J. J. Abert with the explanation that Secretary of War Poinsett had approved the hire of the rooms.

Fourth Quarter, 1841

Voucher No. 1, Springfield, Mass., 22 Oct. 1841
U.S. to Wm. Bond & Son

For a new detent spring, new ruby pellet, adjusting and
cleaning a silver pocket chronometer   20.00

Voucher taken by Capt. W. H. Swift, Corps of Topographical Engineers,
who was then paid by JCF. A manuscript business directory of Springfield
for 1820–53, in the possession of the Springfield Library and Museums Association, shows no listing for William Bond & Son. We cannot connect this
firm with William Cranch Bond (1789–1859), who had a private observatory
in Dorchester, Mass., before moving to Cambridge in 1839 to establish the
Harvard Observatory.

Voucher No. 2, Washington, 20 Oct. 1841
U.S. to A. D. Melcher

To taking down, repairing, and moving drawing table   2.70

A. D. Melcher not identified.

Voucher No. 3, Washington, 13 Dec. 1841
U.S. to J. N. Nicollet

For services rendered to the U.S. as superintendent of Surveys West of the Mississippi from 1 Aug. to 30 Nov. 1841,
122 days @ 8.00 per diem   976.00

Voucher No. 4, Washington, 13 Dec. 1841
U.S. to J. N. Nicollet

For traveling expenses incurred in the following journey,
performed under the direction of the Secretary of War:
From Washington to New York, 225 mi.   22.50
To Albany, 151 mi.   15.10
To Oswego via Syracuse, 172 mi.   17.20
To Kingston and return, 120 mi.   12.00
To Niagara, 120 mi.   12.00
To Buffalo, 26 mi.   2.60
To Chicago round the northern lake, 1000 mi.   100.00
Exploration of the south end of Lake Michigan and return
to Chicago, 325 mi.   32.50
Chicago and Illinois Canal to Peru, 102 mi.   10.20

Exploration of the Illinois coal region, 415 mi.	41.50
From Peru to St. Louis, 400 mi.	40.00
Exploration of the American Bottom and shale mineral region in the state of Missouri, 380 mi.	38.00
From Meramec to White River on the Mississippi, 624 mi.	62.40
To the mouth of Ohio River, 462 mi.	46.20
To Wheeling, 887 mi.	88.70
To Washington, 264 mi.	26.40
	567.30

Endorsement by Albert M. Lea: "It appears that there was no *written* authority or orders given to Mr. Nicollet for the travelling charged for in the within account, and it has been submitted to me, as the late Chief Clerk of the War Department, for a statement of the intentions or directions of the late Secretary of War on the subject. A representation made to the Secretary of War that Mr. Nicollet's duties would not necessarily require his presence in the city during the Autumn of 1841, and that it was important to the completeness of the work then under preparation by him, the Secretary in person and through me directed Mr. Nicollet to perform a tour of observation and exploration. . . . It was intended by the Secretary at the time that *all* Mr. Nicollet's necessary expenses should be paid by the government. . . . Washington, D.C., Feby. 21, 1842."

Albert M. Lea, mentioned briefly in our note for Doc. No. 30, served for a time as chief clerk of the War Department under Secretary John Bell, and was also Acting Secretary for six weeks under President Tyler.

Voucher No. 5, Baltimore, 18 Dec. 1841
U.S. to Auguste Richard

1 Buquet's [?] chronometer	320.00

Auguste Richard was a watchmaker on Fayette Street, Baltimore, in 1842; by 1850 his name had disappeared from the directories.

Voucher No. 6, Washington, 24 Dec. 1841
U.S. to Lemuel Williams

To making slat for drawing table	1.00

Lemuel Williams not identified.

Voucher No. 7, Washington, 10 Jan. 1842
U.S. to J. N. Nicollet

For services to the U.S. as superintendent of Surveys West of the Mississippi, for 31 days, 1 Dec. to 31 Dec. 1841, @ 8.00 per diem	248.00

Voucher No. 8, Washington, 9 Oct. 1841
U.S. to Baltimore & Ohio Railroad

For transportation and charges on the box containing geological specimens from the Des Moines River, from Baltimore to Washington.   .75
Charges paid in Baltimore   2.62
                                                           ―――
                                                           3.37

The vouchers presented above are in DNA-217, Third Auditor's Reports
and Accounts, Acct. Nos. 12245, 13327, and 14900.

37. Frémont to J. J. Abert

WASHINGTON CITY D.C. April 14th 1842

SIR,

Herewith I have the honor to enclose a brief Report, accompanied
by a Map,[1] of the Survey of the Des Moines river, from the Racoon
Fork to the mouth, made conformably to your directions in July
1841. Very respectfully Sir your Obdt. Servt.

J. C. FREMONT
2d Lieut. Topl. Engineers

[Enclosure]

SIR,

In pursuance of orders received at this city in June 1841, I left on
the 27th of the same month the small settlement of Churchville,[2] on
the west Bank of the Mississippi, a few hundred yards below the
mouth of the Des Moines river. The road for about nine miles lay
over a luxuriant prairie bottom, bordered by the timber of the Fox
& Des Moines Rivers,[3] & covered with a profusion of flowers, among
which the characteristic plant was Psoralia Orobrychis [scurf pea].
Ascending the Bluffs & passing about two miles through a wood
where the prevailing growth was Quercus nigra mixed with imbricaria [*Q. marilandica,* black jack oak, and *Q. imbricaria,* shingle
oak], we emerged on a narrow level prairie, occupying the summit
of the ridge between the Fox & Des Moines rivers. It is from one and
a half miles to three miles in width, limited by the timber which
generally commences with the descent of the river hills. Journeying

along this, the remainder of the day & the next brought us at evening to a Farm house on the verge of the prairie about two miles & a half from Chiquest [Chequest] Creek. The route next morning led among, or rather over the river hills, which were broken, wooded & filled with the delicate fragrance of the Ceanothus [redroot], which grew here in great quantities. Crossing Chiquest about four miles from the mouth, we forded the Des Moines at the little town, Portland, about ten miles above the mouth of the creek. The road now led along the northern bank, which was fragrant & white with elder [*Sambucus canadensis* L.] & a ride of about twelve miles brought us to the little village of Iowaville, lying on the line which separates the Indian lands from those to which their title has already been extinguished. After leaving this place we began to fall in with parties of Indians on horseback, & here and there scattered along the river bank, under tents of blankets stretched along the boughs, were Indian families, the men lying about smoking & the women engaged in making baskets & cooking—apparently as much at home as if they had spent their lives on the spot. Late in the evening we arrived at the Post of Mr. Phelps, one of the partners of the American Fur Company.[4] Up to this point there are three plants which more especially characterize the Prairies & which were all in their places very abundant. The Psoralia Orobrychis, which prevailed in the bottom near the mouth of the Des Moines, gave place on the higher prairies to a species of casalia,[5] which was followed, on its disappearance farther up, by Parthenium integrifolium. The Prairie bottoms bordering the river were filled with Lyatris pycnostachya & a few miles above Portland, on the north Bank of the river, were quantities of Liatris resinosa mingled with Rudbackia digitata.

On the Bluffs here the growth was principally Quercus alba, interspersed with tunctoria & macrocarpa & sometimes carya alba. All these now and then appear in the bottoms, with carya oliveformis & Tilia. Ulmus americana & fulvia, Betula rubra with ostrya virginica & Gymnocladus canadensis are found on the bottom land of the creeks. Populus canadensis & Salix form groves in the inundated river bottoms, & the Celtis occidentalis is found every where.

Having been furnished with a guide & other necessaries by the uniform kindness of the American Fur Company, we resumed our journey on the morning of the first of July & late in the evening reached the house of Mr. Jameson,[6] another of the Company's Posts, about twenty miles higher up. Making here the necessary preparations, I commenced on the morning of the third, a survey of the river valley.

A canoe with Instruments & Provisions & manned by five men, proceeded up the river while in conformity to Instructions which directed my attention more particularly to the Topography of the Southern side, I forded the river & proceeded by land. The character of the river rendered the progress of the boat necessarily slow & enabled me generally to join them at night, after having made during the day a satisfactory examination of the neighbouring country. Proceeding in this way we reached the Racoon Fork [7] on the evening of the ninth of July. I had found the whole region densely & luxuriantly timbered. From Mule Creek to the Eastward as far as Chiquest the forests extend with only the interruption of a narrow prairie between the latter & Soap Creek. The most open country is on the uplands bordering Cedar River, which consists of a prairie with a rich soil, covered with the usual innumerable flowers & copses of hazel & wild plum. This prairie extends from the mouth of Cedar river to the top of the Missouri dividing ridge, which is here at its nearest approach to the Des Moines river, the timber of the Chariton or Southern Slope, being not more than twelve miles distant. From this point to the Racoon Fork the country is covered with heavy & dense bodies of timber, with a luxuriant soil & almost impenetrable undergrowth.

Acer saccharinum of an extraordinary size, Juglans cathartica, & nigra, with Celtis crassifolia,[8] were among the prevailing growth, flourishing as well on the broken slopes of the bluffs as on the uplands. With the occasional exception of a small prairie shut up in the forests, the only open land is between the main tributaries of the Des Moines, towards which narrow strips of prairie run down from the main ridge. The heaviest bodies lie on the three rivers where it extends out to the top of the main ridge, about thirty miles. On the northern side of the Des Moines the ridge appeared to be continuously wooded, but with a breadth of only three to five miles as the streams on that side are all short creeks. A very correct idea of the relative quantity & disposition of Forest land & Prairie will be conveyed by the rough sketch annexed [*not printed*].

Having determined the position of the Racoon Fork, which was one of the principal objects of my visit to this country, I proceeded to make a survey of the Des Moines river thence, to the mouth. In the course of the survey which occupied me until the twenty second of July, I was enabled to fix four additional astronomical positions, which I should have preferred had time permitted, to place at the mouth of the principal tributaries.

From the Racoon fork, to its mouth, the Des Moines winds a circuitous length of two hundred & three miles through the level & rich alluvium of a valley a hundred & forty miles long & varying in breadth from one to three & sometimes four miles.

Along its whole course are strips of dense wood, alternate with rich prairies entirely beyond the reach of the highest waters, which seldom rise more than eight feet above the low stage. Acer eriocarpum [9] which is found on the banks of such rivers as have a gravelly bed, is seen almost constantly along the shore, next to the salix and populus canadensis, which border the water's edge.

The bed of the river is sand & gravel & sometimes rock, of which the rapids generally consist. All of these which presented themselves, deserving the name, will be found noted on the accompanying map & two of the more important are represented on a large scale. After these, the most considerable rapid above the Great Bend is at the head of the island above Keokuck's village. The bend in the river here is very sharp, the water swift, with a fall of about one foot, & a bottom of loose rocks with a depth of two feet at the lowest stage. At the mouth of Tohlman's creek[10] is a rocky rapid used as a ford, whose depth at low water is only one foot. The rapid of the Great Bend,[11] $4\frac{1}{4}$ miles below Chiquest creek has a fall of twelve inches & so far as I could ascertain had formerly a depth of eighteen inches at low water. A Dam has been built at this place & the river passes through an opening of about forty feet. Another dam has been built at a rapid twelve miles lower down, where the river is six hundred & fifty feet wide. The fall, which I had no means to ascertain correctly was represented to me as slight, with a depth of eighteen inches at lowest water. Four & a half miles lower down, at Farmington,[12] another dam & mill are in course of construction, but the rapid here is inconsiderable & the low water depth greater than at the other two.

I regret that I had neither the time nor the Instruments requisite, to determine accurately, the velocity & fall of the river, which I estimated at six inches per mile making a total fall of about one hundred feet from the Racoon to the mouth. It is three hundred & fifty

feet wide between the perpendicular banks at the mouth of the Racoon, from which it receives about one third its supply of water &
which is two hundred feet wide a little above the mouth. Its width
increases very regularly to over six hundred feet at Mr. Phelp's post,
between which, & seven hundred feet it varies until it enters the
Mississippi bottom near Francisville[13] where it becomes somewhat
narrower & deeper. At the time of my visit, the water was at one of
its lowest stages, & at the shallowest place above Cedar river, known
as such to the Fur Company boatmen, I found a depth of twenty
inches. The principal difficulties in the navigation, more especially
above the Cedar consist in the sand-bars. These, which are very
variable in position, sometimes extend entirely across the river & often
terminate abruptly, changing from a depth of a few inches, to eight &
twelve feet. From my own observations, joined to the information
obtained from Mr. Phelps who has resided about twenty years on
this river & who has kept boats upon it constantly during that period, I
am enabled to present the following, relative to the navigation, as
data that may be relied upon.

Steamboats drawing four feet water, may run to the mouth of
Cedar river from the 1st of April to the middle of June, & keel boats
drawing two feet, from the 20th of March to the 1st of July, & those
drawing twenty inches again from the middle of October to the 20th
of November. Mr. Phelps ran a Mississippi Steamer to his post, a distance of eighty-seven miles from the mouth, & a company are now
engaged in building one to navigate the river. From these observations it will be seen that this river is highly susceptible of improvement, presenting no where any obstacles that would not yield readily & at slight expense. The removal of loose stone at some points, &
the construction of artificial banks at some few others, to destroy
the abrupt bends, would be all that is required. The variable nature
of the bed & the velocity of the current would keep the channel
constantly clear.

The Botany & Geology of the region visited, occupied a considerable share of my attention. Should it be required by the Bureau these
may form the subject of a separate report. In this I have noticed the
prevailing growth & characteristic plants, & those places at which
coal beds presented themselves will be found noted on the map.
Very Respectfully Sir Your Obdt. Servt.

J. C. Frémont.
2d. Lt. Topl. Engineers.

Table of Distances.

	Miles	Miles
From Racoon Fork to Upper 3 Rivers [North R.]	$13\frac{3}{4}$	
" Upper 3 Rivers to Middle 3 Rivers [Middle R.]	9	$22\frac{3}{4}$
" Middle 3 Rivers to Lowest 3 Rivers [South R.]	$5\frac{1}{4}$	28
" Lowest 3 Rivers to Red Rock Rapids	$16\frac{3}{4}$	$44\frac{3}{4}$
" Red Rock Rapids to White Breast River [White Breast Creek]	$9\frac{1}{4}$	54
" White Breast River to Eagle Nest Rapids	$8\frac{1}{4}$	$62\frac{1}{4}$
" Eagle Nest Rapids to English River[14]	$3\frac{3}{4}$	66
" English River to Cedar River [Cedar Creek]	11	77
" Cedar River to Vessar's Trading House, A. F. C.	17	94
" Vessar's Trading house, A.F.C. to Phelp's Trading House, A.F.C.	22	116
" Phelps T. H., A.F.C. to Soap Creek	$12\frac{3}{4}$	$128\frac{3}{4}$
" Soap Creek to Shoal Creek [Lick Creek]	$15\frac{3}{4}$	$144\frac{1}{2}$
" Shoal Creek to Dam at Rapid of the Great Bend	8	$152\frac{1}{2}$
" Dam at Rapid of the Great Bend to Second Dam	12	$164\frac{1}{2}$
" Second Dam to Indian Creek	6	$170\frac{1}{2}$
" Indian Creek to Sweet Home [?]	$7\frac{1}{4}$	$177\frac{3}{4}$
" Sweet home to [St.] Francisville landing	$9\frac{1}{2}$	$187\frac{1}{4}$
" Francisville's landing to Sugar or Half breed Creek	$7\frac{1}{4}$	$194\frac{1}{2}$
" Half Breed Creek to the Mouth	9	$203\frac{1}{2}$

ALS-JBF, RC (DNA-77, LR). Now that John and Jessie are married, the phrase "autograph letter, signed" becomes a rather vague term. Jessie now begins the lifetime task of writing nearly all of JCF's letters; she does not hesitate to sign them "J. C. Frémont" and let the recipient assume they are in her husband's hand. She will even certify Army vouchers, at a later time, and sign his name to the certification. Our solution is to coin a symbol, ALS-JBF, meaning a letter purportedly written and signed by JCF but actually produced in its entirety by Jessie Benton Frémont. Where variants are significant, they will be noted.

1. JCF is referring to the large map drawn to a scale of 1:200,000 and labeled, "A Survey of the Des Moines River from the Racoon Fork to the Mouth Made in July 1841 by Lieut. J. C. Frémont, Corps Topl. Engineers." The original is in the cartographic records of DNA-77, designated as map Q7-1. It is not reproduced here.

2. A village no longer extant, between Alexandria, Mo., and Keokuk, Iowa.

3. The Fox enters the Mississippi from the west, just below the Des Moines. The Des Moines is a major river, draining a large portion of the state of Iowa and entering the Mississippi below Keokuk, Iowa. All of JCF's survey was made in the state of Iowa.

4. A trading house near the Indian village headed by Keokuk, titular leader of the Sauk and Fox tribes. William Phelps was in charge of this one, and his brother Sumner had a similar establishment in Kansas. For Indian complaints against William, and against P. Chouteau, Jr., and Company, see *Annals of Iowa*, ser. 3, 15:256–57. Listed as residing in Clark County, Mo., he was one of the creditors of the confederated Sauk and Fox tribes at a treaty signed with the Indians 11 Oct. 1842 (*ibid.*, 12:335–81).

5. *Cacalia tuberosa*, Indian plantain. JCF adopted tree names from Michaux, *North American Sylva*. Other plants mentioned in this paragraph and the next include: *Parthenium integrifolium*, wild quinine; *Liatris pycnostachya* and *Liatris spicata* var. *resinosa*, blazing star; *Rudbeckia* sp., coneflower; *Quercus alba*, white oak; *Q. velutina*, black oak; *Q. macrocarpa*, bur oak; *Carya ovata*, shagbark hickory, or *C. glabra*, pignut hickory; *C. illinoensis*, pecan; *Tilia americana*, basswood; *Ulmus americana*, American elm; *U. rubra*, slippery elm; *Betula nigra*, river birch; *Ostrya virginiana*, ironwood; *Gymnocladus dioicus*, Kentucky coffee tree; *Populus deltoides*, eastern cottonwood; *Salix*, willow; *Celtis occidentalis*, hackberry.

6. We have not identified Mr. Jameson, but he must surely turn up some day in the Chouteau or American Fur Company papers if the name is correct. JCF's map shows "Vessar's" trading house about where Jameson's would be, near present Ottumwa, Iowa, and the vouchers show a payment to a man named Vessar [Vauchard?], first name not given.

7. The Raccoon River joins the Des Moines from the west within the city limits of Des Moines, Iowa.

8. For sugar maple, *Acer saccharum*, JCF followed Michaux in "Acer saccharinum"; *Juglans cinerea*, butternut, and *J. nigra*, black walnut; *Celtis occidentalis*, hackberry.

9. Michaux's name for *A. saccharinum*, silver maple.

10. Perhaps Holcomb Creek, entering the Des Moines from the west in Van Buren County, Iowa.

11. This bend is a convolution of the Des Moines in Van Buren County. The town of Keosauqua is located about midway in the so-called Great Bend.

12. In Van Buren County.

13. Now called St. Francisville, in Clark County, Mo.

14. Not identified. The present English River is farther north, the largest affluent of the Iowa.

38. J. J. Abert to Frémont

Bureau of Topogrl. Engineers
Washington, April 25. 1842

Sir

You will repair as soon as practicable to Fort Leavenworth in order to make a Survey of the Platte or Nebraska river, up to the head of the Sweetwater. Having been already employed on such duties, and being well acquainted with the kind of Survey required, it is not necessary to enumerate the objects to which your attention will be directed.

After having completed the Survey of the Platte, should the season be favorable, you will make a similar survey of the Kansas. These duties being completed, you will return to this place in order to prepare the drawings & report.

You will submit without delay the requisite estimate for these duties. Very Respectfully,

J. J. ABERT. C. C. T. E.

Lbk (DNA-77, LS, 5:325). Apparently it was now clear to all concerned that the ailing Nicollet, originally scheduled to lead this survey, no longer had the strength for such an undertaking.

Going to the head of the Sweetwater would lead JCF to South Pass on the Continental Divide, and plainly this is one object of the orders. No other set of orders has been found in letterbooks of the bureau. But in later years, Thomas Hart Benton claimed that the original orders had been too restrictive and that JCF himself had found it necessary to get them altered: "Col. Abert, the chief of the corps, gave him an order to go to the frontier beyond the Mississippi. That order did not come up to his [JCF's] views. After receiving it he carried it back, and got it altered, and the Rocky Mountains inserted as an object of his exploration, and the South Pass in those mountains named as a particular point to be examined, and its position fixed by him" (BENTON [1], 2:478).

39. J. J. Abert to Frémont

Bureau of Topl. Engineers
WASHINGTON, April 25th 1842

SIR

I have to acknowledge the receipt of your estimate of funds for the Survey of the Platte or Nebraska & Kansas rivers, and to inform you that a requisition has been this day made in your favor for $4000, to be remitted to you at St. Louis Missr. Very Respectfully,

J. J. ABERT CL. C. T. E.

Lbk (DNA-77, LS, 5:325-26). JCF's estimate, bearing the same date, is registered in the bureau files but not found. The register entry states he estimated the cost of his survey of the Platte and Kansas at $4,000.

40. J. J. Abert to Frémont

Bureau of Topl. Engineers
WASHINGTON, May 9th 1842

SIR

I have just received your letter of the 5th instt.; there are two errors in it, which it is proper to bring to your notice.

1st. You have no authority to purchase instruments: There is an order prohibiting purchases of this kind without a requisition for the same being previously submitted & approved.

2nd. You have no authority to draw for money, and without special authority for drawing; the practice is strictly prohibited.

Presuming you to be unacquainted with these matters, the purchase of the chronometer is approved and the draft will be paid; but hereafter you must not expect similar indulgence. Very respectflly,

J. J. ABERT. C. C. T. E.

Lbk (DNA-77, LS, 5:342). Entered in the bureau's register but not found, JCF's letter of 5 May in which he writes that he has purchased a box chronometer and drawn on Abert for $310. Also registered is the transmittal of the draft by Arthur Stewart, on 7 May, asking that the amount be remitted.

41. J. J. Abert to Frémont

Bureau of Topl. Engineers
WASHINGTON, May 26th 1842

SIR

You stand charged on the books of this office with the following instruments recvd. from Cpt. [W. G.] Williams, and no return has been received from you since:

1 Sextant
1 Theodolite
2 Surveyor's compasses

2 Boxes drawing instruments

Your immediate attention to this matter is. desirable. Very respectfully,

J. J. ABERT, Cl. C. T. E.

Lbk (DNA-77, LS, 5:375). JCF may have had these instruments since
his work with Williams on the Cherokee survey in 1838. In military parlance,
a "return" is a periodic inventory of equipment, supplies, or personnel.

42. Contract with Honoré Ayot

[26 May 1842]

Before the [*blank*] the undersigned was present.

Honoré Ayot who has voluntarily committed himself and com-
mits himself by these presents to *J. C. Fremont* at this time and accepting for his first assignment to leave this post in the capacity of
voyageur-hunter in order to make the trip, both out and back, and
to winter *during the space of some months more or less, to go on
the Missouri and into the mountains,* free upon his return *to St.
Louis,* subsisting on Indian corn or other sustenance obtained in the
wilderness.

And to have well and duly taken care of, on the road and once at
the said place, all merchandise, furs, victuals, utensils, and all things
necessary for the journeys, trading, and wintering: to serve, obey
and faithfully execute all that the said *J. C. Fremont,* or all persons
to whom the said *Fremont* authorizes by these presents to transfer
this commitment, will order him to make his profit legal and honest,
avoid doing harm, warn him of all things touching his interest
which come to his knowledge, work in the posts, cities, villages and
countrysides not considered as wilderness, so required and generally all that a good [*blank*] should, and is obligated to do, without providing for the carrying out of trade for his own person,
neither with the whites nor with the Indians, nor absenting himself
nor leaving the said service, under the penalties provided by the laws
and the loss of his wages.

This commitment thus made, for and depending upon the sum

of *twenty* piastres, money of the United States, that the said *J. C. Fremont* or to whomever this commitment is transferred promises and binds himself to lease and pay to the said [*blank*] one month after its term has passed.

Made and dispatched at *St. Louis* the *twenty-sixth of May* in the year one thousand eight hundred *forty-two* and signed, with the exception of said [*blank*] having declared not to know how to sign, has made his usual mark after cognizance taken

In the presence of the witness

M. S. CERRE[1]

his

HONORÉ X AYOT

mark

DS (CLSM). The original is in French. A printed form, obviously in common use for the employment of *voyageurs,* etc. In the translation above, penned-in words are shown in italics. For a facsimile reproduction of the original, see WHEAT [2]. No biographical information is available for Honoré, but probably a brother or a cousin was Alexis Ayot, who was with JCF on the expedition of 1843–44 and lost a leg as the result of a gunshot wound (Rudolph Bircher to JCF, 15 Sept. 1844, Sen. Doc. 329, 29th Cong., 1st sess., Serial 476).

1. For a note on Michel Sylvestre Cerré, see under Doc. No. 27.

43. Benjamin Clapp to Andrew Drips

SAINT LOUIS 30 May 1842

DEAR SIR.

This will be presented by our friend Lieut. J. C. Fremont of the U. S. Army, now on his route to the interior to make certain Surveys, &ct. by direction of the Government, whom we beg to introduce to your acquaintance.

As this Gentleman will need some person acquainted with the country, the mode of voyaging &c. we have recommended that he avail of your good services for that purpose, & trust you will consent to accompany him—With this view, & to that effect, we wrote you a few lines the other day by the men who went up with Mr. Fremont's Horses.

You will of course make your own arrangements as regards compensation &c.—Very truly yours &c.

P. Chouteau Junr. & Co.
BENJ. CLAPP

ALS, RC (MoSHi—Drips Papers). The letter was directed to Drips at Westport; the earlier one mentioned in the second paragraph is not on file. Benjamin Clapp (1790–1849) was one of the associates of P. Chouteau, Jr., and Company, having come to St. Louis in 1838. He had earlier been affiliated with John Jacob Astor and, at Mackinac, with Crooks, Abbott & Company (St. Louis *Weekly Reveille,* 2 July 1849). Andrew Drips (1789–1860) was born in Westmoreland County, Pa., and after service in the War of 1812 had migrated to St. Louis. After connections with several firms, he may have worked for a time as clerk for the Missouri Fur Company. By 1822, he was associated with fur trader William H. Vanderburgh. His career in the Missouri country was a long one. JCF planned to hire him but, while en route up the Missouri and before seeing Drips, he met and hired Christopher Carson instead. Probably Drips would have hesitated to go anyway, as he had an application for special Indian agent for the Upper Missouri pending with the government. He learned of his appointment 29 Aug. 1842, while JCF was in the field (ANDERSON, 292–96). See also SUNDER. For a note on Carson, see p. 151.

44. J. J. Abert to Frémont

Bureau of Topl. Engineers
WASHINGTON, July 8th 1842.

SIR

Your letter of the 25th May submitting an estimate for four thousand dollars has been duly received. Such estimates are inadmissible. It is necessary to state in some detail the objects of the estimate, that the Bureau may be able to judge of the propriety of the expenditures contemplated, and whether or not they are kept strictly within the orders which you have received and the duties which have been assigned to you, as it is only to that extent that your expenditures can be approved. Very respectfully,

J. J. ABERT. Cl. C.T.E.

Lbk (DNA-77, LS, 5:417). In a letter registered by the bureau but no longer present, JCF had written that his original estimate of $4,000 for the survey would not be sufficient, and asked for an additional $4,000.

45. J. J. Abert to P. Chouteau, Jr., and Company

Bureau of Topl. Engineers
Washington, July 28th 1842

Gentn.

I have the honor to acknowledge the receipt of your letter of the 17th instt.[1]

Lieut. Fremont has not furnished this office with the least intimation, direct or indirect, of any advances made by you. I have no doubt the advances was made, upon your statement, and am fully sensible of your frequent kindnesses in this respect. But Lieut. Fremont should not have called upon you, as there was a sufficiency of funds to meet his wants, and he was supplied with 4000$ more on the 25th of May, but it was not sent, for reasons which were communicated to him by letter and because it was known that he would be absent if it were sent.[2]

The only duties assigned to him were the Surveys of the Kansas and the Platte, and if he makes these cost the amount of his requisitions, it will be nearly equal to much larger expeditions, and much more extensive Surveys in that quarter.

As soon as Lt. Fremont returns and makes a proper application for funds it will be complied with. Believe me to be

J. J. Abert, Cl. C. T. E.

Lbk (DNA-77, LS, 5:440–41).

1. This letter, calling the Topographical Bureau's attention to the necessity of providing means to meet the expenses of JCF's expedition upon his return to St. Louis, was entered in the register but not found.

2. Abert seems to mean that the money was *allocated* on the basis of JCF's request of 25 May, but held up until the need for it could be clarified.

46. J. J. Abert to P. Chouteau, Jr., and Company

Bureau of Topogrl. Engineers
WASHINGTON, August 1st 1842

GENTN.

Please to inform me when you think Lt. Fremont will return to St. Louis, and what amount will be required to enable him to close his accounts. Very respectfully,

J. J. ABERT, Cl. C. T. E.

Lbk (DNA-77, LS, 5:443). In a letter registered but not found, the Chouteau firm replied 11 Aug. that JCF was expected back in St. Louis by 1 Oct., and that he would need about $4,000 to close his accounts.

47. J. J. Abert to Frémont

Bureau of Topl. Engineers
WASHINGTON Aug. 13th 1842

SIR

I have to inform you that a requisition has been this day made in your favor for 3000$ to meet your payments on account of the Surveys of the Platte & Kansas river. Very respectfully,

J. J. ABERT. Cl. C. T. E.

Lbk (DNA-77, LS, 5:455). Abert has trimmed by $1,000 JCF's estimate of additional funds needed to complete his survey—an estimate confirmed by P. Chouteau, Jr., and Company which had provided the money.

48. Frémont to John Torrey

WASHINGTON D. C. Novr. 16th 1842

SIR

I transmit to you by to-day's Cars a Collection of Plants which I have made during the present year in the course of a Geographical Exploration to the Rocky Mountains. The region, over which the collection was made, extends from the 39th to the 43d. degree of North Latitude & from about the 95th to the 112th degree West Longitude. The labels which are affixed to the plants will enable us to assign them their exact localities on a Topographical Map of the country which I am now engaged in constructing, based upon numerous Astronomical positions, & the Barometrical observations which I succeeded in to the top of the Mountains, will give us their limits. In their present state I am afraid you will find it almost impossible to fix localities from the labels & I regret that I have no means at present to render them more clear.

I think that you will already have heard from Professor Jeager[1] on this subject. It will be necessary for me to annex a catalogue of the plants to my report, which will be required for the use of the Congress early in the Session. Mr. Jeager informed me that it would suit your present engagements to give the necessary time to this examination & that he felt assured you would furnish me with a Catalogue in a few weeks. Should these plants possess any interest for you, I trust that they will be an apology for the liberty I have taken. It is probable that next year I shall be sent to continue these Explorations to the Pacific, & I shall be very much gratified if you will take some interest in my researches & enable me to give to any thing I may find interesting in your science, the authority of your name.

The Box will be left to your order at Mr. Ernest Berthoud's,[2] No. 8 Pine St. When your leisure will permit, I shall be happy to hear from you & in the mean time, am Very Respectfully,

J. C. Frémont
Lieut. Topl. Engineers

ALS, RC (NNNBG). Endorsed, "Recd. Nov. 18." As far as we are aware, this is the earliest surviving letter written after JCF returned from his expedition. Now that he is back in Washington, it would seem logical to present his report of the expedition at this point: but there are compelling reasons to present the documents in chronological order—and JCF did not complete his report and submit it to Abert until 1 March 1843. It is presented as our Doc. No. 61, beginning on p. 168.

John Torrey (1796–1873), professor of chemistry at Columbia and Princeton and "father" of the New York Botanical Garden and the United States National Herbarium, was a pioneer taxonomic botanist. His name is often linked to that of another well-known botanist, Asa Gray, because the two worked for long years to classify and describe plant specimens brought back from the West. They also collaborated on a monumental, flora of North America. See TORREY & GRAY, and for biographies of Torrey, see RODGERS and C. C. ROBBINS.

1. Benedict Jaeger (1789–1869) was professor of German and Italian, and lecturer on natural history, at Princeton (WERTENBAKER, 121, 127; MEISEL, 3:455, 456, 604).

2. Ernest Berthoud not identified.

49. John Torrey to Asa Gray

MY DEAR FRIEND—

. . . .

A few days ago I recd. a letter from Jaeger—formerly of Princeton, giving me an account of some plants collected towards the Rocky Mountains by a Lt. Fremont in the U. S. service. He advised the gentleman to send the whole to me—& this morning a letter arrived from the gentleman himself—informing me that the box was dispatched from Washington on the 16th. It is by this time in N. York. The specimens were collected, he says "the present year, in the course of a geographical exploration to the Rocky. Mountains. The region over which the collection was made, extends from the 39th to the 43d degree of N. Latitude & from the 95th to the 112 deg. W. Longitude. The labels which are affixed to the specimens will enable us to assign them their exact localities on a topographical map of the country which I am now engaged in constructing, based upon numerous Astronomical positions, & the Barometrical observations which I succeeded in to the top of the mountains, will give us their limits." He writes something like a foreigner, but he signs himself J. C. Frémont, Lt. Topog. Engineers. He expects, next year, to continue the exploration to the Pacific & offers me what he collects. So here is a chance for you to get seeds &c. How would it do to send a collector with him. Leavenworth[1] wishes to go somewhere—& this place might suit *him*—but not *us*—in all respects. When I get the box, I will send you the *Compositae* & such duplicates of the other (if there be any) as you may desire for your own herbm.

. . . .

Yours affectionately,

J. TORREY

ALS, RC (MH-G). Asa Gray (1810–88), professor of natural history at Harvard from 1842 until his death, was a founder of the National Academy of Sciences and a regent of the Smithsonian Institution. In addition to the *Flora* he produced with Torrey, he is best known for a work entitled *Manual of the Botany of the Northern United States.* First published in 1848, it is still in use today, in revised form, as *Gray's Manual of Botany.* For a biography, see DUPREE.

1. Melines C. Leavenworth (1796–1862), a botanist and Army surgeon who had collected in the South during his military career. He had resigned from the Army in 1840 and was therefore available "to go somewhere" (HEITMAN; RODGERS, 125, 155, 175–76, 210, 298).

50. Frémont to Joseph N. Nicollet

WASHINGTON, D.C. Nov. 27th 1842

MY DEAR MR. NICOLLET

I have deferred writing to you until I should have something to say decisive of the fate of the Map[1]—immediately after the receipt of yours of the 10th [*not found*] I called on Col. A. & in an incidental conversation he informed that he intended to publish the Map for the present Congress, but seemed to have no objection whatever to engraving the leading Ridges & prominent features of the Country, & said he would send for Mr. Stone & see if sufficient time remained for the Execution of that part of the work. After the lapse of some days I received a note from him, directing me to call on Mr. Stone. The latter informed me that it is entirely impossible to engrave any part of the Topography, & that it had been determined to publish what had been engraved, on the common thin paper, for the *commencement* of this Session; & that an estimate for the Engraving of the Topographical part would be submitted & if the money could be obtained, that work would be executed in the coming year. In answer to my enquiry, why the work had not been executed during the past summer, he told me that you would not permit the Mississippi Sources nor the Southern part of the Map to be engraved, & that it was impossible for him to engrave one portion of the Map without the other, so that you had prevented the engraving of the Topography—This is in substance what passed & will put you clearly in possession of the position of affairs. He gave me one of the sheets for correction, which I made & returned to him the next day. I also corrected the Missouri at Leavenworth, & think that I could improve that river if I had here the large Book which contains the survey; I could then compare places with my late survey, which on the scale of the map is not possible, or rather is very difficult.[2] Write to me on these subjects & think if I can be of any service to the Map—Now of other affairs, I have the pleasure to tell you that I have a fine little daughter,[3] eleven days old to-day. Jessie is sitting up & has got through with her sickness very well indeed. The family send all their regards to you, Col. Benton proposes to go to Baltimore, probably in the morning & told me that he will call to see you. Can you have an occultation calculated for me so that I can get the result next week? If so I will send the data immediately & be very much obliged to you. Give our regards to Dr. Ducatel's[4] family & write me as soon as you can—Most truly yours,

J. C. FRÉMONT

ALS, RC (PHi—Gratz Collection). On the back of the letter in Benton's hand: "With the best wishes of Mr. Benton, and the hope that Mr. Nicollet will soon be able to see his friends in Washington." Addressed to the care of Dr. J. T. Ducatel on Franklin Street, Baltimore.

1. Two versions of the Nicollet map were produced: one dated 1842, printed at a scale of 1:600,000 and distributed to the Senate in an edition of 300 copies; a second one, completely recalculated and re-engraved, done at a scale of 1:1,200,000 to accompany the 1843 *Report*. The 1842 map is quite scarce; we note one copy in DNA and two in DLC and have made no effort to locate others. The 1843 map is reproduced in the Map Portfolio. It is also available with Nicollet's *Report* and in a version reprinted from the original plates by the Minnesota Historical Society in 1965.

For manuscript maps in the cartographic records of DNA-77 which provided copy for the engravers, see:

U.S. 41. "Sources of the Mississippi and North Red River," based on Nicollet's surveys of 1836 and 1837. One sheet.

U.S. 131. Two maps bearing the same file number, each in four sheets, one map measuring 75 × 61 inches and the other 78 × 62½ inches, each entitled "Map of the Hydrographical Basin of the Upper Mississippi River."

2. The "large Book" is the chart of the Missouri. JCF's "late survey" is his 1842 expedition to South Pass.

3. Elizabeth Benton Frémont, born 13 Nov. 1842 in Washington.

4. Julius Timoleon Ducatel (1796–1849), a friend of Nicollet's who was later to become state geologist of Maryland. With J. H. Alexander he made a new map and geological survey of the state (MEISEL, 2:553–57, 619).

51. Asa Gray to John Torrey

[5 Dec. 1842]

. . . .

Saturday afternoon

The parcel of Compositae &c. of the Far West has only just come in. I have looked over the Compos. with some excitement. Some few new, and the old help out Nuttall's[1] scraps &c. very well. Tetradymia's [horsebrush] this side of the Rocky Mts.!! Some new Senecio's [ragworts], especially from the Mountain near the snow line. How I would like to botanize up there! I will give you an account of these Compos. soon, and send back the spec. as you desire, selecting one for myself where it will bear it. Pray remember me in this matter as regards the other families of this collection.

. . . .

Monday morning

I meant to have sent this today in a parcel containing Carey's[2] Compos. (Senecio's & Thistles) from Nuttall: but I will retain them longer, as I shall want to compare some of Nuttall's bits of Artemisia's [wormwood] &c.—with those of this new collection. I hope to send it next week. Is the Lieutenant's name *Fremont?*

I have just looked over the parcel of Lupinus, Rosa & Oenothera.[3] I know nearly all, except the Lupines. If I do not send sooner, I shall hope to bring them all back to you sometime next month. . . .

. . . .

I wish we had a collector to go with Fremont. It is a great chance. If none are to be had, Lieut. F. must be *indoctrinated,* & taught to collect both dried spec. & seeds. Tell him he shall be *immortalized* by having the 999th Senecio called *S. Fremonti,* that's pos., for he has at least two new ones. . . . This letter you see has no beginning, as I have scribbled down memoranda for a day or two past, as they occurred to me. . . . I am deep among thistles, which are thorny. . . .

With kind remembrances to all at Princeton—when you see them —I remain, Yours affectionately,

A. GRAY

Cambridge, 5th Dec. 1842

ALS, RC (NNNBG). Addressed, "Prof. John Torrey, Medical College, 67 Crosby St., New York."

1. Thomas Nuttall (1786–1859), naturalist, botanist, and ornithologist, had explored along the Missouri, Arkansas, and Red rivers, and with the Wyeth expedition of 1834–35 had gone to the mouth of the Columbia. He became professor of botany at Harvard and curator of its botanical garden. Much of JCF's botanizing on his 1842 expedition was in an area already covered by Nuttall, as the catalogue of plants (p. 286) will indicate.

2. John Carey, a good friend of Asa Gray's, had come from England in 1830 to dabble in business and botany. He had botanized with Gray in Virginia and North Carolina in 1841, and worked on the sedges and willows for Gray's manual. After a fire that destroyed his herbarium and took the life of his son, he returned to England (DUPREE, 54, 97, 172, 201, 327).

3. Lupine or blue bonnet, wild rose, and evening primrose (*Oenothera*).

52. Frémont to J. C. Edwards

WASHINGTON CITY, December 10, 1842

SIR:

It will be a reply to a greater part of the questions contained in your favor of the 7th, to say that the survey which I made of the Des Moines in July, 1841, was simply geographical, and principally to determine some astronomical positions, particularly at the mouth of the Rackoon Fork. Any examination, therefore, of the rapids, or other obstructions to the navigation, would be merely incidental; and to those within the territorial line more especially the rapids of the Great Bend, which had been made the subject of a particular survey, I gave very little attention. There are some 10 or 12 rapids in the space between the Rackoon Fork and the Great Bend, a distance of 145 miles. Of the two largest, the Eagle Nest and Red Rock rapids, you will find drawings on an enlarged scale on the map which accompanies my report; the former is 108 and the latter 90 miles above the rapids of the Great Bend. At this last place, I estimated the perpendicular fall to be 12 inches; and it is very probable not less than two feet in 80 or 100 yards. The rapid at Lexington is two miles and 1,000 yards south of that at the Great Bend, and by the river $11\frac{3}{4}$ miles below. Heavy and continuous rains had occasioned a rise of some feet when I made the survey of the lower part of the river, and the rapid at Farmington, which is $15\frac{1}{2}$ miles below that at the Great Bend, and $5\frac{1}{4}$ miles south of it, was then scarcely a ripple, and below this point I remarked no rapids worthy the name.

In the course of surveys on the western tributaries of the upper Mississippi, I found, among their numerous shoals, and in the lower part of their course, one to which was usually given the name of falls or rapids, by way of distinction. The "St. Peter's rapids," which form a serious obstruction to the navigation of that river, occur about 60 miles from the mouth. Those of the Embarras river, of which there are two, about one mile apart, with a perpendicular fall of three feet each, are within the distance above mentioned from the mouth of the river. To this line of falls, extending across these rivers from north to south, and occasioned perhaps by a change in the formation, I supposed that the rapids at the Great Bend might belong.

Very respectfully, your obedient servant,

J. C. FREMONT
Lieut. Top. Engineers

Printed, "Northern Boundary of Missouri," H.R. Doc. 38, at pp. 19–20, 27th Cong., 3rd sess., Serial 420. Democratic Representative John Cummins Edwards (1804–88) was from Missouri and served as governor in 1844 (BIOG. DIR. CONG.).

Also printed in H.R. Doc. 38 are JCF's report of his survey; the report of W. Bowling Guion of 9 Oct. 1841 which came as a result of his instructions of 1 Dec. 1840 to make a survey of the Des Moines and Iowa rivers; and the report of Albert M. Lea, 19 Jan. 1839, to the commissioner of the General Land Office. The object of all this interest was the northern boundary of Missouri, which was in dispute because of the error of John C. Sullivan, a government surveyor, in marking in 1816 the boundaries designated in the Osage Indian treaty of 1808. A confusion of language and perhaps faulty knowledge of geography also was involved, as Congress had authorized the northern boundary to be the Sullivan line, describing it as passing through "the rapids of the river Des Moines." Missourians and Iowans disputed for twelve years the meaning of the term: rapids *in* the Des Moines, or the better-known rapids in the Mississippi just above the mouth of the Des Moines? In 1849, the Supreme Court finally decreed that the old Sullivan line should stand.

There is no evidence in our records to show that JCF's survey was instigated as a result of this dispute, but we suspect that it was—and that Senator Benton of Missouri was somehow involved in having the survey made—just as he surely must, of necessity, have been involved in the boundary dispute.

53. Financial Records, 1842

[31 Dec. 1842]

First and Second Quarters, 1842

Voucher No. 1, Washington, 11 Feb. 1842
U.S. to Charles Preuss

For services rendered to the U.S. as assistant draughtsman in
the Topographical Bureau @ 2.60 per diem, 31 days from
10 Jan. to 10 Feb. 1842   80.60

Charles Preuss (1803–54), a German cartographer, had worked for Ferdinand Hassler before joining Nicollet and JCF early in 1842. His association
with JCF was to extend over many years, and he was to prove himself a
highly skilled and conscientious mapmaker. He was not a happy or well-
adjusted man—he hanged himself in 1854—but the extent of his frequent
miseries was not revealed until the translation and publication of his western
diaries in 1958 (PREUSS). There he comes through as a dour traveler, unhappy
with JCF, unhappy with hardship and inclement weather. Assuming that his
diaries are in part catharsis, we can place some credence in JCF's own recollections of the man (MEMOIRS, 70 and *passim*) as one who had served him
willingly and well. Quotations from the Preuss diaries will appear as notes in
this and subsequent volumes. Erwin G. and Elisabeth K. Gudde present the
best available biographical sketch in their preface to his diaries.

Voucher No. 2, Washington, 14 Feb. 1842
U.S. to E. & G. W. Blunt

1 sextant	120.00
1 circle	150.00
box, freight, etc.	2.00
	272.00

Voucher No. 3, Baltimore, 1 March 1842
U.S. to James Green

18 Aug. 1841

1 mountain barometer repaired	6.00
1 ditto	3.00
1 ditto	3.50
1 thermometer	1.50
1 ditto	.50

2 leather cases for barometer	5.00
20 Aug.	
repairing sextant, 3 shades, eyepiece, &c.	4.00
Case for dipping needle	3.00
23 Aug. 1841	
Strap for leather case	.50
25 Aug.	
1 hydrometer, Beaume	1.00
1 March 1842	
repairing sextant, regraduating, &c.	18.00
repairing horizon box	.50
packing box	.37½
	46.87½

Voucher No. 4, Washington, 25 March 1842
U.S. to John A. Blake

Repairing and binding 2 maps	4.25

John A. Blake was often engaged by the government to bind books and official documents. He may be the same John A. Blake who, in the *Daily National Intelligencer* for 24 Dec. 1839, advertised himself as an auctioneer and commission merchant, with a variety of goods for sale at Centre Market Place.

Voucher No. 5, Washington, 25 March 1842
U.S. to William King, Jr.

Taking down and removing a large drawing table from the office of the Coast Survey, on 20 March	3.50

Voucher No. 6, Washington, 28 March 1842
U.S. to E. & G. W. Blunt

1 Troughton sextant and case	88.00

Voucher No. 7, Washington, 1 April 1842
U.S. to J. N. Nicollet

For services rendered to the U.S. as superintendent of the Surveys West of the Mississippi for 90 days, 1 Jan. to 31 March 1842, @ 8.00 per diem	720.00

Voucher No. 8, Washington, 1 April 1842
U.S. to Charles Preuss

For services rendered the U.S. as assistant to J. N. Nicollet
@ 2.60 per diem, 49 days from 11 Feb. to 31 March 1842   127.40

Endorsed by JCF: "The Hon. J. C. Spencer, Sec. at War, authorized J. N. Nicollet to employ the above named Charles Preuss as assistant in his astronomical & other calculations & drawings."

Voucher No. 9, Philadelphia, 21 April 1842
U.S. to Wm. H. C. Riggs

[ ] March
Refitting the hook inside the main spring, resetting by brazing
anew the cock diamond, polishing pivots, poising the balance, cleaning, reducing, and ascertaining rate of Chronometer by Brockbank No. 739   15.00

William H. C. Riggs, watchmaker and chronometer maker, was located in 1847 at 126 S. Front Street and 13 Dock Street, Philadelphia.

Voucher No. 10, Washington, 26 April 1842
U.S. to Thomas R. Gedney

1 Massey's patent log   40.00

Thomas R. Gedney (d. 1857), a naval commander, lived on F Street N. near Nineteenth W., Washington. He had been an assistant in the Coast Survey and by direction of Ferdinand R. Hassler had surveyed New York harbor and discovered a new channel.

Voucher No. 11, Washington, 27 April 1842
U.S. to F. W. Naylor

1 tin case for maps   2.62

In 1843, Francis Naylor, a turner, was located at $4\frac{1}{2}$ Street W. near C Street S., Washington.

Voucher No. 12, Washington, 28 April 1842
U.S. to William Würdemann

repairing and cleaning a sextant for J. N. Nicollet   5.50
making $1\frac{1}{2}$ doz. silver and German silver draughting pens   2.70
additions to a camera lucida   2.50

138

German silver scale of ³⁄₁₀ meters divided for ¹⁄₂₀₀,₀₀₀	6.00
20 spiral springs for chronometer box	1.50
	18.20

In 1846, William Würdemann was a mathematical instrument maker on the west side of Delaware Avenue, between B and C, in Washington. He had done much work for Hassler in the Coast Survey.

Voucher No. 13, Washington, 28 April 1842
U.S. to William Fischer

½ ream Southworth's linen quarto, ruled	2.75
4 lead pencils	.50
India rubber	.06
inkstand 75¢, ink 19¢	.94
sealing wax 25¢, 1 stick India ink 37¢	.62
2 cards Hayden's pens	.75
2 cards mapping pens	2.00
	7.62

Voucher No. 14, Washington, 29 April 1842
U.S. to John A. Blake

lining with cotton 10 sheets largest size drawing paper	12.50
binding 1 small quarto volume in half morocco	1.00
	13.50

Voucher No. 15, Washington, 29 April 1842
U.S. to Polkinhorn & Campbell

2 cases for instruments	7.00
1 case for spyglass	1.00
	8.00

Voucher No. 16, New York, 30 April 1842
U.S. to E. & G. W. Blunt

1 English nautical almanac	2.50
1 new [. . .], new balance staff and cleaning chronometer	11.00
	13.50

Voucher No. 17, Washington, 30 April 1842
U.S. to Charles Preuss

For services rendered to the U.S. as assistant to J. N. Nicollet,
@ 2.75 per diem for 30 days, 1 April to 30 April 1842   82.50

Voucher No. 18, Washington, 30 April 1842
U.S. to J. N. Nicollet

For services rendered the U.S. as superintendent of the Surveys West of the Mississippi for 30 days, 1 April to 30
April   240.00

Voucher No. 19, Washington, 1 May 1842
U.S. to William King, Jr.

13 Oct. 1841
mirror for camera obscura   .75
portable box to form the above   8.00
30 April 1842
packing box for instruments   11.00
packing 6 instrument boxes   3.00
1 pine table arranged to pack in box, for camp use   9.00
packing the same in a box   1.50
moving table to Coast Survey office   2.00
                                                               _____
                                                               35.25

Voucher No. 20, New York, 4 May 1842
U.S. to Arthur Stewart

1 first class 2-day London chronometer by French, No. 7810   300.00
1 land-carriage outside box, with extra pillows, cushion, &c. 10.00
                                                               _____
                                                               310.00

In 1846, Arthur Stewart's firm, listed as "chronometers, merchant exchange," was on William at the corner of Wall Street, New York.

Voucher No. 21, New York, 5 May 1842
U.S. to American Fur Company

1 three-breadths brown Russia sheeting tent   20.00

Rect. by Ramsay Crooks as president of the company.

Voucher No. 22, New York, 5 May 1842
U.S. to E. & G. W. Blunt

3 May

1 mountain barometer in leather case	35.00
4 best thermometers in mahogany case, graduated to order	9.00
2 lbs. best refined quicksilver 2.00, box and bottle 25¢	4.25
	48.25

Voucher No. 23, New York, 4 May 1842
U.S. to A. Bininger & Co.

6 lbs. Dresden chocolate	4.50

Voucher No. 24, New York, 5 May 1842
U.S. to Horace H. Day

1 air army boat or floater	150.00
2 pieces India rubber cloth	39.98
2 pots rubber composition	1.00
	190.98

Horace H. Day had opened a small factory at New Brunswick, N.J., to manufacture rubber fabrics in 1839. His interests soon conflicted with those of Charles Goodyear, who patented a vulcanization process in 1844. After a series of law suits, Day was permanently enjoined from further rubber manufacture in 1852. For JCF's unfortunate experiences with the rubber boat, see below, pp. 275–79.

Voucher No. 25, New York, 5 May 1842
U.S. to Benjamin Pike & Sons

1 mountain barometer	25.00
1 leather case for same	2.00
1 boat compass	3.00
	30.00

Benjamin Pike & Sons were opticians at 166 Broadway, New York.

Voucher No. 26, New York, 6 May 1842
U.S. to Moore, Baker & Co.

1 pair fine pistols in case	50.00
powder, caps, &c.	1.00
	51.00

Moore, Baker & Co. had a gun and saddlery shop at 204 Broadway, New York.

Voucher No. 27, Chicago, 15 May 1842
U.S. to Frink Walker & Co.

To furnishing an exclusive extra post coach for 2 persons and
14 cases containing instruments from Chicago to Peru   50.00

Frink, Walker, & Co. was a stage proprietor at the corner of Lake and Dearborn Streets, Chicago.

Voucher No. 28, St. Louis, 25 May 1842
U.S. to E. M. Buckingham

For making 1 spirit gas field lamp   3.00

E. M. Buckingham was a dealer in stoves and hollow-ware at 130 N. First Street, St. Louis.

Voucher No. 29, St. Louis, 26 May 1842
U.S. to Dinnies & Radford

6 half-bound blank books	10.75
1 doz. pencils, lead	1.25
1 penknife	.75
1 card steel pens	1.00
1 bottle black ink	.62
1 piece Indian rubber	.13
	15.00

Voucher No. 30, St. Louis, 26 May 1842
U.S. to Hendrick Tisius

2 pair ice shoes	10.00
2 pair iron plates and heels with steel nails	4.00
2 steel pins for sticks	.50
	14.50

Hendrick Tisius not further identified. When the purchase of these items was questioned by the government auditors, JCF wrote in an accompanying explanation: "The articles in this account were for use among the ice-fields in the Survey of the Wind River Mts."

Voucher No. 31, St. Louis, 27 May 1842
U.S. to Carstens & Schuetze

1 lb. Jamaica arrowroot	.50
1 lb. [. . .]	.25
3 oz. purg[ative] pills	4.50
4 oz. laudanum	.75
3¾₆ oz. pure quicksilver	8.00
1 oz. iodine	.75
1 oz. nitric acid	.38
2 lbs. sulphur	.50
24 doses emetic	3.00
24 doses Dover's powder	3.00
2 lancets	2.00
	23.63

Voucher No. 32, St. Louis, 29 May 1842
U.S. to Jacob Blattner

1 best quality French pocket compass	12.00
1 German pocket compass	12.00
1 common pocket compass	4.00
1 best quality thermometer	9.00
1 magnifying glass	.75
1 pair forceps	.75
1 magnet	1.50
	40.00

Voucher No. 33, Baltimore, 1 June 1842
U.S. to J. N. Nicollet

For services to the U.S. as superintendent of the North Western Surveys for 31 days @ 8.00 per diem from 1 May to 31 May 1842   248.00

Voucher No. 34, Westport, Mo., 4 June 1842
U.S. to the Steamboat Rowena

3 June
passage for 17 men from St. Louis to Westport   114.75

freight on 468 lbs.	17.50
freight on 3 kegs powder	1.50
freight on 8 French carts [?]	24.00
	157.75

Voucher No. 35, St. Louis, 10 June 1842
U.S. to C. & F. Chouteau

Bought of Boone & Hamilton:

1 double-barreled shotgun	35.00
2 rifles	30.00
1 coil rope	10.50
6 halters	9.00
12 tug ropes	3.00
8 dressed deerskins	16.00
12 boxes percussion caps	3.00
6 twilled bags	6.00
repairing guns	4.21
	158.71

This document is a subvoucher rendered at Westport on 15 June 1842. The main voucher is nearly illegible, but consists of sundries such as those shown in voucher no. 31 for the second and third quarters, 1842. One entry reads: "amount assumed to Boone & Hamilton, 158.71." The total is $503.00.

Cyprian and Francis Chouteau, sons of Pierre Chouteau, Sr., by Osage mothers, together and separately maintained a number of posts on the Kansas River for trade with the Indians. One joint enterprise was "Four Houses," established between 1813 and 1821 at the site of Bonner Springs, Kan. In 1825, the brothers built a post on the south side of the Kansas, about seven miles from Westport, Mo., and in 1828–29, Cyprian located a post for trade with the Delawares and Shawnees on the north side of the river, six miles west of the Missouri line. It was from this last house that JCF organized his first expedition, and it was also the main outfitting station for caravans engaged in the Santa Fe trade (*Kan. State Hist. Coll.*, 9:573–74).

Albert G. Boone, grandson of frontiersman Daniel Boone, had taken his family to Westport about 1838. With James G. Hamilton, his partner, he obtained a license in 1843 to trade with the Potawatomis, Weas, Ottawas, and Piankeshaws (BARRY, pt. 10, 29:153, pt. 12, 29:474–75).

Voucher No. 36, Westport, Mo. Terr., 10 June 1842
U.S. to P. M. Chouteau

4 mules bought of L. Maxwell	160.00
1 barrel sugar 286 lbs.	28.60
1 sack coffee 188 lbs.	23.70

to blacksmithing	6.95
amount assumed to Boone & Hamilton	79.37
	298.62

A subvoucher is present for the purchase of sundries from Boone & Hamilton. JCF's endorsement explains that some of the purchases from that firm were personal items for his men, "but these bills did not reach my hands until after I had paid off my men, & I respectfully submit that the accidental loss may not fall upon me."

P. M. Chouteau is probably Pierre Menard Chouteau, son of Francis Gesseau Chouteau (b. 1797). He had settled in Westport.

Voucher no. 6, third and fourth quarters of 1842 below, shows Maxwell employed as a hunter for 152 days on the expedition. Lucien Bonaparte Maxwell (1818–75) was the grandson of trader Pierre Menard of Illinois, was related to the Chouteaus, and was a friend of Kit Carson. Probably in 1844, he married the heiress of the vast Beaubien-Miranda tract in New Mexico, and eventually became its sole owner. He would accompany JCF on his expedition to California in 1845 and play a role in the conquest of California (DUNHAM [2]; PEARSON, 10). DUNHAM says that Maxwell had accompanied the Nicollet expedition of 1839 and already was acquainted with JCF; but his name does not appear in the vouchers for that expedition. A *voyageur* named Maxime Maxwell was present on the 1838 expedition, which may be the source of some confusion.

Voucher No. 37, Kansas Ford, Mo. Terr., 15 June 1842
U.S. to Louis Pepin

20 lbs. coffee	5.00
a quantity of pumpkins and beans	3.00
	8.00

Signed with Pepin's mark and witnessed by C. Lambert. Pepin not further identified. The name may be "Papin," and possibly he is the brother of Joseph Papin, who operated a ferry at the site of Topeka from 1840.

Subvoucher, New York, 6 May 1842
U.S. to James R. Chilton

1 set of Daguerreotype apparatus	40.00
25 polished Daguerreotype plates	37.50
1 pocket microscope	.75
	78.25

This document is handled as a subvoucher because it is not carried in the regular abstract of vouchers for the quarter. Dr. James R. Chilton, a physician and chemist at 263 Broadway, New York, supplied daguerreotype apparatus to JCF for the expeditions of 1842 and 1843–44. The device was still very new, and there is little doubt that JCF was among the first to attempt to photograph the West with such equipment. Some of the lithographs appearing in the *Reports* and *Memoirs* are undoubtedly based upon daguerreotypes or on negatives copied by Mathew Brady and others. Apparently no originals have survived.

Charles Preuss, in a belittling mood as always, had no patience when JCF tinkered with the gadget. "Yesterday afternoon and this morning Fremont set up his daguerreotype to photograph the rocks; he spoiled five plates that way. Not a thing was to be seen on them. That's the way it often is with these Americans. They know everything, can do everything, and when they are put to a test, they fail miserably" (2 Aug. 1842, PREUSS, 32). When JCF tried again on 5 Aug., Preuss wrote, "Today he said the air up here is too thin; that is the reason his daguerreotype was a failure. Old boy, you don't understand the thing, that is it" (PREUSS, 35).

Third and Fourth Quarters, 1842

Voucher No. 1, Fort John, Platte River, 17 July 1842
U.S. to Registe Larente

For services as voyageur 48 days @ 1.00 per diem, 27 May to 13 July 1842	48.00

Signed with Larente's mark and witnessed by C. Lambert. Larente apparently was the only employee who chose to leave the expedition when JCF outlined the dangers which lay ahead (see p. 226).

Voucher No. 2, Fort Bissonette, Laramie Fork, 1 Sept. 1842
U.S. to Sibille, Adams & Co.

20 July	
1 tomahawk	1.00
3 Aug.	
A. Lucier and his mule 8 days @ 2.00	16.00
Joseph Bissonnette for guide and interpreter, 8 days @ 13.00 per diem	104.00
1 horse paid to an Indian	36.00
1 Sept.	
12 cups coffee 18.00, 6 cups sugar 9.00	27.00
	254.00
Less 1 cow and calf	50.00
	204.00

Jean Sibille and David Adams had been licensed to trade with the Indians in the vicinity of Laramie as early as 1841, and by Jan. 1842 had started a post they called Fort Adams, apparently upstream from Fort John. They then purchased a new establishment of Lancaster P. Lupton's, called Fort Platte.

Thereafter, one hears no more of Fort Adams, and the new owners had finished construction of Fort Platte by Oct. 1842. A fragmentary diary kept by Adams records finding the fort "oll finished and oll the boys well on 27 October." He also refers to another partner in the firm, John Richard; to "mr. besonat [Bissonette]"; and "mr. shatraw [Chartrain]," a clerk.

Dale L. Morgan, who has supplied the above information from the Adams Papers, MoSHi, also reports that A. Lucier had been an employee of the Sibille & Adams firm. Joseph Bissonette (1818–94), born in St. Louis, had come to the Platte region at the age of eighteen and married into the Sioux tribe. He worked variously as a company trader and free trader, and as an interpreter for Indian agents. He is said to have worked as late as 1875 in persuading Sioux chiefs Red Cloud and Spotted Tail to relinquish the Black Hills in Dakota Territory (J. D. MC DERMOTT [2]).

Voucher No. 3, Bellevue, Mo. Terr., 4 Oct. 1842
U.S. to P. A. Sarpy

An almost illegible voucher for goods received between 26 Sept. and 3 Oct. 1842, including food, the use of four horses and men for four days, etc. The largest item is for a mackinaw boat, $166.00. Total charges, $348.28. In explaining the cost of such items, JCF wrote: "In that country we often found a difficulty in getting anything to eat, & were obliged to take what we could get at any cost." Peter A. Sarpy (1805–65), brother of John B. Sarpy and a skillful barterer with the Indians, was in charge of the post at Bellevue, just north of the junction of the Platte and Missouri rivers. For a biography, see WICKMAN.

Voucher No. 4, St. Louis, 17 Oct. 1842
U.S. to Clément Lambert

For the following articles furnished to Lt. Fremont's party of 25 men on their voyage down the Missouri River, from Bellevue to St. Louis:

apples 1.25, 3 tin cups 25¢, 1 lantern 1.00, coffee mill 1.25	3.75
eggs and milk 1.25, chickens 1.37½, pork 1.00	3.62½
beef 2.00, 2 forks 25¢, butter 50¢, milk 25¢	3.00
turnips 37½¢, coffee 2.00, sugar 1.00, apples 1.00	4.37½
bread 1.75, milk 50¢, eggs 75¢, coffee 75¢	3.75
chickens 1.25, honey 25¢, milk 37½	1.87½
poultry 2.00, butter 75¢, eggs 62½¢, honey 75¢	4.25
milk 50¢, whiskey 1.37½, bacon 3.00	4.87½
sugar 1.25, bread 1.00, whiskey 50¢	2.75
chickens, eggs, milk, potatoes, cabbage	1.75
onions 50¢, whiskey 1.00, candles 75¢, poultry 2.00	4.25

eggs 75¢, butter 1.25, milk 50¢, bread 1.00   3.25
whiskey 2.00, bread 75¢, coffee 1.25, milk 75¢   4.75
eggs 1.00, whiskey 1.00   2.00
                                                              ‾‾‾‾‾
                                                              48.25

Voucher No. 5, St. Louis, 31 Oct. 1842
U.S. to Benjamin Clapp

1 barometer   35.00

Voucher No. 6, St. Louis, 31 Oct. 1842
U.S. to Lucien Maxwell

For services as hunter @ 1.66½ per diem for 152 days, from 1
  July to 31 Oct. 1842   234.75
1 horse   70.00
2 mules   90.00
                                                              ‾‾‾‾‾‾
                                                              414.75

Voucher No. 7, St. Louis, 31 Oct. 1842
U.S. to J. B. L'Esperance

For 12 days' time and expenses going to Lexington, Mo., to
  collect a draft for $3,000 drawn by the U.S. on the Receiver
  of Public Moneys at Lexington in favor of Lt. Fremont   66.25

Endorsed by JCF: "I was not able to cash the above draft in St. Louis, & was obliged to hire a trustworthy person to proceed to Lexington as it was necessary to pay off my men as soon as possible." J. B. L'Esperance not further identified.

Voucher No. 8, St. Louis, 31 Oct. 1842
U.S. to Jean B. Lefevre

For service as voyageur @ 81¾¢ per diem, 153 days from
  26 May to 26 Oct. 1842.   125.07

Signed with Lefevre's mark and witnessed by F. V. Pfister. Pfister was a clerk on Laurel Street in St. Louis, probably working for P. Chouteau, Jr., and Company.

Voucher No. 9, St. Louis, 31 Oct. 1842
U.S. to Jean B. Lefevre

Transportation of 19 horses and a party of men from St. Louis to Chouteau's Landing, 300 mi.   38.00

Signed with Lefevre's mark and witnessed by B. Clapp.

Voucher No. 10, St. Louis, 31 Oct. 1842
U.S. to Benjamin Potra

For services as voyageur @ 66¢ per diem for 153 days, 26 May to 26 Oct. 1842   100.98

Signed with Potra's mark and witnessed by John B. Sarpy. Sarpy (1798–1857) was one of the most active and influential citizens of St. Louis, a partner of Pierre Chouteau, Jr., and an original projector of the Missouri Pacific Railroad (SCHARF, 1:580–83).

Voucher No. 11, St. Louis, 31 Oct. 1842
U.S. to Louis Guion

For services as voyageur @ 87½¢ per diem for 102 days, 20 July to 31 Oct. 1842   89.25
2 horses @ 70.00 each   140.00
                    229.25

Signed with Guion's mark and witnessed by John B. Sarpy.

Voucher No. 12, St. Louis, 31 Oct. 1842
U.S. to Jean Baptiste Dumes

For services as cook @ 75¢ per diem for 153 days, 26 May to 26 Oct. 1842   114.75

No further information on Dumes; voucher not signed or witnessed.

Voucher No. 13, St. Louis, 31 Oct. 1842
U.S. to Basil Lajeunesse

For services as voyageur @ 75¢ per diem for 153 days, from 26 May to 26 Oct. 1842   114.75
1 overcoat lost in the Platte River, in the service of the U.S.   5.00
                    119.75

Signed with Basil Lajeunesse's mark and witnessed by John B. Sarpy. Lajeunesse also accompanied JCF on his second expedition as far as Fort Hall, and on the 1845 expedition. He was killed by the Modocs at Klamath Lake in 1846. A brother, François, who had been one of Sir William Drummond Stewart's employees on his journey of 1837, was with JCF in 1843–44.

Voucher No. 14, St. Louis, 31 Oct. 1842
U.S. to François Tessier

For services as voyageur @ 62½¢ per diem for 153 days,
from 26 May to 26 Oct. 1842   95.62½

Signed with Tessier's mark and witnessed by John B. Sarpy. No further information on Tessier.

Voucher No. 15, St. Louis, 31 Oct. 1842
U.S. to Benjamin Cadot

For services as voyageur @ 62½¢ per diem for 153 days,
from 26 May to 26 Oct. 1842   95.62½

Signed with Cadot's mark and witnessed by John B. Sarpy. A man named Benjamin Cadot, thirty-seven years of age and of Canadian birth, was listed in the census of 1860 at the Yankton agency (see *South Dakota Historical Collections*, 10:436).

Voucher No. 16, St. Louis, 31 Oct. 1842
U.S. to Joseph Clement

For services as voyageur @ 66½¢ per diem for 153 days,
from 26 May to 26 Oct. 1842   101.75

Signed with Clement's mark and witnessed by John B. Sarpy. Clement not further identified.

Voucher No. 17, St. Louis, 31 Oct. 1842
U.S. to Daniel Simonds

For services as voyageur @ 62½¢ per diem for 153 days,
from 26 May to 26 Oct. 1842   95.62½

Signed with Simonds' mark and witnessed by John B. Sarpy. The David Adams Papers, MoSHi, contain a contract between Sibille & Adams and "Daniel Simons," in which Simons signs on as a "common hand" for a Rocky Mountain expedition. He signed by mark in Aug. 1841, came down from the mountains with Adams in the spring of 1842, and evidently signed on with JCF shortly thereafter.

Voucher No. 18, St. Louis, 31 Oct. 1842
U.S. to Leonard Benoist

For services as voyageur @ 75¢ per diem for 153 days, 26
May to 26 Oct. 1842   114.75

Benoist not further identified.

Voucher No. 19, St. Louis, 31 Oct. 1842
U.S. to Christopher Carson

For services as guide and hunter @ 100.00 per month for
3 months, from 1 June to 1 Sept. 1842   300.00
1 mule   40.00
                                                               _____
                                                                340.00

Signed with Carson's mark and witnessed by F. V. Pfister. The acquisition
of Christopher Carson (1809–68) as a guide was a stroke of luck for JCF and
the beginning of a long friendship between the young explorer and the experienced Scotch-Irish trapper and Indian fighter. Although at this time he
was unable to write his name, he could converse in French, Spanish, and several Indian languages. Later he would share honors as a guide with his
former fellow trapper, Thomas "Broken Hand" Fitzpatrick, on JCF's second expedition, and as a member of the third venture he would participate
in the conquest of California. After the Mexican War and the refusal of the
Senate to confirm his commission in the regular Army, Carson settled in
Taos, New Mexico Territory, served as Indian agent for the Utes, and dictated
the story of his life to John Mostin, probably at the persuasion of Jesse B.
Turley. For biographical background, see SABIN and CARSON.

Voucher No. 20, St. Louis, 31 Oct. 1842
U.S. to Michel Marly

For services as voyageur @ 62½¢ per diem for 153 days,
from 26 May to 26 Oct. 1842   95.62½

Michel Marly, born in St. Louis in 1820; no further information.

Voucher No. 21, St. Louis, 31 Oct. 1842
U.S. to Baptiste Bernier

For services as voyageur @ 1.00 per diem for 153 days, from
26 May to 26 Oct. 1842   153.00

Signed with Bernier's mark and witnessed by John B. Sarpy. It is probably
to Baptiste Bernier that Lucien Fontenelle referred when he wrote Andrew
Drips from Fort William, 1 Aug. 1835: "young Provost, Bernier, Bellaire and
others are hired as trappers" (MoSHi—Drips Papers).

Voucher No. 22, St. Louis, 31 Oct. 1842
U.S. to Honoré Ayot

For services as voyageur @ 83¢ per diem for 153 days,
from 26 May to 26 Oct. 1842   126.99

Signed with Ayot's mark and witnessed by John B. Sarpy. For Ayot's contract with JCF, see Doc. No. 42.

Voucher No. 23, Fort John, Platte River, 2 Sept. 1842
U.S. to François Latulipe

For services as voyageur @ 1.00 per diem for 63 days, from
29 June to 1 Sept. 1842   63.00
For one horse   30.00
12 buffalo robes for pack horses   25.00

                                                                118.00

Signed with Latulippe's mark and witnessed by C. Lambert.

Voucher No. 24, St. Louis, 31 Oct. 1842
U.S. to François Badeau

For services as voyageur @ 1.00 per diem for 153 days,
from 26 May to 26 Oct. 1842   153.00

Signed with Badeau's mark and witnessed by John B. Sarpy. Badeau, who also went on the second expedition and was described by JCF as being one of his "most faithful and efficient men," was accidentally killed by his own gun, 23 May 1844, as the expedition was returning home and was buried on the banks of the Sevier River. See p. 697.

Voucher No. 25, St. Louis, 31 Oct. 1842
U.S. to Louis Ménard

For services as voyageur @ 81¾¢ per diem for 153 days,
from 26 May to 26 Oct. 1842   125.07¾

The name Louis Ménard is so common that it is difficult to identify this man, but he is probably the same Louis L. Ménard who contracted his services as a boatman on the upper Missouri in May 1852 (MoSHi—P. Chouteau Maffitt Collection). Louis Ménard was also on Frémont's second expedition.

Voucher No. 26, St. Louis, 31 Oct. 1842
U.S. to C. Lambert

For services as camp conductor @ 1.85¾¢ per diem for
153 days, 26 May to 26 Oct. 1842   278.07

Voucher No. 27, St. Louis, 31 Oct. 1842
U.S. to Joseph Ruelle

For services as voyageur @ 66½¢ per diem for 153 days,
26 May to 26 Oct. 1842   101.75

Signed with Ruelle's mark and witnessed by John B. Sarpy. The name
appears often in the records of Chouteau's American Fur Company (vols. X
and GG) from 1835 to 1845, in the upper Missouri area. According to G. R.
BROOKS he had been with Robert Campbell in 1833 and may also be the Joseph
Ruel who married Jeanne Pichereau on 3 July 1838 in St. Louis. Ruelle obtained a judgment in St. Louis, 21 Nov. 1844, of $40.75 against Frémont for
a gun lost on the expedition (DNA-217, T-135, Statement of Differences on
Settlement of Frémont's Accounts, 6 June 1849, No. 7624, p. 6).

Voucher No. 28, St. Louis, 31 Oct. 1842
U.S. to Auguste Janisse

For services as voyageur @ 87½¢ per diem for 153 days,
from 26 May to 26 Oct. 1842   133.87½

Signed with Janisse's mark and witnessed by John B. Sarpy. The name appears as Auguste Janis in the GG ledger of P. Chouteau, Jr., and Company.
PREUSS and his editors call him Johnny Auguste Janisse, and the editors say
he was the only Negro or mulatto among JCF's men on this expedition. He
was also with Stansbury in 1849.

Voucher No. 29, St. Louis, 31 Oct. 1842
U.S. to Moise Chardonnais

For services as voyageur @ 75¢ per diem for 153 days,
from 26 May to 26 Oct. 1842   144.75

Signed with Chardonnais' mark and witnessed by John B. Sarpy. No further identification of Chardonnais.

Voucher No. 30, St. Louis, 31 Oct. 1842
U.S. to Raphael Proue

For services as voyageur @ 75¢ per diem for 153 days, from
26 May to 26 Oct. 1842   114.75

The faithful Raphael Proue [Proulx, Proux] would continue with JCF on his second and third ventures as well as the disastrous fourth expedition of 1848 and would freeze to death 9 Jan. 1849 in the San Juan Mountains of southwest Colorado.

Voucher No. 31, St. Louis, 31 Oct. 1842
U.S. to P. Chouteau, Jr., and Company

8 French carts	280.00
10 Spanish saddles	60.00
10 bridles	7.50
30 halters	37.50
30 white oak stakes	30.00
11 saddle blankets	8.25
8 sets harness for shaft	100.00
8 sets harness for French carts	68.00
4 Spanish saddles	28.00
3 bridles and martingales	9.75
1 3-pt. blue blanket	10.00
1 piece Russia sheeting	13.00
1 lb. patent thread, 1.00, 1 bundle cord, 75¢	1.75
1 blank memorandum book	.50
1 box tobacco, 148 lbs.	14.80
10 lbs. vermillion	30.00
4 doz. fire steels, 7.00, 1 gross Indians awls 2.20	9.20
6 scalping knives 18.00, 500 gun flints 2.50	20.50
2 buffalo tongues, 12.00, 6 hams, 100 lbs., 6.25	18.25
310 lbs. common bacon	12.40
2 barrels pork 15.00, 2 barrels flour 10.00	25.00
4 barrels pilot bread 16.00, 1 barrel butter crackers 5.00	21.00
50 lbs. coffee	7.75
6 lbs. tea	6.00
100 lbs. sugar and keg	7.75
23 lbs. rice and keg	1.69
3 loaves white sugar, 11½ lbs. @ 20¢	2.30
1 keg 50 proof port wine, 4 gals.	11.50
1 keg brandy, 4 gallons	11.50
10 lbs. common soap	1.00
2 lbs. castile soap	.75
100 lbs. bar lead 5.00, 50 lbs. gunpowder 15.00	20.00
1 bag shot 1.75, 1 ball twine 25¢, 2 doz. tent pins 75¢	2.75

11 yds. Russia sheeting	4.37
spades 2.50, 1 coffee mill 1.50	4.00
½ doz. mustard 3.00, 11 lbs. sperm candles 5.50	8.50
6 lbs. assorted nails 60¢, 1 keg tar 1.00	1.60
1 can 100 proof spirits of wine, 4 gals.	4.13
½ doz. matches	.25
3 reams wrapping paper	7.50
1 file 25¢, 1 pair nippers 1.00, 2 doz. spoons 75¢	2.00
1 piece canvas for cart covers, 33½ yds.	5.03
1 box macaroni	5.38
4 lead lines	2.50
3 bands for bacon	1.87
3 sheet iron kettles	6.60
2 tin kettles	1.50
2 tin pans 1.00, 1 doz. tin plates 1.50	2.50
1 doz. cups 63¢, 1 coffee boiler and 1 lantern 1.00	1.63
6 knives and forks 1.25, 1 lb. pepper 16¢, 2 augers 88¢	2.29
1 drawing knife 75¢, 1 hand saw 1.25	2.00
1 hatchet 1.50, 3 Collins axes, 3.75	5.25
3 balls twine 75¢, 1 teakettle 1.00, 1 ball lampwick 25¢	2.00
1 bag salt 40¢, 1 pineapple cheese 1.25	1.65
1 oven and lid	1.25
1 frying pan	.75
paid for making tent	15.00
5 lbs. saleratus	1.00
1 can linseed oil, 2 gals.	4.00
10 lbs. Spanish brown paint 1.00, 1 brush 1.12	2.12
1 rifle given to Preuss	20.00
2 mosquito bars	8.00
1 powder horn	1.25
drayages	1.50
	1005.85
Commission	48.83
	1054.68

Endorsed by JCF: "At the time when this expenditure was incurred I had not yet received sufficient funds & as the advanced season of the year did not permit me [to] delay the setting out of the expedition, I had recourse to the house of Chouteau & Co. who advanced me money, transacted my business & charged a commission."

Voucher No. 32, St. Louis, 31 Oct. 1842
U.S. to P. Chouteau, Jr., and Company

17 horses and 2 mules	970.62
13 mules	520.00
transportation of the above	103.75
	1591.37

Voucher No. 33, St. Louis, 31 Oct. 1842
U.S. to Bent, St. Vrain & Co.

3 mules	135.00
2 horses	50.00
bunting for flag	25.00
5 lb. coffee	10.00
1 comb	.50
1 piece rope	1.00
	221.50

Bent, St. Vrain & Co., with a branch post (Fort St. Vrain) on the South Platte and Bent's Fort on the Arkansas, ranked next to P. Chouteau, Jr., and Company in the amount of business transacted during this period. The business included trading with the Indians and raising horses and mules.

Voucher No. 34, St. Louis, 31 Oct. 1842
U.S. to J. & S. Hawken

For splicing gun stock	1.50
fly on lock	.50
cleaning double-barreled gun	.75
hind sight on rifle	.50
	3.25

Voucher No. 35, Washington, 1 Nov. 1842
U.S. to Charles Preuss

For transportation of 13 boxes containing instruments for surveys from Washington to New York	2.37½
from New York to Buffalo	6.21¼
from Buffalo to Chicago	3.27½
from Chicago to St. Louis	3.37½
	15.23¾

Voucher No. 36, Washington, 31 Oct. 1842
U.S. to Charles Preuss

For services rendered to the U.S. as assistant to Lt. J. C. Fremont in the survey of the Platte and Kansas rivers for 184 days, from 1 May to 1 Nov. 1842, @ 3.00 per diem   552.00

Voucher No. 37, Washington, 24 Nov. 1842
U.S. to Thomas W. Burch

for making 1 drawing table and shelves   7.00

Thomas W. Burch not further identified.

Voucher No. 38, Washington, 1 Dec. 1842
U.S. to Charles Preuss

For services rendered to the U.S. as assistant to Lt. J. C. Fremont in constructing maps of surveys west of the Mississippi for 30 days, from 1 to 30 Nov. 1842   90.00

Voucher No. 39, Baltimore, 5 Dec. 1842
U.S. to J. N. Nicollet

For services rendered to the U.S. as superintendent of Surveys West of the Mississippi for 92 days, from 1 Aug. to 31 Oct. 1842, @ 8.00 per diem   736.00

Voucher No. 40, St. Louis, 28 Dec. 1842
U.S. to Osea Harmiyo

For services as voyageur @ 50¢ per diem for 113 days, from 9 July to 31 Oct. 1842   36.50

Signed with Harmiyo's mark and witnessed by H[enry] B. Brant. The spelling is phonetic for José Armijo, a young Spaniard hired at Fort St. Vrain. See below, pp. 204–5. Henry B. Brant, the nineteen-year-old son of Lieut. Col. Joshua B. and Sarah Benton Brant, of St. Louis, accompanied the expedition as far as Fort Laramie—together with John Randolph Benton, the twelve-year-old brother of Jessie. Here the two young men were left because of possible encounters with hostile Indians. In the fall, when the expedition returned to the settlements, JCF sold at public auction in Bellevue much of the equipment that was still intact—such as carts, harnesses, horses, mules, rifles, and saddles—and it was Henry B. Brant who later swore to the correctness of the $910 bill of sale (see Bill of Sale, DNA-217, T-135, 9 Feb. 1843).

For services as voyageur @ $1.00 per diem, for 144 days,
from 9 June to 31 October 1842   144.00

Signed with Joseph Bougar's mark and witnessed by H. B. Brant. Bougar
is not listed in JCF's reports or the *Memoirs* as being a part of the expedition; yet he must have joined just as the party was ready to leave Cyprian
Chouteau's trading house on the Kansas River. An order of William Kenceleur
to P. Chouteau, Jr., and Company, to pay Bougar $82.00 indicates that he was
at the Vermillion Post [Kansas] on 11 May 1842 (MoSHi—P. Chouteau
Maffitt Collection).

All the above documents are in DNA-217, Third Auditor's Reports and Accounts, Acct. No. 16962, except voucher nos. 35 and 36 in the first and second
quarters, no. 31 and no. 40 in third and fourth quarters, and the subvoucher
to Chilton, all of which are on roll No. 1 of DNA microfilm T-135—a
special consolidated file of JCF accounts.

54. Asa Gray to John Torrey

Monday Morning [Feb. 1843], CAMBRIDGE

MY DEAR FRIEND

I conclude to send you a small parcel instead of a letter. Enclosed
is a hasty determination of the Fremont plants now in my hands. I
found *ripe seeds* of the first two of the list, which I hope to grow.
Both are worthy of being figured, although the first only is showy.

I found Hooker's[1] letter [*not found*] dated so far back as Nov. 10,
and send it for your perusal. I think some arrangement such as he
desires may be made respecting the Antarctic collections. The Oregon and Califn. I hope will somehow tumble into our hands. Please
send back his letter (by mail if you are not sending a parcel) early
next week, as I must answer it on the 1st prox. . . .

Engelmann writes about his friend Dr. Lindheimer, who wants to
collect in Texas &c.—and offer plants for sale, at $8–10 per hundred.
he & I to vouch for generic names.—advertise in Silliman.—I shall
write to him on the subject, securing that all shall pass thro' our
hands. I think I will advise him to send him to Rky. Mts. with some
of the parties that will be sure to be going if the Oregon bill
passes. As he is a Doctor—a pretty good botanist, I guess, and makes

very good specimens of the right kind—flowers—fruit &c.—why not recommend him to Fremont & Col. Abert, and get him a place? I think we cannot do better. If you think so please act upon the suggestion without delay. The more collectors we can get into the field the better, Buckley[2] & all.

.   .   .   .

Your affectionate,

A. GRAY

ALS, RC (NNNBG).
1. Sir William Jackson Hooker (1785–1865), director of Kew Gardens in London and a highly respected English botanist. He had published a well known work on North American botany, *Flora Boreali-Americana* (London, 1829–40).
2. Persons mentioned in this paragraph include Dr. Ferdinand Jakob Lindheimer (1801–79), a German botanist who was visiting in St. Louis. He had fought in the war for Texan independence and, encouraged by Engelmann, was about to return to Texas on a collecting expedition (GEISER). Benjamin Silliman (1779–1864) was publisher of the *American Journal of Science and Arts,* a pioneer work of its kind in the United States. Samuel Botsford Buckley (1809–83), botanist and field naturalist, later became state geologist of Texas. Gray held Buckley in low esteem (particularly for daring to publish new species, some considered valid today, on his own!) and his remark twitches with feeling.
Asa Gray had proposed that Lindheimer be sent to the Rockies and Oregon for further collecting, possibly with JCF. "Fremont will not take Geyer; but I believe he wants some one. The interesting region (the most so in the world) is the high Rocky Mountains about the sources of the Platte & thence South!!" (Gray to Engelmann, 13 Feb. 1843, MoSB). Gray's enthusiasm for western flora contributed much to botanical knowledge of the region, but it was not until 1872 that he was able to go to the Rockies himself and see the vegetation that he had studied for a lifetime.

55. J. J. Abert to Thomas H. Benton

Bureau of Topographical Engr.
WASHINGTON March 10th 1843

SIR

I have the honor to acknowledge the receipt of your letter of the 7th inst. and to thank you for your suggestions in reference to the Survey now required in the vicinity of the Rocky Mountains. Be assured that they will receive the greatest attention. A sketch embracing your views has been enclosed to Mr. Fremont in order to obtain from him the customary estimate. Very Respectfully Your Obt. Servt.

J. J. ABERT
Cl. C. T. E.

Lbk (DNA-77, LS, 6:152). Benton's letter is not found, but the "sketch" is an enclosure with Doc. No. 56.

56. J. J. Abert to Frémont

Bureau of Topographical Engs.
WASHINGTON March 10th 1843

SIR

You will please to give immediate attention to your accounts, as it is necessary, both by the laws & regulations that these should be adjusted. Before the Bureau can decide upon any orders for your duties during the ensuing season, it is necessary that you should submit an estimate in detail of the probable expence, embracing the whole or a part of the sketch of duties a copy of which is enclosed. Very Respectfully Your Obt. Servt.

J. J. ABERT
C. C. T. E.

[Enclosure]

To proceed to the main forks of the Kansas river, determine their position and thence survey the main stream to its head. From the head of the Kansas to fall directly on to the Arkansas and survey it to its head, crossing the mountains by that prong which forms the *boundary between the United States and Mexico*. Continuing along the western base of the mountains and crossing the heads of all the streams which take their rise in that portion of the mountains, join on to your positions of 1842 on the Colorado of the Gulf of California. Thence continuing north-westwardly across the waters of the Columbia, turn westwardly into the Flat-head Country, and join on to Lieut. Wilkes' Survey. From that point to return by the Oregon road, and on again reaching the mountains, diverge a little and make a circuit of the Wind river chain, which is about eighty miles long.

This circuit would embrace within its limits the heads of the Colorado, the Columbia, some of the heads of the Missouri proper, the Yellowstone and the Platte.

Lbk (DNA-77, LS, 6:151). Senator Benton's influence upon Colonel Abert, and his role as the man behind the scenes in the rise of JCF's career, is evident here. Benton writes JCF's orders, obviously after consultation with the young lieutenant, and Abert—in a sense—merely ratifies them. But Abert is not a cipher, as Benton and the Frémonts later portrayed him; his views happened to correspond to Benton's in the matter of western expansion. "Abert could not, as did Senator Benton, intrigue on behalf of a special policy of imperial aggrandizement, nor could he initiate a legislative policy for the West" (GOETZMANN, 66).

These are the orders for JCF's expedition of 1843–44 which will take him into California. Yet nothing in the orders indicates that he has this discretion; he is, in fact, to return down the eastern side of the Wind River Mountains in Wyoming—having explored the western slopes in 1842.

Charles Wilkes (1798–1877), naval officer and explorer, had just completed a long voyage which had begun in Aug. 1838 and had taken him to the Antarctic, certain islands of the Pacific, and the northwest coast of North America. Benton's interest in Oregon makes him eager to extend Wilkes' coastal observations into the interior.

57. Frémont to John Torrey

WASHINGTON CITY March 11th 1843

MY DEAR SIR,

Your favor of the 27th with the enclosure came safely to hand. I think that it would be unjust to you were I to write a preface to the catalogue of plants and would be assuming for myself a knowledge that I do not possess. I claim no other credit than what may be due to having collected them under circumstances of considerable hardship and privation. From the mouth of the Kansas river to the Red buttes, I had with me a number of carts which afforded means to transport the plants conveniently, but from that place our examination of the country was made on horseback. To accomplish the exploration on which I had been sent required very rapid movements and it was impossible for me to give to the plants the time necessary to arrange them properly. We were in a savage and inhospitable country, sometimes annoyed by the Indians and frequently in great distress from want of provisions, and when you join to these things the various duties which were constantly claiming my attention, you will readily make an allowance for the bad condition of the collection I sent you. It was made under very unfavorable circumstances, and in the intervals of very pressing duties.

Casting your eye on the small sketch I sent you, you will see that our line of road is generally along the bottoms of the Kansas tributaries and sometimes over the upper prairies. The soil of the river bottoms is always rich, and generally well timbered, though the whole region is what is called a prairie country. The upper prairies are an immense deposit of sand and gravel, covered with a good and very generally a rich soil. Along the road on reaching the little stream called Sandy creek, the soil became more sandy. The geological formation of this position is lime—and sand-stone. The Amorpha was the characteristic plant, in many places being as abundant as the grass. From its mouth to the junction of its main forks the valley of the Platte generally about four miles broad is rich and well timbered, covered with luxuriant grasses. The large purple Aster? was here the characteristic, flourishing in great magnificence. From the junction to Laramie's fork the country may be called a sandy one; the valley of the stream is without timber, but still the grasses are fine and plants abundant. On our return in September the whole valley looked like a garden. It was yellow with fields of sunflower which was the characteristic.

Between these two main forks of the Platte, and from the junction to Laramie's fork the formation consists of a calcareous marl, a soft earthy limestone, and a granitic sandstone. In the region traversed from Laramie's fork to the mouth of the Sweet water river the soil is generally sandy, the formation consisting of a variety of sandstones —yellow and gray sandstones a red argillaceous sandstone with compact gypsum or alabaster and fine conglomerates. The Sweet Water valley is a sandy plain about 120 miles long, and generally about 5 miles broad, bounded by ranges of granitic mountains between which the valley formation consists near the Devil's gate of a grayish micaceous sandstone and fine grained conglomerate with a fine grained white sandstone. Proceeding twenty or thirty miles up the valley we find a white sandstone alternating with white clay and white clayey sandstone. At our encampment of August 5th–6th we found a fine white clayey sandstone—a coarse sandstone or puddingstone and white calcareous sandstone. A few miles to the west of that position we reached a point where the sandstone reposed immediately upon the granite, which thenceforward along our line of route alternated with a compact clay slate.

We crossed the dividing ridge on the 8th of August & found the soil of the plains at the foot of the mountains on the western side to be sandy, being the decomposition of the neighbouring granite mountains. From Laramie's fork to this point Artemesia was the characteristic plant, occupying the place of the grasses, and filling the air with its odour of camphor and spirits of turpentine. On the morning of the 10th we entered the defile of the Wind river mountains.

I hope that what I have hastily said above will enable you to write a short preface to the catalogue and I would be exceedingly indebted to you if you could send it with the 2d part of the catalogue in order that I may introduce it into the report. The work is now in the hands of the printer but I will delay its publication some days until I hear from you. Should you find it proper to refer in your preface to heights above the sea I will fill up any blanks you may leave. In a few days I will reply to some other points in your letter and in the mean time beg you to let me hear from you as soon as will suit your convenience, as I am exceedingly pressed & should be very sorry to publish the catalogue incomplete. Very truly yours,

J. C. Frémont.

I had just written the above when I received your note with the 2d part of the catalogue. I am sure I need not tell you how much gratified I am that it has arrived in time for publication. I will put it to-day in the hands of the printer and the proofs shall be forwarded to you at Princeton as soon as they are struck. This letter is already very long & I will not add to it by expressing my thanks of which you are I know assured. Believe me yours truly,

J. C. Frémont.

ALS-JBF, RC (NNNBG). While many letters from JCF to Torrey have survived, we have only a printed excerpt of a letter from Torrey to JCF (July 1848). Torrey's 27 Feb. suggestion that Frémont write the preface to the catalogue of plants was a courteous one, but as the document indicates, JCF refused. Torrey did write the preface, presented with his catalogue as an addendum to the report of the expedition (our Doc. No. 61).

58. J. J. Abert to Frémont

Bureau of Topographical Engineers
WASHINGTON March 14th 1843

SIR

I have to inform you that a requisition has been this day made in your favor for twelve hundred Dollars.

You will please pay Mr. Nicollet the amount that may be due him for services to the 10th inst. inclusive, on which day his employment terminated.

You will repair to Baltimore in order to adjust Mr. Nicollet's account and to receive from him the public instruments which he has to return for which you will please to give the customary receipts, after which you will return to this place and report. Very Respectfully Your Obt. Servt.

J. J. ABERT
Col. C. T. E.

Lbk (DNA-77, LS, 6:161).

59. Thomas H. Benton to Frémont

WASHINGTON CITY, March 20. 1843.

DEAR SIR,

In the very important expedition which you are fitting out to the region beyond the *Rocky Mountains,* and to complete the gap in the Surveys between the South Pass and the head of tidewater in the Columbia, the officer in command has to appear to the Indians as the *representative of the government,* and not as the officer of a bureau. To them he represents the government, and as such he must make presents, or bring both himself and his government into contempt. This is an expense which belongs to the Indian department more than to the Topographical bureau, and I repeat to you, as my opinion, that you should apply to the Secretary at War for a part of the contingencies, or a part of the appropriations for Indian presents, for this object. There is no danger of getting too much, and one or two thousand dollars would be quite small for the number of Indians who will be encountered. On any account, both as it concerns the success of the expedition, the respectability of the government, and the future friendship of the Indians, it is indispensable that the officer who carries the flag of the U. States into these remote regions, should carry presents. All savages expect them: they even demand them; and they feel contempt & resentment if disappointed. Respectfully, Sir Yr. Obt. Servant,

THOMAS H. BENTON

ALS, RC (CSmH).

60. Frémont to John Torrey

WASHINGTON CITY March 21st 1843

MY DEAR SIR,

Yours of the 14th with the enclosure came safely to hand yesterday—I beg you to accept my thanks for the preface to your Catalogue, which I find exceedingly interesting, & am happy to say is in time for the printer. Herewith I send you a corrected sheet, which has still some errors, but I think you will find it more free from them, than proof sheets generally are. The printer desires me to say, that having no Greek characters, he has supplied their place for the moment with the usual letters, but has sent to Baltimore for them, and you will find them inserted in the final sheets, together with some other omissions. It will give me pleasure to furnish you with the number of Catalogues you mention.

There was an error in my letter, relative to the fact of the *clay* slate alternating with granite; it should have been *mica* slate, which is one of the predominant rocks in that quarter. In *Equisetum arvense* of the Catalogue, is *"arvense"* right? Among the plants collected on the Sandy river, (branch of the Colorado) on our return, was a portion of an *artemisia* (?) can you tell me if this *is* an artemisia, & if so, what one? I am anxious to know, as this is the plant with the odour of camphor & spirits of turpentine, which I mentioned in my letter as being highly characteristic. There is one plant among the collection of which I am very desirous to know the name; I met with in fields in full bloom filling the air with fragrance, & almost entirely covering the bottom land of the South Fork of the Platte, within some twenty miles of the Rocky Mts. & at an elevation of between 5, and 6000 feet. I did not see it again until I reached the valley of the Sweetwater near the Devils Gate, which is at about the same elevation. I cannot describe it to you from memory, although I should recognize it immediately. It is about the size of the amorpha & the predominant colour of the flowers, is the purple hue of the amorpha. One perfectly white, which is however seen but rarely, amid the fields of purple flowers, and one of a light blue, almost as frequent as the purple colour. Is it "Lupinus leucophyllus" or is it perhaps an amorpha?

I have purposely delayed replying to an occasional enquiry in some of your letters as to whether or not I should be able to take with me a botanist, in order that I might be in possession of information, which would enable me to give you a definite answer. I find for various strong reasons, that I shall not be able to do so, but still I contemplate doing something for your favourite science. Can we not do something together? Is it not customary sometimes for collectors, unskilled as myself to publish their plants in partnership with, & under the shadow of, the standard names in the science. I do not know if I am asking too much, but if I am not, I should be glad if you would write to me on the subject, and I think something good may be done.[1] The following is a brief outline of my expedition for the present year. I shall leave this city about the 5th of April & before the 1st of May shall be beyond the western frontier of Missouri. I propose crossing the mountains to the South of the Great Pass,— range along their western bases,—visit the mountainous region of the Flathead country, probably go as far down as Fort Vancouver, and return by the heads of the Missouri. This you will see, affords a fine range for botanical researches, and should my veiws meet your approbation, a few words of instruction from you would be very beneficial to me. By the time you return the proof sheets of the Catalogue the whole report will be ready for the Binder.

I should be glad to hear from you on the subject of this letter, & in the meanwhile I am Very truly yours,

J. Charles Frémont

ALS-JBF, RC (NHi).
1. JCF's reluctance to take professional scientists on his expeditions, and

his desire to collaborate with men such as Torrey in describing and naming his collections, eventually became a topic of comment. Asa Gray wrote to Torrey on 8 March 1845 that he believed JCF wanted all the scientific glory. "He ought to be above it, and to aim higher; but indeed, it is hardly to be expected" (NNNBG).

61. *Report* of the First Expedition, 1843

Editorial note: This account was first published in 1843 as Senate Doc. 243, 27th Cong., 3rd sess., under the title: *A Report of an Exploration of the Country Lying between the Missouri River and the Rocky Mountains on the Line of the Kansas and Great Platte Rivers.* It was speedily sent to the Senate after JCF had completed the manuscript, for it had been long delayed. JCF presented it to Colonel Abert on 1 March 1843, and on the following day it went directly to Secretary of War John Canfield Spencer. In a covering letter, Abert explained that the delay "was not owing to any want of industry on the part of Lieut. Frémont, but to the great amount of matter which had to be introduced in the report and the many calculations which had to be made, of the astronomical & barometrical observations, the necessary labor on these accounts has delayed the completion of the report until today" (DNA-77, LS, 6:141).

On 2 March the Senate ordered the report to be printed, and the next day a resolution provided that "nine hundred additional copies be furnished for the use of the Senate, and one hundred copies for the use of the Topographical Bureau." It was later to be combined with the report of the 1843–44 expedition and widely distributed by trade publishers.

"I write more easily by dictation," JCF said many years later, and ". . . therefore the labor of amanuensis, commencing at this early time, has remained with Mrs. Frémont" (MEMOIRS, 163). We have already noted that Jessie did indeed produce a great number of the documents attributed to her husband. There is, however, a surviving manuscript draft of this report in the National Archives (DNA-77) which is much less a joint effort than JCF's comment would indicate. The first nineteen sheets are in Jessie's hand, and the remainder in JCF's with some corrections and refinements in Jessie's. Where the manuscript draft differs materially from the printed version, we indicate the difference in a note.

In a brief explanation to the reader at the beginning of the report, JCF explains: "For the Mineralogical Character of the Rocks mentioned in the course of the following report, I am indebted to Mr. James D. Dana, of the late Exploring Expedition to the South Seas. The Collection of Plants made during my exploration was placed in the hands of Dr. John Torrey, who prepared the catalogue which is annexed to the narrative." James Dwight Dana (1813–95) had recently returned from serving with Charles Wilkes. He was a professor at Yale, author of standard works in geology, and editor of the *American Journal of Science*.

Despite our usual adherence to the policy of presenting documents in chronological order, we have placed this report slightly out of order so that it may appear at the end of this division of the volume.

REPORT

WASHINGTON, *March* 1, 1843

To COL. J. J. ABERT,
  Chief of the Corps of Topographical Engineers:

SIR: Agreeably to your orders to explore and report upon the country between the frontiers of Missouri and the South Pass in the Rocky mountains, and on the line of the Kansas and Great Platte rivers, I sat out from Washington city on the 2d day of May, 1842, arrived at St. Louis, by way of New York, the 22d of May, where the necessary preparations were completed, and the expedition commenced. I proceeded in a steamboat to Chouteau's Landing, about 400 miles by water from St. Louis, and near the mouth of the Kansas river, whence we proceeded twelve miles to Mr. Cyprian Chouteau's trading house, where we completed our final arrangements for the expedition.

Bad weather, which interfered with astronomical observations, delayed us several days in the early part of June at this post, which is on the right bank of the Kansas river, about ten miles above the mouth, and six beyond the western boundary of Missouri. The sky cleared off at length, and we were enabled to determine our position, in longitude 94° 39′ 16″, and latitude 39° 5′ 57″. The elevation above the sea is about 700 feet. Our camp, in the meantime, presented an animated and bustling scene. All were busily occupied in completing the necessary arrangements for our campaign in the wilderness, and profiting by this short delay on the verge of civilization, to provide ourselves with all the little essentials to comfort in the nomadic life we were to lead for the ensuing summer months. Gradually, however, everything, the *materiel* of the camp, men, horses, and even mules, settled into its place, and by the 10th we were ready to depart; but, before we mount our horses, I will give a short description of the party with which I performed this service.

I had collected in the neighborhood of St. Louis twenty-one men, principally Creole and Canadian *voyageurs,* who had become familiar with prairie life in the service of the fur companies in the Indian country. Mr. Charles Preuss, a native of Germany, was my assistant in the topographical part of the survey. L. Maxwell, of Kaskaskia, had been engaged as hunter, and Christopher Carson, more familiarly known, for his exploits in the mountains, as Kit Carson, was our guide. The persons engaged in St. Louis, were:

Clément Lambert, J. B. L'Esperance, J. B. Lefêvre, Benjamin Potra, Louis Gouin, J. B. Dumés, Basil Lajeunesse, François Tessier, Benjamin Cadotte, Joseph Clément, Daniel Simonds, Leonard Benoit, Michel Morly, Baptiste Bernier, Honoré Ayot, François Latulippe, François Badeau, Louis Ménard, Joseph Ruelle, Moise Chardonnais, Auguste Janisse, Raphael Proue.

In addition to these, Henry Brant, son of Col. J. B. Brant, of St. Louis, a young man of nineteen years of age, and Randolph, a lively boy of twelve, son of the Hon. Thomas H. Benton, accompanied me, for the development of mind and body which such an expedition would give.[1] We were all well armed and mounted, with the exception of eight men, who conducted as many carts, in which were packed our stores, with the baggage and instruments, and which were each drawn by two mules. A few loose horses, and four oxen, which had been added to our stock of provisions, completed the

---

1. All the men on the expedition have been mentioned earlier, and some biographical information—usually scant—has been presented. In the present listing, JCF does not mention Registe Larente, who went only as far as Fort John near the mouth of the Laramie; Osea Harmiyo [José Armijo], hired at Fort St. Vrain on 9 July; or a man named Descoteaux who is not mentioned here or in the vouchers but is named later in the report. Latulippe did not start with the expedition, but was encountered with some comrades on 29 June, laden with robes, and was hired on the spot. He had been with Nicollet and JCF on the 1839 expedition.

train. We sat out on the morning of the 10th, which happened to be Friday, a circumstance which our men did not fail to remember and recall during the hardships and vexations of the ensuing journey. Mr. Cyprian Chouteau, to whose kindness during our stay at his house we were much indebted, accompanied us several miles on our way, until we met an Indian, whom he had engaged to conduct us on the first thirty or forty miles, where he was to consign us to the ocean of prairie, which, we were told, stretched without interruption almost to the base of the Rocky Mountains.

From the belt of wood which borders the Kanzas, in which we had passed several good-looking Indian farms, we suddenly emerged on the prairies, which received us at the outset with some of their striking characteristics; for here and there rode an Indian, and but a few miles distant, heavy clouds of smoke were rolling before the fire. In about ten miles we reached the Santa Fé road, along which we continued for a short time, and encamped early on a small stream, having travelled about eleven miles.[2] During our journey,

---

2. JCF is reconnoitering, not trailblazing, and there is little need to document every mile of his progress along an already established trail. When he reaches the South Pass area and strikes out to the north on his own, we shall feel justified in following him more closely. A word is required about our approach to the identification of topographical features, campsites, and other matters of geographical interest. With an expedition as early as, say, the Lewis and Clark expedition of 1804–6, where every bend of the river brought the men into view of hitherto unknown and unnamed features of the land, the places where they camped and the names they devised are of great historical importance. But JCF, half a century later, is no pathfinder—never personally claimed to be—and his eyes seldom fall upon a mountain range or a lake not known by an earlier traveler. This is particularly true when he is on the Oregon Trail.

While we do not feel compelled to annotate every river, lake, or other feature described by JCF, we do it frequently and perhaps not always consistently. We do it to keep track of the expedition on the map, to identify landmarks which have special interest, and to provide modern nomenclature for certain place-names which have changed through the years. We are more attentive to this responsibility when JCF is not following well-worn trails. For detailed information on the early trails, see George R. Stewart, *The California Trail* (New York, 1962), Jay Monaghan, *The Overland Trail* (Indianapolis, 1947), Irene D. Paden, *The Wake of the Prairie Schooner* (New York, 1943), and the "Introductions" by Dale L. Morgan to *The Overland Diary of James A. Pritchard from Kentucky to California in 1849* (Denver, Colo., 1959) and by David Potter to *Trail to California* (New Haven, Conn., 1945). A recent and authoritative work, but following the trail along the Platte and North Platte only as far as Fort Laramie, is Merrill J. Mattes, *The Great Platte River Road* (Lincoln, Nebr., 1969).

it was the customary practice to encamp an hour or two before sunset, when the carts were disposed so as to form a sort of barricade around a circle some eighty yards in diameter. The tents were pitched, and the horses hobbled and turned loose to graze; and but a few minutes elapsed before the cooks of the messes, of which there were four, were busily engaged in preparing the evening meal. At night fall, the horses, mules, and oxen, were driven in, and picketted —that is, secured by a halter, of which one end was tied to a small steel-shod picket, and driven into the ground; the halter being twenty or thirty feet long, which enabled them to obtain a little food during the night. When we had reached a part of the country where such a precaution became necessary, the carts being regularly arranged for defending the camp, guard was mounted at eight o'clock, consisting of three men, who were relieved every two hours; the morning watch being horse guard for the day. At daybreak, the camp was roused, the animals turned loose to graze, and breakfast generally over between six and seven o'clock, when we resumed our march, making regularly a halt at noon for one or two hours. Such was usually the order of the day, except when accident of country forced a variation, which, however, happened but rarely. We travelled the next day along the Santa Fé road, which we left in the afternoon, and encamped late in the evening on a small creek, called by the Indians Mishmagwi. Just as we arrived at camp, one of the horses set off at full speed on his return, and was followed by others. Several men were sent in pursuit, and returned with the fugitives about midnight, with the exception of one man, who did not make his appearance until morning. He had lost his way in the darkness of the night, and slept on the prairie. Shortly after midnight it began to rain heavily, and as our tents were of light and thin cloth, they offered but little obstruction to rain; we were all well soaked, and glad when morning came. We had a rainy march on the 12th, but the weather grew fine as the day advanced. We encamped in a remarkably beautiful situation on the Kanzas Bluffs, which commanded a fine view of the river valley, here from three to four miles wide. The central portion was occupied by a broad belt of heavy timber, and nearer the hills the prairies were of the richest verdure. One of the oxen was killed here for food.

We reached the ford of the Kanzas[3] late in the afternoon of the

3. One of the well-known fording places on the Kansas River, in the vicinity of present Topeka. JCF's route thus far has been the traditional one,

14th, where the river was two hundred and thirty yards wide, and commenced immediately preparations for crossing. I had expected to find the river fordable, but it had been swollen by the late rains, and was sweeping by with an angry current, yellow and turbid as the Missouri. Up to this point, the road we had travelled was a remarkably fine one, well beaten, and level, the usual road of a prairie country. By our route the ford was one hundred miles from the mouth of the Kanzas river. Several mounted men led the way into the stream to swim across. The animals were driven in after them, and in a few minutes all had reached the opposite bank in safety, with the exception of the oxen, which swam some distance down the river, and, returning to the right bank were not got over until the next morning. In the meantime, the carts had been unloaded and dismantled, and an India-rubber boat, which I had brought with me for the survey of the Platte river, placed in the water. The boat was twenty feet long, and five broad, and on it was placed the body and wheels of a cart, with the load belonging to it, and three men with paddles.

The velocity of the current, and the inconvenient freight, rendering it difficult to be managed, Basil Lajeunesse, one of our best swimmers, took in his teeth a line attached to the boat, and swam ahead in order to reach a footing as soon as possible, and assist in drawing her over. In this manner, six passages had been successfully made, and as many carts with their contents, and a greater portion of the party deposited on the left bank; but night was drawing near, and in our anxiety to have all over before darkness closed in, I put upon the boat the remaining two carts, with their accompanying load. The man at the helm was timid in water, and in his alarm

---

starting out along the Santa Fe Trail to avoid some bad crossings, then veering northward in the direction of the Platte. The creek he calls "Mishmagwi" may be Bull Creek or Captain Creek. After his crossing of the Kansas he will be traveling north and west, across northern tributaries of the Little Blue, until he reaches Grand Island at the Platte.

The hunter who visited camp on the evening of 17 June brought news of one of the very earliest wagon trains to journey to Oregon. Dr. Elijah White (d. 1879), of New York, had gone to the Willamette Valley by sea in 1837, on behalf of the Methodist Episcopal Church. Returning to Washington, D.C., he was appointed Indian agent with the understanding that he was to return to Oregon. At the time of his departure he was anticipating the passage of a bill authorizing the president to appoint agents for the territory west of Iowa. (The bill did not pass and White's appointment failed, but this was not known in Oregon until the fall of 1843.)

capsized the boat. Carts, barrels, boxes, and bales, were in a moment floating down the current, but all the men who were on the shore jumped into the water, without stopping to think if they could swim, and almost every thing, even heavy articles, such as guns and lead, were recovered.

Two of the men who could not swim came nigh being drowned, and all the sugar belonging to one of the messes wasted its sweets on the muddy waters; but our heaviest loss was a bag of coffee, which contained nearly all our provision. It was a loss which none but a traveller in a strange and inhospitable country can appreciate; and often afterward, when excessive toil and long marching had overcome us with fatigue and weariness, we remembered and mourned over our loss in the Kanzas. Carson and Maxwell had been much in the water yesterday, and both in consequence were taken ill. The former continuing so, I remained in camp. A number of Kanzas Indians visited us to-day. Going up to one of the groups who were scattered among the trees, I found one sitting on the ground among some of the men, gravely and fluently speaking French, with as much facility and as little embarrassment as any of my own party, who were nearly all of French origin.

On all sides was heard the strange language of his own people, wild, and harmonizing well with their appearance. I listened to him for some time with feelings of strange curiosity and interest. He was now apparently thirty-five years of age; and, on inquiry, I learned that he had been at St. Louis when a boy, and there had learned the French language. From one of the Indian women I obtained a fine cow and calf in exchange for a yoke of oxen. Several of them brought us vegetables, pumpkins, onions, beans, and lettuce. One of them brought butter, and from a half-breed near the river I had the good fortune to obtain some twenty or thirty pounds of coffee. The dense timber in which we had encamped interfered with astronomical observations, and our wet and damaged stores required exposure to the sun. Accordingly, the tents were struck early the next morning, and, leaving camp at six o'clock, we moved about seven miles up the river to a handsome, open prairie some twenty feet above the water, where the fine grass afforded a luxurious repast to our horses.

During the day we occupied ourselves in making astronomical observations, in order to lay down the country to this place, it being our custom to keep up our map regularly in the field, which we found attended with many advantages. The men were kept busy in

174

drying the provisions, painting the cart covers, and otherwise completing our equipage, until the afternoon, when powder was distributed to them, and they spent some hours in firing at a mark. We were now fairly in the Indian country, and it began to be time to prepare for the chances of the wilderness.

Friday, June 17.—The weather yesterday had not permitted us to make the observations I was desirous to obtain here, and I therefore did not move to-day. The people continued their target firing. In the steep bank of the river here were nests of innumerable swallows, into one of which a large prairie snake had got about half his body, and was occupied in eating the young birds. The old ones were flying about in great distress, darting at him, and vainly endeavoring to drive him off. A shot wounded him, and, being killed, he was cut open, and eighteen young swallows were found in his body. A sudden storm that burst upon us in the afternoon cleared away in a brilliant sunset, followed by a clear night, which enabled us to determine our position in longitude 96° 10′ 06″, and in latitude 39° 06′ 40″.

A party of emigrants to the Columbia river, under the charge of Dr. White, an agent of the Government in Oregon Territory, were about three weeks in advance of us. They consisted of men, women, and children. There were sixty-four men and sixteen or seventeen families. They had a considerable number of cattle, and were transporting their household furniture in large heavy wagons. I understood that there had been much sickness among them, and that they had lost several children. One of the party who had lost his child, and whose wife was very ill, had left them about one hundred miles hence on the prairies; and as a hunter who had accompanied them visited our camp this evening, we availed ourselves of his return to the States to write to our friends.

The morning of the 18th was very unpleasant. A fine rain was falling, with cold wind from the north, and mists made the river hills look dark and gloomy. We left our camp at seven, journeying along the foot of the hills which border the Kansas valley, generally about three miles wide, and extremely rich. We halted for dinner, after a march of about thirteen miles, on the banks of one of the many little tributaries to the Kansas, which look like trenches in the prairie, and are usually well timbered. After crossing this stream, I rode off some miles to the left, attracted by the appearance of a cluster of huts near the mouth of the [Little] Vermillion. It was a large but deserted Kansas village, scattered in an open wood along the margin of the stream, on a spot chosen with the customary Indian fondness for beauty and scenery. The Pawnees had attacked it in the early spring. Some of the houses were burnt, and others blackened with smoke, and weeds were already getting possession of the cleared places. Riding up the [Little] Vermillion river, I reached the ford in time to meet the carts, and crossing, encamped on its western side. The weather continued cool, the thermometer being this evening as low as 49°, but the night was sufficiently clear for astronomical observations, which placed us in longitude 96° 36′ 40″, and latitude 39° 15′ 19″.[4] At sunset, the barometer was at 28,845, thermometer 64°.

We breakfasted the next morning at half past five, and left our encampment early. The morning was cool, the thermometer being at 45°. Quitting the river bottom, the road ran along the uplands, over a rolling country, generally in view of the Kansas, from eight to twelve miles distant. Many large boulders of a very compact sandstone of various shades of red, some of them four or five tons in weight, were scattered along the hills; and many beautiful plants in flower, among which the *amorpha canescens* was a characteristic, enlivened the green of the prairie. At the heads of the ravines I remarked occasionally thickets of *salix longifolia,* the most common willow of the country. We travelled nineteen miles, and pitched our tents at evening on the head waters of a small creek, now nearly dry, but having in its bed several fine springs. The barometer indicated a considerable rise in the country—here about fourteen hundred feet above the sea—and the increased elevation appeared already to have some slight influence upon the vegetation. The night was cold, with a heavy dew, the thermometer at ten standing at 46°, barometer 28,483. Our position was in longitude 96° 48′ 05″, and latitude 39° 30′ 40″.

The morning of the 20th was fine, with a southerly breeze and a

---

4. In the manuscript draft, the longitude is the same as that given here, but in the 1845 edition it is changed to 96° 04′ 07″. Although JCF's latitudes remain fairly constant in the various versions, the longitudes—more difficult to fix—were frequently changed by later findings or calculations. In a note on his observations written after his 1843–44 expedition, and placed in the 1845 edition, he explains that his earlier longitudes were thrown too far to the westward by the use of an occultation "which experience has recently shown to be deserving of little comparative confidence." He then adjusted all these 1842 longitudes by referring them chronometrically to those established in 1843–44. His corrected longitudes usually lie to the west of modern readings. The readings used here for the 1842 expedition will be those first published by JCF in the 1843 report.

bright sky, and at 7 o'clock we were on the march. The country to-day was rather more broken, rising still, and covered every where with fragments of siliceous limestone, particularly on the summits, where they were small, and thickly strewed as pebbles on the shore of the sea. In these exposed situations grew but few plants; though, whenever the soil was good and protected from the winds, in the creek bottoms and ravines, and on the slopes, they flourished abundantly; among them, the *amorpha*[5] still retaining its characteristic place. We crossed, at 10, the Big Vermillion [Black Vermillion], which has a rich bottom of about one mile in breadth, one third of which is occupied by timber. Making our usual halt at noon, after a day's march of twenty-four miles, we reached the Big Blue, and encamped on the uplands of the western side, near a small creek, where was a fine large spring of very cold water. This is a clear and handsome stream, about one hundred and twenty feet wide, running, with a rapid current, through a well-timbered valley. To-day antelope were seen running over the hills, and at evening Carson brought us a fine deer. Long. of the camp 97° 06′ 58″, lat. 39° 45′ 08″. Thermometer at sunset 75°. A pleasant southerly breeze and fine morning had given place to a gale, with indications of bad weather, when, after a march of ten miles, we halted to noon on a small creek, where the water stood in deep pools. In the bank of the creek, limestone made its appearance in a stratum about one foot thick. In the afternoon, the people seemed to suffer for want of water. The road led along a high dry ridge; dark lines of timber indicated the heads of streams in the plains below; but there was no water near, and the day was very oppressive, with a hot wind, and the thermometer at 90°. Along our route, the *amorpha* has been in very abundant but variable bloom: in some places, bending beneath the weight of purple clusters; in others, without a flower. It seems to love best the sunny slopes, with a dark soil and southern exposure. Every where the rose is met with, and reminds us of cultivated gardens and civilization. It is scattered over the prairies in small bouquets, and, when glittering in the dews and waving in the pleasant breeze of the early morning, is the most beautiful of the prairie flowers. The *artemisia,* absinthe, or prairie sage, as it is variously called, is increasing in size, and glitters like silver, as the

---

5. The manuscript draft reads, "among them the *Coreopsis palmata* began to cluster in larger yellow patches but the Amorpha still retained its characteristic place."

southern breeze turns up its leaves to the sun. All these plants have their insect inhabitants, variously colored; taking generally the hue of the flower on which they live. The *artemisia* has its small fly accompanying it through every change of elevation and latitude; and wherever I have seen the *asclepias tuberosa,* I have always remarked, too, on the flower, a large butterfly, so nearly resembling it in color, as to be distinguishable at a little distance only by the motion of its wings.[6] Travelling on the fresh traces of the Oregon emigrants relieves a little the loneliness of the road; and to-night, after a march of twenty-two miles, we halted on a small creek, which had been one of their encampments. As we advance westward, the soil appears to be getting more sandy, and the surface rock, an erratic deposite of sand and gravel, rests here on a bed of coarse yellow and gray and very friable sandstone. Evening closed over with rain and its usual attendant, hordes of mosquitoes, with which we were annoyed for the first time.

June 22.—We enjoyed at breakfast this morning a luxury very unusual in this country, in a cup of excellent coffee, with cream from our cow. Being milked at night, cream was thus had in the morning. Our mid-day halt was at Wyeth's creek, in the bed of which, were numerous boulders of dark ferruginous sandstone, mingled with others of the red sandstone already mentioned. Here a pack of cards, lying loose on the grass, marked an encampment of our Oregon emigrants; and it was at the close of the day when we made our bivouac in the midst of some well-timbered ravines near the Little Blue, twenty-four miles from our camp of the preceding night. Crossing the next morning a number of handsome creeks, with clear water and sandy beds, we reached, at 10, a very beautiful wooded stream, about thirty-five feet wide, called Sandy creek, and, sometimes, as the Otoes frequently winter there, the Otoe fork. The country has become very sandy, and the plants less varied and abundant, with the exception of the *amorpha,* which rivals the grass in quantity, though not so forward as it has been found to the eastward.

---

6. In the manuscript draft, a blank is left for *A. tuberosa,* and "butterfly" reads "red butterfly." Inserted after the next sentence: "This party consists of above 100 persons, with cattle, horses, carts, &c." Throughout the remainder of the manuscript version, many of the scientific names of plants are missing, JCF having left blanks to be filled in after Torrey had made the necessary determinations. All of the plants collected by JCF are catalogued, beginning on p. 290, and we make few comments on them in the notes.

At the Big Trees, where we had intended to noon, no water was to be found. The bed of the little creek was perfectly dry, and on the adjacent sandy bottom, *cacti* [prickly pear], for the first time, made their appearance. We made here a short delay in search of water; and, after a hard day's march of twenty-eight miles, encamped, at five o'clock, on the Little Blue, where our arrival made a scene of the Arabian desert. As fast as they arrived, men and horses rushed into the stream, where they bathed and drank together in common enjoyment. We were now in the range of the Pawnees, who were accustomed to infest this part of the country, stealing horses from companies on their way to the mountains, and, when in sufficient force openly attacking and plundering them, and subjecting them to various kinds of insult. For the first time, therefore, guard was mounted to night. Our route the next morning lay up the valley, which, bordered by hills with graceful slopes, looked uncommonly green and beautiful. The stream was about fifty feet wide and three or four deep, fringed by cotton wood and willow, with frequent groves of oak tenanted by flocks of turkeys. Game here, too, made its appearance in greater plenty. Elk were frequently seen on the hills, and now and then an antelope bounded across our path, or a deer broke from the groves. The road in the afternoon was over the upper prairies, several miles from the river, and we encamped at sunset on one of its small tributaries, where an abundance of prêle (*equisetum*) afforded fine forage to our tired animals. We had travelled thirty-one miles. A heavy bank of black clouds in the west came on us in a storm between nine and ten, preceded by a violent wind. The rain fell in such torrents that it was difficult to breathe facing the wind, the thunder rolled incessantly, and the whole sky was tremulous with lightning; now and then illuminated by a blinding flash, succeeded by pitchy darkness. Carson had the watch from ten to midnight, and to him had been assigned our young *compagnons de voyage,* Messrs. Brant and R. Benton. This was their first night on guard, and such an introduction did not augur very auspiciously of the pleasures of the expedition. Many things conspired to render their situation uncomfortable; stories of desperate and bloody Indian fights were rife in the camp; our position was badly chosen, surrounded on all sides by timbered hollows, and occupying an area of several hundred feet, so that necessarily the guards were far apart; and now and then I could hear Randolph, as if relieved by the sound of a voice in the darkness, calling out to the sergeant of the guard, to

179

direct his attention to some imaginary alarm; but they stood it out, and took their turn regularly afterward.

The next morning we had a specimen of the false alarms to which all parties in these wild regions are subject. Proceeding up the valley, objects were seen on the opposite hills, which disappeared before a glass could be brought to bear upon them. A man[7] who was a short distance in the rear came spurring up in great haste, shouting Indians! Indians! He had been near enough to see and count them, according to his report, and had made out twenty-seven. I immediately halted, arms were examined and put in order; the usual preparations made; and Kit Carson, springing upon one of the hunting horses, crossed the river, and galloped off into the opposite prairies to obtain some certain intelligence of their movements.

Mounted on a fine horse, without a saddle, and scouring bareheaded over the prairies, Kit was one of the finest pictures of a horseman I have ever seen. A short time enabled him to discover that the Indian war party of twenty-seven consisted of six elk, who had been gazing curiously at our caravan as it passed by, and were now scampering off at full speed. This was our first alarm, and its excitement broke agreeably on the monotony of the day. At our noon halt, the men were exercised at a target; and in the evening we pitched our tents at a Pawnee encampment of last July. They had apparently killed buffalo here, as many bones were lying about, and the frames where the hides had been stretched were yet standing. The road of the day had kept the valley, which is sometimes rich and well timbered, though the country is generally sandy. Mingled with the usual plants, a thistle (*carduus leucógraphus*) had for the last day or two made its appearance; and along the river bottom, *tradescantia* (*virginica*) and milk plant (*asclepias syriaca**) in considerable quantities.[8]

* "This plant is very odoriferous, and in Canada charms the traveller, especially when passing through woods in the evening. The French there eat the tender shoots in the spring, as we do asparagus. The natives make a sugar of the flowers, gathering them in the morning when they are covered with dew, and collect the cotton from the pods to fill their beds. On account of the silkiness of this cotton, Parkinson calls the plant Virginian silk."—*Loudon's Encyclopedia of Plants*. The Sioux Indians of the Upper Platte eat the young pods of this plant, boiling them with the meat of the buffalo.

---

7. PREUSS, 13, says this man was Henry Brant.

8. At this point in the text, the manuscript draft contains the following deleted paragraphs:

Our march to-day had been twenty-one miles, and the astronomical observations gave us a chronometric longitude of 98° 54' 07", and latitude 40° 26' 50". We were moving forward at seven in the morning, and in about five miles reached a fork of the Blue, where the road leaves that river, and crosses over to the Platte. No water was to be found on the dividing ridge, and the casks were filled and the animals here allowed a short repose. The road led across a high and level prairie ridge, where were but few plants, and those principally thistle (*carduus leucógraphus*), and a kind of dwarf artemisia. Antelope were seen frequently during the morning, which was very stormy. Squalls of rain, with thunder and lightning, were around us in every direction; and while we were enveloped in one of them, a flash, which seemed to scorch our eyes as it passed, struck in the prairie within a few hundred feet, sending up a column of dust.

Crossing on the way several Pawnee roads to the Arkansas, we reached, in about twenty-one miles from our halt on the Blue, what is called the coast of the Nebraska, or Platte river. This had seemed in the distance a range of high and broken hills, but on a nearer approach were found to be elevations of forty to sixty feet, into which the wind had worked the sand. They were covered with the usual fine grasses of the country, and bordered the eastern side of the ridge on a breadth of about two miles. Change of soil and country appeared here to have produced some change in the vegetation. *Cacti* were numerous, and all the plants of the region appeared to flourish among the warm hills. Among them the *amorpha,* in full bloom, was remarkable for its large and luxuriant purple clusters. From the foot of the coast, a distance of two miles across the level

---

"Our cook was very dilatory & I had been obliged to give him an assistant. He thought rather that men lived to eat than that they ate to live, had no idea of the value of time & was never known to hurry except when eating an omelette soufflé which was a dish he said that couldn't bear to wait.

"Descouteaux, the man I had given, was an excellent cook & though but a prairie artist one on whom the mantle of Ade [?] had fallen most becomingly. They did not agree very well & this evening a professional dispute broke into an open fight, with which I did not interfere as it was conducted with their natural weapons, frying-pans & gridirons. Unwilling to fatigue and annoy the men by restraining their natural freedom in the ettiquette of small observances, I had determined to enforce only those points of discipline which really regarded our preservation in a remote country & the success of the Expedition & so long as in their disputes they had no recourse to arms I followed the custom of the country & in no wise interfered with their amusements."

bottom brought us to our encampment on the shore of the river, about twenty miles below the head of Grand island, which lay extended before us, covered with dense and heavy woods. From the mouth of the Kansas, according to our reckoning, we had travelled three hundred and twenty-eight miles; and the geological formation of the country we had passed over consisted of lime and sandstone, covered by the same erratic deposite of sand and gravel which forms the surface rock of the prairies between the Missouri and Mississippi rivers; except in some occasional limestone boulders, I had met with no fossils. The elevation of the Platte valley above the sea is here about two thousand feet. The astronomical observations of the night placed us in longitude 99° 17′ 47″, latitude 40° 41′ 06″.

June 27.—The animals were somewhat fatigued by their march of yesterday, and after a short journey of eighteen miles along the river bottom, I encamped near the head of Grand island,[9] in longitude, by observation, 99° 37′ 45″, latitude 40° 39′ 32″. The soil here was light but rich, though in some places rather sandy; and, with the exception of a scattered fringe along the bank, the timber, consisting principally of poplar (*populus monilifera*), elm, and hackberry (*celtis crassifolia*), is confined almost entirely to the islands.

June 28.— We halted to noon at an open reach of the river, which occupies rather more than a fourth of the valley, here only about four miles broad. The camp had been disposed with the usual precaution, the horses grazing at a little distance, attended by the guard, and we were all sitting quietly at our dinner on the grass, when suddenly we heard the startling cry *"du monde!"* In an instant, every man's weapon was in his hand, the horses were driven in, hobbled and picketted, and horsemen were galloping at full speed in the direction of the new comers, screaming and yelling with the wildest excitement. "Get ready, my lads!" said the leader of the approaching party to his men, when our wild-looking horsemen were discovered bearing down upon them; *"nous allons attraper des coups de baguette."* They proved to be a small party of fourteen, under the

---

9. At the site of present Grand Island, Nebr. When William Marshall Anderson camped there in 1834, he described it as "the longest fresh water river island, perhaps in America. . . . It commences indeed, God knows where, & ends God knows where" (ANDERSON, 204). It still does, as the channelings of the river have broken it into many segments. Early travelers estimated its length at anywhere from 50 to 120 miles. But it was never much more than a band, splitting the river into two main channels (MATTES, 194).

charge of a man named John Lee, and with their baggage and provisions strapped to their backs, were making their way on foot to the frontier. A brief account of their fortunes will give some idea of navigation in the Nebraska. Sixty days since they had left the mouth of Laramie's fork, some three hundred miles above, in barges laden with the furs of the American Fur Company. They started with the annual flood, and drawing but nine inches water, hoped to make a speedy and prosperous voyage to St. Louis; but, after a lapse of forty days, found themselves only one hundred and thirty miles from their point of departure. They came down rapidly as far as Scott's bluffs, where their difficulties began. Sometimes they came upon places where the water was spread over a great extent, and here they toiled from morning until night, endeavoring to drag their boat through the sands, making only two or three miles in as many days. Sometimes they would enter an arm of the river, where there appeared a fine channel, and after descending prosperously for eight or ten miles, would come suddenly upon dry sands, and be compelled to return, dragging their boat for days against the rapid current; and at others, they came upon places where the water lay in holes, and getting out to float off their boat, would fall into water up to their necks, and the next moment tumble over against a sandbar. Discouraged at length, and finding the Platte growing every day more shallow, they discharged the principal part of their cargoes one hundred and thirty miles below Fort Laramie, which they secured as well as possible, and leaving a few men to guard them, attempted to continue their voyage, laden with some light furs and their personal baggage. After fifteen or twenty days more struggling in the sands, during which they made but one hundred and forty miles, they sunk their barges, made a *cache* of their remaining furs and property, in trees on the bank, and, packing on his back what each man could carry, had commenced, the day before we encountered them, their journey on foot to St. Louis.

We laughed then at their forlorn and vagabond appearance, and in our turn a month or two afterwards furnished the same occasion for merriment to others.[10] Even their stock of tobacco, that *sine qua*

---

10. Deleted from the manuscript draft at this point: "In their parti-coloured & motley dresses one was strongly reminded of Hogarth's picture of the Beggars, rendered somewhat dingy by time." Among the forlorn and vagabond of John Lee's party was Rufus B. Sage (1817–93), a young Connecticut-born newspaperman. He had gone west to trap and trade and to

non of a *voyageur,* without which the night fire is gloomy, was entirely exhausted. However, we shortened their homeward journey by a small supply from our own provision. They gave us the welcome intelligence that the Buffalo were abundant some two days' march in advance, and made us a present of some choice pieces, which were a very acceptable change from our salt pork. In the interchange of news, and the renewal of old acquaintanceships, we found wherewithal to fill a busy hour, then we mounted our horses, and they shouldered their packs, and we shook hands and parted. Among them, I had found an old companion on the northern prairie, a hardened and hardly served veteran of the mountains, who had been as much hacked and scarred as an old *moustache* of Napoleon's "old guard." He flourished in the sobriquet of La Tulipe,[11] and his real name I never knew. Finding that he was going to the States only because his company was bound in that direction, and that he was rather more willing to return with me, I took him again into my service. We travelled this day but seventeen miles.

At our evening camp, about sunset, three figures were discovered approaching, which our glasses made out to be Indians. They proved to be Cheyennes, two men and a boy of thirteen. About a month since, they had left their people on the south fork of the river, some three hundred miles to the westward, and a party of only four in number had been to the Pawnee villages on a horse stealing excursion, from which they were returning unsuccessful. They were miserably mounted on wild horses from the Arkansas plains, and had no other weapons than bows and long spears; and had they been discovered by the Pawnees, could not, by any possibility, have escaped. They were mortified by their ill success, and said the Pawnees were cowards who shut up their horses in their lodges at night. I invited

---

gather material for an intended book which he published in 1846 under the title *Scenes in the Rocky Mountains.* . . . The book went through many printings. The first edition included 3,000 copies paperbound and 500 clothbound. Some copies of the clothbound volume included a map which was apparently adapted from Frémont's *Report.* Sage married in 1847 and settled down in the small Connecticut town of his birth, Upper Middletown, where he farmed until his death (SAGE, 1:1–27, 2:41).

11. François Latulippe, previously identified. Perhaps as an added inducement, JCF bought twelve buffalo hides from him (voucher no. 23, p. 152). According to Sage a pack of buffalo robes generally embraced ten skins and weighed about eighty pounds (SAGE, 2:19n). Latulippe was paid off at Fort John on the return trip.

them to supper with me, and Randolph and the young Cheyenne, who had been eyeing each other suspiciously and curiously, soon became intimate friends. After supper we sat down on the grass, and I placed a sheet of paper between us, on which they traced rudely, but with a certain degree of relative truth, the watercourses of the country which lay between us and their villages, and of which I desired to have some information. Their companions, they told us, had taken a nearer route over the hills, but they had mounted one of the summits to spy out the country, whence they had caught a glimpse of our party, and, confident of good treatment at the hands of the whites, hastened to join company. Latitude of the camp 40° 39′ 51″.

We made the next morning sixteen miles. I remarked that the ground was covered in many places with an efflorescence of salt, and the plants were not numerous. In the bottoms was frequently seen *tradescantia,* and on the dry benches were *carduus, cactus,* and *amorpha.* A high wind during the morning had increased to a violent gale from the northwest, which made our afternoon ride cold and unpleasant. We had the welcome sight of two buffaloes on one of the large islands; and encamped at a clump of timber about seven miles from our noon halt, after a day's march of twenty-two miles.

The air was keen the next morning at sunrise, the thermometer standing at 44°, and it was sufficiently cold to make overcoats very comfortable. A few miles brought us into the midst of the Buffalo, swarming in immense numbers over the plains, where they had left scarcely a blade of grass standing. Mr. Preuss, who was sketching at a little distance in the rear, had at first noted them as large groves of timber. In the sight of such a mass of life, the traveller feels a strange emotion of grandeur. We had heard from a distance a dull and confused murmuring, and when we came in view of their dark masses, there was not one among us who did not feel his heart beat quicker. It was the early part of the day, when the herds are feeding; and every where they were in motion. Here and there a huge old bull was rolling in the grass, and clouds of dust rose in the air from various parts of the bands, each the scene of some obstinate fight. Indians and buffalo make the poetry and life of the prairie, and our camp was full of their exhilaration. In place of the quiet monotony of the march, relieved only by the cracking of the whip, and an *"avance donc! enfant de garce!"* shouts and songs resounded from every part of the line, and our evening camp was always the commencement of a feast, which terminated only with our departure on the following morning. At any time of the night might be seen pieces of the most delicate and choicest meat, roasting *en appolas,* on sticks around the fire, and the guard were never without company. With pleasant weather and no enemy to fear, an abundance of the most excellent meat, and no scarcity of bread or tobacco, they were enjoying the oasis of a voyageur's life. Three cows were killed to-day. Kit Carson had shot one, and was continuing the chase in the midst of another herd, when his horse fell headlong, but sprang up and joined the flying band. Though considerably hurt, he had the good fortune to break no bones, and Maxwell, who was mounted on a fleet hunter, captured the runaway after a hard chase. He was on the point of shooting him to avoid the loss of his bridle, a handsomely mounted Spanish one, when he found that his horse was able to come up with him. Animals are frequently lost in this way; and it is necessary to keep close watch over them, in the vicinity of the buffalo, in the midst of which they scour off to the plains, and are rarely retaken. One of our mules took a sudden freak into his head, and joined a neighboring band to-day. As we were not in a condition to lose horses, I sent several men in pursuit and remained in camp, in the hope of recovering him, but lost the afternoon to no purpose, as we did not see him again. Astronomical observations placed us in longitude 100° 38′ 10″, latitude 40° 49′ 55″.

July 1.—Along our road to-day the prairie bottom was more elevated and dry, and the hills which border the right side of the river higher and more broken and picturesque in the outline. The country too was better timbered. As we were riding quietly along the bank, a grand herd of buffalo, some seven or eight hundred in number, came crowding up from the river, where they had been to drink, and commenced crossing the plain slowly, eating as they went. The wind was favorable, the coolness of the morning invited to exercise, the ground was apparently good, and the distance across the prairie, two or three miles, gave us a fine opportunity to charge them before they could get among the river hills. It was too fine a prospect for a chase to be lost, and, halting for a few moments, the hunters were brought up and saddled, and Kit Carson, Maxwell, and I, started together. They were now somewhat less than half a mile distant, and we rode easily along until within about three hundred yards, when a sudden agitation, a wavering in the band, and a galloping to and fro of some which were scattered along the skirts, gave us the intimation that we were discovered. We started together at a

186

hand gallop, riding steadily abreast of each other, and here the interest of the chase became so engrossingly intense, that we were sensible to nothing else.[12] We were now closing upon them rapidly, and the front of the mass was already in rapid motion for the hills, and in a few seconds the movement had communicated itself to the whole herd.

A crowd of bulls, as usual, brought up the rear, and every now and then some of them faced about, and then dashed on after the band a short distance, and turned and looked again, as if more than half inclined to stand and fight. In a few moments, however, during which we had been quickening our pace, the rout was universal, and we were going over the ground like a hurricane. When at about thirty yards we gave the usual shout, the hunter's *pas de charge,* and broke into the herd. We entered on the side, the mass giving way in every direction in their heedless course. Many of the bulls, less active and less fleet than the cows, paying no attention to the ground, and occupied solely with the hunter, were precipitated to the earth with great force, rolling over and over with the violence of the shock, and hardly distinguishable in the dust. We separated on entering, each singling out his game.

My horse was a trained hunter, famous in the west under the name of Proveau, and with his eyes flashing, and the foam flying from his mouth, sprang on after the cow like a tiger. In a few moments he brought me alongside of her, and rising in the stirrups, I fired at the distance of a yard, the ball entering at the termination of the long hair, and passing near the heart. She fell headlong at the report of the gun, and checking my horse, I looked around for my companions. At a little distance Kit was on the ground, engaged in tying his horse to the horns of a cow which he was preparing to cut up. Among the scattered bands at some distance below I caught a glimpse of Maxwell; and while I was looking, a light wreath of white smoke curled away from his gun, of which I was too far to hear the report. Nearer, and between me and the hills, towards which they were directing their course, was the body of the herd, and giving my horse the rein, we dashed after them. A thick cloud of dust hung upon their rear, which filled my mouth and eyes, and

---

12. After this sentence, a prudent deletion in the manuscript draft: "Fifty Indians might have charged upon us and not been seen until they were at our bridles."

nearly smothered me. In the midst of this I could see nothing, and the buffalo were not distinguishable until within thirty feet. They crowded together more densely still as I came upon them, and rushed along in such a compact body, that I could not obtain an entrance—the horse almost leaping upon them. In a few moments the mass divided to the right and left, the horns clattering with a noise heard above every thing else, and my horse darted into the opening. Five or six bulls charged on us as we dashed along the line, but were left far behind, and singling out a cow, I gave her my fire, but struck too high. She gave a tremendous leap, and scoured on swifter than before. I reined up my horse, and the band swept on like a torrent, and left the place quiet and clear.[13] Our chase had led us into dangerous ground. A prairie-dog village so thickly settled that there were three or four holes in every twenty yards square, occupied the whole bottom for nearly two miles in length. Looking around, I saw only one of the hunters, nearly out of sight, and the long dark line of our caravan crawling along, three or four miles distant. After a march of twenty-four miles, we encamped at nightfall, one mile and a half above the lower end of Brady's island.[14] The breadth of this arm of the river was eight hundred and eighty yards, and the water nowhere two feet in depth. The island bears the name of a man killed on this spot some years ago. His party had encamped here, three in company, and one of the number went off to hunt, leaving Brady and his companion together. These two had frequently quarrelled, and on the hunter's return he found Brady dead, and was told that he had shot himself accidentally. He was buried here on the bank, but, as usual, the wolves had torn him out, and some human bones that were lying on the ground we supposed were his. Troops of wolves that were hanging on the skirts of the buffalo, kept up an uninterrupted howling during the night, venturing almost into camp. In the morning, they were sitting at a short distance, barking, and impatiently waiting our departure, to fall upon the bones.

July 2.—The morning was cool and smoky. Our road led closer to

---

13. Deleted from the manuscript draft at this point: "I looked around & saw only one of the hunters nearly out of sight, & the long dark line of our caravan crawling slowly along, three or four miles distant."

14. Brady's Island, about fifteen miles long, lies just below North Platte, Nebr. It apparently was named after a man called Brada or Brady, variously reported to have been killed in 1827 or 1833 (ANDERSON, 190n).

the hills, which here increased in elevation, presenting an outline of conical peaks three hundred to five hundred feet high. Some timber, apparently pine, grew in the ravines, and streaks of clay or sand whiten their slopes. We crossed during the morning a number of hollows, timbered principally with box elder (*acer negundo*), poplar and elm. Brady's island is well wooded, and all the river along which our road led to-day may, in general, be called tolerably well timbered. We passed near an encampment of the Oregon emigrants, where they appear to have reposed several days. A variety of household articles were scattered about, and they had probably disburdened themselves here of many things not absolutely necessary. I had left the usual road before the mid-day halt, and in the afternoon, having sent several men in advance to reconnoitre, marched directly for the mouth of the South fork. On our arrival, the horsemen were sent in and scattered about the river to search the best fording places, and the carts followed immediately. The stream is here divided by an island into two channels. The southern is four hundred and fifty feet wide, having eighteen or twenty inches water in the deepest places. With the exception of a few dry bars, the bed of the river is generally quicksands, in which the carts began to sink rapidly so soon as the mules halted, so that it was necessary to keep them constantly in motion.

The northern channel, 2,250 feet wide, was somewhat deeper, having frequently three feet water in the numerous small channels, with a bed of coarse gravel. The whole breadth of the Nebraska [Platte], immediately below the junction, is 5,350 feet. All our equipage had reached the left bank safely at six o'clock, having to-day made twenty miles. We encamped at the point of land immediately at the junction of the North and South forks. Between the streams is a low rich prairie, extending from their confluence 18 miles westwardly to the bordering hills, where it is 5½ miles wide. It is covered with a luxuriant growth of grass, and along the banks is a slight and scattered fringe of cottonwood and willow. In the buffalo trails and wallows, I remarked saline efflorescences, to which a rapid evaporation in the great heat of the sun probably contributes, as the soil is entirely unprotected by timber. In the vicinity of these places there was a bluish grass, which the cattle refuse to eat, called by the voyageurs "*herbe saleé*," (salt grass). The latitude of the junction is 41° 4′ 47″, and longitude by chronometer and lunar distances, 101° 21′ 24″. The elevation above the sea is about 2,700 feet. The hunters came in with a fat cow, and, as we had labored hard, we enjoyed well a supper of roasted ribs and *boudins,* the *chef d'œuvre* of a prairie cook. Mosquitoes thronged about us this evening; but, by 10 o'clock, when the thermometer had fallen to 47°, they had all disappeared.[15]

July 3.—As this was to be a point in our homeward journey, I made a *cache* (a term used in all this country for what is hidden in the ground) of a barrel of pork. It was impossible to conceal such a proceeding from the sharp eyes of our Cheyenne companions, and I therefore told them to go and see what it was they were burying. They would otherwise have not failed to return and destroy our *cache,* in expectation of some rich booty; but pork they dislike and never eat. We left our camp at 9, continuing up the South fork, the prairie bottom affording us a fair road; but in the long grass we roused myriads of mosquitoes and flies, from which our horses suffered severely. The day was smoky, with a pleasant breeze from the south, and the plains on the opposite side were covered with buffalo. Having travelled twenty-five miles we encamped at 6 in the evening, and the men were sent across the river for wood, as there is none here on the left bank. Our fires were partially made of the *bois de vache,* the dry excrement of the buffalo, which like that of the camel in the Arabian deserts, furnishes to the traveller a very good substitute for wood, burning like turf. Wolves in great numbers surrounded us during the night, crossing and recrossing from the opposite herds to our camp, and howling and trotting about in the river until morning.

July 4.—The morning was very smoky, the sun shining dimly and red, as in a thick fog. The camp was roused with a salute at daybreak, and from our scanty store a portion of what our Indian friends called the "red fire water" served out to the men. While we were at breakfast, a buffalo calf broke through the camp, followed by a couple of wolves. In its fright, it had probably mistaken us for a band of buffalo. The wolves were obliged to make a circuit around the camp, so that the calf got a little the start, and strained every nerve to reach a large herd at the foot of the hills, about two miles distant; but first one and then another and another wolf joined in the chase, until his pursuers amounted to twenty or thirty, and they

---

15. Here the manuscript draft carries the phrase, "Characteristic Plants," but none are named.

ran him down before he could reach his friends. There were a few bulls near the place, and one of them attacked the wolves and tried to rescue him; but was driven off immediately, and the little animal fell an easy prey, half devoured before he was dead. We watched the chase with the interest always felt for the weak, and had there been a saddled horse at hand, he would have fared better. Leaving camp, our road soon approached the hills in which strata of a marl like that of the chimney rock, hereafter described, make their appearance. It is probably of this rock that the hills on the right bank of the Platte, a little below the junction, are composed, and which are worked by the winds and rains into sharp peaks and cones, giving them, in contrast to the surrounding level region, something of a picturesque appearance. We crossed this morning numerous beds of the small creeks which, in the time of rains and melting snow, pour down from the ridge, bringing down with them always great quantities of sand and gravel, which have gradually raised their beds four to ten feet above the level of the prairie which they cross, making each one of them a miniature Po. Raised in this way above the surrounding prairie, without any bank, the long yellow and winding line of their beds resembles a causeway from the hills to the river. Many spots on the prairie are yellow with sunflower (*helianthus*).

As we were riding slowly along this afternoon, clouds of dust in the ravines among the hills to the right, suddenly attracted our attention, and in a few minutes column after column of buffalo came galloping down, making directly to the river. By the time the leading herds had reached the water, the prairie was darkened with the dense masses. Immediately before us, when the bands first came down into the valley, stretched an unbroken line, the head of which was lost among the river hills on the opposite side, and still they poured down from the ridge on our right. From hill to hill the prairie bottom was certainly not less than two miles wide, and allowing the animals to be ten feet apart, and only ten in a line, there were already 11,000 in view. Some idea may thus be formed of their number when they had occupied the whole plain. In a short time they surrounded us on every side, extending for several miles in the rear, and forward, as far as the eye could reach, leaving around us as we advanced, an open space of only two or three hundred yards. This movement of the buffalo indicated to us the presence of Indians on the North fork.

I halted earlier than usual, about forty miles from the junction, and all hands were soon busily engaged in preparing a feast to celebrate the day. The kindness of our friends at St. Louis had provided us with a large supply of excellent preserves and rich fruit cake; and when these were added to a macaroni soup and variously prepared dishes of the choicest buffalo meat, crowned with a cup of coffee, and enjoyed with prairie appetite, we felt, as we sat in barbaric luxury around our smoking supper on the grass, a greater sensation of enjoyment than the Roman epicure at his perfumed feast. But most of all it seemed to please our Indian friends, who in the unrestrained enjoyment of the moment, demanded to know if our "medicine days came often." No restraint was exercised at the hospitable board, and, to the great delight of his elders, our young Indian lad made himself extremely drunk.

Our encampment was within a few miles of the place where the road crosses to the North fork, and various reasons led me to divide my party at this point. The North fork was the principal object of my survey, but I was desirous to ascend the South branch, with a view of obtaining some astronomical positions, and determining the mouths of its tributaries as far as St. Vrain's fort, estimated to be some two hundred miles further up the river, and near to Long's peak. There I hoped to obtain some mules, which I found would be necessary to relieve my horses. In a military point of view, I was desirous to form some opinion of the country relative to the establishment of posts on a line connecting the settlements with the South pass of the Rocky mountains, by way of the Arkansas, the South and Laramie forks of the Platte. Crossing the country northwestwardly from St. Vrain's fort, to the American company's fort at the mouth of Laramie, would give me some acquaintance with the affluents which head in the mountains between the two; I therefore determined to set out the next morning, accompanied by Mr. Preuss and four men, Maxwell, Bernier, Ayot, and Basil Lajeunesse. Our Cheyennes, whose village lay up this river, also decided to accompany us. The party I left in charge of Clément Lambert, with orders to cross to the North fork; and at some convenient place, near to the *Coulée des Frénes* [Ash Hollow], make a *cache* of every thing not absolutely necessary to the further progress of our expedition. From this point, using the most guarded precaution in his march through the country, he was to proceed to the American [Fur] company's fort at the mouth of Laramie's fork, and await my arrival, which would be prior to the 16th, as on that and the following night would occur some occultations which I was desirous to obtain at that place.

July 5.—Before breakfast all was ready. We had one led horse in addition to those we rode, and a pack mule, destined to carry our instruments, provisions, and baggage; the last two articles not being of very great weight. The instruments consisted of a sextant, artificial horizon, &c., a barometer, spy glass, and compass. The chronometer I of course kept on my person. I had ordered the cook to put up for us some flour, coffee, and sugar, and our rifles were to furnish the rest. One blanket, in addition to his saddle and saddle blanket, furnished the materials for each man's bed, and every one was provided with a change of linen. All were armed with rifles or double barrelled guns; and, in addition to these, Maxwell and myself were furnished with excellent pistols. Thus accoutred, we took a parting breakfast with our friends, and set forth.

Our journey the first day afforded nothing of any interest. We shot a buffalo toward sunset, and having obtained some meat for our evening meal, encamped where a little timber afforded us the means of making a fire. Having disposed our meat on roasting sticks, we proceeded to unpack our bales in search of coffee and sugar, and flour for bread. With the exception of a little parched coffee, unground, we found nothing. Our cook had neglected to put it up, or it had been somehow forgotten. Tired and hungry, with tough bull meat without salt, for we had not been able to kill a cow, and a little bitter coffee, we sat down in silence to our miserable fare, a very disconsolate party; for yesterday's feast was yet fresh in our memories, and this was our first brush with misfortune. Each man took his blanket, and laid himself down silently; for the worst part of these mishaps is, that they make people ill-humored. To-day we had travelled about thirty-six miles.

July 6.—Finding that our present excursion would be attended with considerable hardship, and unwilling to expose more persons than necessary, I determined to send Mr. Preuss back to the party. His horse, too, appeared in no condition to support the journey, and accordingly, after breakfast, he took the road across the hills attended by one of my most trusty men, Bernier. The ridge between the rivers is here about fifteen miles broad, and I expected he would probably strike the fork near their evening camp. At all events, he would not fail to find their trail and rejoin them the next day.

We continued our journey, seven in number, including the three

Cheyennes. Our general course was southwest, up the valley of the river, which was sandy, bordered on the northern side of the valley by a low ridge, and on the south, after seven or eight miles, the river hills became higher. Six miles from our resting place we crossed the bed of a considerable stream, now entirely dry, a bed of sand. In a grove of willows, near the mouth, were the remains of a considerable fort, constructed of trunks of large trees. It was apparently very old, and had probably been the scene of some hostile encounter among the roving tribes. Its solitude formed an impressive contrast to the picture which our imaginations involuntarily drew of the busy scene which had been enacted here. The timber appeared to have been much more extensive formerly than now. There were but few trees, a kind of long-leaved willow, standing; and numerous trunks of large trees were scattered about on the ground. In many similar places I had occasion to remark an apparent progressive decay in the timber. Ten miles farther we reached the mouth of Lodge Pole creek,[16] a clear and handsome stream, running through a broad valley. In its course through the bottom it has a uniform breadth of twenty-two feet, and six inches in depth. A few willows on the banks strike pleasantly on the eye, by their greenness, in the midst of the hot and barren sands.

The *amorpha* was frequent among the ravines, but the sunflower (*helianthus*) was the characteristic; and flowers of deep warm colors seem most to love the sandy soil. The impression of the country travelled over to-day was one of dry and barren sands. We turned in towards the river at noon, and gave our horses two hours for food and rest. I had no other thermometer than the one attached to the barometer, which stood at 89°, the height of the column in the barometer being 26.235, at meridian. The sky was clear, with a high wind from the south. At 2, we continued our journey; the wind had moderated, and it became almost unendurably hot, and our animals suffered severely. In the course of the afternoon, the wind rose suddenly, and blew hard from the southwest, with thunder and lightning and squalls of rain; these were blown against us with violence by the wind, and, halting, we turned our backs to the storm until it blew over. Antelope were tolerably frequent, with a large gray hare; but the former were shy, and the latter hardly worth the delay of

16. Called Pole Creek on his map, but now Lodgepole Creek, entering the South Platte from the north at Julesburg, Colo.

stopping to shoot them; so, as the evening drew near, we again had recourse to an old bull, and encamped at sunset on an island in the Platte.

We ate our meat with good relish this evening, for we were all in fine health, and had ridden nearly all of a long summer's day, with a burning sun reflected from the sands. My companions slept rolled up in their blankets, and the Indians lay in the grass near the fire, but my sleeping place generally had an air of more pretension. Our rifles were tied together near the muzzle, the butts resting on the ground, and a knife laid on the rope, to cut away in case of an alarm. Over this, which made a kind of frame, was thrown a large India-rubber cloth, which we used to cover our packs. This made a tent sufficiently large to receive about half of my bed, and was a place of shelter for my instruments; and as I was careful always to put this part against the wind, I could lie here with a sensation of satisfied enjoyment, and hear the wind blow and the rain patter close to my head, and know that I should be at least half dry. Certainly, I never slept more soundly. The barometer at sunset was 26.010, thermometer 81°, and cloudy; but a gale from the west sprang up with the setting sun, and in a few minutes swept away every cloud from the sky. The evening was very fine, and I remained up to take some astronomical observations, which made our position in latitude 40° 51′ 17″, and longitude 103° 35′ 04″.

July 7.—At our camp this morning, at 6 o'clock, the barometer was at 26.183, thermometer 69°, and clear, with a light wind from the southwest. The past night had been squally, with high winds, and occasionally a few drops of rain. Our cooking did not occupy much time, and we left camp early. Nothing of interest occurred during the morning. The same dreary barrenness, except that a hard marly clay had replaced the sandy soil. Buffalo absolutely covered the plain on both sides of the river, and whenever we ascended the hills, scattered herds gave life to the view in every direction. A small drove of wild horses made their appearance on the low river bottoms, a mile or two to the left, and I sent off one of the Indians (who seemed very eager to catch one) on my led horse, a spirited and fleet animal. The savage manoeuvred a little to get the wind of the horses, in which he succeeded; approaching within a hundred yards without being discovered. The chase for a few minutes was animated and interesting. My hunter easily overtook and passed the hindmost of the wild drove, which the Indian did not attempt to *lasso;* all his efforts being directed to the capture of the leader. But the strength of the horse, weakened by the insufficient nourishment of grass, failed in a race, and all the drove escaped. We halted at noon on the bank of the river, the barometer at that time being 26.192, and the thermometer 103°, with a light air from the south and clear weather.

In the course of the afternoon, dust rising among the hills at a particular place, attracted our attention, and riding up we found a band of eighteen or twenty buffalo bulls engaged in a desperate fight. Though butting and goring were bestowed liberally and without distinction, yet their efforts were evidently directed against one, a huge gaunt old bull, very lean, while his adversaries were all fat and in good order. He appeared very weak, and had already received some wounds, and while we were looking on was several times knocked down and badly hurt, and a very few moments would have put an end to him. Of course we took the side of the weaker party, and attacked the herd, but they were so blind with rage that they fought on, utterly regardless of our presence, although on foot and on horseback we were firing in open view within twenty yards of them. But this did not last long. In a very few seconds we created a commotion among them. One or two which were knocked over by the balls jumped up and ran off into the hills, and they began to retreat slowly along a broad ravine to the river, fighting furiously as they went. By the time they had reached the bottom we had pretty well dispersed them, and the old bull hobbled off, to lie down somewhere. One of his enemies remained on the ground where we had first fired upon them, and we stopped there for a short time to cut from him some meat for our supper. We had neglected to secure our horses, thinking it an unnecessary precaution in their fatigued condition; but our mule took it into his head to start, and away he went, followed at full speed by the pack horse, with all the baggage and instruments on his back. They were recovered and brought back, after a chase of a mile. Fortunately every thing was well secured, so that nothing, not even the barometer, was in the least injured.

The sun was getting low, and some narrow lines of timber four or five miles distant, promised us a pleasant camp, where, with plenty of wood for fire, and comfortable shelter, and rich grass for our animals, we should find clear cool springs, instead of the warm water of the Platte. On our arrival we found the bed of a stream fifty to one hundred feet wide, sunk some thirty feet below the level of the prairie, with perpendicular banks, bordered by a fringe of green cottonwood, but not a drop of water. There were several small forks to the stream all in the same condition. With the exception of the Platte bottom, the country seemed to be of a clay formation, dry, and perfectly devoid of any moisture, and baked hard by the sun. Turning off towards the river, we reached the bank in about a mile, and were delighted to find an old tree, with thick foliage and spreading branches, where we encamped. At sunset, the barometer was at 25,950, thermometer 81°, with a strong wind from S. 20° E., and the sky partially covered with heavy masses of cloud, which settled a little towards the horizon by 10 o'clock, leaving it sufficiently clear for astronomical observations, which placed us in latitude 40° 33′ 26″, and longitude 104° 02′ 13″.

July 8.—The morning was very pleasant. The breeze was fresh from S. 50° E. with few clouds; the barometer at 6 o'clock standing at 25,970, and the thermometer at 70°. Since leaving the forks, our route had passed over a country alternately clay and sand, each presenting the same naked waste. On leaving camp this morning, we struck again a sandy region, in which the vegetation appeared somewhat more vigorous than that which we had observed for the last few days, and on the opposite side of the river were some tolerably large groves of timber.

Journeying along, we came suddenly upon a place where the ground was covered with horses' tracks, which had been made since the rain, and indicated the immediate presence of Indians in our neighborhood. The buffalo, too, which the day before had been so numerous, were nowhere in sight, another sure indication that there were people near. Riding on, we discovered the carcass of a buffalo recently killed, perhaps the day before. We scanned the horizon carefully with the glass, but no living object was to be seen. For the next mile or two the ground was dotted with buffalo carcasses, which showed that the Indians had made a surround here, and were in considerable force. We went on quickly and cautiously, keeping the river bottom, and carefully avoiding the hills; but we met with no interruption, and began to grow careless again. We had already lost one of our horses, and here Basil's mule showed symptoms of giving out, and finally refused to advance, being what the Canadians call *resté*. He therefore dismounted, and drove her along before him, but this was a very slow way of travelling. We had inadvertently got about half a mile in advance, but our Cheyennes, who were generally a mile or two in the rear, remained with him. There were some

197

dark looking objects among the hills, about two miles to the left, here low and undulating, which we had seen for a little time, and supposed to be buffalo coming in to water; but happening to look behind, Maxwell saw the Cheyennes whipping up furiously, and another glance at the dark objects showed them at once to be Indians coming up at speed.

Had we been well mounted and disencumbered of instruments, we might have set them at defiance, but as it was, we were fairly caught. It was too late to rejoin our friends, and we endeavored to gain a clump of timber about half a mile ahead; but the instruments and the tired state of our horses did not allow us to go faster than a steady canter, and they were gaining on us fast. At first they did not appear to be more than fifteen or twenty in number, but group after group darted into view at the top of the hills, until all the little eminences seemed in motion, and in a few minutes from the time they were first discovered, two or three hundred, naked to the breech cloth, were sweeping across the prairie. In a few hundred yards we discovered that the timber we were endeavoring to make was on the opposite side of the river, and before we could reach the bank, down came the Indians upon us.

I am inclined to think that in a few seconds more the leading man, and perhaps, some of his companions, would have rolled in the dust, for we had jerked the covers from our guns, and our fingers were on the triggers; men in such cases generally act from instinct, and a charge from three hundred naked savages is a circumstance not well calculated to promote a cool exercise of judgment. Just as he was about to fire, Maxwell recognized the leading Indian, and shouted to him in the Indian language, You're a fool, God damn you, don't you know me? The sound of his own language seemed to shock the savage, and, swerving his horse a little, he passed us like an arrow. He wheeled, as I rode out toward him, and gave me his hand, striking his breast and exclaiming, Arapahó! They proved to be a village of that nation among whom Maxwell had resided as a trader a year or two previously, and recognized him accordingly. We were soon in the midst of the band, answering as well as we could a multitude of questions, of which the very first was, of what tribe were our Indian companions who were coming in the rear? They seemed disappointed to know that they were Cheyennes, for they had fully anticipated a grand dance around a Pawnee scalp that night.

The chief showed us his village at a grove on the river six miles ahead, and pointed out a band of Buffalo, on the other side of the Platte immediately opposite us, which he said they were going to surround. They had seen the band early in the morning from their village, and had been making a large circuit to avoid giving them the wind, when they discovered us. In a few minutes the women came galloping up, astride on their horses, and naked from their knees down, and the hips up. They followed the men to assist in cutting up and carrying off the meat.

The wind was blowing directly across the river, and the chief requested us to halt where we were, for a while, in order to avoid raising the herd. We, therefore, unsaddled our horses, and sat down on the bank to view the scene, and our new acquaintances rode a few hundred yards lower down, and began crossing the river. Scores of wild looking dogs followed, looking like troops of wolves, and having, in fact, but very little of the dog in their composition. Some of them remained with us, and I checked one of the men, whom I found aiming at one, which he was about to kill for a wolf. The day had become very hot. The air was clear, with a very slight breeze, and now, at twelve o'clock, while the barometer stood at 25.920, the attached thermometer was at 108°. Our Cheyennes had learned that with the Arapaho village, were about twenty lodges of their own, including their own families; they, therefore, immediately commenced making their toilette. After bathing in the river, they invested themselves in some handsome calico shirts, which I afterward learned they had stolen from my own men, and spent some time in arranging their hair and painting themselves with some vermillion I had given them. While they were engaged in this satisfactory manner, one of their half wild horses, to which the crowd of prancing animals which had just passed had recalled the freedom of her existence among the wild droves on the prairie, suddenly dashed into the hills at the top of her speed. She was their pack horse, and had on her back all the worldly wealth of our poor Cheyennes, all their accoutrements, and all the little articles which they had picked up among us, with some few presents I had given them. The loss which they seemed to regret most were their spears and shields, and some tobacco which they had received from me. However, they bore it all with the philosophy of an Indian, and laughingly continued their toilette. They appeared, however, a little mortified at the thought of returning to the village in such a sorry plight. "Our people will laugh at us," said one of them, "returning to the village on foot, instead of driving back a drove of Pawnee horses." He demanded to know if I loved my sorrel hunter very much, to which I replied he was the object of my most intense affection. Far from being able to give, I was myself in want of horses, and any suggestion of parting with the few I had valuable, was met with peremptory refusal. In the mean time the slaughter was about to commence on the other side. So soon as they reached it, the Indians separated into two bodies. One party proceeded directly across the prairie toward the hills in an extended line, while the other went up the river; and instantly as they had given the wind to the herd, the chase commenced. The buffalo started for the hills, but were intercepted and driven back toward the river, broken and running in every direction. The clouds of dust soon covered the whole scene, preventing us from having any but an occasional view. It had a very singular appearance to us at a distance, especially when looking with the glass. We were too far to hear the report of the guns, or any sound, and at every instant, through the clouds of dust which the sun made luminous, we could see for a moment two or three buffalo dashing along, and close behind them an Indian with his long spear, or other weapon, and instantly again they disappeared. The apparent silence, and the dimly seen figures flitting by with such rapidity, gave it a kind of dreamy effect, and seemed more like a picture than a scene of real life. It had been a large herd when the *cerne* commenced, probably three or four hundred in number; but, though I watched them closely, I did not see one emerge from the fatal cloud where the work of destruction was going on. After remaining here about an hour, we resumed our journey in the direction of the village.

Gradually, as we rode on, Indian after Indian came dropping along, laden with meat; and by the time we had neared the lodges, the backward road was covered with the returning horsemen. It was a pleasant contrast with the desert road we had been travelling. Several had joined company with us, and one of the chiefs invited us to his lodge. The village consisted of about one hundred and twenty-five lodges, of which twenty were Cheyennes; the latter pitched a little apart from the Arapahoes. They were disposed in a scattering manner on both sides of a broad irregular street, about one hundred and fifty feet wide, and running along the river. As we rode along, I remarked near some of the lodges a kind of tripod frame, formed of three slender poles of birch, scraped very clean, to which were affixed the shield and spear, with some other weapons of a chief. All were scrupulously clean, the spear head was burnished bright, and the shield white and stainless. It reminded me of the days of feudal chivalry; and when as I rode by I yielded to the passing impulse, and touched some of the spotless shields with the muzzle of my gun, I almost expected a grim warrior to start from the lodge and resent my challenge. The master of the lodge spread out a robe for me to sit upon, and the squaws set before us a large wooden dish of buffalo meat. He had lit his pipe in the meanwhile, and when it had been passed around, we commenced our dinner while he continued to smoke. Gradually, five or six other chiefs came in, and took their seats in silence. When we had finished, our host asked a number of questions relative to the object of our journey, of which I made no concealment; telling him simply that I had made a visit to see the country, preparatory to the establishment of military posts on the way to the mountains. Although this was information of the highest interest to them, and by no means calculated to please them, it excited no expression of surprise, and in no way altered the grave courtesy of their demeanor. The others listened and smoked. I remarked, that in taking the pipe for the first time, each had turned the stem upward, with a rapid glance, as in offering to the Great Spirit, before he put it in his mouth. A storm had been gathering for the past hour, and some pattering drops on the lodge warned us that we had some miles to our camp. Some Indian had given Maxwell a bundle of dried meat, which was very acceptable, as we had nothing, and, springing upon our horses, we rode off at dusk in the face of a cold shower and driving wind. We found our companions under some densely foliaged old trees, about three miles up the river. Under one of them lay the trunk of a large cottonwood, to leeward of which the man had kindled a fire, and we sat here and roasted our meat in tolerable shelter. Nearly opposite was the mouth of one of the most considerable affluents of the South fork, *la Fourche aux Castors* (Beaver fork),[17] heading off in the ridge to the southeast.

July 9.—This morning we caught the first faint glimpse of the Rocky Mountains, about sixty miles distant. Though a tolerably

17. Beaver Creek, entering from the south near Brush, Colo.

bright day, there was a slight mist, and we were just able to discern the snowy summit of "Long's peak," (*"les deux oreilles"* of the Canadians,) showing like a small cloud near the horizon. I found it easily distinguishable, there being a perceptible difference in its appearance from the white clouds that were floating about the sky. I was pleased to find that among the traders and voyageurs the name of "Long's peak" had been adopted and become familiar in the country.[18] In the ravines near this place, a light brown sandstone made its first appearance. About 8, we discerned several persons on horseback a mile or two ahead on the opposite side of the river. They turned in towards the river, and we rode down to meet them. We found them to be two white men, and a mulatto named Jim Beckwith,[19] who had left St. Louis when a boy, and gone to live with the Crow Indians. He had distinguished himself among them by some acts of daring bravery, and had risen to the rank of a chief, but had now, for some years, left them. They were in search of a band of horses that had gone off from a camp some miles above, in charge of Mr. Chabonard.[20] Two of them continued down the river, in search of the horses, and the American turned back with us, and we rode on towards the camp. About eight miles from our sleeping place we reached Bijou's fork [Bijou Creek], an affluent of the right bank. Where we crossed it, a short distance from the Platte, it has a sandy bed about four hundred yards broad; the water in various small streams, a few inches deep. Seven miles further brought us to

---

18. Long's Peak in north central Colorado is, at 14,255 feet, the highest peak in the Rocky Mountain National Park. It is named for Stephen H. Long, whose 1820 expedition to the Rockies was the second U.S. Army reconnaissance (the first was Zebulon Pike's in 1806–7) of that general region.

19. James P. Beckwourth (1798–1866) lived among the Crows from about 1829 to 1831, then traded among them for the American Fur Company. He operated on the Upper Missouri until 28 June 1836, when F. A. Chardon reported his departure from Fort Clark at the Mandan villages. He was trading on the upper Arkansas and South Platte when JCF encountered him.

20. Jean Baptiste Charbonneau (1805–66), son of Toussaint Charbonneau and his Shoshoni wife Sacagawea, had accompanied his mother and father on the Lewis and Clark expedition as a child, starting at the Mandan villages. After the expedition, William Clark undertook to educate young Jean Baptiste, and there are records of Clark's involvement as late as 1820. After a stay in Europe (1823–29) with Prince Paul, Duke of Württemburg, he returned to the West and became an employee of various fur companies. In 1843, he would accompany Sir William Drummond Stewart part way to the Rockies, and in 1846 help guide the Mormon Battalion across New Mexico and Arizona (A. HAFEN [1]; ANDERSON, 283–88).

a camp of some four or five whites, New Englanders, I believe, who had accompanied Captain Wyeth[21] to the Columbia river, and were independent trappers. All had their squaws with them, and I was really surprised at the number of little fat buffalo-fed boys, that were tumbling about the camp, all apparently of the same age, about three or four years old. They were encamped on a rich bottom, covered with a profusion of fine grass, and had a large number of fine-looking horses and mules. We rested with them a few minutes, and in about two miles arrived at Chabonard's camp, on an island in the Platte. On the heights above, we met the first Spaniard I had seen in the country. Mr. Chabonard was in the service of Bent and St. Vrain's company, and had left their fort some forty or fifty miles above, in the spring, with boats laden with the furs of the last year's trade. He had met the same fortune as the voyageurs on the North fork, and finding it impossible to proceed, had taken up his summer's residence on this island, which he had named St. Helena. The river hills appeared to be composed entirely of sand, and the Platte had lost the muddy character of its waters, and here was tolerably clear. From the mouth of the South fork, I had found it occasionally broken up by small islands, and at the time of our journey, which was at a season of the year when the waters were at a favorable stage, it was not navigable for anything drawing six inches water. The current was very swift—the bed of the stream a coarse gravel.

From the place at which we had encountered the Arapahoes, the Platte had been tolerably well fringed with timber, and the island here had a fine grove of very large cottonwoods, under whose broad shade the tents were pitched. There was a large drove of horses in the opposite prairie bottom; smoke was rising from the scattered fires, and the encampment had quite a patriarchal air. Mr. C. received us hospitably. One of the people was sent to gather mint, with the aid of which he concocted very good julep; and some boiled buffalo tongue, and coffee with the luxury of sugar, were soon set before us. The people in his employ were generally Spaniards, and among them I saw a young Spanish woman from Taos, whom I found to be Beckwith's wife.

---

21. Capt. Nathaniel Jarvis Wyeth (1802–56), the builder of Fort William at the mouth of the Willamette and Fort Hall on the Snake River in Idaho, had made two overland journeys to Oregon and had done much to publicize the region.

July 10.—We parted with our hospitable host after breakfast the next morning, and reached St. Vrain's fort,[22] about forty-five miles from St. Helena, late in the evening. The post is situated on the South fork of the Platte, immediately under the mountains, about seventeen miles east of Long's peak. It is on the right bank, on the verge of the upland prairie, about forty feet above the river, of which the immediate valley is about six hundred yards wide. The stream is divided into various branches by small islands, among which it runs with a swift current. The bed of the river is sand and gravel, the water very clear, and here may be called a mountain stream. This region appears to be entirely free from the limestones and marls which give to the lower Platte its yellow and dirty color. The Black hills[23] lie between the stream and the mountains, whose snowy peaks glitter a few miles beyond. At the fort we found Mr. St. Vrain,[24] who received us with much kindness and hospitality. Maxwell had spent the last two or three years between this post and the village of Taos, and here he was at home and among his friends. Spaniards frequently came over in search of employment, and several came in shortly after our arrival. They usually obtain about six dollars a month, generally paid to them in goods. They are very useful in a camp in taking care of horses and mules, and I engaged one, who proved to be an active, laborious man, and was of very considerable service to me.[25] The elevation of the Platte here is 5,400 feet above the sea. The neighboring mountains did not appear to enter far the region of perpetual snow, which was generally confined to the northern side of the peaks. On the southern I remarked very little. Here it appeared, so far as I could judge in the

---

22. Fort St. Vrain, about twelve miles below the mouth of St. Vrain Creek, was first called Fort Lookout and was also sometimes called Fort George. It was probably completed after 1837 and closed in 1845, although Bent, St. Vrain & Co. made temporary and seasonal use of it for several years (CARTER [2]).

23. Dale L. Morgan has suggested, and the matter is worth further study, that JCF conceived of this entire area from Fort Laramie south to the Cache la Poudre as comprising a general range of "Black Hills." (There are other formations bearing this name, of course, such as those in South Dakota.) For support of Morgan's suggestion, see Map 2 in the Portfolio, showing such a range extending on as far as the Red Buttes.

24. Marcellin St. Vrain (1815–71), younger brother of the better known Ceran St. Vrain, had taken charge of the fort about 1837 (CARTER [2]).

25. This is the man listed in the vouchers as Osea Harmiyo [José Armijo], who continued on with the exploring party.

distance, to descend but a few hundred feet below the summits.

I regretted that time did not permit me to visit them; but the proper object of my survey lay among the mountains further north; and I looked forward to an exploration of their snowy recesses with great pleasure. The piney region of the mountains to the south was enveloped in smoke, and I was informed had been on fire for several months. Pike's peak is said to be visible from this place, about 100 miles to the southward, but the smoky state of the atmosphere prevented my seeing it. The weather continued overcast during my stay here, so that I failed in determining the latitude, but obtained good observation for time on the mornings of the 11th and 12th. An assumed latitude of 40° 22′ 30″ from the evening position of the 12th, enabled me to obtain, for a tolerably correct longitude, 105° 45′ 13″.

July 12.—The kindness of Mr. St. Vrain had enabled me to obtain a couple of horses and three good mules, and, with a further addition to our party of the Spaniard whom I had hired, and two others, who were going to obtain service at Laramie's fork, we resumed our journey at 10, on the morning of the 12th. We had been able to procure nothing at the post in the way of provision. An expected supply from Taos had not yet arrived, and a few pounds of coffee was all that could be spared to us. In addition to this, we had dried meat enough for the first day; on the next we expected to find buffalo. From this post, according to the estimate of the country, the fort at the mouth of Laramie's fork, which was our next point of destination, was nearly due north, distant about one hundred and twenty-five miles.

For a short distance, our road lay down the valley of the Platte; which resembled a garden in the splendor of fields of varied flowers, which filled the air with fragrance. The only timber I noticed consisted of poplar, birch [alder], cottonwood, and willow. In something less than three miles, we crossed Thompson's creek [Thompson River], one of the affluents to the left bank of the South fork, a fine stream about sixty-five feet wide and three feet deep. Journeying on, the low dark line of the Black hills lying between us and the mountains to the left, in about ten miles from the fort, we reached *Cache à la Poudre* [River], where we halted to noon. This is a very beautiful mountain stream, about one hundred feet wide, flowing with a full swift current over a rocky bed. We halted under the shade of some cottonwoods, with which the stream is wooded scatteringly. In the upper part of its course, it runs amid the wildest mountain scenery, and breaking through the Black Hills falls into the Platte about ten miles below this place. In the course of our late journey, I had managed to become the possessor of a very untractable mule, a perfect vixen, and her I had turned over to my Spaniard. It occupied us about half an hour to-day to get the saddle upon her; but, once on her back José could not be dismounted, realizing the accounts given of Mexican horses and horsemanship; and we continued our route in the afternoon.

At evening, we encamped on Crow (?) creek, having travelled about twenty-eight miles. None of the party were well acquainted with the country, and I had great difficulty in ascertaining what were the names of the streams we crossed between the North and South forks of the Platte. This I supposed to be Crow creek.[26] It is what is called a salt stream, and the water stands in pools, having no continuous course. A fine grained sandstone made its appearance in the banks. The observations of the night placed us in a latitude 40° 42′, longitude 105° 33′ 27″. The barometer at sunset was 25.231; attached thermometer at 66°. Sky clear, except in the east, with a light wind from the north.

July 13.—There being no wood here, we used last night the *bois de vache,* which is very plentiful. At our camp this morning, the barometer was at 25.235, the attached thermometer 60°. A few clouds were moving through a deep blue sky, with a light wind from the west. After a ride of twelve miles, in a northerly direction, over a plain covered with innumerable quantities of *cacti,* we reached a small creek in which there was water, and where several herds of buffalo were scattered about among the ravines, which always afford good pasturage. We seem now to be passing along the base of a plateau of the Black hills, in which the formation consists of marls, some of them white and laminated, the country to the left rising suddenly, and falling off gradually and uniformly to the right. In five or six miles of a northeasterly course, we struck a high

---

26. Not likely. To reach Crow Creek in one day, by the route they are taking, they must travel to the latitude of Cheyenne, Wyo.—an impossible distance. JCF's own reading of latitude is of no help, putting him in the neighborhood of Thompson River. Until he strikes the North Platte, we shall have no clear indication of his location. He is traveling north by northeast, across Crow, Lodgepole, and Horse creeks, and through the Goshen Hole country of Goshen County, Wyo.

ridge, broken into conical peaks, on whose summits large boulders were gathered in heaps. The magnetic direction of the ridge is northwest and southeast, the glittering white of its precipitous sides making it visible for many miles to the south. It is composed of a soft earthy limestone, and marls resembling that hereafter described, in the neighborhood of the Chimney Rock, on the North fork of the Platte, easily worked by the winds and rains, and sometimes moulded into very fantastic shapes. At the foot of the northern slope was the bed of a creek some forty feet wide, coming by frequent falls from the bench above. It was shut in by high perpendicular banks, in which were strata of white laminated marl. Its bed was perfectly dry, and the leading feature of the whole region is one of remarkable aridity, and perfect freedom from moisture. In about six miles we crossed the bed of another dry creek; and continuing our ride over a high level prairie, a little before sundown we came suddenly upon a beautiful creek, which revived us with a feeling of delighted surprise by the pleasant contrast of the deep verdure of its banks, with the parched desert we had passed. We had suffered much to-day, both men and horses, for want of water; having met with it but once in our uninterrupted march of forty miles, and an exclusive meat diet creates much thirst.

"*Las bestias tienen mucha hambre,*" said the young Spaniard, inquiringly; "*y la gente tambien,*" said I, "*amigo,* we'll camp here." A stream of good and clear water ran winding about through the little valley, and a herd of buffalo were quietly feeding a little distance below. It was quite a hunter's paradise; and while some ran down toward the band to kill one for supper, others collected *bois de vache* for a fire, there being no wood; and I amused myself with hunting for plants among the grass.

It will be seen, by occasional remarks on the geological formation, that the constituents of the soil in these regions are good, and every day served to strengthen the impression in my mind, confirmed by subsequent observation, that the barren appearance of the country, is due almost entirely to the extreme dryness of the climate. Along our route, the country had seemed to increase constantly in elevation. According to the indication of the barometer, we were at our encampment, 5,440 feet above the sea.

The evening was very clear, with a fresh breeze from the south, 50° east. The barometer at sunset was 24.862, the thermometer attached showing 68°. I supposed this to be a fork of Lodge Pole creek, so far as I could determine from our uncertain means of information. Astronomical observations gave for the camp a longitude of 105° 13′ 38″, and latitude 41° 08′ 31″.

July 14.—The wind continued fresh from the same quarter in the morning, the day being clear with the exception of a few clouds in the horizon. At our camp at six o'clock, the height of the barometer was 24.830, the attached thermometer 61°. Our course this morning was directly north, by compass, the variation being 15° or 16° easterly. A ride of four miles brought us to Lodge Pole creek, which we had seen at its mouth on the South fork; crossing on the way two dry streams, in eighteen miles from our encampment of the past night, we reached a high bleak ridge, composed entirely of the same earthy limestone and marl previously described. I had never seen anything which impressed so strongly on my mind a feeling of desolation. The valley through which ran the waters of Horse creek, lay in view to the north, but too far to have any influence on the immediate view. On the peak of the ridge where I was standing, some six or seven hundred feet above the river, the wind was high and bleak; the barren and arid country seemed as if it had been swept by fires, and in every direction the same dull ash-colored hue, derived from the formation, met the eye. On the summits were some stunted pines, many of them dead, all wearing the same ashen hue of desolation.[27] We left the place with pleasure; and after we had descended several hundred feet, halted in one of the ravines, which, at the distance of every mile or two, cut the flanks of the ridge with little rushing streams, wearing something of a mountain character. We had already begun to exchange the comparatively barren lands for those of a more fertile character. Though the sandstone formed the broken banks of the creek, yet they were covered with a thin grass; and the fifty or sixty feet which formed the bottom land of the little stream, was clothed with very luxuriant grass, among which I remarked willow and cherry, (*cerasus virginiana;*) and a quantity of gooseberry and currant bushes occupied the greater part.

The creek was three or four feet broad, and about six inches deep, with a swift current of clear water, and tolerably cool. We had

---

27. Deleted from the manuscript draft at this point: "It gave a body to the foetid creations of the internal Regions, & the poet's words come strongly to my mind."

struck it too low down to find the cold water, which we should have enjoyed nearer to its sources. At 2 P. M., the barometer was at 25.050, the attached thermometer 104°. A day of hot sunshine, with clouds, and a moderate breeze from the south. Continuing down the stream, in about four miles we reached its mouth, at one of the main branches of Horse creek. Looking back upon the ridge, whose direction appeared to be a little to the north of east, we saw it seamed at frequent intervals with the dark lines of wooded streams, affluents of the river that flowed so far as we could see along its base. We crossed, in the space of twelve miles from our noon halt, three or four forks of Horse creek, and encamped at sunset on the most easterly.

The fork on which we encamped appeared to have followed an easterly direction up to this place; but here it makes a very sudden bend to the north, passing between two ranges of precipitous hills, called, as I was informed, Goshen's hole. There is somewhere in or near this locality a place so called, but I am not certain that it was the place of our encampment. Looking back upon the spot, at the distance of a few miles to the northward, the hills appear to shut in the prairie, through which runs the creek, with a semi-circular sweep, which might very naturally be called a hole in the hills. The geological composition of the ridge is the same which constitutes the rock of the Court-house and Chimney on the North fork, which appeared to me a continuation of this ridge. The winds and rains work this formation into a variety of singular forms. The pass into Goshen's hole is about two miles wide, and the hill on the western side imitates, in an extraordinary manner, a massive fortified place, with a remarkable fulness of detail. The rock is marl and earthy limestone, white, without the least appearance of vegetation, and much resembles masonry at a little distance; and here it sweeps around a level area two or three hundred yards in diameter, and in the form of a half moon, terminating on either extremity in enormous bastions. Along the whole line of the parapets appear domes and slender minarets, forty or fifty feet high, giving it every appearance of an old fortified town. On the waters of White river, where this formation exists in great extent, it presents appearances which excite the admiration of the solitary voyageur, and form a frequent theme of their conversation when speaking of the wonders of the country. Sometimes it offers the perfectly illusive appearances of a large city, with numerous streets and magnificent buildings, among which the Canadians never fail to see their *cabaret;* and sometimes it takes the form of a solitary house, with many large chambers, into which they drive their horses at night, and sleep in these natural defences perfectly secure from any attack of prowling savages. Before reaching our camp at Goshen's hole, in crossing the immense detritus at the foot of the Castle rock, we were involved amidst winding passages cut by the waters of the hill; and where, with a breadth scarcely large enough for the passage of a horse, the walls rise thirty and forty feet perpendicularly. This formation supplies the discoloration of the Platte. At sunset, the height of the mercurial column was 25.500, the attached thermometer 80°, and wind moderate from S. 38° E. Clouds covered the sky with the rise of the moon, but I succeeded in obtaining the usual astronomical observations, which placed us in latitude 41° 40′ 13″, and longitude 104° 59′ 23″.

July 15.—At 6 this morning, the barometer was at 25.515, the thermometer 72°, the day was fine, with some clouds looking dark on the south, with a fresh breeze from the same quarter. We found that in our journey across the country we had kept too much to the eastward. This morning accordingly we travelled by compass some 15 or 20° to the west of north, and struck the Platte some thirteen miles below Fort Laramie. The day was extremely hot, and among the hills the wind seemed to have just issued from an oven. Our horses were much distressed, as we had travelled hard, and it was with some difficulty that they were all brought to the Platte; which we reached at 1 o'clock. In riding in towards the river, we found the trail of our carts, which appeared to have passed a day or two since.

After having allowed our animals two hours for food and repose, we resumed our journey, and towards the close of the day came in sight of Laramie's fork. Issuing from the river hills, we came first in view of Fort Platte,[28] a post belonging to Messrs. Sybille, Adams & Co., situated immediately in the point of land at the junction of Laramie with the Platte. Like the post we had visited on the South fork, it was built of earth, and still unfinished, being enclosed with walls, or rather houses, on three of the sides, and open on the fourth to the river. A few hundred yards brought us in view of the post

---

28. Fort Platte, at the confluence of the Laramie and the North Platte, was built in 1841 by Lancaster P. Lupton, sold in the spring of 1842 to Sibille & Adams, and abandoned in 1845.

of the American Fur Company, called Fort John, or Laramie.[29] This was a large post, having more the air of military construction than the fort at the mouth of the river. It is on the left bank, on a rising ground some twenty-five feet above the water; and its lofty walls, whitewashed and picketed, with the large bastions at the angles, gave it quite an imposing appearance in the uncertain light of evening. A cluster of lodges, which the language told us belonged to Sioux Indians, was pitched under the walls, and, with the fine back ground of the Black Hills and the prominent peak of Laramie mountain, strongly drawn in the clear light of the western sky, where the sun had already set, the whole formed at the moment a strikingly beautiful picture. From the company at St. Louis I had letters for Mr. Boudeau,[30] the gentleman in charge of the post, by whom I was received with great hospitality and an efficient kindness, which was invaluable to me during my stay in the country. I found our people encamped on the bank, a short distance above the fort. All were well, and in the enjoyment of a bountiful supper, which coffee and bread made luxurious to us, we soon forgot the fatigues of the last ten days.

July 16.—I found that, during my absence, the situation of affairs had undergone some change; and the usual quiet and somewhat monotonous regularity of the camp had given place to excitement and alarm. The circumstances which occasioned this change will be found narrated in the following extract from the journal of Mr.

---

29. William Marshall Anderson provides an eye-witness account of the establishment of Fort Laramie's predecessor, Fort William. It was founded in 1834 by William L. Sublette (of Sublette & Campbell) and was named both for Sublette and his guest, Anderson. The fort was known for a while as Fort Lucien after its sale in 1835 to [Lucien] Fontenelle, Fitzpatrick & Co., but the name Fort William hung on. After the American Fur Company took over the interests of the owners, it was rebuilt as an adobe structure and renamed Fort John. It probably was rebuilt on the same site, though this has not yet been determined archeologically. As JCF indicates, the name Laramie was also in use, and when the Army purchased the structure in 1849 it officially became Fort Laramie. There are many accounts of the post and its history, including JCF's description, p. 218. For William Marshall Anderson's account of its founding as Fort William, see ANDERSON, 35 and passim.

30. James Bordeaux (1814–78), fur trader and interpreter, had come to the Platte region from Fort Pierre where he had worked for the American Fur Company. He served more than once as *bourgeois* at Fort Laramie, and operated a number of trading posts in the area (TRENHOLM; J. D. MC DERMOTT [1]).

Preuss, which commences with the day of our separation on the South fork of the Platte.

Extract from the Journal of Mr. Preuss.[31]

"*July* 6.—We crossed the plateau or highland between the two forks in about six hours. I let my horse go slow as he liked, to indemnify us both for the previous hardship; and about noon we reached the North fork. There was no sign that our party had passed; we rode, therefore, to some pine trees, unsaddled the horses, and stretched our limbs on the grass, awaiting the arrival of our company. After remaining here two hours, my companion [Bernier] became impatient, mounted his horse again, and rode off down the river to see if he could discover our people. I felt so marode [*sic*] yet, that it was a horrible idea to me to bestride that saddle again, so I lay still. I knew they could not come any other way, and then my companion, one of the best men of the company, would not abandon me. The sun went down; he did not come; uneasy I did not feel, but very hungry; I had no provisions, but I could make a fire; and as I espied two doves in a tree, I tried to kill one; but it needs a better marksman than myself to kill a little bird with a rifle. I made a large fire, however, lighted my pipe—this true friend of mine in every emergency—laid down, and let my thoughts wander to the far East. It was not many minutes after when I heard the tramp of a horse, and my faithful companion was by my side. He had found the party, who had been delayed by making their *cache,* about seven miles below. To the good supper which he brought with him I did ample justice. He had forgotten salt, and I tried the soldier's substitute in time of war, and used gunpowder; but it answered badly—bitter enough, but no flavor of kitchen salt.[32] I slept well;

---

31. Preuss apparently produced two accounts, at least for this period. His principal journal covering all his travels with JCF, the original manuscript of which is in DLC and available in translation (PREUSS), is quite different for his journey to Fort Laramie. His editors conjecture that Preuss simply gave JCF the information to cover his trip, and that JCF wrote the "abstract" to harmonize with the rest of his report. This is quite probably true.

32. In his "other" account, Preuss is in his usual dour and ungrateful mood: "After we had walked back to the cedar tree, he exhibited his wares: meat, tongue, bread, and the remainder of Frémont's Fourth of July keg. What a joy, what a delight! Yet a person is never satisfied. When I was eating I thought that those people could have sent along a little salt if they had had anything of a cultured taste" (PREUSS, 20).

and was only disturbed by two owls, which were attracted by the fire, and took their place in the tree under which we slept. Their music seemed as disagreeable to my companion as to myself; he fired his rifle twice, and then they let us alone.

"*July* 7.—At about 10 o'clock, the party arrived; and we continued our journey through a country which offered but little to interest the traveller. The soil was much more sandy than in the valley below the confluence of the forks, and the face of the country no longer presented the refreshing green which had hitherto characterized it. The rich grass was now found only in dispersed spots, on low grounds, and on the bottom land of the streams. A long drought, joined to extreme heat, had so parched up the upper prairies, that they were in many places bald, or covered only with a thin growth of yellow and poor grass. The nature of the soil renders it extremely susceptible to the vicissitudes of the climate. Between the forks, and from their junction to the Black Hills, the formation consists of marl and a soft earthy limestone, with granitic sandstone. Such a formation cannot give rise to a sterile soil; and on our return in September, when the country had been watered by frequent rains, the valley of the Platte looked like a garden; so rich was the verdure of the grasses, and so luxuriant the bloom of abundant flowers. The wild sage begins to make its appearance, and timber is so scarce that we generally made our fires of the *bois de vache*. With the exception of now and then an isolated tree or two, standing like a light-house on the river bank, there is none whatever to be seen.[33]

"*July* 8.—Our road to-day was a solitary one. No game made its appearance, not even a buffalo or a stray antelope; and nothing occurred to break the monotony until about 5 o'clock, when the caravan made a sudden halt. There was a galloping in of scouts and horsemen from every side—a hurrying to and fro in noisy confusion; rifles were taken from their cover; bullet pouches examined: in short, there was the cry of "Indians," heard again. I had become so much accustomed to these alarms, that now they made but little impression on me; and, before I had time to become excited, the new comers were ascertained to be whites. It was a large party of traders and trappers, conducted by Mr. Bridger, a man well

---

33. The entry for this day in his published diary reads only: "Nothing new under this sun" (PREUSS, 20).

known in the history of the country.[34] As the sun was low, and there was a fine grass patch not far ahead, they turned back and encamped for the night with us. Mr. Bridger was invited to supper; and, after the *table cloth* was removed, we listened with eager interest to an account of their adventures. What they had met, we would be likely to encounter; the chances which had befallen them, would probably happen to us; and we looked upon their life as a picture of our own. He informed us that the condition of the country had become exceedingly dangerous. The Sioux, who had been badly disposed, had broken out into open hostility, and in the preceding autumn his party had encountered them in a severe engagement, in which a number of lives had been lost on both sides. United with the Cheyenne and Gros Ventre Indians, they were scouring the upper country in war parties of great force, and were at this time in the neighborhood of the *Red Buttes,* a famous landmark, which was directly on our path. They had declared war upon every living thing which should be found westward of that point; though their main object was to attack a large camp of whites and Snake Indians, who had a rendezvous in the Sweet Water valley. Availing himself of his intimate knowledge of the country, he had reached Laramie by an unusual route through the Black Hills, and avoided coming into contact with any of the scattered parties. This gentleman offered his services to accompany us so far as the head of the Sweet Water; but the absence of our leader, which was deeply regretted by us all,[35] rendered it impossible for us to enter upon such an arrangement. In a camp consisting of men whose lives had been spent in this country, I expected to find every one prepared for occurrences of this nature; but, to my great surprise, I found, on the contrary, that this news had thrown them all into the greatest consternation, and, on every side, I heard only one exclamation, *"Il n'y aura pas de vie pour nous."* All the night scattered groups were assembled around the fires, smoking their pipes, and listening with the greatest eagerness to exaggerated details of Indian hostilities;

---

34. Jim Bridger (1804–81), the famous frontiersman and scout who had been connected with northwestern fur companies since 1822, would in the course of the next year establish a way-station in southwestern Wyoming. For a biography, see ALTER.

35. These can hardly be Preuss' own words. His published diary says: "I feel better because of Frémont's absence" (PREUSS, 21).

and in the morning I found the camp dispirited, and agitated by a variety of conflicting opinions. A majority of the people were strongly disposed to return;[36] but Clément Lambert, with some five or six others, professed their determination to follow Mr. Frémont to the uttermost limit of his journey. The others yielded to their remonstrances; and, somewhat ashamed of their cowardice, concluded to advance at least so far as Laramie fork, eastward of which they were aware no danger was to be apprehended. Notwithstanding the confusion and excitement, we were very early on the road, as the days were extremely hot, and we were anxious to profit by the freshness of the morning. The soft marly formation, over which we were now journeying frequently offers to the traveller views of remarkable and picturesque beauty. To several of these localities where the winds and the rain have worked the bluffs into curious shapes, the voyageurs have given names according to some fancied resemblance. One of these, called the *Courthouse,* we passed about six miles from our encampment of last night, and toward noon came in sight of the celebrated *Chimney Rock.*[37] It looks, at this distance of about thirty miles, like what it is called, the long chimney of a steam-factory establishment, or a shot-tower in Baltimore. Nothing occurred to interrupt the quiet of the day; and we encamped on the river, after a march of twenty-four miles. Buffalo had become very scarce, and but one cow had been killed, of which the meat had been cut into thin slices, and hung around the carts to dry.

"*July* 10.—We continued along the same fine, plainly beaten road, which the smooth surface of the country afforded us for a distance of six hundred and thirty miles, from the frontiers of Missouri to

---

36. And so was Preuss, who says in his published diary: "It would be ridiculous to risk the lives of twenty-five people just to determine a few longitudes and latitudes and to find out the elevation of a mountain range" (PREUSS, 21–22).

37. Courthouse Rock and Chimney Rock, both famous landmarks on the trail along the south bank of the North Platte, in Morrill County, Nebr., bear some relevance to the JCF expedition. A study of trail landmarks by Dale L. Morgan indicates that the name of Courthouse Rock was unknown in the literature before JCF's first *Report* was issued, and the general and early acceptance of that name is one more indication of the impact his *Report* had on an America looking westward. As for Chimney Rock, Preuss made a sketch (p. 216) which is the second oldest on record (MATTES, 385), and said it looked like the chimney of a factory or "a shot-tower in Baltimore." Preuss appears to have been the first to use the name Chimney Rock.

Chimney Rock

the Laramie fork. In the course of the day we met some whites, who were following along in the train of Mr. Bridger; and, after a day's journey of twenty-four miles, encamped about sunset at the Chimney Rock, of which the annexed drawing [p. 216] will render any description unnecessary. It consists of marl and earthy limestone, and the weather is rapidly diminishing its height, which is now not more than two hundred feet above the river. Travellers who visited it some years since placed its height at upwards of five hundred feet.

"*July* 11.—The valley of the North fork is of a variable breadth, from one to four and sometimes six miles. Fifteen miles from the Chimney Rock we reached one of those places where the river strikes the bluffs and forces the road to make a considerable circuit over the uplands. This presented an escarpment on the river of about nine hundred yards in length, and is familiarly known as Scott's bluffs.[38] We had made a journey of thirty miles before we again struck the river, at a place where some scanty grass afforded an insufficient pasturage to our animals. About twenty miles from the Chimney Rock we had found a very beautiful spring of excellent and cold water; but it was in such a deep ravine, and so small, that the animals could not profit by it, and we therefore halted only a few minutes, and found a resting place ten miles further on. The plain between Scott's bluffs and Chimney Rock was almost entirely covered with drift wood, consisting principally of cedar, which, we were informed, had been supplied from the Black Hills, in a flood five or six years since.

"*July* 12.—Nine miles from our encampment of yesterday we crossed Horse creek, a shallow stream of clear water, about seventy yards wide, falling into the Platte on the right bank. It was lightly timbered, and great quantities of drift wood were piled up on the banks, appearing to be supplied by the creek from above. After a journey of twenty-six miles, we encamped on a rich bottom, which afforded fine grass to our animals. Buffalo have entirely disappeared, and we live now upon the dried meat which is exceedingly poor food. The marl and earthy limestone, which constituted the formation for several days past, had changed during the day into a com-

---

38. Scotts Bluff, south of the river near Scottsbluff, Nebr., is a national monument maintained by the National Park Service. Portions of the old wagon trail are still visible near by.

pact white or grayish white limestone, sometimes containing horn-stone; and at the place of our encampment this evening, some strata in the river hills cropped out to the height of thirty or forty feet, consisting of a fine-grained granitic sandstone; one of the strata closely resembling gneiss.

"*July* 13.—To-day, about four o'clock, we reached Fort Laramie, where we were cordially received; we pitched our camp a little above the fort, on the bank of Laramie river, in which the pure and clear water of the mountain stream looked refreshingly cool, and made a pleasant contrast to the muddy, yellow waters of the Platte."[39]

I walked up to visit our friends at the fort, which is a quadrangular structure, built of clay, after the fashion of the Mexicans, who are generally employed in building them. The walls are about fifteen feet high, surmounted with a wooden palisade, and form a portion of ranges of houses, which entirely surround a yard of about one hundred and thirty feet square. Every apartment has its door and window, all, of course, opening on the inside. There are two entrances opposite each other and midway the wall, one of which is a large and public entrance, the other smaller and more private: a sort of postern gate. Over the great entrance is a square tower, with loopholes; and, like the rest of the work, built of earth. At two of the angles, and diagonally opposite each other, are large square bastions, so arranged as to sweep the four faces of the walls.

This post belongs to the American Fur Company, and, at the time of our visit, was in charge of Mr. Boudeau. Two of the company's clerks, Messrs. Galpin and Kellogg,[40] were with him, and he had in the fort about sixteen men. As usual, these had found wives

---

39. The end of the so-called abstract from the Preuss journal. His published version merely reads, "Nothing new, except that we arrived at the Fort to-day" (PREUSS, 23).

40. Charles E. Galpin (d. ca. 1870), was for many years connected with the fur trade on the upper Missouri, and was in charge at Fort Pierre when it was sold to the U.S. government. Fort Pierre was a depot for Fort Laramie at this time (see *South Dakota Historical Collections,* 1:364–65). The other clerk apparently was Philander Kellogg (1810–ca. 1848). When he went to the North Platte region is uncertain, but his brothers Florentine and Benjamin Kellogg encountered him unexpectedly on the trail during a trip to California in 1846 (KORNS, 153). A letter from Fort Pierre, 19 Aug. 1845, from A. R. Bouis to P. Chouteau, Jr., and Company, sheds some light on Kellogg's activities and also illustrates how Fort Pierre served as a shipping

among the Indian squaws; and, with the usual accompaniment of children, the place had quite a populous appearance. It is hardly necessary to say, that the object of the establishment is trade with the neighboring tribes, who, in the course of the year, generally make two or three visits to the fort. In addition to this, traders, with a small outfit, are constantly kept amongst them. The articles of trade consist on the one side almost entirely of buffalo robes, and on the other, of blankets, calicoes, guns, powder, and lead, with such cheap ornaments as glass beads, looking-glasses, rings, vermilion for painting, tobacco, and principally, and in spite of the prohibition, of spirits, brought into the country in the form of alcohol, and diluted with water before sold. While mentioning this fact, it is but justice to the American Fur Company to state, that, throughout the country, I have always found them strenuously opposed to the introduction of spirituous liquors. But in the present state of things, when the country is supplied with alcohol, when a keg of it will purchase from an Indian every thing he possesses—his furs, his lodge, his horses, and even his wife and children—and when any vagabond who has money enough to purchase a mule can go into a village and trade against them successfully—without withdrawing entirely from the trade, it is impossible for them to discontinue its use. In their opposition to this practice, the company is sustained, not only by their obligation to the laws of the country and the welfare of the Indians, but clearly, also, on grounds of policy; for, with heavy and expensive outfits, they contend at manifestly great disadvantage against the numerous independent and unlicensed traders, who enter the country from various avenues, from the United States and from Mexico, having no other stock in trade than some kegs of liquor, which they sell at the modest price of thirty-six dollars per gallon. The difference between the regular trader and the *coureur des bois,* as the French call the itinerant or peddling traders, with respect to the sale of spirits, is here as it always has been, fixed and permanent, and growing out of the nature of their trade. The regular trader looks ahead, and has an interest in the preservation of the Indians,

---

point for Fort Laramie. "Messrs. Lurty, Harper & Farwell arrived yesterday from Fort John [Laramie]. They left Mr. Kellogg on White River with 13 wagons and carts laden with 387 Pack Robes. He is progressing but slowly. . . . I expect him here by 1st September, and soon as possible after his arrival, I will start two mackinaw boats . . . with 550 packs for St. Louis" (DELAND, 205).

Fort Laramie

and in the regular pursuit of their business, and the preservation of their arms, horses, and every thing necessary to their future and permanent success in hunting: the *coureur des bois* has no permanent interest, and gets what he can, and for what he can, from every Indian he meets, even at the risk of disabling him from doing any thing more at hunting.

The fort had a very cool and clean appearance. The great entrance, in which I found the gentlemen assembled, and which was floored, and about fifteen feet long, made a pleasant, shaded seat, through which the breeze swept constantly; for this country is famous for high winds. In the course of conversation, I learned the following particulars, which will explain the condition of the country: For several years the Cheyennes and Sioux had gradually become more and more hostile to the whites, and in the latter part of August, 1841, had had a rather severe engagement with a party of sixty men, under the command of Mr. Frapp,[41] of St. Louis. The Indians lost eight or ten warriors, and the whites had their leader and four men killed. This fight took place on the waters of Snake river; and it was this party, on their return under Mr. Bridger, which had spread so much alarm among my people. In the course of the spring, two other small parties had been cut off by the Sioux; one on their return from the Crow nation, and the other among the Black Hills. The emigrants to Oregon and Mr. Bridger's party met here, a few days before our arrival. Division and misunderstandings had grown up among them; they were already somewhat disheartened by the fatigue of their long and wearisome journey, and the feet of their cattle had become so much worn as to be scarcely able to travel. In this situation, they were not likely to find encouragement in the hostile attitude of the Indians, and the new and unexpected difficulties which sprang up before them. They were told that

---

41. Henry Fraeb, who had been one of the founders and proprietors of the Rocky Mountain Fur Company. After that company was dissolved in 1834, Fraeb engaged in trade both independently and in partnership with various men. In 1840–41 his partner was Jim Bridger. JCF's report of the number of men killed when Fraeb skirmished with the Cheyennes, Arapahos, and Sioux is only one of many differing reports (L. HAFEN [2]). In Dale L. Morgan's sketch of Fraeb (ANDERSON, 312–15), he corrects JCF by pointing out that the Fraeb skirmish probably occurred early in August, not the "latter part." The scene was the stream now called the Little Snake, and JCF has considerably exaggerated the effect of the attack on emigration and the morale of emigrants who learned of the affair.

the country was entirely swept of grass, and that few or no buffalo were to be found on their line of route; and with their weakened animals, it would be impossible for them to transport their heavy wagons over the mountain. Under these circumstances, they disposed of their wagons and cattle at the forts; selling them at the prices they had paid in the States, and taking in exchange coffee and sugar at one dollar a pound, and miserable worn out horses, which died before they reached the mountains. Mr. Boudeau informed me that he had purchased thirty, and the lower fort eighty head of fine cattle, some of them of the Durham breed. Mr. Fitzpatrick,[42] whose name and high reputation are familiar to all who interest themselves in the history of this country, had reached Laramie in company with Bridger; and the emigrants were fortunate enough to obtain his services to guide them as far as the British post of Fort Hall, about two hundred and fifty miles beyond the South Pass of the mountains. They had started for this post on the 4th of July, and immediately after their departure, a war party of three hundred and fifty braves sat out upon their trail. As their principal chief or partisan had lost some relations in the recent fight, and had sworn to kill the first whites on his path, it was supposed that their intention was to attack the party, should a favorable opportunity offer; or, if they were foiled in their principal object by the vigilance of Mr. Fitzpatrick, content themselves with stealing horses and cutting off stragglers. These had been gone but a few days previous to our arrival.

The effect of the engagement with Mr. Frapp had been greatly to irritate the hostile spirit of the savages; and immediately subsequent to that event, the Gros Ventre Indians had united with the Oglallahs and Cheyennes, and taken the field in great force, so far as I could ascertain, to the amount of eight hundred lodges. Their object was to make an attack on a camp of Snake and Crow Indians,

---

42. Thomas Fitzpatrick (1799–1854), called "Broken Hand" by the Indians, was an Irish immigrant who became one of the greatest of the "mountain men." With Bridger, Fraeb, and others he had organized the Rocky Mountain Fur Company in 1830; but when the beaver were depleted he quit trapping to serve as a guide to early emigrant trains or expeditions. He guided the White-Hastings party to Fort Hall from Fort Laramie in 1842. In 1843–45, he would serve as a guide for JCF, and would in 1846 become an Indian agent for tribes on the upper Platte and the Arkansas (DNA-75, LS, 38:357). See the biography by HAFEN & GHENT.

and a body of about one hundred whites, who had made a rendezvous somewhere in the Green river valley, or on the Sweet Water.
After spending some time in buffalo hunting in the neighborhood
of the Medicine Bow mountain, they were to cross over to the Green
river waters, and return to Laramie by way of the South Pass and
the Sweet Water valley. According to the calculation of the Indians,
Mr. Boudeau informed me they were somewhere near the head
of the Sweet Water. I subsequently learned that the party led by Mr.
Fitzpatrick were overtaken by their pursuers, near Rock Independence, in the valley of the Sweet Water; but his skill and resolution saved them from surprise, and small as his force was, they did
not venture to attack him openly. Here they lost one of their party
by an accident, and, continuing up the valley, they came suddenly
upon the large village. From these they met with a doubtful reception. Long residence and familiar acquaintance had given to Mr.
Fitzpatrick great personal influence among them, and a portion of
them were disposed to let him pass quietly; but by far the greater
number were inclined to hostile measures; and the chiefs spent the
whole of one night, during which they kept the little party in the
midst of them, in council, debating the question of attacking them
the next day; but the influence of "the Broken Hand," as they
called Mr. Fitzpatrick (one of his hands having been shattered by
the bursting of a gun), at length prevailed, and obtained for them
an unmolested passage; but they sternly assured him that this path
was no longer open, and that any party of whites which should
hereafter be found upon it, would meet with certain destruction.
From all that I have been able to learn, I have no doubt that the
emigrants owe their lives to Mr. Fitzpatrick.

Thus it would appear that the country was swarming with scattered war parties; and when I heard during the day, the various contradictory and exaggerated rumors which were incessantly repeated
to them, I was not surprised that so much alarm prevailed among
my men. Carson, one of the best and most experienced mountaineers, fully supported the opinion given by Bridger of the dangerous
state of the country, and openly expressed his conviction that we
could not escape without some sharp encounters with the Indians.[43]

---

43. The draft manuscript has Carson saying that "all of us should never
see that fort again."

In addition to this, he made his will, and among the circumstances which were constantly occurring to increase their alarm, this was the most unfortunate; and I found that a number of my party had become so much intimidated, that they had requested to be discharged at this place. I dined to-day at Fort Platte, which has been mentioned as situated at the junction of Laramie river with the Nebraska. Here I heard a confirmation of the statements given above. The party of warriors, which had started a few days since on the trail of the emigrants, was expected back in fourteen days, to join the village with which their families and the old men had remained. The arrival of the latter was hourly expected, and some Indians have just come in who had left them on the Laramie fork, about twenty miles above. Mr. Bissonette, one of the traders belonging to Fort Platte, urged the propriety of taking with me an interpreter and two or three old men of the village, in which case, he thought there would be little or no hazard in encountering any of the war parties. The principal danger was in being attacked before they should know who we were.

They had a confused idea of the numbers and power of our people, and dreaded to bring upon themselves the military force of the United States. This gentleman, who spoke the language fluently, offered his services to accompany me so far as the Red Buttes. He was desirous to join the large party on its return, for purposes of trade, and it would suit his views as well as my own, to go with us to the Buttes; beyond which point it would be impossible to prevail on a Sioux to venture, on account of their fear of the Crows. From Fort Laramie to the Red Buttes, by the ordinary road, is one hundred and thirty-five miles; and, though only on the threshold of danger, it seemed better to secure the services of an interpreter [Joseph Bissonette] for the partial distance, than to have none at all.

So far as frequent interruption from the Indians would allow, we occupied ourselves in making some astronomical calculations, and bringing up the general map to this stage of our journey, but the tent was generally occupied by a succession of our ceremonious visitors. Some came for presents, and others for information of our object in coming to the country; now and then one would dart up to the tent on horseback, jerk off his trappings, and stand silently at the door, holding his horse by the halter, signifying his desire to trade. Occasionally a savage would stalk in, with an invitation to a feast of honor, a dog feast, and deliberately sit down and wait quietly until

I was ready to accompany him.[44] I went to one; the women and children were sitting outside the lodge, and we took our seats on buffalo robes spread around. The dog was in a large pot over the fire in the middle of the lodge, and immediately on our arrival was dished up in large wooden bowls, one of which was handed to each. The flesh appeared very glutinous, with something of the flavor and appearance of mutton. Feeling something move behind me, I looked round and found that I had taken my seat among a litter of fat young puppies. Had I been nice in such matters, the prejudices of civilization might have interfered with my tranquility; but fortunately, I am not of delicate nerves, and continued quietly to empty my platter.

The weather was cloudy at evening, with a moderate south wind, and the thermometer at 6 o'clock 85°. I was disappointed in my hope of obtaining an observation of an occultation, which took place about midnight. The moon brought with her heavy banks of clouds, through which she scarcely made her appearance during the night.

The morning of the 18th was cloudy and calm, the thermometer at 6 o'clock at 64°. About 9, with a moderate wind from the west, a storm of rain came on, accompanied by sharp thunder and lightning, which lasted about an hour. During the day the expected village arrived, consisting principally of old men, women, and children. They had a considerable number of horses, and large troops of dogs. Their lodges were pitched near the fort, and our camp was constantly crowded with Indians of all sizes, from morning until night; at which time some of the soldiers generally came to drive them all off to the village. My tent was the only place which they respected. Here only came the chiefs and men of distinction, and generally one of them remained to drive away the women and children. The numerous strange instruments applied to still stranger uses excited awe and admiration among them, and those which I used in talking with the sun and stars they looked upon with especial reverence, as mysterious things of "great medicine." Of the three barometers which I had brought with me thus far successfully, I found that two were out of order, and spent the greater part of the 19th in repairing them, an operation of no small difficulty in the midst of the incessant inter-

---

44. "These Indians are irksome people, pesky as children. They come into the tent, sit down, and smoke their pipes as if they were at home" (PREUSS, 29).

ruptions to which I was subjected. We had the misfortune to break here a large thermometer, graduated to show fifths of a degree, which I used to ascertain the temperature of boiling water, and with which I had promised myself some interesting experiments in the mountains. We had but one remaining, on which the graduation extended sufficiently high, and this was too small for exact observations. During our stay here the men had been engaged in making numerous repairs, arranging pack saddles, and otherwise preparing for the chances of a rough road and mountain travel. All things of this nature being ready, I gathered them around me in the evening, and told them that "I had determined to proceed the next day. They were all well armed. I had engaged the services of Mr. Bissonette as interpreter, and had taken, in the circumstances, every possible means to insure our safety. In the rumors we had heard I believed there was much exaggeration, and then they were men accustomed to this kind of life and to the country; and that these were the dangers of every day occurrence, and to be expected in the ordinary course of their service. They had heard of the unsettled condition of the country before leaving St. Louis, and therefore could not make it a reason for breaking their engagements. Still I was unwilling to take with me on a service of some certain danger, men on whom I could not rely; and as I had understood that there were among them some who were disposed to cowardice, and anxious to return, they had but to come forward at once and state their desire, and they would be discharged with the amount due to them for the time they had served." To their honor be it said, there was but one among them who had the face to come forward and avail himself of the permission.[45] I asked him some few questions in order to expose him to the ridicule of the men, and let him go. The day after our departure he engaged himself to one of the forts, and set off with a party for the Upper Missouri. I did not think that the situation of the country justified me in taking our young companions, Messrs. Brant and Benton, along with us. In case of misfortune, it would

---

45. Deleted from the manuscript draft: "The same [Registe] Larent whom I have previously had occasion to mention. He was a well-looking, robust man of thirty, & on this occasion pleaded sickness as a reason for not exposing himself to the hardships of the Mountains. His only sickness consisted in overeating himself & I had frequently been obliged to give him medicine, to assist him in getting rid of the enormous quantity of animal food he daily consumed."

have been thought, at the least, an act of great imprudence; and therefore, though reluctantly, I determined to leave them. Randolph had been the life of the camp, and the *"petit garcon"* was much regretted by the men, to whom his buoyant spirits had afforded great amusement. They all, however, agreed in the propriety of leaving him at the fort, because, as they said, he might cost the lives of some of the men in a fight with the Indians.

July 21.—A portion of our baggage, with our field notes and observations, and several instruments, were left at the fort. One of the gentlemen, Mr. Galpin, took charge of a barometer, which he engaged to observe during my absence, and I entrusted to Randolph, by way of occupation, the regular winding up of two of my chronometers, which were among the instruments left. Our observations showed that the chronometer which I retained for the continuation of our voyage had preserved its rate in a most satisfactory manner.[46] As deduced from it, the longitude of Fort Laramie is 7*h*. 01′ 21″, and from lunar distance 7*h*. 01′ 29″, giving for the adopted longitude 105° 21′ 10″. Comparing the barometrical observations made during our stay here with those of Dr. G. Engelman at St. Louis, we find for the elevation of the fort above the Gulf of Mexico 4,470 feet. The winter climate here is remarkably mild for the latitude; but rainy weather is frequent, and the place is celebrated for winds, of which the prevailing one is west. An east wind in summer and a south wind in winter is said to be always accompanied with rain.

We were ready to depart; the tents were struck, the mules geared up, and our horses saddled, and we walked up to the fort to take the *stirrup cup* with our friends in an excellent home-brewed preparation.[47] While thus pleasantly engaged, seated in one of the little cool

---

46. "We left the large chronometer in Laramie; Frémont succeeded in making it run again, and he was jubilant when he heard again the ticking and tick-tocking. In comparing we found, however, that every twenty-four hours it went wrong by about one hour. Oh, you American blockheads!" (PREUSS, 30–31).

47. Oliver P. Wiggins, who was probably born on Grand Island in the Niagara River in 1823, claimed that he and a few friends joined the expedition at Fort Laramie and accompanied it westward "because they could be depended on to fight in Indian dangers" ("Early Far West Notes," F. W. Cragin, Western History Collection, CoU). In CARSON, 20–22, Harvey L. Carter not only points out the preposterous nature of this claim, which had been accepted by such biographers as Edwin L. Sabin and M. Morgan Estergreen, but also questions his whole association with Kit Carson at Taos. In

chambers, at the door of which a man had been stationed to prevent all intrusion from the Indians, a number of chiefs, several of them powerful fine-looking men, forced their way into the room in spite of all opposition. Handing me the following letter, they took their seats in silence:

"FORT PLATTE, *July* 1, 1842.

"Mr. Fremont: Les chefs s'étant assemblés présentement me disent de vous avertir de ne point vous mettre en route, avant que le parti de jeunes gens qui est en dehors, soient de retour. Deplus ils me disent qu'ils sont très certain qu'ils feront feu, à la première rencontre. Ils doivent être de retour dans sept à huit jours; excusez si je vous fais cos observations, mais il me semble qu'il est mon devoir de vous avertir du danger. Même de plus, les chefs sont les porteurs de ce billet, qui vous defendent de partir avant le retour des guerriers.
"Je suis votre ob't servt'r,

"JOSEPH BISSONETTE,
"Par L. B. CHARTRAIN."[48]

Les noms de quelques chefs:
Le Chapeau de Loutre, le Casseur de Flêches, la Nuit Noir, La Queue de Bœuf.

[*Translation*]

"FORT PLATTE, *July* 1, 1842.

"Mr. Fremont: The chiefs having assembled in council, have just told me to warn you not to set out before the party of young men which is now out shall have returned. Furthermore, they tell me that they are very sure they will fire upon you as soon as they meet you. They are expected back in seven or eight days; excuse me for making these observations, but it seems my duty to warn you of

---

fact, Carter is reasonably certain that Wiggins, who has been exposed as a complete charlatan, did not come west before 1850, and then only as far as Scottsbluff, Nebr.

48. L. B. Chartrain probably left Independence with a Sibille & Adams party in the fall of 1841. The fragmentary diaries of Adams (MoSHi) first mention him in December of that year, saying he has gone to trade on Cheyenne waters. He is last mentioned in the diaries in 1845.

danger. Moreover, the chiefs who prohibit your setting out before the return of the warriors are the bearers of this note.

"I am your obedient servant,

"Joseph Bissonette,

"By L. B. Chartrain."

"Names of some of the chiefs:

"The Otter Hat, the Breaker of Arrows, the Black Night, the Bull's Tail."

After reading this, I mentioned its purport to my companions, and seeing that all were fully possessed of its contents, one of the Indians rose up, and, having first shaken hands with me, spoke as follows:

"You have come among us at a bad time. Some of our people have been killed, and our young men, who are gone to the mountains, are eager to avenge the blood of their relations, which has been shed by the whites. Our young men are bad, and if they meet you they will believe that you are carrying goods and ammunition to their enemies, and will fire upon you. You have told us that this will make war. We know that our great father has many soldiers and big guns, and we are anxious to have our lives. We love the whites, and are desirous of peace. Thinking of all these things, we have determined to keep you here until our warriors return. We are glad to see you among us. Our father is rich, and we expected that you would have brought presents to us—horses, and guns, and blankets. But we are glad to see you. We look upon your coming as the light which goes before the sun; for you will tell our great father that you have seen us, and that we are naked and poor, and have nothing to eat, and he will send us all these things." He was followed by others to the same effect.

The observations of the savage appeared reasonable; but I was aware that they had in view only the present object of detaining me, and were unwilling I should go further into the country. In reply, I asked them, through the interpretation of Mr. Boudeau, to select two or three of their number to accompany us until we should meet their people—they should spread their robes in my tent and eat at my table, and on our return I would give them presents in reward of their services. They declined, saying that there were no young men left in the village, and that they were too old to travel so many days on horseback, and preferred now to smoke their pipes in the lodge, and let the warriors go on the war-path. Besides, they had no power over the young men, and were afraid to interfere with them. In my turn I addressed them: "You say that you love the whites; why have you killed so many already this spring? You say that you love the whites, and are full of many expressions of friendship to us, but you are not willing to undergo the fatigue of a few days' ride to save our lives. We do not believe what you have said, and will not listen to you. Whatever a chief among us tells his soldiers to do, is done. We are the soldiers of the great chief, your father. He has told us to come here and see this country, and all the Indians, his children. Why should we not go? Before we came, we heard that you had killed his people, and ceased to be his children; but we came among you peaceably, holding out our hands. Now we find that the stories we heard are not lies, and that you are no longer his friends and children. We have thrown away our bodies, and will not turn back. When you told us that your young men would kill us, you did not know that our hearts were strong, and you did not see the rifles which my young men carry in their hands. We are few, and you are many, and may kill us all; but there will be much crying in your villages, for many of your young men will stay behind, and forget to return with your warriors from the mountains. Do you think that our great chief will let his soldiers die, and forget to cover their graves? Before the snows melt again, his warriors will sweep away your villages as the fire does the prairie in the autumn. See! I have pulled down my *white houses,* and my people are ready: when the sun is ten paces higher, we shall be on the march. If you have anything to tell us, you will say it soon." I broke up the conference, as I could do nothing with these people, and being resolved to proceed, nothing was to be gained by delay. Accompanied by our hospitable friends, we returned to the camp. We had mounted our horses, and our parting salutations had been exchanged, when one of the chiefs, the Bull's Tail, arrived to tell me that they had determined to send a young man with us; and if I would point out the place of our evening camp, he should join us there. "The young man is poor," said he; "he has no horse, and expects you to give him one." I described to him the place where I intended to encamp, and shaking hands, in a few minutes we were among the hills, and this last habitation of whites shut out from our view.

The road led over an interesting plateau between the north fork of the Platte on the right and Laramie river on the left. At the distance of ten miles from the fort we entered the sandy bed of a creek, a kind of defile, shaded by precipitous rocks, down which we wound our way for several hundred yards to a place where, on the left bank, a very large spring gushes with considerable noise and force out of the limestone rock. It is called "the Warm Spring," and furnishes to the hitherto dry bed of the creek a considerable rivulet. On the opposite side, a little below the spring, is a lofty limestone escarpment, partially shaded by a grove of large trees, whose green foliage, in contrast with the whiteness of the rock, renders this a picturesque locality. The rock is fossiliferous, and, so far as I was able to determine the character of the fossils, belongs to the carboniferous limestone of the Missouri river, and is probably the western limit of that formation. Beyond this point I met with no fossils of any description.

I was desirous to visit the Platte near the point where it leaves the Black Hills, and therefore followed this stream, for two or three miles, to the mouth; where I encamped on a spot which afforded good grass and *prêle* (equisetum) for our animals. Our tents having been found too thin to protect ourselves and the instruments from the rains, which in this elevated country are attended with cold and unpleasant weather, I had procured from the Indians at Laramie a tolerably large lodge, about eighteen feet in diameter and twenty feet in height. Such a lodge, when properly pitched, is, from its conical form, almost perfectly secure against the violent winds which are frequent in this region, and with a fire in the centre is a dry and warm shelter in bad weather. By raising the lower part so as to permit the breeze to pass freely, it is converted into a pleasant summer residence, with the extraordinary advantage of being entirely free from mosquitoes, one of which I have never seen in an Indian lodge. While we were engaged very unskilfully in erecting this, the interpreter, Mr. Bissonette, arrived, accompanied by the Indian and his wife. She laughed at our awkwardness, and offered her assistance, of which we were frequently afterward obliged to avail ourselves, before the men acquired sufficient expertness to pitch it without difficulty. From this place we had a fine view of the gorge where the Platte issues from the Black Hills, changing its character abruptly from a mountain stream into a river of the plains.[49] Immediately

---

49. The trail the party has been following has not run directly along the banks of the North Platte, so JCF has come down to the river to inspect the rough country in the vicinity of Guernsey, Wyo. The original course and

around us the valley of the stream was tolerably open, and at the distance of a few miles, where the river had cut its way through the hills, was the narrow cleft, on one side of which a lofty precipice of bright red rock rose vertically above the low hills which lay between us.

July 22.—In the morning, while breakfast was being prepared, I visited this place with my favorite man, Basil Lajeunesse. Entering so far as there was footing for the mules, we dismounted, and, tying our animals, continued our way on foot. Like the whole country, the scenery of the river had undergone an entire change, and was in this place the most beautiful I have ever seen. The breadth of the stream, generally near that of its valley, was from two to three hundred feet, with a swift current, occasionally broken by rapids, and the water perfectly clear. On either side rose the red precipices, vertical, and sometimes overhanging, two and four hundred feet in height, crowned with green summits, on which were scattered a few pines. At the foot of the rocks was the usual detritus, formed of masses fallen from above. Among the pines that grew here and on the occasional banks, were the cherry, (*cerasus virginiana*) currants, and grains de bœuf (*shepherdia argentea.*) Viewed in the sunshine of a pleasant morning, the scenery was of a most striking and romantic beauty, which arose from the picturesque disposition of the objects and the vivid contrast of colors. I thought with much pleasure of our approaching descent in the canoe through such interesting places; and, in the expectation of being able at that time to give to them a full examination, did not now dwell so much as might have been desirable upon the geological formations along the line of the river, where they are developed with great clearness. The upper portion of the red strata consists of very compact clay, in which are occasionally seen imbedded large pebbles. Below was a stratum of compact red sandstone, changing a little above the river into a very hard siliceous limestone. There is a small but handsome open prairie immediately below this place, on the left bank of the river, which would be a

---

nature of the river, west of Guernsey, are now obscured by the Guernsey Reservoir and a smaller man-made body of water, Newell Bay.

Dale L. Morgan, in his correspondence with us, believes it clear from JCF's text that he took what later became known as the Hill Road from Fort Laramie to Warm Spring (thus reaching Warm Spring Canyon above the spring), not the River Road traveled by the Mormons in 1847, which kept to the banks of the North Platte as far as the mouth of Warm Spring Canyon. This Hill Road followed the divide between the Laramie and North Platte rivers.

good locality for a military post. There are some open groves of cottonwood on the Platte. The small stream which comes in at this place is well timbered with pine, and good building rock is abundant.

If it is in contemplation to keep open the communications with Oregon Territory, a show of military force in this country is absolutely necessary; and a combination of advantages renders the neighborhood of Fort Laramie the most suitable place, on the line of the Platte, for the establishment of a military post. It is connected with the mouth of the Platte and the Upper Missouri by excellent roads, which are in frequent use, and would not in any way interfere with the range of the buffalo, on which the neighboring Indians mainly depend for support. It would render any posts on the Lower Platte unnecessary; the ordinary communication between it and the Missouri being sufficient to control the intermediate Indians. It would operate effectually to prevent any such coalitions as are now formed among the Gros Ventres, Sioux, Cheyennes, and other Indians, and would keep the Oregon road through the valley of the Sweet Water and the South Pass of the mountains constantly open. A glance at the map[50] which accompanies this report, will show that it lies at the foot of a broken and mountainous region, along which, by the establishment of small posts, in the neighborhood of St. Vrain's fort, on the South fork of the Platte, and Bent's fort, on the Arkansas, a line of communication would be formed, by good *wagon* roads, with our southern military posts, which would entirely command the mountain passes, hold some of the most troublesome tribes in check, and protect and facilitate our intercourse with the neighboring Spanish settlements. The vallies of the rivers on which they would be situated are fertile; the country which supports immense herds of buffalo is admirably adapted to grazing, and herds of cattle might be maintained by the posts, or obtained from the Spanish country, which already supplies a portion of their provisions to the trading posts mentioned above.

Just as we were leaving the camp this morning our Indian came up, and stated his intention of not proceeding any further until he had seen the horse which I intended to give him. I felt strongly tempted to drive him out of the camp, but his presence appeared to give confidence to my men, and the interpreter thought it absolutely

---

50. See Map 2 (Map Portfolio).

necessary. I was, therefore, obliged to do what he requested, and pointed out the animal, with which he seemed satisfied, and we continued our journey. I had imagined that Mr. Bissonette's long residence had made him acquainted with the country, and, according to his advice, proceeded directly forward without attempting to regain the usual road. He afterward informed me that he had rarely ever lost sight of the fort; but the effect of the mistake was to involve us for a day or two among the hills, where, although we lost no time, we encountered an exceedingly rough road.

To the south, along our line of march to-day, the main chain of the Black or Laramie Hills[51] rises precipitatous [precipitously]. Time did not permit me to visit them, but, from comparative information, the ridge is composed of the coarse sandstone or conglomerate hereafter described. It appears to enter the region of clouds, which are arrested in their course and lie in masses along the summits. An inverted cone of black cloud (cumulus) rested during all the forenoon on the lofty peak of Laramie Mountain, which I estimated to be about two thousand feet above the fort, or six thousand five hundred above the sea. We halted to noon on the *Fourche Amère* [Cottonwood Creek], so called from being timbered principally with the *liard amère* (a species of poplar), with which the valley of the little stream is tolerably well wooded, and which, with large expansive summits, grows to the height of sixty or seventy feet.

The bed of the creek is sand and gravel, the water dispersed over the broad bed in several shallow streams. We found here, on the right bank, in the shade of the trees, a fine spring of very cold water. It will be remarked that I do not mention, in this portion of the journey, the temperature of the air, sand, springs, &c., an omission which will be explained in the course of the narrative. In my search for plants, I was well rewarded at this place.

With the change in the geological formation, on leaving Fort Laramie, the whole face of the country has entirely altered its appearance. Eastward of that meridian, the principal objects which strike the eye of a traveller are the absence of timber, and the immense expanse of prairie, covered with the verdure of rich grasses, and highly adapted for pasturage. Wherever they are not disturbed by the vicinity of man, large herds of buffalo give animation to this

---

51. The Laramie Range of the Rockies.

country. Westward of Laramie river, the region is sandy and apparently sterile; and the place of the grass is usurped by the *artemisia* and other odoriferous plants, to whose growth the sandy soil and dry air of this elevated region seem highly favorable.

One of the prominent characteristics in the face of the country is the extraordinary abundance of the *artemisias*. They grow every where, on the hills, and over the river bottoms, in tough, twisted, wiry clumps; and, wherever the beaten track was left, they rendered the progress of the carts rough and slow. As the country increased in elevation on our advance to the west, they increased in size; and the whole air is strongly impregnated and saturated with the odor of camphor and spirits of turpentine which belongs to this plant. This climate has been found very favorable to the restoration of health, particularly in cases of consumption; and possibly the respiration of air, so highly impregnated by aromatic plants, may have some influence.

Our dried meat had given out, and we began to be in want of food; but one of the hunters killed an antelope this evening, which afforded some relief, although it did not go far among so many hungry men. At 8 o'clock at night, after a march of twenty-seven miles, we reached our proposed encampment on the *Fer-à-Cheval,* or Horse Shoe creek. Here we found good grass, with a great quantity of *prêle,* which furnished good food for our tired animals. This creek is well timbered, principally with *liard amère,* and, with the exception of Deer creek, which we had not yet reached, is the largest affluent of the right bank between Laramie and the mouth of the Sweet Water.

July 23.—The present year had been one of unparalleled drought, and throughout the country the water had been almost dried up. By availing themselves of the annual rise, the traders had invariably succeeded in carrying their furs to the Missouri; but this season, as has already been mentioned, on both forks of the Platte they had entirely failed. The greater number of the springs and many of the streams which made halting places for the *voyageurs,* had been dried up. Every where the soil looked parched and burnt, the scanty yellow grass crisped under the foot, and even the hardiest plants were destroyed by want of moisture. I think it necessary to mention this fact, because to the rapid evaporation in such an elevated region, nearly 5,000 feet above the sea, almost wholly unprotected by timber, should be attributed much of the sterile appearance of the country,

in the destruction of vegetation, and the numerous saline efflorescences which covered the ground. Such I afterward found to be the
case.

I was informed that the roving villages of Indians and travellers
had never met with difficulty in finding an abundance of grass for
their horses; and now it was after great search that we were able to
find a scanty patch of grass, sufficient to keep them from sinking,
and in the course of a day or two they began to suffer very much.
We found none to-day at noon, and, in the course of our search on
the Platte, came to a grove of cottonwood, where some Indian village
had recently encamped. Boughs of the cottonwood yet green covered
the ground, which the Indians had cut down to feed their horses
upon. It is only in the winter that recourse is had to this means of
sustaining them; and their resort to it at this time was a striking
evidence of the state of the country. We followed their example, and
turned our horses into a grove of young poplars. This began to present itself as a very serious evil, for on our animals depended altogether the further prosecution of our journey.

Shortly after we had left this place, the scouts came galloping in
with the alarm of Indians. We turned in immediately toward the river,
which here had a steep high bank, where we formed with the carts a
very close barricade, resting on the river, within which the animals
were strongly hobbled and picketed. The guns were discharged and
reloaded, and men thrown forward, under cover of the bank, in the
direction by which the Indians were expected. Our interpreter, who,
with the Indian, had gone to meet them, came in in about ten
minutes, accompanied by two Sioux. They looked sulky, and we
could obtain from them only some confused information. We learned
that they belonged to the party which had been on the trail of the
emigrants, whom they had overtaken at Rock Independence, on the
Sweet Water. Here the party had disagreed, and came nigh fighting
among themselves. One portion were desirous of attacking the
whites, but the others were opposed to it; and finally they had
broken up into small bands and dispersed over the country. The
greater portion of them had gone over into the territory of the
Crows, and intended to return by way of the Wind river valley, in
the hope of being able to fall upon some small parties of Crow
Indians. The remainder were returning down the Platte in scattered
parties of ten and twenty, and those whom we had encountered belonged to those who had advocated an attack on the emigrants.

Several of the men suggested shooting them on the spot; but I promptly discountenanced any such proceeding. They further informed me that buffalo were very scarce, and little or no grass to be found. There had been no rain, and innumerable quantities of grasshoppers had destroyed the grass. This insect had been so numerous since leaving Fort Laramie, that the ground seemed alive with them; and in walking, a little moving cloud preceded our footsteps. This was bad news. No grass, no buffalo—food for neither horse nor man. I gave them some plugs of tobacco and they went off, apparently well satisfied to be clear of us; for my men did not look upon them very lovingly, and they glanced suspiciously at our warlike preparations, and the little ring of rifles which surrounded them. They were evidently in a bad humor, and shot one of their horses when they had left us a short distance.

We continued our march, and after a journey of about twenty-one miles, encamped on the Platte. During the day, I had occasionally remarked among the hills the *psoralea esculenta,* the bread root of the Indians. The Sioux use this root very extensively, and I have frequently met with it among them, cut into thin slices and dried. In the course of the evening we were visited by six Indians, who told us that a larger party was encamped a few miles above. Astronomical observations placed us in longitude 106° 03′ 40″, and latitude 42° 39′ 25″.

We made the next day twenty-two miles, and encamped on the right bank of the Platte, where a handsome meadow afforded tolerably good grass. There were the remains of an old fort here [Labonte's Camp], thrown up in some sudden emergency, and on the opposite side was a picturesque bluff of ferruginous sandstone. There was a handsome grove a little above, and scattered groups of trees bordered the river. Buffalo made their appearance this afternoon, and the hunters came in shortly after we had encamped, with three fine cows. The night was fine, and observations gave for the latitude of the camp, 42° 47′ 40″.

July 25.—We made but thirteen miles this day, and encamped about noon in a pleasant grove on the right bank. Low scaffolds were erected, upon which the meat was laid, cut up into thin strips, and small fires kindled below. Our object was to profit by the vicinity of the buffalo, to lay in a stock of provisions for ten or fifteen days. In the course of the afternoon, the hunters brought in five or six cows, and all hands were kept busily employed in pre-

237

paring the meat, to the drying of which the guard attended during the night. Our people had recovered their gaiety, and the busy figures around the blazing fires gave a picturesque air to the camp. A very serious accident occurred this morning, in the breaking of one of the barometers. These had been the object of my constant solicitude, and, as I had intended them principally for mountain service, I had used them as seldom as possible; taking them always down at night, and on the occurrence of storms, in order to lessen the chances of being broken. I was reduced to one, a standard barometer of Troughton's construction. This I determined to preserve, if possible. The latitude is 42° 51′ 35″, and by a mean of the results from chronometer and lunar distances, the adopted longitude of this camp is 106° 25′ 10″.

July 26.—Early this morning we were again in motion. We had a stock of provisions for fifteen days, carefully stored away in the carts, and this I resolved should only be encroached upon when our rifles should fail to procure us present support. I determined to reach the mountains, if it were in any way possible. In the meantime, buffalo were plenty. In six miles from our encampment, which, by way of distinction, we shall call Dried Meat camp, we crossed a handsome stream, called *La Fourche Boisée* [Box Elder Creek]. It is well timbered, and among the flowers in bloom on banks, I remarked several *asters*.

Five miles further we made our noon halt, on the banks of the Platte, in the shade of some cottonwoods. There were here, as generally now along the river, thickets of *hippophaæ,* the *grains de bœuf* of the country. They were of two kinds; one bearing a red berry, (the *shepherdia argentia* of Nuttall;) the other a yellow berry, of which the Tartars are said to make a kind of rob [rub].

By a meridian observation, the latitude of the place was 42° 50′ 08″. It was my daily practice to take observations of the sun's meridian altitude, and why they are not given, will appear in the sequel. Eight miles further we reached the mouth of Deer creek, where we encamped. Here was an abundance of rich grass, and our animals were compensated for past privations. This stream was at this time twenty feet broad, and well timbered with cottonwood of an uncommon size. It is the largest tributary of the Platte, between the mouth of the Sweet Water and the Laramie. Our astronomical observations gave for the mouth of the stream a longitude of 106° 43′ 15″, and latitude 42° 52′ 24″.

July 27.—Nothing worthy of mention occurred on this day; we travelled later than usual, having spent some time in searching for grass, crossing and recrossing the river before we could find a sufficient quantity for our animals. Toward dusk, we encamped among some artemisia bushes, two and three feet in height, where some scattered patches of short tough grass afforded a scanty supply. In crossing, we had occasion to observe that the river was frequently too deep to be forded, though we always succeeded in finding a place where the water did not enter the carts. The stream continued very clear, with two or three hundred feet breadth of water, and the sandy bed and banks were frequently covered with large round pebbles. We had travelled this day twenty-seven miles. The main chain of the Black Hills was here only about seven miles to the south, on the right bank of the river, rising abruptly to the height of eight and twelve hundred feet. Patches of green grass in the ravines on the steep sides, marked the presence of springs, and the summits were clad with pines.

July 28.—In two miles from our encampment we reached the place where the regular road crosses the Platte. There was two hundred feet breadth of water at this time in the bed, which has a variable width of eight to fifteen hundred feet. The channels were generally three feet deep, and there were large angular rocks on the bottom, which made the ford in some places a little difficult. Even at its low stages this river cannot be crossed at random, and this has always been used as the best ford. The low stage of the waters the present year had made it fordable in almost any part of its course, where access could be had to its bed.

For the satisfaction of travellers, I will endeavor to give some description of the nature of the road from Laramie to this point. The nature of the soil may be inferred from its geological formation. The limestone at the eastern limit of this section, is succeeded by limestone without fossils, a great variety of sandstone, consisting principally of red sandstone and fine conglomerates. The red sandstone is argillaceous, with compact white gypsum or alabaster, very beautiful. The other sandstones are gray, yellow, and ferruginous, sometimes very coarse. The apparent sterility of the country must therefore be sought for in other causes than the nature of the soil. The face of the country cannot with propriety be called hilly. It is a succession of long ridges, made by the numerous streams which come down from the neighboring mountain range. The ridges have an undulating surface, with some such appearance as the ocean presents in an ordinary breeze.

The road which is now generally followed through this region is, therefore, a very good one, without any difficult ascents to overcome. The principal obstructions are near the river, where the transient waters of heavy rains have made deep ravines with steep banks, which renders frequent circuits necessary. It will be remembered that wagons pass this road only once or twice a year, which is by no means sufficient to break down the stubborn roots of the innumerable artemisia bushes. A partial absence of these is often the only indication of the track, and the roughness produced by their roots in many places gives the road the character of one newly opened in a wooded country. This is usually considered the worst part of the road east of the mountains, and as it passes through an open prairie region, may be much improved, so as to avoid the greater part of the inequalities it now presents.

From the mouth of the Kanzas to the Green river valley, west of the Rocky Mountains, there is no such thing as a mountain road on the line of communication.

We continued our way, and four miles beyond the ford, Indians were discovered again, and I halted while a party were sent forward to ascertain who they were. In a short time they returned, accompanied by a number of Indians of the Oglallah band of Sioux. From them we received some interesting information. They had formed part of the great village, which they informed us had broken up, and was on its way home.[52] The greater part of the village, including the Arapahoes, Cheyennes, and Oglallahs, had crossed the Platte eight or ten miles below the mouth of the Sweet Water, and were now behind the mountains to the south of us, intending to regain the Platte by way of Deer creek. They had taken this unusual route in search of grass and game. They gave us a very discouraging picture of the country. The great drought, and the plague of grasshoppers, had swept it so, that scarce a blade of grass was to be seen, and there was not a buffalo to be found in the whole region. Their people, they further said, had been nearly starved to death, and we would find their road marked by lodges which they had thrown

52. Deleted from the end of this sentence in the manuscript draft: "in a very miserable cond."

away in order to move more rapidly, and by the carcasses of the horses which they had eaten, or which had perished by starvation. Such was the prospect before us.

When he had finished the interpretation of these things, Mr. Bissonette immediately rode up to me and urgently advised that I should entirely abandon the further prosecution of my exploration. *"Le meilleure avis que je pourrais vous donner c'est de virer de suite."* "The best advice I can give you, is to turn back at once." It was his own intention to return, as we had now reached the point to which he had engaged to attend me. In reply, I called up my men, and communicated to them fully the information I had just received. I then expressed to them my fixed determination to proceed to the end of the enterprise on which I had been sent, but as the situation of the country gave me some reason to apprehend that it might be attended with an unfortunate result to some of us, I would leave it optional with them to continue with me or to return.

Among them were some five or six who I know would remain. We had still ten days' provisions; and, should no game be found, when this stock was expended, we had our horses and mules, which we could eat when other means of subsistence failed. But not a man flinched from the undertaking. "We'll eat the mules," said Basil Lajeunesse; and thereupon we shook hands with our interpreter and his Indians, and parted. With them I sent back one of my men, Dumés, whom the effects of an old wound in the leg rendered incapable of continuing the journey on foot, and his horse seemed on the point of giving out. Having resolved to disencumber ourselves immediately of every thing not absolutely necessary to our future operations, I turned directly in toward the river, and encamped on the left bank, a little above the place where our council had been held, and where a thick grove of willows offered a suitable spot for the object I had in view.

The carts having been discharged, the covers and wheels were taken off, and, with the frames, carried into some low places among the willows, and concealed in the dense foliage in such a manner that the glitter of the iron work might not attract the observation of some straggling Indian. In the sand which had been blown up into waves among the willows, a large hole was then dug, ten feet square and six deep. In the meantime, all our effects had been spread out upon the ground, and whatever was designed to be carried along

241

with us separated and laid aside, and the remaining part carried to the hole and carefully covered up.[53] As much as possible, all traces of our proceedings were obliterated, and it wanted but a rain to render our *cache* safe beyond discovery. All the men were now set at work to arrange the pack-saddles and make up the packs.

The day was very warm and calm, and the sky entirely clear, except where, as usual along the summits of the mountainous ridge opposite, the clouds had congregated in masses. Our lodge had been planted, and, on account of the heat, the ground pins had been taken out, and the lower part slightly raised. Near to it was standing the barometer, which swung in a tripod frame; and within the lodge, where a small fire had been built, Mr. Preuss was occupied in observing the temperature of boiling water. At this instant, and without any warning until it was within fifty yards, a violent gust of wind dashed down the lodge, burying under it Mr. Preuss[54] and about a dozen men, who had attempted to keep it from being carried away. I succeeded in saving the barometer, which the lodge was carrying off with itself, but the thermometer was broken. We had no others of a high graduation, none of those which remained going higher than 135° Fahrenheit. Our astronomical observations gave to this place, which we named *Cache* camp, a longitude of 107° 15′ 55″, latitude 42° 50′ 53″.

July 29.—All our arrangements having been completed, we left the encampment at 7 o'clock this morning. In this vicinity the ordinary road leaves the Platte, and crosses over to the Sweet Water river, which it strikes near Rock Independence. Instead of following this road, I had determined to keep the immediate valley of the Platte so far as the mouth of the Sweet Water, in the expectation of finding better grass. To this I was further prompted by the nature of my instructions. To Mr. Carson was assigned the office of guide, as we had now reached a part of the country with which, or a great part of which, long residence had made him familiar. In a few miles we reached the Red Buttes,[55] a famous landmark in this

---

53. Deleted at this point in the manuscript draft, a partial sentence: "Here were deposited the harness of the mules, the greatest part of our clothing, a store of powder and lead. . . ."

54. The Preuss diary skips from 27 to 31 July, and thus we are deprived of his own caustic record of this incident.

55. Another well-known landmark on the trail to South Pass, about fifteen miles southwest of Casper, Wyo., on state highway 220.

country, whose geological composition is red sandstone, limestone, and calcareous sandstone and puddingstone.

The river here cuts its way through a ridge; on the eastern side of it are the lofty escarpments of red argillaceous sandstone, which are called the Red Buttes. In this passage the stream is not much compressed or pent up, there being a bank of considerable though variable breadth on either side. Immediately on entering we discovered a band of buffalo. The hunters failed to kill any of them, the leading hunter being thrown into a ravine, which occasioned some delay, and in the meantime the herd clambered up the steep face of the ridge. It is sometimes wonderful to see these apparently clumsy animals make their way up and down the most rugged and broken precipices. We halted to noon before we had cleared this passage at a spot twelve miles distant from *Cache* camp, where we found an abundance of grass. So far the account of the Indians was found to be false. On the banks were willow and cherry trees. The cherries were not yet ripe, but in the thickets were numerous fresh tracks of the grizzly bear, which are very fond of this fruit. The soil here is red, the composition being derived from the red sandstone. About seven miles brought us through the ridge, in which the course of the river is north and south. Here the valley opens out broadly, and high walls of the red formation present themselves among the hills to the east. We crossed here a pretty little creek, an affluent of the right bank. It is well timbered with cottonwood in this vicinity, and the absinthe [*Artemisia*] has lost its shrub-like character, and becomes small trees six and eight feet in height, and sometimes eight inches in diameter. Two or three miles above this creek we made our encampment, having travelled to-day twenty-five miles. Our animals fared well here, as there is an abundance of grass. The river bed is made up of pebbles, and in the bank at the level of the water is a conglomerate of coarse pebbles about the size of ostrich eggs, and which I remarked in the banks of the Laramie fork. It is overlaid by a soil of mixed clay and sand, six feet thick. By astronomical observations our position is in longitude 107° 29' 06", and latitude 42° 38'.

July 30.—After travelling about twelve miles this morning, we reached a place where the Indian village had crossed the river. Here were the poles of discarded lodges and skeletons of horses lying about. Mr. Carson, who had never been higher up than this point on the river, which has the character of being exceedingly rugged and walled in by precipices above, thought it advisable to camp near this place, where we were certain of obtaining grass, and to-morrow make our crossing among the rugged hills to the Sweet Water river. Accordingly we turned back and descended the river to an island near by, which was about twenty acres in size, covered with a luxuriant growth of grass. The formation here I found highly interesting. Immediately at this island the river is again shut up in the rugged hills, which come down to it from the main ridge in a succession of spurs three or four hundred feet high, and alternated with green level *prairillons* or meadows, bordered on the river banks with thickets of willow, and having many plants to interest the traveller. The island lies between two of these ridges, three or four hundred yards apart, of which that on the right bank is composed entirely of red argillaceous sandstone, with thin layers of fibrous gypsum. On the left bank, the ridge is composed entirely of siliceous puddingstone, the pebbles in the numerous strata increasing in size from the top to the bottom, where they are as large as a man's head. So far as I was able to determine, these strata incline to the northeast, with a dip of about 15°. This puddingstone or conglomerate formation I was enabled to trace through an extended range of country, from a few miles east of the meridian of Fort Laramie to where I found it superimposed on the granite of the Rocky Mountains, in longitude 109° 30′. From its appearance, the main chain of the Laramie mountain is composed of this rock; and in a number of places I found isolated hills, which served to mark a former level, which had been probably swept away.

These conglomerates are very friable and easily decomposed; and I am inclined to think this formation is the source from which was derived the great deposite of sand and gravel which forms the surface rock of the prairie country west of the Mississippi.

Crossing the ridge of red sandstone, and traversing the little prairie which lies to the southward of it, we made in the afternoon an excursion to a place which we have called the Hot Spring Gate. This place has much the appearance of a gate, by which the Platte passes through a ridge composed of a white and calcareous sandstone. The length of the passage is about four hundred yards, with a smooth green prairie on either side. Through this place, the stream flows with a quiet current, unbroken by any rapid, and is about seventy yards wide between the walls, which rise perpendicularly from the water. To that on the right bank, which is the lower, the barometer gave a height of three hundred and sixty feet. Annexed is a view of this place, which will be more particularly described hereafter, as we passed through it on our return.

We saw here numerous herds of mountain sheep, and frequently heard the volley of rattling stones which accompanied their rapid descent down the steep hills. This was the first place at which we had killed any of these animals; and, in consequence of this circumstance, and of the abundance of these sheep or goats (for they are called by each name), we gave to our encampment the name of Goat Island. Their flesh is much esteemed by the hunters, and has very much the flavor of the Allegany [*sic*] mountain sheep. I have frequently seen the horns of this animal three feet long and seventeen inches in circumference at the base, weighing eleven pounds. But two or three of these were killed by our party at this place, and of these the horns were small. The use of these horns seems to be to protect the animal's head in pitching down precipices to avoid pursuing wolves—their only safety being in places where they cannot be followed. The bones are very strong and solid, the marrow occupying but a very small portion of the bone in the leg, about the thickness of a rye straw. The hair is short, resembling the winter color of our common deer, which it nearly approaches in size and appearance. Except in the horns, it has no resemblance whatever to the goat. The longitude of this place, resulting from chronometer and lunar distances, and an occultation of ϵ Arietis, is 107° 37′ 27″, and the latitude is 42° 33′ 27″. One of our horses, which had given out, we left to receive strength on the island, intending to take her, perhaps, on our return.

July 31.—This morning we left the course of the Platte, to cross over to the Sweet Water. Our way for a few miles lay up the sandy bed of a dry creek, in which I found several interesting plants. Leaving this we wound our way to the summit of the hills, of which the peaks are here eight hundred feet above the Platte, bare and rocky. A long and gradual slope led from these hills to the Sweet Water, which we reached in fifteen miles from Goat Island. I made an early encampment here, in order to give the hunters an opportunity to procure a supply from several bands of buffalo, which made their appearance in the valley near by. The stream here is about sixty feet wide, and at this time twelve to eighteen inches deep, with a very moderate current.

The adjoining prairies are sandy; but the immediate river bottom is good soil, which afforded an abundance of soft green grass to

Hot Springs Gate

our horses, and where I found a variety of interesting plants, which made their appearance for the first time. A rain to-night made it unpleasantly cold; and there was no tree here, to enable us to pitch our single tent, the poles of which had been left at *Cache camp*. We had, therefore, no shelter except what was to be found under cover of the *absinthe* bushes, which grew in many thick patches, one or two and sometimes three feet high.

August 1.—The hunters went ahead this morning, as buffalo appeared tolerably abundant, and I was desirous to secure a small stock of provisions, and we moved about seven miles up the valley, and encamped one mile below Rock Independence. This is an isolated granite rock, about six hundred and fifty yards long, and forty in height. Except in a depression of the summit, where a little soil supports a scanty growth of shrubs, with a solitary dwarf pine, it is entirely bare. Everywhere within six or eight feet of the ground, where the surface is sufficiently smooth, and in some places sixty or eighty feet above, the rock is inscribed with the names of travellers. Many a name famous in the history of this country, and some well-known to science, are to be found mixed among those of the traders and of travellers for pleasure and curiosity, and of missionaries among the savages. Some of these have been washed away by the rain, but the greater number are still very legible.[56] The position of this rock is in longitude 107° 56', latitude 42° 29' 36". We remained at our camp of August 1st until noon of the next day, occupied in drying meat. By observation, the longitude of the place is 107° 55', latitude 42° 29' 56".

August 2.—Five miles above Rock Independence we came to a place called the Devil's Gate, where the Sweet Water cuts through the point of a granite ridge. The length of the passage is about three hundred yards, and the width thirty-five yards. The walls of rock are vertical, and about four hundred feet in height; and the stream in the gate is almost entirely choked up by masses which have fallen from above. In the wall, on the right bank, is a dike of trap rock, cutting through a fine-grained gray granite. Near the point of this ridge crop out some strata of the valley formation, consisting of a grayish micaceous sandstone, and fine-grained conglomerate, and marl. We encamped eight miles above the Devil's Gate, of which

---

56. Independence Rock, on Wyoming state highway 220, is now protected from the further carving of *graffiti* by a strong steel fence.

Devil's Gate

a view is given in the annexed plate [p. 248].[57] There was no timber of any kind on the river, but good fires were made of drift wood, aided by the *bois de vache*.

We had tonight no shelter from the rain, which commenced with squalls of wind about sunset. The country here is exceedingly picturesque. On either side of the valley, which is four or five miles broad, the mountains rise to the height of twelve and fifteen hundred, or two thousand feet. On the south side, the range appears to be timbered, and to-night is luminous with fires, probably the work of the Indians, who have just passed through the valley. On the north, broken and granite masses rise abruptly from the green sward of the river, terminating in a line of broken summits. Except in the crevices of the rock, and here and there on a ledge or bench of the mountain, where a few hardy pines have clustered together, these are perfectly bare and destitute of vegetation.

Among these masses, where there are sometimes isolated hills and ridges, green valleys open in upon the river, which sweeps the base of these mountains for thirty-six miles. Everywhere its deep verdure and profusion of beautiful flowers is in pleasing contrast with the sterile grandeur of the rock and the barrenness of the sandy plain, which, from the right bank of the river, sweeps up to the mountain range that forms its southern boundary. The great evaporation on the sandy soil of this elevated plain, and the saline efflorescences which whiten the ground, and shine like lakes reflecting the sun, make a soil wholly unfit for cultivation.

August 3.—We were early on the road the next morning, travelling along the upper part of the valley, which is overgrown with *artemisia*. Scattered about on the plain are occasional small isolated hills. One of these which I examined, about fifty feet high, consisted of white clay and marl, in nearly horizontal strata. Several bands of buffalo made their appearance to-day, with herds of antelope; and a grizzly bear—the only one we encountered during the journey—was seen scrambling up among the rocks. As we passed

---

57. The name Devil's Gate apparently was quite new. Father De Smet went to the mountains in 1840 without mentioning it, but on his second journey, in a letter dated 16 Aug. 1841, he said that "travellers have named this spot the Devil's Entrance" (quoted from ANDERSON, 182n). The appellation, Devil's Gate, came into use soon after the appearance of JCF's *Report*. The view of the formation in this edition (see p. 248) may derive from a daguerreotype, although Preuss did not think that JCF had produced any good plates when he set up his equipment here.

over a slight rise near the river, we caught the first view of the Wind River mountains, appearing at this distance of about seventy miles, to be a low and dark mountainous ridge. The view dissipated in a moment the pictures which had been created in our minds, by many descriptions of travellers, who have compared these mountains to the Alps in Switzerland; and speak of the glittering peaks which rise in icy majesty amidst the eternal glaciers nine or ten thousand feet into the region of eternal snows.[58] The nakedness of the river was relieved by groves of willows, where we encamped at night, after a march of twenty-six miles; and numerous bright-colored flowers had made the river bottom look gay as a garden. We found here a horse, which had been abandoned by the Indians, because his hoofs had been so much worn that he was unable to travel; and, during the night, a dog came into the camp.

August 4.—Our camp was at the foot of the Granite mountains, which we climbed this morning to take some barometrical heights; and here among the rocks was seen the first magpie. On our return, we saw one at the mouth of the Platte river. We left here one of our horses, which was unable to proceed farther. A few miles from the encampment we left the river, which makes a bend to the south, and traversing an undulating country, consisting of a grayish micaceous sandstone and fine-grained conglomerates, struck it again, and encamped after a journey of twenty-five miles. Astronomical observations placed us in latitude 42° 32′ 30″.

August 5.—The morning was dark, with a driving rain, and disagreeably cold. We continued our route as usual, but the weather became so bad that we were glad to avail ourselves of the shelter offered by a small island, about ten miles above our last encampment, which was covered with a dense growth of willows. There was fine grass for our animals, and the timber afforded us comfortable protection and good fires. In the afternoon the sun broke

---

58. Deleted from the manuscript draft here: "As we had been drawing nearer to the mountains, Mr. Preuss had kept constantly before his mind the moment in which he had first seen the Alps; when, turning a corner of the Jura between Basle and Tololburn, the whole ridge, from Mt. Blanc to the Tyrolese Alps, burst upon his view in the glory of a bright sunshine, and his disappointment [in seeing the Wind River Mountains] was proportionably great." In his diary entry for 4 Aug., Preuss mentions his experience in the Alps and is predictably disdainful of the Rockies. "An American has measured them to be as high as 25,000 feet. I'll be hanged if they are half as high, yea, if they are 8,000 feet high" (PREUSS, 33).

through the clouds for a short time, and the barometer at 5 P. M., was at 23.713, the thermometer at 60°, with the wind strong from the northwest. We availed ourselves of the fine weather to make excursions in the neighborhood. The river, at this place, is bordered by hills of the valley formation. They are of moderate height, one of the highest peaks on the right bank being, according to the barometer, one hundred and eighty feet above the river. On the left bank they are higher. They consist of a fine white clayey sandstone, a white calcareous sandstone, and coarse sandstone or puddingstone.

August 6.—It continued steadily raining all the day; but, notwithstanding, we left our encampment in the afternoon. Our animals had been much refreshed by their repose, and an abundance of rich, soft grass, which had been much improved by the rains. In about three miles, we reached the entrance of a *kanyon,* where the Sweet Water issues upon the more open valley we had passed over. Immediately at the entrance, and superimposed directly upon the granite are strata of compact, calcareous sandstone and chert, alternating with fine white and reddish white, and fine gray and red sandstones. These strata dip to the eastward at an angle of about 18°, and form the western limit of the sandstone and limestone formations on the line of our route. Here we entered among the primitive rocks. The usual road passes to the right of this place, but we wound, or rather scrambled, our way up the narrow valley for several hours. Wildness and disorder were the character of this scenery. The river had been swollen by the late rains, and came rushing through with an impetuous current, three or four feet deep, and generally twenty yards broad. The valley was sometimes the breadth of the stream, and sometimes opened into little green meadows, sixty yards wide, with open groves of aspen. The stream was bordered throughout with aspen, beech, and willow; and tall pines grew on the sides and summits of the crags. On both sides, the granite rocks rose precipitously to the height of three hundred and five hundred feet, terminating in jagged and broken pointed peaks; and fragments of fallen rock lay piled up at the foot of the precipices. Gneiss, mica slate, and a white granite, were among the varieties I noticed. Here were many old traces of beaver on the stream, remnants of dams, near which were lying trees, which they had cut down, one and two feet in diameter. The hills entirely shut up the river at the end of about five miles, and we turned up a ravine that led to a high prairie, which seemed to be the general level of the country. Hence, to the summit of the ridge, there is a regular and very gradual rise. Blocks of granite were piled up at the heads of the ravines, and small bare knolls of mica slate and milky quartz protruded at frequent intervals on the prairie, which was whitened in occasional spots with small salt lakes where the water had evaporated, and left the bed covered with a shining incrustation of salt. The evening was very cold, a northwest wind driving a fine rain in our faces, and at nightfall we descended to a little stream on which we encamped, about two miles from the Sweet Water. Here had recently been a very large camp of Snake and Crow Indians, and some large poles lying about afforded the means of pitching a tent, and making other places of shelter. Our fires to-night were made principally of the dry branches of the artemisia, which covered the slopes. It burns quickly, with a clear oily flame, and makes a hot fire. The hills here are composed of hard, compact mica slate, with veins of quartz.

August 7.—We left our encampment with the rising sun. As we rose from the bed of the creek, the *snow* line of the mountains stretched grandly before us, the white peaks glittering in the sun. They had been hidden in the dark weather of the last few days, and it had been *snowing* on them, while it *rained* in the plains. We crossed a ridge, and again struck the Sweet Water; here, a beautiful swift stream, with a more open valley, timbered with beech and cottonwood. It now began to lose itself in the many small forks which make its head, and we continued up the main stream until near noon, when we left it a few miles to make our noon halt on a small creek among the hills, from which the stream issues by a small opening. Within was a beautiful grassy spot, covered with an open grove of large beech trees, among which I found several plants that I had not previously seen.

The afternoon was cloudy, with squalls of rain; but the weather became fine at sunset, when we again encamped on the Sweet Water, within a few miles of the South Pass. The country, over which we have passed to-day, consists principally of the compact mica slate, which crops out on all ridges, making the uplands very rocky and slaty. In the escarpments which border the creeks, it is seen alternating with a light-colored granite, at an inclination of 45°; the beds varying in thickness from two or three feet to six or eight hundred. At a distance, the granite frequently has the appearance of irregular lumps of clay, hardened by exposure. A variety of *asters* may now be numbered among the characteristic plants, and the artemisia continues in full glory; but *cacti* have become rare, and mosses begin to dispute the hills with them. The evening was damp and unpleasant, the thermometer at 10 o'clock being at 36°, and the grass wet with a heavy dew. Our astronomical observations placed this encampment in longitude 109° 51′ 29″, and latitude 42° 27′ 15″.

Early in the morning we resumed our journey, the weather still cloudy, with occasional rain. Our general course was west, as I had determined to cross the dividing ridge by a bridle path among the broken country more immediately at the foot of the mountains, and return by the wagon road two and a half miles to the south of the point where the trail crosses.

About six miles from our encampment brought us to the summit.[59] The ascent had been so gradual that, with all the intimate knowledge possessed by Carson, who had made this country his home for seventeen years, we were obliged to watch very closely to find the place at which we had reached the culminating point. This was between two low hills, rising on either hand fifty or sixty feet. When I looked back at them, from the foot of the immediate slope on the western plain, their summits appeared to be about one hundred and twenty feet above. From the impression on my mind at this time, and subsequently on our return, I should compare the elevation which we surmounted at the pass, to the ascent of the Capitol hill from the avenue, at Washington. It is difficult for me to fix positively the breadth of this pass. From the broken ground where it commences, at the foot of the Wind River chain, the view to the southeast is over a champaign country, broken, at the distance of nineteen miles, by the Table Rock; which, with the other isolated hills in its vicinity, seems to stand on a comparative plain. This I judged to be its termination, the ridge recovering its rugged character with the Table Rock. It will be seen that it in no manner resembles the places to which the term is commonly applied—nothing of the gorge-like character and winding ascents of the Allegany [*sic*] passes in America, nothing of the Great St. Bernard and Simplon passes in Europe. Approaching it from the mouth of the Sweet Water, a sandy plain, one hundred and twenty miles long, conducts,

59. South Pass is not so much a place as an area. JCF is crossing it at the very southern extremity of the Wind River chain. Modern travelers who pull off of Wyoming state highway 220 to read the markers erected by the state, and by the National Park Service, are seven to ten miles south of his route.

by a gradual and regular ascent, to the summit, about seven thousand feet above the sea; and the traveller, without being reminded of any change by toilsome ascents, suddenly finds himself on the waters which flow to the Pacific ocean. By the route we had travelled, the distance from Fort Laramie is three hundred and twenty miles, or nine hundred and fifty from the mouth of the Kanzas.

Continuing our march, we reached, in eight miles from the pass, the Little Sandy, one of the tributaries of the Colorado, or Green river of the Gulf of California.[60] The weather had grown fine during the morning, and we remained here the rest of the day, to dry our baggage and take some astronomical observations. The stream was about forty feet wide, and two or three deep, with clear water and a full swift current, over a sandy bed. It was timbered with a growth of low, bushy and dense willows, among which were little verdant spots, which gave our animals fine grass, and where I found a number of interesting plants. Among the neighboring hills I noticed fragments of granite containing magnetic iron. Longitude of the camp was 110° 07' 46", and latitude 42° 27' 34".

August 9.—We made our noon halt today on Big Sandy, another tributary of Green river. The face of the country traversed was of a brown sand of granite materials, the *detritus* of the neighboring mountains. Strata of the milky quartz cropped out, and blocks of granite were scattered about containing magnetic iron. On Sandy creek the formation was of parti-colored sand, exhibited in escarpments fifty to eighty feet high. In the afternoon we had a severe storm of hail, and encamped at sun set on the first New Fork [East Fork River]. Within the space of a few miles, the Wind mountains supply a number of tributaries to Green river, which are all called the New Forks. Near our camp were two remarkable isolated hills, one of them sufficiently large to merit the name of mountain.[61] They are called the Two Buttes, and will serve to identify the place of our encampment, which the observations of the evening placed in longi-

60. Now JCF has left the wagon trail and struck off to the northwest, to reconnoiter the Wind River Mountains. His camp on the Little Sandy, ignoring his usually faulty astronomical observations, is probably southeast of Little Prospect Mountain.

61. But now called Fremont Butte, and located about seven miles south of Boulder Lake.

tude 110° 29′ 17″, and latitude 42° 42′ 46″. On the right bank of the stream, opposite to the large hill, the strata which are displayed consist of decomposing granite, which supplies the brown sand of which the face of the country is composed to a considerable depth.

August 10.—The air at sunrise is clear and pure, and the morning extremely cold, but beautiful. A lofty snow peak of the mountain is glittering in the first rays of the sun, which has not yet reached us. The long mountain wall to the east, rising two thousand feet abruptly from the plain, behind which we see the peaks, is still dark, and cuts clear against the glowing sky. A fog, just risen from the river, lies along the base of the mountain. A little before sunrise, the thermometer was at 35°, and at sunrise 33°. Water froze last night, and fires are very comfortable. The scenery becomes hourly more interesting and grand, and the view here is truly magnificent; but, indeed, it needs something to repay the long prairie journey of a thousand miles. The sun has just shot above the wall, and makes a magical change. The whole valley is glowing and bright, and all the mountain peaks are gleaming like silver. Though these snow mountains are not the Alps, they have their own character of grandeur and magnificence, and will doubtless find pens and pencils to do them justice. In the scene before us we feel how much wood improves a view. The pines on the mountain seemed to give it much additional beauty. I was agreeably disappointed in the character of the streams on this side of the ridge. Instead of the creeks which description had led me to expect, I find bold broad streams, with three or four feet water, and a rapid current. The fork on which we are encamped is upwards of a hundred feet wide, timbered with groves or thickets of the low willow. We were now approaching the loftiest part of the Wind River chain; and I left the valley a few miles from our encampment, intending to penetrate the mountains as far as possible with the whole party. We were soon involved in very broken ground, among long ridges covered with fragments of granite. Winding our way up a long ravine, we came unexpectedly in view of a most beautiful lake, set like a gem in the mountains. The sheet of water lay transversely across the direction we had been pursuing; and, descending the steep, rocky ridge, where it was necessary to lead our horses, we followed its banks to the southern extremity. Here a view of the utmost magnificence and grandeur burst upon our eyes. With nothing between us and their feet to lessen the effect of the whole height, a grand bed of snow-capped mountains rose before us, pile upon pile, glowing in the bright light of an August day. Immediately below them lay the lake between two ridges covered with dark pines, which swept down from the main chain to the spot where we stood. Here, where the lake glittered in the open sunlight, its banks of yellow sand and the light foliage of aspen groves contrasted well with the gloomy pines. "Never before," said Mr. Preuss, "in this country or in Europe, have I seen such magnificent, grand rocks." I was so much pleased with the beauty of the place, that I determined to make the main camp here, where our animals would find good pasturage, and explore the mountains with a small party of men. Proceeding a little further, we came suddenly upon the outlet of the lake where it found its way through a narrow passage between low hills. Dark pines which overhung the stream and masses of rock where the water foamed along, gave it much romantic beauty. Where we crossed, which was immediately at the outlet, it is two hundred and fifty feet wide, and so deep, that with difficulty we were able to ford it. Its bed was an accumulation of rocks, boulders, and broad slabs, and large angular fragments, among which the animals fell repeatedly.

The current was very swift, and the water cold and of a crystal purity. In crossing this stream, I met with a great misfortune in having my barometer broken. It was the only one; a great part of the interest of the journey for me was in the exploration of these mountains, of which so much had been said that was doubtful and contradictory; and now their snowy peaks rose majestically before me, and the only means of giving them authentically to science, the object of my anxious solicitude by night and day, was destroyed. We had brought this barometer in safety a thousand miles, and broke it almost among the snow of the mountains. The loss was felt by the whole camp—all had seen my anxiety, and aided me in preserving it; the height of these mountains, considered by the hunters and traders the highest in the whole range, had been a theme of constant discussion among them; and all had looked forward with pleasure to the moment when the instrument, which they believed to be true as the sun, should stand upon the summits, and decide their disputes. Their grief was only inferior to my own.

This lake is about three miles long, and of very irregular width, and apparently great depth, and is the head water of the third New Fork, a tributary to Green river, the Colorado of the West. On the map and in the narrative, I have called it Mountain lake.[62] I encamped on the north side, about three hundred and fifty yards from the outlet. This was the most western point at which I obtained astronomical observations, by which this place, called Bernier's encampment, is made in 110° 37' 25" west longitude from Greenwich, and latitude 42° 49' 49". The mountain peaks, as laid down, were fixed by bearings from this and other astronomical points. We had no other compass than the small ones used in sketching the country; but from an azimuth, in which one of them was used, the variation of the compass is 18° east. The correction made in our field work by the astronomical observations indicates that this is a very correct observation.

As soon as the camp was formed, I set about endeavoring to repair my barometer. As I have already said, this was a standard cistern barometer, of Troughton's construction. The glass cistern had been broken about midway; but as the instrument had been kept in a proper position, no air had found its way into the tube, the end of which had always remained covered. I had with me a number of vials of tolerably thick glass, some of which were of the same diameter as the cistern, and I spent the day slowly working on these, endeavoring to cut them of the requisite length; but as my instrument was a very rough file, I invariably broke them. A groove was cut in one of the trees, where the barometer was placed during the night, to be out of the way of any possible danger, and in the morning I commenced again. Among the powder horns in the camp, I found one which was very transparent, so that its contents could be almost as plainly seen as through glass. This I boiled, and stretched on a piece of wood to the requisite diameter, and scraped it very thin, in order to increase to the utmost its transparency. I then secured it firmly in its place on the instrument with strong glue, made from a buffalo, and filled it with mercury, properly heated. A piece of skin, which had covered one of the vials, furnished a good pocket, which was well secured with strong thread and glue, and then the brass cover was screwed to its place. The instrument was left some

---

62. In the 1845 edition of his report, JCF says he called this body of water Mountain Lake both on his map and in his narrative. None of his maps carries this legend, but judging from the description of the lake and from his position at the time, it can only be Boulder Lake—lying transversely across his route between T. 33 N. and T. 34 N. It is about seven air-line miles east of Pinedale, Wyo.

time to dry, and when I reversed it, a few hours after, I had the satisfaction to find it in perfect order; its indications being about the same as on the other side of the lake, before it had been broken. Our success in this little incident diffused pleasure throughout the camp, and we immediately set about our preparations for ascending the mountains.

As will be seen, on reference to a map, on this short mountain chain are the head waters of four great rivers of the continent; namely, the Colorado, Columbia, Missouri, and Platte rivers. It had been my design, after having ascended the mountains, to continue our route on the western side of the range, and crossing through a pass at the northwestern end of the chain, about thirty miles from our present camp, return along the eastern slope, across the heads of the Yellowstone river, and join on the line to our station of August 7, immediately at the foot of the ridge. In this way I should be enabled to include the whole chain, and its numerous waters, in my survey; but various considerations induced me, very reluctantly, to abandon this plan.

I was desirous to keep strictly within the scope of my instructions, and it would have required ten or fifteen additional days for the accomplishment of this object; our animals had become very much worn out with the length of the journey; game was very scarce; and, though it does not appear in the course of the narrative, as I have avoided dwelling upon trifling incidents not connected with the objects of this expedition, the spirits of the men had been much exhausted by the hardships and privations to which they had been subjected. Our provisions had well nigh all disappeared. Bread had been long out of the question, and of all our stock we had remaining two or three pounds of coffee, and a small quantity of macaroni, which had been husbanded with great care for the mountain expedition we were about to undertake. Our daily meal consisted of dry buffalo meat, cooked in tallow; and, as we had not dried this with Indian skill, part of it was spoiled; and what remained of good, was as hard as wood, having much the taste and appearance of so many pieces of bark. Even of this our stock was rapidly diminishing in a camp which was capable of consuming two buffaloes in every twenty-four hours. These animals had entirely disappeared, and it was not probable that we should fall in with them again until we returned to the Sweet Water.

Our arrangements for the ascent were rapidly completed; we

were in a hostile country, which rendered the greatest vigilance and circumspection necessary. The pass at the north end of the mountain was generally infested by Blackfeet, and immediately opposite was one of their forts, on the edge of a little thicket, two or three hundred feet from our encampment. We were posted in a grove of beech, on the margin of the lake, and a few hundred feet long, with a narrow *prairillon* on the inner side, bordered by the rocky ridge. In the upper end of this grove we cleared a circular space about forty feet in diameter, and with the felled timber and interwoven branches surrounded it with a breastwork five feet in height. A gap was left for a gate on the inner side, by which the animals were to be driven in and secured, while the men slept around the little work. It was half hidden by the foliage; and garrisoned by twelve resolute men, would have set at defiance any band of savages which might chance to discover them in the interval of our absence. Fifteen of the best mules, with fourteen men, were selected for the mountain party. Our provisions consisted of dried meat for two days, with our little stock of coffee and some macaroni. In addition to the barometer and a thermometer, I took with me a sextant and spy glass, and we had, of course, our compasses. In charge of the camp I left Bernier, one of my most trustworthy men, who possessed the most determined courage.

August 12.—Early in the morning we left the camp, fifteen in number, well armed of course, and mounted on our best mules. A pack animal carried our provisions, with a coffee pot and kettle, and three or four tin cups. Every man had a blanket strapped over his saddle to serve for his bed, and the instruments were carried by turns on their backs. We entered directly on rough and rocky ground; and, just after crossing the ridge, had the good fortune to shoot an antelope. We heard the roar, and had a glimpse of a waterfall as we rode along; and crossing in our way two fine streams, tributary to the Colorado, in about two hours' ride we reached the top of the first row or range of mountains. Here, again, a view of the most romantic beauty met our eyes. It seemed as if, from the vast expanse of uninteresting prairie we had passed over, nature had collected all her beauties together in one chosen place. We were overlooking a deep valley, which was entirely occupied by three lakes, and from the brink the surrounding ridges rose precipitously five hundred and a thousand feet, covered with the dark green of the balsam pine, relieved on the border of the lake with the light foliage of the aspen. They all communicated with each other, and the green of the waters, common to mountain lakes of great depth, showed that it would be impossible to cross them. The surprise manifested by our guides when these impassable obstacles suddenly barred our progress, proved that they were among the hidden treasures of the place, unknown even to the wandering trappers of the region. Descending the hill, we proceeded to make our way along the margin of the southern extremity. A narrow strip of angular fragments of rock sometimes afforded a rough pathway for our mules, but generally we rode along the shelving side, occasionally scrambling up at a considerable risk of tumbling back into the lake.

The slope was frequently 60°; the pines grew densely together, and the ground was covered with the branches and trunks of trees. The air was fragrant with the odor of the pines; and I realized this delightful morning the pleasure of breathing that mountain air which makes a constant theme of the hunter's praise, and which now made us feel as if we had all been drinking some exhilarating gas. The depths of this unexplored forest were a place to delight the heart of a botanist. There was a rich undergrowth of plants, and numerous gay-colored flowers in brilliant bloom. We reached the outlet at length, where some freshly barked willows that lay in the water showed that beaver had been recently at work. There were some small brown squirrels jumping about in the pines, and a couple of large mallard ducks swimming about in the stream.

The hills on this southern end were low, and the lake looked like a mimic sea, as the waves broke on the sandy beach in the force of a strong breeze. There was a pretty, open spot, with fine grass for our mules, and we made our noon halt on the beach, under the shade of some large hemlocks. We resumed our journey after a halt of about an hour, making our way up the ridge on the western side of the lake. In search of smoother ground, we rode a little inland; and, passing through groves of aspen, soon found ourselves again among the pines. Emerging from these, we struck the summit of the ridge above the upper end of the lake.

We had reached a very elevated point, and in the valley below, and among the hills, were a number of lakes at different levels; some two or three hundred feet above others, with which they communicated by foaming torrents. Even to our great height the roar of the cataracts came up, and we could see them leaping down in lines of snowy foam. From this scene of busy waters, we turned abruptly into the stillness of a forest, where we rode among the open bolls of the pines, over a lawn of verdant grass, having strikingly the air of cultivated grounds. This led us, after a time, among masses of rock which had no vegetable earth but in hollows and crevices, though still the pine forest continued. Toward evening, we reached a defile, or rather a hole in the mountains, entirely shut in by dark pine-covered rocks.

A small stream, with a scarcely perceptible current, flowed through a level bottom of perhaps eighty yards width, where the grass was saturated with water. Into this the mules were turned, and were neither hobbled nor picketed during the night, as the fine pasturage took away all temptation to stray; and we made our bivouac in the pines. The surrounding masses were all of granite. While supper was being prepared, I set out on an excursion in the neighborhood, accompanied by one of my men. We wandered about among the crags and ravines until dark, richly repaid for our walk by a fine collection of plants, many of them in full bloom. Ascending a peak to find the place of our camp, we saw that the little defile in which we lay communicated with the long green valley of some stream, which, here locked up in the mountains, far away to the south, found its way in a dense forest to the plains.

Looking along its upward course, it seemed to conduct, by a smooth gradual slope, directly toward the peak, which, from long consultation as we approached the mountain, we had decided to be the highest of the range. Pleased with the discovery of so fine a road for the next day, we hastened down to the camp, where we arrived just in time for supper. Our table service was rather scant, and we held the meat in our hands; and clean rocks made good plates, on which we spread our macaroni. Among all the strange places on which we had occasion to encamp during our long journey, none have left so vivid an impression on my mind as the camp of this evening. The disorder of the masses which surrounded us; the little hole through which we saw the stars overhead; the dark pines where we slept; and the rocks lit up with the glow of our fires, made a night picture of very wild beauty.

August 13.—The morning was bright and pleasant, just cool enough to make exercise agreeable, and we soon entered the defile I had seen the preceding day. It was smoothly carpeted with a soft grass, and scattered over with groups of flowers, of which yellow was the predominant color. Sometimes we were forced by an occasional difficult pass to pick our way on a narrow ledge along the side of the defile, and the mules were frequently on their knees; but these obstructions were rare, and we journeyed on in the sweet morning air, delighted at our good fortune in having found such a beautiful entrance to the mountains. This road continued for about three miles, when we suddenly reached its termination in one of the grand views which, at every turn, meet the traveller in this magnificent region. Here the defile up which we had travelled, opened out into a small lawn, where, in a little lake, the stream had its source.

There were some fine *asters* in bloom, but all the flowering plants appeared to seek the shelter of the rocks, and to be of lower growth than below, as if they loved the warmth of the soil, and kept out of the way of the winds. Immediately at our feet a precipitous descent led to a confusion of defiles, and before us rose the mountains as we have represented them in the annexed view. It is not by the splendor of far off views, which have lent such a glory to the Alps, that these impress the mind; but by a gigantic disorder of enormous masses, and a savage sublimity of naked rock, in wonderful contrast with innumerable green spots of a rich floral beauty, shut up in their stern recesses. Their wildness seems well suited to the character of the people who inhabit the country.

I determined to leave our animals here, and make the rest of our way on foot. The peak appeared so near, that there was no doubt of our returning before night, and a few men were left in charge of the mules, with our provisions and blankets. We took with us nothing but our arms and instruments, and as the day had become warm, the greater part left our coats. Having made an early dinner, we started again. We were soon involved in the most ragged precipices, nearing the central chain very slowly, and rising but little. The first ridge hid a succession of others, and when with great fatigue and difficulty we had climbed up five hundred feet, it was but to make an equal descent on the other side; all these intervening places were filled with small deep lakes, which met the eye in every direction, descending from one level to another, sometimes under bridges formed by huge fragments of granite, beneath which was heard the roar of the water. These constantly obstructed our path, forcing us to make long *détours;* frequently obliged to retrace our steps, and frequently falling among the rocks. Maxwell was precipitated toward the face of a precipice, and saved himself from going over by throwing himself flat on the ground. We clambered on, always expecting, with every ridge that we crossed, to reach the foot of the peaks, and always disappointed, until about 4 o'clock, when, pretty well worn out, we reached the shore of a little lake, in which there was a rocky island, and from which we obtained the view given in the frontispiece [p. 264]. We remained here a short time to rest, and continued on around the lake, which had in some places a beach of white sand, and in others was bound with rocks, over which the way was difficult and dangerous, as the water from innumerable springs made them very slippery.

By the time we had reached the further side of the lake, we found ourselves all exceedingly fatigued, and much to the satisfaction of the whole party, we encamped. The spot we had chosen was a broad flat rock, in some measure protected from the winds by the surrounding crags, and the trunks of fallen pines afforded us bright fires. Near by was a foaming torrent, which tumbled into the little lake about one hundred and fifty feet below us, and which, by way of distinction, we have called Island lake.[63] We had reached the upper limit of the piney region; as, above this point, no tree was to be seen, and patches of snow lay everywhere around us on the cold sides of the rocks. The flora of the region we had traversed since leaving our mules was extremely rich and, among the characteristic plants, the scarlet flowers of the *dodecatheon dentatum* everywhere met the eye in great abundance. A small green ravine, on the edge of which we were encamped, was filled with a profusion of alpine plants in brillant bloom.[64] From barometrical observations, made during our three days' sojourn at this place, its elevation above the Gulf of Mexico is 10,000 feet.[65] During the day, we had seen no sign of animal life; but among the rocks here, we heard what was supposed to

---

63. Island Lake is about eighteen air-line miles northeast of Pinedale. When the senior editor followed JCF's route in May and June 1967, he left his (JCF's) trail at Boulder Lake. BONNEY & BONNEY take up the trail here at Island Lake, but his route between those two lakes is still conjectural. The current map of the Bridger Division, Bridger National Forest, shows several trails in the area between the two lakes, the most direct passing those lakes now named George, Horseshoe, Barnes, Spruce, Chain, Polecreek, Nelson, and Seneca. Here JCF is traveling almost due north. From Island Lake to the peak which he climbs, we rely mainly on the observations of the Bonneys.

64. Added to this sentence in the manuscript draft: "among which a beautiful auricula delighted us with the associations of civilization."

65. Deleted from the end of this sentence in the manuscript draft: "We had nothing to eat tonight."

View of the Wind River Mountains

be the bleat of a young goat, which we searched for with hungry activity, and found to proceed from a small animal of a gray color, with short ears and no tail; probably the Siberian squirrel. We saw a considerable number of them, and with the exception of a small bird like a sparrow, it is the only inhabitant of this elevated part of the mountains. On our return, we saw, below this lake, large flocks of the mountain goat. We had nothing to eat to-night. Lajeunesse, with several others, took their guns, and sallied out in search of a goat; but returned unsuccessful. At sunset, the barometer stood at 20.522; the attached thermometer 50°. Here we had the misfortune to break our thermometer, having now only that attached to the barometer. I was taken ill shortly after we had encamped, and continued so until late in the night, with violent headache and vomiting. This was probably caused by the excessive fatigue I had undergone, and want of food, and perhaps also in some measure, by the rarity of the air. The night was cold, as a violent gale from the north had sprung up at sunset, which entirely blew away the heat of the fires. The cold, and our granite beds, had not been favorable to sleep, and we were glad to see the face of the sun in the morning. Not being delayed by any preparation for breakfast, we set out immediately.

On every side as we advanced was heard the roar of waters, and of a torrent, which we followed up a short distance, until it expanded into a lake about one mile in length. On the northern side of the lake was a bank of ice, or rather of snow, covered with a crust of ice. Carson had been our guide into the mountains, and agreeably to his advice, we left this little valley, and took to the ridges again; which we found extremely broken, and where we were again involved among precipices. Here were ice fields, among which we were all dispersed, seeking each the best path to ascend the peak. Mr. Preuss attempted to walk along the upper edge of one of these fields, which sloped away at an angle of about twenty degrees; but his feet slipped from under him, and he went plunging down the plane. A few hundred feet below, at the bottom, were some fragments of sharp rock, on which he landed; and though he turned a couple of somersets, fortunately received no injury beyond a few bruises. Two of the men, Clément Lambert and Descoteaux,[66] had been taken ill,

---

66. This man, called de Couteau in PREUSS, 44, does not appear in the vouchers or in JCF's roster of the party. He does appear, however, in a passage deleted from the manuscript draft (note 8, above). A man of this name took passage to St. Louis with Maximilian, Prince of Wied-Neuwied, at Fort Pierre

and laid down on the rocks a short distance below; and at this point I was attacked with headache and giddiness, accompanied by vomiting, as on the day before. Finding myself unable to proceed, I sent the barometer over to Mr. Preuss, who was in a gap two or three hundred yards distant, desiring him to reach the peak, if possible, and take an observation there.[67] He found himself unable to proceed further in that direction, and took an observation, where the barometer stood at 19.401; attached thermometer 50°, in the gap. Carson, who had gone over to him, succeeded in reaching one of the snowy summits of the main ridge, whence he saw the peak towards which all our efforts had been directed, towering eight or ten hundred feet into the air above him. In the mean time, finding myself grow rather worse than better, and doubtful how far my strength would carry me, I sent Basil Lajeunesse, with four men, back to the place where the mules had been left.

We were now better acquainted with the topography of the country, and I directed him to bring back with him, if it were in any way possible, four or five mules, with provisions and blankets. With me were Maxwell and Ayot; and after we had remained nearly an hour on the rock, it became so unpleasantly cold, though the day was bright, that we set out on our return to the camp, at which we all arrived safely, straggling in one after the other. I continued ill during the afternoon, but became better towards sundown, when my recovery was completed by the appearance of Basil and four men, all mounted. The men who had gone with him had been too much fatigued to return, and were relieved by those in charge of the horses; but in his powers of endurance Basil resembled more a mountain goat than a man. They brought blankets and provisions, and we enjoyed well our dried meat and a cup of good coffee. We rolled ourselves up in our blankets, and with our feet turned to a blazing fire, slept soundly until morning.

August 15.—It had been supposed that we had finished with the mountains; and the evening before, it had been arranged that Car-

---

in 1834, and brought a shipment of beaver skins down to Liberty, Mo. (MAXIMILIAN, 24:92–93, 117). In late 1842 or early 1843, a man referred to as Michael Des Coteaux was wounded in a fray at Long Point, sometimes called McKenzie's Point, near the mouth of the Cheyenne River (A. R. Bouis to Andrew Drips, 18 April 1843, MoSHi—Drips Papers).

67. See PREUSS, 39–45, for his own account of the climb. He is sardonic, as usual.

son should set out at daylight, and return to breakfast at the Camp of the Mules, taking with him all but four or five men, who were to stay with me and bring back the mules and instruments. Accordingly, at the break of day they set out. With Mr. Preuss and myself remained Basil Lajeunesse, Clément Lambert, Janisse, and Descoteaux. When we had secured strength for the day by a hearty breakfast, we covered what remained, which was enough for one meal, with rocks, in order that it might be safe from any marauding bird; and, saddling our mules, turned our faces once more towards the peaks. This time we determined to proceed quietly and cautiously, deliberately resolved to accomplish our object if it were within the compass of human means. We were of opinion that a long defile which lay to the left of yesterday's route would lead us to the foot of the main peak.[68] Our mules had been refreshed by the fine grass in the little ravine at the island camp, and we intended to ride up the defile as far as possible, in order to husband our strength for the main ascent. Though this was a fine passage, still it was a defile of the most rugged mountains known, and we had many a rough and steep slippery place to cross before reaching the end. In this place the sun rarely shone, snow lay along the border of the small stream which flowed through it, and occasional icy passages made the footing of the mules very insecure, and the rocks and ground were moist with the trickling waters in this spring of mighty rivers. We soon had the satisfaction to find ourselves riding along the huge wall which forms the central summits of the chain. There at last it rose by our sides, a nearly perpendicular wall of granite, terminating 2,000 to 3,000 feet above our heads in a serrated line of broken, jagged cones.[69] We rode on until we came almost immediately below the main peak, which I denominated the Snow Peak, as it exhibited more snow to the eye than any of the neighboring summits. Here were three small lakes [Titcomb Lakes] of a green color, each of perhaps a thousand yards in diameter, and apparently very deep. These lay in a kind of chasm; and, according to the barometer, we had attained but a few hundred feet above the Island lake. The barometer here stood at 20.450, attached thermometer 70°.

<hr>

68. "The climber who will leave Island Lake and start for Woodrow Wilson [Peak] can follow this route all the way up the Titcomb Valley" (BONNEY & BONNEY, 98).

69. The west wall of Fremont, Sacagawea, and Helen peaks (BONNEY & BONNEY, 98).

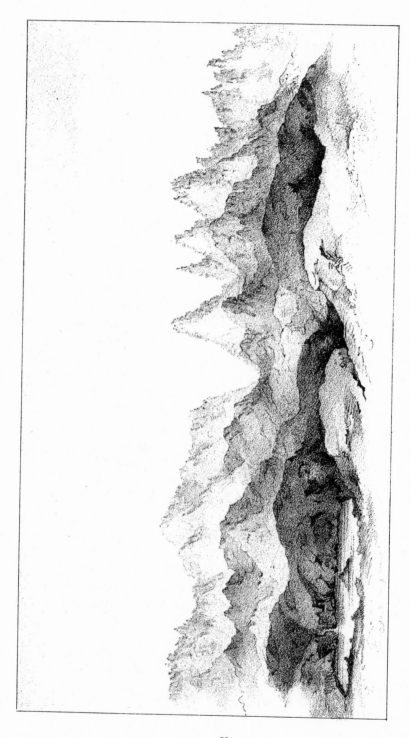

Central chain of the *Wind River Mountains*

We managed to get our mules up to a little bench about a hundred feet above the lakes, where there was a patch of good grass, and turned them loose to graze. During our rough ride to this place, they had exhibited a wonderful surefootedness. Parts of the defile were filled with angular, sharp fragments of rock, three or four and eight or ten feet cube; and among these they had worked their way, leaping from one narrow point to another, rarely making a false step, and giving us no occasion to dismount. Having divested ourselves of every unnecessary encumbrance, we commenced the ascent. This time, like experienced travellers, we did not press ourselves, but climbed leisurely, sitting down so soon as we found breath beginning to fail. At intervals we reached places where a number of springs gushed from the rocks, and about 1,800 feet above the lakes came to the snow line. From this point our progress was uninterrupted climbing. Hitherto I had worn a pair of thick moccasins, with soles of *parflêche;* but here I put on a light thin pair, which I had brought for the purpose, as now the use of our toes became necessary to a further advance. I availed myself of a sort of comb of the mountain, which stood against the wall like a buttress, and which the wind and the solar radiation, joined to the steepness of the smooth rock, had kept almost entirely free from snow. Up this I made my way rapidly. Our cautious method of advancing in the outset had spared my strength; and, with the exception of a slight disposition to headache, I felt no remains of yesterday's illness. In a few minutes we reached a point where the buttress was overhanging, and there was no other way of surmounting the difficulty than by passing around one side of it, which was the face of a vertical precipice of several hundred feet.

Putting hands and feet in the crevices between the blocks, I succeeded in getting over it, and, when I reached the top, found my companions in a small valley below. Descending to them, we continued climbing, and in a short time reached the crest. I sprang upon the summit, and another step would have precipitated me into an immense snow field five hundred feet below. To the edge of this field was a sheer icy precipice; and then, with a gradual fall, the field sloped off for about a mile, until it struck the foot of another lower ridge. I stood on a narrow crest, about three feet in width, with an inclination of about 20° N. 51° E. As soon as I had gratified the first feelings of curiosity I descended, and each man ascended in his turn, for I would only allow one at a time to mount the unstable and precarious slab, which it seemed a breath would hurl into the abyss below. We mounted the barometer in the snow of the summit, and fixing a ramrod in a crevice, unfurled the national flag to wave in the breeze where never flag waved before.[70] During our morning's ascent we had met no sign of animal life except the small sparrow-like bird already mentioned. A stillness the most profound and a terrible solitude forced themselves constantly on the mind as the great features of the place. Here on the summit, where the stillness was absolute, unbroken by any sound, and the solitude complete, we thought ourselves beyond the region of animated life; but while we were sitting on the rock a solitary bee (*bromus, the bumble bee*) came winging his flight from the eastern valley, and lit on the knee of one of the men.[71]

It was a strange place, the icy rock and the highest peak of the Rocky Mountains, for a lover of warm sunshine and flowers, and we pleased ourselves with the idea that he was the first of his species to cross the mountain barrier, a solitary pioneer to foretell the advance of civilization. I believe that a moment's thought would have made us let him continue his way unharmed, but we carried out the law of this country, where all animated nature seems at war; and seizing him immediately, put him in at least a fit place, in the leaves of a large book, among the flowers we had collected on our way. The barometer stood at 18.293, the attached thermometer at 44°, giving for the elevation of this summit 13,570 feet above the Gulf of Mexico, which may be called the highest flight of the bee. It is certainly the highest known flight of that insect. From the description given by Mackenzie[72] of the mountains where he crossed them, with that of

---

70. He is not on Fremont Peak, but probably on one farther north which the Bonneys call Woodrow Wilson Peak, just south of Gannett Peak. A party of the American Alpine Club climbed the peak in 1951, checking JCF's description of his ascent against their own observations, and concluded that he could have been on no other peak in the area. The flag, which JCF presented to Jessie upon the birth of their daughter Elizabeth, was a special variation on the usual stars and stripes. In addition to thirteen stripes and twenty-six stars, it bore an American eagle holding arrows and an Indian peace pipe in its claws. The flag is now in the Southwest Museum, Los Angeles.

71. *Bombus* species, the bumblebee.

72. Sir Alexander Mackenzie (1755?–1820) was the first explorer to cross the North American continent north of Mexico, making the trip in 1793. The French officer of whom JCF speaks may be Gabriel Franchère (1786–1863), one of the Astorians who reached the Columbia on the *Tonquin* in 1811. He

a French officer still farther to the north, and Colonel Long's measurements to the south, joined to the opinion of the oldest traders of the country, it is presumed that this is the highest peak of the Rocky Mountains.[73] The day was sunny and bright, but a slight shining mist hung over the lower plains, which interfered with our view of the surrounding country. On one side we overlooked innumerable lakes and streams, the spring of the Colorado of the Gulf of California; and on the other was the Wind River valley, where were the heads of the Yellowstone branch of the Missouri; far to the north, we just could discover the snowy heads of the *Trois Tetons,* where were the sources of the Missouri and Columbia rivers; and at the southern extremity of the ridge the peaks were plainly visible, among which were some of the springs of the Nebraska or Platte river. Around us the whole scene had one main striking feature, which was that of terrible convulsion. Parallel to its length, the ridge was split into chasms and fissures; between which rose the thin lofty walls, terminated with slender minarets and columns, which is correctly represented in the view from the camp on Island lake. According to the barometer, the little crest of the wall on which we stood was three thousand five hundred and seventy feet above that place, and two thousand seven hundred and eighty above the little lakes at the bottom, immediately at our feet. Our camp at the Two Hills (an astronomical station) bore south 3° east,[74] which, with a bearing afterward obtained from a fixed position, enabled us to locate the peak. The bearing of the *Trois Tetons* was north 50° west, and the

---

returned by land to Montreal in 1814, crossing the main range of the Rockies by way of Athabasca Pass. Franchère's journal was published in French and in several English translations, beginning in 1820. Senator Benton, in a speech on the Oregon question (*Congressional Globe,* 25 May 1846), acknowledged having read it in French, and the chances are good that JCF had seen it, perhaps in the Benton household. The mention of Major Long refers to Stephen H. Long's reconnaissance of a part of the Front Range of the Rockies in 1820.

73. An incautious statement, for the next peak to the north is higher, and so are dozens of others in the Rockies. JCF's measurement of the peak at about 13,500 feet is quite accurate, and it would have been impossible for him to detect with the eye the fact that Gannett Peak is—at 13,785 feet—considerably higher. This is especially true when Woodrow Wilson Peak is ascended by the route which JCF used, and from which it appears to tower above Gannett. At 14,431 feet, Mount Elbert in central Colorado is the highest peak in the Rockies, but there are many more which exceed 14,000 feet.

74. "This bearing checks with Woodrow Wilson, but not with Fremont Peak" (BONNEY & BONNEY, 99).

direction of the central ridge of the Wind River mountains south 39° east. The summit rock was gneiss, succeeded by syenitic gneiss. Syenite and feldspar succeeded in our descent to the snow line, where we found a feldspathic granite. I had remarked that the noise produced by the explosion of our pistols had the usual degree of loudness, but was not in the least prolonged, expiring almost instantaneously. Having now made what observations our means afforded, we proceeded to descend. We had accomplished an object of laudable ambition, and beyond the strict order of our instructions. We had climbed the loftiest peak of the Rocky Mountains, and looked down upon the snow a thousand feet below, and standing where never human foot had stood before, felt the exultation of first explorers. It was about 2 o'clock when we left the summit, and when we reached the bottom the sun had already sunk behind the wall, and the day was drawing to a close. It would have been pleasant to have lingered here and on the summit longer, but we hurried away as rapidly as the ground would permit, for it was an object to regain our party as soon as possible, not knowing what accident the next hour might bring forth.

We reached our deposit of provisions at nightfall. Here was not the inn which awaits the tired traveller on his return from Mont Blanc, or the orange groves of South America, with their refreshing juices and soft fragrant air; but we found our little *cache* of dried meat and coffee undisturbed. Though the moon was bright, the road was full of precipices, and the fatigue of the day had been great. We therefore abandoned the idea of rejoining our friends, and lay down on the rock, and, in spite of the cold, slept soundly.

August 16.—We left our encampment with the daylight. We saw on our way large flocks of the mountain goat looking down on us from the cliffs. At the crack of a rifle they would bound off among the rocks, and in a few minutes make their appearance on some lofty peak, some hundred or a thousand feet above. It is needless to attempt any further description of the country; the portion over which we travelled this morning was rough as imagination could picture it, and to us seemed equally beautiful. A concourse of lakes and rushing waters, mountains of rocks naked and destitute of vegetable earth, dells and ravines of the most exquisite beauty, all kept green and fresh by the great moisture in the air, and sown with brilliant flowers, and every where thrown around all the glory of most magnificent scenes; these constitute the features of the place, and impress themselves vividly on the mind of the traveller. It was not until 11 o'clock that we reached the place where our animals had been left, when we first attempted the mountains on foot. Near one of the still burning fires we found a piece of meat, which our friends had thrown away, and which furnished us a mouthful—a very scanty breakfast. We continued directly on, and reached our camp on the mountain lake at dusk. We found all well. Nothing had occurred to interrupt the quiet since our departure, and the fine grass and good cool water had done much to re-establish our animals. All heard with great delight the order to turn our faces homeward; and toward sundown of the 17th, we encamped again at the Two Buttes.

In the course of this afternoon's march, the barometer was broken past remedy. I regretted it, as I was desirous to compare it again with Dr. Engelman's barometers at St. Louis, to which mine were referred; but it had done its part well, and my objects were mainly fulfilled.

August 19.—We left our camp on Little Sandy river about 7 in the morning, and traversed the same sandy undulating country. The air was filled with the turpentine scent of the various *artemisias,* which are now in bloom, and numerous as they are, give much gaiety to the landscape of the plains. At 10 o'clock, we stood exactly on the divide in the pass, where the wagon road crosses, and descending immediately upon the Sweet Water, halted to take a meridian observation of the sun. The latitude was 42° 24′ 32″.

In the course of the afternoon we saw buffalo again, and at our evening halt on the Sweet Water, the roasted ribs again made their appearance around the fires, and with them, good humor and laughter, and song were restored to the camp. Our coffee had been expended, but we now made a kind of tea from the roots of the wild cherry tree.

August 23.—Yesterday evening we reached our encampment at Rock Independence, where I took some astronomical observations. Here, not unmindful of the custom of early travellers and explorers in our country, I engraved on this rock of the Far West a symbol of the Christian faith. Among the thickly inscribed names, I made on the hard granite the impression of a large cross, which I covered with a black preparation of India rubber, well calculated to resist the influence of wind and rain. It stands amidst the names of many who have long since found their way to the grave, and for whom the huge rock is a giant grave stone.

One George Weymouth was sent out to Maine by the Earl of Southampton, Lord Arundel, and others; and in the narrative of their discoveries, he says: "The next day, we ascended in our pinnace, that part of the river which lies more to the westward, carrying with us a cross—a thing never omitted by any Christian traveller—which we erected at the ultimate end of our route." This was in the year 1605, and in 1842 I obeyed the feeling of early travellers, and left the impression of the cross deeply engraved on the vast rock one thousand miles beyond the Mississippi, to which discoverers have given the national name of *Rock Independence*.[75]

In obedience to my instructions to survey the river Platte, if possible, I had determined to make an attempt at this place. The India-rubber boat was filled with air, placed in the water, and loaded with what was necessary for our operations; and I embarked with Mr. Preuss and a party of men. When we had dragged our boat for a mile or two over the sands, I abandoned the impossible undertaking, and waited for the arrival of the party, when we packed up our boat and equipage, and at 9 o'clock were again moving along on our land journey. We continued along the valley on the right bank of the Sweet Water, where the formation, as already described, consists of a grayish micaceous sandstone, and fine-grained conglomerate, and marl. We passed over a ridge which borders or constitutes the river hills of the Platte, consisting of huge blocks sixty or eighty feet cube of decomposing granite. The cement which united them was probably of easier decomposition, and has disappeared and left them isolate, and separated by small spaces. Numerous horns of the mountain goat were lying among the rocks, and in the ravines were cedars, whose trunks were of extraordinary size. From this ridge we descended to a small open plain at the mouth of the Sweet Water, which rushed with a rapid current into the Platte, here flowing along in a broad, tranquil, and apparently deep stream, which seemed, from its turbid appearance to be considerably swollen. I ob-

---

75. JCF's political opponents will later use this incident as evidence when they "charge" him with being a Roman Catholic during the presidential campaign of 1856.

tained here some astronomical observations, and the afternoon was spent in getting our boat ready for navigation the next day.[76]

August 24.—We started before sunrise, intending to breakfast at Goat island. I had directed the land party, in charge of Bernier, to proceed to this place, where they were to remain, should they find no note to apprise them of our having passed. In the event of receiving this information, they were to continue their route, passing by certain places which had been designated. Mr. Preuss accompanied me, and with us were five of my best men, viz: C. Lambert, Basil Lajeunesse, Honoré Ayot, Benoist, and Descoteaux. Here appeared no scarcity of water, and we took on board, with various instruments and baggage, provisions for ten or twelve days. We paddled down the river rapidly, for our little craft was light as a duck on the water, and the sun had been some time risen, when we heard before us a hollow roar, which we supposed to be that of a fall of which we had heard a vague rumor, but whose exact locality no one had been able to describe to us. We were approaching a ridge, through which the river passes by a place called "cañon" (pronounced *kanyon*), a Spanish word, signifying a piece of artillery, the barrel of a gun, or any kind of tube; and which, in this country, has been adopted to describe the passage of a river between perpendicular rocks of great height, which frequently approach each other so closely overhead as to form a kind of tunnel over the stream, which foams along below, half-choked up by fallen fragments. Between the mouth of the Sweet Water and Goat island, there is probably a fall of three hundred feet, and that was principally made in the cañons before us; as without them, the water was comparatively smooth. As we neared the ridge, the river made a sudden turn, and swept squarely down against one of the walls of the cañon with a great velocity and so steep a descent, that it had to the eye the appearance of an inclined plane. When we launched into this, the men jumped overboard, to check the velocity of the boat, but were soon in water up to their necks, and our boat ran on; but we succeeded in bringing her to a small point of rocks on the right, at the mouth of the cañon. Here was a kind of elevated sand beach, not many yards square, backed by the rocks, and around the point the river swept at

---

76. The confluence of the Platte and the Sweetwater is now obscured by the waters of the Pathfinder Reservoir.

a right angle. Trunks of trees deposited on jutting points twenty or thirty feet above, and other marks, showed that the water here frequently rose to a considerable height. The ridge was of the same decomposing granite already mentioned, and the water had worked the surface, in many places, into a wavy surface of ridges and holes. We ascended the rocks to reconnoitre the ground, and from the summit the passage appeared to be a continued cataract foaming over many obstructions, and broken by a number of small falls. We saw nowhere a fall answering to that which had been described to us as having twenty or twenty-five feet, but still concluded this to be the place in question, as, in the season of floods, the rush of the river against the wall would produce a great rise, and the waters reflected squarely off, would descend through the passage in a sheet of foam, having every appearance of a large fall. Eighteen years previous to this time, as I have subsequently learned from himself, Mr. Fitzpatrick, somewhere above on this river, had embarked with a valuable cargo of beaver. Unacquainted with the stream, which he believed would conduct him safely to the Missouri, he came unexpectedly into this cañon, where he was wrecked, with the total loss of his furs. It would have been a work of great time and labor to pack our baggage across the ridge, and I determined to run the cañon. We all again embarked, and at first attempted to check the way of the boat; but the water swept through with so much violence that we narrowly escaped being swamped, and were obliged to let her go in the full force of the current, and trust to the skill of the boatmen. The dangerous places in this cañon were where huge rocks had fallen from above, and hemmed in the already narrow pass of the river to an open space of three or four and five feet. These obstructions raised the water considerably above, which was sometimes precipitated over in a fall; and at other places, where this dam was too high, rushed through the contracted opening with tremendous violence. Had our boat been made of wood, in passing the narrows she would have been staved; but her elasticity preserved her unhurt from every shock, and she seemed fairly to leap over the falls.

In this way we passed three cataracts in succession, where, perhaps, a hundred feet of smooth water intervened; and finally, with a shout of pleasure at our success, issued from our tunnel into the open day beyond. We were so delighted with the performance of our boat, and so confident in her powers, that we would not have hesitated to leap a fall of ten feet with her. We put to shore for breakfast at some willows on the right bank, immediately below the mouth of the cañon; for it was now eight o'clock, and we had been working since daylight, and were all wet, fatigued, and hungry. While the men were preparing breakfast, I went out to reconnoitre. The view was very limited. The course of the river was smooth, so far as I could see; on both sides were broken hills; and but a mile or two below was another high ridge. The rock at the mouth of the cañon was still the decomposing granite, with great quantities of mica, which made a very glittering sand.

We re-embarked at 9 o'clock, and in about twenty minutes reached the next cañon. Landing on a rocky shore at its commencement, we ascended the ridge to reconnoitre. Portage was out of the question. So far as we could see, the jagged rocks pointed out the course of the cañon, on a winding line of seven or eight miles. It was simply a narrow, dark chasm in the rock; and here the perpendicular faces were much higher than in the previous pass, being at this end two to three hundred, and further down, as we afterwards ascertained, five hundred feet in vertical height. Our previous success had made us bold, and we determined again to run the cañon. Every thing was secured as firmly as possible; and, having divested ourselves of the greater part of our clothing, we pushed into the stream. To save our chronometer from accident, Mr. Preuss took it, and attempted to proceed along the shore on the masses of rock, which in places were piled up on either side; but, after he had walked about five minutes, every thing like shore disappeared, and the vertical wall came squarely down into the water. He, therefore, waited until we came up. An ugly pass lay before us. We had made fast to the stern of the boat a strong rope about fifty feet long; and three of the men clambered along among the rocks, and with this rope let her down slowly through the pass. In several places high rocks lay scattered about in the channel; and in the narrows it required all our strength and skill to avoid staving the boat on the sharp points. In one of these, the boat proved a little too broad, and stuck fast for an instant, while the water flew over us; fortunately it was but for an instant, as our united strength forced her immediately through. The water swept overboard only a sextant and a pair of saddle bags. I caught the sextant as it passed by me; but the saddlebags became the prey of the whirlpools. We reached the place where Mr. Preuss was standing, took him on board, and, with the aid of the boat, put the men with the rope on the succeeding pile of rocks. We found this passage much

277

worse than the previous one, and our position was rather a bad one. To go back was impossible; before us the cataract was a sheet of foam; and, shut up in the chasm by the rocks, which in some places seemed almost to meet overhead, the roar of the water was deafening. We pushed off again; but, after making a little distance, the force of the current became too great for the men on shore, and two of them let go the rope. Lajeunesse, the third man, hung on, and was jerked headforemost into the river from a rock above twelve feet high; and down the boat shot like an arrow, Basil following us in the rapid current, and exerting all his strength to keep in mid channel—his head only seen occasionally like a black spot in the white foam. How far we went I do not exactly know; but we succeeded in turning the boat into an eddy below. " 'Cré Dieu," said Basil Lajeunesse, as he arrived immediately after us, "Je crois bien que j'ai nagé un demi mile." He had owed his life to his skill as a swimmer; and I determined to take him and the two others on board, and trust to skill and fortune to reach the other end in safety. We placed ourselves on our knees, with the short paddles in our hands, the most skilful boatman being at the bow; and again we commenced our rapid descent. We cleared rock after rock, and shot past fall after fall, our little boat seeming to play with the cataract. We became flushed with success and familiar with the danger; and, yielding to the excitement of the occasion, broke forth together into a Canadian boat song. Singing, or rather shouting, we dashed along; and were, I believe, in the midst of the chorus, when the boat struck a concealed rock immediately at the foot of a fall, which whirled her over in an instant. Three of my men could not swim, and my first feeling was to assist them, and save some of our effects; but a sharp concussion or two convinced me that I had not yet saved myself. A few strokes brought me to an eddy, and I landed on a pile of rocks on the left side. Looking around, I saw that Mr. Preuss had gained the shore on the same side, about twenty yards below; and a little climbing and swimming soon brought him to my side. On the opposite side against the wall, lay the boat bottom up; and Lambert was in the act of saving Descoteaux, whom he had grasped by the hair, and who could not swim; "Lache pas," said he, as I afterward learned, "lache pas, cher frère." "Crains pas," was the reply, "Je m'en vais mourir avant que de te lâcher." Such was the reply of courage and generosity in this danger. For a hundred yards below, the current was covered with floating books and boxes, bales of blankets, and scattered articles of clothing; and so strong and boiling was the stream, that even our heavy instruments, which were all in cases, kept on the surface, and the sextant, circle, and the long black box of the telescope, were in view at once. For a moment, I felt somewhat disheartened. All our books; almost every record of the journey—our journals and registers of astronomical and barometrical observations—had been lost in a moment. But it was no time to indulge in regrets; and I immediately set about endeavoring to save something from the wreck. Making ourselves understood as well as possible by signs, for nothing could be heard in the roar of waters, we commenced our operations. Of every thing on board, the only article that had been saved was my double-barrelled gun, which Descoteaux had caught, and clung to with drowning tenacity. The men continued down the river on the left bank. Mr. Preuss and myself descended on the side we were on; and Lajeunesse, with a paddle in his hand, jumped on the boat alone, and continued down the cañon. She was now light, and cleared every bad place with much less difficulty. In a short time, he was joined by Lambert; and the search was continued for about a mile and a half, which was as far as the boat could proceed in the pass.

Here the walls were about five hundred feet high, and the fragments of rocks from above had choked the river into a hollow pass, but one or two feet above the surface. Through this and the interstices of the rock, the water found its way. Favored beyond our expectations, all of our registers had been recovered, with the exception of my journals, which contained the notes and incidents of travel, and topographical descriptions, a number of scattered astronomical observations, principally meridian altitudes of the sun, and our barometrical register west of Laramie. Fortunately, our other journals contained duplicates of the most important barometrical observations which had been taken in the mountains. These, with a few scattered notes, were all that had been preserved of our meteorological observations. In addition to these, we saved the circle; and these, with a few blankets, constituted every thing that had been rescued from the waters.

The day was running rapidly away, and it was necessary to reach Goat island, whither the party had preceded us before night. In this uncertain country, the traveller is so much in the power of chance, that we became somewhat uneasy in regard to them. Should anything have occurred, in the brief interval of our separation, to prevent our rejoining them, our situation would be rather a desperate one. We had not a morsel of provisions, our arms and ammunition were gone; and we were entirely at the mercy of any straggling party of savages, and not a little in danger of starvation. We therefore set out at once in two parties. Mr. Preuss and myself on the left, and the men on the opposite side of the river. Climbing out of the cañon, we found ourselves in a very broken country, where we were not yet able to recognize any locality. In the course of our descent through the cañon, the rock, which at the upper end was of the decomposing granite, changed into a varied sandstone formation. The hills and points of the ridges were covered with fragments of a yellow sandstone, of which the strata were sometimes displayed in the broken ravines which interrupted our course, and made our walk extremely fatiguing. At one point of the cañon, the red argillaceous sandstone rose in a wall of five hundred feet, surmounted by a stratum of white sandstone, and in an opposite ravine a column of red sandstone rose in form like a steeple, about one hundred and fifty feet high. The scenery was extremely picturesque, and notwithstanding our forlorn condition, we were frequently obliged to stop and admire it. Our progress was not very rapid. We had emerged from the water half naked, and on arriving at the top of the precipice, I found myself with only one moccasin. The fragments of rock made walking painful, and I was frequently obliged to stop and pull out the thorns of the *cactus,* here the prevailing plant, and with which a few minutes' walk covered the bottom of my feet. From this ridge the river emerged into a smiling prairie, and descending to the bank for water, we were joined by Benoist. The rest of the party were out of sight, having taken a more inland route. We crossed the river repeatedly, sometimes able to ford it, and sometimes swimming; climbed over the ridges of two more cañons, and towards evening reached the cut, which we here named the Hot Spring Gate. On our previous visit in July we had not entered this pass, reserving it for our descent in the boat; and when we entered it this evening, Mr. Preuss was a few hundred feet in advance. Heated with the long march, he came suddenly upon a fine bold spring, gushing from the rock, about ten feet above the river. Eager to enjoy the crystal water, he threw himself down for a hasty draught, and took a mouthful of water almost boiling hot. He said nothing to Benoist, who laid himself down to drink, but the steam from the water arrested his eagerness, and he escaped the hot draught. We had no thermometer to ascertain the temperature, but I could hold my hand in the water just long enough to count two seconds.[77] There are eight or ten of these springs, discharging themselves by streams large enough to be called runs. A loud hollow noise was heard from the rock, which I supposed to be produced by the fall of the water. The strata immediately where they issue is a fine white and calcareous sandstone, covered with an incrustation of common salt. Leaving this Thermopylae of the West, in a short walk, we reached the red ridge which has been described as lying just above Goat island. Ascending this we found some fresh tracks and a button which showed that the other men had already arrived. A shout from the man who first reached the top of the ridge, responded to from below, informed us that our friends were all on the island, and we were soon among them. We found some pieces of buffalo standing around the fire for us, and managed to get some dry clothes among the people. A sudden storm of rain drove us into the best shelter we could find, where we slept soundly, after one of the most fatiguing days I have ever experienced.

August 25.—Early this morning Lajeunesse was sent to the wreck for the articles which had been saved, and about noon we left the island. The mare which we had left here in July had much improved in condition, and she served us well again for some time, but was finally abandoned at a subsequent part of the journey. At 10 in the morning of the 26th we reached Cache camp, where we found every thing undisturbed. We disinterred our deposit, arranged our carts which had been left here on the way out, and travelling a few miles in the afternoon, encamped for the night at the ford of the Platte.

August 27.—At midday we halted at the place where we had taken dinner on the 27th of July. The country, which when we passed up looked as if the hard winter frosts had passed over it, had now assumed a new face, so much of vernal freshness had been given to it by the late rains. The Platte was exceedingly low, a mere line of water among the sand bars. We reached Laramie fort on the

---

77. "About one mile above Goat Island I found a hot spring under the rocks through which the Platte breaks its course. When I noticed it, I was pleased at the chance of enjoying a clear cold drink; the water of the Platte is always turbid. But how quickly did I withdraw my mouth! I did not tell Benoit, who followed me; why should he not burn his lips a little, too?" (PREUSS, 57).

last day of August, after an absence of forty-two days, and had the pleasure to find our friends all well. The fortieth day had been fixed for our return, and the quick eyes of the Indians, who were on the lookout for us, discovered our flag as we wound among the hills. The fort saluted us with repeated discharges of its single piece, which we returned with scattered volleys of our small arms, and felt the joy of a home reception in getting back to this remote station, which seemed so far off as we went out.

On the morning of the 3d of September we bade adieu to our kind friends at the fort, and continued our homeward journey down the Platte, which was glorious with the autumnal splendor of innumerable flowers in full and brilliant bloom. On the warm sands, among the *helianthi* [sunflower], one of the characteristic plants, we saw great numbers of rattlesnakes, of which five or six were killed in the morning's ride. We occupied ourselves in improving our previous survey of the river; and, as the weather was fine, astronomical observations were generally made at night and at noon.

We halted for a short time in the afternoon of the 5th with a village of Sioux Indians, some of whose chiefs we had met at Laramie. The water in the Platte was extremely low; in many places the large expanse of sands, with some occasional stunted trees on the banks, gave it the air of the seacoast, the bed of the river being merely a succession of sandbars, among which the channel was divided into rivulets a few inches deep.[78] We crossed and recrossed with our carts repeatedly and at our pleasure, and whenever an obstruction barred our way, in the shape of precipitous bluffs that came down upon the river, we turned directly into it, and made our way along the sandy bed, with no other inconvenience than the frequent quicksands, which greatly fatigued our animals. Disinterring on the way the *cache* which had been made by our party when they

---

78. During this dull retracing of the outward trail, Preuss made an assessment of their trip: "What has *he* really done. . . . He has established some latitudes and two longitudes—that is all. Collecting plants and minerals is good and praiseworthy, but it is not part of the commission. If he had returned south via the Arkansas, or north via the [Big] Horn and the Yellowstone, we could make an entirely different map. . . . He cannot quite manage the sextant which is left . . ." (PREUSS, 65). But after he reaches Grand Island, JCF will be covering new ground, at least for him, and probably doing as much justice to his commission as if he were striking out into other territory. He is also laboring within a time schedule which Preuss does not fully understand.

ascended the river, we reached without accident, on the evening of the 12th of September, our old encampment of the 2d of July, at the junction of the forks. Our *cache* of the barrel of pork was found undisturbed, and proved a seasonable addition to our stock of provisions. At this place I had determined to make another attempt to descend the Platte by water, and accordingly spent two days in the construction of a bull boat. Men were sent out on the evening of our arrival, the necessary number of bulls killed, and their skins brought to the camp. Four of the best of them were strongly sewed together with buffalo sinew, and stretched over a basket frame of willow. The seams were then covered with ashes and tallow, and the boat left exposed to the sun for the greater part of one day, which was sufficient to dry and contract the skin, and make the whole work solid and strong. It had a rounded bow, was eight feet long and five broad, and drew with four men about four inches water. On the morning of the 15th we embarked in our hide boat, Mr. Preuss and myself, with two men. We dragged her over the sands for three or four miles, and then left her on a bar, and abandoned entirely all further attempts to navigate this river. The names given by the Indians are always remarkably appropriate; and certainly none was ever more so than that which they have given to this stream, "the Nebraska, or Shallow river." Walking steadily the remainder of the day, a little before dark we overtook our people at their evening camp, about twenty-one miles below the junction. The next morning we crossed the Platte, and continued our way down the river bottom on the left bank, where we found an excellent, plainly beaten road.

On the 18th we reached Grand island, which is fifty-two miles long, with an average breadth of one mile and three quarters. It has on it some small eminences, and is sufficiently elevated to be secure from the annual floods of the river. As has been already remarked, it is well timbered, with an excellent soil, and recommends itself to notice as the best point for a military position on the Lower Platte.

On the 22d we arrived at the village of the Grand Pawnees, on the right bank of the river, about thirty miles above the mouth of the Loup fork. They were gathering in their corn, and we obtained from them a very welcome supply of vegetables.

The morning of the 24th we reached the Loup fork of the Platte. At the place where we forded it, this stream was four hundred and thirty yards broad, with a swift current of *clear* water, in this respect differing from the Platte, which has a yellow muddy color, derived from the limestone and marl formation, of which we have previously spoken. The ford was difficult, as the water was so deep that it came into the body of the carts, and we reached the opposite bank after repeated attempts, ascending and descending the bed of the river in order to avail ourselves of the bars. We encamped on the left bank of the fork, in the point of land at its junction with the Platte. During the two days that we remained here for astronomical observations, the bad weather permitted us to obtain but one good observation for the latitude, a meridian latitude of the sun, which gave for the latitude of the mouth of the Loup fork, 41° 22′ 11″.

Five or six days previously, I had sent forward C. Lambert, with two men, to Bellevue, with directions to ask from Mr. P. Sarpy, the gentleman in charge of the American Company's establishment at that place, the aid of his carpenters in constructing a boat, in which I proposed to descend the Missouri. On the afternoon of the 27th we met one of the men,[79] who had been despatched by Mr. Sarpy with a welcome supply of provisions and a very kind note, which gave us the very gratifying intelligence that our boat was in rapid progress. On the evening of the 30th we encamped in an almost impenetrable undergrowth on the left bank of the Platte, in the point of land at its confluence with the Missouri, three hundred and fifteen miles, according to our reckoning, from the junction of the forks, and five hundred and twenty from Fort Laramie.[80]

From the junction we had found the bed of the Platte occupied with numerous islands, many of them very large, and all well timbered; possessing, as well as the bottom lands of the river, a very excellent soil. With the exception of some scattered groves on the banks, the bottoms are generally without timber. A portion of these consist of low grounds, covered with a profusion of fine grasses, and are probably inundated in the spring; the remaining part is high river prairie, entirely beyond the influence of the floods. The breadth of the river is usually three quarters of a mile, except where it is enlarged by islands. That portion of its course which is occupied by Grand island has an average breadth, from shore to shore,

---

79. Menard, according to PREUSS, 75.

80. JCF is now at the future site of Plattsmouth, Nebr., and the cowbells he will hear tomorrow morning will be sounding from settlements in what is now Mills County, Iowa.

of two and a half miles. The breadth of the valley, with the various accidents of ground—springs, timber, and whatever I have thought interesting to travellers and settlers—you will find indicated on the larger map which accompanies this report.[81]

October 1.—I rose this morning long before daylight, and heard with a feeling of pleasure the tinkling of cow bells at the settlements on the opposite side of the Missouri. Early in the day we reached Mr. Sarpy's residence; and, in the security and comfort of his hospitable mansion, felt the pleasure of being again within the pale of civilization. We found our boat on the stocks; a few days sufficed to complete her; and, in the afternoon of the 4th, we embarked on the Missouri. All our equipage, horses, carts, and the *materiel* of the camp, had been sold at public auction at Bellevue. The strength of my party enabled me to man the boat with ten oars, relieved every hour; and we descended rapidly. Early on the morning of the 10th, we halted to make some astronomical observations at the mouth of the Kanzas, exactly four months since we had left the trading post of Mr. Cyprian Chouteau, on the same river, ten miles above. On our descent to this place, we had employed ourselves in surveying and sketching the Missouri, making astronomical observations regularly at night and at midday, whenever the weather permitted. These operations on the river were continued until our arrival at the city of St. Louis, Missouri, on the 17th; and will be found, imbodied with other results, on the map[82] and in the appendices which accompany this report. At St. Louis, the sale of our remaining effects was made; and, leaving that city by steamboat on the 18th, I had the honor to report to you at the city of Washington on the 29th of October.

Very respectfully, sir, your obedient servant,

J. C. FREMONT,
2d Lieut. Corps of Topographical Engineers.

---

81. See Map 2 (Map Portfolio).
82. *Ibid.*

CATALOGUE OF PLANTS COLLECTED
BY LIEUTENANT FREMONT IN HIS EXPEDITION
TO THE ROCKY MOUNTAINS.
BY JOHN TORREY.

PREFACE.[83]

The collection of plants submitted to me for examination, though made under unfavorable circumstances, is a very interesting contribution to North American Botany. From the mouth of the Kanzas river to the "Red Buttes" on the North fork of the Platte, the transportation was effected in carts; but from that place to and from the mountains, the explorations were made on horseback, and by such rapid movements, (which were necessary, in order to accomplish the objects of the expedition) that but little opportunity was afforded for collecting and drying botanical specimens. Besides, the party was in a savage and inhospitable country, sometimes annoyed by Indians, and frequently in great distress from want of provisions; from which circumstances, and the many pressing duties that constantly engaged the attention of the commander, he was not able to make so large a collection as he desired. To give some general idea of the country explored by Lieut. Fremont, I recapitulate, from his report, a brief sketch of his route. The expedition left the mouth of the Kanzas on the 10th of June, 1842, and proceeding up that river about one hundred miles, then continued its course generally along the "bottoms" of the Kanzas tributaries, but sometimes passing over the upper prairies. The soil of the river bottoms is always rich, and generally well timbered; though the whole region is what is called a prairie country. The upper prairies are an immense deposite of sand and gravel, covered with a good, and, very generally, a rich soil. Along the road, on reaching the little stream called Sandy creek (a tributary of the Kanzas), the soil became

---

83. Torrey's catalogue is printed verbatim, after his preface, using his own binomials and common names. For modern binomials and, usually, common names, consult the index under each species.

more sandy. The rock-formations of this region are limestone and sandstone. The *Amorpha canescens* was the characteristic plant; it being in many places as abundant as the grass.

Crossing over from the waters of the Kanzas, Lieut. F. arrived at the Great Platte, two hundred and ten miles from its junction with the Missouri. The valley of this river, from its mouth to the great forks, is about four miles broad, and three hundred and fifteen miles long. It is rich, well-timbered, and covered with luxuriant grasses. The purple *Liatris scariosa,* and several *Asters,* were here conspicuous features of the vegetation. I was pleased to recognise among the specimens collected near the forks, the fine large-flowered Asclepias, that I described many years ago in my account of James's Rocky Mountain plants, under the name of *A. speciosa,* and which Mr. Geyer also found in Nicollet's expedition. It seems to be the plant subsequently described and figured by Sir W. Hooker, under the name of *A. Douglasii.* On the Lower Platte, and all the way to the Sweet Water, the showy *Cleome integrifolia* occurred in abundance. From the Forks to Laramie river, a distance of about two hundred miles, the country may be called a sandy one. The valley of the North fork is without timber; but the grasses are fine, and the herbaceous plants abundant. On the return of the expedition in September, Lieut. Fremont says the whole country resembled a vast garden; but the prevailing plants were two or three species of *Helianthus* (sunflower). Between the main forks of the Platte, from the junction, as high up as Laramie's fork, the formation consisted of marl, a soft earthy limestone, and a granite sandstone. At the latter place, that singular leguminous plant, the *Kentrophyta montana* of Nuttall was first seen, and then occurred, at intervals, to the Sweet Water river. Following up the North fork, Lieut. Fremont arrived at the mouth of the Sweet Water river, one of the head waters of the Platte. Above Laramie's fork to this place, the soil is generally sandy. The rocks consist of limestone, with a variety of sandstones (yellow, gray, and red argillaceous), with compact gypsum or alabaster, and fine conglomerates.

The route along the North fork of the Platte afforded some of the best plants in the collection. The *Senecio rapifolia,* Nutt., occurred in many places, quite to the Sweet Water; *Lippia (Zapania) cuneifolia* (Torr. in James's plants, only known before from Dr. [Edwin] James's collection;) *Cercocarpus parvifolius,* Nutt.; *Erio-*

gonum parvifolium and *cœspitosum,* Nutt.; *Shepherdia argentea,* Nutt., and *Geranium Fremontii,*[84] a new species (near the Red Buttes), were found in this part of the journey. In saline soils, on the Upper Platte, near the mouth of the Sweet Water, were collected several interesting CHENOPODIACEÆ, one of which was first discovered by Dr. James, in Long's Expedition; and although it was considered as a new genus, I did not describe it, owing to the want of the ripe fruit. It is the plant doubtfully referred by Hooker, in his Flora Boreali Americana, to Batis. He had seen the male flowers only. As it is certainly a new genus, I have dedicated it to the excellent commander of the expedition, as a well-merited compliment for the services he has rendered North American botany.

The Sweet Water valley is a sandy plain, about one hundred and twenty miles long, and generally about five miles broad; bounded by ranges of granitic mountains, between which, the valley formation consists, near the Devil's gate, of a grayish micaceous sandstone, with marl and white clay. At the encampment of August 5th–6th, there occurred a fine white argillaceous sandstone, a coarse sandstone or puddingstone, and a white calcareous sandstone. A few miles to the west of that position, Lieut. F. reached a point where the sandstone rested immediately upon the granite, which thenceforward, along his line of route, alternated with a compact mica slate.

Along the Sweet Water, many interesting plants were collected, as may be seen by an examination of the catalogue; I would, however, mention the curious *Œnothera Nuttallii,* Torr. and Gr.; *Eurotia lanata,* Mocq. (Diotis lanata, *Pursh*), which seems to be distinct from *E. ceratoides; Thermopsis montana,* Nutt.; *Gilia pulchella,* Dougl.; *Senecio spartioides,* Torr. and Gr.; a new species, and four or five species of wild currants (*Ribes irriguum,* Dougl., &c.) Near the mouth of the Sweet Water was found the *Plantago eriophora,*

---

84. *Geranium fremontii* as published by Torrey was a *nomen nudum,* and thus illegitimate by International Rules of Botanical Nomenclature. When the name was validated by Asa Gray in *Memoirs* of the American Academy, ser. 2, 4 (1849):26, a Frémont collection numbered "42" was cited without locality. G. N. and F. F. Jones (*Rhodora,* 45 [1943]:44) suggested when reviewing the genus that the Frémont specimen came from "probably farther north and west" of Lieut. J. W. Abert's collection, also cited by Gray, taken in the Raton Mountains, New Mexico, 7 Aug. 1846. However, this report (p. 292) gives the "Black Hills" as the source of Frémont's collection and so there may have been a second numbered specimen sent to Gray.

Torr., a species first described in my Dr. James's Rocky Mountain Plants. On the upper part, and near the dividing ridge, were collected several species of *Castilleja; Pentstemon micrantha,* Nutt.; several *Gentians;* the pretty little *Androsace occidentalis,* Nutt.; *Solidago incana,* Torr. and Gr.; and two species of *Eriogonum,* one of which was new.

On the 8th of August, the exploring party crossed the dividing ridge or pass, and found the soil of the plains at the foot of the mountains, on the western side, to be sandy. From Laramie's fork to this point, different species of artemisia were the prevailing and characteristic plants; occupying the place of the grasses, and filling the air with the odor of camphor and turpentine. Along Little Sandy, a tributary of the Colorado of the West, were collected a new species of *Phaca* (*P. digitata*), and *Parnassia fimbriata.*

On the morning of the 10th of August, they entered the defiles of the Wind River mountains, a spur of the Rocky Mountains or Northern Andes, and among which they spent about eight days. On the borders of a lake, embosomed in one of the defiles, were collected *Sedum Rhodiola,* DC. (which had been found before, south of Kotzebue's sound, only by Dr. James); *Senecio hydrophilus,* Nutt.; *Vaccinium uliginosum; Betula glandulosa,* and *B. occidentalis,* Hook.; *Eleagnus argentea,* and *Shepherdia Canadensis.* Some of the higher peaks of the Wind River mountains rise 1,000 feet above the limits of perpetual snow. Lieut. Fremont, attended by four of his men, ascended one of the loftiest peaks on the 15th of August. On this he found the snow line 12,500 feet above the level of the sea. The vegetation of the mountains is truly Alpine, embracing a considerable number of species common to both hemispheres, as well as some that are peculiar to North America. Of the former, Lieut. Fremont collected *Phleum alpinum; Oxyria reniformis; Veronica alpina;* several species of *Salix; Carex atrata; C. panicea;* and, immediately below the line of perpetual congelation, *Silene acaulis* and *Polemonium cœruleum,* β Hook. Among the alpine plants peculiar to the western hemisphere, there were found *Oreophila myrtifolia,* Nutt.; *Aquilegia cœrulea,* Torr.; *Pedicularis surrecta,* Benth.; *Pulmonaria ciliata,* James; *Silene Drummondii,* Hook.; *Menziesia empetriformis, Potentilla gracilis,* Dougl.; several species of *Pinus; Frasera speciosa,* Hook.; *Dodecatheon dentatum,* Hook.; *Phlox muscoides,* Nutt.; *Senecio Fremontii,* n. sp., Torr. and Gr.; four or five *Asters,* and *Vaccinium myrtilloides,* Mx.; the last seven or eight very near the snow line. Lower down the mountain were found *Arnica angustifolia,* Vahl; *Senecio triangularis,* Hook.; *S. subnudus,* DC.; *Macrorhynchus troximoides,* Torr. and Gr.; *Helianthella uniflora,* Torr. and Gr.; and *Linosyris viscidiflora,* Hook.

The expedition left the Wind River mountains about the 18th of August, returning by the same route as that by which it ascended, except that it continued its course through the whole length of the Lower Platte, arriving at its junction with the Missouri on the 1st of October.

As the plants of Lieut. Fremont were under examination while the last part of the Flora of North America was in the press, nearly all the new matter relating to the Compositæ was inserted in that work. Descriptions of a few of the new species were necessarily omitted, owing to the report of the expedition having been called for by Congress before I could finish the necessary analyses and comparisons. These, however, will be inserted in the successive numbers of the work to which I have just alluded.

JOHN TORREY.

NEW YORK, *March*, 1843.

CATALOGUE OF PLANTS

CLASS I.—EXOGENOUS PLANTS.

RANUNCULACEÆ.

Clematis Virginiana (Linn.) Valley of the Platte. June, July.
Ranunculus sceleratus (Linn.) Valley of the Sweet Water river. August 18–20.
R. Cymbalaria (Pursh). Upper Platte. July 31, August.
Aquilegia cœrulea (Torr.) Wind river mountains. August 13–16.
Actæa rubra (Bigel.) Upper Platte. August 26–31.
Thalictrum Cornuti (Linn.) Platte.
T. megacarpum, n. sp. Upper Platte. August 26–31.

MENISPERMACEÆ.

Menispermum Canadense (Linn.) Leaves only. On the Platte.

BERBERIDACEÆ.

Berberis Aquifolium (Torr. and Gr.) Wind River mountains. August 13–16.

PAPAVERACEÆ.

Argemone Mexicana β albiflora (DC.) Forks of the Platte. July 2.

CRUCIFERÆ.

Nasturtium palustre (DC.) Black Hills of the Platte. July 26–August.

Erysimum cheiranthoides (Linn.) Black Hills. July 23.

E. asperum (Nutt.) South fork of the Platte. July 4.

Pachypodium (Thelypodium, Endl. gen., p. 876), integrifolium (Nutt.) North fork of the Platte. September 4. *Var.* with longer pods. With the preceding.

Vesicaria didymocarpa (Hook.) Leaves only. North fork of the Platte, above the Red Buttes, July 30.

Braya n. sp. Wind River mountains, near the limits of perpetual snow. August 15.

Lepidium ruderale (Linn.) On the Platte. June 29.

CAPPARIDACEÆ.

Cleome integrifolia (Torr. and Gr.) From the Lower Platte nearly to the mountains. June 29, July 2, August 21.

Polanisia trachysperma, β (Torr. and Gr.) Black Hills of the Platte, July 23.

POLYGALACEÆ.

Polygala alba (Nutt.) P. Beyrichii, (Torr. and Gr.) Forks of the Platte. July 2.

DROSERACEÆ.

Parnassia fimbriata (Banks.) Little Sandy creek, defiles of the Wind River mountains. Aug. 8.

CARYOPHYLLACEÆ.

Arenaria congesta (Nutt.) Highest parts of the Wind River mountains. Aug. 13–16.
Silene Drummondii (Hook.) With the preceding.
S. acaulis (Linn.) Wind River mountains, at the limits of perpetual snow.

PORTULACACEÆ.

Talinum parviflorum (Nutt.) Little Blue river of the Kansas. June 26.

LINACEÆ.

Linum rigidum (Pursh). North fork of the Platte. July 8.
L. perenne (Linn.) Black Hills to the Sweet Water of the Platte. Aug. 2–31.

GERANIACEÆ.

Geranium Fremontii, n. sp. Black Hills. Aug. 26–31.

OXALIDACEÆ.

Oxalis stricta (Linn.) On the Kansas. June.

ANACARDIACEÆ.

Rhus trilobata (Nutt.) Red Buttes. July 29.

MALVACEÆ.

Malva pedata (Torr. and Gr.) Big Blue river of the Kansas. June 21.

M. involucrata (Torr. and Gr.) Little Blue river of the Kansas. June 23.

Sida coccinea (DC.) Little Blue river to the South fork of the Platte. June 22–July 4.

VITACEÆ.

Vitis riparia (Michx.) Grand island of the Platte. Sept. 19.

ACERACEÆ.

Negundo aceroides (Mœnch.) On the lower part of the Platte.

CELASTRACEÆ.

Oreophila myrtifolia (Nutt.) Summit of the Wind River mountains. Aug. 13–14.

RHAMNACEÆ.

Ceanothus velutinus (Dougl.) With the preceding.

C. Americanus, var. sanguineus. C. sanguineus (Pursh). On the Platte.

C. mollissimus, n. sp. Near the Kansas river. June 19.

LEGUMINOSÆ.

Lathyrus linearis (Nutt.) On the Platte, from its confluence with the Missouri, to Fort Laramie. Sept. 2–30.

Amphicarpœa monoica (Torr. and Gr.) North fork of the Platte. Sept. 4.

Apios tuberosa (Mœnch.) Forks of the Platte. Sept. 13.

Glycyrrhiza lepidota (Pursh). From near the Kansas river to the Black Hills of the Platte. June 21–July 25.

Psoralea floribunda (Nutt.) Forks of the Platte. July 2.

P. campestris (Nutt.?) and a more glabrous variety. With the preceding. July 2.

P. lanceolata (Pursh). Black Hills of the Platte. July 24.

P. argophylla (Pursh). Little Blue river. June 23.

P. tenuiflora, (Pursh). (no flowers). Forks of the Platte. Sept. 12.

Petalostemon violaceum (Michx.) Big Blue river of the Kansas, &c. June 21.

P. candidum (Michx.) Red Buttes. July 29.

Amorpha fruticosa (Linn.) From the Lower Platte to the mountains. August 8–Sept. 19.

A. canescens (Nutt.) Kansas and the Lower Platte rivers. June 19–Sept. 20.

Lespedeza capitata (Michx.) Mouth of the Platte. Sept. 30.

Desmodium acuminatum (DC.) Little Blue river of the Kansas. June 22.

Astragalus gracilis (Nutt.) Forks of the Platte. July 2.

A. mollissimus (Torr.) Valley of the Platte. June 29.

A. Hypoglottis (Linn.) Sweet Water of the Platte. Aug. 5.

Oxytropis Lambertii (Pursh). Big Blue river of the Kansas to the forks of the Platte. June 20–July 2.

O. Plattensis (Nutt.?) (no flowers). Goat island of the Upper Platte. July 31.

Phaca astragalina (DC.) Highest summits of the Wind River mountain. Aug. 15.

P. elegans (Hook.) var.? Goat island of the Upper Platte. July 31.

P. (Orophaca) digitata, n. sp. Little Sandy river. Aug. 8.

P. longifolia (Nutt.) (leaves only). Wind River mountains. Aug. 12–17.

Kentrophyta montana (Nutt.) Laramie river to the Sweet Water. July 14–Aug. 5.

Lupinus leucophyllus (Lindl.) Wind River mountains, and Sweet Water of the Platte. Aug. 4–21.

L. ornatus (Dougl.) L. leucopsis (Agardh.) With the preceding.

Baptisia leucantha, (Torr. and Gr.) Kansas river.

Thermopsis montana (Nutt.) Sweet Water river. Aug. 5.

Cassia chamaecrista (Linn.) Mouth of the Platte. Sept 30.

Schrankia uncinata (Willd.) Kansas and Platte rivers. June 19–Sept.

Darlingtonia brachypoda (DC.) On the Platte. Sept. 17.

ROSACEÆ.

Cerasus Virginiana (Torr. and Gr.) Upper North Fork of the Platte. July 30.

Cercocarpus parvifolius (Nutt.) Bitter creek, North Fork of the Platte. July 22.

Purshia tridentata (DC.) Sweet Water river, &c. Aug. 12–Sept.

Geum Virginianum (Linn.) Kansas river. June 20.

Sibbaldia procumbens (Linn.) Wind River mountains, near perpetual snow. Aug. 13–14.

Potentilla gracilis (Dougl.) With the preceding.

P. diversifolia (Lehm.) Sweet Water of the Platte to the mountains. Aug. 4–15.

P. sericea β. glabrata (Lehm.) With the preceding.

P. fruticosa (Linn.) With the preceding.

P. Anserina (Linn.) Black Hills of the Platte. July 26–31.

P. arguta (Pursh). Little Blue river of the Kansas, and Black Hills of the Platte. June 23–Aug. 28.

Rubus strigosus (Michx.) Defiles of the Wind River mountains. Aug. 12–17.

Amelanchier diversifolia, var. alnifolia, (Torr. and Gr.) Sweet Water of the Platte. August 5.

Rosa blanda (Ait.) Lower Platte.

R. foliolosa (Nutt.) var. leiocarpa. With the preceding.

ONAGRACEÆ.

Epilobium coloratum (Muhl.) Black Hills of the Platte to the Sweet Water river. Aug. 4–31.

E. spicatum (Lam.) From the Red Buttes to the Wind River mountains. Aug. 13–31.

Œnothera albicaulis (Nutt.) North fork of the Platte. July 14.

Œ. Missouriensis (Sims.) Big Blue river of the Kansas. June 19–20.

Œ. trichocalyx (Nutt.) North fork of the Platte. July 30.

Œ. serrulata (Nutt.) On the Kansas and Platte. June–July 14.

Œ. rhombipetala (Nutt.) On the Platte. September 18–20.

Œ. biennis (Linn.) Black Hills to the Sweet Water river. July 23–August 4.

Œ. (Taraxia) Nuttallii (Torr. and Gr.) Upper part of the Sweet Water.

Œ. speciosa (Nutt.) Big Blue river of the Kanzas. June 19–20.

Œ. Drummondii (Hook.?) Black Hills. July 26.

Gaura coccinea (Nutt.) Var.? Little Blue river of the Kanzas, and south fork of the Platte. June 26–July 4.

LOASACEÆ.

Mentzelia nuda (Torr. and Gr.) North fork of the Platte. July 14.

GROSSULACEÆ.

Ribes cereum (Lindl.) Sweet Water of the Platte. August 2–4.

R. lacustre (Poir.) With the preceding. *β.* leaves deeply lobed. R. echinatum (Dougl.) Perhaps a distinct species.

R. irriguum (Dougl.) With the preceding.

CACTACEÆ.

Opuntia Missouriensis (DC.) Forks of the Platte. July 2.

CRASSULACEÆ.

Sedum Rhodiola (DC.) On a lake in Wind River mountains. August 12–17.

UMBELLIFERÆ.

Heracleum lanatum (Michx.?) Leaves only. The leaves are more glabrous than in the ordinary form of the plant. Alpine region of the Wind River mountains.

Polytœnia Nuttallii (DC.) On the Kanzas. June 20.

Sium? incisum, n. sp. Stem sulcate; segments of the leaves distant, deeply incised or pinnatified; the lower teeth or divisions often elongated and linear.—North fork of the Platte. July 12.

Edosmia Gairdneri (Torr. and Gr.) Without fruit.

Cicuta maculata (Linn.) Lower Platte.

Musenium tenuifolium (Nutt.) Alpine region of the Wind River mountains.

CORNACEÆ.

Cornus stolonifera (Michx.) On a lake in the Wind River mountains. August 12–17.

C. circinata (L'Her.) On the Platte.

CAPRIFOLIACEÆ.

Symphoricarpus occidentalis (R. Brown). North fork of the Platte. July 10–Aug. 31.

S. vulgaris (Michx.) Defiles of the Wind River mountains. August 13–14.

RUBIACEÆ.

Galium boreale (Linn.) Upper part of the north fork of the Platte. August 12–31.

COMPOSITÆ.

Vernonia fasciculata (Michx.) On the Platte.

Liatris scariosa (Willd.) Lower part of the Platte. Sept. 27.

L. spicata (Willd.) North fork of the Platte. Sept. 4.

L. squarrosa, var. *intermedia* (DC.) A small form of the plant. On the Platte.

L. punctata (Hook.) Black Hills of the Platte. Aug. 29.

Brickellia grandiflora (Nutt.) North fork of the Platte.

Aster integrifolius (Nutt.) Base of the Wind River mountains.

A. adscendens (Lindl.) Wind River Mountains. Var. Fremontii. With the preceding, the highest summits to the limits of perpetual snow. Aug. 16.

A. laevis (Linn.) North fork of the Platte.

A. Novi-Belgii (Linn.) Sweet Water of the Platte. August 22.

A. cordifolius (Linn.) Lower Platte.

A. multiflorus, β. (Torr. and Gr.) Upper Platte, &c.

A. falcatus (Lindl.) Black Hills to the Sweet Water. July 30–Aug.

A. laxifolius (Nees.) On the Platte, from its mouth to the forks. Sept. 12–30.

A. oblongifolius (Nutt.) Lower Platte, &c.

A. Novæ-Angliæ (Linn.) Lower Platte to the Wind River mountains. Aug. 18–Sept. 24.

A. Andinus (Nutt.) Near the snow line of the Wind River mountains. Aug. 16.

A. glacialis (Nutt.) With the preceding.

A. salsuginosus (Richards.) With the preceding.

A. elegans (Torr. and Gr.) Wind River mountains.

A. glaucus (Torr. and Gr.) With the preceding.

Dieteria viscosa (Nutt.) On the Platte.

D. coronopifolia (Nutt.) With the preceding.

D. pulverulenta (Nutt.) Near D. sessiliflora. With the preceding.

Erigeron Canadense (Linn.) On the Platte, from near its mouth to the Red Buttes. Latter part of September to July 30.

E. Bellidiastrum (Nutt.) On the Platte.

E. macranthum (Nutt.) With the preceding.

E. glabellum (Nutt.) With the preceding.

E. strigosum (Muhl.) With the preceding.

Gutierrezia Euthamiæ (Torr. and Gr.) Laramie river, upper north fork of the Platte. Sept. 3.

Solidago rigida (Linn.) North fork of the Platte.

S. Missouriensis (Nutt.) Fort Laramie, north fork of the Platte. July 22, to the mountains.

S. speciosa (Nutt.) Upper Platte.

S. Virga-aurea (Linn.) var. multiradiata, (Torr. and Gr.) Wind River mountain, from the height of 7,000 feet to perpetual snow.

S. incana (Torr. and Gr.) Sweet Water river.

S. gigantea (Linn.) var. β. From the Platte to the mountains.

Linosyris graveolens (Torr. and Gr.) Sweet Water river. Aug. 20.

L. viscidiflora (Hook.) Upper Platte.

Aplopappus spinulosus (DC.) Fort Laramie, north fork of the Platte. Sept. 3.

Grindelia squarrosa (Dunal). Upper north fork of the Platte, and on the Sweet Water. July 22–Aug. 21.

Chrysopsis hispida (Hook.) On the Platte.

C. mollis (Nutt.) With the preceding. Too near *C. foliosa,* (Nutt.)

Iva axillaris (Pursh). Sweet Water river. Aug. 3.

Franseria discolor (Nutt.) Near the Wind River mountains.

Lepachys columnaris (Torr. and Gr.) Little Blue river of the Kansas. June 26.

Balsamorrhiza sagittata (Nutt.) Wind River mountains.

Helianthus petiolaris (Nutt.) Black Hills of the Platte. July 26.

H. Maximiliani (Schrad.) With the preceding.

Helianthella uniflora (Torr. and Gr.) Wind River mountains.

Coreopsis tinctoria (Nutt.) On the Platte.

Cosmidium gracile (Torr. and Gr.) Upper Platte.

Bidens connata (Muhl.) With the preceding.

Hymenopappus corymbosus (Torr. and Gr.) With the preceding.

Actinella grandiflora (Torr. and Gr.) n. sp. Wind River mountains.

Achillea Millefolium (Linn.) A. lanosa. (Nutt.) Upper Platte to the mountains.

Artemisia biennis (Willd.) On the Platte.

A. cana (Pursh). Without flowers. With the preceding.

A. tridentata (Nutt.) On the Sweet Water, near the mountains.

A. filifolia (Torr.) South fork of the Platte, and north fork, to Laramie river. July 4–Sept. 3.

A. Canadensis (Michx.) With the preceding.

A. Ludoviciana, (Nutt.) Black Hills of the Platte. July 26.

A. frigida (Willd.) Black Hills to the mountains.

A. Lewisii (Torr. and Gr.?) No flowers. On the Platte.

Stephanomeria runcinata (Nutt.) Upper Platte.

Gnaphalium uliginosum. (Linn.) Var. foliis angustioribus. Sweet Water river.

G. palustre (Nutt.) β. (Torr. and Gr.) With the preceding.

Arnica angustifolia (Vahl.) A. fulgens, (Pursh). Defiles of the Wind River mountains, from 7,000 feet and upwards. August 13–14.

Senecio triangularis (Hook.) β. (Torr. and Gr.) With the preceding.

S. subnudus (DC.) With the preceding.

S. Fremontii (Torr. and Gr.) n. sp. Highest parts of the mountains, to the region of perpetual snow. Aug. 15.

S. rapifolius (Nutt.) North fork of the Platte and Sweet Water.

S. lanceolatus (Torr. and Gr.) n. sp. With the preceding.

S. hydrophilus (Nutt.) On a lake in the Wind River mountains. Aug. 12–17.

S. spartioides (Torr. and Gr.) n. sp. Sweet Water river. Aug. 21.

Cacalia tuberosa (Nutt.) Upper Platte.

S. filifolius (Nutt.) β. Fremontii, (Torr. and Gr.) Lower Platte.

Tetradymia inermis (Nutt.) Sweet Water river, from its mouth to the highest parts of the Wind River mountains.

Cirsium altissimum (Spreng.) Lower Platte.

Crepis glauca (Hook.) Upper Platte.

Macrorhynchus (*Stylopappus*) *troximoides* (Torr. and Gr.) Defiles of the Wind River mountains. Aug. 13–14.

Mulgedium pulchellum (Torr. and Gr.) Black Hills of the Platte. July 25–31.

Lygodesmia juncea (Don). Upper Platte.

Troximon parviflorum (Nutt.) Sweet Water river, near the mountains.

LOBELIACEÆ.

Lobelia spicata (Lam.) On the Lower Platte. June 28.

L. siphilitica (Linn.) North fork of the Platte. Sept. 4.

CAMPANULACEÆ.

Campanula rotundifolia (Linn.) Lower Platte.

Specularia amplexicaulis (DC.) Little Blue river of the Kansas.

ERICACEÆ.

Phyllodoce empetriformis (D. Don). Defiles of the Wind River mountains. Aug. 13–16.

Vaccinium myrtilloides (Hook.) Wind River mountains, in the vicinity of perpetual snow. Aug. 15.

V. uliginosum (Linn.) With the preceding.

Artostaphylos Uva-ursi (Spreng.) On a lake in the mountains. Aug. 12–17.

PRIMULACEÆ.

Dodecatheon dentatum (Hook.) Defiles of the Wind River mountains. Aug. 13–16.

Androsace occidentalis (Nutt.) Sweet Water river. Aug. 5.

Lysimachia ciliata (Linn.) Forks of the Platte. July 2.

Glaux maritima (Linn.) Upper North fork of the Platte. July 31.

SCROPHULARIACEÆ.

Orthocarpus luteus (Nutt.) Sweet Water river. Aug. 5.

Mimulus alsinoides (Benth.) Defiles of the Wind River mountains. Aug. 13–16.

M. Lewisii (Pursh). With the preceding.

Castilleja pallida (Kunth). Sweet Water river. Aug. 8.

C. miniata (Benth.) Wind River mountains. Aug. 13–16. There are two or three other species of this genus in the collection, which I have not been able to determine.

Veronica alpina β. (Hook.) Alpine region of the Wind River mountains.

Pentstemon albidum (Nutt.) Forks of the Platte. July 2.

P. cæruleum (Nutt.) South fork of the Platte. July 4.

P. micranthum (Nutt.) Sources of the Sweet Water, near the mountains. Aug. 7.

Pedicularis surrecta (Benth.) Defiles of the Wind River mountains. Aug. 13–16.

Gerardia longifolia (Nutt.) Lower Platte. July 22.

OROBANCHACEÆ.

Orobanche fasciculata (Nutt.) South fork of the Platte. July 4.

LABIATÆ.

Monarda fistulosa (Linn.) On the Platte.

Teucrium Canadense (Linn.) With the preceding.

Lycopus sinuatus (Ell.) With the preceding.

Stachys aspera (Michx.) Forks of the Platte. July 2.

Scutellaria galericulata (Linn.) North of the Platte. July 10.

Mentha Canadensis (Linn.) With the preceding.

Salvia azurea (Lam.) Kansas river and forks of the Platte. June 19–29, July 2.

VERBENACEÆ.

Lippia cuneifolia, Zapania cuneifolia (Torr.! in ann. Lyc. Nat. Hist. N. York, 2. p. 234.) N. fork of the Platte. July 12.

Verbena stricta (Vent.) With the preceding.
V. hastata (Linn.) With the preceding.
V. bracteata (Michx.) With the preceding.

BORAGINACEÆ.

Pulmonaria ciliata (James; Torr. in ann. Lyc. N. York, 2. p. 224.)
   Defiles in the Wind River mountains. Aug. 13–15.
Onosmodium molle (Michx.) On the Platte. June 29.
Batschia Gmelini (Michx.) Little Blue river of the Kansas. June 22.
Myosotis glomerata (Nutt.) Forks of the Platte. July 2.

HYDROPHYLLACEÆ.

Eutoca sericea (Lehm.) Wind River mountains!
Phacelia leucophylla, n. sp. White plant strigosely canescent; leaves
   elliptical, petiolate entire; racemes numerous, scorpioid, densely
   flowered.—Goat Island, upper North fork of the Platte. July 30.
   Perennial.—Stems branching from the base. Leaves about two
   inches long, and 6–8 lines wide; radical and lower cauline ones on
   long petioles; the others nearly sessile. Spikes forming a terminal
   crowded sort of panicle. Flowers sessile, about 3 lines long. Sepals
   strongly hispid. Corolla one-third longer than the calyx; the lobes
   short and entire. Stamens much exserted; filaments glabrous. Style
   2-parted to the middle, the lower part hairy. Ovary hispid, incom-
   pletely 2-celled, with 2 ovules in each cell. Capsule, by abortion,
   one-seeded; seed oblong, strongly punctate. Nearly related to P.
   integrifolia (Torr.); but differs in the leaves being perfectly entire,
   the more numerous spikes, one-seeded capsules, as well as in the
   whitish strigose pubescence of the whole plant.

POLEMONIACEÆ.

Phlox muscoides (Nutt.) Immediately below the region of perpetual
   snow, on the Wind River mountains. Aug. 15.
P. Hoodii (Richards.) North fork of the Platte. July 8.
P. pilosa (Nutt.) Big Blue river of the Kansas. June 20.

Polemonium cæruleum (Linn., Hook.) Red Buttes on the Upper N. fork of the Platte. β humile (Hook.) Highest parts of the mountains, near perpetual snow. Aug. 13–15.

Gilia (*Cantua*) *longiflora* (Torr.) Sand Hills of the Platte. Sept. 16.

G. pulchella (Dougl.) Upper part of the Sweet Water, near the mountains. Aug. 7–20.

G. inconspicua (Dougl.?) Goat Island, upper N. fork of the Platte. July 30. This differs from the Oregon plant in its fleshy, simply pinnatifid leaves, with ovate, obtuse segments.

CONVOLVULACEÆ.

Calystegia sepium (R. Br.) Forks of the Platte. July 2.

Ipomœa leptophylla, n. sp. Stems branching from the base, prostrate, glabrous, angular; leaves lanceolate-linear, very acute, entire, attenuate at the base into a petiole; peduncles 1–3-flowered; sepals roundish-ovate, obtuse with a minute mucro.—Forks of the Platte to Laramie river. July 4–Sept. 3. Imperfect specimens of this plant were collected about the sources of the Canadian, by Dr. James, in Long's expedition; but they were not described in my account of his plants. The root, according to Dr. James, is annual, producing numerous thick prostrate, but not twining, stems, which are two feet or more in length. The leaves are from two to four inches long, acute at each end, strongly veined and somewhat coriaceous. Peduncles an inch or more in length, those towards the extremity of the branches only 1-flowered; the lower ones bearing 2–3, and sometimes 4 flowers, which are nearly the size of those of Calystegia sepium, and of a purplish color. Sepals appressed, about five lines long. Corolla campanulate—funnel form, the tube much longer than the calyx. Stamens inserted near the base of the corolla; filaments villous at the base, anthers oblong-linear, large. Style as long as the stamens; stigma 2-lobed; the lobes capitate. Ovary 2-celled, with two ovules in each cell.

SOLANACEÆ.

Nycterium luteum (Donn cat.) South fork of the Platte. July 4.

Physalis pubescens (Willd.) Upper North fork of the Platte. July 23.
P. pumila (Nutt.) With the preceding.

GENTIANACEÆ.

Gentiana arctophila β densiflora (Griseb.? in Hook. fl. Bor.—Am. 2. p. 61.) Sweet Water of the Platte. Aug. 4.

G. affinis (Griseb.) North fork of the Platte. Sept. 9.

G. Pneumonanthe (Linn.) Laramie river to Little Sandy creek in the mountains. July 12–Aug. 8.

G. Fremontii, n. sp. Stem branched at the base; branches 1-flowered; leaves ovate, cuspidate, cartilaginous on the margin, erect; corolla funnel-form; plicæ small, slightly 2-toothed; capsule ovate, at length entirely exserted on its thick stipe.—Wind River mountains.— Annual. Branches several, 2–3 inches long, of nearly equal length. Leaves about three lines long, with a strong whitish cartilaginous border, shorter than the internodes. Flowers as large as those of G. prostrata, pentamerous. Calyx two-thirds the length of the corolla; the teeth about one-third the length of the tube. Plicæ of the coralla scarcely one-third as long as the lanceolate lobes. Stamens included; anthers oblong, somewhat cordate at the base. Capsule in maturity, and after dehiscence (in which state all our specimens were collected), exserted quite beyond the corolla, and, with its long stipe, resembling a style with a large bilamellate stigma. None of the capsules contained any seeds. This species is nearly related to *G. prostrata* (Haenk.) and *G. humilis* (Stev.), but the former has spatulate obtuse recurved leaves, and the latter entire plicæ, which are nearly the length of the corrolla. In *G. humilis,* and in the allied *G. squarrosa* (Ledeb.) the capsule is exserted after discharging the seeds.

Swertia perennis, β obtusa (Hook.) From Laramie river to the Big Buttes.

Frasera speciosa, (Hook.) Defiles of the Wind River mountains. Aug. 13–14.

Lisianthus Russelianus (Hook.) Lower Platte to the Forks. July– Sept.

APOCYNACEÆ.

Apocynum cannabinum (Linn.) On the Platte.

ASCLEPIADACEÆ.

Asclepias speciosa (Torr., in ann. Lyc. N. York, 2. p. 218.—A. Douglasii, Hook. fl. Bor.—Am. 2 p. 53. t. 142.) Forks of the Platte. July 2. Collected also by Mr. Nicollet in his Northwestern expedition. Hooker's plant differs in no essential characters from my A. speciosa, collected by Dr. James in Long's first expedition.

A. verticillata (Linn.) Small variety. With the preceding.

A. tuberosa (Linn.) Kansas river. June 19.

Anantherix viridis (Nutt.) Big Blue river of the Kansas. June 20.

Acerates longifolia (Ell.) Polyotus longifolia. (Nutt.) With the preceding.

A. angustifolius. Polyotus angustifolius. (Nutt.) With the preceding.

OLEACEÆ.

Fraxinus platycarpa (Michx.) Leaves only. Lower Platte.

PLANTAGINACEÆ.

Plantago eriopoda (Torr. in ann. Lyc. N. York, 2, p. 237.) Mouth of the Sweet Water. July 31.

P. gnaphaloides (Nutt.) Little Blue river of the Kansas. June 24.

CHENOPODIACEÆ.

Chenopodium zosterifolium (Hook.) Platte?

C. Album (Linn.) North fork of the Platte. July 12.

Olione canescens (Mocq. Chenop. p. 74.) Atriplex canescens. (Nutt.) Upper north fork of the Platte. July 26.

Cycloloma platyphylla (Mocq. 1. c. p. 18.) Kochia dentata, (Willd.) North fork of the Platte. Sept. 4.

Sueda maritima (Mocq. 1. c. p. 127.) With the preceding.

Eurotia lanata (Mocq. 1. c. p. 81.) *Diotis lanata,* (Pursh). Red Buttes to the mountains. Aug. 18–25.

Fremontia, n. gen. Flowers diclinous, monœcious &? dioicous, heteromorphous. Stam. Fl. in terminal aments. Scales eccentrically peltate, on a short stipe, angular, somewhat cuspidate upward. Stamens 2–3–4 under each scale, naked, sessile; anthers oblong.

Pist. Fl. solitary, axillary. Perigonium closely adhering to the lower half of the ovary, the border entire, nearly obsolete, but in fruit enlarging into a broad horizontal angular and undulate wing. Ovary ovate; styles thick, divaricate; stigmas linear. Fruit a utricle, the lower two-thirds covered with the indurated calyx, compressed. Seed vertical; integument double. Embryo flat-spiral (2–3 turns) green; radicle inferior; albumen none.

F. vermicularis. Batis? vermicularis, (Hook.) Fl. Bor. Amer. 2. p. 128. Upper north fork of the Platte, near the mouth of the Sweet Water. July 30. A low, glabrous, diffusely branched shrub, clothed with a whitish bark. Leaves alternate, linear, fleshy and almost semiterete, 6–12 lines long and 1–2 lines wide. Staminate aments about three-fourths of an inch long, cylindrical, at first dense, and composed of closely compacted angular scales, covering naked anthers. Anthers very deciduous. Fertile flowers in the axils of the rameal leaves. Calyx closely adherent, and at first with only an obscure border or limb, but at length forming a wing 3–4 lines in diameter, resembling that of Salsola. This remarkable plant, which I dedicate to Lieutenant Fremont, was first collected by Dr. James about the sources of the Canadian, (in Long's expedition) but it was omitted in my account of his plants, published in the Annals of the Lyceum of Natural History. It is undoubtedly the Batis? vermicularis of Hooker, (1. c.) collected on the barren grounds of the Oregon river by the late Mr. Douglas, who found it with only the staminate flowers. We have it now from a third locality, so that the plant must be widely diffused in the barren regions towards the Rocky Mountains. It belongs to the sub-order Spirolobeæ of Meyer and Mocquin, but can hardly be referred to either the tribe Suædinæ or to Salsolæ, differing from both in its diclinous heteromorphous flowers, and also from the latter in its flat-spiral, not cochleate embryo.

NYCTAGINACEÆ.

Oxybaphus nyctaginea (Torr. in James' Rocky mountain plants.) = Calymenia nyctaginea (Nutt.) Kansas river, June 20.
Abronia mellifera (Dougl.) North fork of the Platte, July 7–12.
A. (Tripterocalyx) micranthum, n. sp. Viscid and glandularly pubescent; leaves ovate, undulate, obtuse, acute at the base, petiolate;

perianth funnel form, 4-lobed at the summit, 3–4 androus; achenium broadly 3-winged.—Near the mouth of the Sweet Water river. Aug. 1. Annual. Stem diffusely branched from the base, beginning to flower when only an inch high; the branches of the mature plant above a foot long. Leaves 1–1½ inch in length; petioles about as long as the lamina. Heads axillary. Involucre 5-leaved, 8–14-flowered; leaflets ovate, acuminate. Perianth colored (purplish) 3–4 lines long; lobes semi-ovate, obtuse. Stamens inserted in the middle of the tube, unequal; anthers ovate, sagittate at the base. Ovary oblong, clothed with the 3-winged base of the calyx; style filiform; stigma filiform-clavate, incurved. Mature achenium about 7 lines long and 4 wide, the wings broad, nearly equal, membranaceous and strongly reticulated. Seed oblong. Embryo conduplicate, involving the deeply 2-parted mealy albumen; radicle linear-terete; inner cotyledon abortive! outer one oblong, foliaceous, concave, as long as the radicle. This interesting plant differs from its congeners in its funnel-form perianth, 3–4 androus flowers, and broadly 3-winged fruit, but I have not been able to compare it critically with other species of Abronia. It may prove to be a distinct genus.

POLYGONACEÆ.

Polygonum Persicaria (Linn.) North fork of the Platte. Sept. 4.

P. aviculare (Linn.) With the preceding.

P. amphibium (Linn.) Sweet Water river. August 4.

P. viviparum (Linn.) Black Hills. July 26.

Rumex salicifolius (Weinn.) With the preceding.

Oxyria reniformis (Hill.) Alpine region of the Wind River mountains. August 13–16.

Eriogonum ovalifolium (Nutt.) Horse-shoe creek, upper north fork of the Platte. July 22.

E. cæspitosum (Nutt.) With the preceding.

E. umbellatum (Torr.) in ann. Lyc. Nat. Hist. N. York, 2, p. 241. Sweet Water river, Aug. 7.

E. Fremontii, n. sp. With the preceding.

E. annuum (Nutt.) North fork of the Platte. September 4.

ELEAGNACEÆ.

Shepherdia argentea (Nutt.) *"Grains de bœuf."* Upper north fork of the Platte, from the Red Buttes to the mouth of the Sweet Water. Aug. 24–28.

S. Canadensis (Nutt.) On a lake in the Wind River mountains. August 12–17.

Eleagnus argenteus (Pursh). With the preceding.

EUPHORBIACEÆ.

Euphorbia marginata (Pursh). Forks of the Platte. September 11.

E. polygonifolia (Linn). South Fork of the Platte. July 4.

E. corollata (Linn.) On the Kanzas.

E. obtusata (Pursh). Little Blue river of the Kanzas. July 23.

Pilinophytum capitatum (Klotsch in Weigem. arch. Apr. 1842.) Croton capitatum (Michx.) Forks of the Platte.

Hendecandra? (Esch.) *multiflora,* n. sp.; annual canescent, with stellate pubescence, diœcious; stem somewhat diffusely and trichotomously branched; leaves ovate-oblong, petiolate, obtuse, entire; staminate flowers on crowded axillary and terminal compound spikes.—Laramie river, north fork of the Platte. Sept. 3–11.—About a foot high. Fructiferous plant unknown. With larger leaves. Forks of the Platte. July 2. This seems to be the same as the plant of Drummond's Texan Collection, III., No. 266.

SALICIACEÆ.

Salix longifolia (Willd.) On the Platte.

S. Muhlenbergii (Willd.) With the preceding. Several other species exist in the collection—some from the Platte, others from the mountains; but I have had no time to determine them satisfactorily.

Populus tremuloides (Michx.) Lake in the Wind River mountains.

P. angustifolia (Torr. in ann. Lyc. N. Hist. of New York, 2, p. 249.) Sweet Water river. Aug. 21.

P. monilifera (Ait.) Lower Platte.

ULMACEÆ.

Ulmus fulva (Michx.) Lower Platte.
Celtis crassifolia (Nutt.) With the preceding.

BETULACEÆ.

Betula glandulosa (Michx.) On a lake in the Wind River mountains.
Aug. 12–17.
B. occidentalis (Hook.) With the preceding.

CONIFERÆ.

Pinus rigida (Linn.) Lower Platte. Without cones. Leaves in threes,
about 3 inches long.
P. undetermined. Defiles of the Wind River mountains. Aug. 13–14.
Between P. Strobus and P. Lambertiana. Leaves in 5's, $1\frac{1}{2}$–2 inches
long, rigid. No cones.
P. (*Abies*) *alba* (Michx.) With the preceding.
P. near *Balsamea*. With the preceding. Leaves only.
Juniperus Virginiana (Linn.) Lower Platte.

ENDOGENOUS PLANTS.

ALISMACEÆ.

Sagittaria sagittifolia (Linn.) On the Kansas.

ORCHIDACEÆ.

Platanthera leucophæa (Lindl.) Black Hills. July 27.
P. hyperborea (R. Br.) Laramie river to the Red Buttes. Aug. 26–31.
Spiranthes cernua (Rich.) Sweet Water river. Aug. 7.
Aplectrum hyemale (Nutt.) On the Platte. June 29.

IRIDACEÆ.

Sisyrinchium anceps (Linn.) North fork of the Platte. July 12.
Iris Missouriensis (Nutt. in Jour. Acad. Phil. 7, p. 58.) In fruit.

Sweet Water river. Aug. 3. Rhizoma very thick. Leaves narrow, rigid, as long as the scape. Scape nearly naked, 2-flowered, terete, 10 inches high. Capsules oblong obtusely triangular. Flowers not seen.

LILIACEÆ.

Yucca angustifolia (Sims). Laramie river. July 14.
Allium reticulatum (Fras.) Defiles in the Wind River mountains. Aug. 12–17.
Smilacina stellata (Desf.) From the Laramie river to the Red Buttes. Aug. 26–31.

MELANTHACEÆ.

Zigadenus glaucus (Nutt.) Sweet Water river. Aug.

JUNCACEÆ.

Juncus echinatus (Muhl.) North fork of the Platte. Sept. 4.

COMMELYNACEÆ.

Tradescantia Virginica (Linn.) and a narrow-leaved variety. Kansas and Platte.

CYPERACEÆ.

Carex festucacea (Schk.) On the Kansas. June.
C. aurea (Nutt.) Little Blue river of the Kansas. June 22.
C. panicea (Linn.) Alpine region of the Wind River mountains, near perpetual snow. Aug. 15.
C. atrata (Linn.) With the preceding.

GRAMINEÆ.

Spartina cynosuroides, (Willd.) Little Blue river of the Kansas. June 22.

Aristida pallens, (Pursh). On the Platte. June 29.

Agrostis Michauxiana (Trin.) Little Blue river of the Kansas. June 23.

Phleum alpinum, (Linn.) Alpine region of the Wind River mountains. Aug. 13–14.

Bromus ciliatus (Linn.) On the Platte. June–Aug.

Festuca ovina (Linn.) Alpine region of the Wind River mountains. Aug. 13–14.

Festuca nutans, (Willd.) On the Kansas.

Poa laxa (Haenke.) With the preceding.

P. crocata (Michx.?) With the preceding. Spikelets 2-flowered.

P. nervata (Willd.) On the Kansas.

Koeleria cristata (Pers.) Big Blue river of the Kansas, and on the Platte as high as Laramie river. June 20–July 22.

Deschampsia cæspitosa, (Beauv.) Alpine region of the Wind River mountains. Aug. 13–14.

Andropogon scoparius (Michx.) Lower Platte.

A. nutans (Linn.) Laramie river, North fork of the Platte. Sept. 3–4.

Hordeum jubatum (Ait.) Forks of the Platte. July 2.

Elymus Virginicus (Linn.) Big Blue river of the Kansas. June 20.

E. Canadensis (Linn.) Little Blue river of the Kansas. June 22.

Beckmannia eruciformis (Jacq.) North fork of the Platte. July 22.

EQUISETACEÆ.

Equisetum arvense (Linn.) On a lake in the Wind River mountains. Aug. 12–17.

FILICES.

Hypopeltis obtusa (Torr. compend. bot. N. States, p. 380, 1826.) Aspidium obtusum (Willd.) Woodsia Perriniana (Hook. and Grev. Icon. Fil. I. t. 68.) Physematium (Kaulf.) obtusum, (Hook. fl. Bor.—Am. 2, p. 259.) On the Platte.

ASTRONOMICAL OBSERVATIONS.

The maps which accompany this report are on Flamsteed's modified projection, and the longitudes are referred to the meridian of
Greenwich.

For the determination of astronomical positions, we were provided with the following instruments:

    One telescope, magnifying power 120.
    One circle, by Gambey, Paris.
    One sextant, by Gambey, Paris.
    One sextant, by Troughton.
    One box chronometer, No. 7,810, by French.
    One Brockbank pocket chronometer.
    One small watch with a light chronometer balance, No. 4,632,
       by Arnold & Dent.

The rate of the chronometer 7,810, is exhibited in the following
statement:

"New York, May 5, 1842.

"Chronometer No. 7,810, by French, is this day at noon—
    "*Slow* of Greenwich mean time   —   —   11′ 4″
    "Fast of New York mean time   —   — 4h 45′ 1″
    "Loses per day —   —   —   —   —   2″ $\frac{7}{10}$

"ARTHUR STEWART,
"74 Merchants' Exchange."

An accident among some rough ground in the neighborhood of
the Kanzas river, strained the balance of this chronometer (No.
7,810,) and rendered it useless during the remainder of the campaign. From the 9th of June to the 24th of August inclusively, the
longitudes depend upon the Brockbank pocket chronometer; the
rate of which, on leaving St. Louis, was fourteen seconds. The rate
obtained by observations at Fort Laramie, 14″.05, has been used in
calculation.

From the 24th of August until the termination of the journey, No.
4,632 (of which the rate was 35″.79) was used for the same purposes.

The rate of this watch was irregular, and I place but little confidence in the few longitudes which depend upon it, though, so far as we have any means of judging, they appear tolerably correct.

Table of latitudes and longitudes, deduced from the annexed observations.

Date.	Station.	Latitude. deg. min. sec.	Longitude. In time. h. min. sec.	Longitude. In arc. deg. min. sec.
1842.				
May 27	St. Louis—residence of Colonel Brant	38 37 34	6 01 03.7	90 15 55
June 8	Chouteau's lower trading post, Kanzas river	39 05 57	6 18 38	94 39 31
16	Left bank of the Kanzas river, seven miles above the ford	39 06 40	6 24 40	96 10 06
18	Vermillion creek	39 15 19	6 26 26.7	96 36 40
19	Cold Springs (near the road to Laramie)	39 30 40	6 27 12.3	96 48 05
20	Big Blue river	39 45 08	6 28 27.8	97 06 58
25	Little Blue river	40 26 50	6 35 36.5	98 54 08
26	Right bank of Platte river	40 41 06	6 37 11.1	99 17 47
27	Right bank of Platte river	40 39 32	6 38 31	99 37 45
28	Right bank of Platte river	40 39 51		
30	Right bank of Platte river	40 39 55	6 42 32.7	100 33 10
July 2	Junction of North and South forks of the Nebraska or Platte river	41 05 05	6 45 25.6	101 21 24
4	South fork of Platte river—left bank		6 48 11.3	102 08 50
6	South fork of Platte river—island	40 51 17	6 54 20	103 35 04
7	South fork of Platte river—left bank	40 33 26	6 56 08.9	104 02 13
11	South fork of Platte river—St. Vrain's fort	40 22 35	7 03 00.9	105 45 13
12	Crow creek	40 41 59	7 02 13.8	105 33 27
13	On a stream, name unknown	41 08 30	7 00 54.5	105 13 38
14	Horse creek—Goshen's Hole?	41 40 13	6 59 57.6	104 59 23
16	Fort Laramie, near the mouth of Laramie's fork	42 12 10	7 01 24.6	105 21 19
23	North fork of Platte river	42 39 25	7 04 13	106 03 40
24	North fork of Platte river	42 47 40		
25	North fork of Platte river—Dried Meat camp	42 51 35	7 05 40.7	106 25 10
26	North fork of the Platte river—noon halt	42 50 08		
26	North fork of Platte river—mouth of Deer creek	42 52 24	7 06 53	106 43 15
28	North fork of Platte river—Cache camp	42 50 53	7 09 03.7	107 15 55
29	North fork of Platte river—left bank	42 38 01	7 09 56.4	107 29 06
30	North fork of Platte river—Goat island	42 33 27	7 10 30.9	107 37 27
August 1	Sweet Water river—one mile below Rock Independence	42 29 56	7 11 40	107 55 01
4	Sweet Water river	42 32 31		

Date	Locality	°	′	″	h.	m.	s.	°	′	″
7......	Sweet Water river	42	27	15	7	19	26	109	51	29
8......	Little Sandy creek, tributary to the Colorado of the West......	42	27	34	7	20	31	110	07	46
9......	New fork—tributary to the Colorado..........	42	42	46	7	21	57.2	110	29	17
10......	Mountain lake	42	49	49	7	22	29.7	110	37	25
15......	Highest peak of the Wind River mountains									
19......	Sweet Water—noon halt	42	24	32						
19......	Sweet Water river	42	22	22						
20......	Sweet Water river—noon halt	42	31	46						
22......	Sweet Water river	42	26	10						
23......	Sweet Water river—at Rock Independence	42	29	36						
30......	North fork of Platte river—mouth of Sweet Water..........	42	27	18	7	11	01.8	107	45	27
September 3...	Horse Shoe creek—noon halt	42	24	24						
4...	North fork of Platte river—right bank	42	01	40						
5...	North fork of Platte river, near Scott's bluffs	41	54	38						
8...	North fork of Platte river—right bank—six miles above Chimney Rock	41	43	36						
9...	North fork of Platte river—mouth of Ash creek	41	17	19						
10...	North fork of Platte river—right bank	41	14	30						
16...	North fork of Platte river—Cedar bluffs	41	10	16						
16...	Platte river—noon halt	40	54	31						
17...	Platte river—left bank	40	52	34						
18...	Platte river....do....	40	42	38						
19...	Platte river....do....	40	40	21						
20...	Platte river—noon halt—left bank	40	39	44						
20...	Platte river—left bank	40	48	19						
21...	Platte river ....do....	41	05	37						
23...	Platte river—noon halt—left bank	41	20	20						
23...	Platte river—left bank	41	22	52						
25...	Platte river—mouth of Loup fork	41	22	11						
28...	Platte river—mouth of Elk Horn river..........	41	09	34						
29...	Platte river—left bank	41	02	15						
October 2.....	Bellevue—at the post of the American Fur Co., right bank of the Missouri river.	41	08	24	6	23	11	95	47	46
4.....	Left bank of the Missouri—opposite to the right bank of the mouth of the Platte	41	02	11						
5.....	Missouri river..........	40	34	08						
6.....	Bertholet's island—noon halt	40	27	08						
6.....	Missouri river—mouth of Nishnabatona river	40	16	40						
8.....	Missouri river—left bank	39	36	02						
10.....	Missouri river—mouth of the Kanzas river..........	39	06	03	6	18	11.6	94	32	54

METEOROLOGICAL OBSERVATIONS

The elevations which have been given in the course of the preceding report, are founded upon the annexed barometrical observations, and it is scarcely necessary to say are offered only as the best indications we have. The barometers were compared with those of Dr. G. Engelman, of St. Louis, Missouri, whose observations are given for a corresponding period. The following is the result of forty comparative observations of three barometers instituted by him from May 22d, to May 29th, 1842, at St. Louis. Range of barometers during that period 0" .400, temperature 60° to 75°. Barometer E, as observed for and noted in the journal of the academy:

$=$ Fremont's Troughton (T.)$-0''$ .136 $=$ Fremont's Carey (C.) $-0''$ .178.

Range in the differences:

Mean E	$=$ Fremont's Troughton (T.)$-0''$ .136	$=$ Fremont's Carey (C.)$-0''$ .178
Minimum $=$	" " $-0''$ .116 $=$	" " $0''$ .167
Maximum $=$	" " $-0''$ .150 $=$	" " $0''$ .190
Range $=$	" " $0''$ .034 $=$	" " $0''$ .023

In the annexed observations, the barometers, Troughton and Carey, are designated respectively by the letters T. and C. In calculation the observations at the upper stations were referred to the *single* corresponding observations for the relative period of time at the lower station. It would perhaps have been better to refer to the mean of the observations for the month at the lower station. In calculation, the tables used were those of Bessel and of Oltmanns, as given in Humboldt.

On the road from the mouth of the Kanzas to Fort Laramie.

Date.	Hour.	T.	Attached thermometer.	C.	Attached thermometer.	Temperature of the air.	Remarks.
	h. min.						
1842. Camp of June 8-10	8 30 A. M.	29.172	63.3	29.160	64.0	59.0	Very cloudy.
	9 30	29.154	63.5	29.140	67.5	60.7	Entirely overcast.
	12 30 P. M.	29.220	69.0	29.205	75.4	69.2	Some few clouds.
	4 30	29.150	77.7	29.150	83.5	76.0	
	6	29.141	74.0	29.130	77.8	72.4	
	9	29.154	68.0	29.154	72.0	66.2	
	5 30 A. M.	29.189	57.5	29.155	60.5	56.0	Perfectly clear; very fresh breeze from S. 60° W.
	7	29.252	72.5	29.250	79.25	73.0	Perfectly clear; pleasant breeze from SW.
	1 P. M.	29.283	81.7	29.294	88.0	78.0	Clear.
	4 30	29.240	83.0	29.237	89.0	85.0	
	6 30	29.211	75.7	29.210	80.7	75.0	
Camp of June 10-11	7 A. M.	29.272	55.0	29.260	58.5	57.0	
	6 30 P. M.	29.040	75.0			72.0	
	10 A. M.	29.040	57.0			54.0	
	5	29.063	55.0			56.0	Night clear and calm.
	6 A. M.	29.052	54.7			55.7	Cloudy. Wind ENE.
Noon halt.........	12 M.	28.983	76.0				Light breeze, with occasional thunder and lightning.
Camp of June 11-12	7 P. M.	28.792	69.0	28.805	77.7	71.4	Bright and clear. Wind tolerably strong from SE.
	8	28.814	64.7	28.767	72.3		Calm. Stars overhead, and clouds in the horizon, with occasional thunder and lightning.
	10	28.902	58.7	28.765	67.0		
Camp of June 12-13	7 A. M.	29.000	62.0	28.867	62.4	61.0	Entirely clouded. Wind W. 10° N.
	8 P. M.	29.032	56.2			64.7	Clear. Few clouds in the North.
	10	29.044	55.0			54.5	Clear. Wind fresh from NW.
Noon halt.........	6 A. M.					58.3	
Camp of June 13-14	1 P. M.	29.000	73.0				Light wind from NW.
	7	29.010	72.0			57.3	
Camp of June 14-16	6 A. M.	28.962	56.4	29.005	70.4		Bright sun. Slight breeze at intervals from West,
	9 A. M.	29.034	66.0	29.000	76.5	71.5	Calm and cloudy.
	10 30	29.022	70.0			75.0	
	4 30 P. M.	28.974	76.0			72.0	
	7 30	28.920	70.5				

Camp of June 16-18						
10 A.M.	28.970	66.0	......	......	66.4	Calm, cloudy, and sun at intervals.
5 30 P.M.	28.924	60.5	......	......	60.5	Clear. A few white clouds in the horizon.
12 30	29.012	78.3	......	......	81.4	Sky covered with white clouds. Wind West.
4	28.941	78.0	......	......	80.0	Clear.
7	28.920	76.5	......	......	89.0	Sky covered with thin white clouds. Wind West.
11	28.902	66.0	......	......	66.0	A moderate breeze. Some clouds, especially near the horizon. Wind S. 10° E.
6 30 A.M.	28.881	63.0	......	......	73.0	Sun and clouds. Strong breeze from S. 20 F.
10 30	28.844	80.3	......	......	78.2	Clouds; stronger breeze.
11 30 P.M.	28.822	81.0	28.805	86.0	84.0	Sky covered with heavy clouds.
1	28.813	78.0	28.784	......	79.6	Thunder in the NW. Clouds.
5	28.763	73.0	28.715	75.0	69.7	Heavy and dark. Wind moderate from South.
6 30	28.712	66.0	28.676	68.3	65.5	Nearly calm; raining steadily. Sky of a uniform leaden appearance. Thunder frequent and long continued, seeming to travel over all the sky.
Sunset......	28.733	63.5	28.700	66.7	64.0	
h. min. 10 P.M.	28.744	62.0	28.715	64.5	63.0	Light wind from North. Brilliant sunset. Masses of clouds in the sky. Dark in E. Wind N. slight, cloudy.
7 . A.M.	28.762	56.7	28.723	59.5	56.5	Cold wind from the North.

On the road from the mouth of the Kanzas to Fort Laramie—Continued.

Date.	Hour.	T.	Attached thermometer.	Temperature of the air.	Remarks.
Camp of June 18–19	7 P. M.	28.845	64.5	64.0	
	10 P. M.	28.891	51.0	49.0	
Noon halt of June 19	6 30' A. M.	28.982	46.5	45.0	Perfectly clear. Light breeze from NW.
Camp of June 19–20	2 P. M.	28.864	70.0	.....	
	6 30' P. M.	28.502	65.0	77.0	L't breeze from S. Sun bright. Few clouds in zenith and N.
	10 30' P. M.	28.483	49.0	46.5	Clear and bright. Wind fresh from S. 10° E.
Noon halt of June 20	6 30' A. M.	28.490	47.5	54.3	
Camp of June 20–21	2 30' P. M.	28.544	76.0	.....	Wind S. Thin white clouds stretched about the sky.
	7 P. M.	28.711	77.0	75.0	Sun and cloudy. Wind S. 10° E.
	10 P. M.	28.694	60.0	60.0	Wind Strong from W. Sun bright.
Noon halt of June 21	6 35' A. M.	28.613	63.0	63.7	
Camp of June 21–22	1 30' P. M.	28.531	84.5	.....	
	7 P. M.	28.371	78.5	77.0	Wind quite fresh from S. 8° W. Appearance of rain.
	7 30' P. M.	28.362	75.0	.....	
	10 30' P. M.	28.363	69.5	70.8	High wind from S. Cloudy.
	5 30' A. M.	28.344	66.6	.....	
Noon halt of June 22	6 30' A. M.	28.362	68.5	69.0	High wind from E. Cloudy.
Camp of June 22–23	12 30' P. M.	28.513	83.5	.....	Bright sun at intervals.
Noon halt of June 23	6 30' A. M.	28.471	62.7	.....	Cloudy, with appearance of rain. Wind NW.
Camp of June 23–24	2 P. M.	28.000	94.2	.....	Blowing a gale from S. 30° E.
	6 30' P. M.	28.330	80.8	84.3	Wind ESE. fresh, cloudy. A few stars visible.
	10 P. M.	28.280	68.5	69.5	Wind strong from S. 30° E.
Camp of June 24–25	Sunrise	28.191	63.7	65.0	Heavily clouded.
	6 A. M.	28.180	64.6	66.5	Wind S. 30° E, fresh. Sky clear in zenith. Heavy clouds in the W.
	Sunset	27.875	83.0	82.7	Clear. Pleasant breeze from N. 10° E.
Noon halt of June 25	5 A. M.	28.004	63.5	63.5	Clear. Wind light from N. 10° E.
	5 30' A. M.	28.002	63.8	67.3	Clear, Wind moderate from NE.
	6 A. M.	28.012	65.2	70.2	
	2 P. M.	28.020	89.0	.....	Clear, with light wind from NE.
Camp of June 25–26	7 P. M.	27.983	79.8	81.0	Clear and calm. Sun set in a bank of clouds,
	Sunset	27.970	73.5	71.3	
	6 A. M.	28.114	61.0	64.0	Sun and clouds. Wind strong from N,

Noon halt of June 26	12 M.	28.034	67.5	......	Squalls of rain, heavy thunder and lightning.
Camp of June 26-27	Sunset	27.934	68.8	......	Clear and calm.
	11 P.M.	27.912	55.0	55.0	Clear. Light air from S.
	6 A.M.	27.880	60.0	62.0	Clear. Light air from N.
	7 A.M.	27.921	63.0	65.0	Cloudy. Light air from N.
	8 A.M.	27.932	65.3	......	Cloudy. Light wind from S.
Noon halt of June 27	12 M.	27.933	70.8	......	Calm.
Camp of June 27-28	2 P.M.	27.871	80.5	......	Rain ceased, sun shining, and sky partially clear. Wind moderate from S.
	Sunset	27.720	71.0	65.0	Calm, cloudy; bright sunset; banks of clouds in W.
	10 30' P.M.	27.683	63.5	57.0	Cloudy in the horizon; lightning in N.; light wind from E.
	Sunrise	27.651	57.3	69.0	Many light clouds on a blue sky; sun bright; calm.
	6 A.M.	27.660	65.3	84.2	Light breeze from N.
	9 A.M.	27.633	78.2		
Camp of June 28-29	Sunset	27.324	79.0	......	Clear, except in the horizon.
	10 P.M.	27.302	69.5	69.5	Clear in the zenith; lightning in N.; clouds on the whole horizon; wind S.
Noon halt of June 29	6 A.M.	27.373	67.0	68.3	Cloudy; wind light from N. 30° W.
	12 M.	27.362	80.5	......	Wind E.; sun; blue sky and cumuli.
Camp of June 29-30	2 P.M.	27.381	79.5	......	Wind fresh from E.
	6 P.M.	27.473	60.5	......	Cloudy; wind increasing; now violent gale from N. 30° W., with rain.
	Sunset	27.454	52.6	53.3	Cloudy, except in W.
	9 P.M.	27.493	51.5	......	Strong wind from NW.; clearing off.
	Sunrise	27.594	44.0	......	Slight breeze from W 30° S.; eastern sky clouded.
	6 A.M.	27.611	50.5	57.8	Sun and clouds; wind W. 30° S.
Noon halt	12 M.	27.552	62.7	......	Wind strong, N. 50° W.; sun and clouds.
	2 P.M.	27.533	69.0	......	Wind strong, N. 50° W.; sun and clouds.
Camp of June 30 and July 1	6 30' P.M.	27.521	68.8	......	Clear; wind fresh from N. 50° W.
	Sunset	27.513	60.2	58.6	Light wind from N. Clear, except a few clouds over the setting sun.
	10 30' P.M.	27.492	44.3	43.0	Sun, sky mottled with clouds, wind fresh S. 55° W.
	5 30' A.M.	27.450	50.7	49.0	Same wind, more cloudy.
	6 A.M.	27.450	54.3	55.2	Calm, sun, sky not clear.
Camp of July 1-2	Sunset	27.200	68.7	65.5	Calm and clear.
	9 30' P.M.	27.193	53.0	51.0	Calm, sun, foggy.
	5 A.M.	27.163	47.0	46.0	
	5 30' A.M.	27.162	50.0	49.0	
	6 A.M.	27.171	52.4	51.0	Foggy, sun shining as through a mist, and light air from N.
Noon halt of July 2	2 P.M.	27.194	77.5	......	Wind tolerably strong from NW.; sun and smoky.
Camp of July 2-3	7 P.M.	27.173	68.0	68.0	Wind light from N.

On the road from the mouth of the Kanzas to Fort Laramie—Continued.

Date.	Hour.	T.	Attached thermometer.	Temperature of the air.	Remarks.
Camp of July 2–3............	Sunset	27.160	65.5	63.4	Calm, dirty horizon, otherwise clear.
	10 30′ P. M.....	27.151	51.0	47.0	Clear, light wind from NW.
Noon halt of July 3.........	7 A. M.........	27.203	57.0	55.8	Sun and little smoky, calm; very smoky, wind light from S.
	1 P. M.........	27.103	79.0	....	
	2 P. M.........	27.084	84.5	....	
Camp of July 3–4..........	Sunset	26.924	71.0	....	Smoky, wind moderate from S.
	10 P. M........	26.890	64.0	....	Smoky and cloudy; wind light from S.
	5 30′ A. M.....	26.831	51.6	54.5	Wind light from S. 78° W.; sun shining red as through a thick fog.
Noon halt of July 4........	6 A. M.........	26.832	53.3	54.5	Smoky, sky entirely covered; wind tolerably strong from N 7° W.
	12 30′ P. M.....	26.822	76.0	....	
Camp of July 4–5.........	5 30′ P. M.....	26.831	69.0	69.0	Same smoky sky, wind moderate from N.
	6 P. M.........	26.824	67.3	67.2	Same sky, wind light from N.
	9 30′ P. M.....	26.821	53.3	52.6	Sun from between clouds, has been raining; wind E. 15° S.
	6 30′ A. M.....	26.804	52.5	52.0	

On the road from the mouth of the Kanzas to Fort Laramie—Continued.

Date.	Hour.	C.	Attached thermometer.	Remarks.
Camp of July 5–6	Sunset	26.485	66.0	Sky clear; wind S. 67° E.
	6 A. M.	26.455	55.5	Sky clear; high wind from S.
Noon halt of July 6	12 P. M.	26.235	89.2	Cloudy; a gale from W.
Camp of July 6–7	Sunset	26.010	81.5	Clear; wind high from SW. Squally, and high wind with rain.
	6 A. M.	26.183	69.0	Nearly calm; light air from S. 7° W. Clear.
Noon halt of July 7	12	26.192	103.4	Wind strong from S. 20° E.; masses of clouds.
Camp of July 7–8	Sunset	25.950	81.4	Wind fresh from S. 50° E.; sun and a few clouds.
	6 A. M.	25.970	70.0	Sun; calm and clear.
Noon halt of July 8	12 M.	25.920	108.0	Sun a little faint, sometimes obscured by long white clouds.
Noon halt of July 10	12 30' P. M.	25.373	90.5	Calm; sun and clouds.
St. Vrain's fort, July 11	6 30' A. M.	25.100	77.5	Calm; sun and clouds.
	9 A. M.	25.084	79.7	Calm; sun and clouds.
	12 M.	25.042	84.0	Sun and clouds; wind moderate from N. 65° E.
	4 30' P. M.	25.010	85.1	Cloudy; wind moderate from N. 65° E.
	6 30' P. M.	25.014	80.0	Sun and clouds; wind moderate from E.
St. Vrain's fort, July 12	6 A. M.	25.253	76.0	Sun and clouds; wind moderate from E.
	8 A. M.	25.305	77.0	Sun and clouds.
Noon halt of July 12	2 P. M.	25.417	86.0	Clear except in E.; wind light from N.
Camp of July 12–13	Sunset	25.231	66.0	Sun; blue sky and clouds. Light wind from W.
	6 A. M.	25.235	59.8	Clear; fresh wind from S. 50° E.
Camp of July 13–14	Sunset	24.862	67.7	Sun; a few clouds in the horizon. Wind fresh from S. 50° E.
	6 A. M.	24.830	60.6	Sun and clouds; wind moderate from S.
Noon halt of July 14	2 P. M.	25.050	103.6	Light clouds all over the sky, and heavy dark ones in the W. Wind moderate from S. 38° E.
Camp of July 14–15	Sunset	25.560	80.0	Sun and clouds; wind fresh from S. 10° W.
Camp of July 16	6 A. M.	25.515	71.6	Clear; a few clouds in the W. horizon. Wind W.
	6 30' A. M.	25.882	74.3	

Fort Laramie.

Date.	Hour.	T.	Attached thermometer.	C.	Attached thermometer.	Temperature of the air.	Wet bulb.	Remarks.
July 16	9	25.801	87.5					Cloudy; strong west wind.
	12	25.784	89					Sun and clouds; light wind, W. 10° S.
	4	25.744	72.2					Entirely clouded; moderate wind, S. 8° W.
	6	25.734	83.5					Entirely clouded; moderate wind, S. 8° W.
	9	25.761	78.7					Cloudy; wind light NW.; gale from S. during night.
17	7	25.842	72.6	25.831	80.7	92.5	59.5	do
	9	25.852	76.3	25.820	99	89.3	66.1	do
	12	25.840	91.8	25.745	92	85	71	
	4	25.771	86.7	25.743	82	80.4		Wind N. 60° E.
	Sunset	25.782	79	25.785	73.3	74		Wind N. 60° E.; rain in W.; thunder and lightning.
18	6	25.803	70.5	25.762	65.7	77	65	
	9	25.800	63.5	25.840	63.3	96	60	Cloudy; calm. [lightning,
	10	25.821	62	25.826	66.3	90	61.5	Moderate wind W.; showers, with thunder and
	11	25.863	63	25.833	71.3	68.5		
	12	25.881	67	25.851	78.5	64		Light air from SW.; cloudy.
	3	25.900	73.6	25.805	82.3	59.2	66	Wind light from S.
	5	25.813	78.6	25.806	85.7	73		Wind moderate, S. 33° E.
	6	25.835	80.6	25.795	82.7	89	66.5	Wind E.; moderate.
	7	25.832	78.5					Do
19	10	25.840	75	25.810	64	80		do
	6	25.860	64.2	25.803	69	78.3		Calm.
	8	25.904	64.5	25.840	80.4	73.4		Light wind from E.
	10	25.913	73.2	25.877	90.2	63		Calm and clear.
	12	25.890	84	25.846	86.3	68.5		E. wind fresh; sun and clouds.
20	5	25.812	82.3	25.775	78.7	67		Wind light E.; sun and clouds.
	7	25.813	75.8	25.765	73.9	81		Rain in squalls; wind very fresh E.
	9	25.850	71.5	25.805	68.5	76	65.5	Wind moderate S. 70° E.; cloudy.
	6	25.811	65	25.760	64.6	73	65	High wind from E.
	9	25.842	61.3	25.803	88.7	60	64	Light F. wind; cloudy.
	12	25.791	82.6	26.070	94	79	69	Wind fresh from E.; cloudy.
	5	25.753	85.4	26.105	72.3	95	70	Wind very fresh from E.; appearance of rain.
	6	25.724	70.2	26.096	88.5	75	64	Wind SE. very fresh; raining in squalls since three; [sharp thunder and lightning.
			31.7					Calm.

Observations among the Wind River mountains.

Station and date.	Hour.	T.	Therm.	Remarks.
Island Lake of August 13	5 30′ P. M.......	20.532	58	Wind South; clear sky.
....Do.....do............	Sunset	20.522	50	Wind South; at dusk, a gale from NW., continued till late in the night.
....Do......August 14	Between day light and sunrise ...	20.573	39	Wind South, sky bright.
In a gap of the central chain, of August 14............	Noon............	19.401	50	Wind South 40° W.; bright, with clouds.
Camp at Island Lake of August 14.	5 P. M.........	20.643	55.5	Wind light from South; blue sky, much covered with heavy masses of cumuli.
....Do.....do.....do.........	Sunset	20.641	50	Wind South, but the cumuli come over the mountains from N.
....Do......August 15	Between daylight and sunrise....	20.662	40.2	Sky clear; calm.
....Do.....do....do.........	6 A. M.........	20.672	40.3	Do do
Lake below the summit, August 15.	9½ A. M.........	20.450	70.5	Wind N.; clear, some cumuli.
Highest point of the Wind River chain, of August 15......	1 P. M.........	18.320	45.3	Wind South 35° W.; clear and clouds.
Highest point of the Wind River chain, of August 15......	1 P. M.........	18.293	44	Do do do
Camp at Island Lake, of August 15.	Sunset	20.642	52	Wind N.; some clear cumuli.
....Do......do......August 16.	Between daylight and sunrise....	20.651	41.5	Do do do

Register of meteorological observations made by Dr. G. Engelmann, at St. Louis, Missouri.

Barometer (E.) 60 feet above low water mark of the Mississippi; or, according to Mr. Nicollet's observations, 442 feet above the Gulf of Mexico.

Date	Hour	Barometer	Thermometer		Wind	Rain	Memoranda
			Attached.	Free.			
1842. June 1	Sunrise	......	......	Degrees. 56	E.	Inches. 0.10	Nearly clear.
	9	29.31	72	76	SE.	......	Do
	12	29.28	75	81	SE.	......	Do
	3	29.27	76	75		......	Beginning to rain ; thunder.
	9	29.15	73	67		......	Clearing up.
2	Sunrise	......	......	66	S.	0.86	Overcast.
	6½	29.08	71	65		......	Heavy rain ; thunder.
	9	29.01	72	75		......	Clouds; sunshine.
	12	28.91	75	80	SSE.	......	Stormy ; overclouded.
	3	28.79	77	83	S.	......	Nearly clear; few clouds.
	3½	28.78	77	......	SSW.	......	Heavy storm beginning; hurricane at Athens, 40 miles SE.
	4	28.84	77	70	SW.	......	Thunderstorm past.
	9	28.90	76	71		......	Distant thunder.
3	Sunrise	......	......	66	WSW.	......	Overclouded.
	9	29.15	71	68	WNW.	......	Do
	12	29.17	74	75	WNW.	......	Clouds ; sunshine.
	3	29.17	76	81	WNW.	......	Nearly clear.
	9	29.18	76	71		......	Clear.
4	Sunrise	......	......	65	SE.	0.08	Nearly clear; a little hazy.
	9	29.23	77	82	SE.	......	Do do
	12	29.17	82	87	SE.	......	Do do
	3	29.13	85	93	SSE.	......	Do light clouds.
	9	29.12	83	81		......	Overclouded. Thunderstorm, and rain at 11 o'clock.
5	Sunrise	......	......	70	N.	......	Overclouded.
	9	29.32	79	76	N.	......	Clouds ; sunshine.
	12	29.35	79	79.5	NNW.	......	Hazy ; sun faint.

Day	Hour	Bar.	Ther.	Ther.	Wind	Rain	Weather
6	3	29.31	80	81	NNW.		Do
	10	29.38	74	67	NNW.		Clear; windy
7	Sunrise			59	N.		Clear.
	9	29.43	73	69	NE.		Clear; windy.
	12	29.41	74	75	NE.		Nearly clear.
	3	29.39	75	76	NE.		Do
	10	29.38	70	61	NE.		Do
8	Sunrise			51	NE.		Do
	9	29.29	70	57	NE.	0.10	Overclouded; beginning to rain.
	12	29.26	70	61	NE.		Drizzling.
	3	29.25	66	60	NNE.		Do
	10	29.27	65	57	NNE.		Overclouded.
9	Sunrise			55	N.		Overcast.
	9	29.35	64	63	N.		Do
	12	29.37	66	71			Do
	3	29.36	69	74	SW.	0.04	Clearing up; few clouds.
	10	29.35	68	61	NW.		Clear.
10	Sunrise			62	NW.		Clouds; sunshine.
	9½	29.35	70	71	NW.		Thunder storm. Clearing up.
	12	29.33	73	80	W.		Clouds; sunshine; sultry.
	3	29.33	76	82	NW.		Clearing up.
	10	29.35	74	67	NW.		Clear.
11	Sunrise			59	NW.		Do
	9	29.45	75	73	NE.		Clear; few clouds.
	12	29.46	75	88	E.		Nearly clear.
	3	29.48	77	87	E.		Clear.
	10	29.55	70	54	SE.		Nearly clear; clouds.
12	Sunrise	29.57	61	63		0.05	Clear.
	9½	29.55	67	71	SW.		Nearly clear.
	12	29.51	70	77	SW.		Some clouds.
	3	29.45	74	62	W.		Clear.
	10	29.34	71	62	NW.		Nearly clear.
13	Sunrise			56	NW.		Hazy; sun faint.
	9	29.29	72	72	NW.		Cloudy; a little rain.
	12	29.30	72	70	NW.		Cloudy.
	3	29.31	73	70	NW.		Clear.
		29.35	71	62			Clear.
		29.43	72	72			Clear, few clouds,
		29.43	73	77			Do
		29.40	74	79			Do

Date.	Hour.	Barometer.	Thermometer. Attached.	Thermometer. Free.	Wind.	Rain. Inches.	Memoranda.
1842. June 13	10....	29.40	*Degrees.* 74	*Degrees.* 64	NW.	....	Clear.
14	Sunrise....	....	....	58	SW.	....	Do
	9....	29.39	74	76	SE.	....	Hazy.
	12....	29.36	75	81	SW.	....	Nearly clear.
	3....	29.34	77	82	SW.	....	Clouds; sunshine.
	10....	29.32	75	67	....	....	Cloudy; thunder clouds.
15	Sunrise....	....	....	64	SW.	....	Clouds; sunshine.
	9....	29.35	76	78	SW.	....	Do do
	12....	29.32	77	85	SE.	....	Nearly clear.
	3½....	29.29	80	84	SE.	....	Overclouded; drops of rain at sunset.
	10....	29.28	77	71	....	....	Cloudy.
16	Sunrise....	....	....	62	SW.	....	Clear.
	9....	29.33	79	77	SW.	....	Cloudy; sunshine.
	12....	29.31	80	81.5	WSW.	....	do
	3....	29.29	82	85.5	WSW.	....	Nearly clear.
	10....	29.31	80	71	....	....	Clear.
17	Sunrise....	....	....	64	NE.	....	Do
	9....	29.25	81	82	SE.	....	Clouds; sunshine.
	12....	29.19	83	86	....	....	Do do
	3....	29.13	85	88	S.	....	Heavy clouds; sunshine.
	10....	29.11	82	75	....	....	Clouds; moonshine.
18	Sunrise....	....	....	72	W.	....	Cloudy; drops of rain.
	9....	29.08	80	81	W.	....	Cloudy; sunshine.
	12....	29.07	83	77	NW.	0.04	Some rain; some thunder.
	3....	29.07	83	81	NW.	....	Cloudy.
	12....	29.14	77	69	NW.	....	Do
19	Sunrise....	....	....	59	NW.	....	Clear.
	9....	29.22	71	68	NW.	....	Do
	12....	29.27	73	72	NW.	....	Clear; few clouds.
	3....	29.31	75	74	NW.	....	Do

Date	Time	Bar.	Ther.	Ther.	Wind	Rain	Remarks
20	10....	29.36	71	63	NW.		Clear; light clouds.
	Sunrise			55	N.W.		Cloudy; clearing up.
	9....	29.43	73	73	NW.		Clear.
	12....	29.43	74	77.5	N.		Do
	4....	29.39	76	79.5	SE.		Do
	10....	29.42	74	67	SE.		Do
21	Sunrise			63	SE.		Do
	9....	29.43	78	80	SE.		Clear; few clouds.
	12½....	29.39	80	86	SE.		do
	3....	29.34	83	87	SE.		Nearly clear; hazy.
	9....	29.34	81	76	S.		Overclouded; rain at 8 o'clock.
22	Sunrise			70	SW.	0.10	Clouds; heavy rain at 11½.
	9....	29.31	80	84	WNW.	0.42	Cloudy; sunshine.
	12....	29.27	80	75	W.	0.14	Cloudy; some sunshine; thunder storm at 5 o'clock.
	3....	29.24	82	83		0.99	Cloudy; soon after heavy rain for 4 hours.
	12....	29.20	78	73			Overclouded.
23	Sunrise			71	NW.	0.10	Cloudy; rain.
	1....	29.23	80	83	NW.		Clearing up; hot.
	3....	29.23	80	83	N.		Do
	12....	29.24	80	81	N.		Cloudy.
	12....	29.26	76	69	N.		Overclouded.
24	Sunrise			65	NE.		Do
	9....	29.28	74	75	NE.		Nearly clear.
	12....	29.26	79	85	SE.		Cloudy; sunshine.
	3½....	29.23	83	88	SE.		Clear.
	10....	29.18	81	77			Do
25	Sunrise			74	S.		Clear; few light clouds.
	9....	29.18	84	89	SSW.		Do do
	12½....	29.14	90	94	SSW.		Thunder clouds.
	3....	29.13	91	95	SW.	0.14	Thunder storm from 7 to 8.
26	9....	29.16	84	77	W.		Overclouded.
	11½....	29.08	83	75	SW.		Hard storm.
	Sunrise			73	W.		Overclouded.
	9....	29.22	81	82	W.		Nearly clear.
	12....	29.25	81	83	WNW.		Overclouded.
	3....	29.26	82	87	WNW.		Clouds; sunshine.
	10¼....	29.24	84	69			Clear.
		29.31	81	62			
27	Sunrise			69	W.		Do few clouds.
	9....	29.37	77	79	WNW.		do
	12....	29.37	80	84	WNW.		Do

Date.	Hour.	Barometer.	Thermometer.		Wind.	Rain.	Memoranda.
			Attached.	Free.			
1842.			*Degrees.*	*Degrees.*		*Inches.*	
June 27	3	29.37	82	88	WNW.		Clear.
	10	29.36	81	71	WNW.		Do
28	Sunrise			68	SW.		Nearly clear.
	9	29.34	80	84	S.		Somewhat hazy.
	12	29.31	83	89	S.		Nearly clear; some clouds.
	3	29.27	86	91	SSW.		More clouds.
	10	29.28	84	77			Stars dim.
29	Sunrise			74	S.		Hazy; sun faint.
	9	29.21	82	85	S.		Clouds; sunshine.
	12	29.16	83	87	S.		Cloudy; sunshine; wind.
	3	29.14	85.5	90	S.		Nearly clear.
	10	29.13	83	80			Thunder; no rain; heavy thunder at night.
30	Sunrise			66		1.75	Some rain; cloudy.
	9	29.24	77	79	SSW.		Clearing up.
	12	29.29	86	76	W.		Sprinkling of rain; raining.
	3	29.30	81	73	WNW.	0.81	Overclouded; raining hard.
	10	29.34	72	60	NW.		Clear. Rain in the night.
July 1	Sunrise			58	W.	0.19	Overclouded; some rain.
	9	29.37	68	65	W.	0.11	Sprinkling of rain.
	12	29.38	69	67	W.	0.02	Raining.
	3	29.35	68	67	NW.		Overclouded.
	10	29.37	62	60	W.		Clear.
2	Sunrise			56	SW.		Do
	8½	29.38	69	69	SW.		Do
	12	29.37	74	80	SSW.		Do
	3	29.35	76	83	SSW.		Do
	10	29.37	75	70	S.		Do
3	Sunrise			67	SW.		Hazy; sunshine.
	9	29.43	74	76	W.		Overclouded.
	12	29.45	77	82	W.		Hazy; sunshine.

Day	Hour	Bar.	Ther.	Ther.	Wind	Rain	Remarks
4	3	29.44	78	83	S.		Do do
	11	29.43	77	70.5	S.		Nearly clear.
5	Sunrise			68	S.		Hazy; sun a yellow disk.
	9	29.39	75	84	SSW.		Do sun faint.
	12	29.34	78	81	S.		Do do
	3	29.29	78	70	SW.	0.04	Overclouded.
	11	29.28	77	68	W.		Hazy; some stars.
6	Sunrise			68	NW.		Overclouded; thunder storm.
	9	29.30	74	69	NNW.		Overclouded; some rain.
	12	29.32	73	67	N.		Overcast.
	3	29.31	73	61	NE.		Do
	10	29.39	69	54	NE.		Overclouded.
7	Sunrise			67	NE.		Hazy; sunshine.
	9	29.48	70	74	E.		Do
	1	29.46	72	75	SE.		Do nearly clear.
	3	29.44	72	62	SE.		Do do
	10	29.43	69	58	SE.		Stars.
8	Sunrise			71	SSE.		Nearly clear.
	9	29.36	73	83	WNW.		Do
	12	29.28	79	85	NW.		Do
	3	29.22	81.5	77	NW.		Cloudy; some sunshine.
	10	29.17	79	66	NW.		Nearly clear.
	11½	29.26	77	68	NNW.	0.38	Heavy rain and thunder.
9	Sunrise			69	NE.		Cloudy; sunshine,
	9	29.30	76	70	NE.		Sprinkling of rain,
	12	29.33	75	64	ENE.		Cloudy.
	3	29.35	74	57	SE.		Do
	10	29.41	70	71	SSE.		Overclouded.
10	Sunrise			77	SE.		Clear.
	9	29.50	71	79	SE.		Cloudy; sunshine.
	12	29.49	72	67	SE.		Do
	3	29.46	73	62	SE.		Do
	10	29.45	71	78	SE.		Clear.
11	Sunrise			82			Do
	9	29.50	74	85			Clear; few clouds.
	12	29.50	76	71			do
		29.46	78	66			Do
		29.45	77	83			Do
		29.50	81	98			Do
		29.47	82				Do
							Do
							Dq

METEOROLOGICAL OBSERVATIONS AT ST. LOUIS—Continued.

Date	Hour	Barometer	Thermometer		Wind	Rain	Memoranda
			Attached.	Free.			
1842.			Degrees.	Degrees.		Inches.	
July 12	3....	29.45	84	90	SE.	....	Clear.
	10....	39.42	81	74	SE.	....	Do
	Sunrise	....	....	69	SE.	....	Do
	9....	29.45	78	85	SE.	....	Do
	12....	29.41	82	88	SE.	....	Do few light clouds.
	3....	29.38	86	89	SE.	....	Do
	10....	29.38	83	75	SW.	....	Do
13	Sunrise	29.39	....	70	SW.	....	Sunshine; clouds.
	9....	29.39	82	84	SW.	....	Do do
	12....	29.39	84	82	NW.	0.17	Stormy; thunder storm.
	3....	29.42	84	83	N.	....	Clouds; sunshine.
	10....		80	71		....	Clear.
14	Sunrise	29.54	....	60	NW.	....	Do
	9½...	29.53	80	76	NW.	....	Do few clouds.
	12....	29.52	81	82	NNW.	....	Do
	3....	29.54	82	84	NNW.	....	Do
	10....		78	70		....	Do
15	Sunrise	29.61	....	58	N.	....	Do
	8....	29.59	75	68	NNE.	....	Do
	12....	29.55	78	79	NE.	....	Do
	3....	29.56	80	83	NE.	....	Do
	11....		76	70		....	Do
16	Sunrise	29.61	....	60	ENE.	....	Do
	9....	29.58	80	80	ENE.	....	Do
	12....	29.53	83	85	ENE.	....	Do
	3....	29.53	84	86		....	Do light clouds.
	10....		81	73		....	Do
17	Sunrise	29.54	....	66	SW.	....	Do
	9....	29.49	78	79	SW.	....	Do
	12....		82	88	SE.	....	Do

No.	Time	Bar.	Ther.	Ther.	Wind	Rain	Weather
18	3	29.43	84	91	SE.	…	Do
	10	29.43	84	76.3	SE.	…	Nearly clear.
19	Sunrise	…	…	71	SSW.	…	Do
	9	29.43	83	85	SW.	…	Do
	12	29.41	86	89	W.	…	Do
	3	29.40	89	92	W.	…	Do
	10	29.39	86	78	W.	…	Do
20	Sunrise	…	…	70	WSW.	…	Clear.
	9	29.44	84	87	WSW.	…	Do
	12	29.44	88	91	W.	…	Do
	3	29.41	90	95.5	WNW.	…	Nearly clear.
	8½	…	…	81	…	0.03	Thunder and rain.
	10	…	…	74	…	…	Overclouded.
21	Sunrise	29.44	87	84	N.	…	Clear.
	9	29.53	82	89	N.	…	Do
	12	29.56	85	89.5	N.	…	Do
	3	29.55	86	75	N.	…	Do
	10	29.54	88	62	N.	…	Do
22	Sunrise	29.54	83	81	N.	…	Do
	10	29.55	80	87	NNE.	…	Hazy; sun faint.
	12	29.54	82	89	NNE.	…	Nearly clear; light clouds.
	3	29.49	85	77	…	…	Do do
	11	29.49	82	71	…	…	Clear; few clouds.
23	Sunrise	29.48	84	85	SE.	…	Do
	9	29.46	87	91	SE.	…	Do few clouds.
	12	29.43	90	94	SE.	…	Do do
	3	29.44	85	77	SW.	…	Nearly clear.
	10	29.49	82	72	SW.	…	Clouds.
24	Sunrise	29.48	83	84	SW.	…	Hazy; sunshine.
	9	29.44	87	88	S.	…	Overclouded.
	12	29.49	85	90	S.	…	Cloudy.
	3	…	…	79	…	…	Clouds; hot sunshine; thunder storm S. at 6.
	10	29.59	83	73	SW.	…	Cloudy.
25	Sunrise	29.56	86	86	SW.	…	Cloudy.
	9	29.54	88	93	WSW.	…	Nearly clear.
	12	29.57	85	94	NW.	…	Cloudy; sunshine.
	3	29.58	83	78	NE.	…	Clouds; sunshine.
	11	…	…	71	NE.	…	Nearly clear.
	Sunrise	29.56	87	84	E.	…	Do little hazy.
	9	…	…	93	…	…	Somewhat cloudy.

METEOROLOGICAL OBSERVATIONS AT ST. LOUIS—Continued.

Date	Hour	Barometer	Thermometer		Wind	Rain	Memoranda
			Attached.	Free.			
			Degrees.	*Degrees.*			
1842 July 25	3....	29.52	89	92	NE.	....	Somewhat cloudy; hazy; sun hot.
	10....	29.50	86	83	....	0.12	Hazy; moon faint.
26	Sunrise....	....	....	77	SE.	....	Hazy; nearly clear.
	9....	29.53	88	93	SE.	....	Clouds. Thunderstorm at 11 o'clock.
	1....	29.47	85	82	SW.	....	Overclouded.
	4....	29.41	85	84	NW.	....	Do
	10....	29.45	83	76	NW.	....	Do
27	Sunrise....	....	....	74	SE.	....	Nearly clear.
	9....	29.46	83	85	SSE.	....	Nearly clear; few clouds.
	12....	29.44	87	87	SE.	0.01	Sunshine; thunder clouds all round; soon afterward, storm and rain from E.
28	2....	29.40	88	91	E.	....	Overclouded; windy.
	3....	....	....	87	E.	....	Cloudy; stars faint.
	11....	29.42	83	77	SE.	....	Overclouded.
	Sunrise....	....	....	....	SE.	....	
	9....	29.42	82	75	SE.	....	Do
	12....	29.39	85	82	SE.	....	Cloudy; sunshine.
	3....	29.37	84	87	E.	0.08	Thunder and rain between 1 and 2 o'clock.
	6....	....	....	87	SE.	0.06	Heavy but short thunder storm and rain.
29	10....	29.38	83	77	E.	....	Cloudy.
	Sunrise....	....	....	75	SE.	....	Do
	9....	29.37	83	85	SE.	....	Nearly clear; light clouds.
	12....	29.34	87	90	S.	....	Heavy thunder clouds SW.; thunder storm and rain at 1 o'clock.
	3....	29.27	83	82	E.	....	Overclouded.
30	5....	....	83	76	E.	0.05	Heavy thunder storm; rain fifteen minutes.
	9....	29.25	81	76	SSE.	0.25	Cloudy; rain at night.
	Sunrise....	....	....	....	S.	0.16	Cloudy.
	9¼....	29.16	85	86	S.	....	Some clouds; sultry.

Date	Time	Bar.			Wind	Rain	Remarks
31	12....	29.11	85	86	SW.		Overclouded. Rain at 2 o'clock.
	3....	29.12	85	86	NW.		Overclouded.
	6....			67	N.	0.02	Very dark; heavy rain for a few minutes.
	10....	29.25	78	58	NNE.		Windy; very dark.
	Sunrise			65	NNE.	0.07	Overcast.
	9....	29.44	69	71	NNE.		Do
	12....	29.45	71	74	N.		Nearly clear; windy.
	3....	29.45	72	59	N.		Clear; windy.
	10....	29.50	69	52	NE.		Do
August 1	Sunrise			67	NE.		Clear.
	9	29.62	69	74	NE.		Do
	1	29.61	73	75	NE.		Do
	3	29.59	74	61	NE.		Do
	10	29.61	70	52	ENE.		Do
2	Sunrise			69	ENE.		Do
	9	29.71	70	74	NE.		Do
	12....	29.69	73	75	NE.		Do
	3½....	29.65	75	63	NE.		Do
	10....	29.66	72	55	NE.		Do
3	Sunrise			76	NE.		Do
	10....	29.72	75	78.5	NE.		Do
	12....	29.71	76	79	NE.		Do
	3....	29.67	79	67	NE.		Do
	9....	29.65	75	62	E.		Do
4	Sunrise			74	NE.		Light clouds.
	9....	29.65	73	80	ENE.		Do
	12....	29.62	75	78	E.		Overclouded; hazy; sun faint.
	4....	29.58	77	68	E.		Hazy; faint sunshine.
	10....	29.55	76	64	E.		Some clouds; stars.
5	9½....	29.56	77	78	SE.		Clouds; hazy.
	12....	29.53	80	80	SE.		Clouds; hazy; sunshine.
	4....	29.49	82	83	SW.		Clouds.
	10....	29.47	79	69.5	SW.		Nearly clear.
6	Sunrise	29.42	76	58	SW.		Do
	9....	29.47	78	80	SW.		Fog.
	12....	29.46	80	86	SW.		Nearly clear.
	3....	29.41	82	87	SW.		Clouds; sunshine
	10....	29.39	81	73	SW.		Nearly clear.
7	Sunrise	29.35	76	67	SW.		Do
	9¾....	29.37	77	77	NW.		Overclouded.

METEOROLOGICAL OBSERVATIONS AT ST. LOUIS—Continued.

Date.	Hour.	Barometer.	Thermometer		Wind.	Rain.	Memoranda.
			Attached.	Free.			
			Degrees.	*Degrees.*		*Inches.*	
August 7	12....	29.37	79	81.5	W.	....	Overclouded.
	3....	29.36	81	84	....	....	Nearly clear.
	10½...	29.37	80	73	NW.	....	Do
8	Sunrise	....	....	59	NE.	....	Overcast.
	9....	29.39	71	65	NE.	....	Do
	12....	29.40	73	71	NNE.	....	Do
	3....	29.38	75	75	NNW.	....	Clearing up.
	10....	29.37	74	67	NNW.	....	Clear.
9	Sunrise	....	....	61	NNE.	....	Hazy; cloudy.
	9....	29.43	75	73	NNE.	....	Clearing up.
	12....	29.41	77	82	E.	....	Nearly clear; clouds.
	3....	29.40	80	84	ESE.	....	Do do
	10....	29.41	78	71	....	....	Clear.
10	Sunrise	....	....	68	ESE.	....	Overclouded.
	9....	29.46	75	75	E.	....	Do
	12....	29.46	75	77	SE.	0.35	Sprinkling of rain.
	3....	29.45	75	75	S.	....	Raining.
	11....	29.44	74	68	....	....	Do
11	Sunrise	29.43	71	64	NE.	0.19	Some rain; overcast.
	9....	29.44	72	68	E.	....	Raining.
	12....	29.44	72	63	E.	0.32	Raining hard.
	3½...	29.40	73	70	E.	....	Overcast.
	10....	29.40	72	69	....	0.14	Overclouded.
12	Sunrise	29.37	70	67	ENE.	....	Overcast; some rain.
	9....	29.39	72	70.5	ENE.	0.39	Do do
	12....	29.38	73	77	ENE.	....	Do do
	3....	29.34	75	79	NE.	0.05	Overclouded.
	12....	29.31	74	71	E.	....	Do
13	Sunrise	29.29	73	69	E.	0.11	Raining.
	9....	....	....	73	....		

14	12	29.28	76	78.5	E.	0.08	Some rain.
	3	29.26	75	73	E.	0.46	Raining.
	11	29.23	73	70	SE.	0.04	Rain at night.
	Sunrise	....	....	71	SE.		Overcast.
	9	29.19	75	77	SE.	0.10	Rain and sunshine.
	12	29.18	78	78	SE.		Rain again; overcast.
	3	29.15	79	80	SE.		Springling of rain; glimpses of sunshine.
	10	29.16	78	76	....	0.23	Nearly clear; sultry.
15	Sunrise	29.17	76	68	SSW.		Do do
	9	29.16	77	77	SSW.		Overclouded; sultry.
	12	29.16	78	80	SSW.	0.13	Do some rain.
	4	29.18	77	74	W.		Do do
	10	29.21	75	71	....		Clear.
16	Sunrise	29.22	72	61	SW.		Do
	9	29.22	75	72	SW.		Do
	12	29.20	77	77.5	SW.		Light clouds.
	2½	29.17	72	79	W.		Windy; some clouds.
	10	29.13	72	71	SW.		Overclouded.
17	Sunrise	29.09	71	67	SW.		Overcast.
	9	29.11	73	70	SW.		Do
	12	29.14	73	74	WSW.	0.05	Overclouded; sun faint.
	3	29.16	72	73	WSW.		Overclouded; cool; windy; rain between 4 and 5 o'clock.
	10	29.22	....	67	WSW.		Clear.
18	Sunrise	....	....	63	W.		Hazy; sun faint.
	9	29.30	72	72	W.		Nearly clear; somewhat hazy.
	12	29.32	74	79	WNW.		Do do
	3½	29.33	77	80	WNW.		Clear.
	9	29.36	75	69	WNW.		Do
19	Sunrise	....	....	60	SW.		Do
	9	29.45	71	73	SW.		Clear; horizon hazy.
	12	29.46	74	77	SW.		Hazy; cloudy.
	3	29.44	76	81	SW.		Hazy; sunshine.
	9½	29.45	74	66	SW.		Clear.

The Expedition
of 1843–44
to Oregon and California

62. John Torrey to Asa Gray

MY DEAR FRIEND

. . . .

Fremont has at last communicated to me his plans for the ensuing season. He is to leave Washington about the 5th of April—& before the 1st of May he expects [to] be beyond the western frontier of Missouri. He "proposes crossing the mountains to the south of the Great Pass—range along their western bases—visit the mountainous region of the Flat Head Country—probably go as far down as Fort Vancouver—& return by the heads of the Missouri." This will do! I have already given him directions for collection & preserving specimens & he promises to pay attention to what we, of course, consider the main object of the expedition.[1]

. . . .

Yours affectionately,

JOHN TORREY

ALS, RC (MH-G). Addressed, "Prof. A. Gray, Harvard University, Cambridge, Mass."

1. A few weeks later Torrey wrote Gray again, expressing a fear that his catalogue of Frémont's plants would be poorly printed. "I have only received one proof sheet, & that was as bad as it could be. The whole style of the thing was changed from my Mss. I wished it set up like my Rocky Mo[untain] paper but they made it purely Etonian, & employed a very fine type. The extra copies that I requested have not been sent to me & if they are as bad [as] I fear they will be I shall destroy the whole" (RODGERS, 158).

63. J. J. Abert to Frémont

Bureau of Topl Engineers
WASHINGTON April 22 1843

SIR

Allow me to call your attention to certain vouchers which your accounts require, namely the vouchers from the Chouteaus, and the one of the last payment to Mr. Nicollet. These must be forwarded before you start on your expedition to the West. Very Respectfully Sir Your Obt. Servt.,

J. J. ABERT
Col. Corps T. E.

Lbk (DNA-77, LS, 6:225).

64. J. J. Abert to Frémont

Bureau Topographical Engs.
WASHINGTON April 26th 1843

SIR

It appears to me to be no more than a just tribute to your exertions that I should express my great personal as well as official satisfaction with your report which has now been printed, reflecting credit alike upon your good taste as well as intelligence. It is by efforts like these that officers elevate their own character while they also render eminent public services; and while they also contribute to the standing and usefulness of their particular branch of service.

Perseverance in the course you have commenced cannot fail to lead to distinction and to impress you with the gratifying reflection that while your labors bring credit to yourself they also diffuse it to others. Very Respectfully Your Obt. Servt.,

J. J. ABERT
Cl. C. T. E.

Lbk (DNA-77, LS, 6:227).

65. Frémont to Stephen Watts Kearny

[ca. 8 May 1843]

REQUISITION FOR ORDNANCE AND ORDNANCE STORES,
FOR AN EXPEDITION INTO THE OREGON TERRITORY

Oregon Territory.	Mountain howitzer.	Carriage complete, with harness.	Pistols.	Pairs holsters, &c.	Carbines.	Kegs of rifle powder.	Pounds of artillery ammunition.	Tubes filled.
Required May 8, 1843	1	1	4	2	33	5	500	200

Sir: I have been ordered to make an exploration, military and geographical, principally to connect, on the line of communication usually travelled, the frontiers of Missouri with the mouth of the Columbia. In the course of the service I shall be led into countries inhabited by hostile Indians, so that it is absolutely necessary to the performance of this service that my party, consisting of about thirty men, be furnished with every means of defence which may conduce to its safety.

I have accordingly made the above requisition for the necessary arms, which I trust you will be able to issue.

Respectfully, your obedient servant,

J. C. FREMONT,
2d Lieut. Topographical Engineers.

Printed in "Message of the President communicating the correspondence re the mountain howitzer taken by Lieutenant Fremont on the expedition to the Oregon," Senate Doc. 14, 28th Cong., 1st sess., Serial 432. While the requisition is undated it must have been near 8 May, for on that date, Stephen Watts Kearny (1794–1848), who was in command of the Third Military Department with headquarters at Jefferson Barracks, near St. Louis, and who was a friend of the Benton family, ordered Capt. William H. Bell, commanding the St. Louis Arsenal, to issue the requisition as Frémont was "to leave to-morrow and therefore has not time to hear from Washington." He assured

Bell that he (Kearny) assumed "the whole responsibility." Bell obeyed the "positive order" reluctantly and two days later wrote his superior in the Ordnance Office in Washington, Lieut. Col. George Talcott, and asked for his sanction "to this issue" and noted that "if in this matter I have erred, I hope the colonel will perceive that it has been in consequence of being placed in a dilemma of some difficulty and that it has been from a want of anything but a respect for the order and regulations of my department."

66. P. Chouteau, Jr., and Company to Employees of the Company

SAINT LOUIS 10 May 1843

To ANY GENTLEMEN ASSOCIATED WITH OUR HOUSE OR
OTHER PERSON OR PERSONS IN OUR EMPLOYMENT

This will be presented by Lieut. J. C. Fremont of the U. S. Topographical Engineers on a tour to the Pacific Ocean in the service of the Government whom we beg to recommend in a particular manner to your kindness & attention—and to whom we request you will extend such aid & assistance as may from circumstances be necessary.

As the pursuits of the Gentleman are for the public good, we trust you will not hesitate to comply with his wishes & cheerfully attend to the wants & requirements of Lieut. Fremont in case of need. Very truly yours &c.

P. CHOTEAU JUNR. & CO.

ALS, RC (CLSM).

67. J. J. Abert to Frémont

Bureau of Topogl Engineers
WASHINGTON May 15th 1843

SIR

Understanding that you are probably yet at St. Louis, I must call your attention to my letter of the 22d ulto. in reference to certain vouchers & again to repeat the injunction of this office in reference to the limit of the expenditures of your expedition, as I understand from good authority that this amount will be sufficient. Very Respectfully Your Obt. Servt.,

J. J. ABERT
Col. Corps T. E.

Lbk (DNA-77, LS, 6:266).

68. J. J. Abert to Frémont

Duplicate to Fort Leavenworth

Bureau of Topogl. Engs.
WASHINGTON, May 22d. 1843

SIR.

From the reports which have reached the Bureau in reference to the arrangements which you are making for the expedition to the Rocky Mountains, I fear that the discretion and thought which marked your first expedition will be found much wanting in the second.[1]

The limit placed upon your expenditures by the orders of this office, sufficiently indicated the kind of expedition which the Department was willing to authorize. But if reports be true you will much exceed this amount, the consequences of which will be to involve yourself in the most serious difficulties.

I hear also that among other things, you have been calling upon the Ordnance Department for a Howitzer. Now Sir what authority had you to make any such requisition, and of what use can such a piece be in the execution of your duties. Where is your right to increase your party in the numbers & expense, which the management and preservation of such a piece require. If the condition of the Indians in the mountains is such as to require your party to be so warlike in its equipment it is clear that the only objects of your expedition geographical information cannot be obtained.

The object of the Department was a peaceable expedition, similar to the one of last year, an expedition to gather scientific knowledge. If there is reason to believe that the condition of the country will not admit of the safe management of such an expedition, and of course will not admit of the only objects for the accomplishment of which

345

the expedition was planned, you will immediately desist in its further prosecution and report to this office.[2] Very Respectfully Your Obt. Servt.,

J. J. ABERT
Col. Corps T. E.

Lbk (DNA-77, LS, 6:279–80).

1. Captain Bell's letter, with copies of Frémont's requisition (see Doc. No. 65) and Kearny's order, had reached Washington and had been laid before James M. Porter, the Secretary of War *ad interim,* who, in turn referred them to Abert. And when Abert in effect replied that small arms—but not the howitzer—were consistent with JCF's order for a peaceful geographical survey, the Secretary of War wrote: "This whole proceeding appears to have been singularly irregular. If the party of the topographical corps needed arms, they should have applied through the regular channels, and *in season.* Putting off the application to the last hour was ill-advised, and the consequences should have been visited upon those in fault. Order, regularity, and system, must be preserved, and the commandant of the department should not have required, and officers of the ordnance should never have issued, public property in the irregular manner in which this was done. I cannot sanction the proceeding." See "Message of the President communicating the correspondence re the mountain howitzer taken by Lieutenant Fremont on the expedition to the Oregon," Senate Doc. 14, 28th Cong., 1st sess., Serial 432.

2. Abert's letter reached St. Louis after JCF's departure for the West, though later JBF would have us believe that she suppressed the letter and dramatically hurried her husband's departure to prevent his recall by sinister forces. See her article, "The Origin of the Frémont Expeditions," *Century Magazine,* 61 (1891):768–69, and a fragmentary draft of her unpublished memoirs in the Frémont Papers, CU-B. For a treatment of the misrepresentation of Abert's letter, see JACKSON [2].

69. George Engelmann to Asa Gray

Sᴛ. Lᴏᴜɪs June 4th 1843.

Mʏ Dᴇᴀʀ Dᴏᴄᴛᴏʀ,

. . . . .

Fremont was here beginning of May for nearly 2 weeks and I assisted him in his preparations and gave him instructions for geological & botanical researches and collections. He will if possible ascend the Arkansas to its sources, pass over to Lake Bonneville and then to the Columbia. He said he was not authorized to take any botanist with him; but Stewart[1] has taken besides Geyer a gardner and a

"German Scientific gentleman" with him, who says he is also a
botanist & geologist—we will see what they do.[2] I have no doubt
Geyer will do more than all the others together.

With a genus for Geyer & Lindheimer we ought to wait I think
till they send one themselves, it will be more gratifying then.

. . . . .

Yours Entirely,

GEORGE ENGELMANN

ALS, RC (MH-G). Addressed, "Prof. Asa Gray, Cambridge, Mass."
1. Sir William Drummond Stewart (1795–1871), born in Scotland, had
come to America in search of excitement and adventure as early as 1832, and
made several journeys into the wilderness beyond the Missouri River. Alfred
Jacob Miller, a young American artist, went with him on an 1837 trip. John
James Audubon was invited to join the 1843 jaunt to the Rocky Mountains, but
declined, as he had already made arrangements to travel far up the Missouri
in a boat belonging to the American Fur Company. But, as Engelmann notes,
a number of scientists did join the expedition (PORTER & DAVENPORT).
2. The gardener who joined Sir William's expedition was Friedrich George
Jacob Lüders (1813–1904), from Hamburg. As JCF notes later, Lüders lost
the products of his diligent labor in the graveyard of the Columbia (Doc. No.
137, p. 571), but through the kind assistance of the officers at Fort Vancouver he was able to sail for Hamburg in Feb. 1844. Before the year was
over he had returned with a bride to St. Louis where he lived until 1851.
After that time he lived in Sauk County, near Sauk City, Wis., where he
pursued the occupations of gardener and florist (PORTER & DAVENPORT, 216;
HASKINS). Besides Geyer and Lüders, two other plant collectors were attached
to Sir William's expedition: Alexander Gordon, a Scotsman who had long
been resident in America, and who also lost a large part of his collection by
shipwreck soon after his embarkation at New Orleans for England, and
Karl Friedrich Mersch. Mersch (b. 1810) had come to America in 1837 from
a Luxemburg professorship of chemistry, and remained until 1870 (MC-
KELVEY, 785–87, 818–23). Joseph Burke was collecting for the Earl of Derby
and William Jackson Hooker, though he seems to have traveled with the
Hudson's Bay Company's traders for the most part (MC KELVEY, 792–817).

70. J. J. Abert to Robert Campbell

Bureau of Topogl. Engs.
WASHINGTON June 22d 1843.

SIR

Your letter of the 12th instant has been duly received.
In one from Lieut. Freemont dated the 12th of May, he says "I

have made a portion of my purchases at a credit of sixty days and obtained a cash advance of 3000 dollars. Robert Campbell Esq. of this place has been my endorser on this occasion & I have engaged that the funds which you have appropriated to this service and of which there remained to be drawn between Six & seven thousand dollars which the law permits to be drawn from & after the 30th of June."

There is a singular irregularity in this method of doing business, which I feel the less disposed to excuse as Lieut. Freemont had been so frequently admonished of the necessity of great exactness & attention in the expenditure of public money, and also because it seems to me that Lieut. Freemont had time to consult the Bureau & to receive its written advice & directions.

I fully appreciate the enthusiasm with which he encounters these hazardous expeditions, and readily acknowledge the merit which attaches itself to him, for his management of the last, yet these considerations do not relieve him from that exact accountability for expenditures required by the accountant officers, nor do they relieve either himself or this Bureau from the embarrassments consequent upon his irregular course in this respect. There are certain well known regulations for such cases, the neglect of which make serious difficulties.

For the 3000 dollars of Cash advanced for which you are accountable, a requisition will be in due time be made out & transmitted to you. But I do not see how the amount of the purchases can be forwarded. Were you aware of the restrictions upon the sending of public money to any one, you would be conscious of the embarrassments which the circumstances of this case create.

The requisition for the above amount cannot be made till after the 1st July. In addition to this cash advance, if you will please to forward the Bills of Articles purchased, we will see what further can be done. Very Respectfully Your Obt. Servt.,

J. J. ABERT
Col. Corps T. E.

Lbk (DNA-77, LS, 6:317–18). The letter was sent to St. Louis. Scottish-born Robert Campbell (1804–79) came to America in 1822, and soon became active in the fur trade from which he acquired a small fortune and a reputation of straightforward dealing. After 1835, he engaged in mercantile and banking pursuits in St. Louis, became an extensive owner of real estate, and one of the chief suppliers of cash and equipment for JCF's second and third expeditions (SCHARF, 1:369–72).

71. J. J. Abert to Jessie Benton Frémont

Bureau of Topogl. Engs.
WASHINGTON June 23. 1843

MADAM:

I was duly honored by your letter of the 25th of May.[1] The vouchers from Mr. Chouteau and Mr. Nicollet have been received.

Our fears had been excited by reports of Lieut. Freemont['s] arrangements for his second expedition, which from matter made known to the office, looked more to military than to scientific results, hence my letter of the 22d May which you have no doubt seen.

We could not authorize a military expedition under the appropriation for the Survey, and if the danger apprehended from the Indians were such that a peaceable scientific expedition could not be prosecuted it was clearly our duty to avoid changing the one contemplated to an expedition of a military character.

But we hope that our fears have been unnecessarily excited, and that this second expedition will add to the reputation already acquired by Lt. Freemont in his first. Believe me to be with great respect Madam Your Obt. Servt.,

J. J. ABERT
Col. Corps T. E.

Lbk (DNA-77, LS, 6:318–19). This letter does not reflect hostility toward the Frémonts and does not indicate that Abert believed JCF to be on the road to Washington to explain his conduct. And certainly no officer was appointed to proceed to the frontier to take the command from JCF.

1. JBF's letter, registered but not found, seems merely to have stated that she had forwarded letters from JCF to the Topographical Bureau and would communicate such information as might reach her in relation to the expedition to the Rocky Mountains.

72. J. J. Abert to Robert Campbell

SIR:

I have to inform you that a requisition has been this day made in your favor for three Thousand dollars to meet the payment of the loan obtained by Lieut. Fremont, and for which you are responsible. Very Respectfully Your Obt. Servt.

J. J. ABERT
Col. Corps T. E.

Lbk (DNA-77, LS, 6:330). On 13 July, probably before the receipt of this 3 July letter of Abert's, Campbell wrote to say that funds to meet his endorsements for Frémont had not reached St. Louis, and that he was bringing vouchers to Washington to show his advances (entry in Register of Letters Received).

73. J. J. Abert to Thomas H. Benton

SIR:

I have the honor to acknowledge the receipt of your letter of the 27th June.[1]

The error of Lieut. Fremont, was that he kept the authority to which he was responsible, and from which he could have sought advice and directions, and for which he had time, entirely uninformed of his proceedings, wants or views.

No report whatever having been received from him, from the day he left this place for New York, during his stay here on his return, or while at St. Louis, except his letter of the 12th May upon the eve of his departure. Now as the equipment of his party contemplated a serious change in the character of the expedition under his command, one that might involve the Government in Indian hostility, I have no doubt you will admit it to have been a negligence deserving some reproof, that he did not seek the advice and orders of the Department. The Department might under such anticipations have prohibited the expedition, or it might have made it adequate successfully to have encountered the contemplated emergency.

The expedition contemplates Indian hostilities, it may occasion them; need I do more under such a view than to appeal to your Known reputation for discipline when in the Army, and to your experience in public affairs, for justifying the opinion that Lieut. Fremont ought to have made a timely report of Circumstances, and to have sought the advice and orders of the Department.

When the requisitions of Lieut. Freemont upon the Ordnance Department were handed for approval, the course pursued by him, and the equipment were unusual; were without reasons to sustain them, and I was placed in the condition of recommending the approval of what had not been authorized or its necessity shown, or of seriously embarassing [*sic*] a young (and I admit highly promising) officer of my Corps. Under such circumstances I went to the utmost limit of my judgment, waiving all reasoning on account of the irregularity and neglects of the case, I recommended the approval of his requisitions for small arms and ammunition for them, as these were essential under any character of the expedition, but I could not and did not recommend the approval of his requisition for the Howitzer. It appeared to me not only a useless, but an embarrassing weapon to such an expedition, requiring well instructed men for its Management, and a serious increase of means for its transportation; and it will be a more favorable result than I anticipate if the mere embarassments from transportation do not oblige him to leave it and its equipment at the first trading post at which he shall arrive.

Such an equipment had also the aspect of a hostile expedition, which neither the law under which Lieut. Freemont acted, or his orders had authorized, and to meet which the organization of his expedition was not adapted, nor to authorize which had the War Department been consulted. Certainly it seems to me when an Indian War may be the consequence of an expedition, the officer who starts it cannot be blameless, in omitting a reference of all circumstances to the War Department, & in omitting a submission to its decision and orders.

But the only consequence to Lieut. Freemont, by the disapproval of his requisition for the Howitzer, will be that he will be held accountable for its return. There is no other consequence to be apprehended. Of this I am allowed to make you the assurance of the War Department, which under the regulations is obliged to hold Lieut. Freemont, as it would any other officer, responsible for the piece and its equipment. Very Respectfully Sir Your Obt. Servt.,

J. J. ABERT
Col. Corps T. E.

Lbk (DNA-77, LS, 6:341–43).
1. Benton, the chairman of the powerful Senate Committee on Military Affairs, was absent from St. Louis when Abert's 22 May letter arrived, but by 27 June he had returned and seen the letter censuring his son-in-law. While the letter he wrote Abert on that day has not been found, it is entered in the Register of Letters Received in the Office of the Corps of Engineers. The clerk who made the entry, in describing the contents of the letter, wrote that Benton "regrets he [Frémont] should have been censured for the course he pursued in fitting out his expedition." In *Thirty Years' View,* 2:579–80, Benton said he wrote "to the department condemning the recall, repulsing the reprimand which had been lavished upon Frémont, and demanding a court-martial for him when he should return."

74. Jessie Benton Frémont to Adelaide Talbot

SAINT LOUIS, Sep. 16th. 1843

MY DEAR MADAM,

Knowing the anxiety you must feel on account of your son, I take great pleasure in sending you the news which we received a few days since from the party. They had gotten on very prosperously as late as the 26th of June, at which time Mr. Frémont found an opportunity to write by two Indians who brought the letter in. Twenty five of the party were to take one route while the remaining fifteen crossed through the Mexican territory. He does not say in which division your son has been placed, but I assume he is with Mr. Frémont himself, as, knowing him to be an only son he was very anxious to bring him home to you in safety. By the middle or end of December they expect to be in this place & at the New Year's rejoicings Mr. Talbot will I hope be again with you. There are no means of communication with the party & I have therefore retained all the letters for Mr. Talbot which I will give to him on his return. If you see our friend Dr. Martin[1] will you tell him that you heard from us & that all the family beg to be remembered to him?

Should any other intelligence be had of our voyageurs I will do myself the pleasure of communicating it to you instantly. Very respectfully yours,

JESSIE B. FRÉMONT

ALS, RC (DLC—Talbot Papers). Addressed, "Mrs. Talbot, F. Street Washington City D.C." Adelaide Talbot, the widow of Isham Talbot, who had served as U.S. senator from Kentucky, 1815–25, was the mother of young Theodore Talbot, who accompanied JCF as an aide on both the second and third expeditions. Many of the expense vouchers are in Talbot's hand and signatures are often witnessed by him. He also kept a journal (ed. by Charles H. Carey) of the second expedition as far as Fort Boise, the Hudson's Bay Company's post on the Snake River. The letters to his mother and sister Mary provide an interesting source of information for the third expedition. When that expedition became involved in California affairs, Talbot served as lieutenant adjutant in the California Battalion, and after his discharge he reenlisted as an officer in the regular Army, which he then made his career.

1. Dr. J. L. Martin was employed for several months by the Topographical Bureau in translating, and preparing for the press, J. N. Nicollet's unfinished notes on Indian matters (see Abert to Martin, 17 Oct. 1843, Lbk, DNA-77, 6:463; Abert to Martin, 27 April 1844, and Abert to P. Wagner, 27 April 1844, 7:224–25).

75. J. J. Abert to Robert Campbell

Bureau of Topogl. Engs.
WASHINGTON September 18th 1843

SIR

I have the honor to acknowledge the receipt of your letter of the 8th inst.[1] enclosing a copy of one received by you from Lt. Fremont, and to inform you that a requisition has been this day made in your favor for Eight hundred and three $^{14}/_{100}$ dollars, to meet the payment of the several drafts drawn upon you by that officer. Very Respectfully Sir Your Obt. Servt.

J. J. ABERT
Col. Corps T. E.

Lbk (DNA-77, LS, 6:430).
1. Registered but not found. The clerk's entry indicates the St. Louis merchant had requested that a draft for $803.14 on New York or Philadelphia be remitted to him.

76. Frémont to J. J. Abert

$182.31

WASCOPAM, Oregon Territory
Novem: 24th. 1843

SIR,

Ten days after sight, please pay to the order of Dr. Marcus Whitman, the sum of one hundred and eighty-two dollars and thirty-one cents, for supplies furnished to the Exploring party under my command. Very Respectfully Sir, Your Obedt. Servt.,

J. CHARLES FRÉMONT
Lt. Topl. Engineers.

ALS, RC (CLSM). Endorsed on the back: "Oregon 1843. Pay the within Henry Hill Treasurer of the A[merican] B[oard] Ch[ristian] M[issions]. Marcus Whitman. Pay J. T. Smith & Co. on order H. Hill Treasr. Pay Corcoran & Riggs on order John T. Smith & Co. [. . .]."
Although JCF does not mention having seen Marcus Whitman at the Dalles (also called Wascopam) before turning homeward on 25 Nov. (see Doc. No. 137, pp. 552–77), this financial voucher indicates that he had seen him and had purchased supplies from him. In his diary, Preuss writes: "Proposals for the return journey: advice of Dr. Whitman—via Mexico and Vera Cruz. Fitzpatrick—via so-called California to Santa Fé. Frémont's obstinacy—north of Salt Lake, keeping almost to the old trail. I wonder how we shall get through" (PREUSS, 100).

77. Jessie Benton Frémont to Adelaide Talbot

ST. LOUIS Mri. Dec. 3d. 1843.

MY DEAR MADAM,

When I wrote to you a few days since I had not anticipated having the pleasure of sending you any news of our travellers until their arrival here; but last night I saw one of the party who had left them at Fort Hall on the 27th of September. He had a packet of letters and among them one for yourself but in swimming a river they were lost & consequently the gratification of getting news from Mr. Talbot will be denied you. The man gave me many details of the Summer's campaign & a particular account of your son's health. He says he is "fat stout & all the time in a good humour"—and has not been sick an hour since they left the settlements. Mr. Frémont would have accomplished his survey in a week after [Henry] Lee left, & by the middle of October, would be making his way homeward, and in a letter received by Mr. Campbell of this place. Mr. Frémont says that early in January 1844, he will be here. They had had perfect success in all their undertakings but when they arrived at Fort Hall Mr. Frémont found he could not procure provisions enough & therefore gave permission to ten of the least useful of the party to return[1]—to one of these ten our letters were given & by him lost—one or two others were entrusted to a different man & by him brought in safely. You will feel their loss more than I for I have seen the living witness who testified to their health & good progress—but I hope it will be a comfort to you even though it comes at second hand. Very respectfully yours,

JESSIE B. FRÉMONT.

ALS, RC (DLC—Talbot Papers).
1. Actually ten *voyageurs* returned with Henry Lee: Michael Creely, John A. Campbell, William Creuss, Clinton De Forest, Basil Lajeunesse, François Kaskaskai Lajeunesse, Alexis Perrault, Baptiste Tesson, Auguste Vasquez, and Patrick White. The *Daily National Intelligencer*, 15 Dec. 1843, citing the St. Louis *Gazette* as its source of information, reported that ten men had arrived in St. Louis on Sunday, 30 Nov., and brought a "very unfavorable account of their expedition, having been compelled for a portion of the time to subsist on horseflesh" and that the party had not been molested by the Indians, "except at the head of the North Fork, on which occasion the sight of a twelve-pound howitzer soon caused the savages to desist from all hostile movements." The vouchers reveal that each was paid $90.90 for his services as a *voyageur* or $.45 per day for 202 days from 3 May to 20 Nov. 1843, except the Lajeunesse brothers, who received slightly higher rates of compensation. All acknowledged receiving payment at Fort Hall on 20 Sept., an indication that JCF expected the return trip to take approximately two months.

78. J. J. Abert to Robert Campbell

Bureau of Topogl. Engs.
WASHINGTON December 13. 1843.

SIR

I have the honor to acknowledge the receipt of your letter of the 2d. inst.[1] and to inform you that a requisition has been this day made

355

in your favor for five hundred and thirty three $^{98}/_{100}$ dollars, to meet the advances made by you on account of the expedition under Lieut. Fremont. Very Respectfully Sir Your Obt. Servt.

J. J. Abert
Col. Corps T. E.

Lbk (DNA-77, LS, 7:65).
1. Campbell's letter, not found, enclosed a copy of a letter from JCF, who had drawn upon him for funds to pay part of the men of the Oregon expedition, and requested that the government remit the funds.

79. Jessie Benton Frémont to Adelaide Talbot

Saint Louis Feby. 1st 1844.

Your letter has remained unanswered my dear Mrs. Talbot because it found me prostrated by sick headaches occasioned as you will at once conceive by "the sickness of the heart." It made me sorry to see the note to your son for he is not here yet—and I knew that little note contained the welcome home. If our sorrows could be alleviated by knowing that others had as great, yours my dear madam would not seem so insupportable—for although Theodore is an only son yet you have another child & she is with you—whilst my poor mother in law has but one living thing to love. She says "Charles is all that the grave has left me"—and should anything happen to him how utterly desolate must she be; for your own heart would tell you that no daughter in law could replace your son, however much she might love you—and Mr. Fremont's mother has not even the comfort of having me with her so you are not the worst off, although I will admit that you have grief & anxiety enough, & the absence of an only son is cause sufficient for it. My own Mother says I am too young & too perfectly healthy to know all the miseries that attend a separation, & that if I were older and in a nervous state of health this incessant disappointment would wear me out. It is very fortunate for us all that I have elastic spirits for being here I hold a very responsible place & the letters I write my Mother & yourself are I know guides to your thoughts & exert an influence over your feelings.

For the last two weeks I had become so excited & unhappy for every day every hour indeed brought a fresh disappointment, that not then would I have written to you. But last night Mr. Campbell, who has been to Oregon himself twenty years ago nearly, when every difficulty was greater than now, traced out on the map Mr. Frémonts route & gave me the date of his probable arrival at each place, and satisfied me that he would be here in February. As Mr. Campbell says, "They may have a *tedious* journey but I assure *not* a *dangerous* one." If you knew Mr. Campbell you would feel as quiet as I do—for he is an honest man one who in word nor deed *is* untrue. Ma says, I believe, because it is what I want to hear, and although I do not think so yet perhaps it is the case. I do not tell you then my dear Mrs. Talbot to believe as I do in Mr. Campbell, but it would be a very happy thing for you if you could—it is so pleasant to rely implicitly on anyone, especially if they tell you what you love to hear. So this morning I resolved to write and tell you all he had said & hope it would have its influence in tranquilizing your feelings. You only look for your son at regular periods of the day—you cannot estimate that comfort until you are situated as I am. Mr. Frémont may come in any conveyance but a steam car & from the moment I open my eyes in the morning until I am asleep again I look for him. I hurry home from a visit and from church & the first question is "Has he come?" Judge then how the ever recurring *"no"* jars on my ear—it is worse I assure you than it can be to you to see "They have not arrived yet" in the beginning of every letter from me. Still I have the hope that very soon I shall be able to efface all those feelings by telling you "they are here safe and well" and in that little sentence will be healing for every pain.

If it is not asking too much, will you write to me again? but do not tell me I do so much for you—indeed it gratifies me to write much more than it can you to receive them and if I give you an hour of comfort I feel more than compensated. Mother desires me to give her kindest regards to you and I add mine for your daughter whose health is I hope restored. For yourself believe me dear Madam most sincerely your friend,

JESSIE A.[1] B. FRÉMONT

ALS, RC (DLC—Talbot Papers). Addressed, "Mrs. Talbot, F Street, Washington City, D.C."

1. Jessie rarely included in her signature the initial of her middle name "Anne," as she does here.

80. Jessie Benton Frémont to Adelaide Talbot

SAINT LOUIS March 3d. 1844

I have been obliged to leave your letter unanswered for some days my dear Mrs. Talbot for Mother had a return of her fall attack of chills & fever & for ten days has needed such constant attention that I have had no time for writing except to give Father a daily bulletin. My letter giving you the news of the finding of Mr. Frémont's [*blank*] has reached you by this time & has I hope given you the same certainty that it has me—that is, that with his jaded animals he has not ventured to travel in the winter but made a comfortable camp in the buffalo country & gotten through the worse of the winter without exposure. Consequently he cannot be here until the middle of April. I *have* sympathized in your anxieties for your son more than I had expressed for I was aware before they left the frontier, of Mr. Talbot's delicate health. Mr. Frémont sent for Sir William Stuart's [Stewart's] physician, Dr. Tighlman [Tilghman], to attend Mr. Talbot & kept him for that purpose until Sir Wm.'s party left.[1] I know my husband would have mentioned in his letter from Oregon, any sickness of your son's for every one written from the frontier expressed anxiety as to the result of the experiment—for such he felt it—& the responsibility was greater as the Government allows no physician—they are to do or die. The appropriations are doled out from the Department with a view to the praise of Congress for their economy & not with any regard to the comfort of the party. From 10 to 11 thousand was all Col. Abert allowed for this expedition—an expedition to consist of thirty men & last for nine months & to go through the heart of a hostile country, for after the Sioux & Blackfeet are passed they have to encounter the British occupants of Oregon & only those who will not be convinced refuse to believe that they are treacherous and would willingly assist the Indians in case of difficulty. And yet Mr. Frémont has been censured by Col. Abert, Col. Totten[2] & the Secretary at War, separately & collectively for obtaining arms from the arsenal to defend himself, and the arms charged to his private account. Col. Kearny who acted like a generous soldier & gentleman, and ordered their issue has also been censured by Mr. Porter, who I am rejoiced to see was rejected contemptuously by the Senate.[3] I am doing what you apologized for my dear Madam but when I think of the injustice done my husband I have no longer patience with those who have behaved so unjustly towards him. It is hard for a man to leave a family to tremble for him daily, & receiving no reward for his exertions & encounters with danger, but the approval of his Colonel, to be met on his return by a letter equally wounding to him & disgraceful to the writer. It makes me sick to think of its effect upon Mr. Frémont for the bitterest lesson in life is to meet with such miserable behaviour from those who professed friendship. You must pardon me for occupying your time with my own affairs dear Mrs. Talbot but I wish you who have shewn such a kind interest in me to know the truth when you will hear Mr. F. blamed for being displeased with his Colonel. As it is a private affair I have no right perhaps to speak of it, but it will be public when he returns. Will you make my kindest regards to your daughter. I hope to have the pleasure of making her acquaintance in six weeks. As for yourself I feel as if I knew you well already. My poor baby has taken the whooping cough & will need all my time but I will find an opportunity to answer all your letters for they are a great pleasure to me. Very sincerely yours,

JESSIE A. B. FRÉMONT

ALS, RC (DLC—Talbot Papers). Addressed.

1. Dr. Stedman Richard Tilghman, a recent graduate of the Baltimore Medical School, was traveling with Sir William Drummond Stewart on his purely adventurous expedition to the Wind River Mountains. At the Westport staging area, Stewart's "Camp William" near the Shawnee mission was not far from JCF's own camp. It was believed by some at the time that Stewart tried to persuade JCF to accompany him as far as the Rockies (PORTER & DAVENPORT, 218). Even journalist Matthew C. Field, also traveling with Stewart, believed that "young Freemont" was going with them. But this would have been pointless, as Stewart was virtually duplicating JCF's route of the previous year (FIELD, 15).

2. Col. Joseph Gilbert Totten, USMA 1805, was chief engineer, and therefore not only JCF's but also Abert's superior officer. He seems not to have sent a separate letter of censure to JCF.

3. The refusal of the War Department to sanction JCF's taking of the howitzer was now public information, since President Tyler, as requested by a resolution of the Senate on 18 Dec. 1843 (initiated by Benton), had transmitted copies of the interdepartmental correspondence on the howitzer to that body, and on 29 Dec. the Senate had ordered the correspondence printed. Perhaps this played some part in the Senate's refusal by 38 to 3 votes to confirm President Tyler's appointment of James Madison Porter as Secretary of War. Porter, the founder of Lafayette College, left the Cabinet on 30 Jan. 1844. As the question of confirmation was considered in executive sessions after the report of the Senate Committee on Military Affairs, of which Benton was chairman, no debate on Porter was printed (see *Journal of the Executive Proceedings of the Senate of the United States*).

81. Jessie Benton Frémont to Adelaide Talbot

Saint Louis March 24th. 1844.

It is so long since I received your kind letter of congratulation on Father's escape my dear Mrs. Talbot, that I feel ashamed not to have answered it.[1] But in that time I have had a little battle in my mind and it has not been decided until a day or two since—You know I had made my plans to go on with Mother, but as the time drew near to leave St. Louis I felt my resolution leaving me & at last the temptation to remain became so great that like many a better & wiser person I fell before its force. So that I shall not have the pleasure of seeing you as soon as I had supposed but then I shall see your son the sooner & give him your letters & tell him that you have been well during the winter. All the mountaineers agree upon the last of April as the earliest date at which Mr. Frémont can be here, as he can then come swiftly & pleasantly by water.

After Mother leaves I shall be very lonely here and will depend upon you dear Madam for letters to shorten the time of waiting for I shall feel like a sentinel on the look out until Mr. Frémont returns —and then I can give pleasure to you in return for your kindness to me. Then too I can make my letters more agreeable but now I do believe I have but a single idea. Our friend Dr. Martin has a great many & if he were a good Christian he would feel it a charitable act to write to such an unfortunate forlorn person as I will soon be; I think I shall have to resort to some desperate remedy such as plain sewing to relieve the nervous state I shall fall into.

You see Mrs. Talbot I have written you a letter about myself & you must answer in the same way, telling how you feel & think also. There cannot be two more charm[ing] subjects although it might be more selon les règles to leave such speeches to others. Make mine & Mother's kindest regards to your daughter & receive for yourself Mother's warmest thanks for your remembrance of & feeling for her. As she leaves in three days she has no time to write but desires me to say for her that she was much gratified by your writing so kindly. Yours most sincerely,

Jessie A. B. Frémont

ALS, RC (DLC—Talbot Papers). Addressed.
1. Benton was one of the dignitaries aboard the *U.S.S. Princeton*, com-

manded by Robert F. Stockton, which took a Sunday excursion down the Potomac on 28 Feb. 1844. There was exhibition firing of a new cannon which exploded into its audience, killing Secretary of the Navy Thomas Gilmer and Secretary of State Abel Upshur. Benton, who only a few seconds earlier had moved from the ranks of those hit by flying metal, suffered heavy shock and a ruptured eardrum (SMITH, 193).

82. Jessie Benton Frémont to Adelaide Talbot

SAINT LOUIS, June 15th 1844.

You must think it very strange dear Mrs. Talbot that I have not yet answered your two kind letters but since they arrived my little Lilly has been very sick, and I myself have had incessant headaches for the last three weeks. And you know with the headache and a sick child nothing can be done. Lilly is well again now & although I have my usual pain in the head I will no longer defer thanking you for your kindness in writing so often & more especially for the copy of the remarks in the English work you mentioned. Mr. Frémont will be doubly gratified when he reads them for neither of us had any claim to the kindnesses you have shewn us—In return for your attention I can tell you some little news of our party. A Mr. Glasgow has just arrived from California.[1] He saw Mr. Frémont early in November & learned from him that he was to winter at Fort Hall. As Mr. Glasgow came in by the Southern route he of course arrived sooner than our party could as it was probably to return by the Yellowstone. We know that the snows in the mountains are breaking up, for the rivers above are all rising & if after so many disappointments you can still hope, then look for their being here the first of July—How sorry I do feel that neither Mr. Frémonts mother nor yourself can have the certainty of restored happiness as soon as I. It will seem wrong to be so very happy whilst you are still in trembling anxiety. I wish I had Morse's telegraph for that once—it would surely be a better use than disappointing Presidential candidates, and bothering the country about the Texas Treaty.

Nothing but the wish that you might not think harshly of me for not having written before, would have made me write this morning, for I am sure my dear Mrs. Talbot that you will find difficulty in reading my short letter & nothing to reward your trouble when it is read. Remember however that it is a hot Saint Louis day. I have the headache & to add to my troubles my pen is very contrary & refuses to write as I wish it. I will make a second & hope more creditable effort next week & perhaps I may by that time have some news from the mountains. With kindest regards to your daughter I am dear Madam Very sincerely yours,

JESSIE B. FRÉMONT

I find I have omitted what I principally wished to say—that at Fort Hall our friends would have every comfort that fire food & shelter could give. So you need be under no apprehensions as to Theodore's health during the winter for I am sure Mr. Frémont would not let him expose himself.[2]

ALS, RC (DLC—Talbot Papers). A letter of 21 April 1844 from JBF to Mrs. Talbot is not printed, as it gives no information on JCF and merely councils "patience."

1. Possibly Edward J. Glasgow (1820–1908), who had been in business at Mazatlán with his uncle, James Glasgow. This JBF letter implies that Glasgow had seen JCF at Fort Vancouver before returning to St. Louis to engage in the Santa Fe trade.

2. JCF and his party finally arrived at St. Louis on 6 Aug. 1844 in the steamer *Iatan* (see Doc. No. 137, p. 724; *Daily National Intelligencer*, 17 Aug. 1844).

83. Frémont to J. J. Abert

WASHINGTON CITY, August 21. 1845 [1844]

SIR,

I have the honor to submit for your consideration the following statement. Col. Robert Campbell of St. Louis has been in the habit of furnishing funds and supplies for the outfit and maintenance in the field of the different parties under my command in the prosecution of military & geographical surveys west of the Mississippi, from the year 1842 to the present time. Drafts drawn by me upon him in payment of wages and supplies have been always promptly met, and the funds necessary for the discharge of parties furnished by him until the same could be furnished from Washington or was appropriated by Congress. These supplies were furnished in all cases without commissions.

After the return of the recent exploring party from California Mr. Campbell undertook to discharge a part of my liability to the party and thereby to maintain the credit of the government and quiet the clamors of the men. These advances amount to *$6204.44*. They were made on government account and in my name and I have to request that the amount be paid to Col. Campbell out of the appropriations for arrearages, and to be charged to my account, to be sustained hereafter by proper vouchers, which are in my hands, and will be furnished as soon as practicable. Very Respectfully Your Obt. Servt.

J. C. FRÉMONT

Copy (DNA-217, T-135, Roll 1, Accounts and Payments, 1845–49).

84. Frémont to William Wilkins

WASHINGTON CITY
August 28th, 1844.

SIR,

I have read the papers with the perusal of which you honored me,[1] and in addition to the facts contained in them can only add the following, which appear to have any bearing upon the question. The ground on which the action took place is claimed by the Sioux, and undoubtedly belongs to them. On the day previous to the fight a solitary Sioux was surprized & scalped by the Delawares. For the truth of this we have only the word of the Sioux, and it is highly improbable that the Delawares, who are distinguished for their sagacity & skill would have committed such an error in the face[?] of a strong body of their enemies. The Delaware was strictly a hunting party. I saw their traps among the spoils taken by the Sioux. The Delawares were on a customary line of travel for all going to the mountains, both Indians and whites. At this time there are Delaware trappers in the mountains, among them Capt. Swanac's son. The Sioux, Cheyennes, and Arapahoes, appear to enjoy this section of country in common and make no other use of it than to go into it in war parties, principally against the Pawnees. On my return lately from the mountains I met a large war party of Arapahoes on the Smoky Hill Fork of the Kansas. They were returning home and had been down as far as the Pawnee villages. It is customary for Delaware, Kansas, and Pawnee Indians to go into this country for Buffalo as they have none in their own; the Sioux, &c. always had abundance of buffalo in the country which they occupy nearer the mountains. Out of the immediate neighbourhood of their villages the Sioux, Cheyennes, and Arapahoes, never fail to destroy any small parties of Indians and for some years past, of whites also, without any regard whatever as to whom the country may belong where the fight takes place.* They are now, especially the Arapahoes, more hostile than they have been at any period for twenty years. Along the mountains, on the waters of the Arkansas and Platte rivers, the Sioux, Cheyennes and Arapahoes, can bring out three thousand men. Very respectfully sir, Your Obdt. Servt.

J. C. Frémont,
2d. Lieut. Topls. Engineers

* Several acts of this kind have been committed in the present year. My party narrowly escaped being cut off by them and they killed whites in my immediate neighbourhood.

ALS-JBF (DNA-75, LR by the Office of Indian Affairs, Fort Leavenworth Agency). Endorsed, "O. I. A. Ft. Leavenworth Washn. Aug. 28. '44. Lt. J. C. Fremont. Returns letter &c. of Col. Kearny & Th. H. Harvey [. . .] & reports on the killing of Delawares by Sioux & Cheyenne, the subject of them. F 208 Rec Aug 28/44. Indian Office Recd. 30 Augt. 1844." William Wilkins (1779–1865), former U.S. senator and minister to Russia, an expansionist and a supporter of Andrew Jackson's policies, was confirmed as Secretary of War soon after the rejection of his fellow Pennsylvanian, James M. Porter.

1. As the endorsement indicates, these were letters of Colonel Kearny and Thomas H. Harvey, Superintendent of Indian Affairs at St. Louis. Harvey outlined the increasing friction between the Sioux on the one hand and the Delawares, Pawnees, and Omahas on the other, and recommended a strong military establishment above Council Bluffs to keep peace among the western Indians though he knew "too well the strong prejudices of the military to leave civilization to entertain hope of such an establishment until the Government shall be convinced by the most calamitous results to the Indians" (Thomas H. Harvey to the Commissioner of Indian Affairs, St. Louis, 12 Aug. 1844, DNA-75, LR, O. I. A., Fort Leavenworth Agency). The letter of Kearny is not found, but by 1845 he was known to favor biennial or triennial cavalry expeditions rather than permanent forts at remote points (CLARKE, 99–100).

85. Rudolph Bircher to Frémont

Sᴛ. Lᴏᴜɪs, Mo., *September* 15, 1844

Dᴇᴀʀ Sɪʀ:

In the bearer you will recognise Alexis Ayot, one of the men who belonged to your expedition to the Rocky mountains; and who, through accident, was shot during the voyage through his right leg, endangering to all appearances, if not his life, at least the leg itself, to such a degree as to make it uncertain whether amputation would not become necessary.[1] At your request I took the poor fellow under my charge, and I rejoice to be able to send him to you, after careful treatment on my part, in the condition you see him. He is cured, though it is doubtful whether a sort of lameness and permanent weakness will not remain the final result. This has of course subjected the poor man to heavy expenses; his bill for surgical treatment and medicines has amounted to $75, independent of his board, lodging, &c.

When it is taken into consideration that, by this unfortunate accident, his whole object of the voyage was frustrated, his toil, labor, and time lost, (and he stands there at this moment as poor as he started, being crippled besides,) I submit it to your generous and philanthropic heart whether he is not a worthy object of your kindness and protection. There will be, no doubt, various ways to provide for him, should you deem proper to extend aid to him.

With great respect, I am, dear sir, your obedient servant.

Rᴜᴅᴏʟᴘʜ Bɪʀᴄʜᴇʀ

Printed, "Petition for Compensation for Loss of Limb by Alexis Ayot, 27 April 1846," Senate Doc. 329, 29th Cong., 1st sess., Serial 476. In June 1841, Rudolph Bircher had a shop at 87 Main Street, and advertised himself as a hairdresser and barber with capability in "cupping and Leeching" (advertisement in the *Daily Missouri Republican,* 2 June 1841).

1. The accident to the *voyageur* occurred near the end of July as the homeward-bound party was crossing a creek (see p. 723). By a special act of Congress, Ayot was granted a $10 pension per month. He subsequently married an American girl, became a shoemaker in Montpelier, Vt., and voted for JCF in 1856 (see *United States Statutes at Large,* 9:679; ᴍᴇᴍᴏɪʀs, 419).

86. Frémont to John Torrey

My dear Sir,

Your letter arrived yesterday evening and I read it with almost as much pain as gratification. I felt much gratified with the very flattering manner in which you speak of my Report, and at the same time felt regret and mortification at my inability to do any thing just now in furtherance of the plan we had proposed to ourselves when I set out upon the recent campaign. A fatality seemed to attend our plants in this expedition. The collection between Fort Hall (on Lewis' or Snake river) and the bay of San Francisco, in Upper California was entirely lost by a fall of the mule on which it was packed, from a precipice into a torrent. The animal was killed and the bales could not be recovered. From California to the forks of the Kansas river, I had made a collection which would have been full of interest to you. I have never seen anything comparable to the profusion and variety of plants in the country thro' which I passed. I am satisfied that *very* many of the plants & shrubs, as well as several trees were entirely new, & I had with great labor ascertained from the Indians the medicinal qualities of many, and had obtained all those which they used in any way for food. With these latter I was also acquainted from having used them myself, and the use of the former I had witnessed in several important cases. I had carefully studied the vegetation through every mile of the region travelled and made full notes. In addition to our complete publication separate from the body of the Report, I had intended that we should give interest & value to the narrative by inserting in it, & for each day along the line of travel, the characteristic shrubs & plants of the region, which as the country was a waste, desert and mountains, & generally devoid of timber between the Californian & the Rocky Mts. formed a peculiar & highly interesting growth. You will form some idea to yourself of the floral richness of the country from the fact that at a distance of twenty five miles I mistook the fields of red & orange flowers along the slopes at the foot of mountains for strata of parti coloured rocks. Though in the course of our journey the Bales of plants had been twice wet, yet they were in very beautiful order when we encamped on the upper waters of the Kansas on the 13th of July, in the course of which night it began to rain violently & towards morning the river which was 100 yards wide suddenly broke over its banks, becoming in less than 5 minutes more than half a mile in breadth. Everything we had was thoroughly soaked. We were obliged to move camp to the Bluffs in a heavy rain which continued for several days and our fine collection was entirely ruined.[1] I have never had a severer trial of my fortitude. I brought them along and such as they are I send them to you. They are broken up & mouldy and decayed, and to day I tried to change some of them, but found it better to let them alone. Perhaps your familiarity with plants may enable you to make something out of them. You will find them labelled with numbers which correspond to the numbers of notes in my books, which I will copy & send to you in case you can do anything with them.[2] I shall probably be in New York soon & could indicate the localities of such as are not labelled. From the wreck of our Fossil collection I saved some in which the Vegetable impressions seem to me very plain & beautiful. Could you aid me in decyphering them? If so I will send or bring them. From the moment the plants were lost, I had formed a determination which has been strengthened by your letter—to return immediately to the interesting regions I have described to you, with the main and leading object of making anew such collection as will enable us to give a perfect description of the vegetable character of the whole region. Its interest will of course be increased by large additions in Geography & Geology as we shall run an entirely new line in going out. I beg that you will keep this plan in view in your examination of the plants I now send you, as we may possibly be able to connect them with those I shall gather next year. Silence is one of the elements of success, and therefore I know that you will excuse me for telling you that I mention this plan only to yourself & shall speak of it to no one else. I have 60 or 70 fine mules & horses at pasture on the frontier and shall immediately commence my preparations so as to leave the frontier early in April, about the 1st and shall certainly be again at the frontier early in October of next year (1845).

In order to have efficient assistance in preparing & changing the plants &c. I take with me a young German gardener[3] who has the botanical education which they usually receive. We shall also have colored figures of the plants. I trust that you will enter warmly into my enterprise & give me in the course of the winter whatever suggestions may offer themselves to you, tending to ensure our success.

I must not omit to inform you that our geographical labors were attended with a beautiful success. We have passed through a country new & full of interest every mile of which we have sketched in our field books, supported by several volumes of astronomical positions. All my notes of every kind have been preserved and enough remains from the Geological collection to determine much positively & next year will add a great deal. I am very desirous to study these remains with some good Geologist, conversant in fossils & it would be very important to me to endeavor to add something to the little knowledge I have of practical botany. Altogether I shall have a busy winter, in writing a Report of the last campaign which must be presented to Congress before March, & in preparing for another. The plants will leave this place Tuesday morning & I will drop you a note where to find them. You will find a small parcel containing some of the fruit of an accacia (?) of which I have been able to find no description. If not destroyed you will also find the leaves & fruit among the plants in the paper. Among the plants you will [find] the wood of the artemisia (a tridentata)[4] & a salt shrub which I can indicate to you among the plants by the number. The mat I thought would interest you, as it is made from the *Ammoli* a California plant which is in the collection & will be recognized when we compare numbers. I conclude now this disjointed letter & hope to hear from you soon in reply. I am my dear Sir Very truly yours,

J. C. FREMONT.

Dr. Torrey.

ALS, RC (NNNBG—Torrey Correspondence).

1. In the summer of 1844, most if not all of the tributaries of the Kansas River had great floods, possibly record-breaking, due to prolonged and heavy rains in May and June. Almost a month earlier than JCF's 13 July flood, the water had crested at Kansas City and seems to have been considerably higher than the disastrous flood of 1951 from Manhattan to below Lawrence on the Kansas and Marias des Cygnes rivers (FLORA).

2. Torrey in turn sent Frémont's Compositae to Gray, who at first wrote that though the greater part were well known, there did appear to be three or four belonging to genera new to him. All the specimens were so bad that he thought it best not to make an independent report on the collection—"too many puzzles which good specimens another time will settle clearly." Later he decided to characterize the four new genera—"three of which were remarkably distinct ones and curious"—in the *Boston Journal of Natural History* in order to secure them, and his paper was published in Jan. 1845 (5:104–11). See letters of Asa Gray to Torrey, Monday evening, [1844], and 3 Dec.

[1844], NNNBG—Torrey Correspondence. By the time the second *Report* was published, Gray had ascertained a fifth new genus, *Nicolletia,* from the specimens.

3. Not identified.

4. *A. tridentata* Nutt., sagebrush.

87. Asa Gray to John Torrey

Thursday Evening, Oct. 1 [1844]

· · · ·

Dr. Wyman wishes much to accompany Fremont if he goes on another journey—entirely at his own expenses, if need be.[1] As his object is entirely zoology, he will not interfere with Fremont's botanical plans, while the results would redound to Fremont's advantage. He is a most amiable, quiet, and truly gentlemanly fellow, retiring to a fault, but full of nerve, and surely is to be the great man of this country in the highest branches of zoology and comparative anatomy. I therefore very strenuously solicit your influence at court in his behalf.

I am glad that Fremont takes so much personal interest in his botanical collections. He will do all the more. I should like to see his plants, especially the *Compositae* & *Rosaceae.* As to *Coniferae* he should have the *Taxodium sempervirens,* so imperfectly known, and probably a new genus. Look quick at it, for it is probably in Coulter's coll. which Harvey is working at.[2]

· · · ·

With love to all, I remain cordially yours,

A. GRAY

ALS, RC (NNNBG—Torrey Correspondence).

1. At this time Jeffries Wyman (1814–74), who was to become one of America's leading anatomists, was professor of anatomy and physiology, Hampden-Sydney College Medical School, Richmond, Va. In 1847, he was appointed Hersey Professor of Anatomy at Harvard and there built up the anatomical museum. He did not accompany JCF in 1845, but made collecting expeditions to Florida, Surinam, and South America in the 1850s.

2. Thomas Coulter, born near Dublin in 1793, collected plants in Mexico while in the employ of a mining company, and in California in 1831 and 1832. He later became curator of the herbarium in Trinity College, Dublin University, and his successor in this office, Professor W. H. Harvey, worked on Coulter's Mexican and Californian plants in 1844 (MC KELVEY, 428–42).

88. Frémont to John Torrey

My dear Sir,

An absence from the city will account to you for this late reply to your last two letters, which I found here on my return. I am very glad to hear that you will be able to rescue many of the plants & still better satisfied to know that the botanical riches of the country are as great as I had thought. All your suggestions which regard the collection of Cryptogamia [mosses, ferns] shall be particularly attended to & good coloured drawings made of plants & trees, and since reading your letter I am very sanguine that we shall be able to produce a very interesting and valuable work. I have kept myself well informed of the movements of Loeders & Geyer and we must do our best endeavors to anticipate the English botanist. Geyer wrote to me from Fort Hall when I was on the Great Salt Lake. He had made a large collection which he proposed to complete & carry to Europe the present year, embarking at the mouth of the Columbia. He is now in the north or main branch of the Columbia. I met Loeders at the cascades of the Columbia near Vancouver to which he was going. He had made no collection whatever, but proposed doing much work this year. The proposals for the sale of collections which you saw in the European papers were from Engelman of St. Louis. He had made arrangements with Loeder & Geyer to dispose of their collections which should be delivered to him on the condition that Dr. Engelman should fit them out & they enjoy the pecuniary advantage from the sale of the collections which he engaged to dispose of, while all the reputation arising from their description &c. should belong to him.

So far Loeder has not succeeded and Geyer proved entirely faithless to his confidence, carrying off the plants & otherwise behaving very badly.[1] This brings me directly to the gentleman you recommend. He will work for us in good faith for such salary as I can give him, and what profit as may arise from the sale of the plants? If you are certain that he may be relied on for these things I will certainly try to do what you desire & take him with me—tho' I have proceeded somewhat far in an arrangement with another person who would be satisfied to aid me in gathering the plants for a stipulated salary. Still I should like better the gentleman you mention & should take pleasure in aiding him in any way possible as you describe him to be poor & dispirited. I would be glad if you would assist me to determine some fossil remains, belonging to a bituminous coal formation, which I brought among my specimens. They are very interesting & important to me in fixing the geology. If you think you can find leisure I will send them to you. I thank you for your offer to bear a portion of the expense of transporting the plants; but it was small & I beg you will not think of it—Yours very truly,

J. C. FRÉMONT

ALS, RC (NNNBG—Torrey Correspondence). Endorsed, "Upon official business Bureau of Topl. Engrs. J. J. Abert Col. Corps T. E." Addressed to "Dr. John Torrey, Princeton, New Jersey."

1. For Lüders' losses, see Doc. No. 69, note 2, and p. 571. In spite of his written contract with George Engelmann, whereby Geyer gave him disposal rights to his collection in return for his outfit, Geyer returned to London and offered his sets to Sir William Hooker (MC KELVEY, 775, 778).

89. Frémont to George Engelmann

WASHINGTON CITY Octr. 22d. 1844

MY DEAR SIR,

I found the plants in such a miserable condition when I arrived that I could not even change them but sent them direct to Dr. Torrey. The greater part were entirely ruined; he says he thinks he will be able to identify a number of them, & judging from the collection he says we have sustained a great loss as the botanical riches of the country are very great. Among the collection are several specimens of new trees. Dr. Torrey & Dr. Gray are jointly engaged in endeavoring to make what they can out of them. But my misfortune on this occasion will be a safeguard to me on the next trip. I find that the most valuable among the geological specimens have been preserved. These are fossils of vegetable & other remains which fortunately have not been in the least injured while most of the others were entirely ground up. So much therefore we have as certain data & on the next trip may possibly do enough to make a connected work. Will you have the kindness to send me your barometrical observations from May 18th to the 1st of October 1843. I shall be glad to get them soon as by the time they reach here I shall wish to make the calculations. I have been very busy but will find time to write to you occasionally if I have anything of interest to say. Please give my regards to Dr. Wislizenus.[1] Did he in the course of his journey in the mountains see what is given as the mountain goat in Richardson's Fauna—(color white, wool or hair long). The only goat that I have seen is like the animal only in the horns—the body is like a deer & colored like one with short hair—it makes the bleat of a sheep, & the hunters call it the mountain sheep. The naturalist who accompanied Wilkes Exploring expedition[2] tells me that he saw it in the mountains near the head of the Arkansaw but did not get near enough to kill one. Yours very truly & respectfully,

J. C. Frémont

Please put your reply in an envelope addressed to Col. J. J. Abert, Chief of the Topographical Bureau.

ALS, RC (MoSB). Endorsed, "Rec'—Nov. 2d. Ans. Nov. 27th."
1. In 1844, Friedrich Adolph Wislizenus (1810–89) was practicing medicine in St. Louis in partnership with Engelmann. He was already an experienced western traveler and author, for he had accompanied a fur-trading party to the Far West, journeying to a rendezvous on Green River and to Fort Hall, and returning by way of the Laramie plains, the Arkansas River, and the Santa Fe Trail to St. Louis. He published an account of his journey under the title *Ein Ausflug nach der Felsen-Gebirgen in Jahre 1839* (later issued in English). In 1846, he would join a trading caravan for Santa Fe and Chihuahua and make close observations of the fauna, flora, and geology of that region.
2. Titian Ramsay Peale (1799–1885). Peale was much interested in mountain sheep, and some of his sketches of them appear in Jessie Poesch's account of Peale, published as vol. 52 (1961) of the *Memoirs* of the American Philosophical Society.

90. Frémont to John Torrey

Washington D. C. October 28th. 1844

My Dear Sir,

I write you a line to say that constant occupation has prevented my replying to yours as I have been endeavoring day after day to find the time to make you out a copy of notes for the plants. I think I shall be able to carry out many of the suggestions contained in your letter. Col. Abert shewed me a letter from Dr. Grey [Gray] in favor of Dr. Wyman. In case any arrangement should be made with Dr. Wyman, it will be necessary that he receive his salary from the Department and report to it. I have not been able to find a single copy of my Report but if I should succeed in obtaining any I will send them to you. I would be much obliged to you if you could give me the name of the enclosed little plants. It was the first flower I found in bloom on descending from the California Mts. I will write again very soon. Yours truly,

J. C. Frémont

ALS, RC (NNNBG—Torrey Correspondence).

91. Frémont to John Torrey

WASHINGTON CITY Novr 21st. 1844.

MY DEAR SIR,

I send you herewith a list of localities for the plants of 1844. Those for '43 I will send you in a day or two as I did not wish to make one such large package. These are simply the descriptions annexed to the plant when first taken but the greater part of those plants are noticed repeatedly through all my journals, & their localities extended with additional information respecting them—but as I am much pressed for time & this list has already amounted to fifty pages I thought it better to wait—until you ascertained what plants could be recognized, when I will send you the additional information. In the other package the numbers go as high as 800—making about 1500. Nearly all of the plants gathered on the Kansas were not numbered. I was somewhat discouraged by the accident to the others—You will recognize these by the large numbers without labels. If you could conveniently do so, it would give much additional interest to my Report, were you to furnish me with the botanical names of the *grasses* & characteristic plants. For this to be of use it would be necessary for me to have it in a couple of months as my Report must be out by then. I do not know if it is exactly proper to

373

ask this of you but I have met so many losses in my collections on which I relied very much, that I must do all that I can to give some value to my Report. Please let me hear on this subject as soon as you have leisure. Will you let me know how I shall send our Geological specimens to Prof. Hall? or may I send the box to you if he is in New York? There does not now remain much time & I am anxious they should be in his hands as soon as possible. The arrangements for our expedition go on handsomely, I am having excellent instruments made & myself engaged in hard study, among other things descriptive Botany & I am in every possible way forwarding my arrangements, so as to be able to take the field early in the spring. You may depend that I will bring you something handsome before the winter of '45.

We must have the geological formation geographical position & elevation above the sea for all our plants. This with the colored figures of the new specimens will make a solid work. I also send you through the mail, two copies of my Report of '43 which I am glad to have been able to procure for you. Very truly,

J. C. Frémont

ALS, RC (NNNBG—Torrey Correspondence).

92. Frémont to John Torrey

WASHINGTON CITY December 3d. 1844.

MY DEAR SIR,

Having received no reply to my last letters to you, I conclude you must be in Princeton & have not received them as they were directed to New York. The last package contained the catalogue of all the plants except a few hundred for the latter part of 1843—which will be forwarded as soon as you acknowledge the receipt of the others. Will you have the goodness to answer by the return mail that I may know the fate of the Catalogue. Very truly yours,

J. C. Frémont

ALS, RC (NNNBG—Torrey Correspondence).

93. George Engelmann to Asa Gray

St. Louis Dec. 6th. 1844

DEAR DOCTOR

.   .   .   .

I believe I have written you that I had a letter from Geyer from Oregon; he will take his plants directly to England (and not pay his debts here in St. Louis, I expect!). Fremont has seen Lüders on the Columbia, who had lost everything he had in the river. Fremont himself writes me that most of his plants were destroyed. It appeared somewhat singular to me, that during a stay of 8 or 10 days here in St. Louis he would not allow me to open and dry his moulding packages. Did he distrust me? He appears to me rather selfish—I speak confidentially—and disinclined to let any body share in his discoveries, anxious to reap all the honour, as well as undertake all the labour himself. He objected to take any botanist or geologist along with him, though the expense would hardly have been increased and the discoveries certainly greatly augmented, as he himself can not claim any knowledge of either branch, nor of zoology. This however is a private remark. I hope when Government does anything to explore Oregon, some competent men will be sent along, and I must confess I should like much to be of the party.

.   .   .   .

Very truly yours,

G. ENGELMANN

ALS, RC (MH-G). Addressed, "Prof. A. Gray, Cambridge, Near Boston, Mass."

94. Frémont to John Torrey

WASHINGTON CITY Dec. 30th. 1844.

MY DEAR SIR,

I trust that because I delayed answering you for some little time that you will not think that I am not very anxious on the subject of the rocks & plants—on the contrary I am becoming more so as the time at my disposal becomes shorter. I have for some time past been too unwell to devote myself to labor & I have also very many calls upon my attention.

I received your last letter with a great deal of satisfaction as it contained very many agreeable things. The determination of the fossil specimens which I send you, and the botanical information which I hope you will be able to furnish me, will enable me at once to finish my report. These subjects you know are spread over the whole of the work and as their introduction would be to rewrite the Report, I have deferred it until I shall receive it. Could not your friend Dr. Burscheim[1] aid in determining the grasses &c? I would be glad to allow him a proper compensation for it & in that way you might be saved a great deal of trouble & I would get the information in time besides giving him employment which would bring him some little money.

I shall send boxes containing specimens for Dr. Hall by the Transportation line agreeably to the address you gave me & will let you know what time they will be in New York. He will think them a poor collection—but I beg you to tell him that they are merely the wreck of what I had obtained. I send them all to him & he will find among them little pieces & scraps of rock which have no apparent interest—but I consider every geological *fact,* which can be located, of importance in that extensive region & therefore I have held on to every thing. I was desirous that all of the little I would have to say on this subject should be based upon his authority—but if his time should not permit him to examine all of them the box marked No. 1 will contain the fossils & the others might be returned. The numbers attached to each specimen correspond with others in my books & if it would be of any advantage to Dr. Hall I could send him a list of their localities. May I beg you to mention to Dr. Hall the urgent want I have for the results & I must beg you not to be offended at my having so repeatedly pressed you for the botanical knowledge as I am really at a stand on account of it. I am anxious to get through with the business of the last campaign in order that I may prepare earnestly for the next. I enclose you some of the seeds of a species of coniferae (No. 367 of 1844) & found more numerously in 1843. These seeds contribute largely to the sup-

port of Indians & I am anxious to know what the tree is. I shall be
glad to hear from you soon—Yours very truly,

J. C. Frémont

ALS-JBF, RC (NNNBG—Torrey Correspondence).
1. Although there is but slight resemblance to the name "Burscheim," Mrs.
Nesta Ewan believes Dr. Peter Knieskern (1798–1871) was the person intended and that Jessie, who really authored the letter, was confused in recalling the name. Knieskern, who had botanized over the New Jersey Pine
Barrens, was evidently rather friendly with Torrey and interested in grasses.

95. Financial Records, 1 Jan. 1843–31 Dec. 1844

Editorial note: Because of sheer numbers, vouchers for the period
after 1 Jan. 1843 will not be handled as single documents, but will
be presented in summary form with the appropriate notes keyed to
the voucher numbers. Several of the accounts for the second expedition were actually paid by Capt. Thomas J. Cram of the Topographical Engineers at St. Louis, although Frémont, who had returned to Washington, furnished the requisite funds and Thomas
Fitzpatrick helped with the arrangements (see William Henry
Swift to Cram, 2 Sept. 1844, and Abert to Cram, 24 Sept. 1844. Lbk,
DNA-77, LS, 7:391, 432).

The abstract of disbursements for the quarter ending 31 March
1843 is to be found in DNA-217, Third Auditor's Reports and Accounts, Account No. 16962. The abstracts of disbursements for the
remaining quarters plus individual vouchers, statements of differences, and explanations for questioned disbursements are all to be
found on Roll 1 of DNA microfilm T-135, a special consolidated
file of JCF's accounts relating to his expeditions and the California
Battalion. Those pertinent to this period are to be found under two
categories, one of which is too narrowly entitled "Claims and Ac-
knowledgments of Payments, 1842–1845, for the First Expedition"
and the second, "Quarterly Abstracts of Disbursements, 1843–45."

Unless otherwise noted, all payments were made at the locale of
the business firm or at St. Louis.

The editors have added the † and the * to the original documents.

377

The † indicates that the seller became or was a member of the expedition. The * indicates that Theodore Talbot certified that the property was "destroyed, injured, lost, &c." during the expedition. Talbot further certified that of the 224 head of horses and mules purchased for the use of the expedition, 163 were eaten, gave out on the road, died, or were lost or stolen. The remaining 61 were left on the frontier near Westport, Mo.

Abstract of Disbursements on Account of Surveys
West of the Mississippi
for the Quarter Ending 31st March 1843

No. of voucher	Nature of payment	To whom paid	Amount Dollars	Cents
1	Services	Charles Preuss	93	00
2	Services	Joseph Bougar	144	00
3	Services	Charles Preuss	93	00
4	Services	Charles Preuss	84	00
5	Sundries	P. Chouteau, Jr. & Co.	317	00
6	Sundries	P. Chouteau, Jr. & Co.	88	75
7	Postage	J. C. Frémont	1	00
8	Services	J. N. Nicollet	1040	00
			$1860	75[9]

1. Payment at Washington, D.C., for services as assistant, 1 Dec. to 31 Dec. 1842.

2. *Voyageur* on first expedition (see p. 158).

3. Payment at Washington, D.C., for services as assistant, 1 Jan. to 31 Jan. 1843.

4. Payment at Washington, D.C., for services as assistant, 1 Feb. to 28 Feb. 1843.

5. For purchases (such as a lodge skin, ten pack saddles, fifty lbs. of lead, rifle, and powder horn) and services (shoeing horses and repair of guns) made at Fort John on 16 and 18 July 1843.

6. For purchases made at Fort John on the Laramie on 1 and 2 Sept. 1842. Such items as buckskin pants were not permitted and the total had to be reduced to $48.50; yet a statement of "Differences" would indicate that only $28 was not allowed.

7. Postage paid at Washington, D.C., on letter containing public accounts received from Chouteau and Co. in St. Louis.

8. Payment at Baltimore, Md., for services, 1 Nov. 1842 to 10 March 1843.

9. Because of the suspension of items in voucher no. 6, the final total was $1,820.50, and is so shown in the endorsement.

*Abstract of Disbursements on Account of Military and
Geographical Surveys West of the Mississippi for the
Second, Third, and Fourth Quarters of 1843,
and First, Second, and Third Quarters of 1844*

No. of voucher	Nature of expenditure	To whom paid	Amount Dolls.	Cts.
*1	Daguerreotype apparatus	James R. Chilton	78	25
2	Preserved meats, &c	J. E. Flandin	22	31
*3	Daguerreotype apparatus	H. Chilton	68	16
*4	Astl. Instruments &c.	Frye & Shaw	327	50
*5	India Rubber Boat &c.	Horace H. Day	302	10
6	Instruments	Arthur Stewart	215	00
*7	Outfit	Charles Renard	40	00
*8	do	J. & B. Bruce	115	00
9	do	Emory Low	5	63
10	Freight	Steamer Valley Forge	5	00
11	Horses	Louis Lajoie	120	00
12	do	Cyprian Billieau	65	00
13	do	John T. Pigott	110	00
†14	do	Louis Ménard	35	00
15	do	A. Sloan	45	00
16	Provisions	N. Berthoud	47	25
17	Printing blanks	S. Penn, Jr.	10	00
†18	Horse	Auguste Vasquez	25	00
19	do	Wm. G. Sholfield	35	00
20	do	Ewd. Ploudre	35	00
21	Mules	David Goodfellow	90	00
22	Horses	Archibald Sloan	55	00
23	do	A. Gallatin Boone	60	00

No. of voucher	Nature of expenditure	To whom paid	Amount Dolls.	Cts.
*24	Outfit	S. V. Farnsworth & Co.	66	44
25	Horse	George K. McGunegle	20	00
26	Outfit	A. Meier & Co.	52	15
27	do	Jacob Voglesang	6	00
*28	do	J. S. Mathews	2	50
29	do	T. Salorgue	20	00
30	Forage	B. W. Alexander	21	35
*31	Outfit	Edwd. Perry & Co.	172	37
32	Repairing arms	J. & S. Hawken	13	50
33	Stationary	S. W. Meech	28	20
34	Nails	James Conway	6	00
*35	Arms	Wm. Campbell	40	00
*36	Saddles, bridles, harnesses &c.	Thornton Grimsley	438	62
*37	Harness	Ross & Cowe	32	00
38	Equipment	G. W. Rogers	5	00
39	do	Joseph Cailloun	9	00
40	Provisions	N. Devillers & Co.	10	44
41	do	R. O. Taylor	17	78
*42	Making Tents	Z. Prevaud	25	00
*43	Equipment	N. Tiernan	140	00
*44	do	Jos. Murphy	181	20
45	do	John Hobson	30	00
*46	Instruments &c.	Jacob Blattner	27	00
*47	Equipment	N. Phillips	25	00
48	Horse hire and forage	R. Mc O'Blinis	72	52
49	Equipment	K. McKenzie		88
50	do	E. W. & G. Poore	3	00
51	Provisions	F. Leonard	12	07
52	Provisions	E. Sisson	30	94
53	Horse	Benjn. Watson	30	00
54	Mules	D. W. Griffith	70	00
55	do	Thos. Peery	40	00

No. of voucher	Nature of expenditure	To whom paid	Amount Dolls.	Cts.
56	do	Mark R. C. Pulliam	35	00
57	Transportation, pro-visions, &c.	Steamer Col. Woods	150	42
58	Mules	Talton Turner	225	00
59	do	James Foster	25	00
60	do	Lucien Stewart	50	00
61	do	George Wilson	35	00
62	do	Phineas C. Islue	22	50
63	do	A. B. H. Magee	30	00
64	do	F. P. McGee	35	00
65	Repairs &c.	Gabriel Philibert	8	25
66	Horse	Luther M. Carter	40	00
67	Mules	L. D. W. Shaw	205	00
68	do	James M. Weathers	42	50
69	Horse	B. McDermott	25	00
70	Mules	Campbell & Sublette	160	00
71	do	Nathl. Bowman	30	00
72	Horse	Jas. T. Greenfield	26	00
73	Mule	Jas. M. Owen	40	00
74	Forage	Francis Bradley	16	55
75	Mule	S. Wade	25	00
76	Sundries	Boone & Hamilton	184	26
77	Mule	Jas. M. Simpson	40	00
78	Services	Oscar Sarpy	66	00
79	Provisions &c.	J. & E. Walsh	396	63
† *80	Mules &c.	Alex. Godey	200	00
81	Services	Ransom Clark	36	90
82	do	Jas. Power	36	00
83	do	Thos. Rogers	40	26
84	do	Jas. Rogers	40	26
*85	Lodge & poles	A. C. Metcalf	30	00
86	Mules, camp equip-age &c.	Bent & St. Vrain & Co.	667	62
87	Services	Louis Menard	328	66
88	do	Auguste Vasquez	90	90

No. of voucher	Nature of expenditure	To whom paid	Amount Dolls.	Cts.
89	do	François Lajeunesse	126	35
90	do	John Campbell	90	90
91	do	Clinton DeForrest	90	90
92	do	Michael Creely	90	90
93	do	Basil Lajeunesse	164	12
94	do	Alexis Parraw	90	90
95	do	Baptiste Tissant [Tesson]	90	90
96	do	Patrick White	90	90
97	do	Henry Lee	90	90
98	do	William Creuss	90	90
99	Provisions &c.	Hudson Bay Compy.	2038	65
100	Services	John G. Campbell	94	00
101	Provisions &c.	H. B. Brewer	267	89
102	Services	Philibert Cortot	122	65
103	do	Thos. Fallon	129	35
104	do	Jos. Verrot	211	50
105	do	Oliver Beaulieu	122	65
106	[*Incompleted entry scratched*]			
107	Mules & horses	John A. Sutter	2910	00
108	Sundries	John A. Sutter	981	93
109	do	C. W. Flügge	237	25
110	Provisions	Jos. B. Chiles	54	00
111	Services	Saml. Neal	211	00
112	Horses	Archibald Sloan	60	00
†113	do	Baptiste Derosier	18	00
114	Repairing Instruments	Jaccard & Co.	12	00
115	Horse shoes	Milton E. McGee	5	00
116	Mule	W. W. Gett	45	00
117	Services	Francis Parraw	179	10
118	Sundries	A. Robidoux	86	00
119	Services	Chas. Town	342	00
120	do	Christopher Carson	885	00

No. of voucher	Nature of expenditure	To whom paid	Amount Dolls.	Cts.
†121	Mules & Horse	Christopher Carson	140	00
122	Services	Louis Anderson	155	00
123	do	J. R. Walker	165	00
124	Sundries	Bent, St. Vrain & Co.	251	00
125	Provisions	E. T. Peery	37	00
126	Transportation of men	Steamboat Iatan	130	00
127	Services	Thomas Cowie	64	00
128	do	Louis Gouin Admr.	167	85
129	do	Saml. H. Davis	37	00
130	Repg. Instruments	C. D. Sullivan & Co.	4	00
131	Transportation	Chas. Preuss	216	80
132	Services	Chas. Preuss	2076	00
133	Transportation	J. C. Frémont	216	80
134	Services	Jacob Dodson	493	00
†135	Horses	Wm. Perkins	80	00
136	Services	Wm. Perkins	239	16
137	Services	Louis Montreuil	221	85
138	do	Andreas Fuentes	107	50
139	do	Thos. Fitzpatrick	1750	00
140	do	Alexis [Ayot]	328	66
141	do	Tiery Wright	410	83
142	do	Raphael Proue	410	83
†143	do & provisions	Alexis Godare	918	00
144	do	Louis Zindel	573	52
†145	Transportation & c.	Thos. Fitzpatrick	309	50
146	Services	C. Taplin	410	83
147	do	Baptiste Bernier	493	00
148	do	Auguste Archambeau[lt]	190	00
149	[Entry scratched]			
150	[Entry scratched]			
151	Sundries	Robert Campbell	5455	35
152	Stationary	Wm. Fischer	26	39
153	Sundries	Chas. Preuss	38	40
			33092	38

No. of voucher	Nature of expenditure	To whom paid	Amount Dolls.	Cts.
154	Services	Theodore Talbot	986	00
			34078	38
155	do	Admr. Francois Badeau Sep. 19th 1844	387	00
			34465	38[156]

J. C. Frémont
2d. Lt. Topl. Engr.

1. A delayed voucher for the daguerreotype apparatus purchased in New York and used on the first expedition (see p. 145).

2. J. Eugene Flandin, who had accompanied Nicollet and JCF to the Minnesota country in 1838, was working in his father's store when JCF purchased meats, bottled milk, and tomato sauce in New York for his second expedition.

3. H. Chilton, a daguerreotypist in New York, to whom are credited several portraits in the *Democratic Review* (see, for example, *Democratic Review*, 14 [1844], opp. p. 447).

4. The telescope and two artificial horizons survived the hazards of the expedition, but the two pocket compasses, barometer, and five thermometers purchased of Frye & Shaw, a New York firm, were broken.

5. Besides the India rubber boat, payment was made in New York to Horace Day for such items as a tent, water bottles, waterproof cloth, and trunks.

6. Arthur Stewart, of New York, received $15 for repairs for a chronometer which had been purchased for the first expedition (see p. 140) and $200 for a silver pocket two-day chronometer which survived the hazards of the second expedition.

7. Payment was made at Washington, D.C., for a large Swiss rifle.

8. J. and B. Bruce, of Cincinnati, supplied the plain Harrison wagon which was abandoned at the Dalles.

9. Emory Low, on Maine Street between Third and Fourth in Louisville, supplied 4,000 super percussion caps and rifle powder.

16. Mocha coffee.

24. Iron kettles, tin buckets, lanterns, etc.

26. Spades, nails, axes, screws, fish lines and hooks, scissors, etc.

27. Instrument box and frame for the India rubber boat.

28. Goat skin trunk.

29. For making tent poles.

30. The figure on the original voucher is $21.55.

31. Four French carts, pickets, poles, and tent stretchers. Overpaid $0.05.

35. Double-barrelled shotgun.

36. Included three "best Spanish saddles."

37. Two sets of cart harnesses and one chronometer case which became broken and were abandoned at Walla Walla.

38. For making a tent.

39. Three beaver traps.

40. Spices, olive oil, dried apples, and vinegar.

41. The Marketer's House provided fifteen men with 142 meals at 12½ cents per meal. Overpaid $0.03.

42. Three tents and one marquee made by Z. Prevaud.

43. Four horse carts.

44. Four mule carts and forty horse pickets. The twelve carts represented by voucher nos. 31, 43, and 44 either broke down during the journey or were abandoned at the Walla Walla mission.

45. For one mule, and payment apparently made at Williamsburg in Franklin County, Kan.

46. The two pocket compasses, ivory scale, magnet, and two pairs of bellows were either lost or damaged.

47. An ensign made to order.

49. One dozen plough lines.

50. Fifty pounds of lead.

51. Provisions furnished JCF's men at Fort Osage.

52. Provisions furnished JCF's men at Camden, 17 May 1843.

53. Payment made in Boone County.

54. Payment received at Decatur, Howard County, Mo.

55. Payment made at Glasgow, Mo.

56. Payment made in Fayette County, Mo.

57. Passage was for twenty-eight men, and payment was made at Kansas Landing, 18 May 1843.

58–61. Payment made at Glasgow, Mo.

62. Payment made at Westport Landing, 24 May 1843.

63. No place, but probably Westport Landing. The voucher bears JCF's endorsement: "When I was on the frontier this receipt was sent me by the individual & I had no means of having it properly corrected as he left for California immediately afterwards." We cannot fathom the error. A. B. H. Magee has not been identified, but a Milton E. McGee emigrated to California in the Chiles party in 1843 and appears hereafter in JCF's accounts for 1844.

64–65. Payment made at Westport Landing, 24 May 1843.

66. Payment made at Westport, Mo.

67–68. Payment made at Richmond, Mo., 25 May 1843.

69. Payment made at Liberty, Mo., 25 May 1843.

70–71. Payment made at Westport Landing.

72. Payment made at Liberty, Mo.

73. Payment made at Westport Landing, 27 May 1843.

74. No place of payment given, but probably Westport.

75. Payment made at Westport, Mo., 29 May 1843.

76. Payment was made at Westport for a variety of articles, but $24.69 was not admitted as legitimate expenditure, being items for the private use of individuals, such as moccasins for Henry Lee, shoes for Badeau, and a fur cap and silk handkerchief for Fitzpatrick.

77. Payment made in Jackson County, Mo.

78. Paid at Fort St. Vrain for services as a *voyageur* from St. Louis at $1.00 per diem for sixty-six days, 1 May 1843 to 5 July 1843.

79. The original voucher is for $396.33. The supplies were largely food and attached to the voucher was JCF's explanation: "Among the articles in this bill which may require explanation are first *brandy & wine*. These were pur-

chased for medicinal purposes & were used accordingly in the severe weather which the party encountered in the winter. *Macaroni* is one of the best articles, for such a party—it is nutritious, easy to transport & goes farther than flour. *Raisins & Almonds* were taken to be occasionally distributed to the men as in the regular service, they were however but of little use, so with the cheese, but they were issued."

80. Payment made at Fort St. Vrain for two mules and one Spanish saddle and bridle.

81. For services as a *voyageur* from St. Louis to Fort St. Vrain at $0.45 per diem, 3 May to 24 July 1843. Although William S. Clark, the son of Ransom Clark, maintained that his father came to Oregon with JCF, the voucher would indicate that he left the expedition at St. Vrain's and must have gone to Oregon by some other means. He became a permanent settler except for a season in the California gold mines (w. s. CLARK).

82. For services as a *voyageur* from St. Louis to Fort St. Vrain at $0.45 per diem for eighty days, from 3 May to 24 July 1843.

83–84. James and Thomas [Jefferson] Rogers were father and son hunters —either Delaware or Shawnee Indians—who went as far as Fort St. Vrain and were paid for their services at $0.66 per diem each for sixty-one days, 1 June to 31 July 1843.

85. Payment made at Fort St. Vrain, 26 July 1843.

86. Paid at Fort George, River Platte, 24 July 1843. Overcharged $30. Also, items to the value of $40.62 were held to be for private use and not admissible.

87. For services as a *voyageur* at $0.66⅔ per diem for 493 days, 3 May 1843 to 6 Sept. 1844.

88–98. The eleven men listed in these vouchers started with JCF's expedition, but turned back at Fort Hall on 20 Sept. All received pay from 3 May to 20 Nov. 1843, which was the time period calculated to permit their return to St. Louis. All were paid at the rate of $0.45 per diem except Basil and François Lajeunesse, who received $0.81¾ and $0.62½ respectively. A hawk-eyed auditor caught the fact that François had been overpaid by $0.10.

99. For supplies of all kinds, ranging from food to items of equipment received at Forts Hall, Boise, Nez Percé, and Vancouver. Included was $500 for the amount credited to Frederick Dwight at Vancouver per JCF's order. John McLoughlin acknowledged payment by draft of JCF on Abert, 10 Nov. 1843. The $500 to Frederick Dwight was not admissible, of course, as a charge against the U.S.; neither were private items totaling $175.40.

100. For a $4.00 saddle and for services as a *voyageur* from St. Louis to the Dalles at $0.45 per diem for 200 days, 5 May to 21 Nov. 1843.

101. The supplies obtained from the missionary H. B. Brewer at Wascopam, Ore., 23 Nov. 1843, included meal, potatoes, flour, steers, etc. A $2.29 item for John G. Campbell was not permitted as a charge against the U.S.

102. Cortot [Courteau] was paid for services as a *voyageur* from St. Louis to New Helvetia, Calif., at $0.45 per diem for 317 days, 3 May 1843 to 14 March 1844. His pay was docked for forty lbs. of sugar at $0.50 per lb., which he had allegedly stolen from the U.S.

103. For services as a *voyageur* from Fort St. Vrain to New Helvetia, Calif., at $0.45 per diem for 123 days, 24 July to 24 Nov. 1843, and at $0.66⅔ per diem for 111 days, 25 Nov. 1843 to 14 March 1844. For biographical details on Fallon, see Doc. No. 137, p. 453.

104. Paid 14 March 1844 for services as a *voyageur* from St. Louis to New

Helvetia at $0.45 per diem, except from 1 Sept. 1843 to 31 Jan. 1844, when the per diem rate was $0.90.

105. For services as a *voyageur* from St. Louis to New Helvetia at $0.45 per diem for 317 days, 3 May 1843 to 14 March 1844. Like Courteau, his pay was docked for forty lbs. of sugar at $0.50 per lb., stolen from the U.S.

107. $600 of the amount was paid at New Helvetia, 23 March 1844, to Sutter, at his request, in the form of a sight draft drawn in favor of Joseph B. Chiles on Robert Campbell, of St. Louis.

108. Payment was made at New Helvetia, 23 March 1844, by drafts drawn on Colonel Abert. Attached to the voucher is JCF's explanation of some of the items. "The silver plated bridle and sweat cloth including a saddle were purchased by me from Capt. Sutter for my own use. It was a good saddle & I could obtain no other good one; it was necessary to have a Spanish bridle as the horses we rode were wild and unbroken. Accts. Thos. Fallen [Fallon], Joseph Vereau [Verrot], O. Beaulieu were private accounts. The amount paid to Capt. Johnson was on account of the United States & was for the hire of his barge & crew from Capt. Sutter's to the town of Monterrey. The amount paid to H. Chase [for making clothing] was private. Amount paid to Mr. Sinclair [buckskin pants and moccasins] was private. Buck-skin pantaloon's & moccassins for Jacob were private." A total of $182.93 had to be deducted as being for private use.

109. Payment made at New Helvetia, 23 March 1843, by draft drawn on the Topographical Bureau. $80.25 had to be deducted as being the value of items for private use.

110. For flour; payment made at New Helvetia.

111. Paid for services as a *voyageur* from St. Louis to New Helvetia at $0.50 per diem for 246 days, 3 May 1843 to 3 Jan. 1844, and at $1.00 per diem for 88 days, 4 Jan. to 31 March 1844.

113. Payment made at St. Louis, 8 May 1843.

115. This item, dated 17 May 1844, was for one pair of horseshoes, purchased "on the trail from California."

116. Payment was made at Glasgow, Mo., 19 May 1843.

117. Francis Parraw [François Perrault] was paid at Uintah Fort for services as a *voyageur* at $0.45 per diem for 398 days, 3 May 1843 to 3 June 1844.

118. Purchases made at Uintah Fort, 4 June 1844. $15 had to be deducted as being the value of items for private use.

119. Paid at "The Pueblo" for services as an assistant hunter at $1.00 per diem for 342 days, 25 July 1843 to 29 June 1844. Overpaid by $1. See also p. 446.

120. Paid at Bent's Fort as a hunter at $2.00 per diem for 354 days, 15 July 1843 to 2 July 1844.

121. Purchase made at Bent's Fort, 2 July 1844.

122. "For services [*unspecified*] rendered to United States from 'Lesser Youta Lake' to Ft. William [Bent's Fort], Arkansas R.," at $2.50 per diem for forty-two days, 25 May to 5 July 1844, plus an allowance of pay for twenty days to return to the "Snake District."

123. For services as a guide from "The Lesser Youta Lake" to "Ft. William, Arkansas R." at $2.50 per diem for forty-two days, 25 May to 5 July 1844, plus an allowance of twenty days' pay to return to the "Snake District." Frémont also purchased two pair of horseshoes from Walker at $5.00 per pair (see pp. 693 and 720).

124. Payment made at Bent's Fort, Arkansas River, 5 July 1844. $141.00 had to be deducted as being the value of items for private use.

125. Furnished at the Shawnee Indian Manual Labor School, Leavenworth agency, 31 July 1844.

127. For services as a *voyageur* from Uintah Fort to St. Louis at $1.00 per diem for sixty-four days, 5 June to 7 Aug. 1844. For biographical details of Cowie, see second *Report,* our p. 706.

128. Received by Louis Guion, as administrator of Tabeau's estate, for Jean Baptiste Tabeau's services as a *voyageur* at $0.45 per diem for 373 days, 3 May 1843 to 9 May 1844. Tabeau was killed by the Indians (see p. 690). In the abstract for voucher no. 2 of the fourth quarter of 1844, p. 390, Tabeau's estate was paid an additional $150.72 for the period from his death to 6 Sept. 1844, but the government did not recognize this as a legitimate payment and seems to have held JCF responsible for the illegal payment (see note on abstract of disbursements for quarter ending 31 Dec. 1844).

129. Paid at St. Louis for services as a *voyageur* at $1.00 per diem for thirty-seven days, 4 July to 9 Aug. 1844.

131. Paid at Washington, D.C.

132. Paid at Washington for services as a topographical assistant at $4.00 per diem for 519 days, 1 April 1843 to 31 Aug. 1844.

133. For transportation of JCF's baggage from Washington to Westport, 18 April to 17 May 1843, and from Westport to Washington, 2 Aug. to 25 Aug. 1844. Payment made at Washington.

134. Paid at Washington, D.C., for services as a *voyageur* from St. Louis for the round trip at $1.00 per diem for 493 days, 3 May 1843 to 6 Sept. 1844. Dodson was JCF's Negro servant.

135. Payment made at Washington, D.C., for two horses sold at the Dalles, 25 Nov. 1843.

136. Paid at Washington, D.C., for services as a *voyageur* from the Dalles at $0.83⅓ per diem for 287 days, 25 Nov. 1843 to 6 Sept. 1844. The William Perkins in this voucher and the one above is probably William, the Chinook Indian boy (see Doc. Nos. 124 and 128). It would be unusual for a *voyageur* to go all the way to Washington with Frémont. William Perkins went west again with JCF in 1845 and was discharged as a *voyageur* at Johnson's ranch, Upper Calif., 16 June 1847 (DNA-217, T-135, Roll 1, voucher no. 224). On several occasions Talbot mentioned William, the Chinook Indian, as being on the third expedition (see Talbot to Adelaide Talbot, 26 May, 25 June, and 3 July 1845, in the Talbot Papers, DLC).

137. For services as a *voyageur* for the round trip at $0.45 per diem for 493 days, 3 May 1843 to 6 Sept. 1844.

138. For services as a *voyageur* at $0.83⅓ per diem for 129 days, 1 May to 6 Sept. 1844. Fuentes was picked up on the Spanish Trail (p. 677).

139. For services as guide for the round trip at $3.33⅓ per diem for 525 days, 1 April 1843 to 6 Sept. 1844.

140. For services as a *voyageur* for the round trip at $0.66⅔ per diem for 493 days, 3 May 1843 to 6 Sept. 1844.

141. For services as a *voyageur* for the round trip at $0.83⅓ per diem for 493 days from 3 May 1843 to 6 Sept. 1844.

142. For services as a *voyageur* for the round trip at $0.83⅓ per diem for 493 days, 3 May 1843 to 6 Sept. 1844.

143. Paid at St. Louis, $820 for services as a hunter at $2.00 per diem for 410 days, 25 July 1843 to 6 Sept. 1844. $80 of the sum was for a mule which

Godey sold to the expedition at the South Fork of the Platte on 26 July; $18 was for pinoli (ground and parched meal) and dried meat sold to the expedition on 25 May 1844 (for other sales by Godey, see voucher no. 80 above).

144. For services as a *voyageur* for the round trip at $1.16 per diem for 493 days, 3 May 1843 to 6 Sept. 1844.

145. JCF notes that "the item of $109.50 was the amount of expenses made by Mr. Fitzpatrick for board & lodging of a party of men & a drove of horses conducted by himself under my orders from the City of Saint Louis to the frontier town of Westport. The horses mentioned in the bill [$200] were the private property of Mr. Fitzpatrick & purchased from him [at the South Fork of the Platte River on 24 July 1843] for the United States."

146. For the round trip at $0.80⅓ per diem for 493 days, 3 May 1843 to 6 Sept. 1844. Overpaid by $14.79.

147. Bernier, who had been on the first expedition, made the complete trip and received pay for services as a *voyageur* at $1.00 per diem for 493 days, 3 May 1843 to 6 Sept. 1844.

148. For services as a *voyageur* and assistant hunter from Uintah Fort to St. Louis at $2.00 per diem for 95 days, 4 June to 6 Sept. 1844.

151. $1,111.43, actually $1,101.93 as $9.50 was overcredited, purchased goods which JCF stated were "used in making presents to the Indians to facilitate our passage through the country according to the usual custom and in trading with them for horses, provisions & other necessaries & in paying guides. At the missionary post at The Dalles of the Columbia, I purchased with a portion of these goods thirty-seven horses from the Walla Walla Indians. At $40 per head (this being the lowest current price for horses) these amounted to $1480." $4,353.42 of the total was either for goods furnished to members of JCF's expedition or money which Campbell paid to individuals or firms who supplied equipment for the expedition.

152. Purchased at Washington, D.C., 9 Sept. 1844.

153. Paid at Washington, D.C., 10 Sept. 1844, for purchase of small items before the start of the expedition.

154. Paid at Washington for services on the round trip at $2.00 per diem for 493 days, 3 May 1843 to 6 Sept. 1844.

155. For services as a *voyageur* from St. Louis until his accidental death, at $1.00 per diem for 387 days, 3 May 1843 to 23 May 1844. By signed duplicates, Badeau's widow Angeline, with her mark, and Louis Guion, administrator of the estate, acknowledged receipt of the money.

156. The sum, based on the figures as transcribed in this document, should read $34,464.78. The column has been overadded by $0.60, a mistake which JCF's auditor caught. As noted earlier, voucher nos. 30 and 79 were recorded incorrectly, but the incorrect figures are used for the purpose of addition and the document is kept with all of its original figures and errors.

The endorsement on the face of the document indicates that the "overadded," the "overpaid," "personal items," and $4,353.42 of voucher no. 151—all enumerated in the notes above—amounted to a total of $5,562.17, leaving a balance of $28,903.21. In addition $310 and $981.93, represented by unpaid drafts to Sutter, were deducted from voucher nos. 107 and 108, leaving a final balance of $27,611.28 for the quarters represented by the abstract. Thus the total of $34,465.38 appears to be the cost of the second expedition. It is not entirely clear from the surviving documents, however, exactly how much of this total was eventually cleared from JCF's account and paid by the government.

Another voucher pertinent to this second expedition, but not given until 3 June 1845, reflects an advanced payment of $45 to Thérèse Derosier. Her husband had wandered from the expedition's camp in California and was presumed to be dead. When Derosier subsequently showed up in St. Louis, he was paid the balance of $381 due him (see DNA-217, T-135, Roll 1, voucher nos. 146 [3 June 1845] and 301 [12 March 1846]).

Abstract of Disbursements on Account of Military and Geographical Surveys West of the Mississippi for the Quarter Ending 31 Dec. 1844

No. of voucher	Nature of payment	To whom paid	Amount Dollars	Cents
1	Services as Packman	William Martin	98	25
2	" as voyageur	Louis Gouin, admr.	150	72
3	Lining maps &c.	John A. Blake	6	00
4	Binding book	Robt. Connell		75
5	Books	John Downes	10	00
			265	72

1. For services as a packman from New Helvetia to the western frontier of Missouri at $0.75 per diem for 131 days, 21 March to 29 July 1844. William J. Martin, a member of the Oregon emigration group of 1843, which had also included Jesse Applegate and Peter H. Burnett, joined Joseph B. Chiles' party at Fort Hall to travel by horseback to California, and reached Sutter's Fort on 10 Nov. 1843. A voucher submitted much later by JCF indicates that he sold the exploring party flour and skin sacks on 23 March 1844, two days after joining the expedition for the return to Missouri. In 1846, Martin went west again and settled permanently in Oregon. In 1853, he served as Indian agent in the Umpqua Valley, and in 1855 as major of the volunteer northern battalion in the Rogue River Indian War (BARRY, 29:463, 470, 30:344–45; COAN, 33; H. ROBBINS, 345–58).

2. With regard to this entry a note on the voucher reads: "This Vo. No. 2, being wholly suspended, was returned to R. Burgess, attorney for Colo. Frémont, 28 June 1849 per letter of that date." Tabeau's estate had already been paid for his services to the date of his death (see voucher no. 128, p. 383). Even if compensation had been permitted for his widow until the time of the discharge of the men in St. Louis, the amount would have been only $53.55.

3. Paid at Washington, D.C., 7 Sept. 1844.

4. Paid at Washington, D.C., 20 Sept. 1844.

5. Paid at Washington, D.C., 25 Nov. 1844.

96. Asa Gray to John Torrey

Saturday Morning [1845]

DEAR DOCTOR,

. . . .

I have just turned over the Fremontian plants you send. The Malpighiaceae you send are not those fixd. by Bentham—and I should suppose not Malpighiaceae at all. I will look at them and the Œnothera's—some of which are new.

As to the Cruciferous plant, the trifoliate leaves should not stand in the way. Look at Cardamines and Dentarias. And your plant is I doubt not from recollection of the figure (which is not before me) a *Dithraea* perhaps D. Californica, Harvey. That however had a regular terminal raceme, rather low. Is yours in the natural state? Or do the dense axil[lary] clusters come from the top having been bitten off?

. . . .

Yours ever,

A. GRAY

ALS, RC (NNNBG—Torrey Correspondence).

97. Frémont to John Torrey

WASHINGTON CITY Jany. 12th. 1845

MY DEAR SIR,

On Thursday last I sent by the transportation line a box of fossils for Dr. Hall. The Agent informed me that it would be in New York to-morrow but I could not learn whether it would be sent to Mr. Endicott's[1] or whether it was necessary to send for it. I enclose a brief note relative to them which can be extended if it should be of use. The names which I have affixed to some of the vegetable fossils, depend only on my own knowledge as there is no one here to whom I could refer for the least information on the subject, therefore Dr. Hall will know what weight to give them. If it would not be troublesome to him I would be glad to have them again as this year I shall visit the same localities in order to examine as closely as I am able the interesting geology of that country. He had better break up one of the large specimens as he will find several different varieties of plants. Some of these appear to be entirely new. I would have been glad to send him all the different specimens of rocks in order that the little notice that I could make of the Geology on this occasion might depend on his authority—and I am afraid to ask too much of him.

It will be quite a pleasure to hear from you whenever you find time. I hope that in the midst of your labors your health has been good which has not been altogether the case with me. In fact my ill health has taken away much of the energy so necessary for my work, which will account to you for my not having sent the specimens before.

In the box I sent you a cone belonging to the tree from which I sent you the nuts or seeds. You will find one of these contained under each of the scales. I also put in the box a mutilated cone from what I supposed to be Pinus Lambertinai—leaves about 2 inches long—in fives. Cones 6 or 7 inches long. Yours very truly,

J. C. Frémont

ALS-JBF, RC (NNNBG—Torrey Correspondence).
1. Probably George Endicott (1802–48), New York engraver, though sometime in 1845 he was joined by his younger brother William. These lithographers did the original drawings for the botanical illustrations and engraved eight of the plates on stone (voucher no. 232 [16 March 1848], DNA-217, T-135, shows that G. and W. Endicott were paid $95.75 for work done in 1845).

98. Asa Gray to John Torrey

Monday [12 Jan. 1845?]

My dear friend,

Thanks for the numbers from Fremont's list; which came to hand just as the proofs were lying before me.

Have you not made a mistake about No. 414 (1843) "Encampment on the Arkansaw" &c.—and copied from the 1844 list? The plant is not a *shrub,* but a low herb. (Pyrrocoma).[1] *Did Fremont go up the Arkansaw on his way out?

Save me specimens, when they will bear it, from Fremont's plants. At the first collection (except compositae) I only shared after Carey!

. . . . .

I remain faithfully yours,

A. GRAY

ALS, RC (NNNBG—Torrey Correspondence). Torrey's note, added to the bottom of the letter, reads: *"The reference in my letter is correct. Fremont does not call the plant 'a shrub'—but says it forms 'bushes'—which may *mean* an herbaceous plant with a bushy look—(like Lespedeza). He went up the Arkansaw on his way out."
1. Plant evidently described as *Aplopappus fremontii* by Gray in 1864.

99. J. J. Abert to John J. Audubon

[22 Jan. 1845]

MY DEAR SIR:

There was no zoologist with Freemont. The expedition was barren except in its geographical, Geological & Botanical materials. I mean to have the next managed better in these respects & to have some one with it who will attend to birds & beasts—we have now a clever young man here taking lessons in skinning birds and ascertaining their sex[1] although nothing new may be found in these branches, yet it is highly desirable to multiply Specimens. If you can give any hints from your experience in those regions of the best method of preserving skins & of transporting them, you will much oblige me. Most kindly to the family and truly yours,

J. J. ABERT
22 Jan. 1845

Copy (MoSHi—Audubon Papers). A letter to Abert from ornithologist John J. Audubon, written in Dec. 1844 or Jan. 1845, was not found among the "letters received" of the Topographical Bureau, but neither was Abert's reply to Audubon recorded in the letterbook.

1. The name of the "clever young man . . . taking lessons in skinning birds" is not known. John Kirk Townsend (1809–51) was at work in the Great Hall of the Patent Office on bird skins in 1841, when the botanical specimens were arriving from the U.S. Exploring Expedition, but in 1843, as a result of controversies between the National Institution and Captain Wilkes, Townsend was discharged (DAB; GRAUSTEIN, 357–58). He then obtained from JCF some temporary employment, 1 Dec. 1844–8 March 1845, at $2 per day, copying tables and astronomical observations (DNA-217, T-135, voucher no. 13, 8 March 1845). Sometime in 1845 Townsend went back to Philadelphia to study dentistry. It is unlikely that Abert would refer to the author of *Ornithology of the United States of America* as a "clever young man," particularly when writing to Audubon, who had pictured some of Townsend's new birds from Oregon in the last volume of *Birds of America* (New York, 1844).

100. Asa Gray to John Torrey

Tuesday Evening. 28th Jany. [1845]

MY DEAR FRIEND,

. . . .

I have today written to Hooker, directing his attention to your full account of the plant—enquiring whether Fremontia has not the priority, and requesting Hooker, at any rate to reprint your account of the plant, as it completes its history. I do not see that Lindley adds anything even to what they knew abroad, for Schlechtendal in Bot. Zeit. says it is Hooker's Batis vermicularis.

. . . .

There must be some mistake in the numbering of the No. 414. Fremont. It is a very low herb—a new Pyrrocoma—which it is new to find on this side of the Rocky Mts.—tho' not surprising. I let the locality slip by without mentioning it, in my little paper—of which I will send a copy in a few days.

Excuse this way of writing. Goodnight. Yours ever.

A. GRAY

ALS, RC (NNNBG—Torrey Correspondence).

101. Frémont to John Torrey

WASHINGTON CITY February 7th. 1845

MY DEAR SIR,

This will be handed to you by Dr. James McDowell[1] son of the Govr. of Virginia who is to accompany me as surgeon in my next expedition. My Report is about to be ordered in the Senate and as I am obliged to publish it before I go I know you will not feel yourself urged if I beg you to assist me by giving what information you can relative to the botany of the country in order that I may give to it as much interest & value as possible & in some degree proportioned to the interest which has been raised in regard to it. Mr. McDowell happening to have a few days of leisure I prevailed on him to go to New York for the purpose of seeing as he could better explain to you than I how much pressed I am for time & how much indebted I would be for your assistance.

There will be about 10,000 copies of the Report ordered—& as it will be widely disseminated I am exceedingly anxious it will go out with every advantage our limited time can give us. Very truly yours,

J. C. FRÉMONT

ALS-JBF, RC (NNNBG—Torrey Correspondence).
1. Dr. James McDowell was the nephew of Mrs. Thomas Hart Benton. His wife, the daughter of Joshua B. and Sarah Benton Brant, was the great-niece of Thomas Hart Benton. Young McDowell, who had been practicing medicine in St. Louis, was described by Alfred Waugh, the artist who wanted so much to join JCF's third expedition, as being "a tall, well made young man, with rather a handsome face, of a good healthy complexion, and pleasant countenance" (WAUGH, 9, 18).

102. J. J. Abert to Frémont

Bureau of Topogl. Engs.
WASHINGTON Feby. 12. 1845

Brevet Captain J. C. Fremont of the Corps of Topographical Engineers, is hereby assigned to command and direction of the contemplated expedition to the Rocky Mountains. He is assigned thereto, according to his brevet rank, and the pay and allowances of his brevet rank are hereby recognized, by order of the Secretary of War in this order of assignment.

Two Lieutenants of the Corps will also be assigned to the duty.[1] As a Commutation for transportation, fuel and quarters, Captain Fremont will receive $1.50 per day, and each Lieutenant one dollar per day. This commutation to commence on the arrival of each at Independence, Missouri, and to continue during the duties in the field, to be paid out of the appropriation for the expedition and survey.

Mr. Talbott formerly with the expedition can be employed at two dollars per day, and Mr. McDowell as surgeon and Physician, at a compensation of three dollars per day. These allowances to commence on the date of their orders from Captain Fremont. Ten cents per mile for transportation can be paid to each of these persons from Washington to Independence, Missouri, and back to Washington on the termination of the expedition, provided said back transportation shall not exceed the distance from Independence, Mo. to Washington. No other persons will be employed except as engagees and hired men, unless on the special representation of Captain Fremont by letter to the Bureau, and the approval of the War Department.[2] The engagees and hired men of the expedition will not exceed fifty.[3]

The general outline of Captain Fremont's duties are indicated in the annual report from this office. He will strike the Arkansas as soon as practicable, survey that river, and if practicable survey the Red River without our boundary line, noting particularly the navigable properties of each, and will determine as near as practicable the points at which the boundary line of the U. S. the 100th degree of longitude west of Greenwich strikes the Arkansas, and the Red River. It is also important that the Head waters of the Arkansas should be accurately determined. Long journies to determine isolated geographical points are scarcely worth the time and the expense which they occasion; the efforts of Captain Fremont will therefore be more particularly directed to the geography of localities within reasonable distance of Bents Fort, and of the streams which run east from the Rocky Mountains, and he will so time his operations, that his party will come in during the present year.

All specimens collected by the expedition, will be preserved and brought to Washington, subject to the ulterior orders of the War Department; and all reports will be delivered to Captain Fremont; no publications will be permitted by any of the party, except in the report from Captain Fremont.

Captain Fremont is hereby authorized to draw upon the Department, as the duties shall require means.

J. J. ABERT
Col. Corps T.E.

Lbk (DNA-77, LS, 8:211–13). Some of the documents following this one deal wholly or in part with JCF's projected third expedition, which will carry him west again in 1845. As he was planning the third while cleaning up paper work on the second, we have retained such documents to preserve chronological unity.

1. See Doc. No. 118 (10 April 1845), notifying JCF that Lieuts. James W. Abert and William Guy Peck were ordered to report to him.

2. See Doc. No. 106 (5 March 1845), approving the employment of a "Botannical Colourist" for the expedition.

3. See Doc. No. 105 (1 March 1845), noting that an error had been made and that the *engagés* and hired men of the expedition were not to exceed forty. On 10 April, JCF was given permission to detach a party to explore the southern Rocky Mountains and the regions south of the Arkansas, and to increase his party by ten men; on 26 May, he was given greater discretion as to the size of the party, should he find it advantageous to make detachments from his command (see Doc. Nos. 118 and 136).

103. Frémont to John Torrey

WASHINGTON CITY Feby. 26th 1845

MY DEAR SIR,

Will you have the kindness to forward to Prof. Hall, a box which I have sent to Mr. Endicott. I have the pleasure to hear from Dr. Hall, who is getting on well with the fossils.

I enclose a form of the receipts used by the Department & if [you] will please have it receipted for amount paid in the transportation of the boxes I will send on the draft immediately.

I send you a fragment of the Californian poppy, as I suppose it to be, Eschscholtzia Crocea.

I suppose the specimens were so much injured that even this may help. I will send you in an envelope this evening a few plants which I have found among my books—& which were forgotten, (Campanula meda)? Rocky Mts. abundant. (Viola Canina?) Rocky Mts. A strawberry Rocky Mts. In addition to the above will be a fragment (all that is left) of a very interesting leguminous plant with a deep yellow flower. It is highly characteristic in certain portions of the Rocky Mt. region.

The plants will come in a public document.

I have also some additional seed vessels of the new Accacia if you desire them—You will have to search carefully in order to find the plants. Yours truly,

J. C. FRÉMONT

ALS-JBF, RC (NNNBG—Torrey Correspondence).

104. Frémont to John Torrey

367. 1844 A remarkable species. Without cones. Probably a *Pinus* though the leaves are almost all *solitary!*—only two or three being found double in the same sheath.

WASHINGTON CITY Feby. 26. 1845.

MY DEAR SIR,

In looking over the list of plants the words which I have underscored in the above struck me for the first time to-day, & I [have] to tell you that in the first box of fossils which I sent some weeks ago to Dr. Hall, was a cone for you in good preservation belonging to that tree. As there were many specimens of the same tree the cone was probably referred to another number. I also sent you some fruit or seeds of the same in a letter. I am very much interested in this particular tree. Among the plants was a small bundle or sheaf of sweet scented grass from Grand [Colorado] river of the Rocky Mts.[1] It was not labelled. Can you tell me its name? Can you tell me the botanic name of what is commonly called in the west Buffalo grass? A very short succulent curled grass having a small reddish blossom. Yours very truly,

J. C. FRÉMONT

ALS-JBF, RC (NNNBG—Torrey Correspondence).
1. *Hierochloë odorata* (L.) Beauv. Sweetgrass.

105. J. J. Abert to Frémont

Bureau of Topogl. Engs.
WASHINGTON March 1. 1845

SIR

I find an error in my letter to you of the 12th February. It is there said that "the engagees & hired men of the expedition will not exceed fifty." I cannot account for this error, as the understanding between us was that the number of this class should not exceed forty. You will please therefore to understand this number as limited to forty. Respectfully Sir Your Obt. Servt.,

J. J. ABERT
Col. Corps. T. E.

Lbk (DNA-77, LS, 8:234).

106. J. J. Abert to Frémont

Bureau of Topogl. Engs.
WASHINGTON March 5. 1845

SIR,

I have submitted your letter of the 5th inst. to the Secretary of War and in reply have to state that the Secretary approves of the employment of a Botanical Colourist for the expedition at a compensation of three dollars the day.[1] You are therefore hereby authorized to employ one. Very Respectfully Your Obt. Servt.,

J. J. ABERT
Col. Corps. T. E.

Lbk (DNA-77, LS, 8:236).
1. JCF's letter of 5 March not found, but the register indicates that it had merely recommended the employment of a botanical colorist at $3 per day.

107. Frémont to George Talcott

WASHINGTON CITY March 10th 1845

DEAR SIR,

Dr. James McDowell of Virginia, who has been appointed Surgeon to the Expedition will also act incidentally as Naturalist. Several gentlemen of distinguished science from various parts of the country, have made application to accompany the Expedition, but considering the appropriation as purely for Geographical purposes, the Department has declined making any such appointments. Very respectfully Sir Your Obdt. Servt.,

J. C. FRÉMONT

Col. G. Talcott
Ordnance Dept.

ALS-JBF, RC (DNA-156, LR, 10-F-1845). Endorsed, "Returns letter of J. Eights . . ." with summary of letter. James Eights, M.D. (1798–1882), son of Jonathan Eights, was a member of the Albany Institute and a friend of John Torrey.

108. Frémont to John Torrey

[Thursday night, 13 March 1845]

MY DEAR SIR,

I have this moment, near midnight, received your pacquet & thanking you very warmly en passant for it I hasten to tell you that looking first at the end of your letter I was surprised to find the Document on Coals which reached you contained no plants. They were very carefully put between uncut leaves, & most of them were in brown paper envelopes. Did you first open the Document yourself or could it have been opened previously? They were enclosed in the Report on Coals as Col. Benton thought it would be agreeable to you to look over it. I will write to you again soon & in the meantime remain very truly yours,

J. C. FRÉMONT

Thursday night March 13th. [1845]

ALS-JBF, RC (NNNBG—Torrey Correspondence).

109. Frémont to [Edward M. Kern]

WASHINGTON CITY March 20th. 1845

DEAR SIR,

I had already decided, before seeing Mr. Gliddon[1] to give you the appointment of artist to our expedition. I have great confidence in the judgment of Mr. Drayton,[2] who knows perfectly well what qualifications are necessary, & recommended you strongly. I like the specimens you sent & judge from them that you sketch rapidly & correctly. I will send you your appointment in a few days, & should like to see you before you go to the West. I will let you know at what time you had better pass through here. I think it would be well for you to employ what leisure time you have, in making yourself so far instructed, with the structure of plants as to know what particular parts will require most care in your drawings. I need not tell you that in the field your occupations will be constant & laborious but I think that your duties will also in many respects be agreeable. Very respectfully Your Obdt. Servt.

J. C. FRÉMONT

ALS-JBF, RC (NHi). The young Philadelphian Edward Kern (1823–63) served not only as artist but also as topographer and cartographer to the third expedition, and, when many of its members became involved in the conquest of California, Kern was placed in command of the garrison at Sutter's Fort, temporarily called Fort Sacramento. After the court-martial of JCF, Kern persuaded two of his brothers, Richard H., also an artist and drawing teacher, and Benjamin J., a physician, to accompany JCF's fourth expedition to California. Later Edward served with the Navy in the Ringgold-Rodgers and Brooke expeditions to Japan, Siberia, and various Pacific islands, and in the Civil War. For a biography of Kern, see HEFFERNAN; for his role in American expansion, see HINE.

1. George Robbins Gliddon (1809–57), a former U.S. consul at Cairo, was a noted archeologist and lecturer on Egyptian antiquities. Edward M. and Richard H. Kern had prepared the illustrations for Gliddon's hierological lectures (NOTT & GLIDDON, xxxviii).

2. Edward M. Kern's friend, Joseph Drayton, had worked in Philadelphia as an engraver, portrait painter, and artist until 1838, when he joined the Charles Wilkes expedition. At its conclusion in 1842 he went to Washington to work on the illustrations. The 1845 edition of Wilkes' narrative includes sixty-one woodcuts from Drayton's sketches (ARRINGTON; GROCE & WALLACE). Kern sought Drayton's advice on the proper clothing and artist's supplies to take on the western expedition (Kern to Drayton, draft, 20 March 1845, and Drayton to Kern, 22 March 1845, both in CSmH—Fort Sutter Papers).

110. Frémont to John Torrey

Washington City March 23d. 1845

My Dear Sir,

I am delighted to know that you are at Princeton. The letters you have sent since you arrived there have been of great value to me—many of the plants you have determined were characteristic & very many are interesting. Purshia trid[entata] for instance, extends over a great portion of the country west of the Rocky Mts. Fremontia vermicularis with other saline shrubs is very abundant & in many places highly characteristic—the leaves of this plant have a very salty taste which perhaps you do not know. I think that the shrubs of that country, are very great in variety, & form probably the most interesting portion of the plants. Will you not give to the Pinus Piñon the name of your botanical friends—Will you not designate the Acacia by some name. No. 509 1844, is a plant, the root of which is extensively used by the Indians as an article of food, under the names of Racine à Tabac and Black root.[1] It has broad oblong racinal leaves & a bulbous root—many specimens unnumbered—perhaps you might determine it.

No part of my report will go to the press before the end of this month & then I will print very slowly in order that we may avail ourselves as much as possible of your determinations. No. 149—1844. This was from a large oak three feet in diameter[2]—specimen taken in the first days of April—bears a slender acorn three quarters of an inch to an inch & a half long—which has a pleasant flavor. The indians gather it in enormous quantities & I enclose you a rough sketch from our botanical artist that you may judge how we shall do. I will write you a desultory line very frequently & am with much respect truly yours,

J. C. Frémont

ALS-JBF, RC (NNNBG—Torrey Correspondence). In a CLSM manuscript draft of this letter, also in Jessie's hand, JCF speaks of having "been oppressed with a headache for several days."

1. *Valeriana ciliata* Torr. & Gray.
2. *Quercus lobata* Neé; valley oak. First collected in the Monterey region in 1792 by two officers of the Malaspina expedition, Robredo and Esquerra, later praised by Vancouver, and following JCF's contact with the oak, it was described as a new species, *Q. longiglanda* Torr. & Frem., although Torrey could hardly have been ignorant of this beautiful species.

111. J. J. Abert to Frémont

Bureau of Topogl. Engs.
WASHINGTON March 25. 1845

SIR,

A requisition for five thousand dollars was yesterday made in your favor to be placed to your credit in the Bank of Missouri, at St. Louis.

This is the most that can be put to your credit from the appropriation of 1844. The appropriation of 1845 will not be available till on and after the 1st day of July next. For the additional means required for the expedition under your command, you will have to draw on this Bureau payable on the 1st July. Your drafts will be duly paid. Very Respectfully Your Obt. Servt.,

J. J. ABERT

Lbk (DNA-77, LS, 8:270).

112. Frémont to John Torrey

[Thursday, 27 March 1845]
[WASHINGTON CITY]

MY DEAR SIR,

Yours of the 25th from New York, I have this moment received & immediately reply in order that you may lose no time in having the Frémontia engraved—which I beg you will have commenced at once. Will you accompany it with a description? If so I will send you a list of the localities to which it belonged—general & particular.

I will write again by to nights mail & send by the same a Pub. Doc. containing plants. Very truly yours,

J. C. FRÉMONT

Thursday March 27th 1845
Washington City

ALS-JBF, RC (NNNBG—Torrey Correspondence). On the following day, 28 March 1845, Torrey wrote to Gray: "I have run over Fremont's plants, &

furnished him the names of such as could be made out with a cursory examination. There are many interesting shrubs from the mountains, that are quite new to me. What a pity they are in so sad a condition! I recognized Cowania (allied to Purshia) among them & several of which I don't know the natural order! There were roots of Lewisiae evidently alive, & I am putting them in some earth for you. Just now they look pretty vigorous. There were also several bulbs that are now growing finely. You shall have them all in due time. The number of curious Oaks in the Collection is considerable—& some must be quite new . . ." (RODGERS, 165).

113. Frémont to John Torrey

WASHINGTON CITY
March 30th. 1845
MY DEAR SIR,

I was not able to distinguish any difference between the *blue* flax of the Rocky Mt. Country, & the common blue flax of cultivation.[1] Will you tell me if I shall do wrong in calling it Linum Usitatissimum? If you have it at hand please send one when next you write, a little piece of Lynosiris graveolens.[2] With respect I am Very truly yours,

J. C. FRÉMONT

ALS-JBF, RC (NNNBG—Torrey Correspondence).
1. H. G. Baker has discussed "Charles Darwin and the Perennial Flax—a Controversy and Its Implications," involving *Linum perenne* and *L. lewisii* in *Huntia,* 2 (1965):141–61.
2. *Linosyris, Chrysothamnus graveolens* (Nutt.) Greene; rabbit-brush.

114. Frémont to John Torrey

WASHINGTON CITY April 4th 1845
MY DEAR SIR,

I have the pleasure to acknowledge your last letter of the 31st containing your final determinations. I trust with you that we shall not find it necessary to make any sacrifices at the end of the next campaign—at the same time it is really wonderful to me that you have been able to make out so many of this collection, but the beautiful condition in which you will see those of the next, will be some amends for your labor. As we do not publish any appendix, I suppose you will think it not advisable to annex Dr. Grey's pamphlet to the report. I hope that you will succeed with the plate of the Frémontia. You know that can always be put in at the last hour. We shall require certainly ten thousand, & probably twenty thousand impressions. I enclose a little note, on which I beg you to put the answers to the questions, if there are any, and enclose it back to me. They refer to your last determinations. I made some unaccountable mistake in not sending you the missing numbers which shall be forwarded. All my manuscripts are complete. Very truly yours,

J. C. FRÉMONT.

ALS-JBF, RC (NNNBG—Torrey Correspondence).

115. Frémont to Mrs. Townsend

Friday 4th April [1845?]

DEAR MRS. TOWNSEND,

I thank you for your kind enquiry. I have been quite ill but only with the grippe. Its serious results have been the necessity to remain indoors and the incessant headaches it leaves. And I cannot get quite clear of the cough. But Dr. Martin has given me some medicine which acts like a charm and by Monday I shall be out again.

Pray thank Mr. Townsend for me. I would be glad to come over and take my cold with him. Any little excitement is pleasant to the newspapers. I do not easily see how they got me put on the invalid list. Barring this little ailment I am thoroughly sound, as you will see when I report. Sincerely yours,

J. C. FRÉMONT

ALS, RC (James S. Copley Collection, La Jolla, Calif.). The recipient was probably Charlotte Holmes Townsend, wife of John Kirk Townsend.

116. Frémont to John Torrey

WASHINGTON CITY—April 7th. 1845

MY DEAR SIR,

I received safely your letter and the package containing plants, which I delayed acknowledgeing as I had just written you a line. The chenopodiaceous shrubs as you have probably judged form a striking feature in the vegetation of the country, and I will take some pains in having them well figured. There will be a greater number of the Frémontia plate required, than I supposed—I find we shall want 11,335. I am glad that you found a good piece of the plant. Col. Benton says it will give him pleasure to send you any documents that may be of interest. I am my dear Sir Very truly yours,

J. C. FRÉMONT

ALS-JBF, RC (NNNBG—Torrey Correspondence).

117. Frémont to John Torrey

WASHINGTON CITY April 8th 1845.

MY DEAR SIR,

I received your letter of the 4th last night. As we cannot make full use of our botany for the present report I only refer slightly to the plants in the course of the narrative, rarely mentioning any other than are very characteristic—but I suppose it will be well to secure such as the Piñon pine, and the *Spirolobium* and I was desirous to have your advice as to the manner in which I should mention them. That is to say, I should like to know the briefest form, which would shew that you had examined them, & that they rest upon your authority. Will the manner in which you give "*Spirolobium Torr. & Frem.*" be sufficient? In the preface I have stated that all the plants were in your hands and that whatever was said in regard to botany rested on your authority—but that there had not been sufficient time for you to prepare a full botanical account, which would be deferred until the next report.

I think that *S. odorata* is the best name for the tree, as its fragrance is very delightful & remarkable.

I am making every effort to get out at the end of this month but am very much pressed by business. I find it difficult to restrain my impatience when I see every thing coming into bloom & remember how many beautiful things for us [lie] beyond the Mississippi. In the mean time I am organizing my camp on the frontier and collecting my horses there. I go out this time well equipped—I have some beautiful instruments and my longitudes will not have any longer to depend much on chronometers. I will either send you a proof or a copy of the map before I leave. I hope that I shall have an early reply to the question in this & in the meantime remain very respect-fully & truly yours,

J. C. Frémont.

I think that I have seen varieties of the Spirolobium in that coun-try, but will defer being certain until I get there again.

ALS-JBF, RC (NNNBG—Torrey Correspondence).

118. J. J. Abert to Frémont

Bureau of Topogl. Engs.
Washington April 10. 1845

Sir,

On arriving at Bents Fort, if you find it desirable, you will detach a Lieutenant & party to explore the Southern Rocky mountains and the regions South of the Arkansas, under such instructions as your experience shall suggest. You are also authorized to increase your party by 10 or more men, if desirable on arriving at Bents fort, and to make such additional outlay as the condition of the expedition and the duties shall require. It is extremely desirable that you should be in before the adjournment of the next session of Congress in order that if any operations should be required in that Country, the information obtained may be at command.

Lieuts. Abert & Peck have been ordered to report to you.[1]

Your attention will be given to the military peculiarity of the Country which you shall examine, in reference to which you will

probably be required to make a separate report. Respectfully Sir
your Obt. Servt.,

J. J. ABERT
Col. Corps. T. E.

Lbk (DNA-77, LS, 8:296–97).
1. James W. Abert, son of the chief of the Corps of Topographical Engineers and a graduate of Princeton and West Point, would command the detached expedition and leave an account of the journey under the title "Journal
of Lieutenant J. W. Abert, from Bent's Fort to St. Louis, in 1845," published in
1846 as Senate Doc. 438, 29th Cong., 1st sess. A map was included, apparently
engraved from the same plate as the large map in Frémont's *Report*. Resigning from the Army in 1864, Abert became a merchant in Cincinnati, and in
the 1870s a professor of English literature at the University of Missouri. After
William Guy Peck (d. 1892) returned with young Abert, he was attached to
the "Army of the West," under Brigadier General Kearny; he then taught
mathematics at the Military Academy until his resignation from the Army
in 1855. This was followed by a long career as a professor of mathematics,
principally at Columbia College (CULLUM).

119. Frémont to John Bailey

WASHINGTON CITY April 11th. 1845
MY DEAR SIR,

Will you excuse a very brief letter in the pressure of business?
Your pacquet of the 3d. which has been unusually long in coming,
was received only this afternoon. I am very much gratified with
your interesting results, and in the manner of communicating them
I beg you will take the course which you think proper as that will
also be the most agreeable to me—making them known to the
Geological Society will undoubtedly be the best method, & we can
also insert an article in my report and publish with it such plates as
you will be able to prepare. Shall I publish the contents of the letter
you sent me, merely changing the form? or will you write a few
words of a general character, introducing it. You know I am not
at all familiar with this Science—I might make some error, although
I should be very guarded and send you the proof sheets. I shall try to
inform myself a little on this interesting subject—I am reading the
proofs of the first part of the report now—but your reply to this
would be in time as the printer will not reach that part of the Report

for ten days yet, and as the map will not be finished by the Lithographer for six weeks yet, you will have sufficient time to prepare the figures for the engraver. Endicott in New York is engraving some of our fossils and if agreeable to you, you could send the drawings to him.

I shall probably leave the frontier on this expedition, before the work is published but arrangements will be made for these things in my absence. You may be assured that I will bring you a beautiful collection when I return and I expect it will give you a long work, as the specimens will be continuous and from widely extended localities. I am with great respect, very truly yours,

J. C. Frémont

ALS-JBF, RC (Museum of Science, The Library, Science Park, Boston—John Bailey Papers).

120. Frémont to John Torrey

[ca. 15 April 1845]

My dear Sir,

Your letters of the 10th, & 13th, were received together last night. Far from wearying of your letters I never see the handwriting on the address without pleasure and your enthusiasm for botany hardly surpasses my own, although scarcely justified by my slight knowledge. As you know [now] have the most leisure please write whenever you have any suggestion or information to communicate and I will answer as promptly as pressing business will now permit. I [now] answer *seriatim*. Unless *Geyer* be the German botanist I have no idea who it can be, but we will try in the coming expedition to go beyond him. I will send you the notes on the Fremontia to night and will take care about the extra copies, and those of the report. I like your idea of publishing from time to time when I am gone and if I can make a safe opportunity I will send you a collection from the foot of the mountains in the summer. We can arrange to have as many plates paid for as you choose to prepare and I will engage a friend to attend to it in my absence. I send you the only copy of Nicollet's report we have by us—if you mean Espy's report for 1841[1] I can also send you a copy of that. In reply to your note of April 11th I am greatly pleased with your plan for a popular work as supplement to Michaux.[2] I am satisfied that there is a large and extraordinary variety of trees. The Government will pay for the plates.

In reply to April 13th I'll be glad to get your descriptions—they will form what we really want for the present work. A brief notice of the *value* of the Botany and a few descriptions (authorized) of plants that we ought not to lose. I am with great respect Very cordially yours,

J. C. Frémont

Please send me any of the plants you mentioned. The express will bring them to me very carefully. The unnumbered specimens of Tobacco root or black root (valeriana) were not among the Kansas plants—they were gathered about the 26th May 1844, on the Utah lake, west of the Rockies.

ALS-JBF, RC (NNNBG—Torrey Correspondence).
1. Probably James P. Espy (1785–1860), who developed the convectional theory of precipitation and in 1842 became meteorologist to the War Department. It was in 1843—not 1841—that he submitted the first annual weather report. His *Philosophy of Storms* was published in 1841, but by a private firm—C. C. Little and J. Brown of Boston.
2. Silviculturist and botanist François André Michaux (1770–1855) made several voyages of travel and study in the eastern United States and was the author of *Histoire des arbres forestiers de l'Amerique septentrionale* (Paris, 1810–13), better known as *The North American Sylva*. It was later supplemented by Thomas Nuttall.

121. Frémont to John Torrey

Washington City April 18th. 1845.

My dear Sir,

You are perfectly right about the black root, it needed only the smell of the little piece you sent to recognise the plant. In regard to the plates Col. Benton desired me to tell you, that he has no doubt Congress will pay for everything of that kind.

I have always something to ask you. Will you perhaps remember, my having sent you when you were at New York, two little plants, the first I saw in bloom in coming out of the snows of the California Mts.[1] I cannot, after much searching lay my hand on your letter, giving them their names, and I am afraid it will come up, when it is too late, and perhaps you can still tell me what they were.

I have made up my mind to send you from the foot of the mountains, through Bent's Fur Company the plants I shall collect up to that point. I see that many of the trees, particularly some fine oaks, you think are new, and as we have passed over the country several times, we should not let any one anticipate us in publishing them. If you find leisure to send me any pieces of our plants, they will reach me safely through the express, and will be very useful guides to me.

Please let me hear soon in answer to my question: and I will give you any specific information you desire to have in regard to any arrangement you may like to make about the plates.

In that, we may do any thing we like. Yours very truly,

J. C. Frémont

ALS-JBF, RC (NNNBG—Torrey Correspondence).
1. *Sarcodes sanguinea* Torr.; snow plant. Described in *Plantae Frémontianæ* (New York, 1853), 18, and there accompanied by a fine plate executed by Isaac Sprague.

122. Frémont to Stephen Cooper

Washington City April 22d 1845

Dr. Sir:

Col. Benton tells me that you have accepted an appointment in my party, and I am glad to have with me a man for whom he has so high an opinion, as I have no doubt that on this trip we shall need men of the best quality and we must try to have no other.

Dr. McDowell, one of Col. Benton's nephews who goes with us, is about to go into the interior of Missouri to purchase animals, and I would be glad for him to have the benefit of your judgment, as you know exactly what kind we want. He is now at Saint Louis and I write to night to tell him to meet you at Jefferson. Therefore if it is convenient to you, you had better leave home immediately and join him there. Your salary will be $2.00 per diem, and it will commence the day you leave home on this business. Very respectfully Your obedient Servant,

J. C. Frémont
Capt. U. S. Army

ALS-JBF, RC (C). Endorsed, "Received May the 25 1845 left hoam may the 28th [*signed*] Maj. Stephen Cooper." A Kentuckian by birth, Stephen Cooper had been active in the Santa Fe trade in the 1820s, Indian subagent at Council Bluffs in the 1840s, and had just completed a term (representative from Adair County) in the Missouri legislature when JCF's letter arrived. He had a reputation of being "an old and experienced woodsman, and a bold yet cautious man." As he served in Abert's detachment of JCF's third expedition, he returned to Missouri in the fall of 1845, but in 1846 emigrated with his wife and children to California, where he had a varied career as alcalde in Benicia, judge of the Sonoma district, miner at Park's Bar, and justice of the peace in Colusa (*Missouri Republican,* 7 June 1845; PIONEER REGISTER). In view of this letter and the endorsement, it is hard to justify the payment for "extra services or services prior to 28 May 1845" which he received on 2 Nov. 1845 (see DNA-217, T-135, voucher no. 274, 2 Nov. 1845).

123. Asa Gray to John Torrey

Cambridge, Wednesday morning, 23 April [1845]

My Dear Torrey,

. . . .

Now as to the Fremontese plants. I fear I cannot make them a study so as to aid you; certainly not at this moment. I fear I can only answer specific questions.

New gen. Papaveraceæ. That should be noticed. There is a new Gen. Papav. Calif. Coulter described in Lond. Jour. Bot. for Feb., *Romneya,* Harvey. But the plate of it is not yet given. I have been trying for a week to get to Boston to look at the Journal & say if yours be it (my copy is sent to Sullivant.) but have not made out yet. I will try to go tomorrow, yet that is lecture day.

I will then compare your queer Crucifera with *Dithraea, Harv.* If my memory serves the leaves are same (there are plenty of cardamines with compound leaves & the leaflets petiolulate). I remember the figure of that had a loose terminal raceme. I will compare in time.

No. 301 (1843) may well be *Gaura coccinea*—no doubt.

No. 560 (1844)—*Œnothera montana,* Nutt (ex. descr.) The sub-sessile·& not having pods should distinguish it from Œ. marginata (which you have a specm. of).

No number—a starved Œ. Missouriensis. Possibly new; probably not.

751, & 753—Either Œ pallida or albicaulis var. (Nuttall has con-fused the two a little.)

No number—*Œ n. sp.* (place next Jamesii).

81 (1843)—*Œ. Missouriensis.*

337 (1844)—Œ. alyssoides. Hook. Agrees better with a Snake Country specimen I have than with Hooker's figure.

No number—Œnothera (Chylismia) n. sp. diff. from Nuttall's (you can compare). It sustains that section beautifully. Call it Œ. *Fremontii* or *sisymbrioides* or *erysimoides.*

Another without number, with the foliage &c. somewhat of *Gaura coccinea,* the flowers &c. of [?], will form a new subsection (between Kneiffia and Lavauxia—a very distinct plant. *Œ. canescens, Say.* It has an ovate, shapely 4-angled fruit, which is I think septicidal.

782 (1843) Gayophytum diffusum Torr. & Gr.—(but with larger flowers?)

257 (1844) Ribes irriguum.

Your Krameria (no. 425, 1844) is *not* that of Bentham pl. Hart-weg, but most likely it is K. parvifolia, Benth. Voy. Sulphur, p. 6, 1. (he has no flowers: you have no fruit). Did yours come from the Calif. side of mts.

He (Benth. Sulphur) has no Malphigiacea except the two I have already mentioned, neither of which are *yours.*

This is all I can do for you today. You will readily enough gather what ones, thus far, it is worth while to notice.

If you wish me to draw up *characters* of the *Œnothera* I will do so, if you will let me know at once and send with the specimens on Monday next.

The London Hortic. Socy. are about to send Hartweg[1] to collect in Oregon and California.

Is the spec. of Pinus Pigñon [Piñon] to be returned, or no? I don't like the name *Pignon*, which is not *aboriginal,* but voyageur French! In haste. Yours ever.

A. GRAY

I fear I can give you no new light about the Malpighiaceae. Love to all! Why does not Mrs. T. write?

ALS, RC (NNNBG—Torrey Correspondence).
1. Carl Theodor Hartweg (1812–71) and his role in exploration in California and Mexico is noticed by H. R. Fletcher in his *Story of the Royal Horticultural Society, 1804–1968* (London, 1969), 88–89, 152–53, and *passim.*

124. Thomas H. Benton to [William L. Marcy]

WASHINGTON CITY, April 25. 1845

THE HON. SEC. AT WAR,
SIR,

Capt. Fremont brought on with him from Oregon, at the request of some missionaries, a young Indian man of the Chinook tribe, and promised to have him sent back after making some progress in the knowledge of our language and customs, and learning something of our government and people. The time has now come for returning him, which will require some expense to enable him to travel with some emigrant party from the frontiers of Missouri. Two horses at $50. each, and saddle and pack saddle & other horse equipment $50 more—a supply of clothes—means to procure his subsistence along the road, both to purchase and to kill—guns—presents to carry home with him—in all about $500 might be sufficient; and I think the *policy* and the honor of the U. S. requires him to be well treated and sent home favorably impressed in regard to us. He is the son of a chief of a leading tribe on the Pacific, and has come far to see our government & people, and should carry home good accounts. Capt. Fremont could consign him to the excellent Indian agent, Major Cummins,[1] of the Delawares; and the contingent, or *present* fund may furnish the means. Yours truly,

THOMAS H. BENTON.

ALS, RC (DNA-75, LR, Oregon B-2422 1845). Two endorsements: the first is routine, the second reads, "I am induced to advise this expenditure under the existing circumstances of our Territorial Rights in Oregon. They appear to me to justify an appropriation of money to the use of so young an Indian (whose people at home probably do not know what money is,) that in an ordinary state of things would seem to me to be extravagant. 26. Ap. '45 [*signed*] T. Hartley Crawford. Allow $300 in this case. 26 Apl. 45. [*signed*] W. L. Marcy."

1. Richard W. Cummins, a friend of Benton's, was in charge not only of the Delawares but also of the Shawnees, Kickapoos, and other tribes in the Fort Leavenworth agency.

125. J. J. Abert to Frémont

Bureau of Topogl. Engs.
WASHINGTON April 26, 1845

SIR,

Your letter of the 26th was duly received and referred to the Ordnance Department, which Department has recommended that [you] should be relieved from charge on account of the losses of Ordnance stores therein referred to, as lost by unavoidable accident, and the recommendation has been sent to the Auditor Mr. McCalla in order to acquit you of further accountability for them. Respectfully Sir Your Obt. Servt.

J. J. ABERT
Col. Corps T. E.

Lbk (DNA-77, LS, 8:348). JCF's 26 April letter was entered in the register, but is not found. Presumably the relief also included the howitzer.

126. Frémont to Edward M. Kern

WASHINGTON CITY May 1, 1845

SIR

I am authorized to appoint you Artist to the Expedition which is about to visit the region west of the Rocky Mts. Your duties will be arduous but strictly confined to the subjects already enumerated to you.

Your compensation will be three dollars per diem, commencing with the date of this letter and your traveling expenses at the rate of ten cents per mile and reckoned by the usual mail routes, will be paid from this place to Independence Mo. and thence, on your return back to Washington.

Immediately on the receipt of this you will proceed to Saint Louis where the party will be organized, and await further instructions. Very respectfully Your Obdt. Servt.

J. C. FREMONT
Capt. Comdg. Explg. Expedition

Mr. Edwd. M. Kern
Philadelphia
Penna.

City of Philadelphia

Personally appeared before me on the fifth day of May A. D. 1845 Edwd. M. Kern and acknowledged the above to be his act and Deed and desired to the same to be Recorded as such and that this is a true copy of the Original. Witness my hand and Seal the year and day above written.

T[?] Brazu, Alderman of Upper Delaware Wards.

Copy (CSmH). For Edward Kern this was a most welcome letter. It had been more than a month since JCF had written (Doc. No. 109), accepting him for the expedition and promising to "send you your appointment in a few days." For Kern's nervousness over his appointment and Henry Eld's reassurance that JCF was still in Washington—not in St. Louis as some newspapers had reported—and "occupied night and day getting out his report," see Kern to Eld, April 1845, and Eld to Kern, 3 May 1845, CSmH—Fort Sutter Papers.

127. J. J. Abert to Frémont

Bureau of Topogl. Engs.
WASHINGTON May 2. 1845

SIR,

No return of Instruments has been received at this Bureau from you since the 1st quarter 1843. Your attention is invited to the 14th paragraph of the Instructions relative to the "Keeping and rendering the accounts of disbursements under the direction of the Topogl. Bureau," to wit: Quarterly Returns of Instruments, tools, machines and other public property will be regularly made.

You are now charged upon the books of this office with the following instruments to wit

2 Sextants
1 Pocket Compass
1 Reconnoitring or spy glass
1 scale of German silver
1 Box   ⎫
1 Pocket ⎬ chronometer
1 Camera Lucida &c.

Very Respectfully Your Obt. Servt.

J. J. ABERT

Your return of instruments should exhibit all purchases of instruments since the last return.

Lbk (DNA-77, LS, 8:363–64).

128. Caspar Wistar to T. Hartley Crawford

PHILADELPHIA 5th Mo. 5th 1845

RESPECTED FRIEND

William the Chinnook boy on whose account I wrote to thee some time ago has since then come under my medical care with a pretty severe attack of indisposition which has left him much debilitated, and he does not regain his strength and vigor as he should.

He seems drooping & anxious about his return home & says Capt. Fremont promised to take him back this Spring (in April I think). Now my present object in addressing thee is to ascertain something definite as to the intentions of the department & when he may expect to be sent for to join his old friend Captain Fremont to whom he seems much attached. Any information touching this matter will tend to relieve the suspense under which William now labours and will be esteemed a favour by his friends here. With sents. of very high Respect and Esteem I am &c. thy friend,

CASPAR WISTAR

ALS, RC (DNA-75, LR, Oregon W-2635 1845). Routine endorsement with contents of letter summarized. Letter "Recd. 7 My 45, ansd. May 7/45." Caspar Wistar (b. 1801) was the nephew of Philadelphia physician Caspar Wistar and the great-grandson of glass manufacturer Caspar Wistar. Like his famous uncle, this Caspar Wistar also became a physician, and his son, Isaac Jones Wistar, would found and endow the Wistar Institute of Anatomy and Biology in 1892 in honor of his great-uncle (WISTAR).

129. Frémont to John Torrey

WASHINGTON CITY May 7th. 1845
Wednesday morning

MY DEAR SIR,

Yours of the 5th arrived this morning and I reply immediately regretting to hear you are troubled with anything so distressing as toothache. I write hastily to beg you to let me have your Report as early as possible for this reason, which perhaps you have not thought of and that is that I may make the little I say through the Report of Botany, conformable to you, and so avoid contradiction. My notes would enable me to cover the country, but preferring to say nothing, rather than make blunders, I have restricted myself to very little. I will prepare the introductory notice and the proofs of your appendix shall be sent to you by mail for correction. I regret that the appendix to the first report has been all worked off, the whole edition—and we are now reading the proofs of the combined report at the 224th page. You will remember that of the first, only the text and your appendix was reprinted. I shall give you further information respecting the proof sheets as I am endeavoring to get away at the end of the week although I do not like to go until I receive your appendix.

Col. Benton is absent, but I shall still receive everything under cover to him at this place.

Please let me hear immediately—I trust I shall make an early return as I warmly reciprocate your wish for a personal acquaintance. Very truly and cordially yours.

J. C. Frémont

ALS-JBF, RC (NHi).

130. Frémont to J. J. Abert

Washington City. May 9th. 1845

Sir,

I respectfully submit to your consideration the propriety of obtaining for me the authority necessary to make a requisition on the U. S. Arsenal at St. Louis, for arms to equip the Exploring party under my command. The arms required would be a mountain howitzer with about 50 shells: forty pair of holster pistols; with the amount of ammunition necessary for the campaign.

The uncertain and frequently hostile disposition of the people inhabiting the countries along the line of exploration render every advantage of arms which can be afforded, material to the safety of our very small party. I have the honor to be with much respect Your obdt. servt.

J. C. Frémont
Bvt. Capt. Topl. Engineers

LS, RC (DNA-156, LR, 1845). Three endorsements read: (1) "Respectfully submitted to the Chief of the Ord. Dept. with a request that the requisition be complied with. J. J. Abert, Col. Corps. T. E. 9 May 1845." (2) "There is no doubt of the necessity for arming the party of Capt. Fremont, but the orders of the Secretary of War are required for the action of this office. G. Talcott, Lt. Col. Ord., 9 May '45." (3) "The requisition of Capt. Fremont is approved as recommended. W. L. Marcy, Sec War, May 9, '45." A final endorsement reads, "Orders given same day: see letter to Col. Abert of 10 May 1845." A copy of Talcott's letter (10 May 1845, Lbk, DNA-156, Miscl. LS, 65:25) to Abert informing the bureau chief that instructions had been given to Capt. William H. Bell, in command of the St. Louis Arsenal, to issue the mountain howitzer and other stores, was sent to Frémont on 10 May (Abert to JCF, Lbk, DNA-77, LS, 8:385). The howitzer, which had to come from Memphis, did not reach Westport until the expedition had left. Apparently it was intended for the use of Abert's detachment, as an encounter was expected with the Comanche Indians (Talbot to Mary Talbot, St. Louis, 9 June 1845; ABERT, 6).

131. Frémont to John Torrey

WASHINGTON CITY May 14th. 1845

MY DEAR SIR,

I feel ashamed at the disjointed and brief manner in which I have lately been obliged to write to you but I would readily find an excuse if you knew the many harrassing engagements which press upon my mind at this time; on the eve of a long journey I have not been able to find a single quiet hour among my friends—so I hope to be excused by you for any apparent inattention.

Three of the plates were yesterday received from Mr. Endicott; they are really beautiful and the Secretary of the Senate is desirous that Mr. Endicott should also furnish plates for the 11,000 copies ordered by the Senate, and I write to him tonight desiring him to communicate with the Secretary. I was anxious that your appendix should be printed close to the narrative, and before the long astronomical tables. The narrative is all worked off, and the printer is holding back for your sheets, which I have told him I expect every day. I leave positively in the morning, but if you enclose to me as usual under cover to Col. Benton, at this place, the manuscript will be handed immediately to the printer and the proofs will be sent to you for correction. It is expected that the work will be published at the end of this month, and I trust that no accident will prevent your pages from reaching here in time. It would be a pity for us to lose what we have: for the beautiful [. . .] we shall publish at the end of the coming session, we shall have abundant leisure.

Through the narrative in using the words Pinus monophyllus, as the scientific term, I have adopted for the popular name "Nut Pine," instead of Pigñon tree, for which there are good reasons. Will you not do the same.

I cannot in the present hurry find time to write a fit letter to precede your notes. Will you arrange them as to dispense with it. The great length of our journey and the many accidents to which we were exposed will justify any remarks you may make on the condition of the plants, which you will remember were finally ruined at the great floods of the Kansas which deluged the borders of the Missouri and Mississippi rivers.

I send you today a public document in which Mrs. Frémont put a card case for your daughter. In the same I send you a cigar which was brought me from Manilla by the same friend—not because you smoke, neither do I—but as a botanical curiosity. If you happen to smoke it will be quite an enjoyment to you. I trust you received the map safely.[1] You will notice that most of the work laid down on it is new. The published map will extend to the Missouri river inclusive.

The next letter you receive from me will be dated at the foot of the mountains. In the meantime and until I see or hear from you again I am most truly yours,

J. C. FRÉMONT

Any suggestion you have to make, when you send me your notes to this place, will be attended to, as I leave directions to have any letters opened here.

ALS-JBF, RC (NHi).
1. The map appears not to have survived.

132. J. J. Abert to Asbury Dickins

Bureau of Topogl. Engs.
WASHINGTON May 14. 1845

SIR

Captain Fremont handed in a part of his report this morning. In order to save delay in its printing it is now sent to the War Office to be sent to you. The other sheets are in use in the hands of the printer of the House, and will be sent to you as soon as received. But you will probably find it most convenient to print, from the printed (House) copy, which Captain Fremont informed me would be delivered to you as soon as completed for that purpose, and that he had fully explained the matter to you. Although therefore it is spoken of in the letter to this office from Captain Fremont, as well as in the one from this office to the War Department as "the report" it is however as you will perceive from the foregoing, but a part of the report.

The map to illustrate the report is also I understand to be in the hands of the House printer. Very Respectfully Sir Your Obt. Servt.

J. J. ABERT
Col. Corps. T. E.

Lbk (DNA-77, LS, 8:400–401). Asbury Dickins was secretary of the Senate.

133. J. J. Abert to Frémont

Bureau of Topogl. Engs.
WASHINGTON May 14. 1845

SIR,

My letter of the 10th April indicated the propriety of making a detachment from your command on arriving at Bents Fort. To enable this to be done without injury to your operations, Lieut. Abert has been supplied with a sextant and artificial Horizon, and will require from your stock of instruments only a Chronometer, of which instruments as you have four, one at least can be conveniently spared.

It will be proper that Lieut. Abert should be directed, as soon as he has completed your instructions as far as practicable, that he should return with his detachment to the U. S. in order that the expenses of the expedition may be reduced, and funds be left to meet the events of your own efforts for more distant discoveries, which will probably keep you some time longer in the field than he will be. Arrangements should also be made to pay off his party on its return.

It may be proper to remark, that your position is now different from what it has heretofore been. In your first expeditions with Mr. Nicollet, you were in a school of practice under an able hand, and in justice to your intelligence and industry, it is proper that I should say, you proved yourself to be highly apt and meritorious. Your position is now that of principal with two young assistants, and you will have in return to fulfill the duties not merely of Commanding Officer, but of instructor to your assistants in the use of reflecting instruments; a duty performed by every officer similarly situated, and which you will have the best opportunity of performing in the progress of the expedition to the vicinity of Bents Fort.

The strength of the detachment, is of course a matter for your discretion, and will no doubt be supplied with an experienced man among Indians as guide.

Lieut. Abert should be directed on his return to report himself to the Bureau, and to prepare his notes and report ready for you on your return, to be addressed under seal to you and deposited for safe keeping in the Bureau, as the regulations do not admit surveys or parts of surveys to be made public but in the form of a report from the commanding officer of an expedition to the Bureau.

As the artificial Horizon, which Lieut. Abert has (private property) is not a very good one, I would advise that one of the three delivered to you should be turned over to him, for which purpose I have requested Mr. Patten[1] to deliver a third Horizon to you.

Both Lieutenants Abert and Peck will be found well versed in the theories and the mathematics, which the duties require, and in need only of practice in the use of the sextant, which I have no doubt they will soon acquire under your able superintendence. Very Respectfully Your Obt. Servt.

J. J. ABERT
Col. Corps. T. E.

Lbk (DNA-77, LS, 8:398–400).

1. By voucher no. 17, dated 13 May 1845, Richard Patten acknowledged receipt for $84.00 paid to him by JCF for three artificial horizons furnished on 10 May 1845 (DNA-217, T-135, voucher no. 17).

134. Frémont to John Torrey

WHEELING VA. 18th May 1845

MY DEAR SIR,

Fearing that the remark in my last, relative to the use of *"nut pine"* instead of Pigñon Pine, as the popular name for *pinus monophyllus* may not have been clear to you, I think it well again to mention to you that I have used the words *nut pine* in the narrative and that you will also use them on the plates and your "notes." I trust my having failed to prepare the prefatory letter will not possibly prevent your sending the sheets. Remembering how numerous and pressing my engagements are you will have some indulgence for me. I will send back to Mrs. Frémont the three sheets you forwarded to me, and as she will open my letters, they will be returned to you if you need them. You will hear from me from the mountains. Very truly yours,

J. C. FRÉMONT

ALS-JBF, RC (NHi).

135. Frémont to Archibald Campbell

VERSAILLES, KENTUCKY,
May 22d. 1845

MY DEAR CAMPBELL,

I found myself restricted in forming my party solely to the engagement of hired men, having only the farther liberty of procuring the necessary interpreters who may sometimes be had in a portion of the country where we operate. Had I been able to do what we both desired I should have seen you immediately, but, having nothing satisfactory to say, and harrassed [sic] with the pressure of various business, I deferred calling upon you until it entirely escaped my mind in the hurry of leaving the city. Fully intending to have done so, I have to ask your indulgence for the apparent neglect. In arranging the party for the present journey I have very unwillingly created some unpleasant feelings, which should not have been directed to me, but I trust that from you I have nothing of the kind to expect. You perfectly understand the nature of our business and know that any departure from bureau arrangements always exposes to difficulties of a very unpleasant kind. In fact I have not yet found a way to keep myself from such & if there had been a little more time should have committed myself in your case. You must attribute the length of this to my strong wish to preserve your friendly regard. Very truly yours,

J. C. FREMONT

[*Added to the letter in a different handwriting is this note:*]
The foregoing letter is in reply to an application for the appointment of a friend upon the Expedition Fremont was then organizing. Washn. Jany. 2d. 1862.

ARCHIBALD CAMPBELL

ALS, RC (James S. Copley Collection, La Jolla, Calif.). Although Archibald Campbell was a graduate of the Military Academy, he had resigned from the Army in 1836 and was now private secretary to the Secretary of War. Campbell was an old acquaintance of Frémont's; the two young men had served together in a civilian capacity under the direction of Capt. W. G. Williams on a survey of the Cherokee country, before the removal of the Indians beyond the Mississippi River. Campbell was to become chief clerk of the U.S. War Department in April 1846 and later a U.S. commissioner to establish the Northwest Boundary line (MEMOIRS, 24; CULLUM).

136. J. J. Abert to Frémont

Bureau of Topogl. Engs.
WASHINGTON May 26, 1845

SIR,

The limitation which has been placed upon the number of your command will of course be varied according to your discretion, should you find it advantageous to make detachments from your command. Respectfully Your Obt. Servt.

J. J. ABERT
Col. Corps. T. E.

Lbk (DNA-77, LS, 8:428).

137. A Report of the Exploring Expedition to Oregon and North California in the Years 1843–44

WASHINGTON CITY, *March* 1, 1845.

COLONEL J. J. ABERT,

Chief of the Corps of Topographical Engineers:

SIR: In pursuance of your instructions, to connect the reconnoissance of 1842, which I had the honor to conduct, with the surveys of Commander Wilkes on the coast of the Pacific ocean, so as to give a connected survey of the interior of our continent, I proceeded to the Great West early in the spring of 1843, and arrived, on the 17th of May, at the little town of Kansas, on the Missouri frontier, near the junction of the Kansas river with the Missouri river, where I was detained near two weeks in completing the necessary preparations for the extended explorations which my instructions contemplated.

My party consisted principally of Creole and Canadian French, and Americans, amounting in all to 39 men; among whom you will recognize several of those who were with me in my first expedition, and who have been favorably brought to your notice in a former report. Mr. Thomas Fitzpatrick, whom many years of hardship and exposure in the western territories had rendered familiar with a portion of the country it was designed to explore, had been selected as our guide; and Mr. Charles Preuss, who had been my assistant in the previous journey, was again associated with me in the same capacity on the present expedition. Agreeably to your directions, Mr. Theodore Talbot, of Washington City, had been attached to the party, with a view to advancement in his profession; and at St. Louis I had been joined by Mr. Frederick Dwight,[1] a gentleman

---

1. Frederick Dwight (1815–89) had studied law at Harvard and was one of the few survivors of the explosion of the *Moselle* near Cincinnati in the spring

of Springfield, Massachusetts, who availed himself of our overland journey to visit the Sandwich islands and China, by way of Fort Vancouver.

The men engaged for the service were:[2]

Alexis Ayot,	Louis Ménard,
François Badeau,	Louis Montreuil,
Oliver Beaulieu,	Samuel Neal,
Baptiste Bernier,	Alexis Pera [Perrault],
John A. Campbell,	François Pera [Perrault],
John G. Campbell,	James Power,
Manuel Chapman,	Raphael Proue,
Ransom Clark,	Oscar Sarpy,
Philibert Courteau,	Baptiste Tabeau,
Michel Crélis,	Charles Taplin,
William Creuss,	Baptiste Tesson,
Clinton Deforest,	Auguste Vasquez,
Baptiste Derosier,	Joseph Verrot,
Basil Lajeunesse,	Patrick White,
François Lajeunesse,	Tiery Wright,
Henry Lee,	Louis Zindel, and

Jacob Dodson, a free young colored man of Washington city, who volunteered to accompany the expedition, and performed his duty

---

of 1838. Before joining JCF's expedition, he had been interested in land near Prophetstown, Ill. He would leave the Fitzpatrick contingent of the party on 26 Aug. to go on ahead to Fort Hall and then to Vancouver, a departure which caused Talbot to note in his journal, "He is no great loss, for he had not messed with us since we left Fort Laramie" (TALBOT, 40; DWIGHT, 2:893–94; obituary notice in the Massachusetts *Springfield Republican,* 27 Feb. 1889).

2. Except for Manuel Chapman, who settled in Oregon, terms of service and rates of pay for these *voyageurs* are given in notes in the summary of financial vouchers (pp. 379–90). In a letter of 18 June 1850 (DNA-77, LR), JCF asked Abert to pay Chapman. "He left me at the Dalles of the Columbia . . . and he did good service while with me." Abert instructed the Third Auditor to pay Chapman $47.84, the balance remaining in the Treasury for "arrearages of military and geographical surveys west of the Mississippi," and noted that JCF had promised to obtain from Congress the balance due Chapman (DNA-77, LS, 12:395).

Badeau, Bernier, Basil Lajeunesse, Ménard, and Proue had all been on JCF's first western expedition; Zindel had been on the 1839 Nicollet expedition to the Minnesota country; and François Lajeunesse, brother of Basil, had accompanied Sir William Drummond Stewart's western jaunt in 1837.

manfully throughout the voyage.[3] Two Delaware Indians—a fine-looking old man and his son—were engaged to accompany the expedition as hunters, through the kindness of Major Cummins, the excellent Indian agent.[4] L. Maxwell, who had accompanied the expedition as one of the hunters in 1842, being on his way to Taos, in New Mexico, also joined us at this place.

The party was armed generally with Hall's carbines, which, with a brass 12-lb. howitzer, had been furnished to me from the United States arsenal at St. Louis, agreeably to the orders of Colonel S. W. Kearney, commanding the 3d military division. Three men were especially detailed for the management of this piece, under the charge of Louis Zindel, a native of Germany, who had been 19 years a non-commissioned officer of artillery in the Prussian army, and regularly instructed in the duties of his profession. The camp equipage and provisions were transported in twelve carts, drawn each by two mules; and a light covered wagon, mounted on good springs, had been provided for the safer carriage of the instruments. These were:

One refracting telescope, by Frauenhofer.

One reflecting circle, by Gambey.

Two sextants, by Troughton.

One pocket chronometer, No. 837, by Goffe, Falmouth.

One pocket chronometer, No. 739, by Brockbank.

One syphon barometer, by Bunten, Paris.

One cistern barometer, by Frye & Shaw, New York.

Six thermometers, and a number of small compasses.

To make the exploration as useful as possible, I determined, in conformity to your general instructions, to vary the route to the Rocky mountains from that followed in the year 1842. The route then was up the valley of the Great Platte river to the South Pass, in north latitude 42°; the route now determined on was up the valley of the Kansas river, and to the head of the Arkansas, and to some pass in the mountains, if any could be found, at the sources of that river.

---

3. Jacob Dodson, eighteen years old and devoted to the Benton family, was JCF's personal servant on both the second and third expeditions. Later he served as messenger to the U.S. Senate (*Daily National Intelligencer,* 30 March 1849).

4. The names of the "Delawares" (they actually were Shawnees) appear on the financial records as James Rogers and his son Thomas Jefferson Rogers. They traveled with the expedition as far as Fort St. Vrain.

By making this deviation from the former route, the problem of a new road to Oregon and California, in a climate more genial, might be solved; and a better knowledge obtained of an important river, and the country it drained, while the great object of the expedition would find its point of commencement at the termination of the former, which was at that great gate in the ridge of the Rocky mountains called the South Pass, and on the lofty peak of the mountain which overlooks it, deemed the highest peak in the ridge, and from the opposite sides of which four great rivers take their rise, and flow to the Pacific or the Mississippi.

Various obstacles delayed our departure until the morning of the 29th,[5] when we commenced our long voyage, and at the close of a day, rendered disagreeably cold by incessant rain, encamped about four miles beyond the frontier, on the verge of the great prairies.

Resuming our journey on the 31st, after the delay of a day to complete our equipment and furnish ourselves with some of the comforts of civilized life, we encamped in the evening at Elm Grove, in company with several emigrant wagons, constituting a party which was proceeding to Upper California, under the direction of Mr. J. B. Childs, of Missouri.[6] The wagons were variously

---

5. As on his expedition of the previous year, JCF was heading first for Fort St. Vrain on the South Platte, although by a slightly different route. We shall not track him closely until he is past that outpost. His route from 29 May to 4 July will take him over some familiar Oregon Trail country, a part of which he traversed in 1842, but he will stay well south of his old route. As Map 3 in the Map Portfolio shows, he will proceed northwest, angling across Kansas, crossing the main streams and the affluents of the Republican River, the Smoky Hill River, and Solomon's Fork. He will enter the valley of the South Platte 30 June and reach the river about opposite Pawnee Creek, near Atwood, in Logan County, Colo.

It seems desirable to refer here to a statement we made on p. 171 about our approach to the identification of topographical features, campsites, and other matters of geographical interest.

6. Joseph B. Chiles (1810–85) was making a second trip overland. The doughty Missourian had gone to California in 1841 with the John Bartleson party, obtained the promise of a mill site from Mexican authorities, and returned east for the mill machinery. But a portion of his party led by Joseph R. Walker was forced to leave Chiles' mill on the way. The party had divided at Fort Hall, Chiles going on to Fort Boise and reaching the Sacramento Valley by way of the Malheur and Pit rivers. Walker had taken a more southerly route down the Humboldt, over to Walker Lake, then into California by way of Walker Pass. JCF mentions the separation and the routes on pp. 523–25. Chiles went east again in 1847, but returned to California the next year.

Dr. Marcus Whitman and his nephew, Perrin Whitman, spent the night of 1 June with the JCF party near the Kansas Ford. The Whitmans were some-

freighted with goods, furniture, and farming utensils, containing among other things an entire set of machinery for a mill which Mr. Childs designed erecting on the waters of the Sacramento river emptying into the bay of San Francisco.

We were joined here by Mr. William Gilpin, of Missouri, who, intending this year to visit the settlements in Oregon, had been invited to accompany us, and proved a useful and agreeable addition to the party.[7] From this encampment, our route until the 3d of June was nearly the same as that described to you in 1842. Trains of wagons were almost constantly in sight; giving to the road a populous and animated appearance, although the greater portion of the emigrants were collected at the crossing, or already on their march beyond the Kansas river.

Leaving at the ford the usual emigrant road to the mountains, (which you will find delineated with considerable detail on one of the accompanying maps,) we continued our route along the southern side of the Kansas, where we found the country much more broken than on the northern side of the river, and where our progress was much delayed by the numerous small streams, which obliged us to make frequent bridges. On the morning of the 4th, we crossed a handsome stream, called by the Indians Otter creek, about 130 feet wide, where a flat stratum of limestone, which forms the bed, made an excellent ford. We met here a small party of Kansas and Delaware Indians, the latter returning from a hunting and trapping expedition on the upper waters of the river; and on the heights above were five or six Kansas women, engaged in digging prairie potatoes, (*psoralea esculenta*). On the afternoon of the 6th, while busily engaged in crossing a wooded stream, we were thrown into a little confusion by the sudden arrival of Maxwell, who entered the camp at full speed at the head of a war party of Osage Indians, with gay red blankets, and heads shaved to the scalp lock. They had

---

what behind the Chiles group, but overtook them and traveled part of the way to Oregon with them. Whitman was without supplies, and thus dependent upon the hospitality of the emigrants for food, but in return he was able to give medical aid and advice about the route (TALBOT, 9). For the visit of the JCF party to the Whitman mission at Walla Walla, see pp. 551–52.

7. Pennsylvanian William Gilpin (1813–94), soldier, lawyer, and editor, went as far as the Dalles of the Columbia, wintered in the Willamette Valley, and returned to the U.S. in 1844. A keen observer, he made reports on the Oregon country which were much sought after. Later Gilpin would serve as Colorado's first territorial governor, 1861–62. For a biography, see KARNES.

run him a distance of about nine miles, from a creek on which we had encamped the day previous, and to which he had returned in search of a runaway horse belonging to Mr. Dwight, which had taken the homeward road, carrying with him saddle, bridle, and holster pistols. The Osages were probably ignorant of our strength, and, when they charged into the camp, drove off a number of our best horses; but we were fortunately well mounted, and after a hard chase of seven or eight miles, succeeded in recovering them all. This accident, which occasioned delay and trouble, and threatened danger and loss, and broke down some good horses at the start, and actually endangered the expedition, was a first fruit of having gentlemen in company—very estimable, to be sure, but who are not trained to the care and vigilance and self-dependence which such an expedition required, and who are not subject to the orders which enforce attention and exertion. We arrived on the 8th at the mouth of the Smoky-hill fork, which is the principal southern branch of the Kansas; forming here, by its junction with Republican, or northern branch, the main Kansas river.[8] Neither stream was fordable, and the necessity of making a raft, together with bad weather, detained us here until the morning of the 11th; when we resumed our journey along the Republican fork. By our observations, the junction of the streams is in latitude 39° 03′ 38″, longitude 96° 24′ 56″, and at an elevation of 926 feet above the gulf of Mexico. For several days we continued to travel along the Republican, through a country beautifully watered with numerous streams, handsomely timbered; and rarely an incident occurred to vary the monotonous resemblance which one day on the prairies here bears to another, and which scarcely require a particular description. Now and then, we caught a glimpse of a small herd of elk; and occasionally a band of antelopes, whose curiosity sometimes brought them within rifle range, would circle round us, and then scour off into the prairies. As we advanced on our road, these became more frequent; but as we jour-

---

8. Talbot says that on the 10th they crossed the Smoky Hill fork with their carts and baggage on the raft and in the rubber boat, then camped in the point formed by the Republican and the Smoky Hill (TALBOT, 13). This tallies with JCF's account, but Preuss unaccountably says it was 14 June, and does not mention the two river forks, saying only that they crossed the "Kansas" (PREUSS, 6–7). The party will continue along the south side of the Republican River, apparently staying pretty much together (at least in camp) until JCF decides to push ahead with a small party, leaving Thomas Fitzpatrick in charge of the slow-moving heavy equipment.

neyed on the line usually followed by the trapping and hunting parties of the Kansas and Delaware Indians, game of every kind continued very shy and wild. The bottoms which form the immediate valley of the main river were generally about three miles wide; having a rich soil of black vegetable mould, and, for a prairie country, well interspersed with wood. The country was every where covered with a considerable variety of grasses—occasionally poor and thin, but far more frequently luxuriant and rich. We had been gradually and regularly ascending in our progress westward, and on the evening of the 14th, when we encamped on a little creek in the valley of the Republican, 265 miles by our travelling road from the mouth of the Kansas, we were at an elevation of 1,520 feet. That part of the river where we were now encamped is called by the Indians the *Big Timber*. Hitherto our route had been laborious and extremely slow, the unusually wet spring and constant rain having so saturated the whole country that it was necessary to bridge every watercourse, and, for days together, our usual march averaged only five or six miles. Finding that at such a rate of travel it would be impossible to comply with your instructions, I determined at this place to divide the party, and, leaving Mr. Fitzpatrick with 25 men in charge of the provisions and heavier baggage of the camp, to proceed myself in advance, with a light party of 15 men, taking with me the howitzer and the light wagon which carried the instruments.

Accordingly, on the morning of the 16th, the parties separated; and, bearing a little out from the river, with a view of heading some of the numerous affluents, after a few hours travel over somewhat broken ground, we entered upon an extensive and high level prairie, on which we encamped towards evening at a little stream, where a single dry cottonwood afforded the necessary fuel for preparing supper. Among a variety of grasses which to-day made their first appearance, I noticed bunch grass, (*festuca,*) and buffalo grass, (*sesleria dactyloides.*) Amorpha canescens (*lead plant*) continued the characteristic plant of the country, and a narrow-leaved *lathyrus* occurred during the morning in beautiful patches. *Sida coccinea* occurred frequently, with a *psoralia* near *psoralia floribunda,* and a number of plants not hitherto met, just verging into bloom. The water on which we had encamped belonged to Solomon's fork of the Smoky-hill river, along whose tributaries we continued to travel for several days.

The country afforded us an excellent road, the route being generally over high and very level prairies; and we met with no other delay than being frequently obliged to bridge one of the numerous streams, which were well timbered with ash, elm, cottonwood, and a very large oak—the latter being, occasionally, five and six feet in diameter, with a spreading summit. *Sida coccinea* is very frequent in vermilion-colored patches on the high and low prairie; and I remarked that it has a very pleasant perfume.

The wild sensitive plant (*schrankia angustata*) occurs frequently, generally on the dry prairies, in the valleys of streams, and frequently on the broken prairie bank. I remark that the leaflets close instantly to a very light touch. *Amorpha,* with the same *psoralea,* and a dwarf species of *lupinus,* are the characteristic plants.

On the 19th, in the afternoon, we crossed the Pawnee road to the Arkansas, and, travelling a few miles onward, the monotony of the prairies was suddenly dispelled by the appearance of five or six buffalo bulls, forming a vanguard of immense herds, among which we were travelling a few days afterwards. Prairie dogs were seen for the first time during the day; and we had the good fortune to obtain an antelope for supper. Our elevation had now increased to 1,900 feet. *Sida coccinea* was a characteristic on the creek bottoms, and buffalo grass is becoming abundant on the higher parts of the ridges.

June 21.—During the forenoon we travelled up a branch of the creek on which we had encamped, in a broken country, where, however, the dividing ridges always afforded a good road. Plants were few; and with the short sward of the buffalo grass, which now prevailed every where, giving to the prairies a smooth and mossy appearance, were mingled frequent patches of a beautiful red grass, (*aristida pallens,*)[9] which had made its appearance only within the last few days.

We halted to noon at a solitary cottonwood in a hollow, near which was killed the first buffalo, a large old bull.

Antelope appeared in bands during the day. Crossing here to the affluents of the Republican, we encamped on a fork, about forty feet wide and one foot deep, flowing with a swift current over a sandy bed, and well wooded with ash-leaved maple, (*negundo*

---

9. Not identified.

433

fraxinifolium,) elm, cottonwood, and a few white oaks. We were visited in the evening by a very violent storm, accompanied by wind, lightning, and thunder; a cold rain falling in torrents. According to the barometer, our elevation was 2,130 feet above the gulf.

At noon, on the 23d, we descended into the valley of a principal fork of the Republican, a beautiful stream with a dense border of wood, consisting principally of varieties of ash, forty feet wide and four feet deep. It was musical with the notes of many birds, which, from the vast expanse of silent prairie around, seemed all to have collected here. We continued during the afternoon our route along the river, which was populous with prairie dogs, (the bottoms being entirely occupied with their villages,) and late in the evening encamped on its banks. The prevailing timber is a blue-foliaged ash, (*fraxinus,* near *F. Americana,*) and ash-leaved maple. With these were *fraxinus Americana,* cottonwood, and long-leaved willow. We gave to this stream the name of Prairie Dog river. Elevation 2,350 feet. Our road on the 25th lay over high smooth ridges, 3,100 feet above the sea; buffalo in great numbers, absolutely covering the face of the country. At evening we encamped within a few miles of the main Republican, on a little creek, where the air was fragrant with the perfume of *artemisia filifolia,* which we here saw for the first time, and which was now in bloom. Shortly after leaving our encampment on the 26th, we found suddenly that the nature of the country had entirely changed. Bare sand hills every where surrounded us in the undulating ground along which we were moving; and the plants peculiar to a sandy soil made their appearance in abundance. A few miles further we entered the valley of a large stream, afterwards known to be the Republican fork of the Kansas, whose shallow waters, with a depth of only a few inches, were spread out over a bed of yellowish white sand 600 yards wide. With the exception of one or two distant and detached groves, no timber of any kind was to be seen; and the features of the country assumed a desert character, with which the broad river, struggling for existence among quicksands along the treeless banks, was strikingly in keeping. On the opposite side, the broken ridges assumed almost a mountainous appearance; and, fording the stream, we continued on our course among these ridges, and encamped late in the evening at a little pond of very bad water, from which we drove away a herd of buffalo that were standing in and about it. Our encampment this evening was 3,500 feet above the sea. We travelled now for several days through a broken and dry sandy region, about 4,000 feet above the sea, where there were no running streams; and some anxiety was constantly felt on account of the uncertainty of water, which was only to be found in small lakes that occurred occasionally among the hills. The discovery of these always brought pleasure to the camp, as around them were generally green flats, which afforded abundant pasturage for our animals; and here were usually collected herds of buffalo, which now were scattered over all the country in countless numbers.

The soil of bare and hot sands supported a varied and exuberant growth of plants, which were much farther advanced than we had previously found them, and whose showy bloom somewhat relieved the appearance of general sterility. Crossing the summit of an elevated and continuous range of rolling hills, on the afternoon of the 30th of June we found ourselves overlooking a broad and misty valley, where, about ten miles distant, and 1,000 feet below us, the South fork of the Platte was rolling magnificently along, swollen with the waters of the melting snows. It was in strong and refreshing contrast with the parched country from which we had just issued; and when, at night, the broad expanse of water grew indistinct, it almost seemed that we had pitched our tents on the shore of the sea.

Travelling along up the valley of the river, here 4,000 feet above the sea, in the afternoon of July 1 we caught a far and uncertain view of a faint blue mass in the west, as the sun sank behind it; and from our camp in the morning, at the mouth of Bijou [Creek], Long's peak and the neighboring mountains stood out into the sky, grand and luminously white, covered to their bases with glittering snow.

On the evening of the 3d, as we were journeying along the partially overflowed bottoms of the Platte, where our passage stirred up swarms of mosquitoes, we came unexpectedly upon an Indian, who was perched on a bluff, curiously watching the movements of our caravan. He belonged to a village of Oglallah Sioux, who had lost all their animals in the severity of the preceding winter, and were now on their way up the Bijou fork to beg horses from the Arapahoes, who were hunting buffalo at the head of that river.

Several came into our camp at noon; and, as they were hungry, as usual, they were provided with buffalo meat, of which the hunters had brought in an abundant supply.

About noon, on the 4th of July, we arrived at the fort, where Mr. St. Vrain received us with his customary kindness, and invited us to join him in a feast which had been prepared in honor of the day.

Our animals were very much worn out, and our stock of provisions entirely exhausted when we arrived at the fort; but I was disappointed in my hope of obtaining relief, as I found it in a very impoverished condition; and we were able to procure only a little unbolted Mexican flour, and some salt, with a few pounds of powder and lead.

As regarded provisions, it did not much matter in a country where rarely the day passed without seeing some kind of game, and where it was frequently abundant. It was a rare thing to lie down hungry, and we had already learned to think bread a luxury; but we could not proceed without animals, and our own were not capable of prosecuting the journey beyond the mountains without relief.

I had been informed that a large number of mules had recently arrived at Taos, from Upper California; and as our friend, Mr. Maxwell, was about to continue his journey to that place, where a portion of his family resided, I engaged him to purchase for me 10 or 12 mules, with the understanding that he should pack them with provisions and other necessaries, and meet me at the mouth of the *Fontaine qui bouit,* on the Arkansas river, to which point I would be led in the course of the survey.[10]

Agreeably to his own request, and in the conviction that his habits of life and education had not qualified him to endure the hard life of a voyageur, I discharged here one of my party, Mr. Oscar Sarpy, having furnished him with arms and means of transportation to Fort Laramie, where he would be in the line of caravans returning to the States.

At daybreak, on the 6th of July, Maxwell was on his way to Taos; and a few hours after we also had recommenced our journey up the Platte, which was continuously timbered with cottonwood and willow, on a generally sandy soil. Passing on the way the remains of

10. In the fall of 1842, a trading post had been established at the mouth of Fountain Creek by George Simpson, J. B. Doyle, and Alexander Barclay. It became the city of Pueblo, Colo.

two abandoned forts, (one of which, however, was still in good condition,) we reached, in 10 miles, Fort Lancaster, the trading establishment of Mr. Lupton.[11] His post was beginning to assume the appearance of a comfortable farm; stock, hogs, and cattle, were ranging about on the prairie; there were different kinds of poultry; and there was the wreck of a promising garden, in which a considerable variety of vegetables had been in a flourishing condition, but it had been almost entirely ruined by the recent high waters. I remained to spend with him an agreeable hour, and sat off in a cold storm of rain, which was accompanied with violent thunder and lightning. We encamped immediately on the river, 16 miles from St. Vrain's. Several Arapahoes, on their way to the village which was encamped a few miles above us, passed by the camp in the course of the afternoon. Night sat in stormy and cold, with heavy and continuous rain, which lasted until morning.

July 7.—We made this morning an early start, continuing to travel up the Platte; and in a few miles frequent bands of horses and mules, scattered for several miles round about, indicated our approach to the Arapaho village, which we found encamped in a beautiful bottom, and consisting of about 160 lodges. It appeared extremely populous, with a great number of children; a circumstance which indicated a regular supply of the means of subsistence. The chiefs, who were gathered together at the farther end of the village, received us (as probably strangers are always received to whom they desire to show respect or regard) by throwing their arms around our necks and embracing us.

It required some skill in horsemanship to keep the saddle during the performance of this ceremony, as our American horses exhibited for them the same fear they have for a bear or any other wild animal. Having very few goods with me, I was only able to make

---

11. Lancaster P. Lupton (1807–85), a graduate of the U.S. Military Academy, had accompanied Col. Henry Dodge's expedition to the Rocky Mountains in 1835. Resigning from the Army, he built the adobe structure—sometimes called Fort Lupton—on the right bank of the Platte about ten miles above the mouth of the St. Vrain (A. HAFEN [2]; LECOMPTE [2]). Also visiting at Lupton's fort on 6 July 1843 was Rufus B. Sage, whom JCF had encountered on his previous expedition (SAGE, 2:268–69). The two abandoned forts he mentions passing were Fort Vasquez, dating from 1835, of which there are still ruins about a mile south of Platteville, Colo., and Fort Jackson, near Ione, Colo., built in 1837. As we have remarked before in connection with Fort Bridger, JCF was never very interested in the history or identity of the abandoned posts he encountered.

them a meager present, accounting for the poverty of the gift by explaining that my goods had been left with the wagons in charge of Mr. Fitzpatrick, who was well known to them as the White Head, or the Broken Hand. I saw here, as I had remarked in an Arapaho village the preceding year, near the lodges of the chiefs, tall tripods of white poles supporting their spears and shields, which showed it to be a regular custom.

Though disappointed in obtaining the presents which had been evidently expected, they behaved very courteously, and, after a little conversation I left them, and, continuing on up the river, halted to noon on the bluff, as the bottoms are almost inundated; continuing in the afternoon our route along the mountains, which were dark, misty, and shrouded—threatening a storm; the snow peaks sometimes glittering through the clouds beyond the first ridge.

We surprised a grizzly bear sauntering along the river; which, raising himself upon his hind legs, took a deliberate survey of us, that did not appear very satisfactory to him, and he scrambled into the river and swam to the opposite side. We halted for the night a little above Cherry creek; the evening cloudy, with many mosquitoes. Some indifferent observations placed the camp in latitude 39° 43′ 53″, and chronometric longitude 105° 24′ 34″.

July 8.—We continued to-day to travel up the Platte; the morning pleasant, with a prospect of fairer weather. During the forenoon our way lay over a more broken country, with a gravelly and sandy surface; although the immediate bottom of the river was a good soil, of a dark sandy mould, resting upon a stratum of large pebbles, or rolled stones, as at Laramie fork. On our right, and apparently very near, but probably 8 or 10 miles distant, and two or three thousand feet above us, ran the first range of the mountains, like a dark corniced line, in clear contrast with the great snowy chain which, immediately beyond, rose glittering five thousand feet above them. We caught this morning a view of Pike's peak; but it appeared for a moment only, as clouds rose early over the mountains, and shrouded them in mist and rain all the day. In the first range were visible, as at the Red Buttes on the North fork, very lofty escarpments of red rock. While travelling through this region, I remarked that always in the morning the lofty peaks were visible and bright, but very soon small white clouds began to settle around them— brewing thicker and darker as the day advanced, until the afternoon, when the thunder began to roll; and invariably at evening we had more or less of a thunder storm. At 11 o'clock, and 21 miles from St. Vrain's fort, we reached a point in this southern fork of the Platte, where the stream is divided into three forks; two of these (one of them being much the largest) issuing directly from the mountains on the west, and forming, with the easternmost branch, a river of the plains. The elevation of this point is about 5,500 feet above the sea; this river falling 2,800 feet in a distance of 316 miles, to its junction with the North fork of the Platte. In this estimate, the elevation of the junction is assumed as given by our barometrical observations in 1842.

On the easternmost branch, up which we took our way, we first came among the pines growing on the top of a very high bank, and where we halted on it to noon; quaking asp (*populus tremuloides*) was mixed with the cottonwood, and there were excellent grass and rushes for the animals.

During the morning there occurred many beautiful flowers, which we had not hitherto met. Among them, the common blue flowering flax made its first appearance; and a tall and handsome species of *gilia,* with slender scarlet flowers, which appeared yesterday for the first time, was very frequent to-day.

We had found very little game since leaving the fort, and provisions began to get unpleasantly scant, as we had had no meat for several days; but towards sundown, when we had already made up our minds to sleep another night without supper, Lajeunesse had the good fortune to kill a fine deer, which he found feeding in a hollow near by; and as the rain began to fall, threatening an unpleasant night, we hurried to secure a comfortable camp in the timber.

To-night the camp fires, girdled with *appolas* of fine venison, looked cheerful in spite of the stormy weather.

July 9.—On account of the low state of our provisions and the scarcity of game, I determined to vary our route, and proceed several camps to the eastward, in the hope of falling in with the buffalo. This route along the dividing grounds between the South fork of the Platte and the Arkansas, would also afford some additional geographical information. This morning, therefore, we turned to the eastward, along the upper waters of the stream on which we had encamped, entering a country of picturesque and varied scenery; broken into rocky hills of singular shapes; little valleys, with pure crystal water, here leaping swiftly along, and there losing itself in the sands; green spots of luxuriant grass, flowers of all colors, and

439

timber of different kinds—every thing to give it a varied beauty, except game. To one of these remarkably shaped hills, having on the summit a circular flat rock two or three hundred yards in circumference, some one gave the name of Poundcake, which it has been permitted to retain, as our hungry people seemed to think it a very agreeable comparison. In the afternoon a buffalo bull was killed, and we encamped on a small stream, near the road which runs from St. Vrain's fort to the Arkansas.

July 10.—Snow fell heavily on the mountains during the night, and Pike's peak this morning is luminous and grand, covered from the summit as low down as we can see, with glittering white. Leaving the encampment at 6 o'clock, we continued our easterly course over a rolling country, near to the high ridges, which are generally rough and rocky, with a coarse conglomerate displayed in masses, and covered with pines. The rock is very friable, and it is undoubtedly from its decomposition that the prairies derive their sandy and gravelly formation. In 6 miles we crossed a head water of the Kioway river, on which we found a strong fort and *corál* that had been built in the spring, and halted to noon on the principal branch of the river. During the morning our route led over a dark vegetable mould, mixed with sand and gravel, the characteristic plant being *esparcette, (onobrychis sativa,)*[12] a species of clover which is much used in certain parts of Germany for pasturage of stock—principally hogs. It is sown on rocky waste ground, which would otherwise be useless, and grows very luxuriantly, requiring only a renewal of the seed about once in fifteen years. Its abundance here greatly adds to the pastoral value of this region. A species of antennaria[13] in flower was very common along the line of the road, and the creeks were timbered with willow and pine. We encamped on Bijou's fork, the water of which, unlike the clear streams we had previously crossed, is of a whitish color, and the soil of the bottom a very hard, tough clay. There was a prairie dog village on the bottom, and, in the endeavor to unearth one of the little animals, we labored ineffectually in the tough clay until dark. After descending, with a slight inclination, until it had gone the depth of two feet, the hole suddenly turned a sharp angle in another direction for one more foot in depth, when it again turned, taking an ascending direction to

12. *Onobrychis arenaria* (Kit.) DC. Perhaps introduced about trading posts by *voyageurs,* as suggested in EWAN, 28.
13. Probably *Antennaria microphylla* Rydb.

the next nearest hole. I have no doubt that all their little habitations communicate with each other. The greater part of the people were sick to-day, and I was inclined to attribute their indisposition to the meat of the bull which had been killed the previous day.

July 11.—There were no indications of buffalo having been recently in the neighborhood; and, unwilling to travel farther eastward, I turned this morning to the southward, up the valley of Bijou. *Esparcette* occurred universally, and among the plants on the river I noticed, for the first time during this journey, a few small bushes of the *absinthe* of the voyageurs, which is commonly used for fire wood, (*artemisia tridentata.*)[14] Yesterday and to-day the road has been ornamented with the showy bloom of a beautiful *lupinus,* a characteristic in many parts of the mountain region, on which were generally great numbers of an insect with very bright colors, (*litta vesicatoria.*)

As we were riding quietly along, eagerly searching every hollow in search of game, we discovered, at a little distance in the prairie, a large grizzly bear, so busily engaged in digging roots that he did not perceive us until we were galloping down a little hill fifty yards from him, when he charged upon us with sudden energy, that several of us came near losing our saddles. Being wounded, he commenced retreating to a rocky piney ridge near by, from which we were not able to cut him off, and we entered the timber with him. The way was very much blocked up with fallen timber; and we kept up a running fight for some time, animated by the bear charging among the horses. He did not fall until after he had received six rifle balls. He was miserably poor, and added nothing to our stock of provisions.

We followed the stream to its head in a broken ridge, which, according to the barometer, was about 7,500 feet above the sea. This is a piney elevation, into which the prairies are gathered, and from which the waters flow, in almost every direction, to the Arkansas, Platte, and Kansas rivers; the latter stream having here its remotest sources. Although somewhat rocky and broken, and covered with pines, in comparison with the neighboring mountains, it scarcely forms an interruption to the great prairie plains which sweep up to their bases.

The annexed view of Pike's peak from this camp, at the distance

---

14. JCF did not distinguish sagebrush species. Several artemisias of the same habit occur in this region.

of 40 miles, represents very correctly the manner in which this mountain barrier presents itself to travellers on the plains, which sweep almost directly to its bases; an immense and comparatively smooth and grassy prairie, in very strong contrast with the black masses of timber, and the glittering snow above them. This is the picture which has been left upon my mind; and I annex this sketch [p. 444], to convey to you the same impression. With occasional exceptions, comparatively so very small as not to require mention, these prairies are every where covered with a close and vigorous growth of a great variety of grasses, among which the most abundant is the buffalo grass, (*sesleria dactyloides.*) Between the Platte and Arkansas rivers, that part of this region which forms the basin drained by the waters of the Kansas, with which our operations made us more particularly acquainted, is based upon a formation of calcareous rocks. The soil of all this country is excellent, admirably adapted to agricultural purposes, and would support a large agricultural and pastoral population. A glance at the map accompanying this report, along our several lines of travel, will show you that this plain is watered by many streams. Throughout the western half of the plain, these are shallow, with sandy beds, becoming deeper as they reach the richer lands approaching the Missouri river; they generally have bottom lands, bordered by bluffs varying from 50 to 500 feet in height. In all this region the timber is entirely confined to the streams. In the eastern half, where the soil is a deep, rich, vegetable mould, retentive of rain and moisture, it is of vigorous growth, and of many different kinds; and throughout the western half it consists entirely of various species of cottonwood, which deserves to be called the tree of the desert—growing in sandy soils, where no other tree will grow; pointing out the existence of water, and furnishing to the traveller fuel, and food for his animals. Add to this, that the western border of the plain is occupied by the Sioux, Arapaho, and Cheyenne nations and the Pawnees and other half-civilized tribes in its eastern limits, for whom the intermediate country is a war ground, you will have a tolerably correct idea of the appearance and condition of the country. Descending a somewhat precipitous and rocky hill side among the pines; which rarely appear elsewhere than on the ridge, we encamped at its foot, where there were several springs, which you will find laid down upon the map as one of the extreme sources of the Smoky Hill fork of the Kansas. From this place the view extended over the Arkansas valley, and the Spanish peaks in the south beyond. As the greater part of the men continued sick, I encamped here for the day, and ascertained conclusively, from experiments on myself, that their illness was caused by the meat of the buffalo bull.

On the summit of the ridge, near the camp, were several rock-built forts, which in front were very difficult of approach, and in the rear were protected by a precipice entirely beyond the reach of a rifle ball. The evening was tolerably clear, with a temperature at sunset of 63°. Elevation of the camp 7,300 feet.

Turning the next day to the southwest, we reached, in the course of the morning, the wagon road to the settlements on the Arkansas river, and encamped in the afternoon on the *Fontaine-qui-bouit* (or Boiling Spring) river, where it was 50 feet wide, with a swift current. I afterwards found that the spring and river owe their names to the bubbling of the effervescing gas in the former, and not to the temperature of the water, which is cold. During the morning, a tall species of *gilia,* with a slender white flower, was characteristic; and, in the latter part of the day, another variety of *esparcette,* (wild clover,) having the flower white, was equally so. We had a fine sunset of golden brown; and, in the evening, a very bright moon, with the near mountains, made a beautiful scene. Thermometer, at sunset, was 69°, and our elevation above the sea 5,800.

July 13.—The morning was clear, with a northwesterly breeze, and the thermometer at sunrise at 46°. There were no clouds along the mountains, and the morning sun showed very clearly their rugged character.

We resumed our journey very early down the river, following an extremely good lodge trail, which issues by the head of this stream from the bayou Salade, a high mountain valley behind Pike's peak. The soil along the road was sandy and gravelly, and the river well timbered. We halted to noon under the shade of some fine large cottonwoods, our animals luxuriating on rushes (*equisetum hyemale,*)[15] which, along this river, were remarkably abundant. A variety of cactus made its appearance, and among several strange plants were numerous and beautiful clusters of a plant resembling *mirabilis jalapa,*[16] with a handsome convolvulus I had not hitherto seen, (calystegia.) In the afternoon we passed near the encampment

---

15. "Rushes" favored by grazing animals suggests *Juncus* sp., wiregrass, rather than horsetails (*Equisetum*).

16. *Mirabilis multiflora* (Torr.) Gray.

443

View of Pikes Peak

of a hunter named Maurice, who had been out into the plains in pursuit of buffalo calves, a number of which I saw among some domestic cattle near his lodge. Shortly afterwards, a party of mountaineers galloped up to us—fine-looking and hardy men, dressed in skins and mounted on good fat horses; among them were several Connecticut men, a portion of Wyeth's party, whom I had seen the year before, and others were men from the western States.

Continuing down the river, we encamped at noon on the 14th at its mouth, on the Arkansas river. A short distance above our encampment, on the left bank of the Arkansas, is a *pueblo,* (as the Mexicans call their civilized Indian villages,) where a number of mountaineers, who had married Spanish women in the valley of Taos, had collected together, and occupied themselves in farming, carrying on at the same time a desultory Indian trade. They were principally Americans, and treated us with all the rude hospitality their situation admitted; but as all commercial intercourse with New Mexico was now interrupted, in consequence of Mexican decrees to that effect, there was nothing to be had in the way of provisions. They had, however, a fine stock of cattle, and furnished us an abundance of excellent milk. I learned here that Maxwell, in company with two other men, had started for Taos on the morning of the 9th, but that he would probably fall into the hands of the Utah Indians, commonly called the *Spanish Yutes.* As Maxwell had no knowledge of their being in the vicinity when he crossed the Arkansas, his chance of escape was very doubtful; but I did not entertain much apprehension for his life, having great confidence in his prudence and courage. I was further informed that there had been a popular tumult among the *pueblos,* or civilized Indians, residing near Taos, against the *"foreigners"* of that place, in which they had plundered their houses and ill-treated their families. Among those whose property had been destroyed, was Mr. Beaubien,[17] father-in-law of Maxwell, from whom I had expected to obtain supplies, and who had been obliged to make his escape to Santa Fé.

By this position of affairs, our expectation of obtaining supplies from Taos was cut off. I had here the satisfaction to meet our good buffalo hunter of 1842, Christopher Carson, whose services I con-

---

17. Charles Beaubien, an active merchant in the Southwest and one of the two owners of the vast Beaubien-Miranda tract granted by the Mexican government.

sidered myself fortunate to secure again; and as a reinforcement of mules was absolutely necessary, I despatched him immediately, with an account of our necessities, to Mr. Charles Bent, whose principal post is on the Arkansas river, about 75 miles below *Fontaine-qui-bouit*.[18] He was directed to proceed from that post by the nearest route across the country, and meet me with what animals he should be able to obtain at St. Vrain's fort. I also admitted into the party Charles Towns—a native of St. Louis, a serviceable man, with many of the qualities of a good voyageur.[19] According to our observations, the latitude of the mouth of the river is 38° 15′ 23″; its longitude 104° 58′ 30″; and its elevation above the sea 4,880 feet.

On the morning of the 16th, the time for Maxwell's arrival having expired, we resumed our journey, leaving for him a note, in which it was stated that I would wait for him at St. Vrain's fort until the morning of the 26th, in the event that he should succeed in his commission. Our direction was up the Boiling Spring river, it being my intention to visit the celebrated springs from which the river takes its name, and which are on its upper waters, at the foot of Pike's peak. Our animals fared well while we were on this stream, there being every where a great abundance of *prêle. Ipomea leptophylla,* in bloom, was a characteristic plant along the river, generally in large bunches, with two to five flowers on each. Beautiful clusters of the plant resembling *mirabilis jalapa* were numerous, and *glycyrrhiza lepidota* was a characteristic of the bottoms. Currants nearly ripe were abundant, and among the shrubs which covered the bottom was a very luxuriant growth of chenopodiaceous shrubs,[20] four to six feet high.

On the afternoon of the 17th we entered among the broken ridges at the foot of the mountains, where the river made several forks. Leaving the camp to follow slowly, I rode ahead in the afternoon in search of the springs. In the mean time, the clouds, which had been

18. With his brother William, and Ceran St. Vrain, Charles Bent (1799–1847) had built a busy trading post, Bent's Fort, eighty miles northeast of Taos, during 1828–32. Appointed governor of New Mexico in 1846, Charles was killed the following year during an Indian uprising at Taos. For background on the Bents and their enterprise, see LAVENDER, HYDE, TAYLOR, and DUNHAM [1].

19. Charles Town or Towne, a friend of the Bents who had been in the West only since 1841, now joined JCF as a hunter. Town was killed by Apaches and Utes in Manco de Burro Pass, east of Raton, in 1848. Maxwell was wounded in the same fray (LECOMPTE [1]).

20. *Atriplex canescens* (Pursh) Nutt.

gathered all the afternoon over the mountains, began to roll down their sides; and a storm so violent burst upon me, that it appeared I had entered the storehouse of the thunder storms. I continued, however, to ride along up the river until about sunset, and was beginning to be doubtful of finding the springs before the next day, when I came suddenly upon a large smooth rock about twenty yards in diameter, where the water from several springs was bubbling and boiling up in the midst of a white incrustation with which it had covered a portion of the rock. As this did not correspond with a description given me by the hunters, I did not stop to taste the water, but, dismounting, walked a little way up the river, and, passing through a narrow thicket of shrubbery bordering the stream, stepped directly upon a huge white rock, at the foot of which the river, already become a torrent, foamed along, broken by a small fall. A deer which had been drinking at the spring was startled by my approach, and, springing across the river, bounded off up the mountain. In the upper part of the rock, which had apparently been formed by deposition, was a beautiful white basin, overhung by currant bushes, in which the cold clear water bubbled up, kept in constant motion by the escaping gas, and overflowing the rock, which it had almost entirely covered with a smooth crust of glistening white. I had all day refrained from drinking, reserving myself for the spring; and as I could not well be more wet than the rain had already made me, I lay down by the side of the basin, and drank heartily of the delightful water. The annexed sketch [p. 444] is only a rude one, but it will enable you to form some idea of the character of the scenery and the beauty of this spot, immediately at the foot of lofty mountains, beautifully timbered, which sweep closely round, shutting up the little valley in a kind of cove. As it was beginning to grow dark, I rode quickly down the river, on which I found the camp a few miles below.[21]

The morning of the 18th was beautiful and clear, and, all the people being anxious to drink of these famous waters, we encamped immediately at the springs, and spent there a very pleasant day. On the opposite side of the river is another locality of springs, which are

---

21. JCF has reconnoitered the Manitou Springs area near present Colorado Springs, Colo., and is now heading back for Fort St. Vrain, going up Monument Creek, northward to affluents of the Platte, camping for two days on what his map calls Vermillion Creek but which probably was the stream now called East Plum Creek.

entirely of the same nature. The water has a very agreeable taste, which Mr. Preuss found very much to resemble that of the famous Selter springs in the grand duchy of Nassau, a country famous for wine and mineral waters; and it is almost entirely of the same character, though still more agreeable than that of the famous Beer springs, near Bear river of the Great Salt lake. The following is an analysis of an incrustation with which the water had covered a piece of wood lying on the rock:

Carbonate of lime	92.25
Carbonate of magnesia	1.21
Sulphate of lime	
Chloride of calcium }	.23
Chloride of magnesia	
Silica	1.50
Vegetable matter	.20
Moisture and loss	4.61
	100.00

At 11 o'clock, when the temperature of the air was 73°, that of the water in this was 60.5°; and that of the upper spring, which issued from the flat rock, more exposed to the sun, was 69°. At sunset, when the temperature of the air was 66°, that of the lower springs was 58°, and that of the upper 61°.

July 19.—A beautiful and clear morning, with a slight breeze from the northwest; the temperature of air at sunrise being 57.5°. At this time the temperature of the lower spring was 57.8°, and that of the upper 54.3°.

The trees in the neighborhood were birch, willow, pine, and an oak resembling *quercus alba*.[22] In the shrubbery along the river are currant bushes, (*ribes,*)[23] of which the fruit has a singularly piney flavor; and on the mountain side, in a red gravelly soil, is a remarkable coniferous tree, (perhaps an *abies,*)[24] having the leaves singularly long, broad, and scattered, with bushes of *spiraea ariaefolia*.[25] By our observations, this place is 6,350 feet above the sea, in latitude 38° 52′ 10″, and longitude 105° 22′ 45″.

---

22. *Quercus gambelii* Nutt.
23. *Ribes cereum* Dougl.
24. Probably *Pseudotsuga menziesii* (Mirb.) Franco. Douglas fir.
25. *Holodiscus discolor* (Pursh) Maxim.

Resuming our journey on this morning, we descended the river, in order to reach the mouth of the eastern fork, which I proposed to ascend. The left bank of the river here is very much broken. There is a handsome little bottom on the right, and both banks are exceedingly picturesque—strata of red rock, in nearly perpendicular walls, crossing the valley from north to south. About three miles below the springs, on the right bank of the river, is a nearly perpendicular limestone rock, presenting a uniformly unbroken surface, twenty to forty feet high, containing very great numbers of a large univalve shell, which appears to belong to the genus *inoceramus,* and in the appendix is designated by the No. 42.

In contact with this, to the westward, was another stratum of limestone, containing fossil shells of a different character; and still higher up on the stream were parallel strata, consisting of a compact somewhat crystalline limestone, and argillaceous bituminous limestone in thin layers. During the morning, we travelled up the eastern fork of the *Fontaine-qui-bouit* river, our road being roughened by frequent deep gullies timbered with pine, and halted to noon on a small branch of this stream, timbered principally with the narrow-leaved cottonwood, (*populus angustifolia,*) called by the Canadians *liard amère.* On a hill, near by, were two remarkable columns of a grayish-white conglomerate rock, one of which was about twenty feet high, and two feet in diameter. They are surmounted by slabs of a dark ferruginous conglomerate, forming black caps, and adding very much to their columnar effect at a distance. This rock is very destructible by the action of the weather, and the hill, of which they formerly constituted a part, is entirely abraded.

A shaft of the gun carriage was broken in the afternoon; and we made an early halt, the stream being from twelve to twenty feet wide, with clear water. As usual, the clouds had gathered to storm over the mountains, and we had a showery evening. At sunset the thermometer stood at 62° and our elevation above the sea was 6,530 feet.

July 20.—This morning (as we generally found the mornings under these mountains) was very clear and beautiful, and the air cool and pleasant, with the thermometer at 44°. We continued our march up the stream, along a green sloping bottom, between pine hills on the one hand, and the main Black hills on the other, towards the ridge which separates the waters of the Platte from those of the Arkansas. As we approached the dividing ridge, the whole valley was radiant with flowers; blue, yellow, pink, white, scarlet, and purple, vied with each other in splendor. Esparcette was one of the highly characteristic plants, and a bright-looking flower (*gaillardia aristata*) was very frequent; but the most abundant plant along our road today was *geranium maculatum,* which is the characteristic plant on this portion of the dividing grounds. Crossing to the waters of the Platte, fields of blue flax added to the magnificence of this mountain garden; this was occasionally four feet in height, which was a luxuriance of growth that I rarely saw this almost universal plant attain throughout the journey. Continuing down a branch of the Platte, among high and very steep timbered hills, covered with fragments of rock, towards evening we issued from the piney region, and made a late encampment near Poundcake rock, on that fork of the river which we had ascended on the 8th of July. Our animals enjoyed the abundant rushes this evening, as the flies were so bad among the pines that they had been much harassed. A deer was killed here this evening; and again the evening was overcast, and a collection of brilliant red clouds in the west was followed by the customary squall of rain.

Achillea millefolium (milfoil) was among the characteristic plants of the river bottoms to-day. This was one of the most common plants during the whole of our journey, occurring in almost every variety of situation. I noticed it on the lowlands of the rivers, near the coast of the Pacific, and near to the snow among the mountains of the *Sierra Nevada.*

During this excursion, we had surveyed to its head one of the two principal branches of the upper Arkansas, 75 miles in length, and entirely completed our survey of the South fork of the Platte, to the extreme sources of that portion of the river which belongs to the plains, and heads in the broken hills of the Arkansas dividing ridge, at the foot of the mountains. That portion of its waters which were collected among these mountains, it was hoped to explore on our homeward voyage.

Reaching St. Vrain's fort on the morning of the 23d, we found Mr. Fitzpatrick and his party in good order and excellent health, and my true and reliable friend, Kit Carson, who had brought with him ten good mules, with the necessary pack saddles. Mr. Fitzpatrick, who had often endured every extremity of want during the course of his mountain life, and knew well the value of provisions in this country, had watched over our stock with jealous vigilance, and there was an abundance of flour, rice, sugar, and coffee, in the camp; and again we fared luxuriously. Meat was, however, very scarce; and two very small pigs, which we obtained at the fort, did not go far among forty men. Mr. Fitzpatrick had been here a week, during which time his men had been occupied in refitting the camp; and the repose had been very beneficial to his animals, which were now in tolerably good condition.

I had been able to obtain no certain information in regard to the character of the passes in this portion of the Rocky mountain range, which had always been represented as impracticable for carriages, but the exploration of which was incidentally contemplated by my instructions, with the view of finding some convenient point of passage for the road of emigration, which would enable it to reach, on a more direct line, the usual ford of the Great Colorado—a place considered as determined by the nature of the country beyond that river. It is singular that, immediately at the foot of the mountains, I could find no one sufficiently acquainted with them to guide us to the plains at their western base; but the race of trappers, who formerly lived in their recesses, has almost entirely disappeared—dwindled to a few scattered individuals—some one or two of whom are regularly killed in the course of each year by the Indians. You will remember that, in the previous year, I brought with me to their village near this post, and hospitably treated on the way, several Cheyenne Indians, whom I had met on the Lower Platte. Shortly after their arrival here, these were out with a party of Indians, (themselves the principal men,) which discovered a few trappers in the neighboring mountains, whom they immediately murdered, although one of them had been nearly thirty years in the country, and was perfectly well known, as he had grown gray among them.

Through this portion of the mountains, also, are the customary roads of the war parties going out against the Utah and Shoshonee Indians; and occasionally parties from the Crow nation make their way down to the southward along this chain, in the expectation of surprising some straggling lodges of their enemies. Shortly before our arrival, one of their parties had attacked an Arapaho village in the vicinity, which they had found unexpectedly strong; and their assault was turned into a rapid flight and a hot pursuit, in which they had been compelled to abandon the animals they had rode, and escape on their war horses.

Into this uncertain and dangerous region, small parties of three or four trappers, who now could collect together, rarely ventured; and consequently it was seldom visited and little known. Having determined to try the passage by a pass through a spur of the mountains made by the *Câche-à-la-Poudre* river, which rises in the high bed of mountains around Long's peak, I thought it advisable to avoid any encumbrance which would occasion detention, and accordingly again separated the party into two divisions—one of which, under the command of Mr. Fitzpatrick, was directed to cross the plains to the mouth of the Laramie river, and, continuing thence its route along the usual emigrant road, meet me at Fort Hall, a post belonging to the Hudson Bay Company, and situated on Snake river, as it is commonly called in the Oregon Territory, although better known to us as Lewis's fork of the Columbia. The latter name is there restricted to one of the upper forks of the river.[26]

Our Delaware Indians having determined to return to their homes, it became necessary to provide this party with a good hunter; and I accordingly engaged in that capacity Alexander Godey, a young man about 25 years of age, who had been in this country six or seven years, all of which time had been actively employed in hunting for the support of the posts, or in solitary trading expeditions among the Indians.[27] In courage and professional skill he was a formidable rival to Carson, and constantly afterwards was among the best and most efficient of the party, and in difficult situations was of incalculable

---

26. Once again Fitzpatrick and his party (including Talbot) find themselves with the slow equipment-laden party, while JCF with a lighter crew (but with the clumsy howitzer) goes on ahead. Until JCF had returned from his southern excursion to the Pikes Peak region on 24 July, they had not seen him since 16 June, when he left them along the banks of the Republican. The journey of the Fitzpatrick contingent to Fort St. Vrain had been uneventful except for a shortage of water which, on at least one occasion, caused Fitzpatrick himself to make a foray in search of it (and Talbot called the pond he found "execrable"). They had reached the South Platte on 8 July and St. Vrain's on the 14th, where they received instructions sent by JCF that they were to wait for him (TALBOT, 13–29). The Fitzpatrick party now sets off in a northeasterly direction, and will reach the Laramie Fork on 4 Aug.

27. Alexander Godey, French Canadian of St. Louis, would also accompany JCF on his third and fourth expeditions, and may even have been on the fifth. After 1848, he spent most of his life in California, pursuing a variety of occupations. JCF claimed that the first hard-rock gold discovered in California was found on the Mariposa claim by Godey. Godey (whose name on the earliest records we have seen is Godare) served as a guide to Walker's Pass during the Pacific Railroad Survey of 1853. When he died at the Sisters' Hospital in Los Angeles in 1889 at the age of seventy-one, he had been living in Bakersfield with his twenty-one-year-old wife.

value. Hiram Powers, one of the men belonging to Mr. Fitzpatrick's party, was discharged at this place.[28]

A French engagé, at Lupton's fort, had been shot in the back on the 4th of July, and died during our absence to the Arkansas.[29] The wife of the murdered man, an Indian woman of the Snake nation, desirous, like Naomi of old, to return to her people, requested and obtained permission to travel with my party to the neighborhood of Bear river, where she expected to meet with some of their villages. Happier than the Jewish widow, she carried with her two children, pretty little half-breeds, who added much to the liveliness of the camp. Her baggage was carried on five or six pack horses; and I gave her a small tent, for which I no longer had any use, as I had procured a lodge at the fort.

For my own party I selected the following men, a number of whom old associations rendered agreeable to me:

Charles Preuss, Christopher Carson, Basil Lajeunesse, François Badeau, J. B. Bernier, Louis Menard, Raphael Proue, Jacob Dodson, Louis Zindel, Henry Lee, J. B. Derosier, François Lajeunesse, and Auguste Vasquez.

By observation, the latitude of the post is 40° 16′ 33″, and its longitude 105° 12′ 23″, depending, with all the other longitudes along this portion of the line, upon a subsequent occultation of September 13, 1843, to which they are referred by the chronometer. Its distance from Kansas landing, by the road we travelled, (which, it will be remembered, was very winding along the lower Kansas river,) was 750 miles. The rate of the chronometer, determined by observations at this place for the interval of our absence, during this month, was 33.72″, which you will hereafter see did not sensibly change during the ensuing month, and remained nearly constant during the re-

---

28. Probably an error in name, as the financial records indicate that James Power, who had started with the expedition, was discharged at St. Vrain's 24 July 1843. There is no mention of a Hiram Power elsewhere. For a letter written on the 26th by a member of the party, see *Niles Weekly Register,* 65:70–71.

29. The man who died was named Xervier. His assailant, Thomas Fallon, a hand belonging to Fort St. Vrain, was then employed by the Fitzpatrick contingent, while Xervier's widow proceeded with JCF (TALBOT, 24, 28). Fallon was discharged from the expedition in California in March 1844. Later, in 1846, he aided in enlisting men to cooperate with the Bear Flag filibusters. He served in the California Battalion and became mayor of San Jose in 1851 (PIONEER REGISTER).

mainder of our journey across the continent. This was the rate used in referring to St. Vrain's fort, the longitude between that place and the mouth of the *Fontaine-qui-bouit*.

Our various barometrical observations, which are better worthy of confidence than the isolated determination of 1842, give, for the elevation of the fort above the sea, 4,930 feet. The barometer here used was also a better one, and less liable to derangement.

At the end of two days, which was allowed to my animals for necessary repose, all the arrangements had been completed, and on the afternoon of the 26th we resumed our respective routes. Some little trouble was experienced in crossing the Platte, the waters of which were still kept up by rains and melting snow; and having travelled only about four miles, we encamped in the evening on Thompson's creek, where we were very much disturbed by musquitoes.

The following days we continued our march westward over comparative plains, and, fording the Câche-à-la-Poudre on the morning of the 28th, entered the Black hills [of the Cache la Poudre] and nooned on this stream in the mountains beyond them. Passing over a fine large bottom in the afternoon, we reached a place where the river was shut up in the hills; and, ascending a ravine, made a laborious and very difficult passage around by a gap, striking the river again about dusk. A little labor, however, would remove this difficulty, and render the road to this point a very excellent one. The evening closed in dark with rain, and the mountains looked gloomy.

July 29.—Leaving our encampment about 7 in the morning, we travelled until 3 in the afternoon along the river, which, for this distance of about six miles, runs directly through a spur of the main mountains.

We were compelled by the nature of the ground to cross the river eight or nine times, at difficult, deep, and rocky fords, the stream running with great force, swollen by the rains—a true mountain torrent, only forty or fifty feet wide. It was a mountain valley of the narrowest kind—almost a chasm; and the scenery very wild and beautiful. Towering mountains rose round about; their sides sometimes dark with forests of pine, and sometimes with lofty precipices, washed by the river; while below, as if they indemnified themselves in luxuriance for the scanty space, the green river bottom was covered with a wilderness of flowers, their tall spikes sometimes rising above our heads as we rode among them. A profusion of blossoms

454

on a white flowering vine, (*clematis lasianthi,*) which was abundant along the river, contrasted handsomely with the green foliage of the trees. The mountain appeared to be composed of a greenish gray and red granite, which in some places appeared to be in a state of decomposition, making a red soil.

The stream was wooded with cottonwood, box elder, and cherry, with currant and serviceberry bushes. After a somewhat laborious day, during which it had rained incessantly, we encamped near the end of the pass at the mouth of a small creek, in sight of the great Laramie plains.[30] It continued to rain heavily, and at evening the mountains were hid in mists; but there was no lack of wood, and the large fires we made to dry our clothes were very comfortable; and at night the hunters came in with a fine deer. Rough and difficult as we found the pass to-day, an excellent road may be made with a little labor. Elevation of the camp 5,540 feet, and distance from St. Vrain's fort 56 miles.

July 30.—The day was bright again; the thermometer at sunrise 52°; and leaving our encampment at 8 o'clock, in about half a mile we crossed the *Câche-à-la-Poudre* river for the last time; and, entering a smoother country, we travelled along a kind of *vallon,* bounded on the right by red buttes and precipices, while to the left a high rolling country extended to a range of the Black hills, beyond which rose the great mountains around Long's peak.

By the great quantity of snow visible among them, it had probably snowed heavily there the previous day, while it had rained on us in the valley.

We halted at noon on a small branch; and in the afternoon travelled over a high country, gradually ascending towards a range of *buttes,* or high hills covered with pines, which forms the dividing ridge between the waters we had left and those of Laramie river.

Late in the evening we encamped at a spring of cold water, near the summit of the ridge, having increased our elevation to 7,520 feet.[31] During the day we had travelled 24 miles. By some indifferent

---

30. One local historian contends that JCF did not enter Poudre Canyon, nor did he follow the main Poudre as he believed, for it would have been impossible for him to sight the Laramie Plains from any spot on the Poudre River. She believes that on 29 July, JCF was on the North Fork, near Livermore, and not on the main Poudre (BARNES, 185–89). The description of the journey of 29 July seems to describe the canyon of the North Fork of the Cache la Poudre, above Fort Collins.

31. Near the Colorado-Wyoming border.

observations, our latitude is 41° 02′ 19″. A species of *hedeome*[32] was characteristic along the whole day's route.

Emerging from the mountains, we entered a region of bright, fair weather. In my experience in this country, I was forcibly impressed with the different character of the climate on opposite sides of the Rocky mountain range. The vast prairie plain on the east is like the ocean; the rain and clouds from the constantly evaporating snow of the mountains rushing down into the heated air of the plains, on which you will have occasion to remark the frequent storms of rain we encountered during our journey.

July 31.—The morning was clear; temperature 48°. A fine rolling road, among piney and grassy hills, brought us this morning into a large trail where an Indian village had recently passed. The weather was pleasant and cool; we were disturbed by neither musquitoes nor flies; and the country was certainly extremely beautiful. The slopes and broad ravines were absolutely covered with fields of flowers of the most exquisitely beautiful colors. Among those which had not hitherto made their appearance, and which here were characteristic, was a new *delphinium,* of a green and lustrous metallic blue color, mingled with compact fields of several bright-colored varieties of *astragalus,*[33] which were crowded together in splendid profusion. This trail conducted us through a remarkable defile, to a little timbered creek, up which we wound our way, passing by a singular and massive wall of dark red granite. The formation of the country is a red feldspathic granite, overlying a decomposing mass of the same rock, forming the soil of all this region, which every where is red and gravelly, and appears to be of a great floral fertility.

As we emerged on a small tributary of the Laramie river, coming in sight of its principal stream, the flora became perfectly magnificent; and we congratulated ourselves, as we rode along our pleasant road, that we had substituted this for the uninteresting country between Laramie hills and the Sweet Water valley. We had no meat for supper last night or breakfast this morning, and were glad to see Carson come in at noon with a good antelope.

A meridian observation of the sun placed us in latitude 41° 04′ 06″. In the evening, we encamped on the Laramie river, which is here very thinly timbered with scattered groups of cottonwood at con-

32. *Hedeoma hispida* Pursh.
33. By *delphinium* with *astragalus,* JCF probably means *Delphinium geyeri* Greene with *Oxytropis lambertii* Pursh.

siderable intervals. From our camp, we are able to distinguish the gorges, in which are the sources of Câche-à-la-Poudre and Laramie rivers; and the Medicine Bow mountain, toward the point of which we are directing our course this afternoon, has been in sight the greater part of the day. By observation, the latitude was 41° 15′ 02″, and longitude 106° 16′ 54″.[34] The same beautiful flora continued till about 4 in the afternoon, when it suddenly disappeared, with the red soil, which became sandy and of a whitish-gray color. The evening was tolerably clear; temperature at sunset 64°. The day's journey was 30 miles.

August 1.—The morning was calm and clear, with sunrise temperature at 42°. We travelled to-day over a plain, or open rolling country, at the foot of the Medicine Bow mountain;[35] the soil in the morning being sandy, with fragments of rock abundant; and in the afternoon, when we approached closer to the mountain, so stony that we made but little way. The beautiful plants of yesterday reappeared occasionally; flax in bloom occurred during the morning, and esparcette in luxuriant abundance was a characteristic of the stony ground in the afternoon. The camp was roused into a little excitement by a chase after a buffalo bull, and an encounter with a war party of Sioux and Cheyenne Indians about 30 strong. Hares and antelope were seen during the day, and one of the latter was killed. The Laramie peak was in sight this afternoon. The evening was clear, with scattered clouds; temperature 62°. The day's journey was 26 miles.

August 2.—Temperature at sunrise 52°, and scenery and weather made our road to-day delightful. The neighboring mountain is thickly studded with pines, intermingled with the brighter foliage of aspens, and occasional spots like lawns between the patches of snow among the pines, and here and there on the heights. Our route below lay over a comparative plain, covered with the same brilliant vegetation, and the day was clear and pleasantly cool. During the morning, we crossed many streams, clear and rocky, and broad grassy valleys, of a strong black soil, washed down from the mountains, and producing excellent pasturage. These were timbered with the red wil-

---

34. He is a few miles southwest of Laramie, Wyo., just east of Seven-mile Lakes. His latitude reading is close, but a more accurate reading of the longitude would be 105° 40′.

35. JCF's Medicine Bow "mountain" means the entire range rather than the principal crest, Medicine Bow Peak.

low and long-leaved cottonwood, mingled with aspen, as we approached the mountain more nearly towards noon. *Esparcette* was a characteristic, and flax occurred frequently in bloom. We halted at noon on the most western fork of Laramie river [Four Mile Creek] —a handsome stream about sixty feet wide and two feet deep, with clear water and a swift current, over a bed composed entirely of boulders or roll stones. There was a large open bottom here, on which were many lodge poles lying about; and in the edge of the surrounding timber were three strong forts, that appeared to have been recently occupied. At this place I became first acquainted with the *yampah,* (*anethum graveolens,*)[36] which I found our Snake women engaged in digging in the low timbered bottom of the creek. Among the Indians along the Rocky mountains, and more particularly among the Shoshonee or Snake Indians, in whose territory it is very abundant, this is considered the best among the roots used for food. To us, it was an interesting plant—a little link between the savage and civilized life. Here, among the Indians, its root is a common article of food, which they take pleasure in offering to strangers; while with us, in a considerable portion of America and Europe, the seeds are used to flavor soup. It grows more abundantly, and in greater luxuriance, on one of the neighboring tributaries of the Colorado than in any other part of this region; and on that stream, to which the Snakes are accustomed to resort every year to procure a supply of their favorite plant, they have bestowed the name of *Yampah* river. Among the trappers, it is generally known as Little Snake river; but in this and other instances, where it illustrated the history of the people inhabiting the country, I have preferred to retain on the map the aboriginal name. By a meridional observation, the latitude is 41° 45′ 59″.

In the afternoon we took our way directly across the spurs from the point of the mountain, where we had several ridges to cross; and, although the road was not rendered bad by the nature of the ground, it was made extremely rough by the stiff tough bushes of *artemisia tridentata,** in this country commonly called sage.

* The greater portion of our subsequent journey was through a region where this shrub constituted the tree of the country; and, as it will often be mentioned in occasional descriptions, the word *artemisia* only will be used, without the specific name.

36. Yampah, *Carum gairdneri* H. & A., or most recently *Perideridia gairdneri* (H. & A.) Mathias, is distinct from *Anethum graveolens* L., which may have been introduced early in the West.

458

This shrub now began to make its appearance in compact fields; and we were about to quit for a long time this country of excellent pasturage and brilliant flowers. Ten or twelve buffalo bulls were seen during the afternoon; and we were surprised by the appearance of a large red ox. We gathered around him as if he had been an old acquaintance, with all our domestic feelings as much awakened as if we had come in sight of an old farm house. He had probably made his escape from some party of emigrants on Green river; and, with a vivid remembrance of some old green field, he was pursuing the straightest course for the frontier that the country admitted. We carried him along with us as a prize; and, when it was found in the morning that he had wandered off, I would not let him be pursued, for I would rather have gone through a starving time of three entire days, than let him be killed after he had successfully run the gauntlet so far among the Indians. I have been told by Mr. Bent's people of an ox born and raised at St. Vrain's fort, which made his escape from them at Elm grove, near the frontier, having come in that year with the wagons. They were on their way out, and saw occasionally places where he had eaten and lain down to rest; but did not see him for about 700 miles, when they overtook him on the road, travelling along to the fort, having unaccountably escaped Indians and every other mischance.

We encamped at evening on the principal fork of Medicine Bow river, near to an isolated mountain called the Medicine *Butte* [Elk Mountain], which appeared to be about 1,800 feet above the plain, from which it rises abruptly, and was still white, nearly to its base, with a great quantity of snow.[37] The streams were timbered with the long-leaved cottonwood and red willow; and during the afternoon a species of onion was very abundant. I obtained here an immersion of the first satellite of Jupiter, which, corresponding very nearly with the chronometer, placed us in longitude 106° 47′ 25″. The latitude, by observation, was 41° 37′ 16″; elevation above the sea, 7,800 feet; and distance from St. Vrain's fort, 147 miles.

August 3.—There was a white frost last night; the morning is clear and cool. We were early on the road, having breakfasted before sunrise, and in a few miles travel entered the pass of the Medicine *Butte,* through which led a broad trail, which had been recently

---

37. The party has now reached the northern end of the Medicine Bow range and is ready to proceed westward through a pass between the main spurs of that range and an isolated butte now called Elk Mountain.

travelled by a very large party. Immediately in the pass, the road was broken by ravines, and we were obliged to clear a way through groves of aspens, which generally made their appearance when we reached elevated regions. According to the barometer, this was 8,300 feet; and while we were detained in opening a road, I obtained a meridional observation of the sun, which gave 41° 35' 48" for the latitude of the pass. The Medicine *Butte* is isolated by a small tributary of the North fork of the Platte, but the mountains approach each other very nearly; the stream running at their feet. On the south they are smooth, with occasional streaks of pine; but the butte itself is ragged, with escarpments of red feldspathic granite, and dark with pines; the snow reaching from the summit to within a few hundred feet of the trail. The granite here was more compact and durable than that in the formation which we had passed through a few days before to the eastward of Laramie. Continuing our way over a plain on the west side of the pass, where the road was terribly rough with artemisia, we made our evening encampment on the creek, where it took a northern direction, unfavorable to the course we were pursuing.[38] Bands of buffalo were discovered as we came down upon the plain; and Carson brought into the camp a cow which had the fat on the fleece two inches thick. Even in this country of rich pasturage and abundant game, it is rare that the hunter chances upon a finer animal. Our voyage had already been long, but this was the first good buffalo meat we had obtained. We travelled to-day 26 miles.

August 4.—The morning was clear and calm; and, leaving the creek, we travelled towards the North fork of the Platte, over a plain which was rendered rough and broken by ravines. With the exception of some thin grasses, the sandy soil here was occupied almost exclusively by artemisia, with its usual turpentine odor. We had expected to meet with some difficulty in crossing the river, but happened to strike it where there was a very excellent ford, and halted to noon on the left bank, 200 miles from St. Vrain's fort. The hunters brought in pack animals loaded with fine meat. According to our imperfect knowledge of the country, there should have been a small affluent to this stream a few miles higher up; and in the afternoon we continued our way among the river hills, in the expectation of

---

38. Pass Creek turns northward near Overland, Wyo., about five miles east of the Union Pacific tracks.

encamping upon it in the evening. The ground proved to be so exceedingly difficult, broken up into hills, terminating in escarpments and broad ravines 500 or 600 feet deep, with sides so precipitous that we could scarcely find a place to descend, that, towards sunset, I turned directly in towards the river, and, after nightfall, entered a sort of ravine. We were obliged to feel our way, and clear a road in the darkness; the surface being much broken, and the progress of the carriages being greatly obstructed by the artemisia, which had a luxuriant growth of four to six feet in height. We had scrambled along this gully for several hours, during which we had knocked off the carriage lamps, broken a thermometer and several small articles, when, fearing to lose something of more importance, I halted for the night at 10 o'clock.[39] Our animals were turned down towards the river, that they might pick up what little grass they could find; and after a little search, some water was found in a small ravine, and improved by digging. We lighted up the ravine with fires of artemisia, and about midnight sat down to a supper which we were hungry enough to find delightful—although the buffalo meat was crusted with sand, and the coffee was bitter with the wormwood taste of the artemisia leaves.

A successful day's hunt had kept our hunters occupied until late, and they slept out, but rejoined us at daybreak, when, finding ourselves only about a mile from the river, we followed the ravine down, and camped in a cottonwood grove on a beautiful grassy bottom, where our animals indemnified themselves for the scanty fare of the past night. It was quite a pretty and pleasant place; a narrow strip of prairie about five hundred yards long terminated at the ravine where we entered by high precipitous hills closing in upon the river, and at the upper end by a ridge of low rolling hills.

In precipitous bluffs were displayed a succession of strata containing fossil vegetable remains, and several beds of coal. In some of the beds the coal did not appear to be perfectly mineralized; and in some of the seams, it was compact and remarkably lustrous. In these latter places there were also thin layers of a very fine white salts, in powder. As we had a large supply of meat in the camp, which it was necessary to dry, and the surrounding country appeared to be well stocked with buffalo, which it was probable, after a day or

---

39. This camp in the valley of the North Platte was nearly equidistant between Sinclair and Saratoga, Wyo.

two, we would not see again until our return to the Mississippi waters, I determined to make here a provision of dried meat, which would be necessary for our subsistence in the region we were about entering, which was said to be nearly destitute of game. Scaffolds were accordingly soon erected, fires made, and the meat cut into thin slices to be dried; and all were busily occupied, when the camp was thrown into a sudden tumult, by a charge from about 70 mounted Indians, over the low hills at the upper end of the little bottom. Fortunately, the guard, who was between them and our animals, had caught a glimpse of an Indian's head, as he raised himself in his stirrups to look over the hill, a moment before he made the charge; and succeeded in turning the band into the camp, as the Indians charged into the bottom with the usual yell. Before they reached us, the grove on the verge of the little bottom was occupied by our people, and the Indians brought to a sudden halt, which they made in time to save themselves from a howitzer shot, which would undoubtedly have been very effective in such a compact body; and further proceedings were interrupted by their signs for peace. They proved to be a war party of Arapaho and Cheyenne Indians, and informed us that they had charged upon the camp under the belief that we were hostile Indians, and had discovered their mistake only at the moment of the attack—an excuse which policy required us to receive as true, though under the full conviction that the display of our little howitzer, and our favorable position in the grove, certainly saved our horses, and probably ourselves, from their marauding intentions. They had been on a war party, and had been defeated, and were consequently in the state of mind which aggravates their innate thirst for plunder and blood. Their excuse, however, was taken in good part, and the usual evidences of friendship interchanged. The pipe went round, provisions were spread, and the tobacco and goods furnished the customary presents, which they look for even from traders, and much more from Government authorities.

They were returning from an expedition against the Shoshonee Indians, one of whose villages they had surprised, at Bridger's fort, on Ham's [Blacks] fork of Green river,[40] (in the absence of the men,

40. JCF is referring to a horse raid of the Cheyennes against enemy tribes of which we learn more from Theodore Talbot's journal. On 30 July, Talbot was told by "The Blind Chief," a Cheyenne, "that a great portion of their warriors had gone to fight with the Snakes and Crows, their bitter enemies. He hoped we might not encounter them as their hearts were very bad towards

who were engaged in an antelope surround,) and succeeded in carrying off their horses and taking several scalps. News of the attack reached the Snakes immediately, who pursued and overtook them, and recovered their horses; and, in the running fight which ensued, the Arapahos had lost several men killed, and a number wounded, who were coming on more slowly with a party in the rear. Nearly all the horses they had brought off were the property of the whites at the fort. After remaining until nearly sunset, they took their departure; and the excitement which their arrival had afforded subsided into our usual quiet, a little enlivened by the vigilance rendered necessary by the neighborhood of our uncertain visitors. At noon the thermometer was at 75°, at sunset 70°, and the evening clear. Elevation above the sea 6,820 feet; latitude 41° 36′ 00″; longitude 107° 22′ 27″.

August 6.—At sunrise the thermometer was 46°, the morning being clear and calm. We travelled to-day over an extremely rugged country, barren and uninteresting—nothing to be seen but artemisia bushes; and, in the evening, found a grassy spot among the hills, kept green by several springs, where we encamped late. Within a few hundred yards was a very pretty little stream of clear cool water, whose green banks looked refreshing among the dry rocky hills. The hunters brought in a fat mountain sheep, (*ovis montana*).

Our road the next day was through a continued and dense field of *artemisia,* which now entirely covered the country in such a luxuriant growth that it was difficult and laborious for a man on foot to force his way through, and nearly impracticable for our light carriages. The region through which we were travelling was a high plateau, constituting the dividing ridge between the waters of the Atlantic and Pacific oceans, and extending to a considerable distance southward, from the neighborhood of the Table rock, at the southern side of the South Pass. Though broken up into rugged and rocky hills of a dry and barren nature, it has nothing of a mountainous character; the small streams which occasionally occur belonging

---

the whites" (TALBOT, 30). Later, on 30 Aug., Talbot writes that Bridger's people had all been attacked recently by the large party of Cheyennes of whom he, Talbot, had been warned. They had driven off the cavalcade of horses belonging to the fort as well as those belonging to a village of Snakes in the valley below. Traveling with the Stewart party ahead of JCF, journalist Matthew C. Field also learned of the horse raid and said it prompted stricter care in camp (FIELD, 88). Clearly, this raid was influential in prompting Jim Bridger to move the location of his fort (see note 43 below).

neither to the Platte nor the Colorado, but losing themselves either in the sand or in small lakes. From an eminence, in the afternoon, a mountainous range became visible in the north, in which were recognised, some rocky peaks belonging to the range of the Sweet Water valley; and, determining to abandon any further attempt to struggle through this almost impracticable country, we turned our course directly north, towards a pass in the valley of the Sweet Water river. A shaft of the gun carriage was broken during the afternoon, causing a considerable delay; and it was late in an unpleasant evening before we succeeded in finding a very poor encampment, where there was a little water in a deep trench of a creek, and some scanty grass among the shrubs. All the game here consisted in a few straggling buffalo bulls, and during the day there had been but very little grass, except in some green spots where it had collected around springs or shallow lakes. Within fifty miles of the Sweet Water, the country changed into a vast saline plain, in many places extremely level, occasionally resembling the flat sandy beds of shallow lakes. Here the vegetation consisted of a shrubby growth, among which were several varieties of *chenopodiaceous* plants; but the characteristic shrub was *Fremontia vermicularis,* with smaller saline shrubs growing with singular luxuriance, and in many places holding exclusive possession of the ground.

On the evening of the 8th, we encamped on one of these freshwater lakes, which the traveller considers himself fortunate to find; and the next day, in latitude by observation 42° 20′ 06″, halted to noon immediately at the foot of the southern side of the range which walls in the Sweet Water valley, on the head of a small tributary to that river.

Continuing in the afternoon our course down the stream, which here cuts directly through the ridge, forming a very practicable pass, we entered the valley; and, after a march of about nine miles, encamped on our familiar river [the Sweetwater], endeared to us by the acquaintance of the previous expedition; the night having already closed in with a cold rain storm. Our camp was about twenty miles above the Devil's gate,[41] which we had been able to see in com-

41. The site of the camp is now submerged in the waters of the Pathfinder Reservoir, named in JCF's honor. His route for the preceding four days is difficult to determine. However, his course for the next several days is over beaten paths. He is back on the Oregon Trail, and will follow it until he decides to make a side trip to Great Salt Lake.

ing down the plain; and, in the course of the night, the clouds broke away around Jupiter for a short time, during which we obtained an immersion of the first satellite, the result of which agreed very nearly with the chronometer, giving for the mean longitude 107° 50' 07"; elevation above the sea, 6,040 feet; and distance from St. Vrain's fort, by the road we had just travelled, 315 miles.

Here passes the road to Oregon; and the broad smooth highway, where the numerous heavy wagons of the emigrants had entirely beaten and crushed the artemisia, was a happy exchange to our poor animals for the sharp rocks and tough shrubs among which they had been toiling so long; and we moved up the valley rapidly and pleasantly.[42] With very little deviation from our route of the preceding year, we continued up the valley; and on the evening of the 12th encamped on the Sweet Water, at a point where the road turns off to cross to the plains of Green river. The increased coolness of the weather indicated that we had attained a great elevation, which the barometer here placed at 7,220 feet; and during the night water froze in the lodge.

The morning of the 13th was clear and cold, there being a white frost; and the thermometer, a little before sunrise, standing at 26.5°. Leaving this encampment, (our last on the waters which flow towards the rising sun,) we took our way along the upland, towards the dividing ridge which separates the Atlantic from the Pacific waters, and crossed it by a road some miles further south than the one we had followed on our return in 1842. We crossed very near the table mountain, at the southern extremity of the South Pass, which is near twenty miles in width, and already traversed by several different roads. Selecting as well as I could, in the scarcely distinguishable ascent, what might be considered the dividing ridge in this remarkable depression in the mountain, I took a barometrical observation, which gave 7,490 feet for the elevation above the Gulf of Mexico. You will remember that, in my report of 1842, I estimated the elevation of this pass at about 7,000 feet; a correct observation with a good barometer enables me now to give it with more precision. Its importance, as the great gate through which commerce and travelling may hereafter pass between the valley of the Mississippi and the

42. In his journal entry for 10 Aug., Preuss says that the howitzer was used to fire at buffalo: "Shooting buffalo with a howitzer is a cruel but amusing sport" (PREUSS, 84).

north Pacific, justifies a precise notice of its locality and distance from leading points, in addition to this statement of its elevation. As stated in the report of 1842, its latitude at the point where we crossed is 42° 24′ 32″; its longitude 109° 26′ 00″; its distance from the mouth of the Kansas, by the common travelling route, 962 miles; from the mouth of the Great Platte, along the valley of that river, according to our survey of 1842, 882 miles; and its distance from St. Louis about 400 miles more by the Kansas, and about 700 by the Great Platte route; these additions being steamboat conveyance in both instances. From this pass to the mouth of the Oregon is about 1,400 miles by the common travelling route; so that, under a general point of view, it may be assumed to be about half way between the Mississippi and the Pacific ocean, on the common travelling route. Following a hollow of slight and easy descent, in which was very soon formed a little tributary to the Gulf of California, (for the waters which flow west from the South Pass go to this gulf,) we made our usual halt four miles from the pass, in latitude by observation 42° 19′ 53″. Entering here the valley of Green river—the great Colorado of the West—and inclining very much to the southward along the streams which form the Sandy river, the road led for several days over dry and level uninteresting plains; to which a low, scrubby growth of artemisia gave a uniform dull grayish color; and on the evening of the 15th we encamped in the Mexican territory [i.e., south of 42°], on the left bank of Green river, 69 miles from the South Pass, in longitude 110° 05′ 05″, and latitude 41° 53′ 54″, distant 1,031 miles from the mouth of the Kansas. This is the emigrant road to Oregon, which bears much to the southward, to avoid the mountains about the western heads of Green river—the *Rio Verde* of the Spaniards.

August 16.—Crossing the river, here about 400 feet wide, by a very good ford, we continued to descend for seven or eight miles on a pleasant road along the right bank of the stream, of which the islands and shores are handsomely timbered with cottonwood. The refreshing appearance of the broad river, with its timbered shores and green wooded islands in contrast to its dry sandy plains, probably obtained for it the name of Green river, which was bestowed on it by the Spaniards who first came into this country to trade some 25 years ago. It was then familiarly known as the Seeds-ke-dée-agie, or Prairie Hen (*tetrao urophasianus*) river; a name which it received from the Crows, to whom its upper waters belong, and on which this bird is still very abundant. By the Shoshonee and Utah Indians, to whom belongs, for a considerable distance below, the country where we were now travelling, it was called the Bitter Root river, from the great abundance in its valley of a plant which affords them one of their favorite roots. Lower down, from Brown's hole to the southward, the river runs through lofty chasms, walled in by precipices of *red* rock; and even among the wilder tribes who inhabit that portion of its course, I have heard it called by Indian refugees from the Californian settlements the Rio *Colorado*. We halted to noon at the upper end of a large bottom, near some old houses, which had been a trading post,[43] in latitude 41° 46' 54''. At this place the elevation of the river above the sea is 6,230 feet. That of Lewis's fork of the Columbia at Fort Hall is, according to our subsequent observations, 4,500 feet. The descent of each stream is rapid, but that of the Colorado is but little known, and that little derived from vague report. Three hundred miles of its lower part, as it approaches the gulf of California, is reported to be smooth and tranquil; but its upper part is manifestly broken into many falls and rapids. From many descriptions of trappers, it is probable that in its foaming course among its lofty precipices it presents many scenes of wild grandeur; and though offering many temptations, and often discussed, no trappers have been found bold enough to undertake a voyage which has so certain a prospect of a fatal termination. The Indians have strange stories of beautiful valleys abounding with beaver, shut up among inaccessible walls of rock in the lower course of the river; and to which the neighboring Indians, in their occasional

---

43. JCF here makes a very early mention of Jim Bridger's first trading post, on the Green River. Had the contingent he was leading gone up Blacks Fork far enough, they would have encountered Bridger's second fort, already abandoned, and finally the future site of his third. But JCF turns northward along a variant of the Oregon Trail, crossing Muddy Creek (his "salt creek") near Carter, Wyo., and proceeds across the divide to the waters of Bear River. It is Talbot, traveling with the Fitzpatrick contingent, who passes the abandoned second fort and says, "Came nearly west along Black's Fork passing under the bluff on which Vasquez & Bridger's houses are built. We found them deserted and dismantled" (TALBOT, 41).

With Dale L. Morgan's help we can present a capsule history of the three establishments. The first fort was founded in Aug. 1841 on Green River, and lasted until 1843. Then, threatened by raids from the Sioux and Cheyennes, it was moved to the site on Blacks Fork which Talbot saw. But the horse raid we have discussed in note 40 must have convinced Bridger that he had chosen another bad site, so he moved farther west and built again at present Fort Bridger, Wyo. Talbot passed the second abandoned site and may have camped on the future site of the third and final fort the night of 30. Aug.

wars with the Spaniards, and among themselves, drive their herds of cattle and flocks of sheep, leaving them to pasture in perfect security.

The road here leaves the river, which bends considerably to the east; and in the afternoon we resumed our westerly course, passing over a somewhat high and broken country; and about sunset, after a day's travel of 26 miles, reached Black's fork of the Green river—a shallow stream, with a somewhat sluggish current, about 120 feet wide, timbered principally with willow, and here and there an occasional large tree. At 3 in the morning I obtained an observation of an emersion of the first satellite of Jupiter, with other observations. The heavy wagons have so completely pulverized the soil, that clouds of fine light dust are raised by the slightest wind, making the road sometimes very disagreeable.

August 17.—Leaving our encampment at 6 in the morning, we travelled along the bottom, which is about two miles wide, bordered by low hills, in which the strata contained handsome and very distinct vegetable fossils. In a gully a short distance farther up the river, and underlying these, was exposed a stratum of an impure or argillaceous limestone. Crossing on the way Black's [Hams] fork, where it is one foot deep and forty wide, with clear water and a pebbly bed, in nine miles we reached Ham's [Blacks] fork, a tributary to the former stream, having now about sixty feet breadth, and a few inches depth of water. It is wooded with thickets of red willow, and in the bottom is a tolerably strong growth of grass. The road here makes a traverse of twelve miles across a bend of the river. Passing in the way some remarkable hills, two or three hundred feet high, with frequent and nearly vertical escarpments of a green stone, consisting of an argillaceous carbonate of lime, alternating with strata of an iron brown limestone, and worked into picturesque forms by wind and rain, at 2 in the afternoon we reached the river again, having made to-day 21 miles. Since crossing the great dividing ridge of the Rocky mountains, plants have been very few in variety, the country being covered principally with artemisia.

August 18.—We passed on the road, this morning, the grave of one of the emigrants, being the second we had seen since falling into their trail; and halted to noon on the river, a short distance above.

The Shoshonee woman took leave of us here, expecting to find some of her relations at Bridger's fort, which is only a mile or two distant, on a fork of this stream.[44] In the evening we encamped on a salt creek, about fifteen feet wide, having to-day travelled 32 miles.

I obtained an emersion of the first satellite under favorable circumstances, the night being still and clear.

One of our mules died here, and in this portion of our journey we lost six or seven of our animals. The grass which the country had lately afforded was very poor and insufficient; and animals which have been accustomed to grain become soon weak and unable to labor, when reduced to no other nourishment than grass. The American horses (as those are usually called which are brought to this country from the States) are not of any serviceable value until after they have remained a winter in the country, and become accustomed to live entirely on grass.

August 19.—Desirous to avoid every delay not absolutely necessary, I sent on Carson in advance to Fort Hall this morning, to make arrangements for a small supply of provisions. A few miles from our encampment, the road entered a high ridge, which the trappers called the "little mountain," connecting the Utah with the Wind river chain; and in one of the hills near which we passed I remarked strata of a conglomerate formation, fragments of which were scattered over the surface. We crossed a ridge of this conglomerate, the road passing near a grove of low cedar, and descended upon one of the heads of Ham's [Blacks] fork, called Muddy [Little Muddy Creek], where we made our midday halt. In the river hills at this place, I discovered strata of fossilliferous rock, having an *oolitic structure,* which, in connexion with the neighboring strata, authorize us to believe that here, on the west side of the Rocky mountains, we find repeated the modern formations of Great Britain and Europe, which have hitherto been wanting to complete the system of North American geology.

The specimens from this locality are designated in the appendix by the numbers 64, 68, and 74 [p. 754].

In the afternoon we continued our road, and, searching among the hills a few miles up the stream, and on the same bank, I discovered, among alternating beds of coal and clay, a stratum of white indurated clay, containing very clear and beautiful impressions of vegetable remains. This was the most interesting fossil locality I had met in the country, and I deeply regretted that time did not permit

---

44. He is referring to Bridger's second fort, now deserted.

me to remain a day or two in the vicinity; but I could not anticipate the delays to which I might be exposed in the course of our journey —or, rather, I knew that they were many and inevitable; and after remaining here only about an hour, I hurried off, loaded with as many specimens as I could conveniently carry.

Coal made its appearance occasionally in the hills during the afternoon, and was displayed in rabbit burrows in a kind of gap, through which we passed over some high hills, and we descended to make our encampment on the same stream, where we found but very poor grass. In the evening a fine cow, with her calf, which had strayed off from some emigrant party, were found several miles from the road, and brought into camp; and as she gave an abundance of milk, we enjoyed to-night an excellent cup of coffee. We travelled to-day 28 miles, and, as has been usual since crossing the Green river, the road had been very dusty, and the weather smoky and oppressively hot. Artemisia was characteristic among the few plants.

August 20.—We continued to travel up the creek by a very gradual ascent and a very excellent grassy road, passing on the way several small forks of the stream. The hills here are higher, presenting escarpments of parti-colored and apparently clay rocks, purple, dark red, and yellow, containing strata of sandstone and limestone with shells, with a bed of cemented pebbles, the whole overlaid by beds of limestone. The alternation of red and yellow gives a bright appearance to the hills, one of which was called by our people the Rainbow hill; and the character of the country became more agreeable, and travelling far more pleasant, as now we found timber and very good grass. Gradually ascending, we reached the lower level of a bed of white limestone, lying upon a white clay, on the upper line of which the whole road is abundantly supplied with beautiful cool springs, gushing out a foot in breadth and several inches deep, directly from the hill side. At noon we halted at the last main fork of the creek, at an elevation of 7,200 feet, and in latitude, by observation, 41° 39′ 45″; and in the afternoon continued on the same excellent road, up the left or northern fork of the stream, towards its head, in a pass which the barometer placed at 8,230 feet above the sea. This is a connecting ridge between the Utah or Bear river mountains and the Wind river chain of the Rocky mountains, separating the waters of the gulf of California on the east, and those on the west belonging more directly to the Pacific, from a vast interior basin whose rivers are collected into numerous lakes having no outlet to the ocean. From the summit of the pass, the highest which the road crosses between the Mississippi and the Western ocean, our view was over a very mountainous region, whose rugged appearance was greatly increased by the smoky weather, through which the broken ridges were dark and dimly seen. The ascent to the summit of the gap was occasionally steeper than the national road in the Alleghanies; and the descent, by way of a spur on the western side, is rather precipitous, but the pass may still be called a good one. Some thickets of willow in the hollows below deceived us into the expectation of finding a camp at our usual hour at the foot of the mountain; but we found them without water, and continued down a ravine [Bridger Creek], and encamped about dark at a place where the springs again began to make their appearance, but where our animals fared badly; the stock of emigrants having razed the grass as completely as if we were again in the midst of the buffalo.

August 21.—An hour's travel this morning brought us into the fertile and picturesque valley of Bear river, the principal tributary to the Great Salt lake. The stream is here 200 feet wide, fringed with willows and occasional groups of hawthorns. We were now entering a region which for us possessed a strange and extraordinary interest. We were upon the waters of the famous lake which forms a salient point among the remarkable geographical features of the country, and around which the vague and superstitious accounts of the trappers had thrown a delightful obscurity, which we anticipated pleasure in dispelling, but which, in the mean time, left a crowded field for the exercise of our imagination.

In our occasional conversations with the few old hunters who had visited the region, it had been a subject of frequent speculation; and the wonders which they related were not the less agreeable because they were highly exaggerated and impossible.

Hitherto this lake had been seen only by trappers who were wandering through the country in search of new beaver streams, caring very little for geography; its islands had never been visited; and none were to be found who had entirely made the circuit of its shores; and no instrumental observations or geographical survey, of any description, had ever been made any where in the neighboring region. It was generally supposed that it had no visible outlet; but among the trappers, including those in my own camp, were many who believed that somewhere on its surface was a terrible whirlpool,

471

through which its waters found their way to the ocean by some sub-terranean communication. All these things had made a frequent subject of discussion in our desultory conversations around the fires at night; and my own mind had become tolerably well filled with their indefinite pictures, and insensibly colored with their romantic descriptions, which, in the pleasure of excitement, I was well disposed to believe, and half expected to realize.

Where we descended into this beautiful valley, it is three to four miles in breadth, perfectly level, and bounded by mountainous ridges, one above another, rising suddenly from the plain.

Annexed is a map [p. 470] of that portion of the river along which passes the emigrant road. In its character of level bottoms, enclosed between abrupt mountains, it presents a type of the streams of this region.

We continued our road down the river, and at night encamped with a family of emigrants—two men, women, and several children—who appeared to be bringing up the rear of the great caravan. I was struck with the fine appearance of their cattle, some six or eight yoke of oxen, which really looked as well as if they had been all the summer at work on some good farm. It was strange to see one small family travelling along through such a country, so remote from civilization. Some nine years since, such a security might have been a fatal one; but since their disastrous defeats in the country a little north, the Blackfeet have ceased to visit these waters. Indians, however, are very uncertain in their localities; and the friendly feelings, also, of those now inhabiting it may be changed.

According to barometrical observation at noon, the elevation of the valley was 6,400 feet above the sea; and our encampment at night in latitude 42° 03′ 47″, and longitude 111° 10′ 53″, by observation—the day's journey having been 26 miles.[45] This encampment was therefore within the territorial limit of the United States; our travelling, from the time we entered the valley of the Green river, on the 15th of August, having been to the south of the 42d degree

---

45. The party has reached the Bear River and gone northward to a camp near present Cokeville, Wyo. In this area at this time of year, JCF would probably have seen snow on certain elevations of the Wasatch range, north by northwest of his present position. As he proceeded farther north, it would have become apparent that the mountains were timbered to the summits, and not so high as he might have thought earlier.

of north latitude, and consequently on Mexican territory; and this is the route all the emigrants now travel to Oregon.

The temperature at sunset was 65°; and at evening there was a distant thunder storm, with a light breeze from the north.

Antelope and elk were seen during the day on the opposite prairie; and there were ducks and geese in the river.

The next morning, in about three miles from our encampment, we reached Smith's fork,[46] a stream of clear water, about 50 feet in breadth. It is timbered with cottonwood, willow, and aspen, and makes a beautiful debouchement through a pass about 600 yards wide, between remarkable mountain hills, rising abruptly on either side, and forming gigantic columns to the gate by which it enters Bear river valley. The bottoms, which below Smith's fork had been two miles wide, narrowed, as we advanced, to a gap 500 yards wide; and during the greater part of the day we had a winding route, the river making very sharp and sudden bends, the mountains steep and rocky, and the valley occasionally so narrow as only to leave space for a passage through.

We made our halt at noon in a fertile bottom, where the common blue flax was growing abundantly, a few miles below the mouth of Thomas's fork, one of the larger tributaries of the river.

Crossing, in the afternoon, the point of a narrow spur, we descended into a beautiful bottom, formed by a lateral valley, which presented a picture of home beauty that went directly to our hearts. The edge of the wood, for several miles along the river, was dotted with the white covers of emigrant wagons, collected in groups at different camps, where the smokes were rising lazily from the fires, around which the women were occupied in preparing the evening meal, and the children playing in the grass; and herds of cattle,

---

46. Smith's Fork flows into the Bear River from the east near Cokeville. It is logical to assume that this stream, as well as Smith's Fork Creek flowing into Blacks Fork, are named for famed traveler Jedediah Smith. But a trader named Thomas L. "Pegleg" Smith, who in 1848 established a post not far north of this place, had been in the area for twenty years. Born in Garrard County, Ky., in 1801, he had trapped the Southwest and Colorado River areas in the 1820s, later drifting north to trap with Ceran St. Vrain, Milton Sublette, and others (HUMPHREYS, 4:311–30). An overland diary of 1846 by John R. McBride attributes the name of the stream to Thomas L. Smith, but the editor, Dale L. Morgan, believes that Jedediah—who penetrated the area in 1824–25—is the likelier choice (MORGAN [3], 1:97, n. 44).

grazing about in the bottom, had an air of quiet security, and civilized comfort, that made a rare sight for the traveller in such a remote wilderness.

In common with all the emigration, they had been reposing for several days in this delightful valley, in order to recruit their animals on its luxuriant pasturage after their long journey, and prepare them for the hard travel along the comparatively sterile banks of the Upper Columbia. At the lower end of this extensive bottom, the river passes through an open cañon, where there were high vertical rocks to the water's edge, and the road here turns up a broad valley to the right. It was already near sunset; but, hoping to reach the river again before night, we continued our march along the valley, finding the road tolerably good, until we arrived at a point where it crosses the ridge by an ascent of a mile in length, which was so very steep and difficult for the gun and carriage, that we did not reach the summit until dark.

It was absolutely necessary to descend into the valley for water and grass, and we were obliged to grope our way in the darkness down a very steep, bad mountain, reaching the river at about 10 o'clock. It was late before our animals were gathered into camp, several of those which were very weak being necessarily left to pass the night on the ridge; and we sat down again to a midnight supper. The road, in the morning, presented an animated appearance. We found that we had encamped near a large party of emigrants; and a few miles below another party was already in motion. Here the valley had resumed its usual breadth, and the river swept off along the mountains on the western side, the road continuing directly on.

In about an hour's travel we met several Shoshonee Indians, who informed us that they belonged to a large village which had just come into the valley from the mountain to the westward, where they had been hunting antelope and gathering service berries. Glad at the opportunity of seeing one of their villages, and in the hope of purchasing from them a few horses, I turned immediately off into the plain towards their encampment, which was situated on a small stream near the river.

We had approached within something more than a mile of the village, when suddenly a single horseman emerged from it at full speed, followed by another, and another, in rapid succession; and then party after party poured into the plain, until, when the foremost rider reached us, all the whole intervening plain was occupied by a mass of horsemen, which came charging down upon us with guns and naked swords, lances, and bows and arrows—Indians entirely naked, and warriors fully dressed for war, with the long red streamers of their war bonnets reaching nearly to the ground—all mingled together in the bravery of savage warfare. They had been thrown into a sudden tumult by the appearance of our flag, which, among these people, is regarded as an emblem of hostility; it being usually bourne by the Sioux, and the neighboring mountain Indians, when they come here to war; and we had accordingly been mistaken for a body of their enemies. A few words from the chief quieted the excitement; and the whole band, increasing every moment in number, escorted us to their encampment, where the chief pointed out a place for us to encamp, near his own lodge, and made known our purpose in visiting the village. In a very short time we purchased eight horses, for which we gave in exchange blankets, red and blue cloth, beads, knives, and tobacco, and the usual other articles of Indian traffic. We obtained from them also a considerable quantity of berries of different kinds, among which service berries were the most abundant; and several kinds of roots and seeds, which we could eat with pleasure, as any kind of vegetable food was gratifying to us. I ate here, for the first time, the *kooyah*, or *tobacco root, (valeriana edulis,)*[47] the principal edible root among the Indians who inhabit the upper waters of the streams on the western side of the mountains. It has a very strong and remarkably peculiar taste and odor, which I can compare to no other vegetable that I am acquainted with, and which to some persons is extremely offensive. It was characterized by Mr. Preuss as the most horrid food he had ever put in his mouth; and when, in the evening, one of the chiefs sent his wife to me with a portion which she had prepared as a delicacy to regale us, the odor immediately drove him out of the lodge; and frequently afterwards he used to beg that when those who liked it had taken what they desired, it might be sent away. To others, however, the taste is rather an agreeable one, and I was afterwards always glad when it formed an addition to our scanty meals. It is full of nutriment; and in its unprepared state is said by the Indians to have very strong poisonous qualities, of

47. *Valeriana ciliata* T. & G., one of the notable number of aboriginal foods which are poisonous before cooking.

which it is deprived by a peculiar process, being baked in the ground for about two days.

The morning of the 24th was disagreeably cool, with an easterly wind and very smoky weather. We made a late start from the village, and, regaining the road, (on which, during all the day, were scattered the emigrant wagons,) we continued on down the valley of the river, bordered by high and mountainous hills, on which fires are seen at the summit. The soil appears generally good, although, with the grasses, many of the plants are dried up, probably on account of the great heat and want of rain. The common blue flax of cultivation, now almost entirely in seed—only a scattered flower here and there remaining—is the most characteristic plant of the Bear river valley. When we encamped at night on the right bank of the river, it was growing as in a sown field. We had travelled during the day 22 miles, encamping in latitude (by observation) 42° 36′ 56″, chronometric longitude 111° 42′ 05″.

In our neighborhood, the mountains appeared extremely rugged, giving still greater value to this beautiful natural pass.

August 25.—This was a cloudless but smoky autumn morning, with a cold wind from the SE., and a temperature of 45° at sunrise. In a few miles I noticed, where a little stream crossed the road, fragments of *scoriated basalt* scattered about—the first volcanic rock we had seen, and which now became a characteristic rock along our future road. In about six miles travel from our encampment, we reached one of the points in our journey to which we had always looked forward with great interest—the famous *Beer springs*.[48] The sketch annexed [p. 479] will aid in fixing your ideas of the place, which is a basin of mineral waters enclosed by the mountains, which sweep around a circular bend of Bear river, here at its most northern

---

48. Both Beer [Soda] Springs and Steamboat Spring are drowned in the waters of the reservoir at Soda Springs, Idaho. Beer Springs reminded travelers of lager beer because of the acid taste and the effervescent gases of the water. Steamboat Spring made a sound like a high-pressure steam engine.

JCF has already recorded his overtaking emigrant parties below Beer Springs. A young diarist in one of the parties writes on 23 Aug.: "Lieutenant Freemont, of the U.S. Topographical Engineers, with his party, overtook us this morning" (NESMITH, 349). Nesmith's party evidently caught up, as it passed the springs on the 24th. And later, after JCF had sent for supplies to support his trip down to Great Salt Lake, the diarist writes on 26 Aug.: "Kit Carson, of Freemont's company, camped with us, on his return from Fort Hall, having been on express."

point, and which from a northern, in the course of a few miles acquires a southern direction towards the GREAT SALT LAKE. A pretty little stream of clear water enters the upper part of the basin from an open valley in the mountains, and, passing through the bottom, discharges into Bear river. Crossing this stream, we descended a mile below, and made our encampment in a grove of cedar immediately at the Beer springs, which, on account of the effervescing gas and acid taste, have received their name from the voyageurs and trappers of the country, who, in the midst of their rude and hard lives, are fond of finding some fancied resemblance to the luxuries they rarely have the fortune to enjoy.

Although somewhat disappointed in the expectations which various descriptions had led me to form of unusual beauty of situation and scenery, I found it altogether a place of very great interest; and a traveller for the first time in a volcanic region remains in a constant excitement, and at every step is arrested by something remarkable and new. There is a confusion of interesting objects gathered together in a small space. Around the place of encampment the Beer springs were numerous; but, as far as we could ascertain, were entirely confined to that locality in the bottom. In the bed of the river, in front, for a space of several hundred yards, they were very abundant; the effervescing gas rising up and agitating the water in countless bubbling columns. In the vicinity round about were numerous springs of an entirely different and equally marked mineral character. In a rather picturesque spot, about 1,300 yards below our encampment, and immediately on the river bank, is the most remarkable spring of the place. In an opening on the rock, a white column of scattered water is thrown up, in form like a *jet-d'eau,* to a variable height of about three feet, and, though it is maintained in a constant supply, its greatest height is attained only at regular intervals, according to the action of the force below. It is accompanied by a subterranean noise, which, together with the motion of the water, makes very much the impression of a steamboat in motion; and, without knowing that it had been already previously so called, we gave to it the name of the *Steamboat spring.* The rock through which it is forced is slightly raised in a convex manner, and gathered at the opening into an urn-mouthed form, and is evidently formed by continued deposition from the water, and colored bright red by oxide of iron. An analysis of this deposited rock, which I subjoin, will give you some idea of the properties of the water, which, with the exception of the Beer springs, is the mineral water of the place.* It is a hot spring, and the water has a pungent and disagreeable metallic taste, leaving a burning effect on the tongue. Within perhaps two yards of the *jet-d'eau* is a small hole of about an inch in diameter, through which, at regular intervals, escapes a blast of hot air with a light wreath of smoke, accompanied by a regular noise. This hole had been noticed by Doctor Wislizenus, a gentleman who several years since passed by this place, and who remarked, with very nice observation, that smelling the gas which issued from the orifice produced a sensation of giddiness and nausea. Mr. Preuss and myself repeated the observation, and were so well satisfied with its correctness, that we did not find it pleasant to continue the experiment, as the sensation of giddiness which it produced was certainly strong and decided. A huge emigrant wagon, with a large and diversified family, had overtaken us and halted to noon at our encampment; and, while we were sitting at the spring, a band of boys and girls, with two or three young men, came up, one of whom I asked to stoop down and smell the gas, desirous to satisfy myself further of its effects. But his natural caution had been awakened by the singular and suspicious features of the place, and he declined my proposal decidedly, and with a few indistinct remarks about the devil, whom he seemed to consider the *genius loci.* The ceaseless motion and the play of the fountain, the red rock, and the green trees near, make this a picturesque spot.

A short distance above the spring, and near the foot of the same spur, is a very remarkable yellow-colored rock, soft and friable, consisting principally of carbonate of lime and oxide of iron, of regular structure, which is probably a fossil coral. The rocky bank along the shore between the Steamboat spring and our encampment, along which is dispersed the water from the hills, is composed entirely of strata of a calcareous *tufa,* with the remains of moss and reed-like grasses, which is probably the formation of springs. The *Beer* or

*ANALYSIS.

Carbonate of lime	92.55
Carbonate of magnesia	0.42
Oxide of iron	1.05
Silica ⎫	
Alumina ⎬	5.98
Water and loss ⎭	
	100.00

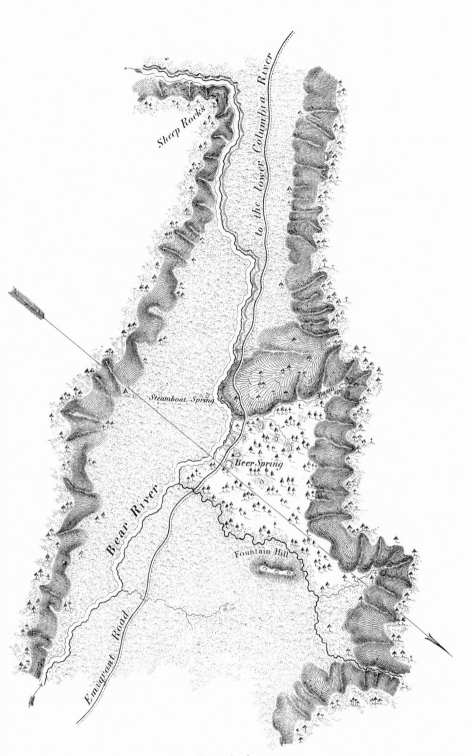

Beer Springs

479

Soda springs, which have given name to this locality, are agreeable, but less highly flavored than the *Boiling springs* at the foot of Pike's peak, which are of the same character. They are very numerous, and half hidden by tufts of grass, which we amused ourselves in removing and searching about for more highly impregnated springs. They are some of them deep, and of various sizes—sometimes several yards in diameter, and kept in constant motion by columns of escaping gas. By analysis, one quart of water contains as follows:

	Grains.
Sulphate of magnesia	12.10
Sulphate of lime	2.12
Carbonate of lime	3.86
Carbonate of magnesia	3.22
Chloride of calcium	1.33
Chloride of magnesium	1.12
Chloride of sodium	2.24
Vegetable extractive matter, &c. . .	0.85
	26.84

The carbonic acid, originally contained in the water, had mainly escaped before it was subjected to analysis; and it was not, therefore, taken into consideration.

In the afternoon I wandered about among the cedars, which occupy the greater part of the bottom towards the mountains. The soil here has a dry and calcined appearance; in some places, the open grounds are covered with saline efflorescences, and there are a number of regularly shaped and very remarkable hills, which are formed of a succession of convex strata that have been deposited by the waters of extinct springs, the orifices of which are found on their summits, some of them having the form of funnel-shaped cones. Others of these remarkably shaped hills are of a red-colored earth, entirely bare, and composed principally of carbonate of lime, with oxide of iron, formed in the same manner. Walking near one of them, on the summit of which the springs were dry, my attention was attracted by an underground noise, around which I circled repeatedly, until I found the spot from beneath which it came; and, removing the red earth, discovered a hidden spring, which was boiling up from below, with the same disagreeable metallic taste as the

Steamboat spring. Continuing up the bottom, and crossing the little stream which has been already mentioned, I visited several remarkable red and white hills, which had attracted my attention from the road in the morning. These are immediately upon the stream, and, like those already mentioned, are formed by the deposition of successive strata from the springs. On their summits, the orifices through which the waters had been discharged were so large that they resembled miniature craters, being some of them several feet in diameter, circular, and regularly formed as if by art. At a former time, when these dried-up fountains were all in motion, they must have made a beautiful display on a grand scale; and nearly all this basin appears to me to have been formed under their action, and should be called the *place of fountains.* At the foot of one of these hills, or rather on its side near the base, are several of these small limestone columns, about one foot in diameter at the base, and tapering upwards to a height of three or four feet; and on the summit the water is boiling up and bubbling over, constantly adding to the height of the little obelisks. In some, the water only boils up, no longer overflowing, and has here the same taste as the Steamboat spring. The observer will remark a gradual subsidence in the water, which formerly supplied the fountains, as on all the summits of the hills the springs are now dry, and are found only low down upon their sides, or on the surrounding plain.

A little higher up the creek, its banks are formed by strata of a very heavy and hard scoriaceous basalt, having a bright metallic lustre when broken. The mountains overlooking the plain are of an entirely different geological character. Continuing on, I walked to the summit of one of them, where the principal rock was a granular quartz. Descending the mountains, and returning towards the camp along the base of the ridge which skirts the plain, I found at the foot of a mountain spur, and issuing from a compact rock of a dark-blue color, a great number of springs having the same pungent and disagreeably metallic taste already mentioned, the water of which was collected into a very remarkable basin, whose singularity, perhaps, made it appear to me very beautiful. It is large—perhaps fifty yards in circumference; and in it the water is contained at an elevation of several feet above the surrounding ground by a wall of calcareous *tufa,* composed principally of the remains of mosses, three or four, and sometimes ten feet high. The water within is very clear and pure, and three or four feet deep, where it could be conveniently measured near the wall; and, at a considerably lower level, is another pond or basin of which the gas was escaping in bubbling columns at many places. This water was collected into a small stream, which, in a few hundred yards, sank under ground, reappearing among the rocks between the two great springs near the river, which it entered by a little fall.

Late in the afternoon I sat out on my return to the camp, and, crossing in the way a large field of a salt that was several inches deep, found on my arrival that our emigrant friends, who had been encamped in company with us, had resumed their journey, and the road had again assumed its solitary character. The temperature of the largest of the *Beer* springs at our encampment was 65° at sunset, that of the air being 62.5°. Our barometric observation gave 5,840 feet for the elevation above the gulf, being about 500 feet lower than the Boiling springs, which are of a similar nature, at the foot of Pike's peak. The astronomical observations gave for our latitude 42° 39′ 57″, and 111° 46′ 00″ for the longitude. The night was very still and cloudless, and I sat up for an observation of the first satellite of Jupiter, the emersion of which took place about midnight; but fell asleep at the telescope, awaking just a few minutes after the appearance of the star.

The morning of the 26th was calm, and the sky without clouds, but smoky; and the temperature at sunrise 28.5°. At the same time, the temperature of the large Beer spring, where we were encamped, was 56°; that of the Steamboat spring 87°; and that of the steam hole, near it, 81.5°. In the course of the morning, the last wagons of the emigration passed by, and we were again left in our place, in the rear.

Remaining in camp until nearly 11 o'clock, we travelled a short distance down the river, and halted to noon on the bank, at a point where the road quits the valley of Bear river, and, crossing a ridge which divides the Great Basin from the Pacific waters, reaches Fort Hall, by way of the Portneuf river, in a distance of probably fifty miles, or two and a half days' journey for wagons. An examination of the great lake which is the outlet of this river, and the principal feature of geographical interest in the basin, was one of the main objects contemplated in the general plan of our survey, and I accordingly determined at this place to leave the road, and, after having completed a reconnoissance of the lake, regain it subsequently at

Fort Hall.[49] But our little stock of provisions had again become extremely low; we had only dried meat sufficient for one meal, and our supply of flour and other comforts was entirely exhausted. I therefore immediately despatched one of the party, Henry Lee, with a note to Carson, at Fort Hall, directing him to load a pack horse with whatever could be obtained there in the way of provisions, and endeavor to overtake me on the river. In the mean time, we had picked up along the road two tolerably well-grown calves, which would have become food for wolves, and which had probably been left by some of the earlier emigrants, none of those we had met having made any claim to them; and on these I mainly relied for support during our circuit to the lake.

In sweeping around the point of the mountain which runs down into the bend, the river here passes between perpendicular walls of basalt [Black Canyon], which always fix the attention, from the regular form in which it occurs, and its perfect distinctness from the surrounding rocks among which it has been placed. The mountain, which is rugged and steep, and, by our measurement, 1,400 feet above the river directly opposite the place of our halt, is called the *Sheep rock*[50]—probably because a flock of the common mountain sheep (*ovis montana*) had been seen on the craggy point.

As we were about resuming our march in the afternoon, I was attracted by the singular appearance of an isolated hill [Alexander Crater] with a concave summit, in the plain, about two miles from the river, and turned off towards it, while the camp proceeded on its way to the southward in search of the lake. I found the thin and stony soil of the plain entirely underlaid by the basalt which forms the river walls; and when I reached the neighborhood of the hill, the surface of the plain was rent into frequent fissures and chasms of

49. From 26 Aug. to 18 Sept. JCF carried out a side trip to Great Salt Lake. Starting down the Bear from Soda Springs, he sheared away from that river at Standing Rock Pass, went up Weston Creek and down Deep Creek to the valley of the Malad. He followed the Malad and the Bear nearly to Great Salt Lake, and just above the mouth of the Bear he crossed to the left bank and went south around Bear River Bay to Weber River. From a base camp west of present Ogden, Utah, he visited Fremont Island in the lake, and then, growing short of provisions, returned northward to Fort Hall. His return route lay up the Malad and Little Malad rivers, crossing over to the Bannock and down that river to the Snake. The route of the excursion to Great Salt Lake will not be detailed here, but may be found discussed in KORNS and in STANSBURY—who describes the terrain in detail.

50. Now Soda Point.

the same scoriated volcanic rock, from forty to sixty feet deep, but which there was not sufficient light to penetrate entirely, and which I had not time to descend. Arrived at the summit of the hill, I found that it terminated in a very perfect crater, of an oval, or nearly circular form, 360 paces in circumference, and 60 feet at the greatest depth. The walls, which were perfectly vertical, and disposed like masonry in a very regular manner, were composed of a brown-colored scoriaceous lava, evidently the production of a modern volcano, and having all the appearance of the lighter scoriaceous lavas of Mount Ætna, Vesuvius, and other volcanoes. The faces of the walls were reddened and glazed by the fire, in which they had been melted, and which had left them contorted and twisted by its violent action.

Our route during the afternoon was a little rough, being (in the direction we had taken) over a volcanic plain, where our progress was sometimes obstructed by fissures, and black beds composed of fragments of the rock. On both sides, the mountains appeared very broken, but tolerably well timbered.

August 26.—Crossing a point of ridge which makes in to the river, we fell upon it again before sunset, and encamped on the right bank, opposite to the encampment of three lodges of Snake Indians. They visited us during the evening, and we obtained from them a small quantity of roots of different kinds, in exchange for goods. Among them was a sweet root of very pleasant flavor, having somewhat the taste of preserved quince. My endeavors to become acquainted with the plants which furnish to the Indians a portion of their support were only gradually successful, and after long and persevering attention; and even after obtaining, I did not succeed in preserving them until they could be satisfactorily determined. In this portion of the journey, I found this particular root cut up into such small pieces, that it was only to be identified by its taste, when the bulb was met with in perfect form among the Indians lower down on the Columbia, among whom it is the highly celebrated kamás. It was long afterwards, on our return through Upper California, that I found the plant itself in bloom, which I supposed to furnish the kamás root, (*camassia esculenta.*) The root diet had a rather mournful effect at the commencement, and one of the calves was killed this evening for food. The animals fared well on rushes.

August 27.—The morning was cloudy, with appearance of rain, and the thermometer at sunrise at 29°. Making an unusually early start, we crossed the river at a good ford; and, following for about three hours a trail which led along the bottom, we entered a labyrinth of hills below the main ridge, and halted to noon in the ravine of a pretty little stream, timbered with cottonwood of a large size, ash-leaved maple, with cherry and other shrubby trees. The hazy weather, which had prevented any very extended views since entering the Green river valley, began now to disappear. There was a slight rain in the earlier part of the day, and at noon, when the thermometer had risen to 79.5°, we had a bright sun, with blue sky and scattered *cumuli*. According to the barometer, our halt here among the hills was at an elevation of 5,320 feet. Crossing a dividing ridge in the afternoon, we followed down another little Bear river tributary, to the point where it emerged on an open green flat among the hills, timbered with groves, and bordered with cane thickets, but without water. A pretty little rivulet, coming out of the hill side, and overhung by tall flowering plants of a species I had not hitherto seen, furnished us with a good camping place. The evening was cloudy, the temperature at sunset 69°, and the elevation 5,140 feet. Among the plants occurring along the line of road during the day, *epinettes des prairies* (grindelia squarrosa) was in considerable abundance, and is among the very few plants remaining in bloom—the whole country having now an autumnal appearance, in the crisped and yellow plants, and dried-up grasses. Many cranes were seen during the day, with a few antelope, very shy and wild.

August 28.—During the night we had a thunder storm, with moderate rain, which has made the air this morning very clear, the thermometer being at 55°. Leaving our encampment at the *Cane spring,* and quitting the trail on which we had been travelling, and which would probably have afforded us a good road to the lake, we crossed some very deep ravines, and, in about an hour's travelling, again reached the river. We were now in a valley of five or six miles wide, between mountain ranges, which, about thirty miles below, appeared to close up and terminate the valley, leaving for the river only a very narrow pass, or cañon, behind which we imagined that we should find the broad waters of the lake. We made the usual halt at the mouth of a small clear stream, having a slightly mineral taste, (perhaps of salt,) 4,760 feet above the gulf. In the afternoon we climbed a very steep sandy hill; and, after a slow and winding day's march of 27 miles, encamped at a slough on the river [on the west side, near Preston, Idaho]. There were great quantities of geese and ducks, of which only a few were shot; the Indians having probably made them very wild. The men employed themselves in fishing, but caught nothing. A skunk, (*mephitis Americana,*) which was killed in the afternoon, made a supper for one of the messes. The river is bordered occasionally with fields of cane, which we regarded as an indication of our approach to a lake country. We had frequent showers of rain during the night, with thunder.

August 29.—The thermometer at sunrise was 54°, with air from the NW., and dark rainy clouds moving on the horizon; rain squalls and bright sunshine by intervals. I rode ahead with Basil to explore the country, and, continuing about three miles along the river, turned directly off on a trail running towards three marked gaps in the bordering range, where the mountains appeared cut through to their bases, towards which the river plain rose gradually. Putting our horses into a gallop on some fresh tracks which showed very plainly in the wet path, we came suddenly upon a small party of Shoshonee Indians, who had fallen into the trail from the north. We could only communicate by signs; but they made us understand that the road through the chain was a very excellent one, leading into a broad valley which ran to the southward. We halted to noon at what may be called the gate of the pass; on either side of which were huge mountains of rock, between which stole a little pure water stream, with a margin just sufficiently large for our passage. From the river, the plain had gradually risen to an altitude of 5,500 feet, and, by meridian observation, the latitude of the entrance was 42°.

In the interval of our usual halt, several of us wandered along up the stream to examine the pass more at leisure. Within the gate, the rocks receded a little back, leaving a very narrow, but most beautiful valley, through which the little stream wound its way, hidden by different kinds of trees and shrubs—aspen, maple, willow, cherry, and elder; a fine verdure of smooth short grass spread over the remaining space to the bare sides of the rocky walls. These were of a blue limestone, which constitutes the mountain here; and opening directly on the grassy bottom were several curious caves, which appeared to be inhabited by root diggers. On one side was gathered a heap of leaves for a bed, and they were, dry, open, and pleasant. On the roofs of the caves I remarked bituminous exudations from the rock.

The trail was an excellent one for pack horses; but, as it sometimes crossed a shelving point, to avoid the shrubbery we were obliged in several places to open a road for the carriage through the wood. A squaw on horseback, accompanied by five or six dogs, entered the pass in the afternoon; but was too much terrified at finding herself in such unexpected company to make any pause for conversation, and hurried off at a good pace—being, of course, no further disturbed than by an accelerating shout. She was well and showily dressed, and was probably going to a village encamped somewhere near, and evidently did not belong to the tribe of *root diggers*. We had now entered a country inhabited by these people; and as in the course of our voyage we shall frequently meet with them in various stages of existence, it will be well to inform you that, scattered over the great region west of the Rocky mountains, and south of the Great Snake river, are numerous Indians whose subsistence is almost solely derived from roots and seeds, and such small animals as chance and great good fortune sometimes bring within their reach. They are miserably poor, armed only with bows and arrows, or clubs; and, as the country they inhabit is almost destitute of game, they have no means of obtaining better arms. In the northern part of the region just mentioned, they live generally in solitary families; and farther to the south, they are gathered together in villages. Those who live together in villages, strengthened by association, are in exclusive possession of the more genial and richer parts of the country; while the others are driven to the ruder mountains, and to the more inhospitable parts of the country. But by simply observing, in accompanying us along our road, you will become better acquainted with these people than we could make you in any other than a very long description, and you will find them worthy of your interest.

Roots, seeds, and grass, every vegetable that affords any nourishment, and every living animal thing, insect or worm, they eat. Nearly approaching to the lower animal creation, their sole employment is to obtain food; and they are constantly occupied in a struggle to support existence.

In the annexed view [p. 488] will be found a sketch of the *Standing rock*—the most remarkable feature of the pass where a huge rock, fallen from the cliffs above, and standing perpendicularly near the middle of the valley, presents itself like a watch tower in the pass. It will give you a tolerably correct idea of the character of the scenery in this country, where generally the mountains rise abruptly up from comparatively unbroken plains and level valleys; but it will

Pass of the Standing Rock

entirely fail in representing the picturesque beauty of this delightful place, where a green valley, full of foliage, and a hundred yards wide, contrasts with naked crags that spire up into a blue line of pinnacles 3,000 feet above, sometimes crested with cedar and pine, and sometimes ragged and bare.

The detention that we met with in opening the road, and perhaps a willingness to linger on the way, made the afternoon's travel short; and about two miles from the entrance we passed through another gate, and encamped on the stream at the junction of a little fork from the southward, around which the mountains stooped more gently down, forming a small open cove.

As it was still early in the afternoon, Basil and myself in one direction, and Mr. Preuss in another, set out to explore the country, and ascended different neighboring peaks, in the hope of seeing some indications of the lake; but though our elevation afforded magnificent views, the eye ranging over a long extent of Bear river, with the broad and fertile *Cache valley* in the direction of our search, was only to be seen a bed of apparently impracticable mountains. Among these, the trail we had been following turned sharply to the northward, and it began to be doubtful if it would not lead us away from the object of our destination; but I nevertheless determined to keep it, in the belief that it would eventually bring us right. A squall of rain drove us out of the mountain, and it was late when we reached the camp. The evening closed in with frequent showers of rain, with some lightning and thunder.

August 30.—We had constant thunder storms during the night, but in the morning the clouds were sinking to the horizon, and the air was clear and cold, with the thermometer at sunrise at 39°. Elevation by barometer 5,580 feet. We were in motion early, continuing up the little stream without encountering any ascent where a horse would not easily gallop, and, crossing a slight dividing ground at the summit, descended upon a small stream, along which we continued on the same excellent road. In riding through the pass, numerous cranes were seen; and prairie hens, or grouse, (*bonasia umbellus,*) which lately had been rare, were very abundant.

This little affluent brought us to a larger stream [Deep Creek], down which we travelled through a more open bottom, on a level road, where heavily-laden wagons could pass without obstacle. The hills on the right grew lower, and, on entering a more open country, we discovered a Shoshonee village; and being desirous to obtain information, and purchase from them some roots and berries we halted on the river, which was lightly wooded with cherry, willow, maple, service berry, and aspen. A meridian observation of the sun, which I obtained here, gave 42° 14′ 22″ for our latitude, and the barometer indicated a height of 5,170 feet. A number of Indians came immediately over to visit us, and several men were sent to the village with goods, tobacco, knives, cloth, vermilion, and the usual trinkets, to exchange for provisions. But they had no game of any kind; and it was difficult to obtain any roots from them, as they were miserably poor, and had but little to spare from their winter stock of provisions. Several of the Indians drew aside their blankets showing me their lean and bony figures; and I would not any longer tempt them with a display of our merchandise to part with their wretched subsistence, when they gave as a reason that it would expose them to temporary starvation. A great portion of the region inhabited by this nation formerly abounded in game; the buffalo ranging about in herds, as we had found them on the eastern waters, and the plains dotted with scattered bands of antelope; but so rapidly have they disappeared within a few years, that now, as we journeyed along, an occasional buffalo skull and a few wild antelope were all that remained of the abundance which had covered the country with animal life.

The extraordinary rapidity with which the buffalo is disappearing from our territories will not appear surprising when we remember the great scale on which their destruction is yearly carried on. With inconsiderable exceptions, the business of the American trading posts is carried on in their skins; every year the Indian villages make new lodges, for which the skin of the buffalo furnishes the material; and in that portion of the country where they are still found, the Indians derive their entire support from them, and slaughter them with a thoughtless and abominable extravagance. Like the Indians themselves, they have been a characteristic of the Great West; and as, like them, they are visibly diminishing, it will be interesting to throw a glance backward through the last twenty years, and give some account of their former distribution through the country, and the limit of their western range.

The information is derived principally from Mr. [Thomas] Fitzpatrick, supported by my own personal knowledge and acquaintance with the country. Our knowledge does not go farther back than the spring of 1824, at which time the buffalo were spread in immense numbers over the Green river and Bear river valleys, and through all the country lying between the Colorado, or Green river of the gulf of California, and Lewis's fork of the Columbia river; the meridian of Fort Hall then forming the western limit of their range. The buffalo then remained for many years in that country, and frequently moved down the valley of the Columbia, on both sides of the river as far as the *Fishing falls* [Salmon Falls]. Below this point they never descended in any numbers. About the year 1834 or 1835 they began to diminish very rapidly, and continued to decrease until 1838 or 1840, when, with the country we have just described, they entirely abandoned all the waters of the Pacific north of Lewis's fork of the Columbia. At that time, the Flathead Indians were in the habit of finding their buffalo on the heads of Salmon river, and other streams of the Columbia; but now they never meet with them farther west than the three forks of the Missouri or the plains of the Yellowstone river.

In the course of our journey it will be remarked that the buffalo have not so entirely abandoned the waters of the Pacific, in the Rocky-mountain region south of the Sweet Water, as in the country north of the Great Pass. This partial distribution can only be accounted for in the great pastoral beauty of that country, which bears marks of having long been one of their favorite haunts, and by the fact that the white hunters have more frequented the northern than the southern region—it being north of the South Pass that the hunters, trappers, and traders, have had their rendezvous for many years past; and from that section also the greater portion of the beaver and rich furs were taken, although always the most dangerous as well as the most profitable hunting ground.

In that region lying between the Green or Colorado river and the head waters of the Rio del Norte, over the *Yampah, Kooyah, White,* and *Grand* rivers—all of which are the waters of the Colorado—the buffalo never extended so far to the westward as they did on the waters of the Columbia; and only in one or two instances have they been known to descend as far west as the mouth of White river. In travelling through the country west of the Rocky mountains, observation readily led me to the impression that the buffalo had, for the first time, crossed that range to the waters of the Pacific only a few years prior to the period we are considering; and in this opinion I am sustained by Mr. Fitzpatrick, and the older trappers in that country. In the region west of the Rocky mountains, we never meet with any of the ancient vestiges which, throughout all the country lying upon their eastern waters, are found in the *great highways,* continuous for hundreds of miles, always several inches and sometimes several feet in depth, which the buffalo have made in crossing from one river to another, or in traversing the mountain ranges. The Snake Indians, more particularly those low down upon Lewis's fork, have always been very grateful to the American trappers, for the great kindness (as they frequently expressed it) which they did to them, in driving the buffalo so low down the Columbia river.

The extraordinary abundance of the buffalo on the east side of the Rocky mountains, and their extraordinary diminution, will be made clearly evident from the following statement: At any time between the years 1824 and 1836, a traveller might start from any given point south or north in the river; and, during the whole distance, his road would be always among large bands of buffalo, which would never be out of his view until he arrived almost within sight of the abodes of civilization.

At this time, the buffalo occupy but a very limited space, principally along the eastern base of the Rocky mountains, sometimes extending at their southern extremity to a considerable distance into the plains between the Platte and Arkansas rivers, and along the eastern frontier of New Mexico as far south as Texas.

The following statement, which I owe to the kindness of Mr. [John F. A.] Sanford, a partner in the American Fur Company, will further illustrate this subject, by extensive knowledge acquired during several years of travel through the region inhabited by the buffalo:

"The total amount of robes annually traded by ourselves and others will not be found to differ much from the following statement:

	Robes.
American Fur Company . . .	70,000
Hudson's Bay Company . . .	10,000
All other companies, probably . .	10,000
Making a total of	90,000

as an average annual return for the last eight or ten years.

"In the northwest, the Hudson's Bay Company purchase from the Indians but a very small number—their only market being Canada, to which the cost of transportation nearly equals the produce of the furs; and it is only within a very recent period that they have received buffalo robes in trade; and out of the great number of buffalo annually killed throughout the extensive regions inhabited by the Camanches and other kindred tribes, no robes whatever are furnished for trade. During only four months of the year, (from November until March,) the skins are good for dressing; those obtained in the remaining eight months being valueless to traders; and the hides of bulls are never taken off or dressed as robes at any season. Probably not more than one-third of the skins are taken from the animals killed, even when they are in good season, the labor of preparing and dressing the robes being very great; and it is seldom that a lodge trades more than twenty skins in a year. It is during the summer months, and in the early part of autumn, that the greatest number of buffalo are killed, and yet at this time a skin is never taken for the purpose of trade."

From these data, which are certainly limited, and decidedly within bounds, the reader is left to draw his own inference of the immense number annually killed.

In 1842, I found the Sioux Indians of the Upper Platte *demontés,* as their French traders expressed it, with the failure of the buffalo; and in the following year, large villages from the Upper Missouri came over to the mountains at the heads of the Platte, in search of them. The rapidly progressive failure of their principal and almost their only means of subsistence had created great alarm among them; and at this time there are only two modes presented to them, by which they see a good prospect for escaping starvation: one of these is to rob the settlements along the frontier of the States; and the other is to form a league between the various tribes of the Sioux nation, the Cheyennes, and Arapahoes, and make war against the Crow nation, in order to take from them their country, which is now the best buffalo country in the west. This plan they now have in consideration; and it would probably be a war of extermination, as the Crows have long been advised of this state of affairs, and say that they are perfectly prepared. These are the best warriors in the Rocky mountains, and are now allied with the Snake Indians; and it is probable that their combination would extend itself to the Utahs, who have long been engaged in war against the Sioux. It is in this section of country that my observation formerly led me to recommend the establishment of a military post.

The farther course of our narrative will give fuller and more de-

493

tailed information of the present disposition of the buffalo in the country we visited.

Among the roots we obtained here, I could distinguish only five or six different kinds; and the supply of the Indians whom we met consisted principally of yampah, (*anethum, graveolens,*) tobacco root, (*valeriana,*) and a large root of a species of thistle, (*circium Virginianum,*) which now is occasionally abundant, and is a very agreeably flavored vegetable.

We had been detained so long at the village, that in the afternoon we made only five miles, and encamped on the same river after a day's journey of 19 miles. The Indians informed us that we should reach the big salt water after having slept twice and travelling in a south direction. The stream had here entered a nearly level plain or valley, of good soil, eight or ten miles broad, to which no termination was to be seen, and lying between ranges of mountains which, on the right, were grassy and smooth, unbroken by rock, and lower than on the left, where they were rocky and bald, increasing in height to the southward. On the creek were fringes of young willows, older trees being rarely found on the plains, where the Indians burn the surface to produce better grass. Several magpies (*pica Hudsonica*) were seen on the creek this afternoon; and a rattlesnake was killed here, the first which had been seen since leaving the eastern plains. Our camp to-night had such a hungry appearance, that I suffered the little cow to be killed, and divided the roots and berries among the people. A number of Indians from the village encamped near.

The weather the next morning was clear, the thermometer at sunrise at 44.5°, and, continuing down the valley, in about five miles we followed the little creek of our encampment to its junction with a larger stream, called *Roseaux,* or Reed [Malad] river. Immediately opposite, on the right, the range was gathered into its highest peak, sloping gradually low, and running off to a point apparently some forty or fifty miles below. Between this (now become the valley stream) and the foot of the mountains, we journeyed along a handsome sloping level, which frequent springs from the hills made occasionally miry, and halted to noon at a swampy spring, where there were good grass and abundant rushes. Here the river was forty feet wide, with a considerable current; and the valley a mile and a half in breadth; the soil being generally good, of a dark color, and apparently well adapted to cultivation. The day had become bright and pleasant, with the thermometer at 71°. By observation, our latitude was 41° 59′ 31″, and the elevation above the sea 4,670 feet. On our left, this afternoon, the range at long intervals formed itself into peaks, appearing to terminate, about forty miles below, in a rocky cape; beyond which, several others were faintly visible; and we were disappointed when at every little rise we did not see the lake. Towards evening, our way was somewhat obstructed by fields of *artemisia,* which began to make their appearance here, and we encamped on the Roseaux, the water of which had acquired a decidedly salt taste, nearly opposite to a cañon gap in the mountains, through which the Bear river enters this valley. As we encamped, the night set in dark and cold, with heavy rain; and the artemisia, which was here our only wood, was so wet that it would not burn. A poor, nearly starved dog, with a wound in his side from a ball, came to the camp, and remained with us until the winter, when he met a very unexpected fate.

September 1.—The morning was squally and cold; the sky scattered over with clouds; and the night had been so uncomfortable, that we were not on the road until 8 o'clock. Travelling between Roseaux and Bear rivers, we continued to descend the valley, which gradually expanded, as we advanced, into a level plain of good soil, about 25 miles in breadth, between mountains 3,000 and 4,000 feet high, rising suddenly to the clouds, which all day rested upon the peaks. These gleamed out in the occasional sunlight, mantled with the snow which had fallen upon them, while it rained on us in the valley below, of which the elevation here was about 4,500 feet above the sea. The country before us plainly indicated that we were approaching the lake, though, as the ground where we were travelling afforded no elevated point, nothing of it as yet could be seen; and at a great distance ahead were several isolated mountains, resembling islands, which they were afterwards found to be. On this upper plain the grass was every where dead; and among the shrubs with which it was almost exclusively occupied, (artemisia being the most abundant,) frequently occurred handsome clusters of several species of *dieteria*[51] in bloom. *Purshia tridentata* was among the frequent shrubs. Descending to the bottoms of Bear river, we found good grass for the animals, and encamped about 300 yards above the mouth of Roseaux, which here makes it junction, without communicating any of its

---

51. *Machaeranthera viscosa* (Nutt.) Greene.

salty taste to the main stream, of which the water remains perfectly pure. On the river are only willow thickets, (*salix longifolia,*)[52] and in the bottoms the abundant plants are canes, solidago, and helianthi, and along the banks of Roseaux are fields of *malva rotundifolia*. At sunset the thermometer was at 54°.5, and the evening clear and calm; but I deferred making any use of it until 1 o'clock in the morning, when I endeavored to obtain an emersion of the first satellite; but it was lost in a bank of clouds, which also rendered our usual observations indifferent.

Among the useful things which formed a portion of our equipage, was an India-rubber boat, 18 feet long, made somewhat in the form of a bark canoe of the northern lakes. The sides were formed by two air-tight cylinders, eighteen inches in diameter, connected with others forming the bow and stern. To lessen the danger from accidents to the boat, these were divided into four different compartments, and the interior space was sufficiently large to contain five or six persons and a considerable weight of baggage. The Roseaux being too deep to be forded, our boat was filled with air, and in about one hour all the equipage of the camp, carriage and gun included, ferried across. Thinking that perhaps in the course of the day we might reach the outlet at the lake, I got into the boat with Basil Lajeunesse, and paddled down Bear river, intending at night to rejoin the party, which in the mean time proceeded on its way. The river was from sixty to one hundred yards broad, and the water so deep, that even on the comparatively shallow points we could not reach the bottom with 15 feet. On either side were alternately low bottoms and willow points, with an occasional high prairie; and for five or six hours we followed slowly the winding course of the river, which crept along with a sluggish current among frequent *détours* several miles around, sometimes running for a considerable distance directly up the valley. As we were stealing quietly down the stream, trying in vain to get a shot at a strange large bird that was numerous among the willows, but very shy, we came unexpectedly upon several families of *Root Diggers,* who were encamped among the rushes on the shore, and appeared very busy about several weirs or nets which had been rudely made of canes and rushes for the purpose of catching fish. They were very much startled at our appearance, but we soon established an acquaintance; and finding that they had

---

52. Probably *Salix interior* Rowlee.

some roots; I promised to send some men with goods to trade with them. They had the usual very large heads, remarkable among the Digger tribe, with matted hair, and were almost entirely naked; looking very poor and miserable, as if their lives had been spent in the rushes where they were, beyond which they seemed to have very little knowledge of any thing. From the few words we could comprehend, their language was that of the Snake Indians.

Our boat moved so heavily, that we had made very little progress; and, finding that it would be impossible to overtake the camp, as soon as we were sufficiently far below the Indians, we put to the shore near a high prairie bank, hauled up the boat, and *cached* our effects in the willows. Ascending the bank, we found that our desultory labor had brought us only a few miles in a direct line; and, going out into the prairie, after a search we found the trail of the camp, which was now nowhere in sight, but had followed the general course of the river in a large circular sweep which it makes at this place. The sun was about three hours high when we found the trail; and as our people had passed early in the day, we had the prospect of a vigorous walk before us. Immediately where we landed, the high arable plain on which we had been travelling for several days past terminated in extensive low flats, very generally occupied by salt marshes, or beds of shallow lakes, whence the water had in most places evaporated, leaving their hard surface encrusted with a shining white residuum, and absolutely covered with very small *univalve* shells. As we advanced, the whole country around us assumed this appearance; and there was no other vegetation than the shrubby chenopodiaceous and other apparently saline plants, which were confined to the rising grounds. Here and there on the river bank, which was raised like a levee above the flats through which it ran, was a narrow border of grass and short black-burnt willows; the stream being very deep and sluggish, and sometimes 600 to 800 feet wide. After a rapid walk of about 15 miles, we caught sight of the camp fires among clumps of willows just as the sun had sunk behind the mountains on the west side of the valley, filling the clear sky with a golden yellow. These last rays, to us so precious, could not have revealed a more welcome sight. To the traveller and the hunter, a camp fire in the lonely wilderness is always cheering; and to ourselves, in our present situation, after a hard march in a region of novelty, approaching the *debouches* of a river, in a lake of almost fabulous reputation, it was doubly so. A plentiful supper of aquatic birds, and the interest of the scene, soon dissipated fatigue; and I obtained during the night emersions of the second, third, and fourth satellites of Jupiter, with observations for time and latitude.

September 3.—The morning was clear, with a light air from the north, and the thermometer at sunrise at 45°.5. At 3 in the morning, Basil was sent back with several men and horses for the boat, which, in a direct course across the flats, was not 10 miles distant; and in the mean time there was a pretty spot of grass here for the animals. The ground was so low that we could not get high enough to see across the river, on account of the willows; but we were evidently in the vicinity of the lake, and the water fowl made this morning a noise like thunder. A pelican (*pelecanus onecrotalus*) was killed as he passed by, and many geese and ducks flew over the camp. On the dry salt marsh here, is scarce any other plant than *salicornia herbacea*.

In the afternoon the men returned with the boat, bringing with them a small quantity of roots, and some meat, which the Indians had told them was bear meat.

Descending the river for about three miles in the afternoon, we found a bar to any further travelling in that direction—the stream being spread out in several branches, and covering the low grounds with water, where the miry nature of the bottom did not permit any further advance. We were evidently on the border of the lake, although the rushes and canes which covered the marshes prevented any view; and we accordingly encamped at the little *delta* which forms the mouth of Bear river; a long arm of the lake stretching up to the north between us and the opposite mountains. The river was bordered with a fringe of willows and canes, among which were interspersed a few plants; and scattered about on the marsh was a species of *uniola,* closely allied to *U. spicata* of our sea coast. The whole morass was animated with multitudes of water fowl, which appeared to be very wild—rising for the space of a mile round about at the sound of a gun, with a noise like distant thunder. Several of the people waded out into the marshes, and we had to-night a delicious supper of ducks, geese, and plover. [They were at Bear River Bay. The mountains were the Promontory range.]

Although the moon was bright, the night was otherwise favorable; and I obtained this evening an emersion of the first satellite, with the usual observations. A mean result, depending on various observations made during our stay in the neighborhood, places the mouth of the river in longitude 112° 19′ 30″ west from Greenwich; latitude 41° 30′ 22″; and, according to the barometer, in elevation 4,200 feet above the gulf of Mexico. The night was clear, with considerable dew, which I had remarked every night since the first of September. The next morning, while we were preparing to start, Carson rode into the camp with flour and a few other articles of light provision, sufficient for two or three days—a scanty but very acceptable supply. Mr. Fitzpatrick had not yet arrived, and provisions were very scarce, and difficult to be had at Fort Hall, which had been entirely exhausted by the necessities of the emigrants. He brought me also a letter from Dr. Dwight, who, in company with several emigrants, had reached that place in advance of Mr. Fitzpatrick, and was about continuing his journey to Vancouver.

Returning about five miles up the river, we were occupied until nearly sunset in crossing to the left bank—the stream, which in the last five or six miles of its course, is very much narrower than above, being very deep immediately at the banks; and we had great difficulty in getting our animals over. The people with the baggage were easily crossed in the boat, and we encamped on the left bank where we crossed the river. At sunset the thermometer was at 75°, and there was some rain during the night, with a thunder storm at a distance.

September 5.—Before us was evidently the bed of the lake, being a great salt marsh, perfectly level and bare, whitened in places by saline efflorescences, with here and there a pool of water, and having the appearance of a very level sea shore at low tide. Immediately along the river was a very narrow strip of vegetation, consisting of willows, helianthi, roses, flowering vines, and grass; bordered on the verge of the great marsh by a fringe of singular plants, which appear to be a shrubby salicornia, or a genus allied to it.

About 12 miles to the southward was one of those isolated mountains now appearing to be a kind of peninsula; and towards this we accordingly directed our course, as it probably afforded a good view of the lake; but the deepening mud as we advanced forced us to return toward the river, and gain the higher ground at the foot of the eastern mountains. Here we halted for a few minutes at noon, on a beautiful little stream of pure and remarkably clear water, with a bed of rock *in situ,* on which was an abundant water plant with a white blossom. There was good grass in the bottoms; and, amidst a rather luxuriant growth, its banks were bordered with a large showy plant (*eupatorium purpureum,*) which I here saw for the first time. We named the stream *Clear* [Willard] *creek.*

We continued our way along the mountain, having found here a broad plainly beaten trail, over what was apparently the shore of the lake in the spring; the ground being high and firm, and the soil excellent and covered with vegetation, among which a leguminous plant (*glycyrrhiza lepidota*) was a characteristic plant. The ridge here rises abruptly to the height of about 4,000 feet; its face being very prominently marked with a massive stratum of rose-colored granular quartz, which is evidently an altered sedimentary rock; the lines of deposition being very distinct. It is rocky and steep; divided into several mountains; and the rain in the valley appears to be always snow on their summits at this season. Near a remarkable rocky point of the mountain, at a large spring of pure water, were several hackberry trees, (*celtis,*) probably a new species, the berries still green; and a short distance farther, thickets of sumach (*rhus.*)

On the plain here I noticed blackbirds and grouse. In about seven miles from Clear creek, the trail brought us to a place at the foot of the mountain where there issued with considerable force ten or twelve hot springs, highly impregnated with salt. In one of these, the thermometer stood at 136°, and in another at 132°.5; and the water, which spread in pools over the low ground, was colored red.*

At this place the trail we had been following turned to the left, apparently with the view of entering a gorge in the mountain, from which issued the principal fork of a large and comparatively well-

---

* An analysis of the red earthy matter deposited in the bed of the stream from the springs, gives the following result:

Peroxide of iron	33.50
Carbonate of magnesia	2.40
Carbonate of lime	50.43
Sulphate of lime	2.00
Chloride of sodium	3.45
Silica and alumina	3.00
Water and loss	5.22
	100.00

[Adding to JCF's note, we can say that the springs he has encountered are Utah Hot Springs. His camp of 5 Sept. was on the Weber River at its northernmost bend, about a mile south of Plain City. The next day he will reach what he calls a butte, now Little Mountain, where at an altitude of 4,673 feet there is a marker to commemorate his passage.]

timbered stream, called Weber's fork. We accordingly turned off towards the lake, and encamped on this river, which was 100 to 150 feet wide, with high banks, and very clear pure water, without the slightest indication of salt.

September 6.—Leaving the encampment early, we again directed our course for the peninsular *butte* across a low shrubby plain, crossing in the way a slough-like creek with miry banks, and wooded with thickets of thorn (*crataegus*) which were loaded with berries. This time we reached the butte without any difficulty, and, ascending to the summit, immediately at our feet beheld the object of our anxious search—the waters of the Inland Sea, stretching in still and solitary grandeur far beyond the limit of our vision. It was one of the great points of the exploration; and as we looked eagerly over the lake in the first emotions of excited pleasure, I am doubtful if the followers of Balboa felt more enthusiasm when, from the heights of the Andes, they saw for the first time the great Western ocean. It was certainly a magnificent object, and a noble *terminus* to this part of our expedition; and to travellers so long shut up among mountain ranges, a sudden view over the expanse of silent waters had in it something sublime. Several large islands raised their high rocky heads out of the waves; but whether or not they were timbered, was still left to our imagination, as the distance was too great to determine if the dark hues upon them were woodland or naked rock. During the day the clouds had been gathering black over the mountains to the westward, and, while we were looking, a storm burst down with sudden fury upon the lake, and entirely hid the islands from our view. So far as we could see, along the shores there was not a solitary tree, and but little appearance of grass; and on Weber's fork, a few miles below our last encampment, the timber was gathered into groves, and then disappeared entirely. As this appeared to be the nearest point to the lake where a suitable camp could be found, we directed our course to one of the groves, where we found a handsome encampment, with good grass and an abundance of rushes, (*equisetum hyemale.*)[53] At sunset, the thermometer was at 55°; the evening clear and calm, with some cumuli.

September 7.—The morning was calm and clear, with a temperature at sunrise at 39°.5. The day was spent in active preparation for our intended voyage on the lake. On the edge of the stream a favor-

---

53. Almost certainly *Juncus* sp.

able spot was selected in a grove, and, felling the timber, we made a strong corál, or horse pen, for the animals, and a little fort for the people who were to remain. We were now probably in the country of the Utah Indians, though none reside upon the lake. The India-rubber boat was repaired with prepared cloth and gum, and filled with air, in readiness for the next day.

The provisions which Carson had brought with him being now exhausted, and our stock reduced to a small quantity of roots, I determined to retain with me only a sufficient number of men for the execution of our design; and accordingly seven were sent back to Fort Hall, under the guidance of François Lajeunesse, who, having been for many years a trapper in the country, was considered an experienced mountaineer. Though they were provided with good horses, and the road was a remarkably plain one of only four days' journey for a horseman, they became bewildered, (as we afterwards learned,) and, losing their way, wandered about the country in parties of one or two, reaching the fort about a week afterwards. Some straggled in of themselves, and the others were brought in by Indians who had picked them up on Snake river, about sixty miles below the fort, travelling along the emigrant road in full march for the Lower Columbia. The leader of this adventurous party was François.

Hourly barometrical observations were made during the day, and, after departure of the party for Fort Hall, we occupied ourselves in continuing our little preparations, and in becoming acquainted with the country in the vicinity. The bottoms along the river were timbered with several kinds of willow, hawthorn, and fine cottonwood trees (*populus canadensis*) with remarkably large leaves, and sixty feet in height by measurement.

We formed now but a small family. With Mr. Preuss and myself, Carson, Bernier, and Basil Lajeunesse, had been selected for the boat expedition—the first ever attempted on this interior sea;[54] and Badeau, with Derosier, and Jacob, (the colored man,) were to be left in charge of the camp. We were favored with the most delightful weather. To-night there was a brilliant sunset of golden orange and green, which left the western sky clear and beautifully pure; but clouds in the east made me lose an occultation. The summer

---

54. Not true. William H. Ashley's men had sailed around the lake in skin canoes in 1826.

frogs were singing around us, and the evening was very pleasant, with a temperature of 60°—a night of a more southern autumn. For our supper we had *yampah,* the most agreeably flavored of the roots, seasoned by a small fat duck, which had come in the way of Jacob's rifle. Around our fire to-night were many speculations on what to-morrow would bring forth, and in our busy conjectures we fancied that we should find every one of the large islands a tangled wilderness of trees and shrubbery, teeming with game of every description that the neighboring region afforded, and which the foot of a white man or Indian had never violated. Frequently, during the day, clouds had rested on the summits of their lofty mountains, and we believed that we should find clear streams and springs of fresh water; and we indulged in anticipations of the luxurious repasts with which we were to indemnify ourselves for past privations. Neither, in our discussions, were the whirlpool and other mysterious dangers forgotten, which Indian and hunter's stories attributed to this unexplored lake. The men had discovered that, instead of being strongly sewed (like that of the preceding year, which had so triumphantly rode the cañons of the Upper Great Platte,) our present boat was only pasted together in a very insecure manner, the maker having been allowed so little time in the construction, that he was obliged to crowd the labor of two months into several days. The insecurity of the boat was sensibly felt by us; and, mingled with the enthusiasm and excitement that we all felt at the prospect of an undertaking which had never before been accomplished, was a certain impression of danger, sufficient to give a serious character to our conversation. The momentary view which had been had of the lake the day before, its great extent and rugged islands, dimly seen amidst the dark waters in the obscurity of the sudden storm, were well calculated to heighten the idea of undefined danger with which the lake was generally associated.

September 8.—A calm, clear day, with a sunrise temperature of 41°. In view of our present enterprise, a part of the equipment of the boat had been made to consist in three air-tight bags, about three feet long, and capable each of containing five gallons. These had been filled with water the night before, and were now placed in the boat, with our blankets and instruments, consisting of a sextant, telescope, spy glass, thermometer, and barometer.

We left the camp at sunrise, and had a very pleasant voyage down the river, in which there was generally eight or ten feet of water, deepening as we neared the mouth in the latter part of the day. In the course of the morning we discovered that two of the cylinders leaked so much as to require one man constantly at the bellows, to keep them sufficiently full of air to support the boat. Although we had made a very early start, we loitered so much on the way—stopping every now and then, and floating silently along, to get a shot at a goose or a duck—that it was late in the day when we reached the outlet. The river here divided into several branches, filled with fluvials, and so very shallow that it was with difficulty we could get the boat along, being obliged to get out and wade. We encamped on a low point among rushes and young willows, where there was a quantity of drift wood, which served for our fires. The evening was mild and clear; we made a pleasant bed of the young willows; and geese and ducks enough had been killed for an abundant supper at night, and for breakfast the next morning. The stillness of the night was enlivened by millions of water fowl. Latitude (by observation) 41° 11′ 26″; and longitude 112° 11′ 30″.

September 9.—The day was clear and calm; the thermometer at sunrise at 49°. As is usual with the trappers on the eve of any enterprise, our people had made dreams, and theirs happened to be a bad one—one which always preceded evil—and consequently they looked very gloomy this morning; but we hurried through our breakfast, in order to make an early start, and have all the day before us for our adventure. The channel in a short distance became so shallow that our navigation was at an end, being merely a sheet of soft mud, with a few inches of water, and sometimes none at all, forming the low-water shore of the lake. All this place was absolutely covered with flocks of screaming plover. We took off our clothes, and, getting overboard, commenced dragging the boat—making, by this operation, a very curious trail, and a very disagreeable smell in stirring up the mud, as we sank above the knee at every step. The water here was still fresh, with only an insipid and disagreeable taste, probably derived from the bed of fetid mud. After proceeding in this way about a mile, we came to a small black ridge on the bottom, beyond which the water became suddenly salt, beginning gradually to deepen, and the bottom was sandy and firm. It was a remarkable division, separating the fresh water of the rivers from the briny water of the lake, which was entirely *saturated* with common salt. Pushing our little vessel across the narrow boundary, we sprang on board, and at length were afloat on the waters of the unknown sea.

We did not steer for the mountainous islands [Promontory range and Antelope Island], but directed our course towards a lower one [in between], which it had been decided we should first visit, the summit of which was formed like the crater at the upper end of Bear river valley. So long as we could touch the bottom with our paddles, we were very gay; but gradually, as the water deepened, we became more still in our frail batteau of gum cloth distended with air, and with pasted seams. Although the day was very calm, there was a considerable swell on the lake; and there were white patches of foam on the surface, which were slowly moving to the southward, indicating the set of a current in that direction, and recalling the recollection of the whirlpool stories. The water continued to deepen as we advanced; the lake becoming almost transparently clear, of an extremely beautiful bright green color; and the spray, which was thrown into the boat and over our clothes, was directly converted into a crust of common salt, which covered also our hands and arms. "Captain," said Carson, who for some time had been looking suspiciously at some whitening appearances outside the nearest islands, "what are those yonder?—won't you just take a look with the glass?" We ceased paddling for a moment, and found them to be the caps of the waves that were beginning to break under the force of a strong breeze that was coming up the lake. The form of the boat seemed to be an admirable one, and it rode on the waves like a water bird; but, at the same time, it was extremely slow in its progress. When we were a little more than half way across the reach, two of the divisions between the cylinders gave way, and it required the constant use of the bellows to keep in a sufficient quantity of air. For a long time we scarcely seemed to approach our island, but gradually we worked across the rougher sea of the open channel, into the smoother water under the lee of the island; and began to discover that what we took for a long row of pelicans, ranged on the beach, were only low cliffs whitened with salt by the spray of the waves; and about noon we reached the shore, the transparency of the water enabling us to see the bottom at a considerable depth.

It was a handsome broad beach where we landed, behind which the hill, into which the island was gathered, rose somewhat abruptly;

and a point of rock at one end enclosed it in a sheltering way; and as there was an abundance of drift wood along the shore, it offered us a pleasant encampment. We did not suffer our fragile boat to touch the sharp rocks; but, getting overboard, discharged the baggage, and, lifting it gently out of the water, carried it to the upper part of the beach, which was composed of very small fragments of rock.

Among the successive banks of the beach, formed by the action of the waves, our attention, as we approached the island, had been attracted by one 10 to 20 feet in breadth, of a dark-brown color. Being more closely examined, this was found to be composed, to the depth of seven or eight and twelve inches, entirely of the *larvae* of insects, or, in common language, of the skins of worms, about the size of a grain of oats, which had been washed up by the waters of the lake.

Alluding to this subject some months afterwards, when travelling through a more southern portion of this region, in company with Mr. Joseph Walker,[55] an old hunter, I was informed by him, that, wandering with a party of men in a mountain country east of the great Californian range, he surprised a party of several Indian families encamped near a small salt lake, who abandoned their lodges at his approach, leaving every thing behind them. Being in a starving condition, they were delighted to find in the abandoned lodges a number of skin bags, containing a quantity of what appeared to be fish, dried and pounded. On this they made a hearty supper; and were gathering around an abundant breakfast the next morning, when Mr. Walker discovered that it was with these, or a similar worm, that the bags had been filled. The stomachs of the stout trappers were not proof against their prejudices, and the repulsive food was suddenly rejected. Mr. Walker had further opportunities of seeing these worms used as an article of food; and I am inclined to think they are the same as those we saw, and appear to be a product of the salt lakes. It may be well to recall to your mind that Mr. Walker was associated with Captain Bonneville in his expedition to the Rocky mountains; and has since that time remained in the country, generally residing in some one of the Snake villages, when not

55. Another allusion to Joseph R. Walker, who would be serving as a guide on the homeward leg of the present journey, from "The Lesser Youta Lake" to Bent's Fort, 25 May to 5 July 1844. Still later he would guide JCF's third expedition into California.

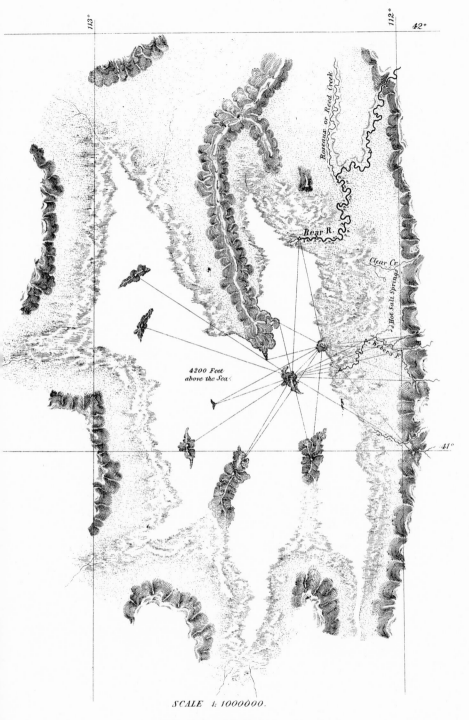

SCALE 1: 1000000.

The Great Salt Lake

507

engaged in one of his numerous trapping expeditions, in which he is celebrated as one of the best and bravest leaders who have ever been in the country.

The cliffs and masses of rock along the shore were whitened by an incrustation of salt where the waves dashed up against them; and the evaporating water, which had been left in holes and hollows on the surface of the rocks, was covered with a crust of salt about one-eighth of an inch in thickness. It appeared strange that, in the midst of this grand reservoir, one of our greatest wants lately had been salt. Exposed to be more perfectly dried in the sun, this became very white and fine, having the usual flavor of very excellent common salt, without any foreign taste; but only a little was collected for present use, as there was in it a number of small black insects.

Carrying with us the barometer and other instruments, in the afternoon we ascended to the highest point of the island—a bare rocky peak, 800 feet above the lake. Standing on the summit, we enjoyed an extended view of the lake, enclosed in a basin of rugged mountains, which sometimes left marshy flats and extensive bottoms between them and the shore, and in other places came directly down into the water with bold and precipitous bluffs. Following with our glasses the irregular shores, we searched for some indications of a communication with other bodies of water, or the entrance of other rivers; but the distance was so great that we could make out nothing with certainty. To the southward, several peninsular mountains, 3,000 or 4,000 feet high, entered the lake, appearing, so far as the distance and our position enabled us to determine, to be connected by flats and low ridges with the mountains in the rear. Although these are probably the islands usually indicated on maps of this region as entirely detached from the shore, we have preferred to represent them, in the small map on the preceding page, precisely as we were enabled to sketch them on the ground, leaving their more complete delineation for a future survey. The sketch, of which the scale is nearly sixteen miles to an inch, is introduced only to show clearly the extent of our operations, which, it will be remembered, were made when the waters were at their lowest stage. At the season of high waters in the spring, it is probable that all the marshes and low grounds are overflowed, and the surface of the lake considerably greater. In several places (which will be indicated to you in the sketch, by the absence of the bordering mountains) the view was of unlimited extent—here and there a rocky islet appearing above the water at a great distance; and beyond, every thing was vague and undefined. As we looked over the vast expanse of water spread out beneath us, and strained our eyes along the silent shores over which hung so much doubt and uncertainty, and which were so full of interest to us, I could hardly repress the almost irresistible desire to continue our exploration; but the lengthening snow on the mountains was a plain indication of the advancing season, and our frail linen boat appeared so insecure that I was unwilling to trust our lives to the uncertainties of the lake. I therefore unwillingly resolved to terminate our survey here, and remain satisfied for the present with what we had been able to add to the unknown geography of the region. We felt pleasure also in remembering that we were the first who, in the traditionary annals of the country, had visited the islands, and broken, with the cheerful sound of human voices, the long solitude of the place. From the point where we were standing, the ground fell off on every side to the water, giving us a perfect view of the island, which is twelve or thirteen miles in circumference, being simply a rocky hill, on which there is neither water nor trees of any kind; although the *Fremontia vermicularis,* which was in great abundance, might easily be mistaken for timber at a distance. The plant seemed here to delight in a congenial air, growing in extraordinary luxuriance seven to eight feet high, and was very abundant on the upper parts of the island, where it was almost the only plant. This is eminently a saline shrub; its leaves have a very salt taste; and it luxuriates in saline soils, where it is usually a characteristic. It is widely diffused over all this country. A chenopodiaceous shrub, which is a new species of OBIONE, (O. rigida, *Torr. & Frem.,*)[56] was equally characteristic of the lower parts of the island. These two are the striking plants of the island, and belong to a class of plants which form a prominent feature in the vegetation of this country. On the lower parts of the island, also, a prickly pear of very large size was frequent. On the shore, near the water, was a woolly species of *phaca;* and a new species of umbelliferous plant (*leptotæmia*) was scattered about in very considerable abundance. These constituted all the vegetation that now appeared upon the island.

I accidentally left on the summit the brass cover to the object end of my spy glass; and as it will probably remain there undisturbed

---

56. *Atriplex canescens* (Pursh) Nutt. Possibly the same as *Pterochiton occidentale* Torr. & Frem., new genus, now interpreted as a form of polymorphic species.

by Indians, it will furnish matter of speculation to some future traveller. In our excursions about the island, we did not meet with any kind of animal; a magpie, and another larger bird, probably attracted by the smoke of our fire, paid us a visit from the shore, and were the only living things seen during our stay. The rock constituting the cliffs along the shore where we were encamped, is a talcous rock, or steatite, with brown spar.

At sunset, the temperature was 70°. We had arrived just in time to obtain a meridian altitude of the sun, and other observations were obtained this evening, which place our camp in latitude 41° 10′ 42″, and longitude 112° 21′ 05″ from Greenwich. From a discussion of the barometrical observations made during our stay on the shores of the lake, we have adopted 4,200 feet for its elevation above the gulf of Mexico. In the first disappointment we felt from the dissipation of our dream of the fertile islands, I called this *Disappointment island.*[57]

Out of the drift wood, we made ourselves pleasant little lodges, open to the water, and, after having kindled large fires to excite the wonder of any straggling savage on the lake shores, lay down, for the first time in a long journey, in perfect security; no one thinking about his arms. The evening was extremely bright and pleasant; but the wind rose during the night, and the waves began to break heavily on the shore, making our island tremble. I had not expected in our inland journey to hear the roar of an ocean surf; and the strangeness of our situation, and the excitement we felt in the associated interests of the place, made this one of the most interesting nights I remember during our long expedition.

In the morning, the surf was breaking heavily on the shore, and we were up early. The lake was dark and agitated, and we hurried through our scanty breakfast, and embarked—having first filled one of the buckets with water from the lake, of which it was intended to make salt. The sun had risen by the time we were ready

---

57. Howard Stansbury gave the island its present name, Fremont Island, when he surveyed it in 1850, "in honor of him who first set foot upon its shore" (STANSBURY, 159). He also came upon a cross carved under a "shelving rock" near the summit of the island, but did not know who had placed it there. It proved to be the work of Carson and perhaps Bernier, passing the time while JCF and Preuss were mapping (CARSON, 88). The cap of the telescope was found by Jacob Miller during the 1860s while he was using the island as a sheep range. For another account of JCF in the Great Salt Lake region, see MILLER.

to start; and it was blowing a strong gale of wind, almost directly off the shore, and raising a considerable sea, in which our boat strained very much. It roughened as we got away from the island, and it required all the efforts of the men to make any head against the wind and sea; the gale rising with the sun, and there was danger of being blown into one of the open reaches beyond the island. At the distance of half a mile from the beach, the depth of water was 16 feet, with a clay bottom; but, as the working of the boat was very severe labor, and during the operation of rounding it was necessary to cease paddling, during which the boat lost considerable way, I was unwilling to discourage the men, and reluctantly gave up my intention of ascertaining the depth, and the character of the bed. There was a general shout in the boat when we found ourselves in one fathom, and we soon after landed on a low point of mud, immediately under the *butte* of the peninsula, where we unloaded the boat, and carried the baggage about a quarter of a mile to firmer ground. We arrived just in time for meridian observation, and carried the barometer to the summit of the butte, which is 500 feet above the lake. Mr. Preuss set off on foot for the camp, which was about nine miles distant; Basil accompanying him, to bring back horses for the boat and baggage.

The rude-looking shelter we raised on the shore, our scattered baggage and boat lying on the beach, made quite a picture; and we called this the *Fisherman's camp. Lynosiris graveolens,* and another new species of OBIONE, (O. confertifolia—*Torr. & Frem.,*) were growing on the low grounds, with interspersed spots of an unwholesome salt grass, on a saline clay soil, with a few other plants.

The horses arrived late in the afternoon, by which time the gale had increased to such a height that a man could scarcely stand before it; and we were obliged to pack our baggage hastily, as the rising water of the lake had already reached the point where we were halted. Looking back as we rode off, we found the place of recent encampment entirely covered. The low plain through which we rode to the camp was covered with a compact growth of shrubs of extraordinary size and luxuriance. The soil was sandy and saline; flat places, resembling the beds of ponds, that were bare of vegetation, and covered with a powdery white salts, being interspersed among the shrubs. Artemisia tridentata was very abundant, but the plants were principally saline; a large and vigorous chenopodiaceous shrub, five to eight feet high, being characteristic, with Fremontia vermicularis, and a shrubby plant which seems to be a new *salicornia*. We reached the camp in time to escape a thunder storm which blackened the sky, and were received with a discharge of the howitzer by the people, who, having been unable to see any thing of us on the lake, had begun to feel some uneasiness.

September 11.—To-day we remained at this camp, in order to obtain some further observations, and to boil down the water which had been brought from the lake, for a supply of salt. Roughly evaporated over the fire, the five gallons of water yielded fourteen pints of very fine-grained and very white salt, of which the whole lake may be regarded as a saturated solution. A portion of the salt thus obtained has been subjected to analysis—giving, in 100 parts, the following proportions:

Analysis of the salt.

Chloride of sodium, (common salt) . .	97.80
Chloride of calcium	0.61
Chloride of magnesium	0.24
Sulphate of soda	0.23
Sulphate of lime	1.12
	100.00

Glancing your eye along the map, you will see a small stream[58] entering the *Utah lake,* south of the Spanish fork, and the first waters of that lake which our road of 1844 crosses in coming up from the southward. When I was on this stream with Mr. Walker in that year, he informed me that on the upper part of the river are immense beds of rock salt of very great thickness, which he had frequently visited. Farther to the southward, the rivers which are affluent to the Colorado, such as the Rio Virgen, and Gila river, near the mouths, are impregnated with salt by the cliffs of rock salt between which they pass. These mines occur in the same ridge in which, about 120 miles to the northward, and subsequently in their more immediate neighborhood, we discovered the fossils belonging to the oolitic period, and they are probably connected with that formation, and are the deposite from which the Great Lake obtains

---

58. The stream he mentions is Salt Creek. JCF's mapping in this area is not his best. The most notorious error of his map, for this region, is the depiction of Utah Lake as an arm of Great Salt Lake. For his speculations on the nature of Utah Lake, see pp. 694 and 698.

its salt. Had we remained longer, we should have found them in its bed, and in the mountains around its shores.

By observation, the latitude of this camp is 41° 15′ 50″, and longitude 112° 06′ 43″.

The observations made during our stay give for the rate of the chronometer 31″.72, corresponding almost exactly with the rate obtained at St. Vrain's fort. Barometrical observations were made hourly during the day. This morning we breakfasted on yampah, and had only kamás for supper; but a cup of good coffee still distinguished us from our *Digger* acquaintances.

September 12.—The morning was clear and calm, with a temperature at sunrise of 32°. We resumed our journey late in the day, returning by nearly the same route which we had travelled in coming to the lake; and, avoiding the passage of Hawthorn creek, struck the hills a little below the hot salt springs. The flat plain we had here passed over consisted alternately of tolerably good sandy soil and of saline plats. We encamped early on Clear creek, at the foot of the high ridge; one of the peaks of which we ascertained by measurement to be 4,210 feet above the lake, or about 8,400 feet above the sea. Behind these front peaks the ridge rises towards the Bear river [Wasatch] mountains, which are probably as high as the Wind river chain. This creek is here unusually well timbered with a variety of trees. Among them were birch (*betula,*) the narrow-leaved poplar (*populus angustifolia,*) several kinds of willow (*salix,*) hawthorn (*crataegus,*) alder (*alnus viridis,*) and *cerasus,* with an oak allied to *quercus alba,*[59] but very distinct from that or any other species in the United States.

We had to-night a supper of sea gulls, which Carson killed near the lake. Although cool, the thermometer standing at 47°, musquitoes were sufficiently numerous to be troublesome this evening.

September 13.—Continuing up the river valley, we crossed several small streams; the mountains on the right appearing to consist of the blue limestone, which we had observed in the same ridge to the northward, alternating here with a granular quartz already mentioned. One of these streams, which forms a smaller lake near the river, was broken up into several channels; and the irrigated bottom of fertile soil was covered with innumerable flowers, among

---

59. *Quercus utahensis* (A. DC.) Rydb. He has evidently ascended Weber River far enough to head First Salt Creek, then traveled northeast toward Utah Hot Springs, passing present Plain City.

which were purple fields of *eupatorium purpureum,* with helianthi, a handsome solidago (*S. canadensis,*) and a variety of other plants in bloom. Continuing along the foot of the hills, in the afternoon we found five or six hot springs gushing out together, beneath a conglomerate, consisting principally of fragments of a grayish-blue limestone, efflorescing a salt upon the surface. The temperature of these springs was 134°, and the rocks in the bed were colored with a red deposite, and there was common salt crystallized on the margin. There was also a white incrustation upon leaves and roots, consisting principally of carbonate of lime. There were rushes seen along the road this afternoon, and the soil under the hills was very black, and apparently very good; but at this time the grass is entirely dried up. We encamped on Bear river, immediately below a cut-off, the cañon by which the river enters this valley bearing north by compass. The night was mild, with a very clear sky; and I obtained a very excellent observation of an occultation of Tau.[1] Arietis, with other observations. Both immersion and emersion of the star were observed; but, as our observations have shown, the phase at the bright limb generally gives incorrect longitudes, and we have adopted the result obtained from the emersion at the dark limb, without allowing any weight to the immersion. According to these observations, the longitude is 112° 05' 12", and the latitude 41° 42' 43". All the longitudes on the line of our outward journey, between St. Vrain's fort and the Dalles of the Columbia, which were not directly determined by satellites, have been chronometrically referred to this place.

The people to-day were rather low-spirited, hunger making them very quiet and peaceable; and there was rarely an oath to be heard in the camp—not even a solitary *enfant de garce.* It was time for the men with an expected supply of provisions from Fitzpatrick to be in the neighborhood; and the gun was fired at evening, to give them notice of our locality, but met with no response.

September 14.—About four miles from this encampment, the trail led us down to the river, where we unexpectedly found an excellent ford—the stream being widened by an island, and not yet disengaged from the hills at the foot of the range. We encamped on a little creek where we had made a noon halt in descending the river. The night was very clear and pleasant, the sunset temperature being 67°.

The people this evening looked so forlorn, that I gave them permission to kill a fat young horse which I had purchased with goods from the Snake Indians, and they were very soon restored to gayety and good humor. Mr. Preuss and myself could not yet overcome some remains of civilized prejudices, and preferred to starve a little longer; feeling as much saddened as if a crime had been committed.

The next day we continued up the valley, the soil being sometimes very black and good, occasionally gravelly, and occasionally a kind of naked salt plains. We found on the way this morning a small encampment of two families of Snake Indians, from whom we purchased a small quantity of *kooyah*. They had piles of seeds, of three different kinds, spread out upon pieces of buffalo robe; and the squaws had just gathered about a bushel of the roots of a thistle, (*circium Virginianum.*) They were about the ordinary size of carrots, and, as I have previously mentioned, are sweet and well flavored, requiring only a long preparation. They had a band of twelve or fifteen horses, and appeared to be growing in the sunshine with about as little labor as the plants they were eating.

Shortly afterwards we met an Indian on horseback who had killed an antelope, which we purchased from him for a little powder and some balls. We crossed the Roseaux, and encamped on the left bank; halting early for the pleasure of enjoying a wholesome and abundant supper, and were pleasantly engaged in protracting our unusual comfort, when Tabeau galloped into the camp with news that Mr. Fitzpatrick was encamped close by us, with a good supply of provisions—flour, rice, and dried meat, and even a little butter. Excitement to-night made us all wakeful; and after a breakfast before sunrise the next morning, we were again on the road, and, continuing up the valley, crossed some high points of hills, and halted to noon on the same stream, near several lodges of Snake Indians, from whom we purchased about a bushel of service berries, partially dried. By the gift of a knife, I prevailed upon a little boy to show me the *kooyah* plant, which proved to be *valeriana edulis.* The root, which constitutes the *kooyah,* is large, of a very bright yellow color, with the characteristic odor, but not so fully developed as in the prepared substance. It loves the rich moist soil of river bottoms, which was the locality in which I always afterwards found it. It was now entirely out of bloom; according to my observation, flowering in the months of May and June. In the afternoon we entered a long ravine leading to a pass in the dividing ridge between the waters of Bear river and the Snake river, or Lewis's fork of the Columbia; our way being very much impeded, and almost entirely blocked up, by compact fields of luxuriant artemisia. Taking leave at this point of the waters of Bear river, and of the geographical basin which encloses the system of rivers and creeks which belong to the Great Salt Lake, and which so richly deserves a future detailed and ample exploration, I can say of it, in general terms, that the bottoms of this river, (Bear,) and some of the creeks which I saw, form a natural resting and recruiting station for travellers, now, and in all time to come. The bottoms are extensive; water excellent; timber sufficient; the soil good, and well adapted to the grains and grasses suited to such an elevated region. A military post, and a civilized settlement, would be of great value here; and cattle and horses would do well where grass and salt so much abound. The lake will furnish exhaustless supplies of salt. All the mountain sides here are covered with a valuable nutritious grass, called bunch grass, from the form in which it grows, which has a second growth in the fall. The beasts of the Indians were fat upon it; our own found it a good subsistence; and its quantity will sustain any amount of cattle, and make this truly a bucolic region.[60]

We met here an Indian family on horseback, which had been out to gather service berries, and were returning loaded. This tree was scattered about on the hills; and the upper part of the pass was timbered with aspen; (*populus trem.,*) the common blue flowering flax occurring among the plants. The approach to the pass was very steep; and the summit about 6,300 feet above the sea—probably only an uncertain approximation, as at the time of observation it was blowing a violent gale of wind from the northwest, with *cumuli* scattered in masses over the sky, the day otherwise bright and clear. We descended, by a steep slope, into a broad open valley—good soil; from four to five miles wide; coming down immediately upon one of the head-waters of the Pannack [Bannock] river, which here loses itself in swampy ground. The appearance of the country here is not very interesting. On either side is a regular range of mountains of the usual character, with a little timber, tolerably rocky on the right, and higher and more smooth on the left, with still higher peaks looking out above the range. The valley afforded a good level road;

---

60. JCF's remarks on the attractions of the Bear River had a great influence on the Mormons in Nauvoo, 1845–46, when they considered a possible place for settlement. Also, when the government sent the Regiment of Mounted Riflemen west in 1849, it was originally thought the regiment would establish itself on Bear River. Instead, they built Cantonment Loring near Fort Hall.

but it was late when it brought us to water, and we encamped at dark. The northwest wind had blown up very cold weather, and the artemisia, which was our fire wood to-night, did not happen to be very abundant. This plant loves a dry, sandy soil, and cannot grow in the good bottoms where it is rich and moist, but on every little eminence, where water does not rest long, it maintains absolute possession. Elevation above the sea about 5,100 feet.

At night scattered fires glimmered along the mountains, pointing out camps of the Indians; and we contrasted the comparative security in which we travelled through this country, with the guarded vigilance we were compelled to exert among the Sioux and other Indians on the eastern side of the Rocky mountains.

At sunset the thermometer was at 50°, and at midnight at 30°.

September 17.—The morning sky was calm and clear, the temperature at daylight being 25°, and at sunrise 20°. There is throughout this mountain country a remarkable difference between the morning and midday temperatures, which at this season was very generally 40° or 50°, and occasionally greater; and frequently, after a very frosty morning, the heat in a few hours would render the thinnest clothing agreeable. About noon we reached the main fork. The Pannack [Bannock] river was before us; the valley being here 1½ mile wide, fertile, and bordered by smooth hills, not over 500 feet high, partly covered with cedar; a high ridge, in which there is a prominent peak, rising behind those on the left. We continued to descend this stream, and found on it at night a warm and comfortable camp. Flax occurred so frequently during the day as to be almost a characteristic, and the soil appeared excellent. The opposite hills on the right are broken here into a great variety of shapes. The evening was gusty, with a temperature at sunset of 59°. I obtained, about midnight, an observation of an emersion of the first satellite; the night being calm and very clear, the stars remarkably bright, and the thermometer at 30°. Longitude, from mean of satellite and chronometer, 112° 29′ 52″; and latitude, by observation, 42° 44′ 40″.

September 18.—The day clear and calm, with a temperature of 25° at sunrise. After travelling seven or eight miles, we emerged on the plains of the Columbia, in sight of the famous *"Three Buttes,"* a well-known landmark in the country, distant about 45 miles. The French word *butte,* which so often occurs in this narrative, is retained from the familiar language of the country, and identifies the objects to which it refers. It is naturalized in the region of the Rocky mountains; and, even if desirable to render it in English, I know of no word which would be its precise equivalent. It is applied to the detached hills and ridges which rise abruptly, and reach too high to be called hills or ridges, and not high enough to be called mountains. *Knob,* as applied in the western States, is the most descriptive term in English. *Cerro* is the Spanish term; but no translation, or paraphrasis, would preserve the identity of these picturesque landmarks, familiar to the traveller, and often seen at a great distance. Covered as far as could be seen with artemisia, the dark and ugly appearance of this plain obtained for it the name of the *Sage Desert;* and we were agreeably surprised, on reaching the Portneuf river, to see a beautiful green valley with scattered timber spread out beneath us, on which, about four miles distant, were glistening the white walls of the fort. The Portneuf runs along the upland plain nearly to its mouth, and an abrupt descent of perhaps 200 feet brought us down immediately upon the stream, which at the ford is 100 yards wide and 3 feet deep, with clear water, a swift current, and gravelly bed; but a little higher up the breadth was only about 35 yards, with apparently deep water.

In the bottom I remarked a very great number of springs and sloughs, with remarkably clear water and gravel beds. At sunset we encamped with Mr. Talbot and our friends, who come on to Fort Hall when we went to the lake, and whom we had the satisfaction to find all well, neither party having met with any mischance in the interval of our separation. They, too, had had their share of fatigue and scanty provisions, as there had been very little game left on the trail of the populous emigration; and Mr. Fitzpatrick had rigidly husbanded our stock of flour and light provisions, in view of the approaching winter and the long journey before us.

September 19.—This morning the sky was very dark and gloomy, and at daylight it began snowing thickly, and continued all day, with cold, disagreeable weather. At sunrise the temperature was 43°. I rode up to the fort, and purchased from Mr. Grant[61] (the officer in charge of the post) several very indifferent horses, and five oxen in

---

61. Born in Montreal, Richard Grant (1794–1862) spent his life in the fur trade. After twenty years in the Saskatchewan, Athabasca, and Peace River districts, he was transferred to the Columbia River district of the Hudson's Bay Company and took charge of the post at Fort Hall. He served there until 1851. The fort was located at a bend of the Snake near the junction of the

very fine order, which were received at the camp with great satisfaction; and, one being killed at evening, the usual gayety and good humor were at once restored. Night came in stormy.

September 20.—We had a night of snow and rain, and the thermometer at sunrise was at 34°; the morning was dark, with a steady rain, and there was still an inch of snow on the ground, with an abundance on the neighboring hills and mountains. The sudden change in the weather was hard for our animals, who trembled and shivered in the cold—sometimes taking refuge in the timber, and now and then coming out and raking the snow off the ground for a little grass, or eating the young willows.

September 21.—Ice made tolerably thick during the night, and in the morning the weather cleared up very bright, with a temperature at sunrise of 29°; and I obtained a meridian observation for latitude at the fort, with observations for time. The sky was again covered in the afternoon, and the thermometer at sunset 48°.

September 22.—The morning was cloudy and unpleasant, and at sunrise a cold rain commenced, with a temperature of 41°.

The early approach of winter, and the difficulty of supporting a large party, determined me to send back a number of the men who had become satisfied that they were not fitted for the laborious service and frequent privation to which they were necessarily exposed, and which there was reason to believe would become more severe in the further extension of the voyage. I accordingly called them together, and, informing them of my intention to continue our journey during the ensuing winter, in the course of which they would probably be exposed to considerable hardship, succeeded in prevailing upon a number of them to return voluntarily. These were:

Blackfoot and Portneuf rivers, on what is now the Fort Hall Indian Reservation. It had been an important port of call on the route to Oregon since 1834, when it was established by Nathaniel Wyeth. Visitors wishing to go to the site might well consider a more comfortable alternative: a replica of the establishment located on the upper level of Ross Park in Pocatello, Idaho. The actual site lies on the reservation, occupied by Shoshoni and Bannock tribes, above the American Falls Reservoir. A stone marker and bronze plaque mark the location, reached by driving first to the agency headquarters at Fort Hall, then west over a succession of progressively less improved roads, to an area of wild hay fields long known as the Bottoms. Visitors to the site are mainly duck hunters. In May 1968, when Dr. Tom Stevens, the Fort Hall agency physician, made a sketch map to direct the senior editor to the site, one of the instructions he set down was "turn right at cow's skull on post."

Charles [Clinton] De Forrest, Henry Lee, J. Campbell, Wm. Creuss, A. Vasquez, A. Pera, Patrick White, B. Tesson, M. Creely, François Lajeunesse, Basil Lajeunesse. Among these, I regretted very much to lose Basil Lajeunesse, one of the best men in my party, who was obliged, by the condition of his family, to be at home in the coming winter. Our preparations having been completed in the interval of our stay here, both parties were ready this morning to resume their respective routes.[62]

Except that there is a greater quantity of wood used in its construction, Fort Hall very much resembles the other trading posts which have been already described to you, and would be another excellent post of relief for the emigration. It is in the low, rich bottom of a valley, apparently 20 miles long, formed by the confluence of Portneuf river with Lewis's fork of the Columbia, which it enters about nine miles below the fort, and narrowing gradually to the mouth of the Pannack river, where it has a breadth of only two or three miles. Allowing 50 miles for the road from the *Beer springs* of Bear river to Fort Hall, its distance along the *travelled* road from the town of Westport, on the frontier of Missouri, by way of Fort Laramie and the great South Pass, is 1,323 miles. Beyond this place, on the line of road along the *barren* valley of the Upper Columbia, there does not occur, for a distance of nearly three hundred miles to the westward, a fertile spot of ground sufficiently large to produce the necessary quantity of grain, or pasturage enough to allow even a temporary repose to the emigrants. On their recent passage, they had been able to obtain, at very high prices and in insufficient quantity, only such assistance as could be afforded by a small and remote trading post—and that a foreign one—which, in the supply of its own wants, had necessarily drawn around it some of the resources of civilization, but which obtained nearly all its supplies from the distant depot of Vancouver, by a difficult water carriage of 250 miles up the Columbia river, and a land carriage by pack horses of 600 miles. An American military post sufficiently strong to give to their road a perfect security against the Indian tribes, who are unsettled in locality and very *uncertain* in their disposition, and which, with the necessary facilities for the repair of their equipage, would be able to afford them relief in stock and grain from the produce of the post,

---

62. The party bound for St. Louis was mounted and had guns and twelve days' provisions to take them into buffalo country (TALBOT, 51).

would be of extraordinary value to the emigration. Such a post (and all others which may be established on the line to Oregon) would naturally form the *nucleus* of a settlement, at which supplies and repose would be obtained by the emigrant, or trading caravans, which may hereafter traverse these elevated, and, in many places, desolate and inhospitable regions.

I subjoin an analysis of the soil in the river bottom near Fort Hall, which will be of assistance in enabling you to form some correct idea of its general character in the neighboring country. I characterize it as good land, but the analysis will show its precise properties.

Analysis of soil.

Silica	68.55
Alumina	7.45
Carbonate of lime	8.51
Carbonate of magnesia	5.09
Oxide of iron	1.40
Organic vegetable matter	4.74
Water and loss	4.26
	100.00

Our observations place this post in longitude 112° 29′ 54″, latitude 43° 01′ 30″, and in elevation above the sea 4,500 feet.

Taking leave of the homeward party, we resumed our journey down the valley, the weather being very cold, and the rain coming in hard gusts, which the wind blew directly in our faces. We forded the Portneuf in a storm of rain, the water in the river being frequently up to the axles, and about 110 yards wide. After the gust, the weather improved a little, and we encamped about three miles below, at the mouth of the Pannack river, on Lewis's fork, which here has a breadth of about 120 yards. The temperature at sunset was 42°; the sky partially covered with dark, rainy clouds.

September 23.—The temperature at sunrise was 32°; the morning dark, and snow falling steadily and thickly, with a light air from the southward. Profited of being obliged to remain in camp, to take hourly barometrical observations from sunrise to midnight. The wind at eleven o'clock set in from the northward in heavy gusts, and the snow changed into rain. In the afternoon, when the sky brightened, the rain had washed all the snow from the bottoms; but the neighboring mountains, from summit to foot, were luminously white—an inauspicious commencement of the autumn, of which this was the first day.

September 24.—The thermometer at sunrise was at 35°, and a blue sky in the west promised a fine day. The river bottoms here are narrow and swampy, with frequent sloughs; and after crossing the Pannack, the road continued along the uplands, rendered very slippery by the soil of wet clay, and entirely covered with artemisia bushes, among which occur frequent fragments of obsidian. At noon we encamped in a grove of willows, at the upper end of a group of islands, about half a mile above the *American falls* of Snake river. Among the willows here, were some bushes of Lewis and Clarke's currant, (*ribes aureum.*)[63] The river here enters between low mural banks, which consist of a fine vesicular trap rock, the intermediate portions being compact and crystalline. Gradually becoming higher in its downward course, these banks of scoriated volcanic rock form, with occasional interruptions, its characteristic feature along the whole line to the Dalles of the Lower Columbia, resembling a chasm which had been rent through the country, and which the river had afterwards taken for its bed. The immediate valley of the river is a high plain, covered with black rocks and artemisias. In the south is a bordering range of mountains, which, although not very high, are broken and covered with snow; and at a great distance to the north is seen the high, snowy line of the Salmon river mountains, in front of which stand out prominently in the plain the three isolated rugged-looking little mountains commonly known as *the Three Buttes*. Between the river and the distant Salmon river range, the plain is represented by Mr. Fitzpatrick

---

63. No edition of the full journals of Lewis and Clark, with their botanical observations, would be available for another half century. But JCF, and surely Torrey, would have had access to the narrative of their expedition prepared by Nicholas Biddle and published in 1814. Seeds and dried plants of several species of *Ribes* were brought back by Lewis and Clark, the seeds going to horticulturist Bernard McMahon. Later, McMahon reported to Thomas Jefferson that he had grown "seven or eight sorts of *gooseberries* & *currants*" from the seeds (JACKSON [1], 389n). Specimens of *R. aureum* and *R. viscosissimum* (yellow and black currants) brought back by Lewis and Clark are in the herbarium of the Academy of Natural Sciences, Philadelphia (CUTRIGHT, 172n).

as so entirely broken up and rent into chasms as to be impracticable for a man even on foot. In the sketch annexed [p. 524], the point of view is low, but it conveys very well some idea of the open character of the country, with the buttes rising out above the general line. By measurement, the river above is 870 feet wide, immediately contracted at the fall in the form of a lock, by jutting piles of scoriaceous basalt, over which the foaming river must present a grand appearance at the time of high water. The evening was clear and pleasant, with dew; and at sunset the temperature was 54°. By observation, the latitude is 42° 47' 05", and the longitude 112° 40' 13". A few hundred yards below the falls, and on the left bank of the river, is the escarpment from which were taken the specimens that in the appendix are numbered, 94, 96, 97, 101, 102, 106, and 107.

September 25.—Thermometer at sunrise 47°. The day came in clear, with a strong gale from the south, which commenced at 11 of the last night. The road to-day led along the river, which is full of rapids and small falls. Grass is very scanty; and along the rugged banks are scattered cedars, with an abundance of rocks and sage. We travelled 14 miles, and encamped in the afternoon near the river, on a rocky creek, the bed of which was entirely occupied with boulders of a very large size. For the last three or four miles the right bank of the river has a palisaded appearance. One of the oxen was killed here for food. The thermometer at evening was at 55°, the sky almost overcast, and the barometer indicated an elevation of 4,400 feet.

September 26.—Rain during the night, and the temperature at sunrise 42°. Travelling along the river, in about 4 miles we reached a picturesque stream, to which we gave the name of Fall creek. It is remarkable for the many falls which occur in a short distance; and its bed is composed of a calcareous tufa, or vegetable rock, composed principally of the remains of reeds and mosses, resembling that at the *Basin spring* on Bear river.

The road along the river bluffs had been occasionally very bad; and imagining that some rough obstacles rendered such a détour necessary, we followed for several miles a plain wagon road leading up this stream, until we reached a point whence it could be seen making directly towards a low place in the range on the south side of the valley, and we became immediately aware that we were on a trail formed by a party of wagons, in company with whom we had

The American Falls of Lewis Fork

encamped at Elm grove, near the frontier of Missouri, and which you will remember were proceeding to Upper California under the direction of Mr. Jos. Chiles. At the time of their departure, no practicable passes were known in the southern Rocky mountains within the territory of the United States; and the probable apprehension of difficulty in attempting to pass near the settled frontier of New Mexico, together with the desert character of the unexplored region beyond, had induced them to take a more northern and circuitous route by way of the Sweet Water pass and Fort Hall. They had still between them and the valley of the Sacramento a great mass of mountains, forming the *Sierra Nevada,* here commonly known as the *Great California mountain,* and which were at this time considered as presenting an impracticable barrier to wheeled carriages. Various considerations had suggested to them a division of the party; and a greater portion of the camp, including the wagons, with the mail and other stores, were now proceeding under the guidance of Mr. Joseph Walker, who had engaged to conduct them, by a long sweep to the southward, around what is called the *point of the mountain;* and, crossing through a pass known only to himself, gain the banks of the Sacramento by the valley of the San Joaquin. It was a long and hazardous journey for a party in which there were women and children. Sixty days was the shortest period of time in which they could reach the point of the mountain, and their route lay through a country inhabited by wild and badly disposed Indians, and very poor in game; but the leader was a man possessing great and intimate knowledge of the Indians, with an extraordinary firmness and decision of character. In the mean time, Mr. Chiles had passed down the Columbia with a party of ten or twelve men, with the intention of reaching the settlements on the Sacramento by a more direct course, which indefinite information from hunters had indicated in the direction of the head waters of the *Rivière aux Malheurs;* and having obtained there a reinforcement of animals, and a supply of provisions, meet the wagons before they should have reached the point of the mountain, at a place which had been previously agreed upon. In the course of our narrative, we shall be able to give you some information of the fortune which attended the movements of these adventurous travellers.

Having discovered our error, we immediately regained the line along the river, which the road quitted about noon, and encamped at 5 o'clock on a stream called Raft river, (*Rivière aux Cajeux,*)[64] having travelled only 13 miles. In the north, the Salmon river mountains are visible at a very far distance; and on the left, the ridge in which Raft river heads is about 20 miles distant, rocky, and tolerably high. Thermometer at sunset 44°, with a partially clouded sky, and a sharp wind from the SW.

September 27.—It was now no longer possible, as in our previous journey, to travel regularly every day, and find at any moment a convenient place for repose at noon or a camp at night; but the halting places were now generally fixed along the road, by the nature of the country, at places where, with water, there was a little scanty grass. Since leaving the American falls, the road had frequently been very bad; the many short, steep ascents, exhausting the strength of our worn-out animals, requiring always at such places the assistance of the men to get up each cart, one by one; and our progress with twelve or fourteen wheeled carriages, though light and made for the purpose, in such a rocky country, was extremely slow; and I again determined to gain time by a division of the camp. Accordingly, to-day the parties again separated, constituted very much as before—Mr. Fitzpatrick remaining in charge of the heavier baggage.

The morning was calm and clear, with a white frost, and the temperature at sunrise 24°.

To-day the country had a very forbidding appearance; and, after travelling 20 miles over a slightly undulating plain, we encamped at a considerable spring, called Swamp creek [Marsh Creek], rising in low grounds near the point of a spur from the mountain. Returning with a small party in a starving condition from the westward 12 or 14 years since [probably the spring of 1836], Carson had met here three or four buffalo bulls, two of which were killed. They were among the pioneers which had made the experiment of colonizing in the valley of the Columbia, and which had failed, as heretofore stated. At sunset the thermometer was at 46°, and the evening was overcast, with a cold wind from the SE., and to-night we had only

---

64. The Raft River joins the Snake in Blaine County, Idaho, after heading in the Raft River Mountains. JCF is one of the few early travelers to correctly render the name *cajeux,* applied at an early date by the French peasantry to small rafts. Lewis and Clark also made a stab at it by mentioning "chaussies" on the Missouri in 1804.

sage for fire wood. Mingled with the artemisia was a shrubby and thorny chenopodiaceous plant.

September 28.—Thermometer at sunrise 40°. The wind rose early to a gale from the west, with a very cold driving rain; and, after an uncomfortable day's ride of 25 miles, we were glad when at evening we found a sheltered camp, where there was an abundance of wood, at some elevated rocky islands covered with cedar, near the commencement of another long cañon of the river. With the exception of a short detention at a deep little stream called Goose creek, and some occasional rocky places, we had to-day a very good road; but the country has a barren appearance, sandy, and densely covered with the artemisias from the banks of the river to the foot of the mountains. Here I remarked, among the sage bushes, green bunches of what is called the second growth of grass. The river to-day has had a smooth appearance, free from rapids, with a low, sandy hill slope bordering the bottoms, in which there is a little good soil. Thermometer at sunset 45°, blowing a gale, and disagreeably cold.

September 29.—The thermometer at sunrise 36°, with a bright sun, and appearance of finer weather. The road for several miles was *extremely* rocky, and consequently bad; but, entering after this a sandy country, it became very good, with no other interruption than the sage bushes, which covered the river plain so far as the eye could reach, and, with their uniform tint of dark gray, gave to the country a gloomy and sombre appearance. All the day the course of the river has been between walls of the black volcanic rock, a dark line of the escarpment on the opposite side pointing out its course, and sweeping along in foam at places where the mountains which border the valley present always on the left two ranges, the lower one a spur of the higher; and, on the opposite side, the Salmon river mountains are visible at a great distance. Having made 24 miles, we encamped about 5 o'clock on Rock creek—a stream having considerable water, a swift current, and wooded with willow.

September 30.—Thermometer at sunrise 28°. In its progress towards the river, this creek soon enters a chasm of the volcanic rock, which in places along the wall presents a columnar appearance; and the road becomes extremely rocky whenever it passes near its banks. It is only about twenty feet wide where the road crosses it, with a deep bed, and steep banks, covered with rocky fragments, with willows and a little grass on its narrow bottom. The soil appears to be full of calcareous matter, with which the rocks are incrusted. The fragments of rock which had been removed by the emigrants in making a road where we ascended from the bed of this creek were whitened with lime; and during the afternoon's march I remarked in the soil a considerable quantity of calcareous concretions. Towards evening the sages became more sparse, and the clear spaces were occupied by tufts of green grass. The river still continued its course through a trough or open cañon; and towards sunset we followed the trail of several wagons which had turned in towards Snake river, and encamped, as they had done, on the top of the escarpment. There was no grass here, the soil among the sage being entirely naked; but there is occasionally a little bottom along the river, which a short ravine of rocks, at rare intervals, leaves accessible; and by one of these we drove our animals down, and found some tolerably good grass bordering the water.

Immediately opposite to us, a subterranean river bursts out directly from the face of the escarpment, and falls in white foam to the river below. In the views annexed, you will find, with a sketch of this remarkable fall [Shoshone Falls], a representation of the mural precipices which enclose the main river, and which form its characteristic feature along a great portion of its course. A melancholy and strange-looking country—one of fracture, and violence, and fire.

We had brought with us, when we separated from the camp, a large gaunt ox, in appearance very poor; but, being killed to-night, to the great joy of the people, he was found to be remarkably fat. As usual at such occurrences, the evening was devoted to gayety and feasting; abundant fare now made an epoch among us; and in this laborious life, in such a country as this, our men had but little else to enjoy. The temperature at sunset was 65°, with a clear sky and a very high wind. By the observation of the evening, the encampment was in longitude 114° 25′ 04″, and in latitude 42° 38′ 44″.

October 1.—The morning clear, with wind from the west, and the thermometer at 55°. We descended to the bottom, taking with us the boat, for the purpose of visiting the fall in the opposite cliffs; and while it was being filled with air, we occupied ourselves in measuring the river, which is 1,786 feet in breadth, with banks 200 feet high. We were surprised, on our arrival at the opposite side, to find a beautiful basin of clear water, formed by the falling river, around which the rocks were whitened by some saline incrustation. Here the Indians had constructed wicker dams, although I was informed that

Outlet of subterranean river

the salmon do not ascend the river so far; and its character below would apparently render it impracticable.

The ascent of the steep hill side was rendered a little difficult by a dense growth of shrubs and fields of cane; and there were frequent hidden crevices among the rocks, where the water was heard rushing below; but we succeeded in reaching the main stream, which, issuing from between strata of the trap rock in two principal branches, produced almost immediately a torrent, 22 feet wide, and white with foam. It is a picturesque spot of singular beauty; overshaded by bushes, from under which the torrent glances, tumbling into the white basin below where the clear water contrasted beautifully with the muddy stream of the river. Its outlet was covered with a rank growth of canes, and a variety of unusual plants, and nettles, (*urtica canabina*,) which, before they were noticed, had set our hands and arms on fire. The temperature of the spring was 58°, while that of the river was 51°. The perpendicular height of the place at which this stream issues is 45 feet above the river, and 152 feet below the summit of the precipice, making nearly 200 feet for the height of the wall. On the hill side here, was obtained the specimen designated by the number 12 in the collection, consisting principally of fragments of the shells of small crustacea, and which was probably formed by deposition from these springs proceeding from some lake or river in the highlands above.

We resumed our journey at noon, the day being hot and bright; and, after a march of 17 miles, encamped at sunset on the river, near several lodges of Snake [Shoshoni] Indians.

Our encampment was about one mile below the *Fishing falls* [Salmon Falls], a series of cataracts with very inclined planes, which are probably so named because they form a barrier to the ascent of the salmon; and the great fisheries from which the inhabitants of this barren region almost entirely derive a subsistence commence at this place. These appeared to be unusually gay savages, fond of loud laughter; and, in their apparent good nature and merry character, struck me as being entirely different from the Indians we had been accustomed to see. From several who visited our camp in the evening, we purchased, in exchange for goods, dried salmon. At this season they are not very fat, but we were easily pleased. The Indians made us comprehend, that when the salmon came up the river in the spring, they are so abundant that they merely throw in their spears at random, certain of bringing out a fish.

These poor people are but slightly provided with winter clothing; there is but little game to furnish skins for the purpose; and of a little animal which seemed to be the most numerous, it required 20 skins to make a covering to the knees. But they are still a joyous talkative race, who grow fat and become poor with the salmon, which at least never fail them—the dried being used in the absence of the fresh. We are encamped immediately on the river bank, and with the salmon jumping up out of the water, and Indians paddling about in boats made of rushes, or laughing around the fires, the camp to-night has quite a lively appearance.

The river at this place is more open than for some distance above; and, for the time, the black precipices have disappeared, and no calcareous matter is visible in the soil. The thermometer at sunset 74°; clear and calm.

October 2.—The sunrise temperature was 48°; the weather clear and calm. Shortly after leaving the encampment, we crossed a stream of clear water, with a variable breadth of 10 to 25 yards, broken by rapids, and lightly wooded with willow, and having a little grass on its small bottom land. The barrenness of the country is in fine contrast to-day with the mingled beauty and grandeur of the river, which is more open than hitherto, with a constant succession of falls and rapids. Over the edge of the black cliffs, and out from their faces, are falling numberless streams and springs; and all the line of the river is in motion with the play of the water. In about seven miles we reached the most beautiful and picturesque fall I had seen on the river.

On the opposite side, the vertical fall is perhaps 18 feet high; and nearer, the sheet of foaming water is divided and broken into cataracts, where several little islands on the brink and in the river above give it much picturesque beauty, and make it one of those places the traveller turns again and again to fix in his memory. There were several lodges of Indians here, from whom we traded salmon. Below this place the river makes a remarkable bend; and the road, ascending the ridge, gave us a fine view of the river below, intersected at many places by numerous fish dams. In the north, about 50 miles distant, were some high snowy peaks of the Salmon river mountains; and in the northeast, the last peak of the range was visible at the distance of perhaps 100 miles or more. The river hills consist of very broken masses of sand, covered every where with the same interminable fields of sage, and occasionally the road is very heavy. We now very frequently saw Indians, who were strung along the river at every little rapid where fish are to be caught, and the cry *haggai, haggai,* (fish,) was constantly heard whenever we passed near their huts, or met them in the road. Very many of them were oddly and partially dressed in overcoat, shirt, waistcoat, or pantaloons, or whatever article of clothing they had been able to procure in trade from the emigrants; for we had now entirely quitted the country where hawk's bells, beads, and vermilion, were the current coin, and found that here only useful articles, and chiefly clothing, were in great request. These, however, are eagerly sought after; and for a few trifling pieces of clothing, travellers may procure food sufficient to carry them to the Columbia.

We made a long stretch across the upper plain, and encamped on the bluff, where the grass was very green and good; the soil of the upper plains containing a considerable proportion of calcareous matter. This green freshness of the grass was very remarkable for the season of the year. Again we heard the roar of a fall in the river below, where the water in an unbroken volume goes over a descent of several feet. The night is clear, and the weather continues very warm and pleasant, with a sunset temperature of 70°.

October 3.—The morning was pleasant, with a temperature at sunrise of 42°. The road was broken by ravines among the hills, and in one of these, which made the bed of a dry creek, I found a fragmentary stratum, or brecciated conglomerate, consisting of flinty slate pebbles, with fragments of limestone containing fossil shells, which will be found described in the appendix under the numbers 16, 21, and 39.

On the left, the mountains are visible at the distance of twenty or thirty miles, appearing smooth and rather low; but at intervals higher peaks look out from beyond, and indicate that the main ridge, which we are leaving with the course of the river, and which forms the northern boundary of the Great Basin, still maintains its elevation. About 2 o'clock we arrived at the ford where the road crosses to the right bank of Snake river. An Indian was hired to conduct us through the ford, which proved impracticable for us, the water sweeping away the howitzer and nearly drowning the mules, which we were obliged to extricate by cutting them out of the harness. The river here is expanded into a little bay, in which there are two islands, across which is the road of the ford; and the emigrants had passed by placing two of their heavy wagons abreast of each other, so as to oppose a considerable mass against the body of water. The Indians informed us that one of the men, in attempting to turn some cattle which had taken a wrong direction, was carried off by the current and drowned. Since their passage, the water had risen considerably; but, fortunately, we had a resource in a boat, which was filled with air and launched; and at seven o'clock we were safely encamped on the opposite bank, the animals swimming across, and the carriage, howitzer, and baggage of the camp, being carried over in the boat. At the place where we crossed, above the islands, the river had narrowed to a breadth of 1,049 feet by measurement, the greater portion of which was from six to eight feet deep. We were obliged to make our camp where we landed, among the Indian lodges, which are semicircular huts made of willow, thatched over with straw, and open to the sunny south. By observation, the latitude of our encampment on the right bank of the river was 42° 55′ 58″; chronometric longitude 115° 04′ 46″, and the travelled distance from Fort Hall 208 miles.[65]

October 4.—Calm pleasant day, with the thermometer at sunrise at 47°. Leaving the river at a considerable distance to the left, and following up the bed of a rocky creek, with occasional holes of water, in about six miles we ascended, by a long and rather steep hill, to a plain 600 feet above the river, over which we continued to travel during the day, having a broken ridge 2,000 or 3,000 feet high on the right. The plain terminates, where we ascended, in an escarpment of vesicular trap rock, which supplies the fragments of the creek below. The sky clouded over, with a strong wind from the northwest, with a few drops of rain and occasional sunlight, threatening a change.

Artemisia still covers the plain, but *Purshia tridentata* makes its appearance here on the hill sides and on bottoms of the creeks—quite a tree in size, and larger than the artemisia. We crossed several hollows with a little water in them, and improved grass; and, turning off from the road in the afternoon in search of water, travelled about three miles up the bed of a willow creek, towards the mountain, and found a good encampment, with wood and grass, and little ponds of water in the bed of the creek [Alkali Creek]; which must be of more importance at other seasons, as we found there several old fix-

---

65. The Oregon Trail crossed the Snake River here at Three Island Crossing, near present Glenns Ferry, Idaho. The route then left the river and took the wagons on a cross-country course toward Fort Boise.

tures for fishing. There were many holes on the creek prairie, which had been made by the diggers in search of roots.

Wind increased to a violent gale from the NW., with a temperature at sunset of 57°.

October 5.—The morning was calm and clear, and at sunrise the thermometer was at 32°. The road to-day was occasionally extremely rocky, with hard volcanic fragments, and our travelling very slow. In about nine miles the road brought us to a group of smoking hot springs,[66] with a temperature of 164°. There were a few helianthi in bloom, with some other low plants, and the place was green round about; the ground warm, and the air pleasant, with a summer atmosphere that was very grateful in a day of high and cold searching wind. The rocks were covered with a white and red incrustation; and the water has on the tongue the same unpleasant effect as that of the Basin spring on Bear river. They form several branches, and bubble up with force enough to raise the small pebbles several inches.

The following is an analysis of the deposite with which the rocks are incrusted:

Analysis.

Silica	72.55
Carbonate of lime	14.60
Carbonate of magnesia	1.20
Oxide of iron	4.65
Alumina	0.70
Chloride of sodium, &c.⎤ Sulphate of soda ⎬ . . . . . Sulphate of lime, &c. ⎦	1.10
Organic vegetable matter⎤ . . . . Water and loss ⎦	5.20
	100.00

These springs are near the foot of the ridge, (a dark and rugged looking mountain,) in which some of the nearer rocks have a reddish appearance, and probably consist of a reddish-brown trap, fragments of which were scattered along the road after leaving the spring. The road was now about to cross the point of this mountain, which we judged to be a spur from the Salmon river range. We

---

66. A well-known landmark to early travelers, Hot Springs lies east of Mountain Home, Idaho.

crossed a small creek, and encamped about sunset on a stream, which is probably Lake river.[67] This is a small stream, some five or six feet broad, with a swift current, timbered principally with willows and some few cottonwoods. Along the banks were canes, rose bushes, and clematis, with Purshia tridentata and artemisias on the upper bottom. The sombre appearance of the country is somewhat relieved in coming unexpectedly from the dark rocks upon these green and wooded watercourses, sunk in chasms; and, in the spring, the contrasted effect must make them beautiful.

The thermometer at sunset 47°, and the night threatening snow.

October 6.—The morning warm, the thermometer 46° at sunrise, and sky entirely clouded. After travelling about three miles over an extremely rocky road, the volcanic fragments began to disappear; and, entering among the hills at the point of the mountain, we found ourselves suddenly in a granite country. Here, the character of the vegetation was very much changed; the artemisia disappeared almost entirely, showing only at intervals towards the close of the day, and was replaced by Purshia tridentata, with flowering shrubs, and small fields of *dieteria divaricata,* which gave bloom and gayety to the hills. These were every where covered with a fresh and green short grass, like that of the early spring. This is the fall or second growth, the dried grass having been burnt off by the Indians; and wherever the fire has passed, the bright-green color is universal. The soil among the hills is altogether different from that of the river plain, being in many places black, in others sandy and gravelly, but of a firm and good character, appearing to result from the decomposition of the granite rocks, which is proceeding rapidly.

In quitting for a time the artemisia (sage) through which we had been so long voyaging, and the sombre appearance of which is so discouraging, I have to remark, that I have been informed that in Mexico wheat is grown upon the ground which produces this shrub; which, if true, relieves the soil from the character of sterility imputed to it. Be this as it may, there is no dispute about the grass, which is almost universal on the hills and mountains, and always nutritious, even in its dry state. We passed on the way masses of granite on the slope of a spur, which was very much weathered and abraded. This

---

67. His 1845 map shows a camp at "R. aux Rochers," and the Preuss map of 1846 identifies it as Rock Creek. He was at the foot of the Sawtooth Mountains, and may have camped on what is now called Rattlesnake Creek.

is a white feldspathic granite, with small scales of black mica; smoky quartz and garnets appear to constitute this portion of the mountain.

The road at noon reached a broken ridge, on which were scattered many boulders or blocks of granite; and, passing very small streams, where, with a little more than the usual timber, was sometimes gathered a little wilderness of plants, we encamped on a small stream, after a march of 22 miles, in company with a few Indians. Temperature at sunset 51°; and the night was partially clear, with a few stars visible through drifting white clouds. The Indians made an unsuccessful attempt to steal a few horses from us—a thing of course with them, and to prevent which the traveller is on perpetual watch.

October 7.—The day was bright, clear, and pleasant, with a temperature of 45°; and we breakfasted at sunrise, the birds singing in the trees as merrily as if we were in the midst of summer. On the upper edge of the hills on the opposite side of the creek, the black volcanic rock reappears; and ascending these, the road passed through a basin, around which the hills swept in such a manner as to give it the appearance of an old crater. Here were strata and broken beds of black scoriated rock, and hills composed of the same, on the summit of one of which there was an opening resembling a rent. We travelled to-day through a country resembling that of yesterday, where, although the surface was hilly, the road was good, being firm, and entirely free from rocks and artemisia. To our left, below, was the great sage plain; and on the right were the near mountains, which presented a smoothly broken character, or rather a surface waved into numberless hills. The road was occasionally enlivened by meeting Indians, and the day was extremely beautiful and pleasant; and we were pleased to be free from the sage, even for a day. When we had travelled about 8 miles, we were nearly opposite to the highest portion of the mountains on the left side of the Smoke [Snake] river valley; and, continuing on a few miles beyond, we came suddenly in sight of the broad green line of the valley of the *Rivière Boisée,* (wooded river,) black near the gorge where it debouches into the plains, with high precipices of basalt, between walls of which it passes, on emerging from the mountains. Following with the eye its upward course, it appears to be shut in among lofty mountains, confining its valley in a very rugged country.

Descending the hills, after travelling a few miles along the high plain, the road brought us down upon the bottoms of the river, which is a beautiful rapid stream, with clear mountain water, and, as the name indicates, well wooded with some varieties of timber— among which are handsome cottonwoods. Such a stream had become quite a novelty in this country, and we were delighted this afternoon to make a pleasant camp under fine old trees again. There were several Indian encampments scattered along the river; and a number of their inhabitants, in the course of the evening, came to the camp on horseback with dried and fresh fish to trade. The evening was clear, and the temperature at sunset 57°.

At the time of the first occupation of this region by parties engaged in the fur trade, a small party of men under the command of ———Reid [John Reed], constituting all the garrison of a little fort on this river, were surprised and massacred by the Indians; and to this event the stream owes its occasional name of *Reid's river*.[68]

On the 8th we travelled about 26 miles, the ridge on the right having scattered pines on the upper parts; and, continuing the next day our road along the river bottom, after a day's travel of 24 miles we encamped in the evening on the right bank of the river, a mile above the mouth, and early the next morning arrived at Fort *Boisé*. This is a simple dwelling-house on the right bank of Snake river, about a mile below the mouth of Rivière Boissée; and on our arrival we were received with an agreeable hospitality by Mr. Payette,[69] an officer of the Hudson Bay Company, in charge of the fort; all of whose garrison consisted in a Canadian *engagé*.

Here the road recrosses the river, which is broad and deep; but, with our good boat, aided by two canoes, which were found at the place, the camp was very soon transferred to the left bank. Here we found ourselves again surrounded by the sage; artemisia tridentata, and the different shrubs which during our voyage had always made their appearance abundantly on saline soils, being here the prevailing and almost the only plants. Among them the surface was

---

68. An unlucky Irish trader, John Reed had gone to the Snake River region as one of the Astorians in the summer of 1813, building a post at the confluence of the Boise and the Snake. He and his party were massacred in Jan. 1814 (PORTER).

69. François Payette (fl. 1810–44), who came to Fort Boise in 1837, had been in the Pacific Northwest for more than thirty years. A French Canadian, he left New York in 1811 as an *engagé* with John Jacob Astor's Pacific Fur Company. When Astor sold his northwest properties to the North West Company, Payette transferred to that enterprise and was with it when it ultimately merged with the Hudson's Bay Company (HAINES [1]).

covered with the usual saline efflorescences, which here consist almost entirely of carbonate of soda, with a small portion of chloride of sodium. Mr. Payette had made but slight attempts at cultivation, his efforts being limited to raising a few vegetables, in which he succeeded tolerably well; the post being principally supported by salmon. He was very hospitable and kind to us, and we made a sensible impression upon all his comestibles; but our principal inroad was into the dairy, which was abundantly supplied, stock appearing to thrive extremely well; and we had an unusual luxury in a present of fresh butter, which was, however, by no means equal to that of Fort Hall—probably from some accidental cause. During the day we remained here, there were considerable numbers of miserable half-naked Indians around the fort, who had arrived from the neighboring mountains. During the summer, the only subsistence of these people is derived from the salmon, of which they are not provident enough to lay up a sufficient store for the winter, during which many of them die from absolute starvation.

Many little accounts and scattered histories, together with an acquaintance which I gradually acquired of their modes of life, had left the aboriginal inhabitants of this vast region pictured in my mind as a race of people whose great and constant occupation was the means of procuring a subsistence; and though want of space, and other reasons, will prevent me from detailing the many incidents which made these things familiar to me, this great feature among the characteristics of the country will gradually be forced upon your mind.

Pointing to a group of Indians who had just arrived from the mountains on the left side of the valley, and who were regarding our usual appliances of civilization with an air of bewildered curiosity, Mr. Payette informed me that, every year since his arrival at this post, he had unsuccessfully endeavored to induce these people to lay up a store of salmon for their winter provision. While the summer weather and the salmon lasted, they lived contentedly and happily, scattered along the different streams where the fish were to be found; and as soon as the winter snows began to fall, little smokes would be seen rising among the mountains, where they would be found in miserable groups, starving out the winter; and sometimes, according to the general belief, reduced to the horror of cannibalism —the strong, of course, preying on the weak. Certain it is, they are driven to any extremity for food, and eat every insect, and every creeping thing, however loathsome and repulsive. Snails, lizards, ants—all are devoured with the readiness and greediness of mere animals.

In common with all the other Indians we had encountered since reaching the Pacific waters, these people use the Shoshonee or Snake language, which you will have occasion to remark, in the course of the narrative, is the universal language over a very extensive region.

On the evening of the 10th, I obtained, with the usual observations, a very excellent emersion of the first satellite, agreeing very nearly with the chronometer. From these observations, the longitude of the fort is 116° 47' 00''; latitude 43° 49' 22'', and elevation above the sea 2,100 feet.

Sitting by the fire on the river bank, and waiting for the immersion of the satellite, which did not take place until after midnight, we heard the monotonous song of the Indians, with which they accompany a certain game of which they are fond. Of the poetry we could not judge, but the music was miserable.

October 11.—The morning was clear, with a light breeze from the east, and a temperature at sunrise of 33°. A part of a bullock purchased at the fort, together with the boat to assist him in crossing, was left here for Mr. Fitzpatrick, and at 11 o'clock we resumed our journey; and directly leaving the river, and crossing the artemisia plain, in several ascents we reached the foot of a ridge, where the road entered a dry sandy hollow, up which it continued to the head; and, crossing a dividing ridge, entered a similar one. We met here two poor emigrants, (Irishmen,) who had lost their horses two days since—probably stolen by the Indians; and were returning to the fort, in hopes to hear something of them there. They had recently had nothing to eat; and I halted to unpack an animal, and gave them meat for their dinner. In this hollow, the artemisia is partially displaced on the hill sides by grass; and descending it —— miles, about sunset we reached the *Rivière aux Malheurs,* (the unfortunate or unlucky river,) a considerable stream, with an average breadth of 50 feet, and, at this time, 18 inches depth of water.[70]

The bottom lands were generally one and a half mile broad, cov-

---

70. The expedition had crossed the present eastern boundary of Oregon and reached the river named the Malheur by Peter Skene Ogden when he traveled in the region in 1825–26. Ogden called it an "unfortunate" stream because property hidden there by employees of the Hudson's Bay Company was stolen by Indians (MAC ARTHUR, 383).

ered principally with long dry grass; and we had difficulty to find sufficient good grass for the camp. With the exception of a bad place of a few hundred yards long, which occurred in rounding a point of hill to reach the ford of the river, the road during the day had been very good.

October 12.—The morning was clear and calm, and the thermometer at sunrise 23°. My attention was attracted by a smoke on the right side of the river, a little below the ford, where I found on the low bank, near the water, a considerable number of hot springs, in which the temperature of the water was 193°. The ground, which was too hot for the naked foot, was covered above and below the springs with an incrustation of common salt, very white and good, and fine grained.

Leading for 5 miles up a broad dry branch of the Malheurs river, the road entered a sandy hollow, where the surface was rendered firm by the admixture of another rock; being good and level until arriving near the head of the ravine, where it became a little rocky, and we met with a number of sharp ascents over an undulating surface. Crossing here a dividing ridge, it became an excellent road of gradual descent down a very marked hollow; in which, after 10 miles, willows began to appear in the dry bed of a head of the *Rivière aux Bouleaux,* (Birch river;) and descending 7 miles, we found, at its junction with another branch, a little water, not very good or abundant, but sufficient in case of necessity for a camp. Crossing Birch river [Birch Creek], we continued for about 4 miles across a point of hill; the country on the left being entirely mountainous, with no level spot to be seen; whence we descended to Snake river—here a fine-looking stream, with a large body of water and a smooth current; although we hear the roar, and see below us the commencement of rapids where it enters among the hills. It forms here a deep bay, with a low sand island in the midst; and its course among the mountains is agreeably exchanged for the black volcanic rock. The weather during the day had been very bright and extremely hot; but, as usual, so soon as the sun went down, it was necessary to put on overcoats.

I obtained this evening an observation of an emersion of the first satellite, and our observations of the evening place this encampment in latitude 44° 17′ 36″, and longitude 116° 56′ 45″, which is the mean of the results from the satellite and chronometer. The elevation above the sea 1,880 feet. At this encampment, the grass is scanty and poor.

October 13.—The morning was bright, with the temperature at sunset 28°. The horses had strayed off during the night, probably in search of grass; and, after a considerable delay, we had succeeded in finding all but two, when, about 9 o'clock, we heard the sound of an Indian song and drum approaching; and shortly after, three Cayuse Indians appeared in sight, bringing with them the two animals. They belonged to a party which had been on a buffalo hunt in the neighborhood of the Rocky mountains, and were hurrying home in advance. We presented them with some tobacco, and other things, with which they appeared well satisfied, and moderating their pace, travelled in company with us.

We were now about to leave the valley of the great southern branch of the Columbia river, to which the absence of timber, and the scarcity of water, give the appearance of a desert, to enter a mountainous region where the soil is good, and in which the face of the country is covered with nutritious grasses and dense forest—land embracing many varieties of trees peculiar to the country, and on which the timber exhibits a luxuriance of growth unknown to the eastern part of the continent and to Europe. This mountainous region connects itself in the southward and westward with the elevated country belonging to the Cascade or California range; and, as will be remarked in the course of the narrative, forms the eastern limit of the fertile and timbered lands along the desert and mountainous region included within the Great Basin[71]—a term which I apply to the intermediate region between the Rocky mountains and the next range, containing many lakes, with their own system of rivers and creeks, (of which the Great Salt is the principal,) and which have no connexion with the ocean, or the great rivers which flow into it. This Great Basin is yet to be adequately explored. And here, on quitting the banks of a sterile river, to enter on arable mountains, the remark may be made, that, on this western slope of our continent, the usual order or distribution of good and bad soil is often reversed; the river and creek bottoms being often sterile, and

---

71. Here JCF mentions for the first time a geographical feature of the western U.S. which he was first to recognize. It must be remembered that his report was written at the completion of the expedition, when he had seen a great deal of the Basin.

darkened with the gloomy and barren artemisia; while the mountain is often fertile, and covered with rich grass, pleasant to the eye, and good for flocks and herds.

Leaving entirely the Snake river, which is said henceforth to pursue its course through cañons, amidst rocky and impracticable mountains, where there is no possibility of travelling with animals, we ascended a long and somewhat steep hill; and crossing the dividing ridge, came down into the valley of *Burnt* river, which here looks like a hole among the hills. The average breadth of the stream here is 30 feet; it is well fringed with the usual small timber; and the soil in the bottoms is good, with better grass than we had lately been accustomed to see.

We now travelled through a very mountainous country; the stream running rather in a ravine than a valley, and the road is decidedly bad and dangerous for single wagons, frequently crossing the stream where the water is sometimes deep; and all the day the animals were fatigued in climbing up and descending a succession of steep ascents, to avoid the precipitous hill sides; and the common trail, which, leads along the mountain side at places where the river strikes the base, is sometimes bad even for a horseman. The mountains along this day's journey were composed, near the river, of a slaty calcareous rock in a metamorphic condition. It appears originally to have been a slaty sedimentary limestone, but its present condition indicates that it has been altered, and has become partially crystalline—probably from the proximity of volcanic rocks. But though travelling was slow and fatiguing to the animals, we were delighted with the appearance of the country, which was green and refreshing after our tedious journey down the parched valley of Snake river. The mountains were covered with good bunch grass, (*festuca;*) the water of the streams was cold and pure; their bottoms were handsomely wooded with various kinds of trees; and huge and lofty and picturesque precipices were displayed where the river cut through the mountains.

We found in the evening some good grass and rushes; and encamped among large timber, principally birch, which had been recently burnt and blackened, and almost destroyed by fire. The night was calm and tolerably clear, with the thermometer at sunset at 59°. Our journey to-day was about 20 miles.

October 14.—The day was clear and calm, with a temperature at sunrise of 46°. After travelling about three miles up the valley, we found the river shut up by precipices in a kind of cañon, and the road makes a circuit over the mountains. In the afternoon we reached the river again, by another little ravine; and, after travelling along it for a few miles, left it enclosed among rude mountains; and, ascending a smaller branch, encamped on it about 5 o'clock, very much elevated above the valley. The view was everywhere limited by mountains, on which were no longer seen the black and barren rocks, but a fertile soil, with excellent grass, and partly well covered with pine. I have never seen a wagon road equally bad in the same space, as this of yesterday and to-day. I noticed where one wagon had been overturned twice, in a very short distance; and it was surprising to me that those wagons which were in the rear, and could not have had much assistance, got through at all. Still, there is no mud; and the road has one advantage, in being perfectly firm. The day had been warm and very pleasant, and the night was perfectly clear.

October 15.—The thermometer at daylight was 42°, and at sunrise 40°; clouds, which were scattered over all the sky, disappeared with the rising sun. The trail did not much improve until we had crossed the dividing grounds between the *Brulé* (Burnt) and Powder rivers. The rock displayed on the mountains, as we approached the summit, was a compact trap, decomposing on the exposed surfaces, and apparently an altered argillaceous sandstone, containing small crystalline nodules of anolcime, apparently filling cavities originally existing. From the summit here, the whole horizon shows high mountains; no high plain or level is to be seen; and on the left, from south around by the west to north, the mountains are black with pines; while, through the remaining space to the eastward, they are bald with the exception of some scattered pines. You will remark that we are now entering a region where all the elevated parts are covered with dense and heavy forests. From the dividing grounds we descended by a mountain road to Powder river, on an old bed of which we encamped. Descending from the summit, we enjoyed a picturesque view of high rocky mountains on the right, illuminated by the setting sun.

From the heights we had looked in vain for a well-known landmark on Powder river, which had been described to me by Mr. Payette as *l'arbre seul* (the lone tree;) and, on arriving at the river, we found a fine tall pine stretched on the ground, which had been felled by some inconsiderate emigrant axe. It had been a beacon on the road for many years past. Our Cayuses had become impatient to reach their homes, and travelled on ahead to-day; and this afternoon we were visited by several Indians, who belonged to the tribes on the Columbia. They were on horseback, and were out on a hunting excursion, but had obtained no better game than a large gray hare, of which each had some six or seven hanging to his saddle. We were also visited by an Indian who had his lodge and family in the mountain to the left. He was in want of ammunition, and brought with him a beaver skin to exchange, and which he valued at six charges of powder and ball. I learned from him that there are very few of these animals remaining in this part of the country.

The temperature at sunset was 61°, and the evening clear. I obtained, with other observations, an immersion and emersion of the third satellite. Elevation 3,100 feet.

October 16.—For several weeks the weather in the daytime has been very beautiful, clear, and warm; but the nights, in comparison, are very cold. During the night there was ice a quarter of an inch thick in the lodge; and at daylight the thermometer was at 16°, and the same at sunrise; the weather being calm and clear. The annual vegetation now is nearly gone, almost all the plants being out of bloom.

Last night two of our horses had run off again, which delayed us until noon; and we made to day but a short journey of 13 miles, the road being very good, and encamped in a fine bottom of Powder river.

The thermometer at sunset was at 61°, with an easterly wind, and partially clear sky; and the day has been quite pleasant and warm, though finer and clearer towards evening.

October 17.—Thermometer at sunrise 25°. The weather at daylight was fine, and the sky without a cloud; but these came up, or were formed with the sun, and at 7 were thick over all the sky. Just now, this appears to be the regular course—clear and brilliant during the night, and cloudy during the day. There is snow yet visible in the neighboring mountains, which yesterday extended along our route to the left, in a lofty and dark-blue range, having much the appearance of the Wind river mountains. It is probable that they have received their name of the *Blue mountains* from the dark-blue appearance given to them by the pines. We travelled this morning across the affluents to Powder river, the road being good, firm, and level; and the country became constantly more pleasant and interesting. The soil appeared to be very deep, and is black and extremely good, as well among the hollows of the hills on the elevated plats, as on the river bottoms; the vegetation being such as is usually found in good ground. The following analytical result shows the precise qualities of this soil, and will justify to science the character of fertility which the eye attributes to it:

Analysis of Powder river soil.

Silica	72.30
Alumina	6.25
Carbonate of lime	6.86
Carbonate of magnesia	4.62
Oxide of iron	1.20
Organic matter	4.50
Water and loss	4.27
	100.00

From the waters of this stream, the road ascended by a good and moderate ascent to a dividing ridge, but immediately entered upon ground covered with fragments of an altered siliceous slate, which are in many places large, and render the road racking to a carriage. In this rock the planes of deposition are distinctly preserved, and the metamorphism is evidently due to the proximity of volcanic rocks. On either side, the mountains here are densely covered with tall and handsome trees; and, mingled with the green of a variety of pines, is the yellow of the European larch (*pinus larix,*) which loses its leaves in the fall. From its present color, we were enabled to see that it forms a large proportion of the forests on the mountains, and is here a magnificent tree, attaining sometimes the height of 200 feet, which I believe is elsewhere unknown. About two in the afternoon we reached a high point of the dividing ridge, from which we obtained a good view of the *Grand Rond*—a beautiful level basin, or mountain valley, covered with good grass, on a rich soil, abundantly watered, and surrounded by high and well-timbered mountains; and its name descriptive of its form—the great circle. It is a place—one of the few we have seen in our journey so far— where a farmer would delight to establish himself, if he were content to live in the seclusion which it imposes. It is about 20 miles in diameter; and may, in time, form a superb county. Probably with the view of avoiding a circuit, the wagons had directly descended into the *Rond* by the face of a hill so very rocky and continuously steep as to be apparently impracticable; and, following down on their trail, we encamped on one of the branches of the Grand Rond river, immediately at the foot of the hill.[72] I had remarked, in descending, some very white spots glistening on the plain, and, going out in that direction after we had encamped, I found them to be the bed of a dry salt lake, or marsh, very firm and bare, which was covered thickly with a fine white powder, containing a large quantity of carbonate of soda, (thirty-three in one hundred parts.)

The old grass had been lately burnt off from the surrounding hills, and, wherever the fire had passed, there was a recent growth of strong, green, and vigorous grass; and the soil of the level prairie, which sweeps directly up to the foot of the surrounding mountains, appears to be very rich, producing flax spontaneously and luxuriantly in various places.

Analysis of the Grand Rond soil.

Silica	70.81
Alumina	10.97
Lime and magnesia	1.38
Oxide of iron	2.21
Vegetable matter, partly decomposed .	8.16
Water and loss	5.46
Phosphate of lime	1.01
	100.00

The elevation of this encampment is 2,940 feet above the sea.

October 18.—It began to rain an hour before sunrise, and continued until 10 o'clock; the sky entirely overcast, and the temperature at sunrise 48°.

We resumed our journey somewhat later than usual, travelling in a nearly north direction across this beautiful valley; and about noon reached a place on one of the principal streams, where I had determined to leave the emigrant trail, in the expectation of finding a more direct and better road across the Blue mountains. At this place the emigrants appeared to have held some consultation as to their further route, and finally turned directly off to the left; reaching the

---

72. The valley and river in Union County, Ore., are properly spelled Grand Ronde. JCF is moving north into what is now southeastern Washington.

foot of the mountain in about three miles, which they ascended by a hill as steep and difficult as that by which we had yesterday descended to the Rond. Quitting, therefore, this road, which, after a very rough crossing, issues from the mountains by the heads of the *Umatilah* [Umatilla] river, we continued our northern course across the valley, following an Indian trail which had been indicated to me by Mr. Payette, and encamped at the northern extremity of the Grand Rond, on a slough-like stream of very deep water, without any apparent current. There are some pines here on the low hills at the creek; and in the northwest corner of the Rond is a very heavy body of timber, which descends into the plain. The clouds, which had rested very low among the mountain sides during the day, rose gradually up in the afternoon; and in the evening the sky was almost entirely clear, with a temperature at sunset of 47°. Some indifferent observations placed the camp in longitude 117° 28' 26", latitude 45° 26' 47"; and the elevation was 2,600 feet above the sea.

October 19.—This morning the mountains were hidden by fog; there was a heavy dew during the night, in which the exposed thermometer at daylight stood at 32°, and at sunrise the temperature was 35°.

We passed out of the Grand Rond by a fine road along the creek, which, for a short distance, runs in a kind of rocky chasm. Crossing a low point, which was a little rocky, the trail conducted into the open valley of the stream—a handsome place for farms; the soil, even of the hills, being rich and black. Passing through a point of pines, which bore evidences of being much frequented by the Indians, and in which the trees were sometimes apparently 200 feet high and 3 to 7 feet in diameter, we halted for a few minutes in the afternoon at the foot of the Blue mountains, on a branch of the Grand Rond river, at an elevation of 2,709 feet. Resuming our journey, we commenced the ascent of the mountain through an open pine forest of large and stately trees, among which the balsam pine made its appearance; the road being good, with the exception of one steep ascent, with a corresponding descent, which might both have been easily avoided by opening a way for a short distance through the timber. It would have been well had we encamped on the stream where we had halted below, as the night overtook us on the mountain, and we were obliged to encamp without water, and tie up the animals to the trees for the night. We had halted on a smooth open place of a narrow ridge, which descended very rapidly to a ravine or piney hollow, at a considerable distance below; and it was quite a pretty spot, had there been water near. But the fires at night look very cheerless after a day's march, when there is no preparation for supper going on; and, after sitting some time around the blazing logs, Mr. Preuss and Carson, with several others, volunteered to take the India rubber buckets and go down into the ravine in search of water. It was a very difficult way in the darkness down the slippery side of the steep mountain, and harder still to climb about half a mile up again; but they found the water, and the cup of coffee (which it enabled us to make) and bread were only enjoyed with greater pleasure.

At sunset the temperature was 46°; the evening remarkably clear; and I obtained an emersion of the first satellite, which does not give a good result, although the observation was a very good one. The chronometric longitude was 117° 28′ 34″, latitude 45° 38′ 07″, and we had ascended to an elevation of 3,830 feet. It appeared to have snowed yesterday on the mountains, their summits showing very white to-day.

October 20.—There was a heavy white frost during the night, and at sunrise the temperature was 37°.

The animals had eaten nothing during the night; and we made an early start, continuing our route among the pines, which were more dense than yesterday, and still retained their magnificent size. The larches cluster together in masses on the sides of the mountains, and their yellow foliage contrasts handsomely with the green of the balsam and other pines. After a few miles we ceased to see any pines, and the timber consisted of several varieties of spruce, larch, and balsam pine, which have a regularly conical figure. These trees appeared from 60 to nearly 200 feet in height; the usual circumference being 10 to 12 feet, and in the pines sometimes 21 feet. In open places near the summit, these trees became less high and more branching, the conical form having a greater base. The instrument carriage occasioned much delay, it being frequently necessary to fell trees and remove the fallen timber. The trail we were following led up a long spur, with a very gradual and gentle rise.

At the end of three miles, we halted at an open place near the summit, from which we enjoyed a fine view over the mountainous country where we had lately travelled, to take a barometrical observation at the height of 4,760 feet.

After travelling occasionally through open places in the forest, we

548

were obliged to cut a way through a dense body of timber, from which we emerged on an open mountain side, where we found a number of small springs, and encamped after a day's journey of 10 miles. Our elevation here was 5,000 feet.

October 21.—There was a very heavy white frost during the night, and the thermometer at sunrise was 30°.

We continued to travel through the forest, in which the road was rendered difficult by fallen trunks, and obstructed by many small trees, which it was necessary to cut down. But these are only accidental difficulties, which could easily be removed, and a very excellent road may be had through this pass, with no other than very moderate ascents or declivities. A laborious day, which had advanced us only six miles on our road, brought us in the afternoon to an opening in the forest, in which there was a fine mountain meadow, with good grass, and a large clear-water stream—one of the head branches of the *Umatilah* river. During this day's journey, the barometer was broken; and the elevations above the sea, hereafter given, depend upon the temperature of boiling water. Some of the white spruces which I measured to-day were twelve feet in circumference, and one of the larches ten; but eight feet was the average circumference of those measured along the road. I held in my hand a tape line as I walked along, in order to form some correct idea of the size of the timber. Their height appeared to be from 100 to 180, and perhaps 200 feet, and the trunks of the larches were sometimes 100 feet without a limb; but the white spruces were generally covered with branches nearly to the root. All these trees have their branches, particularly the lower ones, declining.

October 22.—The white frost this morning was like snow on the ground; the ice was a quarter of an inch thick on the creek, and the thermometer at sunrise was at 20°. But, in a few hours, the day became warm and pleasant, and our road over the mountains was delightful and full of enjoyment.

The trail passed sometimes through very thick young timber, in which there was much cutting to be done; but, after travelling a few miles, the mountains became more bald, and we reached a point from which there was a very extensive view in the northwest. We were here on the western verge of the Blue mountains, long spurs of which, very precipitous on either side, extended down into the valley, the waters of the mountain roaring between them. On our right was a mountain plateau, covered with a dense forest; and to the westward, immediately below us, was the great *Nez Percé* (pierced nose) prairie, in which dark lines of timber indicated the course of many affluents to a considerable stream that was seen pursuing its way across the plain towards what appeared to be the Columbia river. This I knew to be the Walahwalah [Walla Walla] river, and occasional spots along its banks, which resembled clearings, were supposed to be the mission or Indian settlements; but the weather was smoky and unfavorable to far views with the glass. The rock displayed here in the escarpments is a compact amorphous trap, which appears to constitute the mass of the Blue mountains in this latitude; and all the region of country through which we have travelled since leaving the Snake river has been the seat of violent and extensive igneous action. Along the Burnt river valley, the strata are evidently sedimentary rocks, altered by the intrusion of volcanic products, which in some instances have penetrated and essentially changed their original condition. Along our line of route from this point to the California mountains, there seems but little essential change. All our specimens of sedimentary rocks show them to be much altered, and volcanic productions appear to prevail throughout the whole intervening distance.

The road now led along the mountain side, around heads of the precipitous ravines; and, keeping men ahead to clear a road, we passed alternately through bodies of timber and small open prairies, and encamped in a large meadow, in view of the great prairie below.

At sunset the thermometer was at 40°, and the night was very clear and bright. Water was only to be had here by descending a bad ravine, into which we drove our animals, and had much trouble with them, in a very close growth of small pines. Mr. Preuss had walked ahead, and did not get into camp this evening. The trees here maintained their size, and one of the black spruces measured 15 feet in circumference. In the neighborhood of the camp, pines have reappeared here among the timber.

October 23.—The morning was very clear; there had been a heavy white frost during the night, and at sunrise the thermometer was at 31°.

After cutting through two thick bodies of timber, in which I noticed some small trees of *hemlock* spruce, (*perusse,*) the forest became more open, and we had no longer any trouble to clear a way. The pines here were 11 or 12 feet in circumference, and about 110 feet high, and appeared to love the open grounds. The trail now led along one of the long spurs of the mountain, descending gradually towards the plain; and after a few miles travelling, we emerged finally from the forest, in full view of the plain below, and saw the snowy mass of Mount Hood, standing high out above the surrounding country, at the distance of 180 miles. The road along the ridge was excellent, and the grass very green and good; the old grass having been burnt off early in the autumn. About 4 o'clock in the afternoon we reached a little bottom on the Walahwalah river, where we found Mr. Preuss, who yesterday had reached this place, and found himself too far in advance of the camp to return. The stream here has just issued from the narrow ravines, which are walled with precipices, in which the rock has a brown and more burnt appearance than above.

At sunset the thermometer was at 48°; and our position was in longitude 118° 00' 39", and in latitude 45° 53' 35".

The morning was clear, with a temperature at sunrise of 24°. Crossing the river, we travelled over a hilly country with good bunch grass; the river bottom, which generally contains the best soil in other countries, being here a sterile level of rock and pebbles. We had found the soil in the Blue mountains to be of excellent quality, and it appeared also to be good here among the lower hills. Reaching a little eminence, over which the trail passed, we had an extensive view along the course of the river, which was divided and spread over its bottom in a net work of water, receiving several other tributaries from the mountains. There was a band of several hundred horses grazing on the hills about two miles ahead; and as we advanced on the road we met other bands, which Indians were driving out to pasture also on the hills. True to its general character, the reverse of other countries, the hills and mountains here were rich in grass, the bottoms barren and sterile.

In six miles we crossed a principal fork, below which the scattered water of the river was gathered into one channel; and, passing on the way several unfinished houses, and some cleared patches, where corn and potatoes were cultivated, we reached, in about eight miles farther, the missionary establishment of Dr. Whitman,[73] which con-

---

73. Dr. Marcus Whitman (1802–47) had given up a rural medical practice to locate among the Oregon tribes as a missionary. After a preliminary visit to the West in 1835, he had returned to the Oregon country again the following year with his bride Narcissa and the Henry H. Spaldings. Two missions were established, Whitman's at Waiilatpu, twenty-seven miles from the Hud-

sisted, at this time, of one *adobe* house—i.e. built of unburnt bricks, as in Mexico.

I found Dr. Whitman absent on a visit to the *Dalles* of the Columbia; but had the pleasure to see a fine-looking large family of emigrants, men, women, and children, in robust health, all indemnifying themselves for previous scanty fare, in a hearty consumption of potatoes, which are produced here of a remarkably good quality. We were disappointed in our expectation of obtaining corn meal or flour at this station, the mill belonging to the mission having been lately burnt down; but an abundant supply of excellent potatoes banished regrets, and furnished a grateful substitute for bread. A small town of Nez Percé [Cayuse] Indians gave an inhabited and even a populous appearance to the station; and, after remaining about an hour, we continued our route, and encamped on the river about four miles below, passing on the way an emigrant encampment.

Temperature at sunset, 49°.

October 25.—The weather was pleasant, with a sunrise tempera-

---

son's Bay Company's post, Fort Walla Walla, and Spalding's at Lapwai near present Lewiston, Idaho. When dissension arose among the missionaries, and their joint Presbyterian-Congregationalist board ordered a curtailment of their work, Whitman made his famous winter ride east in 1842–43, via Fort Hall and Taos, to visit his mission headquarters in Boston. He had just returned to Oregon when JCF, whom he had seen at the Kansas Ford, arrived.

JCF's comment that he missed seeing Whitman at the mission does not necessarily mean that he failed to see him at all during his stay in the area. Whitman's correspondence mentions JCF several times during this period and expresses apprehension that his party would have to be provisioned from a dwindling supply of food. Writing from Fort Walla Walla, 1 Nov. 1843, to the Rev. David Greene of Boston, Whitman says that JCF, who was then on a trip to Vancouver, would "make his way at once back by the head of the Missouri to the states by this fall & winter in which case I shall write by him; but it seems to me he may still charter a small American Brig which is in the River below & go down to Panama & cross the Isthmus & from thence reach the U States" (HULBERT & HULBERT, 2:318, 319, 322, 328). For a standard biography of Whitman, see DRURY [2].

The mission site is seven miles west of Walla Walla, Wash., near U.S. highway 12, and is a National Historic Site administered by the National Park Service. It has been extensively excavated, and many artifacts uncovered, but the foundations of adobe proved to be so friable that they have been covered over with earth. Outlines of the foundations are now marked by concrete blocks laid level with the ground. Among the artifacts in the museum at the site is a cannon ball thought to have been left by the JCF expedition. But it weighs only eight pounds, and its caliber seems too small for a twelve-pound howitzer.

552

ture of 36°. Our road to-day had in it nothing of interest; and the country offered to the eye only a sandy, undulating plain, through which a scantily timbered river takes its course. We halted about three miles above the mouth, on account of grass; and the next morning arrived at the Nez Percé fort [Fort Walla Walla], one of the trading establishments of the Hudson Bay Company, a few hundred yards above the junction of the Walahwalah with the Columbia river. Here we had the first view of this river, and found it about 1,200 yards wide, and presenting the appearance of a fine navigable stream. We made our camp in a little grove of willows on the Walahwalah, which are the only trees to be seen in the neighborhood; but were obliged to send the animals back to the encampment we had left, as there was scarcely a blade of grass to be found. The post is on the bank of the Columbia, on a plain of bare sands, from which the air was literally filled with clouds of dust and sand, during one of the few days we remained here; this place being one of the several points on the river which are distinguished for prevailing high winds, which come from the sea. The appearance of the post and country was without interest, except that we here saw, for the first time, the great river on which the course of events for the last half century has been directing attention and conferring historical fame. The river is, indeed, a noble object, and has here attained its full magnitude. About nine miles above, and in sight from the heights about the post, is the junction of the two great forks which constitute the main stream—that on which we had been travelling from Fort Hall, and known by the names of Lewis's fork, Shoshonee, and Snake river; and the North fork, which has retained the name of Columbia, as being the main stream.

We did not go up to the junction, being pressed for time; but the union of two large streams, coming one from the southeast, and the other from the northeast, and meeting in what may be treated as the geographical centre of the Oregon valley, thence doubling the volume of water to the ocean, while opening two great lines of communication with the interior continent, constitutes a feature in the map of the country which cannot be overlooked; and, it was probably in reference to this junction of waters, and these lines of communication, that this post was established. They are important lines, and, from the structure of the country, must forever remain so—one of them leading to the South Pass, and to the valley of the Mississippi; the other to the pass at the head of the Athabasca river, and to the countries drained by the waters of the Hudson Bay. The British fur companies now use both lines; the Americans, in their emigration to Oregon, have begun to follow the one which leads towards the United States. Batteaus from tide water ascend to the junction, and thence high up the North fork, or Columbia. Land conveyance only is used upon the line of Lewis's fork. To the emigrants to Oregon, the Nez Percé is a point of interest, as being, to those who choose it, the termination of their overland journey. The broad expanse of the river here invites them to embark on its bosom; and the lofty trees of the forest furnish the means of doing so.

From the South Pass to this place is about 1,000 miles; and as it is about the same distance from that pass to the Missouri river at the mouth of the Kansas, it may be assumed that 2,000 miles is the *necessary* land travel in crossing from the United States to the Pacific ocean on this line. From the mouth of the Great Platte it would be about 100 miles less.

Mr. McKinley,[74] the commander of the post, received us with great civility; and both to myself, and the heads of the emigrants who were there at the time, extended the rites of hospitality in a comfortable dinner to which he invited us.

By a meridional altitude of the sun, the only observation that the weather permitted us to obtain, the mouth of the Walahwalah river is in latitude 46° 03′ 46″; and, by the road we had travelled, 612 miles from Fort Hall. At the time of our arrival, a considerable body of the emigrants under the direction of Mr. Applegate,[75] a man of considerable resolution and energy, had nearly completed the building of a number of Mackinaw boats, in which they proposed to continue their further voyage down the Columbia. I had seen, in descending the Walahwalah river, a fine drove of several hundred cattle, which they had exchanged for Californian cattle, to be received

---

74. Archibald McKinlay (d. 1882), married to a daughter of Peter Skene Ogden, served at Walla Walla until 1846 when he was promoted and sent to Oregon City to take charge of the Hudson's Bay Company's affairs there (ELLIOTT).

75. Jesse Applegate (1811–88), who was to become one of Oregon's leading citizens, had joined the great emigration of 1843 and become captain of the so-called "cow column." Later he took an active part in the organization of the provisional government of 1845, helped to frame the state constitution, and became a farmer and rancher in the Umpqua Valley. In Aug. 1868, he published in *The Overland Monthly* a spirited account of his emigrating experiences entitled "A Day with the Cow Column." See SCHAFER.

at Vancouver, and which are considered a very inferior breed. The other portion of the emigration had preferred to complete their journey by land along the banks of the Columbia, taking their stock and wagons with them.

Having reinforced our animals with eight fresh horses, hired from the post, and increased our stock of provisions with dried salmon, potatoes, and a little beef, we resumed our journey [28 Oct.] down the left bank of the Columbia, being guided on our road by an intelligent Indian boy, whom I had engaged to accompany us as far as the Dalles.

The sketch of a rock which we passed in the course of the morning is annexed, to show the manner in which the basaltic rock, which constitutes the geological formation of the Columbia valley, now presents itself. From an elevated point over which the road led, we obtained another far view of Mount Hood, 150 miles distant. We obtained on the river bank an observation of the sun at noon, which gave for the latitude 45° 58′ 08″. The country to-day was very unprepossessing, and our road bad; and as we toiled slowly along through deep loose sands, and over fragments of black volcanic rock, our laborious travelling was strongly contrasted with the rapid progress of Mr. Applegate's fleet of boats, which suddenly came gliding swiftly down the broad river, which here chanced to be tranquil and smooth. At evening we encamped on the river bank, where there was very little grass, and less timber. We frequently met Indians on the road, and they were collected at every favorable spot along the river.

October 29.—The road continued along the river, and in the course of the day Mount St. Helens, another snowy peak of the Cascade range, was visible. We crossed the Umatilah river at a fall near its mouth. This stream is of the same class as the Walahwalah river, with a bed of volcanic rock, in places split into fissures. Our encampment was similar to that of yesterday; there was very little grass, and no wood. The Indians brought us some pieces for sale, which were purchased to make our fires.[76]

October 31.—By observation, our camp is in latitude 45° 50′ 05″, and longitude 119° 22′ 18″. The night has been cold, and we have

---

76. JCF is camping this night on the Columbia, between the mouths of the Umatilla and John Day rivers. He gives no further indication of his campsites until 2 Nov.

Hill of columnar basalt on the Columbia River

white frost this morning, with a temperature at daylight of 25°, and at sunrise of 24°. The early morning was very clear, and the stars bright; but, as usual since we are on the Columbia, clouds formed immediately with the rising sun. The day continued fine, the east being covered with scattered clouds, but the west remaining clear; showing the remarkable cone-like peak of Mount Hood brightly drawn against the sky. This was in view all day in the southwest, but no other peaks of the range were visible. Our road was a bad one, of very loose deep sand. We met on the way a party of Indians unusually well dressed, wearing clothes of civilized texture and form. They appeared intelligent, and, in our slight intercourse, impressed me with the belief that they possessed some aptitude for acquiring languages.

We continued to travel along the river, the stream being interspersed with many sand bars (it being the season of low water) and with many islands, and an apparently good navigation. Small willows were the only wood; rock and sand the prominent geological feature. The rock of this section is a very compact and tough basalt, occurring in strata which have the appearance of being broken into fragments, assuming the form of columnar hills, and appearing always in escarpments, with the broken fragments strewed at the base and over the adjoining country.

We made a late encampment on the river, and used to-night *purshia tridentata* for fire wood. Among the rocks which formed the bank, was very good green grass. Latitude 45° 44′ 23″, longitude 119° 45′ 09″.

November 1.—Mount Hood is glowing in the sunlight this morning, and the air is pleasant, with a temperature of 38°. We continued down the river, and, passing through a pretty green valley, bounded by high precipitous rocks, encamped at the lower end.

On the right shore, the banks of the Columbia are very high and steep; the river is 1,690 feet broad, and dark bluffs of rock give it a picturesque appearance.

November 2.—The river here entered among bluffs, leaving no longer room for a road; and we accordingly left it, and took a more inland way among the river hills; on which we had no sooner entered, than we found a great improvement in the country. The sand had disappeared, and the soil was good, and covered with excellent grass, although the surface was broken into high hills, with uncommonly deep valleys. At noon we crossed John Day's[77] river, a clear and beautiful stream, with a swift current and a bed of rolled stones. It is sunk in a deep valley, which is characteristic of all the streams in this region; and the hill we descended to reach it well deserves the name of mountain. Some of the emigrants had encamped on the river, and others at the summit of the farther hill, the ascent of which had probably cost their wagons a day's labor; and others again had halted for the night a few miles beyond, where they had slept without water. We also encamped in a grassy hollow without water; but as we had been forewarned of this privation by the guide, the animals had all been watered at the river, and we had brought with us a sufficient quantity for the night.

November 3.—After two hours' ride through a fertile, hilly country, covered as all the upland here appears to be with good green grass, we descended again into the river bottom, along which we resumed our sterile road, and in about four miles reached the ford of the Fall river, (*Rivière aux Chutes,*) [Deschutes] a considerable tributary to the Columbia. We had heard, on reaching the Nez Percé fort, a repetition of the account in regard to the unsettled character of the Columbia Indians at the present time; and to our little party they had at various points manifested a not very friendly disposition, in several attempts to steal our horses. At this place I expected to find a badly disposed band, who had plundered a party of 14 emigrant men a few days before, and taken away their horses; and accordingly we made the necessary preparations for our security, but happily met with no difficulty.

The river was high, divided into several arms, with a rocky island at its outlet into the Columbia, which at this place it rivalled in size, and apparently deserved its highly characteristic name, which is received from one of its many falls some forty miles up the river. It entered the Columbia with a roar of falls and rapids, and is probably a favorite fishing station among the Indians, with whom both banks of the river were populous; but they scarcely paid any attention to us.

---

77. The John Day River, entering the Columbia from the north above the Dalles, is named for a Virginian who became a hunter for the Astorians. With Ramsay Crooks, he was robbed by Indians in the spring of 1812. The river now bearing the name appears not to be the original, but one to which the name was later given. Francis Haines, Jr., believes that Day died on the stream now called Little Lost River, and that early traders and trappers called that stream the John Day (HAINES [2], 6–10).

The ford was very difficult at this time, and, had they entertained any bad intentions, they were offered a good opportunity to carry them out, as I drove directly into the river, and during the crossing the howitzer was occasionally several feet under water, and a number of the men appeared to be more often below than above. Our guide was well acquainted with the ford, and we succeeded in getting every thing safe over to the left bank. We delayed here only a short time to put the gun in order, and, ascending a long mountain hill, left both rivers, and resumed our route again among the interior hills.

The roar of the *Falls of the Columbia* is heard from the heights, where we halted a few moments to enjoy a fine view of the river below. In the season of high water it would be a very interesting object to visit, in order to witness what is related of the annual submerging of the fall under the waters which back up from the basin below, constituting a great natural lock at this place. But time had become an object of serious consideration; and the Falls, in their present state, had been seen and described by many.

After a day's journey of 17 miles, we encamped among the hills on a little clear stream, where, as usual, the Indians immediately gathered round us. Among them was a very old man, almost blind from age, with long and very white hair. I happened of my own accord to give this old man a present of tobacco, and was struck with the impression which my unpropitiated notice made on the Indians, who appeared in a remarkable manner acquainted with the real value of goods, and to understand the equivalents of trade. At evening, one of them spoke a few words to his people, and, telling me that we need entertain no uneasiness in regard to our animals, as none of them would be disturbed, they went all quietly away. In the morning, when they again came to the camp, I expressed to them the gratification we felt at their reasonable conduct, making them a present of some large knives and a few smaller articles.

November 4.—The road continued among the hills, and, reaching an eminence, we saw before us in a little green valley, watered by a clear stream, a tolerably large valley, through which the trail passed.

In comparison with the Indians of the Rocky mountains and the great eastern plain, these are disagreeably dirty in their habits. Their huts were crowded with half-naked women and children, and the atmosphere within any thing but pleasant to persons who had just been riding in the fresh morning air. We were somewhat amused with the scanty dress of one woman, who, in common with the others, rushed out of the huts on our arrival, and who, in default of other covering, used a child for a fig leaf.

The road in about half an hour passed near an elevated point, from which we overlooked the valley of the Columbia for many miles, and saw in the distance several houses surrounded by fields, which a chief, who had accompanied us from the village, pointed out to us as the Methodist missionary station.[78]

In a few miles we descended to the river, which we reached at one of its remarkably interesting features, known as the *Dalles of the Columbia.* The whole volume of the river at this place passed between the walls of a chasm, which has the appearance of having been rent through the basaltic strata which form the valley rock of the region. At the narrowest place we found the breadth, by measurement, 58 yards, and the average height of the walls above the water 25 feet; forming a trough between the rocks—whence the name, probably applied by a Canadian voyageur. The mass of water, in the present low state of the river, passed swiftly between, deep and black, and curled into many small whirlpools and counter currents, but unbroken by foam, and so still that scarcely the sound of a ripple was heard. The rock, for a considerable distance from the river, was worn over a large portion of its surface into circular holes and well-like cavities, by the abrasion of the river, which, at the season of high waters, is spread out over the adjoining bottoms.

In the recent passage through this chasm, an unfortunate event had occurred to Mr. Applegate's party, in the loss of one of their boats, which had been carried under water in the midst of the *Dalles,* and two of Mr. Applegate's children and one man drowned.[79] This misfortune was attributed only to want of skill in the steersman, as at this season there is no impediment to navigation; although the place is entirely impassable at high water, when boats pass safely over the great falls above, in the submerged state in which they then find themselves.

The basalt here is precisely the same as that which constitutes the

---

78. The Rev. Jason Lee (1803–45) and his nephew, Daniel Lee, had gone to Oregon in 1834 with the N. J. Wyeth party to establish an unsuccessful mission among the Flatheads. Later missions were established, including this one at the Dalles.

79. Jesse Applegate lost a twelve-year-old son, Edward, and a nephew in the raft accident to which JCF refers.

rock of the valley higher up the Columbia, being very compact, with a few round cavities.

We passed rapidly three or four miles down the level valley, and encamped near the mission. The character of the forest growth here changed, and we found ourselves, with pleasure, again among oaks and other forest trees of the east, to which we had long been strangers; and the hospitable and kind reception with which we were welcomed among our country people at the mission aided the momentary illusion of home.

Two good-looking wooden dwelling houses, and a large school house, with stables, barn, and garden, and large cleared fields between the houses and the river bank, on which were scattered the wooden huts of an Indian village, gave to the valley the cheerful and busy air of civilization, and had in our eyes an appearance of abundant and enviable comfort.

Our land journey found here its western termination. The delay involved in getting our camp to the right bank of the Columbia, and in opening a road through the continuous forest to Vancouver, rendered a journey along the river impracticable; and on this side the usual road across the mountain required strong and fresh animals, there being an interval of three days in which they could obtain no food. I therefore wrote immediately to Mr. Fitzpatrick, directing him to abandon the carts at the Walahwalah missionary station, and, as soon as the necessary pack saddles could be made, which his party required, meet me at the Dalles, from which point I proposed to commence our homeward journey. The day after our arrival being Sunday, no business could be done at the mission; but on Monday Mr. Perkins[80] assisted me in procuring from the Indians a large canoe, in which I designed to complete our journey to Vancouver, where I expected to obtain the necessary supply of provisions and stores for our winter journey. Three Indians, from the family to whom the canoe belonged, were engaged to assist in working her during the voyage, and, with them, our water party consisted of Mr. Preuss and myself, with Bernier and Jacob Dodson. In charge of the party which was to remain at the Dalles I left Carson, with instructions to occupy the people in making pack saddles and refitting

---

80. H. W. K. Perkins (1812–84) was a member of the second party of reinforcements for the Jason Lee missionaries, and with Daniel Lee had established the Dalles mission. He returned to the East in 1844 (HINES).

their equipage. The village from which we were to take the canoe was on the right bank of the river, about ten miles below, at the mouth of the Tinanens creek; and while Mr. Preuss proceeded down the river with the instruments, in a little canoe paddled by two Indians, Mr. Perkins accompanied me with the remainder of the party by land. The last of the emigrants had just left the Dalles at the time of our arrival, travelling some by water and others by land, making ark-like rafts, on which they had embarked their families and household, with their large wagons and other furniture, while their stock were driven along the shore.

For about five miles below the Dalles, the river is narrow, and probably very deep; but during this distance it is somewhat open, with grassy bottoms on the left. Entering, then, among the lower mountains of the Cascade range, it assumes a general character, and high and steep rocky hills shut it in on either side, rising abruptly in places to the height of 1,500 feet above the water, and gradually acquiring a more mountainous character as the river approaches the Cascades.

After an hour's travel, when the sun was nearly down, we searched along the shore for a pleasant place, and halted to prepare supper. We had been well supplied by our friends at the mission with delicious salted salmon which had been taken at the fattest season; also, with potatoes, bread, coffee, and sugar. We were delighted at a change in our mode of travelling and living. The canoe sailed smoothly down the river; at night we encamped upon the shore, and a plentiful supply of comfortable provisions supplied the first of wants. We enjoyed the contrast which it presented to our late toilsome marchings, our night watchings, and our frequent privation of food. We were a motley group, but all happy; three unknown Indians; Jacob, a colored man; Mr. Preuss, a German; Bernier, creole French; and myself.

Being now upon the ground explored by the South Sea expedition under Captain Wilkes, and having accomplished the object of uniting my survey with his, and thus presenting a connected exploration from the Mississippi to the Pacific, and the winter being at hand, I deemed it necessary to economize time by voyaging in the night, as is customary here, to avoid the high winds, which rise with the morning, and decline with the day.

Accordingly, after an hour's halt, we again embarked, and resumed our pleasant voyage down the river. The wind rose to a gale after several hours; but the moon was very bright, and the wind was fair, and the canoe glanced rapidly down the stream, the waves breaking into foam alongside; and our night voyage, as the wind bore us rapidly along between the dark mountains, was wild and interesting. About midnight we put to the shore on a rocky beach, behind which was a dark-looking pine forest. We built up large fires among the rocks, which were in large masses round about; and, arranging our blankets on the most sheltered places we could find, passed a delightful night.

After an early breakfast, at daylight we resumed our journey, the weather being clear and beautiful, and the river smooth and still. On either side the mountains are all pine-timbered, rocky, and high. We were now approaching one of the marked features of the lower Columbia, where the river forms a great *cascade,* with a series of rapids, in breaking through the range of mountains to which the lofty peaks of Mount Hood and St. Helens belong, and which rise as great pillars of snow on either side of the passage. The main branch of the *Sacramento* river, and the *Tlamath* [Klamath], issue in cascades from this range; and the Columbia, breaking through it in a succession of cascades, gives the idea of cascades to the whole range; and hence the name of the CASCADE RANGE, which it bears, and distinguishes it from the Coast Range lower down. In making a short turn to the south, the river forms the cascades in breaking over a point of agglomerated masses of rock, leaving a handsome bay to the right, with several rocky pine-covered islands, and the mountains sweep at a distance around a cove where several small streams enter the bay. In less than an hour we halted on the left bank, about five minutes' walk above the cascades, where there were several Indian huts, and where our guides signified it was customary to hire Indians to assist in making the *portage.* When travelling with a boat as light as a canoe, which may easily be carried on the shoulders of the Indians, this is much the better side of the river for the portage, as the ground here is very good and level, being a handsome bottom, which I remarked was covered (*as was now always the case along the river*) with a growth of green and fresh-looking grass. It was long before we could come to an understanding with the Indians; but at length, when they had first received the price of their assistance in goods, they went vigorously to work; and, in a shorter time than had been occupied in making our arrangements, the canoe, instruments, and baggage, were carried through (a distance of about half a mile) to the bank below the main cascade, where we again embarked, the water being white with foam among ugly rocks, and boiling into a thousand whirlpools. The boat passed with great rapidity, crossing and recrossing in the eddies of the current. After passing through about 2 miles of broken water, we ran some wild-looking rapids, which are called the Lower Rapids, being the last on the river, which below is tranquil and smooth—a broad, magnificent stream. On a low broad point on the right bank of the river, at the lower end of these rapids, were pitched many tents of the emigrants, who were waiting here for their friends from above, or for boats and provisions which were expected from Vancouver. In our passage down the rapids, I had noticed their camps along the shore, or transporting their goods across the portage. This portage makes a head of navigation, ascending the river. It is about two miles in length; and above, to the Dalles, is 45 miles of smooth and good navigation.

We glided on without further interruption between very rocky and high steep mountains, which sweep along the river valley at a little distance, covered with forests of pine, and showing occasionally lofty escarpments of red rock. Nearer, the shore is bordered by steep escarped hills and huge vertical rocks, from which the waters of the mountain reach the river in a variety of beautiful falls, sometimes several hundred feet in height. Occasionally along the river occurred pretty bottoms, covered with the greenest verdure of the spring. To a professional farmer, however, it does not offer many places of sufficient extent to be valuable for agriculture; and after passing a few miles below the Dalles, I had scarcely seen a place on the south shore where wagons could get to the river. The beauty of the scenery was heightened by the continuance of very delightful weather, resembling the Indian summer of the Atlantic. A few miles below the cascades we passed a singular isolated hill; and in the course of the next six miles occurred five very pretty falls from the heights on the left bank, one of them being of a very picturesque character; and towards sunset we reached a remarkable point of rocks, distinguished, on account of prevailing high winds, and the delay it frequently occasions to the canoe navigation, by the name of *Cape Horn*. It borders the river in a high wall of rock, which comes boldly down into deep water; and in violent gales down the river, and from the opposite shore, which is the prevailing direction of strong winds, the water is dashed against it with considerable violence. It appears to form a serious obstacle to canoe travelling; and I was informed by Mr. Perkins, that in a voyage up the river he had been detained two weeks at this place, and was finally obliged to return to Vancouver.

The winds of this region deserve a particular study. They blow in currents, which show them to be governed by fixed laws; and it is a problem how far they may come from the mountains, or from the ocean through the breaks in the mountains which let out the river.

The hills here had lost something of their rocky appearance, and had already begun to decline. As the sun went down, we searched along the river for an inviting spot; and, finding a clean rocky beach, where some large dry trees were lying on the ground, we ran our boat to the shore; and, after another comfortable supper, ploughed our way along the river in darkness. Heavy clouds covered the sky this evening, and the wind began to sweep in gusts among the trees, as if bad weather were coming. As we advanced, the hills on both sides grew constantly lower; on the right, retreating from the shore, and forming a somewhat extensive bottom of intermingled prairie and wooded land. In the course of a few hours, and opposite to a small stream coming in from the north, called the *Tea Prairie* river, the highlands on the left declined to the plains, and three or four miles below disappeared entirely on both sides, and the river entered the low country. The river had gradually expanded; and when we emerged from the highlands, the opposite shores were so distant as to appear indistinct in the uncertainty of the light. About 10 o'clock our pilots halted, apparently to confer about the course; and, after a little hesitation, pulled directly across an open expansion of the river, where the waves were somewhat rough for a canoe, the wind blowing very fresh. Much to our surprise, a few minutes afterwards we ran aground. Backing off our boat, we made repeated trials at various places to cross what appeared to be a point of shifting sand bars, where we had attempted to shorten the way by a cut-off. Finally, one of our Indians got into the water, and waded about until he found a channel sufficiently deep, through which we wound along after him, and in a few minutes again entered the deep water below. As we paddled rapidly down the river, we heard the noise of a saw mill at work on the right bank; and, letting our boat float quietly down, we listened with pleasure to the unusual sounds; and before midnight encamped on the bank of the river, about a mile above Fort Vancouver. Our fine dry weather had given place to a dark cloudy night. At midnight it began to rain; and we found ourselves suddenly in the gloomy and humid season, which, in the narrow region lying between the Pacific and the Cascade mountains, and for a considerable distance along the coast, supplies the place of winter.

In the morning, the first object that attracted my attention was the barque Columbia, lying at anchor near the landing. She was about to start on her voyage to England, and was now ready for sea; being detained only in waiting the arrival of the express batteaus, which descend the Columbia and its north fork with the overland mail from Canada and Hudson's bay, which had been delayed beyond their usual time. I immediately waited upon Dr. McLaughlin,[81] the executive officer of the Hudson Bay Company in the territory west of the Rocky mountains, who received me with the courtesy and hospitality for which he has been eminently distinguished, and which makes a forcible and delightful impression on a traveller from the long wilderness from which we had issued. I was immediately supplied by him with the necessary stores and provisions to refit and support my party in our contemplated winter journey to the States; and also with a Mackinaw boat and canoes, manned with Canadian and Iroquois voyageurs and Indians, for their transportation to the Dalles of the Columbia. In addition to this efficient kindness in furnishing me with these necessary supplies, I received from him a warm and gratifying sympathy in the suffering which his great experience led him to anticipate for us in our homeward journey, and a letter of recommendation and credit for any officers of the Hudson Bay Company into whose posts we might be driven by unexpected misfortune.

Of course, the future supplies for my party were paid for, bills on

81. The dignified trader and physician, John McLoughlin (1784–1857), known to the Indians as White Eagle, had been in charge of the Columbia district since 1824. He could be merciless in competition, and served his company well, but—as JCF notes—he also could be kind, and he kept many an American settler from perishing by extending credit for provisions and supplies. Although he always encouraged settlement south of the Columbia, he hoped that the country north of the river would remain in British hands. For a biography, see MONTGOMERY. For his letters to the governor and Committee at this time, see RICH.

the Government of the United States being readily taken; but every hospitable attention was extended to me, and I accepted an invitation to take a room in the fort, *"and to make myself at home while I staid."*

I found many American emigrants at the fort; others had already crossed the river into their land of promise—the Walahmette [Willamette] valley. Others were daily arriving; and all of them had been furnished with shelter, so far as it could be afforded by the buildings connected with the establishment. Necessary clothing and provisions (the latter to be afterwards returned in kind from the produce of their labor) were also furnished. This friendly assistance was of very great value to the emigrants, whose families were otherwise exposed to much suffering in the winter rains, which had now commenced, at the same time that they were in want of all the common necessaries of life. Those who had taken a water conveyance at the Nez Percé fort continued to arrive safely, with no other accident than has been already mentioned. The party which had passed over the Cascade mountains were reported to have lost a number of their animals; and those who had driven their stock down the Columbia had brought them safely in, and found for them a ready and very profitable market, and were already proposing to return to the States in the spring for another supply.

In the space of two days our preparations had been completed, and we were ready to set out on our return. It would have been very gratifying to have gone down to the Pacific, and, solely in the interest and in the love of geography, to have seen the ocean on the western as well as on the eastern side of the continent, so as to give a satisfactory completeness to the geographical picture which had been formed in our minds; but the rainy season had now regularly set in, and the air was filled with fogs and rain, which left no beauty in any scenery, and obstructed observations. The object of my instructions had been entirely fulfilled in having connected our reconnoissance with the surveys of Captain Wilkes; and although it would have been agreeable and satisfactory to terminate here also our ruder astronomical observations, I was not, for such a reason, justified to make a delay in waiting for favorable weather.

Near sunset of the 10th, the boats left the fort, and encamped after making only a few miles. Our flotilla consisted of a Mackinaw barge and three canoes—one of them that in which we had descended the river; and a party in all of 20 men. One of the emigrants, Mr. Burnet,[82] of Missouri, who had left his family and property at the Dalles, availed himself of the opportunity afforded by the return of our boats to bring them down to Vancouver. This gentleman, as well as the Messrs. Applegate, and others of the emigrants whom I saw, possessed intelligence and character, with the moral and intellectual stamina, as well as the enterprise, which give solidity and respectability to the foundation of colonies.

November 11.—The morning was rainy and misty. We did not move with the practised celerity of my own camp; and it was near 9 o'clock when our motley crew had finished their breakfast and were ready to start. Once afloat, however, they worked steadily and well, and we advanced at a good rate up the river; and in the afternoon a breeze sprung up, which enabled us to add a sail to the oars. At evening we encamped on a warm-looking beach, on the right bank, at the foot of the high river hill, immediately at the lower end of Cape Horn. On the opposite shore is said to be a singular hole in the mountain, from which the Indians believe comes the wind producing these gales. It is called the Devil's hole; and the Indians, I was told, have been resolving to send down one of their slaves to explore the region below. At dark, the wind shifted into its stormy quarter, gradually increasing to a gale from the southwest; and the sky becoming clear, I obtained a good observation of an emersion of the first satellite; the result of which, being an absolute observation, I have adopted for the longitude of the place.

November 12.—The wind during the night had increased to so much violence, that the broad river this morning was angry and white; the waves breaking with considerable force against this rocky wall of the cape. Our old Iroquois pilot was unwilling to risk the boats around the point, and I was not disposed to hazard the stores of our voyage for the delay of a day. Further observations were obtained during the day, giving for the latitude of the place 45° 33' 09"; and the longitude, obtained from the satellite, is 122° 6' 15".

---

82. Peter Hardeman Burnett (1807–95) was to serve as an Oregon supreme court judge in 1845 and to lead a party to the California gold fields in 1848. He remained in California and was governor from 1849 to 1851. Recalling the trip up the Columbia with JCF many years later, he said the explorer gave his orders with great mildness and simplicity, but he required obedience. When the Indians were slow to work, JCF simply put out their fires (BURNETT, 85–88).

November 13.—We had a day of disagreeable and cold rain; and, late in the afternoon, began to approach the rapids of the cascades. There is here a high timbered island on the left shore, below which, in descending, I had remarked in a bluff on the river the extremities of trunks of trees appearing to be imbedded in the rock. Landing here this afternoon, I found in the lower part of the escarpment a stratum of coal and forest trees, imbedded between strata of altered clay containing the remains of vegetables, the leaves of which indicate that the plants were dicotyledonous. Among these, the stems of some of the ferns are not mineralized, but merely charred, retaining still their vegetable structure and substance; and in this condition a portion also of the trees remain. The indurated appearance and compactness of the strata, as well, perhaps, as the mineralized condition of the coal, are probably due to igneous action. Some portions of the coal precisely resemble in aspect the cannel coal of England, and, with the accompanying fossils, have been referred to the tertiary formation.

These strata appear to rest upon a mass of agglomerated rock, being but a few feet above the water of the river; and over them is the escarpment of perhaps eighty feet, rising gradually in the rear towards the mountains. The wet and cold evening, and near approach of night, prevented me from making any other than a very slight examination.

The current was now very swift, and we were obliged to *cordelle* the boat along the left shore, where the bank was covered with large masses of rocks. Night overtook us at the upper end of the island, a short distance below the cascades, and we halted on the open point. In the mean time, the lighter canoes, paddled altogether by Indians, had passed ahead, and were out of sight. With them was the lodge, which was the only shelter we had, with most of the bedding and provisions. We shouted, and fired guns; but all to no purpose, as it was impossible for them to hear above the roar of the river; and we remained all night without shelter, the rain pouring down all the time. The old voyageurs did not appear to mind it much, but covered themselves up as well as they could, and lay down on the sand beach, where they remained quiet until morning. The rest of us spent a rather miserable night; and, to add to our discomfort, the incessant rain extinguished our fires; and we were glad when at last daylight appeared, and we again embarked.

Crossing to the right bank, we *cordelled* the boat along the shore, there being no longer any use for the paddles, and put into a little bay below the upper rapids. Here we found the lodge pitched, and about twenty Indians sitting around a blazing fire within, making a luxurious breakfast with salmon, bread, butter, sugar, coffee, and other provisions. In the forest, on the edge of a high bluff overlooking the river, is an Indian grave yard, consisting of a collection of tombs, in each of which were the scattered bones of many skeletons. The tombs were made of boards, which were ornamented with many figures of men and animals of the natural size—from their appearance, constituting the armorial device by which, among Indians, the chiefs are usually known.

The masses of rock displayed along the shores of the ravine in the neighborhood of the cascades are clearly volcanic products. Between this cove, which I called Grave-yard bay, and another spot of smooth water above, on the right, called Lüders bay,[83] sheltered by a jutting point of huge rocky masses at the foot of the cascades, the shore along the intervening rapids is lined with precipices of distinct strata of red and variously colored lavas, in inclined positions.

The masses of rock forming the point at Lüders bay consist of a porous trap, or basalt—a volcanic product of a modern period. The rocks belong to agglomerated masses, which form the immediate ground of the cascades, and have been already mentioned as constituting a bed of cemented conglomerate rocks appearing at various places along the river. Here they are scattered along the shores, and through the bed of the river, wearing the character of convulsion, which forms the impressive and prominent feature of the river at this place.

Wherever we came in contact with the rocks of these mountains, we found them volcanic, which is probably the character of the range; and at this time, two of the great snowy cones, Mount Regnier and St. Helens, were in action. On the 23d of the preceding November, St. Helens had scattered its ashes, like a light fall of snow, over the Dalles of the Columbia, 50 miles distant. A specimen of these ashes was given to me by Mr. Brewer, one of the clergymen at the Dalles.[84]

83. The name "Lüders Bay" apparently did not come into general use and soon faded from memory. The bay, named for a German botanist (see p. 571), would have been a short distance below Stevenson, Wash. (HASKINS).

84. Henry Bridgman Brewer (1813–86) and his wife had come by sea in 1839 to join the Oregon Methodist Episcopal Mission, where he served for

The lofty range of the Cascade mountains forms a distinct boundary between the opposite climates of the regions along its western and eastern bases. On the west, they present a barrier to the clouds of fog and rain which roll up from the Pacific ocean and beat against their rugged sides, forming the rainy season of the winter in the country along the coast. Into the brighter skies of the region along their eastern base, this rainy winter never penetrates; and at the Dalles of the Columbia the rainy season is unknown, the brief winter being limited to a period of about two months, during which the earth is covered with slight snows of a climate remarkably mild for so high a latitude. The Cascade range has an average distance of about 130 miles from the sea coast. It extends far both north and south of the Columbia, and is indicated to the distant observer, both in course and position, by the lofty volcanic peaks which rise out of it, and which are visible to an immense distance.

During several days of constant rain, it kept our whole force laboriously employed in getting our barge and canoes to the upper end of the cascades. The portage ground was occupied by emigrant families; their thin and insufficient clothing, bare-headed and bare-footed children, attesting the length of their journey, and showing that they had, in many instances, set out without a due preparation of what was indispensable.

A gentleman named [Friedrich G. J.] Lüders, a botanist from the city of Hamburg, arrived at the bay I have called by his name while we were occupied in bringing up the boats. I was delighted to meet at such a place a man of kindred pursuits; but we had only the pleasure of a brief conversation, as his canoe, under the guidance of two Indians, was about to run the rapids; and I could not enjoy the satisfaction of regaling him with a breakfast, which, after his recent journey, would have been an extraordinary luxury. All of his few instruments and baggage were in the canoe, and he hurried around by land to meet it at the Grave-yard bay; but he was scarcely out of sight, when, by the carelessness of the Indians, the boat was drawn into the midst of the rapids, and glanced down the river, bottom up, with the loss of every thing it contained. In the natural concern I

<hr>

seven years. Later he farmed in the Willamette Valley, then returned to New England by way of the Sandwich Islands (BREWER). It was Mount Baker (not Mount Rainier), far to the north, that had become active in 1842. Many times in the 1840s, Mount St. Helens seems to have been active to a varying degree, with the great eruption taking place in Nov. 1842 (HOLMES).

felt for his misfortune, I gave to the little cove the name of Lüders bay.

November 15.—We continued to-day our work at the portage.

About noon, the two barges of the express from Montreal arrived at the upper portage landing, which, for large boats, is on the right bank of the river. They were a fine-looking crew, and among them I remarked a fresh-looking woman and her daughter, emigrants from Canada. It was satisfactory to see the order and speed with which these experienced watermen effected the portage, and passed their boats over the cascades. They had arrived at noon, and in the evening they expected to reach Vancouver. These batteaus carry the express of the Hudson Bay Company to the highest navigable point of the north fork of the Columbia, whence it is carried by an overland party to lake Winipec [Lake Winnipeg], where it is divided—part going to Montreal, and part to Hudson Bay. Thus a regular communication is kept up between three very remote points.

The Canadian emigrant was much chagrined at the change of climate, and informed me that, only a few miles above, they had left a country of bright blue sky and a shining sun. The next morning the upper parts of the mountains which directly overlook the cascades were white with the freshly fallen snow, while it continued to rain steadily below.

Late in the afternoon we finished the portage, and, embarking again, moved a little distance up the right bank, in order to clear the smaller rapids of the cascades, and have a smooth river for the next morning. Though we made but a few miles, the weather improved immediately and though the rainy country and the cloudy mountains were close behind, before us was the bright sky; so distinctly is climate here marked by a mountain boundary.

November 17.—We had to-day an opportunity to complete the sketch of that portion of the river down which we had come by night, and of which I will not give a particular description, which the small scale of our map would not illustrate. Many places occur along the river, where the stumps, or rather portions of the trunks of pine trees, are standing along the shore, and in the water, where they may be seen at a considerable depth below the surface, in the beautifully clear water. These collections of dead trees are called on the Columbia the *submerged forest,* and are supposed to have been created by the effects of some convulsion which formed the cascades, and which, by damming up the river, placed these trees under water and destroyed them. But I venture to presume that the cascades are older than the trees; and as these submerged forests occur at five or six places along the river, I had an opportunity to satisfy myself that they have been formed by immense land slides from the mountains, which here closely shut in the river, and which brought down with them into the river the pines of the mountain. At one place, on the right bank, I remarked a place where a portion of one of these slides seemed to have planted itself, with all the evergreen foliage, and the vegetation of the neighboring hill, directly amidst the falling and yellow leaves of the river trees. It occurred to me that this would have been a beautiful illustration to the eye of a botanist.

Following the course of a slide, which was very plainly marked along the mountain, I found that in the interior parts the trees were in their usual erect position; but at the extremity of the slide they were rocked about, and thrown into a confusion of inclinations.

About 4 o'clock in the afternoon we passed a sandy bar in the river, whence we had an unexpected view of Mount Hood, bearing directly south by compass.

During the day we used oar and sail, and at night had again a delightful camping ground, and a dry place to sleep upon.

November 18.—The day again was pleasant and bright. At 10 o'clock we passed a rock island, on the right shore of the river, which the Indians use as a burial ground; and, halting for a short time, about an hour afterwards, at the village of our Indian friends, early in the afternoon we arrived again at the Dalles.

Carson had removed the camp up the river a little nearer to the hills, where the animals had better grass. We found every thing in good order, and arrived just in time to partake of an excellent roast of California beef. My friend Mr. Gilpin had arrived in advance of the party. His object in visiting this country had been to obtain correct information of the Walahmette settlements; and he had reached this point in his journey, highly pleased with the country over which he had travelled, and with invigorated health. On the following day he continued his journey, in our returning boats, to Vancouver.

The camp was now occupied in making the necessary preparations for our homeward journey, which, though homeward, contemplated a new route, and a great circuit to the south and southeast, and the exploration of the Great Basin between the Rocky mountains and the *Sierra Nevada*. Three principal objects were indicated, by report or by maps, as being on this route; the character or existence

573

of which I wished to ascertain, and which I assumed as landmarks, or leading points, on the projected line of return. The first of these points was the *Tlamath* lake, on the table land between the head of Fall river, which comes to the Columbia, and the Sacramento, which goes to the bay of San Francisco; and from which lake a river of the same name makes its way westwardly direct to the ocean. This lake and river are often called *Klamet,* but I have chosen to write its name according to the Indian pronunciation. The position of this lake, on the line of inland communication between Oregon and California; its proximity to the demarcation boundary of latitude 42°; its imputed double character of lake, or meadow, according to the season of the year; and the hostile and warlike character attributed to the Indians about it—all made it a desirable object to visit and examine. From this lake our course was intended to be about southeast, to a reported lake called Mary's, at some days' journey in the Great Basin; and thence, still on southeast, to the reputed *Buenaventura* river,[85] which has had a place in so many maps, and countenanced the belief of the existence of a great river flowing from the Rocky mountains to the bay of San Francisco. From the Buenaventura the next point was intended to be in that section of the Rocky mountains which includes the heads of Arkansas river, and of the opposite waters of the Californian gulf; and thence down the Arkansas to Bent's fort, and home. This was our projected line of return—a great part of it absolutely new to geographical, botani-

---

85. It is uncertain whether JCF really believed in the existence of the Buenaventura. Benton says he did, and that Dr. McLoughlin "made out a conjectural manuscript map to show its place and course" (BENTON [1], 2:580). Benton also credits JCF with eliminating the mythical river from the maps, but that had already been done; it does not appear on Albert Gallatin's or B. L. E. Bonneville's important maps. Possibly JCF had seen the map made by Lieut. Charles Wilkes after his survey of the coast by sea and land, though he never acknowledged this in a later controversy with Wilkes over the accuracy of certain cartographic positions. We know from JCF's comments on p. 588 that he had heard of the experiences of Jedediah Smith, and he may also have known of Joseph R. Walker's journey across the Great Basin in 1833–34. These men found no Buenaventura. JCF's recurring journal entries about his search for the fabled river—written *after* the expedition—and his final conclusion that the river did not exist, seem almost like a deliberately introduced element to add continuity and suspense to the *Report*. It is hard to resist the suspicion that Jessie Benton Frémont's flair for the dramatic is somehow involved. For more about the river, see CRAMPTON & GRIFFEN.

cal, and geological science—and the subject of reports in relation to lakes, rivers, deserts, and savages hardly above the condition of mere wild animals, which inflamed desire to know what this *terra incognita* really contained. It was a serious enterprise, at the commencement of winter, to undertake the traverse of such a region, and with a party consisting only of twenty-five persons, and they of many nations—American, French, German, Canadian, Indian, and colored—and most of them young, several being under twenty-one years of age. All knew that a strange country was to be explored, and dangers and hardships to be encountered; but no one blenched at the prospect. On the contrary, courage and confidence animated the whole party. Cheerfulness, readiness, subordination, prompt obedience, characterized all; nor did any extremity of peril and privation, to which we were afterwards exposed, ever belie, or derogate from, the fine spirit of this brave and generous commencement. The course of the narrative will show at what point, and for what reasons, we were prevented from the complete execution of this plan, after having made considerable progress upon it, and how we were forced by desert plains and mountain ranges, and deep snows, far to the south and near to the Pacific ocean, and along the western base of the Sierra Nevada; where, indeed, a new and ample field of exploration opened itself before us. For the present, we must follow the narrative, which will first lead us south along the valley of Fall [Deschutes] river, and the eastern base of the Cascade range, to the Tlamath lake, from which, or its margin, three rivers go in three directions—one west, to the ocean; another north, to the Columbia; the third south, to California [misconception of the Sacramento River].

For the support of the party, I had provided at Vancouver a supply of provisions for not less than three months, consisting principally of flour, peas, and tallow—the latter being used in cooking; and, in addition to this, I had purchased at the mission some California cattle, which were to be driven on the hoof. We had 104 mules and horses —part of the latter procured from the Indians about the mission; and for the sustenance of which, our reliance was upon the grass which we should find, and the soft porous wood, which was to be its substitute when there was none.

Mr. Fitzpatrick, with Mr. Talbot and the remainder of our party, arrived on the 21st; and the camp was now closely engaged in the labor of preparation. Mr. Perkins succeeded in obtaining as a guide to the Tlamath lake two Indians—one of whom had been there, and bore the marks of several wounds he had received from some of the Indians in the neighborhood; and the other went along for company. In order to enable us to obtain horses, he despatched messengers to the various Indian villages in the neighborhood, informing them that we were desirous to purchase, and appointing a day for them to bring them in.

We made, in the mean time, several excursions in the vicinity. Mr. Perkins walked with Mr. Preuss and myself to the heights, about nine miles distant, on the opposite side of the river, whence, in fine weather, an extensive view may be had over the mountains, including seven great peaks of the Cascade range; but clouds, on this occasion, destroyed the anticipated pleasure, and we obtained bearings only to three that were visible: Mount Regnier, St. Helens, and Mount Hood. On the heights, about one mile south of the mission, a very fine view may be had of Mount Hood and St. Helens. In order to determine their positions with as much accuracy as possible, the angular distances of the peaks were measured with the sextant, at different fixed points from which they could be seen.

The Indians brought in their horses at the appointed time, and we succeeded in obtaining a number in exchange for goods; but they were relatively much higher here, where goods are plenty and at moderate prices, than we had found them in the more eastern part of our voyage. Several of the Indians inquired very anxiously to know if we had any *dollars;* and the horses we procured were much fewer in number than I had desired, and of thin, inferior quality; the oldest and poorest being those that were sold to us. These horses, as ever in our journey you will have occasion to remark, are valuable for hardihood and great endurance.

November 24.—At this place one of the men was discharged;[86] and at the request of Mr. Perkins, a Chinook Indian, a lad of nineteen, who was extremely desirous to "see the whites," and make some acquaintance with our institutions, was received into the party, under my special charge, with the understanding that I would again

---

86. John Gill Campbell was discharged. Later he was employed as a clerk by Archibald McKinlay, then became a member of the Oregon Exchange Company which coined "Beaver money" in Oregon City from 1849 to 1854, when U.S. coins from the San Francisco mint came into use (GARY, 392; SCOTT).

return him to his friends. He had lived for some time in the household of Mr. Perkins, and spoke a few words of the English language.[87]

November 25.—We were all up early, in the excitement of turning towards home. The stars were brilliant, and the morning cold—the thermometer at daylight 26°.

Our preparations had been finally completed, and to-day we commenced our journey.[88] The little wagon which had hitherto carried the instruments I judged it necessary to abandon; and it was accordingly presented to the mission. In all our long travelling, it had never been overturned or injured by any accident of the road; and the only things broken were the glass lamps, and one of the front panels, which had been kicked out by an unruly Indian horse. The howitzer was the only wheeled carriage now remaining. We started about noon, when the weather had become disagreeably cold, with flurries of snow. Our friend Mr. Perkins, whose kindness had been active and efficient during our stay, accompanied us several miles on our road; when he bade us farewell, and consigned us to the care of our guides. Ascending to the uplands beyond the southern fork of the *Tinanens* [Fifteenmile] creek, we found the snow lying on the ground in frequent patches, although the pasture appeared good, and the new short grass was fresh and green. We travelled over high, hilly land, and encamped on a little branch of Tinanens creek, where there were grass and timber. The southern bank was covered with snow, which was scattered over the bottom; and the little creek, its borders lined with ice, had a chilly and wintry look. A number of Indians had accompanied us so far on our road, and remained with us during the night. Two bad-looking fellows, who were detected in stealing, were tied and laid before the fire, and guard mounted over them during the night. The night was cold, and partially clear.

November 26.—The morning was cloudy and misty, and but a few stars visible. During the night water froze in the tents, and at sunrise

---

87. The Chinook Indian was known as William, and he did go all the way home with JCF. For his desire to return to his own people, see Doc. Nos. 124 and 128, 25 April and 5 May 1845. He may also be a *voyageur,* William Perkins (see Doc. No. 95, notes 135 and 136). The boy was probably named for the missionary H. W. K. Perkins.

88. JCF now starts south from the Dalles, journeying through central Oregon along the waters of the Deschutes.

the thermometer was at 20°. Left camp at 10 o'clock, the road leading along tributaries of the Tinanens, and being, so far, very good.
We turned to the right at the fork of the trail, ascending by a steep
ascent along a spur to the dividing grounds between this stream and
the waters of Fall river. The creeks we had passed were timbered
principally with oak and other deciduous trees. Snow lies every
where here on the ground, and we had a slight fall during the morning; but towards noon the gray sky yielded to a bright sun. This
morning we had a grand view of St. Helens and Regnier: the latter
appeared of a conical form, and very lofty, leading the eye far up
into the sky. The line of the timbered country is very distinctly
marked here, the bare hills making with it a remarkable contrast.
The summit of the ridge commanded a fine view of the Taih
[Tygh] prairie, and the stream running through it, which is a tributary to the Fall river, the chasm of which is visible to the right. A
steep descent of a mountain hill brought us down into the valley,
and we encamped on the stream after dark, guided by the light of
fires, which some naked Indians belonging to a village on the opposite side were kindling for us on the bank. This is a large branch
[White River] of the Fall river. There was a broad band of thick ice
some fifteen feet wide on either bank, and the river current is swift
and bold. The night was cold and clear, and we made our astronomical observation this evening with the thermometer at 20°.

In anticipation of coming hardship, and to spare our horses, there
was much walking done to-day; and Mr. Fitzpatrick and myself
made the day's journey on foot. Somewhere near the mouth of this
stream are the falls from which the river takes its name.

November 27.—A fine view of Mount Hood this morning; a rose-
colored mass of snow, bearing S. 85° W. by compass. The sky is
clear, and the air cold; the thermometer 2°.5 below zero; the trees
and bushes glittering white, and the rapid stream filled with floating
ice.

Stiletsi and *the White Crane,* two Indian chiefs who had accompanied us thus far, took their leave, and we resumed our journey at
10 o'clock. We ascended by a steep hill from the river bottom, which
is sandy, to a volcanic plain, around which lofty hills sweep in a regular form. It is cut up by gullies of basaltic rock, escarpments of
which appear every where in the hills. This plain is called the Taih
prairie [Tygh Valley], and is sprinkled with some scattered pines.
The country is now far more interesting to a traveller than the route

along the Snake and Columbia rivers. To our right we had always the mountains, from the midst of whose dark pine forests the isolated snowy peaks were looking out like giants. They served us for grand beacons to show the rate at which we advanced in our journey. Mount Hood was already becoming an old acquaintance, and, when we ascended the prairie, we obtained a bearing to Mount Jefferson, S. 23° W. The Indian superstition has peopled these lofty peaks with evil spirits, and they have never yet known the tread of a human foot. Sternly drawn against the sky, they look so high and steep, so snowy and rocky, that it would appear almost impossible to climb them; but still a trial would have its attractions for the adventurous traveller. A small trail takes off through the prairie, towards a low point in the range, and perhaps there is here a pass into the Walahmette valley. Crossing the plain, we descended by a rocky hill into the bed of a tributary [Nena Creek] of Fall river, and made an early encampment. The water was in holes, and frozen over, and we were obliged to cut through the ice for the animals to drink. An ox, which was rather troublesome to drive, was killed here for food.

The evening was fine, the sky being very clear, and I obtained an immersion of the third satellite, with a good observation of an emersion of the first; the latter of which gives for the longitude, 121° 02′ 43″; the latitude, by observation, being 45° 06′ 45″. The night was cold—the thermometer during the observations standing at 9°.

November 28.—The sky was clear in the morning, but suddenly clouded over, and at sunrise began to snow, with the thermometer at 18°.

We traversed a broken high country, partly timbered with pine, and about noon crossed a mountainous ridge, in which, from the rock occasionally displayed, the formation consists of compact lava. Frequent tracks of elk were visible in the snow. On our right, in the afternoon, a high plain, partially covered with pine, extended about ten miles, to the foot of the Cascade mountains.

At evening we encamped in a basin narrowly surrounded by rocky hills, after a day's journey of 21 miles. The surrounding rocks are either volcanic products, or highly altered by volcanic action, consisting of quartz and reddish-colored siliceous masses.

November 29.—We emerged from the basin, by a narrow pass, upon a considerable branch of Fall river, running to the eastward through a narrow valley. The trail, descending this stream, brought us to a locality of hot springs, which were on either bank. Those on the left, which were formed into deep handsome basins, would have been delightful baths, if the outer air had not been so keen, the thermometer in these being at 89°. There were others, on the opposite side, at the foot of an escarpment, in which the temperature of the water was 134°. These waters deposited around the spring a brecciated mass of quartz and feldspar, much of it of a reddish color [on Warm Springs River].

We crossed the stream here, and ascended again to a high plain, from an elevated point of which we obtained a view of six of the great peaks—Mount Jefferson, followed to the southward by two others of the same class; and succeeding, at a still greater distance to the southward, were three other lower peaks, clustering together in a branch ridge. These, like the great peaks, were snowy masses, secondary only to them; and, from the best examination our time permitted, we are inclined to believe that the range to which they belong is a branch from the great chain which here bears to the westward. The trail during the remainder of the day followed near to the large stream on the left, which was continuously walled in between high rocky banks. We halted for the night on a little by-stream.

November 30.—Our journey to-day was short. Passing over a high plain, on which were scattered cedars, with frequent beds of volcanic rock in fragments interspersed among the grassy grounds, we arrived suddenly on the verge of the steep and rocky descent to the valley of the stream we had been following, and which here ran directly across our path, emerging from the mountains on the right. You will remark that the country is abundantly watered with large streams, which pour down from the neighboring range.

These streams are characterized by the narrow and chasm-like valleys in which they run, generally sunk a thousand feet below the plain. At the verge of this plain, they frequently commence in vertical precipices of basaltic rock, and which leave only casual places at which they can be entered by horses. The road across the country, which would otherwise be very good, is rendered impracticable for wagons by these streams. There is another trail among the mountains, usually followed in the summer, which the snows now compelled us to avoid; and I have reason to believe that this, passing nearer the heads of these streams, would afford a much better road.

At such places, the gun carriage was unlimbered, and separately descended by hand. Continuing a few miles up the left bank of the river, we encamped early in an open bottom among the pines, a short distance below a lodge of Indians. Here, along the river the bluffs present escarpments seven or eight hundred feet in height, containing strata of a very fine porcelain clay, overlaid, at the height of about five hundred feet, by a massive stratum of compact basalt one hundred feet in thickness, which again is succeeded above by other strata of volcanic rocks. The clay strata are variously colored, some of them very nearly as white as chalk, and very fine grained. Specimens brought from these have been subjected to microscopical examination by Professor [J. W.] Bailey, of West Point, and are considered by him to constitute one of the most remarkable deposites of fluviatile infusoria on record. While they abound in genera and species which are common in fresh water, but which rarely thrive where the water is even brackish, not one decidedly marine form is to be found among them; and their fresh-water origin is therefore beyond a doubt. It is equally certain that they lived and died at the situation where they were found, as they could scarcely have been transported by running waters without an admixture of sandy particles; from which, however, they are remarkably free. Fossil infusoria of a fresh-water origin had been previously detected by Mr. Bailey in specimens brought by Mr. James D. Dana from the tertiary formation of Oregon. Most of the species in those specimens differed so much from those now living and known, that he was led to infer that they might belong to extinct species, and considered them also as affording proof of an alternation, in the formation from which they were obtained, of fresh and salt water deposites, which, common enough in Europe, had not hitherto been noticed in the United States. Coming evidently from a locality entirely different, our specimens* show very few species in common with those brought by Mr. Dana, but bear a much closer resemblance to those inhabiting the northeastern States. It is possible that they are from a more recent deposite; but the presence of a few remarkable forms which are common to the two localities renders it more probable that there is no great difference in their age.

I obtained here a good observation of an emersion of the second

* The specimens obtained at this locality are designated in the appendix by the Nos. 53, 54, 55, 56, 57, 58, 59, 60. The results obtained by Mr. Bailey, in his examination of specimens from the infusorial strata, with a plate exhibiting some of the most interesting forms, will be found imbodied in the appendix.

satellite; but clouds, which rapidly overspread the sky, prevented the usual number of observations. Those which we succeeded in obtaining are, however, good; and give for the latitude of the place 44° 35′ 23″, and for the longitude from the satellite 121° 10′ 25″.

December 1.—A short distance above our encampment, we crossed this river, which was thickly lined along its banks with ice. In common with all these mountain streams, the water was very clear, and the current swift. It was not every where fordable, and the water was three or four feet deep at our crossing, and perhaps a hundred feet wide. As was frequently the case at such places, one of the mules got his pack, consisting of sugar, thoroughly wet, and turned into molasses. One of the guides informed me that this was a "salmon water," and pointed out several ingeniously contrived places to catch the fish; among the pines in the bottom I saw an immense one, about twelve feet in diameter. A steep ascent from the opposite bank delayed us again; and as, by the information of our guides, grass would soon become very scarce, we encamped on the height of land, in a marshy place among the pines, where there was an abundance of grass. We found here a single Nez Percé family, who had a very handsome horse in their drove, which we endeavored to obtain in exchange for a good cow; but the man "had two hearts," or, rather, he had one and his wife had another: she wanted the cow, but he loved the horse too much to part with it. These people attach great value to cattle, with which they are endeavoring to supply themselves.

December 2.—In the first rays of the sun, the mountain peaks this morning presented a beautiful appearance, the snow being entirely covered with a hue of rosy gold. We travelled to-day over a very stony, elevated plain, about which were scattered cedar and pine, and encamped on another large branch [Metolius River] of Fall river. We were gradually ascending to a more elevated region, which would have been indicated by the rapidly increasing quantities of snow and ice, had we not known it by other means. A mule which was packed with our cooking utensils wandered off among the pines unperceived, and several men were sent back to search for it.

December 3.—Leaving Mr. Fitzpatrick with the party, I went ahead with the howitzer and a few men, in order to gain time, as our progress with the gun was necessarily slower. The country continued the same—very stony, with cedar and pine; and we rode on until dark, when we encamped on a hill side covered with snow, which we used to-night for water, as we were unable to reach any stream.

December 4.—Our animals had taken the back track, although a great number were hobbled; and we were consequently delayed until noon. Shortly after we had left this encampment, the mountain trail from Dalles joined that on which we were travelling. After passing for several miles over an artemisia plain, the trail entered a beautiful pine forest, through which we travelled for several hours; and about 4 o'clock descended into the valley of another large branch, on the bottom of which were spaces of open pines, with occasional meadows of good grass, in one of which we encamped. The stream is very swift and deep, and about 40 feet wide, and nearly half frozen over. Among the timber here, are larches 140 feet high, and over 3 feet in diameter. We had to-night the rare sight of a lunar rainbow.

December 5.—To-day the country was all pine forest; and beautiful weather made our journey delightful. It was too warm at noon for winter clothes; and the snow, which lay every where in patches through the forest, was melting rapidly. After a few hours' ride, we came upon a fine stream in the midst of the forest, which proved to be the principal branch of Fall [Deschutes] river. It was occasionally 200 feet wide—sometimes narrowed to 40 feet; the waters very clear, and frequently deep. We ascended along the river, which sometimes presented sheets of foaming cascades; its banks occasionally blackened with masses of scoriated rock, and found a good encampment on the verge of an open bottom, which had been an old camping ground of the Cayuse Indians. A great number of deer horns were lying about, indicating game in the neighborhood. The timber was uniformly large; some of the pines measuring 22 feet in circumference at the ground, and 12 to 13 feet at six feet above.

In all our journeying, we had never travelled through a country where the rivers were so abounding in falls, and the name of this stream is singularly characteristic. At every place where we come in the neighborhood of the river, is heard the roaring of falls. The rock along the banks of the stream, and the ledge over which it falls, is a scoriated basalt, with a bright metallic fracture. The stream goes over in one clear pitch, succeeded by a foaming cataract of several hundred yards. In the little bottom above the falls, a small stream discharges into an *entonnoir,* and disappears below.

583

We had made an early encampment, and in the course of the evening Mr. Fitzpatrick joined us here with the lost mule. Our lodge poles were nearly worn out, and we found here a handsome set, leaning against one of the trees, very white, and cleanly scraped. Had the owners been here, we would have purchased them; but as they were not, we merely left the old ones in their place, with a small quantity of tobacco.

December 6.—The morning was frosty and clear. We continued up the stream on undulating forest ground, over which there was scattered much fallen timber. We met here a village of Nez Percé Indians, who appeared to be coming down from the mountains, and had with them fine bands of horses. With them were a few Snake Indians of the root-digging species. From the forest we emerged into an open valley ten or twelve miles wide, through which the stream was flowing tranquilly, upward of two hundred feet broad, with occasional islands, and bordered with fine broad bottoms. Crossing the river, which here issues from a great mountain ridge on the right, we continued up the southern and smaller branch [Little Deschutes River], over a level country, consisting of fine meadow land, alternating with pine forests, and encamped on it early in the evening. A warm sunshine made the day pleasant.

December 7.—To-day we had good travelling ground; the trail leading sometimes over rather sandy soils in the pine forest, and sometimes over meadow land along the stream. The great beauty of the country in summer constantly suggested itself to our imaginations; and even now we found it beautiful, as we rode along these meadows, from half a mile to two miles wide. The rich soil and excellent water, surrounded by noble forests, make a picture that would delight the eye of a farmer; and I regret that the very small scale of the map would not allow us to give some representation of these features of the country.

I observed to-night an occultation of η *Geminorum;* which, although at the bright limb of the moon, appears to give a very good result, that has been adopted for the longitude. The occultation, observations of satellites, and our position deduced from daily surveys with the compass, agree remarkably well together, and mutually support and strengthen each other. The latitude of the camp is 43° 30′ 36″; and longitude, deduced from the occultation, 121° 33′ 50″.

December 8.—To-day we crossed the last branch [Little Deschutes] of the Fall river, issuing, like all the others we had crossed, in a southwesterly direction from the mountains. Our direction was a little east of south, the trail leading constantly through pine forests. The soil was generally bare, consisting, in greater part, of a yellowish white pumice stone, producing varieties of magnificent pines, but not a blade of grass; and to-night our horses were obliged to do without food, and use snow for water. These pines are remarkable for the red color of the bolls; and among them occurs a species, of which the Indians had informed me when leaving the Dalles. The unusual size of the cone (16 to 18 inches long) had attracted their attention; and they pointed it out to me among the curiosities of the country. They are more remarkable for their large diameter than their height, which usually averages only about 120 feet. The leaflets are short—only two or three inches long, and five in a sheath; the bark of a red color.

December 9.—The trail leads always through splendid pine forests. Crossing dividing grounds by a very fine road, we descended very gently towards the south. The weather was pleasant, and we halted late. The soil was very much like that of yesterday; and on the surface of a hill, near our encampment, were displayed beds of pumice stone; but the soil produced no grass, and again the animals fared badly.

December 10.—The country began to improve; and about 11 o'clock we reached a spring of cold water on the edge of a savannah, or grassy meadow, which our guides informed us was an arm of the Tlamath lake; and a few miles further we entered upon an extensive meadow, or lake of grass, surrounded by timbered mountains. This was the Tlamath lake.[89] It was a picturesque and beautiful spot, and rendered more attractive to us by the abundant and excellent grass, which our animals, after travelling through pine forests, so much needed; but the broad sheet of water which constitutes a lake was not to be seen. Overlooking it, immediately west, were several snowy knobs, belonging to what we have considered a branch of the Cascade range. A low point covered with pines made out into the lake, which afforded us a good place for an encampment, and for the security of our horses, which were guarded in view on the open meadow. The character of courage and hostility attributed to the Indians of

---

89. The largest body of water in Oregon, now called Upper Klamath Lake, had been JCF's destination, but he failed to reach it. He has now reached Klamath Marsh, some thirty miles to the north of the lake, lying partly inside the Klamath National Forest Wildlife Refuge. He will now turn to the east.

this quarter induced more than usual precaution; and, seeing smokes rising from the middle of the lake (or savannah) and along the opposite shores, I directed the howitzer to be fired. It was the first time our guides had seen it discharged; and the bursting of the shell at a distance, which was something like the second fire of the gun, amazed and bewildered them with delight. It inspired them with triumphant feelings; but on the camps at a distance the effect was different, for the smokes in the lake and on the shores immediately disappeared.

The point on which we were encamped forms, with the opposite eastern shore, a narrow neck, connecting the body of the lake with a deep cove or bay which receives the principal affluent stream, and over the greater part of which the water (or rather ice) was at this time dispersed in shallow pools. Among the grass, and scattered over the prairie lake, appeared to be similar marshes. It is simply a shallow basin, which, for a short period at the time of melting snows, is covered with water from the neighboring mountains; but this probably soon runs off, and leaves for the remainder of the year a green savannah, through the midst of which the river Tlamath,[90] which flows to the ocean, winds its way to the outlet on the southwestern side.

December 11.—No Indians made their appearance, and I determined to pay them a visit. Accordingly, the people were gathered together, and we rode out towards the village in the middle of the lake, which one of our guides had previously visited. It could not be directly approached, as a large part of the lake appeared a marsh; and there were sheets of ice among the grass, on which our horses could not keep their footing. We therefore followed the guide for a considerable distance along the forest; and then turned off towards the village, which we soon began to see was a few large huts, on the tops of which were collected the Indians. When we had arrived within half a mile of the village, two persons were seen advancing to meet us; and, to please the fancy of our guides, we ranged ourselves into a long line, riding abreast, while they galloped ahead to meet the strangers.

We were surprised, on riding up, to find one of them a woman, having never before known a squaw to take any part in the business of war. They were the village chief and his wife, who, in excitement

---

90. The Williamson River.

and alarm at the unusual event and appearance, had come out to meet their fate together. The chief was a very prepossessing Indian, with very handsome features, and a singularly soft and agreeable voice—so remarkable as to attract general notice.

The huts were grouped together on the bank of the river, which, from being spread out in a shallow marsh at the upper end of the lake, was collected here into a single stream. They were large round huts, perhaps 20 feet in diameter, with rounded tops, on which was the door by which they descended into the interior. Within, they were supported by posts and beams.

Almost like plants, these people seem to have adapted themselves to the soil, and to be growing on what the immediate locality afforded. Their only subsistence at this time appeared to be a small fish, great quantities of which, that had been smoked and dried, were suspended on strings about the lodge. Heaps of straw were lying around; and their residence in the midst of grass and rushes had taught them a peculiar skill in converting this material to useful purposes. Their shoes were made of straw or grass, which seemed well adapted for a snowy country; and the women wore on their head a closely woven basket, which made a very good cap. Among other things, were parti-colored mats about four feet square, which we purchased to lay on the snow under our blankets, and to use for table cloths.

Numbers of singular-looking dogs, resembling wolves, were sitting on the tops of the huts; and of these we purchased a young one, which, after its birthplace, was named Tlamath. The language spoken by these Indians is different from that of the Shoshonee and Columbia river tribes; and otherwise than by signs they cannot understand each other. They made us comprehend that they were at war with the people who lived to the southward and to the eastward; but I could obtain from them no certain information. The river on which they live enters the Cascade mountains on the western side of the lake, and breaks through them by a passage impracticable for travellers; but over the mountains, to the northward, are passes which present no other obstacle than in the almost impenetrable forests. Unlike any Indians we had previously seen, these wore shells in their noses. We returned to our camp, after remaining here an hour or two, accompanied by a number of Indians.

In order to recruit a little the strength of our animals, and obtain some acquaintance with the locality, we remained here for the remainder of the day. By observation, the latitude of the camp was 42° 56' 51"; and the diameter of the lake, or meadow, as has been intimated, about 20 miles. It is a picturesque and beautiful spot; and, under the hand of cultivation, might become a little paradise. Game is found in the forest; timbered and snowy mountains skirt it, and fertility characterizes it. Situated near the heads of three rivers, and on the line of inland communication with California, and near to Indians noted for treachery, it will naturally, in the progress of the settlement of Oregon, become a point for military occupation and settlement.

From Tlamath lake, the further continuation of our voyage assumed a character of discovery and exploration, which, from the Indians here, we could obtain no information to direct, and where the imaginary maps of the country, instead of assisting, exposed us to suffering and defeat. In our journey across the desert, Mary's lake, and the famous Buenaventura river, were two points on which I relied to recruit the animals, and repose the party. Forming, agreeably to the best maps in my possession, a connected water line from the Rocky mountains to the Pacific ocean, I felt no other anxiety than to pass safely across the intervening desert to the banks of the Buenaventura, where, in the softer climate of a more southern latitude, our horses might find grass to sustain them, and ourselves be sheltered from the rigors of winter and from the inhospitable desert. The guides who had conducted us thus far on our journey were about to return; and I endeavored in vain to obtain others to lead us, even for a few days, in the direction (east) which we wished to go. The chief to whom I applied alleged the want of horses, and the snow on the mountains across which our course would carry us, and the sickness of his family, as reasons for refusing to go with us.

December 12.—This morning the camp was thronged with Tlamath Indians from the southeastern shore of the lake; but, knowing the treacherous disposition which is a remarkable characteristic of the Indians south of the Columbia, the camp was kept constantly on its guard. I was not unmindful of the disasters which Smith and other travellers had met with in this country,[91] and therefore was equally vigilant in guarding against treachery and violence.

---

91. Jedediah Smith and his party of trappers were on their way from California to Fort Vancouver in 1828 when they were attacked on 14 July by

According to the best information I had been able to obtain from the Indians, in a few days' travelling we should reach another large water, probably a lake, which they indicated exactly in the course we were about to pursue. We struck our tents at 10 o'clock, and crossed the lake [marsh] in a nearly east direction, where it has the least extension—the breadth of the arm being here only about a mile and a half. There were ponds of ice, with but little grass, for the greater part of the way; and it was difficult to get the pack animals across, which fell frequently, and could not get up with their loads, unassisted. The morning was very unpleasant, snow falling at intervals in large flakes, and the sky dark. In about two hours we succeeded in getting the animals over; and, after travelling another hour along the eastern shore of the lake, we turned up into a cove where there was a sheltered place among the timber, with good grass, and encamped. The Indians, who had accompanied us so far, returned to their village on the southeastern shore. Among the pines here, I noticed some five or six feet in diameter.

December 13.—The night has been cold; the peaks around the lake gleam out brightly in the morning sun, and the thermometer is at zero. We continued up the hollow formed by a small affluent to the lake, and immediately entered an open pine forest on the mountain. The way here was sometimes obstructed by fallen trees, and the snow was four to twelve inches deep. The mules at the gun pulled heavily, and walking was a little laborious. In the midst of the wood, we heard the sound of galloping horses, and were agreeably surprised by the unexpected arrival of our Tlamath chief, with several Indians. He seemed to have found his conduct inhospitable in letting the strangers depart without a guide through the snow, and had come, with a few others, to pilot us a day or two on the way. After travelling in an easterly direction through the forest for about four hours, we reached a considerable stream, with a border of good grass; and here, by the advice of our guides, we encamped. It is about thirty feet wide, and two to four feet deep; the water clear, with some current; and, according to the information of our Indians, is

Indians of the Umpqua River region. Fifteen men were killed. Smith and the two men who were away from the camp with him, searching for a road, escaped, as did another who fled the scene. Smith went on to Fort Vancouver, where he was befriended by Dr. McLoughlin (MORGAN [1], 268–70).

the principal affluent to the lake, and the head water of the Tlamath river.

A very clear sky enabled me to obtain here to-night good observations, including an emersion of the first satellite of Jupiter, which give for the longitude 121° 20' 42", and for the latitude 42° 51' 26". This emersion coincides remarkably well with the result obtained from an occultation at the encampment of December 7th to 8th, 1843; from which place, the line of our survey gives an easting of thirteen miles. The day's journey was 12 miles.

December 14.—Our road was over a broad mountain, and we rode seven hours in a thick snow storm, always through pine forests, when we came down upon the head waters of another stream, on which there was grass. The snow lay deep on the ground, and only the high swamp grass appeared above. The Indians were thinly clad, and I had remarked during the day that they suffered from the cold. This evening they told me that the snow was getting too deep on the mountain, and I could not induce them to go any farther. The stream we had struck issued from the mountain in an easterly direction, turning to the southward a short distance below; and, drawing its course upon the ground, they made us comprehend that it pursued its way for a long distance in that direction, uniting with many other streams, and gradually becoming a great river. Without the subsequent information, which confirmed the opinion, we became immediately satisfied that this water formed the principal stream of the *Sacramento* river;[92] and, consequently, that this main affluent of the bay of San Francisco had its source within the limits of the United States, and opposite a tributary to the Columbia, and near the head of the Tlamath river, which goes to the ocean north of 42°, and within the United States.

December 15.—A present, consisting of useful goods, afforded much satisfaction to our guides; and, showing them the national flag, I explained that it was a symbol of our nation; and they engaged always to receive it in a friendly manner. The chief pointed out a course, by following which we would arrive at the big water, where no more snow was to be found. Travelling in a direction N. 60° E. by compass, which the Indians informed me would avoid a

92. An incorrect conclusion. He is still in the Klamath Lake watershed, and has reached a tributary, perhaps Beaver Creek, of the Sycan River. Its waters eventually flow into the Klamath River, issuing from Upper Klamath Lake.

bad mountain to the right, we crossed the Sacramento where it turned to the southward, and entered a grassy level plain—a smaller Grand Rond; from the lower end of which the river issued into an inviting country of low rolling hills. Crossing a hard-frozen swamp on the farther side of the Rond, we entered again the pine forest, in which very deep snow made our travelling slow and laborious. We were slowly but gradually ascending a mountain; and, after a hard journey of seven hours, we came to some naked places among the timber, where a few tufts of grass showed above the snow, on the side of a hollow; and here we encamped. Our cow, which every day got poorer, was killed here, but the meat was rather tough.

December 16.—We travelled this morning through snow about three feet deep, which, being crusted, very much cut the feet of our animals. The mountain still gradually rose; we crossed several spring heads covered with quaking asp; otherwise it was all pine forest. The air was dark with falling snow, which every where weighed down the trees. The depths of the forest were profoundly still; and below, we scarce felt a breath of the wind which whirled the snow through their branches. I found that it required some exertion of constancy to adhere steadily to one course through the woods, when we were uncertain how far the forest extended, or what lay beyond; and, on account of our animals, it would be bad to spend another night on the mountain. Towards noon the forest looked clear ahead, appearing suddenly to terminate; and beyond a certain point we could see no trees. Riding rapidly ahead to this spot, we found ourselves on the verge of a vertical and rocky wall of the mountain. At our feet—more than a thousand feet below—we looked into a green prairie country, in which a beautiful lake, some twenty miles in length, was spread along the foot of the mountains, its shores bordered with green grass.[93] Just then the sun broke out among the clouds, and illuminated the country below, while around us the storm raged fiercely. Not a particle of ice was to be seen on the lake, or snow on its borders, and all was like summer or spring. The glow of the sun in the valley below brightened up our hearts with sudden pleasure; and we made the woods ring with joyful shouts to those behind; and gradually, as each came up, he stopped to enjoy

---

93. Summer Lake, on the eastern edge of Klamath National Forest. It is landlocked, having no external drainage, and its alkaline waters support waterfowl but no fish.

the unexpected scene. Shivering on snow three feet deep, and stiffening in a cold north wind, we exclaimed at once that the names of Summer Lake and Winter Ridge should be applied to these two proximate places of such sudden and violent contrast.

We were now immediately on the verge of the forest land, in which we had been travelling so many days; and, looking forward to the east, scarce a tree was to be seen. Viewed from our elevation, the face of the country exhibited only rocks and grass, and presented a region in which the artemisia became the principal wood, furnishing to its scattered inhabitants fuel for their fires, building material for their huts, and shelter for the small game which ministers to their hunger and nakedness. Broadly marked by the boundary of the mountain wall, and immediately below us, were the first waters of that Great Interior Basin which has the Wahsatch and Bear river mountains for its eastern, and the Sierra Nevada for its western rim; and the edge of which we had entered upwards, of three months before, at the Great Salt lake.

When we had sufficiently admired the scene below, we began to think about descending, which here was impossible, and we turned towards the north, travelling always along the rocky wall. We continued on for four or five miles, making ineffectual attempts at several places; and at length succeeded in getting down at one which was extremely difficult of descent. Night had closed in before the foremost reached the bottom, and it was dark before we all found ourselves together in the valley. There were three or four half dead dry cedar trees on the shore, and those who first arrived kindled bright fires to light on the others. One of the mules rolled over and over two or three hundred feet into a ravine, but recovered himself, without any other injury than to his pack; and the howitzer was left midway the mountain until morning. By observation, the latitude of this encampment is 42° 57′ 22″. It delayed us until near noon the next day to recover ourselves and put every thing in order; and we made only a short camp along the western shore of the lake, which, in the summer temperature we enjoyed to-day, justified the name we had given it. Our course would have taken us to the other shore, and over the highlands beyond; but I distrusted the appearance of the country, and decided to follow a plainly beaten Indian trail leading along the side of the lake. We were now in a country where the scarcity of water and of grass makes travelling dangerous, and great caution was necessary.

December 18.—We continued on the trail along the narrow strip of land between the lake and the high rocky wall, from which we had looked down two days before. Almost every half mile we crossed a little spring, or stream of pure cold water; and the grass was certainly as fresh and green as in the early spring. From the white efflorescence along the shore of the lake, we were enabled to judge the water was impure, like that of lakes we subsequently found; but the mud prevented us from approaching it. We encamped near the eastern point of the lake, where there appeared between the hills a broad and low connecting hollow with the country beyond. From a rocky hill in the rear, I could see, marked out by a line of yellow dried grass, the bed of a stream, which probably connected the lake with other waters in the spring.

The observed latitude of this encampment is 42° 42′ 37″.

December 19.—After two hours' ride in an easterly direction, through a low country, the high ridge with pine forest still to our right, and a rocky and bald but lower one on the left, we reached a considerable fresh-water stream, which issues from the piney mountains. So far as we had been able to judge, between this stream and the lake we had crossed dividing grounds; and there did not appear to be any connexion, as might be inferred from the impure condition of the lake water.

The rapid stream of pure water,[94] roaring along between banks overhung with aspens and willows, was a refreshing and unexpected sight; and we followed down the course of the stream, which brought us soon into a marsh, or dry lake, formed by the expanding waters of the stream. It was covered with high reeds and rushes, and large patches of ground had been turned up by the squaws in digging for roots, as if a farmer had been preparing the land for grain. I could not succeed in finding the plant for which they had been digging. There were frequent trails, and fresh tracks of Indians; and, from the abundant signs visible, the black-tailed hare appears to be numerous here. It was evident that, in other seasons, this place was a sheet of water. Crossing this marsh towards the eastern hills, and passing over a bordering plain of heavy sands, covered with artemisia, we encamped before sundown on the creek, which here was very small, having lost its water in the marshy grounds. We found here tolerably good grass. The wind to-night was high, and

---

94. Probably the Chewaucan River.

we had no longer our huge pine fires, but were driven to our old resource of small dried willows and artemisia. About twelve miles ahead, the valley appears to be closed in by a high, dark-looking ridge.

December 20.—Travelling for a few hours down the stream this morning, we turned a point of the hill on our left, and came suddenly in sight of another and much larger lake, which, along its eastern shore, was closely bordered by the high black ridge which walled it in by a precipitous face on this side. Throughout this region the face of the country is characterized by these precipices of black volcanic rock, generally enclosing the valleys of streams, and frequently terminating the hills. Often in the course of our journey we would be tempted to continue our road up the gentle ascent of a sloping hill, which, at the summit, would terminate abruptly in a black precipice. Spread out over a length of 20 miles, the lake, when we first came in view, presented a handsome sheet of water; and I gave to it the name of Lake Abert,[95] in honor of the chief of the corps to which I belonged. The fresh-water stream we had followed emptied into the lake by a little fall; and I was doubtful for a moment whether to go on, or encamp at this place. The miry ground in the neighborhood of the lake did not allow us to examine the water conveniently, and, being now on the borders of a desert country, we were moving cautiously. It was, however, still early in the day, and I continued on, trusting either that the water would be drinkable, or that we should find some little spring from the hill side. We were following an Indian trail which led along the steep rocky precipice; a black ridge along the western shore holding out no prospect whatever. The white efflorescences which lined the shore like a bank of snow, and the disagreeable odor which filled the air as soon as we came near, informed us too plainly that the water belonged to one of those fetid salt lakes which are common in this region. We continued until late in the evening to work along the rocky shore, but, as often afterwards, the dry inhospitable rock deceived us; and, halting on the lake, we kindled up fires to guide those who

---

95. Lake Abert, about twenty-five air-line miles southwest of Summer Lake, is another of those landlocked bodies of water of the region into which a high concentration of salts has leached from the surrounding land. Like Summer Lake, it supports no fish, and has the typical pale green cast of an alkaline lake. A steep and barren escarpment along the east side, which JCF later describes, is now called Abert Rim.

594

were straggling along behind. We tried the water, but it was impossible to drink it, and most of the people to-night lay down without eating; but some of us, who had always a great reluctance to close the day without supper, dug holes along the shore, and obtained water, which, being filtered, was sufficiently palatable to be used, but still retained much of its nauseating taste. There was very little grass for the animals, the shore being lined with a luxuriant growth of chenopodiaceous shrubs, which burned with a quick bright flame, and made our firewood.

The next morning we had scarcely travelled two hours along the shore when we reached a place where the mountains made a bay, leaving at their feet a low bottom around the lake. Here we found numerous hillocks covered with rushes, in the midst of which were deep holes, or springs of pure water; and the bottom was covered with grass, which, although of a salt and unwholesome quality, and mixed with saline efflorescences, was still abundant, and made a good halting place to recruit our animals; and we accordingly encamped here for the remainder of the day. I rode ahead several miles to ascertain if there was any appearance of a watercourse entering the lake; but found none, the hills preserving their dry character, and the shore of the lake sprinkled with the same white powdery substance, and covered with the same shrubs. There were flocks of ducks on the lake, and frequent tracks of Indians along the shore, where the grass had been recently burnt by their fires.

We ascended the bordering mountain, in order to obtain a more perfect view of the lake in sketching its figure; hills sweep entirely around its basin, from which the waters have no outlet.

December 22.—To-day we left this forbidding lake. Impassable rocky ridges barred our progress to the eastward, and I accordingly bore off towards the south, over an extensive sage plain. At a considerable distance ahead, and a little on our left, was a range of snowy mountains, and the country declined gradually towards the foot of a high and nearer ridge immediately before us, which presented the feature of black precipices, now becoming common to the country. On the summit of the ridge, snow was visible; and there being every indication of a stream at its base, we rode on until after dark, but were unable to reach it, and halted among the sage bushes on the open plain, without either grass or water. The two India-rubber bags had been filled with water in the morning, which afforded sufficient for the camp; and rain in the night formed pools, which relieved the thirst of the animals. Where we encamped on the bleak sandy plain, the Indians had made huts or circular enclosures, about four feet high and twelve feet broad, of artemisia bushes. Whether these had been forts or houses, or what they had been doing in such a desert place, we could not ascertain.

December 23.—The weather is mild; the thermometer at daylight 38°; the wind having been from the southward for several days. The country has a very forbidding appearance, presenting to the eye nothing but sage and barren ridges. We rode up towards the mountain, along the foot of which we found a lake [Anderson], which we could not approach on account of the mud; and, passing around its southern end, ascended the slope at the foot of the ridge, where in some hollows we had discovered bushes and small trees—in such situations, a sure sign of water. We found here several springs, and the hill side was well sprinkled with a species of *festuca*—a better grass than we had found for many days. Our elevated position gave us a good view over the country, but we discovered nothing very encouraging. Southward, about ten miles distant, was another small lake, towards which a broad trail led along the ridge; and this appearing to afford the most practicable route, I determined to continue our journey in that direction.

December 24.—We found the water of the lake tolerably pure, and encamped at the farther end. There were some good grass and canes along the shore, and the vegetation at this place consisted principally of chenopodiaceous shrubs.

December 25.—We were roused, on Christmas morning, by a discharge from the small arms and howitzer, with which our people saluted the day; and the name of which we bestowed on the lake.[96] It was the first time, perhaps, in this remote and desolate region, in which it had been so commemorated. Always, on days of religious or national commemoration, our voyageurs expect some unusual allowance; and, having nothing else, I gave them each a little brandy, (which was carefully guarded, as one of the most useful articles a traveller can carry,) with some coffee and sugar, which here, where every eatable was a luxury, was sufficient to make them

96. The lake which JCF named Christmas Lake was one of those in the Warner Lakes group, perhaps either Hart Lake (as MC ARTHUR believes) or Crump Lake. From personal observation we are inclined to choose the latter one, south of Hart, as the lake which JCF visited. In this view we are supported by staff members in the supervisor's office, Fremont National Forest.

a feast. The day was sunny and warm; and, resuming our journey, we crossed some slight dividing grounds into a similar basin, walled in on the right by a lofty mountain ridge. The plainly beaten trail still continued, and occasionally we passed camping grounds of the Indians, which indicated to me that we were on one of the great thoroughfares of the country. In the afternoon I attempted to travel in a more eastern direction; but, after a few laborious miles, was beaten back into the basin by an impassable country. There were fresh Indian tracks about the valley, and last night a horse was stolen. We encamped on the valley bottom, where there was some cream-like water in ponds, colored by a clay soil and frozen over. Chenopodiaceous shrubs constituted the growth, and made again our fire wood. The animals were driven to the hill, where there was tolerably good grass.

December 26.—Our general course was again south. The country consists of larger or smaller basins, into which the mountain waters run down, forming small lakes; they present a perfect level, from which the mountains rise immediately and abruptly. Between the successive basins, the dividing grounds are usually very slight; and it is probable that, in the seasons of high water, many of these basins are in communication. At such times there is evidently an abundance of water, though now we find scarcely more than the dry beds. On either side, the mountains, though not very high, appear to be rocky and sterile. The basin in which we were travelling declined towards the southwest corner, where the mountains indicated a narrow outlet; and, turning round a rocky point or cape, we continued up a lateral branch valley, in which we encamped at night on a rapid, pretty near the ridge, on the right side of the valley. It was bordered with grassy bottoms and clumps of willows, the water partially frozen. This stream belongs to the basin we had left. By a partial observation to-night, our camp was found to be directly on the 42d parallel [Oregon-Nevada line, ten miles east of the California line]. To-night a horse belonging to Carson, one of the best we had in the camp, was stolen by the Indians.

December 27.—We continued up the valley of the stream, the principal branch of which here issues from a bed of high mountains. We turned up a branch to the left, and fell into an Indian trail, which conducted us by a good road over open bottoms along the creek, where the snow was five or six inches deep. Gradually ascending, the trail led through a good broad pass in the mountain, where we found the snow about one foot deep. There were some remarkably large cedars in the pass, which were covered with an unusual quantity of frost, which we supposed might possibly indicate the neighborhood of water; and as, in the arbitrary position of Mary's lake, we were already beginning to look for it, this circumstance contributed to our hope of finding it near. Descending from the mountain, we reached another basin, on the flat lake bed [Dry or Alkali Lake] of which we found no water, and encamped among the sage on the bordering plain, where the snow was still about one foot deep. Among this the grass was remarkably green, and to-night the animals fared tolerably well.[97]

December 28.—The snow being deep, I had determined, if any more horses were stolen, to follow the tracks of the Indians into the mountains, and put a temporary check to their sly operations; but it did not occur again.

Our road this morning lay down a level valley, bordered by steep mountainous ridges, rising very abruptly from the plain. Artemisia was the principal plant, mingled with Fremontia and the chenopodiaceous shrubs. The artemisia was here extremely large, being sometimes a foot in diameter and eight feet high. Riding quietly along over the snow, we came suddenly upon smokes rising among these bushes; and, galloping up, we found two huts, open at the top, and loosely built of sage, which appeared to have been deserted at the instant; and, looking hastily around, we saw several Indians on the crest of the ridge near by, and several others scrambling up the side. We had come upon them so suddenly, that they had been well nigh surprised in their lodges. A sage fire was burning in the middle; a few baskets made of straw were lying about, with one or two rabbit skins; and there was a little grass scattered about, on which they had been lying. "Tabibo—bo!" they shouted from the hills—a word which, in the Snake language, signifies *white*—and remained looking at us from behind the rocks. Carson and Godey rode towards the hill, but the men ran off like deer. They had been so much pressed, that a woman with two children had dropped behind a sage bush near the lodge, and when Carson accidentally stumbled

---

97. JCF had crossed into what was then Mexican territory, now northern Washoe County, Nev., and had entered the basin of the Mud Lakes. For the next several days he would be making his way toward Pyramid Lake. The bracketed place-names supplied in the text are based mainly on the work of MACK.

598

upon her, she immediately began screaming in the extremity of fear, and shut her eyes fast, to avoid seeing him. She was brought back to the lodge, and we endeavored in vain to open a communication with the men. By dint of presents, and friendly demonstrations, she was brought to calmness; and we found that they belonged to the Snake nation, speaking the language of that people. Eight or ten appeared to live together, under the same little shelter; and they seemed to have no other subsistence than the roots or seeds they might have stored up, and the hares which live in the sage, and which they are enabled to track through the snow, and are very skilful in killing. Their skins afford them a little scanty covering. Herding together among bushes, and crouching almost naked over a little sage fire, using their instinct only to procure food, these may be considered, among human beings, the nearest approach to the mere animal creation. We have reason to believe that these had never before seen the face of a white man.

The day had been pleasant, but about two o'clock it began to blow; and crossing a slight dividing ground we encamped on the sheltered side of a hill, where there was good bunch grass, having made a day's journey of 24 miles. The night closed in, threatening snow; but the large sage bushes made bright fires.

December 29.—The morning mild, and at 4 o'clock it commenced snowing. We took our way across a plain, thickly covered with snow, towards a range of hills in the southeast. The sky soon became so dark with snow that little could be seen of the surrounding country; and we reached the summit of the hills in a heavy snow storm. On the side we had approached, this had appeared to be only a ridge of low hills; and we were surprised to find ourselves on the summit of a bed of broken mountains, which, as far as the weather would permit us to see, declined rapidly to some low country ahead, presenting a dreary and savage character; and for a moment I looked around in doubt on the wild and inhospitable prospect, scarcely knowing what road to take which might conduct us to some place of shelter for the night. Noticing among the hills the head of a grassy hollow, I determined to follow it, in the hope that it would conduct us to a stream. We followed a winding descent for several miles, the hollow gradually broadening into little meadows, and becoming the bed of a stream as we advanced; and towards night we were agreeably surprised by the appearance of a willow grove, where we found a sheltered camp, with water and excellent and abundant grass. The grass, which was covered by the snow on the bottom, was long and green, and the face of the mountain had a more favorable character in its vegetation, being smoother, and covered with good bunch grass. The snow was deep, and the night very cold. A broad trail had entered the valley from the right, and a short distance below the camp [at High Rock Creek] were the tracks where a considerable party of Indians had passed on horseback, who had turned out to the left, apparently with the view of crossing the mountains to the eastward.

December 30.—After following the stream for a few hours in a southeasterly direction, it entered a cañon where we could not follow; but determined not to leave the stream, we searched a passage below, where we could regain it, and entered a regular narrow valley. The water had now more the appearance of a flowing creek; several times we passed groves of willows, and we began to feel ourselves out of all difficulty. From our position, it was reasonable to conclude that this stream would find its outlet in Mary's lake, and conduct us into a better country. We had descended rapidly, and here we found very little snow. On both sides, the mountains showed often stupendous and curious-looking rocks, which at several places so narrowed the valley, that scarcely a pass was left for the camp. It was a singular place to travel through—shut up in the earth, a sort of chasm, the little strip of grass under our feet, the rough walls of bare rock on either hand, and the narrow strip of sky above. The grass to-night was abundant, and we encamped in high spirits.

December 31.—After an hour's ride this morning, our hopes were once more destroyed. The valley opened out, and before us again lay one of the dry basins [Soldier Meadows]. After some search, we discovered a high-water outlet [Soldier Creek], which brought us in a few miles, and by a descent of several hundred feet, into another long broad basin, in which we found the bed of a stream, and obtained sufficient water by cutting the ice. The grass on the bottoms was salt and unpalatable.

Here we concluded the year 1843, and our new year's eve was rather a gloomy one. The result of our journey began to be very uncertain; the country was singularly unfavorable to travel; the grasses being frequently of a very unwholesome character, and the hoofs of our animals were so worn and cut by the rocks, that many of them were lame, and could scarcely be got along [at the western edge of Black Rock Desert].

New Year's day, 1844.—We continued down the valley, between a dry-looking black ridge on the left and a more snowy and high one on the right. Our road was bad along the bottom, being broken by gullies and impeded by sage, and sandy on the hills, where there is not a blade of grass, nor does any appear on the mountains. The soil in many places consists of a fine powdery sand, covered with a saline efflorescence; and the general character of the country is desert. During the day we directed our course towards a black cape, at the foot of which a column of smoke indicated hot springs.

January 2.—We were on the road early, the face of the country hidden by falling snow. We travelled along the bed of the stream, in some places dry, in others covered with ice; the travelling being very bad, through deep fine sand, rendered tenacious by a mixture of clay. The weather cleared up a little at noon, and we reached the hot springs of which we had seen the vapor the day before. There was a large field of the usual salt grass here, peculiar to such places. The country otherwise is a perfect barren, without a blade of grass, the only plants being some dwarf Fremontias. We passed the rocky cape, a jagged broken point, bare and torn. The rocks are volcanic, and the hills here have a burnt appearance—cinders and coals occasionally appearing as at a blacksmith's forge. We crossed the large dry bed of a muddy lake in a southeasterly direction, and encamped at night without water and without grass, among sage bushes covered with snow. The heavy road made several mules give out to-day; and a horse, which had made the journey from the States successfully thus far, was left on the trail.

January 3.—A fog, so dense that we could not see a hundred yards, covered the country, and the men that were sent out after the horses were bewildered and lost; and we were consequently detained at camp until late in the day. Our situation had now become a serious one. We had reached and run over the position where, according to the best maps in my possession, we should have found Mary's lake, or river. We were evidently on the verge of the desert which had been reported to us; and the appearance of the country was so forbidding, that I was afraid to enter it, and determined to bear away to the southward, keeping close along the mountains, in the full expectation of reaching the Buenaventura river. This morning I put every man in the camp on foot—myself, of course, among the rest—and in this manner lightened by distribution the loads of the animals. We travelled seven or eight miles along the ridge bordering the valley, and encamped where there were a few bunches of grass on the bed of a hill torrent, without water. There were some large artemisias; but the principal plants are chenopodiaceous shrubs. The rock composing the mountains is here changed suddenly into white granite [Granite Range]. The fog showed the tops of the hills at sunset, and stars enough for observations in the early evening, and then closed over us as before. Latitude by observation, 40° 48' 15".

January 4.—The fog to-day was still more dense, and the people again were bewildered. We travelled a few miles around the western point of the ridge, and encamped where there were a few tufts of grass, but no water. Our animals now were in a very alarming state, and there was increased anxiety in the camp [in Granite Creek Desert].

January 5.—Same dense fog continued, and one of the mules died in camp this morning. I have had occasion to remark, on such occasions as these, that animals which are about to die leave the band, and coming into the camp, lie down about the fires. We moved to a place where there was a little better grass, about two miles distant. Taplin, one of our best men, who had gone out on a scouting excursion, ascended a mountain near by, and to his great surprise emerged into a region of bright sunshine, in which the upper parts of the mountain were glowing, while below all was obscured in the darkest fog.

January 6.—The fog continued the same, and, with Mr. Preuss and Carson, I ascended the mountain, to sketch the leading features of the country, as some indication of our future route, while Mr. Fitzpatrick explored the country below. In a very short distance we had ascended above the mist, but the view obtained was not very gratifying. The fog had partially cleared off from below when we reached the summit; and in the southwest corner of a basin communicating with that in which we had encamped, we saw a lofty column of smoke, 16 miles distant, indicating the presence of hot springs. There, also, appeared to be the outlet of those draining channels of the country; and, as such places afforded always more or less grass, I determined to steer in that direction. The ridge we had ascended appeared to be composed of fragments of white granite. We saw here traces of sheep and antelope.

Entering the neighboring valley, and crossing the bed of another lake, after a hard day's travel over ground of yielding mud and sand, we reached the springs, where we found an abundance of grass, which, though only tolerably good, made this place, with reference to the past, a refreshing and agreeable spot.

This is the most extraordinary locality of hot springs we had met during the journey. The basin of the largest one has a circumference of several hundred feet; but there is at one extremity a circular space of about fifteen feet in diameter, entirely occupied by the boiling water. It boils up at irregular intervals, and with much noise. The water is clear, and the spring deep; a pole about sixteen feet long was easily immersed in the centre, but we had no means of forming a good idea of the depth. It was surrounded on the margin with a border of *green* grass, and near the shore the temperature of the water was 206°. We had no means of ascertaining that of the center, where the heat was greatest; but, by dispersing the water with a pole, the temperature at the margin was increased to 208°, and in the centre it was doubtless higher. By driving the pole towards the bottom, the water was made to boil up with increased force and noise. There are several other interesting places, where water and smoke or gas escape, but they would require a long description. The water is impregnated with common salt, but not so much as to render it unfit for general cooking; and a mixture of snow made it pleasant to drink [the hot springs at Gerlach, Nev.]

In the immediate neighborhood, the valley bottom is covered almost exclusively with chenopodiaceous shrubs, of greater luxuriance, and larger growth, than we have seen them in any preceding part of the journey.

I obtained this evening some astronomical observations.

Our situation now required caution. Including those which gave out from the injured condition of their feet, and those stolen by Indians, we had lost, since leaving the Dalles of the Columbia, fifteen animals; and of these, nine had been left in the last few days. I therefore determined, until we reach a country of water and vegetation, to feel our way ahead, by having the line of route explored some fifteen or twenty miles in advance, and only to leave a present encampment when the succeeding one was known.

Taking with me Godey and Carson, I made to-day a thorough exploration of the neighboring valleys, and found in a ravine in the bordering mountains a good camping place, where was water in springs, and a sufficient quantity of grass for a night. Overshading the springs were some trees of the sweet cottonwood, which, after a long interval of absence, we saw again with pleasure, regarding them as harbingers of a better country. To us, they were eloquent of green prairies and buffalo. We found here a broad and plainly marked trail, on which there were tracks of horses, and we appeared to have regained one of the thoroughfares which pass by the watering places of the country. On the western mountains [Lake Mountains] of the valley, with which this of the boiling spring communicates, we remarked scattered cedars—probably an indication that we were on the borders of the timbered region extending to the Pacific. We reached the camp at sunset after a day's ride of about forty miles. The horses we rode were in good order, being of some that were kept for emergencies, and rarely used.

Mr. Preuss had ascended one of the mountains, and occupied the day in sketching the country; and Mr. Fitzpatrick had found, a few miles distant, a hollow of excellent grass and pure water, to which the animals were driven, as I remained another day to give them an opportunity to recruit their strength. Indians appear to be every where prowling about like wild animals, and there is a fresh trail across the snow in the valley near.

Latitude of the boiling springs, 40° 39′ 46″.

On the 9th we crossed over to the cottonwood camp. Among the shrubs on the hills were a few bushes of *ephedra occidentalis,* which afterwards occurred frequently along our road, and, as usual, the lowlands were occupied with artemisia. While the party proceeded to this place, Carson and myself reconnoitred the road in advance, and found another good encampment for the following day.

January 10.—We continued our reconnoisance ahead, pursuing a south direction in the basin along the ridge; the camp following slowly after. On a large trail there is never any doubt of finding suitable places for encampments. We reached the end of the basin, where we found, in a hollow of the mountain which enclosed it, an abundance of good bunch grass. Leaving a signal for the party to encamp, we continued our way up the hollow, intending to see what lay beyond the mountain. The hollow was several miles long, forming a good pass [Fremont Pass], the snow deepening to about a foot as we neared the summit. Beyond, a defile between the mountains descended rapidly about two thousand feet; and, filling up all the lower space, was a sheet of green water, some twenty miles broad. It broke upon our eyes like the ocean. The neighboring peaks rose high above us, and we ascended one of them to obtain a better view. The waves were curling in the breeze, and their dark-green color showed it to be a body of deep water. For a long time we sat enjoying the view, for we had become fatigued with mountains, and the free expanse of moving waves was very grateful. It was set like a gem in the mountains, which, from our position, seemed to enclose it almost entirely. At the western end it communicated with the line of basins we had left a few days since; and on the opposite side it swept a ridge of snowy mountains, the foot of the great Sierra. Its position at first inclined us to believe it Mary's lake, but the rugged mountains were so entirely discordant with descriptions of its low rushy shores and open country, that we concluded it some unknown body of water; which it afterwards proved to be.[98]

On our road down, the next day, we saw herds of mountain sheep, and encamped on a little stream at the mouth of the defile, about a mile from the margin of the water, to which we hurried down immediately. The water is so slightly salt, that, at first, we thought it fresh, and would be pleasant to drink when no other could be had. The shore was rocky—a handsome beach, which reminded us of the sea. On some large *granite* boulders that were scattered about the shore, I remarked a coating of a calcareous substance, in some places a few inches and in others a foot in thickness. Near our camp, the hills, which were of primitive rock, were also covered with this substance, which was in too great quantity on the mountains along the shore of the lake to have been deposited by water, and has the appearance of having been spread over the rocks in mass.*

* The label attached to a specimen of this rock was lost; but I append an analysis of that which, from memory, I judge to be the specimen.

Carbonate of lime	77.31
Carbonate of magnesia	5.25
Oxide of iron	1.60
Alumina	1.05
Silica	8.55
Organic matter, water, and loss	6.24
	100.00

98. Pyramid Lake, in Washoe County, northwestern Nevada, inside the boundaries of the Pyramid Lake Indian Reservation. The lake, about twenty-five miles long and from four to eleven miles wide, is fed by the Truckee River and has no outlet. Although the water contains a high concentration of minerals, it does support fish life. The shores are inhabited by the Northern Paiute Indians (but JCF thought he recognized a second tribe also). For a map tracing the probable route of the expedition around the lake, see the frontispiece in WHEELER.

Pyramid Lake

Where we had halted, appeared to be a favorite camping place for Indians.

January 13.—We followed again a broad Indian trail along the shore of the lake to the southward. For a short space we had room enough in the bottom; but, after travelling a short distance, the water swept the foot of precipitous mountains, the peaks of which are about 3,000 feet above the lake. The trail wound along the base of these precipices, against which the water dashed below, by a way nearly impracticable for the howitzer. During a greater part of the morning the lake was nearly hid by a snow storm, and the waves broken on the narrow beach in a long line of foaming surf, five or six feet high. The day was unpleasantly cold, the wind driving the snow sharp against our faces; and, having advanced only about 12 miles, we encamped in a bottom formed by a ravine, covered with good grass, which was fresh and green.

We did not get the howitzer into camp, but were obliged to leave it on the rocks until morning. We saw several flocks of sheep, but did not succeed in killing any. Ducks were riding on the waves, and several large fish were seen. The mountain sides were crusted with the calcareous cement previously mentioned. There were cheno-podiaceous and other shrubs along the beach; and, at the foot of the rocks, an abundance of *ephedra occidentalis,* whose dark-green color makes them evergreens among the shrubby growth of the lake. Towards evening the snow began to fall heavily, and the country had a wintry appearance.

The next morning the snow was rapidly melting under a warm sun. Part of the morning was occupied in bringing up the gun; and, making only nine miles, we encamped on the shore, opposite a very remarkable rock in the lake, which had attracted our attention for many miles. It rose, according to our estimate, 600 feet above the water; and, from the point we viewed it, presented a pretty exact outline of the great pyramid of Cheops. The accompanying drawing presents it as we saw it. Like other rocks along the shore, it seemed to be incrusted with calcareous cement. This striking feature suggested a name for the lake; and I called it Pyramid lake; and though it may be deemed by some a fanciful resemblance, I can undertake to say that the future traveller will find a much more striking resemblance between this rock and the pyramids of Egypt, than there is between them and the object from which they take their name.

The elevation of this lake above the sea is 4,890 feet, being nearly

700 feet higher than the Great Salt lake, from which it lies nearly west, and distant about eight degrees of longitude.[99] The position and elevation of this lake make it an object of geographical interest. It is the nearest lake to the western rim, as the Great Salt lake is to the eastern rim, of the Great Basin which lies between the base of the Rocky mountains and the Sierra Nevada; and the extent and character of which, its whole circumference and contents, it is so desirable to know.

The last of the cattle which had been driven from the Dalles was killed here for food, and was still in good condition.

January 15.—A few poor-looking Indians made their appearance this morning, and we succeeded in getting one into the camp. He was naked, with the exception of a tunic of hare skins. He told us that there was a river at the end of the lake, but that he lived in the rocks near by. From the few words our people could understand, he spoke a dialect of the Snake language; but we were not able to understand enough to know whether the river ran in or out, or what was its course; consequently, there still remained a chance that this might be Mary's lake.

Groves of large cottonwood, which we could see at the mouth of the river, indicated that it was a stream of considerable size; and, at all events, we had the pleasure to know that now we were in a country where human beings could live. Accompanied by the Indian, we resumed our road, passing on the way several caves in the rock where there were baskets and seeds; but the people had disappeared. We saw also horse tracks along the shore.

Early in the afternoon, when we were approaching the groves at the mouth of the river, three or four Indians met us on the trail. We had an explanatory conversation in signs, and then moved on together towards the village, which the chief said was encamped on the bottom.

Reaching the groves, we found the *inlet* of a large fresh-water stream, and all at once were satisfied that it was neither Mary's river nor the waters of the Sacramento, but that we had discovered a large interior lake, which the Indians informed us had no outlet. It is about 35 miles long; and, by the mark of the water line along the

---

99. The elevation which JCF determined by the boiling point of water is much too high. Although the elevation has varied, and is listed at 3,800 feet by the U.S. Geological Survey, it probably has never been higher than 3,950 feet for thousands of years (WHEELER, 38).

shores, the spring level is about 12 feet above its present waters. The chief commenced speaking in a loud voice as we approached; and parties of Indians armed with bows and arrows issued from the thickets. We selected a strong place for our encampment—a grassy bottom, nearly enclosed by the river, and furnished with abundant fire wood. The village, a collection of straw huts, was a few hundred yards higher up. An Indian brought in a large fish to trade, which we had the inexpressible satisfaction to find was a salmon trout; we gathered round him eagerly. The Indians were amused with our delight, and immediately brought in numbers; so that the camp was soon stocked. Their flavor was excellent—superior, in fact, to that of any fish I have ever known. They were of extraordinary size—about as large as the Columbia river salmon—generally from two to four feet in length.[100] From the information of Mr. Walker, who passed among some lakes lying more to the eastward, this fish is common to the streams of the inland lakes. He subsequently informed me that he had obtained them weighing six pounds when cleaned and the head taken off; which corresponds very well with the size of those obtained at this place. They doubtless formed the subsistence of these people, who hold the fishery in exclusive possession.

I remarked that one of them gave a fish to the Indian we had first seen, which he carried off to his family. To them it was probably a feast; being of the Digger tribe, and having no share in the fishery, living generally on seeds and roots. Although this was a time of the year when the fish have not yet become fat, they were excellent, and we could only imagine what they are at the proper season. These Indians were very fat, and appeared to live an easy and happy life. They crowded into the camp more than was consistent with our safety, retaining always their arms; and, as they made some unsatisfactory demonstrations, they were given to understand that they would not be permitted to come armed into the camp; and strong guards were kept with the horses. Strict vigilance was maintained among the people, and one-third at a time were kept on guard during the night. There is no reason to doubt that these dispositions, uniformly preserved, conducted our party securely through Indians famed for treachery.

In the mean time, such a salmon-trout feast as is seldom seen was

---

100. Cutthroat trout (*Salmo clarkii*), a species which tolerates alkaline water.

going on in our camp; and every variety of manner in which fish could be prepared—boiled, fried, and roasted in the ashes—was put into requisition; and every few minutes an Indian would be seen running off to spear a fresh one. Whether these Indians had seen whites before, we could not be certain; but they were evidently in communication with others who had, as one of them had some brass buttons, and we noticed several other articles of civilized manufacture. We could obtain from them but little information respecting the country. They made on the ground a drawing of the river, which they represented as issuing from another lake in the mountains three or four days distant, in a direction a little west of south; beyond which, they drew a mountain; and further still, two rivers; on one of which they told us that people like ourselves travelled. Whether they alluded to the settlements on the Sacramento, or to a party from the United States which had crossed the Sierra about three degrees to the southward, a few years since, I am unable to determine.

I tried unsuccessfully to prevail on some of them to guide us for a few days on the road, but they only looked at each other and laughed.

The latitude of our encampment, which may be considered the mouth of the inlet, is 39° 51′ 13″ by our observations.

January 16.—This morning we continued our journey along this beautiful stream, which we naturally called the Salmon Trout river. Large trails led up on either side; the stream was handsomely timbered with large cottonwoods; and the waters were very clear and pure. We were travelling along the mountains of the great Sierra, which rose on our right, covered with snow; but below the temperature was mild and pleasant. We saw a number of dams which the Indians had constructed to catch fish. After having made about 18 miles, we encamped under some large cottonwoods on the river bottom, where there was tolerably good grass [on the Truckee River near Wadsworth].

January 17.—This morning we left the river, which here issues from the mountains on the west. With every stream I now expected to see the great Buenaventura; and Carson hurried eagerly to search, on every one we reached, for beaver cuttings, which he always maintained we should find only on waters that ran to the Pacific; and the absence of such signs was to him a sure indication that the water had no outlet from the great basin. We followed the Indian trail through a tolerably level country, with small sage bushes, which brought us, after 20 miles journey, to another large stream [Carson River], timbered with cottonwood, and flowing also out of the mountains, but running more directly to the eastward.

On the way we surprised a family of Indians in the hills; but the man ran up the mountain with rapidity; and the woman was so terrified, and kept up such a continued screaming, that we could do nothing with her, and were obliged to let her go.

January 18.—There were Indian lodges and fish dams on the stream. There were no beaver cuttings on the river; but below, it turned round to the right; and, hoping that it would prove a branch of the Buenaventura, we followed it down for about three hours, and encamped.

I rode out with Mr. Fitzpatrick and Carson to reconnoitre the country, which had evidently been alarmed by the news of our appearance. This stream joined with the open valley of another to the eastward; but which way the main water ran, it was impossible to tell. Columns of smoke rose over the country at scattered intervals—signals by which the Indians here, as elsewhere, communicate to each other that enemies are in the country. It is a signal of ancient and very universal application among barbarians.

Examining into the condition of the animals when I returned into the camp, I found their feet so much cut up by the rocks, and so many of them lame, that it was evidently impossible that they could cross the country to the Rocky mountains. Every piece of iron that could be used for the purpose had been converted into nails, and we could make no further use of the shoes we had remaining. I therefore determined to abandon my eastern course, and to cross the Sierra Nevada into the valley of the Sacramento, wherever a practicable pass could be found. My decision was heard with joy by the people, and diffused new life throughout the camp.[101]

---

101. As we have noted earlier, there was nothing in JCF's orders taking him to California. It seems likely that he could have wintered comfortably on the Walker or the Truckee, living off salmon and other game, with ample grass for the animals. Perhaps he had heard so much talk of western expansion, around the Benton fireside, that he could not resist the opportunity to obtain geographical and political information on California. Indeed, Thomas Hart Benton would not have hesitated to give him private, verbal orders which extended or altered the written ones he had received from his superior, Colonel Abert. In any case, it is well to remember that his narrative, containing his own justification for his actions, was written after his return.

Adding to the confusion about when and why JCF decided to enter Cali-

Latitude, by observation, 39° 24′ 16″.

January 19.—A great number of smokes are still visible this morning, attesting at once the alarm which our appearance had spread among these people, and their ignorance of us. If they knew the whites, they would understand that their only object in coming among them was to trade, which required peace and friendship; but they have nothing to trade—consequently, nothing to attract the white man; hence their fear and flight.

At daybreak we had a heavy snow; but sat out, and, returning up the stream, went out of our way in a circuit over a little mountain; and encamped on the same stream, a few miles above, in latitude 39° 19′ 21″ by observation.[102]

January 20.—To-day we continued up the stream, and encamped on it close to the mountains. The freshly fallen snow was covered with the tracks of Indians, who had descended from the upper waters, probably called down by the smokes in the plain.

We ascended a peak of the range, which commanded a view of this stream behind the first ridge, where it was winding its course through a somewhat open valley, and I sometimes regret that I did not make the trial to cross here; but while we had fair weather below, the mountains were darkened with falling snow, and, feeling unwilling to encounter them, we turned away again to the southward.[103] In that direction we travelled the next day over a tolerably level country, having always the high mountains on the west. There was but little snow or rock on the ground; and, after having travelled 24 miles, we encamped again on another large stream, running

---

fornia is a comment by Preuss made 16 Oct., before the party had even reached the Walla Walla. First he wrote, "Since it is now certain that we shall not get home this winer, I am making plans in my spare time of how to spend all the money I shall have earned by next spring." And later, "The latest plan now is to turn south from Fort Vancouver through Mexican territory. There we shall have to find the route from Monterey to Santa Fé and follow it. We hope to find sufficient grass for the animals there" (PREUSS, 93–94).

There is also to be considered Marcus Whitman's belief that JCF was returning home at once "by the head of the Missouri" unless he decided to charter a vessel and go home by way of Panama (see note 73 above).

102. The camp on 19 Jan. was near the site of Fort Churchill.

103. The "winding stream" and the "open valley" were Carson River and Carson Valley. Had JCF gone westward instead of turning south, he would have been following Walker's route of 1833 and 1843 up the Carson River and would have saved a long and futile detour to the south (FLETCHER, 121).

off to the northward and eastward, to meet that we had left. It ran through broad bottoms, having a fine meadow-land appearance.[104]

Latitude 39° 01' 53".

January 22.—We travelled up the stream for about 14 miles to the foot of the mountains, from which one branch issued in the south-west, the other flowing from SSE. along their base. Leaving the camp below, we ascended the range through which the first stream passed, in a cañon; on the western side was a circular valley, about 15 miles long, through which the stream wound its way, issuing from a gorge in the main mountain, which rose abruptly beyond. The valley looked yellow with faded grass; and the trail we had followed was visible, making towards the gorge, and this was evidently a pass; but again, while all was bright sunshine on the ridge and on the valley where we were, the snow was falling heavily in the mountains. I determined to go still to the southward, and encamped on the stream near the forks; the animals being fatigued and the grass tolerably good.[105]

The rock of the ridge we had ascended is a compact lava, assuming a granitic appearance and structure, and containing, in some places, small nodules of obsidian. So far as composition and aspect are concerned, the rocks in other parts of the ridge appears to be granite; but it is probable that this is only a compact form of lava of recent origin.

---

104. The party was on the Walker River a few miles north of present Yerington, Nev.

105. Here JCF takes the East Walker and begins a period of confused traveling. A week later he will be camping on the other branch, the West Walker, not far from his present position.

The movements of the expedition before and during the Sierra crossing have been the subject of much speculation. Neither JCF's nor Preuss' journal, nor the 1845 map, are of much help in solving the problem. The senior editor of this edition has visited the area and has traced the possible routes of the men on U.S.G.S. quadrangle maps, but in the end he finds himself relying upon published and unpublished researches of others.

SMITH, DELLENBAUGH, and FARQUHAR are among those who have attempted to clarify the matter. Relying in part upon those writers, but supplementing his research with actual observation, Vincent P. Gianella published a study of the subject in 1959. In the annotations that follow, we cite Gianella and others, and also rely upon an exchange of correspondence with Fred I. Green, of Reno, Nev., who has spent a lifetime in the area and has some interesting points of view. He has not published his own version of the crossing, which differs from Gianella's, but marked maps and other exhibits of his work are available at the Nevada State Museum, Carson City.

By observation, the elevation of the encampment was 5,020 feet; and the latitude 38° 49′ 54″.

January 23.—We moved along the course of the other branch towards the southeast, the country affording a fine road; and, passing some slight dividing grounds, descended towards the valley of another stream. There was a somewhat rough-looking mountain ahead, which it appeared to issue from, or to enter—we could not tell which; and as the course of the valley and the inclination of the ground had a favorable direction, we were sanguine to find here a branch of the Buenaventura; but were again disappointed, finding it an inland water, on which we encamped after a day's journey of 24 miles. It was evident that, from the time we descended into the plain at Summer lake, we had been flanking the great range of mountains which divided the Great Basin from the waters of the Pacific; and that the continued succession, and almost connexion, of lakes and rivers which we encountered, were the drainings of that range. Its rains, springs, and snows, would sufficiently account for these lakes and streams, numerous as they were.

January 24.—A man was discovered running towards the camp as we were about to start this morning, who proved to be an Indian of rather advanced age—a sort of forlorn hope, who seemed to have been worked up into the resolution of visiting the strangers who were passing through the country.[106] He seized the hand of the first man he met as he came up, out of breath, and held on, as if to assure himself of protection. He brought with him in a little skin bag a few pounds of the seeds of a pine tree, which to-day we saw for the first time, and which Dr. Torrey has described as a new species, under the name of *pinus monophyllus;* in popular language, it might be called the *nut pine.* We purchased them all from him. The nut is oily, of very agreeable flavor, and must be very nutritious, as it constitutes the principal subsistence of the tribes among which we were now travelling. By a present of scarlet cloth, and other striking articles, we prevailed upon this man to be our guide of two days' journey. As clearly as possible by signs, we made him understand our object; and he engaged to conduct us in sight of a good pass which he knew. Here we ceased to hear the Shoshonee language; that of this man being perfectly unintelligible. Several Indians, who had been

---

106. Probably a member of the Washo tribe.

waiting to see what reception he would meet with, now came into camp; and, accompanied by the new comers, we resumed our journey.

The road led us up the creek, which here becomes a rather rapid mountain stream, fifty feet wide, between dark-looking hills without snow; but immediately beyond them rose snowy mountains on either side, timbered principally with the nut pine. On the lower grounds, the general height of this tree is twelve to twenty feet, and eight inches the greatest diameter; it is rather branching, and has a peculiar and singular but pleasant odor. We followed the river for only a short distance along a rocky trail, and crossed it at a dam which the Indians made us comprehend had been built to catch salmon trout. The snow and ice were heaped up against it three or four feet deep entirely across the stream.

Leaving here the stream, which runs through impassable cañons, we continued our road over a very broken country, passing through a low gap between the snowy mountains. The rock which occurs immediately in the pass has the appearance of impure sandstone, containing scales of black mica. This may be only a stratified lava; on issuing from the gap, the compact lava, and other volcanic products usual in the country, again occurred. We descended from the gap into a wide valley, or rather basin, and encamped on a small tributary to the last stream, on which there was very good grass. It was covered with such thick ice, that it required some labor with pickaxes to make holes for the animals to drink. The banks are lightly wooded with willow, and on the upper bottoms are sage and Fremontia with *ephedra occidentalis,* which begins to occur more frequently. The day has been a summer one, warm and pleasant; no snow on the trail, which, as we are all on foot, makes travelling more agreeable. The hunters went into the neighboring mountains, but found no game. We have five Indians in camp to-night.

January 25.—The morning was cold and bright, and as the sun rose the day became beautiful. A party of twelve Indians came down from the mountains to trade pine nuts, of which each one carried a little bag. These seemed now to be the staple of the country; and whenever we met an Indian, his friendly salutation consisted in offering a few nuts to eat and to trade; their only arms were bows and flint-pointed arrows. It appeared that, in almost all the valleys, the neighboring bands were at war with each other; and we had some

615

difficulty in prevailing on our guides to accompany us on this day's journey, being at war with the people on the other side of a large snowy mountain which lay before us.

The general level of the country appeared to be getting higher, and we were gradually entering the heart of the mountains. Accompanied by all the Indians, we ascended a long ridge, and reached a pure spring at the edge of the timber, where the Indians had waylaid and killed an antelope, and where the greater part of them left us. Our pacific conduct had quieted their alarms; and though at war among each other, yet all confided in us. Thanks to the combined effects of power and kindness—for our arms inspired respect, and our little presents and good treatment conciliated their confidence. Here we suddenly entered snow six inches deep, and the ground was a little rocky with volcanic fragments, the mountain appearing to be composed of such rock. The timber consists principally of nut pines, (*pinus monophyllus,*) which here are of larger size—12 to 15 inches in diameter; heaps of cones lying on the ground, where the Indians have gathered the seeds.

The snow deepened gradually as we advanced. Our guides wore out their moccasins; and, putting one of them on a horse, we enjoyed the unusual sight of an Indian who could not ride. He could not even guide the animal, and appeared to have no knowledge of horses. The snow was three or four feet deep in the summit of the pass; and from this point the guide pointed out our future road, declining to go any further. Below us was a little valley; and beyond this, the mountains rose higher still, one ridge above another, presenting a rude and rocky outline. We descended rapidly to the valley; the snow impeded us but little; yet it was dark when we reached the foot of the mountain.

The day had been so warm, that our moccasins were wet with melting snow; but here, as soon as the sun begins to decline, the air gets suddenly cold, and we had great difficulty to keep our feet from freezing—our moccasins being frozen perfectly stiff. After a hard day's march of 27 miles, we reached the river some time after dark, and found the snow about a foot deep on the bottom—the river being entirely frozen over. We found a comfortable camp, where there were dry willows abundant, and we soon had blazing fires.[107] A

107. DELLENBAUGH, 215, places the party on the East Walker River, just downstream from Bridgeport, Calif.

little brandy, which I husbanded with great care, remained, and I do not know any medicine more salutary, or any drink (except coffee) more agreeable, than this in a cold night after a hard day's march. Mr. Preuss questioned whether the famed nectar even possessed so exquisite a flavor. All felt it to be a reviving cordial.

The next morning, when the sun had not yet risen over the mountains, the thermometer was 2° below zero; but the sky was bright and pure, and the weather changed rapidly into a pleasant day of summer. I remained encamped, in order to examine the country, and allow the animals a day of rest, the grass being good and abundant under the snow.

The river is fifty to eighty feet wide, with a lively current, and very clear water. It forked a little above our camp, one of its branches coming directly from the south. At its head appeared to be a handsome pass; and from the neighboring heights we could see, beyond, a comparatively low and open country, which was supposed to form the valley of the Buenaventura. The other branch issued from a nearer pass, in a direction S. 75° W., forking at the foot of the mountain, and receiving part of its waters from a little lake. I was in advance of the camp when our last guides had left us; but, so far as could be understood, this was the pass which they had indicated, and, in company with Carson, to-day I set out to explore it. Entering the range, we continued in a northwesterly direction up the valley, which here bent to the right. It was pretty, open bottom, locked between lofty mountains, which supplied frequent streams as we advanced. On the lower part they were covered with nut-pine trees, and above with masses of pine, which we easily recognised, from the darker color of the foliage. From the fresh trails which occurred frequently during the morning, deer appeared to be remarkably numerous in the mountain.

We had now entirely left the desert country, and were on the verge of a region which, extending westward to the shores of the Pacific, abounds in large game, and is covered with a singular luxuriance of vegetable life.

The little stream grew rapidly smaller, and in about twelve miles we had reached its head, the last water coming immediately out of the mountain on the right; and this spot was selected for our next encampment. The grass showed well in sunny places; but in colder situations the snow was deep, and began to occur in banks, through which the horses found some difficulty in breaking a way.

To the left, the open valley continued in a southwesterly direction, with a scarcely perceptible ascent, forming a beautiful pass; the exploration of which we deferred until the next day, and returned to the camp.

To-day an Indian passed through the valley, on his way into the mountains, where he showed us was his lodge. We comprehended nothing of his language; and, though he appeared to have no fear, passing along in full view of the camp, he was indisposed to hold any communication with us, but showed the way he was going, and pointed for us to go on our road.

By observation, the latitude of this encampment was 38° 18′ 01″, and the elevation above the sea 6,310 feet.

January 27.—Leaving the camp to follow slowly, with directions to Carson to encamp at the place agreed on, Mr. Fitzpatrick and myself continued the reconnoissance. Arriving at the head of the stream, we began to enter the pass—passing occasionally through open groves of large pine trees, on the warm side of the defile, where the snow had melted away, occasionally exposing a large Indian trail. Continuing along a narrow meadow, we reached in a few miles the gate of the pass, where there was a narrow strip of prairie, about fifty yards wide, between walls of granite rock. On either side rose the mountains, forming on the left a rugged mass, or nucleus, wholly covered with deep snow, presenting a glittering and icy surface. At the time, we supposed this to be the point into which they were gathered between the two great rivers,[108] and from which the waters flowed off to the bay. This was the icy and cold side of the pass, and the rays of the sun hardly touched the snow. On the left, the mountains rose into peaks; but they were lower and secondary, and the country had a somewhat more open and lighter character. On the right were several hot springs, which appeared remarkable in such a place. In going through, we felt impressed by the majesty of the mountain, along the huge wall of which we were riding. Here there was no snow; but immediately beyond was a deep bank, through which we dragged our horses with considerable effort. We then immediately struck upon a stream, which gathered itself rapidly, and descended quick; and the valley did not preserve the open character of the other side, appearing below to form a cañon. We therefore climbed one of

---

108. Apparently he means the San Joaquin and the Sacramento.

the peaks on the right,[109] leaving our horses below; but we were so much shut up, that we did not obtain an extensive view, and what we saw was not very satisfactory, and awakened considerable doubt. The valley of the stream pursued a northwesterly direction, appearing below to turn sharply to the right, beyond which further view was cut off. It was, nevertheless, resolved to continue our road the next day down this valley, which we trusted still would prove that of the middle stream between the two great rivers. Towards the summit of this peak, the fields of snow were four or five feet deep on the northern side; and we saw several large hares, which had on their winter color, being white as the snow around them.

The winter day is short in the mountains, the sun having but a small space of sky to travel over in the visible part above our horizon; and the moment his rays are gone, the air is keenly cold. The interest of our work had detained us long, and it was after nightfall when we reached the camp.

January 28.—To-day we went through the pass with all the camp, and, after a hard day's journey of twelve miles, encamped on a high point where the snow had been blown off, and the exposed grass afforded a scanty pasture for the animals. Snow and broken country together made our travelling difficult: we were often compelled to make large circuits, and ascend the highest and most exposed ridges, in order to avoid snow, which in other places was banked up to a great depth.

During the day a few Indians were seen circling around us on snow shoes, and skimming along like birds; but we could not bring them within speaking distance. Godey, who was a little distance from the camp, had sat down to tie his moccasins, when he heard a low whistle near, and, looking up, saw two Indians half hiding behind a rock about forty yards distant; they would not allow him to approach, but, breaking into a laugh, skimmed off over the snow, seeming to have no idea of the power of fire arms, and thinking themselves perfectly safe when beyond arm's length.[110]

---

109. Fred I. Green (letter of 8 June 1968) believes that JCF and Fitzpatrick made their observations from an unnamed elevation of 8,422 feet, three miles north of Burcham Flat.

110. Green believes that JCF was now on Mill Creek, a stream which joins the West Walker at the head of Antelope Valley. The Indians were Mill Creek Washo whose village was at the mouth of the creek. They may have

To-night we did not succeed in getting the howitzer into camp. This was the most laborious day we had yet passed through; the steep ascents and deep snow exhausting both men and animals. Our single chronometer had stopped during the day, and its error in time occasioned the loss of an eclipse of a satellite this evening. It had not preserved the rate with which we started from the Dalles, and this will account for the absence of longitudes along this interval of our journey.

January 29.—From this height we could see, at a considerable distance below, yellow spots in the [Antelope] valley, which indicated that there was not much snow. One of these places we expected to reach to-night; and some time being required to bring up the gun, I went ahead with Mr. Fitzpatrick and a few men, leaving the camp to follow, in charge of Mr. Preuss. We followed a trail down a hollow where the Indians had descended, the snow being so deep that we never came near the ground; but this only made our descent the easier, and, when we reached a little affluent to the river at the bottom, we suddenly found ourselves in presence of eight or ten Indians. They seemed to be watching our motions, and, like the others, at first were indisposed to let us approach, ranging themselves like birds on a fallen log on the hill side above our heads, where, being out of reach, they thought themselves safe. Our friendly demeanor reconciled them, and, when we got near enough, they immediately stretched out to us handfulls of pine nuts, which seemed an exercise of hospitality. We made them a few presents, and, telling us that their village was a few miles below, they went on to let their people know what we were. The principal stream still running through an impracticable cañon, we ascended a very steep hill, which proved afterwards the last and fatal obstacle to our little howitzer, which was finally abandoned at this place.[111] We passed through a small

---

been on the way to Summit Meadows, where they caught hares in the deep snow during the winter months.

111. The late Carl P. Russell wrote (RUSSELL, 275) that the howitzer was abandoned on the East Walker River. But if we are to follow the theory of Fred I. Green, which we are inclined to do, we must place the location on Mill Creek. Certainly the weapon was not left on Lost Cannon Creek, a stream farther west. A howitzer on display at the Nevada State Museum is also a brass twelve-pounder, one of a dozen made in 1836 for the Army. It might be the one which JCF had to leave behind, and there is a local tradition that the JCF weapon was found several decades ago. But the museum staff cannot trace their specimen back in an unbroken line; there is a gap in the records.

meadow a few miles below, crossing the river, which depth, swift current, and rock, made it difficult to ford; and, after a few more miles of very difficult trail, issued into a larger prairie bottom, at the farther end of which we encamped, in a position rendered strong by rocks and trees. The lower parts of the mountain were covered with the nut pine. Several [Mill Creek Washo] Indians appeared on the hill side, reconnoitring the camp, and were induced to come in; others came in during the afternoon; and in the evening we held a council. The Indians immediately made it clear that the waters on which we were also belong to the Great Basin, in the edge of which we had been since the 17th of December; and it became evident that we had still the great ridge on the left to cross before we could reach the Pacific waters.

We explained to the Indians that we were endeavoring to find a passage across the mountains into the country of the whites, whom we were going to see; and told them that we wished them to bring us a guide, to whom we would give presents of scarlet cloth, and other articles, which were shown to them. They looked at the reward we offered, and conferred with each other, but pointed to the snow on the mountain, and drew their hands across their necks, and raised them above their heads, to show the depth; and signified that it was impossible for us to get through. They made signs that we must go to the southward, over a pass through a lower range, which they pointed out; there, they said, at the end of one day's travel, we would find people who lived near a pass in the great mountain; and to that point they engaged to furnish us a guide. They appeared to have a confused idea, from report, of whites who lived on the other side of the mountain; and once, they told us, about two years ago, a party of twelve men like ourselves had ascended their river, and crossed to the other waters. They pointed out to us where they had crossed; but then, they said, it was summer time; but now it would be impossible. I believe that this was a party led by Mr. Chiles, one of the only two men whom I know to have passed through the California mountains from the interior of the Basin—Walker being the other; and both were engaged upwards of twenty days, in the summer time, in getting over.[112] Chiles's destination was the bay of San

Museum Director James Calhoun suggests that the howitzer in his care may have been brought west by dragoons.

112. Green plausibly suggests that this was Joseph R. Walker and a party of twelve who appeared in Los Angeles in Feb. 1841 (not in the summer, as

Francisco, to which he descended by the Stanislaus river; and Walker subsequently informed me that, like myself, descending to the southward on a more eastern line, day after day he was searching for the Buenaventura, thinking that he had found it with every new stream, until, like me, he abandoned all idea of its existence, and, turning abruptly to the right, crossed the great chain. These were both western men, animated with the spirit of exploratory enterprise which characterizes that people.

The Indians brought in during the evening an abundant supply of pine nuts, which we traded from them. When roasted, their pleasant flavor made them an agreeable addition to our now scanty store of provisions, which were reduced to a very low ebb. Our principal stock was in peas, which it is not necessary to say contain scarcely any nutriment. We had still a little flour left, some coffee, and a quantity of sugar, which I reserved as a defence against starvation.

The Indians informed us that at certain seasons they have fish in their waters, which we supposed to be salmon trout; for the remainder of the year they live upon the pine nuts, which form their great winter subsistence—a portion being always at hand, shut up in the natural storehouse of the cones. At present, they were presented to us as a whole people living upon this simple vegetable.

The other division of the party did not come in to-night, but encamped in the upper meadow, and arrived the next morning. They had not succeeded in getting the howitzer beyond the place mentioned, and where it had been left by Mr. Preuss in obedience to my orders; and, in anticipation of the snow banks and snow fields still ahead, foreseeing the inevitable detention to which it would subject us, I reluctantly determined to leave it there for the time. It was of the kind invented by the French for the mountain part of their war in Algiers; and the distance it had come with us proved how well it was adapted to its purpose. We left it, to the great sorrow of the whole party, who were grieved to part with a companion which had made the whole distance from St. Louis, and commanded respect for us on some critical occasions, and which might be needed for the same purpose again.

JCF says). Walker's presence in the Los Angeles area is documented by passages in the Stearns Papers, CSmH. It is also possible that the Indians had seen, or heard of, a part of the Bartleson-Bidwell caravan which crossed the Sierra north of Sonora Pass in 1841.

January 30.—Our guide, who was a young man, joined us this morning; and, leaving our encampment late in the day, we descended the river, which immediately opened out into a broad valley, furnishing good travelling ground. In a short distance we passed the village, a collection of straw huts; and a few miles below, the guide pointed out the place where the whites had been encamped before they entered the mountain. With our late start we made but ten miles, and encamped on the low river bottom, where there was no snow, but a great deal of ice; and we cut piles of long grass to lay under our blankets, and fires were made of large dry willows, groves of which wooded the stream. The river took here a northeasterly direction, and through a spur from the mountains on the left was the gap where we were to pass the next day.[113]

January 31.—We took our way over a gently rising ground, the dividing ridge being tolerably low; and travelling easily along a broad trail, in twelve or fourteen miles reached the upper part of the pass, when it began to snow thickly, with very cold weather. The Indians had only the usual scanty covering, and appeared to suffer greatly from the cold. All left us, except our guide. Half hidden by the storm, the mountains looked dreary; and, as night began to approach, the guide showed great reluctance to go forward. I placed him between two rifles, for the way began to be difficult. Travelling a little farther, we struck a ravine, which the Indian said would conduct us to the river; and as the poor fellow suffered greatly, shivering in the snow which fell upon his naked skin, I would not detain him any longer; and he ran off to the mountain, where he said there was a hut near by. He had kept the blue and scarlet cloth I had given him tightly rolled up, preferring rather to endure the cold than to get them wet. In the course of the afternoon, one of the men had his foot frost bitten; and about dark we had the satisfaction to reach the bottoms of a stream timbered with large trees, among which we found a sheltered camp, with an abundance of such grass as the season afforded for the animals. We saw before us, in descending from the pass, a great continuous range, along which stretched the valley of the river; the lower parts steep, and dark with pines, while above it was hidden in clouds of snow. This we felt instantly satisfied was the central ridge of the Sierra Nevada, the

113. The expedition is in Antelope Valley, which it entered from the mouth of West Walker Canyon.

great California mountain, which only now intervened between us and the waters of the bay. We had made a forced march of 26 miles, and three mules had given out on the road. Up to this point, with the exception of two stolen by Indians, we had lost none of the horses which had been brought from the Columbia river, and a number of these were still strong and in tolerably good order. We had now 67 animals in the band.

We had scarcely lighted our fires, when the camp was crowded with nearly naked Indians; some of them were furnished with long nets in addition to bows, and appeared to have been out on the sage hills to hunt rabbits. These nets were perhaps 30 to 40 feet long, kept upright in the ground by slight sticks at intervals, and were made from a kind of wild hemp, very much resembling in manufacture those common among the Indians of the Sacramento valley. They came among us without any fear, and scattered themselves about the fires, mainly occupied in gratifying their astonishment. I was struck by the singular appearance of a row of about a dozen, who were sitting on their haunches perched on a log near one of the fires, with their quick sharp eyes following every motion.

We gathered together a few of the most intelligent of the Indians, and held this evening an interesting council. I explained to them my intentions. I told them that we had come from a very far country, having been travelling now nearly a year, and that we were desirous simply to go across the mountain into the country of the other whites. There were two who appeared particularly intelligent—one, a somewhat old man. He told me that, before the snows fell, it was six sleeps to the place where the whites lived, but that now it was impossible to cross the mountain on account of the deep snow; and showing us, as the others had done, that it was over our heads, he urged us strongly to follow the course of the river, which he said would conduct us to a lake in which there were many large fish. There, he said, were many people; there was no snow on the ground; and we might remain there until the spring. From their descriptions, we were enabled to judge that we had encamped on the upper water of the Salmon Trout river.[114] It is hardly necessary to

---

114. The route today, according to Green, has taken them through the swampy area which is now Topaz Lake in Antelope Valley. They are still on the waters of the Walker River, not the "Salmon Trout" or East Carson, Green believes. But GIANELLA, 55, who picks up the route at this point, places the expedition several miles northwest of Antelope Valley, on the East Carson.

say that our communication was only by signs, as we understood nothing of their language; but they spoke, notwithstanding, rapidly and vehemently, explaining what they considered the folly of our intentions, and urging us to go down to the lake. *Tah-ve,* a word signifying snow, we very soon learned to know, from its frequent repetition. I told him that the men and the horses were strong, and that we would break a road through the snow; and spreading before him our bales of scarlet cloth, and trinkets, showed him what we would give for a guide. It was necessary to obtain one, if possible; for I had determined here to attempt the passage of the mountain. Pulling a bunch of grass from the ground, after a short discussion among themselves, the old man made us comprehend, that if we could break through the snow, at the end of three days we would come down upon grass, which he showed us would be about six inches high, and where the ground was entirely free. So far, he said, he had been in hunting for elk; but beyond that, (and he closed his eyes) he had seen nothing; but there was one among them who had been to the whites, and, going out of the lodge, he returned with a young man of very intelligent appearance. Here, said he, is a young man who has seen the whites with his own eyes; and he swore, first by the sky, and then by the ground, that what he said was true. With a large present of goods, we prevailed upon this young man to be our guide, and he acquired among us the name Mélo—a word signifying friend, which they used very frequently. He was thinly clad, and nearly barefoot; his moccasins being about worn out. We gave him skins to make a new pair, and to enable him to perform his undertaking to us. The Indians remained in the camp during the night, and we kept the guide and two others to sleep in the lodge with us— Carson lying across the door, and having made them comprehend

---

It seems superfluous in an edition of this kind to present the detailed notes needed to set forth, and perhaps to reconcile, the two versions of the route as seen by Green and Gianella. This is a task for historians of the region who like to climb. Green's route, for example, passes north of Red Lake and Gianella's passes south of it. Green proposes that JCF viewed Lake Tahoe from Stevens Peak; Gianella says it was Red Lake Peak. Only the most avid reader of the *Sierra Club Bulletin* can ponder all these speculations with complete interest. Since Gianella's observations are published and readily available, and since our correspondence with Green does not give us a clear picture of his views on the actual crossing of the summit of the Sierra, we shall annotate mainly from Gianella. We regret that an injury cut short Mr. Green's correspondence with us and that publication could not await his recovery.

the use of our fire arms. The snow, which had intermitted in the evening, commenced falling again in the course of the night, and it snowed steadily all day. In the morning I acquainted the men with my decision, and explained to them that necessity required us to make a great effort to clear the mountains. I reminded them of the beautiful valley of the Sacramento, with which they were familiar from the descriptions of Carson, who had been there some fifteen years ago, and who, in our late privations, had delighted us in speaking of its rich pastures and abounding game, and drew a vivid contrast between its summer climate, less than a hundred miles distant, and the falling snow around us. I informed them (and long experience had given them confidence in my observations and good instruments) that almost directly west, and only about 70 miles distant, was the great farming establishment of Captain [John Augustus] Sutter—a gentleman who had formerly lived in Missouri, and, emigrating to this country, had become the possessor of a principality. I assured them that, from the heights of the mountain before us, we should doubtless see the valley of the Sacramento river, and with one effort place ourselves again in the midst of plenty. The people received this decision with the cheerful obedience which has always characterized them; and the day was immediately devoted to the preparations necessary to enable us to carry it into effect. Leggings, moccasins, clothing—all were put into the best state to resist the cold. Our guide was not neglected. Extremity of suffering might make him desert; we therefore did the best we could for him. Leggings, moccasins, some articles of clothing, and a large green blanket, in addition to the blue and scarlet cloth, were lavished upon him, and to his great and evident contentment. He arrayed himself in all his colors; and, clad in green, blue, and scarlet, he made a gay-looking Indian; and, with his various presents, was probably richer and better clothed than any of his tribe had ever been before.

I have already said that our provisions were very low; we had neither tallow nor grease of any kind remaining, and the want of salt became one of our greatest privations. The poor dog which had been found in the Bear river valley, and which had been a *compagnon de voyage* ever since, had now become fat, and the mess to which it belonged requested permission to kill it. Leave was granted. Spread out on the snow, the meat looked very good; and it made a strengthening meal for the greater part of the camp. Indians brought in two or three rabbits during the day, which were purchased from them.

The river was 40 to 70 feet wide, and now entirely frozen over. It was wooded with large cottonwood, willow, and *grain de boeuf*. By observation, the latitude of this encampment was 38° 37' 18".

February 2.—It had ceased snowing, and this morning the lower air was clear and frosty; and six or seven thousand feet above, the peaks of the Sierra now and then appeared among the rolling clouds, which were rapidly dispersing before the sun. Our Indian shook his head as he pointed to the icy pinnacles, shooting high up into the sky, and seeming almost immediately above us. Crossing the river on the ice, and leaving it immediately, we commenced the ascent of the mountain along the vally of a tributary stream. The people were unusually silent; for every man knew that our enterprise was hazardous, and the issue doubtful.

The snow deepened rapidly, and it soon became necessary to break a road. For this service, a party of ten was formed, mounted on the strongest horses; each man in succession opening the road on foot, or on horseback, until himself and his horse became fatigued when he stepped aside; and, the remaining number passing ahead, he took his station in the rear. Leaving this stream, and pursuing a very direct course, we passed over an intervening ridge to the river we had left. On the way we passed two low huts entirely covered with snow, which might very easily have escaped observation. A family was living in each; and the only trail I saw in the neighborhood was from the door hole to a nut-pine tree near, which supplied them with food and fuel. We found two similar huts on the creek where we next arrived; and, travelling a little higher up, encamped on its banks in about four feet depth of snow. Carson found near, an open hill side, where the wind and the sun had melted the snow, leaving exposed sufficient bunch grass for the animals to-night.

The nut pines were now giving way to heavy timber, and there were some immense pines on the bottom, around the roots of which the sun had melted away the snow; and here we made our camps and built huge fires.[115] To-day we had travelled sixteen miles, and our elevation above the sea was 6,760 feet.

February 3.—Turning our faces directly towards the main chain,

---

115. "The route was southwesterly up Long Valley, and probably into Diamond Valley, then south across the low hills until they again came upon the East Carson. They went into camp in the meadow where Markleeville Creek joins the river, about a mile northeast of Markleeville" (GIANELLA, 55).

we ascended an open hollow along a small tributary to the river, which, according to the Indians, issues from a mountain to the south. The snow was so deep in the hollow, that we were obliged to travel along the steep hill sides, and over spurs, where wind and sun had in places lessened the snow, and where the grass, which appeared to be in good quality along the sides of the mountains, was exposed. We opened our road in the same way as yesterday, but made only seven miles; and encamped by some springs at the foot of a high and steep hill, by which the hollow ascended to another basin in the mountain.[116] The little stream below was entirely buried in snow. The springs were shaded by the boughs of a lofty cedar, which here made its first appearance; the usual height was 120 to 130 feet, and one that was measured near by was 6 feet in diameter.

There being no grass exposed here, the horses were sent back to that which we had seen a few miles blow. We occupied the remainder of the day in beating down a road to the foot of the hill, a mile or two distant; the snow being beaten down when moist, in the warm part of the day, and then hard frozen at night, made a foundation that would bear the weight of the animals the next morning. During the day several Indians joined us on snow shoes. These were made of a circular hoop, about a foot in diameter, the interior space being filled with an open network of bark.

February 4.—I went ahead early with two or three men, each with a led horse, to break the road. We were obliged to abandon the hollow entirely, and work along the mountain side, which was very steep, and the snow covered with an icy crust. We cut a footing as we advanced, and trampled a road through for the animals; but occasionally one plunged outside the trail, and slided along the field to the bottom, a hundred yards below. Late in the day we reached another bench in the hollow, where, in summer, the stream passed over a small precipice. Here was a short distance of dividing ground between the two ridges, and beyond an open basin [Faith Valley], some ten miles across, whose bottom presented a field of snow. At the further or western side rose the middle crest of the mountain, a dark-looking ridge of volcanic rock [Elephant's Back].

The summit line presented a range of naked peaks, apparently

---

116. The route was up Markleeville Creek and the camp at Grovers Springs. "The difficulty of ascending the steep mountain was to detain the main party at Grovers Springs until February 16" (GIANELLA, 56).

destitute of snow and vegetation; but below, the face of the whole country was covered with timber of extraordinary size. Annexed you are presented with a view of this ridge from a camp on the western side of the basin [p. 636].

Towards a pass which the guide indicated here, we attempted in the afternoon to force a road; but after a laborious plunging through two or three hundred yards, our best horses gave out, entirely refusing to make any further effort; and, for the time, we were brought to a stand. The guide informed us that we were entering the deep snow, and here began the difficulties of the mountain; and to him, and almost to all, our enterprise seemed hopeless. I returned a short distance back, to the break in the hollow, where I met Mr. Fitzpatrick.[117]

The camp had been all the day occupied in endeavoring to ascend the hill, but only the best horses had succeeded. The animals, generally, not having sufficient strength to bring themselves up without the packs; and all the line of road between this and the springs was strewed with camp stores and equipage, and horses floundering in snow. I therefore immediately encamped on the ground with my own mess, which was in advance, and directed Mr. Fitzpatrick to encamp at the springs, and send all the animals, in charge of Tabeau, with a strong guard, back to the place where they had been pastured the night before. Here was a small spot of level ground, protected on one side by the mountain, and on the other sheltered by a little ridge of rock. It was an open grove of pines, which assimilated in size to the grandeur of the mountain, being frequently six feet in diameter.

To-night we had no shelter, but we made a large fire around the trunk of one of the huge pines; and covering the snow with small boughs, on which we spread our blankets, soon made ourselves comfortable. The night was very bright and clear, though the thermometer was only at 10°. A strong wind, which sprang up at sundown, made it intensely cold; and this was one of the bitterest nights during the journey.

Two Indians joined our party here; and one of them, an old man, immediately began to harangue us, saying that ourselves and ani-

---

117. Going up Markleeville Creek and passing along Charity Valley, JCF camped on the east side of Faith Valley and but a few miles from the main ridge of the Sierra Nevada.

mals would perish in the snow; and that if we would go back, he would show us another and a better way across the mountain. He spoke in a very loud voice, and there was a singular repetition of phrases and arrangement of words, which rendered his speech striking, and not unmusical.

We had now begun to understand some words, and, with the aid of signs, easily comprehended the old man's simple ideas. "Rock upon rock—rock upon rock—snow upon snow—snow upon snow," said he; "even if you get over the snow, you will not be able to get down from the mountains." He made us a sign of precipices, and showed us how the feet of the horses would slip, and throw them off from the narrow trails which led along their sides. Our Chinook, who comprehended even more readily than ourselves, and believed our situation hopeless, covered his head with his blanket, and began to weep and lament. "I wanted to see the whites," said he; "I came away from my own people to see the whites, and I wouldn't care to die among them; but here"—and he looked around into the cold night and gloomy forest, and, drawing his blanket over his head, began again to lament.

Seated around the tree, the fire illuminating the rocks and the tall bolls of the pines round about, and the old Indian haranguing, we presented a group of very serious faces.

February 5.—The night had been too cold to sleep, and we were up very early. Our guide was standing by the fire with all his finery on; and seeing him shiver in the cold, I threw on his shoulders one of my blankets. We missed him a few minutes afterwards, and never saw him again. He had deserted. His bad faith and treachery were in perfect keeping with the estimate of Indian character, which a long intercourse with this people had gradually forced upon my mind.

While a portion of the camp were occupied in bringing up the baggage to this point, the remainder were busied in making sledges and snow shoes. I had determined to explore the mountain ahead, and the sledges were to be used in transporting the baggage.

The mountains here consisted wholly of a white micaceous granite.

The day was perfectly clear, and, while the sun was in the sky, warm and pleasant.

By observation, our latitude was 38° 42′ 26″; and elevation, by the boiling point, 7,400 feet.

February 6.—Accompanied by Mr. Fitzpatrick, I sat out to-day with a reconnoitring party, on snow shoes. We marched all in single file, trampling the snow as heavily as we could. Crossing the open basin, in a march of about ten miles we reached the top of one of the peaks, to the left of the pass indicated by our guide. Far below us, dimmed by the distance, was a large snowless valley, bounded on the western side, at the distance of about a hundred miles, by a low range of mountains, which Carson recognised with delight as the mountains bordering the coast. "There," said he, "is the little mountain—it is 15 years ago since I saw it; but I am just as sure as if I had seen it yesterday."[118] Between us, then, and this low coast range, was the valley of the Sacramento; and no one who had not accompanied us through the incidents of our life for the last few months could realize the delight with which at last we looked down upon it. At the distance of apparently 30 miles beyond us were distinguished spots of prairie; and a dark line, which could be traced with the glass, was imagined to be the course of the river; but we were evidently at a great height above the valley, and between us and the plains extended miles of snowy fields and broken ridges of pine-covered mountains.

It was late in the day when we turned towards the camp; and it grew rapidly cold as it drew towards night. One of the men became fatigued, and his feet began to freeze, and, building a fire in the trunk of a dry old cedar, Mr. Fitzpatrick remained with him until his clothes could be dried, and he was in a condition to come on. After a day's march of 20 miles, we straggled into camp, one after another, at night fall; the greater number excessively fatigued, only two of the party having ever travelled on snow shoes before.

All our energies were now directed to getting our animals across the snow; and it was supposed that, after all the baggage had been drawn with the sleighs over the trail we had made, it would be sufficiently hard to bear our animals. At several places, between this point and the ridge, we had discovered some grassy spots, where the wind and sun had dispersed the snow from the sides of the hills, and these were to form resting places to support the animals for a night in their passage across. On our way across, we had set on fire

---

118. Mount Diablo. Carson had been in California in 1829–30 with a party of trappers under the leadership of Ewing Young.

several broken stumps, and dried trees, to melt holes in the snow for the camps. Its general depth was 5 feet; but we passed over places where it was 20 feet deep, as shown by the trees.

With one party drawing sleighs loaded with baggage, I advanced to-day [7 Feb.] about four miles along the trail, and encamped at the first grassy spot, where we expected to bring our horses. Mr. Fitzpatrick, with another party remained behind, to form an intermediate station between us and the animals.

February 8.—The night has been extremely cold; but perfectly still, and beautifully clear. Before the sun appeared this morning, the thermometer was 3° below zero; 1° higher, when his rays struck the lofty peaks; and 0° when they reached our camp.

Scenery and weather, combined, must render these mountains beautiful in summer; the purity and deep-blue color of the sky are singularly beautiful; the days are sunny and bright, and even warm in the noon hours; and if we could be free from the many anxieties that oppress us, even now we would be delighted here; but our provisions are getting fearfully scant. Sleighs arrived with baggage about 10 o'clock; and leaving a portion of it here, we continued on for a mile and a half, and encamped at the foot of a long hill on this side of the open bottom.

Bernier and Godey, who yesterday morning had been sent to ascend a higher peak, got in, hungry and fatigued.[119] They confirmed what we had already seen. Two other sleighs arrived in the afternoon; and the men being fatigued, I gave them all tea and sugar. Snow clouds began to rise in the SSW.; and, apprehensive of a storm, which would destroy our road, I sent the people back to Mr. Fitzpatrick, with directions to send for the animals in the morning. With me remained Mr. Preuss, Mr. Talbot, and Carson, with Jacob.

Elevation of the camp, by the boiling point, is 7,920 feet.

February 9.—During the night the weather changed, the wind rising to a gale, and commencing to snow before daylight; before morning the trail was covered. We remained quiet in camp all day, in the course of which the weather improved. Four sleighs arrived

---

119. Bernier and Godey probably climbed a peak on the ridge rising above Winnemucca Lake, a peak one mile south of and 300 feet higher than Elephant's Back. GIANELLA, 58, rejects Farquhar's suggestion that the men may have climbed Round Top, Red Lake Peak, or Stevens Peak, all over 10,000 feet in elevation. Had this been the case they would have been able to see Lake Tahoe, a discovery which did not occur until six days later.

toward evening, with the bedding of the men. We suffer much from the want of salt; and all the men are becoming weak from insufficient food.

February 10.—Taplin was sent back with a few men to assist Mr. Fitzpatrick; and continuing on with three sleighs carrying a part of the baggage, we had the satisfaction to encamp within two and a half miles of the head of the hollow, and at the foot of the last mountain ridge.[120] Here two large trees had been set on fire, and in the holes, where the snow has been melted away, we found a comfortable camp.

The wind kept the air filled with snow during the day; the sky was very dark in the southwest, though elsewhere very clear. The forest here has a noble appearance; the tall cedar[121] is abundant; its greatest height being 130 feet, and circumference 20, three or four feet above the ground; and here I see for the first time the white pine,[122] of which there are some magnificent trees. Hemlock spruce[123] is among the timber, occasionally as large as 8 feet in diameter four feet above the ground; but, in ascending, it tapers rapidly to less than one foot at the height of 80 feet. I have not seen any higher than 130 feet, and the slight upper part is frequently broken off by the wind. The white spruce[124] is frequent; and the red pine, (*pinus colorado* of the Mexicans,)[125] which constitutes the beautiful forest along the flanks of the Sierra Nevada to the northward, is here the principal tree, not attaining a greater height than 140 feet, though with sometimes a diameter of 10. Most of these trees appeared to differ slightly from those of the same kind on the other side of the continent.

The elevation of the camp, by the boiling point, is 8,050 feet. We are now 1,000 feet above the level of the South Pass in the Rocky mountains; and still we are not done ascending. The top of a flat

120. The party was at the foot of Elephant's Back, on the western side of Faith Valley, probably near Forestdale Creek (GIANELLA, 58). SMITH, 144, and DELLENBAUGH, 218, both place the camp at the head of Hope Valley.

121. *Libocedrus decurrens* Torr., incense cedar, later described from the JCF collection at the headwaters of the Sacramento on the third expedition, 1846, and illustrated with a handsome plate in *Plantae Frémontianæ* (1853).

122. *Pinus lambertiana* Dougl., sugar pine.

123. *Tsuga mertensiana* (Bong.) Carr., mountain hemlock.

124. *Abies concolor* (Gord. & Glend.) Lindl., white fir.

125. *Pinus ponderosa,* Dougl., yellow or ponderosa pine. JCF's vernacular name and the Spanish folk name allude to the reddish bark plates.

ridge near was bare of snow, and very well sprinkled with bunch grass, sufficient to pasture the animals two or three days; and this was to be their main point of support. This ridge is composed of a compact trap, or basalt, of a columnar structure; over the surface are scattered large boulders of porous trap. The hills are in many places entirely covered with small fragments of volcanic rock.

Putting on our snow shoes, we spent the afternoon in exploring a road ahead. The glare of the snow, combined with great fatigue, had rendered many of the people nearly blind; but we were fortunate in having some black silk handkerchiefs, which, worn as veils, very much relieved the eye.

February 11.—High wind continued, and our trail this morning was nearly invisible—here and there indicated by a little ridge of snow. Our situation became tiresome and dreary, requiring a strong exercise of patience and resolution.

In the evening I received a message from Mr. Fitzpatrick, acquainting me with the utter failure of his attempt to get our mules and horses over the snow—the half-hidden trail had proved entirely too slight to support them, and they had broken through, and were plunging about or lying half buried in snow. He was occupied in endeavoring to get them back to his camp; and in the mean time sent to me for further instructions. I wrote to him to send the animals immediately back to their old pastures; and, after having made mauls and shovels, turn in all the strength of his party to open and beat a road through the snow, strengthening it with branches and boughs of the pines.

February 12.—We made mauls, and worked hard at our end of the road all the day. The wind was high, but the sun bright, and the snow thawing. We worked down the face of the hill, to meet the people at the other end. Towards sundown it began to grow cold, and we shouldered our mauls, and trudged back to camp.

February 13.—We continued to labor on the road; and in the course of the day had the satisfaction to see the people working down the face of the opposite hill, about three miles distant. During the morning we had the pleasure of a visit from Mr. Fitzpatrick, with the information that all was going on well. A party of Indians had passed on snow shoes, who said they were going to the western side of the mountain after fish. This was an indication that the salmon were coming up the streams; and we could hardly restrain our impatience as we thought of them, and worked with increased vigor.

The meat train did not arrive this evening, and I gave Godey leave to kill our little dog, (Tlamath,) which he prepared in Indian fashion; scorching off the hair, and washing the skin with soap and snow, and then cutting it up into pieces, which were laid on the snow. Shortly afterwards, the sleigh arrived with a supply of horse meat; and we had to-night an extraordinary dinner—pea soup, mule, and dog.

February 14.—Annexed [p. 636] is a view of the dividing ridge of the Sierra, taken from this encampment. With Mr. Preuss, I ascended to-day the highest peak to the right; from which we had a beautiful view of a mountain lake at our feet, about fifteen miles in length, and so entirely surrounded by mountains that we could not discover an outlet.[126] We had taken with us a glass; but, though we enjoyed an extended view, the valley was half hidden in mist, as when we had seen it before. Snow could be distinguished on the higher parts of the coast mountains; eastward, as far as the eye could

---

126. The lake was certainly Tahoe, but the peak from which JCF viewed it is far from certain. Stevens Peak is the choice of SMITH, 145, and FARQUHAR, 83, and it has the advantage of being closer and perhaps providing a more unobstructed view of the lake than Gianella's choice—which is Red Lake Peak. He explains that what JCF called "volcanic conglomerate" is now designated volcanic agglomerate, or breccia, of the Sierran andesites. "The volcanic agglomerate lies on the surface eroded across the edges of the steeply dipping, metamorphosed, Mesozoic rocks. These old . . . rocks have acquired a reddish cast, and this color has influenced the naming of the peak, as well as the beautiful little [Red] lake lying in the glaciated canyon at the southern base of the mountain" (GIANELLA, 59). The large lake which JCF sighted was called Mountain Lake on the maps in the early editions of his *Report*. Later he named it Lake Bonpland in honor of Aimé Bonpland, the French botanist who accompanied Baron Alexander von Humboldt to South America. It is so labeled on Preuss' map of 1848 accompanying the *Geographical Memoir*. In the 1850s, the friends of California's governor John Bigler succeeded in naming the lake in his honor. But during the Civil War, Unionists in California sponsored a move to restore to the lake its Washo Indian name, understood to be Tahoe. This became the popular name but was not made official until 1945 (GUDDE [1]).

The sketch made by Preuss (p. 636) while at the "Long Camp" is used by Gianella to support his assertion that JCF climbed Red Lake Peak. In reproducing the sketch he gives it this caption: "Summit of the Sierra Nevada, Alpine County, California. To the left is Elephant's Back. On the right is Red Lake Peak rising above the canyon leading up to Carson Pass . . ." (GIANELLA, 60).

Pass in the Sierra Nevada of California

extend, it ranged over a terrible mass of broken snowy mountains, fading off blue in the distance. The rock composing the summit consists of a very coarse dark volcanic conglomerate; the lower parts appeared to be of a slaty structure. The highest trees were a few scattering cedars and aspens. From the immediate foot of the peak, we were two hours in reaching the summit, and one hour and a quarter in descending. The day had been very bright, still, and clear, and spring seems to be advancing rapidly. While the sun is in the sky, the snow melts rapidly, and gushing springs cover the face of the mountain in all the exposed places; but their surface freezes instantly with the disappearance of the sun.

I obtained to-night some observations; and the result from these, and others made during our stay, gives for the latitude 38° 41′ 57″, longitude 120° 25′ 57″, and rate of the chronometer 25″.82.

February 16.—We had succeeded in getting our animals safely to the first grassy hill; and this morning I started with Jacob on a reconnoitring expedition beyond the mountain. We travelled along the crests of narrow ridges, extending down from the mountain in the direction of the valley, from which the snow was fast melting away. On the open spots was tolerably good grass; and I judged we should succeed in getting the camp down by way of these. Towards sundown we discovered some icy spots in a deep hollow; and, descending the mountain, we encamped on the head water of a little creek, where at last the water found its way to the Pacific.

The night was clear and very long. We heard the cries of some wild animals, which had been attracted by our fire, and a flock of geese passed over during the night. Even these strange sounds had something pleasant to our senses in this region of silence and desolation.

We started again early in the morning. The creek acquired a regular breadth of about 20 feet, and we soon began to hear the rushing of the water below the ice surface, over which we travelled to avoid the snow; a few miles below we broke through, where the water was several feet deep, and halted to make a fire and dry our clothes. We continued a few miles farther, walking being very laborious without snow shoes.

I was now perfectly satisfied that we had struck the stream on which Mr. Sutter lived; and, turning about, made a hard push, and reached the camp at dark. Here we had the pleasure to find all the remaining animals, 57 in number, safely arrived at the grassy hill near the camp; and here, also, we were agreeably surprised with the sight of an abundance of salt. Some of the horse guard had gone to a neighboring hut for pine nuts, and discovered unexpectedly a large cake of very white fine-grained salt, which the Indians told them they had brought from the other side of the mountain; they used it to eat with their pine nuts, and readily sold it for goods.

On the 19th, the people were occupied in making a road and bringing up the baggage; and, on the afternoon of the next day, *February* 20, 1844, we encamped with the animals and all the *materiel* of the camp, on the summit of the Pass in the dividing ridge, 1,000 miles by our travelled road from the Dalles of the Columbia.[127]

The people, who had not yet been to this point, climbed the neighboring peak to enjoy a look at the valley.

The temperature of boiling water gave for the elevation of the encampment 9,338 feet above the sea.

This was 2,000 feet higher than the South Pass in the Rocky mountains, and several peaks in view rose several thousand feet still higher. Thus, at the extremity of the continent, and near the coast, the phenomenon was seen of a range of mountains still higher than the great Rocky mountains themselves. This extraordinary fact accounts for the Great Basin, and shows that there must be a system of small lakes and rivers here scattered over a flat country, and which the extended and lofty range of the Sierra Nevada prevents from escaping into the Pacific ocean. Latitude 38° 44′; longitude 120° 28′.

Thus this Pass in the Sierra Nevada, which so well deserves its name of snowy mountain, is eleven degrees west and about four degrees south of the South Pass.

February 21.—We now considered ourselves victorious over the mountain; having only the descent before us, and the valley under our eyes, we felt strong hope that we should force our way down. But this was a case in which the descent was *not* facile. Still deep fields of snow lay between, and there was a large intervening space of rough-looking mountains, through which we had yet to wind our way. Carson roused me this morning with an early fire, and we were all up long before day, in order to pass the snow fields before the sun should render the crust soft. We enjoyed this morning a scene, at sunrise, which even here was unusually glorious and beauti-

---

127. It is now generally conceded that the party traveled not through Carson Pass, but an unidentified and unnamed pass lying farther south.

ful. Immediately above the eastern mountains was repeated a cloud-formed mass of purple ranges, bordered with bright yellow gold; the peaks shot up into a narrow line of crimson cloud, above which the air was filled with a greenish orange; and over all was the singular beauty of the blue sky. Passing along a ridge which commanded the lake on our right, of which we began to discover an outlet through a chasm on the west, we passed over alternating open ground and hard-crusted snow fields which supported the animals, and encamped on the ridge after a journey of 6 miles. The grass was better than we had yet seen, and we were encamped in a clump of trees twenty or thirty feet high, resembling white pine. With the exception of these small clumps, the ridges were bare; and, where the snow found the support of the trees, the wind had blown it up into banks ten or fifteen feet high. It required much care to hunt out a practicable way, as the most open places frequently led to impassable banks.[128]

We had hard and doubtful labor yet before us, as the snow appeared to be heavier where the timber began further down, with few open spots. Ascending a height, we traced out the best line we could discover for the next day's march, and had at least the consolation to see that the mountain descended rapidly. The day had been one of April; gusty, with a few occasional flakes of snow; which, in the afternoon, enveloped the upper mountain in clouds. We watched them anxiously, as now we dreaded a snow storm. Shortly afterwards we heard the roll of thunder, and, looking towards the valley, found it all enveloped in a thunder storm. For us, as connected with the idea of summer, it had a singular charm; and we watched its progress with excited feelings until nearly sunset, when the sky cleared off brightly, and we saw a shining line of water directing its course towards another, a broader and larger sheet. We knew that these could be no other than the Sacramento and the bay of San Francisco; but, after our long wandering in the rugged moun-

---

128. The crossing was a trying experience for the animals. PREUSS, 111, says that of the 104 horses and mules with the party when it left the Columbia, only fifty-three had now survived. Actually, only thirty-three reached Sutter's Fort. The descent from the summit, as described in GIANELLA, 62, was northwest and down the high ridge between Silver Fork and the headwaters of the Upper Truckee River. Farther down, Strawberry Creek was on the left and Sayles Canyon on the right. The expedition finally reached the American River at Strawberry Valley.

tains, where so frequently we had met with disappointments, and where the crossing of every ridge displayed some unknown lake or river, we were yet almost afraid to believe that we were at last to escape into the genial country of which we had heard so many glowing descriptions, and dreaded again to find some vast interior lake, whose bitter waters would bring us disappointment. On the southern shore of what appeared to be the bay could be traced the gleaming line where entered another large stream; and again the Buenaventura rose up in our minds.

Carson had entered the valley along the southern side of the bay, and remembered perfectly to have crossed the mouth of a very large stream, which they had been obliged to raft; but the country then was so entirely covered with water from snow and rain, that he had been able to form no correct impression of watercourses.

We had the satisfaction to know that at least there were people below. Fires were lit up in the valley just at night, appearing to be in answer to ours; and these signs of life renewed, in some measure, the gayety of the camp. They appeared so near, that we judged them to be among the timber of some of the neighboring ridges; but, having them constantly in view day after day, and night after night, we afterwards found them to be fires that had been kindled by the Indians among the *tulares,* on the shore of the bay, 80 miles distant.

Among the very few plants that appeared here, was the common blue flax. To-night, a mule was killed for food.

February 22.—Our breakfast was over long before day. We took advantage of the coolness of the early morning to get over the snow, which to-day occurred in very deep banks among the timber; but we searched out the coldest places, and the animals passed successfully with their loads the hard crust. Now and then, the delay of making a road occasioned much labor and loss of time. In the after part of the day, we saw before us a handsome grassy ridge point; and, making a desperate push over a snow field 10 to 15 feet deep, we happily succeeded in getting the camp across; and encamped on the ridge, after a march of three miles. We had again the prospect of a thunder storm below; and to-night we killed another mule— now our only resource from starvation.

We satisfied ourselves during the day that the lake had an outlet between two ranges on the right; and with this, the creek on which I had encamped probably effected a junction below. Between these, we were descending.

We continued to enjoy the same delightful weather; the sky of the same beautiful blue, and such a sunset and sunrise as on our Atlantic coast we could scarcely imagine. And here among the mountains, 9,000 feet above the sea, we have the deep-blue sky and sunny climate of Smyrna and Palermo, which a little map before me shows are in the same latitude.[129]

The elevation above the sea, by the boiling point, is 8,565 feet.

February 23.—This was our most difficult day: we were forced off the ridges by the quantity of snow among the timber, and obliged to take to the mountain sides, where, occasionally, rocks and a southern exposure afforded us a chance to scramble along. But these were steep, and slippery with snow and ice; and the tough evergreens of the mountain impeded our way, tore our skins, and exhausted our patience. Some of us had the misfortune to wear moccasins with *parflêche* soles, so slippery that we could not keep our feet, and generally crawled across the snow beds. Axes and mauls were necessary to-day, to make a road through the snow. Going ahead with Carson to reconnoitre the road, we reached in the afternoon the river which made the outlet of the lake. Carson sprang over, clear across a place where the stream was compressed among rocks, but the *parflêche* sole of my moccasin glanced from the icy rock, and precipitated me into the river. It was some few seconds before I could recover myself in the current, and Carson, thinking me hurt, jumped in after me, and we both had an icy bath. We tried to search a while for my gun, which had been lost in the fall, but the cold drove us out; and making a large fire on the bank, after we had partially dried ourselves we went back to meet the camp. We afterwards found that the gun had been slung under the ice which lined the banks of the creek.

Using our old plan of breaking the road with alternate horses, we reached the creek in the evening and encamped on a dry open place in the ravine. Another branch, which we had followed, here comes in on the left; and from this point the mountain wall, on which we had travelled to-day, faces to the south along the right bank of the river, where the sun appears to have melted the snow; but the opposite ridge is entirely covered. Here, among the pines, the hill side

---

129. Preuss, the usually dour cartographer, was in a mood which for him can only be described as rapturous: "But what an atmosphere! One does not [often] see such sunrises and morning and evening glows. . . . We are in the latitude of Smyrna and Palermo. The sky is as blue as forget-me-nots" (PREUSS, 112).

produces but little grass—barely sufficient to keep life in the animals. We had the pleasure to be rained upon this afternoon; and grass was now our greatest solicitude. Many of the men looked badly; and some this evening were giving out.

February 24.—We rose at three in the moning, for an astronomical observation, and obtained for the place a latitude of 38° 46′ 58″; longitude 120° 34′ 20″. The sky was clear and pure, with a sharp wind from the northeast, and the thermometer 2° below the freezing point.

We continued down the south face of the mountain; our road leading over dry ground, we were able to avoid the snow almost entirely. In the course of the morning, we struck a foot path, which we were generally able to keep; and the ground was soft to our animal's feet, being sandy or covered with mould. Green grass began to make its appearance, and occasionally we passed a hill scatteringly covered with it. The character of the forest continued the same; and, among the trees, the pine with sharp leaves and very large cones was abundant, some of them being noble trees. We measured one that had 10 feet diameter, though the height was not more than 130 feet. All along, the river was a roaring torrent, its fall very great; and, descending with a rapidity to which we had long been strangers, to our great pleasure oak trees appeared on the ridge, and soon became very frequent; on these I remarked unusually great quantities of mistletoe. Rushes began to make their appearance; and at a small creek where they were abundant, one of the messes was left with the weakest horses, while we continued on.

The opposite mountain side was very steep and continuous—unbroken by ravines, and covered with pines and snow; while on the side we were travelling, innumerable rivulets poured down from the ridge. Continuing on, we halted a moment at one of these rivulets, to admire some beautiful evergreen trees,[130] resembling live oak, which shaded the little stream. They were forty to fifty feet high, and two in diameter, with a uniform tufted top; and the summer green of their beautiful foliage, with the singing birds, and the sweet summer wind which was whirling about the dry oak leaves, nearly intoxicated us with delight; and we hurried on, filled with excitement, to escape entirely from the horrid region of inhospitable snow, to the perpetual spring of the Sacramento.

---

130. *Quercus wislizenii* A. DC., canyon oak.

When we had travelled about ten miles, the valley opened a little to an oak and pine bottom, through which ran rivulets closely bordered with rushes, on which our half-starved horses fell with avidity; and here we made our encampment. Here the roaring torrent has already become a river, and we had descended to an elevation of 3,864 feet.

Along our road to-day the rock was a white granite, which appears to constitute the upper part of the mountains on both the eastern and western slopes; while between, the central is a volcanic rock.

Another horse was killed to-night, for food.

February 25.—Believing that the difficulties of the road were passed, and leaving Mr. Fitzpatrick to follow slowly, as the condition of the animals required, I started ahead this morning with a party of eight, consisting (with myself) of Mr. Preuss and Mr. Talbot, Carson, Derosier, Towns, Proue, and Jacob. We took with us some of the best animals, and my intention was to proceed as rapidly as possible to the house of Mr. Sutter, and return to meet the party with a supply of provisions and fresh animals.

Continuing down the river, which pursued a very direct westerly course through a narrow valley, with only a very slight and narrow bottom land, we made twelve miles, and encamped at some old Indian huts, apparently a fishing place on the river. The bottom was covered with trees of deciduous foliage, and overgrown with vines and rushes. On a bench of the hill near by, was a field of fresh green grass, six inches long in some of the tufts which I had the curiosity to measure. The animals were driven here; and I spent part of the afternoon sitting on a large rock among them, enjoying the pauseless rapidity with which they luxuriated in the unaccustomed food.

The forest was imposing to-day in the magnificence of the trees; some of the pines, bearing large cones, were 10 feet in diameter; cedars also abounded, and we measured one $28\frac{1}{2}$ feet in circumference four feet from the ground. This noble tree seemed here to be in its proper soil and climate. We found it on both sides of the Sierra, but most abundant on the west.

February 26.—We continued to follow the stream, the mountains on either hand increasing in height as we descended, and shutting up the river narrowly in precipices, along which we had great difficulty to get our horses.

It rained heavily during the afternoon, and we were forced off the river to the heights above; whence we descended, at night-fall, the point of a spur between the river and a fork of nearly equal size, coming in from the right. Here we saw, on the lower hills, the first flowers in bloom, which occurred suddenly, and in considerable quantity; one of them a species of *gilia*.

The current in both streams (rather torrents than rivers) was broken by large boulders. It was late, and the animals fatigued; and not succeeding to find a ford immediately, we encamped, although the hill side afforded but a few stray bunches of grass, and the horses, standing about in the rain, looked very miserable.

February 27.—We succeeded in fording the stream, and made a trail by which we crossed the point of the opposite hill, which, on the southern exposure, was prettily covered with green grass, and we halted a mile from our last encampment. The river was only about sixty feet wide, but rapid, and occasionally deep, foaming among boulders, and the water beautifully clear. We encamped on the hill slope, as there was no bottom level, and the opposite ridge is continuous, affording no streams.

We had with us a large kettle; and a mule being killed here, his head was boiled in it for several hours, and made a passable soup for famished people.

Below, precipices on the river forced us to the heights, which we ascended by a steep spur 2,000 feet high. My favorite horse, Proveau, had become very weak, and was scarcely able to bring himself to the top. Travelling here was good, except in crossing the ravines, which were narrow, steep, and frequent. We caught a glimpse of a deer, the first animal we had seen; but did not succeed in approaching him. Proveau could not keep up, and I left Jacob to bring him on, being obliged to press forward with the party, as there was no grass in the forest. We grew very anxious as the day advanced and no grass appeared, for the lives of our animals depended on finding it to-night. They were in just such a condition that grass and repose for the night enabled them to get on the next day. Every hour we had been expecting to see open out before us the valley, which, from the mountain above, seemed almost at our feet. A new and singular shrub,[131] which had made its appearance since crossing the mountain, was very frequent to-day. It branched out near the ground, forming a clump eight to ten feet high, with pale-green leaves of an oval form, and the body and branches had a naked appearance, as

---

131. *Arctostaphylos* sp., manzanita.

if stripped of the bark, which is very smooth and thin, of a chocolate color, contrasting well with the pale green of the leaves. The day was nearly gone; we had made a hard day's march, and found no grass. Towns became light-headed, wandering off into the woods without knowing where he was going, and Jacob brought him back.

Near night-fall we descended into the steep ravine of a handsome creek thirty feet wide, and I was engaged in getting the horses up the opposite hill, when I heard a shout from Carson, who had gone ahead a few hundred yards—"Life yet," said he, as he came up, "life yet; I have found a hill side sprinkled with grass enough for the night." We drove along our horses, and encamped at the place about dark, and there was just room enough to make a place for shelter on the edge of the stream. Three horses were lost to-day—Proveau; a fine young horse from the Columbia, belonging to Charles Towns; and another Indian horse which carried our cooking utensils; the two former gave out, the latter strayed off into the woods as we reached the camp.

February 29.—We lay shut up in the narrow ravine, and gave the animals a necessary day; and men were sent back after the others. Derosier volunteered to bring up Proveau, to whom he knew I was greatly attached, as he had been my favorite horse on both expeditions. Carson and I climbed one of the nearest mountains; the forest land still extended ahead, and the valley appeared as far as ever. The pack horse was found near the camp, but Derosier did not get in.

March 1.—Derosier did not get in during the night, and leaving him to follow, as no grass remained here, we continued on over the uplands, crossing many small streams, and camped again on the river, having made 6 miles. Here we found the hill side covered (although lightly) with fresh green grass; and from this time forward we found it always improving and abundant.

We made a pleasant camp on the river hill, where were some beautiful specimens of the chocolate-colored shrub, which were a foot in diameter near the ground, and fifteen to twenty feet high. The opposite ridge runs continuously along, unbroken by streams. We are rapidly descending into the spring, and we are leaving our snowy region far behind; every thing is getting green; butterflies are swarming; numerous bugs are creeping out, wakened from their winter's sleep; and the forest flowers are coming into bloom. Among those which appeared most numerously to-day was *dodecatheon dentatum.*

We began to be uneasy at Derosier's absence, fearing he might have been bewildered in the woods. Charles Towns, who had not yet recovered his mind, went to swim in the river, as if it were summer, and the stream placid, when it was a cold mountain torrent foaming among rocks. We were happy to see Derosier appear in the evening. He came in, and, sitting down by the fire, began to tell us where he had been. He imagined he had been gone several days, and thought we were still at the camp where he had left us; and we were pained to see that his mind was deranged. It appeared that he had been lost in the mountain, and hunger and fatigue, joined to weakness of body, and fear of perishing in the mountains, had crazed him. The times were severe when stout men lost their minds from extremity of suffering—when horses died—and when mules and horses, ready to die of starvation, were killed for food. Yet there was no murmuring or hesitation.

A short distance below our encampment, the river mountains terminated in precipices, and, after a fatiguing march of only a few miles, we encamped on a bench where there were springs and an abundance of the freshest grass. In the mean time, Mr. Preuss continued on down the river, and, unaware that we had encamped so early in the day, was lost. When night arrived, and he did not come in, we began to understand what had happened to him; but it was too late to make any search.

March 3.—We followed Mr. Preuss's trail for a considerable distance along the river, until we reached a place where he had descended to the stream below and encamped. Here we shouted and fired guns, but received no answer; and we concluded that he had pushed on down the stream. I determined to keep out from the river, along which it was nearly impracticable to travel with animals, until it should form a valley. At every step the country improved in beauty; the pines were rapidly disappearing, and oaks became the principal trees of the forest. Among these, the prevailing tree was the evergreen oak, (which, by way of distinction, we shall call the *live oak;*) and with these, occurred frequently a new species of oak bearing a long slender acorn, from an inch to an inch and a half in length, which we now began to see formed the principal vegetable food of the inhabitants of this region. In a short distance we crossed a little rivulet, where were two old huts, and near by were heaps of acorn hulls. The ground round about was very rich, covered with an

646

exuberant sward of grass; and we sat down for a while in the shade of the oaks, to let the animals feed. We repeated our shouts for Mr. Preuss; and this time we were gratified with an answer. The voice grew rapidly nearer, ascending from the river; but when we expected to see him emerge, it ceased entirely. We had called up some straggling Indian—the first we had met, although for two days back we had seen tracks—who, mistaking us for his fellows, had been only undeceived on getting close up. It would have been pleasant to witness his astonishment; he would not have been more frightened had some of the old mountain spirits they are so much afraid of suddenly appeared in his path. Ignorant of the character of these people, we had now an additional cause of uneasiness in regard to Mr. Preuss; he had no arms with him, and we began to think his chance doubtful. We followed on a trail, still keeping out from the river, and descended to a very large creek, dashing with great velocity over a pre-eminently rocky bed and among large boulders. The bed had sudden breaks, formed by deep holes and ledges of rock running across. Even here, it deserves the name of *Rock* creek, which we gave to it. We succeeded in fording it, and toiled about three thousand feet up the opposite hill. The mountains now were getting sensibly lower; but still there is no valley on the river, which presents steep and rocky banks; but here, several miles from the river, the country is smooth and grassy; the forest has no undergrowth; and in the open valleys of rivulets, or around spring heads, the low groves of live oak give the appearance of orchards in an old cultivated country. Occasionally we met deer, but had not the necessary time for hunting. At one of these orchard grounds, we encamped about noon to make an effort for Mr. Preuss. One man took his way along a spur leading into the river, in hope to cross his trail; and another took our own back. Both were volunteers; and to the successful man was promised a pair of pistols—not as a reward, but as a token of gratitude for a service which would free us all from much anxiety.

We had among our few animals a horse which was so much reduced, that, with travelling, even the good grass could not save him; and, having nothing to eat, he was killed this afternoon. He was a good animal, and had made the journey round from Fort Hall.

Dedecatheon dentatum continued the characteristic plant in flower; and the naked-looking shrub already mentioned continued characteristic, beginning to put forth a small white blossom. At evening the men returned, having seen or heard nothing of Mr. Preuss; and I determined to make a hard push down the river the next morning, and get ahead of him.

March 4.—We continued rapidly along on a broad plainly-beaten trail, the mere travelling and breathing the delightful air being a positive enjoyment. Our road led along a ridge inclining to the river, and the air and the open grounds were fragrant with flowering shrubs; and in the course of the morning we issued on an open spur, by which we descended directly to the stream. Here the river issues suddenly from the mountains, which hitherto had hemmed it closely in; these now become softer, and change sensibly their character; and at this point commences the most beautiful valley in which we had ever travelled. We hurried to the river, on which we noticed a small sand beach, to which Mr. Preuss would naturally have gone. We found no trace of him, but, instead, were recent tracks of barefooted Indians, and little piles of muscle shells, and old fires where they had roasted the fish. We travelled on over the river grounds, which were undulating, and covered with grass to the river brink. We halted to noon a few miles beyond, always under the shade of the evergreen oaks, which formed open groves on the bottoms.

Continuing our road in the afternoon, we ascended to the uplands, where the river passes round a point of great beauty, and goes through very remarkable dalles, in character resembling those of the Columbia river, and which you will find mentioned on the map annexed. Beyond, we again descended to the bottoms, where we found an Indian village, consisting of two or three huts; we had come upon them suddenly, and the people had evidently just run off. The huts were low and slight, made like beehives in a picture, five or six feet high, and near each was a crate, formed of interlaced branches and grass, in size and shape like a very large hogshead. Each of these contained from six to nine bushels. These were filled with the long acorns already mentioned, and in the huts were several neatly made baskets, containing quantities of the acorns roasted. They were sweet and agreeably flavored, and we supplied ourselves with about half a bushel, leaving one of our shirts, a handkerchief, and some smaller articles, in exchange. The river again entered for a space among hills, and we followed a trail leading across a bend through a handsome hollow behind. Here, while engaged in trying to circumvent a deer, we discovered some Indians on a hill several hundred yards ahead, and gave them a shout, to which they responded by loud and rapid talking and vehement gesticulation, but made no stop, hurrying up the mountain as fast as their legs could carry them. We passed on, and again encamped in a grassy grove.

The absence of Mr. Preuss gave me great concern; and, for a large reward, Derosier volunteered to go back on the trail. I directed him to search along the river, travelling upward for the space of a day and a half, at which time I expected he would meet Mr. Fitzpatrick, whom I requested to aid in the search; at all events, he was to go no farther, but return to this camp, where a *cache* of provisions was made for him.

Continuing the next day down the river, we discovered three squaws in a little bottom, and surrounded them before they could make their escape. They had large conical baskets, which they were engaged in filling with a small leafy plant (*erodium cicutarium*)[132] just now beginning to bloom, and covering the ground like a sward of grass. These did not make any lamentations, but appeared very much impressed with our appearance, speaking to us only in a whisper, and offering us smaller baskets of the plant, which they signified to us was good to eat, making signs also that it was to be cooked by the fire. We drew out a little cold horse meat, and the squaws made signs to us that the men had gone out after deer, and that we could have some by waiting till they came in. We observed that the horses ate with great avidity the herb which they had been gathering; and here also, for the first time, we saw Indians eat the common grass— one of the squaws pulling several tufts, and eating it with apparent relish. Seeing our surprise, she pointed to the horses; but we could not well understand what she meant, except, perhaps, that what was good for the one was good for the other.

We encamped in the evening on the shore of the river, at a place where the associated beauties of scenery made so strong an impression on us that we have given it the name of the Beautiful Camp. The undulating river shore was shaded with the live oaks, which formed a continuous grove over the country, and the same grassy sward extended to the edge of the water; and we made our fires near some large granite masses which were lying among the trees. We had seen several of the acorn *caches* during the day; and here there were two which were very large, containing each, probably,

132. *Erodium cicutarium* (L.) L'Her. Filagree. Here the Indians were making domestic use of a plant almost certainly introduced by Spanish explorers and Franciscan missionaries during the previous century.

ten bushels. Towards evening we heard a weak shout among the hills behind, and had the pleasure to see Mr. Preuss descending towards the camp. Like ourselves, he had travelled to-day 25 miles, but had seen nothing of Derosier. Knowing, on the day he was lost, that I was determined to keep the river as much as possible, he had not thought it necessary to follow the trail very closely, but walked on, right and left, certain to find it somewhere along the river, searching places to obtain good views of the country. Towards sunset he climbed down towards the river to look for the camp; but, finding no trail, concluded that we were behind, and walked back until night came on, when, being very much fatigued, he collected drift wood and made a large fire among the rocks. The next day it became more serious, and he encamped again alone, thinking that we must have taken some other course. To go back would have been madness in his weak and starved condition, and onward towards the valley was his only hope, always in expectation of reaching it soon. His principal means of subsistence were a few roots, which the hunters call sweet onions, having very little taste, but a good deal of nutriment, growing generally in rocky ground, and requiring a good deal of labor to get as he had only a pocket knife. Searching for these, he found a nest of big ants, which he let run on his hand, and stripped them off in his mouth; these had an agreeable acid taste. One of his greatest privations was the want of tobacco; and a pleasant smoke at evening would have been a relief which only a voyageur could appreciate. He tried the dried leaves of the live oak, knowing that those of other oaks were sometimes used as a substitute; but these were too thick, and would not do. On the 4th he made seven or eight miles, walking slowly along the river, avoiding as much as possible to climb the hills. In little pools he caught some of the smallest kind of frogs, which he swallowed, not so much in the gratification of hunger, as in the hope of obtaining some strength. Scattered along the river were old fire-places, where the Indians had roasted muscles and acorns; but though he searched diligently, he did not there succeed in finding either. He had collected fire wood for the night, when he heard at some distance from the river the barking of what he thought were two dogs, and walked in that direction as quickly as he was able, hoping to find there some Indian hut, but met only two wolves; and, in his disappointment, the gloom of the forest was doubled.

Travelling the next day feebly down the river, he found five or six

Indians at the huts of which we have spoken; some were painting themselves black, and others roasting acorns. Being only one man, they did not run off, but received him kindly, and gave him a welcome supply of roasted acorns. He gave them his pocket knife in return, and stretched out his hand to one of the Indians, who did not appear to comprehend the motion, but jumped back, as if he thought he was about to lay hold of him. They seemed afraid of him, not certain as to what he was.

Travelling on, he came to the place where we had found the squaws. Here he found our fire still burning, and the tracks of the horses. The sight gave him sudden hope and courage; and, following as fast as he could, joined us at evening.

March 6.—We continued on our road, through the same surpassingly beautiful country, entirely unequalled for the pasturage of stock by any thing we had ever seen. Our horses had now become so strong that they were able to carry us, and we travelled rapidly—over four miles an hour; four of us riding every alternate hour. Every few hundred yards we came upon a little band of deer; but we were too eager to reach the settlement which we momentarily expected to discover, to halt for any other than a passing shot. In a few hours we reached a large fork, the northern branch of the river, and equal in size to that which we had descended. Together they formed a beautiful stream, 60 to 100 yards wide; which at first, ignorant of the nature of the country through which that river ran, we took to be the Sacramento.[133]

We continued down the right bank of the river, travelling for a while over a wooded upland, where we had the delight to discover tracks of cattle. To the southwest was visible a black column of smoke, which we had frequently noticed in descending, arising from the fires we had seen from the top of the Sierra. From the upland we descended into broad groves on the river, consisting of the evergreen, and a new species of white oak with a large tufted top, and three to six feet in diameter. Among these was no brushwood; and the grassy surface gave to it the appearance of parks in an old settled country. Following the tracks of the horses and cattle in search of people, we discovered a small village of Indians. Some of these had on shirts of civilized manufacture, but were otherwise naked, and we

---

133. The American River at last. They had been traveling on its tributaries for several days.

could understand nothing from them; they appeared entirely astonished at seeing us.

We made an acorn meal at noon, and hurried on; the valley being gay with flowers, and some of the banks being absolutely golden with the Californian poppy, (*eschscholtzia crocea.*) Here the grass was smooth and green, and the groves very open; the large oaks throwing a broad shade among sunny spots. Shortly afterwards we gave a shout at the appearance on a little bluff of a neatly built *adobe* house with glass windows. We rode up, but, to our disappointment, found only Indians. There was no appearance of cultivation, and we could see no cattle, and we supposed the place had been abandoned. We now pressed on more eagerly than ever; the river swept round in a large bend to the right; the hills lowered down entirely; and, gradually entering a broad valley, we came unexpectedly into a large Indian village, where the people looked clean, and wore cotton shirts and various other articles of dress. They immediately crowded around us, and we had the inexpressible delight to find one who spoke a little indifferent Spanish, but who at first confounded us by saying there were no whites in the country; but just then a well-dressed Indian came up, and made his salutations in very well spoken Spanish. In answer to our inquiries, he informed us that we were upon the *Rio de los Americanos,* (the river of the Americans,) and that it joined the Sacramento river about 10 miles below. Never did a name sound more sweetly! We felt ourselves among our countrymen; for the name of *American,* in these distant parts, is applied to the citizens of the United States. To our eager inquiries he answered, "I am a *vaquero* (cow herder) in the service of Capt. Sutter, and the people of this *rancheria* work for him." Our evident satisfaction made him communicative; and he went on to say that Capt. Sutter was a very rich man, and always glad to see his country people. We asked for his house. He answered, that it was just over the hill before us; and offered, if we would wait a moment, to take his horse and conduct us to it. We readily accepted his civil offer. In a short distance we came in sight of the fort; and, passing on the way the house of a settler on the opposite side, (a Mr. Sinclair,) we forded the river; and in a few miles were met a short distance from the fort by Capt. Sutter himself.[134] He gave us a most frank and cordial re-

---

134. Scotsman John Sinclair (d. 1849) had been in the employ of the Hudson's Bay Company in Oregon, and editor of a paper in Honolulu, before coming to California in 1839. When JCF met him he was occupying the

ception—conducted us immediately to his residence—and under his hospitable roof we had a night of rest, enjoyment, and refreshment, which none but ourselves could appreciate. But the party left in the mountains with Mr. Fitzpatrick were to be attended to; and the next morning, supplied with fresh horses and provisions, I hurried off to meet them. On the second day we met, a few miles below the forks of the Rio de los Americanos; and a more forlorn and pitiable sight than they presented cannot well be imagined. They were all on foot —each man, weak and emaciated, leading a horse or mule as weak and emaciated as themselves. They had experienced great difficulty in descending the mountains, made slippery by rains and melting snows, and many horses fell over precipices, and were killed; and with some were lost the *packs* they carried. Among these, was a mule with the plants which we had collected since leaving Fort Hall, along a line of 2,000 miles travel. Out of 67 horses and mules with which we commenced crossing the Sierra, only 33 reached the valley of the Sacramento, and they only in a condition to be led along. Mr. Fitzpatrick and his party, travelling more slowly, had been able to make some little exertion at hunting, and had killed a few deer. The

El Paso rancho, north of New Helvetia, for Eliab Grimes, to whom it was granted in 1844. He later was alcalde of the Sacramento district (PIONEER REGISTER). "Capt. Sutter" is, of course, the prominent John Augustus Sutter (1803–80), a Swiss emigrant whose fame in California renders annotation needless. His colony on the American River, at its juncture with the Sacramento, was to become one of the principal places of call for American settlers coming into the area. Biographies include GUDDE [2] and DILLON.

In addition to treating Frémont's debilitated party with civility and generosity, Sutter felt it his duty to report the matter to the U.S. consul at Monterey, Thomas Oliver Larkin. Larkin commented upon JCF's presence in a letter to the Secretary of State, 12 April 1844 (DNA-59), and enclosed an extract from Sutter's letter to him. Sutter had said, in part: "On the 6 instant [March] Lieut. J. C. Fremont from the U. States exploring expedition arrived here in distress, having been forced to deviate from his course on account of deep snows, loss of Animals and want of Provisions. He informed me of having left the Columbia River a short distance above Fort Vancouver with the intention of crossing to the head waters of the Arkansas River eastward, through the lower or southern part of Oregon Territory, but finding a succession of high mountains covered with snow which with the distressed condition of his company forced him to abandon his route and strike for the settlements of California, refit and cross the mountains farther to the South. . . . The visit of this exploring expedition I attribute entirely to accident. . . . The starvation and fatigue they had endured rendered them truly deplorable objects."

Larkin's letter thus provided direct news of JCF to Washington long before the expedition had returned. It was received in Washington 2 May 1845.

scanty supply was a great relief to them; for several had been made sick by the strange and unwholesome food which the preservation of life compelled them to use. We stopped and encamped as soon as we met; and a repast of good beef, excellent bread, and delicious salmon, which I had brought along, were their first relief from the sufferings of the Sierra, and their first introduction to the luxuries of the Sacramento. It required all our philosophy and forbearance to prevent *plenty* from becoming as hurtful to us now, as *scarcity* had been before.

The next day, March 8th, we encamped at the junction of the two rivers, the Sacramento and Americanos; and thus found the whole party in the beautiful valley of the Sacramento. It was a convenient place for the camp; and, among other things, was within reach of the wood necessary to make the pack saddles, which we should need on our long journey home, from which we were farther distant now than we were four months before, when from the Dalles of the Columbia we so cheerfully took up the homeward line of march.

Captain Sutter emigrated to this country from the western part of Missouri in 1838–'39, and formed the first settlement in the valley, on a large grant of land which he obtained from the Mexican Government. He had, at first, some trouble with the Indians; but, by the occasional exercise of well-timed authority, he has succeeded in converting them into a peaceable and industrious people. The ditches around his extensive wheat fields, the making of the sun-dried bricks, of which his fort is constructed; the ploughing, harrowing, and other agricultural operations, are entirely the work of these Indians, for which they receive a very moderate compensation— principally in shirts, blankets, and other articles of clothing. In the same manner, on application to the chief of a village, he readily obtains as many boys and girls as he has any use for. There were at this time a number of girls at the fort, in training for a future woollen factory; but they were now all busily engaged in constantly watering the gardens, which the unfavorable dryness of the season rendered neccessary. The occasional dryness of the seasons, I understood to be the only complaint of the settlers in this fertile valley, as it sometimes renders the crops uncertain. Mr. Sutter was about making arrangements to irrigate his lands by means of the Rio de los Americanos. He had this year sown, and altogether by Indian labor, three hundred fanegas of wheat.

A few years since, the neighboring Russian establishment of

Ross,[135] being about to withdraw from the country, sold to him a large number of stock, with agricultural and other stores, with a number of pieces of artillery and other munitions of war; for these, a regular yearly payment is made in grain.

The fort is a quadrangular *adobe* structure, mounting 12 pieces of artillery, (two of them brass,) and capable of admitting a garrison of a thousand men; this, at present, consists of 40 Indians, in uniform —one of whom was always found on duty at the gate. As might naturally be expected, the pieces are not in very good order. The whites in the employment of Capt. Sutter, American, French and German, amount, perhaps, to 30 men. The inner wall is formed into buildings comprising the common quarters, with blacksmith and other workshops; the dwelling house, with a large distillery house, and other buildings, occupying more the centre of the area.

It is built upon a pond-like stream, at times a running creek communicating with the Rio de los Americanos, which enters the Sacramento about two miles below. The latter is here a noble river, about three hundred yards broad, deep and tranquil, with several fathoms of water in the channel, and its banks continuously timbered. There were two vessels belonging to Capt. Sutter at anchor near the landing—one a large two-masted lighter, and the other a schooner, which was shortly to proceed on a voyage to Fort Vancouver for a cargo of goods.

Since his arrival, several other persons, principally Americans, have established themselves in the valley. Mr. Sinclair, from whom I experienced much kindness during my stay, is settled a few miles distant, on the Rio de los Americanos. Mr. Coudrois,[136] a gentleman from Germany, has established himself on Feather river, and is associated with Captain Sutter in agricultural pursuits. Among other improvements, they are about to introduce the cultivation of rape

---

135. "Ross," which because of its fortifications became known to the Californians as Fuerto de los Rusos and to the Americans as Fort Ross, was begun by the Russians in 1812 and formed the nucleus of their Californian activities in agriculture, sealing, and the fur trade to 1841 (ESSIG).

136. Theodor Cordua (1796–1857), born in Mecklenburg and probably of Spanish descent. Like Sinclair and Sutter, he had been in Honolulu before coming to California. In 1844, he received Mexican citizenship and grants of land on the Feather River. After running a store at the mines during the gold rush, and losing his wealth, he returned to Hawaii and ultimately to Germany (CORDUA).

seed, (*brassica rapus,*)[137] which there is every reason to believe is admirably adapted to the climate and soil. The lowest average produce of wheat, as far as we can at present know, is 35 fanegas for one sown; but, as an instance of its fertility, it may be mentioned that Señor Val[l]ejo obtained, on a piece of ground where sheep had been pastured, 800 fanegas for eight sown. The produce being different in various places, a very correct idea cannot be formed.

An impetus was given to the active little population by our arrival, as we were in want of every thing. Mules, horses, and cattle, were to be collected; the horse mill was at work day and night, to make sufficient flour; the blacksmith's shop was put in requisition for horse shoes and bridle bitts; and pack saddles, ropes, and bridles, and all the other little equipment of the camp, were again to be provided.

The delay thus occasioned was one of repose and enjoyment, which our situation required, and, anxious as we were to resume our homeward journey, was regretted by no one. In the mean time, I had the pleasure to meet with Mr. Chiles, who was residing at a farm on the other side of the river Sacramento, while engaged in the selection of a place for a settlement, for which he had received the necessary grant of land from the Mexican Government.

It will be remembered that we had parted near the frontier of the States, and that he had subsequently descended the valley of Lewis's fork, with a party of 10 or 12 men, with the intention of crossing the intermediate mountains to the waters of the bay of San Francisco. In the execution of this design, and aided by subsequent information, he left the Columbia at the mouth of *Malheur* river; and, making his way to the head waters of the Sacramento with a part of his company, travelled down that river to the settlements of Nueva Helvetia. The other party, to whom he had committed his wagons, and mill irons and saws, took a course farther to the south, and the wagons and their contents were lost.

On the 22d we made a preparatory move, and encamped near the settlement of Mr. Sinclair, on the left bank of the Rio de los Americanos. I had discharged five of the party: Neal, the blacksmith, (an excellent workman, and an unmarried man, who had done his duty faithfully, and had been of very great service to me,) desired to remain, as strong inducements were offered here to mechanics. Although at considerable inconvenience to myself, his good conduct

---

137. An error for *Brassica napus* L.

induced me to comply with his request; and I obtained for him, from Captain Sutter, a present compensation of two dollars and a half per diem, with a promise that it should be increased to five, if he proved as good a workman as had been represented. He was more particularly an agricultural blacksmith. The other men were discharged with their own consent.[138]

While we remained at this place, Derosier, one of our best men, whose steady good conduct had won my regard, wandered off from the camp, and never returned to it again; nor has he since been heard of.[139]

March 24.—We resumed our journey with an ample stock of provisions and a large cavalcade of animals, consisting of 130 horses and mules, and about thirty head of cattle, five of which were milch cows. Mr. Sutter furnished us also with an Indian boy, who had been trained as a *vaquero,* and who would be serviceable in managing our cavalcade, a great part of which were nearly as wild as buffalo; and who was, besides, very anxious to go along with us.[140] Our direct course home was east; but the Sierra would force us south, above five hundred miles of travelling, to a pass at the head of the San Joaquin river.[141] This pass, reported to be good, was discovered by Mr. Joseph Walker, of whom I have already spoken, and whose name it might therefore appropriately bear. To reach it, our course lay along the valley of the San Joaquin—the river on our right, and the lofty wall of the impassable Sierra on the left. From that pass we were to move southeastwardly, having the Sierra then on the

138. The others discharged included Oliver Beaulieu, Philibert Courteau, Thomas Fallon, and Joseph Verrot. Beaulieu and Courteau were accused of stealing sugar from the party's supplies, and deductions were made from their final pay. JCF encountered them again in California in 1846, when he bought supplies from Beaulieu and hired Courteau as a cattle guard. See bill of Beaulieu to JCF, 8 March 1846 (CSmH), and Courteau voucher (no. 4), 30 Sept. 1846, DNA-217, T-135. As we have already noted, Fallon took an active part in the Bear Flag Revolt and for a short time was mayor of San Jose.

139. Baptiste Derosier wandered on the plains for many days before returning to Sutter's establishment. He finally reached Jefferson, Mo., 21 Nov. 1845, more than a year after the main party had returned. His wife Thérèse had already been paid $45 of the amount due him, and he was paid the rest when he returned (DNA-217, T-135, voucher no. 301).

140. According to Sutter, Lieut. Col. Rafael Tellez, a captain, a lieutenant, and twenty-five dragoons arrived on 27 March to inquire about JCF's activities in California (GUDDE [2], 100–101).

141. JCF means Tehachapi Pass, but we shall see soon that he did not use it.

right, and reach the *"Spanish trail,"* deviously traced from one watering place to another, which constituted the route of the caravans from *Puebla de los Angeles,* near the coast of the Pacific, to *Santa Fé* of New Mexico. From the pass to this trail was 150 miles. Following that trail through a desert, relieved by some fertile plains indicated by the recurrence of the term *vegas,* until it turned to the right to cross the Colorado, our course would be northeast until we regained the latitude we had lost in arriving at the Eutah lake, and thence to the Rocky mountains at the head of the Arkansas. This course of travelling, forced upon us by the structure of the country, would occupy a computed distance of two thousand miles before we reached the head of the Arkansas; not a settlement to be seen upon it; and the names of places along it, all being Spanish or Indian, indicated that it had been but little trod by *American* feet. Though long, and not free from hardships, this route presented some points of attraction, in tracing the Sierra Nevada—turning the Great Basin, perhaps crossing its rim on the south—completely solving the problem of any river, except the Colorado, from the Rocky mountains on that part of our continent—and seeing the southern extremity of the Great Salt lake, of which the northern part had been examined the year before.

Taking leave of Mr. Sutter, who, with several gentlemen, accompanied us a few miles on our way, we travelled about eighteen miles, and encamped on the *Rio de los Cosumnes,* a stream receiving its name from the Indians who live in its valley.[142] Our road was through a level country, admirably suited to cultivation, and covered with groves of oak trees, principally the evergreen oak, and a large oak already mentioned, in form like those of the white oak. The weather, which here, at this season, can easily be changed from the summer heat of the valley to the frosty mornings and bright days nearer the mountains, continued delightful for travellers, but unfavorable to the agriculturists, whose crops of wheat began to wear a yellow tinge from want of rain.

March 25.—We travelled for 28 miles over the same delightful country as yesterday, and halted in a beautiful bottom at the ford of

---

142. The route from 24 March through 31 March takes the party to the Cosumnes the first night and the Mokelumne the next. By 26 March, they are on the Calaveras not far from Stockton. On 28 March, they camp on the Stanislaus near Ripon. Next day they travel seventeen miles without finding a crossing, finally ferrying across in the vicinity of the San Joaquin.

the *Rio de los Mukelemnes,* receiving its name from another Indian tribe living on the river. The bottoms on the stream are broad, rich, and extremely fertile; and the uplands are shaded with oak groves. A showy *lupinus* of extraordinary beauty, growing four to five feet in height, and covered with spikes in bloom, adorned the banks of the river, and filled the air with a light and grateful perfume.

On the 26th we halted at the *Arroyo de las Calaveras,* (Skull creek,) a tributary to the San Joaquin—the previous two streams entering the bay between the San Joaquin and Sacramento rivers. This place is beautiful, with open groves of oak, and a grassy sward beneath, with many plants in bloom; some varieties of which seem to love the shade of the trees, and grow there in close small fields. Near the river, and replacing the grass, are great quantities of *ammole,* (soap plant,)[143] the leaves of which are used in California for making, among other things, mats for saddle cloths. A vine with a small white flower, (*melothria?*)[144] called here *la yerba buena,* and which, from its abundance, gives name to an island and town in the bay, was to-day very frequent on our road—sometimes running on the ground or climbing the trees.

March 27.—To-day we travelled steadily and rapidly up the valley; for, with our wild animals, any other gait was impossible, and making about five miles an hour. During the earlier part of the day, our ride had been over a very level prairie, or rather a succession of long stretches of prairie, separated by lines and groves of oak timber, growing along dry gullies, which are filled with water in seasons of rain; and, perhaps, also, by the melting snows. Over much of this extent, the vegetation was sparse; the surface showing plainly the action of water, which, in the season of flood, the Joaquin spreads over the valley. About 1 o'clock we came again among innumerable flowers; and a few miles further, fields of the beautiful blue-flowering *lupine,* which seems to love the neighborhood of water, indicated that we were approaching a stream. We here found this beautiful shrub in thickets, some of them being 12 feet in height. Occasionally three or four plants were clustered together, forming a grand bouquet, about 90 feet in circumference, and 10 feet high; the whole

---

143. *Chlorogalum pomeridianum* (DC.) Kunth. Evidently widely used by native Indians as food, either raw or cooked, and by settlers as a convenient soap. Its use for saddle mats is seldom mentioned.

144. *Satureja douglasii* (Benth.) Briq., yerba buena, gave San Francisco its name. A mixed reference here involving cucurbit *Echinocystis watsoni.*

summit covered with spikes of flowers, the perfume of which is very sweet and grateful. A lover of natural beauty can imagine with what pleasure we rode among these flowering groves, which filled the air with a light and delicate fragrance. We continued our road for about half a mile, interspersed through an open grove of live oaks, which, in form, were the most symmetrical and beautiful we had yet seen in this country. The ends of their branches rested on the ground, forming somewhat more than a half sphere of very full and regular figure, with leaves apparently smaller than usual.

The Californian poppy, of a rich orange color, was numerous to-day. Elk and several bands of antelope made their appearance.

Our road was now one continued enjoyment; and it was pleasant, riding among this assemblage of green pastures with varied flowers and scattered groves, and out of the warm green spring, to look at the rocky and snowy peaks where lately we had suffered so much. Emerging from the timber, we came suddenly upon the Stanislaus river, where we hoped to find a ford, but the stream was flowing by, dark and deep, swollen by the mountain snows; its general breadth was about 50 yards.

We travelled about five miles up the river, and encamped without being able to find a ford. Here we made a large *corál,* in order to be able to catch a sufficient number of our wild animals to relieve those previously packed.

Under the shade of the oaks, along the river, I noticed *erodium cicutarium* in bloom, eight or ten inches high. This is the plant which we had seen the squaws gathering on the Rio de los Americanos. By the inhabitants of the valley, it is highly esteemed for fattening cattle, which appear to be very fond of it. Here, where the soil begins to be sandy, it supplies to a considerable extent the want of grass.

Desirous, as far as possible, without delay, to include in our examination the San Joaquin river, I returned this morning down the Stanislaus for 17 miles, and again encamped without having found a fording place. After following it for 8 miles further the next morning, and finding ourselves in the vicinity of the San Joaquin, encamped in a handsome oak grove, and, several cattle being killed, we ferried over our baggage in their skins. Here our Indian boy, who probably had not much idea of where he was going, and began to be alarmed at the many streams which we were rapidly putting between him and the village, deserted.

Thirteen head of cattle took a sudden fright, while we were driving them across the river, and galloped off. I remained a day in the endeavor to recover them; but, finding they had taken the trail back to the fort, let them go without further effort. Here we had several days of warm and pleasant rain, which doubtless saved the crops below.

On the 1st of April, we made 10 miles across a prairie without timber, when we were stopped again by another large river, which is called the *Rio de la Merced,* (river of our Lady of Mercy.)[145] Here the country had lost its character of extreme fertility, the soil having become more sandy and light; but, for several days past, its beauty had been increased by the additional animation of animal life; and now, it is crowded with bands of elk and wild horses; and along the rivers are frequent fresh tracks of grizzly bear, which are unusually numerous in this country.

Our route had been along the timber of the San Joaquin, generally about 8 miles distant, over a high prairie.

In one of the bands of elk seen to-day, there were about 200; but the larger bands, both of these and wild horses, are generally found on the other side of the river, which, for that reason, I avoided crossing. I had been informed below, that the droves of wild horses were almost invariably found on the western bank of the river; and the danger of losing our animals among them, together with the wish of adding to our reconnoissance the numerous streams which run down from the Sierra, decided me to travel up the eastern bank.

April 2.—The day was occupied in building a boat, and ferrying our baggage across the river; and we encamped on the bank. A large fishing eagle, with white head and tail, was slowly sailing along, looking after salmon; and there were some pretty birds in the timber, with partridges, ducks, and geese innumerable in the neighborhood. We were struck with the tameness of the latter bird at Helvetia, scattered about in flocks near the wheat fields, and eating grass on the prairie; a horseman would ride by within 30 yards, without disturbing them.

April 3.—To-day we touched several times the San Joaquin river —here a fine-looking tranquil stream, with a slight current, and apparently deep. It resembled the Missouri in color, with occasional points of white sand; and its banks, where steep, were a kind of

---

145. Actually the Tuolumne, which will require all the next day to cross.

sandy clay; its average width appeared to be about eighty yards. In the bottoms are frequent ponds, where our approach disturbed multitudes of wild fowl, principally geese. Skirting along the timber, we frequently started elk; and large bands were seen during the day, with antelope and wild horses. The low country and the timber rendered it difficult to keep the main line of the river; and this evening we encamped on a tributary stream,[146] about five miles from its mouth. On the prairie bordering the San Joaquin bottoms, there occurred during the day but little grass, and in its place was a sparse and dwarf growth of plants; the soil being sandy, with small bare places and hillocks, reminded me much of the Platte bottoms; but, on approaching the timber, we found a more luxuriant vegetation; and at our camp was an abundance of grass and pea vines.

The foliage of the oak is getting darker; and every thing, except that the weather is a little cool, shows that spring is rapidly advancing; and to-day we had quite a summer rain.

April 4.—Commenced to rain at daylight, but cleared off brightly at sunrise. We ferried the river without any difficulty, and continued up the San Joaquin. Elk were running in bands over the prairie and in the skirt of the timber. We reached the river again at the mouth of a large slough, which we were unable to ford, and made a circuit of several miles around. Here the country appears very flat; oak trees have entirely disappeared, and are replaced by a large willow, nearly equal to it in size. The river is about a hundred yards in breadth, branching into sloughs, and interspersed with islands. At this time it appears sufficiently deep for a small steamer, but its navigation would be broken by shallows at low water. Bearing in towards the river, we were again forced off by another slough; and, passing around, steered towards a clump of trees on the river, and, finding there good grass, encamped. The prairies along the left bank are alive with immense droves of wild horses; and they have been seen during the day at every opening through the woods which afforded us a view across the river. Latitude, by observation, 37° 08' 00"; longitude 120° 45' 22".

April 5.—During the earlier part of the day's ride, the country presented a lacustrine appearance; the river was deep, and nearly on a level with the surrounding country; its banks raised like a levee, and fringed with willows. Over the bordering plain were inter-

---

146. The Merced, which will be ferried the following day.

spersed spots of prairie among fields of *tulé* (bulrushes,) which in this country are called *tulares,* and little ponds. On the opposite side, a line of timber was visible, which, according to information, points out the course of the slough, which, at times of high water, connects with the San Joaquin river—a large body of water in the upper part of the valley, called the Tulé lakes [Tulare Lake]. The river and all its sloughs are very full, and it is probable that the lake is now discharging. Here elk were frequently started, and one was shot out of a band which ran around us. On our left, the Sierra maintains its snowy height, and masses of snow appear to descend very low towards the plains; probably the late rains in the valley were snow on the mountains. We travelled 37 miles, and encamped on the river. Longitude of the camp, 120° 28′ 34″, and latitude 36° 49′ 12″.

April 6.—After having travelled 15 miles along the river, we made an early halt, under the shade of sycamore trees. Here we found the San Joaquin coming down from the Sierra with a westerly course, and checking our way, as all its tributaries had previously done. We had expected to raft the river; but found a good ford, and encamped on the opposite bank, where droves of wild horses were raising clouds of dust on the prairie. Columns of smoke were visible in the direction of the Tulé lakes to the southward—probably kindled in the tulares by the Indians, as signals that there were strangers in the valley.

We made, on the 7th, a hard march in a cold chilly rain from morning until night—the weather so thick that we travelled by compass. This was a *traverse* from the San Joaquin to the waters of the Tulé lakes, and our road was over a very level prairie country. We saw wolves frequently during the day, prowling about after the young antelope, which cannot run very fast. These were numerous during the day, and two were caught by the people.

Late in the afternoon we discovered timber, which was found to be groves of oak trees on a dry *arroyo.* The rain, which had fallen in frequent showers, poured down in a storm at sunset, with a strong wind, which swept off the clouds, and left a clear sky. Riding on through the timber, about dark we found abundant water in small ponds, 20 to 30 yards in diameter, with clear deep water and sandy beds, bordered with bog rushes (*juncus effusus,*) and a tall rush (*scirpus lacustris*) 12 feet high, and surrounded near the margin with willow trees in bloom; among them one which resembled *salix myricoides*.[147] The oak of the groves was the same already mentioned, with small leaves, in form like those of the white oak, and forming, with the evergreen oak, the characteristic trees of the valley.

April 8.—After a ride of two miles through brush and open groves, we reached a large stream, called the River of the Lake [King's River], resembling in size the San Joaquin, and being about 100 yards broad. This is the principal tributary to the Tulé lakes, which collect all the waters in the upper part of the valley. While we were searching for a ford, some Indians appeared on the opposite bank, and, having discovered that we were not Spanish soldiers, showed us the way to a good ford several miles above.

The Indians of the Sierra make frequent descents upon the settlements west of the Coast Range, which they keep constantly swept of horses; among them are many who are called Christian Indians, being refugees from Spanish missions. Several of these incursions occurred while we were at Helvetia. Occasionally parties of soldiers follow them across the Coast Range, but never enter the Sierra.

On the opposite side we found some forty or fifty Indians, who had come to meet us from the village below. We made them some small presents, and invited them to accompany us to our encampment, which, after about three miles through fine oak groves, we made on the river. We made a fort, principally on account of our animals. The Indians brought otter skins, and several kinds of fish, and bread made of acorns, to trade. Among them were several who had come to live among these Indians when the missions were broken up, and who spoke Spanish fluently. They informed us that they were called by the Spaniards *mansitos*, (tame,) in distinction from the wilder tribes of the mountains. They, however, think themselves very insecure, not knowing at what unforeseen moment the sins of the latter may be visited on them. They are dark-skinned, but handsome and intelligent Indians, and live principally on acorns and the roots of the tulé, of which also their huts are made.

By observation, the latitude of the encampment is 36° 24′ 50″, and longitude 119° 41′ 40″.

April 9.—For several miles we had very bad travelling over what is called rotten ground, in which the horses were frequently up to their knees. Making towards a line of timber, we found a small ford-

---

147. Probably *Salix melanopsis* Nutt.

able stream, beyond which the country improved, and the grass became excellent; and, crossing a number of dry and timbered *arroyos,* we travelled until late through open oak groves, and encamped among a collection of streams. These were running among rushes and willows; and, as usual, flocks of blackbirds announced our approach to water. We have here approached considerably nearer to the eastern Sierra, which shows very plainly, still covered with masses of snow, which yesterday and to-day has also appeared abundant on the Coast Range.

April 10.—To-day we made another long journey of about forty miles, through a country uninteresting and flat, with very little grass and a sandy soil, in which several branches we crossed had lost their water. In the evening the face of the country became hilly; and, turning a few miles up towards the mountains, we found a good encampment on a pretty stream [White River] hidden among the hills, and handsomely timbered, principally with large cottonwoods, (*populus,* differing from any in Michaux's Sylva.) The seed vessels of this tree were now just about bursting.

Several Indians came down the river to see us in the evening; we gave them supper, and cautioned them against stealing our horses; which they promised not to attempt.

April 11.—A broad trail along the river here takes out among the hills. "Buen camino," (good road,) said one of the Indians, of whom we had inquired about the pass; and, following it accordingly, it conducted us beautifully through a very broken country, by an excellent way, which, otherwise, we should have found extremely bad. Taken separately, the hills present smooth and graceful outlines, but, together, make bad travelling ground. Instead of grass, the whole face of the country is closely covered with *erodium cicutarium,* here only two or three inches high. Its height and beauty varied in a remarkable manner with the locality, being, in many low places which we passed during the day, around streams and springs, two and three feet in height. The country had now assumed a character of aridity; and the luxuriant green of these little streams, wooded with willow, oak, or sycamore, looked very refreshing among the sandy hills.

In the evening we encamped on a large creek [Poso Creek], with abundant water. I noticed here in bloom, for the first time since leaving the Arkansas waters, the *mirabilis Jalapa.*

April 12.—Along our road to-day the country was altogether sandy, and vegetation meager. *Ephedra occidentalis,* which we had first seen in the neighborhood of the Pyramid lake, made its appearance here, and in the course of the day became very abundant, and in large bushes. Towards the close of the afternoon, we reached a tolerably large river, which empties into a small lake at the head of the valley; it is about thirty-five yards wide, with a stony and gravelly bed, and the swiftest stream we have crossed since leaving the bay.[148] The bottoms produced no grass, though well timbered with willow and cottonwood; and, after ascending it for several miles, we made a late encampment on a little bottom, with scanty grass. In greater part, the vegetation along our road consisted now of rare and unusual plants, among which many were entirely new.

Along the bottoms were thickets consisting of several varieties of shrubs, which made here their first appearance; and among these was *Garrya elliptica,* (Lindley,) a small tree belonging to a very peculiar natural order, and, in its general appearance, (growing in thickets,) resembling willow. It now became common along the streams, frequently supplying the place of *salix longifolia.*

April 13.—The water was low, and a few miles above we forded the river at a rapid, and marched in a southeasterly direction over a less broken country. The mountains were now very near, occasionally looming out through fog. In a few hours we reached the bottom of a creek without water, over which the sandy beds were dispersed in many branches. Immediately where we struck it, the timber terminated; and below, to the right, it was a broad bed of dry and bare sands. There were many tracks of Indians and horses imprinted in the sand, which, with other indications, informed us was the creek issuing from the pass, and which on the map we have called Pass [Tehachapi] creek. We ascended a trail for a few miles along the creek, and suddenly found a stream of water five feet wide, running with a lively current, but losing itself almost immediately. This little stream showed plainly the manner in which the mountain waters lose themselves in sand at the eastern foot of the Sierra, leaving only a parched desert and arid plains beyond. The stream enlarged rapidly, and the timber became abundant as we descended. A new species of pine made its appearance, with several kinds of oaks, and a variety of trees; and the country changing its

---

148. JCF later named this river and lake Kern River and Kern Lake, after Edward M. Kern, the topographer and artist for the third expedition.

appearance suddenly and entirely, we found ourselves again travelling among the old orchard-like places. Here we selected a delightful encampment in a handsome green oak hollow, where, among the open bolls of the trees, was an abundant sward of grass and pea vines. In the evening a Christian Indian rode into the camp, well dressed, with long spurs, and a *sombrero,* and speaking Spanish fluently. It was an unexpected apparition, and a strange and pleasant sight in this desolate gorge of a mountain—an Indian face, Spanish costume, jingling spurs, and horse equipped after the Spanish manner. He informed me that he belonged to one of the [former] Spanish missions to the south, distant two or three days' ride, and that he had obtained from the priests leave to spend a few days with his relations in the Sierra. Having seen us enter the *pass,* he had come down to visit us. He appeared familiarly acquainted with the country, and gave me definite and clear information in regard to the desert region east of the mountains. I had entered the pass with a strong disposition to vary my route, and to travel directly across towards the Great Salt lake, in the view of obtaining some acquaintance with the interior of the Great Basin, while pursuing a direct course for the frontier; but his representation, which described it as an arid and barren desert, that had repulsed by its sterility all the attempts of the Indians to penetrate it, determined me for the present to relinquish the plan; and, agreeably to his advice, after crossing the Sierra, continue our intended route along its eastern base to the Spanish trail. By this route, a party of six Indians, who had come from a great river in the eastern part of the desert to trade with his people, had just started on their return. He would himself return the next day to *San Fernando;* and as our roads would be the same for two days, he offered his services to conduct us so far on our way. His offer was gladly accepted. The fog, which had somewhat interfered with views in the valley, had entirely passed off, and left a clear sky. That which had enveloped us in the neighborhood of the pass proceeded evidently from fires kindled among the tulares by Indians living near the lakes, and which were intended to warn those in the mountains that there were strangers in the valley. Our position was in latitude 35° 17′ 12″, and longitude 118° 35′ 03″.

April 14.—Our guide joined us this morning on the trail; and, arriving in a short distance at an open bottom where the creek forked, we continued up the right-hand branch, which was enriched by a profusion of flowers, and handsomely wooded with sycamore, oaks, cottonwood, and willow, with other trees, and some shrubby plants. In its long strings of balls, this sycamore differs from that of the United States, and is the *platanus occidentalis* of Hooker—a new species, recently described among the plants collected in the voyage of the Sulphur. The cottonwood varied its foliage with white tufts, and the feathery seeds were flying plentifully through the air. Gooseberries, nearly ripe, were very abundant on the mountain; and as we passed the dividing grounds, which were not very easy to ascertain, the air was filled with perfume, as if we were entering a highly cultivated garden; and, instead of green, our pathway and the mountain sides were covered with fields of yellow flowers, which here was the prevailing color. Our journey to-day was in the midst of an advanced spring, whose green and floral beauty offered a delightful contrast to the sandy valley we had just left. All the day, snow was in sight on the butt of the mountain, which frowned down upon us on the right; but we beheld it now with feelings of pleasant security, as we rode along between green trees and on flowers, with humming birds and other feathered friends of the traveller enlivening the serene spring air. As we reached the summit of this beautiful pass,[149] and obtained a view into the eastern country, we saw at once that here was the place to take leave of all such pleasant scenes as those around us. The distant mountains were now bald rocks again; and below, the land had any color but green. Taking into consideration the nature of the Sierra Nevada, we found this pass an excellent one for horses; and with a little labor, or perhaps with a more perfect examination of the localities, it might be made sufficiently practicable for wagons. Its latitude and longitude may be considered that of our last encampment, only a few miles distant. The elevation was not taken—our half-wild cavalcade making it too troublesome to halt before night, when once started.[150]

We here left the waters of the bay of San Francisco, and, though

---

149. Apparently not Tehachapi Pass, but rather Oak Creek Pass, five or six air-line miles farther south. Preuss told R. S. Williamson, during the Pacific Railroad Survey of 1853, that the party had used Oak Creek Pass, and an inspection of the area by a later investigator (see JOHNSON) seems to bear him out. Certainly it was not Walker Pass, some two degrees to the north, as JCF called it and as earlier historians believed it to be.

150. On 18 April, Preuss, recording that the cavalcade consisted of 124 head of stock and twenty-one men (only seventeen of whom could be counted on to care for the animals), wondered why the party was burdened with so much livestock (PREUSS, 125).

forced upon them contrary to my intentions, I cannot regret the necessity which occasioned the deviation. It made me well acquainted with the great range of the Sierra Nevada of the Alta California, and showed that this broad and elevated snowy ridge was a continuation of the Cascade Range of Oregon, between which and the ocean there is still another and a lower range, parallel to the former and to the coast, and which may be called the Coast Range. It also made me well acquainted with the basin of the San Francisco bay, and with the two pretty rivers and their valleys, (the Sacramento and San Joaquin,) which are tributary to that bay; and cleared up some points in geography on which error had long prevailed. It had been constantly represented, as I have already stated, that the bay of San Francisco opened far into the interior, by some river coming down from the base of the Rocky mountains, and upon which supposed stream the name of Rio Buenaventura had been bestowed. Our observations of the Sierra Nevada, in the long distance from the head of the Sacramento [Klamath] to the head of the San Joaquin, and of the valley below it, which collects all the waters of the San Francisco bay, show that this neither is nor can be the case. No river from the interior does, or can, cross the Sierra Nevada— itself more lofty than the Rocky mountains; and as to the Buenaventura, the mouth of which seen on the coast gave the idea and the name of the reputed great river, it is, in fact, a small stream of no consequence [Salinas River], not only below the Sierra Nevada, but actually below the Coast Range—taking its rise within half a degree of the ocean, running parallel to it for about two degrees, and then falling into the Pacific near Monterey. There is no opening from the bay of San Francisco into the interior of the continent. The two rivers which flow into it are comparatively short, and not perpendicular to the coast, but lateral to it, and having their heads towards Oregon and southern California. They open lines of communication north and south, and not eastwardly; and thus this want of interior communication from the San Francisco bay, now fully ascertained, gives great additional value to the Columbia, which stands alone as the only great river on the Pacific slope of our continent which leads from the ocean to the Rocky mountains, and opens a line of communication from the sea to the valley of the Mississippi.

Four *compañeros* joined our guide at the pass; and two going back at noon, the others continued on in company. Descending from the hills, we reached a country of fine grass, where the *erodium cicutarium* finally disappeared, giving place to an excellent quality of bunch grass. Passing by some springs where there was a rich sward of grass among groves of large black oak, we rode over a plain on which the guide pointed out a spot where a refugee Christian Indian had been killed by a party of soldiers which had unexpectedly penetrated into the mountains. Crossing a low sierra, and descending a hollow where a spring gushed out, we were struck by the sudden appearance of *yucca* trees,[151] which gave a strange and southern character to the country, and suited well with the dry and desert region we were approaching. Associated with the idea of barren sands, their stiff and ungraceful form makes them to the traveller the most repulsive tree in the vegetable kingdom. Following the hollow, we shortly came upon a creek timbered with large black oak, which yet had not put forth a leaf. There was a small rivulet of running water, with good grass.

April 15.—The Indians who had accompanied the guide returned this morning, and I purchased from them a Spanish saddle and long spurs, as reminiscences of the time; and for a few yards of scarlet cloth they gave me a horse, which afterwards became food for other Indians.

We continued a short distance down the creek, in which our guide informed us that the water very soon disappeared, and turned directly to the southward along the foot of the mountain; the trail on which we rode appearing to describe the eastern limit of travel, where water and grass terminated. Crossing a low spur, which bordered the creek, we descended to a kind of plain among the lower spurs; the desert being in full view on our left, apparently illimitable. A hot mist lay over it to-day, through which it had a white and glistening appearance; here and there a few dry-looking *buttes* and isolated black ridges rose suddenly upon it. "There," said our guide, stretching out his hand towards it [the Mojave Desert], "there are the great *llanos,* (plains;) *no hay agua; no hay zacaté—nada:* there is neither water nor grass—nothing; every animal that goes out upon them, dies." It was indeed dismal to look upon, and hard to conceive so great a change in so short a distance. One might travel the world over, without finding a valley more fresh and verdant—more floral

---

151. *Yucca brevifolia* Engelm. Joshua tree. It is historically notable that the tree yucca was not described by botanists until 1857, when it was made a variety of *Yucca draconis,* the dragon tree of Teneriffe, by Torrey. Engelmann gave it its present botanical name in 1871.

and sylvan—more alive with birds and animals—more bounteously watered—than we had left in the San Joaquin: here, within a few miles ride, a vast desert plain spread before us, from which the boldest traveller turned away in despair.

Directly in front of us, at some distance to the southward, and running out in an easterly direction from the mountains, stretched a sierra, having at the eastern end (perhaps 50 miles distant) some snowy peaks, on which, by the information of our guide, snow rested all the year [San Gabriel and San Bernardino Mountains].

Our cavalcade made a strange and grotesque appearance; and it was impossible to avoid reflecting upon our position and composition in this remote solitude. Within two degrees of the Pacific ocean; already far south of the latitude of Monterey; and still forced on south by a desert on one hand, and a mountain range on the other; guided by a civilized Indian, attended by two wild ones from the Sierra; a Chinook from the Columbia; and our own mixture of American, French, German—all armed; four or five languages heard at once; above a hundred horses and mules, half wild; American, Spanish, and Indian dresses and equipments intermingled—such was our composition. Our march was a sort of procession. Scouts ahead, and on the flanks; a front and rear division; the pack animals, baggage, and horned cattle, in the centre; and the whole stretching a quarter of a mile along our dreary path. In this form we journeyed; looking more like we belonged to Asia than to the United States of America.

We continued in a southerly direction across the plain, to which, as well as to all the country so far as we could see, the *yucca* trees gave a strange and singular character. Several new plants appeared, among which was a zygophyllaceous shrub (*zygophyllum Californicum,* Torr. & Frem.) sometimes 10 feet in height; in form, and in the pliancy of its branches, it is rather a graceful plant. Its leaves are small, covered with a resinous substance; and, particularly when bruised and crushed, exhale a singular but very agreeable and refreshing odor.[152] This shrub and the *yucca,* with many varieties of cactus, make the characteristic features in the vegetation for a long distance to the eastward. Along the foot of the mountain, 20 miles to the southward, red stripes of flowers were visible during the morning, which we supposed to be variegated sandstones. We rode

---

152. *Larrea glutinosa* Engelm. Creosote bush.

rapidly during the day, and in the afternoon emerged from the *yucca* forest at the foot of an *outlier* of the Sierra before us, and came among the fields of flowers we had seen in the morning, which consisted principally of the rich orange-colored Californian poppy, mingled with other flowers of brighter tints. Reaching the top of the spur, which was covered with fine bunch grass, and where the hills were very green, our guide pointed to a small hollow in the mountain before us, saying, *"á este piedra hay agua."* He appeared to know every nook in the country. We continued our beautiful road, and reached a spring in the slope, at the foot of the ridge, running in a green ravine, among granite boulders; here nightshade, and borders of buckwheat,[153] with their white blossoms around the granite rocks, attracted our notice as familiar plants. Several antelopes were seen among the hills, and some large hares. Men were sent back this evening in search of a wild mule with a valuable pack, which had managed (as they frequently do) to hide itself along the road.

By observation, the latitude of the camp is 34° 41′ 42″; and longitude 118° 20′ 00″. The next day the men returned with the mule.

April 17.—Crossing the ridge by a beautiful pass of hollows, where several deer broke out of the thickets, we emerged at a small salt lake [Elizabeth Lake] in a *vallon* lying nearly east and west, where a trail from the mission of *San Buenaventura* comes in. The lake is about 1,200 yards in diameter; surrounded on the margin by a white salty border, which, by the smell, reminded us slightly of Lake Abert. There are some cottonwoods, with willow and elder, around the lake; and the water is a little salt, although not entirely unfit for drinking. Here we turned directly to the eastward, along the trail, which, from being seldom used, is almost imperceptible; and, after travelling a few miles, our guide halted, and, pointing to the hardly visible trail, *"aqui es camino,"* said he, *"no se pierde—va siempre."* He pointed out a black *butte* on the plain at the foot of the mountain, where we could find water to encamp at night; and, giving him a present of knives and scarlet cloth, we shook hands and parted. He bore off south, and in a day's ride would arrive at San Fernando, one of several missions in this part of California, where the country is so beautiful that it is considered a paradise, and the

---

153. The nightshade is *Solanum xanti* Gray, and the buckwheat *Eriogonum fasciculatum* Benth.

name of its principal town (*Puebla de los Angeles*) would make it angelic. We continued on through a succession of valleys, and came into a most beautiful spot of flower fields: instead of green, the hills were purple and orange, with unbroken beds, into which each color was separately gathered. A pale straw color, with a bright yellow, the rich red orange of the poppy mingled with fields of purple, covered the spot with a floral beauty; and, on the border of the sandy deserts, seemed to invite the traveller to go no farther. Riding along through the perfumed air, we soon after entered a defile overgrown with the ominous *artemisia tridentata*, which conducted us into a sandy plain covered more or less densely with forests of *yucca*.

Having now the snowy ridge on our right, we continued our way towards a dark *butte* belonging to a low sierra in the plain, and which our guide had pointed out for a landmark. Late in the day the familiar growth of cottonwood, a line of which was visible ahead, indicated our approach to a creek, which we reached where the water spread out into sands, and a little below sank entirely. Here our guide had intended we should pass the night; but there was not a blade of grass, and, hoping to find nearer the mountain a little for the night, we turned up the stream. A hundred yards above, we found the creek a fine stream, 16 feet wide, with a swift current. A dark night overtook us when we reached the hills at the foot of the ridge, and we were obliged to encamp without grass; tying up what animals we could secure in the darkness, the greater part of the wild ones having free range for the night. Here the stream was two feet deep, swift and clear, issuing from a neighboring snow peak. A few miles before reaching this creek, we had crossed a broad dry river bed, which, nearer the hills, the hunters had found a bold and handsome stream.

April 18.—Some parties were engaged in hunting up the scattered horses, and others in searching for grass above; both were successful, and late in the day we encamped among some spring heads of the river, in a hollow which was covered with only tolerably good grasses, the lower ground being entirely overgrown with large bunches of the coarse stiff grass, (*carex sitchensis.*)

Our latitude, by observation, was 34° 27′ 03″; and longitude 117° 13′ 00″.

Travelling close along the mountain, we followed up, in the afternoon of the 19th, another stream, in hopes to find a grass patch like that of the previous day, but were deceived; except some scattered bunch grass, there was nothing but rock and sand; and even the fertility of the mountain seemed withered by the air of the desert. Among the few trees was the nut pine, (*pinus monophyllus.*)

Our road the next day was still in an easterly direction along the ridge, over very bad travelling ground, broken and confounded with crippled trees and shrubs; and, after a difficult march of 18 miles, a general shout announced that we had struck the object of our search—THE SPANISH TRAIL—which here was running directly north.[154] The road itself, and its course, were equally happy discoveries to us. Since the middle of December we had continually been forced south by mountains and by deserts, and now would have to make six degrees of *northing,* to regain the latitude on which we wished to cross the Rocky mountains. The course of the road, therefore, was what we wanted; and, once more, we felt like going homewards. A *road* to travel on, and the *right* course to go, were joyful consolations to us; and our animals enjoyed the beaten track like ourselves. Relieved from the rocks and brush, our wild mules started off at a rapid rate, and in 15 miles we reached a considerable river,[155] timbered with cottonwood and willow, where we found a bottom of tolerable grass. As the animals had suffered a great deal in the last few days, I remained here all next day, to allow them the necessary repose; and it was now necessary, at every favorable place, to make a little halt. Between us and the Colorado river we were aware that the country was extremely poor in grass, and scarce for water, there being many *jornadas,* (days' journey,) or long stretches of 40 to 60 miles, without water, where the road was marked by bones of animals.

Although in California we had met with people who had passed over this trail, we had been able to obtain no correct information about it; and the greater part of what we had heard was found to be only a tissue of falsehoods. The rivers that we found on it were never mentioned, and others, particularly described in name and

---

154. JCF struck the Spanish Trail a few miles north of Cajon Pass, where the trail came through from Los Angeles. Because the Hafens have carefully annotated the JCF route as far as Little Salt Lake, we shall cite their work and offer locations more frequently than we might otherwise do on an established trail. We have also profited, as always, from our correspondence with Dale L. Morgan.

155. He is now on the Mojave River, which he reached just above present Oro Grande, about six miles northwest of Victorville (HAFEN & HAFEN, 287). JCF calls the river the Mohahve.

locality, were subsequently seen in another part of the country. It was described as a tolerably good sandy road, with so little rock as scarcely to require the animals to be shod; and we found it the roughest and rockiest road we had ever seen in the country, and which nearly destroyed our band of fine mules and horses. Many animals are destroyed on it every year by a disease called the foot evil; and a traveller should never venture on it without having his animals well shod, and also carrying extra shoes.

Latitude 34° 34′ 11″; and longitude 117° 13′ 00″.

The morning of the 22d was clear and bright, and a snowy peak to the southward shone out high and sharply defined. As has been usual since we crossed the mountains and descended into the hot plains, we had a gale of wind. We travelled down the right bank of the stream [Mojave River], over sands which are somewhat loose, and have no verdure, but are occupied by various shrubs. A clear bold stream, 60 feet wide, and several feet deep, had a strange appearance, running between perfectly naked banks of sand. The eye, however, is somewhat relieved by willows, and the beautiful green of the sweet cottonwoods with which it is well wooded. As we followed along its course, the river, instead of growing constantly larger, gradually dwindled away, as it was absorbed by the sand. We were now careful to take the old camping places of the annual Santa Fé caravans, which, luckily for us, had not yet made their yearly passage. A drove of several thousand horses and mules would entirely have swept away the scanty grass at the watering places, and we should have been obliged to leave the road to obtain subsistence for our animals. After riding 20 miles in a northeasterly direction, we found an old encampment, where we halted.[156]

By observation, the elevation of this encampment is 2,250 feet.

April 23.—The trail followed still along the river, which, in the course of the morning, entirely disappeared. We continued along the dry bed, in which, after an interval of about 16 miles, the water reappeared in some low places, well timbered with cottonwood and willow, where was another of the customary camping grounds.[157]

---

156. About sixteen miles southwest of Barstow, Calif., near a railway station named Wild.

157. Although he mentions marching only sixteen miles, his table of distances records thirty-three. He passed the sites of Barstow and Daggett, Calif., to a point about five miles below Daggett, southeast of present Yermo. His map shows that he crossed to the north bank at present Barstow.

Here a party of six Indians came into camp, poor and hungry, and quite in keeping with the character of the country. Their arms were bows of unusual length, and each had a large gourd, strengthened with meshes of cord, in which he carried water. They proved to be the Mohahve Indians mentioned by our recent guide; and from one of them, who spoke Spanish fluently, I obtained some interesting information, which I would be glad to introduce here. An account of the people inhabiting this region would undoubtedly possess interest for the civilized world. Our journey homeward was fruitful in incident; and the country through which we travelled, although a desert, afforded much to excite the curiosity of the botanist; but limited time, and the rapidly advancing season for active operations, oblige me to omit all extended descriptions, and hurry briefly to the conclusion of this report.

The Indian who spoke Spanish had been educated for a number of years at one of the Spanish missions, and, at the breaking up of those establishments, had returned to the mountains, where he had been found by a party of *Mohahve* (sometimes called *Amuchaba*) Indians, among whom he had ever since resided.

He spoke of the leader of the present party as *"mi amo,"* (my master.) He said they lived upon a large river in the southeast, which the "soldiers called the Rio Colorado;" but that, formerly, a portion of them lived upon this river, and among the mountains which had bounded the river valley to the northward during the day, and that here along the river they had raised various kinds of melons. They sometimes came over to trade with the Indians of the Sierra, bringing with them blankets and goods manufactured by the Monquis [Hopi] and other Colorado [River] Indians. They rarely carried home horses, on account of the difficulty of getting them across the desert, and of guarding them afterwards from the Pa-utah Indians, who inhabit the Sierra, at the head of the *Rio Virgen,* (river of the Virgin.)

He informed us that, a short distance below, this river finally disappeared. The two different portions in which water is found had received from the priests two different names; and subsequently I heard it called by the Spaniards the *Rio de las Animas,* but on the map we have called it the *Mohahve* river.

April 24.—We continued down the stream (or rather its bed) for about eight miles, where there was water still in several holes, and encamped.[158] The caravans somtimes continued below, to the end of the river, from which there is a very long *jornada* of perhaps sixty miles, without water. Here a singular and new species of acacia, with spiral pods or seed vessels, made its first appearance; becoming henceforward, for a considerable distance, a characteristic tree. It was here comparatively large, being about 20 feet in height, with a full and spreading top, the lower branches declining towards the ground. It afterwards occurred of smaller size, frequently in groves, and is very fragrant. It has been called by Dr. Torrey *spirolobium odoratum*.[159] The zygophyllaceous shrub had been constantly characteristic of the plains along the river; and here, among many new plants, a new and very remarkable species of eriogonum (*eriogonum inflatum*, Torr. & Frem.) made its first appearance.

Our cattle had become so tired and poor by this fatiguing travelling, that three of them were killed here, and the meat dried. The Indians had now an occasion for a great feast, and were occupied the remainder of the day and all the night in cooking and eating. There was no part of the animal for which they did not find some use, except the bones. In the afternoon we were surprised by the sudden appearance in the camp of two Mexicans—a man and a boy. The name of the man was *Andreas Fuentes;* and that of the boy, (a handsome lad, 11 years old,) *Pablo Hernandez*. They belonged to a party consisting of six persons, the remaining four being the wife of Fuentes, the father and mother of Pablo, and Santiago Giacome, a resident of New Mexico.[160] With a cavalcade of about thirty horses, they had come out from Puebla de los Angeles, near the coast, under the guidance of Giacome, in advance of the great caravan, in order to travel more at leisure, and obtain better grass. Having advanced as far into the desert as was considered consistent with their safety, they

---

158. Leaving the Spanish Trail temporarily, the expedition today continues down the river to the site of what was later Camp Cady, east of the railroad station of Harvard (HAFEN & HAFEN, 288).

Dale L. Morgan says that JCF's reference to caravans continuing down to the end of the river—Soda Lake—then making a *jornada* (perhaps northward to the Amargosa River), is the only reference he has seen on the subject.

159. Now *Prosopis odorata*, with a number of common names such as screwbean mesquite, screwpod mesquite, and tornillo (MC KELVEY, 873).

160. Santiago Giacome we have not identified. There is little additional information on Andreas Fuentes and Pablo Hernandez, but see p. 724, notes 193 and 194.

halted at the *Archilette,* one of the customary camping grounds, about 80 miles from our encampment, where there is a spring of good water, with sufficient grass; and concluded to await there the arrival of the great caravan. Several Indians were soon discovered lurking about the camp, who, in a day or two after, came in, and, after behaving in a very friendly manner, took their leave, without awakening any suspicions. Their deportment begat a security which proved fatal. In a few days afterwards, suddenly a party of about one hundred Indians appeared in sight, advancing towards the camp. It was too late, or they seemed not to have presence of mind to take proper measures of safety; and the Indians charged down into their camp, shouting as they advanced, and discharging flights of arrows. Pablo and Fuentes were on horse guard at the time, and mounted, according to the custom of the country. One of the principal objects of the Indians was to get possession of the horses, and part of them immediately surrounded the band; but, in obedience to the shouts of Giacome, Fuentes drove the animals over and through the assailants, in spite of their arrows; and, abandoning the rest to their fate, carried them off at speed across the plain. Knowing that they would be pursued by the Indians, without making any halt except to shift their saddles to other horses, they drove them on for about sixty miles, and this morning left them at a watering place on the trail, called Agua de Tomaso. Without giving themselves any time for rest, they hurried on, hoping to meet the Spanish caravan, when they discovered my camp. I received them kindly, taking them into my own mess, and promised them such aid as circumstances might put it in my power to give.

April 25.—We left the river abruptly, and, turning to the north, regained in a few miles the main trail, (which had left the river sooner than ourselves,) and continued our way across a lower ridge of the mountain, through a miserable tract of sand and gravel. We crossed at intervals the broad beds of dry gullies, where in the season of rains and melting snows there would be brooks or rivulets; and at one of these, where there was no indication of water, were several freshly-dug holes, in which there was water at the depth of two feet. These holes had been dug by the wolves [coyotes], whose keen sense of smell had scented the water under the dry sand. They were nice little wells, narrow, and dug straight down, and we got pleasant water out of them.

The country had now assumed the character of an elevated and mountainous desert; its general features being black, rocky ridges, bald, and destitute of timber, with sandy basins between. Where the sides of these ridges are washed by gullies, the plains below are strewed with beds of large pebbles or rolled stones, destructive to our soft-footed animals, accustomed to the grassy plains of the Sacramento valley. Through these sandy basins sometimes struggled a scanty stream, or occurred a hole of water, which furnished camping grounds for travellers. Frequently in our journey across, snow was visible on the surrounding mountains; but their waters rarely reached the sandy plain below, where we toiled along, oppressed with thirst and a burning sun. But, throughout this nakedness of sand and gravel, were many beautiful plants and flowering shrubs, which occurred in many new species, and with greater variety than we had been accustomed to see in the most luxuriant prairie countries; this was a peculiarity of this desert. Even where no grass would take root, the naked sand would bloom with some rich and rare flower, which found its appropriate home in the arid and barren spot.

Scattered over the plain, and tolerably abundant, was a handsome leguminous shrub, three or four feet high, with fine bright-purple flowers. It is a new *psoralea,* and occurred frequently henceforward along our road.[161]

Beyond the first ridge, our road bore a little to the east of north, towards a gap in a higher line of mountains; and, after travelling about twenty-five miles, we arrived at the *Agua de Tomaso*—the spring where the horses had been left; but, as we expected, they were gone. A brief examination of the ground convinced us that they had been driven off by the Indians. Carson and Godey volunteered with the Mexican to pursue them; and, well mounted, the three set off on the trail. At this stopping place there were a few bushes and very little grass. Its water was a pool; but near by was a spring, which had been dug out by Indians or travellers. Its water was cool—a great refreshment to us under a burning sun.[162]

In the evening Fuentes returned, his horse having failed; but Carson and Godey had continued the pursuit.

---

161. Instead of a new *Psoralea* it was a *Dalea,* and probably *D. fremontii,* a species collected in about the same region by the later Death Valley expedition (PARISH, 61).

162. Back to the main Spanish Trail, ascending the shoulder of Alvord Mountain via Spanish Canyon and traveling twenty-five miles to Agua de Tomaso [Bitter Spring].

I observed to-night an occultation of a^2 *Cancri,* at the dark limb of the moon, which gives for the longitude of the place 116° 23′ 28″; the latitude, by observation, is 35° 13′ 08″. From Helvetia to this place, the positions along the intervening line are laid down with the longitudes obtained from the chronometer, which appears to have retained its rate remarkably well; but henceforward, to the end of the journey, the few longitudes given are absolute, depending upon a subsequent occultation and eclipses of the satellites.

In the afternoon of the next day, a war-whoop was heard, such as Indians make when returning from a victorious enterprise; and soon Carson and Godey appeared, driving before them a band of horses, recognized by Fuentes to be part of those they had lost. Two bloody scalps, dangling from the end of Godey's gun, announced that they had overtaken the Indians as well as the horses. They informed us, that after Fuentes left them, from the failure of his horse, they continued the pursuit alone, and towards nightfall entered the mountains, into which the trail led. After sunset the moon gave light, and they followed the trail by moonshine until late in the night, when it entered a narrow defile, and was difficult to follow. Afraid of losing it in the darkness of the defile, they tied up their horses, struck no fire, and lay down to sleep in silence and in darkness. Here they lay from midnight till morning. At daylight they resumed the pursuit, and about sunrise discovered the horses; and, immediately dismounting and tying up their own, they crept cautiously to a rising ground which intervened, from the crest of which they perceived the encampment of four lodges close by. They proceeded quietly, and had got within thirty or forty yards of their object, when a movement among the horses discovered them to the Indians; giving the war shout, they instantly charged into the camp, regardless of the number which the *four* lodges would imply. The Indians received them with a flight of arrows shot from their long bows, one of which passed through Godey's shirt collar, barely missing the neck; our men fired their rifles upon a steady aim, and rushed in. Two Indians were stretched on the ground, fatally pierced with bullets; the rest fled, except a lad that was captured. The scalps of the fallen were instantly stripped off; but in the process, one of them, who had two balls through his body, sprung to his feet, the blood streaming from his skinned head, and uttering a hideous howl. An old squaw, possibly his mother, stopped and looked back from the mountain side she was climbing, threatening and lamenting. The frightful spectacle appalled the stout hearts of our men; but they did what humanity required, and quickly terminated the agonies of the gory savage. They were now masters of the camp, which was a pretty little recess in the mountain, with a fine spring, and apparently safe from all invasion. Great preparations had been made to feast a large party, for it was a very proper place for a rendezvous, and for the celebration of such orgies as robbers of the desert would delight in. Several of the best horses had been killed, skinned, and cut up; for the Indians living in mountains, and only coming into the plains to rob and murder, make no other use of horses than to eat them. Large earthen vessels were on the fire, boiling and stewing the horse beef; and several baskets, containing fifty or sixty pairs of moccasins, indicated the presence, or expectation, of a considerable party. They released the boy, who had given strong evidence of the stoicism, or something else, of the savage character, in commencing his breakfast upon a horse's head as soon as he found he was not to be killed, but only tied as a prisoner. Their object accomplished, our men gathered up all the surviving horses, fifteen in number, returned upon their trail, and rejoined us at our camp in the afternoon of the same day. They had rode about one hundred miles in the pursuit and return, and all in thirty hours. The time, place, object, and numbers, considered, this expedition of Carson and Godey may be considered among the boldest and most disinterested which the annals of western adventure, so full of daring deeds, can present. Two men, in a savage desert, pursue day and night an unknown body of Indians into the defiles of an unknown mountain—attack them on sight, without counting numbers—and defeat them in an instant—and for what? To punish the robbers of the desert, and to avenge the wrongs of Mexicans whom they did not know. I repeat: it was Carson and Godey who did this—the former an *American,* born in the Boonslick country of Missouri; the latter a Frenchman, born in St. Louis—and both trained to western enterprise from early life.[163]

---

163. While JCF rejoiced that Carson and Godey had been able to give a "useful lesson to these American Arabs" (p. 684), Preuss thought such butchery disgusting. "Are these whites not much worse than Indians? The more noble Indian takes from the killed enemy only a piece of the scalp as large as a dollar, somewhat like the tonsure of a priest. These two heroes, who shot the Indians [while] creeping up on them from behind, brought along the entire scalp. The Indians are braver in a similar situation. Before they shoot, they raise a yelling war whoop. Kit and Alex sneaked, like cats, as close as possible. Kit shot an Indian in the back . . ." (PREUSS, 127).

By the information of Fuentes, we had now to make a long stretch of forty or fifty miles across a plain which lay between us and the next possible camp; and we resumed our journey late in the afternoon, with the intention of travelling through the night, and avoiding the excessive heat of the day, which was oppressive to our animals. For several hours we travelled across a high plain, passing, at the opposite side, through a cañon by the bed of a creek running *northwardly* into a small lake beyond, and both of them being dry. We had a warm, moonshiny night; and, travelling directly towards the north star, we journeyed now across an open plain between mountain ridges; that on the left being broken, rocky, and bald, according to the information of Carson and Godey, who had entered here in pursuit of the horses. The plain appeared covered principally with the *zygophyllum Californicum* already mentioned; and the line of our road was marked by the skeletons of horses, which were strewed to a considerable breadth over the plain. We were afterwards always warned, on entering one of these long stretches, by the bones of these animals, which had perished before they could reach the water. About midnight we reached a considerable stream bed, now dry, the discharge of the waters of this basin, (when it collected any,) down which we descended in a *northwesterly* direction. The creek bed was overgrown with shrubbery, and several hours before day it brought us to the entrance of a cañon, where we found water, and encamped. This word *cañon* is used by the Spaniards to signify a defile or gorge in a creek or river, where high rocks press in close, and make a narrow way, usually difficult, and often impossible to be passed.

In the morning we found that we had a very poor camping ground: a swampy, salty spot, with a little long, unwholesome grass; and the water, which rose in springs, being useful only to wet the mouth, but entirely too salt to drink. All around was sand and rocks, and skeletons of horses which had not been able to find support for their lives. As we were about to start, we found, at the distance of a few hundred yards, among the hills to the southward, a spring of tolerably good water, which was a relief to ourselves; but the place was too poor to remain long, and therefore we continued on this morning. On the creek were thickets of *spirolobium odoratum* (acacia) in bloom, and very fragrant.

Passing through the cañon, we entered another sandy basin, through which the dry stream bed continued its northwesterly course, in which direction appeared a high snowy mountain [Amargosa Range].

We travelled through a barren district, where a heavy gale was blowing about the loose sand, and, after a ride of eight miles, reached a large creek of salt and bitter water, running in a westerly direction, to receive the stream bed we had left. It is called by the Spaniards *Amargosa*—the bitter water of the desert. Where we struck it, the stream bends; and we continued in a northerly course up the ravine of its valley, passing on the way a fork from the right, near which occurred a bed of plants, consisting of a remarkable new genus of *cruciferae.*

Gradually ascending, the ravine opened into a green valley, where, at the foot of the mountain, were springs of excellent water. We encamped among groves of the new *acacia,* and there was an abundance of good grass for the animals.[164]

This was the best camping ground we had seen since we struck the Spanish trail. The day's journey was about 12 miles.

April 29.—To-day we had to reach the *Archilette,* distant seven miles, where the Mexican party had been attacked; and, leaving our encampment early, we traversed a part of the desert, the most sterile and repulsive that we had yet seen. Its prominent features were dark *sierras,* naked and dry; on the plains a few straggling shrubs—among them, cactus of several varieties. Fuentes pointed out one called by the Spaniards *bisnada,* which has a juicy pulp, slightly acid, and is eaten by the traveller to allay thirst. Our course was generally north; and, after crossing an intervening ridge, we descended into a sandy plain, or basin, in the middle of which was the grassy spot, with its springs and willow bushes, which constitutes a camping place in the desert, and is called the *Archilette.* The dead silence of the place was ominous; and, galloping rapidly up, we found only the corpses of the two men: every thing else was gone. They were naked, mutilated, and pierced with arrows. Hernandez had evidently fought, and with desperation. He lay in advance of the willow half-faced tent, which sheltered his family, as if he had come out to meet dan-

---

164. During 26–28 April, JCF made afternoon and nighttime passages to the east of the Avawatz Mountains, then north through a broad valley with two dry lakes, then northwest to the Salt Creek Spring on the edge of Amargosa Valley. His last twenty miles were on the present route of highway 127, proceeding north from Baker toward Shoshone and Death Valley (HAFEN & HAFEN, 291).

ger, and to repulse it, from that asylum. One of his hands, and both his legs, had been cut off. Giacome, who was a large and strong-looking man, was lying in one of the willow shelters, pierced with arrows. Of the women no trace could be found, and it was evident they had been carried off captive. A little lap-dog, which had belonged to Pablo's mother, remained with the dead bodies, and was frantic with joy at seeing Pablo: he, poor child, was frantic with grief; and filled the air with lamentations for his father and mother. *Mi padre! Mi madre!*—was his incessant cry. When we beheld this pitiable sight, and pictured to ourselves the fate of the two women, carried off by savages so brutal and so loathsome, all compunction for the scalped-alive Indian ceased; and we rejoiced that Carson and Godey had been able to give so useful a lesson to these American Arabs, who lie in wait to murder and plunder the innocent traveller.

We were all too much affected by the sad feelings which the place inspired, to remain an unnecessary moment. The night we were obliged to pass there. Early in the morning we left it, having first written a brief account of what had happened, and put it in the cleft of a pole planted at the spring, that the approaching caravan might learn the fate of their friends. In commemoration of the event, we called the place *Agua de Hernandez*—Hernandez's spring.[165] By observation, its latitude was 35° 51′ 21″.

April 30.—We continued our journey over a district similar to that of the day before. From the sandy basin, in which was the spring, we entered another basin of the same character, surrounded every where by mountains. Before us stretched a high range, rising still higher to the left, and terminating in a snowy mountain.

After a day's march of 24 miles, we reached at evening the bed of a stream from which the water had disappeared; a little only remained in holes, which we increased by digging; and about a mile above, the stream, not yet entirely sunk, was spread out over the sands, affording a little water for the animals.[166] The stream came out of the mountains on the left, very slightly wooded with cotton-wood, willow, and acacia, and a few dwarf oaks; and grass was nearly as scarce as water. A plant with showy yellow flowers (*Stan-*

---

165. The place later came to be called Resting Springs.

166. Still on the Spanish Trail, across the Nopah Range via the steep canyon now known as Emigrant Pass, and moving across the Pahrump Valley to a dry steam bed. Camp was made at Stump Spring, with Charleston Peak dominating the northeast skyline (HAFEN & HAFEN, 292).

leya integrifolia) occurred abundantly at intervals for the last two days, and *eriogonum inflatum* was among the characteristic plants.

May 1.—The air is rough, and overcoats pleasant. The sky is blue, and the day bright. Our road was over a plain, towards the foot of the mountain; *zygophyllum Californicum,* now in bloom with a small yellow flower, is characteristic of the country; and *cacti* were very abundant, and in rich fresh bloom which wonderfully ornaments this poor country. We encamped at a spring in the pass, which had been the site of an old village. Here we found excellent grass, but very little water. We dug out the old spring, and watered some of our animals. The mountain here was wooded very slightly with the nut pine, cedars, and a dwarf species of oak; and among the shrubs were *Purshia tridentata, artemisia,* and *ephedra occidentalis.* The numerous shrubs which constitute the vegetation of the plains are now in bloom, with flowers of white, yellow, red, and purple. The continual rocks, and want of water and grass, begin to be very hard on our mules and horses; but the principal loss is occasioned by their crippled feet, the greater part of those left being in excellent order, and scarcely a day passes without some loss; and, one by one, Fuentes's horses are constantly dropping behind. Whenever they give out, he dismounts and cuts off their tails and manes, to make saddle girths; the last advantage one can gain from them.

The next day, in a short but rough ride of 12 miles, we crossed the mountain; and, descending to a small valley plain, encamped at the foot of the ridge, on the bed of a creek, where we found good grass in sufficient quantity, and abundance of water in holes. The ridge is extremely rugged and broken, presenting on this side a continued precipice, and probably affords very few passes. Many *digger* tracks are seen around us, but no Indians were visible.

May 3.—After a day's journey of 18 miles, in a northeasterly direction, we encamped in the midst of another very large basin, at a camping ground called *las Vegas*—a term which the Spaniards use to signify fertile or marshy plains, in contradistinction to *llanos,* which they apply to dry and sterile plains.[167] Two narrow streams of

167. On 1 May, JCF crossed the eastern part of Pahrump Valley and ascended a long slope to Mountain Spring, near the summit of the pass over a section of the Spring Mountains. On 2 May, he reached Cottonwood Spring near the present village of Blue Diamond, Nev., and on 3 May arrived at Las Vegas (The Meadows). Cottonwood Spring also has been called Pearl Spring and Ojo de Cayetana (HAFEN & HAFEN, 292–93; AVERETT, 31). At Las Vegas

clear water, four or five feet deep, gush suddenly, with a quick current, from two singularly large springs; these, and other waters of the basin, pass out in a gap to the eastward. The taste of the water is good, but rather too warm to be agreeable; the temperature being 71° in the one, and 73° in the other. They, however, afforded a delightful bathing place.

May 4.—We started this morning earlier than usual, travelling in a northeasterly direction across the plain. The new acacia (*spirolobium odoratum*) has now become the characteristic tree of the country; it is in bloom, and its blossoms are very fragrant. The day was still, and the heat, which soon became very oppressive, appeared to bring out strongly the refreshing scent of the zygophyllaceous shrubs and the sweet perfume of the acacia. The snowy ridge we had just crossed looked out conspicuously in the northwest. In about five hours' ride, we crossed a gap in the surrounding ridge, and the appearance of skeletons of horses very soon warned us that we were engaged in another dry *jornada,* which proved the longest we had made in all our journey—between fifty and sixty miles without a drop of water.

Travellers through countries affording water and timber can have no conception of our intolerable thirst while journeying over the hot yellow sands of this elevated country, where the heated air seems to be entirely deprived of moisture. We ate occasionally the *bisnada,* and moistened our mouths with the acid of the sour dock, (*rumex venosus.*) Hourly expecting to find water, we continued to press on until towards midnight, when, after a hard and uninterrupted march of 16 hours, our wild mules began running ahead; and in a mile or two we came to a bold running stream—so keen is the sense of that animal, in these desert regions, in scenting at a distance this necessary of life.

According to the information we had received, Sevier river was a tributary of the Colorado; and this, accordingly, should have been one of its affluents. It proved to be the *Rio de los Angeles* (river of the Angels)—a branch of the *Rio Virgen* (river of the Virgin.)[168]

---

he regained the present U.S. route 91 and Interstate 15, from which he had separated on 25 April.

168. After a hard daytime journey, the expedition reached what is now the Muddy River. The route from Las Vegas was essentially that now followed by U.S. 91 and Interstate 15, except for the last few miles when the party descended California Wash, striking the river about midway between present

May 5.—On account of our animals, it was necessary to remain to-day at this place. Indians crowded numerously around us in the morning; and we were obliged to keep arms in hand all day, to keep them out of the camp. They began to surround the horses, which, for the convenience of grass, we were guarding a little above, on the river.. These were immediately driven in, and kept close to the camp.

In the darkness of the night we had made a very bad encampment, our fires being commanded by a rocky bluff within 50 yards; but, notwithstanding, we had the river and small thickets of willows on the other side. Several times during the day the camp was insulted by the Indians; but, peace being our object, I kept simply on the defensive. Some of the Indians were on the bottoms, and others haranguing us from the bluffs; and they were scattered in every direction over the hills, Their language being probably a dialect of the *Utah,* with the aid of signs some of our people could comprehend them very well. They were the same people who had murdered the Mexicans; and towards us their disposition was evidently hostile, nor were we well disposed towards them. They were barefooted, and nearly naked; their hair gathered up into a knot behind; and with his bow, each man carried a quiver with thirty or forty arrows partially drawn out. Besides these, each held in his hand two or three arrows for instant service. Their arrows are barbed with a very clear translucent stone, a species of opal, nearly as hard as the diamond; and, shot from their long bow, are almost as effective as a gunshot. In these Indians, I was forcibly struck by an expression of countenance resembling that in a beast of prey; and all their actions are those of wild animals. Joined to the restless motion of the eye, there is a want of mind—an absence of thought—and an action wholly by impulse, strongly expressed, and which constantly recalls the similarity.

A man who appeared to be a chief, with two or three others, forced himself into camp, bringing with him his arms, in spite of

---

Moapa and Glendale, Nev. The Indians encountered were the Southern Paiutes. The next dry drive of 6 May, Dale L. Morgan believes, was along a route across Mormon Mesa, heading all the branches of Halfway Wash, and still following approximately the present federal highway to a point on the Virgin a few miles below present Riverside, Nev. Corroboration comes from JCF himself, who states that after reaching the Virgin he ascended it twenty-eight miles. This would have put him in the vicinity of Littlefield, Ariz., where he left the river.

my orders to the contrary. When shown our weapons, he bored his ear with his fingers, and said he could not hear. "Why," said he, "there are none of you." Counting the people around the camp, and including in the number a mule which was being shod, he made out 22. "So many," said he, showing the number "and we—we are a great many;" and he pointed to the hills and mountains round about. "If you have your arms," said he, twanging his bow, "we have these." I had some difficulty in restraining the people, particularly Carson, who felt an insult of this kind as much as if it had been given by a more responsible being. "Don't say that, old man," said he; "don't you say that—your life's in danger"—speaking in good English; and probably the old man was nearer to his end than he will be before he meets it.

Several animals had been necessarily left behind near the camp last night; and early in the morning, before the Indians made their appearance, several men were sent to bring them in. When I was beginning to be uneasy at their absence, they returned with information that they had been driven off from the trail by Indians; and, having followed the tracks in a short distance, they found the animals cut up and spread out upon bushes. In the evening I gave a fatigued horse to some of the Indians for a feast; and the village which carried him off refused to share with the others, who made loud complaints from the rocks of the partial distribution. Many of these Indians had long sticks, hooked at the end, which they used in hauling out lizards, and other small animals, from their holes. During the day they occasionally roasted and ate lizards at our fires. These belong to the people who are generally known under the name of *Diggers;* and to these I have more particularly had reference when occasionally speaking of a people whose sole occupation is to procure food sufficient to support existence. The formation here consists of fine yellow sandstone, alternating with a coarse conglomerate, in which the stones are from the size of ordinary gravel to six or eight inches in diameter. This is the formation which renders the surface of the country so rocky, and gives us now a road alternately of loose heavy sands and rolled stones, which cripple the animals in a most extraordinary manner.

On the following morning we left the *Rio de los Angeles,* and continued our way through the same desolate and revolting country, where lizards were the only animal, and the tracks of the lizard eaters the principal sign of human beings. After twenty miles' march

688

through a road of hills and heavy sands, we reached the most dreary river I have ever seen—a deep rapid stream, almost a torrent, passing swiftly by, and roaring against obstructions. The banks were wooded with willow, acacia, and a frequent plant of the country already mentioned, (*Garrya elliptica,*) growing in thickets, resembling willow, and bearing a small pink flower. Crossing it, we encamped on the left bank, where we found a very little grass. Our three remaining steers, being entirely given out, were killed here. By the boiling point, the elevation of the river here is 4,060 feet; and latitude by observation, 36° 41′ 33″. The stream was running towards the southwest, and appeared to come from a snowy mountain in the north. It proved to be the *Rio Virgen*—a tributary to the Colorado. Indians appeared in bands on the hills, but did not come into camp. For several days we continued our journey up the river, the bottoms of which were thickly overgrown with various kinds of brush; and the sandy soil was absolutely covered with the tracks of *Diggers,* who followed us stealthily, like a band of wolves; and we had no opportunity to leave behind, even for a few hours, the tired animals, in order that they be brought into camp after a little repose. A horse or mule, left behind, was taken off in a moment. On the evening of the 8th, having travelled 28 miles up the river from our first encampment on it, we encamped at a little grass plat, where a spring of cool water issued from the bluff. On the opposite side was a grove of cottonwoods at the mouth of a fork, which here enters the river. On either side the valley is bounded by ranges of mountains, every where high, rocky, and broken. The caravan road was lost and scattered in the sandy country, and we had been following an Indian trail up the river. The hunters the next day were sent out to reconnoitre, and in the mean time we moved about a mile farther up, where we found a good little patch of grass. There being only sufficient grass for the night, the horses were sent with a strong guard in charge of Tabeau to a neighboring hollow, where they might pasture during the day; and, to be ready in case the Indians should make any attempt on the animals, several of the best horses were picketed at the camp. In a few hours the hunters returned, having found a convenient ford in the river, and discovered the Spanish trail on the other side.

I had been engaged in arranging plants; and, fatigued with the heat of the day, I fell asleep in the afternoon, and did not awake until sundown. Presently Carson came to me, and reported that

Tabeau, who early in the day had left his post, and, without my knowledge, rode back to the camp we had left, in search of a lame mule, had not returned. While we were speaking, a smoke rose suddenly from the cottonwood grove below, which plainly told us what had befallen him; it was raised to inform the surrounding Indians that a blow had been struck, and to tell them to be on their guard. Carson, with several men well mounted, was instantly sent down the river, but returned in the night without tidings of the missing man. They went to the camp we had left, but neither he nor the mule was there. Searching down the river, they found the tracks of the mule, evidently driven along by Indians, whose tracks were on each side of those made by the animal. After going several miles, they came to the mule itself, standing in some bushes, mortally wounded in the side by an arrow, and left to die, that it might be afterwards butchered for food. They also found, in another place, as they were hunting about the ground for Tabeau's tracks, something that looked like a puddle of blood, but which the darkness prevented them from verifying. With these details they returned to our camp, and their report saddened all our hearts.

May 10.—This morning, as soon as there was light enough to follow tracks, I set out myself, with Mr. Fitzpatrick and several men, in search of Tabeau. We went to the spot where the appearance of puddled blood had been seen; and this, we saw at once, had been the place where he fell and died.[169] Blood upon the leaves, and beaten down bushes, showed that he had got his wound about twenty paces from where he fell, and that he had struggled for his life. He had probably been shot through the lungs with an arrow. From the place where he lay and bled, it could be seen that he had been dragged to the river bank, and thrown into it. No vestige of what had belonged to him could be found, except a fragment of his horse equipment. Horse, gun, clothes—all became the prey of these Arabs of the New World.

Tabeau had been one of our best men, and his unhappy death spread a gloom over our party. Men, who have gone through such

---

169. Tabeau was killed in the vicinity of Littlefield, Ariz. The Spanish Trail crossed and recrossed the Virgin in this reach of the river, but JCF's map shows that he kept to the south bank all the way (and thus lost the trail). It appears that Tabeau was killed before the party crossed to the north bank and to the site of Littlefield.

dangers and sufferings as we had seen, become like brothers, and feel each other's loss. To defend and avenge each other, is the deep feeling of all. We wished to avenge his death; but the condition of our horses, languishing for grass and repose, forbade an expedition into unknown mountains. We knew the tribe who had done the mischief—the same which had been insulting our camp. They knew what they deserved, and had the discretion to show themselves to us no more. The day before, they infested our camp; now, not one appeared; nor did we ever afterwards see but one who even belonged to the same tribe, and he at a distance.

Our camp was in a basin below a deep cañon—a gap of two thousand feet deep in the mountain—through which the *Rio Virgen* passes, and where no man or beast could follow it. The Spanish trail, which we had lost in the sands of the basin, was on the opposite side of the river. We crossed over to it, and followed it northwardly towards a gap which was visible in the mountain. We approached it by a defile, rendered difficult for our barefooted animals by the rocks strewed along it; and here the country changed its character. From the time we entered the desert, the mountains had been bald and rocky; here they began to be wooded with cedar and pine, and clusters of trees gave shelter to birds—a new and welcome sight—which could not have lived in the desert we had passed.

Descending a long hollow, towards the narrow valley of a stream, we saw before us a snowy mountain, far beyond which appeared another more lofty still. Good bunch grass began to appear on the hill sides, and here we found a singular variety of interesting shrubs. The changed appearance of the country infused among our people a more lively spirit, which was heightened by finding at evening a halting place of very good grass on the clear waters of the *Santa Clara* fork of the *Rio Virgen*.

May 11.—The morning was cloudy and quite cool, with a shower of rain—the first we have had since entering the desert, a period of twenty-seven days; and we seem to have entered a different climate, with the usual weather of the Rocky mountains. Our march to-day was very laborious, over very broken ground, along the Santa Clara river; but then the country is no longer so distressingly desolate. The stream is prettily wooded with sweet cottonwood trees—some of them of large size; and on the hills, where the nut pine is often seen, a good and wholesome grass occurs frequently. This cottonwood, which is now in fruit, is of a different species from any in Michaux's Sylva. Heavy dark clouds covered the sky in the evening, and a cold wind sprang up, making fires and overcoats comfortable.[170]

May 12.—A little above our encampment, the river forked; and we continued up the right-hand branch, gradually ascending towards the summit of the mountain. As we rose towards the head of the creek, the snowy mountain on our right showed out handsomely—high and rugged with precipices, and covered with snow for about two thousand feet from their summits down. Our animals were somewhat repaid for their hard marches by an excellent camping ground on the summit of the ridge, which forms here the dividing chain between the waters of the *Rio Virgen,* which goes south to the Colorado, and those of Sevier river, flowing northwardly, and belonging to the Great Basin. We considered ourselves as crossing the rim of the basin; and, entering it at this point, we found here an extensive mountain meadow, rich in bunch grass, and fresh with numerous springs of clear water, all refreshing and delightful to look upon. It was, in fact, that *las Vegas de Santa Clara,*[171] which had been so long presented to us as the terminating point of the desert, and where the annual caravan from California to New Mexico halted and recruited for some weeks. It was a very suitable place to recover from the fatigue and exhaustion of a month's suffering in the hot and sterile desert. The meadow was about a mile wide, and some ten miles long, bordered by grassy hills and mountains— some of the latter rising two thousand feet, and white with snow down to the level of the *vegas.* Its elevation above the sea was 5,280 feet; latitude, by observation, 37° 28' 28"; and its distance from where we first struck the Spanish trail about four hundred miles. Counting from the time we reached the desert, and began to skirt, at our descent from Walker's [Oak Creek] Pass in the Sierra Nevada, we had travelled 550 miles, occupying twenty-seven days, in that inhospitable region. In passing before the great caravan, we had the ad-

170. The march of 10 and 11 May has taken the party away from the Virgin at the mouth of Beaver Dam Wash, back onto the Spanish Trail, which they had lost in the sand, and along the route of U.S. highway 91, to pass over the Beaver Dam Mountains down to Santa Clara River (HAFEN & HAFEN, 297).

171. Up the Santa Clara River and its northern fork, Magotsu Creek, to the place now called Mountain Meadows in southwestern Utah. In 1857, this spot would be the site of the massacre by fanatic Mormons of a train of emigrants from Missouri and Arkansas (J. BROOKS).

vantage of finding more grass, but the disadvantage of finding also the marauding savages, who had gathered down upon the trail, waiting the approach of that prey. This greatly increased our labors, besides costing us the life of an excellent man. We had to move all day in a state of watch, and prepared for combat—scouts and flankers out, a front and rear division of our men, and baggage animals in the centre. At night, camp duty was severe. Those who had toiled all day, had to guard, by turns, the camp and the horses all night. Frequently one-third of the whole party were on guard at once; and nothing but this vigilance saved us from attack. We were constantly dogged by bands, and even whole tribes of the marauders; and although Tabeau was killed, and our camp infested and insulted by some, while swarms of them remained on the hills and mountain sides, there was manifestly a consultation and calculation going on, to decide the question of attacking us. Having reached the resting place of the *Vegas de Santa Clara,* we had complete relief from the heat and privations of the desert, and some relaxation from the severity of camp duty. Some relaxation, and relaxation only—for camp guards, horse guards, and scouts, are indispensable from the time of leaving the frontiers of Missouri until we return to them.

After we left the *Vegas,* we had the gratification to be joined by the famous hunter and trapper, Mr. Joseph Walker,[172] whom I have before mentioned, and who now became our guide. He had left California with the great caravan, and perceiving, from the signs along the trail, that there was a party of whites ahead, which he judged to be mine, he detached himself from the caravan, with eight men, (Americans,) and ran the gauntlet of the desert robbers, killing two, and getting some of the horses wounded, and succeeded in overtaking us. Nothing but his great knowledge of the country, great courage and presence of mind, and good rifles, could have brought him safe from such a perilous enterprise.

---

172. Mountaineer Joseph Reddeford Walker (1798–1876) had been reared in Roane County, Tenn. In 1819, he moved to Missouri, and after trading and trapping out of Independence, he joined Captain Bonneville's company which left for the mountains in 1832. From the Green River rendezvous in 1833 he set out westward, first to Great Salt Lake, then to the Humboldt River, and on to what is known as Walker Lake. His group crossed the Sierra and reached Monterey, Calif. On his return east in 1834 he recrossed the mountains by what is now Walker Pass, and rejoined Bonneville in Idaho. As noted earlier, he joined Chiles' emigrant company at Fort Bridger in Aug. 1843 and led a part of it into California.

May 13.—We remained one day at this noted place of rest and refreshment; and, resuming our progress in a northeastwardly direction, we descended into a broad valley, the water of which is tributary to Sevier lake. The next day we came in sight of the Wah-satch range of mountains on the right, white with snow, and here forming the southeast part of the Great Basin. Sevier lake, upon the waters of which we now were, belonged to the system of lakes in the eastern part of the Basin—of which, the Great Salt lake, and its southern limb, the Utah lake,[173] were the principal—towards the region of which we were now approaching. We travelled for several days in this direction, within the rim of the Great Basin, crossing little streams which bore to the left for Sevier lake; and plainly seeing, by the changed aspect of the country, that we were entirely clear of the desert, and approaching the regions which appertained to the system of the Rocky mountains. We met, in this traverse, a few mounted Utah Indians, in advance of their main body, watching the approach of the great caravan.

May 16.—We reached a small salt lake, about seven miles long and one broad, at the northern extremity of which we encamped for the night.[174] This little lake, which well merits its characteristic

---

173. Utah Lake is not the southern limb of Great Salt Lake, but a separate body of water, connected to Great Salt Lake by the Jordan River. Although JCF does express some puzzlement over the fact that it is not salt water (p. 698), he leaves little doubt—on his map as well as in his narrative—that he considers Utah Lake a part of the larger one to the north.

174. As Dale L. Morgan has pointed out during his patient and much-appreciated consultations with us, JCF was careless with his narrative after leaving Mountain Meadows. His narrative says he lay over one day to rest; his table of distances says that he went on to Pinto Creek at present Newcastle on the 13th and rested there on the 14th. Pinto Creek is almost certainly where he met Walker.

From Pinto Creek he passed north of the Antelope Range and east to Iron Springs, and his map shows but does not name either stream—both of which soon fade into the sands. On the 16th, he reached Ojo de San Jose at present Enoch, Utah, near the divide between Cedar and Parowan (Little Salt Lake) valleys near the southern end of Little Salt Lake—not the northern end as his narrative states.

If the route on the map is to be accepted, we must believe that he traveled north from Ojo de San Jose and passed *west* of Little Salt Lake, missing a chance to strike several creeks if he had passed east of the lake. He then continued on from Enoch, west of the hills which run north-northeast from there, to a point west of the southwestern end of Little Salt Lake, and then on to a night camp at Buckhorn Springs, the only tolerable watering place before Beaver Valley.

name, lies immediately at the base of the Wah-satch range, and nearly opposite a gap in that chain of mountains through which the Spanish trail passes; and which, again falling upon the waters of the Colorado, and crossing that river, proceeds over a mountainous country to Santa Fé.

May 17.—After 440 miles of travelling on a trail, which served for a road, we again found ourselves under the necessity of exploring a track through the wilderness. The Spanish trail had borne off to the southeast, crossing the Wah-satch range. Our course led to the northeast, along the foot of that range, and leaving it on the right. The mountain presented itself to us under the form of several ridges, rising one above the other, rocky, and wooded with pine and cedar; the last ridge covered with snow. Sevier river, flowing northwardly to the lake of the same name, collects its principal waters from this section of the Wah-satch chain. We had now entered a region of great pastoral promise, abounding with fine streams, the rich bunch grass, soil that would produce wheat, and indigenous flax growing as if it had been sown. Consistent with the general character of its bordering mountains, this fertility of soil and vegetation does not extend far into the Great Basin. Mr. Joseph Walker, our guide, and who has more knowledge of these parts than any man I know, informed me that all the country to the left was unknown to him, and that even the *Digger* tribes, which frequented Lake Sevier, could tell him nothing about it.

May 20.—We met a band of Utah Indians, headed by a well-known chief, who had obtained the American or English name of Walker, by which he is quoted and well known. They were all mounted, armed with rifles, and use their rifles well. The chief had a fusee, which he had carried slung, in addition to his rifle. They were journeying slowly towards the Spanish trail, to levy their usual tribute upon the great Californian caravan. They were robbers of a higher order than those of the desert. They conducted their depredations with form, and under the color of trade and toll for passing through their country. Instead of attacking and killing, they affect

---

On 19 May, he camped north of the Beaver River. From there he traveled north into Wildcat Canyon and across a divide to Pine Creek, perhaps to camp there or at Cove Fort farther north on the 20th, and on Chalk Creek at present Fillmore on the 21st. He was in Round or Scipio Valley on the night of 22 May; on the 23rd at the site of Yuba Dam on the Sevier River; on the 24th, Salt Creek at Nephi; and then on to the Spanish Fork River on 25 May.

to purchase—taking the horses they like, and giving something nominal in return. The chief was quite civil to me. He was personally acquainted with his namesake, our guide, who made my name known to him. He knew of my expedition of 1842; and, as tokens of friendship, and proof that we had met, proposed an interchange of presents. We had no great store to choose out of; so he gave me a Mexican blanket, and I gave him a very fine one which I had obtained at Vancouver.

May 23.—We reached Sevier river—the main tributary of the lake of the same name—which, deflecting from its northern course, here breaks from the mountains to enter the lake. It was really a fine river, from eight to twelve feet deep; and, after searching in vain for a fordable place, we made little boats (or, rather, rafts) out of bulrushes, and ferried across. These rafts are readily made, and give a good conveyance across a river. The rushes are bound in bundles, and tied hard; the bundles are tied down upon poles, as close as they can be pressed, and fashioned like a boat, in being broader in the middle and pointed at the ends. The rushes, being tubular and jointed, are light and strong. The raft swims well, and is shoved along by poles, or paddled, or pushed and pulled by swimmers, or drawn by ropes. On this occasion, we used ropes—one at each end—and rapidly drew our little float backwards and forwards, from shore to shore. The horses swam. At our place of crossing, which was the most northern point of its bend, the latitude was 39° 22′ 19″. The banks sustained the character for fertility and vegetation which we had seen for some days. The name of this river and lake was an indication of our approach to regions of which our people had been the explorers. It was probably named after some American trapper or hunter, and was the first American name we had met with since leaving the Columbia river.[175] From the *Dalles* to the point where we turned across the Sierra Nevada, near 1,000 miles, we heard In-

---

175. Not true, as JCF will acknowledge in his *Geographical Memoir* of 1848. The name is a corruption of the Spanish version, Río Severo. Reaching the Sevier and crossing it near the present Yuba Dam, the expedition here loses François Badeau in the accident which JCF next describes. When Arthur Shearer, with one of the first wagon companies to travel the Salt Lake–to–Los Angeles road, was at the site on 6 Oct. 1849, he wrote: "We are encamped on the same ground that Fremont occupied when here and found and burned some wood cut & left by him. Saw grave of Bourdouxe who was accidentally shot at this place" (CU-B). There seem to have been no subsequent references to Badeau's gravesite.

dian names, and the greater part of the distance none; from Nueva Helvetia (Sacramento) to *las Vegas de Santa Clara,* about 1,000 more, all were Spanish; from the Mississippi to the Pacific, French and American or English were intermixed; and this prevalence of names indicates the national character of the first explorers.

We had here the misfortune to lose one of our people, François Badeau, who had been with me in both expeditions; during which he had always been one of my most faithful and efficient men. He was killed in drawing towards him a gun by the muzzle; the hammer being caught, discharged the gun, driving the ball through his head. We buried him on the banks of the river.

Crossing the next day a slight ridge along the river, we entered a handsome mountain valley [Tintic Valley] covered with fine grass, and directed our course towards a high snowy peak, at the foot of which lay the Utah lake. On our right was a bed of high mountains, their summits covered with snow, constituting the dividing ridge between the Basin waters and those of the Colorado. At noon we fell in with a party of Utah Indians coming out of the mountain, and in the afternoon encamped on a tributary to the lake, which is separated from the waters of the Sevier by very slight dividing grounds.

Early the next day we came in sight of the lake; and, as we descended to the broad bottoms of the Spanish fork, three horsemen were seen galloping towards us, who proved to be Utah Indians—scouts from a village, which was encamped near the mouth of the river. They were armed with rifles, and their horses were in good condition. We encamped near them, on the Spanish fork, which is one of the principal tributaries to the lake. Finding the Indians troublesome, and desirous to remain here a day, we removed the next morning farther down the lake, and encamped on a fertile bottom near the foot of the same mountainous ridge which borders the Great Salt lake, and along which we had journeyed the previous September. Here the principal plants in bloom were two, which were remarkable as affording to the Snake Indians—the one an abundant supply of food, and the other the most useful among the applications which they use for wounds. These were the kooyah plant, growing in fields of extraordinary luxuriance, and *convollaria stellata,* which, from the experience of Mr. Walker, is the best remedial plant known among those Indians. A few miles below us was another village of Indians, from which we obtained some fish—among them a few salmon trout, which were very much inferior in size to those along the Californian mountains. The season for taking them had not yet arrived; but the Indians were daily expecting them to come up out of the lake [to spawn].

We had now accomplished an object we had in view when leaving the Dalles of the Columbia in November last; we had reached the Utah lake; but by a route very different from what we had intended, and without sufficient time remaining to make the examinations which were desired. It is a lake of note in this country, under the dominion of the Utahs, who resort to it for fish. Its greatest breadth is about 15 miles, stretching far to the north, narrowing as it goes, and connecting with the Great Salt lake. This is the report, and which I believe to be correct; but it is fresh water, while the other is not only salt, but a saturated solution of salt; and here is a problem which requires to be solved. It is almost entirely surrounded by mountains, walled on the north and east by a high and snowy range, which supplies to it a fan of tributary streams. Among these, the principal river is the *Timpan-ogo* [Provo River]—signifying Rock river—a name which the rocky grandeur of its scenery, remarkable even in this country of rugged mountains, has obtained for it from the Indians. In the Utah language, *og-wáh-be,* the term for river, when coupled with other words in common conversation, is usually abbreviated to *ogo; timpan* signifying rock. It is probable that this river furnished the name which on the older maps has been generally applied to the Great Salt lake; but for this I have preferred a name which will be regarded as highly characteristic, restricting to the river the descriptive term Timpan-ogo, and leaving for the lake into which it flows the name of the people who reside on its shores, and by which it is known throughout the country.

The volume of water afforded by the Timpan-ogo is probably equal to that of the Sevier river; and, at the time of our visit, there was only one place in the lake valley at which the Spanish fork was fordable. In the cove of mountains along its eastern shore, the lake is bordered by a plain, where the soil is generally good, and in greater part fertile; watered by a delta of prettily timbered streams. This would be an excellent locality for stock farms; it is generally covered with good bunch grass, and would abundantly produce the ordinary grains.

In arriving at the Utah lake, we had completed an immense circuit of twelve degrees diameter north and south, and ten degrees east and west; and found ourselves, in May, 1844, on the same sheet of water which we had left in September, 1843. The Utah is the southern limb of the Great Salt lake; and thus we had seen that remarkable sheet of water both at its northern and southern extremity, and were able to fix its position at these two points. The circuit which we had made, and which had cost us eight months of time, and 3,500 miles of travelling, had given us a view of Oregon and of North California from the Rocky mountains to the Pacific ocean, and of the two principal streams which form bays or harbors on the coast of that sea. Having completed this circuit, and being now about to turn the back upon the Pacific slope of our continent, and to recross the Rocky mountains, it is natural to look back upon our footsteps, and take some brief view of the leading features and general structure of the country we had traversed. These are peculiar and striking, and differ essentially from the Atlantic side of our country. The mountains are all higher, more numerous, and more distinctly defined in their ranges and directions; and, what is so contrary to the natural order of such formations, one of these ranges, which is near the coast, (the Sierra Nevada and the Coast Range,) presents higher elevations and peaks than any which are to be found in the Rocky mountains themselves. In our eight months' circuit, we were never out of sight of snow; and the Sierra Nevada, where we crossed it, was near 2,000 feet higher than the South Pass in the Rocky mountains. In height, these mountains greatly exceed those of the Atlantic side, constantly presenting peaks which enter the region of eternal snow; and some of them volcanic, and in a frequent state of activity. They are seen at great distances, and guide the traveller in his courses.

The course and elevation of these ranges give direction to the rivers and character to the coast. No great river does, or can, take its rise below the Cascade and Sierra Nevada range; the distance to the sea is too short to admit of it. The rivers of the San Francisco bay, which are the largest after the Columbia, are local to that bay, and lateral to the coast, having their sources about on a line with the Dalles of the Columbia, and running each in a valley of its own, between coast range and the Cascade and Sierra Nevada range. The Columbia is the only river which traverses the whole breadth of the country, breaking through all the ranges, and entering the sea. Drawing its waters from a section of ten degrees of latitude in the Rocky mountains, which are collected into one stream by three main forks (Lewis's, Clark's, and the North fork) near the centre of the

Oregon valley, this great river thence proceeds by a single channel to the sea, while its three forks lead each to a pass in the mountains, which opens the way into the interior of the continent. This fact in relation to the rivers of this region gives an immense value to the Columbia. Its mouth is the only inlet and outlet to and from the sea; its three forks lead to the passes in the mountains; it is therefore the only line of communication between the Pacific and the interior of North America; and all operations of war or commerce, of national or social intercourse, must be conducted upon it. This gives it a value beyond estimation, and would involve irreparable injury if lost. In this unity and concentration of its waters, the Pacific side of our continent differs entirely from the Atlantic side, where the waters of the Allegany mountains are dispersed into many rivers, having their different entrances into the sea, and opening many lines of communication with the interior.

The Pacific coast is equally different from that of the Atlantic. The coast of the Atlantic is low and open, indented with numerous bays, sounds, and river estuaries, accessible every where, and opening by many channels into the heart of the country. The Pacific coast, on the contrary, is high and compact, with few bays, and but one that opens into the heart of the country. The immediate coast is what the seamen call *iron bound*. A little within, it is skirted by two successive ranges of mountains, standing as ramparts between the sea and the interior country; and to get through which, there is but one gate, and that narrow and easily defended. This structure of the coast, backed by these two ranges of mountains, with its concentration and unity of waters, gives to the country an immense military strength, and will probably render Oregon the most impregnable country in the world.

Differing so much from the Atlantic side of our continent, in coast, mountains, and rivers, the Pacific side differs from it in another most rare and singular feature—that of the Great interior Basin, of which I have so often spoken, and the whole form and character of which I was so anxious to ascertain. Its existence is vouched for by such of the American traders and hunters as have some knowledge of that region; the structure of the Sierra Nevada range of mountains requires it to be there; and my own observations confirm it. Mr. Joseph Walker, who is so well acquainted in those parts, informed me that, from the Great Salt lake west, there was a succession of lakes and rivers which have no outlet to the sea, nor any connexion with the Columbia, or with the Colorado of the Gulf of California. He described some of these lakes as being large, with numerous streams, and even considerable rivers, falling into them. In fact, all concur in the general report of these interior rivers and lakes; and, for want of understanding the force and power of evaporation, which so soon establishes an equilibrium between the loss and supply of waters, the fable of whirlpools and subterraneous outlets has gained belief, as the only imaginable way of carrying off the waters which have no visible discharge. The structure of the country would require this formation of interior lakes for the waters which would collect between the Rocky mountains and the Sierra Nevada, not being able to cross this formidable barrier, nor to get to the Columbia or the Colorado, must naturally collect into reservoirs, each of which would have its little system of streams and rivers to supply it. This would be the natural effect; and what I saw went to confirm it. The Great Salt lake is a formation of this kind, and quite a large one; and having many streams, and one considerable river, four or five hundred miles long, falling into it. This lake and river I saw and examined myself; and also saw the Wah-satch and Bear River mountains which enclose the waters of the lake on the east, and constitute, in that quarter, the rim of the Great Basin. Afterwards, along the eastern base of the Sierra Nevada, where we travelled for forty-two days, I saw the line of lakes and rivers which lie at the foot of that Sierra; and which Sierra is the western rim of the Basin. In going down Lewis's fork and the main Columbia, I crossed only inferior streams coming in from the left, such as could draw their water from a short distance only; and I often saw the mountains at their heads, white with snow; which, all accounts said, divided the waters of the *desert* from those of the Columbia, and which could be no other than the range of mountains which form the rim of the Basin on its northern side. And in returning from California along the Spanish trail, as far as the head of the Santa Clara fork of the Rio Virgen, I crossed only small streams making their way south to the Colorado, or lost in sand—as the Mo-hah-ve; while to the left, lofty mountains, their summits white with snow, were often visible, and which must have turned water to the north as well as to the south, and thus constituted, on this part, the southern rim of the Basin. At the head of the Santa Clara fork, and in the Vegas de Santa Clara, we crossed the ridge which parted the two systems of waters. We entered the Basin at that point, and have travelled in it ever since, having its southeastern rim (the Wah-satch mountain) on the right, and crossing the streams which flow down into it. The existence of the Basin is therefore an established fact in my mind; its extent and contents are yet to be better ascertained. It cannot be less than four or five hundred miles each way, and must lie principally in the Alta California; the demarcation latitude of 42° probably cutting a segment from the north part of the rim. Of its interior, but little is known. It is called a *desert,* and, from what I saw of it, sterility may be its prominent characteristic; but where there is so much water, there must be some *oasis.* The great river, and the great lake, reported, may not be equal to the report; but where there is so much snow, there must be streams; and where there is no outlet, there must be lakes to hold the accumulated waters, or sands to swallow them up. In this eastern part of the Basin, containing Sevier, Utah, and the Great Salt lakes, and the rivers and creeks falling into them, we know there is good soil and good grass, adapted to civilized settlements. In the western part, on Salmon Trout river, and some other streams, the same remark may be made.

The contents of this Great Basin are yet to be examined. That it is peopled, we know; but miserably and sparsely. From all that I heard and saw, I should say that humanity here appeared in its lowest form, and in its most elementary state. Dispersed in single families; without fire arms; eating seeds and insects; digging roots, (and hence their name)—such is the condition of the greater part. Others are a degree higher, and live in communities upon some lake or river that supplies fish, and from which they repulse the miserable *Digger.* The rabbit is the largest animal known in this desert; its flesh affords a little meat; and their bag-like covering is made of its skins. The wild sage is their only wood, and here it is of extraordinary size—sometimes a foot in diameter, and six or eight feet high. It serves for fuel, for building material, for shelter to the rabbits, and for some sort of covering for the feet and legs in cold weather. Such are the accounts of the inhabitants and productions of the Great Basin; and which, though imperfect, must have some foundation, and excite our desire to know the whole.

The whole idea of such a desert, and such a people, is a novelty in our country, and excites Asiatic, not American ideas. Interior basins, with their own systems of lakes and rivers, and often sterile, are common enough in Asia; people still in the elementary state of families, living in deserts, with no other occupation than the mere animal search for food, may still be seen in that ancient quarter of the globe; but in America such things are new and strange, unknown and unsuspected, and discredited when related. But I flatter myself that what is discovered, though not enough to satisfy curiosity, is sufficient to excite it, and that subsequent explorations will complete what has been commenced.

This account of the Great Basin, it will be remembered, belongs to the Alta California, and has no application to Oregon, whose capabilities may justify a separate remark. Referring to my journal for particular descriptions, and for sectional boundaries between good and bad districts, I can only say, in general and comparative terms, that, in that branch of agriculture which implies the cultivation of grains and staple crops, it would be inferior to the Atlantic States, though many parts are superior for wheat; while in the rearing of flocks and herds it would claim a high place. Its grazing capabilities are great; and even in the indigenous grass now there, an element of individual and national wealth may be found. In fact, the valuable grasses begin within one hundred and fifty miles of the Missouri frontier, and extend to the Pacific ocean. East of the Rocky mountains, it is the short curly grass, on which the buffalo delight to feed, (whence its name of buffalo,) and which is still good when dry and apparently dead. West of those mountains it is a larger growth, in clusters, and hence called bunch grass, and which has a second or fall growth. Plains and mountains both exhibit them; and I have seen good pasturage at an elevation of ten thousand feet. In this spontaneous product, the trading or travelling caravans can find subsistence for their animals; and in military operations any number of cavalry may be moved, and any number of cattle may be driven; and thus men and horses be supported on long expeditions, and even in winter in the sheltered situations.

Commercially, the value of the Oregon country must be great, washed as it is by the north Pacific ocean—fronting Asia—producing many of the elements of commerce—mild and healthy in its climate —and becoming, as it naturally will, a thoroughfare for the East India and China trade.

Turning our faces once more eastward, on the morning of the 27th we left the Utah lake, and continued for two days to ascend the Spanish fork, which is dispersed in numerous branches among very rugged mountains, which afford few passes, and render a familiar acquaintance with them necessary to the traveller. The stream can scarcely be said to have a valley, the mountains rising often abruptly from the water's edge; but a good trail facilitated our travelling, and there were frequent bottoms, covered with excellent grass. The streams are prettily and variously wooded; and every where the mountain shows grass and timber.

At our encampment on the evening of the 28th, near the head of one of the branches we had ascended, strata of bituminous limestone were displayed in an escarpment on the river bluffs, in which were contained a variety of fossil shells of new species.

It will be remembered, that in crossing this ridge about 120 miles to the northward in August last, strata of fossiliferous rock were discovered, which have been referred to the oolitic period; it is probable that these rocks also belong to the same formation.

A few miles from this encampment we reached the head of the stream; and crossing by an open and easy pass, the dividing ridge which separates the waters of the Great Basin from those of the Colorado, we reached the head branches of one of its larger tributaries, which, from the decided color of its waters, has received the name of White [Price] river. The snows of the mountains were now beginning to melt, and all the little rivulets were running by in rivers, and rapidly becoming difficult to ford. Continuing a few miles up a branch of White river, we crossed a dividing ridge between its waters and those of the *Uintah*. The approach to the pass, which is the best known to Mr. Walker, was somewhat difficult for packs, and impracticable for wagons—all the streams being shut in by narrow ravines, and the narrow trail along the steep hill sides allowing the passage of only one animal at a time. From the summit we had a fine view of the snowy Bear River range; and there were still remaining beds of snow on the cold sides of the hills near the pass. We descended by a narrow ravine, in which was rapidly gathered a little branch [Strawberry] of the Uintah, and halted to noon about 1,500 feet below the pass, at an elevation, by the boiling point, of 6,900 feet above the sea.

The next day [30 May] we descended along the river, and about noon reached a point where three forks come together. Fording one of these with some difficulty, we continued up the middle branch, which, from the color of its waters, is named the Red [Strawberry] river. The few passes, and extremely rugged nature of the country, give to it great strength, and secure the Utahs from the intrusion of their enemies. Crossing in the afternoon a somewhat broken highland, covered in places with fine grasses, and with cedar on the hill sides, we encamped at evening on another tributary to the *Uintah,* called the *Duchesne* fork. The water was very clear, the stream not being yet swollen by the melting snows; and we forded it without any difficulty. It is a considerable branch, being spread out by islands, the largest arm being about a hundred feet wide; and the name it bears is probably that of some old French trapper.

The next day we continued down the river, which we were twice obliged to cross; and, the water having risen during the night, it was almost every where too deep to be forded. After travelling about sixteen miles, we encamped again on the left bank.[176]

I obtained here an occultation of δ *Scorpii* at the dark limb of the moon, which gives for the longitude of the place 112° 18′ 30″, and the latitude 40° 18′ 53″.

June 1.—We left to-day the Duchesne fork, and, after traversing a broken country for about sixteen miles, arrived at noon at another considerable branch, a river of great velocity, to which the trappers have improperly given the name of Lake Fork. The name applied to it by the Indians signifies great swiftness, and is the same which they use to express the speed of a race horse. It is spread out in various channels over several hundred yards, and is every where too deep and swift to be forded. At this season of the year, there is an uninterrupted noise from the large rocks which are rolled along the bed. After infinite difficulty, and the delay of a day, we succeeded in getting the stream bridged, and got over with the loss of one of our

---

176. JCF's narrative and map do not agree here, and the narrative is in error. The route from 27 through 31 May has taken the party to the headwaters of Spanish Fork in the Wasatch Mountains, across the divide at Soldier Summit into the Colorado River basin, to the waters of what was then the South White and is now the Price. Ascending a small branch of the Price, JCF's expedition reached the headwaters of the "Uinta" on 29 May. He then descended Avintaquin Creek to its confluence with the Strawberry River, nearly opposite the mouth of Red Creek. Then he crossed the Strawberry and went up the northern branch, Red Creek. To have ascended the "middle" branch would have taken him up the Strawberry through its canyons into Strawberry Valley, then back across the Wasatch to Utah Valley. According to present usage, the Duchesne is considered the main river, the Strawberry and the Uinta affluents.

animals. Continuing our route across a broken country, of which the higher parts were rocky and timbered with cedar, and the lower parts covered with good grass, we reached, on the afternoon of the 3d, the Uintah fort, a trading post belonging to Mr. A. Roubideau, on the principal fork of the Uintah river.[177] We found the stream nearly as rapid and difficult as the Lake fork, divided into several channels, which were too broad to be bridged. With the aid of guides from the fort, we succeeded, with very great difficulty, in fording it; and encamped near the fort, which is situated a short distance above the junction of two branches which make the river.

By an immersion of the 1st satellite, (agreeing well with the result of the occultation observed at the Duchesne fork,) the longitude of the post is 109° 56′ 42″, the latitude 40° 27′ 45″.

It has a motley garrison of Canadian and Spanish *engagés* and hunters, with the usual number of Indian women. We obtained a small supply of sugar and coffee, with some dried meat and a cow, which was a very acceptable change from the *pinoli* on which we had subsisted for some weeks past. I strengthened my party at this place by the addition of Auguste Archambeau, an excellent voyageur and hunter, belonging to the class of Carson and Godey.[178]

On the morning of the 5th we left the fort* and the Uintah river,

* This fort was attacked and taken by a band of the Utah Indians since we passed it; and the men of the garrison killed, the women carried off. Mr. Roubideau, a trader of St. Louis, was absent, and so escaped the fate of the rest.

---

177. Antoine Robidoux (1794–1860), a naturalized Mexican citizen from Florissant, Mo. After 1825, he became associated with the fur trade around Santa Fe, Taos, and the intermontane corridor northwest of New Mexico. The last years of his life were spent in St. Joseph, Mo., a town founded by his brother, Joseph Robidoux III. Antoine Robidoux actually had two forts, and authorities differ as to the dates of establishment as well as the mode of destruction. WALLACE, his biographer, thinks that Fort Uintah (sometimes known as Fort Wintey or Fort Robidoux) was established in the early 1840s at the fork of Uinta River and White Rocks Creek, and was attacked by Indians in the winter of 1844–45, as JCF indicates below. On the other hand, MORGAN [2], 216, 218, believes it was established as early as 1837 and contends it was Fort Uncompagre (on the Gunnison) which was attacked by Utes. After the destruction of Fort Uncompagre, Robidoux abandoned Fort Uintah and it was eventually burned by mountain man Jim Baker to prevent renewed competition for the Ute trade.

178. François Perrault was discharged here. Thomas Cowie, who had emigrated to California in 1843 with the Chiles-Walker party, was—along with Archambeault—added to the expedition. Cowie was probably one of the eight men traveling with Walker when he joined JCF as a guide on 25 May,

and continued our road over a broken country, which afforded, how-ever, a rich addition to our botanical collection;[179] and, after a march of 25 miles, were again checked by another stream, called Ashley's fork, where we were detained until noon of the next day.

An immersion of the 2d satellite gave for this place a longitude of 109° 27' 07", the latitude by observation being 40° 28' 07".

In the afternoon of the next day we succeeded in finding a ford; and, after travelling fifteen miles, encamped high up on the moun-tain side, where we found excellent and abundant grass, which we had not hitherto seen. A new species of *elymus*,[180] which had a purgative and weakening effect upon the animals, had occurred abundantly since leaving the fort. From this point, by observation 7,300 feet above the sea, we had a view of the Colorado [Green] below, shut up amongst rugged mountains, and which is the re-cipient of all the streams we had been crossing since we passed the rim of the Great Basin at the head of the Spanish fork.

On the 7th we had a pleasant but long day's journey, through beautiful little valleys and a high mountain country, arriving about evening at the verge of a steep and rocky ravine, by which we de-scended to *"Brown's hole."*[181] This is a place well known to trappers in the country, where the cañons through which the Colorado runs expand into a narrow but pretty valley, about sixteen miles in length. The river was several hundred yards in breadth, swollen to the top of its banks, near to which it was in many places fifteen to twenty feet deep. We repaired a skin boat which had been purchased at the fort, and, after a delay of a day, reached the opposite banks with much less delay than had been encountered on the Uintah waters. According to information, the lower end of the valley is the most

---

and only now becomes a paid member of the party. In Feb. 1844, Walker had applied to the Mexican authorities in California for a pass for Cowie. Cowie later returned to California, joined the Bear Flaggers, and was killed near Santa Rosa.

179. JCF became, in 1844 and again in 1845, the first man to make botani-cal collections in the Uinta Basin. Not until the twentieth century were collec-tions again made there (MC KELVEY, 878).

180. Not identified.

181. Now Brown's Park, an area lying within the boundaries of Dinosaur National Monument in northwestern Colorado and northeastern Utah. Local residents distinguish between Brown's Park (a large valley) and Brown's Hole, a smaller valley within the park. JCF camped a mile or so above the point where the Green River disappears through the Gate of Lodore into Lodore Canyon.

eastern part of the Colorado; and the latitude of our encampment, which was opposite to the remains of an old fort[182] on the left bank of the river, was 40° 46′ 27″, and, by observation, the elevation above the sea 5,150 feet. The bearing to the entrance of the cañon below was south 20° east. Here the river enters between lofty precipices of red rock, and the country below is said to assume a very rugged character; the river and its affluents passing through cañons which forbid all access to the water. This sheltered little valley was formerly a favorite wintering ground for the trappers, as it afforded them sufficient pasturage for their animals, and the surrounding mountains are well stocked with game.

We surprised a flock of mountain sheep as we descended to the river, and our hunters killed several. The bottoms of a small stream called the Vermillion creek, which enters the left bank of the river a short distance below our encampment, were covered abundantly with *F. vermicularis,* and other chenopodiaceous shrubs. From the lower end of Brown's hole we issued by a remarkably dry cañon, fifty or sixty yards wide, and rising, as we advanced, to the height of six or eight hundred feet. Issuing from this, and crossing a small green valley, we entered another rent of the same nature, still narrower than the other, the rocks on either side rising in nearly vertical precipices perhaps 1,500 feet in height. These places are mentioned, to give some idea of the country lower down on the Colorado, to which the trappers usually apply the name of a cañon country. The cañon opened upon a pond of water, where we halted to noon. Several flocks of mountain sheep were here among the rocks, which rung with volleys of small arms. In the afternoon we entered upon an ugly, barren, and broken country, corresponding well with that we had traversed a few degrees north, on the same side of the Colorado. The Vermillion creek afforded us brackish water and indifferent grass for the night.

A few scattered cedar trees were the only improvement of the country on the following day; and at a little spring of bad water, where we halted to noon, we had not even the shelter of these from the hot rays of the sun. At night we encamped in a fine grove of

---

182. Fort Davy Crockett, according to L. HAFEN [1]. Carson had spent much time there and must have been able to tell his chief something of the fort's history, but nothing of this is recorded by JCF.

cottonwood trees, on the banks of the Elk Head river, the principal fork of the Yampah river, commonly called by the trappers the Bear river. We made here a very strong *corál* and fort, and formed the camp into vigilant guards. The country we were now entering is constantly infested by war parties of the Sioux and other Indians, and is considered among the most dangerous war grounds in the Rocky mountains; parties of whites having been repeatedly defeated on this river.

On the 11th we continued up the river, which is a considerable stream, fifty to a hundred yards in width, handsomely and continuously wooded with groves of the narrow-leaved cottonwood, (*populus angustifolia;*) with these were thickets of willow and *grain du beouf*. The characteristic plant along the river is *F. vermicularis,* which generally covers the bottoms; mingled with this, are saline shrubs and artemisia. The new variety of grass which we had seen on leaving the Uintah fort had now disappeared. The country on either side was sandy and poor, scantily wooded with cedars, but the river bottoms afforded good pasture. Three antelopes were killed in the afternoon, and we encamped a little below a branch of the river, called St. Vrain's fork.[183] A few miles above was the fort at which Frapp's [Fraeb's] party had been defeated two years since; and we passed during the day a place where Carson had been fired upon so close that one of the men had five bullets through his body. Leaving this river the next morning, we took our way across the hills, where every hollow had a spring of running water, with good grass.

Yesterday and to-day we have had before our eyes the high mountains which divide the Pacific from the Mississippi waters; and entering here among the lower spurs, or foot hills of the range, the face of the country began to improve with a magical rapidity. Not only the river bottoms, but the hills, were covered with grass; and among the usual varied flora of the mountain region, these were occasionally blue with the showy bloom of a *lupinus*. In the course of the morning we had the first glad view of buffalo, and welcomed the appear-

---

183. The route of 8–11 June has taken the expedition from Brown's Park, up Vermillion Creek for two nights of camping on the Little Snake, which JCF mistakenly calls the Elk Head (another tributary of the Yampa, farther south). He camps on Battle Creek, at the mouth of which, in Routt County, Colo., just below the Wyoming line, Henry Fraeb was killed.

ance of two old bulls with as much joy as if they had been messengers from home; and when we descended to noon on St. Vrain's fork, an affluent of Green river, the hunters brought in mountain sheep and the meat of two fat bulls. Fresh entrails in the river showed us that there were Indians above; and, at evening, judging it unsafe to encamp in the bottoms, which were wooded only with willow thickets, we ascended to the spurs above, and forted strongly in a small aspen grove, near to which was a spring of cold water. The hunters killed two fine cows near the camp. A band of elk broke out of a neighboring grove; antelopes were running over the hills; and on the opposite river plains, herds of buffalo were raising clouds of dust. The country here appeared more variously stocked with game than any part of the Rocky mountains we had visited; and its abundance is owing to the excellent pasturage, and its dangerous character as a war ground.

June 13.—There was snow here near our mountain camp, and the morning was beautiful and cool. Leaving St. Vrain's fork, we took our way directly towards the summit of the dividing ridge. The bottoms of the streams and level places were wooded with aspens; and as we neared the summit, we entered again the piney region. We had a delightful morning's ride, the ground affording us an excellent bridle path, and reached the summit towards midday, at an elevation of 8,000 feet. With joy and exultation we saw ourselves once more on the top of the Rocky mountains, and beheld a little stream taking its course towards the rising sun. It was an affluent of the Platte, called *Pullam's* fork, and we descended to noon upon it. It is a pretty stream, twenty yards broad, and bears the name of a trapper who, some years since, was killed here by the *Gros Ventre* Indians.

Issuing from the pines in the afternoon, we saw spread out before us the valley of the Platte, with the pass of the Medicine Butte beyond, and some of the Sweet Water mountains; but a smoky haziness in the air entirely obscured the Wind River chain.

We were now about two degrees south of the South Pass, and our course home would have been eastwardly; but that would have taken us over ground already examined, and therefore without the interest which would excite curiosity. Southwardly there were objects worthy to be explored, to wit: the approximation of the head waters of three different rivers—the Platte, the Arkansas, and the

Grand River fork of the Rio Colorado of the gulf of California; the Passes at the heads of these rivers; and the three remarkable mountain coves, called Parks, in which they took their rise. One of these Parks was, of course, on the western side of the dividing ridge; and a visit to it would require us once more to cross the summit of the Rocky mountains to the west, and then to re-cross to the east; making, in all, with the transit we had just accomplished, three crossings of that mountain in this section of its course. But, no matter. The coves, the heads of the rivers, the approximation of their waters, the practicability of the mountain passes, and the locality of the THREE PARKS, were all objects of interest, and, although well known to hunters and trappers, were unknown to science and to history. We therefore changed our course, and turned up the valley of the Platte instead of going down it.

We crossed several small affluents, and again made a fortified camp in a grove. The country had now become very beautiful—rich in water, grass, and game; and to these were added the charm of scenery and pleasant weather.[184]

June 14.—Our route this morning lay along the foot of the mountain, over the long low spurs which sloped gradually down to the river, forming the broad valley of the Platte. The country is beautifully watered. In almost every hollow ran a clear, cool mountain stream; and in the course of the morning we crossed seventeen, several of them being large creeks, forty to fifty feet wide, with a swift current, and tolerably deep. These were variously wooded with groves of aspen and cottonwood, with willow, cherry, and other shrubby trees. Buffalo, antelope, and elk, were frequent during the day; and, in their abundance, the latter sometimes reminded us slightly of the Sacramento valley.

We halted at noon on Potter's fork—a clear and swift stream, forty yards wide, and in many places deep enough to swim our animals; and in the evening encamped on a pretty stream, where there were several beaver dams, and many trees recently cut down by the beaver. We gave to this the name of Beaver Dam creek, as now they are becoming sufficiently rare to distinguish by their name the streams on which they are found. In this mountain they occurred

---

184. JCF has crossed the Continental Divide in the Sierra Madre range, and descended to the valley of the North Platte along one of its affluents in Carbon County, Wyo.

more abundantly than elsewhere in all our journey, in which their vestiges had been scarcely seen.

The next day we continued our journey up the valley, the country presenting much the same appearance, except that the grass was more scanty on the ridges, over which was spread a scrubby growth of sage; but still the bottoms of the creeks were broad, and afforded good pasture grounds. We had an animated chase after a grizzly bear this morning, which we tried to lasso. Fuentes threw the lasso upon his neck, but it slipped off, and he escaped into the dense thickets of the creek, into which we did not like to venture. Our course in the afternoon brought us to the main Platte river, here a handsome stream, with a uniform breadth of seventy yards, except where widened by frequent islands. It was apparently deep, with a moderate current, and wooded with groves of large willow.

The valley narrowed as we ascended, and presently degenerated into a gorge, through which the river passed as through a gate. We entered it, and found ourselves in the New Park—a beautiful circular valley of thirty miles diameter, walled in all round with snowy mountains, rich with water and with grass, fringed with pine on the mountain sides below the snow line, and a paradise to all grazing animals. The Indian name for it signifies *"cow lodge,"* of which our own may be considered a translation; the enclosure, the grass, the water, and the herds of buffalo roaming over it, naturally presenting the idea of a park. We halted for the night just within the gate, and expected, as usual, to see herds of buffalo; but an Arapahoe village had been before us, and not one was to be seen. Latitude of the encampment 40° 52′ 44″. Elevation by the boiling point, 7,720 feet.[185]

It is from this elevated *cove,* and from the gorges of the surrounding mountains, and some lakes within their bosoms, that the Great Platte river collects its first waters, and assumes its first form; and certainly no river could ask a more beautiful origin.

June 16.—In the morning we pursued our way through the Park, following a principal branch of the Platte, and crossing, among many smaller ones, a bold stream, scarcely fordable, called Lodge Pole fork, and which issues from a lake in the mountains on the right,

---

185. Up the North Platte Valley on 14 and 15 June. His Potter's Fork may be present Encampment River, and Beaver Dam Creek now Beaver Creek. On the 15th, he entered "New Park," now North Park, where the river passes between Independence Mountain and Watson Mountain, not far from Colorado highway 125.

ten miles long. In the evening we encamped on a small stream, near the upper end of the Park.[186] Latitude of the camp 40° 33' 22".

June 17.—We continued our way among the waters of the Park, over the foot hills of the bordering mountains, where we found good pasturage, and surprised and killed some buffalo. We fell into a broad and excellent trail, made by buffalo, where a wagon would pass with ease; and, in the course of the morning, we [re]crossed the summit of the Rocky mountains, through a pass which was one of the most beautiful we had ever seen. The trail led among the aspens, through open grounds, richly covered with grass, and carried us over an elevation of about 9,000 feet above the level of the sea.

The country appeared to great advantage in the delightful summer weather of the mountains, which we still continued to enjoy. Descending from the pass, we found ourselves again on the western waters; and halted to noon on the edge of another mountain valley, called the Old Park, in which is formed Grand river, one of the principal branches of the Colorado of California. We were now moving with some caution, as, from the trail, we found the Arapahoe village had also passed this way. As we were coming out of their enemy's country, and this was a war ground, we were desirous to avoid them. After a long afternoon's march, we halted at night on a small creek, tributary to a main fork of Grand river, which ran through this portion of the valley.[187] The appearance of the country in the Old Park is interesting, though of a different character from the New; instead of being a comparative plain, it is more or less broken into hills, and surrounded by the high mountains, timbered on the lower parts with quaking asp and pines.

June 18.—Our scouts, who were as usual ahead, made from a *butte* this morning the signal of Indians, and we rode up in time to meet a party of about 30 Arapahoes. They were men and women going into the hills—the men for game, the women for roots—and informed us that the village was encamped a few miles above, on the main fork of Grand river, which passes through the midst of the valley. I made

---

186. The campsite for today is not determined, but the stream he calls Lodge Pole Fork may be the north fork of the North Platte, which is joined by Lake Creek before it reaches the main North Platte. A lake now called Lake John, and some smaller ones, lie in the foothills to the right.

187. Recrossing the Divide about where it is intersected by U.S. highway 40, the expedition has camped on Muddy Creek, an affluent of the Colorado. The party is now in Middle Park.

them the usual presents; but they appeared disposed to be unfriendly, and galloped back at speed to the village. Knowing that we had trouble to expect, I descended immediately into the bottoms of Grand river, which were overflowed in places, the river being up, and made the best encampment the ground afforded. We had no time to build a fort, but found an open place among the willows, which was defended by the river on one side and the overflowed bottoms on the other. We had scarcely made our few preparations, when about 200 of them appeared on the verge of the bottom, mounted, painted, and armed for war. We planted the American flag between us; and a short parley ended in a truce, with something more than the usual amount of presents. About 20 Sioux were with them—one of them an old chief, who had always been friendly to the whites. He informed me that, before coming down, a council had been held at the village, in which the greater part had declared for attacking us—we had come from their enemies, to whom we had doubtless been carrying assistance in arms and ammunition; but his own party, with some few of the Arapahoes who had seen us the previous year in the plains, opposed it. It will be remembered that it is customary for this people to attack the trading parties which they meet in this region, considering all whom they meet on the western side of the mountains to be their enemies. They deceived me into the belief that I should find a ford at their village, and I could not avoid accompanying them; but put several sloughs between us and their village, and forted strongly on the banks of the river, which was every where rapid and deep, and over a hundred yards in breadth. The camp was generally crowded with Indians; and though the baggage was carefully watched and covered, a number of things were stolen.

The next morning we descended the river for about eight miles, and halted a short distance above a cañon, through which Grand river issues from the Park.[188] Here it was smooth and deep, 150 yards in breadth, and its elevation at this point 6,700 feet. A frame for the boat being very soon made, our baggage was ferried across; the horses, in the mean time, swimming over. A southern fork of Grand river here makes its junction, nearly opposite to the branch by which

188. JCF has descended the Colorado through Middle Park and is now camping near Gore Canyon in the vicinity of Kremmling, Colo., near where the present Blue River comes in from the south.

we had entered the valley, and up this we continued for about eight miles in the afternoon, and encamped in a bottom on the left bank, which afforded good grass. At our encampment it was 70 to 90 yards in breadth, sometimes widened by islands, and separated into several channels, with a very swift current and bed of rolled rocks.

On the 20th[189] we travelled up the left bank, with the prospect of a bad road, the trail here taking the opposite side; but the stream was up, and nowhere fordable. A piney ridge of mountains, with bare rocky peaks, was on our right all the day, and a snowy mountain appeared ahead. We crossed many foaming torrents with rocky beds, rushing down to the river; and in the evening made a strong fort in an aspen grove. The valley had already become very narrow, shut up more closely in densely timbered mountains, the pines sweeping down the verge of the bottoms. The *coq de prairie* (*tetrao europhasianus*) was occasionally seen among the sage.

We saw to-day the returning trail of an Arapahoe party which had been sent from the village to look for Utahs in the Bayou Salade, (South Park;) and it being probable that they would visit our camp with the desire to return on horseback, we were more than usually on the alert.

Here the river diminished to 35 yards, and, notwithstanding the number of affluents we had crossed, was still a large stream, dashing swiftly by, with a great continuous fall, and not yet fordable. We had a delightful ride along a good trail among the fragrant pines; and the appearance of buffalo in great numbers indicated that there were Indians in the Bayou Salade, (South Park,) by whom they were driven out. We halted to noon under the shade of the pines, and the weather was most delightful. The country was literally alive with buffalo; and the continued echo of the hunter's rifles on the other

189. Here, for the next several days, JCF does not always provide dates. Starting on the 20th, he goes up the Blue to Hoosier Pass, then down the valley of the Middle Fork of the South Platte—not the South Fork, as he surmises. He has the rugged Mosquito Range on his right, and correctly assumes that beyond it to the left lie the headwaters of the Arkansas. He enters the Arkansas River watershed via a rough country that gave Zebulon Pike trouble in the winter of 1806–7. But, unlike Pike, he avoids the treacherous Royal Gorge of the Arkansas, an indication that he probably went down Fourmile Creek and struck the Arkansas well below the gorge. His camp on 28 June was in the vicinity of Canon City, Colo., and he reached Pueblo on the 29th.

side of the river for a moment made me uneasy, thinking perhaps they were engaged with Indians; but in a short time they came into camp with the meat of seven fat cows.

During the earlier part of the day's ride, the river had been merely a narrow ravine between high piney mountains, backed on both sides, but particularly on the west, by a line of snowy ridges; but, after several hours' ride, the stream opened out into a valley with pleasant bottoms. In the afternoon the river forked into three apparently equal streams; broad buffalo trails leading up the left hand, and the middle branch indicating good passes over the mountains; but up the right-hand branch, (which, in the object of descending from the mountain by the main head of the Arkansas, I was most desirous to follow,) there was no sign of a buffalo trace. Apprehending from this reason, and the character of the mountains, which are known to be extremely rugged, that the right-hand branch led to no pass, I proceeded up the middle branch, which formed a flat valley bottom between timbered ridges on the left and snowy mountains on the right, terminating in large *buttes* of naked rock. The trail was good, and the country interesting; and at nightfall we encamped in an open place among the pines, where we built a strong fort. The mountains exhibit their usual varied growth of flowers, and at this place I noticed, among others, *thermopsis montana,* whose bright yellow color makes it a showy plant. This has been a characteristic in many parts of the country since reaching the Uintah waters. With fields of iris were *aquilegia cœrulea,* violets, esparcette, and strawberries.

At dark, we perceived a fire in the edge of the pines, on the opposite side of the valley. We had evidently not been discovered, and, at the report of a gun, and the blaze of fresh fuel which was heaped on our fires, those of the strangers were instantly extinguished. In the morning, they were found to be a party of six trappers, who had ventured out among the mountains after beaver. They informed us that two of the number with which they started had been already killed by the Indians—one of them but a few days since—by the Arapahoes we had lately seen, who had found him alone at a camp on this river, and carried off his traps and animals. As they were desirous to join us, the hunters returned with them to their encampment, and we continued up the valley, in which the stream rapidly diminished, breaking into small tributaries—every hollow affording water. At our noon halt, the hunters joined us with the trappers.

While preparing to start from their encampment they found themselves suddenly surrounded by a party of Arapahoes, who informed them that their scouts had discovered a large Utah village in the Bayou Salade, (South Park,) and that a large war party, consisting of almost every man in the village, except those who were too old to go to war, were going over to attack them. The main body had ascended the left fork of the river, which afforded a better pass than the branch we were on; and this party had followed our trail, in order that we might add our force to theirs. Carson informed them that we were too far ahead to turn back, but would join them in the bayou; and the Indians went off apparently satisfied. By the temperature of boiling water, our elevation here was 10,430 feet; and still the pine forest continued, and grass was good.

In the afternoon, we continued our road—occasionally through open pines, with a very gradual ascent. We surprised a herd of buffalo, enjoying the shade at a small lake among the pines; and they made the dry branches crack, as they broke through the woods. In a ride of about three-quarters of an hour, and having ascended perhaps 800 feet, we reached the SUMMIT OF THE DIVIDING RIDGE, which would thus have an estimated height of 11,200 feet. Here the river spreads itself into small branches and springs, heading nearly in the summit of the ridge, which is very narrow. Immediately below us was a green valley, through which ran a stream; and a short distance opposite rose snowy mountains, whose summits were formed into peaks of naked rock. We soon afterwards satisfied ourselves that immediately beyond these mountains was the main branch of the Arkansas river—most probably heading directly with the little stream below us, which gathered its waters in the snowy mountains near by. Descriptions of the rugged character of the mountains around the head of the Arkansas, which their appearance amply justified, deterred me from making any attempt to reach it, which would have involved a greater length of time than now remained at my disposal.

In about a quarter of an hour, we descended from the summit of the Pass into the creek below, our road having been very much controlled and interrupted by the pines and springs on the mountain side. Turning up the stream, we encamped on a bottom of good grass near its head, which gathers its waters in the dividing crest of the Rocky mountains, and, according to the best information we could obtain, separated only by the rocky wall of the ridge from the head of the main Arkansas river. By the observations of the evening, the latitude of our encampment was 39° 20′ 24″, and south of which, therefore, is the head of the Arkansas river. The stream on which we had encamped is the head of either the *Fontaine-qui-bouit,* a branch of the Arkansas, or the remotest head of the south fork of the Platte; as which, you will find it laid down on the map. But descending it only through a portion of its course, we have not been able to settle this point satisfactorily.

In the evening, a band of buffalo furnished a little excitement, by charging through the camp.

On the following day, we descended the stream by an excellent buffalo trail, along the open grassy bottom of the river. On our right, the bayou was bordered by a mountainous range, crested with rocky and naked peaks; and below, it had a beautiful park-like character of pretty level prairies, interspersed among low spurs, wooded openly with pine and quaking asp, contrasting well with the denser pines which swept around on the mountain sides. Descending always the valley of the stream, towards noon we descried a mounted party descending the point of a spur, and, judging them to be Arapahoes— who, defeated or victorious, were equally dangerous to us, and with whom a fight would be inevitable—we hurried to post ourselves as strongly as possible on some willow islands in the river. We had scarcely halted when they arrived, proving to be a party of Utah women, who told us that on the other side of the ridge their village was fighting with the Arapahoes. As soon as they had given us this information, they filled the air with cries and lamentations, which made us understand that some of their chiefs had been killed.

Extending along the river, directly ahead of us, was a low piney ridge, leaving between it and the stream a small open bottom, on which the Utahs had very injudiciously placed their village, which, according to the women, numbered about 300 warriors. Advancing in the cover of the pines, the Arapahoes, about daylight, charged into the village, driving off a great number of their horses, and killing four men; among them, the principal chief of the village. They drove the horses perhaps a mile beyond the village, to the end of a hollow, where they had previously forted at the edge of the pines. Here the Utahs had instantly attacked them in turn, and, according to the report of the women, were getting rather the best of the day. The women pressed us eagerly to join with their people, and would immediately have provided us with the best horses at the village; but it was not for us to interfere in such a conflict. Neither party were our friends, or under our protection; and each was ready to prey upon us that could. But we could not help feeling an unusual excitement at being within a few hunderd yards of a fight, in which 500 men were closely engaged, and hearing the sharp cracks of their rifles. We were in a bad position, and subject to be attacked in it. Either party which we might meet, victorious or defeated, was certain to fall upon us; and, gearing up immediately, we kept close along the pines of the ridge, having it between us and the village, and keeping the scouts on the summit, to give us notice of the approach of Indians. As we passed by the village, which was immediately below us, horsemen were galloping to and fro, and groups of people were gathered around those who were wounded and dead, and who were being brought in from the field. We continued to press on, and, crossing another fork, which came in from the right, after having made fifteen miles from the village, fortified ourselves strongly in the pines, a short distance from the river.

During the afternoon, Pike's Peak had been plainly in view before us, and, from our encampment, bore N. 87° E. by compass. This was a familiar object, and it had for us the face of an old friend. At its foot were the springs, where we had spent a pleasant day in coming out. Near it were the habitations of civilized men; and it overlooked the broad smooth plains, which promised us an easy journey to our home.

The next day we left the river, which continued its course towards Pike's Peak; and taking a southeasterly direction, in about ten miles we crossed a gentle ridge, and issuing from the South Park, found ourselves involved among the broken spurs of the mountains which border the great prairie plains. Although broken and extremely rugged, the country was very interesting, being well watered by numerous affluents to the Arkansas river, and covered with grass and a variety of trees. The streams, which, in the upper part of their course, ran through grassy and open hollows, after a few miles all descended into deep and impracticable cañons, through which they found their way to the Arkansas valley. Here the buffalo trails we had followed were dispersed among the hills, or crossed over into the more open valleys of other streams.

During the day our road was fatiguing and difficult, reminding us much, by its steep and rocky character, of our travelling the year before among the Wind river mountains; but always at night we found some grassy bottom, which afforded us a pleasant camp. In the deep seclusion of these little streams, we found always an abundant pasturage, and a wild luxuriance of plants and trees. Aspens and pines were the prevailing timber; on the creeks, oak was frequent; but the narrow-leaved cottonwood, (*populus angustifolia,*) of unusually large size, and seven or eight feet in circumference, was the principal tree. With these were mingled a variety of shrubby trees, which aided to make the ravines almost impenetrable.

After several days' laborious travelling, we succeeded in extricating ourselves from the mountains, and on the morning of the 28th encamped immediately at their foot, on a handsome tributary to the Arkansas river. In the afternoon we descended the stream, winding our way along the bottoms, which were densely wooded with oak, and in the evening encamped near the main river. Continuing the next day our road along the Arkansas, and meeting on the way a war party of Arapahoe Indians, (who had recently been committing some outrages at Bent's fort, killing stock and driving off horses,) we arrived before sunset at the Pueblo, near the mouth of the *Fontaine-qui-bouit* river, where we had the pleasure to find a number of our old acquaintances. The little settlement appeared in a thriving condition; and in the interval of our absence another [Hardscrabble] had been established on the river, some thirty miles above.

June 30.—Our cavalcade moved rapidly down the Arkansas, along the broad road which follows the river, and on the 1st of July we arrived at Bent's fort, about 70 miles below the mouth of the *Fontaine-qui-bouit*. As we emerged into view from the groves on the river, we were saluted with a display of the national flag and repeated discharges from the guns of the fort, where we were received by Mr. George Bent[190] with a cordial welcome and a friendly hospitality, in the enjoyment of which we spent several very agreeable days. We were now in the region where our mountaineers were accustomed to live; and all the dangers and difficulties of the road being considered past, four of them, including Carson and Walker, remained at the fort.[191]

190. George Bent (1814–47), brother of the better known Charles and William Bent, was really the builder of Fort St. Vrain on the South Platte, and for a time it was called Fort George in his honor. In April 1844, George was left in charge of Bent's Fort by William, who went back to St. Louis and stayed several months (CARTER [1]).

191. The other two were Charles Town, who was actually discharged at "The Pueblo," and Louis Anderson, who had been traveling with Walker. Cowie and Walker had both been members of the Chiles-Walker emigrant party to California in 1843, and Anderson's rate of pay, $2.50 per day (which

On the 5th we resumed our journey down the Arkansas, travelling along a broad wagon road, and encamped about twenty miles below the fort. On the way we met a very large village of Sioux and Cheyenne Indians, who, with the Arapahoes, were returning from the crossing of the Arkansas, where they had been to meet the Kioway and Camanche Indians. A few days previous they had massacred a party of fifteen Delawares, whom they had discovered in a fort on the Smoky Hill river, losing in the affair several of their own people. They were desirous that we should bear a pacific message to the Delawares on the frontier, from whom they expected retaliation; and we passed through them without any difficulty or delay. Dispersed over the plain in scattered bodies of horsemen, and family groups of women and children, with dog trains carrying baggage, and long lines of pack horses, their appearance was picturesque and imposing.

Agreeably to your instructions, which required me to complete, as far as practicable, our examinations of the Kansas, I left at this encampment the Arkansas river, taking a northeasterly direction across the elevated dividing grounds which separate that river from the waters of the Platte. On the 7th we crossed a large stream, about forty yards wide, and one or two feet deep, flowing with a lively current on a sandy bed. The discolored and muddy appearance of the water indicated that it proceeded from recent rains; and we are inclined to consider this a branch of the Smoky Hill river, although, possibly, it may be the Pawnee fork of the Arkansas. Beyond this stream we travelled over high and level prairies, halting at small ponds and holes of water, and using for our fires the *bois de vache,* the country being without timber. On the evening of the 8th we encamped in a cottonwood grove on the banks of a sandy stream bed, where there was water in holes sufficient for the camp. Here several hollows, or dry creeks with sandy beds, met together, forming the head of a stream which afterwards proved to be the Smoky Hill fork of the Kansas river.

The next morning, as we were leaving our encampment, a number of Arapahoe Indians were discovered. They belonged to a war

---

was also the rate for Walker), indicates he was no ordinary *voyageur.* JCF allowed both Anderson and Walker an additional twenty days to return to the "Snake District" (DNA-217, T-135, voucher nos. 122 and 123, 5 July 1844; PIONEER REGISTER).

party which had scattered over the prairie in returning from an expedition against the Pawnees.

As we travelled down the valley, water gathered rapidly in the sandy bed from many little tributaries; and at evening it had become a handsome stream, fifty to eighty feet in width, with a lively current in small channels, the water being principally dispersed among quicksands.

Gradually enlarging, in a few days' march it became a river eighty yards in breadth, wooded with occasional groves of cottonwood. Our road was generally over level uplands bordering the river, which were closely covered with a sward of buffalo grass.

On the 10th we entered again the buffalo range, where we had found these animals so abundant on our outward journey, and halted for a day among numerous herds, in order to make a provision of meat sufficient to carry us to the frontier.

A few days afterwards, we encamped, in a pleasant evening, on a high river prairie, the stream being less than a hundred yards broad. During the night we had a succession of thunder storms, with heavy and continuous rain, and towards morning the water suddenly burst over the banks, flooding the bottoms, and becoming a large river, five or six hundred yards in breadth. The darkness of the night and incessant rain had concealed from the guard the rise of the water; and the river broke into the camp so suddenly, that the baggage was instantly covered, and all our perishable collections almost entirely ruined, and the hard labor of many months destroyed in a moment.

On the 17th we discovered a large village of Indians encamped at the mouth of a handsomely wooded stream on the right bank of the river.[192] Readily inferring, from the nature of the encampment, that they were Pawnee Indians, and confidently expecting good treatment from a people who receive regularly an annuity from the Government, we proceeded directly to the village, where we found assembled nearly all the Pawnee tribe, who were now returning from the crossing of the Arkansas, where they had met the Kioway and Camanche Indians. We were received by them with the unfriendly rudeness and characteristic insolence which they never fail to display whenever they find an occasion for doing so with impunity. The little that remained of our goods was distributed among them,

---

192. The Indians were encamped at Big Timber Creek, which enters the Smoky Hill River near the present Ellis–Rush County line in Kansas.

but proved entirely insufficient to satisfy their greedy rapacity; and, after some delay, and considerable difficulty, we succeeded in extricating ourselves from the village, and encamped on the river about fifteen miles below.*

The country through which we had been travelling since leaving the Arkansas river, for a distance of 260 miles, presented to the eye only a succession of far-stretching green prairies, covered with the unbroken verdure of the buffalo grass, and sparingly wooded along the streams with straggling trees and occasional groves of cottonwood; but here the country began perceptibly to change its character, becoming a more fertile, wooded and beautiful region, covered with a profusion of grasses, and watered with innumerable little streams, which were wooded with oak, large elms, and the usual varieties of timber common to the lower course of the Kansas river.

As we advanced, the country steadily improved, gradually assimilating itself in appearance to the northwestern part of the State of Missouri. The beautiful sward of the buffalo grass, which is regarded as the best and most nutritious found on the prairies, appeared now only in patches, being replaced by a longer and coarser grass, which covered the face of the country luxuriantly. The difference in the character of the grasses became suddenly evident in the weakened condition of our animals, which began sensibly to fail as soon as we quitted the buffalo grass.

The river preserved a uniform breadth of eighty or a hundred yards, with broad bottoms continuously timbered with large cottonwood trees, among which were interspersed a few other varieties.

While engaged in crossing one of the numerous creeks which frequently impeded and checked our way, sometimes obliging us to ascend them for several miles, one of the people (Alexis Ayot) was shot through the leg by the accidental discharge of a rifle—a mortifying and painful mischance, to be crippled for life by an accident, after having nearly accomplished in safety a long and eventful journey. He was a young man of remarkably good and cheerful temper, and had been among the useful and efficient men of the party.

After having travelled directly along its banks for two hundred

* In a recent report to the department, from Major [Clifton] Wharton, who visited the Pawnee villages with a military force some months afterwards, it is stated that the Indians had intended to attack our party during the night we remained at this encampment, but were prevented by the interposition of the Pawnee Loups.

and ninety miles, we left the river, where it bore suddenly off in a northwesterly direction, towards its junction with the Republican fork of the Kansas, distant about sixty miles; and, continuing our easterly course, in about twenty miles we entered the wagon road from Santa Fé to Independence, and on the last day of July encamped again at the little town of Kansas, on the banks of the Missouri river.

During our protracted absence of fourteen months, in the course of which we had necessarily been exposed to great varieties of weather and of climate, no one case of sickness had ever occurred among us.

Here ended our land journey; and the day following our arrival, we found ourselves on board a steamboat rapidly gliding down the broad Missouri. Our travel-worn animals had not been sold and dispersed over the country to renewed labor, but were placed at good pasturage on the frontier, and are now ready to do their part in the coming expedition.

On the 6th of August we arrived at St. Louis, where the party was finally disbanded; a great number of the men having their homes in the neighborhood.

Andreas Fuentes also remained here, having readily found employment for the winter, and is one of the men engaged to accompany me the present year.[193]

Pablo Hernandez remains in the family of Senator Benton, where he is well taken care of, and conciliates good will by his docility, intelligence, and amiability.[194] General Almonte, the Mexican minister at Washington, to whom he was of course made known, kindly offered to take charge of him, and to carry him back to Mexico; but the boy preferred to remain where he was until he got an education, for which he shows equal ardor and aptitude.

---

193. JCF paid Fuentes for services as a *voyageur* from the time he was picked up on the trail [1 May] to 6 Sept. 1844. See Doc. No. 95.

194. In his MEMOIRS, 409, JCF noted that this early promise of Hernandez was misleading, and that he was led into wrong courses and away from his friends. For a time he was in Mexico, but "after some years the report came to us," Frémont wrote, "that he was the Joaquin who for some years was so well known as a robber chief in the San Joaquin Valley and the mountain country. Whether or not this was so, it was the last that I heard of Pablo." If Frémont means to suggest that Pablo Hernandez was the shadowy bandit Joaquín Murrieta, who became the folk hero of John Rollins Ridge's sensational and mythical tale, he is almost certainly in error (see J. H. Jackson's introduction to RIDGE).

Our Chinook Indian had his wish to see the whites fully gratified. He accompanied me to Washington, and, after remaining several months at the Columbia college, was sent by the Indian department to Philadelphia, where, among other things, he learned to read and write well, and speak the English language with some fluency.

He will accompany me in a few days to the frontier of Missouri, whence he will be sent with some one of the emigrant companies to the village at the Dalles of the Columbia.

Very respectfully, your obedient servant,

J. C. FREMONT,
Bt. Capt. Topl. Engineers.

TABLE OF DISTANCES

THE ROAD TRAVELLED BY THE EXPEDITION IN 1843 AND 1844.

OUTWARD JOURNEY.

From Kansas Landing to Fort Vancouver.

Date.	Distance travelled each day.	Distance from Kansas landing.	Localities.	Date.	Distance travelled each day.	Distance from Kansas landing.	Localities.
1843.	*Miles.*	*Miles.*		1843.	*Miles.*	*Miles.*	
May 29	7	7		July 29	6	807	
30	22	29		30	24	831	
31	26	55		31	30	861	
June 1	23	78		Aug. 1	26	887	
2	22	100		2	31	918	Medicine Bow river.
3	23	123		3	26	944	
4	18	141		4	18	962	North fork.
5	19	160		6	19	981	
6	14	174		7	30	1,011	
7	8	182		8	29	1,040	
8	5	187	Junction of Smoky Hill and Republican forks.	9	26	1,066	Sweet Water.
				10	23	1,089	
10	1	188		11	29	1,118	
11	24	212		12	25	1,143	
12	28	240		13	9	1,152	South Pass.
13	18	258			15	1,167	
14	17	275		14	25	1,192	
16	21	296		15	29	1,221	Green river, or Rio Colorado.
17	14	310		16	26	1,247	
18	23	333		17	21	1,268	
19	18	351		18	32	1,300	
20	26	377		19	28	1,328	
21	27	404		20	30	1,358	
22	26	430		21	26	1,384	
23	26	456		22	37	1,421	
24	34	490		23	12	1,433	
25	26	516	Crossing of the Republican.	24	22	1,455	
				25	8	1,463	Beer Springs.
26	24	540		26	21	1,484	
27	27	567		27	21	1,505	
28	30	597		28	27	1,532	
29	21	618		29	17	1,549	
30	26	644	South fork.	30	19	1,568	
July 1	32	676		31	26	1,594	
2	29	705		Sept. 1	22	1,616	
3	28	733		2	17	1,633	
4	18	751	St. Vrain's fort.	3	3	1,636	Mouth of Bear river.
26	4	755		4	6	1,642	
27	26	781		5	27	1,669	
28	20	801		6	25	1,694	

Date.	Distance travelled each day.	Distance from Kansas landing.	Localities.	Date.	Distance travelled each day.	Distance from Kansas landing.	Localities.
1843.	*Miles.*	*Miles.*		1843.	*Miles.*	*Miles.*	
Sept. 8	20	1,714	Shore of the Salt lake.	Oct. 9	24	2,254	
				10	2	2,256	Fort Boise.
9	8	1,722	Island in the Salt lake.	11	20	2,276	
				12	27	2,303	
10	28	1,750		13	20	2,323	
12	13	1,763		14	22	2,345	
13	27	1,790		15	26	2,371	
14	24	1,814		16	13	2,384	
15	19	1,833		17	21	2,405	
16	26	1,859		18	20	2,425	
17	24	1,883		19	21	2,446	
18	23	1,906	Fort Hall.	20	12	2,458	
22	12	1,918		21	5	2,463	
24	10	1,928	American falls on Lewis's fork.	22	16	2,479	
				24	18	2,497	
25	13	1,941		25	18	2,515	
26	17	1,958		26	3	2,518	Fort Nez Percé, at the mouth of Walahwalah river.
27	20	1,978					
28	25	2,003					
29	24	2,027		28	19	2,537	
30	26	2,053		29	19	2,556	
Oct. 1	16	2,069		30	21	2,577	
2	29	2,098		31	26	2,603	
3	16	2,114		Nov. 1	23	2,626	
4	19	2,133		2	19	2,645	
5	26	2,159		3	17	2,662	
6	22	2,181		4	14	2,676	Dalles.
7	23	2,204		6 & 7	90	2,766	Fort Vancouver.
8	26	2,230					

HOMEWARD JOURNEY.

From the Dalles to the Missouri river.

Date.	Distance travelled each day.	Distance from the Dalles.	Localities.	Date.	Distance travelled each day.	Distance from the Dalles.	Localities.
1843.	*Miles.*	*Miles.*		1843.	*Miles.*	*Miles.*	
Nov. 25	12	12		Dec. 4	9	147	
26	22	34		5	11	158	
27	13	47		6	19	177	
28	21	68		7	25	202	
29	21	89		8	19	221	
30	10	99		9	14	235	
Dec. 1	6	105		10	15	250	Tlamath lake.
2	11	116		12	5	255	
3	22	138		13	12	267	

Table of distances—Continued.

Date.	Distance travelled each day.	Distance from the Dalles.	Localities.	Date.	Distance travelled each day.	Distance from the Dalles.	Localities.
1843.	*Miles.*	*Miles.*		1844.	*Miles.*	*Miles.*	
Dec. 14	21	288		Feb. 20	3	1,001	Summit of the Sierra
15	21	309					Nevada.
16	9	318	Summer lake.	21	5	1,006	
17	6	324		22	3	1,009	
18	20	344		23	5	1,014	
19	21	365		24	12	1,026	
20	26	391	Lake Abert.	25	14	1,040	
21	6	397		26	14	1,054	
22	29	426		27	1	1,055	
23	7	433		28	10	1,065	
24	13	446	Christmas lake.	March 1	6	1,071	
25	14	460		2 & 3	10	1,081	
26	21	481		4	7	1,088	
27	24	505		5	20	1,108	
28	16	521		6	34	1,142	Nueva Helvetia.
29	15	536		24	16	1,158	
30	17	553		25	18	1,176	
31	18	571		26	21	1,197	
				27	42	1,239	
1844.				28	17	1,256	
Jan. 1	20	591		29	8	1,264	
2	25	616		April 1	10	1,274	
3	7	623		3	22	1,296	
4	7	630		4	18	1,314	
5	2	632		5	37	1,351	
6	15	647	Great Boiling spring.	6	15	1,366	
9	11	658		7	50	1,416	
10	10	668		8	6	1,422	
11	10	678		9	31	1,453	
12	6	684	Pyramid lake.	10	40	1,493	
13	12	696		11	24	1,517	
14	9	705		12	15	1,532	
15	12	717		13	27	1,559	Pass in the Sierra
16	18	735					Nevada.
17	22	757		14	32	1,591	
18	8	765		15	32	1,623	
19	18	783		17	39	1,662	
20	5	788		18	3	1,665	
21	24	812		19	15	1,680	
22	14	826		20	33	1,713	Spanish trail at Mo-
23	25	851					hahve river.
24	20	871		22	20	1,733	
25	25	896		23	33	1,766	
27	12	908		24	8	1,774	
28	12	920		25	25	1,799	
29	7	927		27	43	1,842	
30	11	938		28	12	1,854	
31	26	964		29	7	1,861	
Feb. 2	16	980		30	24	1,885	
3	7	987		May 1	15	1,900	
4	3	990		2	12	1,912	
7	4	994		3	18	1,930	
8	1	995		4	57	1,987	
10	3	998		6	18	2,005	Rio Virgen.

Table of distances—Continued.

Date.	Distance travelled each day.	Distance from the Dalles.	Localities.
1844.	Miles.	Miles.	
May 7	10	2,015	
8	18	2,033	
9	1	2,034	
10	24	2,058	
11	12	2,070	
12	14	2,084	Vegas de Santa Clara.
13	15	2,099	
15	21	2,120	
16	17	2,137	
17	17	2,154	
19	27	2,181	
20	22	2,203	
21	31	2,234	
22	23	2,257	
23	12	2,269	Sevier river.
24	23	2,292	
25	32	2,324	
26	9	2,333	Utah lake.
27	22	2,355	
28	25	2,380	
29	25	2,405	
30	31	2,436	
31	16	2,452	
June 1	16	2,468	
2	8	2,476	
3	21	2,497	Uintah fort.
5	26	2,523	
6	15	2,538	
7	30	2,568	Green river, (Brown's hole.)
9	36	2,604	
10	30	2,634	
11	30	2,664	
12	26	2,690	
13	26	2,716	
14	23	2,739	
15	25	2,764	New Park.
16	26	2,790	
17	33	2,823	Old Park.
18	13	2,836	
19	16	2,852	
20	27	2,879	

Date.	Distance travelled each day.	Distance from the Dalles.	Localities.
1844.	Miles.	Miles.	
June 21	19	2,898	
22	15	2,913	Bayou Salade, (South Park.)
23	36	2,949	
24	21	2,970	
25	21	2,991	
26	11	3,002	
27	10	3,012	
28	21	3,033	
29	30	3,063	Pueblo, on the Arkansas.
30	37	3,100	
July 1	33	3,133	Bent's fort.
5	20	3,153	
6	31	3,184	
7	31	3,215	
8	28	3,243	Head water of Smoky Hill fork of the Kansas.
9	27	3,270	
10	28	3,298	
12	24	3,322	
13	30	3,352	
15	10	3,362	
16	23	3,385	
17	32	3,417	
18	24	3,441	
19	29	3,470	
20	29	3,499	
21	23	3,522	
22	17	3,539	
23	26	3,565	
24	22	3,587	
25	19	3,606	
26	24	3,630	
27	18	3,648	
28	22	3,670	
29	12	3,682	
30	12	3,694	
31	8	3,702	Kansas landing
Aug. 1	7	3,709	Missouri river.

APPENDIX.

A.

Geological Formations

Nature of the geological formations occupying the portion of Oregon and North California, included in a geographical survey under the direction of Captain Frémont: by James Hall, palæontologist to the State of New York.

The main geographical features of every country, as well as its soils and vegetable productions, depend upon the nature of its geological formations. So universally true is this, that a suite of the rocks prevailing in any country, with their mineral and fossil contents, will convey more absolute information regarding the agricultural and other capabilities of that country, than could be given by a volume written without reference to these subjects. Indeed, no survey of any unknown region should be made, without at the same time preserving collections of the prevailing rocks, minerals, and fossils. The attention given to this subject in the foregoing report renders the information of the highest value, and perfectly reliable in reference to opinions or calculations regarding the resources of the country.

The specimens examined present a great variety of aspect and composition; but calcareous rocks prevail over a large portion of the country traversed between longitude 98° and the mouth of the Columbia river, or 122° west from Greenwich. That portion of the route embraced in this notice, varies in latitude through seven degrees, viz: 38° to 45° north; and specimens are presented in nearly every half degree of latitude. Such a collection enables us to form a very satisfactory conclusion regarding this portion of the country 7° in width and 24° in length; having an extent east and west equal to the distance between the Atlantic coast of New York and the Mississippi river, and lying in the temperate latitudes which extend from Washington city to the northern limit of the State of New York.

Although we are far from being able to fix the minute or detailed geology, this collection presents us with sufficient materials to form some probable conclusions regarding the whole region from this side of the Rocky mountains westward to the mouth of the Columbia river. But it is not within my province to dwell upon the advan-

730

tages opened to us in the vast field which the researches of Captain Frémont have made known. I therefore proceed to a description of the specimens as they occur, taking them in the order from east to west. This, in connexion with the section of altitudes on which the rocks are marked, will show the comparative extent of different formations.

Longitude $96\frac{1}{4}°$, latitude $38\frac{3}{4}°$; *Otter creek.*—The single specimen from this locality is a yellowish, impure limestone, apparently containing organic remains, whose structure is obliterated by crystallization. From its position relatively to the formations farther east, I am inclined to refer it to the cretaceous formation.

Longitude $98°$, latitude $39°$; *Smoky Hill river.*—The specimens from this locality are numbered 26, 29, 31, 33, and 88. They all bear a similar character, and the fossils are alike in each. The rock is an impure limestone, pretty compact, varying in color from dull yellowish to ashy brown, and abounding in shells of a species of Inoceramus. (See description.)

This rock probably belongs to the cretaceous formation; the lower part of which has been indicated by Dr. Morton as extending into Louisiana, Arkansas, and Missouri.

Although the specimens from this locality bear a more close resemblance to the upper part of the formation, I do not feel justified in referring them to any other period. This formation evidently underlies large tracts of country, and extends far towards the base of the Rocky mountains.

Longitude $105°$, latitude $39°$.—The specimens from this locality are a somewhat porous, light-colored limestone, tough and fine grained. One or two fragments of fossils from this locality still indicate the cretaceous period; but the absence of any perfect specimens must deter a positive opinion upon the precise age of the formation. One specimen, however, from its form, markings, and fibrous structure, I have referred to the genus inoceramus.

It is evident, from the facts presented, that little of important geological change is observed in travelling over this distance of 7 degrees of longitude. But at what depths beneath the surface the country is underlaid by this formation, I have no data for deciding. Its importance, however, must not be overlooked. A calcareous formation of this extent is of the greatest advantage to a country; and the economical facilities hence afforded in agriculture, and the uses of civilized life, cannot be overstated.

The whole formation of this region is probably, with some variations, an extension of that which prevails through Louisiana, Arkansas, and Missouri.

The strata at the locality last mentioned are represented as being vertical, standing against the eastern slope of the Rocky mountains, immediately below Pike's Peak.

Longitude 106°, latitude 41°.—At this point, although only one degree west of the last-named specimens, we find a total change in the geology of the region. The specimens are of a red feldspathic granite, showing a tendency to decomposition; and, from the information accompanying the same, this rock overlies a mass of similar granite, in more advanced stages of decomposition. The specimens present nothing peculiar in their appearance; and the only apparent difference between these and the ordinary red feldspathic granites of more eastern localities, is their finer grain and dingy color.

Longitude 107°, latitude 41½°.—The specimens from this locality are of crystalline feldspathic granite, of a flesh-red color, apparently not acted on by the weather, and presenting the common appearance of this kind of granite in other localities.

No. 95, "above the third bed of coal, in the lower hill, North fork of the Platte river," is a siliceous clay slate, having a saline taste.

Longitude 110°, latitude 41½°; Nos. 99 and 104.—No. 99 is a fine-grained, soft, argillaceous limestone, of a light ash color, evidently a modern formation; but, from the absence of fossils, it would be unsatisfactory to assign it any place in the scale of formations. The other specimen, No. 104, is a compact serpentine, having the aspect of a greenstone trap; and, from the account given, is probably interstratified with the limestone. The limestone is more friable and chalky than any specimen previously noticed.

Longitude 110¼°, latitude 41½°.—The specimens from this locality are very peculiar and remarkable. The first is a friable or pulverulent green calcareous sand, unctuous to the touch, but remaining unaltered on exposure to the atmosphere. Its character is very similar to the green sands of New Jersey; but it is of a brighter color, and less charged with iron. The second specimen is of similar composition, but quite solid—being, in fact, a green limestone. The singularity of the specimen, and that which first attracted my attention, was the efflorescence of a salt upon its surface, which appears to be, in part, chloride of sodium. Supposing this to be accidental, I broke a specimen, and, after a day or two, a similar efflorescence appeared from the fresh fracture; leaving no doubt but the salt arise from decomposition of substances within the stone itself.

Longitude 111°, latitude 41½°; *Muddy river.*—These specimens are of a yellowish-gray oolitic limestone, containing turbo, cerithium, &c. The rock is a perfect oolite; and, both in color and texture, can scarcely be distinguished from specimens of the Bath oolite. One of the specimens is quite crystalline, and the oolitic structure somewhat obscure. In this instance, the few fossils observed seem hardly sufficient to draw a decisive conclusion regarding the age of the formation; but, when taken in connexion with the oolitic structure of the mass, its correspondence with the English oolites, and the modern aspect of the whole, there remains less doubt of the propriety of referring it to the oolitic period. A further collection from this interesting locality would doubtless develop a series of fossils, which would forever settle the question of the relative age of the formation.

A few miles up this stream, Captain Frémont has collected a beautiful series of specimens of fossil ferns. The rock is an indurated clay, wholly destitute of carbonate of lime, and would be termed a "fire clay." These are probably, geologically as well as geographically, higher than the oolite specimens, as the rocks at this place were observed to dip in the direction of N. 65° W. at an angle of 20 degrees. This would show, conclusively, that the vegetable remains occupy a higher position than the oolite. Associated with these vegetable remains, were found several beds of coal, differing in thickness. The section of strata at this place is as follows:

	ft.	in.
Sandstone	1	0
Coal	1	3
Coal	1	3
Indurated clay, with vegetable remains .	20	0
Clay	5	0
Coal		
Clay	5	0
Coal		
Clay	5	0
Coal		

The stratum containing the fossil ferns is about 20 feet thick; and above it are two beds of coal, each about 15 inches. These are succeeded by a bed of sandstone. Below the bed containing the ferns, there are three distinct beds of coal, each separated by about 5 feet of clay. Before examining the oolitic specimens just mentioned, I compared these fossil ferns with a large collection from the coal measures of Pennsylvania and Ohio, and it was quite evident that this formation could not be of the same age. There are several specimens which I can only refer to the Glossopteris Phillipsii, (see description,) an oolitic fossil; and this alone, with the general character of the other species, and the absence of the large stems so common in the coal period, had led me to refer them to the oolitic period. I conceive, however, that we have scarcely sufficient evidence to justify this reference; and though among the fossil shells there are none decidedly typical of the oolite, yet neither are they so of any other formation; and the lithological character of the mass is not reliable evidence. Still, viewed in whatever light we please, these fossil ferns must, I conceive, be regarded as mostly of new species, and in this respect form a very important addition to the flora of the more modern geological periods.

In passing from this locality westward to the Bear river, Captain Frémont crossed a high mountain chain, which is the dividing ridge between the waters of Muddy river flowing eastward, and those of Muddy creek flowing into Bear river on the west. The gap where the ridge was crossed is stated to be 8,200 feet above the level of the sea. In this ridge, 115 miles to the southward of the locality of the fossils last mentioned, were collected the specimens next to be named. These were obtained near the summit of the ridge, and probably higher than the point where Captain Frémont's party crossed.

The collection from this locality (longitude 111°, latitude 40°) consists of several specimens of an argillaceous, highly bituminous, and somewhat slaty limestone, loaded with fossils. It is very brittle, and easily shivered into small fragments by a blow of the hammer. Its natural color is a light sepia, but it bleaches on exposure to the atmosphere. In structure, it is not unlike some of the limestones of the lias or oolite formations. The fossils are chiefly one species of Cerithium and one of Mya; and besides these another species of Cerithium and a Nucula can be identified. So far as I am able to ascertain, these fossils are undescribed, and will therefore be regarded as new species.

It may be considered premature to decide upon the geological position of this mass. It may belong to the same period, though far higher in the series than those in the same longitude, which have

734

just been described. In the locality of the fossil plants, the strata dip W. by N.; but, from the structure of the country, it is evident that there is a change in the direction of the dip before reaching the high ridge from which the specimens under consideration were taken. Further examination, I have no doubt, will set this question at rest.

I may here notice the interesting fact of the wide extent of these formations, showing the existence, in this longitude, of these calcareous beds, of a nature precisely like those of the modern formations of western Europe.

A few miles south of the locality of these fossils, Captain Frémont describes the occurrence of an immense stratum of fossil salt; and the same ridge is represented as bounding the Great Salt lake. There would therefore seem no doubt that the salt in question is associated with the strata of this period, and probably coeval with the same.

I may remark, in the same connexion, that the surfaces of the specimens containing the fossil ferns also effloresce a salt, which is apparently chloride of sodium. This fact seems to indicate the presence of fossil salt at this distance north of the known locality, and is a circumstance which we naturally appropriate as part of the evidence of identity in the age of the formations.

This region is unquestionably one of the highest interest, both as regards its economical resources, and equally so in the contributions which it will yield to geological science. In the specimens from the vegetable locality, I have been able to indicate seven or eight species of fossil ferns, most of which are new. Further researches will doubtless greatly multiply this number. Besides these, as new species probably peculiar to our continent, they have a higher interest, inasmuch as they show to us the wide extent and the nature of the vegetation of this modern coal period. In the broad fields of the west, we shall have an opportunity of tracing it over large and unbroken areas, and many highly interesting results may follow its comparison with the vegetation of the true carboniferous period.

Again: since these deposites have evidently been made over large tracts of country, it is not unreasonable to suppose that the quantity of materials accumulated will be very great, and that we may expect to find profitable coal beds in the rocks of this age. This subject, besides being of high interest to science, is of some prospective economical importance, though perhaps too remote to dwell upon, while the country remains so little explored as at present.

Longitude 112°, latitude 42°.—The specimen No. 72 is a grayish-blue limestone, efflorescing a salt upon the surface, "from the Hot Salt Springs of September 13, 1843." No. 108 is a siliceous limestone of a brownish-gray color; where exposed, the surface becomes porous, from the solution and removal of the lime, while the siliceous particles remain. From the general lithological characters of the specimen, it is probably a modern rock, but its precise age cannot be decided.

Longitude 112°, latitude 41½°.—The single specimen from this locality is, in its present state, "granular quartz." It is, however, very evidently, an altered sedimentary rock, with the lines of deposition quite distinctly preserved. This rock probably comes out from under the siliceous limestone last described, both having been altered by modern igneous action. The character of the specimens from the next locality—three-quarters of a degree farther west—may perhaps throw some light upon the present condition of those last named.

Longitude 112¾°, latitude 42¾°; *at the American Falls of Snake river.*—The collection from this point presents the following, in a descending order. These specimens are numbered 94, 96, 97, 101, 102, 106, and 107:

1. A botryoidal or concretionary lava, No. 94.
2. Obsidian, No. 102.
3. Vitrified sandstone, No. 106.
4. A whitish ash-colored chalk or limestone, No. 107.
5. A light ashy volcanic sand, No. 97.
6. Brown sand, volcanic. (?)

These are all apparently volcanic products, with, probably, the exception of Nos. 106 and 107, which may be sedimentary products; the first altered by heat. The two lower deposites are evidently volcanic sand or "ashes;" the upper of these, or No. 5, has all the characters of pulverized pumice stone, and is doubtless of similar origin.

No. 107 is an impure limestone, but little harder than common chalk; and, but for its associations, would be regarded as of similar origin.*

* Since this was written, a specimen of No. 107 has been submitted to the examination of Professor Bailey, who finds it highly charged with "calcareous polythalamia" in excellent preservation. He remarks, that "the forms are, many of them, such as are common in chalk and cretaceous marls; but as these forms are still living in our present oceans, their presence does not afford conclusive evidence as to the age of the deposite in which they occur.

No. 106 is apparently a vitrified sandstone, the grains all rounded, and the surfaces of the mass highly polished.

No. 102 is a beautiful black obsidian.

No. 94 is a mammillary or botryoidal lava; the concretions having a radiated structure, the mass is easily frangible, and readily separates into small angular fragments.

The whole of this series, with the exception of No. 107, may be regarded as of volcanic origin; for the apparently vitrified sandstone may be, in its composition, not very distinct from trap or basalt, though it is more vitreous, and its fracture fresher and brighter.

Longitude $114\frac{1}{2}°$, latitude $42\frac{1}{2}°$.—The specimens marked No. 3 are of light-colored tufaceous limestone and siliceous limestone. The specimens appear as if from some regular formation, broken up and thinly coated by calcareous matter from springs. From the fact observed by Captain Frémont, that these fragments enter largely into the composition of the soil, we may presume that the same is highly calcareous.

The specimen No. 12, from the same locality, consists mainly of small fragments of the crust, claws, &c., of some crustacean—probably of fresh-water origin. There are also some vertebræ and ribs of fishes. The whole is so unchanged, and of such recent appearance, as to induce a belief that the deposit is of fresh-water origin, and due to the desiccation of some lake or stream. Should such a deposite be extensive, its prospective value to an agricultural community will be an important consideration. But, as before remarked, there is evidently a preponderance of calcareous matter throughout the whole extent of country traversed.

Longitude $115°$, latitude $43°$.—The specimens from this locality are numbered 16, 21, and 39. Nos. 16 and 21 are angular fragments of impure limestone of some recent geological period, and No. 39 consists of an aggregation of pebbles and gravel. The pebbles are of black siliceous slate, which are represented as forming a conglomerate with the limestone fragments just mentioned. The limestone specimens are probably broken fragments from some stratum *in situ*

I have, however, invariably found that in our tertiary deposites, the chalk polythalamia are accompanied by large species of genera *peculiar* to the tertiary. Now, as these are entirely wanting in the specimen from Captain Frémont, the evidence, *as far as it goes,* is in favor of the view that the specimen came from a cretaceous formation."

in the same vicinity, and the conglomerate is one of very recent formation. The slate pebbles are from a rock of much older date, and worn very round and smooth, while the limestone bears little evidence of attrition.

The gray siliceous limestone specimens contain a species of Turritella, and a small bivalve shell. (See descriptions and figures.)

Longitude 115½°, latitude 43½°.—The two specimens from this locality are of volcanic origin. No. 46 is a reddish compact trap or lava, with small nodules or cavities filled with analcime and stilbite. No. 52 is a coarse and porous trap, or ancient lava.

Longitude 116°, latitude 43½°.—The single specimen from this place is a white feldspathic granite, with a small proportion of quartz, and black mica in small scales. The specimen contains a single garnet. The structure is somewhat slaty, and from appearances it is rapidly destructible from atmospheric agency.

Longitude 117°, latitude 44½°.—These specimens from Brulé river are numbered 4, 19, 41, and 48.

No. 4 is a slaty limestone, partially altered, probably from the proximity of igneous rocks.

No. 41 is of similar character, very thinly laminated, and of a dark color.

No. 19 is of similar character, but more altered, and partially crystalline. The lines of deposition are, however, preserved.

No. 48 has the appearance of a compact gray feldspathic lava; but there are some apparent lines of deposition still visible, which incline me to the opinion that it is an altered sedimentary rock.

Longitude 117½°, latitude 45°.—The specimen is a compact, dark-colored basalt, showing a tendency to desquamate upon the exposed surfaces. This rock forms the mountains of Brulé river.

Longitude 117½°, latitude 45½°.—The specimen No. 110 is a fine-grained basalt or trap, with a few small cells filled with analcime. This is of the rock forming the Blue mountain.

Longitude 118°, latitude 45°.—The single specimen (No. 43) from this locality is apparently an altered siliceous slate. It is marked by what appear to be lines of deposition, the thin laminæ being separated by layers of mica.

Longitude 119°, latitude 38½°.—The specimens Nos. 14, 23, 45, and 51, are all from this locality.

No. 14 appears to be a decomposed feldspar, having a slightly porous structure; it is very light, and adheres strongly to the tongue.

No. 23. A friable, argillaceous sandstone, somewhat porous upon the exposed surfaces.

No. 45. A compact lava of a sienitic structure, containing obsidian. This specimen appears much like some of the porous portions of trap dikes which cut through the sienitic rocks of New England.

No. 51. Feldspar, with a little black mica. The specimen is probably from a granite rock, though its structure is that of compact feldspar.

Longitude 120°, latitude 45½°.—The single specimen (No. 20) from this locality is a compact, fine-grained trap, or basalt, with a few round cavities of the size of peas.

Longitude 120½°, latitude 38½°.—The specimens are numbered 91, 109, and 117.

No. 91 has the appearance of a porous trap, or basalt, though possibly the production of a modern volcano. It is thickly spotted with crystals of analcime, some apparently segregated from the mass, and others filling vesicular cavities.

No. 117 is a compact basalt, the specimen exhibiting the character of the basalt of the Hudson and Connecticut river valleys.

No. 109 is a fine-grained granite, consisting of white quartz and feldspar, with black mica. Captain Frémont remarks that this rock forms the eastern part of the main California mountain. From its granular and rather loose structure, it is to be inferred that it would undergo rapid decomposition in a climate like ours.

Longitude 121°, latitude 44½°.—The specimens from this locality are numbered 53, 54, 55, 56, 57, 58, 59, 60, and 61. These are characteristic specimens of the strata composing a bluff 700 feet high, and are numbered in the descending order.

The specimens 59, 60, and 61, are three specimens of what appear to be very fine clay, perfectly free from carbonate of lime, and nearly as white as ordinary chalk. These three specimens, which are understood to be from three distinct strata, vary but slightly in their characters—No. 61 being of the lightest color.

No. 58 is a specimen of grayish volcanic breccia, the larger portion consisting of volcanic sand or ashes.

Nos. 55, 56, and 57, are of the same character, being, however, nearly free from fragments or pebbles, and composed of light volcanic sand, or scoria, with an apparently large admixture of clay from the strata below. The whole is not acted on by acids, and, so far as can be judged, is of volcanic origin.

No. 58 is of similar character to the preceding three specimens, but contains more fragments, and has a generally coarser aspect.*

Longitude 121°, latitude 45°.—These specimens are numbered 7, 35, 40, 47, and 49.

* The specimens Nos. 59, 60, and 61, which are from three different but contiguous strata, have since been examined by Professor J. W. Bailey, of West Point, who finds them charged with fluviatile infusoria of remarkable forms.

Below are descriptions (accompanied by a plate) of some of the most interesting forms, which were sketched by him with a camera-lucida attached to his microscope. It has not been considered necessary to distinguish, particularly, to which of the strata the individuals figured belong, as no species occur in one, which are not present in the others. They are evidently deposites of the same epoch, and differ very slightly in their characters.

Figs. 1, 2, and 3. Side views of *Eunotia librile* of Ehrenberg—The species is figured and described by Ehrenberg, who received it from Real del Monte, Mexico. It resembles *Eunotia Westermanni*, (Ehr.,) but differs in its granulations. The three figures are from individuals of different age.

Figs. 4 and 5. *Eunotia gibba*, (Ehr.)—Identical with a common freshwater species now living at West Point.

Fig. 6. *Pinnularia pachyptera?* (Ehr.)—Ehrenberg's figure of P. pachyptera from Labrador is very similar to the Oregon species here represented.

Figs. 7, 8, and 9. *Cocconema cymbiforme?* (Ehr.)—These are probably merely varieties of the same species. Fig. 8 is rather larger than C. cymbiforme usually grows at West Point.

Fig. 10. *Gomphonema clavatum?* (Ehr.)—Front view.

Fig. 11. *Gomphonema clavatum?* (Ehr.)—Side view.

Fig. 12 *Gomphonema minutissimum*, (Ehr.)—A cosmopolite species.

Fig. 13. *Gallionella (new species, a.)*—This is evidently identical with a large species which I have described and figured as occurring at Dana's locality. (See Silliman's Journal for April, 1845.)

Figs. 14 and 15. *Gallionella, new species?* δ (*a*—edge view; *b*—side view.) —This species presents remarkably compressed frustules, which are marked on their circular bases with radiant lines. It is particularly abundant in Nos. 59 and 61.

Fig. 16. *Gallionella distans?*—This very minute species constitutes the chief mass of No. 60, but also abounds in Nos. 59 and 61.

Figs. 17 and 18. *Cocconeis prætexta*, (Ehr.)—Appears to agree with a species from Mexico figured by Ehrenberg.

Fig. 19. *Fragillaria* ——.

Fig. 20. *Surirella* ——.—A fragment only. I have seen several fragments of beautiful Surirellæ, but have not yet found a perfect specimen to figure.

Fig. 21. *Fragillaria rhabdosoma?*—Fragment.

Figs. 22 and 23. *Spiculæ of fresh-water sponges.*—Spongilla.

Fig. 24. Four-sided crystal of ——?

Fig. 25. Scale = 10-100ths of millimetre magnified equally with the drawings.

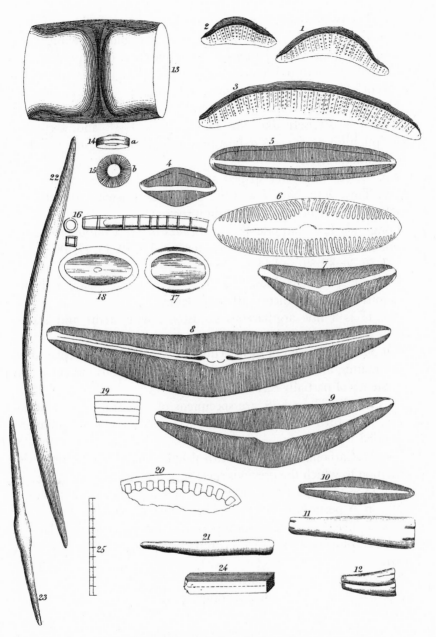

Fossil fresh-water infusoria from Oregon

No. 7 is a siliceous sinter, coated externally with hydrate of iron.

No. 35. A reddish, rather compact lava. The color is owing to the presence of iron, which hastens its decomposition on exposure.

No. 40. A reddish brecciated feldspathic lava, embracing fragments of light-colored siliceous sandstone or lava.

No. 47. Compact trap, or basalt, with a few rounded cavities. This specimen is precisely like No. 20, longitude 120°; and, from the description given, appears to be a prevailing rock along the valley of the Columbia river.

No. 49. An imperfect striped agate, with the centre of siliceous sinter. This, with Nos. 7 and 40, is doubtless associated with the basalt, No. 47, which is the prevailing rock.

Longitude 122°, latitude 45½°; *Cascades of the Columbia river.*— From this place are the specimens numbered 9, 10, 13, 17, 18, 22, 24, 25, 27, 30, 36, 37, 38, and 44.

Of these specimens, Nos. 13 and 24 are indurated clay, with impressions of leaves of dicotyledonous plants.

No. 17 is a fine argillaceous sandstone, with stems and leaves, which still retain their fibrous structure.

No. 30 is a specimen of dicotyledonous wood, partially replaced by stony matter, and a portion still retaining the fibrous structure and consistency of partially carbonized wood.

Nos. 10, 25, 27, and 38, are specimens of coal from the same locality. (For further information of these, see analysis of specimens appended.)

No. 22. Carbonaceous earth, with pebbles, evidently a part of the formation to which the previous specimens are referred.

No. 18 is a compact trap, apparently having a stratified structure.

No. 36. A porus basaltic lava, with crystals of analcime, &c.

No. 37. Two specimens—one a porous or rather scoriaceous lava of a reddish color; and the other a compact gray lava, with a few small cavities.

No. 44. A brown scoriaceous lava.

No. 44*a*. A small specimen of compact lava.

Miscellaneous specimens.

No. 62. A coral in soft limestone; the structure too much obliterated to decide its character. (From the dividing ridge between Bear creek and Bear river, at a point 8,200 feet above tide water.)

No. 71. Calcareous tufa, containing the remains of grasses, twigs, moss, &c.

No. 81. Calcareous tufa stained with iron.

No. 98. Ferruginous calcareous tufa, containing remains of twigs, &c.

These three last-named specimens are evidently the calcareous deposites from springs holding carbonate of lime in solution.

APPENDIX.

B.

Organic Remains.

Descriptions of organic remains collected by Captain J. C. Frémont, in the geographical survey of Oregon and North California: by James Hall, palæontologist to the State of New York.

Plates I and II.

Fossil ferns, etc.

The specimens here described are all from one locality, in longitude 111°, latitude 41½°. They occur in a light-gray indurated clay, which is entirely free from calcareous matter, very brittle, and having a very imperfect slaty structure. Nearly all the species differ from any described in Brongniart's *"Hist. Veg. Foss.,"* in Goppert's *"Systema Filicum Fossilium,"* or in Phillips's *"Geology of Yorkshire."*

1. Sphenopteris Fremonti. Pl. 2, figs. 3, 3 *a*. (No. 118 of collection.) Compare *sphenopteris crenulata;* Brong. Hist. Veg. Foss. i, p. 187, t. 56, f. 3.

Description.—Frond bipinnate, (or tripinnate?) rachis moderately strong, striated; pinnæ oblique to the rachis, rigid, moderately approximate, alternate; pinnules subovate, somewhat decurrent at the base, about three or four lobed; fructification very distinct in round dots (capsules) of carbonaceous matter upon the margins of the pinnules. 3 *a,* a portion twice magnified.

I have named this beautiful and unique species in honor of Captain Frémont, and as a testimony of the benefits that science has derived from his valuable explorations on the west of the Rocky mountains.

2. Sphenopteris triloba. Pl. 1, fig. 8. (Nos. 65, 79, and 80, of collection.)

Description.—Frond bipinnate, or tripinnate; rachis slender, flexuous; pinnæ long, flexuous, distant, opposite, perpendicular to the rachis; pinnules oblong, sub-trilobate, opposite or alternate, narrow at base, distant, perpendicular.

The distant, long, and flexuous pinnæ, with the small trilobate pin-

744

nules, distinguish this species. In general features, it approaches somewhat the *sphenopteris rigida*, (Brong.,) but differs essentially in the smaller pinnules, which are usually nearly opposite, and in never being more than sub-trilobate, while in *S. rigida* they are often deeply 5-lobed.

3. Sphenopteris (?) paucifolia Pl. 2, figs. 1, 1 *a*, 1 *b*, 1 *c*, 1 *d*. (No. 118 of collection.)

Description.—Frond tripinnate; rachis rather slender, with long, lateral, straight branches, which are slightly oblique; pinnæ slender, nearly at right angles, alternate and opposite; pinnules minute, oval-ovate, somewhat distant, opposite or alternate, expanded or attenuate at base, sometimes deeply bilobed or digitate; midrib not apparent.

This species was evidently a beautiful fern of large size, with slender, sparse foliage, giving it a peculiarly delicate appearance. In some of its varieties, (as figure 1 *b*,) it resembles *Sphenopteris digitata;* Phillips's Geol. Yorkshire, p. 147, pl. S, figs. 6 and 7; *Sphen. Williamsoni,* Brong. Hist. Veg. Foss., i, p. 177, t. 49, figs. 6, 7, and 8. The fossil under consideration, however, is quite a different species. In the figure 1 *a*, the branches and pinnules are more lax; figure 1 *d* is a magnified portion.

In its general aspect, this fossil resembles the genus *Pachypteris*, to which I had been inclined to refer it, but for the digitate character of the pinnules manifested by some specimens.

4. Sphenopteris (?) trifoliata. Pl. 2, figs. 2, 2 *a*. (No. 86 of collection.)

Description.—Frond bipinnate; pinnæ trifoliate; pinnules elliptic, narrowing at the base; rachis slender, flexuous; fructification terminal, raceme-like, from the pinnules gradually becoming single and fructiferous.

Fig. 2 *a*—part of the fructiferous portion enlarged, showing the capsules, apparently immersed in a thickened pinnule. This is a most beautiful and graceful species, approaching in some respects to the S. paucifolia just described.

5. Glossopteris Phillipsii? Pl. 2, figs. 5, 5 *a*, 5 *b*, 5 *c*. (Nos. 69, 82, and 86, of the collection.) Compare *Glossopteris Phillipsii,* Brong. Hist. Veg. Foss., p. 225, t. 61 bis, fig. 2; *Pecopteris paucifolia,* Phillips's Geol. Yorkshire, p. 119, pl. viii, fig. 8.

Description.—"Leaves linear lanceolate, narrow, narrowing towards the base and apex; nervules oblique, dichotomous, lax, scarcely distinct, subimmersed in the thick parenchyma." Brong. *ut sup.,* p. 225.

The specimen fig. 5 corresponds precisely with the figure of Brongniart, pl. 61 bis, fig. 5, both in form of the leaf and arrangement of the nervules, so as to leave little doubt of their identity. Figure 5 is a nearly perfect leaf of this species; fig. 5 *a* is the base of another specimen, having a long foot-stalk; fig. 5 *b* is the base of another leaf with fructification (?); fig. 5 *c* the same magnified. This structure is so partial, that it can only with doubt be referred to the fructification of the plant; and it is not improbable that the same may be some parasitic body, or the eggs of an insect which have been deposited upon the leaf. Whatever this may have been, it does not appear to have been calcareous; and the total absence of calcareous matter in the rock is an objection to referring the same to *flustra,* or any of the parasitic corals. The ferns are abundant in the rock at this point, and many of them unbroken, and evidently not far or long transported, which, had they been, would have given support to the supposition of this body being coral.

I have referred this species to the Glossopteris Phillipsii, as being the only description and figure accessible to me, to which this fossil bears any near resemblance. The geological position of that fossil is so well ascertained to be the schists of the upper part of the oolitic period, that, relying upon the evidence offered by a single species, we might regard it as a strong argument for referring all the other specimens to the same geological period.

The two following species, or varieties of the same species, have been referred with doubt to the genus *pecopteris;* but a close examination shows the midrib only partially distinct, and in some cases scarcely visible, while the nervules radiate from the base. In other cases, the midrib appears well marked at the base, but disappears in numerous ramifications before reaching the apex. The character, therefore, given by Brongniart, of *"nervo medio valde notato, nec apice evanescente,"* is inapplicable to these species; but the same feature may be observed in some figured by Brongniart himself.

6. PECOPTERIS UNDULATA. Pl. 1, figs. 1, 1 *a.* (Nos. 83 and 118 of collection.)

Description.—Frond bipinnate; rachis slender; pinnæ long, slightly oblique to the rachis, opposite and alternate; pinnules oblique,, oval-ovate, broad at the base, and the lower ones sometimes lobed, gradually becoming coadunate towards the extremity of the pinnæ.

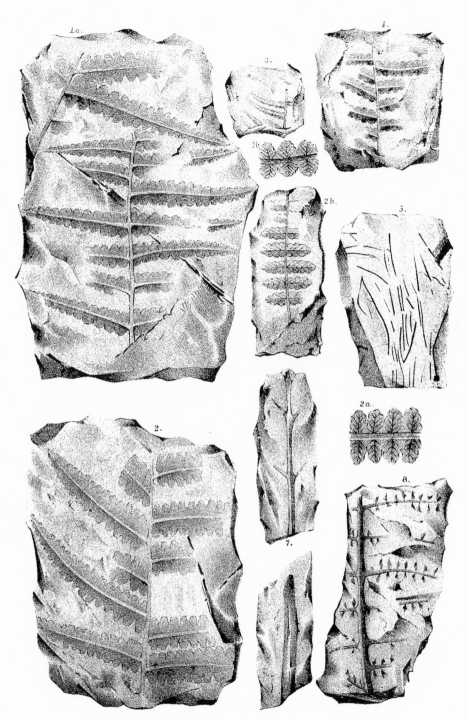

Fossil ferns, Plate 1

747

The pinnules have often an apparently continuous smooth outline; but, on closer examination, they appear undulated, or indented upon the margin; and many of them are obviously so.

7. Pecopteris undulata; *var*. Pl. 1, figs. 2, 2 *a*, 2 *b*. (No. 78 of collection.)

Description.—Frond bipinnate; rachis slender; pinnæ numerous, long, and gradually tapering, oblique to the rachis; pinnules oval-ovate, broad at base; midrib evanescent; nervules strong, bifurcating towards the apex; margins lobed or indented, particularly in those near the base of the pinnæ.

This species may be regarded as a variety of the last, though the pinnules are longer and less broad proportionally; but the general aspect is similar, and the habit of the plant precisely the same.

The specimen fig. 2 *b* can only be regarded as an extreme variety of the same species, which is approached in some of the enlarged pinnules, as fig. 2 *a*.

8. Pecopteris (?) odontopteroides. Pl. 1, figs. 3 and 4. (Nos. 78 and 118 of collection.)

Description.—Frond bipinnate? pinnæ long and slender; secondary pinnæ sub-distant, gradually tapering, nearly perpendicular; pinnules subrotund, obtuse, small, approximate, oblique, alternate, and coadunate at base; nervules strong, diverging from base; no distinct midrib.

Fig. 4. A few of the pinnæ near the termination of a frond.

The arrangement of the pinnules and nerves in this species strongly reminds one of the *Odontopteris Schlotheimii,* Brong. Hist. Veg. Foss., p. 256, t. 78, fig. 5—a fossil fern of the Pennsylvania coal measures; but this is essentially different.

The aspect of the three last-named plants is more like that of the true coal-measure ferns than any of the others; but the whole association, and their fossil condition, demand that they should be referred to a very modern period.

New genus—Trichopteris.

Character.—Frond slender, flexuous, in tufts or single, branching or pinnate; branches long, very slender.

9. Trichopteris filamentosa. Pl. 2, fig. 6. (No. 78 of collection.) Compare *Fucoides æqualis,* Brong. Hist. Veg. Foss., p. 58, t. 5, figs. 3 and 4.

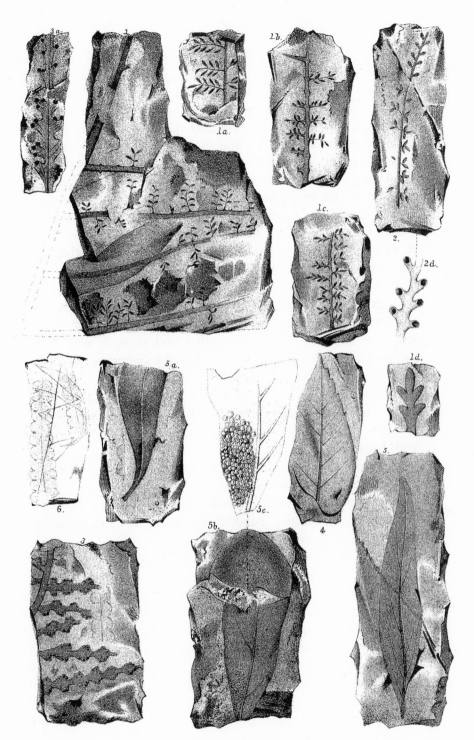

Fossil ferns, Plate 2

749

Description.—Frond pinnate or bipinnate; rachis long, and almost equally slender throughout; branches numerous, regular, alternate, simple, elongated, very slender, and flexuous.

The branches are frequently folded back upon themselves, and undulated, lying like the finest thread upon the surface of the stone. This species is very delicate and graceful, and can scarcely be examined without the aid of a magnifier. This fossil is very similar to the *Fucoides æqualis* of Brong., (from the lower chalk,) except that the branches are longer and undivided.

10. Trichopteris gracilis. Pl. 1, fig. 5. (No. 84 of collection.)

Description.—Slender, stems numerous, flexuous, in a tuft, branched; branches numerous, slender, oblique, stronger than in the last species.

This species is more robust than the first described, but evidently belongs to the same genus. I had first supposed that this might be a collection of fern stems, stripped of their foliage; but their slender structure, long branches, and peculiar arrangement, with the appropriate proportion of all the parts, forbid its reference to any thing of this kind; it is therefore placed in a new genus.

11. Stems of ferns. Pl. 1, fig. 7.

The stems of ferns, denuded of leaves, and portions only of the branches remaining. Great numbers of these stems occur, mingled with fragments of leaves and other portions of ferns still perfect.

12. Leaf of a dycotyledonous plant. (?) Pl. 2, fig. 4. (Fr. Aug. 17, and No. 201 of collection.)

Description.—Leaf ovate-lanceolate, lobed, lobes acute, mucronate; midrib straight, distinct, dichotomous; principal divisions going to the mucronate points.

This leaf has the aspect of the leaf of a dicotyledonous plant, and approaches remotely only to the character of species of the genus *Phlebopteris* of Brongniart, which are regarded as such by Phillips, and by Lindley and Hutton. The specimen was not observed soon enough to make a satisfactory comparison.

Locality, in the neighborhood of the specimens containing the preceding fossils, and regarded by Captain Frémont as belonging to the same formation. The rock containing them is a soft or very partially indurated clay, very unlike the hard and brittle mass containing the other species.

PLATE III.

Fossil shells, &c.

Figures 1, 2, 3, 4, 5, 6, and 7, are from longitude 111°, latitude 40°.
Figures 11, 12, and 13, are from longitude 111°, latitude 41½°.
Figures 8, 9, and 10, are from longitude 115°, latitude 43°.
Figures 14 and 15, leaves, from longitude 122°, latitude 45½°.

13. MYA TELLINOIDES.* Pl. 3, figs. 1 and 2. Compare *unio peregri-nus;* Phillips's Geol. Yorkshire, pl. 7, fig. 12. (Nos. 8, 28, and 32, of collection.)

Description.—Ovate, posterior side extended, slope gentle, rounded at the extremity; anterior side regularly rounded; surface nearly smooth, or marked only by lines of growth; beaks slightly wrinkled; moderately prominent.

The specimen fig. 1 is an entire shell; fig. 2 is a cast of the two valves of a smaller specimen, retaining a small portion of the shell. Another specimen, larger than either of these, presents the inside of both valves, with the hinge broken.

Locality in longitude 111°, latitude 40°, in slaty bituminous limestone.

14. NUCULA IMPRESSA (?) G. Pl. 3, fig. 3. (No. 32 of collection.)

Description.—Sub-elliptical; posterior extremity somewhat expanded; surface smooth. A few of the teeth are still visible on the anterior hinge margin, but the greater part of the hinge line is obscured.

Locality in longitude 111°, latitude 40°, in slaty bituminous limestone.

15. CYTHEREA PARVULA. Pl. 3, figs. 10 and 10 *a*. (No. 21 of collection.) Compare *Isocardia angulata?* Phillips's Geol. Yorkshire, pl. 9, fig. 9.

Description.—Ovate trigonal; umbones elevated; beaks incurved; surface marked by regular concentric lines of growth; umbones and beaks with a few stronger wrinkles. The umbones of this shell are

---

* The species, where no authority is given, are regarded as new, and will be so understood.

scarcely diverging or involute enough to place it in the genus *Iso-cardia,* where it would otherwise very naturally belong.

Locality in longitude 115°, latitude 43°, in gray argillaceous lime-stone. Two other specimens of the same shell were noticed.

16. PLEUROTOMARIA UNIANGULATA. Pl. 3, figs. 4 and 5. (Nos. 8 and 32 of collection.)

Description.—Turbinate: whorls, about six, gradually enlarging; convex below, and angular above; suture plain; surface marked by fine lines of growth. Aperture round-oval; shell thin, fragile.

The specimens are all imperfect, and more or less crushed; the figures, however, are good representations of the fossil. It is readily distinguished by its fine lines of growth, resembling a species of Helix, and by the angular character of the upper part of each whorl.

Locality in longitude 111°, latitude 40°, in a dark slaty bituminous limestone.

17. CERITHIUM TENERUM. Pl. 3, figs. 6, 6 *a.* (Nos. 8, 32, and 34, of collection.)

Description.—Elongated, subulate; whorls, about 10, marked with strong ridges, which are again crossed by finer lines in the direction of the whorls. The strong vertical ridges are often obsolete on the last whorl, as in fig. 6 *a,* and the spiral lines much stronger.

This shell is very strongly marked, and its external aspect is sufficient to distinguish it: it is easily fractured, and, from the nature of the matrix, it has been impossible to obtain a specimen exhibiting the mouth perfectly.

Locality, same as the preceding.

18. CERITHIUM FREMONTI. Pl. 3, figs. 7, 7 *a.* (No. 28 of collection.)

Description.—Shell terete, ovate, acute; whorls, about nine, convex; summit of each one coronated; surface marked by regular rows of pustular knobs, often with smaller ones between; beak small, sharp; mouth not visible in the specimen.

This is a very beautifully marked shell, with the summit of each whorl crowned with a row of short spines.

Locality, same as the preceding.

19. NATICA (?) OCCIDENTALIS. Pl. 3, figs. 8, 8 *a.* (Nos. 16 and 21 of collection.)

Description.—Depressed, conical, or sub-globose; spire short, consisting of about five whorls, the last one comprising the greater part of the shell; aperture semi-oval, rounded at both extremities; umbilicus small. Surface marked by lines of growth.

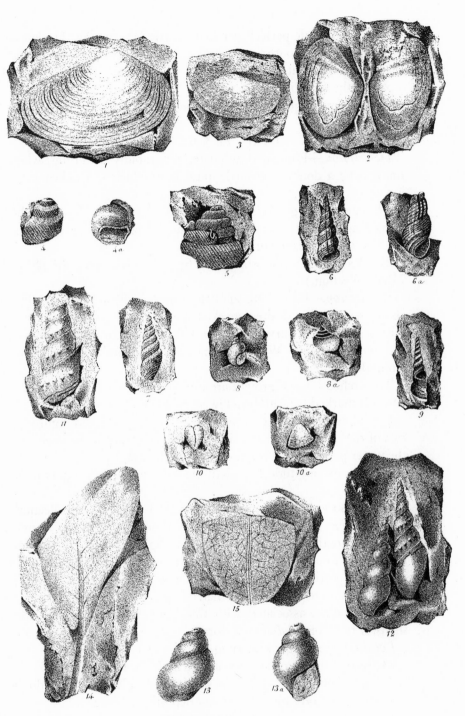

Fossil shells, Plate 3

There is a single perfect specimen and several casts of this delicate little shell. The mouth is not entire, but enough remains to show that the lip was a little expanded; but whether the columella covered a part of the umbilicus is uncertain.

Locality in longitude 115°, latitude 43°, in a gray siliceous limestone.

20. TURRITELLA BILINEATA. Pl. 3, fig. 9. (No. 21 of collection.)

Description.—Elongated, subulate, spire rapidly ascending; whorls marked by a double, elevated, spiral line, which is notched in the lower whorls.

The specimen figured is imperfect, only the upper part of the shell remaining. Several casts of the same species occur in the specimens.

Locality, same as the preceding.

21. CERITHIUM NODULOSUM. Pl. 3, figs. 11 and 12. (Nos. 64, 68, and 74, of collection.)

Description.—Elongated, subulate; spire rapidly ascending; whorls about seven; the sutures marked by a spiral band; surface of whorls marked by curved striæ, or elevated lines, in the direction of the lines of growth. Whorls carinated with a row of protuberances along the centre.

The arched lines of growth are more distinct upon the last whorl, and it is marked beneath by a few spiral lines.

Fig. 11 is a perfect specimen. Fig. 12. The left-hand figure is a cast of the same species; the right-hand figure retains the shell upon the upper part, while it is removed from the lower part.

Locality in longitude 111°, latitude 41½°, in yellowish-gray oolitic limestone.

22. TURBO PALUDINÆFORMIS. Pl. 3, fig. 13. (No. 64 of collection.)

Description.—Whorls, about four, rapidly enlarging, convex, smooth; mouth round-oval; columella slightly reflected; volutions marked by fine arched striæ in the direction of the lines of growth.

A small portion only of the shell remains upon the specimen figured, but it is retained in the matrix. This fossil occurs in gray or yellowish oolite, associated with *Cerithium nodulosum,* and other shells. It resembles *Paludina* in form.

Locality, same as the preceding.

23. LEAVES OF DICOTYLEDONOUS PLANTS. Pl. 3, figs. 14 and 15.

The specimens have not been satisfactorily identified, but doubtless belong to a very modern tertiary deposite.

Locality, Cascades of the Columbia river.

PLATE IV.

24. INOCERAMUS ———? Pl. 4, figs. 1 and 1 *a*. (Nos. 26, 29, 31, 33, and 38, of collection.) Compare *Inoceramus mytiloides,* Sow. Min. Con., tab. 442.

Description.—Inequavalved, depressed, and elongated; surface marked by numerous waved lines and ridges; convex towards the beaks; beaks short and obtuse, somewhat obsolete in old specimens; hinge line oblique.

In the old specimens, the shell appears much flattened, except towards the beaks; while in the younger specimens it is more convex, and particularly so towards the beaks. The youngest specimens are finely lined, and the whole surface of one valve quite convex.

This fossil apparently exists in great numbers, as in the specimens examined there were individuals in all stages of growth; though mostly broken or separated valves. The same species was collected by the late Mr. Nicollet, near the Great Bend of the Missouri.

Locality, Smoky Hill river, longitude 98°, latitude 38°, in yellowish and gray limestone of the cretaceous formation.

25. INOCERAMUS ———? Pl. 4, fig. 2. (No. 42 of collection.) Compare *Inoceramus involutus,* Sow. Min. Con., tab. 583.

Description.—Semicircular; surface flat, with the margin deflected; marked by strong, regular concentric ridges, which become attenuated on either side, and are nearly obsolete towards the beak; beak of one valve small, not elevated; hinge line nearly rectangular.

The strong concentric ridges distinguish this fossil from any other species. The specimen figured is probably the flat valve, as a fragment of a large and much more convex valve accompanies this one, from the same locality. The shell, particularly towards the margin, is very thick and fibrous.

Locality, near the eastern slope of the Rocky mountains, in longitude 105°, latitude 39°, in light yellowish-gray limestone, probably of the cretaceous formation.

NOTE.—The specimens figured on plate III, Nos. 1, 2, 4, 5, and 6, have the appearance of fluviatile shells, and would have been so regarded but for the occurrence of fig. 3, which appears to be a Nucula, and fig. 7, in the same association, the sculpturing of which is unlike any of the Melania known to me. It is not improbable, however, that this may prove a fresh-water deposite of vast interest, as it appears to be of great extent, and occurs at a great elevation. The researches of Capt. Frémont, in his future explorations, will doubtless set this question at rest, by a larger collection of fossils from the same region.

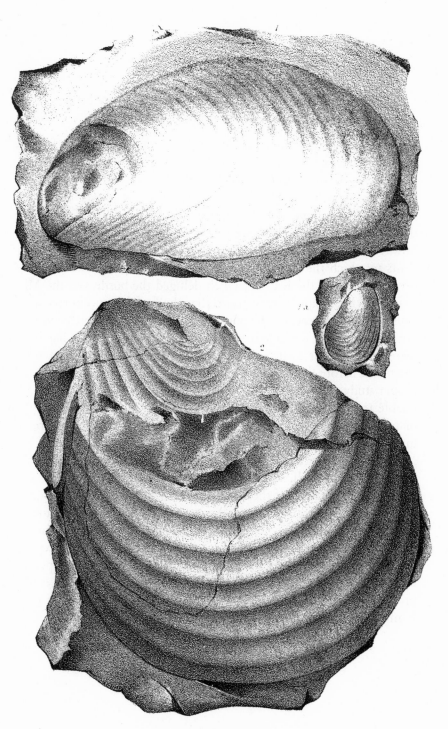

Fossil shells, Plate 4

APPENDIX.

C.

NOTE CONCERNING THE PLANTS COLLECTED IN THE SECOND EXPEDITION OF CAPTAIN FREMONT.

When Captain Frémont set out on his second expedition, he was well provided with paper and other means for making extensive botanical collections; and it was understood that, on his return, we should, conjointly, prepare a full account of his plants, to be appended to his report. About 1,400 species were collected, many of them in regions not before explored by any botanist. In consequence, however, of the great length of the journey, and the numerous accidents to which the party were exposed, but especially owing to the dreadful flood of the Kansas, which deluged the borders of the Missouri and Mississippi rivers, more than half of his specimens were ruined before he reached the borders of civilization. Even the portion saved was greatly damaged; so that, in many instances, it has been extremely difficult to determine the plants. As there was not sufficient time before the publication of Captain Frémont's report for the proper study of the remains of his collection, it has been deemed advisable to reserve the greater part of them to incorporate with the plants which we expect he will bring with him on returning from his third expedition, upon which he has just set out.

The loss sustained by Captain Frémont, and, I may say, by the botanical world, will, we trust, be partly made up the present and next seasons, as much of the same country will be passed over again, and some new regions explored. Arrangements have also been made, by which the botanical collections will be preserved, at least from the destructive effects of water; and a person accompanies the expedition, who is to make drawings of all the most interesting plants. Particular attention will be given to the forest trees and the vegetable productions that are useful in the arts, or that are employed for food or medicine.

JOHN TORREY.

Descriptions of some new genera and species of plants, collected in Captain J. C. Frémont's exploring expedition to Oregon and North California, in the years 1843–'44: By John Torrey and J. C. Frémont.

CLEOMELLA (?) OBTUSIFOLIA. *Torr. and Frém.*[195]

Branching from the base, and diffuse; leaflets cuneate-obovate, obtuse; style filiform.

Annual, stem smooth, the branches spreading, about a span long, hairy in the axils. Leaves, or petioles, an inch or more in length; the lamina of the leaflets 4–6 lines long, apiculate with a deciduous bristle, nearly smooth above, sparsely strigose underneath. Pedicels solitary and axillary, in the upper part of the branches, longer than the petioles. Calyx much shorter than the corolla; the sepals lacerately 3–5-toothed. Petals yellow, oblong-lanceolate, obtuse, about 3 lines in length. Stamens 6, unequal, a little exserted; anthers linear-oblong, recurved when old. Torus hemispherical. Ovary on a long slender stipe, obovate; style longer than the ovary.

On the American fork of the Sacramento river; March. The specimens are not in fruit, so that we cannot be certain as to the genus; but it seems to be a Cleomella.

MECONELLA CALIFORNICA. *Torr. and Frém.*

Leaves obovate-spatulate; stamens 11–12.
On the American fork of the Sacramento river.

This species is intermediate between Meconella and Platystigma. It is a slender annual, 3–4 inches high, with the radical leaves in rosulate clusters, and more dilated at the extremity than in *M. Oregana.* The flowers also are much larger. The torus, which is like that of Eschschotzia, is very distinct.

ARCTOMECON. *Torr. and Frém.—n. gen.*[196]

Calyx of 3 smooth imbricated caducous sepals. Petals 4, obovate, regular. Stamens numerous; anthers oblong-linear: the cells opening

---

195. Mohave stinkweed. Type undoubtedly from the Mojave Desert, certainly not collected on the "American fork of the Sacramento River." Torrey again correctly interpreted genus from incomplete material.

196. JCF's discovery of this spectacular genus growing in the wastes of the Amargosa reminds the botanist of Bartram's chancing upon the highly localized *Franklinia* on the banks of the Altamaha River of Georgia.

longitudinally. Ovary obovoid, composed of 6 carpels, with as many narrow intervalvular placentæ: styles none: stigmas coalescing into a small hemispherical 6-angled sessile head, the angles of which are opposite the placentæ, not forming a projecting disk. Capsule (immature) ovoid, the placentæ almost filiform, opening at the summit by 6 valves, which separate from the persistent placentæ. Seeds oblong, smooth, strophiolate.—A perennial herb, with a thick woody root. Leaves numerous, mostly crowded about the root, flabelliform-cuneate, densely clothed with long gray upwardly barbellate hairs, 3–5 lobed at the summit; the lobes with 2–3 teeth, which are tipped with a rigid pungent upwardly scabrous bristle. Stem scape-like, about a foot high, furnished about the middle with one or two small bract-like leaves, smooth above, rough towards the base. Flowers in a loose, somewhat umbellate, simple or somewhat compound panicle; the peduncles elongated, erect. Petals about an inch long, yellow.

ARCTOMECON CALIFORNICUM. *Torr. and Frém.*[197]

This remarkable plant was found in only a single station in the Californian mountains, on the banks of a creek; flowering early in May. The soil was sterile and gravelly. Although very near Papaver, it differs so much in habit and in the strophiolate seeds, as well as in other characters, that it must be a distinct genus.

KRAMERIA.

A shrubby species of this genus was found on the Virgen river, in California. It seems to be *K. parvifolia* of Bentham, described in the voyage of the Sulphur. His plant, however, was only in fruit, while our specimens are only in flower. Ours grows in thick bunches 1–2 feet high, of a gray aspect, with numerous very straggling and somewhat spinescent branches. Leaves scarcely one-third of an inch long, obovate-spatulate. The flowers are scarcely more than half as large as in *K. lanceolata*. Sepals 5, unequal; claws of the 3 upper petals united into a column below; lamina more or less ovate; the two lower petals short and truncate. Stamens shorter than the upper petals; the filaments united at the base with the column of the petals: anthers one-

197. *Arctomecon californica* Torr. & Frem. Localized endemic poppy yet to be found in California, despite its specific name.

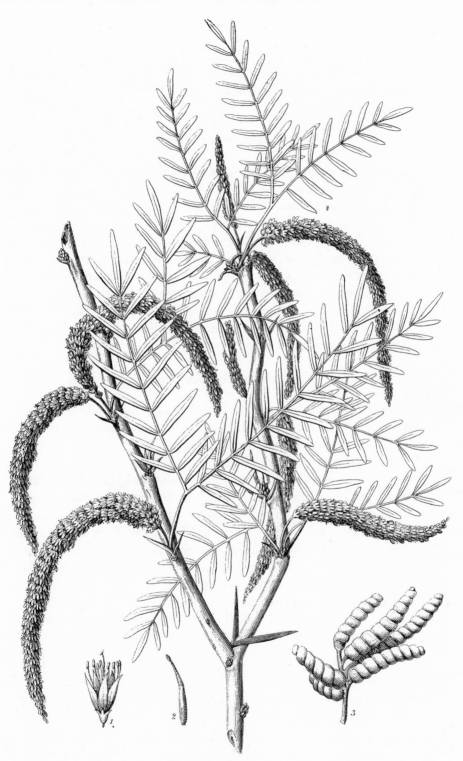

Prosopis odorata

761

celled, with a membranaceous summit, the orifice of which is somewhat dilated, and finally lacerated. Ovary hairy and spinulose; style rigid, declined.

Oxystylis. *Torr. and Frém.—n. gen.*

Sepals linear; petals ovate, somewhat unguiculate; ovary 2-celled; the cells subglobose, each with two ovules: style pyramidal, much larger than the ovary. Silicle didymous: the carpels obovoid-globose, one-seeded, (or rarely two-seeded,) indehiscent, separating from the base of the persistent subulate spinescent style: pericarp crustaceo-coriaceous. Seed ovate, somewhat compressed; testa membranaceous, the lining much thickened and fleshy. Cotyledons incumbent, linear-oblong; radicle opposite the placentæ.—A smooth annual herb. Leaves ternately parted, on long petioles; the leaflets ovate or oblong, entire petiolulate. Flowers in numerous axillary crowded short capitate racemes, small and yellow.

Oxystylis lutea. *Torr. and Frém.*

On the Margoza river, at the foot of a sandy hill; only seen in one place, but abundant there. The specimens were collected on the 28th of April, and were in both flower and fruit.

A rather stout plant; the stem erect, a foot or 15 inches high, simple or a little branching below, leafy. Leaflets 1–1½ inch long, obtuse. Heads of flowers about half an inch in diameter, not elongating in fruit. Calyx shorter than the corolla; the sepals acute, yellowish, tipped with orange. Petals about two lines long. Fruit consisting of two roundish indehiscent carpels, which at maturity separate by a small base, leaving the indurated pointed style. The epicarp is thin, membranaceous, and slightly corrugated.

This remarkable plant seems to connect Cruciferæ with Capparidaceæ. The clusters of old flower stalks, with their numerous crowded spinescent styles, present a singular appearance.

Thamnosma. *Torr. and Frém.—n. gen.*

Flowers hermaphrodite, (or polygamous?) Calyx 4-cleft. Corolla 4-petalled, much longer than the calyx; the æstivation valvate. Stamens 8, in a double series, all fertile. Ovaries 2, sessile and connate at the summit of a stipe, each with 5 or 6 ovules in 2 series; styles united into one; stigma capitate. Capsules 2, sessile at the summit of the stipe, subglobose, united below, (one of them sometimes abortive,) coriaceous, 1–3-seeded. Seeds curved, with a short beak, black and minutely wrinkled; the radicle inferior. Embryo curved; cotyledons broadly linear, incumbent.

THAMNOSMA MONTANA. *Torr. and Frém.*

A shrub of the height of one or two feet, branching from the base, with simple, very small linear wedge-shaped leaves. The flowers are apparently dark purple, in loose terminal clusters. The whole plant has a strong aromatic odor, and every part of it is covered with little glandular dots. Although nearly allied to Xanthoxylum, we regard it as a peculiar genus. It grows in the passes of the mountains, and on the Virgen river in Northern California. The greater part of it was already in fruit in the month of May.

PROSOPIS ODORATA. *Torr. and Frém.*[198]

Branches and leaves smooth; spines stout, mostly in pairs, straight; pinnæ a single pair; leaflets 6–8 pairs, oblong-linear, slightly falcate, somewhat coriaceous, rather obtuse; spikes elongated, on short peduncles; corolla three times as long as the calyx; stamens exserted; legume spirally twisted into a compact cylinder.

A tree about 20 feet high, with a very broad full head, and the lower branches declining to the ground; the thorns sometimes more than an inch long. Leaves smooth; the common petiole 1–2 inches long, and terminated by a spinescent point; leaflets from half an inch to an inch long, and 1–2 lines broad, somewhat coriaceous, sparingly but prominently veined underneath. Spikes 2–4 inches long, and about one-third of an inch in diameter. Flowers yellow, very fragrant, nearly sessile on the rachis. Calyx campanulate, somewhat equally 5-toothed, smooth. Petals ovate-oblong, hairy inside. Stamens 10, one-third longer than the corolla. Anthers tipped with a slightly stipitate gland. Ovary linear-oblong, villous; style smooth; stigma capitate, concave at the extremity. Legumes clustered, spirally twisted

---

198. *Prosopis juliflora* var. *torreyana* L. Benson. JCF mistakenly mixed the leaves of common mesquite and legumes of screwpod mesquite, leading Torrey to propose a binomial which has had to be abandoned.

into a very close rigid cylinder, which is from an inch to an inch and a half long, and about two lines in diameter, forming from ten to thirteen turns, many seeded. Sarcocarp pulpy; the two opposite sides of the firm endocarp are compressed together between the seeds, forming a longitudinal kind of septum, which divides the pulp into two parts. Seeds ovate, kidney-form, compressed, very smooth and hard. Embryo yellowish, surrounded with a thin albumen.

A characteristic tree in the mountainous part of Northern California, particularly along the Mohahve and Virgen rivers, flowering the latter part of April.

This species belongs to the section *strombocarpa* of Mr. Bentham,[*] which includes the *Acacia strombulifera* of Wildenow. In the structure of the pod it is so remarkable that we at one time regarded it as a distinct genus, to which we gave the name of Spirolobium.

There are numerous other Leguminosæ in the collection, including, as might be expected, many species of Lupinus, Astragalus, Oxytropis, and Phaca, some of which are new; also, Thermopsis rhombifolia and montana, and a beautiful shrubby Psoralea (or some allied genus) covered with bright violet flowers.

Cowania plicata. *D. Don.* (?)[199]

Specimens of this plant, without a ticket, were in the collection; doubtless obtained in California. It may prove to be a distinct species from the Mexican plant, for the leaves are more divided than they are described by Don, and the flowers are smaller. The genus Cowania is very nearly allied to Cercocarpus and Purshia, notwithstanding its numerous ovaries. The lobes of the calyx are imbricated, as in those genera, and not valvate, as in *Eudryadeæ,* to which section it is referred by Endlicher.

Purshia tridentata formed a conspicuous object in several parts of the route, not only east of the mountains, but in Oregon and California. It is covered with a profusion of yellow flowers, and is quite ornamental. Sometimes it attains the height of twelve feet.

[*] In Hooker's Journal of Botany, iv, p. 351.

199. This might possibly have been what Torrey later described as *Emplectocladus fasciculatus.* When he published this name in *Plantae Frémontianæ* (1853), he stated that the label of origin had been lost.

Spiræa ariæfolia, var. *discolor,* was found on the upper waters of the Platte, holding its characters so well that it should perhaps be regarded as a distinct species.

Œnothera clavæformis. *Torr. and Frém.*

Leaves ovate or oblong, denticulate or toothed, pinnatified at the base, with a long naked petiole; scape with several small leaves, 8–12-flowered; segments of the calyx longer than the tube; capsules clavate-cylindrical, nearly twice as long as the pedicel. Flowers about as large as in *Œ. pumila.* Grows with the preceding.

This new species belongs to the section *Chylismia* of Nutt. (*Torr. and Gr. Fl. N. Am. 1, p. 506.*)

Œnothera deltoides. *Torr. and Frém.*

Annual: canescently strigose; stem low and stout; leaves rhombi-covate, repandly denticulate, acute; flowers (large) clustered at the summit of the short stem; tube of the calyx nearly twice the length of the segments: petals entire, one-third longer than the slightly de-clined stamens; anthers very long, fixed by the middle; style ex-serted; capsules prismatic-cylindrical.

Allied to *Œ. Jamesii, Torr. and Gr.,* and belongs, like that species, to the section Euœnothera and sub-section *Onagra.*

Œnothera canescens. *Torr. and Frém.*

Strigosely canescent; leaves narrowly lanceolate, rather obtuse, remotely denticulate; flowers in a leafy raceme; tube of the calyx rather slender, three times as long as the ovary, and one third longer than the segments; petals broadly ovate, entire.

This species was collected (we believe) on the upper waters of the Platte. It belongs to the section Euœnothera, and to a sub-section which may be called Gauropsis, and characterized as follows: Peren-nial diffuse herbs; tube of the calyx linear; capsule obovate, sessile, with 4-winged angles and no intermediate ribs, tardily opening; seeds numerous, horizontal; the testa membranaceous; leaves opaque.

Besides these new species, many other Œnothera were collected;

among which may be mentioned *Œ. albicaulis, alyssoides, montana,* and *Missouriensis.* Also, *Gayophytum diffusum,* (from the Snake country, growing about 2 feet high,) *Stenosiphon virgatum,* and *Gaura coccinea.*

COMPOSITÆ.

The plants of this family were placed in the hands of Dr. Gray for examination; and he has described some of them (including four new genera) in the Boston Journal of Natural History for January, 1845. He has since ascertained another new genus among the specimens; and we fully concur with him in the propriety of dedicating it to the late distinguished J. N. Nicollet, Esq., who spent several years in exploring the country watered by the Mississippi and Missouri rivers, and who was employed by the United States Government in a survey of the region lying between the sources of those rivers. This gentleman exerted himself to make known the botany of the country which he explored, and brought home with him an interesting collection of plants, made under his direction, by Mr. Charles Geyer, of which an account is given in the report of Mr. N. The following is the description of this genus by Dr. Gray:

NICOLLETIA. *Gray.*

"Heads heterogamous, with few rays, many flowered. Involucre campanulate, consisting of about 8 oval membranaceous scales in a single series; the base calyculate, with one or two smaller scales. Receptacle convex, alveolate. Corolla of the disk flowers equally 5-toothed. Branches of the style terminated by a subulate hisped appendage. Achenia elongated, slender, canescently pubescent. Pappus double, scarcely shorter than the corolla; the exterior of numerous scabrous, unequal bristles; the inner of 5 linear-lanceolate chaffy scales, which are entire, or 2-toothed at the summit, and furnished with a strong central nerve, which is produced into a short scabrous awn.—A humble, branching (and apparently annual) herb. Leaves alternate, pinnatified, and somewhat fleshy, (destitute of glands?); the lobes and rachis linear. Heads terminal, solitary, nearly sessile, large, (about an inch long,) with one or two involucrate leaves at the base. Corolla yellow."

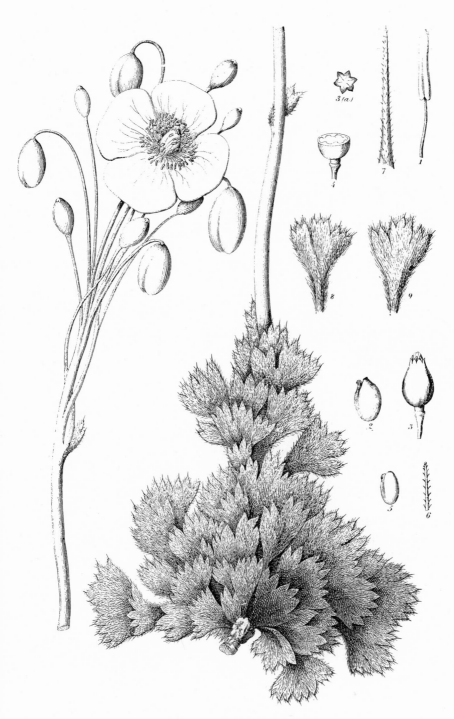

Arctomecon californica

767

NICOLLETIA OCCIDENTALIS. *Gray.*[200]

On the banks of the Mohahve river, growing in the naked sands; flowering in April. The plant has a powerful and rather agreeable odor. This interesting genus (which is described from imperfect materials) belongs to the tribe SENECIONIDEÆ, and the sub-tribe TAGITINEÆ. It has the habit of Dissodia, and exhibits both the chaffy pappus of the division *Tageteæ,* and the *pappus pilosus* of *Porophyllum.**— Gray.*

FRANSERIA DUMOSA. *Gray.*

Shrubby, much branched; leaves pinnatified, canescent on both sides, as are the branchlets; the divisions 3–7, oval, entire, and somewhat lobed; heads rather loosely spiked; involucre of the sterile flowers 5–7 cleft, strigosely canescent; of the fertile, ovoid, 2-celled, 2-flowered.

A shrub, 1–2 feet high, with divaricate rigid branches. Leaves scarcely an inch long. Fertile (immature) involucre clothed with straight soft lanceolate subulate prickles, which are short and scale-like.

On the sandy uplands of the Mohahve river, and very common in all that region of North California. Flowering in April.

AMSONIA TOMENTOSA. *Torr. and Frém.*

Suffrutescent; clothed with a dense whitish pubescence; leaves lanceolate and ovate-lanceolate, acute at each end; segments of the calyx lanceolate-subulate; corolla slightly hairy externally.

Stems numerous, erect, 12 to 18 inches high, woody, below simple or branching. Leaves alternate; the lowest small and spatulate, or reduced to scales; the others about 2 inches long, and varying from 4 to 8 lines in breadth; entire, acuminate at the base. Flowers in rather dense, somewhat fastigiate terminal clusters, nearly three-fourths of

* It should be stated here, that the notice of this genus by Dr. Gray was drawn up in Latin; but we have given it in English, that it may be uniform with our own description.

---

200. *Nicolletia occidentalis* Gray, named, of course, for JCF's former mentor. Two other deserticolous genera based on JCF collections, *Monoptilon* and *Amphipappus,* were described at the same time by Asa Gray.

an inch long. Calyx about one-third the length of the corolla, 5-parted to the base; the segments narrow and hairy. Corolla with the tube ventricose above; the segments ovate-oblong. Stamens included; filaments short; anthers ovate-sagittate. Ovaries oblong, united below, distinct above, smooth; style slender; stigma capitate, with a membranaceous collar at the base.

The specimens of this plant were without tickets; but they were probably collected west of the Rocky mountains. They were without fruit.

ASCLEPIAS SPECIOSA. *Torr. in Ann. Lyc. New York, ii, p. 218.*

This (as was stated in the first report) is *A. Douglasii* of Hooker, well figured in his Flora Boreali Americana, 2, t. 142. It has a wide range, being found on both sides of the Rocky mountains, and from the sources of the St. Peter's to those of the Kansas and Canadian. The fruit was collected from specimens on the banks of the Snake river. It is almost exactly like that of *A. Cornuti,* being inflated, woolly, and covered with soft spines.

ACERATES LATIFOLIA. *Torr. and Frém.*

Stem simple, erect, smooth; leaves roundish-ovate, nearly sessile, obtuse, with a small mucro, smooth on both sides; umbel solitary, on a terminal peduncle, few-flowered; pedicels slender; segments of the corolla ovate-lanceolate; lobes of the crown semilunar-ovate, as long as the column, rather obtuse, cucullate.

On Green river, a tributary of the Colorado of the West; June. About a span high. Leaves about an inch and a half long, and more than an inch wide. Flowers few, very large, apparently yellowish. Fruit not seen.

ERIOGONUM INFLATUM. *Torr. and Frém.*[201]

Smooth, bi-trichotomous; the lower part, and sometimes the two primary divisions of the stem, much inflated and calvate; peduncles

---

201. Seven *Eriogonum* species were described by Torrey and by Bentham, based in whole or part on JCF's collections. Either JCF paid special attention to an inconspicuous plant group, or Torrey solicited his collecting a favorite genus.

divaricately branched, the ultimate divisions filiform and solitary; involucre few-flowered, smooth; the teeth equal, erect.

The specimens of this plant are imperfect, being destitute of leaves, which are probably wholly radical. It is a foot or more high. The first joint of the stem, or rather scape, is remarkably dilated and fistular upward. This divides into three or more branches, the two primary ones of which are sometimes inflated like the first; the subdivisions are dichotomous, with a pedicellate involucre in each fork. The involucres are about a line in diameter, smooth, 5–6-flowered; and, in all the specimens that I examined, only 5-toothed. The plant was found on barren hills in the lower part of North California.

ERIOGONUM RENIFORME. *Torr. and Frém.*

Annual; leaves radical, on long petioles, reniform, clothed with a dense hoary tomentum; stem scape-like naked, 3-forked from the base, glaucous, and nearly smooth; the divisions divaricately 2–3-forked; involucres 2–4 together, on slender peduncles, smooth, campanulate, 5-toothed, the teeth nearly equal, obtuse; perigonium smooth.

On the Sacramento river; March. Allied to *E. vimineum* of Bentham. A small species, with very minute flowers.

ERIOGONUM CORDALUM. *Torr. and Frém.*

Annual; leaves all radical, on long petioles, roundish-ovate, cordate, very obtuse, slightly pubescent above, hairy underneath; scape naked, slender, smooth and glaneous, divaricately branched, the divisions slender; involucres solitary, on filiform peduncles, campanulate, smooth, 5-toothed, the teeth nearly equal, rather obtuse; perigonium hairy.

With the preceding, from which it is easily distinguished by the form of its leaves and color of the pubescence.

Many other species of this genus were collected in California and the Snake country, some of which are probably new, and will be described in the next report.

FREMONTIA VERMICULARIS. *Torr. in Frém. 1st report.*

This curious plant is always found in saline soils, or where the atmosphere is saline. Its greatest height is eight feet. It is a char-

Fremontia vermicularis

acteristic feature of the vegetation throughout a great part of Oregon and North California. About Brown's Hole, on Green river, it occupies almost exclusively the *bottoms* of the neighboring streams. It is abundant also on the shores of a salt lake in lat. 38° and long. 113°; and constantly occurs in the desert region south of the Columbia, and between the Cascade range and the Rocky mountains, as far south as lat. 34°. The branches, when old, become spiny, as in many other plants of this family.

Since the description of this genus was published in the first report, (March, 1843,) Nees has given it the name of Sarcobatus; and Dr. Seubert has published an account of it, with a figure, in the *Botanische Zeitung* for 1844. This we have not yet seen; but, from the remarks of Dr. Lindley, who has given a note on the genus in Hooker's Journal of Botany for January, 1845, it would seem that some doubt existed among European botanists as to its affinities, as they had not seen the ripe seeds. These we have long possessed, and unhesitatingly referred it to Chenopodiaciæ. We regret that our sketches of the staminate flowers were mislaid when the artist was engraving the figure.

Obione confertifolia. *Torr. and Frém.*

Stem pubescent, much branched, erect; leaves alternate, ovate, rather obtuse, petiolate, much crowded, entire, somewhat coriaceous, white with a mealy crust; bracts broadly ovate, obtuse, entire, and the sides without appendages or tubercles.

A small shrub, with rigid crooked and somewhat spinescent branches, and of a whitish aspect. Leaves varying from one-third to half an inch in length, abruptly narrowed at the base into a petiole, thickly clothed with a white mealy substance.

Flowers apparently diœcious. Sterile not seen. Bracts of the fruit 3–4 lines long, united about half way up, distinct above, indurated at the base. Styles distinct. Pericarp very thin. Seed roundish ovate, rostellate upward; the testa coriaceous. Embryo two-thirds of a circle.

On the borders of the Great Salt lake. From the description of *O. coriacea,* Moq., our plant seems to be a near ally of that species.

Pterochiton. *Torr. and Frém.—n. gen.*

Flowers diœcious. Staminate . . . . Pistillate. Perigonium ovoid-tubular, 4-winged, 2-toothed at the summit. Ovary roundish; style short; stigmas 2, linear. Ovule solitary, ascending from the base of the ovary, campulitropous. Fructiferous perianth indurated, broadly 4-winged, closed, minutely 2-toothed at the summit; the wings veined and irregularly toothed. Utricle very thin and membranaceous, free. Seed ovate, somewhat compressed; the podosperm lateral and very distinct, rostrate upward. Integument double, the exterior somewhat coriaceous, brownish, the inner one thin. Embryo nearly a circle, surrounding copious mealy albumen.

PTEROCHITON OCCIDENTALE. *Torr. and Frém.*

An unarmed shrub, 1–2 feet high, with numerous slender branches, which are clothed with a grayish nearly smooth bark. Leaves alternate or fasciculate, linear oblanceolate, narrowed at the base, flat, entire, covered with a whitish mealy crust, flowers somewhat racemose, on short, pedicels. Fructiferous calyx, with the wings 2–3 lines wide, semi-orbicular, coriaceo-membranaceous, mealy like the leaves, strongly veined; the margin more or less toothed. Utricle free from the indurated cavity of the perianth, extremely thin and transparent. Seed conformed to the utricle, the conspicuous podosperm passing along its side; the beak pointing obliquely upward.

This is one of the numerous shrubby plants of the Chenopodiaceous family, that constitute a large part of the vegetation in the saline soils of the west. The precise locality of this plant we cannot indicate, as the label was illegible; but it was probably from the borders of the Great Salt lake. It is allied to Grayia of Hooker and Arnott, a shrub of the same family, which was found in several places on both sides of the Rocky mountains, often in great abundance.

PINUS MONOPHYLLUS. *Torr. and Frém.* (*The nut pine.*)

Leaves solitary, or very rarely in pairs, with scarcely any sheaths, stout and rigid, somewhat pungent; cones ovoid, the scales with a thick obtusely pyramidal and protuberant summit, unarmed; seeds large, without a wing.
A tree with verticillate branches and cylindrical-clavate buds, which are about three-fourths of an inch in length. The leaves are from an inch to two and a half inches long: often more or less curved, scattered, very stout, terete, (except in the very rare case of their being in pairs, when they are semi-cylindrical,) ending in a

spiny tip. Cones about $2\frac{1}{2}$ inches long, and $1\frac{3}{4}$ inch broad in the widest part. The scales are of a light-brown color, thick; the summit obtusely pyramidal and somewhat recurved, but without any point. The seeds are oblong, about half an inch long, without a wing; or rather the wing is indissolubly adherent to the scale. The kernel is of a very pleasant flavor, resembling that of *Pinus Pembra*.[202]

This tree, which is remarkable among the true pines for its solitary leaves, is extensively diffused over the mountains of Northern California, from long. 111° to 120°, and through a considerable range of latitude. It is alluded to repeatedly, in the course of the narrative, as the *nut pine*.

The Coniferæ of the collection were numerous, and suffered less than most of the other plants. Some of them do not appear to have been hitherto described. There was also an Ephedra, which does not differ essentially from *E. occidentalis,* found in great plenty on the sandy uplands of the Mohahve river.

Description of the plates.

Plate 1. ARCTOMECON CALIFORNICUM. *Fig.* 1, a stamen, *magnified; fig.* 2, an ovule, *mag.; fig.* 3, capsule, *nat. size; fig.* 3, (*a,*) stigma, *mag.; fig.* 4, the same cut horizontally, showing the sutures; *fig.* 5, a seed, *mag.; fig.* 6, portion of a hair from the leaf, *mag.; fig.* 7, bristle from the extremity of a leaf lobe, *mag.; figs.* 8 and 9, leaves, *nat. size.*

Plate 2. PROSOPIS ODORATA. *Fig.* 1, a flower, *mag.; fig.* 2, pistil, *mag.; fig.* 3, cluster of ripe legumes, *nat. size.*

Plate 3. FREMONTIA VERMICULARIS. *Fig.* 1, a very young fertile flower, *mag.; fig.* 2, an ovule, *mag.; fig.* 3, a fertile flower more advanced, *mag.; fig.* 4, a fertile flower at maturity, showing the broad-winged border of the calyx, *mag.; fig.* 5, the same cut vertically; *fig.* 6, the same cut horizontally; *fig.* 7, a seed, *mag.; fig.* 8, embryo, *mag.*

Plate 4. PINUS MONOPHYLLUS. *Fig.* 1, a bud, *nat. size; figs.* 2, 3, 4, and 5, leaves, *nat. size; fig.* 2, (*a,*) section of a single leaf; *fig.* 5, (*a,*) section of a pair of leaves; *fig.* 6, a cone, *nat. size; fig.* 7, a scale, as seen from the outside; *fig.* 8, inside view of the same.

---

202. An error for *Pinus cembra,* an ally of *P. monophylla* Torr. & Frem.

Pinus monophyllus

775

The map which accompanies this report is constructed upon Flamsteed's modified projection, on a scale of 1 : 2,000,000, and based upon the astronomical observations made during the campaigns of 1842 and 1843–'44. The longitudes are referred to the meridian of Greenwich, and depend upon eighteen principal stations; four of which are determined by occulations of fixed stars, and the remaining fourteen by eclipses of the satellites of Jupiter. All the longitudes on the map have been chronometrically referred to these positions.

In the course of the last exploration, it became evident that the longitudes established during the campaign of 1842 were collectively thrown too far to the westward, by the occultation of a^2 Arietis, to which they had been referred by the chronometer. This occultation took place at the bright limb of the moon, which experience has recently shown to be deserving of little comparative confidence. This position has therefore been abandoned, and the longitudes depending upon it have been referred chronometrically to those established in 1843 and 1844. The course of the ensuing expedition will intersect the line established by our previous operations, at various points, which it is proposed to correct in longitude by lunar culminations, and such other absolute observations as may be conveniently obtained. Such a position at the mouth of the Fontaine-qui-bouit, on the Arkansas river, will be a good point of reference for the longitudes along the foot of the mountains. In passing by the Utah, to the southern portion of the Great Salt lake, we shall have an opportunity to verify our longitudes in that quarter; and as in the course of our exploration we shall touch upon several points previously determined along the western limit of our recent journey, we shall probably be able to form a reasonably correct frame on which to base the construction of a general map of the country. In that now presented, we have carefully avoided to lay down any thing as certain which may not be found in the field books of our surveys, which were greatly facilitated by the character of the country in which we were operating.

---

203. Pages 330–558 of the *Report,* which constitute the detailed tables of astronomical observations made during the expedition of 1843–44, are not reprinted here.

To the kindness of Captain Wilkes I am indebted for the longitudes of Fort Vancouver and Nueva Helvetia, which were furnished to me before the publication of his map. Our reconnoissance is connected with his surveys by those positions.

The coast line of the Pacific is laid down according to the survey of Vancouver; and the bay of San Francisco is reduced from the copy of a manuscript map of a detailed survey, in the possession of Mr. Sutter.

J. C. Frémont.

Table of latitudes and longitudes deduced from the annexed observations.

Date.	Latitudes.			Longitudes.			Localities.
1843.							
May 30	38° 49′	41″		94° 25′	31″		Elm grove.
June 1	39 01	16		95 11	09		Small tributary to the Kansas.
4	39 11	17		95 56	30		Buck creek, tributary of the Kansas.
5	39 08	24		96 06	02		Elk creek, tributary of the Kansas.
10	39 03	38		96 24	56		Encampment on the Smoky Hill fork, half a mile from its junction with the Republican.
12	39 22	12		97 05	32		Tributary to the Republican fork.
15	39 32	54		98 11	41		Tributary to the Republican fork.
17	39 37	38		98 46	50		Tributary to Solomon's fork of the Republican.
19	39 42	35		99 22	03		Tributary to Solomon's fork of the Republican.
22	39 53	59		100 31	30		Tributary to Republican fork.
23	39 49	28		100 52	00		Prairie Dog river, Republican fork.
25	40 05	08		101 39	23		Small tributary to the Republican.
28	40 29	04		102 44	47		Encampment on a small lake in the sandy plain between the Republican and South fork of the Platte river.
30	40 31	02		103 23	29		South fork of the Platte river.
July 1	40 17	21		104 02	00		South fork, 9 miles above mouth of Beaver fork.
7	39 43	53		105 24	34		South fork, near Cherry creek.
15	38 15	23		104 58	30		Junction of Arkansas and Boiling Spring rivers.
18	38 52	10		105 22	45		Boiling Springs.
21	39 41	45		105 25	38		South fork.
23	40 16	52		105 12	23		St. Vrain's fort.
30	41 02	19		105 35	17		High prairie, broken by buttes and boulders, with scattered cedars, forming dividing grounds between Laramie and Cache à la Poudre rivers.
31	41 04	06		–			Near the preceding.
31	41 15	02		106 16	54		Laramie river.
August 1	41 23	08		–			Stream discharging into a lake.
2	41 45	59		–			Fork of Laramie river.
2	41 37	16		106 47	25		Medicine Bow river.
3	41 35	48		–			Tributary to the North fork.
5	41 35	59		107 22	27		North fork of the Platte river.

Table of latitudes and longitudes—Continued.

Date.	Latitudes.			Longitudes.			Localities.
1843. August 8	42° 02′		03″	–			High plateau between the waters of the Atlantic and the gulf of California.
9	42 20		06	–			Gap in the Sweet Water mountains.
9	–			107° 50′		07″	Sweet Water river.
10	42 31		17	–			Sweet Water river.
13	42 19		53	–			Near South pass, on a small affluent to the Sandy fork of Green river.
13	42 18		08	109 25		55	Small stream, tributary to the Little Sandy river.
14	42 15		11	–			Little Sandy river.
15	41 53		54	110 05		05	Green river, left bank.
16	41 46		54	–			Green river, near old trading post, at point where the road to the Columbia leaves the river.
16	41 37		38	110 10		28	Black's fork of Green river.
17	41 29		53	110 25		06	Black's fork.
18	41 26		08	110 45		58	Small stream, tributary to Ham's fork.
19	41 34		24	–			Muddy river of Ham's fork.
20	41 39		45	–			Muddy river.
21	41 53		55	–			Bear river.
21	42 03		47	111 10		53	Bear river.
22	42 10		27	–			Bear river, above Thomas's fork.
24	42 29		05	–			Tullick's fork of Bear river
24	42 36		56	111 42		08	Bear river.
25	42 39		57	111 46		00	Beer springs.
29	42 07		18	–			Entrance of the beautiful pass with the remarkable rock.
30	42 14		22	–			Branch of Roseaux or Reed river.
31	41 59		31	–			Swampy place, a little distance from Roseaux creek.
Sept. 2	41 30		21	112 15		46	Bear river, near the mouth.
3	41 30		22	112 19		30	Mouth of Bear river.
7, 12	41 15		50	112 06		43	Weber's fork.
8	41 11		26	112 11		30	Weber's fork, very near the mouth.
9	41 10		42	112 21		05	Island in the Great Salt lake.
10	41 14		17	–			Halt in the Mud.

Table of latitudes and longitudes—Continued.

Date.	Latitudes.	Longitudes.	Localities.
1843.			
Sept. 13	41° 42′ 43″	112° 05′ 12″	Bear river, south of the gap—a main station.
15	42 12 57	112 15 04	Roseaux or Reed river.
17	42 44 40	112 29 52	Pannack river.
21	43 01 30	112 29 54	Fort Hall.
24	42 47 05	112 40 13	Snake river, above the American falls.
28	42 29 57	–	Snake river.
29	42 26 21	114 06 04	Rock creek, of Snake river.
30	42 38 44	114 25 04	Snake river, opposite to the River spring.
Oct. 1	42 40 11	114 35 12	Snake river, 2 miles below Fishing falls.
2	42 53 40	114 53 04	Snake river.
3	42 55 58	115 04 46	Ford where road crosses the Snake river.
7	43 35 21	115 54 46	Big Wood river, or Rivière Boisée.
8	43 40 53	116 22 40	Big Wood river, or Rivière Boisée.
10	43 49 22	116 47 03	Fort Boisée.
12	44 17 36	116 56 45	Snake river, below Birch creek.
14	44 37 44	117 09 49	Head water of Burnt river, (Rivière Brulee.)
15	44 50 32	117 24 21	Old bed of Powder river.
16	44 59 29	117 29 22	Powder river.
18	45 26 47	117 28 26	Grand Rond.
19	45 38 07	117 28 34	Blue mountains, east of the summit.
23	45 53 35	118 00 39	Walahwalah river, foot of the mountains.
26	46 03 46	–	Fort Nez Percé.
28	45 58 08	–	Noon halt—left bank of the Columbia.
30	45 50 05	119 22 18	Left bank of the Columbia.
31	45 44 23	119 45 09	Left bank of the Columbia.
Nov. 5	45 35 55	120 55 00	Missionary station at the Dalles of the Columbia.
5	45 35 21	120 53 51	Station on hills in rear of the mission.
11	45 33 09	122 06 15	Right bank of the Columbia, 15 miles below the cascades.
26	45 14 24	–	Large branch of Fall river, (*Rivière aux Chutes.*)

Table of latitudes and longitudes—Continued.

Date.	Latitudes.			Longitudes.			Localities.
1843. Nov. 27	45°	06′	45″	121°	02′	43″	South end of Taih prairie.
30	44	35	23	121	10	25	Main branch of Fall river.
Dec. 5	43	55	20		–		Fall river, (Union Falls.)
6	43	44	15		–		Fall river, (Union falls.)
7	43	30	36	121	33	50	Fall river, (Union Falls.)
8	43	17	49		–		Camp in a pine forest.
10	42	56	51		–		Tlamath lake.
13	42	51	26	121	20	42	Tributary to the lake and head water of the Tlamath river.
16	42	57	22		–		Summer lake.
18	42	42	37		–		Summer lake.
24	42	23	25		–		Christmas lake.
26	42	00	09		–		Desert valley among black rocky hills.
29	41	27	50		–		Camp of the 29th to 30th.
31	41	19	55		–		New-year's Eve camp.
1844. Jan. 3	40	48	15		–		Camp near the Mud lake.
6	40	39	46		–		Camp near Great Boiling spring.
15	39	51	13		–		Pyramid lake, mouth of Salmon Trout river.
18	39	24	16		–		Camp on a river of the Sierra Nevada.
19	39	19	21		–		Camp on a river of the Sierra Nevada.
21	39	01	53		–		Camp on a river of the Sierra Nevada.
22	38	49	54		–		Camp on a river, near a gap.
23	38	36	19		–		Camp on a southern branch of stream of encampment of 22d to 23d.
24	38	24	28		–		Head waters of a stream.
26	38	18	01		–		Camp on a large stream.
30	38	37	18		–		Camp on the same stream which we encamped upon on the night of the 18th to 19th January.
Feb. 5	38	42	26		–		First camp in the pass of the Sierra Nevada.
14, 19	38	41	57	120	25	57	The Long camp.
24	38	46	58	120	34	20	Rio de los Americanos, (high in the mountain.)
Mar. 10, 22	38	34	42		–		Nueva Helvetia.

Date.	Latitudes.	Longitudes.	Localities.
1844. March 25	38° 08′ 23″	121° 23′ 03″	Rio de los Mukelemnes.
26	38 02 48	121 16 22	Rio de las Calaveras.
28	37 42 26	121 07 13	Stanislaus river.
31	37 15 43	120 46 30	Stanislaus river.
April 3	37 22 05	120 58 03	Large tributary of the San Joaquin, (no name.)
4	37 08 00	120 45 22	San Joaquin river.
5	36 49 12	120 28 34	San Joaquin river.
8	36 24 50	119 41 40	Lake fork, (of the Tulares.)
9	36 08 38	119 22 02	Small stream affluent to the lake, (Tulares.)
10	35 49 10	118 56 34	Small stream affluent to the lake, (Tulares.)
13	35 17 12	118 35 03	Near Pass creek in the mountains, (Sierra Nevada.)
14	35 03 00	118 18 09	Small stream east of the Sierra Nevada.
15	34 41 42	118 20 00	Rock spring.
18	34 27 03	117 43 21	Spring heads of a stream among foot hills of the mountain.
21	34 34 11	117 13 00	Mohahve river, on the Spanish trail from Pueblo de los Angeles to Santa Fé.
24	34 56 00	116 29 19	Mohahve river, on the Spanish trail from Pueblo de los Angeles to Santa Fé.
25	35 13 08	116 23 28	Agua de Tomaso, on the Spanish trail.
29	35 51 21	–	Hernandez spring.
May 1	35 58 19	–	Deep Spring hole on a river which loses itself in the sands.
3	36 10 20	–	Las Vegas, (the plains.)
5	36 38 56	–	Branch of the Rio Virgen.
6	36 39 33	–	Rio Virgen.
8	36 53 03	–	Rio Virgen.
9	36 53 40	–	Rio Virgen.
12	37 28 28	–	Vegas de Santa Clara.
19	38 18 20	–	A fine rolling prairie at the spring head of a tributary to Sevier lake.
23	39 22 19	–	Sevier river.
24	39 42 15	–	First stream of Utah lake.
27	40 04 27	–	Right-hand branch of Spanish fork.
28	39 55 11	–	Head of Spanish fork.

Table of latitudes and longitudes—Continued.

Date.		Latitudes.			Longitudes.			Localities.
1844.								
May	29	40°	00'	07"		–		Head of Uintah river.
	30	40	18	52	112°	18'	30"	Duchesne fork.
June	3	40	27	45	109	56	42	Uintah fort.
	5	40	28	07	109	27	07	Ashley's fork.
	7	40	46	27		–		Brown's Hole on Green river.
	8	40	46	27		–		Green river in Brown's Hole.
	10	41	01	48		–		Elk Head river.
	11	41	01	11		–		Elk Head river.
	13	41	18	48		–		Valley of the North fork of Platte, (foot of the mountains.)
	14	41	08	16		–		Valley of the North fork of Platte, (higher.)
	15	40	52	44		–		New Park.
	16	40	33	22		–		New Park.
	19	39	57	26		–		Old Park, fork of Grand river.
	22	39	20	24		–		Entrance of bayou Salade—head of Fontaine-qui-bouit? South fork of the Platte?
	26	38	39	22		–		Small affluent to the Arkansas.
	28	38	23	48		–		A larger affluent to the Arkansas.
	29	38	15	23		–		Junction of Arkansas and Fontaine-qui-bouit rivers.
July	2	38	02	08		–		Near Bent's fort on the Arkansas river.
	9	38	51	15		–		Smoky Hill river.
	10	38	52	22		–		Smoky Hill river.
	13	38	45	57		–		Smoky Hill river.
	17	38	42	33		–		Smoky Hill river, below Pawnee village.
	19	38	43	32	98	17	31	Smoky Hill river.
	21	38	28	38		–		Three miles south of Smoky Hill fork.
	22	38	31	38		–		Between Smoky Hill fork and the Santa Fé trail.
	23	38	33	22		–		Santa Fé road.
	28	38	46	50	98	04	34	*Black jack* on the Santa Fé road.

METEOROLOGICAL OBSERVATIONS
MADE DURING THE JOURNEY.

Comparison of barometers.

According to three observations made at the observatory of Paris, Lieutenant Frémont's barometer, constructed by Bunten, is 0.23 millimetres higher than the standard of the observatory.

The result of forty-three comparative observations of both barometers of Mr. Frémont with both my barometers, gives the following:

Barometer E (English) = E (French) — 0.051 inch = Fr. (N. Y.) — 0.034 inch = Fr. (Bunten) — 0.091 inch.

Barometer E (French) = E (English) + 0.051 inch = Fr. (N. Y.) + 0.017 inch = Fr. (Bunten) — 0.040 inch.

Barometer Fr. (Bunten) = Fr. (N. Y.) + 0.057 inch.

Observations from May 1 to May 11, 1843.

Range of barometer during the time, $= 0''.4$.
Range of thermometer, $= 60°$ to $80°$ Fahrenheit.

G. ENGELMANN.

St. Louis, *May,* 13, 1843.

Table of meteorological observations.

Date.	Time.	Barom.	Thermometer. Attached.	Thermometer. Free.	Altitudes.	Remarks.
1843.		*Millim.*	*Cent.*	*Fahr.*	*Feet.*	
June 10	Sunrise -	733.74	5.0	39.3	900	Clear sky ; fog ; wind N.
	1h. 41m. p. m.	735.43	22.0	69.0	938	NE. wind; clear, and fine cumuli.
	Sunset -	733.95	14.8	55.4	933	Slight breeze from NW.; clear.
11	Sunrise -	734.00	8.8	48.6	933	Clear; cumuli; slight breeze from SW.
12	Sunrise -	728.95	12.9	55.0	1,036	Wind S.; clear; clouds in E. horizon.
	Noon -	726.02	24.9	75.4	1,331	Wind S.; clear; few cumuli.
13	Sunrise -	726.15	15.6	59.5	1,267	Wind N.
	1h. p. m. -	726.19	25.1	76.0	1,329	Wind N.; clear; cumuli.
	Sunset -	724.96	22.0	67.0	1,406	Sky covered with scattered clouds; calm; bright sunset.
14	Sunrise -	723.79	16.3	60.0	1,406	Thunder and rain; rainbow in the W.
15	5h. 55m. a. m.	721.67	17.8	61.6	1,486	At sunset last night a very violent and continuous rain commenced, wind NW., with thunder and lightning, for half an hour, and continued moderate all the night. This morning calm and cloudy.
	Sunset -	724.34	24.0	74.0	1,555	Gentle breeze from NW.; clear, and cumuli.
16	Sunset -	724.72	19.1	64.0	1,401	Wind N. 60° E.; heavy rains during the fore part of the day; clouds and sun in the afternoon; clouds, with the appearance of fair weather.
17	4h. 47m. a. m.	725.45	16.5	60.0	1,347	Sky covered; a misty rain; wind S. 60° E.
	Noon -	723.42	21.1	71.0	1,464	Heavy squalls of rain during the morning; wind shifting from SE. to N., and settled SE. with clouds and sun.
	Sunset -	721.19	19.9	69.0	1,535	Clear, and some cumuli; slight breeze from N.
18	Sunrise -	720.80	16.1	61.2	1,535	Clear; some clouds in W. horizon; wind slight from SE.
	Sunset -	713.33	25.7	78.2	1,911	Wind NE.; sky nearly overcast with clouds.
19	Sunrise -	712.07	20.4	69.0	1,911	Clear; breeze moderate from NE.
	Noon -	715.46	31.5	86.0	1,868	Clear; breeze SE.
	Sunset -	712.53	27.0	80.3	1,903	Clear; breeze SE.
20	Sunrise -	714.15	20.8	69.0	1,903	Clear sky; wind SE.
	Noon -	714.29	31.1	88.0	1,930	Clear; few cumuli; wind S.
	Sunset -	707.07	25.3	77.0	2,135	Clear; clouds in NW.; wind S. 25° E.
21	Sunrise -	708.49	19.7	67.0	2,135	Clear and cloudy; wind SE.
	Noon -	703.23	28.4	83.8	2,386	Clear and clouds; wind SE.
22	Sunset -	701.15	16.0	61.0	2,262	Clear, and some clouds; slight breeze from NW.
23	Sunrise -	704.09	9.0	47.4	2,262	Sky partially overcast, wind N. 70° W.; clear in NW.
	Noon -	703.04	22.7	70.8	2,316	Clear; wind N. 70° W.
	Sunset -	699.78	18.6	65.4	2,354	Clear and calm.
24	Sunrise -	698.49	10.0	49.0	2,354	Clear; light breeze from S. 60° W.
25	Sunrise -	689.19	15.7	59.5	2,822	Clear; wind S. 20° W.

Date.	Time.	Barom.	Thermometer. Attached.	Thermometer. Free.	Altitudes.	Remarks.
1843.		*Millim.*	*Cent.*	*Fahr.*	*Feet.*	
June 25	Noon -	686.60	30.1	90.5	3,087	Clear; wind S. 35° E.
	Sunset -	685.00	21.1	70.0	3,037	Clear; slight breeze from S.; a few clouds.
26	Sunrise -	684.08	15.8	59.5	3,037	Calm and clear.
	Noon (?) -	681.02	31.9	88.3	3,322	Clear; wind S.
27	Sunrise -	672.33	12.0	53.5	3,486	Clear; overcast from NW. to NE.; slight breeze from E.
	Noon -	670.97	29.4	83.0	3,732	Overcast; breeze from N. 20° E.
	Sunset -	667.20	22.9	73.0	3,757	Clear and cumuli; breeze N.
28	Sunrise -	667.75	11.7	52.0	3,757	Clear; slight breeze from W.; a few clouds.
	Sunset -	661.63	25.8	77.0	4,070	Clear; breeze from SE.
29	Sunrise -	659.73	16.8	68.4	4,070	Clear; breeze moderate from N. 80° W.
	1h. 26m. p. m.	653.94	30.0	85.2	4,532	Clear; breeze moderate from N. 80° W.
	Sunset -	650.92	23.9	74.5	4,590	Clear; some clouds.
		650.29	19.3	66.7	4,562	Clear; light air from E.
30	Sunrise -	647.75	14.8	58.0	4,621	Clear; slight breeze from SW.
	3h. 48m. p. m.	655.76	26.5	76.0	4,402	Clear and clouds in the horizon; strong wind from NE.
	Sunset -	657.39	20.6	69.4	4,089	Heavy clouds arising since an hour; sky partially covered; appearance of bad weather; gale of wind from SE., and lightning from the same quarter.
July 1	Sunrise -	663.74	12.6	54.0	4,089	Clear; some clouds; moderate wind from N.
	Noon -	663.60	21.2	70.0	4,015	Clear; wind N.; moderate.
	Sunset -	662.02	15.8	59.0	3,976	Clear; wind NE.; moderate.
2	Sunrise -	661.75	6.6	43.0	3,976	Slight breeze from NE.
	Noon -	658.32	27.7	80.0	4,336	Clear; strong wind from S.60°E.
	Sunset -	654.05	21.9	72.0	4,419	Clear; moderate breeze from S. 35° E.
3	Sunrise -	652.49	10.0	47.0	4,419	Calm and clear.
	Noon -	649.91	31.0	87.5	4,771	Calm and clear.
	Sunset -	646.46	25.5	78.0	4,760	Slight breeze from NW.; sky covered with heavy clouds; a thunder storm passing by.
4	Sunrise -	646.19	10.6	51.5	4,760	Air SW.; clear and clouds.
	1h. 53m. p. m.	643.55	33.3	85.5	5,068	Moderate breeze from E.; clear and clouds.
	3h. 53m. p. m.	642.69	34.2	92.2	5,143	Moderate breeze from E.; clear and clouds.
	Sunset -	641.34	23.1	74.0	4,947	Calm; clear; clouds in horizon.
5	Sunrise -	642.85	14.0	53.0	4,947	Calm and clear; some clouds.
	7h. 53m. a. m.	644.51	23.7	84.4	–	Calm and clear; some clouds.
	Noon -	645.41	29.4	85.0	4,947	Slight breeze from NW.; clear; clouds; big clouds over the mountains.
	1h. 57m. p. m.	645.14	31.6	88.6	–	Slight breeze from NW.; clear; clouds; big clouds over the mountains.
	3h. 57m. p. m.	643.96	31.3	88.2	5,027	Slight breeze from NW.; thunder storm approaching.
6	5h. 3m. a. m. -	646.96	17.4	62.6	4,721	Cloudy; air from S.

Table of meteorological observations—Continued.

Date.	Time.	Barom.	Thermometer. Attached.	Thermometer. Free.	Alti-tudes.	Remarks.
1843. July 6	6h. 58m. a. m.	*Millim.* 647.91	*Cent.* 24.0	*Fahr.* 82.4	*Feet.* 4,899	Clear and clouds; slight breeze or air from S W.
7	Noon	639.55	22.0	73.0	5,103	Clear; clouds in horizon; moderate breeze from N.
	1h. 13m. p. m.	638.84	23.5	78.5	5,192	Clear; clouds in horizon; moderate breeze from N.
	5h. 43m. p. m.	635.13	21.7	69.2	5,305	Overcast with clouds; a little rain; air from N.
	Sunset -	635.93	18.0	64.0	5,203	Clear over head; cloudy horizon; mountains covered with dark clouds.
8	Sunrise -	635.61	14,0	55.5	5,203	Air S.; clear; cloudy horizon.
	Noon -	631.43	21.8	72.0	5,497	Overcast; rainy appearance; slight breeze from N. 60° W.
	1h. 29m. p. m.	630.89	22.3	73.5	5,531	Overcast; rainy appearance; slight breeze from N. 60° W.
9	Sunrise -	623.05	13.7	55,0	5,756	Overcast; air from E.
	0h. 45m. p. m.	604.64	24.2	70.1	6,759	Clear and clouds; moderate breeze from N. 25° E.
	2h. 45m. p. m.	603.49	20.0	66.5	6,770	Overcast; moderate breeze from N. 25° E.
	Sunset -	601.96	14.1	57.0	6,750	Overcast; calm; moderate breeze from N. 25° E.
10	Sunrise -	600.59	10.2	49.0	6,750	Overcast with rainy clouds; wind S. 30° E.
	Noon -	609.20	20.4	68.0	6,517	Overcast, and some blue sky, wind moderate from E.
	0h. 45m. p. m.	608.90	20.2	66.2	6,520	Overcast, and some blue sky; wind moderate from E.
	5h. 30m. p. m.	615.86	20.1	74.0	6,238	Clear; some clouds; wind slight from E.
	Sunset -	615.85	17.1	63.0	–	Clear; some clouds; wind slight from E.
	Sunset -	615.85	17.1	63.0	6,135	Clear; some clouds, wind slight from E.
11	Sunrise -	614.65	10.9	51.0	6,135	Wind SE.; clear.
	2h. 5m. p. m.	589.80	21.1	70.0	7,464	Overcast; moderate wind SE.
	Sunset -	589.46	18.8	65.0	7,305	Clear and clouds; slight breeze from S W.
12	Sunrise -	588.13	7.8	44.0	7,305	Clear; slight wind from NE.
	1h. 20m. p. m.	611.99	32.0	87.5	6,544	Clear; slight wind from NE.
	3h. 20m. p. m.	611.61	32.4	89.5	6,577	Clear; moderate wind from S.
	Sunset -	620.79	21.5	69.5	5,797	Clouds, and some clear sky; calm.
13	Sunrise -	621.40	8.1	46.0	5,797	Clear; breeze from N W.
	Noon .	633.51	30.8	87.0	5,518	Clear, and some clouds; wind SE.
	4h. 28m. p. m.	633.00	30.8	85.0	5,533	Clear, and some clouds; wind SE.
14	Sunrise (?) -	639:60	13.8	58.2	5,086	Clear and calm.
	Noon -	648.84	32.1	90.0	4,885	Clear and clouds; calm.
	1h. 30m. p. m.	648.20	35.7	88.5	5,030	Fresh breeze from E.
	4h. p. m. -	646.51	28.0	82.5	5,038	Calm; thunder storm approaching.
15	Sunrise -	647.85	15.8	59.3	4,655	Clear; a few clouds; calm.
	8h. 50m. p. m.	648.39	25.9	83.0	4,795	Clear and clouds; flaws of wind from SW.
	Noon -	648.08	32.9	91.0	4,881	Clear; clouds; calm.

Date.	Time.	Barom.	Thermometer. Attached.	Thermometer. Free.	Altitudes.	Remarks.
1843.		*Millim.*	*Cent.*	*Fahr.*	*Feet.*	
July 15	2h. 20m. p. m.	647.49	33.9	94.2	4,929	Clear and clouds; flaws from SW.
	4h. 20m. p. m.	646.69	28.7	83.5	4,890	Overcast; moderate breeze from SW.
	Sunset -	646.70	24.0	74.8	4,774	Overcast; calm; dark clouds in E.
16	Sunrise -	646.36	13.3	57.0	4,774	Calm; clear; few cumuli.
	Noon -	637.37	28.2	82.0	5,324	Strong wind from N. 20° E.; squall of rain just passing over; masses of cumuli.
	1h. 50m. p. m.	637.37	29.2	84.5	5,456	Weather growing worse.
17	Sunrise -	634.19	15.6	58.2	5,292	Cloudy; some clear sky; calm.
	Noon -	625.37	26.5	77.0	5,851	Wind E.; clear; some cumuli; dark clouds above the mountains.
	1h. 6m. p. m.	625.37	27.1	78.5	5,863	Wind E.; clear; some cumuli; dark clouds above the mountains.
18	Sunrise -	617.88	10.6	49.0	5,958	Clear; slight breeze from W.
	5h. 27m. a. m.	617.35	12.4	54.0	6,020	Clear; slight breeze from W.
	10h. 50m. a. m.	615.17	27.8	73.0	6,318	Clear and calm; temperature of upper spring = 69°.0 Fahr., lower spring = 60°.5 Fahr.
	Noon -	615.25	29.2	78.6	6,351	Clear; some cumuli; darker clouds over the mountains; slight breeze SE.
	Sunset -	613.90	20.3	66.0	6,260	Cloudy; wind NW., but changing every instant; temperature of upper spring = 61°.0, lower spring = 58°.0 Fahr.
19	Sunrise -	613.04	13.6	57.5	6,260	Clear; a slight breeze from NW.; temperature of upper spring = 57°.8, lower spring 54°.3 Fahr.
	Noon -	614.04	29.7	86.0	6,337	Moderate breeze from N.; clouds; some clear sky; thunder storm in N.
	1h. 50m. p. m.	613.26	26.0	77.5	6,391	Cloudy over the mountains; clear in N.; breeze NE.
	Sunset -	606.80	18.6	62.5	6,527	Cloudy; thunder storm has passed; clear above the mountains; breeze from S., but changing every moment to every quarter.
20	Sunrise -	604.94	7.6	44.2	6,527	Clear and calm.
	1h. 22m. p. m.	608.56	26.9	77.2	6,613	Clear; few cumuli; slight breeze from N.
	2h. 52m. p. m.	608.16	28.2	78.5	6,647	Clear; few cumuli; slight breeze from N.
	Sunset -	615.34	20.6	69.2	6,122	Cloudy; calm.
21	Sunrise -	614.60	7.4	44.8	6,122	Slight breeze from SE.; clear.
	1h. 4m. p. m.	633.30	28.5	83.5	5,488	Clear; some cumuli; slight breeze from NW.
	2h. 32m. p. m.	632.57	24.3	75.0	5,457	Thunder storm, with rain, advancing from NW.
	Sunset -	636.25	21.8	71.0	5,192	Cloudy; some clear sky; calm.
22	Sunrise -	634.50	7.2	44.4	5,192	Clear; air from SE.
	0h. 37m. p. m.	641.03	31.9	85.0	5,161	Clear; air from NW.
	2h. 8m. p. m.	641.03	31.6	86.0	5,163	Clear; air from NW.
	Sunset -	641.19	22.7	73.0	4,974	Clear; slight breeze from E.

Date.	Time.	Barom.	Thermometer. Attached.	Thermometer. Free.	Altitudes.	Remarks.
1843.		*Millim.*	*Cent.*	*Fahr.*	*Feet.*	
July 23	Sunrise -	639.62	7.4	45.0	4,974	Clear; air from E.
	Noon -	645.29	29.8	85.0	4,959	Clear; slight breeze from E.
	2h. p. m. -	645.09	36.6	90.0	5,026	Clear; slight breeze from E.
	4h. p. m. -	644.49	30.4	88.3	5,080	Clear; slight breeze from E.
	Sunset	643.35	21.8	74.0	4,940	Clear and calm.
24	5h. 54m. a. m.	642.95	13.0	55.0	4,940	Clear; air from W.
	2h. 4m. p. m.	641.70	32.8	89.0	5,143	Clear; air from W.; clouds in horizon.
	4h. 4m. p. m.	640.95	33.4	88.5	5,179	Clear; wind from E.
25	Sunrise -	641.39	13.4	55.0	4,965	Clear and clouds; wind N.
	10h. 5m. a. m.	643.74	27.7	81.5	4,991	Clear and clouds; wind N.
	2h. 5m. p. m.	643.00	28.6	82.0	5,032	Clear and clouds; wind N.
	4h. 5m. p. m.	642.48	27.8	81.5	5,048	Clear and clouds; wind N.
	Sunset -	643.50	20.8	69.0	4,857	Clear and clouds; breeze from S.
26	Sunrise -	644.35	14.4	58.0	4,857	Overcast; air from N.
	Sunset -	644.00	17.8	64.0	4,866	Clear and clouds; air from E.
27	1h. 16m. p. m.	642.29	31.4	87.0	5,128	Clear and clouds; breeze from N.
	3h. p. m. -	641.54	32.7	87.2	5,170	Clear and clouds; thunder storm coming up from N.
	Sunset -	636.00	24.4	70.0	5,184	Clear and clouds; breeze from N.
28	Sunrise -	643.11	15.0	58.8	5,184	Overcast; calm.
	Noon -	637.78	22.1	71.0	5,210	Overcast; breeze S. 25° W.
	1h. 26m. p. m.	637.40	21.2	68.2	5,201	Beginning to rain.
29	4h. 26m. a. m.	631.85	12.0	53.0	5,336	Fine rain; calm.
	6h. 56m. p. m.	627.50	14.0	55.5	5,557	Rainy.
30	5h. 11m. a. m.	627.64	11.6	52.5	5,530	Misty; rainy appearance; calm.
	Noon -	612.53	20.0	64.5	6,339	Clear and clouds; slight breeze from SE.
	1h. 26m. p. m.	612.24	20.6	65.3	6,359	Clear and clouds; slight breeze from SE.
	Sunset -	585.52	12.3	54.0	7,521	Clear; moderate breeze from S.
31	Sunrise -	584.40	10.8	48.0	7,521	Clear; mist still in horizon; breeze W.
	Noon -	582.29	22.6	69.0	7,844	Clear and clouds; wind N. 24° W.
	0h. 36m. p. m.	582.29	22.5	69.5	7,847	Clear and clouds; wind N. 24° W.
	Sunset -	592.70	17.7	64.0	7,178	Clear; cloudy in horizon; wind E.
Aug. 1	Sunrise -	592.20	6.2	42.4	7,178	Clear and calm.
	Noon -	592.19	24.0	72.0	7,382	Clouds; a little rain; a little clear; slight breeze from NE.
	0h. 54m. p. m.	592.06	24.8	74.0	7,408	Clouds; a little rain; a little clear; slight breeze from NE.
	Sunset -	582.75	16.4	62.0	7,730	Clear and clouds; breeze from NE.
2	Sunrise -	580.55	11.0	51.6	7,730	Clear; wind W.
	Noon -	579.79	22.2	73.0	7,994	Clear; clouds; strong wind from W.
	1h. 24m. p. m.	579.40	22.2	70.5	7,995	Clear; clouds; strong wind from W.
3	Sunrise -	573.37	1.2	33.0	7,602	Clear and calm.
	9h. 52m. a. m.	572.37	19.0	68.8	8,314	Sky covered with thin misty clouds; breeze S. 70° W.
	Sunset -	592.95	18.4	66.0	7,143	Clear; clouds; moderate breeze from W.
4	Sunrise -	593.64	6.2	33.5	7,143	Clear; few cumuli; calm.
	0h. 32m. p. m.	602.88	26.3	79.5	6,951	Cloudy; some clear sky; slight breeze from S.
	1h. 42m. p. m.	602.88	28.1	80.0	6,963	Cloudy; strong breeze from S.
5	8h. 50m. a. m.	604.71	17.5	64.0	6,727	Clear and calm.
	9h. 50m. a. m.	604.80	19.6	67.2	6,755	Clear and calm.
	10h. 50m. a. m.	604.60	21.3	69.5	6,786	Clear and calm.

Date.	Time.	Barom.	Thermometer. Attached.	Thermometer. Free.	Altitudes.	Remarks.
1843.		*Millim.*	*Cent.*	*Fahr.*	*Feet.*	
Aug. 5.	Noon -	604.65	24.4	75.0	6,825	Clear; calm; cloudy.
	0h. 50m. p. m.	604.45	25.5	79.5	6,881	Clear; calm; cloudy.
	1h. 50m. p. m.	604.45	25.8	78.2	6,875	Clear; calm; cloudy.
	2h. 50m. p. m.	604.45	26.0	77.5	6,871	Clear; calm; cloudy,
	3h. 50m. p. m.	603.85	26.5	75.2	6,888	Clear; W. wind in squalls.
	4h. 50m. p. m.	603.44	25.8	95.0	–	Free thermometer in the sun.
	Sunset -	603.09	20.8	70.0	6,743	Clear; some clouds; W. wind in squalls.
6	Sunrise -	602.70	7.5	46.0	6,743	Clear and calm.
	Sunset -	588.40	19.3	63.5	7,490	Cloudy; thunder storm approaching; air from E.; temperature of spring, 46° Fahr.
7	Sunrise -	587.19	8.0	43.0	6,040	Air from W.; clear.
	1h. 50m. p. m.	597.59	27.0	79.5	7,196	Clear and clouds; breeze from W.
	Sunset -	596.70	21.4	69.8	7,000	Clear and cloudy; slight breeze from W.
8	Sunrise -	596.40	12.6	52.0	7,000	Cloudy; wind from E.
	2h. 28m. p. m.	606.81	25.5	78.0	6,784	Cloudy; wind from S.
9	Sunrise -	603.84	11.1	51.0	6,594	Cloudy; rain last night; wind from N.
	Noon -	611.16	24.8	77.0	6,483	Clouds and clear; wind NW.
	1h. 7m. p. m. -	610.77	26.5	78.0	6,517	Clouds and clear; wind NW.
10	Sunrise -	614.05	6.8	41.0	6,028	Clear; some clouds; calm.
	Noon -	610.80	26.6	78.0	6,502	Clear; squalls from all points.
	Sunset -	607.77	22.0	71.8	6,557	Moderate breeze from W.; clear; horizon dirty.
11	Sunrise -	605.56	12.8	56.5	6,557	Clear; fresh breeze from W.
	2h. 8m. p. m. -	600.30	22.6	71.0	6,926	Hazy; fresh breeze from W.
	Sunset -	599.39	16.8	61.2	6,720	Clear and clouds; moderate wind from NW.
12	Sunrise -	600.14	1.6	31.8	–	Clear; calm; white frost.
	1h. 20m. p. m.	587.45	17.5	60.5	7,446	Clear; calm; moderate wind from NW.
	Sunset -	587.76	11.6	52.8	7,221	Calm and clear.
13	Sunrise -	587.74	— 1.5	28.0	7,221	Calm and clear; white frost.
	10h. 2m. a. m.	587.03	17.9	64.2	7,489	At the divide; moderate breeze from NW.
	Noon -	592.92	21.6	67.0	7,242	Moderate breeze from NW.
	0h. 40m. p. m,	592.65	22.1	68.0	7,265	Moderate breeze from NW.
	Sunset -	595.20	19.8	67.2	6,951	Clear and calm.
14	Sunrise -	595.27	1.2	32.2	6,951	Clear; air from NW.
	10h. 50m. a. m.	602.45	24.8	75.2	6,846	Clear; slight breeze from S.
	Noon -	602.44	29.2	86.1	6,941	Clear; slight breeze from S.
	Sunset -	602.52	23.8	75.0	6,667	Clear; slight breeze from NW.
15	Sunrise -	604.45	2.4	34.0	6,667	Clear; wind from N.
	2h. p. m.	611.50	29.2	84.2	6,546	Clear over head; dirty horizon; calm.
	3h. p. m. -	611.28	29.8	86.5	6,516	Clear over head; dirty horizon; calm.
	Sunset -	610.94	19.0	65.2	6,238	Clear over head; dirty horizon; calm.
16	Sunrise -	610.36	3.2	37.0	6,238	Clear and calm.
	Noon -	613.34	30.1	82.0	6,399	Clear over head; horizon dirty; wind squally from N.
	Sunset -	613.31	23.6	74.3	6,150	Clear over head; horizon dirty; slight breeze from N.
17	Sunrise -	614.24	3.9	38.4	6,150	Clear; foggy horizon; air from SW.

Date.	Time.	Barom.	Thermometer.		Alti-tudes-	Remarks.
			Attached.	Free.		
1843.		*Millim.*	*Cent.*	*Fahr.*	*Feet.*	
Aug. 17	2h. 3m. p. m.	610.45	29.1	84.0	6,558	Clear; foggy horizon; calm.
	Sunset -	610.68	18.1	64.0	6,234	Clear; horizon more pure; calm.
18	Sunrise -	611.83	5.3	38.1	6,234	Clear; air from N. 80° W.; hazy horizon.
	2h. p. m. -	607.04	31.5	82.6	6,735	Clear; slight breeze from W.
	3h. p. m. -	607.04	31.9	82.0	6,732	Clear; slight breeze from W.
19	Sunrise -	606.30	4.6	38.6	6,361	Smoky horizon; calm and clear.
	Noon -	608.85	32.9	88.0	6,640	Clear; few cumuli; breeze in squalls from SW.
	0h. 46m. p. m.	608.54	33.2	89.0	6,719	Clear; few cumuli; breeze in squalls from SW.
	Sunset -	602.75	25.0	72.2	6,661	Clear and calm; horizon not pure.
20	Sunrise -	602.05	4.2	37.0	6,661	Clear, and dirty horizon; breeze from NW.
	Noon -	596.33	27.7	80.5	7,227	Moderate wind N. 60° W.; hazy sun.
	1h. p. m.	596.33	30.0	82.5	7,257	Moderate wind N. 60° W.; hazy sun.
	4h. 10m. p. m.	575.87	27.2	79.2	8,234	Dividing ridge; smoky; sun faint; scattered cumuli; thunder storm some distance in E.; high wind N. 60° W.
21	Sunrise -	607.06	6.6	43.8	6,358	Smoky; sun faint; cumuli; air SE.
	Noon -	614.45	31.6	89.0	6,416	Smoky; sun faint; calm.
	1h. 5m. p. m.	613.93	31.0	87.0	6,425	Smoky; sun faint; wind in squalls from S.
	Sunset -	612.41	18.8	65.0	6,185	Cumuli; thunder storm at a distance; slight breeze from N.
22	Sunrise -	612.29	4.6	36.5	6,185	Smoky; scattered cumuli; calm.
	Noon -	616.50	28.7	84.8	6,281	Very smoky; sun faint; cumuli; calm.
	1h. 30m. p. m.	616.02	27.2	79.0	6,264	Very smoky; high wind from N. 10° W.; rainy appearance.
23	Sunrise -	616.03	8.6	47.2	5,989	Smoky; clear; cold breeze from S.
24	Noon -	614.88	25.2	75.2	6,290	Wind in squalls from NW.
	0h. 45m. p. m.	614.88	25.7	74.5	6,288	Clear; very smoky.
	Sunset -	618.77	14.2	56.4	5,843	Clear and calm; very smoky.
25	Sunrise -	621.22	7.7	45.4	5,843	Clear; hazy; cold wind from SE.
	Noon -	624.34	26.0	72.2	5,841	Clear; hazy; breeze in squalls from SE.
	Sunset -	621.83	16.8	62.5	5,738	Clear; hazy; calm; temperature of Big Spring = 65°.0 Fahr.
26	Sunrise -	620.84	0.	28.5	5,738	Clear; smoky; calm; temperature of { Big Spring = 56°.0 Fahr. Steam hole = 81°.5 " Steamboat = 87°.0 "
	Noon -	623.64	31.4	83.3	5,958	Clear; smoky; moderate breeze from S. 25° E.
	Sunset -	638.67	22.6	68.3	5,012	Clear; smoky; calm.
27	Sunrise -	637.64	0.	29.0	5,012	Clear; smoky; some cumuli; calm.
	Noon -	635.86	24.7	77.0	5,320	Cloudy; rainy appearance; not quite so smoky; breeze S. 70° W.
		635.70	26.1	79.5	5,347	Partly clouded sky.

Date.	Time.	Barom.	Thermometer.		Alti-tudes.	Remarks.
			Attached.	Free.		
1843.		*Millim.*	*Cent.*	*Fahr.*	*Feet.*	
Aug. 27	Sunset -	636.25	20.8	69.2	5,142	Dark clouds; very little blue; slight breeze from S.
28	Sunrise -	638.33	14.6	55.0	5,142	Slight breeze from N.; light clouds all over the sky; thunder storm last night, with moderate rain, which has made the air clear.
	2h. p. m. -	648.50	28.3	78.0	4,764	Fresh breeze S. 20° E.; clear over head; clouds; rain in the horizon.
	Sunset -	647.77	20.3	65.0	4,681	Calm; clear; cumuli.
29	Sunrise -	646.70	14.1	54.0	4,681	Air from NW.; dark rainy clouds moving on the horizon; over head not so dark; considerable rain last night; thunder and wind.
	Noon -	629.32	21.8	71.0	5,561	Clear and clouds; wind from E.
	1h. p. m. -	629.55	25.1	76.0	5,595	Clear and clouds; wind from E.
30	Sunrise -	623.40	4.2	39.0	5,570	Clear; clouds in horizon; constant thunder storms, with rain last night; calm.
	Noon -	637.29	19.8	67.0	5,169	Wind SW.; clouds and blue sky.
	1h. 30m. p. m.	636.95	22.7	73.0	5,228	Strong wind SW.; clouds and blue sky.
	Sunset -	644.49	19.8	64.0	4,723	Calm; almost overcast with heavy clouds.
31	Sunrise -	646.04	8.2	44.5	4,723	Clear; slight breeze from S. 70° W.
	Noon -	649.63	26.6	71.0	4,666	Clear; clouds; calm; began to rain at sunset, and continued almost the whole night.
Sept. 1	4h. 48m. p. m.	659.55	20.2	65.0	4,189	Clear and clouds; fresh breeze from S.
	Sunset -	658.91	12.8	54.5	4,093	Clear and calm; few clouds.
2	Sunrise -	659.04	6.2	41.2	4,093	Clear and calm.
3	5h. 30m. a. m.	658.39	8.5	45.5	4,113	Clear; air from N.
	8h. 50m. a. m.	660.14	22.6	61.3	4,170	Clear; air from S.
	9h. 50m. a. m.	660.04	22.0	66.0	4,190	Clear; air from S.
	10h. 50m. a. m.	660.15	23.2	69.0	4,195	Clear; air from S.
	Noon -	660.27	25.2	72.5	4,222	Clear; slight breeze from S.
	2h. p. m. -	659.28	23.7	79.0	4,282	Clear; slight breeze from S.
	Sunset -	656.83	16.2	60.5	4,247	Clear and calm.
4	5h. 33m. a. m.	655.78	7.5	42.0	4,247	Clear and calm.
	Sunset -	653.10	22.8	75.5	4.526	Calm; clear, and clouds in the horizon.
5	Sunrise -	652.39	18.0	64.5	4,526	Wind brisk from SE.; clouds; rainy appearance; there was a thunder storm at a distance, and some rain last night.
	Sunset -	650.11	18.8	65.0	4,496	Clear over head; dark clouds in horizon; thunder storm, with rain in the afternoon.
6	Sunrise -	652.03	8.6	45.5	4,496	Clear and calm; some cumuli in the horizon.
	Sunset -	656.25	15.7	55.0	4,173	Clear and some cumuli; calm; thunder storm, with some rain and a gale this afternoon.
7	Sunrise -	658 21	5.3	39.5	4,173	Clear and calm.

Date.	Time.	Barom.	Thermometer. Attached.	Thermometer. Free.	Altitudes.	Remarks.
1843.		*Millim.*	*Cent.*	*Fahr.*	*Feet.*	
Sept. 7	6h. 50m. a. m.	658.95	8.6	47.0	4,086	Clear and calm.
	7h. 50m. a. m.	659.44	12.8	55.7	4,119	Clear and calm.
	8h. 50m. a. m.	659.89	15.0	59.2	4,125	Clear and calm.
	9h. 50m. a. m.	660.09	17.8	64.5	4,152	Clear and calm.
	10h. 50m. a. m.	660.10	19.6	67.2	4,172	Clear, and gentle breeze from N. 25° E.
	Noon -	659.88	24.6	70.0	4,218	Clear, and wind in squalls from same quarter.
	0h. 50m. p. m.	659.42	23.3	71.2	4,235	Clear, and wind in squalls from S. 25° W.
	1h. 50m. p. m.	659.66	27.0	75.0	4,258	Clear, and wind in squalls from S. 25° W.
	2h. 50m. p. m.	659.40	27.8	74.3	4,271	Clear, and wind in squalls from S. 25° W.
	3h. 50m. p. m.	659.12	26.9	72.0	4,270	Clear, and some clouds in the horizon.
	4h. 50m. p. m.	659.03	26.8	73.0	4,276	Clear, and some clouds in the horizon.
	Sunset -	657.69	15.7	61.5	4,181	Clear over head; light clouds in horizon; calm.
8	Sunrise -	656.59	5.8	40.9	4,181	Clear; clouds in the horizon; calm.
	4h. p. m. -	657.22	23.2	73.0	4,320	Clear over head; clouds in the horizon; air from SW.
	Sunset -	656.71	18.7	64.0	4,226	Clear over head; clouds in the horizon; air from SW.; calm.
9	Sunrise -	656.39	10.0	49.2	4,226	Clear and calm.
	0h. 18m. p. m.	658.39	28.2	75.0	4,276	Clear over head; clouds in horizon; air from SE.
	4h. 40m. p. m.	638.82	27.1	–	5,159	On the peak of Crater island; air from SE.
	5h. 23m. p. m.	656.05	24.6	72.0	4,336	On the shore of the lake; air from SE.
10	Sunrise -	654.11	15.2	59.0	4,336	Clear; scattered cumuli; a gale of wind S. 55° E.
	0h. 52m. p. m.	654.22	30.3	86.8	4,508	At the foot of the peninsula; very violent gale.
	1h. 36m. p. m.	643.16	31.0	89.5	5,020	At the top of the peninsula; blue sky, with scattered fleecy clouds; heavy near the horizon; wind S. 20° E.
11	6h. 50m. a. m.	652.04	13.0	53.0	4,360	The whole sky covered with rainy clouds; thunder, lightning, and rain almost all the night.
	8h. a. m. -	652.57	14.2	58.0	4,363	Clearing up; calm.
	9h. a. m. -	652.65	11.9	53.0	4,354	Strong wind from N. 25° E.; rainy clouds.
	10h. a. m. -	653.01	12.7	55.0	4,324	Strong wind from N. 25° E.; rainy clouds.
	11h. a. m. -	653.60	13.7	57.0	4,313	Strong wind from N. 25° E.; some blue sky.
	Noon -	653.62	12.2	54.0	4,293	Sky covered with rainy clouds; strong wind from N. 25° E.
	1h. p. m. -	654.06	14.8	60.9	4,315	Sky covered with rainy clouds; some blue sky.
	2h. p. m. -	655.33	22.7	80.0	4,353	More clear sky; sun; moderate wind from N. 25° E. Free thermometer in the sun.

Date.	Time.	Barom.	Thermometer. Attached.	Thermometer. Free.	Altitudes.	Remarks.
1843.		*Millim.*	*Cent.*	*Fahr.*	*Feet.*	
Sept. 11	3h. p. m. -	655.88	22.7	64.0	4,289	Clear; clouds scattered; moderate wind from N. 25° E.
	4h. p. m. -	656.65	21.8	63.0	4,247	Clear; clouds scattered; sun; moderate wind from N. 25° E.
	5h. p. m. -	656.76	20.6	60.2	4,222	Clear; clouds scattered; sun; moderate wind from N. 25° E.
	Sunset -	655.50	9.8	52.2	4,080	Clear.
12	Sunrise -	657.56	2.3	33.0	4,080	Clear and calm.
	Sunset -	655.48	9.2	47.2	4,119	Clear and clouds; calm.
13	Sunrise -	654.88	3.0	35.5	4,119	Clear and clouds; calm.
	4h. 50m. p. m.	657.51	27.2	82.0	4,283	Clear; scattered clouds; sun; calm.
	Sunset -	656.76	18.8	66.5	4,179	Clear; scattered clouds; sun; calm.
14	Sunrise -	655.12	8.2	46.4	4,179	Clear; few scattered clouds; slight breeze from NW.
	3h. 50m. p. m.	651.38	30.0	80.0	4,564	Clear and clouds; sun; moderate breeze from SE.
	Sunset -	650.25	20.6	67.5	4,444	Clear; moderate breeze from SE.
15	Sunrise -	648.28	3.5	37.5	4,444	Clear; horizon partly covered with cumuli; air from NW.
	3h. 43m. p. m.	640.15	30.3	83.0	5,081	Clear and scattered clouds; sun; fresh wind from S.
	Sunset -	638.80	22.6	74.0	5,028	Clear and scattered clouds; sun; fresh wind from S.
16	Sunrise -	637.07	11.1	52.0	5,028	Calm and clear.
	3h. 56m. p. m.	604.04	14.6	58.0	6,280	Dividing ridge, 70 feet below the summit; violent gale from N. 65° W.; cumuli in same quarter.
	6h. 20m. p. m.	630.79	11.1	50.5	5,144	In a valley below the divide; sky clear; cold wind from NW.
17	6h. 9m. a. m.	631.37	—5.5	21.5	5,144	Sky clear and calm.
	3h. 56m. p. m.	642.85	20.0	65.2	4,849	Sky clear; wind from W.
	Sunset -	642.35	15.0	58.6	4,667	Sky clear; wind from W.
18	Sunrise -	643.43	—2.9	25.1	4,667	Clear; calm; bank of fog in N.
	Sunset -	643.31	16.4	60.5	4,779	Fort Hall; clear and calm.
19	Sunset -	645.12	6.3	43.0	4,764	Sky covered with rainy dark clouds; strong wind from S. 25° W.
20	Sunrise -	645.81	3.7	34.0	4,764	Rain and snow during the whole night; wind N.
	0h. 13m. p. m.	649.12	8.6	44.8	4,434	Wind N.; sky covered with clouds.
21	Sunrise -	651.48	—0.2	29.5	4,239	Clear and calm; rain last night.
	9h. 50m. a. m.	652.48	12.0	50.2	4,342	Clear and calm; clouds in horizon.
	10h. 50m. a. m.	652.59	17.2	55.6	4,387	Almost cloudy all over; air SE.
	Sunset -	649.94	9.5	48.0	4,501	
22	Sunrise -	646.00	5.6	41.0	4,504	Wind S.; overcast with rainy clouds; begins to rain.
	Sunset -	646.39	6.0	42.5	4,519	Moderate wind from S.; sky partly clear; partly covered with rainy clouds for the greatest part of the day.
23	Sunrise -	647.50	0.8	32.0	4,519	Calm; overcast; snow falling thick.
	7h. a. m. -	647.76	6.1	32.0	4,487	Calm; overcast; snow falling thick.

Table of meteorological observations—Continued.

Date.	Time.	Barom.	Thermometer.		Alti. tudes.	Remarks.
			Attached.	Free.		
1843.		*Millim.*	*Cent.*	*Fahr.*	*Feet.*	
Sept. 23	8h. a. m. -	649.12	12.8	32.0	4,463	Calm; overcast; snow falling thick.
	9h. a. m. -	648.90	10.2	35.0	4,380	Calm; overcast; snow falling thick.
	10h. a. m. -	648.31	8.8	40.0	4,511	Air from N. 20° W.; snow falling not so thick.
	11h. a. m. -	649.29	18.3	43.0	4,531	Heavy wind from N.; snow turned into rain.
	Noon -	649.16	17.8	43.0	4,534	A little rain; somewhat clearer in the N. and E. horizon.
	1h. p. m. -	648.95	20.2	47.0	4,566	More clearing up in *that* corner; a little blue spot.
	2h. p. m. -	648.65	16.4	47.5	4,567	More moderate; no rain; more clear sky in N.
	3h. p. m. -	649.44	18.6	49.5	4,554	More moderate; no rain; more clear sky in N.
	4h. p. m. -	649.43	17.8	49.5	4,550	More moderate; no rain; more clear sky in N.
	5h. p. m. -	649.50	18.2	49.5	4,550	Wind N.; sky improving from NW. to NE.
	Sunset -	649.99	19.8	45.5	4,520	Nearly calm; clear over head; clouds scattered.
	7h. p. m. -	649.80	19.0	45.0	4,521	Moderate wind from N.; sky cloudy; clear spots between.
	8h. p. m. -	649.80	17.0	42.5	4,499	Air from N.; sky cloudy; some clear spots.
	9h. p. m. -	651.14	14.2	41.0	4,428	More clear.
	10h. p. m. -	650.88	12.9	40.0	4,422	Cloudy; a few stars peeping out.
	11h. p. m. -	650.94	12.7	37.0	4,406	Air from NE.; sky bright, except in E.
	Midnight -	650.51	8.6	37.0	4,403	Air from NE.; southern sky nearly overcast; northern sky partly bright, partly covered with scattered clouds.
24	Sunrise -	651.55	15.6	35.0	4,388	Calm; overcast; clear in the W. horizon.
	Noon -	653.60	13.0	53.2	4,357	Breeze from S.; sky clear; some scattered clouds.
	Sunset -	654.85	10.5	54.0	4,240	Clear; breeze from S.
25	Sunrise -	655.96	15.7	46.8	4,240	Clear; gale from S.
	2h. p. m. -	655.25	17.8	64.0	4,297	Clear and clouds; sun; wind S.
	3h. p. m. -	654.69	16.5	61.5	4,305	Clear and clouds; wind S. 72° E.
	4h. p. m. -	653.99	15.6	60.0	4,324	More clouds.
	5h. p. m. -	653.62	14.0	57.0	4,319	More clouds; dark in the W.
	Sunset -	653.07	12.8	55.0	4,252	Almost overcast.
26	6h. 20m. a. m.	653.39	6.0	40.2	4,252	Cloudy; clear; rain last night; wind S. 25° W.
	Noon -	650.84	9.8	49.2	4,340	Cloudy; rainy appearance; fresh wind from SW.
	Sunset -	654.28	8.0	44.5	4,045	Clouds and clear; wind sharp from SW.
27	Sunrise -	656.35	—1.5	24.0	4,045	Clear and calm; white frost last night.
	Sunset -	651.46	8.0	46.5	4,367	Overcast with clouds; cold wind from SE.
28	Sunrise -	646.16	6.4	40.0	4,367	Overcast with rainy clouds; slight breeze from S.
	Sunset -	654.60	6.8	45.0	3,990	Gale from S. 70° W.; clouds and clear; thunder in N.

Date.	Time.	Barom.	Thermometer. Attached.	Thermometer. Free.	Altitudes.	Remarks.
1843.		*Millim.*	*Cent.*	*Fahr.*	*Feet.*	
Sept. 29	Sunrise -	660.54	4.2	36.4	3,990	Cloudy and clear overhead; wind S. 70° W.
30	Sunrise -	663.35	12.0	28.5	3,727	Light clouds; air from SE.
	Sunset -	682.21	18.6	65.5	3,173	Clear; few clouds; wind squally from W.
Oct. 1	Sunrise -	677.10	19.5	55.5	3,173	Clear; wind from W.
	Sunset -	688.21	21.8	74.0	2,761	Clear and calm.
2	Sunrise -	689.56	16.0	48.0	2,761	Clear and calm.
	Sunset -	684.90	20.5	70.0	2,902	Clear and calm.
·3	Sunrise -	684.81	20.2	42.0	2,902	Air from S. 65° E.; light clouds and clear.
4	Sunrise -	689.87	14.2	47.0	2,649	Calm; cumuli; clear.
	Sunset -	673.04	13.0	57.5	3,172	Cloudy; gale from NW.
5	Sunrise -	677.65	—0.2	32.0	3,172	Calm and clear.
	Sunset -	672.65	9.2	47.0	3,226	Overcast; wind NW.
6	Sunrise -	675.99	7.7	46.0	3,226	Overcast; rainy appearance; wind from NW.
	Sunset -	678.41	10.7	50.8	3,061	Clear; some scattered cumuli; sun; wind NW.
7	Sunrise -	679.09	7.9	45.5	3,061	Clear; wind NW.
	Sunset -	698.91	14.8	57.0	2,302	Clear; breeze from NW.
8	Sunrise -	697.85	4.8	38.2	2,302	Calm and clear.
	Sunset -	702.65	16.9	62.0	2,197	Calm; clear, but cloudy in the horizon.
9	Sunrise -	699.76	2.3	36.0	2,197	Clear and calm.
	Sunset -	702.26	20.6	68.5	2,192	Clear and scattered cumuli; calm.
10	Sunrise -	704.11	8.3	43.0	2,192	Clear over head; cumuli in the horizon; calm.
	Sunset -	706.21	17.3	62.5	1,998	Clear and calm.
11	Sunrise -	706.44	0.8	33.0	1,998	Clear; air from E.
	Sunset -	706.85	19.2	64.0	2,000	Clear and calm; few scattered cumuli.
12	Sunrise -	704.78	—4.3	23.0	2,000	Clear and calm.
	Sunset -	709.43	17.2	62.0	1,879	Clear and calm.
13	Sunrise -	709.08	—0.8	28.8	1,879	Clear; few cumuli; air from W.
	Sunset -	703.46	15.5	59.0	2,144	Clear and light clouds; calm.
14	Sunrise -	705.46	9.0	46.0	2,144	Clear and calm.
	Sunset -	684.68	10.8	50.0	2,802	Clear and calm.
15	Sunrise -	685.25	5.0	40.0	2,802	Clear; few light clouds; calm.
	Sunset -	678.00	16.2	61.0	3,100	Clear, and some cumuli; calm.
16	Sunrise -	674.73	—6.6	16.0	3,100	Calm; clear, with few cumuli.
	Sunset -	676.85	16.0	60.8	3,092	Wind E.; clear and clouds.
17	Sunrise -	677.66	—2.3	25.0	3,092	Clear and clouds; calm.
	Sunset -	682.34	17.0	62.5	2,940	Cloudy; wind SE.
18	Sunrise -	684.65	18.6	48.0	2,940	Overcast; rain began an hour before sunrise; calm.
	Sunset -	690.40	10.0	47.0	2,607	Cloudy; rain in the morning; air from N.
19	Sunrise -	688.72	3.5	35.0	2,607	Misty; dew point = 32°.5 Fahr.; calm.
	0h. 44m. p. m.	688.72	12.4	52.0	2,700	At the foot of Blue mountains.
	Sunset -	657.20	7.6	46.5	3,831	Blue mountains.
20	Sunrise -	659.61	4.3	37.5	3,831	Clear and calm; a bank of clouds in SE. horizon.
	8h. 26m. a. m.	636.82	10.6	47.6	4,766	Blue mountains.
	Sunset -	628.54	2.8	36.3	4,989	Blue mountains; clear and calm.
21	Sunrise -	628.65	0.8	30.0	4,989	Blue mountains; clear and calm.

Table of observations with the thermometer.

Date.		Time.		Thermometer.	Remarks.
1843.				Deg. Fahr.	
Oct.	27	Sunrise	-	-	Fort Walahwalah.
		Sunset	-	66.0	
	28	Sunrise	-	52.0	
		Sunset	.	59.0	
	29	Sunrise	-	38.0	
		Sunset	-	50.0	
	30	Sunrise	-	28.0	
		Sunset	-	53.0	
	31	Sunrise	-	24.0	
		Sunset	-	54.0	
Nov.	1	Sunrise	-	34.0	
		Sunset	-	56.3	
	2	Sunrise	-	36.0	
		Sunset	-	46.0	
	3	Sunrise	-	32.0	
		Sunset	-	44.0	
	4	Sunrise	-	30.0	
		Sunset	-	52.0	
	5	Sunrise	-	36.0	
		Sunset	-	50.0	
	6	Sunrise	-	34.0	
	7	Sunset	-	49.0	
	8	Sunrise	-	42.0	
	12	Sunrise	-	44.0	
		Sunset	-	50.0	
	13	Sunrise	-	42.0	
		Sunset	-	51.5	
	23	Sunrise	-	36.0	
		Sunset	-	41.0	
	24	Sunrise	-	38.0	
		Sunset	-	40.5	
	25	Sunrise	-	26.0	
	26	Sunrise	-	20.0	
	27	Sunrise	-	—2.5	
		Sunset	-	28.0	
	28	Sunrise	-	18.0	
		Sunset		28.0	
	29	Sunrise	-	21.0	
	30	Sunrise	-	37.0	
		Sunset	-	30.0	
Dec.	1	Sunrise	-	32.0	
		Sunset	-	42.0	
	2	Sunrise	-	28.0	
		Sunset	-	34.0	
	3	Sunrise	-	18.5	
	4	Sunrise	-	19.6	
		Sunset	-	34.0	
	5	Sunrise	-	38.0	
		Sunset	.	28.2	
	6	Sunrise	-	26.0	
		Sunset	-	40.0	
	7	Sunset	-	42.0	
	8	Sunrise	-	10.0	
		Sunset	-	42.0	
	9	Sunrise	-	21.0	
		Sunset	-	39.0	
	10	Sunrise	-	10.0	
		Sunset	-	38.5	
	11	Sunrise	-	18.5	
		Sunset	-	39.5	
	12	Sunrise	-	32.0	

Date.	Time.	Thermometer.	Remarks.
1843.		*Deg. Fahr.*	
Dec. 12	Sunset -	39.5	
13	Sunrise -	0.0	
	Sunset -	26.0	
14	Sunrise -	10.0	
	Sunset -	32.0	
15	Sunrise -	25.0	
	Sunset -	36.0	
16	Sunrise -	32.0	
17	Sunrise -	39.0	
	Sunset -	52.0	
18	Sunrise -	34.0	
	Sunset -	48.0	
19	Sunrise -	29.0	
	Sunset -	46.0	
20	Sunrise -	36.0	
	Sunset -	39.0	
21	Sunrise -	33.0	
	Sunset -	43.0	*Spring* 61°; brisk SE. wind all day.
22	Daylight -	39.0	Wind S.; overcast.
23	Daylight -	38.0	
	Sunset -	39.0	Cloudy; little rain.
24	Daylight -	31.0	
	Sunset -	37.0	Fair day; light breeze from S.
25	Daylight -	32.0	
	Sunset -	33.0	Wind S.; fair.
26	Daylight -	22.0	Clouds rising around the horizon.
	Sunset -	30.0	Cloudy; light SE. wind.
27	Daylight -	20.0	Clear; wind SE.
	Sunset -	23.0	Calm; sun faint.
28	Daylight -	18.0	Calm; reddish clouds.
	Sunset -	34.0	Gentle SE. breeze.
29	Daylight -	33.0	Light snow falling.
	Sunset -	19.0	Clear; wind WSW.
30	Daylight -	14.0	
	Sunset -	19.0	Fair; wind S. 80° W.
31	Daylight -	17.0	
	Sunset -	27.0	Fair; moderate SW. wind.
1844.			
Jan. 1	Daylight -	24.0	Fair; light clouds in E.
	Sunset -	28.0	
2	Daylight -	26.0	Thick snow falling.
3	Daylight -	20.0	Heavy mist.
	Sunset -	23.0	Still misty.
4	7h. 12m. a. m.	20.0	
	Sunset -	24.0	Dense mist all day.
5	6h. 25m. a. m.	12.0	
	Sunset -	22.0	Wind NE.; dense mist as on the two previous days.
6	Sunrise -	8.0	Mist breaking away; clear bright sunshine.
	Sunset -	21.0	Clear; nearly calm.
7	7h. 12m. a. m.	6.0	Slight mist.
	Noon -	31.0	
	Evening -	24.0	Clear sunset.
8	7h. 45m. a. m.	20.0	Brisk NE. breeze; bright clouds in W.
	Noon -	35.0	
	Evening -	30.0	Clear; wind from SW.—*Temperature of the main spring at its edge* 206°; *the centre is doubtless at the boiling point.*
9	7h. 25m. a. m.	23.0	
	Sunset -	33.0	A little snow falling.
10	7h. 15m. a. m.	22.0	
	Sunset -	29.0	Overcast.

Date.	Time.	Thermometer.	Remarks.
1844.		*Deg. Fahr.*	
Jan. 11	Sunrise -	15.0	
	Sunset ..	20.0	Day fair; bright sun.
12	Sunrise -	33.0	
	Sunset .	28.0	Partially overcast; wind SW.
13	Sunrise -	29.0	Overcast; wind S. 20° E.
	Sunset -	31.0	Snow falling thick; wind variable.
14	Sunrise ..	26.0	Nearly clear; wind N. 10° W.
		28.0	*Temperature of boiling water* 204°.4; wind N. 6°W.
	Sunset -	26.0	Cloudy; snow falling; wind W.
15	Sunrise -	31.0	
	Sunset -	34.0	Clear; fair.
16	Sunrise -	34.0	
	Sunset -	35.0	Fair; light wind N. 50° W. all day.
17	Sunrise -	17.0	
	Sunset -	42.0	Calm; sun bright.
18	Sunrise -	28.0	Reddish clouds in E.
	3h. 14m. p. m.	49.5	*Temperature of boiling water* 303°.7; wind S.20°W.
	Sunset -	39.0	
19	Sunrise -	37.0	Snow falling from 9h. till 11h. a. m; sun faint.
	Sunset -	35.0	
20	Sunrise -	14.0	
	0h. 55m. p. m.	41.0	*Temperature of boiling water* 204°.3; wind W.
	Sunset -	32.0	Overcast; wind SW.
21	Sunrise -	30.0	Snow falling fast from SW.; snow ceased at 10h. a. m.; sun shone out.
	Sunset -	29.0	Calm; clear sky.
22	Sunrise -	30.0	Wind S. 25° W.; clouds rising in horizon; light snow falling from 9h. a. m. to 1h. p. m.
	4h. 5m. p. m.	37.0	*Temperature of boiling water* 204°.2; wind high from SW.
	Sunset -	36.0	Sky clear; high SW. wind.
23	Sunrise -	40.0	Moderate W. wind; dark clouds in N.
	Sunset -	42.0	Calm; sky nearly clear.
24	Sunrise -	45.0	
	Sunset -	36.0	Sky clear; sun bright.
25	Sunrise -	2.0	Fair day; nearly calm.
26	Sunrise -	2.0	Perfectly clear; calm.
	11h. 15m. a.m.	30.0	*Temperature of boiling water* 202°.2; calm.
	Sunset -	47.0	
27	Sunrise -	12.0	
	Sunset .	33.0	Sky unclouded all the day.
	4h. 25m. p. m.	34.0	*Temperature of boiling water* 202°; light breeze from NW.
28	Sunrise -	27.0	
	Sunset -	40.0	Clear; sun bright; moderate SE. wind.
29	Sunrise -	34.0	Reddish clouds in horizon to E. and N.; wind SE.
30	Sunrise -	31.0	Calm and cloudy.
	Sunset -	39.0	Clouds breaking away.
31	Sunrise -	25.0	Cumuli in SE. and N.
Feb. 1	Sunrise -	27.0	Overcast; snow falling.
	Noon -	40.0	Snowing all day.
	Sunset -	24.0	
2	Sunrise -	24.0	
	Sunset -	35.0	Calm; clear; bright sunshine.
	6h. 15m. p. m.	31.0	*Temperature of boiling water* 201°.5; calm.
3	Sunrise -	14.0	Nearly clear; calm.
	Sunset -	26.0	Overcast.
	3h. 45m. p. m.	28.0	*Temperature of boiling water* 201°.5; nearly calm.
4	Sunrise -	20.0	Light white clouds in E.
	Sunset -	40.0	
	9h. p. m. -	12.0	Strong SW. wind.

Date.	Time.	Thermometer.	Remarks.
1844.		*Deg. Fahr.*	
Feb. 5	Sunrise -	10.0	
	Noon -	48.0	Clear; moderate S. wind.
	Sunset -	24.0	
6	Sunrise -	16.0	Sky unclouded; light breeze SW.
	Noon -	37.0	Sky unclouded; calm.
	Sunset -	26.0	
	0h. 25m. p. m. -	37.5	*Temperature of boiling water* 200°.5; calm.
7	Sunrise -	9.5	
	Sunset -	28.0	Sky perfectly clear the whole day; light variable wind.
8	Sunrise -	— 2.5	
		— 2.0	Sun shining full on high peaks.
		0.0	Sun shining full on valley; sky cloudless; calm.
	3h. 40m. p. m. -	38.0	*Temperature of boiling water* 199°.7; light easterly breeze; nearly clear.
	Sunset -	36.0	Wind E.; whitish clouds rising in the horizon.
9	- - -	28.5	Just before sunrise.
	Sunrise -	29.0	Strong SW. wind; light scud, driving rapidly.
	Noon -	44.0	Moderate WSW. wind; nearly clear; a few wind clouds in W.
	Sunset -	24.0	Wind variable; nearly clear; a few wind clouds in W.
10	- - -	36.0	30m. before sunrise.
	Sunrise -	35.0	Nearly calm; cloudy in SW.
	Noon -	42.0	Wind SE.; white clouds in W.
	0h. 55m p. m. -	42.5	*Temperature of boiling water* 199°.5; moderate SE. wind; sky nearly clear.
	Sunset -	37.0	Moderate SE. wind; sky partially overcast.
	8h. p. m. -	39.0	
11	Sunrise -	33.0	Entirely overcast; wind shifting.
	Noon -	35.0	Clouds breaking away; violent gusts of wind from W.
	Sunset -	33.5	Clearing off; moderate wind N. 80° W.
12	Sunrise -	32.5	Calm; sky nearly clear.
	Sunset -	35.0	Sky clear; gentle W. breeze.
	8h. p. m. -	33.0	
13	- - -	34.0	30m. before sunrise.
	Sunrise -	33.0	Calm; cumuli in E.; sun faint.
	Sunset -	35.0	Overcast; calm.
14	Sunrise -	21.0	Sky clear; moderate westerly wind.
	Sunset -	32.5	Calm; sky nearly clear.
15	Sunrise -	31.0	Calm; clouds in SW.; sun faint.
	Noon -	41.0	Calm; watery clouds moving from SW. to NE.
	Sunset -	31.5	Calm; sky nearly clear.
16	Sunrise -	30.0	Wind SW.; rain clouds in E.
	Sunset -	33.0	Clear; moderate S. wind.
17	Sunrise -	23.0	Entirely clear; calm.
	Sunset -	32.0	Entirely clear; calm.
18	Sunrise -	22.5	Sky very clear; nearly calm.
	Sunset -	31.0	Calm; rain clouds in W.
19	Sunrise -	23.0	Cloudless sky; calm.
	Sunset -	32.0	Cloudless sky; gentle breeze S. 60° E.
20	Sunrise -	22.0	Clear; calm.
	Sunset -	37.0	Sky clear; brisk wind S. 70° W.
	1h. 41m. p. m. -	47.0	*Temperature of boiling water* 197°.5; moderate wind S. 68° W.
21	Sunrise -	32.0	Moderate W. wind; scattered watery clouds.
	Noon -	46.0	Cumuli all over the heavens; nearly calm; snow falling on the mountains behind; rain on the edge of the valley beyond.
	Sunset -	30.0	Sky still cloudy; strong breeze N. 65° E.

Date.	Time.	Thermometer.	Remarks.
1844.		*Deg. Fahr.*	
Feb. 22	Sunrise -	29.0	Sun faint; moderate wind N. 55° E.
	Noon - -	40.0	Light watery clouds in S.; wind N. 40° E.
	1h. 15m. p. m.	37.5	*Temperature of boiling water* 198°.7; watery clouds in S.; calm.
	Sunset -	31.0	Sky nearly clear; wind N. 50° E.
23	Sunrise -	26.0	Cumuli around the horizon; moderate S. wind.
	Sunset -	48.0	Sky clear; calm.
24	Sunrise -	27.0	Sky clear; wind E.
	2h. 45m. p. m.	60.0	*Temperature of boiling water* 206°; sky clear; light breeze from N.
March 9	Sunset -	62.0	Light grayish clouds in S.; moderate SE. wind.
10	Sunrise -	34.0	Light grayish clouds; sky clear; calm.
	Sunset -	63.0	Sky cloudy; wind SW.
	4h. 20m. p. m.	64.0	*Temperature of boiling water* 211°.6; brisk S. wind; sky nearly clear.
11	Sunrise -	45.0	Sky partially overcast; slight rain falling.
	Sunset -	56.0	Sky clear; no air stirring.
12	Sunrise -	31.0	Sky unclouded; calm.
	Sunset -	63 0	Clear sky; brisk SW. wind.
13	Sunrise -	35.0	No clouds visible; calm.
	Noon -	75.0	Strong westerly breeze.
	Sunset -	68.0	Light watery clouds floating in hor.; wind from NW.
14	Sunrise -	45.0	Moderate wind N. 10° W.; unclouded.
	Sunset -	76.0	Clear; perfectly calm.
15	Sunrise -	44.0	Calm and cloudless.
	Sunset -	74.0	Reddish clouds around the setting sun.
16	Sunrise -	40.0	No wind; sky clear.
	Noon -	84.0	
	Sunset -	58.0	No air stirring; clear.
17	Sunrise -	46.0	Sky clear; calm.
	Sunset -	63.0	Slight haze in N.; calm.
18	Sunrise -	38.0	Clear; calm.
	Sunset - -	64.0	Clear; calm.
19	Sunrise -	41.0	Sky unclouded; no wind.
	Sunset -	68.0	Few scattering clouds in W.
20	Sunrise -	40.0	Calm; unclouded.
	Noon -	81.0	In shade; white clouds in E.
	Noon -	96.0	In sun; slight breeze N. 10° E.
	Sunset -	70.0	Clear sky; no wind.
21	Sunrise -	41.0	Sky cloudy; calm.
	Sunset -	64.0	Dark clouds in E.; wind N. 70° W.
22	Sunrise -	36.0	Scattered wind clouds; wind W.
	Sunset -	64.0	Very cloudy; wind S. 10° E.
23	Sunrise -	44.0	Sky nearly clear; moderate SW. wind.
	Sunset -	63.0	Reddish clouds in W.; wind SW.
24	Sunrise -	42.0	Sky clear; calm.
	Sunset -	54.0	Clear; wind S. 80° W.
25	Sunrise -	45.0	Cloudy in E.; sun faint; calm.
	Sunset -	63.0	Cloudy in horizon; gentle westerly breeze.
26	Sunrise -	36.0	Sun faint; partially overcast.
	Sunset -	58.0	Calm; nearly clear.
27	Sunrise -	45.0	Sky overcast; no wind.
	Sunset -	60.0	Very cloudy; appearance of rain; high W. wind.
28	Sunrise -	44.0	Calm; clear.
29	Sunrise -	36.0	Few dark clouds in E.; calm.
	Sunset -	60.0	Cloudy; sun faint.
30	Sunrise -	53.0	Overcast; slight rain falling.
	Noon -	55.0	Incessant rain; moderate wind S. 15° W.
	Sunset -	56.0	Sky clouded; wind SW.
31	Sunrise -	54.0	Heavy rain; wind S. 80° W.
	Noon -	62.0	

Date.	Time.	Thermometer.	Wet bulb.	Remarks.
1844.		*Deg. Fahr.*	*Deg.*	
Mar. 31	Sunset -	58.0	–	Clearing off; wind SW.
April 1	Sunrise -	52.0	–	Sky nearly clear; calm.
	Sunset -	60.0	–	Dark clouds coming up in W.; calm.
2	Sunrise -	48.0	–	Cloudy; light easterly wind.
	Noon -	62.0	–	Rain from SW.; overcast.
	Sunset -	54.0	–	Brisk wind S. 15° E.; clearing off.
3	Sunrise -	43.0	–	Sky nearly clear; wind E.
	Sunset -	56.0	–	Few clouds in SE.; strong breeze N. 60° W.
4	Sunrise -	41.0	–	Slight rain falling; wind S. 60° W.
	Sunset -	60.0	–	Raining; wind from SW.
5	Sunrise -	37.0	–	Sky clear, calm.
	Sunset -	68.0	–	Sky clear, calm.
6	Sunrise -	35.0	–	Sky cloudless; no wind.
	Noon -	90.0	–	In shade.
	Noon -	98.0	–	In sun; sky nearly clear; light SE. breeze.
	Sunset -	72.0	–	Wind S. 40° E.; cloudy in NE.
7	Sunrise -	49.0	–	Raining; overclouded.
8	Sunrise -	55.0	–	Wind N. 60° W.; sky nearly clear.
	Sunset -	52.0	–	Heavy clouds in W.; moderate wind S. 80° W.
9	Sunrise -	38.0	–	Sky clear and calm.
	Sunset -	52.0	–	Dark cumuli in W.; light breeze N. 55° W.
10	Sunrise -	36.0	–	Perfectly clear; no air stirring.
	Sunset -	56.0	–	Nearly clear; calm.
11	Sunrise -	37.0	–	Sky overcast; calm.
	Sunset -	57.0	–	Cloudy in horizon; high wind in N. 45° W.
12	Sunrise -	32.0	–	Smoky; sun faint; calm.
	Sunset -	62.0	⌐	Dense smoke; sun obscured.
13	Sunrise -	45.0	–	Smoky appearance continues; sun faint.
	Sunset -	52.0	–	Sky nearly clear; calm.
14	Sunrise -	40.0	–	Clear and calm.
	Sunset -	53.0	–	Moderate wind N. 80° W.; clear.
15	Sunrise -	40.0	–	Clear sky; no wind.
	Sunset -	56.0	–	High wind S. 15° E.; unclouded.
16	Sunrise -	48.0	–	Clear; moderate wind S. 20° E.
	Sunset -	54.0	–	Brisk breeze S. 30° E.; clear.
17	Sunrise -	40.0	–	Moderate wind S. 30° E.; cloudy in E.
18	Sunrise -	52.0	–	Masses of clouds over the sky; light breeze S. 60° W.
	Sunset -	48.0	–	Clouds over setting sun; wind S. 80° W.
19	Sunrise -	30.0	–	Moderate wind S. 80° W.; sky nearly clear.
	Sunset -	54.9	–	Sky overcast; clouds in NW.; wind S. 60° W.
20	Sunrise -	47.0	–	Dark cumuli in E.; moderate wind S. 70° W.
				Dense mist greater part of the day; cold SW. wind.
21	Sunrise -	47.0	–	Hazy; sun faint; strong wind N. 80° W.
	Noon -	74.0	–	In shade.
	Noon -	82.0	–	In sun; sky clear; wind N. 80° W.
	Sunset -	53.0	–	Sky clear; brisk wind N. 80° W.
22	Sunrise -	47.0	–	Perfectly clear; gentle westerly breeze.
	Sunset -	60.0	–	Bright sunset; moderate west wind.
	Sunset -	–	–	*Temperature of boiling water* 208°.5.
23	Sunrise -	38.5	38.0	Clear except in E.; cold wind N. 70° W.
	Sunset -	54.0	50.0	Sky covered with watery cl'ds; wind W.

Date.	Time.	Thermometer.	Wet bulb.	Remarks.
1844.		*Deg. Fahr.*	*Deg.*	
April 24	Sunrise -	48.0	45.0	Clouds in E.; moderate W. wind.
	Noon -	76.0	69.0	Clear; brisk wind S. 80° W.
	Sunset -	66.0	58.5	Clouds breaking away after a sprinkling of rain.
25	Sunrise -	51.5	48.0	Nearly clear; calm.
	Sunset -	62.0	57.0	Clouds in N.; calm.
26	Sunrise -	42.0	43.0	Perfectly clear; calm.
	Noon -	90.0	85.0	Sky clear; shifting breeze.
	Sunset -	80.5	71.0	Dark clouds in the N.; calm.
27	Sunrise -	44.0	45.0	Clear; calm.
	Noon -	90.5	78.0	Thin white clouds in horizon; southerly breeze at intervals.
28	Sunrise -	66.0	59.5	Nearly clear; calm.
	Sunset -	52.0	48.5	Heavy clouds in NE.; strong wind S. 15° W.
29	Sunrise -	46.0	47.5	Scattered clouds; calm; *temperature of spring used* 66°.
	Noon -	69.0	58.0	Clouds; wind brisk S. 30° W.
	Sunset -	57.0	54.5	Cloudy; moderate wind S. 20° W.
30	Sunrise -	44.5	43.0	Cloudy in E.; cold wind S. 80° E.
	Sunset -	60.5	54.0	Bright sunset; calm; cumuli on near mountains.
May 1	Sunrise -	40.5	42.0	Very clear; calm.
	Sunset -	56.0	48.0	Calm; brilliant sunset.
2	Sunrise -	32.0	35.5	Clear; calm.
	Sunset -	55.5	50.0	Clear; calm.
3	Sunrise -	30.0	34.0	Clear; calm.
	Sunset -	67.0	63.0	Clear; calm.
4	Sunrise -	38.0	41.5	Clear; light breeze N. 70° W.
		52.0	–	*Temperature of* { *Large spring* 73°. *Smaller spring* 71°.
5	Sunrise -	42.0	41.0	Clear; calm.
	Noon -	104.0	85.0	Clear; breeze at intervals.
	Sunset -	56.0	50.0	Clear; shifting breeze.
	Sunrise -	41.0	40.0	Clear; calm.
	6h. 20m. p. m.	70.0	–	*Temperature of boiling water* 205°.7.
	Sunset -	70.5	69.0	
7	Sunrise -	42.0	40.0	Light white clouds in E.; calm.
	Sunset -	76.0	67.0	Clear; calm.
8	Sunrise -	42.5	42.0	Calm; slight haze.
	Sunset -	76.0	69.0	Clear; moderate wind S. 40° W.
9	Sunrise -	68.0	56.5	Clouds in E.; calm.
		70.0	–	*Temperature of spring* 76°.
	Noon -	94.0	85.5	Large masses of white cloud in NE.; high wind S. 70° W.
	Sunset -	70.0	60.0	Clear; slight breeze S. 75° W.
10	Sunrise -	35.0	41.5	Clear; calm.
		35.0	–	*Temperature of river* 48°.
	Sunset -	56.0	53.0	Clear; nearly calm.
11	Sunrise -	53.5	52.0	Sky mottled with dark purple clouds; moderate wind N. 80° W.; shower of rain between 6h. and 7h. a. m.
	Sunset -	53.0	50.0	Dark clouds over the sky; brisk wind N. 10° E.
12	Sunrise -	44.0	45.5	Eastern sky clouded; breeze N. 15° E.
		70.0	–	*Temperature of boiling water* 203°.8; few white clouds on blue sky; moderate wind N. 40° E.
	Sunset -	46.0	45.0	Clear; calm.
13	Sunrise -	31.5	33.0	Sky perfectly clear; calm.
	Sunset -	56.0	53.0	Bright sunset; southerly breeze.

Date.		Time.		Thermometer.	Wet bulb.	Remarks.
1844.				*Deg. Fahr.*	*Deg.*	
May	14	Sunrise	-	42.0	41.5	Clear; moderate wind S. 30° W.
		Noon	-	83.0	68.5	White bank of clouds in N.; strong wind S. 30° W.
		Sunset	-	55.0	50.0	Sky nearly clear; wind high, S. 30° W.
	15	Sunrise	-	41.5	41.0	Scattered clouds; calm.
		Sunset	-	61.0	58.0	Cloudy in horizon; moderate S. wind.
	16	Sunrise	-	32.0	32.5	Nearly clear; wind S.
		Sunset	-	52.0	48.0	Very cloudy; few drops of rain; high N. wind.
	17	Sunrise	-	33.0	36.0	Cloudy in horizon; calm.
		Sunset	-	52.0	48.0	Very cloudy; appearance of rain; wind S. 70° W.
	18	Sunrise	-	45.0	42.5	Overcast; heavy rain; wind S. 65° W.
		Noon	-	48.0	52.0	Heavy and incessant rain; wind S. 65° W.
		Sunset	-	53.0	50.5	Clearing off; wind N. 30° E.
	19	Sunrise	-	29.5	32.0	Nearly clear; wind N. 20° E.
		Sunset	-	50.0	48.0	Cloudy in horizon; calm.
	20	Sunrise	-	39.0	39.0	Perfectly clear; calm.
		Noon	-	88.5	–	*Temperature of boiling water* 203°; sky clear; breeze S. 30° W.
		Sunset	-	48.5	47.5	Nearly clear; calm.
	21	Sunrise	-	45.5	46.5	Clear; calm.
		Sunset	-	70.0	61.0	Very cloudy; mild S. wind.
	22	Sunrise	-	56.0	52.0	Reddish clouds in E.; brisk S. wind.
		Sunset	-	55.0	50.0	Cloudy; wind S.
	23	Sunrise	-	44.0	43.5	Cloudy in horizon; cold S. wind.
		Sunset	-	45.0	41.0	Scattered clouds; calm.
	24	Sunrise	-	41.5	42.5	Sky overcast, few drops of rain.
		Sunset	-	47.5	48.0	Sky nearly clear; calm.
	25	Sunrise	-	30.5	36.0	Perfectly clear; calm.
		Sunset	-	65.0	62.0	Sky clear; calm; Utah lake.
	26	Sunrise	-	44.0	45.5	Sky overcast; calm.
		Sunset	-	64.0	60.0	Very cloudy; high wind N. 20° E.
	27	Sunrise	-	44.0	46.0	Clouded; appearance of rain; calm.
		Sunset	-	45.0	46.0	Bright sunset; clear.
	28	Sunrise	-	35.0	39.5	Clear; calm.
		Sunset	-	46.0	46.5	Sky very clear; calm.
	29	Sunrise	-	29.5	33.0	Clear and calm.
		0h. 15m. p. m.		66.0	–	Station on Uintah waters, 1,500 feet below the pass in the dividing ridge between the waters of White and Uintah rivers; *temperature of boiling water* 201°.3; sky very clear and calm.
		Sunset	-	45.0	45.5	Perfectly clear; calm.
	30	Sunrise	-	36.0	35.0	Sky clear; calm.
		Sunset	-	58.0	54.5	Clear; no air stirring.
	31	Sunrise	-	31.5	36.0	Clear; calm.
		Sunset	-	54.0	53.5	Clear; calm.
June	1	Sunrise	-	48.5	49.0	Clouded in E.; calm.
		Sunset	-	62.0	50.0	Very cloudy; sprinkling of rain; brisk wind N. 70° W.
	2	Sunrise	-	46.0	45.0	Scattered clouds; calm.
		Sunset	-	64.0	58.0	Clouds in horizon; moderate wind N. 30° W.
	3	Sunrise	-	42.0	41.0	Clear and calm.
	4	Sunrise	-	43.0	42.0	Clear and calm.
		Sunset	-	66.0	62.0	Bright sunset; calm.
	5	Sunrise	-	48.0	47.0	Clear; calm.
		Sunset	-	68.0	62.0	Clear; calm.
	6	Sunrise	-	44.5	44.5	Clear; calm.
		Sunset	-	72.0	61.0	Clear; moderate wind N. 45° E.

Date.	Time.	Thermometer.	Wet bulb.	Remarks.
1844.		*Deg. Fahr.*	*Deg.*	
June 6	7h. 45m. p. m.	71.0	–	*Temperature of boiling water* 200°.7; sky clear; moderate wind N. 45° E.
7	Sunrise	52:0	50.0	Sky clear; moderate wind N. 45° E.
	Sunset	75.0	72.0	*Temperature of boiling water* 204°; very cloudy.
8	Sunrise	45.0	48.0	Very clear; calm.
	Noon	80.0	75.0	Sky nearly clear; moderate wind S. 80° W.
	Sunset	70.0	68.0	Dark heavy clouds over the sky.
9	Sunrise	44.5	44.0	Clear; calm.
	Sunset	72.0	68.0	Dark clouds in the western horizon; light breeze S. 70° W.
10	Sunrise	33.0	38.0	Sky clear; calm.
	Sunset	65.0	59.0	Clouds in horizon; moderate wind N. 40° E.
11	Sunrise	32.0	37.5	Sky nearly clear; calm.
	Sunset	60.0	57.0	Sky mottled with clouds; moderate wind S. 65° W.
12	Sunrise	40.0	42.0	Sky clear; calm.
	Sunset	60.0	57.0	Few clouds in W.; moderate wind S. 40° W.
13	Sunrise	36.0	38.0	Sky clear; calm.
	1h. p. m	76.5	–	*Temperature of boiling water* 199°.5; calm; thin white clouds in horizon.
14	Sunrise	44.0	43.0	Sky very clear; calm.
	Sunset	76.0	66.0	Bright sunset; calm.
15	Sunrise	42.0	42.5	Sky clear; calm.
	Sunset	54.5	53.0	*Temperature of boiling water* 200°; sky clear; slight westerly breeze.
16	Sunrise	34.0	36.0	Clear; calm.
	Sunset	54.0	52.0	Bright sunset; calm.
17	Sunrise	29.0	36.0	Perfectly clear; calm.
18	Sunrise	42.0	42.5	Sky clear; calm.
19	- -	63.0	–	*Temperature of boiling water* 201°.6; clear; slight westerly breeze.
	Sunset	68.0	64.0	Sky nearly clear; calm..
20	Sunrise	30.0	36.0	Clear; calm.
	Sunset	49.5	48.5	Bright sunset; calm.
21	Sunrise	40.0	39.0	Slight mist; southerly breeze.
	Sunset	60.5	–	Sky mottled with clouds; shifting breeze.
22	Noon	76.0	–	Fork of Grand river, 1,600 feet below the divide; *temperature of boiling water* 195°.8; clear; southerly breeze.
	Sunset	49.0	49.0	Masses of white clouds; wind variable.
23	Sunrise	33.0	34.0	Sky perfectly clear; calm.
26	Sunset	46.0	50.0	Clear; calm.
27	Sunrise	38.0	40.0	Clear; calm.
	Sunset	62.0	57.5	Bright sunset; calm.
28	Sunrise	42.0	44.0	Cloudless sky; calm.
	Sunset	74.0	71.5	Nearly clear; calm.
29	Sunrise	44.0	46.0	Sky clear; calm.
	Sunset	74.5	72.5	Clear; shifting breeze.
30	Sunrise	56.0	55.0	Clear; calm.
	Sunset	78.5	76.0	Clouds in NE.; moderate wind N. 60° E.
July 1	Sunrise	61.0	61.0	Sky clear; calm.
	Sunset	81.0	80.0	Sky clear, southerly breeze.
2	Sunrise	60.0	60.0	Clear; calm.
	Noon	85.0	84.0	Nearly clear; calm.
	Sunset	84.0	80.0	Dark threatening clouds in W.; high wind S. 50° E.
3	Sunrise	66.0	66.5	Masses of clouds over the whole sky; calm.

Table of observations with the thermometer—Continued.

Date.	Time.	Thermometer.	Wet bulb.	Remarks.
1844.		*Deg. Fahr.*	*Deg.*	
July 3	Sunset -	80.0	76.5	Sky cloudy; thunder and lightning.
4	Sunrise -	70.5	70.5	Clouds in E.; calm.
	Sunset -	82.0	77.0	Few drops of rain; calm.
5	Sunrise -	66.0	66.0	Clear and calm.
	Sunset -	–	–	Heavy rain; NW. wind.
6	Sunrise -	62.0	63.0	Sky overcast; calm.
	Sunset -	75.0	73.5	Clouds in horizon; calm.
7	Sunrise -	65.5	65.5	Very cloudy; calm.
	Sunset -	80.0	78.0	Western sky clouded; calm.
8	Sunrise -	64.5	64.5	Fair; calm.
	Noon -	91.0	89.0	Sky clear and calm.
	Sunset -	81.0	80.0	Sky partially overcast; calm; thunder and lightning, with heavy rain between 10h. and 11h. p. m.
9	Sunrise -	68.0	66.5	Nearly clear; calm.
	Sunset -	79.5	76.0	Clear; no air stirring.
10	Sunrise -	63.0	61.0	Few clouds; calm.
	Sunset -	82.5	80.0	Clouds passing off after a thunder shower.
11	Sunrise -	68.0	70.0	Sky clear; calm.
	Sunset -	79.0	76.5	Storm coming up from westward.
12	Sunrise -	70.0	70.0	Thin watery clouds moving from SW. to NE; breeze variable.
	Sunset -	88.0	86.0	Cumuli in W; wind S. 10° E.
13	Sunrise -	73.0	72.0	Sky nearly clear; moderate wind S. 30° E.
	Sunset -	80.0	79.5	Scattered clouds; calm.
14	Sunset -	82.0	80.0	Clouded every where except in the zenith; slight breeze S. 46° E.
15	Sunrise -	72.0	70.0	Sky cloudy; sun faint.
	Noon -	79.0	78.5	Sky entirely overcast; calm.
	Sunset -	76.0	75.0	Sun and clouds; calm.
16	Sunrise -	70.5	70.0	Cloudy; appearance of rain.
	Sunset -	73.5	74.0	Cloudy every where except around the setting sun; drops of rain; calm.
17	Sunrise -	68.0	68.0	Partially overcast; calm.
	Sunset -	80.0	79.0	Sky clear; moderate wind S. 25° W.
18	Sunrise -	68.5	68.0	White clouds in horizon; moderate S. 15° W.
	Sunset -	72.0	71.5	Clouds rising in eastward; high wind S. 40° W.
19	Sunrise -	60.0	61.5	Sun faint; partially overcast; cold wind S. 45° E.
	Sunset -	69.0	66.0	Sky nearly clear; calm.
20	Sunrise -	53.0	54.5	Sky clear, except in horizon; calm.
	Sunset -	73.5	71.0	Sky nearly clear; slight breeze S. 35° E.
21	Sunrise -	60.0	61.0	Sky clear; calm.
	Sunset -	78.0	76.0	Sky almost clear; calm.
22	Sunrise -	68.0	69.0	Cloudy, except in the zenith; calm.
	Sunset -	80.0	78.0	Wind clouds in W.; moderate wind S. 30° E.
23	Sunrise -	65.0	64.0	Clear and calm.
	Sunset -	74.0	74.5	Low dark clouds in N.; high wind S. 45° E.
24	Sunrise -	64.0	64.0	Sky clear; calm.
	Sunset (?) -	82.0	81.0	Few clouds; moderate wind S.
25	Sunrise -	68.0	67.0	Overcast; shifting breeze.
	2h. p. m. -	83.0		
26	Sunrise -	70.0	70.5	Very clouded; calm.
	2h. p. m. -	82.0	–	Clear; slight breeze.
27	Sunrise -	70.0	71.0	Very much overcast; calm.
	2h. p. m. -	84.0		
28	Sunrise -	70.0	70.5	Misty and calm.
	2h. p. m. -	100.0	–	Clear; no breeze.
29	Sunrise -	72.0	71.0	Clear; calm.

BIBLIOGRAPHY

ABEL   Abel, Annie H., ed. *Chardon's Journal at Fort Clark, 1834–1839.* Pierre, S.D., 1932.

ABERT   Abert, Lt. James W. *Journal of . . . from Bent's Fort to St. Louis, in 1845,* Senate Doc. 438, 29th Cong., 1st sess. Washington, D.C., 1846, [Serial 477].

ACKERMANN   Ackermann, Gertrude W. "Joseph Renville of Lac qui Parle," *Minnesota History,* 12 (Sept. 1931) : 231–46.

ALLEN   Allen, Miss A. J. *Ten Years in Oregon. Travels and Adventures of Doctor E. White and Lady, West of the Rocky Mountains. . . .* Ithaca, N.Y., 1850.

ALMANAC   *American Almanac and Repository of Useful Knowledge* [for the Years 1838–41]. Boston.

ALTER   Alter, J. Cecil. *Jim Bridger, Trapper, Frontiersman, Scout, and Guide.* Columbus, Ohio, 1951.

AMER. FUR CO.   *Calendar of the American Fur Company's Papers.* 2 vols. (*Annual Report* of the American Historical Association for the Year 1944, vols. 2–3.) Washington, D.C., 1945.

ANDERSON   Morgan, Dale L., and Eleanor T. Harris, eds. *The Rocky Mountain Journals of William Marshall Anderson: The West in 1834.* San Marino, Calif., 1967.

ARAGO   Arago, Dominique François Jean. "The History of My Youth: An Autobiography," *Annual Report* of the Smithsonian Institution, 25 (1870) : 145–96.

ARRINGTON   Arrington, Joseph E. "Skirving's Moving Panorama: Colonel Frémont's Western Expeditions Pictorialized," *Oregon Historical Quarterly,* 65 (June 1964) : 133–72.

ASHLEY   Morgan, Dale L., ed. *The West of William H. Ashley: The International Struggle for the Fur Trade . . . 1828–1838.* Denver, Colo., 1964.

AVERETT   Averett, Walter R. *Directory of Southern Nevada Place Names.* Revised ed. [Las Vegas, Nev.], 1963.

BABCOCK   Babcock, Willoughby M. "Louis Provencalle, Fur Trader," *Minnesota History,* 20 (Sept. 1939) : 259–68.

BARNES   Barnes, Gertrude. "Following Frémont's Trail through Northern Colorado," *Colorado Magazine,* 19 (Sept. 1942) : 185–89.

BARRY   Barry, Louise, comp. "Kansas before 1854: A Revised Annals," *Kansas Historical Quarterly,* vols. 28–31 (1962–65).

BEK   Bek, William G. "George Engelmann, Man of Science," *Missouri Historical Review,* vols. 23 (1928–29): 167–206, 427–46, 515–35, and 24 (1929–30): 66–86.

BENTON [1]   Benton, Thomas H. *Thirty Years' View.* . . . 2 vols. New York, 1854–57.

BENTON [2]   ——. *Thrilling Sketch of the Life of Col. J. C. Fremont . . . with an Account of His Expedition to Oregon and California, across the Rocky Mountains, and Discovery of the Great Gold Mines.* London, [1850].

BIGELOW   Bigelow, John. *Memoir of the Life and Public Services of John Charles Fremont.* . . . New York, 1856.

BILLON   Billon, Frederic L. *Annals of St. Louis in Its Territorial Days from 1804 to 1821.* St. Louis, 1888.

BIOG. DIR. CONG.   *Biographical Directory of the American Congress.* Washington, D.C., 1961.

BONNEY & BONNEY   Bonney, Orin H., and Lorraine Bonney. *Guide to the Wyoming Mountains and Wilderness Areas.* Denver, Colo., 1960.

BREWER   Brewer, Henry B. "Diary, Log of the Lausanne, and Time Book of the Dalles Mission," *Oregon Historical Quarterly,* vols. 29 (1928) and 30 (1929).

G. R. BROOKS   Brooks, George R., ed. "The Private Journal of Robert Campbell," *Bulletin* of the Missouri Historical Society, 20 (Oct. 1963 and Jan. 1964): 3–24, 107–18.

J. BROOKS   Brooks, Juanita. *The Mountain Meadows Massacre.* Stanford, Calif., 1950.

BURNETT   Burnett, Peter H. "Recollections and Opinions of an Old Pioneer," *Oregon Historical Quarterly,* 5 (1904): 64–99, 139–98, 272–305, 370–402.

CAJORI   Cajori, Florian. *The Chequered Career of Ferdinand Rudolph Hassler, First Superintendent of the United States Coast Survey.* . . . Boston, 1929.

CALLAHAN   Callahan, Edward W., ed. *List of Officers of the Navy of the United States and of the Marine Corps from 1775 to 1900.* New York, 1901.

CARSON   Carter, Harvey L. *"Dear Old Kit": The Historical Christopher Carson with a New Edition of the Carson Memoirs.* Norman, Okla., 1968.

CARTER [1]   Carter, Harvey L. "George Bent," in *The Mountain Men and the Fur Trade of the Far West,* ed. by LeRoy R. Hafen. 7 vols. to date. Glendale, Calif., 1965—. 4:39–43.

CARTER [2]   ———. "Marcellin St. Vrain," in *The Mountain Men and the Fur Trade of the Far West,* ed. by LeRoy R. Hafen. 7 vols. to date. Glendale, Calif., 1965—. 3:272–77.

CATH. ALMANAC   *The Metropolitan Catholic Almanac and Laity's Directory for 1850.* Baltimore, 1849.

CHITTENDEN   Chittenden, Hiram M. *The American Fur Trade of the Far West.* 3 vols. New York, 1902. Reprinted, 2 vols., Stanford, Calif., 1954.

CHRISTOPHER & HAFEN   Christopher, Adrienne T., and LeRoy R. Hafen. "William F. May," in *The Mountain Men and the Fur Trade of the Far West,* ed. by LeRoy R. Hafen. 7 vols. to date. Glendale, Calif., 1965—. 4:207–16.

P. C. CLARK   Clark, Patricia C., ed. "Obituaries from the *Family Visitor,* April 6, 1822–April 3, 1824," *Virginia Magazine of History and Biography,* 68 (Jan. 1960): 58–91.

W. S. CLARK   Clark, William S. "Pioneer Experience in Walla Walla," *Washington Historical Quarterly,* 24 (1933): 9–24.

CLARKE   Clarke, Dwight L. *Stephen Watts Kearny, Soldier of the West.* Norman, Okla., 1961.

COAN   Coan, C. F. "The Adoption of the Reservation Policy in Pacific Northwest, 1853–1855," *Oregon Historical Quarterly,* 23 (1922): 1–38.

COAST & GEODETIC SURVEY   *Report of the Superintendent of the United States Coast and Geodetic Survey,* [1884]. Washington, D.C., 1885.

CORDUA   Cordua, Theodor. "The Memoirs of Theodor Cordua, the Pioneer of New Mecklenburg in the Sacramento Valley," ed. by Erwin G. Gudde in *California Historical Society Quarterly,* 12 (Dec. 1933): 279–311.

CRAMPTON & GRIFFEN   Crampton, C. Gregory, and Gloria G. Griffen. "The San Buenaventura, Mythical River of the West," *Pacific Historical Review,* 25 (May 1956): 163–71.

CRAWFORD   Crawford, Medorum. "Journal," in *Sources of the History of Oregon.* Eugene, Ore., 1897. 1, no. 1: 5–26.

CULLUM   Cullum, George W. *Biographical Register of the Officers and Graduates of the U.S. Military Academy . . . , 1802 to 1890.* 3rd ed. 3 vols. Boston, 1891. Supplementary vols. under various editors to 1950.

CUTRIGHT   Cutright, Paul Russell. *Lewis and Clark, Pioneering Naturalists.* Urbana, Ill., 1969.

DELAND   Deland, Charles E., ed. "Fort Tecumseh and Fort Pierre Journals," *South Dakota Historical Collections,* 9 (1918): 72–239.

DELLENBAUGH   Dellenbaugh, Frederick S. *Frémont and '49.* New York, 1914.

DAB   *Dictionary of American Biography.* 22 vols. New York, 1928–58.

DNB   *Dictionary of National Biography.* 27 vols. London, 1908–59.

DICT. WIS. BIOG.   *Dictionary of Wisconsin Biography.* Madison, Wis., 1960.

DILLON   Dillon, Richard. *Fool's Gold: The Decline and Fall of Captain John Sutter of California.* New York, 1967.

DRURY [1]   Drury, Clifford M. "Botanist in Oregon in 1843–44 for Kew Gardens, London," *Oregon Historical Quarterly,* 41 (June 1940): 182–88.

DRURY [2]   ———. *Marcus Whitman, M.D.: Pioneer and Martyr.* Caldwell, Idaho, 1937.

DUNHAM [1]   Dunham, Harold H. "Governor Charles Bent [1799–1847]: Pioneer and Martyr," *Westerners Brand Book* (Denver), 7 (1951): 219–67.

DUNHAM [2]   ———. "Lucien B[onaparte] Maxwell [1818–93]: Frontiersman and Businessman," *Westerners Brand Book* (Denver), 5 (1949, pub. 1950): 269–95.

DUPREE   Dupree, A. Hunter. *Asa Gray, 1810–1888.* Cambridge, Mass., 1959.

DWIGHT   Dwight, Benjamin W. *The History of the Descendants of John Dwight of Dedham, Mass.* 2 vols. New York, 1874.

EASTERBY   Easterby, J. H. *A History of the College of Charleston.* Charleston, S.C., 1935.

ELLIOTT   Elliott, T. C. "Richard ('Captain Johnny') Grant," *Oregon Historical Quarterly,* 36 (March 1935): 1–13.

ESSIG   Essig, E. O. "The Russian Settlement at Ross," *California Historical Society Quarterly,* 12 (Sept. 1933): 191–216.

ESTERGREEN   Estergreen, M. Morgan. *Kit Carson, a Portrait in Courage.* Norman, Okla., 1962.

EWAN   Ewan, Joseph. *Rocky Mountain Naturalists.* Denver, Colo., 1950.

FARB   Farb, Peter. *Face of North America: The Natural History of a Continent.* New York, 1963.

FARQUHAR   Farquhar, Francis P. "Frémont in the Sierra Nevada," *Sierra Club Bulletin,* 15 (Feb. 1930): 74–95.

FERRIS   Ferris, Warren Angus. *Life in the Rocky Mountains.* Ed. by Paul C. Phillips. Denver, Colo., 1940.

FIELD   Field, Matthew C. *Prairie and Mountain Sketches.* Ed. by Kate L. Gregg and John Francis McDermott. Norman, Okla., 1957.

FLETCHER   Fletcher, F. N. *Early Nevada: The Period of Exploration, 1776–1848.* Reno, Nev., 1929.

FLORA   Flora, S. D. "The Great Flood of 1844 along the Kansas and Marias des Cygnes Rivers," *Kansas Historical Quarterly,* 20 (1952): 73–81.

FOLWELL   Folwell, William W. *A History of Minnesota.* 4 vols. St. Paul, 1921.

FOSTER Foster, James W. "Fielding Lucas, Jr., Early Nineteenth Century Publisher of Fine Books and Maps," *Proceedings* of the American Antiquarian Society, 65 (1955) : 161–212.

E. B. FRÉMONT Martin, I. T., comp. *Recollections of Elizabeth Benton Frémont.* New York, 1912.

J. B. FRÉMONT Frémont, Jessie B. "The Origin of the Frémont Expeditions," *Century Magazine,* 61 (1891) : 768–69.

FRÉMONT [1] Frémont, Lieut. J. C. *Geographical Memoir upon Upper California, in Illustration of His Map of Oregon and California.* Senate Misc. Doc. 148, 30th Cong., 1st sess. Washington, D.C., 1848, [Serial 511].

FRÉMONT [2] ———. *A Report on an Exploration of the Country Lying between the Missouri River and the Rocky Mountains, on the Line of the Kansas and Great Platte Rivers.* Senate Doc. 243, 27th Cong., 3rd sess. Washington, D.C., 1843, [Serial 416].

FRÉMONT [3] ———. *Report of the Exploring Expedition to the Rocky Mountains in the Year 1843, and to Oregon and North California in the Years 1843–'44.* Washington, D.C., 1845.
See also MEMOIRS.

GARTH Garth, Thomas R. "The Archeological Excavation of Waiilatpu Mission," *Oregon Historical Quarterly,* 49 (June 1948) : 117–36.

GARY Gary, George. "Diary of Reverend George Gary—Part IV," ed. by Charles H. Carey in *Oregon Historical Quarterly,* 24 (Dec. 1923) : 386–433.

GEISER Geiser, Samuel Wood. *Naturalists of the Frontier.* Dallas, Tex., 1937.

GIANELLA Gianella, Vincent P. "Where Frémont Crossed the Sierra Nevada in 1844," *Sierra Club Bulletin,* 44, no. 7 (1959) : 54–63.

GOETZMANN Goetzmann, William H. *Exploration and Empire: The Explorer and the Scientist in the Winning of the American West.* New York, 1966.

GRAUSTEIN Graustein, Jeannette E. *Thomas Nuttall, Naturalist; Explorations in America, 1808–1841.* Cambridge, Mass., 1967.

GROCE & WALLACE Groce, George C., and David H. Wallace. *The New-York Historical Society's Dictionary of Artists in America, 1564–1860.* New Haven, Conn., 1957.

GUDDE [1] Gudde, Erwin G. *California Place Names: The Origin and Etymology of Current Geographical Names.* 3rd ed. Berkeley, Calif., 1969.

GUDDE [2] ———. *Sutter's Own Story.* New York, 1936.

A. HAFEN [1] Hafen, Ann W. "Jean Baptiste Charbonneau," in *The Mountain Men and the Fur Trade of the Far West,* ed. by LeRoy R. Hafen. 7 vols. to date. Glendale, Calif., 1965—. 1:205–24.

A. HAFEN [2] ———. "Lancaster P. Lupton," in *The Mountain Men and the Fur Trade of the Far West,* ed. by LeRoy R. Hafen. 7 vols. to date. Glendale, Calif., 1965—. 2:207–16.

L. HAFEN [1] Hafen, LeRoy R. "Fort Davy Crockett, Its Fur Men and Visitors," *Colorado Magazine,* 29 (Jan. 1952): 17–33.

L. HAFEN [2] ———. "Henry Fraeb," in *The Mountain Men and the Fur Trade of the Far West,* ed. by LeRoy R. Hafen. 7 vols. to date. Glendale, Calif., 1965—. 3:131–39.

L. HAFEN [3] ———. "Étienne Provost," in *The Mountain Men and the Fur Trade of the Far West,* ed. by LeRoy R. Hafen. 7 vols. to date. Glendale, Calif., 1965—. 6:371–85.

HAFEN & GHENT Hafen, LeRoy R., and W. J. Ghent. *Broken Hand: The Life Story of Thomas Fitzpatrick, Chief of the Mountain Men.* Denver, Colo., 1931.

HAFEN & HAFEN Hafen, LeRoy R., and Ann W. Hafen. *Old Spanish Trail: Santa Fé to Los Angeles.* Glendale, Calif., 1954.

HAINES [1] Haines, Francis D., Jr. "François Payette, Master of Fort Boise," *Pacific Northwest Quarterly,* 47 (April 1956): 57–63.

HAINES [2] ———. "The Lost River of John Day," *Idaho Yesterdays,* 2, no. 2 (1958–59): 6–10.

HALL Hall, Carroll D. "New Light on Sutter's Fort," *Quarterly News Letter,* Book Club of California, 26 (Spring 1961): 36–38.

HARLAN Harlan, A. W. "Journal . . . While Crossing the Plains in 1850," *Annals of Iowa,* ser. 3, 11 (1913–15): 32–62.

HASKINS Haskins, Leslie L. "Frederick George Jacob Lueders: Pioneer Botanist," *Oregon Historical Quarterly,* 43 (Dec. 1942): 357–61.

HASTINGS Hastings, Lansford W. *The Emigrants' Guide to Oregon and California.* Cincinnati, 1845. Reprinted, New York, 1969.

HEFFERNAN Heffernan, William Joseph. *Edward M. Kern: The Travels of an Artist-Explorer.* Bakersfield, Calif., 1953.

HEITMAN Heitman, Francis B. *Historical Register and Dictionary of the United States Army.* 2 vols. Washington, D.C., 1903. Reprinted, Urbana, Ill., 1965.

HINE Hine, Robert V. *Edward Kern and American Expansion.* New Haven, Conn., 1962.

HINES Hines, H. K. *Missionary History of the Pacific Northwest, Containing the Wonderful Story of Jason Lee, with Sketches of Many of His Co-laborers All Illustrating Life on the Plains and in the Mountains in Pioneer Days.* Portland, Ore., 1899.

HOFFMANN Hoffmann, M. M. "New Light on Old St. Peter's and Early St. Paul," *Minnesota History,* 8 (March 1927): 27–51.

HOLMES Holmes, Kenneth L. "Mount St. Helens' Recent Eruptions," *Oregon Historical Quarterly,* 56 (Sept. 1955): 197–210.

HULBERT & HULBERT   Hulbert, Archer B., and Dorothy Printup Hulbert, eds. *Marcus Whitman, Crusader,* vols. 6–8 of *Overland to the Pacific.* Denver, Colo., 1936–37.

HUMPHREYS   Humphreys, Alfred Glen. "Thomas L. (Peg-leg) Smith," in *The Mountain Men and the Fur Trade of the Far West,* ed. by LeRoy R. Hafen. 7 vols. to date. Glendale, Calif., 1965—. 4:311–30.

HYDE   Hyde, George E. *Life of George Bent.* Ed. by Savoie Lottinville. Norman, Okla., 1968.

JACKSON [1]   Jackson, Donald, ed. *Letters of the Lewis and Clark Expedition.* Urbana, Ill., 1962.

JACKSON [2]   ——. "The Myth of the Frémont Howitzer," *Bulletin* of the Missouri Historical Society, 23 (April 1967): 205–14.

JACKSON [3]   ——. "Old Fort Madison, 1808–1813," *Palimpsest,* 39 (Jan. 1958): 1–64.

JOHNSON   Johnson, Henry Warren. "Where Did Frémont Cross the Tehachapi Mountains in 1844?" *Annual Publications* of the Historical Society of Southern California, 13, pt. 4 (1927): 365–73.

JONES   Jones, Evan. *Citadel in the Wilderness: The Story of Fort Snelling and the Old Northwest Frontier.* New York, 1966.

JORSTAD   Jorstad, Erling T. "The Life of Henry Hastings Sibley." Doctoral dissertation, University of Wisconsin, 1957.

KARNES   Karnes, Thomas L. *William Gilpin, Western Nationalist.* Austin, Tex., 1970.

KORNS   Korns, J. Roderic, ed. "West from Fort Bridger: The Pioneering of the Immigrant Trails across Utah, 1846–1850," *Utah Historical Quarterly,* 19 (1951): 1–297.

LAVENDER   Lavender, David. *Bent's Fort.* New York, 1954.

LECOMPTE [1]   Lecompte, Janet. "Charles Town," in *The Mountain Men and the Fur Trade of the Far West,* ed. by LeRoy R. Hafen. 7 vols. to date. Glendale, Calif., 1965—. 1:391–97.

LECOMPTE [2]   ——. "The Hardscrabble Settlement, 1844–1848," *Colorado Magazine,* 31 (April 1954): 81–98.

MC ARTHUR   McArthur, Lewis A. *Oregon Geographical Names.* 3rd ed. Portland, Ore., 1952.

J. D. MC DERMOTT [1]   McDermott, John Dishon. "James Bordeaux," in *The Mountain Men and the Fur Trade of the Far West,* ed. by LeRoy R. Hafen. 7 vols. to date. Glendale, Calif., 1965—. 5:65–80.

J. D. MC DERMOTT [2]   ——. "Joseph Bissonette," in *The Mountain Men and the Fur Trade of the Far West,* ed. by LeRoy R. Hafen. 7 vols. to date. Glendale, Calif., 1965—. 4:449–60.

J. F. MC DERMOTT [1]   McDermott, John Francis, ed. *Frenchmen and French Ways in the Mississippi Valley.* Urbana, Ill., 1969.

813

J. F. MC DERMOTT [2] ———. *Private Libraries in Creole Saint Louis.* Baltimore, 1938.

MACK Mack, Effie Mona. *Nevada, a History of the State from the Earliest Times through the Civil War.* Glendale, Calif., 1936.

MC KELVEY McKelvey, Susan D. *Botanical Exploration of the Trans-Mississippi West, 1790–1850.* Jamaica Plain, Mass., 1955.

MAHAN Mahan, Bruce E. *Old Fort Crawford and the Frontier.* Iowa City, Iowa, 1926.

MARTIN Martin, Morgan L. "Narrative of Morgan L. Martin," *Wisconsin Historical Collections,* 11 (1888) : 385–415.

MATTES Mattes, Merrill J. *The Great Platte River Road.* Lincoln, Nebr., 1969.

MAXIMILIAN Maximilian, Prince of Wied-Neuwied. *Travels in the Interior of North America,* vols. 22–25 of *Early Western Travels, 1748–1846,* ed. by Reuben G. Thwaites. 32 vols. Cleveland, Ohio, 1905. Reprinted, New York, 1966.

MEISEL Meisel, Max. *A Bibliography of American Natural History: The Pioneer Century, 1769–1865.* 3 vols. New York, 1924–29.

MEMOIRS Frémont, John Charles. *Memoirs of my Life . . . Including in the Narrative Five Journeys of Western Exploration during the Years 1842, 1843–4, 1845–7, 1848–9, 1853–4. Together with a Sketch of the Life of Senator Benton in Connection with Western Expansion by Jessie Benton Frémont.* Only vol. 1 published. Chicago, 1887.

MILLER Miller, David E. "John C. Frémont in the Great Salt Lake Region," *Historian,* 11 (Autumn 1948) : 14–28.

MINN. COLL. Upham, Warren, and Rose B. Dunlap, comp. "Minnesota Biographies, 1655–1912," *Minnesota Historical Collections,* vol. 14 (1912).

MONTGOMERY Montgomery, R. G. *The White-headed Eagle, John McLoughlin, Builder of an Empire.* New York, 1934.

MORGAN [1] Morgan, Dale L. *Jedediah Smith and the Opening of the West.* Indianapolis, Ind., 1953.

MORGAN [2] ———. "Miles Goodyear and the Founding of Ogden," *Utah Historical Quarterly,* 21 (July and Oct. 1953) : 194–218, 307–29.

MORGAN [3] ———. *Overland in 1846: Diaries and Letters of the California-Oregon Trail.* 2 vols. Georgetown, Calif., 1963.

NESMITH Nesmith, James W. "Diary of the Emigration of 1843," *Oregon Historical Quarterly,* 7 (Dec. 1906) : 329–59.

NEVINS Nevins, Allan. *Frémont: Pathmarker of the West.* New York, 1955.

NICOLLET Nicollet, J. N. *Report Intended to Illustrate a Map of the Hydrographical Basin of the Upper Mississippi River.* Senate Report 237, 26th Cong., 2nd sess. Washington, D.C., 1843, [Serial 380].

NOTT & GLIDDON   Nott, J. C., and George R. Gliddon. *Types of Mankind; or, Ethnological Researches, Based upon the Ancient Monuments, Paintings, Sculptures, and Crania of races, and upon Their Natural, Geographical, Philological, and Biblical History: Illustrated by Selections from the Inedited Papers of Samuel George Morton, M.D. . . .* London, 1854.

NUTE   Nute, Grace Lee. " 'Botanizing' Minnesota in 1838–39," *Conservation Volunteer*, 8 (Jan.–Feb. 1945) : 5–8.

OLIPHANT   Oliphant, J. Orin. "The Library of Archibald McKinlay," *Washington Historical Quarterly*, 25 (1934) : 23–36.

OSBORNE   Osborne, R. B. "The Professional Biography of Moncure Robinson," *William and Mary College Quarterly*, ser. 2, 1 (Oct. 1921) : 237–60.

PADEN   Paden, Irene D. *The Wake of the Prairie Schooner.* New York, 1943.

PARISH   Parish, S. B. "Frémont in Southern California," *Muhlenbergia*, 4 (Sept. 1908) : 57–62.

PEARSON   Pearson, Jim Berry. *The Maxwell Land Grant.* Norman, Okla., 1961.

PIONEER REGISTER   Bancroft, Hubert Howe. *Register of Pioneer Inhabitants of California, 1542–1848.* Reprinted from vols. 2–5 of the *History of California,* published in 1885 and 1886. Los Angeles, 1964.

PORTER   Porter, Kenneth W. "Roll of Overland Astorians, 1810–1812," *Oregon Historical Quarterly*, 34 (June 1933) : 103–12.

PORTER & DAVENPORT   Porter, Mae Reed, and Odessa Davenport. *Scotsman in Buckskin: Sir William Drummond Stewart and the Rocky Mountain Fur Trade.* New York, 1963.

PREUSS   Preuss, Charles. *Exploring with Frémont.* Trans. and ed. by Erwin G. and Elisabeth K. Gudde. Norman, Okla., 1958.

RICH   Rich, E. E., ed. *The Letters of John McLoughlin from Fort Vancouver to the Governor and Committee.* Publications of the Champlain Society, Hudson's Bay Company Series. 3 vols. Toronto, 1941–44.

RIDGE   [Ridge, John Rollins]. *The Life and Adventures of Joaquin Murieta: The Celebrated California Bandit by Yellow Bird.* Introd. by Joseph Henry Jackson. Norman, Okla., 1955.

C. C. ROBBINS   Robbins, Christine Chapman. "John Torrey (1796–1873): His Life and Times," *Bulletin* of the Torrey Botanical Club, 95 (Nov.–Dec. 1968) : 519–645.

H. ROBBINS   Robbins, Harvey. "Journal of Rogue River War, 1855." *Oregon Historical Quarterly*, 34 (1932) : 345–58.

ROBERTON   Roberton, Dr. J. *The First and Second Books of Xenophon's "Anabasis."* Philadelphia, 1850.

ROBINSON Robinson, Doane. "Our First Family," *South Dakota Historical Collections,* 13 (1926) : 46–68.

RODGERS Rodgers, Andrew Denny. *John Torrey: A Story of North American Botany.* Princeton, N.J., 1942.

ROY [1] Roy, Pierre-Georges. "Les ancêtres du general Frémont," *Bulletin des recherches historiques,* 4 (1898) : 277–78.

ROY [2] ———. "Louis-René Frémont," *Mid-America,* new ser., 5 (1933–34) : 235–41.

RUSSELL Russell, Carl Parcher. "Frémont's Cannon," *California Historical Quarterly,* 36 (Dec. 1957) : 359–63.

SABIN Sabin, Edwin L. *Kit Carson Days.* Chicago, 1914.

SAGE Sage, Rufus B. *Rufus B. Sage: His Letters and Papers, 1836–47, with an Annotated Reprint of His "Scenes in the Rocky Mountains. . . ."* Ed. by LeRoy R. and Ann W. Hafen. 2 vols. Glendale, Calif., 1956.

SCHAFER Schafer, Joseph. "Jesse Applegate: Statesman and Philosopher," *Washington Historical Quarterly,* 1 (1907) : 217–33.

SCHARF Scharf, J. Thomas. *History of Saint Louis and County, from the Earliest Periods to the Present Day: Including Biographical Sketches of Representative Men.* 2 vols. Philadelphia, 1883.

SCOTT Scott, Leslie M. "Pioneer Gold Money, 1849," *Oregon Historical Quarterly,* 33 (March 1932) : 25–30.

SIBLEY [1] Sibley, Henry H. "Memoir of Hercules L. Dousman," *Minnesota Historical Collections,* 3 (1870–80) : 192–200.

SIBLEY [2] ———. "Memoir of Jean Baptiste Faribault," *Minnesota Historical Collections,* 3 (1870–80) : 168–79.

SIBLEY [3] ———. "Reminiscences of the Early Days of Minnesota," *Minnesota Historical Collections,* 3 (1870–80) : 242–82.

SMITH Smith, Elbert T. *Magnificent Missourian: The Life of Thomas Hart Benton.* Philadelphia, 1958.

STANSBURY U.S. Army Corps of Topographical Engineers. *Exploration and Survey of the Valley of the Great Salt Lake of Utah, Including a Reconnaissance of a New Route through the Rocky Mountains, by Howard Stansbury.* Philadelphia, 1852.

STEVENS Stevens, O. A. "Nicollet's Expedition of 1839," *North Dakota History,* 21 (1954) : 75–82.

SUNDER Sunder, John E. *The Fur Trade on the Upper Missouri, 1840–65.* Norman, Okla., 1965.

TALBOT Talbot, Theodore. *The Journals of Theodore Talbot, 1843 and 1849–52, with the Fremont Expedition of 1843 and with the First Military Company in Oregon Territory, 1849–1852.* Ed. by Charles H. Carey. Portland, Ore., 1931.

TAYLOR Taylor, Creswell. "Charles Bent Has Built a Fort," *Bulletin* of the Missouri Historical Society, 11 (Oct. 1954) : 82–84.

THOMPSON Thompson, Erwin. *Whitman Mission: National Historical Site,* National Park Service Historical Handbook Series No. 37. Washington, D.C., 1964.

TORREY & GRAY Torrey, John, and Asa Gray. *A Flora of North America: Containing Abridged Descriptions of All the Known Indigenous and Naturalized Plants Growing North of Mexico.* 2 vols. New York, 1838–43.

TRENHOLM Trenholm, Virginia. "The Bordeaux Story," *Annals of Wyoming,* 26 (July 1954) : 119–27.

VAN RAVENSWAAY Van Ravensway, Charles. "The Anglo-American Cabinetmakers of Missouri, 1800–1850," *Bulletin* of the Missouri Historical Society, 14 (1957–58) : 231–57.

WALLACE Wallace, William S. "Antoine Robidoux," in *The Mountain Men and the Fur Trade of the Far West,* ed. by LeRoy R. Hafen. 7 vols to date. Glendale, Calif., 1965—. 4:261–73.

WAUGH Waugh, Alfred S. *Travels in Search of the Elephant: The Wanderings of Alfred S. Waugh, Artist, in Louisiana, Missouri and Santa Fé, in 1845–1846.* Ed. by John F. McDermott. St. Louis, 1951.

WERTENBAKER Wertenbaker, Thomas J. *Princeton, 1746–1896.* Princeton, N.J., 1946.

WHEAT [1] Wheat, Carl I. *Mapping the Transmississippi West, 1540–1861.* 5 vols. San Francisco, 1957–63.

WHEAT [2] ———. "An Unusual Frémont Document," *Annual Publications* of the Historical Society of Southern California, 16 (1934) : 56–57.

WHEELER Wheeler, Sessions S. *The Desert Lake: The Story of Nevada's Pyramid Lake.* Caldwell, Idaho, 1967.

WICKMAN Wickman, John E. "Peter A. Sarpy," in *The Mountain Men and the Fur Trade of the Far West,* ed. by LeRoy R. Hafen. 7 vols. to date. Glendale, Calif., 1965—. 4:284–96.

WILLIAMS [1] Williams, J. Fletcher. *A History of the City of Saint Paul, and of the County of Ramsey, Minnesota.* St. Paul, 1876.

WILLIAMS [2] ———. "Memoir of Capt. Martin Scott," *Minnesota Historical Collections,* 3 (1870–80) : 180–87.

WILSON Wilson, Frederick T. "Fort Pierre and Its Neighbors," *South Dakota Historical Collections,* 1 (1902) : 263–79.

WIS. HIS. REC. SUR. *Wisconsin Historical Records Survey, Wisconsin Territorial Papers.* County series. Crawford County. Proceedings of the County Board of Supervisors, 29 Nov. 1821–19 Nov. 1850.

WISTAR Wistar, Isaac Jones. *Autobiography of Isaac Jones Wistar, 1827–1905.* Philadelphia, 1937.

INDEX

The following abbreviations are used: JCF for John Charles Frémont; 1842 expedition for the 1842 Expedition to South Pass; 1843–44 expedition for the Expedition to Oregon and California; MP for Map Portfolio (followed by appropriate page number).

Abert, Lt. James W.: and 1845 expedition, 397n, 407; biographical data, 408n; re southern Rocky Mountains, 422–23; uses JCF's 1845 map, MP 13

Abert, Col. John James: letters from, 3, 25, 28–29, 44–45, 46–48, 85, 94–95, 96, 101, 121–22, 123–24, 126, 128, 159–60, 164, 342, 344–46, 347–48, 349, 351–52, 353, 355–56, 393, 395–97, 398, 403, 415, 416–17, 421, 422–23, 425; biographical data, 3n; letters to, 44, 84, 115, 354, 363–64, 419; re JCF and Nicollet surveys, 45; orders Des Moines River survey, 96; orders 1842 expedition, 121–22; and Rocky Mountain survey, 159–60; re JCF and howitzer, 345–46, 351–52; and expedition zoologist, 393; plans 1845 expedition, 395–97

Abies concolor, 309, 633n
Abies lasiocarpa, 309
A. Bininger & Co.: vouchers to, 70, 141
Abronia fragrans, 306
Abronia mellifera. See *A. fragrans*
Abronia micrantha, 306–7
Abronia § (Tripterocalyx) micranthum. See *A. micrantha*
Absinthe. *See Artemisia tridentata*
Acacia. See *Prosopis pubescens*
Acacia strombulifera. See *Prosopis strombulifera*
Acerates angustifolius. See *Asclepias stenophylla*
Acerates latifolia. See *Asclepias cryptocera*

Acerates longifolia. See *Asclepias longifolia*
Acer saccharinum, 121n
Acer saccharum, 121n
Achillea millefolium, 299, 450
Ackerman, L.: voucher to, 82
Actaea rubra, 290
Actinella grandiflora. See *Rydbergia grandiflora*
Adam and Eve. *See Amplectrum hyemale*
Adams, David, 146n, 147
Adolphus Meier & Co.: vouchers to, 107, 380; identified, 108n
Agoseris aurantiaca, 290, 300
Agoseris glauca var. *parviflora,* 300
Agrostis michauxiana. See *A. perennans*
Agrostis perennans, 311
Alder. *See Alnus tenuifolia*
Alexander, B. W.: voucher to, 380
Alexander, J. H., 132n
Alexander Crater: geology of, 483–84
Alkali Creek, 533
Alkali (Dry) Lake, 598
Allium, 459
Allium reticulatum. See *A. textile*
Allium textile, 310, 459
Almonte, Gen.: re Pablo Hernandez, 724
Alnus tenuifolia, 513
Alnus viridis. See *A. tenuifolia*
Alpine bilberry. *See Vaccinium scoparium*
Alvord Mountain, 679

Amarella arctophila, 304
Amargosa Range, 683
Amargosa River, 677n, 683
Amargosa Valley, 683n
Amelanchier alnifolia, 295, 455, 474, 475, 516
Amelanchier diversifolia var. *alnifolia.* See *A. alnifolia*
American Fur Company, 9n, 24, 43n, 50, 51; assists Nicollet 1838 expedition, 7; vouchers to, 32, 33, 34, 35–36, 37, 39, 40, 41, 80, 81, 140; furnishes guide, 116; trapping party, 183–84; re buffalo robes, 492. *See also* Fort Laramie; P. Chouteau, Jr., and Company
American Journal of Science, 169
American Journal of Science and Arts, 159n
American River, 639, 651, 653n, 654, 656; Indians along, 651, 652
Ammole (ammoli). See *Chlorogalum pomeridianum*
Amorpha canescens, 176, 177, 178, 181, 185, 194, 287, 294, 432
Amorpha fruticosa, 294
Ampetu-washtoy (Sioux maiden), 7
Amphicarpa comosa, 293
Amphicarpoea monica. See *Amphicarpa comosa*
Amplectrum hyemale, 309
Amsonia tomentosa, 768
Anantherix viridis. See *Asclepias viridis*
Anderson, Louis: voucher to, 383; at Bent's Fort, 720–21
Anderson, William Marshall: re Grand Island, 182n; re Fort William, 211n
Andropogon nutans. See *Sorghastrum nutans*
Andropogon scoparius, 311
Androsace occidentalis, 289, 300
Anethum graveolens. See *Carum gairdneri; Perideridia gairdneri*
Angelrodt, Eggers & Barth: voucher to, 108
Animals, game: abundant on prairies, 179, 180, 181, 431, 433; and Sweetwater River, 249; in California, 658–62, 667; in Rocky Mountains, 710, 711. *See also* Buffalo
Antelope (steamboat), 48, 50, 68n; voucher to, 90
Antelope brush. *See Purshia tridentata*

Antelope Island, 505
Antelope Range, 694n
Antelope Valley, 619n, 620, 623n–25
Antennaria. *See Antennaria microphylla*
Antennaria microphylla, 440
Apios americana, 293
Apios tuberosa. See *A. americana*
Aplectrum hyemale. See *Amplectrum hyemale*
Aplopappus fremontii, 393n
Aplopappus spinulosus. See *Sideranthus spinulosus*
Apocynum cannabinum, 304
Applegate, Jesse: identified, 554n; and fleet of boats, 554–55; and river disaster, 560, 561n
Aquilegia coerulea, 289, 290, 716
Arago, Dominique François, 5, 9n
Arapaho Indians, 240; war parties, 198–99, 363–64, 714–20 *passim;* buffalo hunt, 199–200; villages described, 200–201, 437–38; hostile, 709. *See also* Indians
Arcand (Ascaud), Majese, 36
Archambeault, Auguste (*voyageur*): voucher to, 383; joins 1843–44 expedition, 706
Arctomecon californica, 760
Arctostaphylos sp., 644
Arctostaphylos uva-ursi, 300
Arenaria congesta, 292
Argemone hispida, 291
Argemone mexicana albiflora. See *A. hispida*
Aristida longiseta, 311, 433
Aristida pallens. See *A. longiseta*
Arkansas River, 446; survey planned, 160, 396; watershed, 393n, 445; headwaters of, 396, 710, 715n, 717; valley of, 442, 720
Armijo, José (Harmiyo, Osea): voucher to, 157; identified, 157n; joins 1842 expedition, 204, 206, 207
Arms and ammunition, 31–43 *passim,* 69–83 *passim,* 85–94 *passim,* 104–15 *passim,* 136–58 *passim,* 343, 346, 351, 358, 415, 419; on 1842 expedition, 279; on 1843–44 expedition, 428, 432, 462, 577, 620, 641
Arnica. *See Arnica fulgens*
Arnica angustifolia. See *A. fulgens*
Arnica fulgens, 290

Arrowhead. *See Sagittaria sagittifolia*
Artemisia biennis, 299
Artemisia campestris, 299
Artemisia cana, 299
Artemisia canadensis. See *A. campestris*
Artemisia filifolia, 299, 434, 527
Artemisia frigida, 299
Artemisia lewisii, 299
Artemisia ludoviciana, 299
Artemisia tridentata, 299, 368, 441, 458, 511, 537, 542, 582, 594, 595, 604, 615, 673, 685, 709
Artists, 347, 392, 395, 399, 401, 415
Asclepias cornuti. See *A. syriaca*
Asclepias cryptocera, 769
Asclepias longifolia, 305
Asclepias speciosa, 287, 305, 769
Asclepias stenophylla, 305
Asclepias syriaca, 180n, 769
Asclepias tuberosa, 178, 305
Asclepias verticillata, 305
Asclepias viridis, 305
Ashes: *see Fraxinus platycarpa;* blue-foliaged, *see F. pennsylvanica;* green, *see F. pennsylvanica;* white, *see F. americana*
Ash Hollow (Coulée de Frénes), 192
Ashley, William, 68n, 83
Aspens: *see Populus tremuloides;* quaking, *see P. tremuloides*
Assiniboine River, 64
Aster adscendens, 297
Aster adscendens var. *Fremontii.* See *A. fremontii*
Aster andinus, 298
Aster commutatus, 297
Aster cordifolius, 297
Aster elegans, 298
Aster ericoides, 297
Aster falcatus. See *A. commutatus*
Aster fremontii, 297
Aster glacialis, 298
Aster glaucus, 298
Aster integrifolius, 297
Aster laevis, 297
Aster laxifolius. See *A. longifolius*
Aster longifolius, 297
Aster multiflorus. See *A. ericoides*
Aster nova-angliae. See *A. novae-angliae*
Aster novae-angliae, 298
Aster novi-belgii, 297
Aster oblongifolius, 297

Aster salsuginosus. See *Erigeron salsuginosus*
Asters: *see Aster adscendens; A. andinus; A. cordifolius; A. elegans; A. ericoides; A. fremontii; A. glacialis; A. glaucus; A. integrifolius; A. longifolius; A. novi-belgii; A. oblongifolius;* golden, *see Chrysopsis foliosa;* New England, *see A. novae-angliae;* smooth, *see A. laevis*
Astor, John Jacob, 9n, 537n
Astragalus. *See Astragalus kentrophyta; Oxytropis lambertii*
Astragalus agrestis, 294
Astragalus alpinus, 294
Astragalus eucosmus, 294
Astragalus gracilis, 294
Astragalus hypoglottis. See *A. agrestis*
Astragalus kentrophyta, 287
Astragalus mollissimus, 294
Astragalus tridactylicus, 294
Astronomical observations: 1842 expedition, 312–13; 1843–44 expedition, 776–77
Athabasca Pass, 271n, 553
Atriplex canescens, 189, 305, 406, 446, 497, 509, 511, 527, 595, 708; as fuel, 597
Atriplex confertifolia, 511, 773
Audubon, John James, 68n, 347n; letter to, 393
Avawatz Mountains, 683
Avens. *See Geum canadense*
Avintaquin Creek, 705n
Ayot, Alexis (*voyageur*): injured, 125n, 723; pension to, 365n; voucher to, 383; on 1843–44 expedition, 427
Ayot, Honoré (*voyageur*): contract with, 124–25; on 1842 expedition, 170, 192, 266, 275–78
Ayres, B. W.: voucher to, 109

Badeau, François (*voyageur*), 385n, 502; voucher to estate, 384, 389n; death, 389n, 696n, 697; on 1843–44 expedition, 427; with JCF to Snake River, 453
Bailey, John W., 581, 740n; letter to, 408–9
Baker, Jim, 706n
Balsamorrhiza sagittata, 298
Balsam root. *See Balsamorrhiza sagittata*

Baltimore & Ohio Railroad: voucher to, 115

Bannock (Pannack) River, 483n, 516–17; JCF re military post, 516, 519–20; valley of, 516–17, 521

Baptisia leucantha, 294

Baptisia leucanthia. See *B. leucantha*

Baptisier. *See* Gea, Jean Baptiste

Barberry. *See Berberis aquifolium*

Barclay, Alexander, 436n

Bartleson, John: emigrant train, xix

Basswood. *See Tilia americana*

Batschia gmelini. See *Lithospermum gmelini*

Battle Creek, 709n, 710

Bayou Salade, 265–67, 443, 715. *See also* Colorado Park country

Beale, Lieut. Edward F., MP 16

Bear, grizzly, 243, 661; sighted, 249, 438, 712; killed, 441

Bearberry. *See Arctostaphylos uva-ursi*

Bearded tongues. *See Penstemon albidum; P. angustifolius; P. procerus*

Bear Flag Revolt, 463, 657n, 707n

Bear River, 448, 467n, 472n, 473n, 476, 483n, 496, 498; bay, 498

Bear River valley, 505; described, 471–82; observations taken, 476, 514, 516; JCF re military post, 516

Beaubien, Charles, 445

Beaulieu, Oliver (*voyageur*): voucher to, 382; identified, 387n; on 1843–44 expedition, 427; discharged at Sutter's Fort, 657n

Beaver, traces of, 251, 260, 711

Beaver Creek, 201, 712n

Beaver Dam Mountains, 692n

Beaver Dam Wash, 692n

Beaver River, 695n

Beaver Valley, 694n

Beckmannia eruciformis. See *B. syzigachne*

Beckmannia syzigachne, 311

Beckwourth (Beckwith), James P., 202

Bedstraw. *See Galium boreale*

Beer (Soda) Springs, 448, 476; described, 477; analysis of, 480; temperature of, 482

Beggarticks. *See Bidens connata*

Belford and Clark and Co. (publishers), xxxvi

Bell, John, 98, 99n

Bell, Capt. William H.: re JCF's request for arms, 243–44n, 346, 419n

Bellevue (trading post), 284, 285

Belligny, Gaspard de, 52, 69n; identified, 19n

Benoist (Benoit), Leonard (*voyageur*), 170; voucher to, 151; on Platte River run, 275–78

Bent, Charles, 446

Bent, George: hospitality of, 720

Bent, William, 446n

Benton, John Randolph, 157n; on 1842 expedition, 170; and Cheyenne youth, 185; remains at Fort Laramie, 227

Benton, Thomas Hart, xviii, xxvi, xxxiii, 96, 271n, 406, 410, 411, 418, 611n; and William Perkins, 44; and Jessie's marriage, 103n; re western surveys, 122n, 135n; and Des Moines River survey, 135; letters to, 159–60, 351–52; re presents for Indians, 164–65; letters from, 164–65, 414; JCF and criticism, 352; and ship disaster, 360–61n; and coal deposits, 400; re 1848 map, MP 15–16

Bent, St. Vrain & Co., 203, 204n; vouchers to, 156, 381, 383

Bent's Fort, 156n, 233, 446; and 1845 expedition, 407, 422–23; attacked, 720

Berberis aquifolium, 291

Bernier, Baptiste (*voyageur*), 632; voucher to, 383; on 1843–44 expedition, 427; with JCF to Snake River, 453; on Salt Lake, 502; on Columbia River trip, 561

Berthoud, Ernest, 129, 130n

Berthoud, N.: voucher to, 379

Berula erecta, 296

Betula glandulosa, 289, 309

Betula nigra, 121n

Betula occidentalis, 289, 309

Biddle, Nicholas, 522n

Bidens connata, 299

Big Blue River, 177

Bigler, John, 635

Big root. *See Ipomoea leptophylla*

Big Sandy Creek, 254

Big Sioux River, 19n, 58, 59, 67

Big Stone Lake, 67

Big Swan Lake (Marah-tanka), 14

Big Timber Creek, 722n

Bijou Creek, 202, 435

Billieau, Cyprian: voucher to, 379
Birch Creek, 540
Bircher, Rudolph: letter from, 365
Birches: dwarf, *see Betula glandulosa;* mountain, *see B. occidentalis;* river, *see B. nigra*
Bissonette, Joseph, 146; identified, 147n; as interpreter, 224, 226; letter from, 228–29; leaves 1842 expedition, 241
Bistort. *See Polygonum viviparum*
Bitter Spring, 678, 679n
Black Canyon, 483
Blackfeet Indians: hostile, 259
Black Hills (Colo. and Wyo.), 204, 238; exploration of, 205–10; geology of, 206, 207, 208, 209–10; observations taken in, 206, 207, 208, 210; Sioux attacks in, 221; Platte River in, 231
Black Night (Sioux chief), 229
Black Rock Desert, 600
Blacks Fork, 462, 467n, 468, 469, 473n
Black (Big) Vermillion River: observations taken at, 177
Black walnut. *See Juglans nigra*
Blair and Rives, xix
Blake, John A.: vouchers to, 137, 139, 390
Blanket flower. *See Gaillardia aristata*
Blattner, Jacob: vouchers to, 109, 143, 380
Blazing stars. *See Liatris glabrata; L. scariosa; L. spicata; L. spicata* var. *resinosa; Mentzelia nuda*
Bluebells. *See Campanula rotundifolia; Mertensia ciliata*
Blue bonnets. *See Lupinus leucophyllus; L. sericeus*
Blue cardinal flower. *See Lobelia siphilitica*
Blue Earth River, 17, 18n, 24
Blue flag. *See Iris missouriensis*
Blue Mountains, 544, 546, 547, 549, MP 13
Blue River, 714n, 715n
Blue stem. *See Andropogon scoparius*
Blunt, Edmund and George W.: vouchers to, 70, 136, 137, 139, 141
Blunt-lobed woodsia. *See Woodsia obtusa*
Boat, India rubber: on Kansas River, 173–74; on Platte River, 275–78; on Great Salt Lake, 502–11
Boatmen. *See Voyageurs*

Boiling springs. *See* Manitou Springs
Bois de vache: as fuel, 190, 206, 213, 249, 721
Boise River, 536, 537n
Bombus sp., 270
Bond, William, & Son: voucher to, 113
Bonneville, Capt. B. L. E., 195, 506, 693
Bonpland, Aimé: JCF names lake for, 635n
Books, carried and consulted: American nautical almanacs, 42, 70; English nautical almanacs, 70, 139; logarithm tables, 71
Boone, Albert Gallatin: as trader, 144n; voucher to, 379
Boone & Hamilton, 144, 145; voucher to, 381
Bordeaux (Boudeau), James, 211, 218, 222; as interpreter, 229
Botanical specimens: collected on 1842 expedition, 15, 130, 158–59, 161, 165, 261, 270, 282; and Nicollet's expeditions, 45; Torrey and, 128–29, 163, 169, 286–311, 758–75; Gray and, 133, 158; JCF and, 163, 165–66, 653; collected on 1843–44 expedition, 341, 346, 347, 366–76 *passim*, 391, 394, 397–98, 400, 402, 406, 409–14 *passim*, 522, 689, 707. *See also* individual species by modern binomial
Boucher, Pierre (*voyageur*), 36
Bougar, Joseph (*voyageur*): vouchers to, 158, 378
Bouis, A. R., 218n
Boulder Lake, 257
Boundary, U.S.–Mexican: JCF to reach (1843), 160; to survey (1845), 396; and western travel, 525, 598n
Bowman, Nathl.: voucher to, 381
Box Elder Creek, 238
Bradley, Francis: voucher to, 381
Brady, Mathew, xxxiii, 146n
Brady's Island, 188, 189
Brant, Henry B., 157n, 158n; on 1842 expedition, 170; remains at Fort Laramie, 227
Brassica napus, 656
Brassica rapus. See B. napus
Braya. See Smelowskia americana
Brazu, T.[?], 416
Breadroots. *See Psoralea campestris; P. collina*

823

Breaker of Arrows (Sioux chief), 229

Bredell, Edward and John C.: voucher to, 76

Breese, Samuel, MP 9

Brewer, Henry Bridgman: voucher to, 382; identified, 570–71n

Brickellia grandiflora, 297

Bridger, Jim: and 1843–44 expedition, 213–14, 221; trading posts, 467; Indian attack on, 462–63n

Bridger Creek, 471

British colony, 52. *See also* Douglas, Thomas

Bromus ciliatus, 311

Brooke, Brig.-Gen. George M.: letter from, 49; identified, 50n

Broom rape. *See Orobanche fasciculata*

Brown, Mrs. George, xxxvi

Brown, Joseph Renshaw, 20, 21n

Brown's Hole, 707, 708

Brown's Park, 707n, 709n

Brownweed. *See Gutierrezia sarothrae*

Bruce, J. and B.: voucher to, 379

Brunelle, Joseph (*voyageur*), 36, 41; identified, 36n

Buchloë dactyloides, 432, 433, 442, 709

Buckhorn Springs, 694n

Buckingham, E. M.: voucher to, 142

Buckley, Samuel Botsford, 159n

Buckwheat. *See Eriogonum fasciculatum*

Buenaventura River, 588, 601, 617; survey planned, 574, 610, 640; declared a myth, 669, MP 12

Buffalo: herds, 51, 52, 56, 61, 65, 66, 185–86, 433, 434–35; hunting of, 53–54, 63, 186, 190, 237–38; "Indian surround," 61, 62; abundance of, 184, 185, 191, 195, 710; as food, 186, 190, 237–38; battle, 196; scarcity of, 273; disappearance of, 490–92; robes, value of, 492; and Indian economy, 492–94; and intertribal wars, 493

Buffalo bean. *See Thermopsis montana*

Buffalo berries. *See Shepherdia argentea*

Buffalo bur. *See Solanum rostratum*

Bull Creek, 173n

Bull's Tail (Sioux chief), 229, 230

Bumblebee. *See Bombus sp.*

Bundle flower. *See Desmanthus leptolobus*

Burch, Thomas W.: voucher to, 157

Burcham Flat, 619n

Bureau of Topographical Engineers. *See* Abert, Col. John James; United States Corps of Topographical Engineers

Burke, Joseph, 347n

Burlington (steamboat), 9n, 43n

Burnett, Peter Hardeman: JCF on, 568; identified, 568n

Burnt (Brulé) River: geology along, 542, 543

Burscheim, Dr. *See* Knieskern, Peter

Butte: defined, 517–18

Butte aux Os (Bone Hill): observations taken at, 60

Buttercup. *See Ranunculus cymbalaria*

Butterflyweed. *See Gaura coccinea*

Butternut. *See Juglans cinerea*

Button snakeroot. *See Liatris spicata*

Cacalia tuberosa, 121n, 299

Cache la Poudre River, 205, 452, 454, 455n

Cache camp, 281; observations taken at, 242

Cadot, Benjamin (*voyageur*): voucher to, 150; on 1842 expedition, 170

Cailloun, Joseph: voucher to, 380

Cajon Pass, 674n

Calaveras River, 658n, 659

California Battalion, 377, 453

California Indians: speak Spanish, 664; assist JCF, 667–72. *See also* Mohave Indians

California Wash, 686n

Callirhoë involucrata, 293

Callirhoë digitata, 293

Calystegia sepium, 303

Camass: death, *see Zigadenus glaucus;* white, *see Z. glaucus*

Camassia esculenta, 475, 484, 494

Cameron, 111

Campanula rotundifolia, 300

Campbell, Archibald: letter to, 424; identified, 424n

Campbell, John A. (*voyageur*): returns at Fort Hall, 355n, 386n, 520; voucher to, 382; on 1843–44 expedition, 427

Campbell, John Gill (*voyageur*): voucher to, 382; on 1843–44 expedition, 427; discharged, 576; identified, 576n

Campbell, Marguerite Menager, 33; identified, 34n

Campbell, Col. Robert: letters to, 347–

48, 350, 353, 355–56; identified, 348–49; JCF requests voucher to, 362–63; voucher to, 383
Campbell, Scott, 34n
Campbell, Wm.: voucher to, 380
Campbell & Sublette: voucher to, 381
Camp Cady, 677n
Campions. See *Silene acaulis; S. drummondii*
Canaigre. See *Rumex hymenosepalus*
Canyons: defined, 275, 682; described, 275–77, 280
Captain Creek, 173n
Carex atrata, 289, 310
Carex aurea, 310
Carex barbarae, 673
Carex festucacea, 310
Carex panicea, 289, 310
Carex sitchensis. See *C. barbarae*
Carey, John, 134n
Carpetweed. See *Chamaesyce polygonifolia*
Carson, Christopher (Kit), 145, 174, 177, 179, 227n, 242, 243, 253, 265, 266–67, 456, 548, 561, 573; JCF hires, 126n; vouchers to, 151, 382; identified, 151n; on 1842 expedition, 170; horsemanship of, 180; on buffalo hunt, 186–87; re hostile Indians, 233–34, 688; joins 1843–44 expedition, 445; and mule mission, 450; to Snake River, 453; to Fort Hall, 469; brings supplies to JCF, 499; on Great Salt Lake, 502; re California, 626, 631; to Sutter's Fort, 643; and Spanish Trail massacre, 679, 680–81, 684; leaves expedition at Bent's Fort, 720
Carson Pass, 635n, 638n
Carson River, 611, 612n; valley of, 612
Carstens & Schuetze: vouchers to, 78, 143
Carter, Luther M.: voucher to, 381
Cartography: JCF's training in, xxix–xxx; and 1842 expedition, 15, 27, 52, 224; surveying, 17, 47, 59, 118, 129, 130, 257; and 1843–44 expedition, 574; experts in western American, MP 5–7; JCF's 1845 map used by others, MP 13. *See also* Maps; Preuss, Charles
Carum gairdneri, 296, 458, 494
Carvalho, Solomon Nunes, xxxiii
Carya glabra, 121n

Carya illinoensis, 121n
Carya ovata, 121n
Cascade range, 555n, 562, 563, 571
Cassia, golden. See *Cassia fasciculata*
Cassia chamaecrista. See *C. fasciculata*
Cassia fasciculata, 294
Castilleja linariaefolia, 288, 301
Castilleja miniata, 288, 301
Castilleja pallida. See *C. linariaefolia*
Catchfly. See *Silene drummondii*
Cat's ear. See *Pachystima myrsinites*
Cattle: exchange industry, 554–55; on route to California, 575, 639n, 653
Cayuse Indians: presents to, 541; at Whitman mission, 552; JCF and, 583
C. D. Sullivan & Co.: voucher to, 383
Ceanothus americanus. See *C. sanguineus*
Ceanothus mollissimus. See *C. ovatus*
Ceanothus ovatus, 293
Ceanothus sanguineus, 293
Ceanothus velutinus, 293
Cedar River, 119, 177
Cedars: incense, *see Libocedrus decurrens;* red, *see Juniperus scopulorum*
Cedar Valley, 694n
Celtis crassifolia. See *C. reticulata*
Celtis occidentalis, 121n
Celtis reticulata, 182, 309, 500
Centrocercus urophasianus, 715
Cerasus. See *Prunus melanocarpa*
Cerasus Virginiana. See *Prunus serotina*
Cercocarpus parvifolius, 287, 295
Cerré, Michel Sylvestre: identified, 86n; as witness, 86, 87, 125
Chalk Creek, 695n
Chamaesyce polygonifolia, 308
Chapman, Manuel (*voyageur*): on 1843–44 expedition, 427; voucher to, 427n
Charbonneau (Chabonard), Jean Baptiste, 202; identified, 202n; camp, 203
Chardon, F. A., 202n
Chardonnais, Moise (*voyageur*): voucher to, 153; on 1842 expedition, 170
Charity Valley, 629n
Charleston Peak, 684n
Chartran (Chartrand), Joseph (*voyageur*), 68n, 83; voucher to, 86
Chartrain, L. B., 228–29
Chenopodium album, 305
Chenopodium zosterifolium, 305
Chequest (Chiquest) Creek, 116, 117, 118

Common horsetail. *See Equisetum arvense*

Common yarrow. *See Achillea millefolium*

Compositae, 369, 766

Coneflowers: *see Rudbeckia* sp.; prairie, *see Ratibida columnaris*

Congressional Globe, xix

Connell, Robt.: voucher to, 390

Convollaria stellata. See *Smilacina stellata*

Conway, James: voucher to, 380

Conyza canadense, 298

Cooper, Maj. Stephen: letter to, 411–12; and 1845 expedition, 411–12; biographical data, 412

Coq de Prairie. See *Centrocercus urophasianus*

Coralberry. *See Symphoricarpus oreophilus*

Cordua (Coudrois), Theodor, 655

Coreopsis tinctoria, 299

Cornus circinata. See *C. rugosa*

Cornus rugosa, 297

Cornus stolonifera, 297

Cosmidium gracile. See *Thelesperma gracile*

Cosumnes River, 658

Coteau des Prairies: named by *voyageurs*, 24; described, 67, 98

Cottonwood Creek, 234

Cottonwood Spring, 685n

Cottonwood River, 14, 15, 18n

Cottonwoods: *see Populus angustifolia; P. deltoides;* eastern, *see P. deltoides;* narrow-leaved, *see P. angustifolia;* tree, *see P. sargentii*

Coulter, Thomas, 369n

Coureurs des bois (traders), 219, 220

Cournoyer, George, 41

Courteau (Cortot), Philibert (*voyageur*): voucher to, 382; identified, 386n; on 1843–44 expedition, 427; discharged at Sutter's Fort, 657n

Courthouse Rock, 215

Cove Fort, 695n

Cowania plicata. See *Emplectocladus fasciculatus*

Cowie, Thomas (*voyageur*): voucher to, 383; joins 1843–44 expedition, 706n

Cow parsnip. *See Heracleum maximum*

Coyotes: water holes of, 678

Cram, Capt. Thomas J., 377

Crawford, T. Hartley: letter to, 417–18

Creely (Crélis), Michael (*voyageur*): returns at Fort Hall, 355n, 386n, 520; voucher to, 382; on 1843–44 expedition, 427

Creosote bush. *See Larrea glutinosa*

Crepis glauca, 300

Creuss, William (*voyageur*): returns at Fort Hall, 355n, 386n, 520; voucher to, 382; on 1843–44 expedition, 427

Crooks, Ramsay: identified, 9n, 19n; letters to, 99–100

Crooks, Abbott & Company, 126n

Croton. *See Croton texensis*

Croton capitatus, 308

Croton texensis, 308

Crow Creek, 206

Crowfoot. *See Ranunculus scleratus*

Crow Indians, 221, 222, 224; Beckwourth with, 202n; intertribal wars, 451, 462; as warriors, 493

Cruciferae, 391, 412, 683

Crump (Christmas) Lake, 596n

Cudweeds. *See Gnaphalium palustre; G. uliginosum*

Cummings, Mary, 102; identified, 103n

Cummings, Mary Jane: as JCF's landlady, 103n; vouchers to, 104, 110, 112

Cummins, Maj. Richard W., 428; identified, 415n

Currants: *see Ribes cereum;* bush, *see R. aureum, R. cereum;* black, *see R. montigerum, R. viscosissimum;* swamp, *see R. echinatum;* yellow, *see R. aureum*

Cycloloma atriplicifolium, 305

Cycloloma platyphylla. See *C. atriplicifolium*

Daily National Intelligencer, xix; re 1843–44 expedition, 355n

Dakota Central Railway, 59

Dalea fremontii, 679

The Dalles. *See* Columbia River

Dana, James D.: re minerals, 169, 581

Darlingtonia brachypoda. See *Desmanthus leptolobus*

Davis, Saml. H. (*voyageur*): voucher to, 383

Day, Horace: vouchers to, 141, 379; identified, 141n

Day, John: identified, 558n

Ducatel, Julius Timoleon, 132n
Duchesne River, 705
Duckbill. *See Pedicularis groenlandica*
Dumes, Jean Baptiste: voucher to, 149; on 1842 expedition, 170; leaves expedition, 241
Dwight, Frederick, 430, 499; and 1843–44 expedition, 426; identified, 427n
Dyomme, Benjamin, 35

Eagle Nest rapids, 120, 134
Eakin, Constant M.: voucher to, 93
Earl of Selkirk. *See* Douglas, Thomas
East Carson River, 624n, 627n
East Fork River, 254
East Plum Creek, 447n
East Walker River, 613n, 616n
Echinocystis watsoni, 659n
Edosmia Gairdneri. See Carum gairdneri
Edwards, John Cummins, 134–35
Edwd. Perry & Co.: voucher to, 380
1842 expedition, 169–285; planned, 121–28 *passim;* men on, 170; JCF re fortification of area of, 192, 201, 233; area covered, 286–90. *See also* Financial records for 1842 expedition; Kansas River survey; Platte River survey; South Pass
1843–44 expedition, 426–725; men on, 427–28; purpose of, 428–29, 574–75, 698–703. *See also* Columbia River; Financial records for 1843–44 expedition; Great Basin country; Great Salt Lake; Sierra Nevada Mountains; Snake River; Spanish Trail
1845 expedition: plans for, 367, 374; Abert outlines, 395–97, 399, 403, 407–8, 422–23, 424, 425
Eld, Henry: re Kern's appointment, 416n
Elders: *see Sambucus canadensis;* box, *see Negundo aceroides*
Eleagnus argentea, 289, 308
Eleagnus argenteus. See *E. argentea*
Elephant head. *See Pedicularis groenlandica*
Elephant's Back, 628, 632n, 633n, 635n
Elizabeth Lake: salt, 672
Elk Head River, 709
Elk Mountain (Medicine Butte), 459–60; observations taken at, 459

Elm Grove, 429, 525
Elms: American, *see Ulmus americana;* slippery, *see U. rubra*
Elymus, 707
Elymus canadensis, 311
Elymus virginicus, 311
Emigrant Pass, 684n
Emigrants encountered: on 1842 expedition, 175, 236; on 1843–44 expedition, 429, 468, 473, 476, 478, 516, 525, 526, 532–33, 539, 546, 552, 554, 558, 560, 567, 568, 571, 572, 677
Emplectocladus fasciculatus, 404n, 764
Encampment River, 712n
Enchanted Hill: observations taken at, 65
Endicott, George, 391, 397, 409; identified, 392n
Endicott, William, 392n
Engagés. See *Voyageurs*
Engelmann, George, 670; vouchers to, 77, 78; re Lindheimer, 158; barometer check, 227, 273, 317, 372; meteorological observations, 317–37; re JCF and botanists, 346, 375; letters from, 346–47, 375; letter to, 371–72; re Lüders and Geyer collections, 371n, 375
Ephedra nevadensis, 604, 607, 615, 666, 685
Ephedra occidentalis. See *E. nevadensis*
Epilobium adenocaulon, 295
Epilobium angustifolium, 295
Epilobium coloratum. See *E. adenocaulon*
Epilobium spicatum. See *E. angustifolium*
Epinettes des prairies. See *Grindelia squarrosa*
Equipment: on 1842 expedition, 11, 31–43 *passim,* 50, 55, 69–83 *passim,* 85–94 *passim,* 104–15 *passim,* 123, 136–58 *passim,* 193, 227, 231, 257, 259; breakage and loss of, 226, 238, 242, 256, 265, 273, 277, 279, 377–90 *passim,* 415, 449, 549; on 1843–44 expedition, 349, 352, 377–90 *passim,* 417, 428, 496, 526, 561, 566, 567, 577, 620, 784
Equisetum arvense, 179, 231, 235, 311, 443, 446
Equisetum hyemale, 443, 501
Erigeron bellidiastrum, 298
Erigeron canadensis. See *Conyza canadense*

Flügge, C. W.: voucher to, 382
Fontenelle, Lucien, 151n
Fontenelle, Fitzpatrick & Co., 211n
Food: feasting and enjoyment of, 17, 61, 181, 190, 192, 245, 273, 451, 503, 514, 528, 538, 562, 596, 617; shortages and hunger, 174, 212, 235, 241, 258, 355, 439, 483, 502, 513, 552, 608, 626, 632, 633, 640. *See also* Indian foods; Supplies
Forestdale Creek, 633n
Forget-me-not. *See Myosotis glomerata*
Fort Adams, 146n, 147n
Fort Boise, 533, 537; and supplies, 538; Indians of, 538
Fort Bridger, 467n, 468–69n, 693n. *See also* Bridger, Jim
Fort Churchill, 612n
Fort Clark, 202n
Fort Crawford, 50n
Fort Davy Crockett, 708
Fort George. *See* Fort St. Vrain
Fort Hall, 149n, 222, 452, 483; location of, 453; history of, 518–19; described, 520; JCF re, 520, 521
Fort Jackson: abandoned, 437n
Fort John, 83, 146n. *See also* Fort Laramie
Fort Lancaster, 437
Fort Laramie, 183, 232n; described, 211, 218–19; history of, 211n; Preuss reaches, 218; suitable for military post, 233; welcomes JCF party, 281–82, 284
Fort Leavenworth, 122
Fort Leavenworth–Fort Snelling road: survey of, 96
Fort Lookout. *See* Fort St. Vrain
Fort Lucien. *See* Fort Laramie
Fort Nez Percé. *See* Fort Walla Walla
Fort Pierre, 51, 55, 68n, 211n, 218n, 265n; observations taken at, 52, 59
Fort Platte, 146, 147, 210, 224
Fort Ross, 654–55n
Fort St. Vrain, 156n, 157n, 233, 447, 450; trip to, 192–204; described, 204; observations taken at, 205; and 1843–44 expedition, 436
Fort Snelling, 7, 8, 12, 19n, 21n, 34n, 38, 49, 69n; location of, 18n
Fort Uintah: history of 706n. *See also* Uintah Fort
Fort Uncompagre, 706n

Fort Union, 68n
Fort Vancouver, 341, 612n; 1843–44 expedition and, 166, 341, 566–67
Fort Vasquez: abandoned, 437n
Fort Walla Walla, 553; and emigrant trains, 554; JCF and supplies, 555
Fort William (Ore.), 203n
Fort William (Wyo.). *See* Fort Laramie
Fossil specimens: of 1843–44 expedition, 744–56
Foster, James: voucher to, 381
Fountain Creek (Fontaine-qui-bouit), 436, 449, 718; described, 443; observations taken at, 443
Four Mile Creek: observation taken at, 458
Fourmile Creek, 715n
Fournaise, Joseph (*voyageur*), 68n, 82, 83n; voucher to, 86
Fox Indians, 15, 121n
Fox River, 115, 121n
Foxtail. *See Hordeum jubatum*
Fraeb (Frapp), Henry: killed, 221, 222, 709; identified, 221n
Fragaria virginiana, 398
Franchère, Gabriel, 19, 270–71n
Francis, H., 37
Franseria discolor. See *F. tomentosa*
Franseria dumosa, 768
Franseria tomentosa, 298, 768
Frasera speciosa. See *Swertia radiata*
Fraxinus. See *F. pennsylvanica*
Fraxinus americana, 434
Fraxinus pennsylvanica, 434
Fraxinus platycarpa, 305
Frederick Gebhardt and Co., 19n
Fremon, Ann Beverly Whiting Pryor (mother): biographical data, xxii–xxiv. *See also* Hale, Mrs. Ann B.
Fremon, Charles (father): ancestry, xxii; as teacher, xxii; elopement, xxiii; death, xxiv
Fremon, Elizabeth (sister), xxiv; died, xxvi
Fremon, Frank (brother), xxiv, 11–12n, 22
Fremon, Nina (niece and ward), 12n
Fremon-Pryor scandal, xxii–xxiv
Frémont, Elizabeth Benton (daughter), xxxi, xxxv, xxxvi, 132n, 270n, 361
Frémont, Frank (son), xxxiv, xxxvi
Frémont, Jessie Benton, xxi, xxxiii, xxxiv, xxxvi, 102, 132, 270n; marriage to

Frémont, Jessie Benton (*cont.*)
  JCF, xvii, 103n; writings of, xvii,
  xviii, xxxvi, xxxviii; as amanuensis for
  JCF, xviii, 75, 81–82, 96, 111, 120n,
  377n, 574n; and howitzer, 346n; letter
  to, 349; letters from, 352–53, 354–55,
  356–57, 358–59, 360, 361–62; re 1843–
  44 expedition's progress, 354–55, 356–
  57, 360, 361–62; re JCF and criticism,
  358–59
Frémont, John Charles: published reports of, xvii, xix, xxxi, xxxii, xxxiii,
  xxxiv, xxxvi; court-martial, xvii, xx,
  xxxii, 50n, 401n; in politics, xvii, xxi;
  and Lincoln, xvii; gold mines of, xvii;
  death of, xvii, xxxvi; in Civil War,
  xvii, xx, xxxiv; marriage, xviii, 103n;
  poem quoted, xx–xxi; parentage, xxi–
  xxiii; spelling of name, xxiin, xxxiii;
  education, xxiv, xxv; appearance, xxv;
  as surveyor, xxvi, xxix, xxx; naval
  career, xxvi, xxvii, xxviii; and Topographical Engineers, xxix, xxx, 3, 9n,
  24, 44, 395; as governor of California,
  xxxii; letters from, 10, 12–13, 20–24,
  44, 48–49, 83–84, 99–100, 115, 128–29,
  131–32, 134–35, 161–63, 165–66, 343,
  354, 362–64, 366–68, 370–74, 375–77,
  391–92, 395, 397–98, 400–412, 415–16,
  418–19, 420–21, 423, 424; hunting
  trip, 17–18, 19n; vouchers to, 38–39,
  378, 383; romance, 96, 98, 99n; re
  military significance of exploration,
  233, 343, 345, 349, 351, 364, 407, 520,
  588, 700; letters to, 342, 344–46, 365,
  395–97, 398, 399, 403, 415, 416–17,
  422–23; and maps, MP 5–16. *See also*
  Des Moines River survey; 1842 expedition; 1843–44 expedition; 1845 expedition; Nicollet's 1838 expedition;
  Nicollet's 1839 expedition
Fremont Butte, 254n, 273; observations
  taken at, 255
Fremontia. See Sarcobatus vermicularis
*Fremontia vermicularis. See Sarcobatus
  vermicularis*
Fremont Island, 483n, 510n
Fremont Pass, 604
Fremont Peak, 267n, 270n, 271n
Fremont's geranium. *See Geranium fre-
  montii*
French Academy of Sciences, 5

Frenière (Frenier), Louison, 52, 53, 61,
  65, 66, 82, 89; rescues JCF, 55, 56;
  described, 57; identified, 69n; voucher
  to, 79; listed, 82, 89
Fringed loosestrife. *See Steironema ciliatum*
Frink, Walker, & Co.: voucher to, 142
Frog fruit. *See Lippia cuneifolia*
Fronchet, Desiré (François Dezirie), 36,
  37n
Frye & Shaw: voucher to, 379; identified, 384n
Fuentes, Andreas, 724; voucher to, 383;
  and Spanish Trail massacre, 677–79
Funding: for 1842 expedition, 3, 24, 28,
  29, 43–49, 94, 100, 122, 123, 126, 127,
  128, 164; for 1843–44 expedition, 345,
  348, 350, 353, 354, 355–56, 358, 362,
  396, 403. *See also* Financial records

Gaillardia aristata, 449, 450
Gales and Seaton, xix
Galium boreale, 297
Gallatin, Albert, MP 12
Galpin, Charles E., 218, 227
Gannett Peak, 270n, 271n
Garrya elliptica. See *G. fremontii*
Garrya fremontii, 666, 689
Gate of Lodore, 707n
Gaty, Samuel, 77n
Gaty, Coonce & Beltshoover: voucher to,
  77
Gaura coccinea, 296, 413, 766
Gauropsis, 765
Gavin, Daniel, 28n
Gayophytum diffusum, 413, 766
Gea, Jean Baptiste (*voyageur*), 25, 26,
  27n, 41
Gedney, Thomas R.: voucher to, 138;
  identified, 138n
Geese, 27, 661, 662
Gentiana affinis, 304
Gentiana arctophila densiflora. See *Ama-
  rella arctophila*
Gentiana calycosa, 304
Gentiana fremontii. See *G. prostrata*
Gentiana pneumonanthe. See *G. calycosa*
Gentiana prostrata, 304
Gentians: *see Amarella arctophila; Gen-
  tiana affinis; G. calycosa;* moss, *see G.
  prostrata;* prairie, *see Eustoma russel-
  lianum*

Geological specimens: collected on 1842 expedition, 99; on 1843–44 expedition, 392, 395, 408, 469, 581, 730–56

Geranium fremontii, 288, 292

Geranium maculatum. See *G. richardsonii*

Geranium richardsonii, 450

Gerardia. See *Gerardia tenuifolia*

Gerardia longifolia. See *G. tenuifolia*

Gerardia tenuifolia, 301

Gerdes, Ferdinand H.: letter from, 101–2; identified, 103n

Gerlach, Nev., 603

Gett, W. W.: voucher to, 382

Geum canadense, 295

Geum virginianum. See *G. canadense*

Geyer, Charles A., 10, 45, 46, 52; identified, 11n; on Nicollet's 1838 expedition, 14, 27; salary, 45, 74; vouchers to, 74, 75, 82, 85, 112; financial difficulties, 97, 99n; and Nicollet geological specimens, 98; JCF re, 159n, 370–71; and Stewart expedition, 347n

Giacome, Santiago: death of, 677–84

Gibbs, George: and JCF's 1845 map, MP 13

Gilia. See *Gilia aggregata*

Gilia aggregata, 288, 303, 439, 443

Gilia (Cantua) longiflora. See *G. longiflora*

Gilia inconspicua, 303

Gilia longiflora, 303

Gilia pulchella. See *G. aggregata*

Gilmer, Thomas, 361n

Gilpin, William: on 1843–44 expedition, 430; identified, 430n; at the Dalles, 573

Girardin, L. H.: academy of, xxii; re Fremon-Pryor scandal, xxii, xxiii; and pamphlet, xxiiin

Glasgow, Edward J.: re 1843–44 expedition, 361; identified, 362n

Glaux maritima, 300

Gliddon, George Robbins, 401n

Glyceria striata, 311

Glycyrrhiza lepidota, 293, 446, 500

Gnaphalium palustre, 299

Gnaphalium uliginosum, 299

Goat, mountain. See *Ovis canadensis*

Goat Island, 245, 275; return to, 281

Godey (Godare), Alexander, 619, 632, 635; voucher to, 383; identified, 452n;

and Spanish Trail massacre, 679–81, 684

Goebel, David, 99

Gold: region of on 1848 map, MP 16

Goldenrods: see *Solidago incana; S. missouriensis; S. rigida;* late, see *S. serotina;* showy, see *S. speciosa*

Goodfellow, David: voucher to, 379

Gooseberries: see *Ribes irriguum; R. speciosum;* fuchsia-flowered, see *R. speciosum*

Goose Creek, 527

Goosefoot. See *Chenopodium zosterifolium*

Gordon, Alexander, 347n

Gore Canyon, 714

Goshen's Hole, 209

Grain de Boeuf. See *Shepherdia argentea*

Grand Island, 182; JCF re military post at, 283

Grand Ronde (Rond) River: JCF re farming, 545; valley of, 545–47; soil analysis, 546

Granite Creek Desert, 602

Granite mountains: observations taken in, 250

Granite Range, 602

Grant, Richard: at Fort Hall, 518–19n

Grant, Ulysses S.: *Personal Memoirs,* xxxvi, 15

Grapes: see *Vitis riparia;* Oregon, see *Berberis aquifolium*

Grasses: autumn bent, see *Agrostis perennans;* beargrass, see *Yucca glauca;* blue-eyed, see *Sisyrinchium anceps;* bluegrass, see *Poa fernaldiana, P. palustris;* brome, see *Bromus ciliatus;* buffalo, see *Buchloë dactyloides;* bunch, see *Festuca;* "coarse stiff," see *Carex barbarae;* crested hair, see *Koeleria cristata;* fescue, see *Festuca obtusa;* hair, see *Deschampsia caespitosa;* Indian, see *Sorghastrum nutans;* manna, see *Glyceria striata;* peppergrass, see *Lepidium virginicum;* poverty, see *Aristida longiseta;* salt, see *Distichlis spicata;* slough, see *Beckmannia syzigachne;* sweet, see *Hierochloë odorata;* wire, see *Aristida longiseta, Juncus echinatus*

Grasshopper plague, 237, 240

Gray, Asa, 405; letters to, 130, 341, 346–

Gray, Asa (*cont.*)
  47, 375; identified, 130–31n; letters from, 133, 158–59, 369, 391, 393, 394, 412–14; re JCF's botanical collection, 133, 158, 391, 392–93, 394, 412–14; re Lindheimer, 158–59; re Jeffries Wyman, 369; re catalogue of plants, 393; and pamphlet for catalogue, 393
Greasewood. *See Sarcobatus vermicularis*
Great Basin, 541, 573, 614, 621, 638, 667; explored, 694–709; on 1845 map, MP 13
Great Bend: rapids, 118, 120, 134, 135
"Great Events during the Life of Major General John C. Frémont," xxin, xxxii, 11n
Great Salt Lake, 471–72; trip to, 482–501; boat expedition, 502–11; and water worms, 506; analysis of, 512; on 1845 map, MP 12. *See also* Fremont Island
Greek valerian. *See Polemonium caeruleum*
Green, James: vouchers to, 43, 71, 106, 136; identified, 43n
Greene, David: re JCF's route, 552n
Greenfield, Jas. T.: voucher to, 381
Green River, 459, 467n; tributaries of, 254, 256; names for, 466–67; observations taken at, 467; sighted, 707. *See also* Colorado River
Greenthread. *See Thelesperma gracile*
Griffith, D. W.: voucher to, 380
Grimes, Eliab, 653n
Grimsley, Thornton: voucher to, 380
Grimsley and Young: vouchers to, 79, 109
Grindelia squarrosa, 298, 485
Gromwells: *see Lithospermum gmelini;* false, *see Onosmodium occidentale*
Gros Ventre Indians: as hostiles, 214, 222, 710
Groundnut. *See Apios americana*
Groundsel. *See Senecio triangularis*
Grovers Springs, 628n
Guernsey, Wyo., 231n
Guion (Gouin), Louis (*voyageur*): vouchers to, 149, 383, 388n, 390; on 1842 expedition, 170
Guion, Capt. William Bowling: survey of, 96, 135n
Gumplant. *See Grindelia squarrosa*

Gumweeds: *see Grindelia squarrosa;* curlycup, *see G. squarrosa*
Gutierrezia euthamiae. See *G. sarothrae*
Gutierrezia sarothrae, 298
Gymnocladus dioicus, 121n

Habenaria hyperborea, 309
Habenaria leucophaea, 309
Hackberries: *see Celtis occidentalis;* tree, *see C. reticulata;* net-leaved, *see C. reticulata;* western, *see C. reticulata*
Hale, Mrs. Ann B.: letter to, 10; identified, 11n
Half-breeds: defined, 63; hunting party of, 63–65; Kildonan colony massacre, 64; trade, 65
Halfway Wash, 687n
Hall, [James], 374, 391, 397, 398
Hall, L. W., xix
Halsey, Jacob: voucher to, 90
Hamilton, James G., xxxiii
Hams Fork, 462, 468
Hannah (JCF's nurse), xxiv
Harebell. *See Campanula rotundifolia*
Harmiyo, Osea. *See* Armijo, José
Hartweg, Carl Theodor, 413; identified, 414n
Harvey, Thomas H., 364n
Harvey, W. H., 369
Hassler, Ferdinand Rudolph, 94, 136, 138, 139; identified, 4n, 30n; letter to, 30
Hawken, Jacob and Samuel: vouchers to, 42, 156, 380; identified, 42n
"Hawken rifle," 42n
Haymarket Gardens, xxiiin
Hayne, Robert Young, xxix
Hedeoma hispida, 456
Hedeome. *See Hedeoma hispida*
Hedge nettle. *See Stachys palustris*
Helen Peak, 267n
Helgenberg, Henry: voucher to, 75
Helianthella uniflora, 287, 290, 299
Helianthi, 282, 514
Helianthus maximiliani. See *H. maximilianus*
Helianthus maximilianus, 287, 299
Helianthus petiolaris, 191, 194, 282, 287, 299
Hemlocks: mountain, *see Tsuga mertensiana;* water, *see Cicuta maculata;* western, *see T. heterophylla*

Hemp dogbane. *See Apocynum canna-binum*

Hendecandra (?) *multiflora*. See *Croton texensis*

Heracleum lanatum. See *H. maximum*

Heracleum maximum, 296

Herbe saleé. See *Distichlis spicata*

Hernandez, Pablo, 724, 725n; and Spanish Trail massacre, 677–84

Hickories: pignut, *see Carya glabra;* shagbark, *see C. ovata*

Hierochloë odorata, 398

High Rock Creek, 600

Hitchcock, Capt. Ethan Allen, 9n

Hitz, John: voucher to, 105

Hobson, John: voucher to, 380

Hog peanut. *See Amphicarpa comosa*

Hogweed. *See Conyza canadense*

Hogwort. *See Croton capitatus*

Holcomb Creek, 121n

Holodiscus discolor, 448n, 764

Hooker, William Jackson, 159n, 287, 288, 394

Hoosier Pass, 715n

Hope Valley, 633n

Hopi (Monquis) Indians: and trade goods, 676

Hordeum jubatum, 311

Horsebrush. *See Tetradymia inermis*

Horse Creek, 205, 206n, 209, 217

Horsemint. *See Monarda fistulosa*

Horse Shoe Creek, 235

Horseweed. *See Conyza canadense*

Hot Spring Gate, 244; temperature of, 280–81

Hot springs: in Colorado, 448; of Great Salt Lake, 500; in Idaho, 534, 540; in Nevada, 603. *See also* Beer Springs; Steamboat Spring

Howitzer, xxxix; JCF's requests for, 343, 345–46n, 351, 419; Abert re, 345–46, 349; and hostile Indians, 355n, 462; and War Department, 359n, 415; on 1843–44 expedition, 428, 512, 533, 577, 592, 596, 607; abandoned, 620, 622

Hudson's Bay Company: and Kildonan colony, 64; voucher to, 382; and buffalo robes, 492; and river express, 572. *See also* Fort Hall; Fort Vancouver; Fort Walla Walla

Humbert, John J.: voucher to, 107

Humboldt, Alexander von, xxxiii, 635n

Humboldt River, 693n

Hummingbird trumpet. *See Gilia aggregata*

Hurst, Decatur, xxvii

Hymenopappus corimbosus. See *H. corymbosus*

Hymenopappus corymbosus, 299

Hypopeltis obtusa. See *Woodsia obtusa*

Iatan (steamboat): returns 1843–44 expedition, 362n; voucher to, 383

Independence Mountain, 712n

Independence Rock, 223, 236, 240, 242; names on, 247; observations taken at, 273; JCF engraves cross on, 273–74n

Indian balsam. *See Leptotaenia multifida*

Indian foods: acorns, 648; filagree, 649; kamás root, 484; kooyah, 475; lizards, 688; pine nuts, 614–21; prairie potatoes, 58; roots, 593; salmon, 529–31; thistle, 494; trout, 697; yampah, 296, 458, 494

Indian paint brush. *See Castilleja linariaefolia; C. miniata*

Indian plantain. *See Cacalia tuberosa*

Indians: and 1842 expedition, 51, 61, 116, 174, 184, 198, 240, 283; gifts for, 52, 57, 164–65, 224; hostile, 179, 180, 214, 221, 228–29, 236, 237, 364, 678, 687, 720; and alcohol, 190, 219, 221; dogs, 199, 225; pipe smoking, 201; portable lodge, 231, 242; and 1843–44 expedition, 430, 435, 437, 445, 462, 474, 487–90, 496, 506, 515, 516, 530, 532, 538, 541, 544, 557, 559, 582, 584, 586, 598, 608–29 *passim*, 634, 647–52, 664–67, 676, 695, 697, 713–14, 717, 718, 721, 722; snow shoes, 628. *See also* Indian foods; individual tribes

Indian turnips. *See Psoralea campestris; P. collina*

Indigoes: bush, *see Amorpha fruticosa;* false, *see A. fruticosa;* white false, *see Baptisia leucantha*

Inland Jersey tea. *See Ceanothus ovatus*

Ipomea [*Ipomoea*] *leptophylla*, 303, 446

Iris. *See Iris missouriensis*

Irish, Charles W.: letter from, 58–59; identified, 69n

Iris missouriensis, 309

Iron plant. *See Sideranthus spinulosus*
Iron Springs, 694n
Ironweed. *See Vernonia fasciculata*
Ironwood. *See Ostrya virginiana*
Island Lake, 263, 267n, 271; observations taken at, 263
Islue, Phineas C.: voucher to, 381
Iva axillaris, 298

Jaccard, Louis, 78n
Jaccard & Co.: vouchers to, 77–78, 108, 382
Jaeger, Benedict, 129, 130; identified, 130n
James, Edwin, 287, 288, 289
Jameson, Mr., 116, 121n
James River, 20, 50, 56, 57, 60, 67, 69n
Janisse (Janis), Auguste (*voyageur*): identified, 153n; on 1842 expedition, 170, 267
Jenkins, Edward, and Sons: voucher to, 71
John Day River, 555n, 558
Jordan River, 694n
Joshua tree. *See Yucca brevifolia*
"Journal of Lieutenant J. W. Abert, from Bent's Fort to St. Louis, in 1845," 408n
Juglans cinerea, 121n
Juglans nigra, 121n
Juncus echinatus, 310, 443
Juncus effusus, 663
Juneberry. *See Amelanchier alnifolia*
Juniper. *See Juniperus scopulorum*
Juniperus scopulorum, 309
Juniperus virginiana. See *J. scopulorum*

Kamás root. *See Camassia esculenta*
Kane, Elisha Kent, xxxiii
Kansas Indians: provide JCF with food, 174; intertribal wars, 364
Kansas River valley: geology of, 162, 287; described, 171–81, 432–33; observations taken in, 175, 176, 285, 431; soil of, 286; floods of, 366–67, 368n; re settlements in, 442; 1843–44 expedition returns through, 723–24
Kansas River survey, 170–81, 286. *See also* 1842 expedition
Kearny, Stephen Watts, xvii, 141, 144n, 167; letter to, 343; and JCF re arms, 343, 344n, 346n

Kellogg, Benjamin, 218n
Kellogg, Florentine, 218n
Kellogg, Philander, 218, 219n
Kenceleur, William, 158n
Kenner, Jacob: voucher to, 107
Kentrophyta montana. See *Astragalus kentrophyta*
Kentucky coffee tree. *See Gymnocladus dioicus*
Keokuk (Indian chief), 121n; village of, 118
Kern, Benjamin J., 401n
Kern, Edward M., xxxiii; letters to, 401, 415–16; and 1845 expedition, 401, 415, 666n; biographical data, 401n; re payment, 415–16
Kern, Richard H., 401n
Kern Lake, 666
Kern River, 666
Kildonan settlement: massacre at, 64
King, Nicholas, MP 12
King, William, Jr.: vouchers to, 93, 137, 140
King's River, 664
Kinnikinnick. *See Arctostaphylos uva-ursi*
Kiowa River, 440
Kipp, James, 68n
Klamath Indians: village of, 586–87; and shell adornments, 587; provide guides, 589–90
Klamath (Tlamath) Lake, 574, 575, 585, 590n
Klamath Marsh, 585n
Klamath River, 568, 586
Knieskern, Peter, 377n
Knotweed. *See Polygonum aviculare*
Koeleria cristata, 311
Kooyah. *See Valeriana ciliata*
Kraft, Christopher: voucher to, 105
Krameria. See *K. parvifolia*
Krameria canescens, 760
Krameria lanceolata. See *K. canescens*
Krameria parvifolia, 413, 760
Kruger, A. W.: voucher to, 73

Labonte's Camp, 237
Lacey, Capt. Edgar Martin: death of, 49, 50n
Lac qui Parle (trading post), 16, 19n, 32, 33, 42, 48, 50, 69n; entertainment at, 17

Lactuca pulchella, 300
Ladies' tresses. *See Habenaria hyperborea; H. leucophaea*
Lady's thumb. *See Polygonum persicaria*
Laframboise, Joseph: vouchers to, 35, 36; identified, 35n
Laidlaw, William, 68n
Lajeunesse, Basil *(voyageur),* 279, 281; vouchers to, 149, 382; identified, 149–50n; on 1842 expedition, 170, 241, 264, 266, 267; and rubber boat, 173; on South Platte trip, 192, 197; JCF's companion, 232; on Platte River run, 275–78; returns at Fort Hall, 355n, 386n, 520; on 1843–44 expedition, 427; with JCF to Snake River, 453; on Salt Lake, 502; JCF re, 520
Lajeunesse, François *(voyageur),* 150n; returns at Fort Hall, 355n, 386n, 502, 520; on 1843–44 expedition, 427; with JCF to Snake River, 453
Lajoie, Louis: voucher to, 379
Lake Abert: saline, 594–95
Lake Anderson, 596
Lake Benton, 58
Lake Creek, 713n
Lake Fremont, 19n
Lake Hendricks, 58
Lake Itasca, 4n
Lake Jessie, 69n, MP 9
Lake John, 713n
Lake Kampeska, 59
Lake Mountains, 604
Lake of the Four Hills, 66
"Lake of the Scattered Small Wood," 58, 59
Lake of the Serpents, 66
Lake Pepin, 25–26, 27n, 28n
Lake Poinsett, 59
Lake Preston, 58, 59
Lake Shetek complex, 18n
Lake Tahoe, 625n, 632n, 635
Lake Te-tonka-ha, 58
Lake Thompson, 58, 59
Lake Travers trading post: Indian hostilities, 13
Lake Whitewood, 58
Lake Winnipeg, 64, 572
Lambert, Clément *(voyageur),* 145, 146, 152, 278, 279, 284; vouchers to, 110, 147–48, 153; identified, 110–11n; on 1842 expedition, 170; conducts Fort

Laramie group, 192–93, 215, 265, 267; on Platte River run, 275–78
Lamb's quarter. *See Chenopodium album*
Lanctot, Eusebe *(voyageur),* 36
Lanoix, Pierre, 41
Laramie Fork, 452n
Laramie Mountain, 211, 234, 244, 457
Laramie Plains, 455
Laramie Range, 234; composition of, 244
Laramie River, 192, 243; geology along, 162; headwaters of, 177; observations taken on, 456
Larente, Registe *(voyageur):* voucher to, 146; on 1842 expedition, 170n; leaves expedition, 226n
Larix occidentalis, 549, 554
Larkin, Thomas Oliver: and 1843–44 expedition, 653n
Larrea glutinosa, 671, 677, 682
Las Vegas, 685–86n
Lathyrus linearis. See *L. palustris*
Lathyrus palustris, 293, 432
Lathyrus strictus, 662, 667
Latourville, Mrs., 40
Latulippe, François *(voyageur),* 68n; listed, 83; identified, 83n; vouchers to, 86, 152; and 1842 expedition, 170; joins JCF on prairies, 184
Lea, Albert M., 96, 135n; identified, 114n
Lead plant. *See Amorpha canescens*
Leavenworth, Melines C., 130; identified, 131n
Lee, Daniel, 560n, 561n
Lee, Elizabeth Blair, xxxiii, xxxiv
Lee, Henry *(voyageur):* and JCF's letters, 354–55; returns at Fort Hall, 355n, 386n, 520; voucher to, 382; shoes for, 385n; on 1843–44 expedition, 427; with JCF to Snake River, 453
Lee, Jason, 560n
Lee, John: and river disaster, 183
Lee, Gen. Robert E.: and Mississippi River navigation, 6, 9n
Lefevre, Jean B. *(voyageur):* vouchers to, 148, 149; on 1842 expedition, 170
Leonard, F.: voucher to, 380
Lepachys columnaris. See *Ratibida columnaris*
Lepidium ruderale. See *L. virginicum*
Lepidium virginicum, 291

P. *odorata;* screwpod, *see P. odorata;*
tornillo, *see P. odorata*

Metcalf, A. C.: voucher to, 381

Meteorological observations: on 1842 expedition, 317; on 1843–44 expedition, 784

Metolius River, 582

Michaux, François André, 410

Middle Park, 713n

Mile (Chippeway) River, 27

Milfoil. *See Achillea millefolium*

Milkweeds: *see Asclepias longifolia; A. speciosa; A. stenophylla;* butterfly, *see A. tuberosa;* horsetail, *see A. verticillata;* spider, *see A. viridis*

Milkwort. *See Polygala alba*

Mill Creek, 619n, 620, 621

Miller, Alfred Jacob, 347n

Miller & Kinzpeter: voucher to, 73

Mimulus alsinoides. See *M. moschatus*

Mimulus lewisii, 301

Mimulus moschatus, 301

Minnesota River, 7, 14, 23, 43, 44; headwaters of, 67, 69n

Mint. *See Mentha arvensis*

Mirabilis froebelii, 446, 665

Mirabilis jalapa. See *M. froebelii; M. multiflora*

Mirabilis multiflora, 665

Mirabilis nyctaginea, 306

Missions: Methodist, 560, 561; in California, 664–76 *passim*

Missouri (state) boundary survey, 135n

Missouri River: headwaters of, 67, 258; JCF's chart of, 68n; topography of, 98; boat on, 285

Missouri River Valley survey. *See* Nicollet's 1839 expedition

Mitchell, John W., xxiv, xxv

Mitchell, L. B.: voucher to, 110

Mohave Indians: as Indian traders, 676; water gourd of, 676. *See also* California Indians

Mohave stinkweed. *See Cleomella obtusifolia*

Mojave Desert, 670, 672, 759, MP 13

Mojave River, 674–77; observations taken at, 675

Mokelumne River, 658n, 659

Monarda fistulosa, 301

Monkey flowers. *See Mimulus lewisii; M. moschatus*

Monsoon (steamboat): vouchers to, 107, 109

Montmort, Count de, 13, 27, 44; identified, 19n

Montreuil, Louis (*voyageur*): voucher to, 383; on 1843–44 expedition, 427

Monument Creek, 447n

Moore, Baker & Co.: voucher to, 142

Mormon Mesa, 687n

Mormons: and JCF re Bear River, 516; and massacre of emigrants, 692n

Mormon tea. *See Ephedra nevadensis*

Morning glories: bush, *see Ipomoea leptophylla;* wild, *see Calystegia sepium*

Mosquitoes: as problem, 62, 178, 190, 231, 438, 454

Mosquito Range, 715n

Mountain balm. *See Ceanothus velutinus*

Mountain dandelion. *See Agoseris aurantiaca*

Mountain heath. *See Phyllodoce empetriformis*

Mountain Lake. *See* Boulder Lake

Mountain mahogany. *See Cercocarpus parvifolius*

Mountain Meadows, 692–94n

Mount Baker, 571n

Mount Diablo: Carson sights, 631

Mount Hood: sighted, 551, 555, 557, 573, 578, 579

Mount Jefferson, 579, 580

Mount Rainier (Regnier), 570, 571, 576, 577

Mount St. Helens: sighted, 555, 563, 577; eruptions of, 570, 571n

Muddy Creek, 467n, 713n

Muddy River, 686n

Mule Creek, 117

Mulgedium pulchellum. See *Lactuca pulchella*

Müller, Ludolph: vouchers to, 91, 92, 93

Murphy, Jos.: voucher to, 380

Murrieta, Joaquín, 724n

Musenium tenuifolium, 296

Mustards: *see Thelypodium integrifolium; T. linearifolium;* wormseed, *see Erysimum cheiranthoides*

Myosotis glomerata, 302

Narrow-leaved lathyrus. *See Lathyrus palustris*

Plantago gnaphaloides. See *P. purshii*
Plantago purshii, 305
Plantains. *See Plantago eriopoda; P. purshii*
Platanus occidentalis. See *P. racemosa*
Platanus racemosa, 668
Platanthera hyperborea. See *Habenaria hyperborea*
Platanthera leucophaea. See *Habenaria leucophaea*
Platte River, 169, 450; geology along, 182, 239–49 *passim,* 274–81 *passim;* navigation on, 183, 283; rapids of, 183, 283; quicksand in, 189, 282; warm springs, 231, 280, 281n; headwaters of, 258, 710; river run, 275–78; forded, 283–84, 454; valley of described, 284–85
Platte River survey, 170–284, 287, 288; to South Platte, 192–243; to Black Hills country, 205–10; to Sweetwater River, 249–52; in Wind River Mountains, 254–71; and Nicollet's 1843 map, MP 9. *See also* 1842 expedition
Plattesmouth, Nebr., 284n
Ploudre, Edward: vouchers to, 107, 379
Plympton, Maj. Joseph, 21, 24; identified, 21n
Poa crocata. See *P. palustris*
Poa fernaldiana, 311
Poa laxa. See *P. fernaldiana*
Poa nervata. See *Glyceria striata*
Poa palustris, 311
Poinsett, Joel R., xxvn, xxvi, xxix, 4, 5, 10, 11n, 43n; re JCF and Topographical Engineers, 4, 24; letters to, 12–13, 21–24, 83–84, 94–95; letter from, 95
Poinsett, Mrs. Joel, 13, 84
Polanisia trachysperma, 291
Polemonium caeruleum, 289, 303
Polkinhorn, H., xix
Polkinhorn and Campbell: vouchers to, 109, 139
Polygala. See *P. alba*
Polygala alba, 291
Polygonum amphibium, 307
Polygonum aviculare, 307
Polygonum persicaria, 307
Polygonum viviparum, 307
Polyotus angustifolius. See *Asclepias stenophylla*

Polyotus longifolia. See *Asclepias longifolia*
Polytaenia nuttallii, 296
Poore, E. W. and G.: voucher to, 380
Poppies: *see Arctomecon californica;* California, *see Eschscholtzia californica;* prickly, *see Argemone hispida;* purple poppy mallow, *see Callirhoë involucrata*
Populus angustifolia, 308, 449, 455, 459, 513, 709
Populus canadensis. See *P. sargentii*
Populus deltoides, 179, 182, 189, 203, 205, 233, 236, 238, 243, 252, 308
Populus monilifera. See *P. deltoides*
Populus sargentii, 502
Populus tremuloides, 251, 256, 259, 260, 308, 439, 451, 458
Porter, James M., 346n, 359n
Portneuf River, 482, 518, 519n, 520
Poso Creek, 665
Potatoes: prairie, *see Psoralea esculenta;* swamp, *see Sagittaria sagittifolia*
Potentilla anserina, 295
Potentilla arguta, 295
Potentilla diversifolia, 295
Potentilla fruticosa, 295
Potentilla gracilis, 289, 295
Potentilla sericea β glabrata, 295
Potra, Benjamin (*voyageur*): voucher to, 149; on 1842 expedition, 170
Poundcake Rock, 440, 450
Povertyweed. *See Iva axillaris*
Powder River, 543, 544; soil analysis of valley of, 545
Power, James (*voyageur*): voucher to, 381; on 1843–44 expedition, 427; discharged, 453
Prairie dog, 433; villages, 188, 440–41
Prairie du Chien, 19n, 27, 44, 50n, 67, 69n, 81
Prairie Dog River, 434
Prairie mimosa. *See Desmanthus leptolobus*
Prairie parsley. *See Polytaenia nuttallii*
Prairies: fire in, 18; description of, 56–57; soil of, 162, 178, 189; wolves in, 180, 190–91; drought on, 235, 236, 240. *See also* Animals, game; Buffalo
Pratte, Bernard, 9n
Pratte, Chouteau and Company: letters to, 25, 28–29, 46; voucher to, 37; re

844

expedition finances, 45, 46. *See also* American Fur Company

Prêle. See Equisetum arvense

Preston, Idaho, 485

Preuss, Charles, 69, 73, 192, 193, 242, 267, 283, 548, 550, 551, 617, 632, 633; vouchers to, 136, 138, 140, 156, 378, 383; identified, 136n; re JCF and daguerreotype, 146n; gun to, 155; and Nicollet's map, 157; on 1842 expedition, 170, 185, 378n; from journal of, 212–18; and hostile Indians, 214–15; re scenery, 250n, 256, 265, 266; on Platte River run, 275–78; and Hot Springs, 280, 281n; re JCF's achievement, 282; on 1843–44 expedition, 370, 372, 426, 595, 604, 635; re Manitou Springs, 448; to Snake River, 453; re howitzer, 465n; and tobacco root, 475; on Great Salt Lake, 502–11; on Columbia River trip, 561–66; re California, 641; lost, 646–51; re Carson's Indian scalping, 681n; cartographic work of, MP 10–16

Prevaud, Z.: voucher to, 380

Prevost, Chs., 41

Price River, 209, 704, 705n

Prickly pear. *See Opuntia polyacantha*

Primroses: evening, *see Oenothera drummondii, O. fremontii, O. nuttallii, O. pallida, O. rhombipetala, O. serrulata, O. strigosa;* rock, *see Androsace occidentalis;* white evening, *see O. nuttallii, O. speciosa*

Promontory range, 498, 505

Prosopis juliflora var. *torreyana,* 763

Prosopis odorata, 677, 682, 683, 684, 688. *See also P. juliflora* var. *torreyana*

Prosopis pubescens, 368, 398, 407

Prosopis strombulifera, 764

Proue (Proulx, Proux), Raphael (*voyageur*), 643; vouchers to, 153, 383; identified, 153–54n; on 1842 expedition, 172; on 1843–44 expedition, 427; with JCF to Snake River, 453; discharged at Sutter's Fort, 657n

Provencalle, Louis, 34

Provo (Timpan-ogo) River, 698

Provost (Provinceau), Etienne, 151n; listed, 50, 83; identified, 68n; voucher to, 87

Prunus melanocarpa, 455

Prunus serotina, 208, 232, 243, 455, 513

Pryor, John: and wife's desertion, xxii–xxiii; biographical data, xxiii

Pseudotsuga menziesii, 448n

Psoralea argophylla, 294

Psoralea campestris, 294

Psoralea collina, 294

Psoralea esculenta, 58, 237, 294, 430, 679

Psoralea floribunda, 294, 432

Psoralea lanceolata, 294

Psoralea onobrychis, 115

Psoralia Orobrychis. See Psoralea onobrychis

Pterochiton, 772–73

Pterochiton occidentale. See Atriplex canescens

Ptiloria ramosa, 299

Puebla de los Angeles, 622n, 658, 673, 674n, 677

Pueblo, Colo.: trading post at, 436, 715n, 720; described, 445

Pullam's Fork, 710

Pulliam, Mark R. C.: voucher to, 381

Pulmonaria ciliata. See Mertensia ciliata

Purple heather. *See Phyllodoce empetriformis*

Purshia tridentata, 294, 402, 495, 533, 535, 685; as fuel, 557

Putty root. *See Amplectrum hyemale*

Pyramid Lake, 598n, 605n; water analysis of, 605; boulders in, 605–7

Quenon, Louis, 41

Quercus alba, 121n. *See also Q. gambelii; Q. utahensis*

Quercus gambelii, 434, 448n, 513, 651, 658

Quercus imbricaria, 115

Quercus kelloggii, 646, 647, 648, 660

Quercus lobata, 402n

Quercus macrocarpa, 121n

Quercus marilandica, 115

Quercus utahensis, 513n

Quercus velutina, 121n

Quercus wislizenii, 642

Quinine, wild. *See Parthenium integrifolium*

Rabbit brushes. *See Chrysothamnus graveolens; C. viscidiflora*

Rabbits: method of hunting, 624

Raccoon (River) fork. *See* Des Moines River survey

848

Smith, Thomas L. ("Pegleg"), 473n
Smith's Fork: history of name, 473n
Smith's Fork Creek, 473n
Smoky Hill River, 429n, 431, 442, 721, 722n
Snakeberry. *See Actaea rubra*
Snake Indians, 214, 222; intertribal wars, 451, 462–63; and yampah, 458; on Oregon Trail, 474; and expedition flag, 475; food of, 475, 484, 494; in Salt Lake area, 484, 486; village described, 489–90; condition of, 490. *See also* Snake River Indians
Snake Indian woman: joins 1843–44 expedition, 453; leaves near Bridger's fort, 468
Snake River, 203n, 452, 453, 483, 520, 522–40; geology of, 522–23; American Falls of, 522–26; forded, 532; observations taken on, 533, 540; valley of, 536n
Snake River Indians: salmon fisheries of, 529–31; described, 531–32; condition of, 538–39, 544
Snakeroot. *See Liatris punctata*
Snakes: prairie, 175; rattlesnakes, 282, 494
Snakeweed. *See Gutierrezia sarothrae*
Snowberry. *See Symphoricarpus occidentalis*
Snow-on-the-mountain. *See Euphorbia marginata*
Snow Peak, 267
Snow plant. *See Sarcodes sanguinea*
Soapberry. *See Shepherdia canadensis*
Soap Creek, 117
Soap plant. *See Chlorogalum pomeridianum*
Soapweed. *See Yucca glauca*
Soda Lake, 677n
Soda Point, 483n
Soda Springs. *See* Beer Springs
Solanum rostratum, 303
Solanum xanti, 672
Soldier Creek, 600
Soldier Meadows, 600
Soldier Summit, 705n
Solidago gigantea. See *S. serotina*
Solidago incana, 289, 298
Solidago missouriensis, 298
Solidago rigida, 298
Solidago serotina, 298
Solidago speciosa, 298

Solidago virga-aurea, 298
Solomon's Fork, 429n
Sorghastrum nutans, 311
Sorrels: *see Rumex mexicanus;* mountain, *see Oxyria digyna;* sheep, *see Oxalis stricta;* yellow wood, *see Oxalis stricta*
Sour-top bilberry. *See Vaccinium oreophilum*
Southern Paiute Indians: JCF re, 687; hostile, 687–88. *See also* Digger Indians
South Park. *See* Colorado Park country
South Pass, 252, 710; described, 253–54, 463; importance of, 465, 553; distances from, 466
South Platte River, 429n, 435, 450, 452n, 715n
Southwest Museum, xxin
Spalding, Henry H., 552n
Spanish: in Colorado, 203–4
Spanish Canyon, 679n
Spanish Fork River, 695n, 697, 703, 705n
Spanish Peaks: sighted, 443
Spanish Trail, 658, 667; 1843–44 expedition along, 674–92; massacre on, 677–84; observations taken on, 680; camps on, 683, 685, 692–93
Spartina cynosuroides, 189, 310
Specularia amplexicaulus. See *S. perfoliata*
Specularia perfoliata, 300
Speedwell. *See Veronica wormskjoldii*
Spencer, John Canfield, 168
Sphaeralcea coccinea, 293, 432, 433
Spiderwort. *See Tradescantia occidentalis*
Spiraea ariaefolia. See *Holodiscus discolor*
Spiranthes cernua, 309
Spirolobium odorata. See *Prosopis pubescens*
Spotted Tail (Sioux chief), 147n
Sprague, Isaac, 411n
Spring Mountains, 685n
Spruces: hemlock, *see Tsuga mertensiana, T. heterophylla;* white, *see Abies concolor*
Spurges: *see Chamaesyce polygonifolia; Euphorbia obtusata;* flowering, *see E. corollata*
Squaw bush. *See Rhus trilobata*
Squirrel, Siberian, 265
Squirreltail. *See Hordeum jubatum*

849

Stachys aspera. See *S. palustris*
Stachys palustris, 301
Stafftree. *See Pachystima myrsinites*
Stambaugh, Samuel C., 34n
Stambaugh and Sibley: voucher to, 33; listed, 39
Standing Rock Pass, 483n, 487
Stanislaus River, 622, 658, 660
Stanleya integrifolia. See *S. pinnata*
Stanleya pinnata, 684–85
Steamboat Spring, 476n, 477; water analysis of, 478; temperature of, 482
Steironema ciliatum, 300
Stenosiphon linifolius, 766
Stenosiphon virgatum. See *S. linifolius*
Stephanomeria runcinata. See *Ptiloria ramosa*
Stevens, Maj. Simon, xxivn
Stevens Peak, 625n, 632n, 635n
Stewart, Arthur, 123n, 140n; vouchers to, 140, 379; and astronomical observations, 312–13
Stewart, Lucien: voucher to, 381
Stewart, William Drummond, 150n, 202n, 347n, 359n
Stiletsi (Indian chief), 578
Stockton, Robert F., xxxii
Stockton and Falls and Co.: voucher to, 72
Stone, W. J., 94, 95, 98, 131; identified, 95n; re Nicollet's map, 131
Stonecrop. *See Rhodiola integrifolia*
Strawberry. *See Fragaria virginiana*
Strawberry Creek, 639n
Strawberry River, 704, 705n
Strawberry Valley, 639n, 705n
Strombocarpa. See *Prosopis pubescens*
Stump Spring, 684n
Suaeda erecta, 305
Sublette, Milton, 473n
Sublette, William L., 211n
Sueda maritima. See *Suaeda erecta*
Sullivan, John C.: survey of, 135n
Sulphur-flower. *See Eriogonum umbellatum*
Sumach. *See Rhus glabra*
Summer Lake, 591–92
Summit Meadows, 620n
Sunflowers: *see Helianthella uniflora;* Maximilian's, *see Helianthus maximilianus;* prairie, see *Helianthus petiolaris*
Supplies: for 1842 expedition, 10, 31–43

passim, 69–83 *passim,* 85–94 *passim,* 104–15 *pasism,* 136–58 *passim,* 205, 284–85; for 1843–44 expedition, 377–90 *passim,* 436, 462, 469, 575, 657. *See also* Financial records
Sutter, John Augustus: vouchers to, 382, 387n; re 1843–44 expedition, 652–53n; biographical data, 654; ships of, 655. *See also* Sutter's Fort
Sutter's Fort: community of, 654–56; 1843–44 expedition at, 654
S. V. Farnsworth & Co.: voucher to, 380
Sweet goldenweed. *See Sideranthus spinulosus*
Sweetwater River: Sioux attacks near, 214, 223; route along, 242, 249–52; valley of described, 249, 464; geology along, 249, 250, 251, 252, 288; observations taken on, 251, 253, 273, 465; confluence with Platte, 274, 275n
Swertia. *See Swertia perennis; S. radiata*
Swertia perennis, 304
Swertia perennis β obtusa. See *S. perennis*
Swertia radiata, 289, 304
S. Wing & Co.: voucher to, 78
Sycamore. *See Platanus racemosa*
Sycan River, 590n
Symphoricarpus occidentalis, 297
Symphoricarpus oreophilus, 297
Symphoricarpus vulgaris. See *S. oreophilus*

Tabeau, Jean Baptiste (*voyageur*), 629; vouchers to estate, 383, 388n, 390n; on 1843–44 expedition, 427; killed, 689–91
Table Rock, 253
Talbot, Adelaide: letters to, 352–53, 354–55, 358–59; identified, 353n; JCF and son of, 354, 356–57, 362
Talbot, Isham, 353n
Talbot, Theodore: re JCF's writings, xxxii–xxxiii; identified, 353n; health, 358, 362; and 1843–44 expedition, 378, 426; voucher to, 384; and 1845 expedition, 396; re Dwight, 427n; with Fitzpatrick, 453; re hostile Indians, 462–63n
Talcott, Lieut. Col. George: letter to, 400; re arms and 1845 expedition, 419n
Taliaferro, Lawrence, 9n, 12, 19n, 28n; and Indian peace, 13n

Talinum parviflorum, 292
Talle de Chênes: observations taken at, 60
Taos, N.M., 203, 204, 205; trouble in, 445
Taplin, Charles (voyageur), 602, 633; voucher to, 383; on 1843–44 expedition, 427
Taylor, Franck: voucher to, 92
Taylor, R. O.: voucher to, 380
Taylor and Marshall: voucher to, 77
Taylor, Wilde, & Co., xix
Tea Prairie River, 565
Tehachapi Creek, 666
Tehachapi Pass, 657n, 668n
Tellez, Lieut. Col. Rafael, 657n
Tessier, François (voyageur): voucher to, 150; on 1842 expedition, 170
Tesson (Tissant), Baptiste (voyageur): returns at Fort Hall, 355n, 386n, 520; voucher to, 382; on 1843–44 expedition, 427
Teton Indians. See Sioux Indians
Tetradymia inermis, 133, 299
Tetrao europhasianus. See Centrocercus urophasianus
Teucrium canadense, 301
Thalictrum megacarpum, 290
Thalictrum cornuti, 290
Thamnosma, 762
Thamnosma montana, 763
Thelesperma gracile, 299
Thelypodium integrifolium, 291
Thelypodium linearifolium, 291
Thermopsis montana, 288, 294, 764
Thermopsis rhombifolia, 764
Thistles: see Cirsium altissimum; tall, see C. altissimum
Thomas's Fork, 473
Thompson River, 205, 454
Thoroughwort. See Brickellia grandiflora
Three Buttes, 517, 522
Three Island Crossing, 533n
Tickseed. See Coreopsis tinctoria
Tick trefoil. See Desmodium glutinosum
Tiernan, N.: voucher to, 380
Tilghman, Stedman Richard, 358, 359n
Tilia americana, 121n
Tillot, H., 89
Timothy. See Phleum alpinum

Tintic Valley, 697
Tisius, Hendrick: voucher to, 142
Titcomb Lakes, 267
Titcomb Valley, 267n
Tobacco: and voyageurs, 183–84
Tobacco root. See Valeriana ciliata
Torrey, John, 146, 230; letters to, 128–29, 133, 158–59, 161–63, 165–66, 366–68, 370–71, 372–74, 375–77, 391–92, 395, 397–98, 400, 402, 403, 404–5, 406–7, 409–11, 412–14, 418–19, 420–21, 423; botanical collection to, 128–29, 130, 370, 373–74, 375–77, 403–5, 410–11; identified, 129n; re JCF, 130; letters from, 130, 341; geological data to, 161–63; and botanical catalogue, 341, 374, 404–5, 409–10, 420–21, 423; re writing preface, 287–90; re route of 1842 expedition, 286–89; told of 1845 expedition, 367, 374; and 1843–44 expedition report, 395
Totten, Col. Joseph Gilbert, 358, 359n
Town, Charles, 643, 645, 646, 720; voucher to, 382; on 1843–44 expedition, 446
Townsend, Charlotte Holmes: letter to, 405
Townsend, John Kirk: biographical data, 394n
Tradescantia occidentalis, 180, 185, 310
Tradescantia virginica. See T. occidentalis
Trappers and traders, 183, 203, 213, 445. See also individual names
Traverse des Sioux: described, 14
Triplett, Thomas: voucher to, 93
Trout, cutthroat. See Salmo clarkii
Troximon parviflorum. See Agoseris glauca var. parviflora
Truckee River, 605n, 610, 611, 615
Tsuga heterophylla, 633
Tsuga mertensiana, 633
Tulare (tulé). See Scirpus acutus
Tulare Lake, 663
Tuolumne River, 661
Turner, Talton: voucher to, 381
Twinpod. See Physaria australis
Two Buttes. See Fremont Butte
Tygh Valley, 578

Uintah Fort, 387n, 388n, 389n. See also Fort Uintah

Uinta River, 704–5n, 706n; basin of, 707
Ulmus americana, 121n
Ulmus fulva. See U. rubra
Ulmus rubra, 121n, 189, 309
Umatilla (Umatilah) River, 555; JCF re farming, 547; valley of, 547–49
United States Corps of Topographical Engineers, xxix, xxx, 3n, 4, 6, 9n, 24, 44, 47n. See also Abert, Col. John James
United States Magazine and Democratic Review, xix
United States Post Office: voucher to, 92
U.S.S. Independence, xxix
U.S.S. Natchez, xxvi, xxvii, xxviii
U.S.S. Princeton, 360–61n
United States War Department: and western expeditions, 46, 47, 85, 346, 351, 359n, 396, 397
University of Illinois: and JCF letter, 99n
Upper Truckee River, 639n
Upshur, Abel, 361n
Utah Hot Springs, 500–501, 513n
Utah Indians. See Ute Indians
Utah Lake, 512n, 694, 697, 698, 699, 703; on 1845 map, MP 13
Utah Valley, 705n
Ute Indians: as hostiles, 445; and intertribal wars, 451, 718, 719; and Spanish caravans, 694, 695

Vaccinium myrtilloides. See V. oreophilum
Vaccinium oreophilum, 289, 300
Vaccinium scoparium, 289, 300
Vaccinium uliginosum. See V. scoparium
Valeriana ciliata, 402, 410, 475, 494, 515, 697
Valeriana edulis. See V. ciliata
Valley Forge (steamboat): voucher to, 379
Vancouver, George: JCF and his map, MP 12
Vanderburgh, William H., 126n
Van Horseigh, Father, 103n
Vasquez, Auguste (voyageur): returns at Fort Hall, 355n, 386n, 520; vouchers to, 379, 381; on 1843–44 expedition, 427; with JCF to Snake River, 453
Vauchard, Charles, 112n. See also Vessar
Vauchard, Louis, 112n. See also Vessar

Venus' looking-glass. See Specularia perfoliata
Verbena bracteata, 302
Verbena hastata, 302
Verbena stricta, 302
Vermillion Creek, 708, 709
Vernonia fasciculata, 297
Veronica alpina. See V. wormskjoldii
Veronica wormskjoldii, 289, 301
Verot, Jean Marcel Pierre Auguste, 26; identified, 27–28n
Verrot, Joseph (voyageur): voucher to, 382; on 1843–44 expedition, 427; discharged at Sutter's Fort, 657n
Vervains: see Verbena bracteata; V. stricta; blue, V. hastata
Vesicaria didymocarpa. See Physaria australis
Vessar, 111; identified, 112n, 121n
Vetches: see Astragalus agrestis; A. tridactylicus; alpine, see A. alpinus; milk, see A. gracilis, A. kentrophyta
Vetchling. See Lathyrus palustris
Viola, 398
Violet. See Viola
Virginia Patriot, xxiin, xxiiin
Virgin River, 676, 686–87n, 690, 691
Virgin's bower. See Clematis ligusticifolia
Vitis riparia, 293
Voglesang, Jacob: voucher to, 380
Volcanic rock, 527–34 passim, 536, 570, 580, 601, 634
Voyageurs: on Nicollet expeditions, 7, 13; re Coteau des Prairies, 15; on Des Moines River survey, 115; on 1842 expedition, 170; and tobacco, 183–84; on Platte River run, 275–78; on 1843–44 expedition, 427. See also Financial records

Wade, S.: voucher to, 381
Wasatch Mountains, 472n, 513, 592, 694, 695, 702, 705n
Walker, Joseph Reddeford, 506n, 621n, 622n, 657; voucher to, 383; and wagon train, 429n; worms, eating of, 506; re Great Salt Lake, 512; joins 1843–44 expedition, 693; biographical data, 693n; leaves expedition at Bent's Fort, 720
Walker (Ute chief): JCF and, 695–96; exchanges gifts, 696

Walker Lake, 693n
Walker Pass, 668n, 693n
Walker River, 613n, 624n
Walla Walla River, 550, 551, 612. *See also* Fort Walla Walla; Whitman, Marcus
Walsh, J. and E.: voucher to, 381
Ward, Edward C., xxviii
War Department. *See* United States War Department
Warm Spring, 231, 232n
Warm Spring Canyon, 232n
Warm Springs River, 580
Warren, Gouverneur, xxxivn
Washington, D.C.: in 1838, 4–5
Washo Indians: JCF among, 614–30; snow shoes, 619, 634; refuse guides, 621; salt gatherers, 638
Water cress. *See Rorippa islandica*
Water horehound. *See Lycopus americanus*
Water parsnip. *See Berula erecta*
Water smartweed. *See Polygonum amphibium*
Watson, Benjn.: voucher to, 380
Watson Mountain, 712n
Waugh, Alfred: re James McDowell, 395
Weathers, James M.: voucher to, 381
Weber River, 483n, 500n, 501, 513n
Wells, James, 25, 26; identified, 27n
Western mugwort. *See Artemisia ludoviciana*
Western wallflower. *See Erysimum asperum*
Weston Creek, 483n
West Walker Canyon, 623n
West Walker River, 613n, 619n
Weymouth, George, 274
Wharton, Maj. Clifton: re Pawnee war party, 268, 728
White, Elijah: and Hastings emigrant party, xviii, 222n; in Oregon, 173; precedes JCF, 175
White, Patrick (*voyageur*): returns at Fort Hall, 355n, 386n, 520; voucher to, 382; on 1843–44 expedition, 427
White Crane (Indian chief), 578
White River, 209, 578, 665
White Rocks Creek, 706n
Whitman, Marcus, 612n; voucher to, 354; assists 1843–44 expedition, 354n; wagon train, 429–30n; mission, 551, 552

Whitman, Perrin, 429n
Wiggins, Oliver P., 227–28n
Wild alfalfa. *See Psoralea floribunda*
Wild bean. *See Apios americana*
Wild bergamot. *See Monarda fistulosa*
Wildcat Canyon, 695n
Wild four o'clock. *See Mirabilis nyctaginea*
Wild horses, 195–96, 661–62
Wild lettuce. *See Lactuca pulchella*
Wild lilac. *See Ceanothus sanguineus*
Wild roses. *See Rosa blanda; R. foliolosa*
Wild sensitive plants. *See Schrankia microphylla; S. nuttallii*
Wiley & Putnam, xix
Wilkes, Capt. Charles, 161n, 169; survey of, 160; expedition, 401n, 426; JCF and, 562
Wilkins, William: letter to, 363–64; identified, 364n
Willamette River, 203n, 567
Willard (Clear) Creek, 500, 513
Williams, Lemuel: voucher to, 114
Williams, Capt. William G., xxix, xxx, 10, 123, 124n, 424n
Williamson, R. S., 668n
Williamson River, 586n
Willow herbs. *See Epilobium adenocaulon; E. angustifolium*
Willows: *see Salix tristis;* thicket, *see S. interior;* red, *see S. tristis;* sandbar, *see S. interior*
Wilson, George: voucher to, 381
Wind River Mountains: described, 250, 255, 256, 259–71; route in, 254–71; geology of, 254; ascent of north pass, 259–72; observations taken in, 266, 270, 271; flag planted, 270; JCF's locations questioned, 271n
Winged pigweed. *See Cycloloma atriplicifolium*
Winnemucca Lake, 632n
Winterfat. *See Eurotia lanata*
Wislizenus, Friedrich Adolph, 372, 478
Wistar, Caspar: letter from, 417–18; identified, 418n
Wolfberry. *See Symphoricarpus occidentalis*
Wolves, 188, 190–91, 650, 663
Wood, John: re Fremon-Pryor scandal, xxiii

853